February 4–8, 2017
Austin, Texas, USA

Association for Computing Machinery

Advancing Computing as a Science & Profession

PPoPP'17

Proceedings of the 22nd ACM SIGPLAN Symposium on

Principles and Practice of Parallel Programming

Sponsored by:

ACM SIGPLAN

Supported by:

NSF, Oracle, Hewlett Packard Labs, Two Sigma, Huawei, & WeGreened.com

Association for
Computing Machinery

Advancing Computing as a Science & Profession

The Association for Computing Machinery
2 Penn Plaza, Suite 701
New York, New York 10121-0701

ISBN: 978-1-4503-4493-7 (Digital)

ISBN: 978-1-4503-5440-0 (Print)

Additional copies may be ordered prepaid from:

ACM Order Department
PO Box 30777
New York, NY 10087-0777, USA

Phone: 1-800-342-6626 (USA and Canada)
+1-212-626-0500 (Global)
Fax: +1-212-944-1318
E-mail: acmhelp@acm.org
Hours of Operation: 8:30 am – 4:30 pm ET

Printed in the USA

Message from the Chairs

It is our great pleasure to welcome you to PPoPP 2017, the 22nd ACM SIGPLAN Symposium on Principles and Practice of Parallel Programming held in Austin, Texas during February 4-8, 2017, and co-located with the CGO 2017 and HPCA 2017 conferences. This year's symposium continues and reinforces the PPoPP tradition of publishing leading work on all aspects of parallel programming, including foundational and theoretical aspects, techniques, languages, compilers, runtime systems, tools, and practical experiences. Given the pervasiveness of parallel architectures in the general consumer market, PPoPP, with its interest in new parallel workloads, techniques and productivity tools for parallel programming, is becoming more relevant than ever to the computer science community.

PPoPP 2017 received 132 submissions from countries all over the world. The submitted papers underwent a rigorous two-phase review process. To maintain fairness and uniform standards, the review process was double-blind, throughout. Almost all of the 132 submissions were reviewed in the first phase by four members of the combined PC and ERC. (A very small fraction received three reviews in the first phase.) All papers were assigned a discussion lead from the PC. After the first rebuttal phase and ongoing online discussions, reviewers reached a consensus to relegate half of the submissions. Their authors were subsequently notified and given the choice of withdrawing their papers. The submissions for which there was no clear consensus or that had only three reviews (very few) were retained for the second evaluation stage. In the second phase, the remaining papers received at least two additional reviews exclusively from PC members and some external specialists. After a second rebuttal period, PC and ERC members continued their online discussions and grouped papers in *top*, *bottom* and *discuss* categories. Finally, 35 PC members met in person over two half days from noon, November 5th through the afternoon of November 6th at the Department of Computer Science in Rice University, Houston, TX, and concluded the meeting by accepting (or conditionally accepting) a total of 29 papers. The 14 conditionally accepted papers were shepherded by volunteer PC members, and the final version was made available to all original reviewers for their approval. All in all, this process resulted in a manageable average load of 12 papers for PC members, 6 papers for ERC members, offered all authors the possibility to respond to all reviews, and helped ensure that reviewing efforts were focused on where they were needed the most.

Because many quality papers could not be accommodated as regular contributions, all papers retained for the second review phase were invited to be presented as posters at the conference. As a result, 17 posters were included in the proceedings as 2 page abstracts. The posters were presented during a special two-hour late afternoon session. All authors of accepted papers were given the option of participating in a joint CGO-PPoPP Artifact Evaluation (AE) process. The AE process is intended to encourage researchers to conduct experiments in a reproducible way, to package experimental work-flows and all related materials for broad availability, and ultimately, to enable fair comparison of published techniques. This year saw a considerable increase in the amount of submitted artifacts: 27 versus 18 two years ago, almost equally split between CGO and PPoPP. The Artifact Evaluation Committee of 41 researchers and engineers spent two weeks validating and evaluating the artifacts. Each submission received at least three reviews and only eight of them fell below acceptance criteria. To help educate authors about result reproducibility, these papers were shepherded during a week's time by the AE Committee. Concurrently, the AE committee successfully tried an "open reviewing model", i.e., asked the community to publicly evaluate several artifacts already available at Github, Gila and other project hosting services. This enabled us to find additional external reviewers with access to HPC servers or proprietary benchmarks and tools. At the end of this process all submissions qualified to receive the AE seal and their authors were encouraged to submit a two page Artifact Appendix to document the process.

The success of a major conference like PPoPP very much depends on the hard work of all members of the organizing committee who volunteer their time in this service. We thank all PC and ERC members for their thoughtful reviews and extensive online discussions, with special thanks to the PC members who came from all over the world to the meeting in Houston and deliberated for two half days and read additional papers overnight to produce the PPoPP 2017 program. Several of the PC members volunteered to shepherd papers, and deserve special thanks for their efforts. The AE process was lengthy and demanding, and the AE Chairs, Wonsun Ahn (for PPoPP) and Joe Devietti (for CGO) and their team did an amazing job on that Herculean task.

The Workshops and Tutorials Chair. Rajkishore Barik, did an excellent job on complementing the main conference program with workshops and tutorials relevant to PPoPP. The Treasurer, I-Ting Angelina Lee, worked tirelessly on processing sponsorships and other financial aspects of the conference. We thank Vivek Kumar and Louis-Noel Pouchet for all their hard work as Web Chair and Registration Chair respectively, and are also grateful to our four Publicity Chairs — Jeff Huang, Hironori Kasahara, V.~Krishna Nandivada, and Chenggang Wu — for all their efforts. A special thank you goes to the graduate students (Arghya Chatterjee, Rabimba Karanjai, Sriraj Paul, Yuhan Peng, Jonathan Sharman, Nick Vrvilo) and postdoctoral researchers (Tiago Cogumbreiro, Farzad Khorasani, Martin Kong) at Rice University who assisted with the PC meeting.

We are grateful to ACM SIGPLAN and to the PPoPP steering committee for giving us the opportunity to organize this conference, and for providing guidance and historical perspectives, and thank all corporations who generously supported this conference. We also very much appreciate all the cooperation and support from the organizing committees of the co-located CGO and HPCA conferences. Finally, we wish to thank the authors and all the participants who make PPoPP a unique and vibrant technical forum every year.

Lawrence Rauchwerger
PPoPP'17 Program Chair
Texas A&M University

Vivek Sarkar
PPoPP'17 General Chair
Rice University

Table of Contents

Session 5: Best Papers

Session 6: Languages & Compilers

Session 7: Data Analytics

Session 8: Fault Tolerance

Session 9: Posters

PPoPP 2017 Symposium Organization

General Chair: Vivek Sarkar *(Rice University, USA)*

Program Chair: Lawrence Rauchwerger *(Texas A&M University, USA)*

Tutorials & Workshops Chair: Rajkishore Barik *(Intel Labs, USA)*

Registration Chair: Louis-Noel Pouchet *(Colorado State University, USA)*

Web Chair: Vivek Kumar *(IIIT Delhi, India)*

Publicity Chairs: Jeff Huang *(Texas A&M University, USA)*
Hironori Kasahara *(Waseda University, Japan)*
V. Krishna Nandivada *(IIT Madras, India)*
Chenggang Wu *(Chinese Academy of Sciences, China)*

Treasurer: I-Ting Angelina Lee *(Washington University, USA)*

Steering Committee Chair: Calin Cascaval *(Barefoot Networks, Inc., USA)*

Steering Committee: Rafael Asenjo *(Universidad de Málaga, Spain)*
Albert Cohen *(INRIA, France)*
David Grove *(IBM Research, USA)*
Mary Hall *(University of Utah, USA)*
Timothy Harris *(Oracle Labs, UK)*
James Larus *(EPFL, Switzerland)*
Jose Moreira *(IBM Research, USA)*
David Padua *(University of Illinois at Urbana-Champaign, USA)*
Keshav Pingali *(University of Texas, Austin, USA)*

Program Committee: Nancy Amato *(Texas A&M University, USA)*
Mark Batty *(University of Kent, UK)*
George Bosilca *(University of Tennessee, USA)*
Milind Chabbi *(Hewlett Packard Labs, USA)*
Robert Clay *(Sandia National Laboratories, USA)*
Albert Cohen *(INRIA, France)*
David Dice *(Oracle Labs, USA)*
Sandhya Dwarkadas *(University of Rochester, USA)*
Mootaz Elnozahy *(KAUST, Saudi Arabia)*
Maria Jesus Garzaran *(UIUC and Intel Corporation, USA)*
Seth Copen Goldstein *(Carnegie Mellon University, USA)*
R. Govindarajan *(Indian Institute of Science, India)*
Mary Hall *(University of Utah, USA)*
Timothy Harris *(Oracle Labs, UK)*

Program Committee (continued):

Akihiro Hayashi *(Rice University, USA)*
Yuxiong He *(Microsoft Research, USA)*
Bruce Hendrickson *(Sandia National Laboratories, USA)*
Jeff Huang *(Texas A&M University, USA)*
Paul H J Kelly *(Imperial College, London, UK)*
Alex Kogan *(Oracle Labs, USA)*
Doug Lea *(SUNY Oswego, USA)*
I-Ting Angelina Lee *(Washington University, USA)*
Jaejin Lee *(Seoul National University, Korea)*
Paul McKenney *(IBM, USA)*
Kathryn S McKinley *(Microsoft Research, USA)*
John Mellor-Crummey *(Rice University, USA)*
Samuel Midkiff *(Purdue University, USA)*
Adam Morrison *(Tel Aviv University, Israel)*
Satish Narayanasamy *(University of Michigan, USA)*
Cosmin Oancea *(University of Copenhagen, Denmark)*
Kunle Olukotun *(Stanford University, USA)*
David Padua *(University of Illinois at Urbana-Champaign, USA)*
Erez Petrank *(Technion, Israel)*
Keshav Pingali *(University of Texas, Austin, USA)*
Lawrence Rauchwerger *(Texas A&M University, USA)*
Martin Rinard *(Massachusetts Institute of Technology, USA)*
P. (Saday) Sadayappan *(Ohio State University, USA)*
Michael Scott *(University of Rochester, USA)*
Tatiana Shpeisman *(Intel Labs, USA)*
Armando Solar-Lezama *(Massachusetts Institute of Technology, USA)*
Jeffrey Vetter *(Oak Ridge National Laboratory, USA)*
Uzi Vishkin *(University of Maryland, USA)*
Chenggang Wu *(Chinese Academy of Sciences, China)*

PPoPP 2017 Sponsor & Supporters

Sponsor:

acm SIGPLAN

Gold Supporters:

NSF

ORACLE

Bronze Supporters:

Hewlett Packard Labs

2σ TWO SIGMA

HUAWEI

WeGreened.com

Greencard for PhD/PostDoc/professor/researcher
5,000+ success cases

It's Time for a New Old Language

Guy L. Steele Jr.
Oracle Labs
Burlington, Massachusetts
guy.steele@oracle.com

ABSTRACT

The most popular programming language in computer science has no compiler or interpreter. Its definition is not written down in any one place. It has changed a lot over the decades, and those changes have introduced ambiguities and inconsistencies. Today, dozens of variations are in use, and its complexity has reached the point where it needs to be re-explained, at least in part, every time it is used. Much effort has been spent in hand-translating between this language and other languages that do have compilers. The language is quite amenable to parallel computation, but this fact has gone unexploited.

In this talk we will summarize the history of the language, highlight the variations and some of the problems that have arisen, and propose specific solutions. We suggest that it is high time that this language be given a complete formal specification, and that compilers, IDEs, and proof-checkers be created to support it, so that all the best tools and techniques of our trade may be applied to it also.

ACM Classification Keywords

• Social and professional topics ~ History of programming languages • Theory of computation ~ Grammars and context-free languages • Computing methodologies ~ Parallel programming languages • Software and its engineering ~ Formal language definitions

Author Keywords

programming languages; compilers; specifications

PPoPP'17, February 4–8, 2017, Austin, TX, USA.
ACM ISBN 978-1-4503-4335-0/17/02.
http://dx.doi.org/10.1145/3018743.3018773

BIOGRAPHY

Guy L. Steele Jr. is a Software Architect at Oracle. He received his A.B. in applied mathematics from Harvard College (1975), and his S.M. and Ph.D. in computer science and artificial intelligence from M.I.T. (1977 and 1980). He has also been an assistant professor of computer science at Carnegie-Mellon University; a member of technical staff at Tartan Laboratories in Pittsburgh, Pennsylvania; and a senior scientist at Thinking Machines Corporation in Cambridge, Massachusetts. He joined Sun Microsystems Laboratories in 1994 as a Distinguished Engineer and was named a Sun Fellow in 2003. Sun Microsystems was acquired by Oracle in 2010, and he is now a member of Oracle Labs.

The Association for Computing Machinery awarded him the 1988 Grace Murray Hopper Award and named him an ACM Fellow in 1994. He was elected a Fellow of the American Association for Artificial Intelligence in 1990. He led the team that received a 1990 Gordon Bell Prize honorable mention for achieving the fastest speed to that date for a production application: 14.182 Gigaflops. He was also awarded the 1996 ACM SIGPLAN Programming Languages Achievement Award. In 2001 he was elected to the National Academy of Engineering of the United States of America. In 2002 he was elected to the American Academy of Arts and Sciences. In 2007 he received the IEEE Computer Society Harry H. Goode memorial Award, and in 2011 he was named an IEEE Fellow.

He has served on accredited standards committees X3J11 (C language) and X3J3 (Fortran), and served as chairman of X3J13 (Common Lisp). He was also a member of the IEEE committee that produced the IEEE Standard for the Scheme Programming Language, IEEE Std 1178-1990. He was a representative to the High Performance Fortran Forum, which produced the High Performance Fortran specification in May, 1993. He is a co-author of *The Java Language Specification.*

At Oracle Labs, he is responsible for research in language design and implementation strategies, and architectural and software support for programming languages.

EffiSha: A Software Framework for Enabling Efficient Preemptive Scheduling of GPU

Guoyang Chen, Yue Zhao, Xipeng Shen
Computer Science, North Carolina State University
{gchen11, yzhao30, xshen5}@ncsu.edu

Huiyang Zhou
Electrical and Computer Engineering, North Carolina State University
hzhou@ncsu.edu

Abstract

Modern GPUs are broadly adopted in many multitasking environments, including data centers and smartphones. However, the current support for the scheduling of multiple GPU kernels (from different applications) is limited, forming a major barrier for GPU to meet many practical needs. This work for the first time demonstrates that on existing GPUs, efficient preemptive scheduling of GPU kernels is possible even without special hardware support. Specifically, it presents *EffiSha*, a pure software framework that enables preemptive scheduling of GPU kernels with very low overhead. The enabled preemptive scheduler offers flexible support of kernels of different priorities, and demonstrates significant potential for reducing the average turnaround time and improving the system overall throughput of programs that time share a modern GPU.

1. Introduction

As a kind of massively parallel architectures, GPUs have attained broad adoptions in modern computing systems. Most of these systems are multitasking with more than one application running and requesting the usage of GPU simultaneously. In data centers, for instance, many customers may concurrently submit their requests, multiple of which often need to be serviced simultaneously by a single node in the data center. How to manage GPU usage effectively in such environments is important for the responsiveness of the applications, the utilization of the GPU, and the quality of service of the computing system.

The default management of GPU is through the undisclosed GPU drivers and follows a first-come-first-serve policy. Under this policy, the system-level shared resource, GPU, may get unfairly used: Consider two requests from applications A and B; even though A may have already used the GPU for many of its requests recently and B has only issued its first request, the default GPU management—giving no consideration of the history usage of applications—may still assign the GPU to A and keep B waiting if A's request comes just slightly earlier than B's request. Moreover, the default scheduling is oblivious to the priorities of kernels. Numerous studies [1–4] have shown that the problematic way to manage GPU causes serious unfairness, response delays, and low GPU utilizations.

Latest GPUs (e.g., Pascal from NVIDIA) are equipped with the capability to evict a GPU kernel at an arbitrary instruction. However, the kernel eviction incurs substantial overhead in state saving and restoring. Some recent work [2, 4, 5] proposes some hardware extensions to help alleviate the issue. But they add hardware complexities.

Software solutions may benefit existing systems immediately. Prior efforts towards software solutions fall into two classes. The first is for trackability. They propose some APIs and OS intercepting techniques [1, 3] to allow the OS or hypervisors to track the usage of GPU by each application. The improved trackability may help select GPU kernels to launch based on their past usage and priorities. The second class of work is about granularity. They use kernel slicing [6, 7] to break one GPU kernel into many smaller ones. The reduced granularity increases the flexibility in kernel scheduling, and may help shorten the time that a kernel has to wait before it can get launched.

Although these software solutions may enhance GPU management, they are all subject to one important shortcoming: None of them allow the eviction of a running GPU kernel before its finish—that is, none of them allows preemptive GPU schedules. The request for GPU from an application, despite its priority, cannot get served before the finish of the GPU kernel that another application has already launched. The length of the delay depends on the length of the running kernel. To reduce the delay, some prior proposals (e.g., kernel slicing [6, 7]) attempt to split a kernel into many smaller kernels such that the wait for a kernel to finish

PPoPP '17, February 04-08, 2017, Austin, TX, USA

DOI: http://dx.doi.org/10.1145/3018743.3018748

gets shortened. They however face a dilemma: The resulting increased number of kernel launches and the reduced parallelism in the smaller kernels often cause some substantial performance loss (as much as 58% shown in our experiments in Section 8).

In this work, we propose a simple yet effective way to solve the dilemma. The key is a novel software approach that, for the first time, enables efficient preemptions of kernels on existing GPUs. Kernels need not be sliced anymore; they voluntarily suspend and exit when it is time to switch kernels on GPU.

How to enable efficient kernel preemption is challenging for the large overhead of context savings and restoration for the massive concurrent GPU threads. Before this work, all previously proposed solutions have relied on special hardware extensions [2, 4].

Our solution is pure software-based, consisting of some novel program transformations and runtime machinery. We call our compiler-runtime synergistic framework EffiSha (for efficient sharing). As a pure software framework, it is immediately deployable in today's systems. Instead of slicing a kernel into many smaller kernels, EffiSha transforms the kernel into a form that are amenable for efficient voluntary preemptions. Little if any data need to be saved or restored upon an eviction. Compared to prior kernel slicing-based solutions, EffiSha reduces the runtime eviction overhead from 58% to 4% on average, and removes the need for selecting an appropriate kernel size in kernel slicing.

EffiSha opens the opportunities for preemptive kernel scheduling on GPU. We implement two priority-based preemptive schedulers upon EffiSha. They offer flexible support for kernels of different priorities, and demonstrate significant potential for reducing the average turnaround time (18-65% on average) and improving the overall system throughput of program executions (1.35X-1.8X on average) that time-share a GPU.

This work makes the following major contributions:

1) It presents EffiSha, a compiler-runtime framework that, for the first time, makes beneficial preemptive GPU scheduling possible without hardware extensions.

2) It proposes the first software approach to enabling efficient preemptions of GPU kernels. The approach consists of multi-fold innovations, including the *preemption enabling program transformation*, the creation of GPU proxies, and a three-way synergy among applications, a CPU daemon, and GPU proxies.

3) It demonstrates the potential of EffiSha-based schedulers for supporting kernel priorities and improving kernel responsiveness and system throughput.

2. Terminology and Granularity

We use CUDA terminology for our discussion, but note that the problem and solution discussed in this paper also apply to other GPU programming models (e.g., OpenCL).

```
Kernel of matrix addition:
%threadIdx.x: the index of a thread in its block;
%blockIdx.x: the global index of the thread block;
%blockDim.x: the number of threads per thread block

  idx = threadIdx.x + blockIdx.x * blockDim.x;
  C[idx] = A[idx] + B[idx];
```

Figure 1. A kernel for matrix addition.

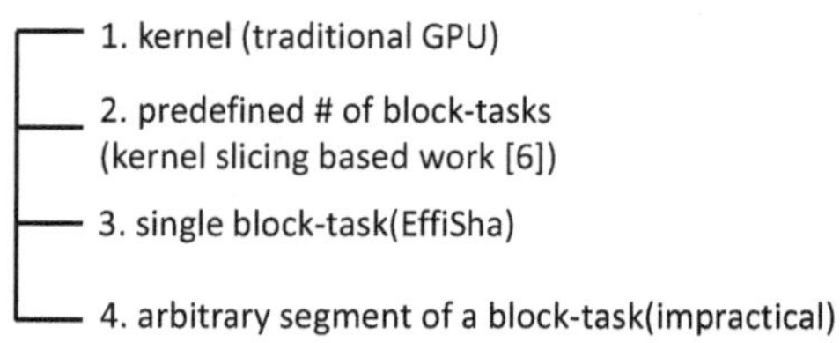

Figure 2. Four levels of GPU scheduling granularity.

A GPU kernel launch usually creates a large number of GPU threads. They all run the same kernel program, which usually includes some references to thread IDs to differentiate the behaviors of the threads and the data they work on. These threads are organized into groups called *thread blocks*.

Note that in a typical GPU program[1], no synchronizations across different thread blocks are supported. Different thread blocks can communicate by operating on the same data locations on the global memory (e.g., reduction through atomic operations), but the communications must not cause dependence hazards (i.e., execution order constraints) among the thread blocks. Otherwise, the kernel could suffer deadlocks due to the hardware-based thread scheduling.

We call the set of work done by a thread block a **block-task**. For the aforementioned GPU property, the block-tasks of a kernel can run in an arbitrary order (even if they operate on some common locations in the memory). Different block-tasks do not communicate through registers or shared memory. The execution of each block-task must first set up the states of their registers and shared memory. Typically, the ID of a thread block is taken as the ID of its block-task. Figure 1 shows the kernel for matrix addition.

Existing GPUs do not allow the eviction of running computing kernels. A newly arrived request for GPU by a different application must wait for the currently running kernel to finish before it can use the GPU [2].

Scheduling Granularity. Scheduling granularity determines the time when a kernel switch can happen on GPU. This section explains the choice we make.

[1] Exceptions are GPU kernels written with persistent threads [8], which are discussed later in this paper.

[2] On some recent GPUs (e.g., the K40m used in our experiments), the hardware sometimes evicts a kernel, but the undisclosed control is entirely oblivious to the priorities of the kernels, OS control, and QoS requirements.

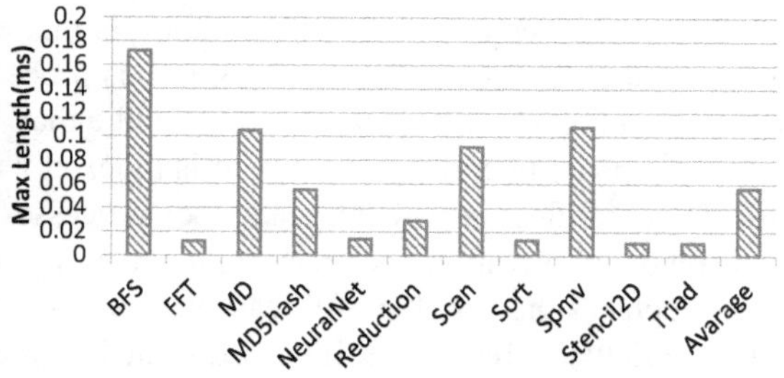

Figure 3. The maximum length of a task in SHOC benchmarks (the largest input in the benchmark suite are used).

Figure 2 lists four granularities for GPU scheduling. At the top is an entire kernel execution; kernel switches can happen only at the end of the entire kernel. This is what traditional GPUs support. All previously proposed software solutions have tried to support a level-2 granularity. The *preemptive kernel model (PKM)* [6], for instance, breaks the original kernel into many smaller kernels, with each processing a pre-defined number (K) of the block-tasks in the original kernel. Even though with this approach the GPU still switches kernels at the boundary of a kernel, the slicing reduces the size of the kernel and hence the granularity. A challenge at this level is to determine the appropriate value of K. Previous work has relied on profiling to do so, feasible to restricted real-time environment, but not for data center-like general sharing environments. It further suffers a dilemma between responsiveness and overhead as Section 8 will show.

The level most flexible for scheduling is the lowest level in Figure 2, where, GPU may switch kernels at an arbitrary point in the execution. The latest generation of GPU, Pascal, supports this level of preemption through hardware. However, the feature is rarely usable in practice due to the tremendous overhead in saving and restoring the state of massive GPU threads [2, 4]. Moreover, the decisions for the preemptions are not software-controllable.

In this work, we design EffiSha to offer the level-3 scheduling granularity. GPU kernel switch can happen at the end of an arbitrary block-task. This choice has several appealing properties. It offers more scheduling flexibility than level 1 or level 2 does. It requires no kernel slicing, and hence, circumvents the difficulty of level 2 for selecting the appropriate K value and the overhead associated with kernel slicing. And finally, unlike level-4, no thread states are needed to save or restore at this level, since preemptions do not happen in the middle of a thread execution.

The size of a block-task determines the worst kernel eviction delay (i.e., the time between the eviction flag is set and the time when the kernel gets actually evicted). Figure 3 shows the maximum length of a block-task in the level-1 SHOC benchmark suite [9]. All block-tasks are shorter than 0.8 milliseconds. The actual eviction delay is even shorter, only 0.08ms on average (detailed in Section 8), much shorter than a typical context switch period in Linux. For the rare

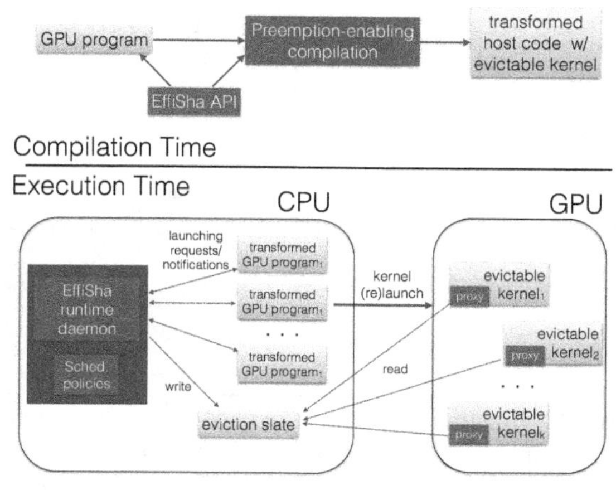

Figure 4. Overview of EffiSha.

cases where a block-task is too large, it is possible to develop some compiler techniques to reduce the granularity by reforming a block-task; the study is left to future.

Terminology clarification: In some (real-time systems) literatures, "preemptive scheduling" exclusively refers to Level-4 scheduling (eviction at an arbitrary instruction). In this article, we adopt a broader meaning of the term, calling a scheduling scheme preemptive if it makes a running kernel evict before its finish.

3. Overview of EffiSha

EffiSha is the first software framework that offers the level 3 scheduling granularity efficiently. As Figure 4 shows, EffiSha consists of four major components, working at the times of both compilation and execution. The compilation step is through a source-to-source compiler that transforms a given GPU program into a form amenable for runtime management and scheduling. It replaces some GPU-related function calls in the host code with some APIs we have introduced, such that at the execution time, those API calls will pass the GPU requests and related information to the EffiSha runtime. It reforms the GPU kernels such that they can voluntarily stop and evict during their executions. The eviction points in the kernels are identified by the compiler such that little if any data would need to be saved and restored upon an eviction.

The EffiSha APIs are mostly intended to be used by the compiler, but could be also used by programmers in a GPU kernel for offering optional hints to the compiler and runtime. Some high-level APIs are designed to allow users to specify the intended priority of kernels.

The EffiSha runtime consists of a daemon on the host side, and a "proxy" of the daemon on the GPU side. The latter is in form of a special thread block of the executing GPU kernel; its creation is facilitated by the *preemption-*

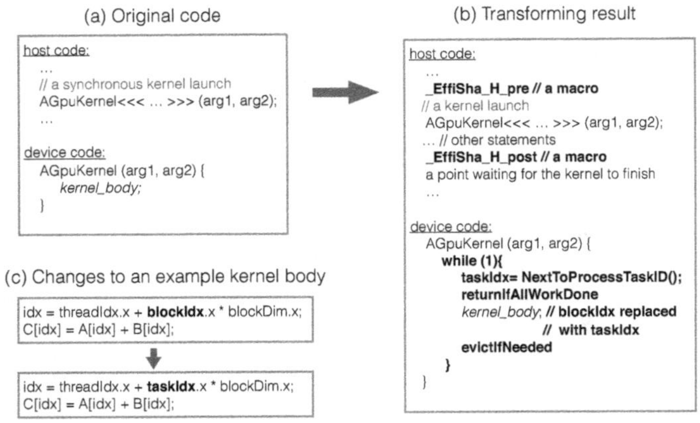

Figure 5. Illustration of the effects of *preemption-enabling* code transformation. Graphs (a) and (b) show the code of a GPU program before and after the transformation; graph (c) uses matrix addition as an example to show the changes to the body of the kernel: from the default thread-block ID indexed form to a block-task ID indexed form.

enabling code transformation done by the compiler. This novel design is key to the low runtime overhead of EffiSha.

The EffiSha daemon receives all the GPU requests from the applications. These requests could be of different priorities. The EffiSha daemon organizes the requests in queues. Based on the scheduling policy that we have designed, it decides when to evict the current running kernel and which kernel to launch next. The interplay between the daemon and the "proxy" of the daemon efficiently notifies the executing GPU kernel when it is time for it to get evicted. Those kernels, thanks to the reformation of their code by the compiler, then voluntarily exit from the GPU. They are recorded in the scheduling queues of EffiSha. When the EffiSha daemon decides that it is time for a kernels to start or resume their executions on GPU, it notifies the hosting process of the kernel, which launches or relaunches the kernels accordingly.

The design of EffiSha ensures a very low overhead of a GPU kernel preemption. We next use an example to first explain how the essential machinery of EffiSha works, and then describe the implementations in the compiler module and the runtime.

4. Preemption-Enabling Code Transformation

Figure 5 illustrates the effects of the *preemption-enabling* transformation to a GPU program. It converts the GPU kernel into a form that uses persistent threads [8] (explained later), and inserts some assistant code into the host side to help with scheduling.

The statements in bold font in Figure 5 are inserted by the EffiSha compiler. A transformation critical for enabling the low-overhead preemption is the changes applied to the device code, shown by Figure 5 (c), which replaces the reference to thread block ID with a block-task ID. An important observation underlying the transformation is that even though in most GPU kernels the ith block-task is processed by the ith thread block, it does not have to be like that. The block-task keeps its integrity as long as it is indexed with i (its task ID), regardless of which thread block processes it.

Based on the observation, the preemption-enabling transformation replaces the variable of thread-block ID in a kernel with a variable of block-task ID as illustrated by the replacement of "blockIdx" with "taskIdx" in Figure 5 (c). By eliminating the tie between a block-task and a thread block ID, it offers the freedom for an arbitrary thread block to process an arbitrary block-task.

With that freedom, in an execution of our transformed GPU kernel, each thread block typically processes not one but a number of block-tasks. That is materialized by the second part of the transformation. As illustrated in the device code in Figure 5 (b), the transformation adds a *while* loop around the body of the kernel such that when a thread block finishes processing a block-task, it tries to process more yet-to-process block-tasks, until all block-tasks are finished or it is time for the kernel to get evicted. Because the threads stay alive across block-tasks, they are called *persistent threads* [8].

An important benefit from using persistent threads is that the transformed program can set the number of thread blocks of a GPU kernel to be just enough to keep the GPU fully utilized. All thread blocks can then be active throughout the kernel execution; global synchronizations among them (e.g., through global memory) hence become possible. It offers some important support to EffiSha as shown later.

Our description has been for the typical GPU kernels that are data-parallel kernels. In some rare cases where the original kernel is already in the form of persistent threads, the compiler can recognize that based on the outmost loop structure, skip this step of code transformation, and move on to the next step.

Low-Overhead Kernel Preemption With the kernel in the form of persistent threads, *preemption-enabling transformation* puts the eviction point at the end of the block-task loop (i.e., the *while* loop in Figure 5 (b).) It gives an appealing property: Upon preemptions, no extra work is needed for saving or restoring threads states. The reason is that since the current block-tasks have finished, there is no need for restoring the threads states. For the block-tasks yet to process, later relaunches of the kernel can process them based on the memory state left by the previous launch of the kernel. (The memory data of the evicted kernel are not copied out or removed from the GPU memory.) The memory state contains the effects left by the earlier block-tasks, including the counter indicating the next block-task to process. If later block-tasks depend on some values produced by earlier block-tasks (e.g., for a reduction), they can find the values on the memory. No extra data saving or restoring is needed upon evictions.

It is worth noting that EffiSha does not cause extra overhead in setting up the states of GPU shared memory. On GPU, by default, the data in shared memory loaded by a thread block cannot be accessed by another thread block. Therefore, in a typical GPU program, each block-task must first load their needed data into shared memory in order to use such memory. It is the same in our transformed code; such load instructions are enclosed inside the "while" loop in Figure 5 (b) as part of the kernel body. Because evictions happen only at the end of a block-task, the shared memory for that block-task needs to be set up only once just as in the default case, regardless of kernel evictions.

The placement of eviction points offer the level-3 scheduling granularity as Section 2 has discussed. This level of scheduling granularity offers more flexibilities than previous software methods do.

As typical as in time-sharing systems, the evicted unfinished kernels and the next-to-run kernel may contend for the space of device memory. Section 6.4 gives further discussions.

In addition to the described code changes, the *Preemption-Enabling* transformation adds two predefined macros respectively at the points before and after the kernel invocation in the host code. It also injects code to create a proxy of the EffiSha runtime daemon on GPU. For their close connections with the EffiSha runtime, we postpone their explanations to the next section where the runtime is explained.

5. EffiSha API and Runtime: Basic Design

The main functionality of the EffiSha runtime is to manage the usage of GPU, making a kernel get launched, evicted, or relaunched at appropriate times. With GPU drivers remaining undisclosed, it is hard for the EffiSha daemon to directly manipulate a GPU kernel inside the context of another process. The runtime management hence involves the cooperations among the EffiSha daemon, the GPU threads, and the CPU processes that host the GPU kernels. A careful design is necessary to ensure that they work together smoothly and efficiently.

To ease the understanding, our description starts with a basic design. It conveys the basic idea, but lacks the support to multiple GPU streams, and suffers large overhead. Section 6 describes the enhanced design and optimizations that address those limitations. For now, the description assumes that each application has only one GPU stream (i.e., one sequence of GPU kernels to run on the GPU).

5.1 GPU-Stubs and State Transitions

We first introduce a runtime data structure named *GPU-stubs* and the states that a GPU kernel could have and their transitions. They are essential for understanding the runtime cooperations.

The EffiSha daemon hosts a number of *GPU-stubs*. Each stub holds a record for a kernel that is yet to finish. As

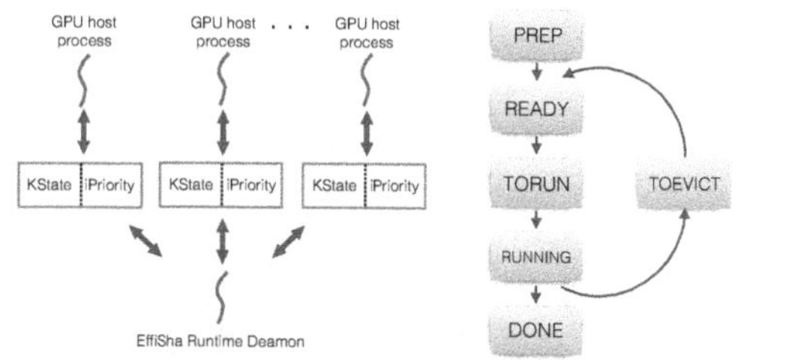

(a) GPU-stubs that reside on pinned memory facilitate the coordinations. (b) Kernel states (i.e. values of KState) and possible state transitions of a kernel

Figure 6. GPU-stubs and the possible state transitions of a GPU kernel.

Figure 6 (a) shows, a GPU-stub contains two fields: One is *KState*, which indicates the current state of the kernel, the other is *iPriority*, which indicates the initial priority of the kernel.

Each GPU-stub is a small piece of (CPU-side) shared memory created by the EffiSha daemon. When an application requests a GPU-stub for a GPU kernel call (through an EffiSha API call), the daemon allocates a stub for it, maps the stub to the address space of the host thread, and returns the address to the host thread. The usage of shared memory allows the stub to be both read and written by the daemon and the host thread directly. We have also considered an alternative design which leaves the stub in the daemon space; the host thread then must access the stub through system calls. It incurs much more overhead because the stubs are frequently read by the host thread as we shall see in the next section.

The field *KState* in a GPU-stub can have one of six values, corresponding to all the six states that a GPU kernel can possibly have. Figure 6 (b) shows the set of states and the possible transitions among them. A GPU-stub is created before the host thread reaches kernel invocations; it is in a preparation state (PREP). Before a kernel invocation, it transits to the READY state, indicating that a kernel is ready to be launched. When the EffiSha daemon changes its state to TORUN, the host thread may launch the kernel and the state of the kernel becomes RUNNING. When the EffiSha daemon changes its state to TOEVICT, the GPU kernel evicts from GPU voluntarily and the kernel goes back to the READY state. When the GPU kernel finishes, the kernel state turns to DONE and the GPU-stub gets reclaimed for other usage.

5.2 Basic Implementation of the Runtime

We now explain the basic implementation of the EffiSha runtime, and how it supports the state transitions for kernel scheduling. Our description follows the computation stages and state transitions shown in Figure 7. On the right side of Figure 7, there is the transformed GPU program code, which reveals the details of some macros showed in Figure 5; on the left side of Figure 7 are the states of the kernel corresponding to each of the computation stages.

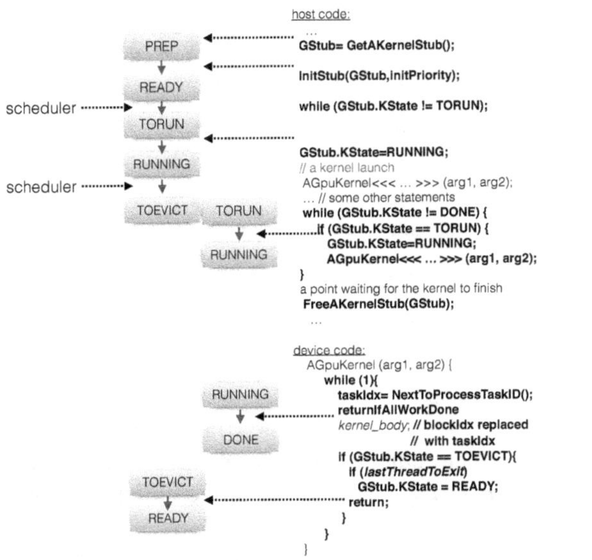

Figure 7. Changes of the KState of a kernel in each stage of the execution of a GPU program (bold font shows the code inserted by the EffiSha compiler).

The host thread calls the API "GetAKernelStub" to obtain a GPU-stub for the next kernel call. At the creation time, the KState in the stub equals "PREP". The API "initStub" sets the "iPriority" field of the GPU-stub with the initial priority (also called static priority) of the kernel; if it is "null", the kernel uses the default priority. The call also changes the state of the kernel to "READY". After that, the host thread starts to poll the *KState* in the stub until the EffiSha runtime daemon changes its value to "TORUN". The host thread then changes the *KState* to "RUNNING" and launches its kernel.

The bottom of Figure 7 shows the device code and state transitions. During the execution of a GPU kernel, when a GPU thread finds no more block-tasks left, it changes the field *KState* of the stub to "DONE". Otherwise, it processes its work, and then before it tries to process a new task, it checks whether the *KState* is now "TOEVICT". If so, the thread exits; the last thread to exit, changes the *KState* to "READY" such that the kernel can be relaunched later. The voluntary evictions require no saving of the GPU thread states as they happen only at the finish of some block-task. In the implementation, GPU-stubs are mapped to pinned memory such that GPU threads can also access it.

After launching the GPU kernel, the host thread continues its execution[3]. Right before it reaches the next waiting point, it gets into a *while* loop, in which, it repeatedly checks the *KState* until it becomes "DONE". During the check, the kernel may get evicted and later get scheduled by the EffiSha runtime to resume, in which case, the runtime changes *KState* to "TORUN"[4], and as soon as the host thread sees it, it relaunches the kernel.

6. Enhanced Design and Optimized Implementation

The basic design and implementation enables evictions and relaunches of GPU kernels, but is subject to two-fold limitations: applicability and efficiency.

6.1 Enhancing Applicability

The most important limitation in applicability is that the basic design cannot work with GPU streams. Modern GPU introduces streams for allowing concurrent executions of multiple kernels (of the same application) on a GPU. Each stream may contain a sequence of kernel launch events. Kernels in different streams can run concurrently on a GPU while kernels in the same stream get launched in serial. The basic design of EffiSha tracks the state of an individual kernel but is oblivious to streams. It cannot maintain the execution properties of multiple streams (e.g., letting multiple kernels from different streams run concurrently). Our enhanced design extends the basic design.

In our design, all streams of an application share a single priority. The choice comes from the property of current GPUs. On current GPUs, kernels from two different GPU applications cannot run concurrently on a GPU, and hence, at an eviction time, all streams of an application have to get evicted before another application can use that GPU. The single-priority restriction could get relaxed for future GPUs when more advanced co-run support is introduced.

In the enhanced design, a GPU-stub is for the entire GPU application rather than for each individual kernel. Its *KState* field now indicates the status of the GPU request from that whole application. Moreover, GPU-stub contains an array of queues besides *KState* and the initial priority. We call the queues *kernelQ*s. The host code is transformed such that a *kernelQ* is created in the GPU-stub right before the creation of a GPU stream. And right before the code for launching a GPU kernel, the ID of the kernel is added into the *kernelQ* of that kernel's stream[5]. As kernel launch commands are asynchronous, the host thread may execute multiple such commands in a sequence, leaving multiple kernel IDs in a *kernelQ*.

There are three other changes: (1) At a kernel launch point, the compiler does not make the code transformations as in the basic design. Instead, it replaces CUDA kernel launch calls with calls to a customized launch API, the implementation of which puts the ID of the to-be-launched ker-

[3] Here, we assume asynchronous kernel launches. If the original kernel launch is synchronous, the compiler changes it to asynchronous and adds a waiting point right after it.

[4] Through atomic operations, it first checks to ensure that *KState* is "READY" state.

[5] In CUDA, stream ID is part of the launching parameters. When it is omitted, the default stream (stream 0) is used. For CUDA 7, each host thread has its own stream 0; on earlier CUDA, one application has only one stream 0.

```
while (GStub.kernelQ[s]!=empty){
   if (GStub.KState == TORUN){
      GStub.KState = RUNNING;
      launch the kernels residing at the heads of all kernelQs.
   }
}
```

Figure 8. Implementation of the customized API for a synchronization on stream s.

nel into the corresponding *kernelQ* and records the kernel parameters for later launches or relaunches to use. That API does not actually launch the kernel as launch time is determined by the runtime scheduler. (2) When the current kernel is done, the device code dequeues that kernel from the *kernelQ* of its stream. It does not set *KState* to DONE unless all *kernelQ*s of the GPU-stub become empty. (3) At synchronization points, the compiler does not insert the code as those inserted in the basic design. Instead, it replaces all GPU device synchronization calls with our customized synchronization API. CUDA has two kinds of stream synchronizations: one is to wait for all the kernels in a particular stream to finish, the other for all streams of the program. For the former, the implementation of our API is as shown in Figure 8. As long as the runtime scheduler permits (indicated by *GStub.KState*), it lets all the streams of the program run on GPU until the *kernelQ* of the to-be-synchronized stream becomes empty (i.e., all kernels in that stream have finished). For the other kind of synchronizations, the implementation is similar except that the exit condition of the "while" loop is that *GStub.KState==DONE*. It is worth mentioning that this enhanced design also avoids some code analysis complexities facing the basic design: The code transformations in the basic design at synchronization points need to know which kernel invocation the points correspond to. It could be complex to figure out if the synchronization points are in a different device function or compilation unit.

6.2 Improving Efficiency

The second main issue of the basic implementation is that it adds some substantial runtime overhead, causing significant slowdowns (up to 97X) to a program execution (shown in Section 8). To make it work efficiently, we have developed three optimizations as follows.

Proxy on GPU In the basic implementation, *KState* is made visible to all three parties: the daemon, the host thread, and the GPU threads. That simplifies the coordinations among them, but is not quite efficient. The main issue is on the repeated accesses to *KState* by each GPU thread. Because the accesses have to go through the connections between CPU and GPU (e.g., through a PCIe link), they cause significant slowdowns to some kernels, especially those that have small block-tasks (e.g., 97x slowdown on a Triad kernel).

We optimize the implementation by creating a special kernel on a special stream for each GPU application. The kernel serves as the proxy of the EffiSha runtime, running on the GPU along with the other streams. In this implementation, there is a copy of *KState* on the GPU memory. The proxy keeps reading the *KState* on the host memory and updates the copy on the GPU accordingly. With that, the threads in other GPU streams just need to read the local copy to find out the time to get evicted. The other job of the proxy is to monitor the status of the kernel (e.g., by reading the block-task counter) and to update the *KState* on the host memory when necessary. The proxy only needs one GPU thread, consuming the minimum resource. It is launched whenever a kernel of the application gets launched.

Adaptive Checking The use of the proxy frees the other thread blocks from accessing the remote host memory repeatedly, which reduces the overhead substantially. But we still observe 15% overhead for kernels with fine-grained block-tasks. We add the feature of adaptive checking to further reduce the overhead. The idea is to let a GPU thread check the local copy of *KState* in every k iterations of the device-side *while* loop in Figure 7, where, k is set to $r * L/l$, L is the length of the scheduling time slice, l is the estimated length of each iteration of the device *while* loop, and the factor r is a positive integer, which helps amortize the influence of the errors in the estimation of l by making several checks per time slice (we use 10 in our experiments). There could be various ways to make the estimation, through performance models, offline or online profiling, or program analysis. Our implementation uses simple online sampling, which, at runtime, measures the length of the first iteration of the *while* loop executed by the first thread of each thread block and uses the average as the estimated value of l.

Together, these optimizations reduce the overhead by 11.06% as detailed in the evaluation section.

Asynchronous Checking In the enhanced design, at a device/stream synchronization point, there is a *while* loop which continuously checks *KState* or *kernelQ* to relaunch the kernels if they are evicted. One potential issue is that if there is a lot of CPU work existing between the original kernel launch point and the synchronization point, the kernel could have got evicted long before the host thread reaches the *while* loop, and hence suffers a long delay in the relaunch. The situation is rare according to our observations. Still, to alleviate the potential consequence, the EffiSha compiler inserts a custom signal handler into the GPU program. When the runtime daemon sees a long delay (about 100 microsec) for *KState* to turn into RUNNING from TORUN, it sends a signal to the host thread. The signal handling function changes *KState* to RUNNING and launches the kernel.

6.3 Setting Priority

The *iPriority* of a GPU-stub has a default value. A programmer may use an EffiSha API call (*setIPriority*) to alter the priority. The call is mainly to pass the info to the compiler, which uses it as the second parameter of the inserted call of *initStub* to set the actual *iPriority* field of the GPU-stub at run time.

Similar to the priority control in Linux for CPU threads, only the superuser (root) may set a higher priority than the default. A caveat is that even though EffiSha runtime daemon respects the priority when scheduling kernels, the actual effect is also related with the priority of the host thread because (re)launches are through them. For instance, if when the EffiSha daemon changes the *KState* to TORUN, the host thread is in CPU waiting queue, the kernel cannot get relaunched until the host thread resumes running. A low-priority host thread could hence result in much (re)launch delay. To avoid it, a suggestion to superusers is to ensure that the host thread has a priority no lower than the kernel.

6.4 Memory Size and Dynamic Parallelism

As in many time-sharing systems, the evicted unfinished kernels and the next-to-run kernel may contend for the space of device memory. It is an issue only if the remaining memory cannot meet the requests of a GPU program. The solution is to let the compiler replace GPU memory allocation calls in the host code with a customized API. Through it, upon the failure of a memory allocation, the runtime scheduler puts that application into a waiting queue, and resumes it when an unfinished application has finished and hence released some space. If there are no unfinished applications, upon an allocation error, the API returns the error immediately as the shortage is due to the device limit.

Modern GPUs support dynamic parallelism (i.e., kernel launch inside a kernel). EffiSha gives no explicit treatment to dynamic parallelism, for two reasons. First, dynamic parallelism on GPU is rarely used in practice due to its large overhead (as much as 60X) [10, 11]. Second, a recent work [10] shows that dynamic parallelism in a kernel can be automatically replaced with thread reuse through *free launch* transformations, and yields large speedups. Therefore, for code with dynamic parallelism, one may apply *free launch* first to remove the dynamic parallelism and then apply Effisha.

7. Scheduling Policies

The support provided by EffiSha opens up the opportunities for the development of various preemptive schedulers for GPU. We demonstrate it by implementing the following two scheduling policies.

1) Static priority-based preemptive schedule. In this schedule, the EffiSha runtime daemon schedules kernels purely based on their initial priorities. The scheduler maintains a waiting queue for applications that are waiting to use GPU. The applications in the queue are ordered in their priorities. When the GPU becomes available, the scheduler always chooses the head of the queue (i.e., the one with the highest priority) to launch. If a new coming kernel has a higher priority than a currently running kernel, the scheduler immediately has the current kernel evicted and has the new kernel launched. Otherwise, the currently running kernel runs to completion.

2) Dynamic priority-based preemptive schedule. The schedule policy is similar to the CPU scheduling policy used by recent Linux systems. It maintains two waiting queues, one active queue and one inactive queue. This schedule uses dynamic priority. The dynamic priority of the GPU request from an application (including all of its streams) equals to its initial (static) priority when its kernels just arrive, but gets increased by one for every millisecond the request waits in the active queue. The increase is capped at 20. In each of the two queues, requests are ordered by their dynamic priorities. A new coming request is put into the active queue (positioned based on its priority).

Every time a request is scheduled to be met, it gets a time slice (or called *quota*). The length of the time slice is weighted by the priority; it is set to $(p+1)/2$ ms, where p is the priority of the kernel. At the expiration of its time quota, the GPU request goes into the inactive waiting queue and its dynamic priority is reset to its initial (static) priority. When a GPU becomes available, the scheduler chooses to meet the request at the head of the active waiting queue. When the active queue becomes empty, the two queues switch the role: The inactive queue becomes active, and the old active queue becomes the inactive queue. The dynamic priority can help prevent starvations facing the static priority-based scheduler.

8. Evaluation

We implement the EffiSha system based on Clang [12], a source-code analysis and transformation tool. We conduct a set of experiments, including comparisons to PKM [6], a prior kernel slicing-based software solution. We try to answer the following main questions:

1) *Preemption.* Can EffiSha indeed enable preemptions? How much delay does the restriction on preemption granularity cause for an eviction to take place?

2) *Priority.* Can an preemptive scheduler based on EffiSha indeed support the different priorities of different kernels? Can it help improve the overall responsiveness and throughput?

3) *Overhead.* How much time overhead does EffiSha add to GPU executions? What is the breakdown?

4) *Comparison.* How doe EffiSha compare with the state-of-art software approach?

8.1 Methodology

Our experiments use all the programs in the level-1 folder of the SHOC CUDA benchmark suite [9]. Table 1 lists the benchmarks.

We design an experimental setting to emulate the scenarios where the requests for GPU from different applications may have different priorities, and some requests may arrive while the GPU is serving for other applications. In our experimental setting, the 11 benchmarks issue their requests

Table 1. Benchmarks

Benchmark	Description
BFS	Breadth-first Search in a graph
FFT	1D Fast Fourier Transform
MD	Molecular dynamics
MD5Hash	MD5 Hash
NeuralNet	A Neural Network
Reduction	Summation of numbers
Scan	An exclusive parallel prefix sum of floating data
Sort	A radix sort on unsigned integer key-value pairs
Spmv	Sparse matrix-dense vector multiplication
Stencil2D	2D 9-point stencil computation
Triad	A version of the stream triad

Table 2. Kernel lengths and priorities.

Benchmark	Standalone time (ms)	Priorities random	group	SJF
NeuralNet	14.25	2	2	1
Sort	5.46	17	2	4
Reduction	2.06	17	2	7
MD5Hash	3.29	22	5	6
MD	13.8	22	5	2
Scan	1.41	7	5	8
Triad	1.22	3	8	9
Stencil2D	28.4	20	8	0
FFT	1.17	24	11	10
Spmv	4.57	7	11	5
BFS	5.99	1	11	3

for GPU (i.e., launching a GPU kernel) in turns. Another application issues the request 3ms after the previous application issues its request. The launch order is chosen arbitrarily, as shown as the top-down order in Table 2. (The priority settings are explained later.)

We run the experiments on a machine equipped with an NVIDIA K40m GPU running CUDA 7 and an Intel Xeon E5-2697 processor. Without noting otherwise, in the experiments, the baseline of the comparisons is always the executions of the original benchmarks without any modifications[6].

8.2 Support for Preemptions and Priorities

We run the 11 benchmarks in all the settings under the preemptive schedule. The programs all run correctly, and kernels get evicted as expected by the scheduling policies.

We further conduct the following experiment to validate the appropriate support of priorities by EffiSha-based preemptive scheduling. We launch the 11 benchmarks for 1000 times and measure the total number of evictions for each kernel. Every launch is assigned with a random priority from 1 to 9 (the higher the more important the kernel is). Initially, all the kernels are launched at the same time. A kernel gets invoked again a certain time period (which is called "wait_time") after the finish of its previous invocation. We change the wait_time from 1ms to 64ms. We use the static-priority–based preemptive scheduling policy for this experiment; the fixed priority makes it easy to analyze the results.

[6] We observed that when multiple kernels request a GPU, the K40m GPU, by default, periodically switch its tenants. The details are not disclosed officially; our observation is that it uses an SM-draining mechanism. It offers no software controllability.

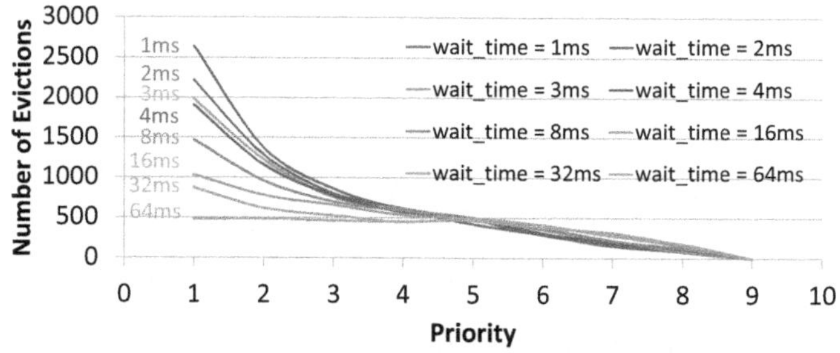

Figure 9. Total Number of Evictions for Different Priorities

Figure 9 shows the number of evictions that happen on the kernels at each level of priority. Because every launch gets a random priority, the total lengths of the kernels at the various priorities are similar. However, the kernels at lower priorities gets clearly more evictions than those at higher priorities. When "wait_time" is 1ms, the launches of kernels are dense, and there are a large number of evictions for kernels at the low priorities. As "wait_time" increases, fewer conflicts happen among the requests for GPU, and the numbers of evictions drop. For a given "wait_time", the higher the priority of a kernel is, the less frequently the kernel gets evicted. These observations are consistent with the objective of the priority-based scheduling policy, confirming the feasibility enabled by EffiSha for scheduling GPU kernels to accommodate kernels of different priorities. Extra evidences are shown in the experiments on the dynamic priority-based scheduling (which will be presented later in Section 8.4).

8.3 Eviction Delay

Since the preemption happens at the end of a block-task, there could be some delay between the setting of the eviction flag and the exit of the kernel from GPU. We call it *eviction delay*. The delay indicates how quickly the running kernel can act on an eviction request. This part reports the eviction delay of each kernel observed in our experiments. To measure it, we keep each kernel doing the same work on GPU as it does in its normal runs, but repeatedly. At some moment, the eviction flag is set to true. An inserted cudaStreamSynchronize() call in the host code makes the host thread wait for the kernel to exit to measure the latency. Figure 10 shows the observed eviction delay of each kernel. *MD* has the longest eviction delay (0.4ms) because of its relatively large block-task, while *BFS, FFT, NeuralNet* and *Triad* have delays less than 0.015ms. The average delay is about 0.08ms, much smaller than the typical length of a context switch period in Linux.

Besides eviction delay, there are some other overhead in the preemptive executions, including relaunch overhead, state checking overhead, and so on. We next report the experimental results of EffiSha-enabled priority-based preemptive scheduling, which shows that these delays do not prevent the scheduler from working profitably. And Section 8.5 analyzes the delays in detail.

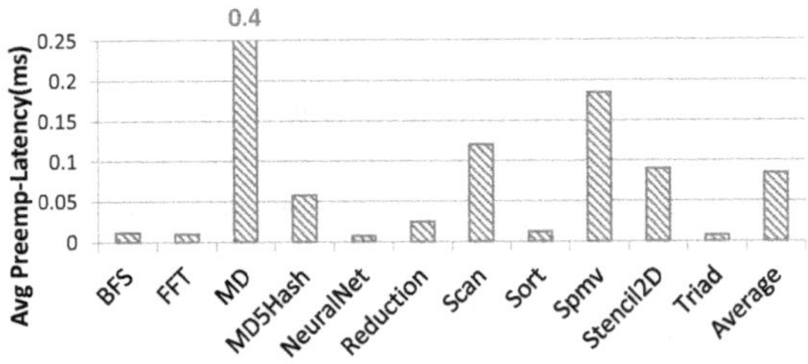

Figure 10. Eviction delay of each kernel.

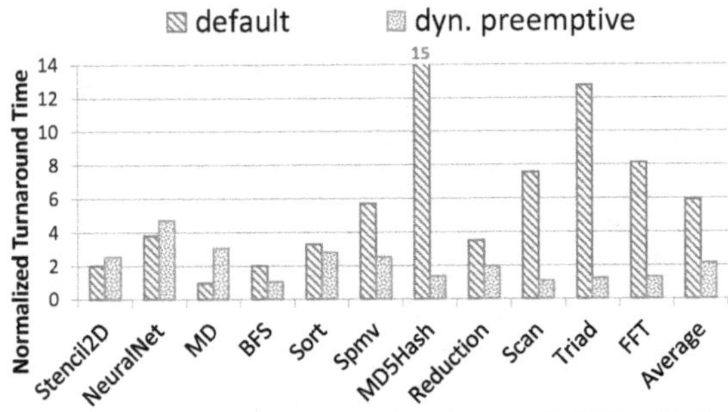

Figure 11. Normalized turnaround time; SJF priorities are used. The benchmarks are put in an increasing order of their priorities (from left to right).

8.4 Benefits from Preemptive Scheduling

The efficient preemption enabled by EffiSha opens the opportunities for the design of various preemptive schedules for GPU kernels. In this part, we use the aforementioned dynamic priority-based preemptive schedule as an example to illustrate the substantial potential benefits of such schedules. The reported timing results include all runtime overhead.

Metrics Following common practice [13], we use two metrics to characterize co-run performance:

1) Average normalized turnaround times (ANTT). NTT is defined as follows [13]:

$$NTT_i = T_i^{MP}/T_i^{SP},$$

where, T_i^{SP} and T_i^{MP} are the execution time of a kernel in its standalone run and its co-run. NTT is usually greater than 1, the smaller the more responsive the kernel is. ANTT is the average of NTTs of a set of programs.

2) System overall throughput (STP). STP is defined as follows. STP is from 0 to n (the number of programs); the larger, the better.

$$STP = \sum_{i=1}^{n} T_i^{SP}/T_i^{MP}.$$

Results In our experiments with the scheduling, we launch the benchmarks one by one by following the scheme described in Section 8.1. We use three settings of priority assignments. The first is to assign priorities to the kernels in a shortest job first (SJF) manner, in which, the priority of a kernel is based on its length (i.e., "standalone time" in Table 2); the longer, the lower, as shown in the "SJF" column in Table 2.

It is well known that an SJF schedule minimizes the total waiting time of a set of jobs, giving superior responsiveness [14]. However, without priority-based preemption support, the default scheduler on GPU fails in harvesting the benefits. As the "default" bars in Figure 11 show, the NTT of the kernels range from 2 to 15, and the high-priority kernels (towards the right end in the graph) tend to suffer the largest NTTs. It is because they have the shortest lengths (i.e., smallest T^{SP}) and hence their NTTs are more sensitive to waiting times. The EffiSha-enabled preemptive scheduler substantially reduces the NTTs for most of the kernels. As the "preemptive" bars in Figure 11 show, the NTTs are lowered to below two for most of the kernels. The reduction is especially significant for the high-priority kernels which receive a high priority treatment in the preemptive scheduler. For instance, when *FFT* requests GPU, the preemptive scheduler immediately raises up the preemption flag and the currently running kernel gets evicted quickly; the *FFT* kernel gets to run and finish on GPU soon after its request is issued. Its NTT is lowered from 8.1 to 1.15. The NTTs of some kernels on the left end in Figure 11 increase slightly, for the low priority treatment they get in the scheduling.

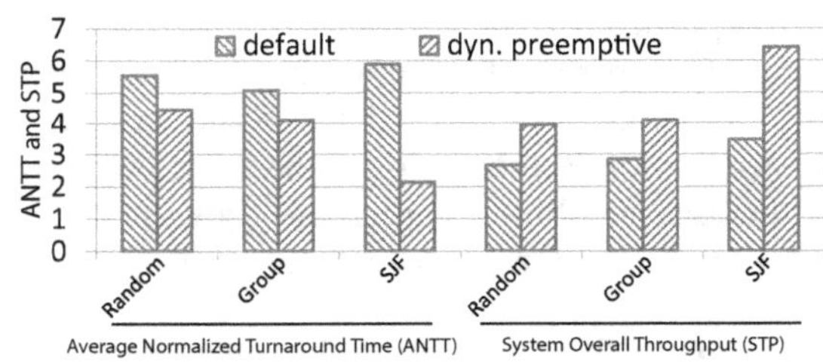

Figure 12. Average normalized turnaround time (ANTT) and overall system throughput (STP) under three priority settings.

On average, the preemptive scheduler cuts the ANTT by 65% (from 6 to 2), and improves the overall throughput by a factor of 1.8 (from 3.5 to 6.3), as reported in Figure 12. Figure 12 also reports the overall results under two other settings of priorities. The "random" scheme assigns an application with a random integer between 0 and 30 as the priority of its kernel. The "group" scheme assigns adjacent two or three applications with the same priority. The priorities of the kernels in both settings are shown in Table 2. Although the benefits of the preemptive scheduler in these settings are not as large as in the "SJF" setting, the improvements are still substantial: 18% ANTT reduction and 1.35X throughput enhancement in the "random" case, and 24% and 1.42X in the "group" case.

8.5 Overhead and Comparison

EffiSha may introduce several sources of overhead. We categorize the overhead into two classes:

1) Transformation overhead: Overhead incurred by code changes, including the usage of persistent kernels, the creation of the GPU proxy, the checks on the eviction flag, and other changes and their effects that the EffiSha compiler makes to the host code and kernels.

2) Scheduling overhead: Overhead incurred by preemptive scheduling. It mainly includes the time taken by kernel evictions and resumptions, and their side effects on the runtime executions.

We measure the overhead of each class respectively.

Transformation Overhead Transformation overhead refers to the overhead brought by the transformed code and the introduced runtime daemon and proxy. For this measurement, we run each of the transformed benchmarks alone; during the execution, the daemon (and proxy) works as normal, except that there is no kernel evictions since no other kernels request the GPU. We compare the execution time with that of the original unmodified kernels to compute the overhead.

Figure 13 reports the transformation overhead in three cases: the basic EffiSha design, the design with the use of proxy, the design with the use of proxy and all other optimizations that have been mentioned in Section 6. The first group of bars in Figure 13 show the overhead of the basic EffiSha implementation. The overhead differs for different applications, due to the differences in their memory access intensities and the length of each block-task. But overall, the overhead is large (up to 97X). The overhead is primarily due to the fact that every GPU thread has to frequently poll the state variable on the host memory through the PCIe bus.

The second group of bars in Figure 13 show that the usage of proxy cuts the overhead dramatically. The average overhead reduces from 10X to 15%. However, for *stencil2D*, the overhead is still over 100%. The reason is that every block-task in that kernel is short. Since the polling of the flag is done in every block-task, the overhead is large. The third group of bars indicate that the adaptive polling method helps address the problem. The overhead of *stencil2D* is reduced to 8%, and the average overhead becomes 4%. We note that the host-side overhead due to the code transformations is negligible.

Compare with Kernel Slicing-based Methods Before EffiSha, kernel slicing is the main approach designed for increasing GPU kernel schedule flexibility. PKM [6] is a representative of the approach. PKM partitions an original kernel into many smaller kernels, with each processing a predefined number (K) of the block-tasks in the original kernel. Preemptions are not supported in PKM, but the reduced size of a kernel could help reduce the time that a kernel needs to wait before getting access to GPU.

A challenge to PKM is to decide the appropriate value of K. A large K leads to slow response to other kernel launch requests, while a small K reduces the thread-level parallelism and incurs additional kernel launching overhead. We measure the overhead of PKM under a spectrum of responsiveness requirements (the objective kernel launch delay ranges from 1ms to 0.0625ms) by tuning K till meeting each level of responsiveness requirement. Figure 14 reports the observed PKM execution overhead. As the objective delay decreases, the overhead of PKM becomes increasingly significant (average 45%, up to 98%, slowdown for 0.0625ms delay requirement).

To compare the overhead of PKM with EffiSha, we tune the K value of PKM such that the launch delay for each kernel is the same as that in EffiSha. The launch delay of EffiSha for each kernel is showed in Figure 10. The last bar in Figure 13 shows the overhead of PKM. As we can see, the average overhead in EffiSha with all optimizations is 4% (up to 8% for *Triad*). For PKM, the average overhead is 58% (up to 140%). Compared to PKM, EffiSha has a much lower overhead. Moreover, EffiSha does not require fine-tuning to determine the appropriate K value as PKM does.

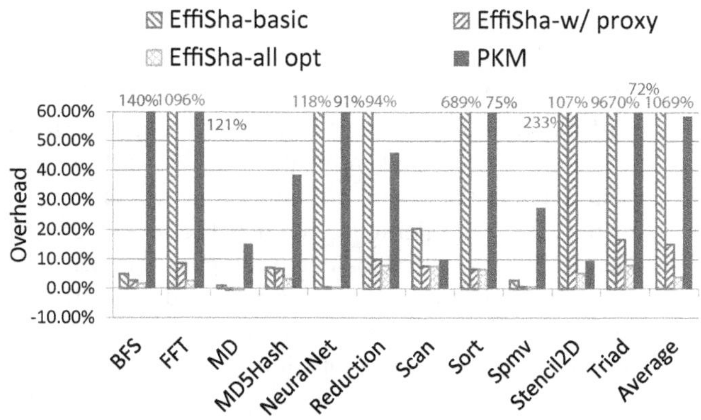

Figure 13. Transformation overhead.

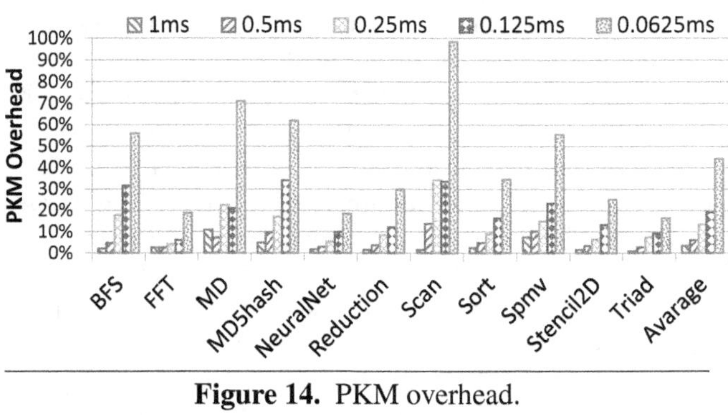

Figure 14. PKM overhead.

Scheduling Overhead We measure scheduling overhead as follows. We launch the original unmodified benchmarks one by one in the scheme mentioned in Section 8 without using EffiSha, and record the time spanning (denoted as T)

from the start of the first kernel to the end of the last kernel. (Notice that because the time between the launches of two adjacent kernels is short, at any moment during the period of T, the GPU is working on some kernel.) We then redo the measurement but with each of the two preemptive schedulers deployed. Let T' be the measured time got in one of the experiments. The scheduling overhead in that experiment is computed as $(T' - T)/T$.

Figure 15 reports the overhead of the two preemptive schedulers under each of the three priority settings. The "dynamic priority" scheduler has overhead larger than the "static priority" scheduler has for its extra complexities. But all the overhead is less than 5%.

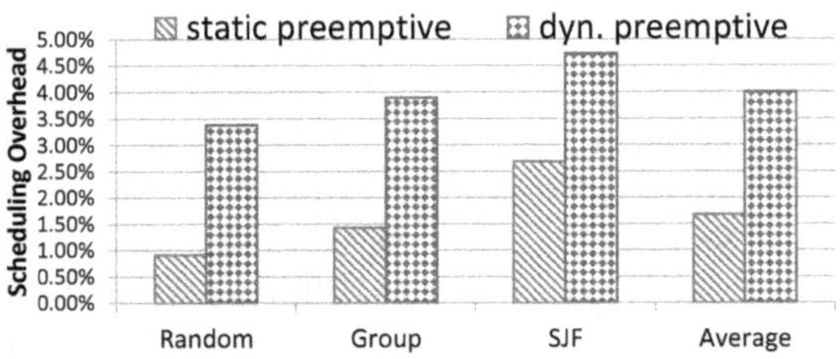

Figure 15. Scheduling overhead.

9. Discussions

To use EffiSha or a scheduler based on it, there is no need to change either the hardware or the OS. One just need to create an alias in the system to redirect the invocations of the default GPU compiler to a customized script, which first invokes the EffiSha source-to-source compiler and then calls the default GPU compiler on the transformed code. To add preemption support to a GPU library, the library developers would need to do the recompilation. An alternative is to implement the EffiSha code transformations at the assembly (PTX) level, which could avoid the need for the source code of a GPU program or library.

Upon a preemption, the memory data of the preempted kernel remain on the GPU memory. There is a possibility that the next kernel on GPU could observe some leftover data on the memory on GPUs that has no virtual memory support. But it is important to note that as observed in prior work [15], such security issue exists even on the default GPU executions. Upon the finish of a default GPU kernel execution, the data typically remain on the GPU memory before the parent CPU process terminates and are hence subject to the same potential issues. The virtual memory support on latest GPUs could help alleviate the security concern.

The sharing of the memory space among multiple GPU applications could cause potential space contention, causing difficulties to some large-footprint kernels to run. Swapping some data of an evicted kernel to the host memory could be an option to alleviate the problem. Extensions of portable data placement optimizers (e.g., PORPLE [16–18]) to both host and device memory could facilitate the process. It is left to study in the future.

10. Related Work

With GPUs becoming an important computing resource, there is a strong interest in making GPUs first-class resource to be managed by operating systems (OS). Gdev [19] integrates the GPU runtime support into the OS. It allows GPU memory to be shared among multiple GPU contexts and virtualizes the GPU into multiple logic ones. GPUfs [20] enables GPUs with the file I/O support. It allows the GPU code to access file systems directly through high-level APIs. GPUvm [1] investigates full- and para-virtualization for GPU virtualization. Wang and others [21] proposed OS-level management for GPU memory rather than letting it managed by applications. Chen and others have recently studied runtime QoS control in data centers equipped with accelerators [22]. None of these studies have considered kernel preemptions.

Some hardware schemes have been proposed to reduce preemption overhead on GPU. Tanasic and others [2] have proposed a hardware-based SM-draining scheme. Park and others [4] have proposed to select different hardware-based preemption techniques based on the progress of a thread block. Lin and others have proposed the use of compression to reduce kernel switch overhead [5]. Wang and others [23] have designed simultaneous multi-kernel (SMK), a hardware method to support incremental kernel evictions. Although these schemes have shown high promises, they require new hardware support. In a certain sense, our solution could be regarded as a software-based approach to materialize SM-draining efficiently. Without hardware extensions needed, it enables preemption on existing GPU devices, and meanwhile, offers software with the rich controllabilities of kernel preemptive scheduling.

Existing proposals of software schemes to enable preemption is to use kernel slicing as mentioned in the introduction. The scheme has been studied in real-time community, represented by the recent proposals of GPES [7], and PKM [6]. A challenge in this scheme is to select the appropriate slice size. As Section 8 has shown, there is an inherent overhead-responsiveness dilemma. For real-time systems where the set of workload is predefined, one could use profiling to find slice sizes suitable to these applications. But For general-purpose systems (e.g., data centers and cloud) with a large, dynamically changing set of workload, the approach is difficult to use. In comparison, our solution requires no kernel slicing and hence is not subject to such a dilemma. Moreover, with Kernel Slicing, the preemption boundaries are still at kernel boundaries; but for EffiSha, the preemption boundaries are at the boundary of a basic block. It is designed to fit the needs of general-purpose systems.

The problem EffiSha addresses is to enable flexible time sharing of GPU among different applications. Orthogonal to it is the support of spatial sharing of GPU. The problem there is how to maximize the GPU efficiency by better controlling the resource usage of each kernel when multiple GPU kernels run at the same time on one GPU. Techniques, such as Elastic Kernel [24] and Kernelet-based co-scheduling [25]. A recent work proposes to partition SMs among kernels for efficient resource usage through SM-centric program transformations [26]. There are also some hardware proposals for a similar purpose [27]. Spatial sharing and time sharing are orthogonal in the sense that both are needed to make GPU better serve for a multi-user shared environment.

Another layer of scheduling is about the tasks within a GPU kernel or between CPU and GPU [8, 28–32]. They are complementary to the scheduling of different kernels on GPU.

Persistent threads have been used in numerous previous studies. For instance, Chen and Shen have used it in *Free Launch* [10] to mitigate the large overhead of dynamic kernel launches. Effisha leverages persistent threads to gain the controllability of GPU task scheduling.

11. Conclusion

In this work, through EffiSha, we demonstrate a software solution that enables preemptive scheduling for GPU without the need for hardware extensions. Experiments show that EffiSha is able to support kernel preemptions with less than 4% overhead on average. It opens up the opportunities for priority-based preemptive management of kernels on existing GPUs. Enabled by EffiSha, a dynamic priority-based preemptive scheduler demonstrates significant potential for reducing the average turnaround time (18-65% on average) and improving the overall system throughput of program executions (1.35X-1.8X on average) that time-share a GPU.

We thank the anonymous reviewers for the helpful comments. This material is based upon work supported by DOE Early Career Award (DE-SC0013700), the National Science Foundation (NSF) under Grant No. 1455404, 1455733 (CAREER), 1525609, 1216569, and 1618509, and Google Faculty Award. Any opinions, findings, and conclusions or recommendations expressed in this material are those of the authors and do not necessarily reflect the views of DOE, NSF, or Google.

References

[1] Y. Suzuki, S. Kato, H. Yamada, and K. Kono, "Gpuvm: Why not virtualizing gpus at the hypervisor?," in *Proceedings of the 2014 USENIX Conference on USENIX Annual Technical Conference*, USENIX ATC'14, (Berkeley, CA, USA), pp. 109–120, USENIX Association, 2014.

[2] I. Tanasic, I. Gelado, J. Cabezas, A. Ramirez, N. Navarro, and M. Valero, "Enabling preemptive multiprogramming on gpus," in *Proceeding of the 41st annual international symposium on Computer architecuture*, pp. 193–204, IEEE Press, 2014.

[3] K. Menychtas, K. Shen, and M. L. Scott, "Disengaged scheduling for fair, protected access to computational accelerators," in *Proceedings of the international conference on Architectural support for programming languages and operating systems*, 2014.

[4] J. J. K. Park, Y. Park, and S. Mahlke, "Chimera: Collaborative preemption for multitasking on a shared gpu," in *Proceedings of the Twentieth International Conference on Architectural Support for Programming Languages and Operating Systems*, pp. 593–606, ACM, 2015.

[5] Z. Lin, L. Nyland, and H. Zhou, "Enabling efficient preemption for simt architectures with lightweight context switching," in *the International Conference on High Performance Computing, Networking, Storage, and Analysis (SC16)*, 2016.

[6] C. Basaran and K. Kang, "Supporting preemptive task executions and memory copies in gpgpus," in *Proceedings of the 24th Euromicro Conference on Real-Time Systems*, 2012.

[7] H. Zhou, G. Tong, and C. Liu, "Gpes: a preemptive execution system for gpgpu computing," in *Real-Time and Embedded Technology and Applications Symposium (RTAS), 2015 IEEE*, pp. 87–97, IEEE, 2015.

[8] K. Gupta, J. A. Stuart, and J. D. Owens, "A study of persistent threads style gpu programming for gpgpu workload s," in *Innovative Parallel Computing*, 2012.

[9] A. Danalis, G. Marin, C. McCurdy, J. S. Meredith, P. C. Roth, K. Spafford, V. Tipparaju, and J. S. Vetter, "The scalable heterogeneous computing (shoc) benchmark suite," in *GPGPU*, 2010.

[10] G. Chen and X. Shen, "Free launch: Optimizing gpu dynamic kernel launches through thread reuse," in *Proceedings of the Annual IEEE/ACM International Symposium on Microarchitecture*, 2015.

[11] Y. Yang and H. Zhou, "Cuda-np: Realizing nested thread-level parallelism in gpgpu applications," *SIGPLAN Not.*, vol. 49, pp. 93–106, Feb. 2014.

[12] "http://clang.llvm.org."

[13] S. Eyerman and L. Eeckhout, "System-level performance metrics for multiprogram workloads," *IEEE micro*, no. 3, pp. 42–53, 2008.

[14] A. S. Tanenbaum, *Modern Operating Systems*. Pearson, 2007.

[15] R. D. Pietro, F. Lombardi, and A. Villani, "Cuda leaks: A detailed hack for cuda and a (partial) fix," *ACM Trans. Embed. Comput. Syst.*, vol. 15, pp. 15:1–15:25, Jan. 2016.

[16] G. Chen, B. Wu, D. Li, and X. Shen, "Porple: An extensible optimizer for portable data placement on gpu," in *Proceedings of the 47th International Conference on Microarchitecture*, 2014.

[17] G. Chen and X. Shen, "Coherence-free multiview: Enabling reference-discerning data placement on gpu," in *Proceedings of the 2016 International Conference on Supercomputing*, ICS '16, (New York, NY, USA), pp. 14:1–14:13, ACM, 2016.

[18] G. Chen, X. Shen, B. Wu, and D. Li, "Optimizing data placement on gpu memory: A portable approach," *IEEE Transactions on Computers*, vol. PP, no. 99, 2016.

[19] S. Kato, M. McThrow, C. Maltzahn, and S. Brandt, "Gdev: First-class gpu resource management in the operating system," in *Proceedings of the 2012 USENIX Conference on Annual Technical Conference*, USENIX ATC'12, (Berkeley, CA, USA), pp. 37–37, USENIX Association, 2012.

[20] M. Silberstein, B. Ford, I. Keidar, and E. Witchel, "Gpufs: Integrating a file system with gpus," *ACM Trans. Comput. Syst.*, vol. 32, pp. 1:1–1:31, Feb. 2014.

[21] K. Wang, X. Ding, R. Lee, S. Kato, and X. Zhang, "Gdm: Device memory management for gpgpu computing," in *The 2014 ACM International Conference on Measurement and Modeling of Computer Systems*, SIGMETRICS '14, (New York, NY, USA), pp. 533–545, ACM, 2014.

[22] Q. Chen, H. Yang, J. Mars, and L. Tang, "Baymax: Qos awareness and increased utilization for non-preemptive accelerators in warehouse scale computers," in *International Conference on Architectural Support for Programming Languages and Operating Systems*, 2016.

[23] Z. Wang, J. Yang, R. Melhem, B. Childers, Y. Zhang, and M. Guo, "Simultaneous multikernel gpu: Multi-tasking throughput processors via fine-grained sharing," in *Proceedings of the 2016 IEEE International Symposium on High Performance Computer Architecture*, HPCA'16, 2016.

[24] S. Pai, M. J. Thazhuthaveetil, and R. Govindarajan, "Improving GPGPU Concurrency with Elastic Kernels," in *International Conference on Architectural Support for Programming Languages and Operating Systems*, 2013.

[25] J. Zhong and B. He, "Kernelet: High-throughput gpu kernel executions with dynamic slicing and scheduling," *CoRR*, vol. abs/1303.5164, 2013.

[26] B. Wu, G. Chen, D. Li, X. Shen, and J. Vetter, "Enabling and exploiting flexible task assignment on gpu through sm-centric program transformations," in *Proceedings of the International Conference on Supercomputing*, ICS '15, 2015.

[27] J. T. Adriaens, K. Compton, N. S. Kim, and M. J. Schulte, "The Case for GPGPU Spatial Multitasking," in *International Symposium on High Performance Computer Architecture*, 2012.

[28] L. Chen, O. Villa, S. Krishnamoorthy, and G. Gao, "Dynamic load balancing on single-and multi-gpu systems," in *IPDPS*, 2010.

[29] S. Xiao and W. chun Feng, "Inter-block gpu communication via fast barrier synchronization," in *IPDPS*, 2010.

[30] T. Aila and S. Laine, "Understanding the efficiency of ray traversal on gpus," in *Proceedings of the Conference on High Performance Graphics 2009*, HPG '09, 2009.

[31] S. Tzeng, A. Patney, and J. D. Owens, "Task management for irregular-parallel workloads on the gpu," in *Proceedings of the Conference on High Performance Graphics*, 2010.

[32] M. Steinberger, M. Kenzel, P. Boechat, B. Kerbl, M. D. okter, and D. Schmalstieg, "Whippletree: Task-based scheduling of dynamic workloads on the gpu," *ACM Transactions on Computer Systems*, vol. 33, no. 6, 2014.

Layout Lock: A Scalable Locking Paradigm for Concurrent Data Layout Modifications *

Nachshon Cohen
Technion
nachshonc@gmail.com

Arie Tal
Technion
arietal@cs.technion.ac.il

Erez Petrank
Technion
erez@cs.technion.ac.il

Abstract

Data-structures can benefit from dynamic data layout modifications when the size or the shape of the data structure changes during the execution, or when different phases in the program execute different workloads. However, in a modern multi-core environment, layout modifications involve costly synchronization overhead. In this paper we propose a novel layout lock that incurs a negligible overhead for reads and a small overhead for updates of the data structure. We then demonstrate the benefits of layout changes and also the advantages of the layout lock as its supporting synchronization mechanism for two data structures. In particular, we propose a concurrent binary search tree, and a concurrent array set, that benefit from concurrent layout modifications using the proposed layout lock. Experience demonstrates performance advantages and integration simplicity.

Keywords Synchronization, Concurrent Data Structures, Data Layout

1. Introduction and Motivation

With the proliferation of multi-core machines, the need for high performance concurrent data structures is becoming acute. Much work has studied avenues for making concurrent data structures more performant and responsive. But some techniques for improving data structure performance are still limited to sequential data structures as their complexity in a concurrent setting seems too high. One such technique is *layout modification* (Wael et al. 2015; Wael 2015; Xu 2013; Sung et al. 2010; Li et al. 2013), which allows modifying the underlying structure of the data to achieve better performance when program behaviors evolve during the execution. Such layout changes are used in various scenarios, e.g., by compilers when parts of the program make limited use of data (Kennedy and Ziarek 2015; Kandemir et al. 1999a; Mannarswamy 2009; Ding and Kennedy 1999), improving data locality and reducing false sharing through data type layout modification (Chakrabarti and Chow 2008; Raman et al. 2007; Eizenberg et al. 2016) or in order to improve matrix multiplication performance (Kandemir et al. 1999b; Lu et al. 2004), etc. But all these uses are limited in existing concurrent data structure designs due to the seemly high complexity of designing a concurrent layout modification and the cost of synchronization.

In this paper we propose a paradigm and a synchronization mechanism for layout modification in a concurrent setting. The new synchronization paradigm (and its supporting mechanism) is called *layout lock* and it enables layout changes during concurrent execution. The paradigm involves three types of operations executed on the data structures: *read*, *write*, and *layout change*. Readers perform read-only accesses; writers may read and update data; and layout changers can modify the internal representation of the data.

Adding a layout lock to an existing data structure implementation requires some care. First, the read operation is executed optimistically, and so a mechanism for handling failed reads must be devised. Second, care must be taken by the layout changer to ensure that (failing) optimistic reads do not reach a bad execution state (e.g., segmentation fault). Finally, in order to obtain performance advantages from layout modifications, one must design data structures for which layout modifications indeed improve performance. In essence, one needs to implement "Just-in-Time" data structures, that can dynamically adapt to usage patterns (Wael 2015; Xu 2013). Using the proposed layout lock typically requires the addition of the appropriate lock acquisitions and releases before and after each of the operations (i.e., read, write, and layout change), and the handling of failed optimistic reads. We discovered that, for data structures that can deal with optimistic reads, adding the layout lock was simple and fast.

Based on the layout lock paradigm, we developed an efficient concurrent binary tree that outperforms known concur-

*This work was supported by the Israel Science Foundation grant No. 274/14 and by the Nechemya LevZion VATAT scholarship.

PPoPP '17, February 04-08, 2017, Austin, TX, USA

DOI: http://dx.doi.org/10.1145/3018743.3018753

rent tree implementations on large trees. Our key observation is that nodes in the high levels of a tree (closer to the root) change infrequently compared to nodes closer to the leaves. Based on this observation, the proposed tree packs sets of neighboring nodes in high levels of the tree into small arrays. The packing improves locality and search speed. Interestingly, the design process was surprisingly simple. We first designed and built this efficient tree in the (simpler) sequential setting, and then we added the layout lock mechanism in almost no time to allow concurrent layout change. This yielded a highly scalable and efficient concurrent tree.

In addition, we also study an array-based implementation of a concurrent set, where only part of the set is sorted. Concurrent layout changes allow occasionally merging the unsorted part into the sorted part, thus speeding up searches. The resulting set is extremely simple to design (using the layout lock) yet provides excellent scalability and performance for small to medium sized sets.

The layout lock paradigm focuses on the problem of synchronizing layout changes with other accesses (i.e, with reads and writes). Synchronization between readers and writers is not the main focus of this paper. We assume that readers and writers are synchronized by some state-of-the-art technique and that readers are extremely fast, so that the overhead of additional synchronization makes a difference.

The layout lock implementation that we propose incurs a negligible overhead on reads of the data structure and a small overhead on updates of the data structure. It assumes that typical uses of the layout lock execute layout modifications infrequently (or even rarely); they execute writes more frequently; and they execute reads most frequently. We believe this behavior is typical in practice, and it holds in the examples presented in this paper.

A possible naïve implementation for a layout lock is to use a reader-writer lock (Mellor-Crummey and Scott 1991; Hsieh and Weihl 1992; Lev et al. 2009; Calciu et al. 2013) to coordinate layout changes. In this setting, a layout changer plays the writer role and all other accesses to the data structures (either reads or writes) play the role of the reader in the reader-writer lock. The drawback of this solution is the cost of reading the data structure. Any thread that reads the data structure needs to announce that it is doing so, and typically also execute a memory fence to make sure that other threads are aware of its announcement. Note that this overhead is imposed even when no layout change actually occurs.

Recently, the idea of *StampedLock* (Lea and JSR-166) was proposed and incorporated into Java 8. The StampedLock is conceptually based on the *SeqLock* (Lameter 2005; Boehm 2012) used in the Linux kernel. It allows readers to proceed optimistically by letting them record a stamp (sequence number) at the beginning of the operation and compare the recorded stamp to the current stamp at the end. This lets readers run without any (hardware) memory fence.

Our proposed layout lock implementation also offers optimistic reads, but further optimizes their performance for the case of rare layout changes and frequent reads by multiple reader threads. Reads of the data structure, which are typically most frequent, are executed with no interference, except for checking a local flag (after the read) to verify that the read value is correct. This reduces the overhead of synchronization to a negligible cost.

For writers we allow a slightly higher overhead, to make sure they do not interfere with a layout change. Yet the overhead is still small and the write operations are scalable.

Organization: The rest of the paper is organized as follows. We present the layout lock, its interface, and implementation in Section 2. In Section 3 we present two data structures that can benefit from layout modifications. We present performance evaluations of these data structures with the layout lock in Section 4. Related work is discussed in Section 5, and we conclude in Section 6.

2. Layout Lock

The layout lock paradigm and mechanism is a synchronization methodology for allowing layout modifications concurrently with reads and writes of a data structure. A layout change is a significant modification to the data representation, such as moving the data (content) to a different location in memory, or changing the way the data is organized.

2.1 Paradigm and Interface

The layout lock interface is similar to Java's StampedLock (Lea and JSR-166) interface and bears a resemblance to the well-known reader-writer lock (Mellor-Crummey and Scott 1991; Hsieh and Weihl 1992; Lev et al. 2009; Calciu et al. 2013). That is, the lock distinguishes between the different types of participants by using separate access methods for each type of participant. The standard reader-writer lock recognizes two types of participants: a *reader* and a *writer*. The layout lock interface acknowledges three types of participants: a *reader*, a *writer* and a *layout changer*, and provides a different set of access methods for each type accordingly. Each of the participants may acquire or release the lock appropriately, yet, the layout lock interface diverges from the standard locking interface for the readers. In particular, releasing a read lock returns a boolean value that indicates the validity of the data that was read. If the data is invalid, the read operation may be retried.

A writer operation may contain several accesses to the data structure, some of them can be reads and other can be updates of the data structure. A reader operation may execute several actual read accesses to the data structure, but it does not update the data structure. A reader operation should have no effect visible by other threads.

Semantically, the layout lock provides guarantees that are similar to a read-write lock, where the layout changer plays the role of the writer (of the read-write lock) and the readers and writers play the role of the reader (of the read-write lock). Specifically, it is guaranteed that read and write operations do not occur concurrently with a layout change and that two layout change operations do not overlap. The writer operation appears to happen either before or after the layout change takes place. For readers, it is guaranteed that a reader operation succeeds (i.e., returns TRUE) only if the read operation can be viewed as happening before or after a layout change, but not concurrently.

Combining the layout lock with other synchronization methods (e.g. between readers and writers) while avoiding deadlocks, requires keeping a strict order between the synchronization mechanisms. For example, always start by acquiring the layout lock and then acquiring the other lock required for synchronization. In the rest of this paper we ignore any additional synchronization and focus only on the synchronization mechanism for enabling a layout change.

The standard way for readers to use the layout lock appears in Listing 1. The term *llock* in the code stands for an instance of a layout lock used to protect the data structure.

Listing 1. Reader

```
start:
llock.startRead();
//execute reader code
if(!llock.endRead()) {
    goto start;
}
```

The interface for writers and layout changers is similar to a standard lock. Acquiring or releasing the layout lock in write mode or layout change mode cannot fail. The code is presented in Listing 2 and Listing 3.

Listing 2. Writer

```
llock.startWrite();
//execute writer code
llock.endWrite();
```

Listing 3. Layout changer

```
llock.startLayoutChange();
//execute layout changer code
llock.endLayoutChange();
```

2.2 Implementation

The proposed implementation starts from any standard (efficient) reader-writer lock, which coordinates the accesses of writers and layout changers. Denote this lock by RW-LOCK. We then add a specialized mechanism to synchronize the readers with the layout changers and facilitate a fast path for them. More specifically, a layout-changer acquires the writer lock of the RW-LOCK, and releases it upon completing the layout change. A writer acquires the reader lock of the RW-LOCK and it releases it after completing the operation. This ensures that writers do not conflict with layout changers and that two different layout changers do not execute simultaneously. It remains to describe the synchronization of readers with the layout change operation. To this end, we assume that it is possible to (quickly) check whether the RW-LOCK is being held in the write mode, which in our case means an active layout change. Such a check can be easily added to reader-writer locks that are available in the literature.

The main idea for obtaining fast readers execution is the use of optimistic execution. A reader executes its reads regardless of whether a layout lock is being held or not. In other words, the *startRead* implementation is empty. When the lock is released, the reader checks whether a layout change operation may have overlapped the reader execution. If it did, the *endRead* method returns FALSE signaling that the read value may be stale. However, if it can be determined that no part of the reader operation overlapped with a layout change, then the *endRead* returns TRUE.

To check whether a layout change might have overlapped with a read operation, a per-thread flag, denoted the *dirty flag*, is maintained. The dirty flag signifies a possible concurrent layout change execution. A reader on the fast path execution simply reads the dirty flag during *endRead* and if the dirty flag is off, the reader completes its execution successfully. On the other hand, if the dirty flag is set, then the reader clears the dirty flag. It then checks whether a layout change is still active and if yes it sets again its dirty flag to make sure that it does not return TRUE until the layout change completes. Finally, the reader returns FALSE to signify that the data that was read may be invalid and indicate that the read operation should be retried. The reader can tell that a layout change has completed by checking that the reader-writer lock is no longer being held in the writer mode.

This implementation relies on the reader executing a memory fence when clearing its dirty flag, before checking whether a layout change is currently active. The strict order is required to ensure that the dirty flag is kept TRUE during a layout change. Therefore, if a reader resets its dirty flag and observes an active layout change, it sets the dirty flag back to TRUE. Without the memory fence, the following race is possible: a reader finds that no layout change is active, then a layout change sets the reader's dirty flag, and finally, the reader clears its dirty flag and continue its execution.

A second important ordering that this implementation relies on, is that reading the dirty flag happens after all the reads in the reader code completed. If the underlying machine has a (very) relaxed memory model, then a read memory fence is required. On standard memory models, such as Total Store Order (TSO) or Partial Store Order (PSO) used with x86 or SPARC, a hardware memory fence is not required. However, a compiler fence is always required to restrict the compiler from changing the order of these reads.

The layout changer first acquires the underlying reader-writer lock in write mode. This prevents writers, who acquired the RW-LOCK in the read mode, and other layout changers from accessing the data structure. Then, before executing the layout change, it sets the dirty flags of all threads as TRUE. From that point and on, readers that have not completed a read operation, must return FALSE. This holds until the layout changer completes and releases the reader-writer lock. The code is presented in Listing 4.

Listing 4. layout lock Implementation

```
class layoutLock{
    ReadWriteLock rwlock;
    bool dirty[MAX_THREADS];
}
void startRead(){
}
bool endRead(){
    //read memory fence if needed
    if (dirty[tid]) {
        dirty[tid] = false;
        __memory_fence();
        if(rwlock.isWriterActive())
            dirty[tid] = true;
        return false;
    }
    return true;
}
void startWrite(){
    rwlock.startRead();
}
void endWrite(){
    rwlock.endRead();
}
void startLayoutChange(){
    rwlock.startWrite();
    for thread in THREADS {
        dirty[thread] = true;
    }
    __memory_fence();
}
void endLayoutChange(){
    rwlock.endWrite();
}
```

2.3 Malformed Pointers and Memory Management

In the layout lock mechanism, in order to achieve better performance, readers are not required to announce their operation. This implies that sometimes readers execute while a layout changer is active, until they find out at the end of the read that the read operation must repeat. However, a read operation may consist of several accesses to the data structure, including reading and dereferencing pointers. This places a restriction that the layout changer must modify the data structure in a way that would allow readers to reach the endRead operation without crashing. For example, the layout changer should install only valid pointers in the data structure. Otherwise, a reader may read and dereference a malformed pointer, causing a crash before reaching the end of the read operation. The layout changer may insert NULL pointers if readers can handle them properly.

Memory management. Freeing memory space that the layout changer vacates requires some care. Since readers may still read from the old version of the object, a layout changer cannot immediately free unused memory after the layout change.

The freeing of unused memory can be handled safely in various ways. The easiest is to use automatic memory reclamation (i.e. garbage collection). If garbage collection is not available on the platform, then memory reclamation can be executed using mechanisms designed for lock-free data structures which deal with similar concerns, such as (Cohen and Petrank 2015b,a; Alistarh et al. 2015; Brown 2015). Alternatively, the following adaptation of the epoch-based memory management can be used. Following a layout change, when all dirty flags have been reset, it is possible to recycle memory freed by the layout change as it is guaranteed that none of the threads are accessing stale memory.

3. Layout Change Usage Examples

In this section we first present a novel concurrent tree design denoted DLTree, which uses the layout lock paradigm to build a highly concurrent binary search tree. The tree changes its layout to allow faster access. Next, we present an array-based implementation of a concurrent set, where layout changes allow most contain operations to finish as a simple binary search.

3.1 DLTree: A Fast Concurrent Binary Tree

Concurrent binary trees were extensively studied in the literature (Bronson et al. 2010; Morrison and Arbel 2015; Natarajan and Mittal 2014; Braginsky and Petrank 2012; Drachsler et al. 2014; Ellen et al. 2010). In this subsection we propose a new concurrent binary tree design, called a *dynamic-layout tree (DLTree)*, which employs a layout change and the layout lock paradigm and implementation to obtain high performance. A core observation used in this design is that nodes of low-depth (which are closer to the root) change infrequently, whereas the set of nodes of higher depth (which are closer to leaves) change frequently. We use this observation is by noting that the almost-immutable high levels of the tree can be compacted to provide better cache utilization and faster traversals. The details of this compaction are described in Subsection 3.1.2 below. In what follows, we explain how this all leads to a faster concurrent tree implementation.

The DLTree maintains lower-depth nodes in a compacted form. The compacted form can be traversed quickly but it is hard to modify. Since the tree size changes during the execution, we should be able to change the number of levels we consider "low depth" and so it should be possible to move parts of the tree from non-compacted form to compacted form and vice versa. The DLTree algorithm deals with mod-

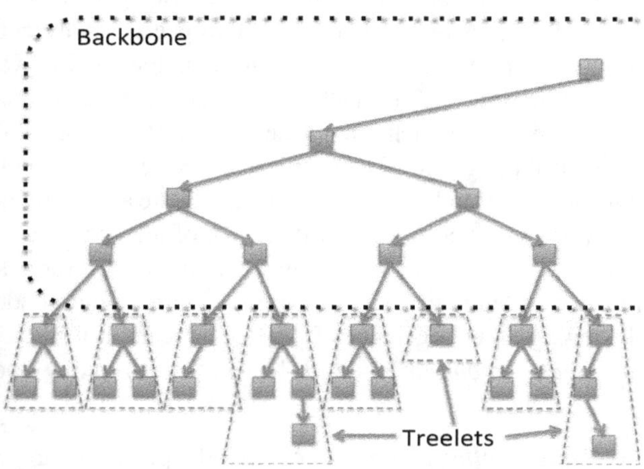

Figure 1. The structure of an DLTree. (Right hand side of the root is similar and omitted for lack of space.) The dotted black (half) rectangle shows the backbone. Each green trapezoid is a treelet.

ifications of the lower-depth nodes by using a layout lock. The majority of tree modifications occur on non-compacted higher-depth nodes and can be modified locally. The occasional lower-depth modifications are handled by acquiring the layout lock in the layout change mode. This implies serializing such modifications, but as lower-depth node modifications are relatively rare, this serialization does not impact the parallelism of the tree data structure in general.

The DLTree algorithm divides the tree into two parts. The *backbone* part of the tree retains all the compacted nodes at the lower-depth levels, and the rest of the tree consists of *treelets*. These are all the subtrees whose roots are descendants of the backbone leaves. An illustration of this structure appears in Figure 1 where the backbone is marked in a big black dotted rectangle. As can be seen in the figure, the backbone is a complete binary tree of four levels in this case. The descendants of a backbone leaf form a treelet, marked by a green trapezoid. While the backbone is a balanced complete tree maintained by the algorithm, the treelets are not necessarily balanced (or complete). The treelet leaves contain the actual data that is stored the DLTree.

Operations on the tree start by searching the backbone for the appropriate treelet, and finish by executing the operation on the relevant treelet. The algorithm's pseudo-code and a discussion appear in Subsection 3.1.3, but let us first explain the simple synchronization that makes this tree concurrent.

3.1.1 Synchronizing Tree Accesses

The two parts of the tree are used to optimize the synchronization on tree access. The backbone is designed to support very frequent reads, and rare layout changes. Thus, it is protected using the layout lock. The treelets receive frequent modifications, but these modifications are typically distributed among the many treelets, thus the treelets rarely need to handle contention. In our implementation we attempt to keep each treelet small and we synchronize each treelet using a simple coarse-grained lock (i.e., one lock per treelet).

While the proposed design is extremely simple, care is needed at the point in which a search moves from the synchronization mechanism of the backbone to the lock of the treelet. To this end, we acquire the lock of the treelet *before* releasing the read lock of the layout lock. This follows the spirit of the well-known hand-over-hand algorithms. However, doing so breaks the invariant that a read operation of the layout lock does not write to a global state. The read operation writes to the treelet lock while acquiring it. If the release of the read lock (of the layout lock) returns FALSE, then this means that a layout change has occurred and the read values cannot be trusted. Luckily, the treelet lock is not part of the backbone and is not protected by the layout lock. Therefore, we can simply continue by releasing the treelet lock and restarting the whole operation.

While composing the two locks is non-trivial, it is still significantly simpler than using fine-grained synchronization. Interestingly, it took less than half an hour to make the basic sequential tree concurrent, by adding the layout lock and the lock-per-treelet synchronization. This stands in contrast to building any of the known concurrent trees. They all employ sophisticated complex synchronization mechanisms.

3.1.2 Backbone Implementation

The treelets are implemented in a very straightforward manner. Their nodes contains a key, a data pointer, two next (left and right) child pointers, and a type field explained below. The backbone tree structure is more complex and in this subsection we present its implementation. We start with the underlying data structure. The backbone tree is implemented as a complete (perfect) external binary tree, whose depth is divisible by 4. Each set of 15 nodes, starting at a node at level $4i$ and including all its descendant of depth 3, i.e., up to its 8 descendants at level $4i+3$, are compacted into a single object called *BigNode*. A complete binary tree of depth $4d$ yields a complete tree of BigNodes of depth d, where each BigNode has 16 BigNode descendants. The leaves of the backbone tree point to treelets. We only implement a search through the backbone. There are no insert or delete operations to specific nodes, as this structure only serves as a backbone directory into the treelets where the actual insert and remove operations take effect. A modification of the backbone occurs when it needs to be enlarged or shrunk. This modification is executed as a layout change and will be discussed below.

BigNodes are organized in memory with care for locality. A BigNode consists of 15 keys, 16 next pointers, and a type field to distinguish a BigNode descendant from a treelet descendant. The type and the 15 keys reside on one cache line (assuming a 4-byte key and a 64-byte cache line), and the next pointers reside on two additional cache lines (assum-

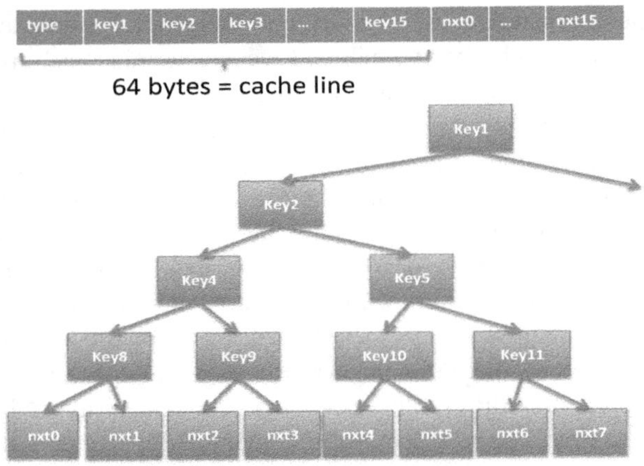

Figure 2. BigNode. (Right hand side of the root is similar and omitted for lack of space.) The top depicts the actual representation of a node in memory starting with the type and proceeding with 15 keys (filling the first cache line), and then the 16 next pointers filling the next two cache lines. Logically, this structure represents four layers of a complete binary tree.

ing a 64-bit platform). The BigNode structure is illustrated in Figure 2.

Traversing the tree of BigNodes is efficient because it allows traversing four layers of the tree on a single cache line, and because it replaces the memory access for dereferencing the left (or right) child pointer with an index computation. The root key is at index one of the BigNode's keys array. To find the correct next child index one multiplies the index by 2, and then adds 1 if the searched key is larger than the root's key. The operation is repeated four times until a leaf is reached. The backbone therefore yields very efficient searches. However, modifying it may be costly. Therefore, the backbone is only modified when the size of the (entire) tree increases or decreases substantially. In order to keep modifications rare, the backbone is enlarged or shrunk by four levels at a time, implying the addition of sixteen BigNodes below every leaf BigNode, or the elimination of all leaf BigNodes. Such enlargement (or shrinkage) means that the number of leaves the backbone has is multiplied (or divided) by sixteen during each such change. The trigger for enlarging or shrinking the backbone is a substantial increase or decrease of the full tree size. In order to avoid the overhead associated with maintaining an accurate size of the tree, each thread keeps a thread-local counter of its own insertions and removals. It then updates the global tree size only when the absolute value of the local counter reaches a predetermined threshold. Enlarging (resp. shrinking) the tree is done when the approximate global tree size nears sixteen times the backbone size (resp. nears one fourth the backbone size).

When enlarging (or shrinking) the tree, we take the opportunity to rebalance the tree. We start by acquiring the layout lock in the layout change mode. Then, we gather all data from all treelets in a sorted vector. This is done by executing the following for each treelet: acquire its lock and move its data to the vector. After gathering all data in a sorted vector, a balanced tree (which is not necessarily full) is built with the existing data. The levels that are closer to the root are built as the backbone, and the rest of the levels create a set of treelets. Finally, the layout lock and the locks of all treelets are released[1]. Since the layout change operation occurs rarely, we made no attempt to optimize this procedure. Pseudo-code illustrating an enlargement of the tree appears in the method *enlargeBackbone* in Listing 6 below. The shrinking operation is similar.

Avoiding Malformed Pointers Read operations are executed concurrently while layout changes take place. Since a read operation may contain several actual read accesses to the global data, it is possible that some of these accesses will happen after a layout change took place. The data structure algorithm must be aware of this problem and make sure this does not cause a crash. For the tree, a problem may arise if a stale pointer is read and then dereferenced. We resolve this problem by maintaining an invariant that a next pointer of a BigNode points either to a valid treelet or to another BigNode. Thus, when the backbone is enlarged, new BigNodes are added only after their next pointers are populated.

3.1.3 Pseudo-Code for the Tree Operations

The DLTree structure is provided in pseudo-code in Listing 5. The tree consists of two types of objects: treelets and BigNodes. It is possible to distinguish between the two using the type field of the node. A treelet contains a lock and a tree. The BigNode underlying structure is as discussed in Section 3.1.2. Traversing the four layers of a BigNode and returning the next pointer is implemented as the *get* method of the BigNode class. Finding the appropriate pointer to descend on each level of the BigNode involves multiplying the index by two, and then adding 1 if the input key is larger than the node key.

Listing 5. DLTree

```
class base{
    enum {BIG_NODE, TREELET} type;
}
class BigNode:public base{
    keys[15];
    base *nexts[16];
public:
    base *get(key){
        keys = &this->keys[-1];
        idx=1;
        idx=2*idx + (key>keys[idx]);
```

[1] Actually, it is possible to simplify this process by releasing the lock of each treelet after copying its values. Arguing that this provides a coherent snapshot of the tree is a bit more involved and left out of this short version of the paper.

```
        idx=2*idx + (key>keys[idx]);
        idx=2*idx + (key>keys[idx]);
        idx=2*idx + (key>keys[idx]);
        return nexts[idx−16];
    }
} attribute=cache line aligned;
class Treelet:public base{
    standardLock lock;
    tree::node root;
}
class Backbone{
    BigNode *head;
}
class layoutTree{
    Backbone backbone;
    LayoutLock llock;
    bool insert(key);
    bool remove(key);
    bool contains(key);
}
```

The DLTree operations (search, insert, and remove) are presented in Listing 6. Each of the operations start by finding the appropriate treelet to execute the operation, and acquiring the lock for this treelet. Finally, the treelet lock is released. The operation that returns the required treelet after acquiring its lock is called *getLockedTreelet*.

The *getLockedTreelet* method searches the backbone to find the relevant treelet. The traversal is executed using the BigNode *get* method. The entire search is enclosed with the layout lock held in the read mode. The backbone traversal is completed when a non-BigNode node is discovered (thus, a Treelet). The treelet lock is then acquired. Finally, if releasing the layout lock returns FALSE, the treelet lock is released and the operation is restarted. If releasing the layout lock returns TRUE, the locked treelet is returned.

After executing an insert operation (or a remove operation) a heuristic is used to determine if it is beneficial to enlarge (or shrink, resp.) the backbone. If it needs to be enlarged (or shrunk), the layout lock is acquired in layout change mode and the modification is performed as discussed in Subsection 3.1.2. Finally, the layout lock is released.

Listing 6. DLTree operations

```
Treelet* layoutTree::getLockedTreelet(key){
start:
    llock.startRead();
    base *tl=this−>head;
    do{
        tl=((BigNode*)tl)−>get(key);
    }while(tl−>type == BIG_NODE);
    Treelet *tll=(Treelet*)tl;
    tll−>lock();
    if(llock.endRead()==false){
        tll−>unlock();
        goto start;
    }
    return tll;
}
bool layoutTree::search(key){
    Treelet *tl=backbone.getLockedTreelet(key);
    bool res = tl−>search(key);
    tl−>unlock();
    return res;
}
bool layoutTree:insert(key){
    Treelet *tl=backbone.getLockedTreelet(key);
    bool res = tl−>insert(key);
    tl−>unlock();
    if(heuristic()) enlargeBackbone();
    return res;
}
bool layoutTree::remove(key){
    Treelet *tl=backbone.getLockedTreelet(key);
    bool res = tl−>remove(key);
    tl−>unlock();
    if(heuristic()) shrinkBackbone();
    return res;
}
void layoutTree::enlargeBackbone(){
    llock.startLayoutChange();
    sortedvector v;
    for each treelet tl in backbone do{
        tl−>acquire();
        v.addItems(tl);
    }
    for each treelet tl in backbone do
        tl−>release();
    BuildBalancedTree(v);
    llock.endLayoutChange();
}
```

3.1.4 Assumptions

While the DLTree is always correct, it provides performance benefits assuming some (realistic) behavior of the application. First, although the DLTree balances treelets during layout changes, it does not provide a balancing guarantee. Thus, like any unbalanced tree, it will not work well for workloads that significantly deviate from uniform.

In addition, the DLTree performs best when the tree layout (backbone) is static for the majority of the time. It is less effective when the tree size changes drastically during execution. For example, for a workload of 100% insertions, layout changes would consume a significant part of the execution time.

Of course, if the layout is completely fixed throughout the execution, then there is no need for the layout lock. The layout never changes. However, this extreme stability is not very realistic. Usually, data structures are allocated empty and items are inserted thereafter. In some cases, the stable running range of keys is not even known when the first element is inserted into the data structure. Thus, a design that does not deal with layout changes is impractical.

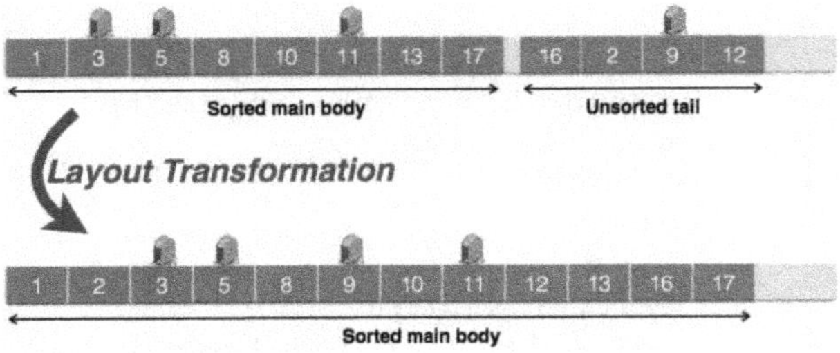

Figure 3. ConcurrentArraySet layout transformation. The unsorted tail is occasionally sorted and merged into the sorted array, thus keeping the tail small.

3.2 Concurrent Array Set

In this subsection we consider an even simpler implementation of an ordered set, using an array. Sorted arrays are well known for their ease of use and provide excellent performance for binary search. However, inserting and removing elements from a sorted array usually requires costly modifications of large parts of the array. Thus, sorted arrays are typically not used to implement sets. In this subsection we utilize the layout lock to propose a concurrent implementation of a set using an extended sorted array.

To avoid frequent costly modifications to the sorted array, we apply the following two ideas. First, insertions are applied into a side buffer, which absorbs multiple insert operations before the changes are merged into the sorted array. Occasional merging of the side buffer into the sorted set helps shift most of the search work towards the easily searchable sorted part.

Second, we designed our sorted array to work best with distributions in which elements tend to recur, i.e., there is good a chance that removed elements will be re-inserted to the set again. Thus, in our set we optimistically keep deleted elements (for a limited time) in the sorted array marked as deleted, but without actually removing their entries, allowing them to be easily resurrected.

In order to correctly merge the side buffer into the sorted array, the threads concurrently accessing the array are synchronized by considering the merge operation as a layout change. This operation is illustrated in Figure 3. In the frequent case, the layout lock allows normal operations to treat the sorted array as if it was read-only, thus avoiding complex synchronization. This way, the proposed algorithm is able to keep the initial simplicity of a sorted array.

Similarly to the DLTree, the Concurrent Array Set also performs best in cases where the layout does not change frequently over time. In the case of Concurrent Array Set, a merge (i.e. layout change) is triggered when the side buffer reaches its full capacity. Therefore, frequent merges are avoided when elements are added to the side buffer at a slow rate, which is indeed the case when most inserted objects are handled by resurrection.

4. Measurements

In this section, we study two questions. First, we ask whether layout modifications are worthwhile for the examples of section 3. We then turn to look at concurrent executions with layout changes, and check whether the proposed layout lock provides good performance when compared against available synchronization mechanisms such as StampedLock (Lea and JSR-166), SeqLock (Lameter 2005), and a standard reader-writer lock. Thus, for each of the data structures provided in Section 3 we consider two sets of competitors. First, we consider state-of-the-art designs for concurrent sets. Second, we consider synchronizing the proposed algorithm by one of the available synchronization techniques.

We ran measurements on a 64-cores machine, featuring 4 AMD Opteron(TM) 6376 2.3GHz processors, each with 16 cores. The machine has 128GB RAM, an L1 cache of 16KB per core, an L2 cache of 2MB for every two cores, and an L3 cache of 6MB per half a processor (8 cores). An Ubuntu 14.04 (kernel version 3.16.0) is used. Each execution was repeated 10 times and lasted for 5 seconds. We report the average number of executed operations (throughput).

The concurrent array set was implemented in Java and run on OpenJDK 1.8.0_91 JVM. Results on HotSpot 1.8.0_91 are similar. The DLTree was implemented in C++ since it requires cache-aligned allocation, which is not currently supported by Java. It was compiled using the g++ compiler version 4.9.3 with the -O3 optimization flag.

4.1 Measuring the DLTree

We incorporated the DLTree into the framework of (David et al. 2015), and used their stress-test benchmark. The percentage of search operations (contains) was set to 80%; and insert and remove operations were chosen with a probability of 10% each. We varied the key ranges between 8K, 128K, and 2M, and also measured a key range of 32K to demonstrate an additional interesting behavior. The key to be searched, inserted, or deleted was chosen uniformly at random in the key range. Thus, the tree size was approximately half of the key range. The tree was populated to its approximated size before the measurement started. We varied the number of threads as powers-of-two between 1 and 64.

Since the tree is pre-populated, the benchmark measures the steady-state performance of the DLTree, when there are no layout changes. Yet, the readers and writers execute their layout synchronizations to make sure that they ran safe even if a layout change does occur. We also added a benchmark that measures the build time of a tree with one million elements. This benchmark executes 100% insertions that triggers several layout changes.

For the tree micro-benchmark we consider four state-of-the-art concurrent trees: Bronson et al. (2010) relaxed balanced AVL tree (denoted *bronson*), Natarajan and Mittal (2014) lock-free tree (denoted *natarajan*) , Drachsler et al. (2014) logical-ordering binary search tree (denoted *drach-*

sler), and Ellen et al. (2010) lock-free tree (denoted *ellen*). For all these trees we took the implementations provided by (David et al. 2015). To the best of our knowledge, these are among the best performing concurrent tree designs. In addition to the DLTree algorithm synchronized by the layout lock (denoted *DLTree*), we consider the same algorithm of the DLTree when synchronized by a reader-writer lock (denoted *DL_RW*) and the same algorithm synchronized by SeqLock (denoted *DL_SeqL*). The SeqLock implementation was taken from the Linux kernel implementation version 4.6. Note that this Linux implementation of the SeqLock does not support concurrent writers, but only optimistic readers and a single layout changer. However, this is sufficient for the DLTree implementation because the backbone (which uses the layout lock) is modified only via a layout change.

Results The results for the tree benchmark are presented in Figure 4 as ratios between the throughput of the given implementation and that of Bronson's tree. Namely, a result of 200% means 2x faster than *bronson*. The absolute throughput values of the baseline are presented in Figure 4 (e).

The performance of the DLTree compared to the other implementations varies between the different tree sizes. It turns out to be excellent for trees of large size. For trees of size 4K, the DLTree performs similarly to the lock-free tree *natarajan*, and better than most other competitors. For trees of size 64K, the DLTree is consistently faster than *natarajan* with 13% improvement for 64 threads. Finally, for large trees of size 1M, the DLTree performs much better than all competitors (35% faster than the *bronson*, the second-best implementation for this configuration, for 64 threads.) The DLTree performs better on larger trees due to the fast traversal of the backbone. But we also added trees of size 16K, where the DLTree performs close to Bronson's tree, but is less efficient than *natarajan*. Interestingly, the discrepancy between the 4K and the 16K sizes represent a general trend, which is determined by the average treelet size. The smaller the treelet, the faster the algorithm, as it spends most of its time in the fast backbone. The average treelet size is 1 for trees of size 4K, 64K, and 1M, but the average treelet size is 4 for trees of size 16K. This dependency on the average treelet size is shown clearly in Figure 5, where we present performance results for 64 threads with varying tree sizes. As can be seen, the DLTree performance is best when its size is a power of 16, where the size of each treelet is 1 on average, and it deteriorates when this size increases.

Note that we could use a more aggressive heuristic for enlarging the tree, making the backbone larger than the number of elements just to make sure that each treelet is small on average all the time. This leads to a memory vs. performance trade-off, which we did not pursue further in this paper.

Comparing the DLTree that uses the layout lock implementation to enable layout modifications with a reader-writer lock implementation, the latter is doing quite well for one or two threads, but deteriorates quickly as the number of threads increases. Compared to the SeqLock, it again performs excellently for a few threads (in some cases even slightly better than layout lock), but is 24% – 30% slower for 64 threads. It should be noted, that the SeqLock requires that an optimistic reader starts by reading the version number and storing it in a local field (a register or a stack location). When it finishes, it re-reads the version and compares it to the stored version. Thus, it requires two loads instructions per read operation (the layout lock requires only one) and occupies a register for the duration of the read. In addition, both of these loads limit the compiler's ability to re-order load instructions, while the layout lock limits it only once. Furthermore, accessing a single location by all threads may be slower than accessing a location per thread as is reported elsewhere (Lin et al. 2015). This may explain the observed performance benefits of the layout lock over SeqLock.

Finally, we created a workload with a 100% insertion rate, which stops immediately after the backbone size reaches a million elements. As discussed in Section 3.1.4, 100% insertions represent a worst case scenario for the DLTree. In addition, a million elements represents a worst case stopping condition, as the workload stops immediately after the entire tree is restructured. That is, the measurement stops immediately after the backbone size is enlarged from 2^{16} treelets to 2^{20} treelets. In this case, the DLTree built the tree in 440 ms while other concurrent trees built such a tree in 180 – 200 ms. The layout changes took approximately 250ms in this case, explaining the performance gap. This demonstrates that layout changes are effective only if a lot of operations are able to benefit from the new layout.

4.2 Measuring the Concurrent Array Set

Similar to the DLTree benchmark, the Concurrent Array Set was measured using 80% searches, 10% insertions, and 10% deletions. The Concurrent Array Set works well with uniform workload over a small to medium range (up to 256K) because all the keys in the range are eventually placed in the sorted array (recall that removed values are only logically removed). To avoid a best case scenario test, we also ran the Concurrent Array Set with a workload of a normal distribution (with a theoretically unlimited range).

The Concurrent Array Set was compared against the concurrent skip list set of the standard Java library as well as the Java implementation of Bronson's tree from (Gramoli 2015). In addition, to demonstrate the benefits of the layout lock in the design of the Concurrent Array Set, we implemented the layout changes synchronization using StampedLock (that is provided by the Java standard library), as follows. Readers use the StampedLock's optimistic readers interface. Writers use the non-optimistic readers interface since they do not modify the layout but must prevent it from being modified during the write. Finally, layout changers use the writer interface since they modify the layout.

Furthermore, in order to demonstrate the benefit of optimistic reads for synchronized layout changes, we have also

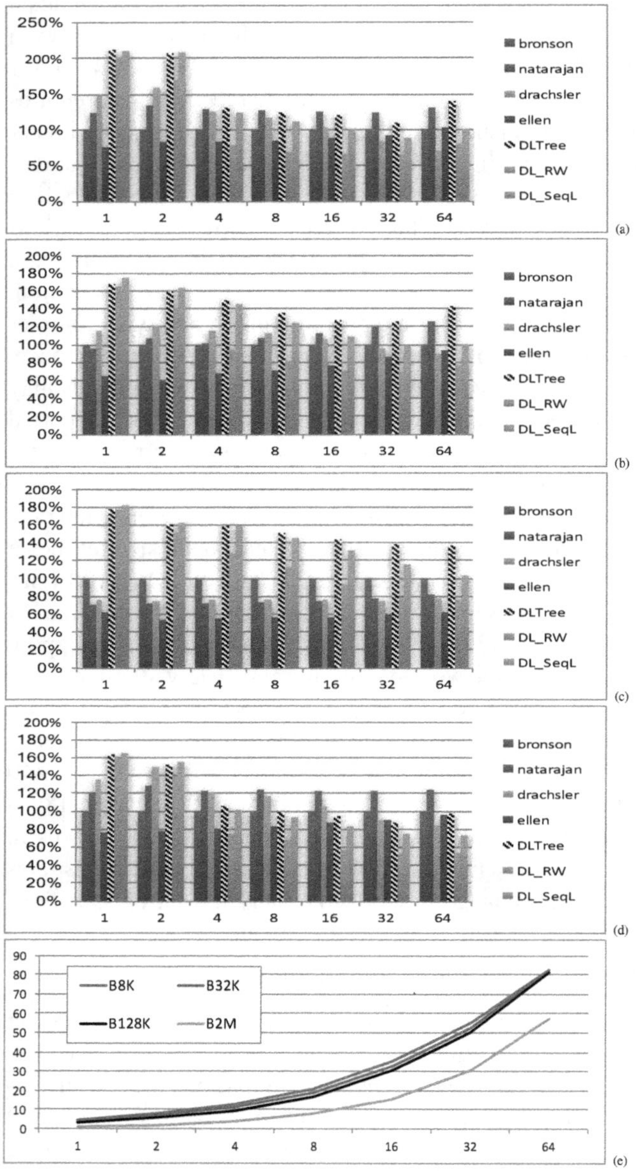

Figure 4. Concurrent tree measurements compared to *bronson* (higher means better performance). Range varies between 8K (a), 128K (b), 2M (c), and 32K (d). (e) shows the absolute throughput of the baseline (bronson) for the different ranges.

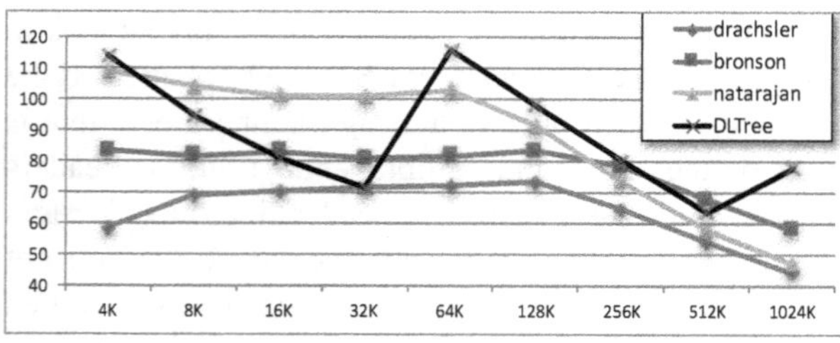

Figure 5. Concurrent tree measurements. Throughput (in millions of operation per second) as a function of tree size. Number of threads is fixed to 64.

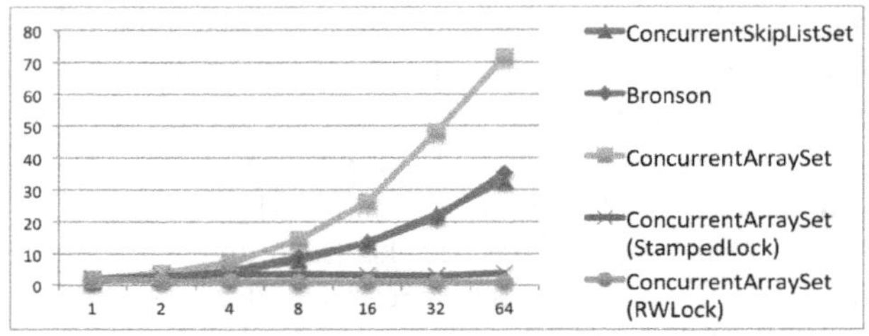

Figure 6. Concurrent Array Set measurements on normally distributed keys ($\sigma = 16384$), with absolute throughput rates in millions of operations per second as functions of the number of threads.

implemented the standard (naïve) solution of using a reader-writer lock to synchronize layout changes. That is, a read lock was used for read and write operations, and a write lock was used for layout change operations.

Results The results of the Concurrent Array Set benchmark are presented in Figure 6 for normally distributed keys with $\sigma = 16K$. Compared to Java's concurrent skip list, the Concurrent Array Set performs 87% faster on a single thread, and 2.7x faster on 64 threads. This demonstrates excellent performance of binary searches over a sorted array, which is enabled by using the layout lock. Results for the uniform distribution with a key range of 256K are presented in Figure 7, and show a similar trend to that of the normal distribution. Results for smaller key ranges (shown in Figure 7(b)) also exhibit similar or stronger relative performance of the Concurrent Array Set, while for large enough sets, the overhead of layout changes becomes too high and performance degrades significantly. Hence, the benefits of the Concurrent Array Set depend on achieving a slow rate of layout changes, which, in turn, depends on the stable running range of keys and the execution time.

Figures 6 and 7 also compare the Concurrent Array Set that uses the layout lock to Concurrent Array Set implementations that use a reader-writer lock (RWLock) or StampedLock for the layout change synchronization. Both latter implementations perform poorly compared to the one using the layout lock when the number of threads is high. Thus, the same performance benefits that we see for the Concurrent Array Set with layout lock are not achieved with current locking mechanisms, even when optimistic locking is applied (in the case of StampedLock) in a manner similar to our proposed paradigm.

5. Related Works

Compiler optimizations that generate code that modifies the memory layout are well known (Kennedy and Ziarek 2015; Kandemir et al. 1999a; Mannarswamy 2009; Ding and Kennedy 1999). But they are avoided when parallel accesses are involved. The layout lock may be used to enable such optimizations with concurrent programs as well.

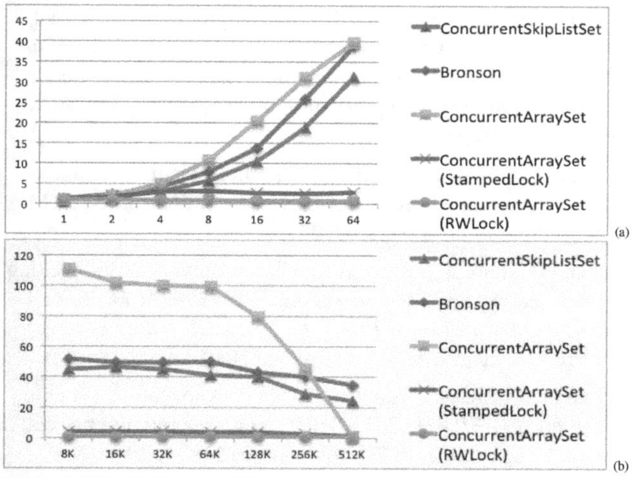

Figure 7. Concurrent Array Set measurements on uniformly distributed keys with (a) absolute throughput rates in millions of operations per second as functions of the number of threads (range = 256K), and (b) absolute throughput rates on 64 threads in millions of operations per second as a function of the key range size.

A scheme for internal modifications of data structure layouts was proposed by (Xu 2013). There, the underlying representation of the data structure is modified dynamically. The scheme was able to support data structures synchronized by a global lock, but with no finer-grained synchronization.

The layout lock paradigm and implementation extends the reader-writer lock. Mellor-Crummey and Scott (1991) propose a scalable design, using a list of waiting processes, where upon releasing the lock it is passed to the next process in the list. Hsieh and Weihl (1992) proposed a design that is very efficient for infrequent writes, and we used it as the base for the layout lock implementation. Many other implementations exist in the literature, e.g., (Lev et al. 2009; Brandenburg and Anderson 2010; Calciu et al. 2013). A recent paper (Liu et al. 2014) presented a very fast reader-writer lock for the TSO memory model. But this design relies on strong kernel support, not always available.

The layout lock interface bears a resemblance to the SeqLock (Lameter 2005) and StampedLock (Lea and JSR-166), which are synchronization techniques that allow optimistic readers. Both of these techniques were discussed in the introduction. As shown in the Measurements section, the layout lock provides better scalability than both of these methods.

Read-Copy-Update (RCU) is a technique for synchronizing readers and writers that avoids blocking readers. Soules et al. (2003) describe RCU-based layout changes for the K42 kernel. They defined a protocol for the state transfer and exemplify layout changes for various file-system operations. This solution requires kernel support. Triplett et al. (2010) used a user-space RCU solution to build a dynamically growing hash map. They used RCU primitives to move nodes between buckets while ensuring that a reader of a bucket in the old table would observe the appropriate data. An RCU-based implementation for adjusting the size of a vector (of semaphore pointers) was considered by (Arcangeli et al. 2003).

There are multiple RCU variants for user-level code (Desnoyers et al. 2012). Quiescent-State-Based Reclamation (QSBR) provides the least overhead for reads (practically none) and is widely used for kernel-level implementation. However, user space libraries, such as ones providing concurrent data structures, cannot generally use the QSBR variant, as they cannot identify quiescent states in the entire application. Other RCU-variants include *general-purpose RCU* and *bullet-proof RCU*. These variants can be used in user-level libraries, but typically result in high overhead for readers. Hence we did not consider using these.

Recently, it was show that it is possible to avoid the expensive memory fence on readers by infrequently issuing a process-wide memory fence, either by OS support such as the Linux sys_membarrier call (McKenney et al.) or via hardware support (Dice et al. 2016). This RCU-variant can be used on user level libraries and exploring its usage for modifying the layout of data structures is an interesting avenue for future work.

The technique used in this paper, of using a thread local flag for detecting optimistic executions going astray, was first introduce by Cohen and Petrank (2015a,b) in the context of memory management for lock-free data structures.

6. Conclusions

This paper studied concurrent layout modifications as a means to improving performance of concurrent algorithms. We introduced the layout lock paradigm and a layout lock implementation which allows concurrently modifying the layout during the execution with a negligible overhead for read operations and with a small overhead for write operations on the shared data.

We demonstrated the benefits of the layout lock implementation by presenting new algorithms that benefit from layout modifications. Measurements show that performance improvements can be significant. One of these constructions, which is of an independent interest, is a concurrent tree design that performs fast on large trees.

References

D. Alistarh, W. M. Leiserson, A. Matveev, and N. Shavit. ThreadScan. In *Proceedings of the 27th ACM on Symposium on Parallelism in Algorithms and Architectures - SPAA '15*, pages 123–132. ACM Press, jun 2015.

A. Arcangeli, M. Cao, P. E. McKenney, and D. Sarma. Using Read-Copy-Update Techniques for System V IPC in the Linux 2.5 Kernel. In *USENIX Annual Technical Conference, FREENIX Track*, pages 297–309, 2003.

H. Boehm. Can seqlocks get along with programming language memory models? *Proceedings of the 2012 ACM SIGPLAN Workshop on Memory Systems Performance and Correctness - MSPC'12*, pages 12 – 20, 2012.

A. Braginsky and E. Petrank. A lock-free B+tree. In *Proceedinbgs of the 24th ACM symposium on Parallelism in algorithms and architectures - SPAA '12*, page 58, New York, New York, USA, jun 2012. ACM Press.

B. Brandenburg and J. Anderson. Spin-based reader-writer synchronization for multiprocessor real-time systems. *Real-Time Systems*, 2010.

N. G. Bronson, J. Casper, H. Chafi, and K. Olukotun. A practical concurrent binary search tree. *Proceedings of the 15th ACM SIGPLAN Symposium on Principles and Practice of Parallel Programming - PPoPP'10*, pages 257–268, may 2010. ISSN 03621340.

T. A. Brown. Reclaiming Memory for Lock-Free Data Structures. In *Proceedings of the 2015 ACM Symposium on Principles of Distributed Computing - PODC '15*, pages 261–270. ACM Press, jul 2015.

I. Calciu, D. Dice, Y. Lev, V. Luchangco, V. Marathe, and N. Shavit. NUMA-aware reader-writer locks. *Proceedings of the 18th ACM SIGPLAN symposium on Principles and practice of parallel programming - PPoPP'13*, pages 157–166, 2013.

G. Chakrabarti and F. Chow. Structure Layout Optimizations in the Open64 Compiler : Design , Implementation and Measurements. *Open64 workshop*, 2008.

N. Cohen and E. Petrank. Efficient Memory Management for Lock-Free Data Structures with Optimistic Access. In *Proceedings of the 27th ACM on Symposium on Parallelism in Algorithms and Architectures - SPAA '15*, pages 254–263, jun 2015a.

N. Cohen and E. Petrank. Automatic memory reclamation for lock-free data structures. *Proceedings of the 2015 ACM SIGPLAN International Conference on Object-Oriented Programming, Systems, Languages, and Applications - OOPLSA'15*, pages 260–279, oct 2015b.

T. David, R. Guerraoui, and V. Trigonakis. Asynchronized Concurrency. In *Proceedings of the Twentieth International Conference on Architectural Support for Programming Languages and Operating Systems - ASPLOS'15*, pages 631–644, mar 2015.

M. Desnoyers, P. E. McKenney, A. S. Stern, M. R. Dagenais, and J. Walpole. User-Level Implementations of Read-Copy Update. *IEEE Transactions on Parallel and Distributed Systems*, 23(2): 375–382, feb 2012.

D. Dice, M. Herlihy, and A. Kogan. Fast non-intrusive memory reclamation for highly-concurrent data structures. In *Proceedings of the 2016 ACM SIGPLAN International Symposium on Memory Management - ISMM 2016*, pages 36–45, New York, New York, USA, 2016. ACM Press. ISBN 9781450343176. doi: 10.1145/2926697.2926699.

C. Ding and K. Kennedy. Improving cache performance in dynamic applications through data and computation reorganization at run time. *Proceedings of the ACM SIGPLAN 1999 conference on Programming language design and implementation - PLDI'99*, 1999.

D. Drachsler, M. Vechev, and E. Yahav. Practical concurrent binary search trees via logical ordering. In *Proceedings of the 19th ACM SIGPLAN symposium on Principles and practice of parallel programming - PPoPP '14*, pages 343–356. ACM Press, feb 2014.

A. Eizenberg, S. Hu, G. Pokam, and J. Devietti. Remix: online detection and repair of cache contention for the JVM. *Proceedings of the 37th ACM*, 2016.

F. Ellen, P. Fatourou, E. Ruppert, and F. van Breugel. Non-blocking binary search trees. In *Proceeding of the 29th ACM SIGACT-SIGOPS symposium on Principles of distributed computing - PODC '10*, page 131. ACM Press, jul 2010.

V. Gramoli. More than you ever wanted to know about synchronization. *PPoPP, Feb*, 2015. URL `http://ssrg.nicta.com.au/publications/nictaabstracts/8487.pdf`.

W. Hsieh and W. Weihl. Scalable reader-writer locks for parallel systems. *Proceedings of the Sixth International Parallel Processing Symposium*, 1992.

M. Kandemir, A. Choudhary, J. Ramanujam, and P. Banerjee. A framework for interprocedural locality optimization using both loop and data layout transformations. In *Proceedings of the 1999 International Conference on Parallel Processing*, pages 95–102. IEEE Comput. Soc, 1999a.

M. Kandemir, J. Ramanujam, and A. Choudhary. Improving cache locality by a combination of loop and data transformations. *IEEE Transactions on Computers*, 48(2):159–167, 1999b.

O. Kennedy and L. Ziarek. Just-In-Time Data Structures. *Proceedings. of the 7th Biennial Conference on Innovative Data Systems Research - CIDR'15*, 2015.

C. Lameter. Effective synchronization on Linux/NUMA systems. *Gelato Conference*, pages 1–23, 2005. URL `http://www.kde.ps.pl/mirrors/ftp.kernel.org/linux/kernel/people/christoph/gelato/gelato2005-paper.pdf`.

D. Lea and JSR-166. StampedLock. URL `http://grepcode.com/file/repository.grepcode.com/java/root/jdk/openjdk/8u40-b25/java/util/concurrent/locks/StampedLock.java`.

Y. Lev, V. Luchangco, and M. Olszewski. Scalable reader-writer locks. *Proceedings of the twenty-first annual symposium on Parallelism in algorithms and architectures - SPAA'09*, pages 101–110, 2009.

Y. Li, Y. Tan, W. Wang, Q. Zhang, and Z. Wang. A Cache-conscious Structure Definition for List. *Journal of Applied Sciences*, 13(8):1192–1198, 2013.

Y. Lin, K. Wang, S. Blackburn, and A. Hosking. Stop and go: understanding yieldpoint behavior. *Proceedings of the 2015 International Symposium on Memory Management - ISMM'15*, pages 70 – 80, 2015.

R. Liu, H. Zhang, and H. Chen. Scalable read-mostly synchronization using passive reader-writer locks. *Proceedings of the 2014 USENIX Annual Technical Conference - USENIX ATC'14*, pages 219–230, 2014.

Q. Lu, X. Gao, and S. Krishnamoorthy. Empirical performance-model driven data layout optimization. *17th International Workshop on Languages and Compilers for High Performance Computing, LCPC'04*, pages 72–86, 2004.

S. Mannarswamy. Region based structure layout optimization by selective data copying. *18th International Conference on Parallel Architectures and Compilation Techniques - PACT '09*, pages 338–347, 2009.

P. E. McKenney, M. Desnoyers, and L. Jiangshan. User-space RCU. URL `https://lwn.net/Articles/573424/`.

J. Mellor-Crummey and M. Scott. Scalable reader-writer synchronization for shared-memory multiprocessors. *Proceedings of the third ACM SIGPLAN symposium on Principles and practice of parallel programming - PPoPP'91*, pages 106–113, 1991.

A. Morrison and M. Arbel. Predicate RCU : An RCU for Scalable Concurrent Updates. In *Proceedings of the 20th ACM SIGPLAN Symposium on Principles and Practice of Parallel Programming - PPoPP'15*, pages 21–30, 2015.

A. Natarajan and N. Mittal. Fast concurrent lock-free binary search trees. *Proceedings of the 19th ACM SIGPLAN Symposium on Principles and Practice of Parallel Programming - PPoPP'14*, pages 317–328, 2014. doi: 10.1145/2555243.2555256.

E. Raman, R. Hundt, and S. Mannarswamy. Structure layout optimization for multithreaded programs. In *International Symposium on Code Generation and Optimization, CGO 2007*, pages 271–282. IEEE, mar 2007. ISBN 0769527647. doi: 10.1109/CGO.2007.36.

C. A. N. Soules, J. Appavoo, K. Hui, R. W. Wisniewski, D. Da Silva, G. R. Ganger, O. Krieger, M. Stumm, M. Auslander, M. Ostrowski, B. Rosenburg, and J. Xenidis. System Support for Online Reconfiguration. In *USENIX Annual Technical Conference. Proceedings of the 2003 Conference on*, pages 141–154, 2003. ISBN 1-931971-10-2.

I. Sung, J. Stratton, and W. Hwu. Data layout transformation exploiting memory-level parallelism in structured grid many-core applications. *Proceedings of the 19th international conference on Parallel architectures and compilation techniques - PACT'10*, pages 513–522, 2010.

J. Triplett, P. E. McKenney, and J. Walpole. Scalable concurrent hash tables via relativistic programming. *ACM SIGOPS Operating Systems Review*, 44(3):102, 2010. ISSN 01635980. doi: 10.1145/1842733.1842750.

M. D. Wael. Just-in-time data structures: towards declarative swap rules. *Proceedings of the 13th International Workshop on Dynamic Analysis - WODA'15*, pages 33–34, 2015.

M. D. Wael, S. Marr, and J. D. Koster. Just-in-time data structures. *2015 ACM International Symposium on New Ideas, New Paradigms, and Reflections on Programming and Software - Onward!'15*, pages 61–75, 2015.

G. Xu. CoCo: Sound and adaptive replacement of java collections. *27th European Conference Object-Oriented Programming - ECOOP'13*, pages 1–26, 2013.

Understanding the GPU Microarchitecture to Achieve Bare-Metal Performance Tuning

Xiuxia Zhang[1,2] Guangming Tan[1,2] Shuangbai Xue[1,2] Jiajia Li[3] Keren Zhou[1,2] Mingyu Chen[1,2]

[1] State Key Laboratory of Computer Architecture, Institute of Computing Technology, Chinese Academy of Sciences
[2] University of Chinese Academy of Sciences
[3] Georgia Institute of Technology

{zhangxiuxia,tgm,xueshuangbai,cmy}@ict.ac.cn jiajiali@gatech.edu zhoukeren@ncic.ac.cn

Abstract

In this paper, we present a methodology to understand GPU microarchitectural features and improve performance for compute-intensive kernels. The methodology relies on a reverse engineering approach to crack the GPU ISA encodings in order to build a GPU assembler. An assembly microbenchmark suite correlates microarchitectural features with their performance factors to uncover instruction-level and memory hierarchy preferences. We use SGEMM as a running example to show the ways to achieve bare-metal performance tuning. The performance boost is achieved by tuning `FFMA` throughput by activating dual-issue, eliminating register bank conflicts, adding non-`FFMA` instructions with little penalty, and choosing proper width of global/shared load instructions. On NVIDIA Kepler K20m, we develop a faster SGEMM with 3.1Tflop/s performance and 88% efficiency; the performance is 15% higher than cuBLAS7.0. Applying these optimizations to convolution, the implementation gains 39%-62% performance improvement compared with cuDNN4.0. The toolchain is an attempt to automatically crack different GPU ISA encodings and build an assembler adaptively for the purpose of performance enhancements to applications on GPUs.

Categories and Subject Descriptors D.1.3 [*Programming Techniques*]: Concurrent Programming---parallel programming; D.3.2 [*Programming Languages*]: Language Classifications---assembly languages

General Terms Performance, Benchmarking

Keywords SGEMM, Assembler, GPU, Performance, Convolution, Reverse-engineering GPU ISA encoding

PPoPP '17, February 04–08, 2017, Austin, TX, USA.
 ISBN 978-1-4503-4493-7/17/02...$15.00
DOI: http://dx.doi.org/10.1145/3018743.3018755

1. Introduction

As GPUs provide higher peak floating-point performance and memory bandwidth than CPUs, researchers tend to adopt GPUs to accelerate compute-intensive data-parallel programs. Hardware vendors provide performance-critical libraries tuned on their specific processors, such as Intel MKL [14] and AMD ACML [3] for multicore x86 CPUs and NVIDIA cuBLAS [14] and AMD clMath [2] for GPUs. However, third-party implementations consistently outperform these vendor libraries. For example, OpenBLAS [30], based on the hand-tuned assembly, achieves better performance than AMD ACML on AMD Piledriver processors and Intel MKL on Intel Sandy Bridge processors. Although a comprehensive OpenBLAS-like library is not available for GPUs, several efforts [6, 11, 16, 25, 29] were invested to achieve better performance than cuBLAS's GEMM by tuning assembly on NVIDIA GPUs. However, these works leave **two open questions** to be addressed for diligent performance tuning on the microarchitecture of every GPU generation. Since single-precision general matrix multiply (SGEMM) is extensively used in scientific applications and deep learning related domains, we use SGEMM as a running example for a concise presentation throughout this paper.

- *A toolchain that can identify GPU microarchitectural features and guide performance tuning is lacking.* Unlike the general-purpose CPU community, where a series of toolchains is available to tune performance in a bare-metal way, only the CUDA model is encouraged in the GPU community. NVIDIA engineers hand tune their supported libraries in GPU assembly language; thus, this leaves other unsupported algorithms poorly optimized. Fortunately, researchers have made some initial progress on performance tuning tools, including benchmarking [18, 29, 31] and the design of assemblers on particular GPU architectures [5, 10, 12, 27]. In this paper, we develop a methodology to systematically identify microarchitectural features by automatically cracking ISA encoding, building a GPU assembler, and benchmarking.

- *There is a lack of comprehensive understanding of the computational kernels' performance behavior in terms of the low-level GPU microarchitecture.* Most SGEMM analyses are circumscribed at the CUDA or PTX level due to the shortage of GPU bare-metal tools. Therefore, these studies cannot directly diagnose compiler deficiencies or hardware defects. By observing the disassembled codes of CUDA SGEMM, we find out that control codes generated by the CUDA compiler NVCC are inefficient in exploiting the FP32 Fused Multiply Add (`FFMA`) dual-issue feature on a Kepler GPU (details in Section 4.2). This implies that the binary codes generated by NVCC cannot utilize GPU cores efficiently. In addition, the compiler deficiencies can lead to a biased estimation of the performance bound.

In this paper, we automate the ISA-to-binary mapping and build a Kepler GPU assembler. Due to the compatible syntax with disassembly generated by `cuobjdump` [21], we can use NVCC to compile CUDA codes to a cubin file and then disassemble it to generate assembly. This approach allows users to optimize any code segment based on the generated assembly instead of coding from scratch. With this assembler, a microbenchmark suite is designed to understand and analyze a plenty of GPU microarchitectural features such as instruction throughput, warp scheduling, and register bank distribution. These features are helpful to understand and optimize the performance of a computational program. More specifically, we make the following contributions:

- We propose a GPU ISA encoding solver to crack ISA encodings of diverse GPU microarchitectures automatically by feeding disassembly codes. A Kepler GPU assembler is developed to tune the assembly codes generated by the CUDA compiler directly.
- We design a microbenchmark suite to explore the undocumented microarchitecture features of NVIDIA GPUs, such as control codes regulating `FFMA` instruction dual-issue and register bank indices influencing instruction throughput. These features are necessary to understand and tune GPU programs.
- We implement both SGEMM and convolution kernels on an NVIDIA Kepler GPU by applying the microarchitecture-level optimizations. The optimized SGEMM achieves up to 88% of the machine's peak floating-point performance, which is 15% higher than cuBLAS7.0. The optimized convolution kernel gains 39%-62% performance improvement compared with cuDNN4.0.

Our methodology is suitable for other NVIDIA GPU architectures with minor adjustments of the instruction solver, assembler, and benchmarking. The experience of exploring bare-metal optimizations is helpful for compiler development and performance tuning [33].

The rest of this paper is organized as follows. Section 2 introduces the SGEMM algorithm on a GPU and the CUDA binary utilities. Section 3 presents the instruction solver algorithms and microbenchmarking insights. In Section 4, a series of microarchitectural optimizations are applied to SGEMM. We report the experimental results in Section 5. Section 6 discusses the generality and portability of our methodology for different GPUs and diverse algorithms. Section 7 summarizes the related work. Finally, Section 8 concludes this work.

2. Background

This section first highlights tunable factors that determine SGEMM performance on the GPU architecture; it then introduces some CUDA binary utilities related to SGEMM optimizations at the assembly level for self-containment.

2.1 Performance Factors of SGEMM

The state-of-the-art SGEMM implementations on GPUs [11, 16, 19, 25] use two-level blocking, register and shared memory blockings, to exploit data reuse through the GPU memory hierarchy. The operation of SGEMM is defined as $C = beta * C + alpha * AB$, where A, B, and C are $m \times k$, $k \times n$, and $m \times n$ matrices, respectively, while $alpha$ and $beta$ are scalar constants.

Algorithm 1 shows the skeleton of the blocked SGEMM algorithm. Task partitioning is based on the result matrix C. Every $t_x \times t_y$ thread block is responsible for computing a $b_m \times b_n$ matrix block of C by reading a $b_m \times b_k$ block of A and a $b_k \times b_n$ block of B, where b_k is the unrolling factor. Therefore, A, B, and C are divided into $M * K$, $K * N$ and $M * N$ grids with $b_m \times b_k$, $b_k \times b_n$, and $b_m \times b_n$ blocks, where $M = \left\lfloor \frac{m+b_m-1}{b_m} \right\rfloor$, $K = \left\lfloor \frac{k+b_k-1}{b_k} \right\rfloor$, and $N = \left\lfloor \frac{n+b_n-1}{b_n} \right\rfloor$.

Algorithm 1 has $2 \times r_x \times r_y \times b_k$ floating-point operations (flops) on each thread for one iteration of the while loop. Table 1 estimates the data movement volume through registers, shared memory, and global memory correspondingly. These parameters demonstrate that SGEMM performance is determined by the hierarchical memory blocking and the unrolling factor of the inner for loop. Tuning these factors relies on GPU memory bandwidth and latency. According to previous work [19, 25], tuning proper parameters to overcome memory bandwidth limits is relatively easy with the estimates in Table 1. Performance tuning for memory latency is much more difficult since latency is closely coupled with particular microarchitectural features such as the instruction sequence and instruction types, which depends on a GPU toolchain and an assembler to identify.

2.2 CUDA Binary Utilities

Though no official GPU assembler is publicly available, NVIDIA provides a PTX assembly compiler `PTXAS` and

Algorithm 1 Blocked SGEMM algorithm of a $t_x \times t_y$ thread block. b_m, b_n, b_k are shared memory blocking sizes, r_x and r_y are register blocking sizes.

▷ Shared memory variables: sm_A, sm_B, sm'_A, sm'_B
▷ Registers variables: $accum[r_x \times r_y]$, $r_A[r_x]$, $r_B[r_y]$, $r'_A[r_x]$, $r'_B[r_y]$.
$sm_A \leftarrow$ a $b_m \times b_k$ block of A
$sm_B \leftarrow$ a $b_k \times b_n$ block of B
$r_A \leftarrow$ a column of sm_A
$r_B \leftarrow$ a row of sm_B
do
    sync
    ▷ Shared memory double buffering
    $sm'_A \leftarrow$ another $b_m \times b_k$ block of A
    $sm'_B \leftarrow$ another $b_k \times b_n$ block of B
    ▷ Thread-local computation
    for $i \leftarrow 0, \ldots b_k - 1$ **do** ▷ loop unrolling
        $r'_A \leftarrow$ a column of sm_A
        $r'_B \leftarrow$ a row of sm_B
        if i is even **then** ▷ Register double buffering
            $accum \leftarrow accum + r_A \circ r_B$ ▷ $\circ$: outer-product
        else
            $accum \leftarrow accum + r'_A \circ r'_B$
        end if
    end for
    $sm_A \leftrightarrow sm'_A$; $sm_B \leftrightarrow sm'_B$ ▷ swap shared memory pointers
while one more valid $b_k \times b_n$ block of B exists
store $accum$ with $b_m \times b_n$ block of C to global memory

Table 1: Data movement volume of each thread for one while loop iteration.

Data path	Volume (in words)
global⇒register (LDG)	$\frac{r_x \times r_y \times b_k}{b_m} + \frac{r_x \times r_y \times b_k}{b_n}$
register⇒shared (STS)	$\frac{r_x \times r_y \times b_k}{b_m} + \frac{r_x \times r_y \times b_k}{b_n}$
shared⇒register (LDS)	$r_x \times b_k + r_y \times b_k$

disassembly tools `cuobjdump` and `nvdisasm`, which make it possible to build a GPU third-party assembler. Both `cuobjdump` and `nvdisasm` disassemble *cubin* files to *sass* files, which are a human-readable disassembly for examining potential performance issues in CUDA programs. Every instruction in the disassembly is composed of an instruction address in hexadecimal, instruction content, and the 64-bit instruction encoding in hexadecimal. For example, an `IADD` instruction in disassembly is recorded as follows:

$$/*0048*/\ \ IADD\ R0,\ R2,\ R0;\ /*0x4800000000201c03*/ \quad (1)$$

Unfortunately, no tools are available to modify the assembly directly for performance tuning; the CUDA codes can only be refined and the newly generated disassembly is reexamine iteratively.

NVIDIA provides its pseudo-assembly language PTX and its compiler `PTXAS`, where PTX targets a stable machine-independent ISA that could span multiple GPU generations. Its machine-independent property is convenient for compiler design, but also brings several performance drawbacks. First, PTX uses pseudo-registers; programmers cannot control its register allocation, so register bank conflicts cannot be avoided. Second, PTX has no control code information which is used in Kepler and Maxwell GPUs to optimize warp scheduling. Thus, dual-issue on Kepler and warp scheduling on both Kepler and Maxwell optimizations cannot be controlled by the PTX programmer. Therefore, an assembler is required to manipulate the assembly. Although NVIDIA hasn't released their internal assembler and instruction encoding format, the disassembled codes in *sass* files and the pseudo-assembly references [22] provide clues to crack its instruction format in order to build our own assembler (details in Section 3). This paper uses disassembly generated from PTX as the input of the GPU ISA encoding solver.

3. Identifying Microarchitectural Features

We first illustrate the methodology to understand microarchitectural features and then explain the three major components: a GPU ISA encoding solver, an assembler, and benchmarks.

3.1 Methodology

We propose a methodology to understand GPU microarchitectural features and correlate them with microbenchmark performance. The workflow in Figure 1 consists of three major components: a GPU ISA encoding solver, a GPU assembler, and the microbenchmarks. The sample programs in Figure 1 are synthetic PTX files which generate specific instructions as the input of the instruction solver. Microbenchmarks are designed in assembly to figure out the correlation between microarchitecture and performance.

We write a simple generator to produce PTX instructions with various modifiers as the PTX samples. The generated PTX files are compiled to `cubin` files by `PTXAS`, and then disassembled by `cuobjdump` to generate native disassembly (around 2300 instruction variants). The ISA encoding solver takes the disassembly *sass* file as the input to decode each field of 64-bit instructions. A set of algorithms are designed to solve all the fields of a binary instruction. The fields include *operands*, *opcodes*, and *modifiers*. `cuobjdump` or `nvdisasm` is used to disassemble the binaries generated from the solver algorithms. Our assembler translates every instruction field to obtain 64-bit binaries and then encapsulates them with an ELF header to generate an executable cubin file. In the benchmarking workflow (dashed arrows in Figure 1), assembly microbenchmarks are tuned to explore GPU microarchitectural features such as register banking, instruction throughput, control codes, and load/store width.

3.2 GPU ISA Encoding Solver

The ISA encoding information that is necessary to build an assembler is not released by GPU vendors. Previous third-party work on building GPU assemblers [10, 12, 27] also involves cracking GPU ISA encodings, whereas no cracking process is explicitly reported. Our solver is proposed to make cracking GPU ISA encodings simple, automatic, and portable to future GPUs.

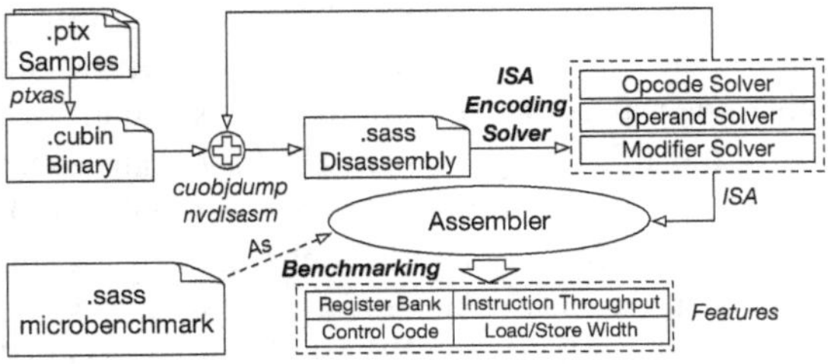

Figure 1: A schematic diagram in which GPU microarchitectural features are demystified by leveraging CUDA binary tools. The solid arrows represent the workflow of the instruction solver, while the dashed arrow represents benchmarking to determine the correlation between microarchitectures and performance.

Operands could be registers (e.g., `R5`), global memory (e.g., `[R6+0x20]`), constant memory (e.g., `C[0x2][0x40]`), shared memory (e.g., `[0x50]`), immediate values (e.g., `0x9` and `1.5`), or predicate registers (e.g., `P3`) [22]. We observe that an operand name always includes a number; thus, an operand can be inferred by its name. Since a number's encoding can be exactly explained, the operand encoding is relatively easy to recognize. For example, the register operand `R5` can be inferred from 101 in binary format, while the immediate value `0x9` is 1001. Opcodes and modifiers are mnemonic symbols, whose encodings cannot be literally explained; a heuristic algorithm is designed to crack their positions. In addition, modifiers are instruction-specific. Modifiers of the same type may have different encodings for different instructions. As an example, masks of the type-size modifier for instructions `LD` and `LDG` are in different binary positions. Hence, the modifier of every instruction needs to be processed independently.

3.2.1 Opcode and Modifier Solvers

We design a heuristic algorithm (Algorithm 2) to crack `opcode` encodings by detecting their bit positions. The opcode solver takes N disassembly instructions generated from PTX samples as the input and outputs all opcode bit positions as $opBits$. Each disassembly instruction $inst$ integrates its 64-bit binary code, name, operand types, and operand values as a structure. Take the `IADD` instruction in Equation 1 as an example; its binary code is $0x4800000000201c03$; the name is `IADD`; the types of operands are represented as a string "RRR"; and the values of operands are represented as a tuple $\{0, 2, 0\}$. By flipping the 64 bits one by one, we determine if each bit belongs to opcodes. Each flip generates a new binary code $\widehat{enc}$, which is disassembled by nvdisasm to a new instruction $\widehat{inst}$. If $\widehat{inst}$ is valid, and its instruction name is different from that of $inst$, this bit is in the opcode field.

From our results on a NVIDIA Tesla K20m, we find that the highest 10 bits and the lowest 2 bits represent opcodes of GPU Kepler architecture. The time complexity of the opcode solver is $O(64N)$, where N is the number of instructions in the disassembly file generated from PTX samples ($N \approx 2300$). This algorithm narrows the opcode enumeration space from 2^{64} to 2^{12}. We only enumerate possible opcodes in the pruned 12 bits and identify all the valid ones.

A modifier defines a specific behavior of an instruction. For example, `LD` instruction has type-size modifiers, such as `.u8`, `.s8`, `.u16`, `.32`, `.64` and `.128`, and cache operation modifiers, such as `.CS` (cache streaming) and `.CG` (cache at global level). We use a similar solver by flipping bit-by-bit to observe whether the bit controls an instruction modifier.

Algorithm 2 Opcode Solver

Input: instSet, N disassembly instructions generated from PTX samples
Onput: opBits, opcode positions in the 64-bit encoding
for $i \leftarrow 0, \dots, N-1$ **do**
  ▷ $inst$ structure: {enc64, name, oprdType, oprd}
  $inst$ = instSet[i]
  ▷ the 64-bit encoding of the instruction
  $enc \leftarrow$ inst.enc64
  ▷ check each bit of enc for opcode
  for $j \leftarrow 0, \dots, 63$ **do**
    ▷ flip the jth bit of the encoding
    $\widehat{enc}$ = xorAt(enc, j)
    ▷ disassemble new encoding $\widehat{enc}$
    $\widehat{inst}$=`nvdisasm`($\widehat{enc}$)
    ▷ bit-j is in the opcode field if $\widehat{inst}$ is a different instruction.
    if isvalid($\widehat{inst}$) and inst.$name \neq \widehat{inst}.name$ **then**
      put(j, $opBits$)
    end if
  end for
end for
Return opBits

3.2.2 Operand Solver

Algorithm 3 shows our algorithm of cracking operand encodings. Since each instruction may have different numbers and types of operands, we identify operand positions as a tuple of its name and operand type. The operand types of an instruction are represented as a string. For example, oprdType of the instruction `IADD` R1, R2, C[0x0][0x40] is "RRC" and oprdType of `IADD` R1, R2, 0x8 is "RRI", where R, C, and I represent registers, constant memory and immediates, respectively. For each instruction with the known opcode, we flip each bit to obtain a new instruction $\widehat{inst}$. We compare $inst$ with $\widehat{inst}$ using a simple function "whichChange". This function confirms which operand value is changed by its position, if any; otherwise, it returns a negative integer. An entry in the visited dictionary is marked as 1 to avoid duplicated probing. The time complexity of Algorithm 3 is $O(52N)$, where N is the number of disassembly instructions with different opcodes.

3.3 Benchmarking

We design a microbenchmark suite to explore NVIDIA GPU microarchitectural features. As shown in Figure 1, we write GPU kernel codes in assembly and compile them into `cubin` by our assembler. The assembly instructions inside the kernel are unrolled without exceeding the L1 instruction cache

Algorithm 3 Operand Solver

```
Input: instSet, N disassembly instructions with different opcodes
Onput: pos, operand positions for each opcode, a 2D array.
visited={ }    ▷ A dictionary to record the visited information of an operand bit, key:⟨name, oprdType⟩
for i ← 0, ..., N − 1 do
    ▷ inst structure: {enc64, name, oprdType, oprd}
    inst = instSet[i]
    ▷ check the rest bits of enc for operand by excluding opcode bits
    for j ← 2, ..., 53 do
        ▷ flip j^th bit of enc
        enc~ = xorAt(enc, j)
        ▷ disassemble new encoding enc~
        inst~=nvdisasm(enc~)
        ▷ If bit-j is an operand bit, return the operand position.
        p = whichChange(inst,inst~)
        if p > 0 then
            put(j, pos[⟨inst.name,inst.oprdType⟩][p])
            ▷ Mark ⟨name, oprdType⟩ as visited
            visited[⟨inst.name,inst.oprdType⟩] = 1
        end if
    end for
end for
Return pos
```

size to cover the branch overhead. The kernel code is tested hundreds of times, and the average time is used for accuracy. Timing ticks are recorded by the `S2R R0, SR_CLOCKLO` instruction, in which `S2R` moves the value from the special clock register `SR_CLOCKLO` to a general purpose register. Time is calculated in the general register, and then written into the global memory. Two metrics are benchmarked: latency and throughput. Latency is tested by a succession of *dependent* instructions by launching only one thread block with 32 threads. Throughput is tested by a succession of *independent* instructions by launching enough threads to make full use of the CUDA cores and memory bandwidth.

In this benchmarking process, we correlate microarchitectural features with the benchmark performance and obtain some meaningful observations in four microarchitectural features: register bank, control code, arithmetic throughput, and memory operation. These observations are useful for optimizing program snippets of real-world applications.

Observation 1–[Register Bank]: *Source register combinations may cause register bank conflicts that degrade instruction throughput.*

Shared memory bank conflicts are recognized as an important performance factor for CUDA programming. Recent research [16] has observed that register bank conflicts are also non-negligible. To probe register bank distribution, our microbenchmarks measure the instruction throughput for different combinations of `FFMA` register operands. Table 2 shows that different register combinations result in various levels of efficiency and throughput. The rightmost column represents the number of register bank conflicts recorded in our experiments. This experiment is conducted in single-issue mode by setting the control code to 0x20. Theoretically, without dual-issue, the peak efficiency is $4 \times 32/192 = 66.67\%$, in which 4 is the number of warp schedulers and 32 is the number of threads in a warp. In fact, we observe that the single-issue and dual-issue modes produce similar throughput behavior with bank conflicts. From our experiments on the Kepler architecture, we observe that:

- The destination register does not contribute to bank conflicts, so they are free to be assigned to any bank.
- When source registers have 2-way or 3-way register bank conflicts, the throughput of float instructions drops by 2.33% and 17.17% respectively, in single-issue mode.
- A proper register distribution is found through benchmarking to eliminate bank conflicts. Table 3 lists partial registers and their corresponding banks on NVIDIA Tesla K20m, which is consistent with the distribution on GTX680 [16]. Although they have different maximal numbers of registers per thread and instruction encodings.

Table 2: The efficiency of instruction throughput varies with different register combinations. Inst: instruction, Th/SM: instruction throughput per SM, Eff: throughput efficiency, Conf: register bank conflicts.

Inst	Th/SM	Eff	Conf
FFMA R5,R4,R1,R0	127.50	66.40%	0
FFMA R2,R4,R1,R0	127.50	66.40%	0
FFMA R5,R2,R1,R0	119.18	62.07%	2-way
FFMA R3,R2,R1,R0	119.18	62.07%	2-way
FFMA R5,R9,R3,R1	94.52	49.23%	3-way
FFMA R11,R9,R3,R1	94.52	49.23%	3-way
FMUL R4,R1,R0	127.50	66.40%	0
FMUL R4,R2,R0	119.17	62.06%	2-way

Table 3: Partial register index to register bank mapping.

Bank0	R0	R2	R8	R10	R16	R18	R24	R26
Bank1	R1	R3	R9	R11	R17	R19	R25	R27
Bank2	R4	R6	R12	R14	R20	R22	R28	R30
Bank3	R5	R7	R13	R15	R21	R23	R29	R31

Observation 2–[Control Code]: *Warp scheduling and issue mode are tunable by modifying control codes that regulate instruction issue.*

Starting with the Kepler architecture, NVIDIA has moved some control logics off the chip and into the kernel instructions to save power [10, 16]. This evolution provides programmers with the opportunity to make globally optimal scheduling decisions and other control optimizations if an assembler is available. The disassembly codes from sample programs indicate that a 64-bit binary control code controls 7 instructions is shown in Figure 7. We determine that the highest 6 bits and the lowest 2 bits are the *opcode* field of the scheduling instructions, and the middle 56 bits are used to control the execution of the following 7 instructions, each of which is assigned to an 8-bit control code.

We figure out the control code meanings by benchmarking the instruction sequences of different control codes. Bit 4, 5, and 7 represent shared memory, global memory, and the texture cache dependency barrier, respectively. We crack

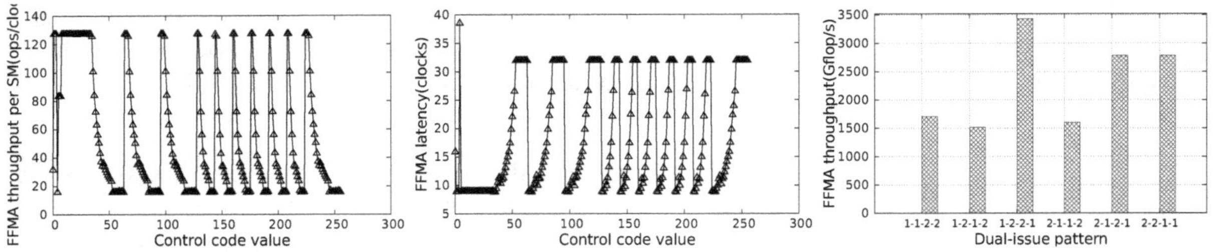

(a) (b) (c)

Figure 2: Different control codes impact on performance(subfigure(c), 1→single-issue, 2→dual-issue).

the meanings of bits 0-3 by testing the latency of FFMA instructions. Figure 2(a) and Figure 2(b) show FFMA's throughput and latency when its control code varies from 0 to 255. After 0x20, both the throughput and latency show obvious periodicity. For each period, by increasing the value of bits 0-3, FFMA throughput drops, and its latency increases at different rates. This phenomenon implies that bits 0-3 indicate the number of stall cycles before issuing the next instruction. Our microbenchmarking reveals some specific patterns of control codes:

- When the control code is set to 0x00, the scheduler suspends a warp of instructions for 16 cycles.
- 0x2n means a warp is suspended for n cycles before issuing the next instruction, where $n = 0, 1, \ldots, 15$.
- 0x20 means the single-issue mode, while 0x04 means the dual-issue mode. When two consecutive instructions are controlled by 0x04 and 0x05, the throughput could reach its maximum.

Observation 3–[Arithmetic Throughput]*: With a proper control code pattern and register allocation,* FFMA *instruction throughput could approach its theoretical peak in dual-issue mode.*

It's very intricate to tune the efficiency of FFMA throughput on Kepler due to the dual-issue mode. Previous work [16] reports the maximal FFMA throughput per SM as 132, which is only 68.75% of the theoretical throughput. Our microbenchmarks reveal several key points of tuning FFMA throughput to 97% efficiency. First, the control codes must be set properly to dual issue adjacent instructions. Second, the ratio and interval of dual issued FFMA instructions must be tuned into a specific pattern. Third, the first instruction of the core loop needs to be aligned by 8 instructions (seven normal instructions plus one scheduling instruction). This restriction is caused by the control code pattern in the seven normal instruction sequences. Finally, each FFMA requires three source registers; thus, in dual-issue mode, two FFMAs require six source registers. However, a Kepler GPU only provides four register banks. The instruction order must be adjusted to use Kepler's operand collector mechanism [7, 26] to avoid register bank conflicts.

Figure 3 illustrates the mapping of FFMA instructions to CUDA cores in dual-issue mode on one SM. There are $32 \times 6 = 192$ cores on one SM; among them, 32 cores are shared by two warp schedulers, and four warp schedulers are available for each SM. In single-issue mode, each warp scheduler can issue one float instruction to 32 cores per cycle, which yields $4 \times 32/192 = 66.67\%$ float computation efficiency. In dual-issue mode, two warp schedulers must use the shared cores alternately to avoid resource conflicts. The jagged white and gray blocks in Figure 3 show a proper phase shift between the executing pace of two warps to get access to the shared computing units in turn. The theoretical optimal ratio of dual-issue to single-issue is $2:2$, $\binom{4}{2} = 6$ combinations for mixed single-issue and dual-issue pattern inside a 7-instruction scheduling block (Figure 2(c)). We choose the best 1-2-2-1 pattern for our SGEMM implementation. As shown in Table 4, these optimizations together improve FFMA throughput to 186 ops/cycle, which is very close to the theoretical peak 192 ops/cycle.

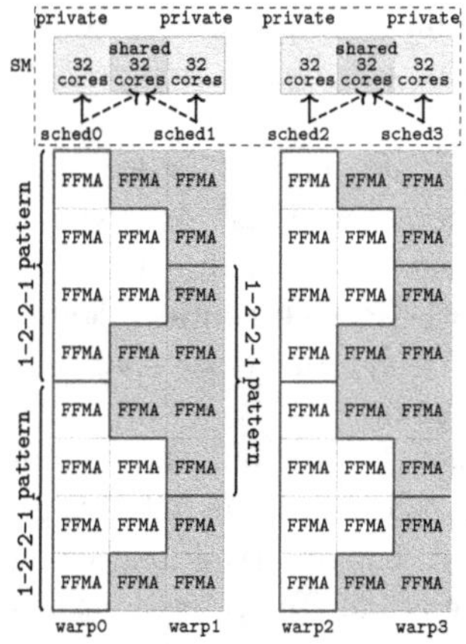

Figure 3: An illustration of FFMA dual-issue on one SM to achieve peak throughput

Table 4: Floating-point instruction throughput on Kepler

Inst	operation	single-issue	dual-issue
FFMA	c=a*b+c	127.52	186.35
FMUL	c=a*b	127.52	186.35
FADD	c=a+b	127.52	186.50

Observation 4–[Memory]: *For high memory bandwidth, shared memory prefers* 64*-bit load instruction* `LDS.64` *while global memory prefers texture cached* 128*-bit load instruction* `LDG.128`.

Regarding the GPU memory hierarchy, we focus on the programmer-controllable memory resources, shared memory and global memory. Different memory access widths (32-, 64-, or 128-bit) and paths (through L2 or texture cache) exist on NVIDIA GPUs. Intuitively, a wider load operation should achieve greater bandwidth. We test the bandwidth of shared memory instructions with different widths, i.e., `LDS.32`, `LDS.64`, and `LDS.128`. The instructions are arranged to avoid shared memory bank conflicts. Figure 4 compares the sequential memory access bandwidth of the three instructions by increasing the data volume. `LDS.64` achieves the highest bandwidth 137GB/s, which is about 76% of the peak shared memory bandwidth[1].

Two paths are used to load data from global memory, through the L2 cache by a `LD` instruction or the texture cache by a `LDG` instruction. We launch 26 thread blocks each with 512 threads, and specify that each thread accesses four words in a stride of $4 \times blockDim.x \times gridDim.x$. The total accessed global memory is 256MB. We benchmark that a `LDG.128` achieves 131GB/s, while `LD.128` only achieves 76GB/s.

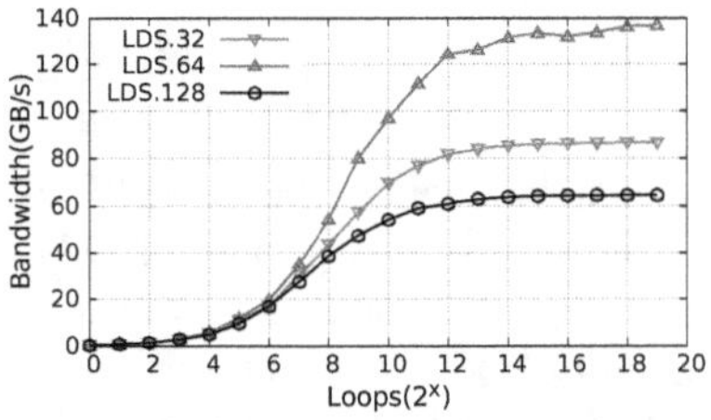

Figure 4: The bandwidth of `LDS.32`, `LDS.64`, and `LDS.128`

4. Optimizing SGEMM

The understanding of GPU microarchitectural features provides us with a larger tuning space for computational kernels. We apply a series of incremental optimizations to improve SGEMM performance on the Kepler architecture. The optimization strategies go through the architectural hierarchy from CUDA cores and registers to memory. All the optimization strategies are inspired by the observations from the benchmarking in Section 3.3.

- At the GPU core level, we promote `FFMA` instruction throughput to approach its peak through dual-issue by setting proper control codes.
- At the register level, we meticulously map operands to registers to avoid bank conflicts in the inner loop of Algorithm 1.
- At the memory level, we select the appropriate shared memory load/store width and global memory data path to achieve high bandwidth.

4.1 Register Allocation

To allocate registers for A column, B row, and C matrix block as in Algorithm 1, we have three objectives: correctness, no bank conflict, and tight register indices. `LDS.128` restricts four-word alignment for registers. Since the NVIDIA GPU does not have a 128-bit register, four consecutive 32-bit registers `RN`, `RN+1`, `RN+2`, and `RN+3` will be an equivalence for a 128-bit register, where N is a register index. We discover an undocumented restriction that N must be divisible by 4; otherwise, illegal instruction errors will be reported. The four-word alignment restriction for `LDS.128` simplifies hardware logic and cuts down power. Since we use `LDS.128` to load A and B, there are two bank allocation choices under this restriction and Kepler's bank distribution (Table 3). We use four colors to represent the four banks and show the register allocation when computing a 12×12 block of C in Figure 5. We assume allocating banks of A as $\begin{bmatrix} 0 \\ 1 \end{bmatrix}$, banks of B as $\begin{bmatrix} 2 & 3 \end{bmatrix}$ as in Figure 5, and two choices remain for C, $\begin{bmatrix} 1 & 2 \\ 3 & 0 \end{bmatrix}$ and $\begin{bmatrix} 3 & 1 \\ 0 & 2 \end{bmatrix}$. The $2 \times 2 = 4$ bank patterns of SGEMM are equivalent in performance. Then, we arbitrarily choose $\begin{bmatrix} 0 \\ 1 \end{bmatrix}$ $\begin{bmatrix} 2 & 3 \end{bmatrix}$ $\begin{bmatrix} 1 & 2 \\ 3 & 0 \end{bmatrix}$ for A, B, and C, respectively. For actual register index allocation, we choose continuous register indices to avoid exceeding 255. Every matrix block C_{ij}, column A_i, and row B_j have different banks in Figure 5; thus, register bank conflicts are completely avoided.

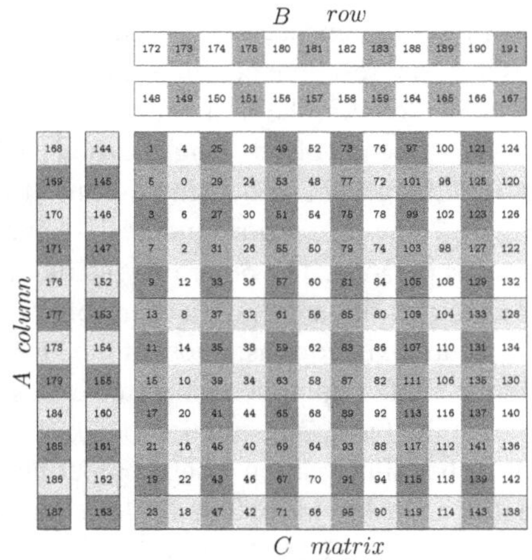

Figure 5: Register allocation in SGEMM. Every number in a cell is a register index. Different colors denote the mapping of register banks: green→bank0, blue→bank1, gray→bank2, red→bank3.

4.2 FFMA Dual-Issue

It is unrealistic to keep warp schedulers dual issuing the same kind of arithmetic instructions (e.g., `FFMA`) all the time.

[1] The theoretical shared memory bandwidth of an SM is calculated as $Bandwidth = f_{core} \times Width \times Warpsize$ in bytes, where f_{core} is the core frequency, $Width$ is the width of each shared memory bank.

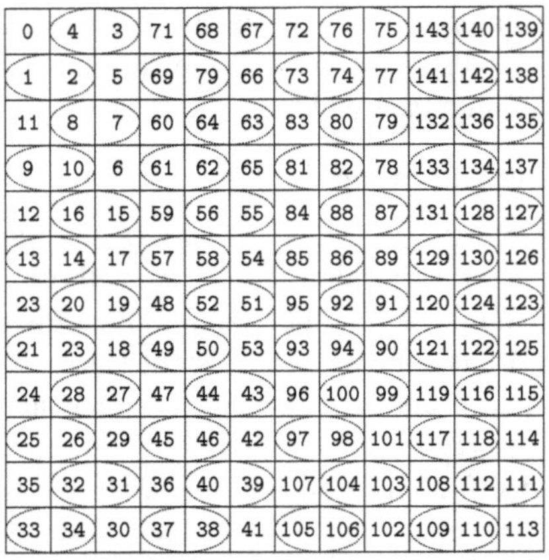

Figure 6: FFMAs instruction scheduling to compute a 12×12 block of C. The numbers in cells denote the FFMA execution order. Dashed ellipses across two adjacent cells indicate that two adjacent FFMA instructions are dual issued in one clock cycle.

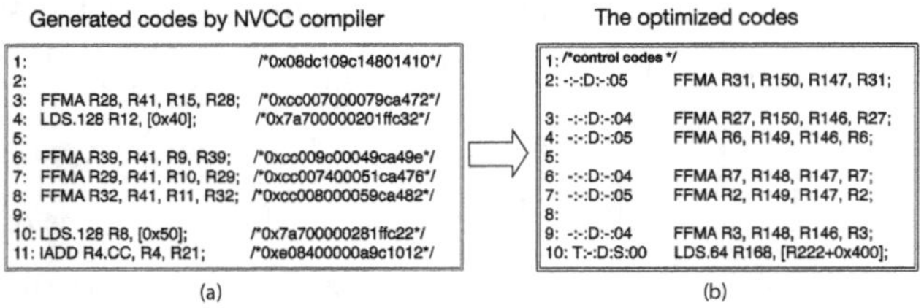

Figure 7: A comparison of compiler generated codes and our tuned assembly codes.

On a Kepler GPU, each warp is privately assigned 32 cores, and four warp schedulers consume 128 cores. The remaining $192 - 128 = 64$ cores are divided into two 32-core groups; each group of 32 cores is shared by two warp schedulers. Two warp schedulers need to negotiate for the extra 32 shared cores to avoid resource conflicts. As noted from *Observation 3* in Section 3.3, the best pattern of FFMA instructions block is a sequence of one single-issue (1 FFMA), two dual-issues (4 FFMAs), and another single-issue (1 FFMA). As shown in Figure 7, the instructions in lines 3-4 and lines 6-7 are dual issued separately. The other two instructions in line 8 and line 11 are two single-issues in terms of floating-point instruction execution. In contrast, most of the FFMAs are single issued in the CUDA compiler generated codes.

By extending the basic 7-instruction block (Section 3.3), we depict the scheduling pattern when computing a 12×12 block of matrix C in Figure 6. The FFMA to calculate C_{00} is issued first, then two FFMAs to compute C_{10} and C_{11} are simultaneously issued.

Another advantage of this execution order is less register pressure due to register reuse by facilitating the operand collector mechanism [7]. The operand collector allows operands to be cached and reused in subsequent instructions. The assembly code in Figure 7 lists the instructions calculating $C_{32}, C_{22}, C_{21}, C_{30}, C_{31}, C_{20}$ which correspond to the orders of $6, 7, 8, 9, 10, 11$ in Figure 5. With the elaborately designed computing order and register allocation, the reuse happens as follows. The FFMA in Line 3 uses cached operand R150 of Line 2, while Line 3 and Line 4 share R146. Thus, in the dual-issue mode, FFMAs of Line 3 and 4 need to read four registers R146, R27, R149, R6 instead of six. The corresponding banks of these registers are $0, 1, 3, 2$ based on Table 3, so no bank conflicts occur. Similarly, Line 7 uses the cached operand R149 from Line 4. In dual-issue mode, two FFMAs of Line 6 and Line 7 need to read 4 registers R148, R147, R7 and R2.

4.3 Schedule non-FFMA Instructions

After setting the order of FFMAs, non-FFMA instructions need to be inserted in proper positions to ensure correctness without losing performance. To tolerate instruction latency, the distance of dependent instructions needs to be larger than their latency. The distance is approximated as

$$distance = \frac{4 \times \#instructions}{7}. \quad (2)$$

A 7-instruction scheduling block costs four clock cycles in dual-issue mode. Therefore, given the distance L of two interleaved instructions, at least $\frac{L*7}{4}$ instructions are needed. In addition, the number of the rest slots to insert these non-FFMA instructions is estimated as

$$\#slots = \frac{r_x \times r_y \times b_k}{ffmas\_in\_schedule\_block} = \frac{12 \times 12 \times 4}{6} = 24 \times 4.$$

$r_x \times r_y \times b_k$ yields the total number of FFMAs for one thread inside the innermost loop in Algorithm 1, where r_x and r_y are register blocking sizes and b_k is the unrolling factor. *ffmas_in_schedule_block* is the number of FFMA instructions of one scheduling block, which is six by the 1-2-2-1 dual-issue pattern in Section 3.3. According to these principles, we first arrange LDS, STS, LDG because of their long latencies. The schedule slots are illustrated in a table. Note that we use double-buffering to hide the LDG latency from global memory, which is around 120 clock cycles. Every four loops require two LDGs to load data from global memory to registers, and four STSs to store data from registers to shared memory. A read after write (RAW) dependency exists between LDG and STS. From Equation 2, $\frac{120 \times 7}{4} = 210$ instructions are needed between them. We put LDG and STS in position $P[77][3]$ and $P[65][2]$, respectively, in Table 5. Thus, the in-between $143 - 77 + 144 \times 2 + 65 = 419\ (> 210)$ instructions are enough to hide the latency of LDGs.

The arrangement of LDS instructions, which load data from shared memory for double buffering A and B, follows the same approach with LDGs. The LDS latency is 28 clock cycles; thus, $\frac{28 \times 7}{4} = 49$ instructions are needed to interleave a LDS and an FFMA. In Table 5, LDS in $P[11][3]$ reads data from STS in $P[65][2]$; the distance between them is more than 28 cycles. At the end, a BAR.SYNC is inserted after STS but before LDS to make sure that data in shared memory is ready. Other instructions such as XOR, IADD, and ISETP are inserted according to data dependency; they do not influence the performance because of their short latencies.

Table 5: The position table of `non-FFMA` instructions. The inner-loop is unrolled four times. The first column records slot numbers, and the first row represents iteration numbers.

slot \ unroll	0	1	2	3
5	ISET P0	IADD A0		XOR smB
11	LDS.64 smA	LDS.64 smA	LDS.64 smA	LDS.64 smA
17	LDS.64 smA	LDS.64 smA	LDS.64 smA	LDS.64 smA
23	LDS.64 smA	LDS.64 smA	LDS.64 smA	LDS.64 smA
29	LDS.64 smA	LDS.64 smA	LDS.64 smA	LDS.64 smA
35	IADD K, -4	IADD A1	TEXDEPBAR	
41	LDS.64 smB	LDS.64 smB	LDS.64 smB	LDS.64 smB
47	LDS.64 smB	LDS.64 smB	LDS.64 smB	LDS.64 smB
53	LDS.64 smB	LDS.64 smB	LDS.64 smB	LDS.64 smB
59	LDS.64 smB	LDS.64 smB	LDS.64 smB	LDS.64 smB
65			STS.64 writeS	ISETP P2
71				
77		IADD B0		LDG A
83	LDS.64 smA	LDS.64 smA	LDS.64 smA	LDS.64 smA
89	ISETP P3			
95	LDS.64 smA	LDS.64 smA	LDS.64 smA	LDS.64 smA
101			STS.64 loadB0	LDG B
107			STS.64 loadB2	XOR writeS
113				
119	LDS.64 smB	LDS.64 smB	LDS.64 smB	LDS.64 smB
125			XOR smA	
131	LDS.64 smB	LDS.64 smB	LDS.64 smB	LDS.64 smB
137				
143		IADD B1	BAR.SYNC	BAR Loop

4.4 Memory Movement

According to our benchmarking observations, we use `LDG.128` to load data from texture cached global memory and `LDS.64` to load data from shared memory. Additional reasons to adopt them in SGEMM kernel are as follows: First, `LDG.128` reduces load instructions, and hence reduces `non-FFMAs`. In the inner loop of Algorithm 1, we need three `LDG.128`s instead of twelve `LDG.32`s to read twelve words from a column of A . Second, the shared memory transaction size of a warp is at most 256 bytes, which forces `LDS.128` memory requests to be split into multiple transactions. As we analyzed in Section 5, `LDS.128` has a lower bandwidth than `LDS.64`, which bounds the SGEMM performance.

5. Evaluation

In this section, we compare the performance of our optimized SGEMM with NVIDIA cuBLAS. Then, we present quantitative analysis on the effect of each optimization strategy and an estimation of the performance upper bound using a roofline model.

The experiments are conducted on an NVIDIA Tesla K20m GPU (refer to [20] for detailed specifications). We compare cuBLAS from CUDA 7.0 by testing both square matrices and rectangle matrices. The size of the square matrices varies from 384 to 12288 with a step 384. The smallest dimension of the rectangle matrices varies from 192 to 3072 with a step 192.

5.1 Overall Performance

We use $[M, K, N]$ to denote size of matrix A to be $M \times K$ and size of matrix B to be $K \times N$. Figure 8 shows the SGEMM performance of five different matrix shapes, $[W, W, W]$, $[W, 2W, 4W]$, $[W, 4W, W]$, $[4W, W, 4W]$, and $[4W, 2W, W]$, where the values of W are shown on the x-axis. The results demonstrate that our 12×12 and 8×8 register blocking implementations are better than cuBLAS in most cases. While 12×12 is the best one when the matrix size is greater than 1000, and 8×8 blocking is better when the matrix size is small. The performance of both cuBLAS and our SGEMM for the matrix shape $[W, 4W, W]$ fluctuates more seriously than other shapes because its parallelism is coarser, and each thread iteration is much longer ($K = 4W$). In contrast, $[4W, W, 4W]$, with the finest parallelism of the four shapes, has the smoothest results. When the matrix size is 12288×12288, the optimized SGEMM achieves 3.1 Tflop/s with 88% efficiency, while cuBLAS gets 2.7 Tflop/s with 76% efficiency. Our SGEMM achieves a $1.15\times$ performance speedup over cuBLAS. SGEMM performance increases with matrix size. One reason is that a larger matrix has a higher ratio of floating-point operations to the store operations of matrix C.Another reason is that a larger matrix has a better load balance on GPU because of the increase in the workload of each CUDA core. The number of thread blocks ranges from $2 \times 2, 8 \times 8, \ldots, 64 \times 64$ from left to right in Figure 8. Since Kepler has 13 SMs, matrix 384×384 suffers more from load imbalance because there are only 4 thread blocks. This explains the significant performance improvement when the size grows from 384 to 1536. With respect to the performance improvement over cuBLAS, our optimizations benefit more from larger matrices. The higher arithmetic intensity of larger matrices makes their performance increasingly bounded by the GPU microarchitecture rather than its memory hierarchy. Therefore, our microarchitecture-level optimization plays an important role in tuning SGEMM performance.

5.2 Performance Analysis

5.2.1 Influence of Register Blocking Sizes

Table 1 summarizes the data movement volume of the blocked SGEMM algorithm. The volume of data moving from shared memory to register is $r_x \times b_k + r_y \times b_k$, and the floating-point computation volume is $r_x \times r_y \times b_k$. The shared memory arithmetic intensity (sAI) is defined as the ratio between them:

$$sAI = \frac{r_x \times r_y \times b_k}{r_x \times b_k + r_y \times b_k} = \frac{1}{\frac{1}{r_x} + \frac{1}{r_y}}. \quad (3)$$

Register blocking sizes r_x and r_y are limited by the register counts per thread. Each thread needs $r_x \times r_y$, $2 \times r_x$ and $2 \times r_y$ registers to store the result of a matrix block of C, two columns of A (double-buffering), and two rows of B (double-buffering), respectively, in one single iteration of the innermost loop in Algorithm 1. Since the total number of registers must be less than the maximum register counts per thread (256 on Kepler), we have

$$r_x \times r_y + 2r_x + 2r_y < 256. \quad (4)$$

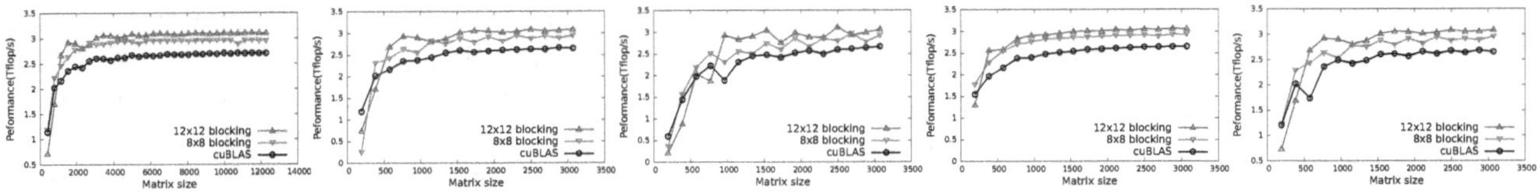

(a) [W,W,W] (b) [W, 2W, 4W] (c) [W, 4W, W] (d) [4W, W, 4W] (e) [4W, 2W, W]

Figure 8: Performance comparison of cuBLAS and the optimized SGEMM on different matrices

Equation 3 implies that larger register blocking yields a higher shared memory arithmetic intensity, and the optimal solution lies at $r_x = r_y$ with restriction by Equation 4. We use 8×8 and 12×12 blockings as a case study. In Figure 8, 12×12 blocking has better performance than 8×8 blocking because 12×12 blocking has higher sAI and instruction level parallelism. With respect to instruction scheduling optimization in Table 5, it has more slots to insert non-FFMA instructions, and latency can be better hidden. $12 * 12 + 4 * 12 = 192$ registers are used by LD and FFMA instructions, and a total of 236 registers with other address indices. The register counts per SM restricts us to launch up to 256 threads/block, which is in our implementation. Each thread block computes a matrix block $C_{192,192}$ by multiplying $A_{192,4}$ and $B_{4,192}$, where 4 is the unrolling factor.

Only one thread block per SM is active due to register limitation; thus, the thread occupancy is $256/2048 = 12.5\%$. With higher instruction level parallelism by using larger register blocking, the thread parallelism becomes low. However, the high performance of our SGEMM confirms that instruction level parallelism also plays an important role in GPU performance. A similar conclusion is offered by Volkov in [28].

5.2.2 Profiling Microarchitectural Optimizations

To examine the performance gains of different optimization strategies, we construct several intermediate implementations by incrementally applying our microarchitectural optimizations.

Baseline: The baseline has adopted conventional optimizations including register blocking, global and shared memory double bufferings, and unrolling, although without the assembly level optimizations. For example, the baseline uses default 32-bit LD rather than 128-bit LDG instructions to load data from global memory. Registers are allocated first for C from 0 to 143, then for A and B. In this case, FFMAs have $368/(144 * 4) = 63.89\%$ 2-way bank conflicts and $64/(144 * 4) = 11.11\%$ 3-way bank conflicts. In addition, the baseline cannot apply dual-issue optimization either.

+Reg: The register allocation pattern described in Section 4.1 is applied to eliminate register bank conflicts.

+LD128: Use wide global load instruction LD.128 with L2-cached. Although Kepler has an L1 data cache, it is designed for local rather than global memory access [20].

+LDG128: Use the faster texture cached LDG instead of L2-cached LD along with TEXDEPBAR before data access due to the weak consistency of the texture cache [17].

+Dual: Use the dual-issue control fully enabled by utilizing the pattern described in Section 3. In dual-issue mode, NOP may be inserted for 7-instruction alignment.

Figure 9 shows the performance gains of each optimization strategy. As long as the number of instructions changes, instruction rescheduling is necessary to achieve good performance. Compared with the baseline implementation, SGEMM can achieve a $2.6\times$ speedup by applying all the optimizations. The elimination of register bank conflicts leads to performance improvement of approximately 10%. Wide load instruction LD.128 contributes 27%-35% to performance, and texture-cached load instruction LDG.128 leads to an improvement of 5%-12%. Dual-issue achieves the highest performance improvement with 84%-106%.

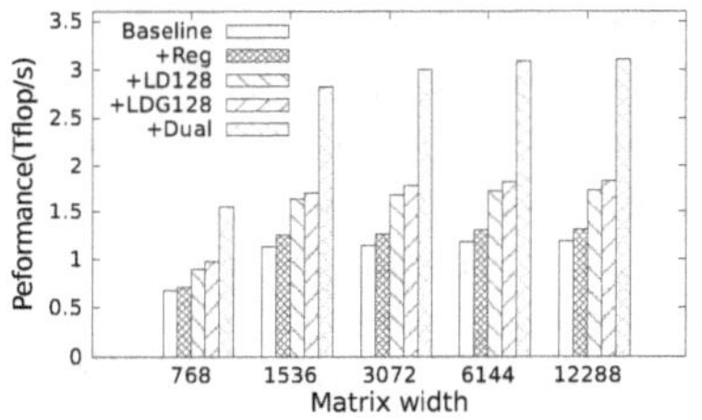

Figure 9: Evaluation of incremental optimizations.

5.2.3 Bounding Factor Analysis

We estimate the upper bound factors: shared memory, global memory, and computation power. In the innermost loop of Algorithm 1, each thread block computes $b_m \times b_n \times b_k$ operations and reads $b_m \times b_k + b_n \times b_k$ words. The upper bound of SGEMM by global memory bandwidth can be modeled as:

$$\frac{2 \times b_m \times b_n \times b_k}{4(b_m \times b_k + b_n \times b_k)} \geq \frac{PeakFlops}{Bandwidth_{global}} \tag{5}$$

According to the parameters in our SGEMM implementation, $b_m = b_n = 192$, $b_k = 4$, $PeakFlops = 3520$Gflop/s, so 73GB/s is the minimum requirement for the global memory bandwidth to achieve the theoretical peak of 3520Gflop/s. Inside each loop, $(r_x \times b_k + r_y \times b_k) \times t_x \times t_y$ words are read from shared memory, where t_x and t_y are thread block sizes, and r_x and r_y are register blocking sizes. The computation flops is $b_m \times b_n \times b_k$; thus, the ratio of computation to shared memory access is

$$\frac{2 \times b_m \times b_k \times b_n}{4t_x \times t_y \times (r_x \times b_k + r_y \times b_k)} \geq \frac{PeakFlops}{Bandwidth_{shared}} \quad (6)$$

The minimum shared memory bandwidth requirement of SGEMM is 1173GB/s on the Tesla K20m, which is $1173/13 = 90$GB/s for each SM. Theoretically, hardware provides 200GB/s of global memory bandwidth and 2349GB/s of shared memory bandwidth, both of which are higher than the requirements; hence, neither of them are the bottleneck.

SGEMM has a different computation to memory access ratio in terms of global memory and shared memory, so we demonstrate two roofline models in Figure 10. The slant line in Figure 10(a) represents attainable performance with different arithmetic intensities when bounded by global bandwidth. The x-axis represents the flops:bytes ratios, which are 48 for 192×192 and 32 for 128×128 shared memory blocking of SGEMM based on Equation 5. Horizontal lines show the machine's peak performance and the performance of our optimized SGEMM with or without dual-issue. This figure demonstrates that SGEMM is not bounded by global memory bandwidth for either 128×128 or 192×192 shared memory blockings. The slant line in Figure 10(b) represents attainable performance with different arithmetic intensities when bounded by shared memory bandwidth. The x-axis represents the flops:bytes ratios, which are 3 for 12×12 and 2 for 8×8 register blocking of SGEMM based on Equation 6. This figure shows SGEMM is not bounded by shared memory through our `LDS` optimization. However, if we use `LDS.128` instead of `LDS.64`, SGEMM will be bounded by shared memory even for 12×12 blocking.

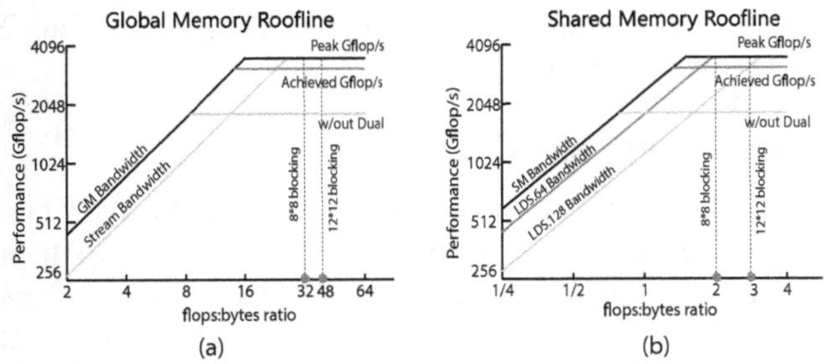

Figure 10: Memory roofline model using log-log scale. "GM/SM Bandwidth" indicates global/shared memory's theoretical bandwidth.

The loss of peak performance can be explained as follows. As we have shown in Section 3, `FFMA` throughput can achieve 97.67% efficiency. The loss is about 2.33%, which may be the result of overhead of the warp scheduler in `FFMA` dual-issue mode. The double-buffering algorithm can amortize the latency of `LDS`. With 12×12 register blocking and unrolling of 4, there are $144 * 4 = 576$ `FFMA`s in the loop. With our designed `FFMA` dual-issue pattern, every six `FFMA`s need four clock cycles in the pipeline. The innermost loop needs $4 \times 144 \times 4/6 = 384$ cycles for each thread, and two `LDG.128`s are also needed. We observe that each `LDG` has 10 cycles of penalty; the total `LDG` causes a $2 \times 10/384 = 5.2\%$ loss. Other penalties may be caused by synchronization and writing C matrix in the block.

6. Generality

Although this paper examines the methodology on GPU Kepler architecture and shows performance optimizations for SGEMM, we argue that the developed toolchains can be easily extended to other NVIDIA GPUs and that the explored optimization strategies are applicable to other floating-point computation-intensive applications.

Portability of Toolchains: For a particular GPU architecture, users only need to regenerate disassembly codes from the PTX samples and microbenchmarks with CUDA binary utilities and then feed them to the ISA encoding solver. The opcode, modifier, and operand solvers are portable among GPU architectures. We have validated the solver functionalities on the Fermi, Kepler, and Maxwell GPUs [33]. A corresponding assembler can be obtained by modifying the instruction grammar definition decoded by the solver, which could be done automatically with an assembler template [4].

Generality of Optimization Methods: The optimization strategies include FFMA dual-issue, register allocation, memory load/store width, and instruction scheduling. Note that the bare-metal tunings are more microarchitectural specific than application specific. With the support of assembly, our scheduling optimization is totally derived from instruction dependency and latency, which is not specific to SGEMM. With a proper blocking algorithm, multiple float computation instructions reside in a single loop iteration; then, register allocation and dual-issue optimization can be used to improve floating-point computation throughput.

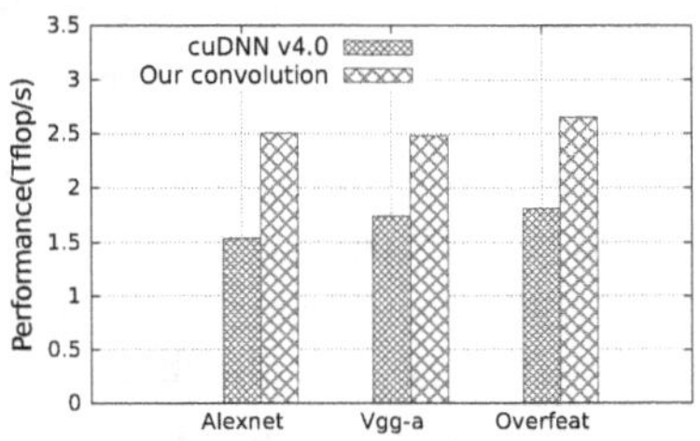

Figure 11: Performance comparison of cuDNN and our optimized convolution on GPU Tesla K20m (batch size is 128).

Applying Optimizations to Convolution Algorithm: Our convolution algorithm implementation uses 128×128 shared memory blocking and 8×8 register blocking. We optimize it at the assembly level by using the method described in section 4. We benchmark three popular convolutional neural networks: Alexnet [15], Vgg [24], and Overfeat [23]. The configuration of each convolutional layer can be found in corresponding papers. Figure 11 presents the performance of our optimized convolution and cuDNN by comparing the average performance of all the convolutional layers in a neural network. Our optimized convolution implementations are 39%, 46%, and 62% higher than cuDNN V4.0 for the three CNN configurations respectively on Tesla K20m.

7. Related Work

This section briefly discusses related work in reverse engineering ISA encoding, GPU assembler, microbenchmarking, and SGEMM optimization.

ISA Encoding Solver and GPU Assembler: CPU ISA encoding reverse engineering work [8, 13] broadly exists by using a MIPS, SPARC, Alpha, PowerPC, ARM, or x86 assembler to crack CPU instruction sets and extract bit-level instruction encoding information. These works output C declarations that can be used by binary tools. However, NVIDIA does not have an available GPU assembler, but a disassembler instead. The lack of a GPU assembler for public use makes our reverse engineering on GPUs more meaningful.

The absence of a GPU assembler motivates a series of works that develop toolchains to facilitate tuning codes at the assembly level. For the early architecture G80, Decuda [27] demonstrated the feasibility of operating assembly instructions. After that, for almost every generation of GPU architecture, there are several efforts to develop assembly toolchains. Asfermi [12], and cudaasm-qhasm [5] are assemblers for the Fermi architecture, and MaxAs [10] assembler is for the Maxwell architecture. Envytools [1] supports the translation of PTX instructions to 64-bit binaries for several GPU architectures; it is not able to generate a compatible `cubin` that can be directly used by the CUDA driver APIs. Although all their work involves reverse engineering GPU ISA encodings, detailed descriptions are not provided nor is a general tool developed to crack a new GPU ISA encoding. We provide a general toolchain to automatically crack different GPU ISA encodings and an assembler for the Kepler architecture.

Benchmarking: Fog [9] did sound work on benchmarking instruction latency and throughput of several generations of Intel and AMD CPUs, and Intel Xeon Phi accelerators. Wong et al. [31] performed a comprehensive benchmarking study on GT200 and provided pipeline latency data and memory features. Mei et al. [18] benchmarked memory hierarchy including cache, and shared memory on Fermi, Kepler, and Maxwell GPUs. However, they did not benchmark the dual-issue mode of arithmetic instructions or vectorized load instructions such as `LD` and `LDS`, which leaves non-negligible unexplored performance space. We leverage the complete assembler to crack control codes that reveal more microarchitecture details for tuning application performance.

Matrix Multiplication Tuning: With respect to GEMM optimization in the microarchitectural level, some work inspires our GPU implementations. Tan et al. [25] implemented a fast DGEMM by using assembly-level optimization, such as software pipelining, vector memory operations, and instruction scheduling. Lai et al. [16] presented performance analysis and optimization work of SGEMM on both Fermi and GTX680 GPUs. Gray [11] presented SGEMM optimization in assembly on a Maxwell GPU. We adopt the proved effective optimization techniques such as shared memory/register blocking and double-buffering [25, 29]. However, it is difficult to tune all possible microarchitectural optimizations well without a useful toolchain. In this work, we present a complete case study of applying microarchitectural features by combining register allocation, dual issuing, memory access paths, and instruction scheduling by using our toolchains.

8. Conclusion

We presented a methodology to understand GPU microarchitectural features and demonstrated its application on tuning SGEMM and convolution algorithms. The methodology includes a GPU ISA solver to crack its ISA encoding, a GPU assembler, and microbenchmarks at the assembly level to correlate architectural features with performance. Based on the disclosed insights, we implemented the fastest SGEMM, 3.1Tflop/s with 88% efficiency on an NVIDIA Tesla K20m, which is 15% faster than cuBLAS. We also build roofline models to analyze its performance upper bound. Applying these optimizations on convolution, the optimized implementations outperform cuDNN4.0 by 39%-62% on the Tesla K20m. Our work brings GPU optimizations to a deeper native machine level, which may shed light on developments in compilers or other performance-critical kernels. In the future, we will apply our methodology to the latest Pascal GPU to reveal its microarchitectural features. We also intend to apply our GPU microarchitectural insights and assembly optimization to optimize code generation of the open source GPU compiler GPUCC [32].

Acknowledgments

We would like to thank Prof. Mary Hall and other reviewers for the very useful comments and suggestions which help us improve the quality of our paper. This work is supported by the National Key Research and Development Program of China (2016YFB0201305, 2016YFB0200504, 2016YFB0200803, 2016YFB1000400), National 863 Foundation of China (2015AA01A301, 2015AA015303), National Natural Science Foundation of China, under grant no. (91430218, 31327901, 61472395, 61272134, 61432018, 61521092), the joint deep learning lab of Institute of Computing Technology and Sugon, and CAS Holdings.

References

[1] Envytools. `https://github.com/envytools/envytools`.

[2] AMD. clMath. `https://github.com/clMathLibraries`.

[3] ACML AMD. AMD Core Math Library (ACML), 2014.

[4] Alexandro Baldassin, Paulo Cesar Centoducatte, and Sandro Rigo. Extending the archc language for automatic generation of assemblers. In *17th International Symposium on Computer Architecture and High Performance Computing (SBAC-PAD'05)*, pages 60–67. IEEE, 2005.

[5] Daniel J Bernstein, Hsieh-Chung Chen, Chen-Mou Cheng, Tanja Lange, Ruben Niederhagen, Peter Schwabe, and Bo-Yin Yang. Usable assembly language for GPUs: a success story. *IACR Cryptology ePrint Archive*, 2012:137, 2012.

[6] Lung-Sheng Chien. Hand tuned SGEMM on GT200 gpu. Technical report, Tech. rep., Department of Mathematics, Tsing Hua University, Taiwan, 2010.

[7] Jack Hilaire Choquette, Manuel Olivier Gautho, and John Erik Lindholm. Methods and apparatus for source operand collector caching, January 28 2014. US Patent 8,639,882.

[8] Christian S Collberg. Reverse interpretation+ mutation analysis= automatic retargeting. In *ACM SIGPLAN Notices*, volume 32, pages 57–70. ACM, 1997.

[9] Agner Fog. Instruction tables: Lists of instruction latencies, throughputs and micro-operation breakdowns for Intel, AMD and VIA CPUs. *Denmark (Lyngby): Technical University of Denmark*, 2012.

[10] Scott Gray. MaxAs. `https://github.com/NervanaSystems/maxas`.

[11] Scott Gray. NervanaGPU. `https://github.com/NervanaSystems/maxas/wiki/SGEMM`.

[12] Yunqing Hou. AsFermi. `https://code.google.com/archive/p/asfermi/wikis`.

[13] Wilson C Hsieh, Dawson R Engler, and Godmar Back. Reverse-engineering instruction encodings. In *USENIX Annual Technical Conference, General Track*, pages 133–145, 2001.

[14] MKL Intel. Intel Math Kernel Library, 2007.

[15] Alex Krizhevsky, Ilya Sutskever, and Geoffrey E Hinton. Imagenet classification with deep convolutional neural networks. In *Advances in neural information processing systems*, pages 1097–1105, 2012.

[16] Junjie Lai and André Seznec. Performance upper bound analysis and optimization of sgemm on Fermi and Kepler GPUs. In *Code Generation and Optimization (CGO), 2013 IEEE/ACM International Symposium on*, pages 1–10. IEEE, 2013.

[17] M. Lukyanov, B. Beylin, R.S. Glanville, and A. Grosul. Efficient placement of texture barrier instructions, February 20 2014. US Patent App. 13/590,075.

[18] Xinxin Mei, Kaiyong Zhao, Chengjian Liu, and Xiaowen Chu. Benchmarking the memory hierarchy of modern GPUs. In *Network and Parallel Computing*, pages 144–156. Springer, 2014.

[19] R Nath, S Tomov, and J Dongarra. An improved MAGMA GEMM for Fermi GPUs, university of tennessee computer science technical report. Technical report, UTCS-10-655, July, 2010.

[20] Nvidia. Nvidias next generation CUDA compute architecture: Kepler GK110, the fastest, most efficient HPC architecture ever built. White Paper, 2012.

[21] NVidia. CUDA binary utilities. September 2015.

[22] NVIDIA. Parallel thread execution ISA v4.3. `http://docs.nvidia.com/cuda/parallel-thread-execution/#axzz42f7ftJVy`, September 2015.

[23] Pierre Sermanet, David Eigen, Xiang Zhang, Michaël Mathieu, Rob Fergus, and Yann LeCun. Overfeat: Integrated recognition, localization and detection using convolutional networks. *arXiv preprint arXiv:1312.6229*, 2013.

[24] Karen Simonyan and Andrew Zisserman. Very deep convolutional networks for large-scale image recognition. *arXiv preprint arXiv:1409.1556*, 2014.

[25] Guangming Tan, Linchuan Li, Sean Triechle, Everett Phillips, Yungang Bao, and Ninghui Sun. Fast implementation of dgemm on fermi gpu. In *Proceedings of 2011 International Conference for High Performance Computing, Networking, Storage and Analysis*, page 35. ACM, 2011.

[26] D. Tarjan and K. Skadron. Policy based allocation of register file cache to threads in multi-threaded processor, June 12 2012. US Patent 8,200,949.

[27] Wladimir J. van der Laan. Decuda. `https://github.com/laanwj/decuda`.

[28] Vasily Volkov. Better performance at lower occupancy. In *Proceedings of the GPU technology conference, GTC*, volume 10, page 16. San Jose, CA, 2010.

[29] Vasily Volkov and James W Demmel. Benchmarking GPUs to tune dense linear algebra. In *High Performance Computing, Networking, Storage and Analysis, 2008. SC 2008. International Conference for*, pages 1–11. IEEE, 2008.

[30] Qian Wang, Xianyi Zhang, Yunquan Zhang, and Qing Yi. Augem: automatically generate high performance dense linear algebra kernels on x86 cpus. In *Proceedings of the International Conference on High Performance Computing, Networking, Storage and Analysis*, page 25. ACM, 2013.

[31] Henry Wong, Misel-Myrto Papadopoulou, Maryam Sadooghi-Alvandi, and Andreas Moshovos. Demystifying GPU microarchitecture through microbenchmarking. In *Performance Analysis of Systems & Software (ISPASS), 2010 IEEE International Symposium on*, pages 235–246. IEEE, 2010.

[32] Jingyue Wu, Artem Belevich, Eli Bendersky, Mark Heffernan, Chris Leary, Jacques Pienaar, Bjarke Roune, Rob Springer, Xuetian Weng, and Robert Hundt. gpucc: an open-source GPGPU compiler. In *Proceedings of the 2016 International Symposium on Code Generation and Optimization*, pages 105–116. ACM, 2016.

[33] Xiuxia Zhang. KeplerAs. `https://github.com/PAA-NCIC/PPoPP2017_artifact`.

Checking Concurrent Data Structures Under the C/C++11 Memory Model

Peizhao Ou and Brian Demsky

University of California, Irvine, USA

{peizhaoo,bdemsky}@uci.edu

Abstract

Concurrent data structures often provide better performance on multi-core processors but are significantly more difficult to design and test than their sequential counterparts. The C/C++11 standard introduced a weak memory model with support for low-level atomic operations such as compare and swap (CAS). While low-level atomic operations can significantly improve the performance of concurrent data structures, they introduce non-intuitive behaviors that can increase the difficulty of developing code.

In this paper, we develop a correctness model for concurrent data structures that make use of atomic operations. Based on this correctness model, we present CDSSPEC, a specification checker for concurrent data structures under the C/C++11 memory model. We have evaluated CDSSPEC on 10 concurrent data structures, among which CDSSPEC detected 3 known bugs and 93% of the injected bugs.

Categories and Subject Descriptors D.1.3 [*Programming Techniques*]: Concurrent Programing; D.2.4 [*Software Engineering*]: Software/Program Verification

Keywords Relaxed Memory Models; Concurrent Data Structure Specifications

1. Introduction

Concurrent data structures can improve scalability by supporting multiple simultaneous operations, reducing cache coherence traffic, and reducing the time taken by individual data structure operations. Researchers have developed many concurrent data structures with these goals [24, 35, 38]. Concurrent data structures often use sophisticated techniques including low-level atomic instructions (e.g., compare and swap), careful reasoning about the order of memory operations, and fine-grained locking. Developing correct concurrent data structures requires subtle reasoning about the data structure and the memory model, and there are numerous examples of incorrect concurrent data structures [40, 41].

PPoPP '17, February 04 - 08, 2017, Austin, TX, USA

ACM 978-1-4503-4493-7/17/02. . . $15.00

DOI: http://dx.doi.org/10.1145/3018743.3018749

1.1 Concurrent Data Structure Specifications

Researchers have developed several techniques for specifying correctness properties of concurrent data structures written for the sequential consistency memory model. While these techniques cannot handle the behaviors exhibited by data structure implementations under relaxed memory models, they provide insight into intuitive approaches for specifying concurrent data structure behavior.

A common approach for specifying the correctness of concurrent data structures is in terms of sequential executions of either the concurrent data structure or a simplified sequential version. The problem then becomes how do we map a concurrent execution to a sequential execution? A common criterion is *linearizability* — linearizability states that a concurrent operation can be viewed as taking effect at some time between its invocation and its response [32].

An *equivalent sequential data structure* is a sequential version of a concurrent data structure that can be used to express correctness properties by relating executions of the concurrent data structure to executions of the equivalent sequential data structure. The equivalent sequential data structure is often simpler, and in many cases, one can simply use existing well-tested implementations from libraries.

A *history* is a total order of the method invocations and responses in an execution. A *sequential history* is one where all invocations are immediately followed by the corresponding responses. A concurrent object is linearizable if for all executions: (1) the invocations and responses can be reordered to yield a sequential history under the constraint that an invocation cannot be reordered before the preceding responses and (2) the concurrent execution yields the same behavior as this sequential history.

A weaker variation of linearization is *sequential consistency*[1]. Sequential consistency only requires that there exists a sequential history that is consistent with the *program order* (intra-thread order). This order does not need to be consistent with the order that operations were actually issued in.

Unfortunately, efficient implementations of many common data structures, e.g., RCU [24], MS Queue [38], etc., for the C/C++ memory model are neither linearizable [29] nor sequentially consistent!

[1] Note that the term sequential consistency in the literature is applied to both the consistency model that data structures expose to clients as well as the guarantees that the memory system provides for loads and stores.

1.2 New Challenges from the C/C++ Memory Model

The C/C++ memory model [1, 2] brings the following two challenges that prevent the application of previous approaches for specifying the correctness of concurrent data structures:

Relaxed Executions Break Existing Data Structure Consistency Models: C/C++ data structures often expose clients to weaker (non-SC) behaviors to gain performance. A common guarantee is to provide happens-before synchronization between operations that perform updates and the operations that read those updates. These data structures often do not guarantee that different threads observe updates in the same order. For example, even when one uses the relatively strong `release` and `acquire` (i.e., `std::memory_order_release` and `std::memory_order_acquire`) memory orderings in C++, it is possible for two different threads to observe two stores happening in different orders. Thus, many data structures legitimately admit executions for which there are no sequential histories that preserve program order.

Like many other relaxed memory models, the C/C++ memory model does not define a total order over all memory operations. Instead of a total order, the C/C++ memory model is formulated as a graph of memory operations with edges representing several partial orders. This complicates the application of traditional approaches to correctness, e.g., linearization cannot be applied. Specifically, approaches that relate the behaviors of concurrent data structures to analogous sequential data structures break down due to the absence of a total ordering of the memory operations. While many dynamic tools [40, 50] for exploring code behavior under relaxed models do as a practical matter print out an execution in some order, this order insufficient as relaxed memory models generally make it possible for a data structure operation (1) to see the effects of operations that appear later in any such order (e.g., a load can read from a store that appears later in the order) and (2) to see the effects of older, stale updates.

Constraining Reorderings (Specifying Synchronization Properties): Synchronization[2] in C/C++ orders memory operations to different locations. Concurrent data structures often establish synchronization to avoid exposing their users to highly non-intuitive behaviors that may break client code. The C/C++ memory model formalizes synchronization in terms of the *happens-before* relation. The happens-before relationship is a partial order over memory accesses. If memory access x happens before memory access y, it means that the effects of x must be ordered before the effects of y.

To illustrate the meaning of synchronization in this context, consider a concurrent queue that does not properly establish synchronization between corresponding pairs of enqueue and dequeue operations. Figure 1 shows a problematic execution of such a queue: (1) thread A initializes the fields of a new object X; (2) thread A enqueues the reference to X; (3) thread B dequeues the reference to X; (4) thread B reads the fields of X through the dequeued reference. In (4), thread B could fail to see the initializing writes from (1). This surprising behavior could occur if the compiler or CPU reorders the initializing writes to be executed after the enqueue operation, i.e., reordering (1) after (2).

Thread A	Thread B
`X->field1=1;` // (1)	`Obj *r1=q->deq();` // (3)
...	if (r1!=NULL)
`q->enq(X);` // (2)	`int r2=r1->field1;` // (4)

Figure 1. The problematic execution of a concurrent queue in which the load in (4) does not see the initialization in (1) (i.e., `r2!=1`) when the dequeue operation in (3) dequeues from the enqueue operation in (2)

1.3 Specification Language and Tool Support

This paper presents CDSSPEC, a specification checking tool that is designed to be used in conjunction with model checking tools. We have implemented it as a plugin for the CDSCHECKER model checker. After implementing a concurrent data structure, developers annotate their code with a CDSSPEC specification. To test their implementation, developers compile the data structure with the CDSSPEC specification compiler to extract the specification and generate code that is instrumented with specification checks. Then, developers compile the instrumented program with a standard C/C++ compiler. Finally, developers run the binary under the CDSSPEC checker. CDSSPEC then exhaustively explores the behaviors of the unit test and generates diagnostic reports for executions that violate the specification.

Researchers have developed tools for exploring the behavior of code under the C/C++ memory model including CDSCHECKER [40], CPPMEM [13], and Relacy [50], and also under a revised C/C++ memory model [11]. While these tools can be used to explore executions, they can be challenging to use for testing as they don't provide support beyond assertions for specifying data structure behavior.

1.4 Contributions

This paper makes the following contributions:

- **Correctness Model:** It presents a non-deterministic correctness model that captures the relaxed behaviors of concurrent data structures as a set of non-deterministic behaviors for a sequential data structure.
- **Specification Language:** It introduces a specification language that enables developers to write specifications of concurrent data structures developed for relaxed memory models in a simple fashion that captures key correctness properties. Our specification language is the first to our knowledge that supports concurrent data structures that use C/C++ atomic operations.

[2] Synchronization here is not mutual exclusion, but rather a lower-level property that captures which stores must be visible to a thread. Effectively, it constrains which reorderings can be performed by a processor or compiler.

- **A Tool for Checking C/C++ Data Structures Against Specifications:** CDSSPEC is the first tool to our knowledge that can check concurrent data structures that exhibit relaxed behaviors against specifications that are specified in terms of intuitive sequential executions.
- **Evaluation:** It shows that the CDSSPEC specification language can express key correctness properties for a set of real-world concurrent data structures, that CDSSPEC can detect bugs, and that CDSSPEC tool can unit test real world data structures with reasonable performance. Specifically, CDSSPEC detected 3 known bugs, 93% of the injected bugs, and one overly strong memory order parameter claimed to be necessary in a paper.

2. Example

Figure 2 presents a simple blocking queue that we will use to motivate our correctness model. In this example, enqueuers enqueue natural numbers, and they compete to insert a new node at the tail of the list by performing a CAS (i.e., `compare_exchange_strong`) operation on the `next` field of the `tail`. If one enqueuer succeeds, all other competing enqueuers will spin waiting for it to update the `tail`. Similarly, dequeuers compete to update the `head` to the next node it points to with a CAS operation if the `next` field of the `head` node is not `NULL`. A dequeuer returns the natural number it dequeues or `-1` if it fails. For illustration purposes, dequeuers do not recycle nodes.

```
1  class Queue {
2  public: atomic<Node*> tail, head;
3  Queue() { tail = head = new Node(); }
4  void enq(int val) {
5    Node *n = new Node(val);
6    while (1) {
7      Node *t = tail.load(acquire);
8      Node *old = NULL;
9      if (t->next.CAS(old, n, release)) {
10       tail.store(n, release);
11       return;
12     }
13   }
14 }
15 int deq() {
16   while (1) {
17     Node *h = head.load(acquire);
18     Node *n = h->next.load(acquire);
19     if (n == NULL) return -1;
20     if (head.CAS(h, n, release))
21       return n->data;
22   }
23 }};
```

Figure 2. Simple blocking queue example

The queue uses release/acquire synchronization (provided by the C/C++11 memory model) that practitioners are likely to use for this scenario. This ensures that `enq` and `deq` method calls[3] are first in-first out (FIFO) ordered, and that `deq` method calls dequeue fully initialized nodes. Under the sequential consistency memory model, the SC counterpart of this queue is linearizable. The CAS operation on the `next` field in line 9 would be the linearization point[4] for the `enq` method if it succeeds, while the load of the `next` field in line 18 from the last iteration of the loop would be the linearization point for the `deq` method.

Figure 3 presents an example execution that violates linearizability under release consistency [5]. In this execution, the loads of the `next` field (line 18) in the `deq` method from threads `T1` and `T2` both read from old values, and thus we get an execution that has no equivalent sequential history. Figure 4(a)[5] shows a sequential history for this problematic execution, in which *hb* represents the *happens-before* relation. Note that in this sequential history, the method call `x.deq` returns the value `-1`, deviating from the behavior of the corresponding sequential execution.

There are three approaches to maintaining the simplicity of the traditional approach to specifying the behavior of concurrent data structures by analogy to sequential executions:

- **Strengthen the Atomics:** We can pay extra runtime overhead and change all of the atomic operations to use the memory order `memory_order_seq_cst` and use linearizability. Figure 4(b) shows a sequential history in which the stronger *sc* order forces the `deq` method call on queue `x` to return `1`. Developers often avoid this solution because of the extra runtime overhead.
- **Constrain the Valid Usage Patterns:** Alternatively, we can constrain the situations under which the queue can be used. If we require that there is always a *happens-before* relationship between conflicting queue operations (i.e., `enq` and `deq` calls on the same queue), then the problematic execution is no longer a legal usage of the queue; hence, we only obtain executions that are linearizable. Figure 4(c) shows a sequential history of such executions.

  Although this approach by itself may excessively limit the usage scenarios of a data structure, it provides the useful insight that a data structure design can encompass specifying *admissibility* conditions, conditions under which the data structure has well-defined behavior. This approach has been used in the context of defining memory models — the C/C++ memory model states that programs with data races have undefined behavior and guarantees sequential consistency for race-free programs that correctly make use of `memory_order_seq_cst` atomics and mutexes.
- **Weaken the Specification:** It turns out that the problematic execution for the queue example occurs only when `deq` returns that the queue is empty (`-1`). We can weaken the sequential specification for the `deq` method to allow it to spuriously return `-1`. As a result, the sequential history shown in Figure 4(d) becomes legal. A similar solution is taken by the C/C++ memory model for the `trylock` method.

[3] Hereafter, the phrase "method call" or "call" refers to the invocation of a method in an execution.

[4] Under linearizability, a linearization point is the point in the execution at which the method call can be viewed as taking effect.

[5] The notations `x.enq(1)` means enqueuing `1` to queue `x`, and `x.deq(-1)` means the `deq` call on queue `x` returns `-1`.

T1	T2
`x.enq(1)`	`y.enq(1)`
`r1=y.deq()`	`r2=x.deq()`

Figure 3. A non-linearizable execution in which queues x and y are initially empty, and r1=r2=-1

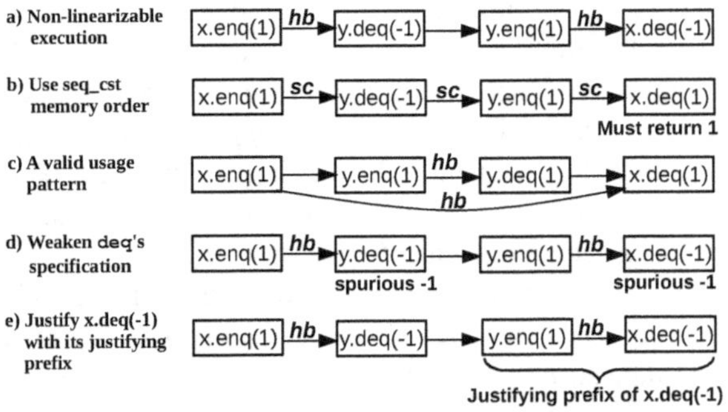

Figure 4. Sequential histories of the non-linearizable execution (shown in Figure 3) and some potential solutions

2.1 Constraining Non-determinism in the Specification

Although weakening the specification by itself works, it is not a perfect solution. One drawback is that the specification can permit uncontrolled non-determinism (i.e., the specification is too loose) so that it misses detecting even trivial correctness properties. For example, we may want to forbid the single-thread execution in which a `deq` method call following an `enq` method call returns `-1`. However, the proposed weakened specification permits such executions. It is worth noting that linearizability and sequential consistency for data structures can use non-deterministic specifications, but they also suffer from this drawback.

Upon closer examination of the problematic execution, we find a fundamental difference between the execution shown in Figure 4(d) and the execution where a `deq` call (after an `enq` call) returns `-1` in a single-thread execution. In the latter case, the program has established the *happens-before* relationship between the `enq` call and the subsequent `deq` call. Hence, under the C/C++11 memory model, the `deq` call will see the effects of the `enq` call. However, in Figure 4(d), the `enq` call on queue `x` does not *happen-before* the `deq` call on queue `x` (i.e., no *hb* between the two method calls), and thus it is acceptable for the `deq` call to return `-1`.

Therefore, CDSSPEC combines non-deterministic specifications for methods with a mechanism for justifying non-deterministic behaviors. Under the C/C++ memory model, a memory operation is required to observe the effects of the memory operations that *happen before* it. Thus, by the nature of the *hb* relation, for C/C++11 data structures, the effects of the subsequence of operations that are ordered before an operation o by the *hb* relation (or in some cases the *sc* relation) are required to be visible to o; and we call this subsequence (ending with o) a *justifying prefix* of o. The behavior of an operation in a justifying prefix justifies the operation's non-deterministic selection of behaviors in the sequential history. The sequential history shown in Figure 4(e) becomes acceptable since for the `deq` call on queue `x`, only the `enq` call on queue `y` is ordered before it in its justifying prefix (and the `enq` call on queue `y` has no effects on queue `x`), and hence the `deq` call on queue `x` is allowed to return -1.

2.2 Handling Concurrent Operations and Multiple Justifying Prefixes

The problem is unfortunately still more complicated. To illustrate this, consider one of the simplest data structures — a C/C++11 atomic register accessed by relaxed operations. A register is an object that encapsulates a value that can be read by a `read` call and updated by a `write` call. The C/C++ memory model allows a read a to return not only (1) the value written by any write $b \xrightarrow{hb} a$ such that $\neg\exists c.\texttt{iswrite}(c), b \xrightarrow{hb} c \xrightarrow{hb} a$, but also (2) the value written by any concurrent write. The solutions we have explored so far cannot specify such properties for the following reasons: for a `read` call, 1) there can be multiple `write` calls that *happen-before* the `read` call that it can read from (and a justifying prefix may not order those write calls appropriately); and 2) it can read from any `write` call that happens concurrently with it.

Thus, we define a method call m_c to be a *concurrent method call* of m if $\neg(m \xrightarrow{r} m_c \vee m_c \xrightarrow{r} m)$, where $\xrightarrow{r}$ is an ordering relation for individual atomic operations that corresponds to the ordering guarantee the implementation relies on (discussed in more detail in Section 3.1). In this example, we use the *happens-before* relation as $\xrightarrow{r}$. We can now handle registers by having a non-deterministic specification that allows a `read` call to read from a write that is not the most recent. More importantly, however, we constrain the non-determinism in the specification by extending our approach to allow accessing concurrent method calls. As a result, in the atomic register example, the non-deterministic behavior that a `read` returns the value written by a `write` that it *happens-before* is disallowed.

Thus, one can view our approach as follows: our specification specifies admissibility conditions under which a data structure has well-defined behaviors; then for all admissible executions, there exists an equivalent sequential execution on all sequential histories (that respect $\xrightarrow{r}$) with respect to a non-deterministic specification; and for each method call m with non-deterministic behaviors, m's behaviors have to be enabled by some equivalent sequential execution on one of its justifying prefixes or a concurrent method call.

2.3 Key Correctness Properties of the Queue Example

We show how our approach can capture the key correctness properties of the queue in Figure 2. Using a sequential FIFO queue as the sequential data structure, we have two options for writing a specification for the queue:

1. Deterministic Specification with Admissibility Constraints: Admissibility specifies whether a given execution satisfies a data structure's assumptions and thus the data structure's specification should hold for the given execution. We specify admissibility with a set of *admissibility rules* that specify the conditions under which two method calls are required to be ordered relative to each other. Thus, we can simply state that a failed `deq` call should be ordered relative to other `enq` calls on the same queue, and then we have a deterministic specification with respect to the sequential FIFO.

2. Non-deterministic Specification: Another option is a non-deterministic specification (i.e., `deq` calls can spuriously fail) that applies unconditionally. We need to specify the following key correctness properties:

I. Correct Synchronization: In the example, a successful `deq` should return a fully initialized item. The sequential FIFO queue ensures that when a `deq` call d dequeues an item from a corresponding `enq` call e, d must synchronize with e; otherwise, there would exist a sequential history in which d can be ordered before e, which would violate the sequential FIFO's semantics.

II. `enq` and `deq` calls take effect in a FIFO order: We can weaken the specification for the sequential FIFO queue by allowing `deq` calls to return empty (`-1`). As a result, the weakened sequential queue ensures that `enq` and successful `deq` calls take effect in FIFO order.

III. Constrain `deq`'s non-determinism: In this case, we can state that a `deq` call d can only return empty when the corresponding `deq` call in the execution of the sequential FIFO on one of d's justifying prefixes also returns empty.

3. Correctness Model

In this section, we describe the approach in more detail and discuss the composability properties of our approach. Readers who are not interested in formalisms may wish to skip ahead to Section 4. Readers who are unfamiliar with formalisms but would like to learn may find the following references helpful: (1) readers interested in execution-oriented approaches can read Maranget *et al.* on ARM and POWER [36] and then read Mark Batty's thesis [9] as a bridge to C/C++11; (2) readers interested in an axiomatic approach can read Algave *et al.* [7] and the work of Batty *et al.* on overhauling SC; and (3) readers coming from a Java viewpoint can read Shipilëv's blog [43, 44].

3.1 Formalizing the Approach

We begin with a concurrent execution $E = (M, \xrightarrow{r})$ of a concurrent object O_c. The set M is the set of method calls in the execution E. The relation $\xrightarrow{r}$ is an acyclic, transitive ordering relation that orders atomic operations. For a C/C++11 data structure, this is in general either *hb* or *sc* and corresponds to the ordering guarantee the implementation relies on. Since methods can be composed of many atomic operations, the ordering relation $\xrightarrow{r}$ is not directly applicable to method calls. To extend the relation $\xrightarrow{r}$ to order the set of method calls M, we provide *ordering point* annotations that the developer uses to select the specific atomic operation instances that order method calls.

In order to map a concurrent execution to an execution on an equivalent sequential data structure, we first define a non-deterministic, sequentialized version of the concurrent object O_c as O_s. We then define the set of concurrent methods calls for a method call $m \in M$ in execution $E = (M, \xrightarrow{r})$ as $concurrent(m) = \{m_c \mid m_c \in M \wedge m_c \neq m \wedge \neg(m_c \xrightarrow{r} m \vee m \xrightarrow{r} m_c)\}$.

We next define the set of executions for which a concurrent object's behavior is well defined. Given a concurrent object O_c, we define an admissibility function $\circ$. For method calls $m_1, m_2 \in M$, if the admissibility condition $m_1 \circ m_2$ returns `true`, then m_1 and m_2 are not required to be ordered by $\xrightarrow{r}$. Consider the queue example. To write a deterministic specification for it, we can require an `enq` call e and a `deq` call d on the same queue that returns empty (`-1`) to be ordered by $\xrightarrow{r}$ (i.e., $e \circ d$ returns false).

Thus, the specification S for a concurrent object O_c is a tuple — $S = (O_s, \circ)$. We next define the notion of an *admissible* execution with respect to S below. Recall that an admissible execution is an execution that meets the requirements of the concurrent object's design and thus for which the concurrent object's behavior is well-specified.

Definition 1 (Admissibility). *An execution $E = (M, \xrightarrow{r})$ of a concurrent object O_c is admissible for a specification $S = (O_s, \circ)$ iff: $\forall m_1, m_2 \in M, m_1 \neq m_2 \Rightarrow m_1 \xrightarrow{r} m_2 \vee m_2 \xrightarrow{r} m_1 \vee m_1 \circ m_2$.*

We next develop the framework for specifying the behaviors of admissible executions. As is the case for linearizability, we first define the corresponding sequential histories for an execution E.

Definition 2 (Valid Sequential History). *Given an execution $E = (M, \xrightarrow{r})$ on a concurrent object O_c and a corresponding total order of method calls H, we say that H is a valid sequential history of E iff:*

1. *E and H contain the same set of method calls, and*
2. *$\forall m_1, m_2 \in M. m_1 \xrightarrow{r} m_2 \Rightarrow m_1$ must appear before m_2 in the total order H (i.e., $m_1 \xrightarrow{H} m_2$).*

Our specifications are non-deterministic — they may admit several behaviors for a given method call. To further constrain the specifications, we introduce the notion of a justifying subhistory, a portion of the execution E that justifies a method call exhibiting a given non-deterministic behavior.

Definition 3 (Justifying Subhistory). *Given an execution $E = (M, \xrightarrow{r})$ and a method call $m \in M$, we say that an ordered list of method calls J taken from M is a justifying subhistory of m iff:*

1. *$m \in J$, and*
2. *$\forall m' \in M, m' \xrightarrow{r} m \Rightarrow m' \in J$, and*
3. *$\forall m' \in M, m' \neq m \wedge \neg(m' \xrightarrow{r} m) \Rightarrow m' \notin J$, and*
4. *$\forall m_1, m_2 \in J, m_1 \xrightarrow{r} m_2 \Rightarrow m_1$ appears before m_2 in J.*

Definition 4 (Justified Behaviors). *We say that the behavior of a method call m in an execution E is justified for a specification S iff: 1) There exists at least one justifying subhistory J for m, the behavior of every method call $m' \in J$ where $m' \neq m$ is justified, and m in J returns the same value as the corresponding method call in E; or 2) the return value of m is determined by the $concurrent(m)$ set.*

Note that the process of determining the return value of m by the $concurrent(m)$ set can be viewed as a non-deterministic function that takes the $concurrent(m)$ set as input and non-deterministically outputs a value. Consider the C/C++11 atomic register (accessed by relaxed operations) as an example. According to Definition 4, a `read` operation r is justified if r returns a value stored by either: (1) the most recent `write` operation in one of r's justifying histories; or (2) one of the `write` operations in the $concurrent(r)$ set. Now that we have defined what it means for given method call's behavior to be justified, we can define the correctness criteria for a concurrent object O_c.

Definition 5 (Non-deterministic Linearizability for a Valid Sequential History). *We say that a concurrent object O_c is non-deterministic linearizable on a valid sequential history H for a specification S iff each method call in H (1) is justified and (2) returns a value that is the same as the corresponding method call in E or as specified in its non-deterministic specification.*

Take the execution of the blocking queue in Figure 3 as an example. Consider one of the valid sequential histories of this execution, denoted as H: `x.enq(1)` $\rightarrow$ `y.enq(1)` $\rightarrow$ `r1=x.deq()` $\rightarrow$ `r2=y.deq()`, where `r1` and `r2` are both `-1`. First, both `deq` calls are justified since there does not exist any `enq` call in any of their justifying subhistories (so they are allowed to return `-1`). Secondly, both `deq` calls return the value `-1`, which is allowed by the non-deterministic specification (spuriously returning `-1`). Thus, according to Definition 5, both objects `x` and `y` are non-deterministic linearizable on H for the non-deterministic specification. Next, we extend the notion of non-deterministic linearizability to executions and concurrent objects.

Definition 6 (Non-deterministic Linearizability for an Execution). *We say that a concurrent object O_c is non-deterministic linearizable on an execution E for a specification S iff O_c is non-deterministic linearizable on all valid sequential histories of E for S.*

Definition 7 (Non-deterministic Linearizability for a Concurrent Object O_c). *We say that a concurrent object O_c is non-deterministic linearizable for a specification S iff O_c is non-deterministic linearizable on all admissible executions of O_c for S.*

3.2 Composability

We next discuss the composability properties of this approach. In other words, if each object in a system is non-deterministic linearizable for its specification, then the system composed of these objects is non-deterministic linearizable for the composition of the each object's specification. This is generally a desirable property in modular design since one can reason about the correctness of each data structure in isolation. Next, we define how to compose specifications and executions.

Definition 8 (Specification Composability). *The composition $S_A \oplus S_B$ of two specifications $S_A = (O_{s_A}, \circ_A)$ and $S_B = (O_{s_B}, \circ_B)$ applies O_{s_A} to operations on O_{c_A} and applies O_{s_B} to operations on O_{c_B}, and the composition of the admissibility functions $\circ_A \oplus \circ_B$ returns the value:*

1. *$m_1 \circ_A m_2$, if m_1 and m_2 are both called on O_{c_A}, or*
2. *$m_1 \circ_B m_2$, if m_1 and m_2 are both called on O_{c_B}, or*
3. *true.*

Definition 9 (Execution Composability). *An execution E on the composition of two concurrent objects O_{c_A} and O_{c_B} has two partial executions $E_A = (M_A, \xrightarrow{r_A})$ and $E_B = (M_B, \xrightarrow{r_B})$. The ordering relation $\xrightarrow{r}$ for E can be expressed as the union of three disjoint sets $\xrightarrow{r} = \xrightarrow{r_A} \cup \xrightarrow{r_B} \cup \xrightarrow{r_{AB}}$, where $\xrightarrow{r_A}$ is the ordering relation between methods calls in M_A, $\xrightarrow{r_B}$ is the ordering relation between methods calls in M_B, and $\xrightarrow{r_{AB}}$ is the ordering relation between method calls in M_A and M_B. We say that such compositions are valid if $\xrightarrow{r_A} \cup \xrightarrow{r_B} \cup \xrightarrow{r_{AB}}$ is acyclic.*

It is useful to note that $\xrightarrow{hb} \cup \xrightarrow{sc}$ in C/C++11 is always acyclic, and $\xrightarrow{r_A} \cup \xrightarrow{r_B} \cup \xrightarrow{r_{AB}}$ is acyclic if $\xrightarrow{r_A}$ and $\xrightarrow{r_B}$ are a subset of $\xrightarrow{hb} \cup \xrightarrow{sc}$. This requirement places minor limitations on the ordering relation; for example, it makes using modification order (C/C++'s per memory location order) problematic. Given these definitions, we next prove the following composability theorem.

Theorem 1 (Composability). *Suppose the concurrent object O_{c_A} is non-deterministic linearizable for a specification S_A; the concurrent object O_{c_B} is non-deterministic linearizable for a specification S_B; and the composition of any two admissible executions from O_{c_A} and O_{c_B} gives an acyclic ordering relation $\xrightarrow{r}$. Then the composition of O_{c_A} and O_{c_B} is non-deterministic linearizable for $S_A \oplus S_B$.*

Proof. Proof by contradiction. Suppose $E = (M, \xrightarrow{r})$ is an admissible execution that violates $S_A \oplus S_B$. Then, there must exist at least one of the object calls in E whose behavior violates its specification.

Without loss of generality, assume the object was O_{c_A}. Since E was admissible, by the definition of $S_A \oplus S_B$, $E_A = (M_A, \xrightarrow{r_A})$, where $\xrightarrow{r_A}$ is the part of $\xrightarrow{r}$ that orders methods calls to M_A, is also admissible. Now, since E violates the specification, there exist two possible cases:

1) There exists at least one sequential history H of E that violates the specification, meaning that there exists at least a method call $m_A \in M_A$ that violates the specification. Now consider H_A, H projected onto the object O_{c_A}. H_A is a valid sequential history of E_A since $\xrightarrow{r_A}$ is a subset of $\xrightarrow{r}$. Also,

since $S_A \oplus S_B$ applies O_{s_A} on O_{c_A}, m_A in the execution of H_A also violates O_{s_A}, meaning that H_A violates S_A.

2) There exists a method call m_A that was not justified. This means that all of its justifying subhistories J and its concurrent method calls violate the specification. Since $\xrightarrow{r_A}$ is a subset of $\xrightarrow{r}$, the concurrent set $concurrent(m_A)$ in E is the union of the concurrent set in E_A and a set of method calls on O_{c_B}. Since only the concurrent method calls on O_{c_A} matter in E for m_A, the $concurrent(m_A)$ sets have the same effect in E and E_A, meaning that $concurrent(m_A)$ also cannot justify m_A's behavior in E_A. Then consider J'_A, the set of all possible justifying subhistories of m_A in E_A; and J_A, the set of subhistories comprised of all of J projected onto O_{c_A}. For any justifying subhistory $j \in J'_A \Rightarrow j \in J$ because in the relation $\xrightarrow{r}$, $\xrightarrow{r_B} \cup \xrightarrow{r_{AB}}$ does not constrain the ordering of method calls on O_{c_A}. Thus, J'_A is a subset of J_A, meaning that all of m_A's justifying subhistories violate the specification.

Thus, O_{c_A} must violate its specification, and we have a contradiction. □

A key restriction is that developers must be sure that their application only generates admissible executions. Otherwise, the program may observe surprising behaviors as it generates executions outside of the correctness model.

Application to Relaxed Atomics One limitation of our approach is that it rules out using *modification-order* relation as $\xrightarrow{r}$. It is still however applicable to many data structures that intentionally use relaxed atomics to achieve performance. For example, our model generally fits data structures that extensively use relaxed atomics but provide synchronization for committing operations, e.g., the ticket lock in our benchmark. Our model can even be useful in more extreme cases. Consider a counter implemented exclusively with relaxed atomics that has two operations — `read` and `increment`. We can write a very weak specification with a sequential counter in which the `increment` or `read` call may non-deterministically return older values. If, however, after a period of time, the program reaches a synchronization point (e.g., thread join), the specification would guarantee that a `read` call must be consistent with the number of `increment` calls before the synchronization.

4. Specification Language Design

The CDSSPEC specification language captures the correctness of concurrent data structures by establishing a correspondence with an equivalent sequential data structure. Figure 5 presents the core grammar of the CDSSPEC specification language. It defines three types of specification annotations: *structure annotations*, *method annotations*, and *ordering point annotations*, discussed in Section 4.1, 4.2 and 4.3, respectively. Annotations are embedded in C/C++ comments. This format does not affect the semantics of the original program and allows the same source to be used by both a standard C/C++ compiler to generate production code and the CDSSPEC specification compiler to extract the

```
Structure        →  (admissibility)*  stateDefine
stateDefine      →  "@DeclareState:" (code)?
                    ("@Initial:" code)?
                    ("@Copy:" code)?
                    ("@Clear:" code)?
admissibility    →  "@Admit:" label "<->" label "(" cond ")"
Method           →  ("@PreCondition:" code)?
                    ("@JustifyingPrecondition:" code)?
                    ("@SideEffect:" code)?
                    ("@JustifyingPostcondition:" code)?
                    ("@PostCondition:" code)?
OrderingPoint    →  "@OPDefine:" cond |
                    "@PotentialOP(" label "):" cond |
                    "@OPCheck(" label "):" cond |
                    "@OPClear:" cond |
                    "@OPClearDefine:" cond
code             →  <Legal C/C++ code>
cond             →  <A legal C/C++ boolean expression>
label            →  <A legal C/C++ variable name>
```

Figure 5. The core grammar for the CDSSPEC specification language

CDSSPEC specification from the comments. In the following discussion, we use Figure 6 to illustrate how to apply CDSSPEC to write a non-deterministic specification for the blocking queue example from Figure 2.

```
/** @DeclareState: IntList *q; */

/** @SideEffect: STATE(q)->push_back(val); */
void enq(int val) {
  Node *n = new Node(val);
  while (1) {
    Node *t = tail.load(acquire);
    Node *old = NULL;
    if (t->next.CAS(old, n, release)) {
      /** @OPDefine: true */
      tail.store(n, release);
      return;
    }
  }
}
/** @SideEffect:
S_RET=STATE(q)->empty()?-1:STATE(q)->front();
if(S_RET!=-1&&C_RET!=-1) STATE(q)->pop_front();
@PostCondition:
    return C_RET==-1?true:C_RET==S_RET;
@JustifyingPostcondition: if (C_RET==-1)
    return S_RET==-1;*/
int deq() {
  while (1) {
    Node *h = head.load(acquire);
    Node *n = h->next.load(acquire);
    /** @OPClearDefine: true */
    if (n == NULL) return -1;
    if (head.CAS(h, n, release))
      return n->data;
  }
}
```

Figure 6. Annotated blocking queue specification example

4.1 Structure Annotations

Each data structure needs a structure annotation to specify:
Admissibility: Developers specify the admissibility of executions by using the `Admit` annotation to write a set of admissibility rules. In the absence of an admissibility rule, a pair of methods is not required to be ordered with respect

to each other. The construct takes in two method names and then takes a guard expression that specifies whether two method calls are required to be ordered with respect to each other. The admissibility guard expression can access the return value and arguments of a method call. Since Figure 6 presents a non-deterministic specification that applies to all executions, we do not need to write any admissibility rules.

Suppose we instead wanted to write a stronger, deterministic specification for the blocking queue that applies conditionally, we would write an admissibility rule: "`@Admit:deq<->enq(M1->C_RET==-1)`", where the key word `M1` refers to the first method call (i.e., the `deq` call) in the rule, and `C_RET` refers to the return value of the concurrent method call. This means whenever a `deq` call returns empty, it must be ordered relative to other `enq` calls in order for the deterministic specification to apply. Note that admissibility criteria are evaluated on pairs of concrete method calls that are not ordered relative to each other when the CDSSPEC checker checks sequential histories.

Equivalent sequential data structure: In the structure annotation, the developer can specify the internal state of the equivalent sequential data structure using a `DeclareState` annotation. The developer specifies the internal state by writing a list of variable declarations. CDSSPEC includes several useful pre-defined types — an ordered list, a set, and a hashmap so that developers can use them to specify the key properties of the data structure more conveniently. For example, we just need one line to declare an ordered list to represent a sequential FIFO in line 1 of Figure 6.

The `Initial`, `Copy`, and `Clear` annotations specify how the CDSSPEC checker should initialize, copy, and destroy the state structure when it checks an execution, respectively. They are usually empty since the CDSSPEC specification has useful defaults for the pre-defined types. For example, an ordered list is initially empty by default.

4.2 Ordering Point Annotations

In real-world data structures, API methods can generally be classified into two types, *primitive* API methods and *aggregate* API methods. Consider a concurrent hashtable as an example. It provides primitive API methods such as `put` and `get` that implement the core functionality of the data structure, and it also has aggregate API methods such as `putAll` that call primitive API methods internally. In our experience working with our benchmark set, it is generally possible to generate sequential histories and justifying subhistories for primitive API method calls for real-world data structures as they generally serialize on a single memory location; however, it is possible to observe partially completed aggregate API method calls, which unfortunately breaks the correctness criteria of linearizability and sequential consistency for data structures. Considering this issue, we design our specification language to primarily target specifying the correctness of primitive API methods of concurrent data structures that have linearizable or sequentially consistent counterparts[6].

As discussed in Section 3, the ordering relation $\xrightarrow{r}$ over method calls is the key to establishing valid sequential histories and justifying subhistories to check concurrent executions against the equivalent sequential data structure. Recall that while the *hb* or *sc* relations form the order relation $\xrightarrow{r}$ for atomic operations, data structure operations are often comprised of many atomic operations. Thus, it is important to specify which atomic operations should order method calls relative to each other.

Borrowing from VYRD's [27] concept of commit points, we allow developers to specify *ordering points* — the specific atomic operations between method invocation and response events that order method calls. Ordering points are a generalization of commit points as there can be more than one ordering point and they can include memory operations that do not commit the data structure operation. In the example, line 10 specifies that a successful CAS operation on the `next` field is the ordering point for an `enq` call, while line 27 specifies that the load operation from the last loop iteration as the ordering point of a `deq` call. Thus, when a `deq` call d returns an item enqueued by an `enq` call e, the ordering points of d and e establish a *hb* relation, which is consistent with the ordering relation between d and e (i.e., $e \xrightarrow{r} d$).

Ordering points are evaluated in each method call when the CDSSPEC checker constructs sequential histories. Thus, in the CDSSPEC specification language, we use ordering point annotations to inform the CDSSPEC checker which atomic operation invocations are ordering points for API method calls. Each ordering point annotation has a condition (that can access any variables visible at the point of the annotation) and takes effect when its condition is satisfied. We next present the individual annotations shown in Figure 5:

OPDefine: In most cases, we immediately know whether a memory operation is an ordering point. We then use the `OPDefine` annotation to specify that the atomic operation that immediately precedes the annotation is an ordering point. For example, in Figure 6, the successful CAS operation on the `next` field (line 9) is the ordering point for an `enq` call. Thus, we specify an `OPDefine` annotation in line 10 with a condition `true`. When an `enq` call is executed to line 10, the successful CAS operation, which immediately precedes the annotation, becomes the ordering point.

OPClear & OPClearDefine: In some cases, the same line of code in a method will be executed multiple times, e.g., an atomic operation in a loop. It is often the case that an atomic operation from the last iteration serves as the ordering point. To support this common programming idiom, we can use an `OPClear` annotation, which removes all previously observed ordering points in the current method call. Then we can

[6] Since the CDSSPEC checker allows developers to combine and check both CDSCHECKER's assertions and the CDSSPEC specifications at the same time, developers can still use assertions to check aggregate methods.

use an `OPDefine` annotation (discussed above) to define the atomic operation from the last iteration as the ordering point. To make it even more convenient to use, we introduce the syntactic sugar `OPClearDefine` to combine the effect of an `OPClear` annotation followed by an `OPDefine` annotation.

For example, in line 27 of Figure 6, we use the `OPClearDefine` annotation to specify that only the load operation on the `next` field from the last iteration of the `while` loop is an ordering point since only the last iteration is effective (i.e., returns either an item or `-1`).

PotentialOP & **OPCheck**: In some cases, it is not possible to determine whether a given atomic operation is an ordering point until later in the execution. For example, some internal methods may be called by multiple API methods. In this case, the same atomic operation can be identified as a potential ordering point for multiple API methods, and each API method later has a checking annotation to verify whether it was the actual ordering point. For example, assume that A is an atomic operation that is potentially an ordering point under some specific condition. The developer would then write a `PotentialOP` annotation with the label `LabelA` to label it as a potential ordering point, and then use the label `LabelA` in an `OPCheck` annotation at a later point.

4.3 Method Annotations

Once we establish a sequential history for an execution or a justifying subhistory for a method call, we use this component to relate the behavior of the concurrent execution to a sequential execution on the sequential history or justifying subhistory in a design-by-contract (DbC) fashion — with a set of *side effects* and *assertions* that describe the desired behavior of each API method call. Note that the method annotations can access the internal variables and methods of the equivalent sequential data structure. Additionally, they can reference the values available at the method invocation and response, i.e., the parameter values and the return value. For each API method, we require a method annotation and provide three types of annotations for this purpose:

SideEffect: After defining the internal state of the equivalent data structure, we use the `SideEffect` annotation to define the corresponding action to be performed on the equivalent sequential data structure. The `SideEffect` annotation corresponds to the sequential executions on both valid sequential histories and justifying subhistories. When this annotation is omitted for a specific API method, the method call will have no side effects on the sequential data structure.

In the example, lines 3 and 17-18 in Figure 6 specify that the `enq` and `deq` methods for the equivalent sequential data structure (i.e., the ordered list) should push an item to the back of the list and pop an item from the front of the list when the ordered list is not empty, respectively. The notation `STATE(q)` refers to the ordered list `q`, and the keyword `S_RET` refers to the return value of the sequential `deq` call.

PreCondition & **PostCondition**: In CDSSPEC, we use the `PreCondition` and `PostCondition` annotations to specify conditions to be checked before and after the execution of an API method call in the sequential execution on a valid sequential history. For example, lines 19-20 in Figure 6 state that after we execute a `deq` call in an execution on a sequential history, we should check that the corresponding concurrent `deq` call returns either empty (`-1`) or the same item as the front of the ordered list. The keyword `C_RET` here refers to the return value of the concurrent `deq` call.

JustifyingPrecondition & **JustifyingPostcondition**: For an API method call m, we use the `JustifyingPrecondition` and `JustifyingPostcondition` annotations to constrain m's non-deterministic behaviors by specifying the condition to be checked before and after we execute m in the sequential execution on m's justifying subhistories. In this annotation, developers can use the primitive `CONCURRENT`, which represents the set of concurrent method calls (of m), to write many types of non-deterministic specifications.

For example, lines 21-22 in Figure 6 state that when a `deq` call spuriously returns empty (`-1`), there must exist an execution on one of its justifying subhistories such that the `deq` call in that execution also returns empty.

Nested API Method Call When an API method calls another API method, CDSSPEC only treats the outermost method call as an API method call and any other API method calls as internal calls. Thus, only the precondition, postcondition, justifying precondition, and justifying postcondition of the outermost API method call must be satisfied.

5. Implementation

Many concurrent data structures have an unbounded space of executions, meaning that we cannot verify correctness by checking individual executions. However, many bugs can be exposed by using the specifications to check executions generated by model checking unit tests. We have implemented the CDSSPEC checker as the combination of a specification compiler and a plugin for the CDSCHECKER framework. CDSSPEC can exhaustively explore (with a few limitations) behaviors for unit tests and provide diagnostic reports for executions that violate the specifications.

5.1 Specification Compiler

The specification compiler translates an annotated C/C++ program into an instrumented C/C++ program that will generate execution traces containing the dynamic information needed to construct the sequential history (and justifying subhistories) and check the specification assertions. We next describe the key annotation actions and methods that the CDSSPEC compiler inserts into the instrumented program.

Ordering Points: Ordering point annotation actions are inserted where they appear with a corresponding conditional guard expression.

Method Boundary: To identify a method's boundaries, CDSSPEC inserts *method_begin* and *method_end* annotation actions at the beginning and end of API methods. Since checking occurs after CDSCHECKER has completed an execution, we store the dynamic information of API method calls (i.e., the arguments and return value) that the CDSSPEC checker can access.

Side Effects, Assertions and Admissibility Checks: These are all compiled into methods which can be called by the CDSSPEC checker. The side effect and assertion methods can access the equivalent sequential data structure's state. The admissibility methods take two method call instances as arguments and return whether they are required to be ordered with respect to each other.

5.2 Dynamic Checking

At this point, we have an execution trace with the necessary annotations to construct a sequential history (and thus the justifying subhistory of each method call) and to check the execution's correctness. Before constructing the sequential history, the CDSSPEC plugin first collects the necessary information for each method call, which is the boundaries for the method call, the ordering point annotations, and the dynamic information (i.e., the arguments and return value).

Extracting the Ordering Relation $\xrightarrow{r}$: The CDSSPEC checker uses the *hb* and *sc* ordering of the ordering points to establish $\xrightarrow{r}$. Therefore, given two atomic operations X and Y that are both ordering points of two method calls A and B: $X \xrightarrow{hb} Y \vee X \xrightarrow{sc} Y \Rightarrow A \xrightarrow{r} B$.

Checking Admissibility: After establishing the ordering relation $\xrightarrow{r}$ for an execution, the CDSSPEC checker checks that for any two method calls, they are either ordered by $\xrightarrow{r}$ or that the admissibility does not require them to be ordered relative to each other. If there exists an execution that does not satisfy this criterion, our tool does not check the correctness properties and prints a warning.

Generating and Checking Sequential Histories: Since the C/C++11 memory model requires that the union of the *hb* and *sc* relation is acyclic, when each API method call has no more than one ordering point, which is the case for all of our benchmarks, the CDSSPEC checker guarantees that $\xrightarrow{r}$ is acyclic.

The CDSSPEC checker then topologically sorts $\xrightarrow{r}$ to generate a sequential history and checks that all method calls in the sequential history return the same value as in the concurrent execution. When multiple histories satisfy $\xrightarrow{r}$, by default we generate and check all possible histories. Since the set of all possible topological sortings can be large in some cases, we also provide the option of randomly generating and checking a user-customized number of sequential histories.

Checking Constrained Non-deterministic Behaviors: When a method call m has non-deterministic behaviors, the CDSSPEC checker then topologically sorts $\xrightarrow{r}$ to generate m's justifying subhistories, and ensure that there must exist at least one justifying subhistory against which the sequential execution satisfies the justifying condition.

Satisfaction Cycles One limitation of CDSCHECKER is that it may not generate executions with satisfaction cycles (i.e., out-of-thin-air executions) [10, 12, 15]. In the context of CDSSPEC, we believe that this limitation is reasonable in that we can still find many data structure bugs. Moreover, as others note [10], it is unclear whether satisfaction cycles are observable in practice, and thus bugs involving satisfaction cycles may be unlikely to affect deployed systems.

6. Evaluation

We have evaluated CDSSPEC on a contention-free lock, a port of the Linux kernel's reader-writer spinlock, two types of concurrent queues, a work stealing deque [34], and the Michael Scott queue from the CDSCHECKER benchmark suite; several data structures which were originally ported for AUTOMO [41] — an RCU implementation, a sequential lock, a ticket lock [42]; and a concurrent hashtable ported from Doug Lea's Java ConcurrentHashMap [35]. We report execution times on an Intel Xeon E3-1246 v3 machine. We have made both the CDSSPEC checker framework and benchmarks publicly available at `http://plrg.eecs.uci.edu/cdsspec`.

6.1 Expressiveness

We first report our experiences writing specifications. Due to space constraints, we describe the specifications in detail for a select set of benchmarks.

Concurrent hashtable: The concurrent hashtable was ported from the Java ConcurrentHashMap. The implementation uses an array of atomic variables to store the key/-value slots, which are divided into multiple concurrent segments protected by different locks. This implementation uses `seq_cst` atomics to establish strong orderings between the `get` and `put` methods on the same key. Thus, we can simply map it to a sequential deterministic hashtable.

In this implementation, the `put` method immediately acquires a lock. If a `get` method finds an entry in the first search, it performs a `seq_cst` load on the value, which will form a *sc* edge with the corresponding `seq_cst` update on the value in the `put` method; otherwise, the `get` method will acquire the lock and search the list again. As a result, a `get` method call will be ordered with a `put` method call on either the write/read of the value or the release/acquire of the lock. Thus, we annotate these operations as the ordering points for the `get` and `put` methods.

Chase-Lev Deque: This is a bug-fixed version of a published C11 adaptation of the Chase-Lev deque [34]. This implementation establishes *hb* ordering between all successful `steal` method calls and allows `steal` method calls to execute concurrently with the `take` and `push` method calls. Since `take` and `push` methods should be called from the same thread, we specify an admissibility condition that `take` and `push` calls should be ordered with respect to each other. Our specification allows `steal` and `take` method calls to spuriously return empty. We maintain the state as an ordered list. A `push` call pushes back its value to the list, and a `steal` or `take` call pops the first or last item from the list (when the list is not empty) and checks whether that item is consistent with their return values. In order to make the specification tighter, for the `take` method, we impose a justifying condition that ensures that when it fails and the maintained list is not empty, there must exist concurrent `steal` method calls that take each element in the list.

If a successful `steal` method call reads a value from the deque, it should be ordered after the `push` method call that wrote that value to the deque. Therefore, we specified the store and load operations to the array in the `steal` and `push` methods as their ordering points. Since `take` and `push` calls are intended to be from the same thread, we specified the last operation in the `take` method as its ordering point.

Linux Reader-Writer Lock: A reader-writer lock allows either multiple concurrent readers or one exclusive writer to hold a lock. We abstract it with a boolean variable `writer_lock` to store whether the write lock is held and an integer variable `reader_cnt` to store the number of threads that currently hold the read lock.

Initially, we did not allow `write_trylock` to spuriously fail, and CDSSPEC checker reports a specification violation. We then analyzed the code and found that `write_trylock` has a transient side effect (i.e., subtract and then restore a bias if it fails), thus causing racing `write_trylock` calls to fail while the sequential specification would force it to succeed. We then modified the specification of `write_trylock` to allow spurious failures so that our correctness model fits this data structure. This shows CDSSPEC can help developers iteratively refine the specifications of data structures.

Ticket Lock: This is a synchronization mechanism that controls which thread can enter a critical section. The data structure maintains two atomic variables — `nowServing` and `curTicket`. The `lock` method first grabs a ticket by atomically executing a `fetch_add` operation on `curTicket` and then spins until `nowServing` is equal to its ticket number, and the `unlock` method increases `nowServing`.

It is noteworthy that the `fetch_add` operation (read-modify-write) in the `lock` method has `relaxed` memory order, and hence the `lock` methods do not establish synchronization at the `fetch_add` operation on the `curTicket` variable, making us unable to use the accesses on `curTicket` to establish the ordering relation $\xrightarrow{r}$. However, the data structure actually establishes proper synchronization elsewhere — on the update/read of the `nowServing` variable. Thus, we can still write a CDSSPEC specification for the ticket lock.

6.2 Ease of Use

While existing model-checking tools support various relaxed memory models, they either do not support the C/C++11 memory model or only provide simple user-specified assertions (e.g., `assert()`) [4, 6, 40]. In this sense, CDSSPEC is complementary to these tools. Conceptually, CDSSPEC can be extended to support other relaxed memory models (such as TSO, PSO, etc.) and used along with these model checking tools as long as we can define an equivalent ordering relation to the *hb* and *sc* relations in other relaxed memory models.

On average, using CDSSPEC to specify our benchmarks required us to write 11.5 lines of specifications for each benchmark, indicating the CDSSPEC is easy to use. We summarize why each CDSSPEC component is easy to write: (1) specifying sequential data structures is easy and straightforward, and developers can often just use an off-the-shelf implementation from a library. Even the sequential specification of those with non-deterministic behaviors are easy to understand. For example, the non-blocking Michael & Scott queue has the same justifying condition for the `dequeue` method as our simple blocking queue. (2) When developers specify ordering points, they only need to know what operations order method calls without needing to specify the subtle reasoning about the corner cases involving interleavings and reorderings introduced by relaxed memory models. In fact, all of the ordering points that we specify in our benchmarks are consistent with the commit points for their linearizable counterparts under the SC memory model. In a total of 27 API methods, we only specified 33 ordering points (1.22 per method on average), and each ordering point only takes 1 line of specification. (3) For admissibility rules, the fact that we express them at the abstraction of methods makes them easy to both reason about and write. Overall, we only used 7 lines to specify admissibility rules in a total 1,253 lines of code (omitting blank lines and comments).

Specification Errors While it is possible for developers to write incorrect CDSSPEC specifications against which the CDSSPEC checker reports no violations, in our experience specification errors typically cause the CDSSPEC checker to report violations (and thus help with refining specifications) for the following reasons:

- Admissibility: Admissibility in CDSSPEC specifications defaults to allowing all possible executions. This ensures that specification writers have to explicitly identify executions in which the specification should not hold, and by default the CDSSPEC checker will assume the specification should be checked on all executions.
- Assertions & Side Effects: The CDSSPEC checker generates and checks all possible sequential histories, so in practice, unless developers do not specify any assertions or specify very trivial assertions, the probability of writing incorrect assertions and side effects for which all histories pass is low. Our experience in refining the Linux Reader-Writer Lock's specification discussed in Section 6.1 conforms this.
- Ordering points: Ordering points can be viewed as an efficient way to construct sequential histories and justifying subhistories. Viewed in this context, mistakes specifying ordering points typically result in spurious errors being reported by the CDSSPEC checker.

Benchmark	# Executions	# Feasible	Total Time (s)
Chase-Lev Deque	893	158	0.10
SPSC Queue	18	15	0.01
RCU	47	18	0.01
Lockfree Hashtable	6	6	0.01
MCS Lock	21,126	13,786	3.00
MPMC Queue	2,911	1,274	4.83
M&S Queue	296	150	0.03
Linux RW Lock	69,386	1,822	13.71
Seqlock	89	36	0.01
Ticket Lock	1,790	978	0.17

Figure 7. Benchmark results

6.3 Performance

Figure 7 presents performance results for CDSSPEC on our benchmark set. We list the number of the total executions that CDSCHECKER has explored, the number of the feasible executions that we checked the specification for, and the time the benchmark took to finish. All of our benchmarks finished within 14 seconds, and 9 out of 10 finished within 5 seconds, and most took less than 1 second to finish.

6.4 Finding Bugs

We also examine the effectiveness of CDSSPEC for detecting known bugs, injected bugs, and potentially overly strong memory order parameters with these benchmarks.

6.4.1 Known Bugs

M&S queue: In this benchmark, two bugs were found by AUTOMO [41], one in the `enqueue` method and the other in the `dequeue` method. Both bugs use weaker than necessary memory order parameters so that the queue behaves incorrectly. We ran the buggy implementation with our specification, and the CDSSPEC checker exposed both bugs by showing specification violations in which a dequeue either incorrectly returns empty or violates the FIFO order. Note that neither bug was found by CDSChecker, and this shows that by writing specifications, we detect more real bugs.
Chase-Lev deq: CDSCHECKER found a bug (using a weaker than necessary ordering parameter) in this benchmark, in which a load in the `steal` method can read from an uninitialized memory location when a steal and push concurrently execute and the push resizes the queue [40]. In order to show that our specification can also expose the same bug, we turn off the CDSCHECKER uninitialized load report by initializing the new array created by the resize operation. We then ran the buggy implementation under our specification, and CDSSPEC checker reported the bug when a `steal` method call returned the wrong item.

6.4.2 Injected Bugs

To further evaluate CDSSPEC, we injected bugs in our benchmarks by weakening the ordering parameters of atomic operations to the next weaker parameters, i.e., changing `seq_cst` to `acq_rel`, `acq_rel` to `release/acquire`, and `acquire/release` to `relaxed`. We weakened one operation per each trial and covered all of the atomic operations that our tests exercise. While this injection strategy may not reproduce all types of errors that developers make, it does simulate errors caused by misunderstanding the complicated semantics of relaxed memory models. More importantly, these errors not only exist in real-world data structures (e.g., all the known bugs mentioned in Section 6.4.1 and the overly strong parameters mentioned in Section 6.4.3 involve using incorrect/inappropriate parameters) but also are exceedingly difficult to reason and find even by experts (e.g., the Chase-Lev deque C11 implementation).

Figure 8 shows the results of the injection detection experiment, which introduces three types of bugs: (1) the column *Built-in* represents specification-independent bugs detected by CDSCHECKER built-in check (i.e., data races and uninitialized loads); and (2) the column *Admissibility* represents a failure to satisfy the admissibility condition once all executions pass the built-in check; and (3) the column *Assertion* represents a specification violation once all executions pass the built-in check and the admissibility condition. The detection rate is the number of injections for which we detected a bug divided by the total number of injections. Strictly speaking, a data structure implementation that allows inadmissible executions may still exhibit correct behaviors under certain usage scenarios; however, it may very well violate the original design intention of the data structure. For example, an MPMC queue without proper synchronization works correctly when only used in a single thread, but this is by no means what such a data structure is designed for.

Benchmark	# Injection	# Built-in	# Admissibility	# Assertion	# Rate
Chase-Lev Deque	7	3	0	4	100%
SPSC Queue	2	0	0	2	100%
RCU	3	3	0	0	100%
Lockfree Hashtable	4	2	0	2	100%
MCS Lock	8	4	0	4	100%
MPMC Queue	8	0	4	0	50%
M&S Queue	10	3	0	7	100%
Linux RW Lock	8	0	0	8	100%
Seqlock	5	0	0	5	100%
Ticket Lock	2	0	0	2	100%
Total	57	15	4	34	93%

Figure 8. Bug injection detection results

Although the CDSSPEC checker is a unit testing tool and limited to small-scale tests to explore common usage scenarios, CDSSPEC was able to find 100% of injections for most data structures (9/10) and to find 93% of the injections on average. For our 57 injections, 15 of them were detected by checks in CDSCHECKER and 38 additional injections were detected by CDSSPEC. This shows that by writing specifications, we detect significantly more fault injections.
MPMC Queue: This is an array-based implementation with read/write counters. Strictly speaking, it is buggy; but the bug requires a load to read from a store from a previous counter epoch (and thus the bug may be acceptable in practice). Several atomic operations have stronger orders than strictly necessary, which only serves to make triggering the bug more difficult (with the condition that the bug requires >100,000 threads and a counter rollover). Our test cases are small enough not to trigger a 16-bit counter rollover.

6.4.3 Overly Strong Parameters

In the injection detection experiment, we found that in the Chase-Lev deq C11 implementation, weakening one `seq_cst` CAS operation on the `Top` variable to `relaxed` triggers no specification violation. We then carefully reviewed the code and believe this is unnecessarily strong. We contacted the paper's authors, and they confirmed that the stronger parameter is not necessary. This shows that CDSSPEC specification can help developers (even experts) avoid overly strong memory ordering parameters and as a result can potentially increase performance.

Limitation of Unit Tests The CDSSPEC checker framework relies on developers providing unit tests. While certain bugs cannot be easily caught by unit tests, in our experience, writing simple unit tests to exercise each corner case (e.g., dequeuing from an empty queue, triggering resize, and racing for the last element) is an effective way to find bugs. To detect both the existing and injected bugs, we only used test cases with 3 or fewer threads, and each thread contained fewer than 2 API method calls on average (5 at most). For example, we detected an existing bug in the Chase-Lev deq implementation by using only 2 threads — a main thread that pushes 3 items and takes 2 items, and a worker thread that tries to steal two items. This shows that simple unit tests can help detect tricky bugs involving the complicated semantics of relaxed memory models.

7. Related Work

Researchers have proposed and designed specifications and approaches to find bugs in concurrent data structures based on linearization. Early work [51] proposed using linearizability to test and verify concurrent objects. Line-up [17] builds on the Chess [39] model checker to automatically check deterministic linearizability. Paraglider [49] supports checking with and without linearization points using SPIN [33]. VYRD [27] is conceptually similar to CDSSPEC— developers specify commit points for concurrent code. These approaches assume the SC memory model and a trace that provides an ordering for method invocation and response events. Our work extends the notion of equivalence to sequential executions to the relaxed memory models used by real systems.

Amit *et al.* [8] present a static analysis based on TVLA for verifying linearizability of concurrent linked data structures. Hemed *et al.* [30] have generalized linearizability to formally describe concurrency-aware objects. Researchers have designed techniques that can automatically prove linearizability [25, 46, 47]. Thread quantification can also verify data structure linearizability [14]. Colvin *et al.* formally verified a list-based set [22]. While these approaches provide stronger guarantees than CDSSPEC, they target the SC memory model and were typically used to check simpler data structures.

Researchers have proposed specification languages for concurrent data structures. Refinement mapping [3] provides the theoretical basis for designing and using specifications. Commit atomicity [28] can verify atomicity properties. Concurrit [26] is a domain-specific language that allows writing scripts to specify thread schedules to reproduce bugs and is useful when developers already have some knowledge about a bug. NDetermin [19] infers non-deterministic sequential specifications to model the behaviors of parallel code.

Batty *et al.* [10] present an approach to specifying the behavior of C/C++11 code in terms of abstractions that also support composability. Their specifications utilize relaxed atomic operations to specify the behaviors of C/C++11 code and thus may not be much easier to reason about than the original implementation. Tassarotti *et al.* [45] verify an RCU implementation using a logic for weak memory models. They capture the correctness of the values returned by reads in terms of an evolution of states, and they require that a read return a value that is at least as new as the specified state.

Bounded relaxation of data structure specifications has been proposed as an approach that allows increasing the performance of concurrent data structures [31]. Unfortunately, this approach does not model the release-acquire synchronization behavior of C/C++11 as there is in general no fixed bound for how far traces for data structure like our example queue can diverge from the traditional specification.

GAMBIT [23] uses a prioritized search technique that combines stateless model checking and heuristic-guided fuzzing to unit test code under the SC memory model. RELAXED [21] explores SC executions to identify executions with races and then re-executes the program under the PSO or TSO memory model to test whether the relaxations expose bugs. CheckFence [16] is a tool for verifying data structures against relaxed memory models and takes a SAT-based approach instead of the stateless model checking approach.

Researchers have developed verification techniques for code that admits only SC executions under the TSO and PSO memory models [18, 20]. Researchers have developed tools to infer memory orderings for C/C++ code that ensure that all executions are equivalent to SC executions [37, 41]. Vafeiadis *et al.* [48] have extended the concurrent separation logic to reason C/C++11 programs.

8. Conclusion

CDSSPEC makes it easier to unit test concurrent data structures written for the C/C++11 memory model. It extends and modifies classic approaches to defining the desired behaviors of concurrent data structures with respect to sequential versions of the same data structure to apply to the C/C++ memory model. Our evaluation shows that the approach can be used to specify and test correctness properties for a wide range of data structures.

References

[1] ISO/IEC 14882:2011, Information technology – programming languages – C++.

[2] ISO/IEC 9899:2011, Information technology – programming languages – C.

[3] M. Abadi and L. Lamport. The existence of refinement mapping. *Theoretical Computer Science*, 82(2):253–284, May 1991.

[4] P. A. Abdulla, S. Aronis, M. F. Atig, B. Jonsson, C. Leonardsson, and K. Sagonas. Stateless model checking for TSO and PSO. In *Proceedings of the 21st International Conference on Tools and Algorithms for the Construction and Analysis of Systems*, 2015.

[5] S. V. Adve and K. Gharachorloo. Shared memory consistency models: A tutorial. *Computer*, 29:66–76, 1996.

[6] J. Alglave, D. Kroening, and M. Tautschnig. Partial orders for efficient bounded model checking of concurrent software. In *Proceedings of the 25th International Conference on Computer Aided Verification*, 2013.

[7] J. Alglave, L. Maranget, and M. Tautschnig. Herding cats: modelling, simulation, testing, and data-mining for weak memory. In *Proceedings of the 2014 ACM SIGPLAN Conference on Programming Language Design and Implementation*, 2014.

[8] D. Amit, N. Rinetzky, T. Reps, M. Sagiv, and E. Yahav. Comparison under abstraction for verifying linearizability. In *Proceedings of the 19th International Conference on Computer Aided Verification*, 2007.

[9] M. Batty. The C11 and C++11 concurrency model. *Ph.D. thesis, University of Cambridge*, 2014.

[10] M. Batty, M. Dodds, and A. Gotsman. Library abstraction for C/C++ concurrency. In *Proceedings of the Symposium on Principles of Programming Languages*, 2013.

[11] M. Batty, A. F. Donaldson, and J. Wickerson. Overhauling SC atomics in C11 and OpenCL. In *Proceedings of the Symposium on Principles of Programming Languages*, 2016.

[12] M. Batty, K. Memarian, K. Nienhuis, J. Pichon-Pharabod, and P. Sewell. The problem of programming language concurrency semantics. In *Proceedings of the 2015 European Symposium on Programming*, 2015.

[13] M. Batty, S. Owens, S. Sarkar, P. Sewell, and T. Weber. Mathematizing C++ concurrency. In *Proceedings of the Symposium on Principles of Programming Languages*, 2011.

[14] J. Berdine, T. Lev-Ami, R. Manivich, G. Ramalingam, and M. Sagiv. Thread quantification for concurrent shape analysis. In *Proceedings of the 20th International Conference on Computer Aided Verification*, 2008.

[15] H. Boehm and B. Demsky. Outlawing Ghosts: Avoiding out-of-thin-air results. In *Proceedings of the 2014 ACM SIGPLAN Workshop on Memory Systems Performance and Correctness*, 2014.

[16] S. Burckhardt, R. Alur, and M. M. K. Martin. CheckFence: Checking consistency of concurrent data types on relaxed memory models. In *Proceedings of the 2007 ACM SIGPLAN Conference on Programming Language Design and Implementation*, 2007.

[17] S. Burckhardt, C. Dern, M. Musuvathi, and R. Tan. Line-up: A complete and automatic linearizability checker. In *Proceedings of the 2010 ACM SIGPLAN Conference on Programming Language Design and Implementation*, 2010.

[18] S. Burckhardt and M. Musuvathi. Effective program verification for relaxed memory models. In *Proceedings of the 20th International Conference on Computer Aided Verification*, 2008.

[19] J. Burnim, T. Elmas, G. Necula, and K. Sen. NDetermin: Inferring nondeterministic sequential specifications for parallelism correctness. In *Proceedings of the 17th ACM SIGPLAN Symposium on Principles and Practice of Parallel Programming*, 2012.

[20] J. Burnim, K. Sen, and C. Stergiou. Sound and complete monitoring of sequential consistency for relaxed memory models. In *Proceedings of the 17th International Conference on Tools and Algorithms for the Construction and Analysis of Systems*, 2011.

[21] J. Burnim, K. Sen, and C. Stergiou. Testing concurrent programs on relaxed memory models. In *Proceedings of the 2011 International Symposium on Software Testing and Analysis*, 2011.

[22] R. Colvin, L. Groves, V. Luchangco, and M. Moir. Formal verification of a lazy concurrent list-based set algorithm. In *Proceedings of the 18th International Conference on Computer Aided Verification*, 2006.

[23] K. E. Coons, S. Burckhardt, and M. Musuvathi. GAMBIT: Effective unit testing for concurrency libraries. In *Proceedings of the 15th ACM SIGPLAN Symposium on Principles and Practice of Parallel Programming*, 2010.

[24] M. Desnoyers, P. E. McKenney, A. S. Stern, M. R. Dagenais, and J. Walpole. User-level implementations of read-copy update. *IEEE Transactions on Parallel and Distributed Systems*, 2012.

[25] C. Drăgoi, A. Gupta, and T. Henzinger. Automatic linearizability proofs of concurrent objects with cooperating updates. In *Proceedings of the 25th International Conference on Computer Aided Verification*, 2013.

[26] T. Elmas, J. Burnim, G. Necula, and K. Sen. CONCURRIT: A domain specific language for reproducing concurrency bugs. In *Proceedings of the 2013 ACM SIGPLAN Conference on Programming Language Design and Implementation*, 2013.

[27] T. Elmas, S. Tasiran, and S. Qadeer. VYRD: Verifying concurrent programs by runtime refinement-violation detection. In *Proceedings of the 2005 ACM SIGPLAN Conference on Programming Language Design and Implementation*, 2005.

[28] C. Flanagan. Verifying commit-atomicity using model-checking. In *Proceedings of the 11th International SPIN Workshop on Model Checking Software*, 2004.

[29] A. Haas, C. M. Kirsch, M. Lippautz, and H. Payer. How FIFO is your concurrent FIFO queue? In *Proceedings of the 2012 ACM Workshop on Relaxing Synchronization for Multicore and Manycore Scalability*, 2012.

[30] N. Hemed, N. Rinetzky, and V. Vafeiadis. Modular verification of concurrency-aware linearizability. In *Proceedings of the 29th International Symposium on Distributed Computing*, 2015.

[31] T. A. Henzinger, C. M. Kirsch, H. Payer, A. Sezgin, and A. Sokolova. Quantitative relaxation of concurrent data structures. In *Proceedings of the 40th Annual ACM SIGPLAN-SIGACT Symposium on Principles of Programming Languages*, 2013.

[32] M. Herlihy and J. Wing. Linearizability: A correctness condition for concurrent objects. *ACM Transactions on Programming Languages and Systems*, 12(3):463–492, July 1990.

[33] G. J. Holzmann. *The SPIN Model Checker: Primer and Reference Manual.* Addison-Wesley Professional, 1st edition, 2003.

[34] N. M. Lê, A. Pop, A. Cohen, and F. Zappa Nardelli. Correct and efficient work-stealing for weak memory models. In *Proceedings of the 18th ACM SIGPLAN Symposium on Principles and Practice of Parallel Programming*, 2013.

[35] D. Lea. util.concurrent.ConcurrentHashMap in java.util.concurrent the Java Concurrency Package. `http://docs.oracle.com/javase/8/docs/api/java/util/concurrent/ConcurrentHashMap.html`.

[36] L. Maranget, S. Sarkar, and P. Sewell. A tutorial introduction to the ARM and POWER relaxed memory models. `http://www.cl.cam.ac.uk/~pes20/ppc-supplemental/test7.pdf`, 2012.

[37] Y. Meshman, N. Rinetzky, and E. Yahav. Pattern-based synthesis of synchronization for the C++ memory model. In *Formal Methods in Computer-Aided Design*, 2015.

[38] M. M. Michael and M. L. Scott. Simple, fast, and practical non-blocking and blocking concurrent queue algorithms. In *Proceedings of the Fifteenth Annual ACM Symposium on Principles of Distributed Computing*, 1996.

[39] M. Musuvathi, S. Qadeer, P. A. Nainar, T. Ball, G. Basler, and I. Neamtiu. Finding and reproducing Heisenbugs in concurrent programs. In *Proceedings of the 8th Symposium on Operating Systems Design and Implementation*, 2008.

[40] B. Norris and B. Demsky. CDSChecker: Checking concurrent data structures written with C/C++ atomics. In *Proceeding of the 28th ACM SIGPLAN Conference on Object-Oriented Programming, Systems, Languages, and Applications*, 2013.

[41] P. Ou and B. Demsky. AutoMO: Automatic inference of memory order parameters for C/C++11. In *Proceeding of the 30th ACM SIGPLAN Conference on Object-Oriented Programming, Systems, Languages, and Applications*, 2015.

[42] D. P. Reed and R. K. Kanodia. Synchronization with eventcounts and sequencers. *Communications of the ACM*, 22(2):115–123, 1979.

[43] A. Shipilëv. `https://shipilev.net/`. Oct. 2016.

[44] A. Shipilëv. Java memory model pragmatics. `https://shipilev.net/blog/2014/jmm-pragmatics/`. Sep. 2016.

[45] J. Tassarotti, D. Dreyer, and V. Vafeiadis. Verifying read-copy-update in a logic for weak memory. In *Proceedings of the 36th ACM SIGPLAN Conference on Programming Language Design and Implementation*, 2015.

[46] V. Vafeiadis. Shape-value abstraction for verifying linearizability. In *Proceedings of the 2009 Conference on Verification, Model Checking, and Abstract Interpretation*, 2009.

[47] V. Vafeiadis. Automatically proving linearizability. In *Proceedings of the 22th International Conference on Computer Aided Verification*, 2010.

[48] V. Vafeiadis and C. Narayan. Relaxed separation logic: A program logic for c11 concurrency. In *Proceeding of the 28th ACM SIGPLAN Conference on Object-Oriented Programming, Systems, Languages, and Applications*, 2013.

[49] M. Vechev, E. Yahav, and G. Yorsh. Experience with model checking linearizability. In *International SPIN Workshop on Model Checking Software*, 2009.

[50] D. Vyukov. Relacy race detector. `http://relacy.sourceforge.net/`, 2011 Oct.

[51] J. M. Wing and C. Gong. Testing and verifying concurrent objects. *Journal of Parallel and Distributed Computing - Special issue on parallel I/O systems*, 17(1-2):164–182, Jan./Feb. 1993.

An Efficient Abortable-locking Protocol for Multi-level NUMA Systems

Milind Chabbi
Hewlett Packard Labs
milind.chabbi@hpe.com

Abdelhalim Amer
Argonne National Laboratory
aamer@anl.gov

Shasha Wen, Xu Liu
College of William and Mary
{swen, xl10}@cs.wm.edu

Abstract

The popularity of Non-Uniform Memory Access (NUMA) architectures has led to numerous locality-preserving hierarchical lock designs, such as HCLH, HMCS, and cohort locks. Locality-preserving locks trade fairness for higher throughput. Hence, some instances of acquisitions can incur long latencies, which may be intolerable for certain applications. Few locks admit a waiting thread to abandon its protocol on a timeout. State-of-the-art abortable locks are not fully locality aware, introduce high overheads, and unsuitable for frequent aborts. Enhancing locality-aware locks with lightweight timeout capability is critical for their adoption. In this paper, we design and evaluate the HMCS-T lock, a Hierarchical MCS (HMCS) lock variant that admits a timeout. HMCS-T maintains the locality benefits of HMCS while ensuring aborts to be lightweight. HMCS-T offers the progress guarantee missing in most abortable queuing locks. Our evaluations show that HMCS-T offers the timeout feature at a moderate overhead over its HMCS analog. HMCS-T, used in an MPI runtime lock, mitigated the poor scalability of an MPI+OpenMP BFS code and resulted in 4.3× superior scaling.

Keywords Synchronization, Spin lock, Queuing lock, MCS lock, Hierarchical lock, Abortable lock, Timeout lock.

1. Introduction

Multi-socket systems have become a norm rather than an exception in modern server and HPC establishments. State-of-the-art shared memory machines such as SGI UV [22] and HP Integrity Superdome X [10] are not only multi-socket but also multi-node. Multi-node, multi-socket systems along with the deep processor cache hierarchy lead to Non-Uniform Memory Access (NUMA) latencies. Maintaining locality of reference is critical to achieving high performance on NUMA architectures.

The emergence of NUMA architectures has propelled researchers to develop various "locality-aware" locking algorithms. Locality-aware locks prefer to handover a lock from the lock holder to the "nearest" lock requester instead of the "earliest" lock requester. This kind of locality bias reduces the indiscriminate migration of shared cache lines (accessed in the critical section and the lock's internal data structures) among different locality domains.

Hierarchical locks sacrifice fairness [5] to exploit locality. In a hierarchical lock, on a highly contended system with a deep NUMA hierarchy, a lock requester may have to wait for an unusually long time when a distant NUMA domain holds the lock. While spinning for a short time to acquire the lock from a neighbor is desirable to enhance locality and throughput, idle waiting for a long time hurts parallelism. The following use cases motivate the need for allowing a waiting thread to timeout and abandon the protocol: (1) A thread in an application with sufficient parallel slackness [9, 24] may desire to discontinue a work chunk blocked on long lock waiting and instead take up a different work chunk not subjected to serialization, (2) A low-priority process may want to temporarily abandon (or permanently abort) its lock request to expedite the lock handoff to a high-priority process, and (3) Database systems assume a deadlock when no progress is observed for a long time, and they require the timeout capability in their locks to unroll a transaction.

State-of-the-art abortable locks suffer from various limitations. They introduce blocking wait (e.g., [20]), have unbounded space and time complexities (e.g., [19] and [8]), lack full locality awareness (e.g., [20], [19], [8]), do not ensure starvation freedom (e.g., [8]), and incur high memory management costs (e.g., [19], [8]). Hierarchical queue-based spin locks with a timeout would offer greater flexibility for application programmers to exploit locality of shared data when available and abandon a long wait to exploit parallelism that exists elsewhere in the system. However, state-of-the-art hierarchical queue-based locks (e.g., [5]) lack the timeout capability. Few, if any, verify their correctness.

PPoPP '17 February 04 - 08, 2017, Austin, TX, USA

ACM 978-1-4503-4493-7/17/02. . . $15.00
DOI: http://dx.doi.org/10.1145/3018743.3018768

We have designed the HMCS-T lock, which allows a waiting thread to abandon on timeout. The HMCS-T lock addresses the aforementioned challenges while being mindful of the principles of the HMCS lock—exploiting locality. It is challenging to incorporate the timeout capability in the HMCS lock because of the dependency of successors at each level on their predecessors to hand-off the lock through the hierarchical tree. A timeout may happen when a thread is waiting to acquire a lock at any level in the tree. Abandoning from an interior node in the tree is particularly challenging since it involves releasing already acquired lower-level locks. Wait loops at various places in the protocol pose daunting challenges in making the protocol non-blocking on timeout. Furthermore, attention needs to be paid to maintain locality in every step of the design. A design that addresses these complications needs rigorous correctness (mutual exclusion and livelock and deadlock freedom) and progress (starvation freedom) guarantees.

The key idea in the HMCS-T lock is that an abandoning thread leaves its queue node record [5] (aka `QNode`) intact in the MCS queue structure with a special status flag indicating that the owner has abandoned. When a lock holder notices an abandoned successor, it passes the lock to the next unabandoned successor. If no unabandoned successor is found at a level, the release proceeds to find a waiting thread at an ancestral level, if any, in the hierarchical tree. A disciplined, locality-preserving abandonment policy handles timeout while retaining the high performance of HMCS.

In HMCS-T, when an abandoned thread requests the same lock again, instead of bringing a new `QNode` record, it reuses its abandoned `QNode`. This design ensures a space complexity linear in the number of participants. This "reuse" design allows an abandoned thread to re-secure its original position in the queue where it had previously abandoned. Such thread can resume its wait notwithstanding its prior abandonment if the lock was not already passed beyond its position. A consequence of this design is that a thread can opportunistically express its "locking intent" well before the lock may be actually needed, *possibly* reducing the waiting time when the need for the lock becomes imminent.

The HMCS-T lock ensures starvation freedom for threads that can wait and ensures a bounded number of steps to abandon (on timeout) or release the lock. Having all these traits is uncommon in lock designs that admit a timeout [8, 19, 20]. For threads that do not admit a timeout, HMCS-T retains the same starvation freedom and fairness guarantees as the HMCS lock, even when intermixed with threads that admit timeouts. We have proved the correctness of HMCS-T via formal verification using the Spin [12] model checker.

The contributions of this paper are the following:

1. Design of a high-throughput queue-based hierarchical spin lock with a timeout capability, which exploits locality and ensures low overheads for abort and reentry.
2. Formal verification of correctness and progress guarantees of the intricate algorithm.
3. Demonstration of the superiority of HMCS-T over other abortable locks and demonstration of 34% speedup and 4.3× superior scaling in an MPI+OpenMP Graph500 BFS kernel by using the HMCS-T lock.

2. Background and Related Work

MCS [17] and CLH [15] queue-based locks do not allow abandoning once a thread has enqueued itself. Scott and Scherer [20] devised MCS and CLH locks with a timeout, which were not non-blocking. Scott designed the non-blocking variants (*MCS_NB* and *CLH_NB* locks [19]), which, unfortunately, introduced an unbounded worst-case space and time complexity for a given number of threads. The designs in [19] need explicit memory management before each acquisition with potential remote memory accesses, which becomes a bottleneck as we show later in our experiments (cf. § 6.2). In contrast, HMCS-T ensures starvation freedom—the threads that do not timeout eventually acquire the lock, and the threads that timeout terminate their protocol in a bounded number of steps. HMCS-T has no loop that cannot admit a timeout; it has a bounded space complexity, and it does not require continuous memory management. The improvements come with an intricate design and slightly reduced performance compared to the baseline HMCS.

Jayanti [14] proposed a token-based abortable lock with linear space bounds and logarithmic time bounds. Pareek et al. [18] proposed a randomized algorithm to abortable locks that can achieve sub-logarithmic remote memory references. Marathe et al. [16] combined a fixed-length queue lock with a back-off lock, relieving the design from expensive memory management. None of these locks are NUMA aware.

Cohort locks [8] employ two levels of locks, treating a system as a two-level NUMA hierarchy. The authors present two timeout-capable cohort locks—a 2-level backoff lock and a global backoff lock coupled with a local CLH lock (A_C_BO_CLH). Aborting a 2-level backoff lock is straightforward since there is no per-thread state. To abort an A_C_BO_CLH lock, the authors use Scott's CLH_NB lock [19] at the local level, which also suffers from repeated memory management but isolates the problem to a socket. These two abortable locks neither ensure starvation freedom (for threads do not abort) nor bound the steps after timeout (for threads that abort), unlike HMCS-T.

HMCS lock [5]. Since we are concerned with the timeout capability in the HMCS lock [5], we provide the details of HMCS first. HMCS employs a tree of MCS locks to leverage multiple levels of locality in a NUMA hierarchy (Figure 1). The tree structure mirrors the underlying NUMA hierarchy; each locality domain has an MCS lock of its own, which is contested by its subdomains. For example, all SMT threads on a core may compete for an MCS lock designated for that CPU core. Not all NUMA levels need be mirrored in the tree.

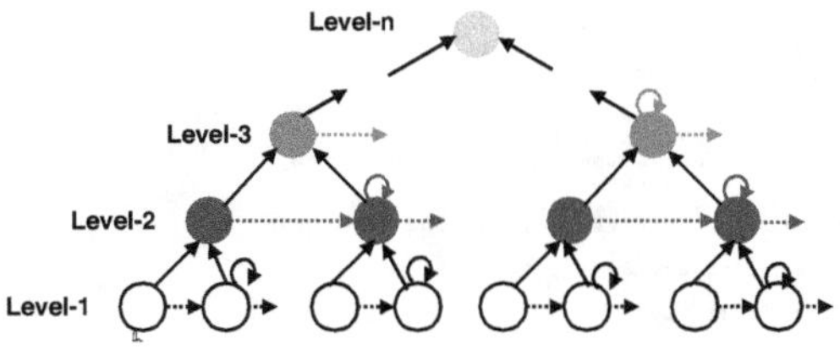

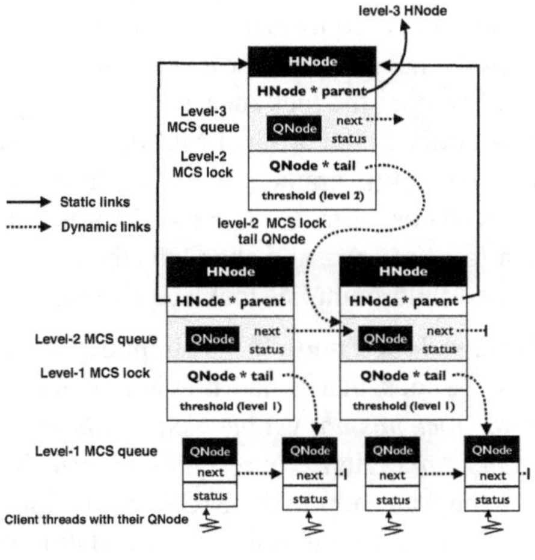

Figure 2: HMCS data structures.

Lock acquisition for each thread begins with competing for a designated leaf-level lock that corresponds to the thread's innermost NUMA domain. When a thread acquires an MCS lock in the tree in an uncontended manner (no predecessor), it proceeds to contend for its parent lock (if any) in the tree. A thread that acquires the lock at the root of the tree immediately enters the critical section. Any thread that fails in immediately acquiring a lock in the tree waits and receives that lock from its predecessor. The release protocol also starts at a leaf of the tree implicitly passing all locks held by the owner to its local successor, if any. A waiting thread at the deepest node on a thread's path to the root, typically, inherits all locks held by its predecessor. As a result, when a successor is granted a lock, it immediately enters the critical section *without explicitly contending for other locks along its path to the root.* To prevent starvation, threads may pass an HMCS lock within a locality domain for a bounded number of times. HMCS does not admit a timeout.

Each interior node of the HMCS tree (`HNode`) encapsulates an MCS lock, a queue node (`QNode`), and a pointer to its parent `HNode` (Figure 2). Each `HNode` is pre-allocated in the corresponding NUMA domain. Threads arrive with their own `QNode`s and a reference to their leaf-level `HNode`. When competing for a non-leaf-level lock, a thread uses a `QNode` present inside the `HNode` dedicated for that domain.

Terminology. We consider a leaf lock of HMCS to be at *level* 1 and the root lock to be at *level n*. We represent an arbitrary level with the letter l. The *tail pointer* of an MCS lock refers to the lock word [5, 17]. The tail pointer is `null` when the lock is free and *non-`null`* otherwise. Although a level-l MCS lock's tail pointer is physically placed a level-$l+1$ `HNode` data structure, for the ease of prose, level-l lock, level-l queue, and level-l `QNode` refer to the lock at level-l, the MCS queue used for competing for the level-l lock, and the constituent `QNode`s in that queue, respectively. For example, a level-1 `QNode` is inside a level-1 queue, which is used to compete for a level-1 lock. An HMCS lock that has n lock levels is represented as HMCS$\langle n \rangle$ and the analogous HMCS-T lock is represented as HMCS-T$\langle n \rangle$. MCS$\approx$HMCS$\langle 1 \rangle$.

Two or more `QNode`s (and hence their owner threads) are *peer*s at level l, if their lowest common ancestral lock is at level l. Two or more `QNode`s *belong* to the same domain at level l, if they share a common lock at level $\leq l$. In a sequence of locks $(l)(l+1)\cdots(m)$, where $1 \leq l < m \leq n$, from level-1 to the root, a lock *prefix* refers to the sequence $(l)(l+1)\cdots(k)$, where $l \leq k \leq m$, and a lock *suffix* refers to the sequence $(k+1)\cdots(m)$. If a lock holder hands off the lock to a waiting thread, we refer to it as "lock passing". A thread "relinquishes" the lock if no thread is waiting during the lock-passing attempt. A "release" refers to either lock passing or relinquishing. `SWAP` refers to an atomic exchange operation. `CAS` refers to an atomic compare exchange operation. On timeout a thread "aborts" or "abandons".

3. Design of One-level HMCS-T

We first describe the HMCS-T$\langle 1 \rangle$ protocol, which allows abandoning in an MCS lock (i.e., HMCS$\langle 1 \rangle$). In §4, we generalize the design to an n-level HMCS-T lock.

Overview. The key idea of HMCS-T is that a thread can abandon by updating its already enqueued `QNode` by `SWAP`ing a special flag, leaving the `QNode` behind in the MCS queue. On noticing an abandoned successor, a lock-releasing predecessor takes the additional responsibility of passing the lock to an unabandoned successor in the queue. The protocol provisions readmission of a previously abandoned requestor into its earlier secured position, if possible. Figure 3 depicts some important steps in the protocol.

Details. The HMCS-T$\langle 1 \rangle$ encodes special values—waiting (`W`), unlocked (`U`), abandoned (`A`), and recycled (`R`)—in the status field of a `QNode`. Every `QNode` is initialized with `R` value for its status field and `null` for its `next` field on creation. *Typically*, a thread waiting to acquire the lock has a `W` status in its `QNode`; a lock holder passes the lock to its successor by `SWAP`ing an `U` into its successor's status field. Symmetrically, a waiting thread on observing its `QNode`'s status change from `W` to `U` infers the lock ownership; a thread updates its `QNode` status to `A` when it aborts on a timeout. A lock releaser that observes an `A` in its successor's status while passing the lock infers successor's abandonment and performs the additional work of releasing the lock to an unabandoned successor, if any.

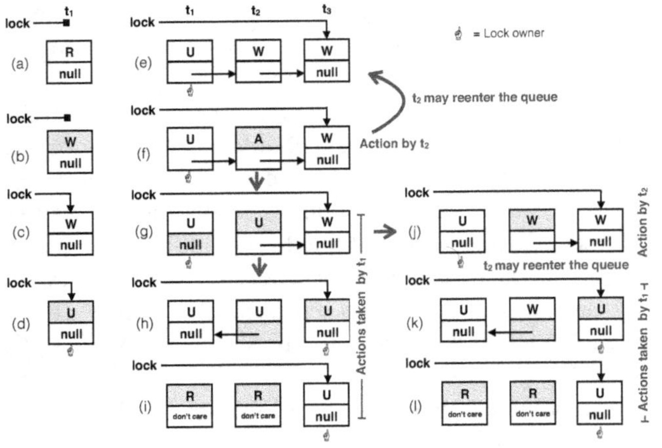

Figure 3: (a) The lock is free, and the thread t_1 arrives with a virgin QNode. (b) t_1 swaps its status to W. (c) t_1 swaps the tail pointer to itself. (d) Since t_1 has no predecessor, it updates its status flag to unlocked (U) and becomes the lock owner. (e) Threads t_2 and t_3 follow a similar protocol and get enqueued. (f) t_2 times out and CASes A in its status flag. (g) t_1 begins releasing the lock by swapping t_2's status and notices that t_2 has abandoned. (h) t_1 proceeds to t_2's successor and passes the lock to t_3. Also, t_1 updates the next pointers to point to their predecessors in steps (g) and (h). (i) t_1 updates the status of t_2 and t_1 to R indicating their readiness for next round of acquisition. After (f), t_2 may re-enter the queue and transition the system back to (e). Also, t_2 may re-enter after (g) by swapping its status to W in (j) but it cannot acquire the lock or reuse the QNode until t_1 has passed the lock to t_3 as shown in (k) and updated t_2's status to R as shown in (l).

QNode maintenance. In HMCS-T, the `next` and `status` fields of a QNode will be accessed by a predecessor even after the owner thread has aborted its acquisition. Hence, an owner thread may not deallocate its QNode until the node is marked for recycling. We use the C++ destructor to ease the QNode maintenance. For convenience, each participating thread allocates an object (QNodeObject) that encapsulates a QNode along with a reference to the parent lock. The object's destructor waits until the object is marked for recycling. The object's constructor initializes the `next` and `status` fields and sets the parent pointer. The acquire and release protocols use a reference to this per-thread object. A thread can reuse the same object across multiple episodes of lock requests without having to reinitialize; for high performance, the reuse is necessary. Listing 1 shows an example usage model, which is applicable to any n-level HMCS-T. The object can reside anywhere—stack, heap, or thread-local storage. Heap allocation allows returning from a callee stack frame without waiting (in the destructor) for the object to be recycled. When used in C, the user must explicitly call the constructor and destructor routines after allocation and before deallocation, respectively.

Acquisition. A thread t begins its lock entry protocol by SWAPing the value W to the status field of the thread's QNode q. The previous value of the status field distinctly indicates the state of the QNode, which governs the next action taken by t. Depending on whether the QNode is ready to use, abandoned previously, or in an intermediate state of being updated by a predecessor, the following three scenarios arise:

```
// Initialize the lock giving it the machine topology
HMCST<3> hmcstLock (machineTopology);
#pragma omp parallel
{
//Assume threads are pinned to cores.
//Create and initialize the per-thread QNode object.
 QNodeObject ctxt(hmcstLock);
 for ( ... ) { // ctxt is reused many times
   if (hmcstLock.Acquire(&ctxt, timeout)==SUCCESS) {
     CriticalSection();
     hmcstLock.Release(&ctxt, timeout);
   } else {
     NonCriticalSection();
   }
 } // end for-loop
} // The destructor ensures ctxt is ready to free.
```

Listing 1: An example 3-level HMCS-T lock in an OpenMP C++ code.

Recycled node (R): The QNode q is ready for use. In this case, t, by-and-large, follows the MCS lock's enqueue protocol: swaps the tail pointer to point to q and if t has no predecessor, it becomes the lock owner, overwriting the status flag to U (not done in the original MCS), otherwise, t spins either until the lock is granted (some predecessor changes `q.status` to U) or a timeout occurs. On timeout, t CASes the value A to `q.status` and abandons the protocol if CAS succeeds. CAS failure implies lock acquisition.

Previously abandoned node (A): It implies t is attempting to re-acquire a lock that it had previously abandoned. *In this case, the lock has not yet been passed beyond t by any of its predecessors.* Hence, t resumes its wait by directly jumping to the wait loop in the MCS acquisition protocol. Note that swapping the tail pointer and updating the predecessor's `next` field are elided. While waiting for the lock, if t times out once again, it CASes an A into its `q.status` and exits if CAS succeeds. CAS failure implies lock acquisition.

Node unlocked after abandonment (U): It implies t must have abandoned previously, and some predecessor p must have tried to grant the lock to t by SWAPing a U value. Since t had already abandoned the node, p is now in the process of passing the lock to a waiting successor in-line past t. Once, p has passed or relinquished the lock, it will change the status of t's QNode q to R. In this case, t waits for `q.status` to change to R. After `q.status` becomes R, t goes through the full enqueue process following the steps listed for a "recycled node". While waiting for the status to change to R, however, if t times out, it CASes an U to revert `q.status` and abandons the wait on CAS success. Failure to CAS implies q is recycled, and t may choose one of the following options: **(1) [optimistic]** follow the steps listed in the "recycled node" case and attempt to acquire the lock hoping to get it immediately without waiting or **(2) [pessimistic]** return as if the lock waiting timed out. We have implemented the optimistic strategy.

The status flag shall never be W when SWAPing at the entry.

Release. A lock releasing thread performs actions that allow abandoned QNodes in the queue to become reusable by their owner threads. When a thread, r, is releasing the lock by updating the status field of its successor s with a value U, the successor could be simultaneously updating its status field with an A in an effort to abandon. *HMCS-T's release protocol is modified to use a SWAP on successor's status fi unlike an unconditional store used in the original MCS lc* The releaser r may have one of the following cases based the previous value observed in the status field of the succ sor:

Waiting successor (W): It implies r successfully granted lock to s, which was still waiting.

Abandoned successor (A): It implies s abandoned the l before r performed its release. In this case, r "impers ates" as if s were releasing the lock to its successor an repeats one of these two steps, if s has a successor.

In case the releaser r finds no waiting successor in MCS queue, it CASes the tail pointer to `null`, similai the MCS lock. In the "abandoned successor" case abc once a releaser takes the role of its successor, it uncoı tionally overwrites its successor's `next` field to its pre cessor, which aids in the reverse traversal. Thus, the `next` pointer is reused as a predecessor pointer. It is legal to trash the next pointer and reuse for another purpose since no one will be using it beyond this point. Once r has successfully passed or relinquished the lock, it follows the chain of predecessor pointers (now stored in the `next` fields of abandoned `QNodes`), unconditionally setting the status in each abandoned `QNode` to R. This step essentially marks abandoned (and potentially re-entered) `QNodes` to be ready for reuse. Any attempt to reuse an U marked `QNodes` by their owning threads for an acquisition during this intermediate state will result in the acquire protocol to land into the "node unlocked after abandonment (U)" case.

The order of recycling the abandoned `QNodes` is LIFO. One can remember the first node and the last node and follow FIFO ordering; we chose LIFO with the intention of allowing newcomers a better opportunity since they will have more time left to reenqueue and likely succeed. The releaser r, does not eagerly flip the status of abandoned `QNodes` to R during its left-to-right forward journey because doing so allows abandoned threads to reenqueue and abandon repeatedly making r's time complexity unbounded. Marking the `QNodes` after the lock release bounds the release protocol's time complexity to linear in the number of participants.

Non-blocking release. The MCS lock has an unbounded wait in its release protocol. In MCS, if a lock releaser, r, notices no successor, it CASes the tail pointer to `null`. However, in the meantime, a new thread, s, might have swapped the tail pointer, and s may be in the process of enqueueing. On CAS failure, while the original MCS protocol waits indefinitely until the successor advertises itself by updating the `next` field of its predecessor, *HMCS-T deviates from this behavior and makes the release protocol non-blocking.* To accomplish the non-blocking release, HMCS-T obeys the following protocol (see Figure 4 for an example):

Release: On failure to CAS the tail pointer to `null`, the releaser r attempts to CAS a special value M (`iMpatient`)

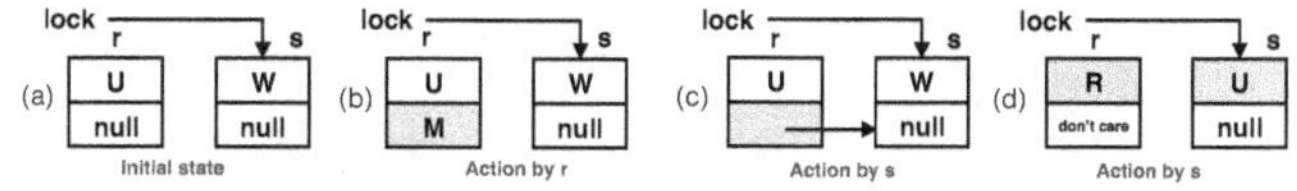

Figure 4: (a) Thread r owning the `QNode` q_r is releasing the lock when another thread s arrives, but s is slow in updating q_r's next pointer to itself. (b) r times out and CASs a special value M in q_r`.next` and leaves. (c) Later s SWAPs a pointer to itself into q_r`.next`. (d) Having observed the special value M, s updates q_r`.status` to R indicating that q_r can now be reused. Also, s updates its status to unlocked (U) and becomes the lock owner.

on to the next field of its `QNode` q_r. Note that q_r may not be owned by r; if successors of r had abandoned, r would be impersonating the last one in the chain of abandoners.

If the CAS succeeds, r's forward journey is over. However, r does not toggle q_r`.status` to R on its return journey through the predecessors because it is unsafe to recycle q_r until s has published itself by updating q_r`.next`. If the CAS fails, because s published itself by updating q_r`.next` in the meantime, then r follows the next pointer to s and SWAPs q_s`.status` to U. The procedure may recur if s aborts before r updates q_s`.status`.

Acquire: To perform a symmetric handshake with the release protocol, the acquire protocol of a successor s performs a SWAP on the next field of its predecessor. If s sees the special value M in its predecessor's `next` field (i.e., q_r`.next`), it infers that the predecessor abandoned having become impatient waiting for its successor. Consequently, s updates its predecessor `QNode`'s status to R indicating that the predecessor node (i.e., q_r) can now be recycled. Also, since s had no "legal" predecessor, it implies lock acquisition. s updates its status to U and enters the critical section.

4. Design of N-level HMCS-T

In principle, if a thread wants to abort in HMCS-T$\langle n \rangle$, it updates the status flag of the `QNode` it is waiting on to A and releases all of its lower-level locks. Symmetrically, if a lock releaser encounters an abandoned successor, it continues looking for a waiting thread until it has found one at the current level; otherwise, it continues to search at the parent level. The details are more involved. Figure 5 presents the key steps of the HMCS-T protocol; we provide the detailed description below.

Details. If a thread (say α) times out while waiting for a level-l lock, it updates the status of its `QNode` (the one it used for competing for the level-l lock) to A. A level-l predecessor of α will ensure passing the level-l (and above) locks to a level-l waiting successor past α, similar to HMCS-T$\langle 1 \rangle$.

If α times out while competing for a level $l > 1$ lock, it must have already acquired the locks at levels $[1, l-1]$. By now, there could be other threads waiting at these lower levels (possibly some already abandoned) relying on α to pass the global lock, which α failed to acquire. Hence, after abandoning at level l, α should release locks at levels $[1, l-1]$ (see Figure 5(a)). Naively, α could release all locks

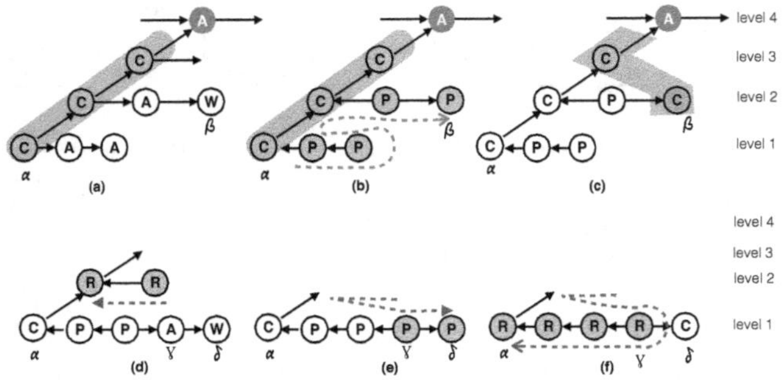

Figure 5: (a) The thread α abandons at level 4 having acquired the level 1-3 locks. Every QNode in the left frontier has the C status. There are several abandoned QNodes in the same domain as α under level 4. (b) α attempts to pass the level 1-3 locks to a successor at level 1 but finds none. α ascends to level 2 and passes the level 2 and 3 locks to the waiting successor β. α marks the status of all QNodes along the path to P, temporarily disallowing their reuse. (c) β updates its status from P to C. β recognizes (not shown) that it owns the level 3 lock by observing the QNode status of C on ascending to level 3. (d) concurrently, α traverses the predecessors in level 2 and marks them ready for reuse. By the time α descends to level 1, γ and δ enqueue at level 1 with γ already abandoned. (e) α passes the level-1 lock to the first waiting successor δ, (f) α traverses the predecessors in level 1 and marks them ready for reuse. Concurrently, δ updates its status to C and proceeds to compete at level 2.

from level $l-1$ to 1, in that order, to a first waiting successor, forcing all of its successors at each level to compete at their parent levels. This naive design, however, suffers from the following problems: 1) releasing all $l-1$ locks is extra work for α compared to simply passing a prefix of locks (suffix from α's viewpoint) to the lowest common descendent, 2) top-down traversal makes high-latency releases compulsory, and 3) every successor at each level has the additional work of competing at the next level.

Our solution is a disciplined, two-pass lock-passing arrangement that exploits locality and minimizes work. In a forward pass, starting from leaf to level $l-1$, α finds the lowest common waiting descendent β and passes all locks it has held starting from that level till level $l-1$ to β. For example, in Figure 5, α abandons at level 4 and passes the already acquired level 2 and 3 locks to β, which was waiting at level 2. β, now, skips acquisitions at levels that it inherited from α by noticing the special value (C) left by α in the status fields of the QNodes at levels that are already acquired. If α found β at a level $i < l-1$, α's forward journey stops at level i. In a reverse path from the level $i-1$ down to level 1, α releases the locks it had not passed during its upward journey. During the forward pass, α would have marked every abandoned successor along the way as temporarily not reusable; it marks them as reusable during its reverse pass.

Deviation in internals from HMCS. HMCS protocol uses its status field to encode the *passing count*—the number of times the lock has been circulated locally [5]. The passing count is incremented on each successive passing to a peer, and the global lock is passed to a successor s by signaling it with a symbolic value $\texttt{V} \in [2, \theta]$, where θ is the threshold of local passing. A releaser signals its successor s with a special value ACQUIRE_PARENT (P), either when the threshold (θ) of local passing is reached or when s arrives after the releaser already released the global lock at an enclosing level. A waiting thread s that is signaled with the special value (P), immediately resets its status to COHORT_BEGIN (C, numerically equal to 1), which indicates: (1) s's ownership of the local lock alone and hence the need to compete at the parent level, and (2) the start of a new round of local passing.

In HMCS-T, the meaning of P is generalized to signal a successor s that it now inherits a *prefix* of locks (instead of the local lock alone) starting at the current level on s's path to the root. Symmetrically, the status C is generalized to indicate that the thread owns a *prefix* of locks starting at the current level but *not all locks on the path to the root.* The value P can be used either when a thread aborted at an ancestor level (and hence passing a lock prefix) or when it reached the local passing threshold. In either case, the successor does not inherit the global lock; the successor turns its status to C and proceeds to compete at ancestral levels, similar to HMCS.

Acquisition. Acquisition begins with competing for a designated level-1 lock. The acquisition protocol of any level-l lock starts by SWAPing the value W to the status field of the QNode q; remember that the leaf-level QNodes are provided by the client threads and the interior QNodes at each level are pre-allocated within HNodes. The previous value of the status field of the QNode governs the subsequent actions taken by the acquire protocol for a thread t. HMCS-T's non-root-level lock has more status flags to handle. The following four cases arise based on the previous value of the status flag:

Recycled node (R): This implies q is reusable. HMCS-T enqueues q by SWAPing the tail pointer of the corresponding level-l lock. Subsequently, one of the following ensues:

1. *Uncontended acquisition (tail was null): t* updates the q.status to C (the beginning of a new cohort) and proceeds to compete for the parent level lock,
2. *Inheritance of all locks (status becomes a legal passing value, V):* acquisition ends successfully,
3. *Acquisition of a prefix of locks (status becomes P): t* updates q.status to C and proceeds to the next level,
4. *Timeout: t* CASes an A into q.status and returns failure if CAS succeeds. CAS failure means successful acquisition.

Previously abandoned node (A): This implies the QNode q was previously abandoned either by t itself or a thread belonging to the same domain. HMCS-T, in this case, skips enqueuing q and resumes the spin wait on q.status.

Inherited ancestral lock (C): This happens when the current level (l) lock was already acquired by a thread p belonging to t's domain at level l or below. Since q.status was C, p must have started a new round of local passing at level l, which implies p did not inherit all locks on its path to the root, and instead it must have proceeded to compete at higher levels (see "Recycled node" case 1, 3). Also, p must have abandoned at some level $j > l$ and subsequently, p found t as its lowest-common descendent at a level $k < l$

and passed a prefix of locks to it. Hence, t already owns the lock at level l. Since t swapped a W during its entry, it reverts `q.status` to C and proceeds to level $l+1$. Reverting is necessary to allow a subsequent thread to acquire this level lock if t also were to abort at a higher level.

Node unlocked after abandonment (V and P): V $\in [2, \theta]$ symbolizes that a predecessor already stepped upon an abandoned node. This case is analogous to the U case of HMCS-T$\langle 1 \rangle$: either t itself or some other thread belonging to the same domain as t at level l must have previously abandoned at level l; t's predecessor p (a level l peer) must have tried to pass the lock to t; p, having noticed that t had abandoned, is now in the process of passing the lock to a waiting successor past t. p will, eventually, revert `q.status` to R once it releases the lock. Hence, t waits for `q.status` to change to R and then re-enqueues q afresh into the MCS queue at level l obeying the protocol already listed under "recycled node". While waiting for `q.status` to become R, if t times out, it CASes the value P into `q.status` and aborts if CAS succeeds. CAS failure happens iff `q.status` becomes R allowing t to reenqueue q optimistically hoping to acquire the lock without waiting.

The status flag shall never be W when SWAPing at the entry. Also, if a thread ends up acquiring the lock at a level when it is about to abandon but does not inherit all locks, it continues to attempt for the next level lock, optimistically hoping to acquire the next level lock in an uncontended manner. If, however, it fails to acquire the next level lock, it begins the abandonment process at that level.

Abandonment. To abandon, while waiting for a lock at level l, the abandoner α obeys the following protocol:

1. α, first, SWAPs the value A into the status flag of its QNode used for competing at level l.
2. If at non-leaf level (that is $l > 1$), α attempts to pass its already acquired locks (levels $[1, l-1]$) to the lowest common waiting descendent thread. That is, to retain maximum locality, α starts looking for a waiting successor starting at the leaf level (`curLevel=1`). Lock passing is similar to HMCS-T$\langle 1 \rangle$, looking for the first unabandoned successor. α SWAPs the special value P into its successor s's status field, which signals s (if waiting) to acquire the necessary suffix locks on its path to the root starting at `curLevel+1`.
3. If α succeeds in passing the lock prefix to a waiting peer at `curLevel`, it goes to Step #4, otherwise (the `next` pointer of the right-most peer is `null`), α ascends to the next level (if any) and recursively performs Step #3 with `curLevel=curLevel+1`.
4. By now, α either passed its lock to a waiting successor or relinquished the lock by CASing the tail pointer to `null`. α traverses the QNodes at the `curLevel` from right to left flipping the flags of each QNode to R, indicating that those QNodes can now be recycled.
5. If `curLevel>1`, α descends to its children level (`curLevel=curLevel-1`). Having already passed its acquired locks at levels $>$ `curLevel`, α now needs to release the lock at `curLevel`. Let m be the QNode that had its `next` pointer `null` when α ascended to the next level in Step #3. It is possible for more threads to have enqueued past m when α was busy passing the upper-level locks. Starting at `m.next`, if any, α attempts to pass the `curLevel` lock to a waiting `curLevel` peer. Since passing the lock at `curLevel` in this phase does not correspond to passing all upper-level locks (which were already released by now), α SWAPs the special status flag P, indicating the successor to compete at the next level. If no peer is found, α relinquishes the `curLevel` lock by CASing the tail pointer to `null`. Having released the `curLevel` lock, α performs a right-to-left traversal of all QNodes whose flags it had SWAPed to P and flips them to R, indicating that they can now be recycled. Figure 5(d)-(f) captures this case. α now repeats Step #5.

At any point, if a lock releasing thread times out while waiting for a successor to update its next pointer, it uses the aforementioned non-blocking technique. Also, at each level, once a releasing thread steps past its abandoned successor node, it uses the next pointer to serve as a predecessor pointer for its return journey.

Release. Lock release is analogous to the steps followed in the abandonment process, except,

1. The ascendance continues till the tree root if no waiting successor is found, and
2. If the value V of the releaser r's representative QNode's status flag is less than the local passing threshold at level l, then r signals its successor with V+1, similar to HMCS. If the passing threshold has reached, then the r releases the parent lock followed by signaling the successor with P to indicate that the successor should compete at the next level.

5. Discussion

Fast-path optimization. To avoid the overhead of multiple levels of lock acquisitions under no contention, we have adapted the *fast-path* strategy described in [6] into HMCS-T. We omit the details of the adaptation for brevity.

Atomic operations. Our use of SWAP and CAS operations may look heavy handed, but they are applied on nearer neighbors, which do not generate remote coherence traffic. Recent studies [7] show that the atomic operations introduce no more than $1.15\times$ overhead compared to loads and stores. Not all atomic operations are on the critical path. Uncontended acquisition in HMCS-T$\langle 1 \rangle$ is same as the uncontended acquisition in MCS with an additional SWAP on the status field. Uncontended release in HMCS-T$\langle 1 \rangle$ is same as the uncontended release in MCS. Uncontended acquisitions in deeper HMCS-T locks cost no more than HMCS-T$\langle 1 \rangle$ due to the fast path optimization.

Memory overhead and lock abuse. HMCS-T, like other hierarchical locks, trades memory for speed. A prior work [19] on abortable locks traded speed for memory. Our evaluation shows that the node recycling is so time consuming on NUMA machines that the locks described in [19] offer little competition to HMCS-T. Preallocated `QNodes` achieve a lower memory footprint compared to [19] under high abort rates. However, one must use precaution when using a deep HMCS-T. HMCS-T must be curated for a given architecture. HMCS-T is not a universal replacement for all locks in a program. One should opt into HMCS-T when contention is expected. A contended HMCS-T's memory consumption is no worse than that of a contended MCS lock since in the worst case HMCS-T would require 2× more space; much less in practice. Modern many-core processors with 10s of MBs of cache can accommodate thousands of HMCS-T locks in less than 1% of their last-level cache.

Design options. On finding an abandoned successor, instead of traversing subsequent successors, one may choose to ascend to ancestral levels to increase the chance of finding a successor and reduce the critical path length. However, the cost of remote access is often much higher than several local accesses. The naive design of releasing ancestral locks instead of releasing the peers first causes up to 3.2× performance loss compared to our optimized strategy. It is straightforward to enforce a bound on how many peers to inspect before ascending to the parent level based on an analytical machine model similar to the one discussed in [5].

Hierarchical locks are best served when threads are pinned to cores. Thread migration makes HMCS-T start its new acquisition in its new domain iff the leaf-level `QNode` is already recycled.

IsLocked() Interface. One can expose an `IsLocked()` API over HMCS, which returns the boolean `LOCKED` or `NOT_LOCKED` based on whether or not any thread already holds the lock. A "try lock" can be built using such interface. If `IsLocked()` returns `NOT_LOCKED`, the user still has to decide whether to acquire the lock with a timeout (HMCS-T) or wait until the lock is granted (HMCS). In summary, the timeout capability is indispensable.

Correctness. HMCS-T is a very involved protocol; the system is stateful. HMCS-T guarantees mutual exclusion, livelock and deadlock freedom under any situation, and starvation freedom for non-aborting threads. We follow a multi-step approach to prove these guarantees. We provide a detailed proof in a separate document: `http://github.com/HMCST/hmcst`, which relies on the Spin [12] model checker.

Complexity of HMCS-T. Let us assume the system has n lock levels and each lock at a level i is contested by k_i descendants. Hence, the total number of participants (maximum threads) in the system is $N = \prod_{i=1}^{n} k_i$.

Space complexity: The space complexity depends on the pre-allocated `HNodes` in the tree. A deeper tree has a larger space complexity. For a given number of participants, the tree depth depends on the machine topology. A loose bound assumes a binary tree. Hence, for a system with N participating threads, there can be at most N pre-allocated `HNodes` and the protocol does not allocate any more `HNodes`. Hence, the space complexity per lock is $O(N)$.

Time complexity: Discussion about time complexity is useful only in light of timeout. Once a timeout occurs, we would like to know how many steps are needed to either abandon or release the lock. Due to its optimistic design, a thread that times out waiting for a leaf-level lock may acquire all locks in n steps followed by releasing all n locks. Releasing n locks, in the worst case, can take k_i steps in each of ith level from 1 to n in a bottom-to-top sweep and k_i more steps in a top-to-bottom sweep. Hence, the worst case acquire followed by a release after timeout is bounded by $n + \sum_{i=1}^{n} 2k_i$ steps. The worst case abandonment happens when a thread that times out waiting for a leaf-level lock acquires $n-1$ locks but fails to acquire the root-level lock and subsequently releases all $n-1$ locks. Hence, the worst case abandonment is bounded by $n - 1 + \sum_{i=1}^{n-1} 2k_i$ steps.

The asymptotic cost on the critical path when all threads, except the lock holder, have aborted is $\sum_{i=1}^{n} k_i$. The bound can be tightened to $(n-1) + k_n$ via the previously proposed alternative of ascending to the parent level on finding an aborted successor.

6. Evaluation of HMCS-T

In this section, we evaluate HMCS-T by comparing it with various locks. We use an 8-blade, 16-socket HP Integrity Superdome X [10] shared-memory machine. Each socket is an 18-core, 2-way SMT Intel Xeon E7-8890V3 processor clocked at 2.5GHz. Blades are interconnected with a custom ASIC. The system has a total of 576 hardware threads. L1, L2, and L3 cache sizes are respectively 32KB, 256KB, and 45MB. A pair of sockets on the same blade are connected over QPI [13]. The system has two on-chip, 2-channel DDR4 memory for a total of 12TB. We used `g++ v4.8.3` compiler and parallelized code via `OpenMP`. Unless stated otherwise, all experiments use a compact binding of threads to cores; a thread will not be bound to another NUMA domain until the current domain is fully populated; the next chosen NUMA domain will be the nearest possible one.

Locks: We use the HMCS-T locks of 1, 2, 3, and 4 levels of hierarchy in our studies. A shallower lock, HMCS-T$\langle 1\rangle$ does not respect locality. An HMCS-T$\langle 2\rangle$ exploits the locality within a node shared by two sockets but ignores the locality within a socket. An HMCS-T$\langle 3\rangle$ exploits the locality within a socket shared by 18 cores, in addition to the behavior of HMCS-T$\langle 2\rangle$ but ignores the locality of SMTs sharing a core. An HMCS-T$\langle 4\rangle$ exploits the locality within a core shared by two SMTs, in addition to the behavior of HMCS-T$\langle 3\rangle$. An HMCS$\langle n\rangle$ has a symmetric configuration as an HMCS-T$\langle n\rangle$ but lacks the timeout capability.

We also compare with a Test-And-Test-And-Set lock with timeout (TATAS-T), CLH_NB and MCS_NB locks [19, 21], and A_C_BO_CLH lock [8]. Our A_C_BO_CLH lock mimics the implementation described in [8]; we form a 2-level hierarchy where cores sharing the same socket form a cohort. For the locks with a cohort property (HMCS, HMCS-T, and A_C_BO_CLH), we set the passing threshold to 64 [8].

§6.1 compares HMCS-T with HMCS using a micro benchmark. §6.2 compares HMCS-T with other abortable locks via a splay tree case study. §6.4 demonstrates the virtue of HMCS-T by exploiting parallel slackness in an MPI+OpenMP Graph500 code and improves its communication-computation overlap.

6.1 HMCS vs. HMCS-T

An HMCS$\langle n \rangle$ serves as an upper (lower) bound for the throughput (latency) of HMCS-T$\langle n \rangle$ when the timeout is infinite. To assess the overhead that HMCS-T adds atop HMCS, we compare them via a micro benchmark: a tight loop of lock acquire and conditional release. We precisely measure the CPU cycles for acquire and release via the x86 `rdtsc` instruction. The benchmark while synthetic is appropriate for the intended comparison.

Figure 6 and 7, respectively, show the throughput and round trip latency (successful acquisition plus release) when the timeout is set to 1K, 10K, and infinite CPU cycles. It is evident from Figure 6 that every HMCS-T instantiation closely follows the throughput of its corresponding HMCS counterpart. The gap narrows as the timeout increases. Figure 7 shows that the latency for successfully acquiring a lock is strictly bounded by the chosen timeout. If lock acquisition is not possible within a given timeout, thread aborts in HMCS-T, and thus the latency of successful acquisitions reaches a plateau, unlike HMCS. At infinite timeout, HMCS-T$\langle n \rangle$'s latency is very close to that of its HMCS$\langle n \rangle$ counterpart. In-general, the throughput of HMCS$\langle 4 \rangle$ > HMCS-T$\langle 4 \rangle$ > HMCS$\langle 3 \rangle$ > HMCS-T$\langle 3 \rangle$ > HMCS$\langle 2 \rangle$ > HMCS-T$\langle 2 \rangle$ > HMCS$\langle 1 \rangle$ > HMCS-T$\langle 1 \rangle$. Not all latency appears on the critical path. The wait time during an acquire is not on the critical path. Once global lock is handed over to a legal successor, rest of the release protocol is not on the critical path. Hence, the throughput is unaffected after 10K CPU cycles timeout.

Table 1 shows the throughput degradation in HMCS-T$\langle n \rangle$ over the corresponding HMCS$\langle n \rangle$ at timeout=∞. The data shows the pure protocol overhead that an HMCS-T incurs to support the abort feature. Under no contention (1 thread), the overhead is fairly low (about 1.25×) in any HMCS-T lock; the degradation does not increase noticeably with the increase in the depth of the lock, which is due to the aforementioned fast path. The worst case degradation is 3.85× observed for HMCS-T$\langle 4 \rangle$ at four threads. This is because of the often missed opportunity to pass to an SMT peer and the presence of subsequent lock levels leads to a lengthy path of relinquishing parent locks preventing local passing benefits. HMCS-T$\langle 4 \rangle$ is an overkill at such low thread count setting.

Table 1: Throughput degradation in HMCS-T$\langle n \rangle$ wrt HMCS$\langle n \rangle$ at timeout=∞.

Threads:	1	2	4	8	18	36	72	144	288	576	GeoMean
HMCS-T<1>	1.22x	1.32x	1.12x	0.97x	0.99x	0.97x	1.04x	0.85x	1.11x	1.09x	**1.06x**
HMCS-T<2>	1.27x	1.79x	1.1x	0.99x	0.97x	0.97x	1.21x	1.19x	1.19x	1.19x	**1.17x**
HMCS-T<3>	1.26x	1.92x	1.21x	1.02x	1.00x	0.95x	0.98x	1.00x	1.00x	1.00x	**1.11x**
HMCS-T<4>	1.27x	2.47x	3.85x	1.68x	1.73x	1.75x	1.74x	1.75x	1.76x	1.79x	**1.89x**

All other locks incur no more than 1.92× overhead. The average overhead is under 1.11×, except for HMCS-T$\langle 4 \rangle$.

To further understand the overheads involved, Figure 8 and Figure 9 decompose the round-trip latency into the latency for successful acquisition and release. We make the following observations:

1. Comparing Figures 8 and 9, acquisition accounts for the bulk of the latency (up to 10^6 cycles) and outweighs the latency for release (under 10^3 cycles) by orders of magnitude between the same pairs of HMCS and HMCS-T locks .
2. Figure 9 shows that the difference in release latency between an HMCS and the corresponding HMCS-T can be high. While HMCS stabilizes at about 25 cycles, HMCS-T$\langle 3 \rangle$ and HMCS-T$\langle 4 \rangle$ stabilize at about 200 cycles (8× higher). The worst case happens for HMCS-T$\langle 1 \rangle$ at 576 threads, which is up to 28× more than HMCS$\langle 1 \rangle$. Most importantly, the latency does *not* grow either with the increase in the number of threads or by changing the timeout. We note that the release latency of 200 cycles for HMCS-T$\langle 3 \rangle$ and HMCS-T$\langle 4 \rangle$ despite their longer critical paths is faster than MCS_NB and CLH_NB, which respectively take about 2300 and 1100 CPU cycles (not shown).
3. Figure 9 shows that the release latency of a shallower HMCS-T is higher than the release latency of a deeper HMCS-T despite the additional cost of releasing parent-levels in a deeper HMCS-T. This is because of two reasons: (1) it is faster to release the lock in a deeper HMCS-T due to the locality of successors, and (2) ascending to ancestral levels in the tree during lock release exponentially increases the chances of finding a waiting successor and avoids inspecting aborted threads in a peer domain.

With zero timeout (not shown), the time to abandon the protocol from the start of acquisition is under 140 cycles for HMCS-T$\langle 1 \rangle$, HMCS-T$\langle 2 \rangle$, and HMCS-T$\langle 3 \rangle$ and 1K cycles for HMCS-T$\langle 4 \rangle$. Beyond 1K cycles timeout, all HMCS-T locks accurately honor the client-chosen timeout. Overall, the HMCS-T locks maintain their competence even after adding the abort feature and offer high timing fidelity.

6.2 HMCS-T vs. Other Abort Locks on Splay Trees

Splay trees [23] are self-adjusting binary search trees with a caching behavior—the last searched item is brought to the tree root and recently searched items appear near the root. Any operation on a splay tree, including a lookup, may involve tree rotations; hence locks are necessary.

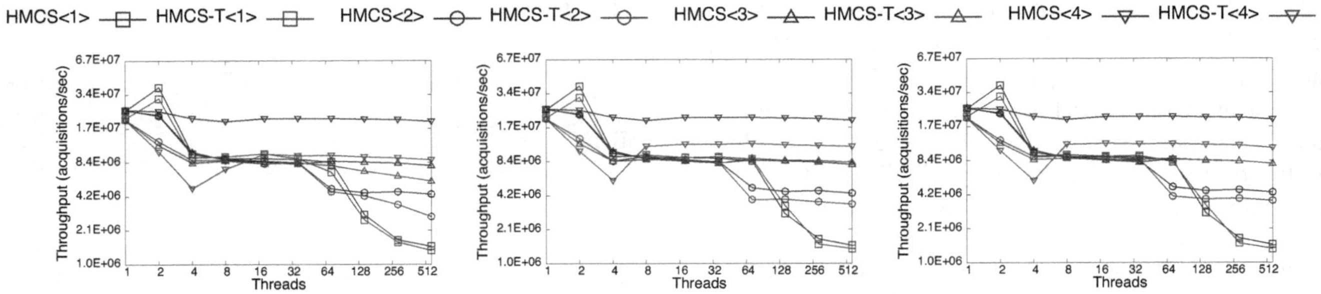

(a) Timeout:1K CPU cycles. (b) Timeout:10K CPU cycles. (c) Timeout:∞ CPU cycles.

Figure 6: Lock throughput of HMCS-T vs. HMCS. Each HMCS-T closely follows its HMCS counterpart.

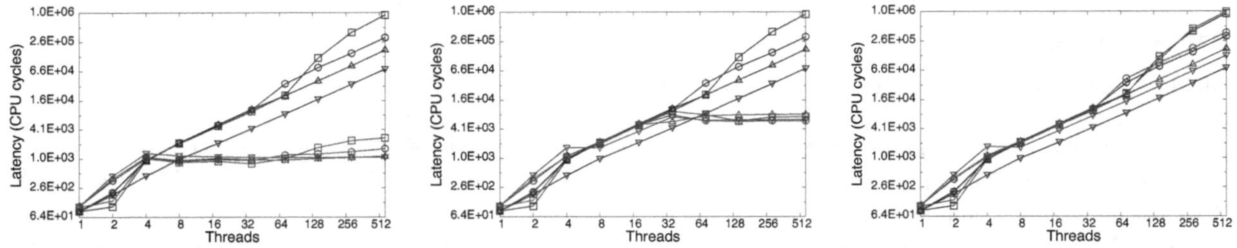

(a) Timeout:1K CPU cycles. (b) Timeout:10K CPU cycles. (c) Timeout:∞ CPU cycles.

Figure 7: Round trip latency of HMCS-T vs. HMCS. Each HMCS-T closely follows its HMCS counterpart at ∞ timeout and offers bounded latency at other timeout values.

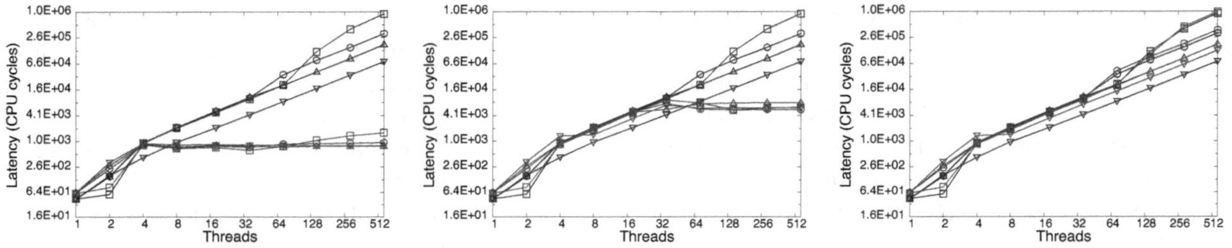

(a) Timeout:1K CPU cycles. (b) Timeout:10K CPU cycles. (c) Timeout:∞ CPU cycles.

Figure 8: Acquisition only latency of HMCS-T vs. HMCS. Acquisition latency governs the total latency.

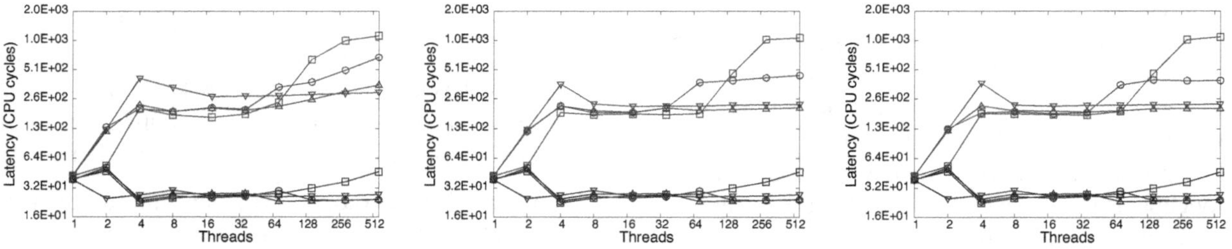

(a) Timeout:1K CPU cycles. (b) Timeout:10K CPU cycles. (c) Timeout:∞ CPU cycles.

Figure 9: Release only latency of HMCS-T vs. HMCS. The lock release in HMCS-T is slower than HMCS but its contribution to the overall latency is insignificant.

We create a setup where all threads attempt to perform a lookup operation on a *global* splay tree when holding a lock (*critical work*). On lock timeout, a thread performs some "other" work (*non-critical work*). The non-critical work is a *thread-local* splay tree and hence it does not require any locking. Using splay tree lookups both inside and outside the critical section allows us to compare both critical and non-critical work accomplished by various locks in a uniform way. Also, instead of idle spinning outside the critical section, switching to a different work chunk pollutes the cache, which represents real world situations.

Our global and thread-local splay trees each have 8K nodes. For both kinds of trees, 90% of the lookups are served by the same key, and the remaining 10% are for the 64 numerically adjacent keys (not necessarily nearby in the tree organization). Note, however, that not all the 90% of the global tree lookups hit at the root since a previous lookup, either by the same thread or by another thread, could have rotated the tree. Furthermore, we change the "hot node" every second to a randomly chosen node from the tree.

A superior lock should deliver high lock throughput and abort swiftly on a timeout; that is, *it shoud show high throughput on both global and local tree operations.* Figure 10(a) compares the throughput of various abortable locks at 10K CPU-cycle timeout. Throughput is measured as total tree lookup operations performed per second, which includes both local and global tree operations. Figure 10(b) and Figure 10(c) respectively decompose the throughput into global (critical) and local (non-critical) work components. We have clipped the lines when the throughput fell below 10K acquisitions per second for the global tree.

We notice that a deeper HMCS-T lock offers higher throughput than a shallower HMCS-T on the global tree. The global-tree throughput drops with increasing concurrency (Figure 10(b)) because the working set increases linearly with the number of threads, which causes the threads compete for the shared cache. For locks that can abort swiftly on timeout (HMCS-T, TATAS, and A_C_BO_CLH) the throughput of the local tree operations increases linearly as the number of threads increase beyond 18. All locks except MCS_NB and CLH_NB show comparable throughput on their local-tree operations.

CLH_NB and MCS_NB [19] locks have dramatically lower throughput compared to HMCS-T locks both on the global tree and local trees. This is because their memory management overhead is excessive. Frequent aborts severely affect node recycling. In the CLH_NB lock, for example, when a thread aborts, it leaves its `QNode` in the CLH queue to be freed by its successor. However, if the successor also aborts, the `QNode` is not freed, and the task is delegated to some other successor. When aborts are common, many `QNodes` are left unreclaimed in the CLH queue. Each thread maintains a list of `QNodes` it allocated (`local_list`). Every new acquisition sweeps its `local_list` looking for a recycled node. When successors keep aborting, none of the previously allocated `QNode` become available for reuse, and hence almost every new acquisition allocates a new `QNode` (via malloc) and appends it to its `local_list` The `local_lists` keep growing increasing both memory footprint and time spent unsuccessfully searching for a free node on each acquisition. Since the `local_list` searching time keeps growing, the timeout happens immediately after allocation, leaving no time to recycle an aborted predecessor. Frequent abort and lengthy allocation time feed back into each other further aggravating the problem.

The average time to sweep the list and allocate a new `QNode` took ~900K CPU cycles in CLH_NB at 10K and 100K cycle timeout thresholds. The code spent more than 90% of the time trying to recycle `QNodes` in the `alloc_local_qnode` procedure incurring more than 97% of its L2 cache misses in the same procedure. As a result, CLH_NB and MCS_NB locks are unsuccessful in acquiring the lock within 10K CPU cycles. The allocation time reduced to 700 cycles only after the timeout was above 10^6 CPU cycles. Since the lock overhead consumes most of the execution time, it results in reduced throughput of non-critical work also. In contrast, HMCS-T's preallocated `QNodes` and their reuse keep the protocol overhead small.

The memory usage and its overhead wrt TATAS-T at 10K timeout with 576 threads is shown in the left half of Table 2. CLH_NB and MCS_NB locks have very high memory usage due to repeated allocations when the nodes cannot be recycled. The numbers remain the same at 100K timeout (not shown). We measured that TATAS-T has a huge skew in the lock distribution—on 70% occasions, the lock holder is the same as the previous one causing thread starvation [19, 20]. A_C_BO_CLH also suffers from starvation.

To quantify the readmission into a previously abandoned `QNode`, we profiled how often a thread resumes from its abandoned node. HMCS-T$\langle 1\rangle$, HMCS-T$\langle 2\rangle$, HMCS-T$\langle 3\rangle$, and HMCS-T$\langle 4\rangle$ resumed their wait from a previously abandoned node on 99%, 97%, 92%, and 47% occasions, respectively at 10K timeout. A shallower lock is slow and has a longer queue, which provides more chance of readmitting an abandoned thread. The readmission fraction progressively reduces with increased depth. HMCS-T$\langle 4\rangle$ offers the least opportunity since the leaf-level queue length is at most two in our setting.

Figure 11(a) and 11(b) respectively show the throughput of both global and local tree operations at different abort thresholds ranging from 10^1 to 10^8 CPU cycles for a 576-threaded experiment. HMCS$\langle 4\rangle$ has the highest global-tree throughput followed by the other shallower hierarchical locks. Throughput over the global tree can drop by about 2$\times$ between 10^1 to 10^6 cycles timeout. MCS_NB and CLH_NB become competitive for the global-tree operations only beyond 10^6 CPU cycles, which is a very high threshold. The local-tree throughput drops as the timeout value increases because few acquisitions timeout and hence few local-tree operations are performed.

6.3 Lock Efficiency

To gain a unified view of the total work accomplished by a lock among a set of locks under study, we compute the following relative metrics for each lock k. $\boldsymbol{\mathcal{G}(k)}$: the ratio of lock k's global-tree throughput (critical work) to the maximum global-tree throughput by any lock under study with the same settings, and $\boldsymbol{\mathcal{L}(k)}$: the ratio of lock k's local-tree throughput (non-critical work) to the maximum local-tree throughput by any lock under study with the same settings. The sum of these two metrics can reach a theoretical maximum of 200%. We normalize it to 100%, which represents the efficiency $\boldsymbol{\mathcal{E}(k)}$ of a lock k. $\mathcal{E}$ quantifies the ability of

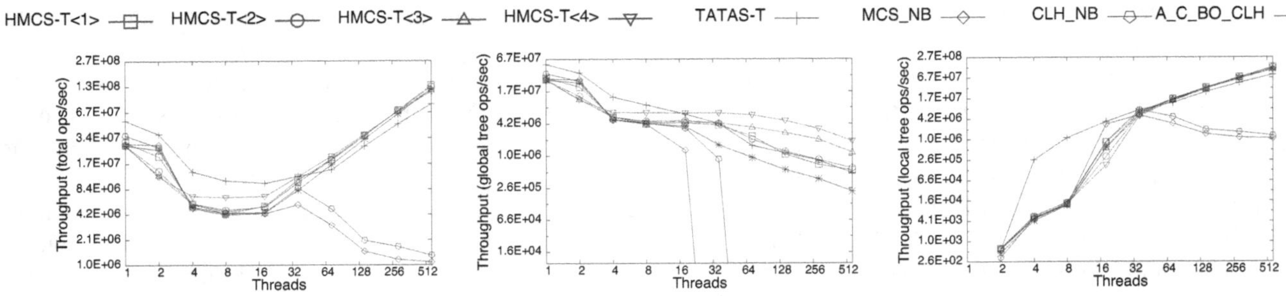

(a) Total splay operations. (b) Global splay operations. (c) Local splay operations.

Figure 10: Lock throughput of different abortable locks. Timeout=10K CPU cycles.

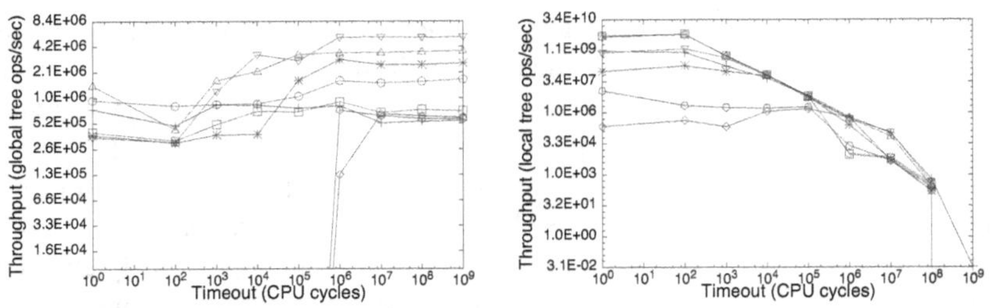

(a) Throughput of global tree operations. (b) Throughput of local tree operations.

Figure 11: Impact of timeout on the throughput of local and global tree operations. The experiment has 576 threads.

Table 2: Left: resident memory and memory overhead w.r.t. a TATAS-T lock. Right: efficiency ($\mathcal{E}$) of locks— a unified metric of critical and non-critical work accomplished. In both experiments, the timeout is set to 10K CPU cycles, and both experiments use 576 threads.

	Resident memory		% peak throughput		Efficiency
	KB	Overhead	Global (G)	Local (L)	E = (G+L)/2
HMCS-T<1>	271,060	1x	29%	100%	64%
HMCS-T<2>	271,160	1x	31%	96%	64%
HMCS-T<3>	271,192	1x	62%	88%	75%
HMCS-T<4>	271,188	1x	100%	84%	92%
TATAS-T	271,020	1x	25%	60%	43%
MCS_NB	3,746,764	14x	1.62E-06%	0.83%	0.41%
CLH_NB	1,783,500	6.6x	1.62E-06%	1%	0.50%
A_C_BO_CLH	271,170	1x	11%	90%	51%

a lock to deliver high throughput of successful lock acquisitions and also to expeditiously exit on timeout.

We computed $\mathcal{G}$, $\mathcal{L}$, and $\mathcal{E}$ metrics at 576 threads among eight locks at 10K cycle timeout (right side of Table 2). HMCS-T$\langle 4\rangle$ has the highest critical path throughput ($\mathcal{G}$ is 100%). Deep hierarchy helps in higher lock throughput, and the throughput falls off for shallower locks. CLH_NB and MCS_NB achieve only a small fraction of the peak throughput. TATAS-T and A_C_BO_CLH, respectively, achieve 25% and 11% of HMCS-T$\langle 4\rangle$'s global tree throughput.

HMCS-T$\langle 1\rangle$ has the highest throughput on the non-critical work ($\mathcal{L}$ is 100%). This is because HMCS-T$\langle 1\rangle$ is the quickest to abandon on timeout and switch to perform local tree operations. Abandoning in HMCS-T$\langle 1\rangle$ is a simple local swap operation at one level, whereas abandoning in an interior node of a deeper HMCS-T may involve more operations. $\mathcal{L}$ decreases for a deeper HMCS-T lock; HMCS$\langle 4\rangle$ achieves 84% of HMCS$\langle 1\rangle$'s non-critical work. Surprisingly, TATAS-T has lower $\mathcal{L}$ despite the fact that an abort takes no memory operation. This is because the CAS operation in TATAS-T has a very high latency. If a thread issues a CAS closer to its timeout, the CAS may complete thousands of cycles after the timeout, which leads to a high protocol overhead.

In the combined metric ($\mathcal{E}$), the deeper hierarchical locks—HMCS-T$\langle 3\rangle$ and HMCS$\langle 4\rangle$—deliver higher efficiency due to their exceeding superiority in critical work over shallower locks. TATAS-T and A_C_BO_CLH have respectable efficiency, but both are unfair locks. CLH_NB and MCS_NB have the lowest efficiency.

6.4 HMCS-T in an MPI+Threads BFS

Parallel breadth-first search (BFS) is an irregular, dynamic, sparse data exchange (DSDE) algorithm. A process communicates with a small subset of processes (neighbors) while the neighborhoods change dynamically over iterations. One of the best-known algorithms for solving DSDE problems is $\mathcal{NBX}$ [11]. In $\mathcal{NBX}$, most of the data exchanges rely on nonblocking point-to-point primitives and a process has to poll manually for communication progress via APIs such as `MPI_Iprobe` or `MPI_Test` in the context of MPI. We use Amer et al. [2]'s multi-threaded $\mathcal{NBX}$ implementation of the Graph500 BFS kernel, where threads in a process perform both computation and communication.

We use the MPICH-3.2 [1] MPI implementation, which has a single lock to protect its core functionality [3, 4]. In a highly threaded BFS run, the MPICH global lock becomes a point of contention because of repeated calls to `MPI_Test` by different threads. Since `MPI_Test` is only a progress checking API, it can be aborted in favor of computation or non-polling APIs, such as `MPI_Isend`. With this intuition, we substituted the MPICH-3.2 Pthread mutex lock with various abortable locks allowing the `MPI_Test` implementation to abort; *rest of the APIs do not abort.* On abort, `MPI_Test` behaves as if the communication has not yet completed. While the progress semantics of MPI require a continuously checking thread to succeed if a matching operation has been posted, such progress guarantee is conceivable in HMCS-T by bounding the number of successive aborts by a thread.

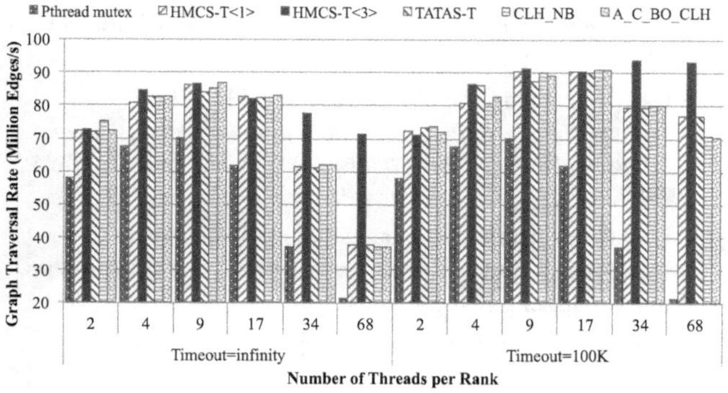

Figure 12: Scalability of BFS with 2^{25} vertices using 4 MPI processes and varying number of threads per MPI process. Pthread mutex, used by the original MPICH, does not support timeout but is only shown for a comparison. HMCS-T$\langle 3 \rangle$ has the best absolute performance and superior scaling at 10K timeout.

We partition the 8-node shared-memory machine into four MPI processes each with 72 cores; we do not use SMTs. Further, we do not load all sockets fully to leave some cores to run MPI daemons and scripts. We measured the BFS graph traversal rate from 16 different root vertices and report the average rate per root vertex in Figure 12 for various locks (including the baseline Pthread mutex) at two timeout values: 100K CPU cycles and infinity (for comparison with the traditional lock waiting regime). Our analysis showed that the overall performance is strongly correlated to the time spent in `MPI_Test` and that changing the lock implementation has little effect on the other parts of the algorithm, e.g., the computation or the amount of data transferred. The degree of computation-communication overlap dictates the performance variation across lock implementations.

At an infinite timeout, the performance peaks at nine threads for all locks. Beyond 17 threads, the performance collapses since more threads cause more wait in `MPI_Test`, hence more polling and less real communication. The only lock that proved to be more robust is HMCS-T$\langle 3 \rangle$, which exploits locality, however, it still suffers 17% performance loss at full concurrency compared to its peak.

With a timeout of 100K, every abortable lock performs superior to its timeout=∞ counterpart (the base Pthread mutex shown only for reference). At 100K timeout, the locks reach their peaks at 17 cores but this time the peaks are higher than those at timeout=∞. This indicates that bounding the lock wait time improves the ability to overlap communication with computation. All locks except HMCS-T$\langle 3 \rangle$ collapse in their performance beyond 17 cores since: 1) the cost of aborts is expensive in other locks due to inter-socket and inter-node communication, and 2) when the lock is passed to a remote requester, the locality is lost. HMCS-T$\langle 3 \rangle$ by virtue of its fast abort and locality-aware lock hand-off scales to a higher throughput (93.2 M edges/s) at 34 and 68 threads and alleviates the performance collapse seen in the other locks. In particular, HMCS-T$\langle 3 \rangle$ with a 100K timeout achieves 30% higher peak performance than its unbounded counterpart. Furthermore, HMCS-T$\langle 3 \rangle$ with 100K timeout retains the same 30% speedup even when compared against HMCS$\langle 3 \rangle$ (not shown) although HMCS$\langle 3 \rangle$ is expected to have slightly less protocol overhead compared to HMCS-T$\langle 3 \rangle$ with infinite timeout.

The top performance of HMCS-T$\langle 3 \rangle$ (at 34-68 threads) is 34% higher than the top performance of the original Pthread mutex (at 9 threads). At full concurrency, HMCS-T$\langle 3 \rangle$ delivers 88% and 21% higher throughput than the next best performing abortable lock (HMCS-T$\langle 1 \rangle$) with an infinite and 100K timeout values, respectively. This justifies the virtue of both locality awareness and abortability. HMCS-T$\langle 3 \rangle$ at a 100K timeout (with 93.2×10^6 edges/s) shows an impressive 330% (4.3$\times$) speedup over the original Pthread mutex-based MPICH (with 21.5×10^6 edges/s) at full concurrency. We also experimented with a `CAS`-based try-lock (not shown) and observed a very poor scalability and a very low peak performance since it is locality agnostic and generates indiscriminate cache coherency traffic.

We experimented the previously mentioned `IsLocked()` primitive with both HMCS-T$\langle 3 \rangle$ (at several timeout values) and HMCS$\langle 3 \rangle$. We invoked the underlying lock iff the `IsLocked()` returned `NOT_LOCKED`. We observed that the graph traversal rate initially increased up to 140 million edges/sec, but once the number of threads crossed a socket, the throughput collapsed dramatically down to below 90 million edges/sec because of the lost data locality. `IsLocked()`+HMCS-T$\langle 3 \rangle$ showed slightly worse performance than merely using HMCS-T$\langle 3 \rangle$ for the same timeout values. `IsLocked()`+HMCS$\langle 3 \rangle$ performed worse than HMCS-T$\langle 3 \rangle$ with $\leq$ 10K cycles timeout regardless of the thread count.

These results clearly indicate that bounding lock waiting times through an abort feature can help scale an otherwise non-scalable code by exploiting parallel slackness.

7. Conclusions

In this paper, we designed the HMCS-T lock, a hierarchical queuing lock that can abandon the lock wait on a timeout. Hierarchical queue-based locks combined with the timeout feature offer two key advantages on many-core NUMA systems—data locality and enhanced concurrency. HMCS-T has bounded space and time complexity together with starvation freedom, which are rare in other abortable locks. HMCS-T has high timing fidelity and outperforms several state-of-the-art abortable locks in latency and throughput.

8. Acknowledgments

John Mellor-Crummy and Karthik Murthy shared their model checking experience, which inspired us to develop our solution. Ram Swaminathan made valuable editorial suggestions. This research was supported by the National Science Foundation under grant number 1464157 and by the U.S. Department of Energy, Office of Science, under contract DE-AC02-06CH11357.

References

[1] A. Amer, P. Balaji, W. Bland, W. Gropp, R. Latham, H. Lu, L. Oden, A. Pena, K. Raffenetti, S. Seo, T. Rajeev, and Z. Junchao. MPICH User's Guide, Version 3.2. `http://www.mpich.org/static/downloads/3.2/mpich-3.2-userguide.pdf`, 2015.

[2] A. Amer, H. Lu, P. Balaji, and S. Matsuoka. Characterizing MPI and Hybrid MPI+Threads Applications at Scale: Case Study with BFS. In *Cluster, Cloud and Grid Computing (CCGrid), 2015 15th IEEE/ACM International Symposium on*, pages 1075–1083. IEEE, 2015.

[3] A. Amer, H. Lu, Y. Wei, P. Balaji, and S. Matsuoka. MPI+Threads: Runtime Contention and Remedies. In *Proceedings of the 20th ACM SIGPLAN Symposium on Principles and Practice of Parallel Programming*, PPoPP 2015, pages 239–248, New York, NY, USA, 2015. ACM.

[4] A. Amer, H. Lu, Y. Wei, H. Jeff, S. Matsuoka, and P. Balaji. Locking Aspects in Multithreaded MPI Implementations. Technical Report ANL/MCS-P6005-0516, 2016.

[5] M. Chabbi, M. Fagan, and J. Mellor-Crummey. High Performance Locks for Multi-level NUMA Systems. In *Proceedings of the 20th ACM SIGPLAN Symposium on Principles and Practice of Parallel Programming*, pages 215–226, 2015.

[6] M. Chabbi and J. Mellor-Crummey. Contention-conscious, Locality-preserving Locks. In *Proceedings of the 21st ACM SIGPLAN Symposium on Principles and Practice of Parallel Programming*, PPoPP '16, pages 22:1–22:14, New York, NY, USA, 2016. ACM.

[7] T. David, R. Guerraoui, and V. Trigonakis. Everything You Always Wanted to Know About Synchronization but Were Afraid to Ask. In *Proceedings of the Twenty-Fourth ACM Symposium on Operating Systems Principles*, SOSP '13, pages 33–48, New York, NY, USA, 2013. ACM.

[8] D. Dice, V. J. Marathe, and N. Shavit. Lock Cohorting: A General Technique for Designing NUMA Locks. In *Proceedings of the 17th ACM SIGPLAN Symposium on Principles and Practice of Parallel Programming*, pages 247–256, 2012.

[9] M. Frigo, C. E. Leiserson, and K. H. Randall. The Implementation of the Cilk-5 Multithreaded Language. In *Proceedings of the ACM SIGPLAN 1998 Conference on Programming Language Design and Implementation*, PLDI '98, pages 212–223, New York, NY, USA, 1998. ACM.

[10] Hewlett Packard Enterprise. HP Integrity Superdome X. `http://www8.hp.com/h20195/v2/GetPDF.aspx/c04383189.pdf`.

[11] T. Hoefler, C. Siebert, and A. Lumsdaine. Scalable Communication Protocols for Dynamic Sparse Data Exchange. In *Proceedings of the 15th ACM SIGPLAN Symposium on Principles and Practice of Parallel Programming*, PPoPP '10, pages 159–168, New York, NY, USA, 2010. ACM.

[12] G. J. Holzmann. The Model Checker SPIN. *IEEE Transactions on Software Engineering — Special issue on formal methods in software practice*, 23(5):279–295, May 1997.

[13] Intel Corp. An Introduction to the Intel® QuickPath Interconnect. `http://www.intel.com/content/www/us/en/io/quickpath-technology/quick-path-interconnect-introduction-paper.html`, 2009.

[14] P. Jayanti. Adaptive and Efficient Abortable Mutual Exclusion. In *Proceedings of the Twenty-second Annual Symposium on Principles of Distributed Computing*, PODC '03, pages 295–304, New York, NY, USA, 2003. ACM.

[15] P. S. Magnusson, A. Landin, and E. Hagersten. Queue Locks on Cache Coherent Multiprocessors. In *Proceedings of the 8th International Symposium on Parallel Processing*, pages 165–171, 1994.

[16] V. Marathe, M. Moir, and N. Shavit. Composite Abortable Locks. In *Parallel and Distributed Processing Symposium, 2006. IPDPS 2006. 20th International*, pages 1–10, April 2006.

[17] J. M. Mellor-Crummey and M. L. Scott. Algorithms for Scalable Synchronization on Shared-memory Multiprocessors. *ACM Transactions on Computer Systems*, 9(1):21–65, February 1991.

[18] A. Pareek and P. Woelfel. RMR-efficient Randomized Abortable Mutual Exclusion. In *Proceedings of the 26th International Conference on Distributed Computing*, DISC'12, pages 267–281, Berlin, Heidelberg, 2012. Springer-Verlag.

[19] M. L. Scott. Non-blocking Timeout in Scalable Queue-based Spin Locks. In *Proceedings of the Twenty-first Annual Symposium on Principles of Distributed Computing*, PODC '02, pages 31–40, New York, NY, USA, 2002. ACM.

[20] M. L. Scott and W. N. Scherer. Scalable Queue-based Spin Locks with Timeout. In *Proceedings of the Eighth ACM SIGPLAN Symposium on Principles and Practices of Parallel Programming*, PPoPP '01, pages 44–52, New York, NY, USA, 2001. ACM.

[21] Scott, Michael. Non-Blocking Timeout in Scalable Queue-Based Spin Locks. `https://www.cs.rochester.edu/research/synchronization/pseudocode/nb_timeout.html`.

[22] SGI. SGI UV The World's Most Powerful In-Memory Supercomputers. `https://www.sgi.com/products/servers/uv/`.

[23] D. D. Sleator and R. E. Tarjan. Self-adjusting Binary Search Trees. *Journal of the ACM*, 32(3):652–686, July 1985.

[24] L. G. Valiant. A Bridging Model for Parallel Computation. *Communications of the ACM*, 33(8):103–111, Aug. 1990.

Contention in Structured Concurrency: Provably Efficient Dynamic Non-Zero Indicators for Nested Parallelism

Umut A. Acar[*†] Naama Ben-David[*] Mike Rainey[†]
[*]Carnegie Mellon University, USA [†]Inria, France
umut@cs.cmu.edu, nbendavi@cs.cmu.edu, mike.rainey@inria.fr

Abstract

Over the past two decades, many concurrent data structures have been designed and implemented. Nearly all such work analyzes concurrent data structures empirically, omitting asymptotic bounds on their efficiency, partly because of the complexity of the analysis needed, and partly because of the difficulty of obtaining relevant asymptotic bounds: when the analysis takes into account important practical factors, such as contention, it is difficult or even impossible to prove desirable bounds.

In this paper, we show that considering structured concurrency or relaxed concurrency models can enable establishing strong bounds, also for contention. To this end, we first present a dynamic relaxed counter data structure that indicates the non-zero status of the counter. Our data structure extends a recently proposed data structure, called SNZI, allowing our structure to grow dynamically in response to the increasing degree of concurrency in the system.

Using the dynamic SNZI data structure, we then present a concurrent data structure for series-parallel directed acyclic graphs (sp-dags), a key data structure widely used in the implementation of modern parallel programming languages. The key component of sp-dags is an *in-counter* data structure that is an instance of our dynamic SNZI. We analyze the efficiency of our concurrent sp-dags and in-counter data structures under nested-parallel computing paradigm. This paradigm offers a structured model for concurrency. Under this model, we prove that our data structures require amortized $O(1)$ shared memory steps, including contention. We present an implementation and an experimental evaluation that suggests that the sp-dags data structure is practical and can perform well in practice.

PPoPP '17 Feb. 04–08, 2017, Austin, Texas, USA.

ISBN 978-1-4503-4493-7/17/02. . . $15.00

DOI: http://dx.doi.org/10.1145/3018743.3018762

1. Introduction

Non-blocking data structures are commonly used in practical concurrent systems because such data structures allow multiple processes to access the structure concurrently while guaranteeing that the whole system will make progress. As discussed by the survey of Moir and Shavit [38], many non-blocking data structures have been designed and implemented for various problems, such as shared counters [22; 42], non-zero indicator counters [14], stacks [45], queues [37], doubly ended queues [7], and binary search trees [9; 13].

The theoretical efficiency of non-blocking data structures, however, has received relatively little attention. One reason for this lack of attention is that in a non-blocking data structure, some processes may get stuck, leading to seemingly infinite execution times. Another reason is that the common shared-memory models, under which concurrent data structures are analyzed, usually do not account for an important practical concern: the effects of memory contention. These effects can be significant especially as the degree of concurrency increases [12; 38; 43].

We are interested in the design and analysis of provably efficient non-blocking data structures in realistic models of concurrency that account for the cost of contention. This goal represents a major challenge, because contention often factors into the running time as a linear additive factor (e.g., [13; 18; 16; 39]). A series of papers have also established linear-time lower bounds [27; 30; 16] when contention is taken into account by using models that allow only one process to access a memory object [11; 12; 5]. For example, Fich, Hendler, and Shavit [16] show that, when accounting for contention, a number of concurrent data structures, including counters, stacks, and queues, require $\Omega(n)$ time, where n is the number of processes/threads in the system, a.k.a., the *degree* of concurrency.

In this paper, we show that a relaxation of the general concurrency model can unlock the design and analysis of provably efficient concurrent data structures, accounting also for contention. As a relaxation, we consider a structured concurrent programming paradigm, nested parallelism, where concurrency is created under the control of programming primitives, such as fork-join and async-finish. Nested parallelism is broadly available in a number of modern programming languages and language extensions, such as OpenMP, Cilk [19], Fork/Join Java [34], Habanero Java [28], TPL [35], TBB [29], X10 [10], parallel ML [17], and parallel Haskell [32]. In these systems, nested-parallel programs can be expressed by using a primitives such as **fork–join** (a.k.a., **spawn–sync**), and **async–finish**. When executed, a nested parallel program can create many threads, leading to a high degree of concurrency, but in a structured fashion: threads may be created by other threads via a **async** (or **fork**) operation and can also terminate and synchronize at known **join** (or **finish**) points. The **fork–join** primitives allow only two threads to synchronize at a **join**. In contrast, with **async–finish** primitives, any number of threads can terminate and synchronize at a single **finish** point. This structured nature of thread creation, termination, and synchronization is the key difference between nested parallelism and general concurrency.

Our starting point is prior work on relaxed concurrent counters, also called *indicators*, that indicate whether a counter is positive or not. Indicators contrast with exact counters as, for example, those considered by Herlihy, Shavit, and Waarts [27]. In prior work, Ellen et al. [14] present the *SNZI* (read "snazzy"), short for Scalable Non-Zero Indicator, data structure, prove it to be linearizable, and evaluate it empirically. They do not, however, provide any analytical upper bounds. Indeed, SNZI data structure could experience contention as multiple operations climb up the SNZI tree. In this paper, we present an extension to the SNZI data structure to allow it to grow dynamically at run time, perhaps in response to increasing degree of concurrency and thus increasing potential for contention (Section 2).

We then consider an application of our dynamic SNZI data structure to nested parallel computations, specifically for representing series-parallel directed acyclic graphs or *sp-dags* with unbounded in-degree vertices, which arise for example with parallel loops and **async–finish** primitives. Variants of dag data structures are used broadly in the implementation of modern parallel programming systems [19; 34; 28; 35; 29; 10; 17; 32]. These languages and systems typically represent the computation as a dag where each vertex corresponds to a fine-grained thread and schedule the vertices of the dag over the processors to minimize completion time. For efficiency reasons, it is important for the dag data structure to be non-blocking and low-contention, because a nested parallel program can create a dynamically varying set of fine-grained threads, consisting of anywhere from several threads to millions or more, depending on the input size.

The crux of the sp-dags problem is determining when a vertex in the dag becomes *ready*, i.e., all of its dependencies have been executed. Such readiness detection requires a concurrent dependency counter, which we call *in-counter*, that counts the number of incoming dependencies for each thread. When a dependency between a thread u and v is created, the in-counter of v is incremented; when u terminates its in-counter is decremented; when its in-counter reaches zero,vertex v becomes ready and can be executed. We show that in-counters can be implemented efficiently by using our dynamic SNZI data structure (Section 3). We prove that by managing carefully the growth of our dynamic SNZI data structure, we can guarantee that all operations require amortized $O(1)$ time, including also contention (Section 4).

Finally, we present an implementation and perform an experimental evaluation in comparison to prior work (Section 5). Our results offer empirical evidence for the practicality of our proposed techniques, showing that our approach can perform well in practice.

Placed in the context of previously proven lower bounds for non-blocking data structures, the key to our result is the structured concurrency model that we consider. Our contributions are as follows.

- Dynamic SNZI: an extension to the original SNZI data structure that allows it to grow varying numbers of threads.
- Non-blocking low-contention sp-dags: a non-blocking data structure for series-parallel dags that can be used to represent nested-parallel computations provably efficiently and with low contention.
- Analysis: proofs that our series-parallel dag data structure experiences low contention under a nested parallel programming model.
- Evaluation: implementation and empirical evaluation that shows that our data structure is practical and that it can perform well in practice.

Due to space restrictions, we present some proof details and more experiments in the full version of the paper, which is available as a technical report [1].

1.1 Model

We consider a standard model of asynchronous shared memory where threads can communicate through taking atomic read-modify-write steps such as read, write and compare-and-swap (CAS). Threads can use these primitives to implement high-level *operations*. We define the *contention* experienced by an operation as the maximum number of non-trivial, shared memory steps that concurrently access the same memory location over all executions. A *non-trivial step* is one that might change the value of the memory location to which it is applied, and a *non-trivial operation* is an operation that takes at least one non-trivial step.

Our definition of contention is similar to *stalls* as defined by Fich et al. in [16]. Their definition, inspired by Dwork et al.'s work on contention models [12], considers a model in which each non-trivial memory step on a memory location must operate in isolation, and the rest of the operations stall.

For our bounds, we consider computations that are structured in a nested-parallel fashion, where threads execute independently in parallel or serially and synchronize at their termination points. A series-parallel computation starts with a single root thread and constructs, as it executes, a series-parallel directed acyclic graph (sp-dag) of vertices where each vertex represents a thread of control, and edges represent dependencies between threads.

2. Dynamic SNZI

Concurrent counters are an important data structure used in many algorithms but can be challenging to implement efficiently when accounting for contention, as shown by the linear (in the degree of concurrency) lower bound of Fich et al [16]. Observing that the full strength of a counter is unnecessary in many applications, Ellen et al proposed *non-zero indicators* as relaxed counters that allow querying not the exact value of the counter but its sign or *non-zero status* [14]. Their non-zero indicator data structure, called SNZI, achieves low-contention by using a tree of *SNZI nodes*, each of which can be used to increment or decrement the counter. Determining the non-zero status of the counter only requires accessing the root of the tree. The tree is updated by increment and decrement operations. These operations are filtered on the way up to the root so that few updates reach the root.

The SNZI data structure is flexible. Each SNZI node interacts with its parent and its children, and will retain its correctness regardless of how many children it has. Thus, a SNZI tree can have any shape but it can be difficult to know the optimal shape of the tree a priori. In this section, we present a simple extension to SNZI that allows the tree to be grown dynamically, and show that our extension preserves correctness. In Section 3, we demonstrate how to use dynamic SNZI in a specific application—namely, to keep track of dependencies in an sp-dag efficiently.

Figure 1 illustrates the interface for the SNZI data structure and pseudo-code for the SNZI node **struct** `snzi_node`, the basic building block of the data structure from [14]. A SNZI node contains a counter c, a version number v, an array of children (two in our example), and a parent. The value at the counter indicates the *surplus* of arrivals with respect to the departures. The `arrive` and `depart` operations increment and decrement the value of the counter at the specified SNZI node a respectively, and `query`, which must be called at the root of the tree, indicates whether the number of `arrive` operations in the whole tree is greater than number of `depart` operations since creation of the tree.

To ensure efficiency and low contention, the SNZI implementation carefully controls the propagation of an arrival or departure at a node up the tree. The basic idea is to propagate a change to a node's parent only if the surplus at that node flips from zero to positive or vice versa. More specifically, an `arrive` at node a is called on a's parent if and only if a had surplus 0 at the beginning of the operation. Similarly, a `depart` at a node a is recursively called on a's parent if and only if a's surplus became 0 due to this `depart`. We say that node *a has surplus due to its child* if there was an `arrive` operation on a that started in a's child's subtree.

```
type snzi_node =
struct {
  (* counter *)
  c : ℕ ∪ {1/2}; initially 0
  (* version number *)
  v : ℕ; initially 0
  children : array of 2 snzi nodes; initially [null, null]
  parent : snzi_node
}

void fun snzi_arrive (snzi_node a) = ...
void fun snzi_depart (snzi_node a) = ...
bool fun snzi_query (snzi_node a) = ...
```

Figure 1: Partial pseudocode for the SNZI data structure; full description can be found in original SNZI paper [14].

The correctness and linearizability of the SNZI data structure as proven relies on two important invariants [14]: (1) a node has surplus due to its child if and only if its child has surplus, and (2) surplus due to a child is never negative. Together, these properties guarantee that the root has surplus if and only if there have been more `arrive` than `depart` operations on the tree.

The SNZI data structure does not specify the shape of the tree that should be used, instead allowing the application to determine its structure. For example, if the counter is being used by p threads concurrently, then we may use a perfectly balanced tree with p nodes, each of which is assigned to a thread to perform its `arrive` and `depart` operations. This approach, however, only supports a *static* SNZI tree, i.e., unchanging over time. While a static SNZI tree may be sufficient for some computations, where a small numbers of coarse-grained threads are created, it is not sufficient for nested parallel computations, where the number of fine-grained threads vary dynamically over a wide range from just a few to very large numbers, such as millions or even billions, depending on the input size. The problem is that, with a fixed-sized tree, it is impossible to ensure low contention when the number of threads increase because many threads would have to share the same SNZI node. Conversely, it is impossible to ensure efficiency when the number of threads is small, because there may be many more nodes than necessary.

To support re-sizing the tree dynamically, we extend the SNZI data structure with a simple operation called `grow`, whose code is shown in Figure 2. The operation takes a SNZI node as argument, determines whether to extend the node (if the node has no children), and returns the (possibly newly created) children of the node. If the node already

```
(snzi_node, snzi_node)
fun grow (a: snzi_node, p: probability) =
  heads ← flip(p) (* flip a p−biased coin. *)
  if heads then
    left ← new snzi_node(0)
    right ← new snzi_node(0)
    CAS(a.children, null, [left, right])
  children ← a.children
  if children = null then
    return (a, a)
  return children
```

Figure 2: Pseudo-code for the probabilistic SNZI `grow`.

has children, pointers to them are returned, but they are left unchanged. If the node does not have children, then they are locally allocated, and then the process tries to atomically link them to the tree. They are initialized with surplus 0 so that their addition to the tree does not affect the surplus of their parent. The `grow` operation also takes a probability p, which dictates how likely it is to create new children for the node. The operation only attempts to create new children if the node does not already have children and it flipped heads in a coin toss with probability p for heads. The idea is that this probabilistic growing allows an application to control the rate at which a SNZI tree grows without changing the protocol for some of the threads using it. Such probabilistic growing is useful when one wants a balance between low contention and frequent memory allocation. The right probability threshold to use, however, may depend not only on the application, but also on the system.

If node a does not have any children at the end of a `grow` operation, we have the operation return two pointers to a itself. This return value is convenient for the in-counter application that we present in the rest of the paper. Other applications using dynamic SNZI may return anything else in that case.

The `grow` operation may be called at any time on any SNZI node. To keep the flexible structure of the SNZI data structure, we do not specify when to use the `grow` operation on the tree, instead leaving it to the application to specify how to do so. For example, in Section 3.3, we show how to use the `grow` operation to implement a low-contention dependency counter for dags. It is easy to see that the operation does not break the linearizability of the SNZI structure; it is completely independent from the *count*, *version number*, and *parent* fields of nodes already in the tree, which are the only fields that affect the correctness and linearizability.

We note a key property of the `grow` operation. We would like to ensure that, given a probability p, when `grow` is called on a childless node, only $1/p$ such calls will return no children in expectation, regardless of the timing of the calls. That is, even if all calls to `grow` are concurrent, we want only $1/p$ of them to return no children. This property is ensured by having the coin flip happen *before* reading the value of the *children* array to be returned. This guarantees that any adversary that does not know the result of local coin flips cannot cause more than $1/p$ calls to return no children in expectation.

Dynamically shrinking the SNZI tree is more difficult, because we need to be sure that no operation could access a deallocated node. In general, one may easily and safely delete a SNZI node from the tree if the following two conditions hold: (1) its surplus is 0, and (2) no thread other than the one deleting the node can reach it. The second condition is much trickier to ensure. In Section 4 we show how to deallocate nodes in our dependency counter data structure.

3. Series-Parallel Dags

A nested-parallel program can be represented as a series-parallel dag, or an sp-dag, of threads, where vertices are pieces of computation, and edges represent dependencies between them. In fact, to execute such a program, modern programming languages construct an sp-dag and schedule it on parallel hardware. We present a provably low-contention sp-dag data structure that can be used to execute nested-parallel programs. After defining sp-dags, we present in Section 3.1 a data structure for sp-dags by assuming an *in-counter* data structure that enables keeping track of the dependencies of a dag vertex (thread). We then present our data structure for in-counters in Section 3.3.

A *serial-parallel dag*, or an *sp-dag* for short, is a directed-acyclic graph (dag) that has a unique *source* vertex, which has indegree 0, and a unique *terminal* vertex, which has out-degree 0 and that can be defined iteratively. In the base case, an sp-dag consists of a source vertex u, a terminal vertex v, and the edge (u, v). In the iterative case, an sp-dag $G = (V, E)$ with source s and terminal t is defined by serial or parallel composition of two disjoint sp-dags G_1 and G_2, where $G_1 = (V_1, E_1)$ with source s_1 and terminal t_1 and $G_2 = (V_2, E_2)$ with source s_2 and terminal t_2, and $V_1 \cap V_2 = \emptyset$:

- **serial composition:** $s = s_1$, $t = t_2$, $V = V_1 \cup V_2$, $E = E_1 \cup E_2 \cup (t_1, s_2)$.
- **parallel composition:** $s, t \notin (V_1 \cup V_2)$, $V = V_1 \cup V_2 \cup \{s, t\}$, and $E = E_1 \cup E_2 \cup \{(s, s_1), (s, s_2), (t_1, t), (t_2, t)\}$.

For any vertex v in an sp-dag, there is a path from s to t that passes through v. We thus define the *finish vertex* of v as the vertex u which is the closest proper descendant of v such that every path from v to the terminal t passes through u.

3.1 The sp-dag data structure

Figure 3 shows our data structure for sp-dags. We represent an sp-dag as a graph G consisting of a set of vertices V and a set of edges E. The data structure assigns to each vertex of the dag an in-counter data structure, which counts the number of (unsatisfied) dependencies of the vertex. As the code for a dag vertex executes, it may dynamically insert and delete dependencies by using several *handles*. These handles can be thought of, in the abstract, as in-counters, but they are implemented as pointers to specific parts of an in-counter data structure.

More precisely, a `vertex` consists of

- a query handle (`query`), an increment handle (`inc`), and a decrement handle (`dec`),
- a flag `first_dec` indicating whether the first or the second decrement handle should be used,
- a flag `dead` indicating whether vertex has been executed,
- the finish vertex `fin` of the vertex, and
- a `body`, which is a piece of code that will be run when the scheduler executes the vertex.

The sp-dag uses an in-counter data structure `Incounter`, whose implementation is described in the Section 3.3. The in-counter data structure supplies the following operations:

- `make`: takes an integer n, creates an in-counter with n as the initial count and returns a handle to the in-counter;
- `increment`: takes a vertex v, increments its in-counter, and returns two decrement and two increment handles;
- `decrement`: takes a vertex v and decrements its in-counter;
- `is_zero`: takes a vertex v and returns true iff that in-counter of v is zero.

Inspired by recent work on formulating a calculus for expressing a broad range of parallel computations [3], our dag data structure provides several operations to construct and schedule dags dynamically at run time. The operation `new_vertex` creates a vertex. It takes as arguments a finish vertex u, an increment handle i, a decrement handle d, and a number n indicating the number of dependencies it starts with. It allocates a fresh vertex, sets its `dead` and `first_dec` flags to `false`, and sets the `body` for the vertex to be a dummy placeholder. It then creates an in-counter and a handle to it. The operation returns the new vertex along with the handle to its in-counter. The handle becomes the query handle. The operation `make` creates an sp-dag consisting of a root u and its finish vertex z and returns the root u. As can be seen in the function `make`, the increment and decrement handles of a vertex v always belong to the in-counter of v's finish vertex.

A vertex u and its finish vertex z can be thought as a computation in which u executes the code specified by its `body` and then returns to z. This constraint implies that z serially depends on u because z can only be executed after u. As it executes, a vertex u can use the functions `chain` and **spawn** to "nest" another sequential or parallel computation (respectively) within the current computation.

The `chain` operation, which corresponds to serial composition of sp-dags, nests a sequential computation within the current computation. When a vertex u calls `chain`, the call creates two vertices v and w such that w serially depends on v.

```
module Incounter = ... (* As defined in Figure 5 *)
module Dag =
G = (V, E)
type handle = Incounter.handle
struct {
  handle query, inc, dec[2];
  boolean first_dec, dead;
  vertex fin;
  (void → void) body;
} vertex;

(vertex, handle)
fun new_vertex (vertex u, handle i, handle d, int n) =
  V ← V ∪ {v}, v ∉ V
  (v.firstDec, v.dead) ← (false, false)
  v.body ← { return }
  v.query ← Incounter.make (n)
  (v.fin, v.inc, v.dec)  ←  (u, i, d)
  return (v, v.query)

(vertex,vertex)
fun make ()
  V ← {v}
  E ← ∅
  (v.firstDec, v.dead) ← (false, false)
  v.body ← { return }
  v.query ← Incounter.make (1)
  u ← new_vertex (u, v.query, v.query, 0)
  return (u, v)

(vertex, vertex)
fun chain (vertex u) =
  (w, h) ← new_vertex (u.fin, u.inc, u.dec, 1)
  (v, h) ← new_vertex (w, h, [h, h], 0)
  E ← E ∪ {(u, v)}
  u.dead ← true
  return (v, w)

(vertex, vertex)
fun spawn (vertex u) =
  (d, i, j) ← Incounter.increment (u.fin)
  (v, _) ← new_vertex (u.fin,  i, d, 0)
  (w, _) ← new_vertex (u.fin, j, d, 0)
  E ← E ∪ {(u, v), (u, w)}
  u.dead ← true
  return (v, w)

void
fun signal (u: vertex) =
  Incounter.decrement (u.fin)
  E ← E ∪ {(u,u.fin)}
```

Figure 3: The pseudo-code for our sp-dag data structure.

Furthermore, v serially depends on u, and z serially depends on w. After calling `chain`, u terminates and thus dies. The initial in-counters of v and w are set to 0 and 1 respectively (to indicate that v is ready for execution, but w is waiting on one other vertex). The edge (u, v) is inserted to the dag to indicate a satisfied dependency between u and v.

The **spawn** operation, which corresponds to parallel composition of sp-dags, nests a parallel computation with the current computation. When a vertex u calls **spawn**, the call creates two vertices, v and w, which depend serially on u, but are themselves parallel. The operation increments the in-counter of u's finish node, to indicate a serial dependency between u's finish vertex and the new vertices v and w. Even though two new vertices are created, the in-counter is incremented once, because one of the vertices can be thought of as a continuation of u. The `increment` operation returns two new increment handles i and j and a decrement-handle pair d. The **spawn** operation then creates the two vertices v and w using the two increment handles, one for each, and the decrement-handle pair d as a shared argument. Assigning each of v and w their own separate increment handles enables controlling contention at the in-counter of u's finish node. As described in Section 3.3, sharing of the decrement handles by the new vertices (v, w) is critical to the efficiency. As with the `chain` operation, **spawn** must be the last operation performed by u. It therefore completes by creating the edges from u to v and w, and marking u dead.

The operation `signal` indicates the completion of its argument vertex u by decrementing the in-counter for its finish vertex v, and inserting the edge (u, v).

In terms of efficiency, apart from calls to `Incounter`, the operations of sp-dags involve several simple, constant time, operations. The asymptotic complexity of the sp-dags is thus determined by the complexity of the in-counter data structure.

3.2 An Example

Although simple, the sp-dag data structure can be used to create any nested-parallel computation. As an example, we consider the classic parallel Fibonacci program, which computes n^{th} Fibonacci number by recursively and in parallel computing the $(n-1)^{th}$ and $(n-2)^{nd}$ numbers. Figure 4 illustrates the code for this example based on the sp-dag data structure and a `Scheduler` module that implements a standard parallel scheduler, such as work stealing [8; 2]. The function `fib_main` initializes the system by calling the function `Scheduler.initialize` and then creates the root and the final vertex of the dag. It then sets the body of the root to run `fib`, passing the arguments n and *result*. The vertices *root* and *final* are then given to the scheduler to be executed. The scheduler returns when the computation is finished, which leads to the return of the result.

The function `fib` implements the parallel Fibonacci function. The function start by creating a chain (u, v), passing `this_vertex`, which is the variable indicating the currently executing vertex, as the parent to the root of the chain. The body of u is set to spawn the two recursive calls and the

```
fib (n: int, dest: int ref) =
  if n <= 1 then
    dest ← n
  else
    res1 = alloc ()
    res2 = alloc ()
    (u, v) ← Dag.chain (this_vertex)
    u.body ← lambda (). {
                (w1, w2) = Dag.spawn (this_vertex)
                w1.body ← lambda ().fib (n − 1, res1)
                w2.body ← lambda ().fib (n − 2, res2)
                Scheduler.add (w1, w2)
              }
    v.body ← lambda (). *dest ← *res1 + *res2
    Scheduler.add (u, v)

fib_main (n: int) =
    int result;
    Scheduler.initialize ()
    (root, final) ← Dag.make ()
    root.body ← lambda ().fib (d, &result)
    Scheduler.add (root, final)
    return result
```

Figure 4: Fibonnacci example. The parallel recursive function at the top and the main function, where execution starts, at the bottom.

body of v is set to compute the final result by summing the return values of the recursive calls. Note that when spawning vertices the body of u uses `this_vertex` as a parent for the vertices created. Since the body is executed when u is executed, at the point of execution `this_vertex` is equal to u.

3.3 Incounters

We present the in-counter: a time and space efficient low-contention data structure for keeping track of pending dependencies in sp-dags. When a new dependency for vertex v is created in the dag, its in-counter is incremented. When a dependency vertex in the dag terminates, v's in-counter is decremented.

Our goal is to ensure that the increment and decrement operations are quick; that is, that they access few memory locations and encounter little contention. These goals could seem contradictory at first—if operations access few memory locations then they would conflict often. Our in-counter data structure circumvents this issue by ensuring that each operation accesses few memory locations that are mostly *disjoint* from those of others.

The in-counter is fundamentally a dynamic SNZI tree. To ensure disjointness of memory accesses, the data structure assigns different *handles* to different dag vertices. These handles are pointers to SNZI nodes within the in-counter, dictating where in the tree an operation should begin. Thus,

```
1  module Incounter =
2  type handle = snzi_node (* A handle is a snzi node *)
3
4  (* Growth probability: architecture specific constant. *)
5  p  ← ...
6
7  (* Make a new counter with surplus n. *)
8  handle
9  fun make (n) = snzi_make (n)
10
11 (* Auxiliary function: select decrement handle. *)
12 handle
13 fun claim_dec (vertex u) =
14   if CAS (u.firstDec, false, true) then u.dec[0]
15   else u.dec[1]
16
17 (* Increment u's target dependency counter. *)
18 (handle[2], handle, handle)
19 fun increment (vertex u) =
20   (a, b) ← grow (u.inc, p)
21   (i1,i2) ← (a, b)
22   if u is a left child then  d2 ← a
23   else  d2 ← b
24   snzi_arrive (d2)
25   d1 ← claim_dec (u)
26   return [[d1,d2],i1,i2]
27
28 (* Decrement u's counter. *)
29 void
30 fun decrement (vertex u) =
31    d ← claim_dec (u)
32    snzi_depart (d)
33
34 (* Check that u's counter is zero. *)
35 boolean
36 fun is_zero (u) = return snzi_isZero(u.query)
```

Figure 5: The pseudo-code for the in-counter data structure.

if two threads have different handles, their operations will access different memory locations.

The in-counter data structure ensures the invariant that only the leaves have a surplus of zero. This allow us to exploit an important property of SNZI: operations complete when they visit a node with positive surplus, effectively stopping propagation of the change up the tree. Specifically, an increment that starts at a leaf completes quickly when it visits the parent. To maintain this invariant, we have to be careful about which SNZI nodes are decremented.

Figure 5 shows the pseudo-code for the in-counter data structure. The in-counter's interface is similar to the original SNZI data structure: the operation `make` creates an instance of the data structure and returns a handle to it. The operation `increment` is meant to be used when a dag vertex spawns. It takes in a dag vertex, and uses its increment handle to increment the SNZI node's surplus. Before doing so, it calls the `grow` operation. Intuitively, this growth request notifies the tree of possible contention in the future and gives it a chance to grow to accommodate a higher load. The `increment` operation returns handles to other nodes in the SNZI tree, that is, two decrement handles and two increment handles, indicating where the newly spawned children of the dag vertex should perform their increment or decrement. The operation `decrement` is meant to be used when a dag vertex signals the end of its computation. It takes in dag vertex, and uses its decrement handle to decrement the surplus of a previously incremented node.

Since the `increment` operation is the only thing that can cause growth in the SNZI tree, the structure of the tree is determined by the operations performed on the in-counter structure. The tree is therefore not necessarily balanced. However, as we establish in Section 4, the operations' running time does not depend on the depth of the tree. In fact, we show that the operations complete in constant amortized time and also lead to constant amortized contention.

To understand the implementation, it is helpful to consider the way the sp-dag structure uses the in-counter operations. The `increment` operation is called by a dag vertex when the vertex calls the **spawn** operation, which uses the vertex's increment handle to determine the node in the SNZI tree, where an arrive operation will start. To find the place, the `increment` operation first uses a `grow` operation to check whether the SNZI node pointed at by the handle has children. Additionally, the operation creates new children if necessary (line 20). Intuitively, we create new SNZI nodes to reduce contention by using more space. Thus, if the increment handle has children, we should make use of them and start our `arrive` operation there. This is exactly what the `increment` operation does (line 24). Note that, in case the `grow` operation does not return new children, we simply have the `arrive` operation start at the increment handle. The `increment` operation returns two increment handles and two decrement handles; one of each for each of the dag vertex's new children.

The in-counter algorithm makes use of an important SNZI property: decrements at the top of the tree do not affect any node below them. Furthermore, if there is a depart operation at SNZI node a, it cannot cause a to phase change as long there is surplus anywhere in a's subtree. These observations lead to the following intuition: to minimize phase changes in the SNZI tree, priority should be given to decrementing nodes closer to the root.

Thus, each dag vertex stores two decrement handles rather than just one. These two decrement handles are shared with the vertex's sibling, and they are ordered: the first handle always points to a SNZI node that is higher in the tree than the second. Decrement handle is needed by the `decrement` operation (line 31) and the `increment` operation. Recall that an `increment` always returns two decrement handles. One of these decrement handles always points to the SNZI node on which the `increment` operation started its `arrive`. However, the other one is inherited from the parent dag vertex (the one that invoked the `increment`). To preserve the invariant, the incrementing vertex needs to claim a decrement handle (line 25). The two decrement handles returned are always ordered as follows: first, the one inherited from the parent, and, then, the one pointing at the freshly incremented SNZI node. In this way, we guarantee that the first decrement handle in any pair points higher in the tree than its counterpart. When a decrement handle is needed, the two dag vertices determine which handle to use through a test-and-set. The first of the two to make use of a decrement handle will take the first handle, thus ensuring that higher SNZI nodes are decremented earlier. We rely on this property to prove our bounds in Lemma 4.6.

Note that, in an `increment` operation, the decrement handle is claimed only *after* the `arrive` has completed. This key invariant helps to ensure that phase changes rarely occur in the SNZI tree, thus leading to fast operations.

4. Correctness and Analysis

We first prove that our in-counter data structure is linearizable and then establish its time and space efficiency. Due to lack of space, we only present the proof for the case where the probability used for the `grow` operation is 1, i.e., the SNZI tree grows on every `increment` operation. The proof for different growth probabilities is similar (and leads to contention that depends on the probability given) but more intricate, and is therefore left for the journal version of this paper.

We say that the in-counter is correct if any `is_zero` operation at the root of the tree correctly indicates whether there is a surplus of `increment` operations over `decrement` operations. To prove correctness, we establish a symmetry with the original SNZI data structure. Note that each `increment`, `decrement`, and `is_zero` operation calls the corresponding SNZI operation (i.e., `arrive`, `depart`, `query` respectively) exactly once. We define the linearization points of each operation as that of the corresponding SNZI operation.

Since the correctness condition for the in-counter and for SNZI are the same, we have the following observation.

Observation 1. *An execution of the in-counter is linearizable if the corresponding SNZI execution is linearizable.*

At this point, we recall that any SNZI run is linearizable if there are never more departs than arrives on any node, i.e., surplus at any node is never negative [14]. We show that this invariant indeed holds for any valid execution of the in-counter data structure, and therefore that any valid execution is linearizable. We define a valid execution as follows.

Definition 1. *An in-counter execution is* valid *if any handle passed as argument to the* `decrement` *operation was returned by a prior* `increment` *operation. Furthermore, that handle is passed to at most one* `decrement` *operation.*

Lemma 4.1. *Any valid in-counter execution is linearizable.*

Proof. Observe that every `increment` operation generates one new decrement handle, and that handle points to the node at which this `increment`'s arrive operation was called. Thus, in valid executions, any `depart` on the underlying SNZI data structure (which is always called by the `decrement` operation) has a corresponding `arrive` at an earlier point in time. Therefore, there are never more departs than arrives at any SNZI node, and the corresponding SNZI execution is linearizable. From Observation 1, the in-counter execution is linearizable as well. □

It is easy to see that any execution of the in-counter that only accesses the object as prescribed by the sp-dag algorithm is valid. From this observation, the main theorem follows immediately.

Theorem 4.2. *Any execution of the in-counter through sp-dag accesses is linearizable.*

4.1 Running Time

To prove that the in-counter is efficient, we analyze shared-memory steps and contention separately: we first show that every operation takes an amortized constant number of shared memory steps, and then we show that each shared memory location experiences constant amortized contention at any time. In our analysis, we do not consider `is_zero`, since it does not do any non-trivial shared memory steps.

For the analysis, consider an execution on an sp-dag, starting with a dag, consisting of a single root vertex and its corresponding finish vertex. Further, observe that this finish vertex has a single SNZI node as the root of its in-counter. Note that all shared memory steps in the execution are on the in-counter. We begin by making an important observation.

Lemma 4.3. *There exist at most one increment and one decrement handle pointing to any given SNZI node.*

To prove this lemma, note that every `increment` operation creates new children for the SNZI node whose handle is used, and thus does not produce another handle to that node. A simple induction, starting with the fact that the root node only has one handle pointing to it, yields the result.

We now want to show that every operation on the in-counter performs an amortized constant number of shared memory steps. First, note that the only calls in the in-counter operations that might result in more than a constant number of steps are their corresponding SNZI operations. The SNZI operations do a constant number of shared memory steps per node they reach, but they can be recursively called up an arbitrarily long path in the tree, as long as nodes in that path phase change due to the operation. That is, frequent phase changing in the SNZI nodes will cause operations on the data structure to be slower. In fact, we show that on average, the length of the path traversed by an `arrive` or `depart` operation is constant, when those SNZI operations are called only through the in-counter operations.

We say that a dag vertex is *live* if it is not marked dead and a handle is live if it is owned by a live vertex. We have the following lemma about live vertices.

Lemma 4.4. *If dag vertex v is live, then it has not used* `claim_dec` *to claim a decrement handle.*

Keeping track of live vertices in the dag is important in the analysis, since by Lemma 4.4, these are the vertices that can use their handles and potentially cause more contention.

To show that operations on SNZI nodes are fast, we begin by considering executions in which only increment operations are allowed, and no decrements happen on the in-counter. Our goal is to show that the in-counter's SNZI tree is relatively saturated, so that `arrive` operations that are called within a `increment` only access a constant number of nodes. After we establish that increment operations are fast when decrements are not allowed, we bring back the decrement operations and see that they cannot slow down the increments.

Lemma 4.5. *Without any decrement operations, when there are no* `increments` *mid-execution, only leaves of the in-counter's SNZI tree can have surplus 0.*

Proof. The proof is by induction on the number of increment operations called on the in-counter. The tree is initialized with one node with surplus 1. Thus, when there have been 0 increments, no node has surplus 0. Assume that the lemma holds for in-counters that have had up to k increments on them. Consider an in-counter that has had k increments, and consider a new `increment` operation invoked on node a in the tree. If a is not a leaf, the `grow` operation does not create new children for a, and the tree does not grow. Thus, the lemma still holds. If a is a leaf, the `increment` operation creates two children for a and starts an arrive operation on one of the children. As a consequence of the SNZI invariant, we know that the surplus of a increased by 1. After the `increment`, regardless of what its surplus was before this operation, a cannot have surplus 0, and the lemma still holds. □

By Lemma 4.5, we know that, ignoring any effect that decrements may have, the tree has surplus in all non-leaf nodes. Recall that an `arrive` operation that reaches a node with positive surplus will terminate at that node. Thus, any `arrive` operation invoked on this tree will only climb up a path until it reaches the first node that was not a leaf before this `increment` started. That is, since each `increment` only expands the tree by at most one level, any `arrive` operation will reach at most 3 nodes.

We now bring back the `decrement` operations. The danger with decrements is that they could potentially cause non-leaf nodes to phase change back to 0 surplus, meaning that an `arrive` operation in that node's subtree might have to traverse a long path up the SNZI tree. Our main lemma shows that traversal of a long path can never happen; if a decrement causes a vertex's surplus to go back to 0, then no subsequent increment operation will start in that node's subtree. We present the proof in the full version.

Lemma 4.6. *If an in-counter node a at any point had a surplus and then phase changed to* 0 *surplus, then no live vertices in the dag point anywhere in its subtree.*

Note that Lemma 4.5 and Lemma 4.6 immediately give us the following important property.

Corollary 4.7. *No* `increment` *operation can invoke more than 3 arrive operations on the SNZI tree.*

Proof. We already saw that by Lemma 4.5, if no decrements happen, then each `increment` operation can invoke at most 3 `arrive` operations.

Now consider decrements as well. Note that if a non-leaf node has surplus 0 and there is no `increment` mid-operation at that node, then it must have previously had surplus (again by Lemma 4.5). By Lemma 4.6, no new `increment` operations can happen on that node's subtree. Thus, even allowing for decrement operations, no `increment` operation can invoke more than 3 arrives on the SNZI tree. □

To finish the proof, we amortize the number of `departs` invoked by `decrements` against the `arrives` invoked by `increments`. Recall that the number of `departs` invoked on a SNZI tree is at most the number of `arrives` invoked on it. We get the following theorem:

Theorem 4.8. *Any operation performed on the in-counter itself calls an amortized $O(1)$ operations on the SNZI tree.*

We now move on to analyzing the amount of contention a process experiences when executing an operation on the in-counter. Note that there have been several models suggested to account for contention, as discussed in Section 6. In our contention analysis, we say that an operation contends with a shared memory step if that step is non-trivial, and it could, in any execution, be concurrent with the operation at the same memory location. Our results are valid in any contention model in which trivial operations do not affect contention (i.e. such as stalls [16], the CRQW model [21], etc.).

Theorem 4.9. *Any operation executed on the in-counter experiences $O(1)$ amortized contention.*

Proof. We show something stronger: the maximum number of operations that access a single SNZI node over the course of an entire dag computation (other than `is_zero` operations on the root) is constant.

Consider a node a in the SNZI tree. By Lemma 4.3, only one `increment` operation ever starts its `arrive` at a. That `increment` has exactly one corresponding `decrement` whose `depart` starts at a. By the SNZI algorithm, an `arrive` at a's child only propagates up to a if that child's surplus was 0 before the `arrive`. By Lemma 4.6, this situation can only happen once; if a's child's surplus returns to 0 after being higher, the counter will never be incremented again. Thus, each of a's children can only ever be responsible for at most two operations that access a; the initial `arrive` and the final `depart` from that subtree.

In total, we get a maximum of 6 operations that access a over the course of the computation. Note also that the first `arrive` at a node always strictly precedes any other operation in that node's subtree. Thus, concurrent `arrive` operations are not an issue. Therefore, any operation on the in-counter can be concurrent with at most 4 other operations per SNZI node it accesses. By Theorem 4.8, every operation on the in-counter accesses amortized $O(1)$ nodes. Therefore, any such operation experiences amortized $O(1)$ contention. □

4.2 Space bounds

Shrinking the tree by removing unnecessary nodes is tricky because, in its most general form, an ideal solution likely requires knowing the future of the computation. Knowing where in the tree to shrink requires knowing which nodes are not likey to be incremented in the future. For the specific case of the `grow` probability of 1, we establish a safety property that makes it possible to keep the data structure compact by removing SNZI nodes that correspond to deleted subgraphs of the sp-dag. Due to space constraints, we present the details in the full version [1].

5. Experimental evaluation

We report an empirical comparison between our in-counter algorithm, the simple fetch-and-add counter, and an algorithm using fixed-size SNZI trees. Our implementation consists of a small, C++ a library that uses a state-of-the-art, implementation of a work-stealing scheduler [2]. Overall, our results show that the simple, fetch-and-add counter performs well only when there is one core, the fixed-size SNZI trees scale better, but our in-counter algorithm outperforms the others when the core count is two or more.

Implementation. Our implementation of core SNZI operations `snzi_arrive` and `snzi_depart` follows closely the algorithm presented in the original SNZI paper, except for two differences. First, we do not need `snzi_query` because readiness detection is performed via the return result of `snzi_depart`. This method suffices because only the caller of `snzi_depart` can bring the count to zero. Second, our `snzi_depart` returns `true` if the call brought the counter to zero. To control the grain of contention, we use the probabilistic technique presented in Section 2, with probability $p := \frac{1}{25c}$, where c is the number of cores. The idea of using c is to try to keep contention the same as the number of cores increase. We chose the constant factor 25, because it yields good results, but as our Threshold study, described below, shows many other constants also yield good results, e.g., any constant in the range $2.5c \le p \le 25c$ yields qualitatively the same results. The implementation of the sp-dags and in-counter data structures (Section 3) build on the SNZI data structure. The sp-dags interface enables writing nested-parallel programs, using various constructs, such as fork-join and async-finish; we use the latter in our experiments.

```
fun fanin_rec(n)
  if n >= 2
    async fanin_rec(n/2)
    async fanin_rec(n/2)

fun fanin(n)
  finish {fanin_rec(n)}
```

Figure 6: Fan-in benchmark.

```
fun indegree2(n)
  if n >= 2
    finish {
      async indegree2(n/2)
      async indegree2(n/2)
    }
```

Figure 7: Indegree-2 benchmark.

We compare our in-counter with an atomic, fetch-and-add counter because the fetch-and-add counter is optimal for very small numbers of cores. For higher number of cores, we designed a different, SNZI-based algorithm that uses a fixed-depth SNZI tree. This algorithm gives us another point of comparison, by offering a data structure that uses the existing state of the art more directly. The fixed-depth SNZI algorithm allocates for each finish block a SNZI tree of $2^{d+1} - 1$ nodes, for a given depth d. To maintain the critical SNZI invariant that the surplus of a SNZI node never becomes negative, the fixed-depth SNZI algorithm ensures that every `snzi_depart` call targets the same SNZI node that was targeted by a matching `snzi_arrive` call. To determine which SNZI node to be targeted by a `snzi_arrive` call, we map DAG vertices to SNZI nodes using a hash function to ensure that operations are spread evenly across the SNZI tree.

Experimental setup. We compiled the code using GCC `-O2 -march=native` (version 5.2). Our machine has four Intel E7-4870 chips and 1Tb of RAM and runs Ubuntu Linux kernel v3.13.0-66-generic. Each chip has ten cores (40 total) and shares a 30Mb L3 cache. Each core runs at 2.4Ghz and has 256Kb of L2 cache and 32Kb of L1 cache. The machine has a non-uniform memory architecture (NUMA), whereby RAM is partitioned into four banks. Pages are, by default in our Linux distribution, allocated to banks according to the first-touch policy, which assigns a freshly allocated page to the bank of the processor that first accesses the page. An alternative policy assigns pages to banks in a round-robin fashion. We determined that, for the purposes of our experiments, the choice of NUMA policy has no significant impact on our main results. The experiment we performed to back this claim is described in more detail in the full paper [1]. For all other experiments, we used the round-robin policy.

Benchmarks: `fanin` and `indegree2`. To study scalability, we use the two small benchmarks shown in Figures 6 and 7. The `fanin` benchmark performs n async calls, all of which

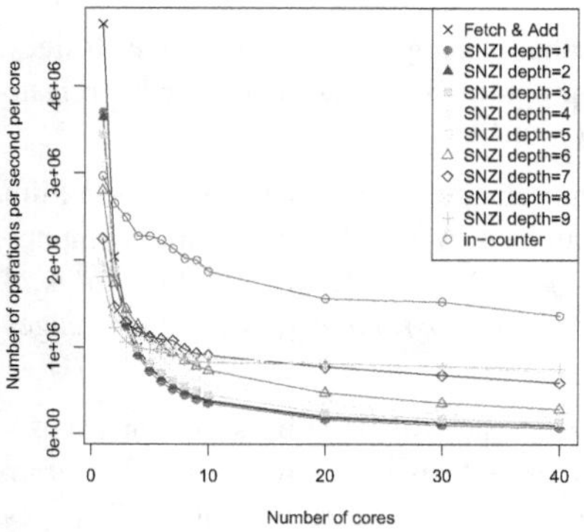

Figure 8: Fanin benchmark with $n = 8$ million, & varying number of processors. Higher is better.

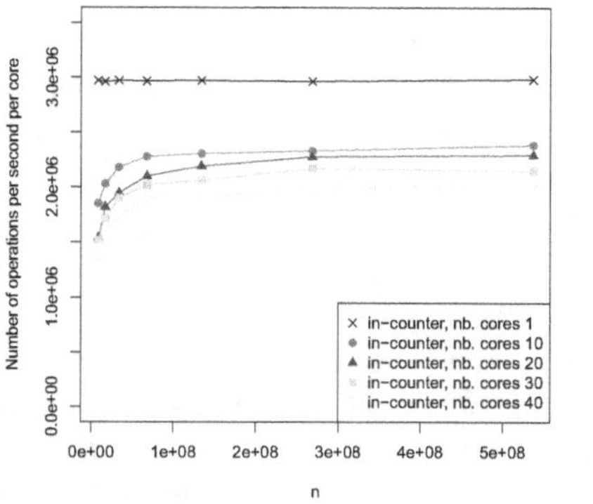

Figure 9: Fanin benchmark, varying the number of operations n. Higher is better.

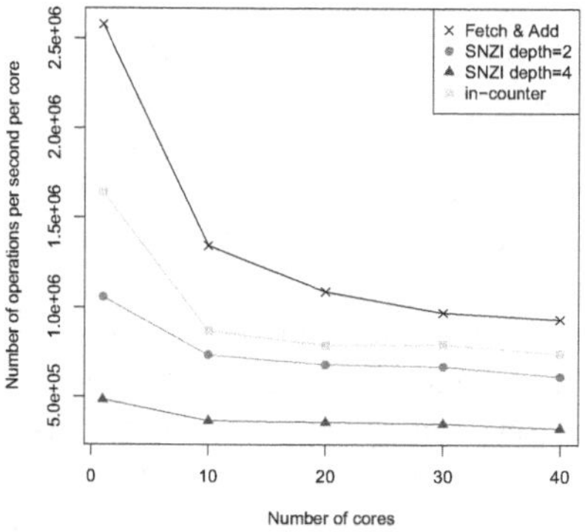

Figure 10: Indegree-2 benchmark, using number of operations $n = 8$ million. Higher is better.

synchronize at a single finish block, making the finish block a potential source of contention. The `fanin` benchmark implements a common pattern, such as a parallel-for, where a number of independent computations are forked to execute in parallel and synchronize at termination. Our second benchmark, `indegree2` implements the same pattern as in `fanin` but by using binary fork join. This program yields a computation dag in which each finish vertex has indegree 2.

Scalability study. Figure 8 shows the scalability of the `fanin` benchmark using different counter data structures. With one core, the Fetch & Add counter performs best because there is no contention, but with more, Fetch & Add gives worst performance for all core counts (this pattern is occluded by the other curves). For more than one core, our in-counter performs the best. The fixed-depth SNZI algorithm scales poorly when depth is small, doing best at the tree depth of 8, where there are enough nodes to deal with contention among 40 cores. Increasing the depth further does not improve the performance, however.

Size-invariance study. Theorem 4.9 shows that the amortized contention of our in-counter is constant. We test this result empirically by measuring the running time of the `fanin` benchmark for different input parameters n. As shown in Figure 9, for all input sizes considered and for all core counts, the throughput is within a factor 2 of the single-core (no-contention) Fetch & Add counter. The throughput suffers a bit for the smaller values of n because, at these values, there is not enough useful parallelism to feed the available cores.

Low-indegree study. Our next experiment examines the overhead imposed by the in-counter by using the `indegree2` benchmark shown in Figure 7. The results, illustrated in Figure 10, show that our in-counter data structure is within a factor 2 of the best performer, the fetch-and-add counter. For SNZI, we only considered small-depths, since larger ones took too long to run. With the fixed-depth SNZI, the

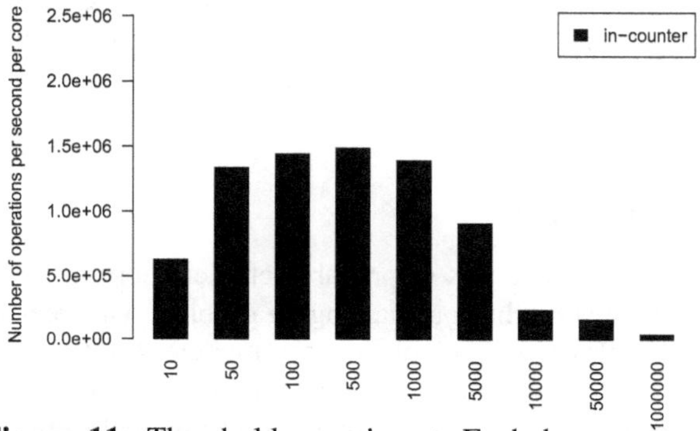

Figure 11: Threshold experiment. Each bar represents a different setting for $p = \frac{1}{threshold}$. All runs were performed using 40 cores. Higher is better.

benchmark creates many finish blocks and thus many SNZI trees, becoming inefficient for large trees.

Threshold study. In Section 2, we presented a technique to control the grain of contention by expanding the SNZI tree dynamically. Here, we report, using the `fanin` benchmark, the results of varying the range of probabilities $p = \frac{1}{threshold}$ for different settings of *threshold*. As shown in Figure 11, essentially any threshold between 50 and 1000 works well. We separately checked that on our test machine using a constant threshold such as 100 or 1000 yields good results when using any number of cores. On a machine, perhaps with many more cores, the best setting might be different or might also depend on the number of cores used.

6. Related Work

Upper bounds for several non-blocking data structures, accounting also for contention, have been proven for several tree- and list-based search structures [13; 18; 39]. In these upper bounds, contention factors in as a linear additive term, which is consistent with established lower bounds for many problems in the general concurrency model [27; 30; 15; 16].

In contrast, for relaxed counters, we show that contention for series-parallel programs can be upper bounded by a constant.

Complexity models for analyzing contention and techniques for designing algorithms for reducing contention has also been important subject of study [36; 31; 12; 20; 21] Contention has also been identified as an important practical performance issue in multiprocessor systems. Techniques that reduce contention by detecting and introducing wait periods or using tokens to be passed between threads proved to be essential for reducing detrimental effects of contention [4; 6]. Managing contention in software-transactional memory may require contention managers that schedule transactions carefully to minimize aborted transactions [41; 23; 26; 40].

In this paper, we consider non-blocking, or lock-free algorithms. Since our upper bounds are quite good, $O(1)$, our algorithms guarantee that each operation completes quickly in our relaxed concurrency model. Wait-free data structures can guarantee similar properties in the general concurrency model [24; 25]. Such data structures were traditionally considered to be impractical, though recent results show that they may be also be practical [33; 44].

7. Conclusion

The design and analysis of provably efficient non-blocking data structures has been a challenging problem. One reason is the complexity of the concurrency models. Another reason is the difficulty of accounting for important practical concerns, such as contention, that can significantly impact performance. In this paper, we show that it is possible to design provably efficient data structures under a slightly more restrictive but still important concurrency model: nested-parallel computations. Our results take advantage of certain structural invariants in nested parallel computations, specifically those that concern the creation, termination, and synchronization of threads. Interesting future research directions include the design and analysis of other concurrent data structures for the nested-parallel concurrency model and consideration of more general, but still restricted, models of concurrency, such as those based on futures.

Acknowledgments

This research is partially supported by the a fellowship from Natural Sciences and Engineering Research Council of Canada (NSERC), and grants from National Science Foundation (CCF-1320563 and CCF-1408940) and European Research Council (grant ERC-2012-StG-308246). We are grateful to Doug Lea for his feedback on the paper.

References

[1] Umut A. Acar, Naama Ben-David, and Mike Rainey. Contention in structured concurrency: Provably efficient dynamic nonzero indicators for nested parallel computation. Technical Report CMU-CS-16-133, Department of Computer Science, Carnegie Mellon University, 2016.

[2] Umut A. Acar, Arthur Charguéraud, and Mike Rainey. Scheduling parallel programs by work stealing with private deques. In *PPoPP '13*, 2013.

[3] Umut A. Acar, Arthur Charguéraud, Mike Rainey, and Filip Sieczkowski. Dag-calculus: A calculus for parallel computation. In *Proceedings of the 21st ACM SIGPLAN International Conference on Functional Programming*, ICFP 2016, pages 18–32, 2016.

[4] A. Agarwal and M. Cherian. Adaptive backoff synchronization techniques. In *Proceedings of the 16th Annual International Symposium on Computer Architecture*, ISCA '89, pages 396–406, 1989.

[5] James H. Anderson and Yong-Jik Kim. An improved lower bound for the time complexity of mutual exclusion. *Distrib. Comput.*, 15(4):221–253, December 2002.

[6] T. E. Anderson. The performance of spin lock alternatives for shared-memory multiprocessors. *IEEE Trans. Parallel Distrib. Syst.*, 1(1):6–16, January 1990.

[7] Nimar S. Arora, Robert D. Blumofe, and C. Greg Plaxton. Thread scheduling for multiprogrammed multiprocessors. In *Proceedings of the tenth annual ACM symposium on Parallel algorithms and architectures*, SPAA '98, pages 119–129. ACM Press, 1998.

[8] Robert D. Blumofe and Charles E. Leiserson. Scheduling multithreaded computations by work stealing. *J. ACM*, 46:720–748, September 1999.

[9] Trevor Brown, Faith Ellen, and Eric Ruppert. A general technique for non-blocking trees. In *Proceedings of the 19th ACM SIGPLAN Symposium on Principles and Practice of Parallel Programming*, PPoPP '14, pages 329–342, 2014.

[10] Philippe Charles, Christian Grothoff, Vijay Saraswat, Christopher Donawa, Allan Kielstra, Kemal Ebcioglu, Christoph von Praun, and Vivek Sarkar. X10: an object-oriented approach to non-uniform cluster computing. In *Proceedings of the 20th annual ACM SIGPLAN conference on Object-oriented programming, systems, languages, and applications*, OOPSLA '05, pages 519–538. ACM, 2005.

[11] Robert Cypher. The communication requirements of mutual exclusion. In *Proceedings of the Seventh Annual ACM Symposium on Parallel Algorithms and Architectures*, SPAA '95, pages 147–156, 1995.

[12] Cynthia Dwork, Maurice Herlihy, and Orli Waarts. Contention in shared memory algorithms. *Journal of the ACM (JACM)*, 44(6):779–805, 1997.

[13] Faith Ellen, Panagiota Fatourou, Joanna Helga, and Eric Ruppert. The amortized complexity of non-blocking binary search trees. In *Proceedings of the 2014 ACM Symposium on Principles of Distributed Computing*, PODC '14, pages 332–340, 2014.

[14] Faith Ellen, Yossi Lev, Victor Luchangco, and Mark Moir. Snzi: Scalable nonzero indicators. In *Proceedings of the Twenty-sixth Annual ACM Symposium on Principles of Distributed Computing*, PODC '07, pages 13–22, 2007.

[15] Faith Fich and Eric Ruppert. Hundreds of impossibility results for distributed computing. *Distrib. Comput.*, 16(2-3):121–163, September 2003.

[16] Faith Ellen Fich, Danny Hendler, and Nir Shavit. Linear lower bounds on real-world implementations of concurrent objects. In *Foundations of Computer Science, 2005. FOCS 2005. 46th Annual IEEE Symposium on*, pages 165–173. IEEE, 2005.

[17] Matthew Fluet, Mike Rainey, John Reppy, and Adam Shaw. Implicitly threaded parallelism in Manticore. *Journal of Functional Programming*, 20(5-6):1–40, 2011.

[18] Mikhail Fomitchev and Eric Ruppert. Lock-free linked lists and skip lists. In *Proceedings of the Twenty-third Annual ACM Symposium on Principles of Distributed Computing*, PODC '04, pages 50–59, 2004.

[19] Matteo Frigo, Charles E. Leiserson, and Keith H. Randall. The implementation of the Cilk-5 multithreaded language. In *PLDI*, pages 212–223, 1998.

[20] Phillip B Gibbons, Yossi Matias, and Vijaya Ramachandran. Efficient low-contention parallel algorithms. In *Proceedings of the sixth annual ACM symposium on Parallel algorithms and architectures*, pages 236–247. ACM, 1994.

[21] Phillip B Gibbons, Yossi Matias, Vijaya Ramachandran, et al. The queue-read queue-write pram model: Accounting for contention in parallel algorithms. *SIAM Journal on Computing*, pages 638–648, 1997.

[22] James R. Goodman, Mary K. Vernon, and Philip J. Woest. Efficient synchronization primitives for large-scale cache-coherent multiprocessors. In *Proceedings of the Third International Conference on Architectural Support for Programming Languages and Operating Systems*, ASPLOS III, pages 64–75, 1989.

[23] Tim Harris and Keir Fraser. Language support for lightweight transactions. In *Proceedings of the 18th Annual ACM SIGPLAN Conference on Object-oriented Programing, Systems, Languages, and Applications*, OOPSLA '03, pages 388–402, 2003.

[24] Maurice Herlihy. Wait-free synchronization. *ACM Trans. Program. Lang. Syst.*, 13:124–149, January 1991.

[25] Maurice Herlihy. A methodology for implementing highly concurrent data objects. *ACM Trans. Program. Lang. Syst.*, 15(5):745–770, November 1993.

[26] Maurice Herlihy, Victor Luchangco, Mark Moir, and William N Scherer III. Software transactional memory for dynamic-sized data structures. In *Proceedings of the twenty-second annual symposium on Principles of distributed computing*, pages 92–101. ACM, 2003.

[27] Maurice Herlihy, Nir Shavit, and Orli Waarts. Linearizable counting networks. *Distributed Computing*, 9(4):193–203, 1996.

[28] Shams Mahmood Imam and Vivek Sarkay. Habanero-java library: a java 8 framework for multicore programming. In *2014 International Conference on Principles and Practices of Programming on the Java Platform Virtual Machines, Languages and Tools, PPPJ '14, Cracow, Poland, September 23-26, 2014*, pages 75–86, 2014.

[29] Intel. Intel threading building blocks. 2011. `https://www.threadingbuildingblocks.org/`.

[30] Prasad Jayanti, King Tan, and Sam Toueg. Time and space lower bounds for nonblocking implementations. *SIAM Journal on Computing*, 30(2):438–456, 2000.

[31] Richard M Karp and Yanjun Zhang. Randomized parallel algorithms for backtrack search and branch-and-bound computation. *Journal of the ACM (JACM)*, 40(3):765–789, 1993.

[32] Gabriele Keller, Manuel M.T. Chakravarty, Roman Leshchinskiy, Simon Peyton Jones, and Ben Lippmeier. Regular, shape-polymorphic, parallel arrays in haskell. In *Proceedings of the 15th ACM SIGPLAN international conference on Functional programming*, ICFP '10, pages 261–272, 2010.

[33] Alex Kogan and Erez Petrank. A methodology for creating fast wait-free data structures. In *Proceedings of the 17th ACM SIGPLAN Symposium on Principles and Practice of Parallel Programming*, PPoPP '12, pages 141–150, 2012.

[34] Doug Lea. A java fork/join framework. In *Proceedings of the ACM 2000 conference on Java Grande*, JAVA '00, pages 36–43, 2000.

[35] Daan Leijen, Wolfram Schulte, and Sebastian Burckhardt. The design of a task parallel library. In *Proceedings of the 24th ACM SIGPLAN conference on Object oriented programming systems languages and applications*, OOPSLA '09, pages 227–242, 2009.

[36] Pangfeng Liu, William Aiello, and Sandeep Bhatt. An atomic model for message-passing. In *Proceedings of the fifth annual ACM symposium on Parallel algorithms and architectures*, pages 154–163. ACM, 1993.

[37] Maged M. Michael and Michael L. Scott. Nonblocking algorithms and preemption-safe locking on multiprogrammed shared memory multiprocessors. *J. Parallel Distrib. Comput.*, 51(1):1–26, May 1998.

[38] Mark Moir and Nir Shavit. Concurrent data structures. *Handbook of Data Structures and Applications*, pages 47–14, 2007.

[39] Rotem Oshman and Nir Shavit. The skiptrie: Low-depth concurrent search without rebalancing. In *Proceedings of the 2013 ACM Symposium on Principles of Distributed Computing*, PODC '13, pages 23–32, 2013.

[40] William N. Scherer, III and Michael L. Scott. Advanced contention management for dynamic software transactional memory. In *Proceedings of the Twenty-fourth Annual ACM Symposium on Principles of Distributed Computing*, PODC '05, pages 240–248, 2005.

[41] Nir Shavit and Dan Touitou. Software transactional memory. In *Proceedings of the Fourteenth Annual ACM Symposium on Principles of Distributed Computing*, PODC '95, pages 204–213, 1995.

[42] Nir Shavit and Asaph Zemach. Combining funnels. *J. Parallel Distrib. Comput.*, 60(11):1355–1387, November 2000.

[43] Julian Shun, Guy E. Blelloch, Jeremy T. Fineman, and Phillip B. Gibbons. Reducing contention through priority updates. In *Proceedings of the Twenty-fifth Annual ACM Symposium on Parallelism in Algorithms and Architectures*, SPAA '13, pages 152–163, 2013.

[44] Shahar Timnat and Erez Petrank. A practical wait-free simulation for lock-free data structures. In *Proceedings of the 19th ACM SIGPLAN Symposium on Principles and Practice of Parallel Programming*, PPoPP '14, pages 357–368, 2014.

[45] R Kent Treiber. Systems programming: Coping with parallelism. Technical report, International Business Machines Incorporated, Thomas J. Watson Research Center, 1986.

Noise Injection Techniques to Expose Subtle and Unintended Message Races

Kento Sato, Dong H. Ahn, Ignacio Laguna, Gregory L. Lee,
Martin Schulz and Christopher M. Chambreau

Lawrence Livermore National Laboratory
7000 East Ave. Livermore, CA
{kento, ahn1, ilaguna, lee218, schulzm, chambreau1}@llnl.gov

Abstract

Debugging intermittently occurring bugs within MPI applications is challenging, and message races, a condition in which two or more sends race to match with a receive, are one of the common root causes. Many debugging tools have been proposed to help programmers resolve them, but their runtime interference perturbs the timing such that subtle races often cannot be reproduced with debugging tools. We present novel noise injection techniques to expose message races even under a tool's control. We first formalize this race problem in the context of non-deterministic parallel applications and use this analysis to determine an effective noise-injection strategy to uncover them. We codified these techniques in NINJA (Noise INJection Agent) that exposes these races without modification to the application. Our evaluations on synthetic cases as well as a real-world bug in Hypre-2.10.1 show that NINJA significantly helps expose races.

Categories and Subject Descriptors D.2.5 [*Software*]: Distributed debugging; F.1.2 [*Theory of Computation*]: Alternation and nondeterminism

Keywords debugging; non-determinism; MPI

1. Introduction

The path towards exascale computing involves significant increases in the amount and type of parallelism, and applications have begun to adopt more asynchronous algorithms to exploit them efficiently. The Message Passing Interface (MPI) is today's workhorse to build large-scale high-performance computing (HPC) applications. While this programming model will remain dominant in the foreseeable future, its usage is increasingly embracing more asynchronous algorithms.

While asynchronous communication allows flexible communication patterns and enables applications to overlap communication with computation [20] for higher performance, it comes at an expense: it often introduces *non-determinism* in communication patterns, e.g., by waiting for any message (e.g. `MPI_ANY_SOURCE`) to arrive and processing them in any order. While this by itself is not problematic, non-determinism is generally hard to reason about, raising the level of difficulty in correctly implementing such algorithms. Even worse, incorrect usage can often produce subtle and hard-to-track non-deterministic bugs that intermittently emerge during production runs, but rarely (or never) occur in testing and debug runs.

A common cause of a non-deterministic bug is an unintended message race, a condition in which two or more message sends race to match with a message receive and at least one of them is unintended. Such an incorrect match only occurs with under a specific message arrival timing, and therefore they can be particularly challenging to reproduce and to diagnose during debug runs, which typically have a different timing behavior caused by different compilation flags, additional instrumentation or other factors. Further, timing is often determined also by external factors in MPI applications, in particular the level of congestion on the network paths.

Unintended message races can significantly increase the debugging cost because programmers must often run the application many times until the races finally manifest. While many parallel debugging tools exist for HPC, they mainly focus on helping programmers in *finding* the cause of a bug by inspecting, tracing, profiling or printing the application's program state once a bug has manifested. Consequently, these tools are effective *only when the bug is observed*. However, *observing* the bug itself, especially under a tool's control, is as difficult as *finding* the root cause of the bug for unintended message races (More details in Sec-

PPoPP '17, Feb. 4–8, 2017, Austin, Texas, USA..

http://dx.doi.org/10.1145/http://dx.doi.org/10.1145/3018743.3018767

tion 2). Further, these tools typically exhibit noticeable runtime overhead, which distorts and thereby potentially masks message race bugs.

In this paper, we present NINJA (Network noise INJection Agent), which injects network noise in order to expose unintended message races more frequently and quickly to *complement* existing debugging tools. The noise amounts are carefully selected to cause delays only on certain message sends to expose the condition akin to when the application intermittently failed.

NINJA provides two network injection modes: system-centric and application-centric. In the system-centric mode, NINJA is configured with system-specific noise parameters to emulate a congested network with no knowledge on the application's messaging patterns. In the application-centric mode, NINJA first obtains the application's own messaging patterns from an initial run in the system-centric mode and then uses them to determine more precise amounts of noise and injection patterns. NINJA uses the MPI profiling interface (PMPI) to inject network noise, and thus existing applications can run under NINJA without code modifications or even without being aware of the tool's existence. Specifically, this paper makes the following contributions:

- An analysis of unintended message races in non-deterministic message-passing applications;
- Two novel network noise injection techniques: one system- and application-centric approach, which use the above analysis to uncover subtle message races;
- A prototype of NINJA that embodies these techniques;
- An empirical evaluation of the effectiveness and overhead of NINJA on synthetic message races as well as a real-world bug in a large sparse matrix solver.

Our evaluation on synthetic cases shows that NINJA can help expose unintended message races frequently and quickly. Further, our evaluation on a real-world bug in Hypre-2.10.1 shows that NINJA can consistently expose message races that had not been fixed (due in large part to their rare occurrence) for over 14 years of its history, i.e., since the first version of Hypre 1.6.0 was released[1].

2. Background

2.1 Motivational Case Study

Two scientists developing a production engineering application in our organization engaged our research team to ask for debugging assistance as their application intermittently hung. They had spent about two months on the hangs in a period of 18 months, but its intermittent nature had been making their effort nearly fruitless. Our research team began to tackle this problem by first lightly sprinkling `printf` statements into code and running it on one of our HPC clusters. However, we found that the bug became even harder to reproduce in our debug runs (more details in Section 3.3).

When our team found and fixed the bugs, our job submission logs showed that our team had to spend two weeks in the period of three months, and submitted 291 jobs (10,392 compute-node hours or 433 compute-node days in total) for diagnosing this single non-deterministic bug. We were able to observe the hang only in 9 jobs, and wasted resources for the remaining 282 jobs. Even when the hang was reproduced in the 9 jobs, it took a few hours before the application got hung. Another phenomena, which hampered our debugging efforts, was that this bug never manifested in another cluster (More details in Section 6.1).

Once we sufficiently captured the hang in debug runs, fixing it was rather easy: it required only about ten lines of code. The root cause was due to an unintended message race between two communication routines within the Hypre solver (Ver. 2.10.1) used in this application. We learned in this investigation that debugging non-deterministic bugs requires frequent and quick manifestations of the target bug.

2.2 Existing Approaches to Message Races

Because of its non-deterministic nature, `printf` debugging is a common technique: programmers add `printf` statements in specific places of the code to log program states including destinations and sources of the messages being exchanged.

Other attractive approaches are record-and-replay [16, 20, 26], MPI deadlock detection [12] and message race detection tools [19]. A record-and-replay tool records a communication trace of all MPI processes. Once the tool captures an incorrect message matching in the record phase, the tool can then repeatedly reproduce the identical incorrect execution, significantly facilitating debugging. However a record-and-replay tool needs to observe untended message matching at lease once and under tool control in order to replay it.

MPI deadlock and message race detection tools can identify where a deadlock or message race occurred in the code. However, these tools also need to observe a deadlock or message race to identify the code location. When it comes to non-deterministic bugs, a new tool, which can make the target bug manifest itself more frequently and quickly so as to complement other existing debugging tools, can be a significant aid.

3. Conceptualizing Message Races

In this section, we present our high-level execution model for MPI applications in order to describe message races in conceptual terms. Using this model, we also explain a common phenomenon where simply applying a debugging tool to this problem often makes it even harder to expose this class of bugs.

[1] The corrected functions, which our research team found and fixed, were incorporated into the next version, Hypre-2.11.0.

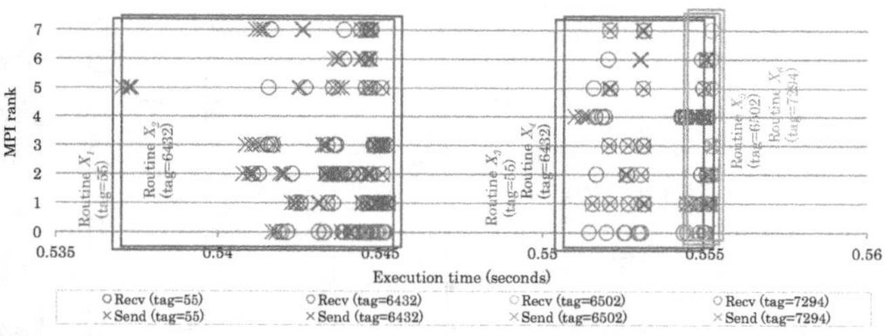

Figure 1. Communication segments in MCB (# of send messages: 205)

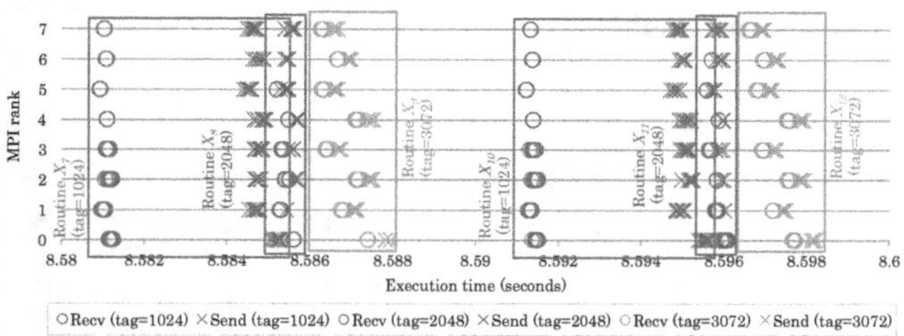

Figure 2. Communication segments in Lulesh (# of send messages: 131)

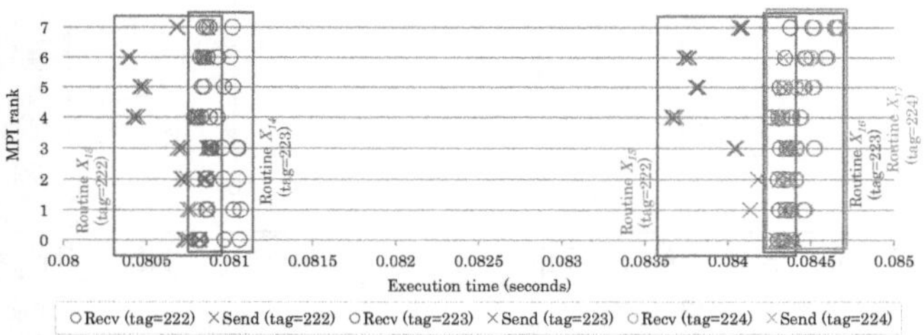

Figure 3. Communication segments in Hypre (# of send messages: 190)

3.1 Execution Model

A majority of today's large-scale parallel applications are written in the Single Program, Multiple Data (SPMD)-based message-passing paradigm. One key pattern of this paradigm is that each MPI process repetitively executes a series of *communication routines*. For example, Figures 1, 2 and 3 show this pattern in terms of receives (e.g., MPI_Recv) and sends (e.g., MPI_Send) on timeline plots of two well-known CORAL benchmark codes (MCB and Lulesh) and the Hypre library. Here, a communication routine represents a self-contained communication instance consisting of sends and receives that often use the same MPI tag and communicator for isolation.

Messages sent in a communication routine are intended to be received by the same communication routine. In our figures, we denote the communication routines as Routine $X_1, X_2 \ldots X_{17}$. If isolation is guaranteed, a communication routine can be overlapped with other communication routines for better performance. However, reasoning about this isolation can often be difficult in particular when program complexity is high, which can lead to extremely hard to debug errors.

Figure 3 shows one such bug in Hypre: the programmer did not intend the messages sent in Routine X_{15} to be received by Routine X_{13}, but there was no isolation between them. In fact, the rarely occurring hang described in Section 2.1 was caused by this unintended message matching where a message sent in Routine X_{15} was received by Routine X_{13}. Because another routine, in this case, Routine X_{14}, and other relatively intense computations occur between Routine X_{13} and X_{15}, this message race did not normally occur. However, when the code was run under significant network congestion, an overlapping of Routine X_{13} and X_{15} occurred. In order to prevent this, these two routines would have needed to use proper isolation mechanisms.

3.2 Unintended Message Race Model

Figure 4-(a) generalizes our target message race problem. Routine X consists of either multiple or none of communication routines and other computations. In the Hypre case, for example, Routine A, X and B correspond to Routine "X_{13}", "X_{14} and other computations" and "X_{15}", respectively. Even if individual routines are free of bugs, the developer must also ensure that unintended message races do not occur across different routines or different invocations of the same routine.

One mechanism to provide the necessary isolation between Routine A and B is to use unique message tags with respect to a communicator within each routine: *matching ID*. Here, each process can receive only the messages designated by the matching ID in the routine (Condition C_{msgid}). Another mechanism is to build a unique epoch (i.e., a period of logical time that *happens before* the subsequent routine) directly into a routine by means of global synchronization (e.g., `MPI_Barrier`) without in-flight messages as shown in Figure 4-(b) (Condition C_{sync}). Typically, the same communication routines are called multiple times either in an iteration or across different iterations, therefore we must ensure that condition C_{sync} is held whenever the same communication routines are called.

In general, when developing MPI applications, the programmer must ensure that either condition is satisfied, $C_{msgid} \cup C_{sync}$, to avoid message races for all communication routines. If there is any communication routine violating both C_{msgid} and C_{sync} condition, i.e., $\overline{C_{msgid}} \cap \overline{C_{sync}}$, then that the communication routines is considered *unsafe*, and the application can *potentially* encounter unintended message races if a specific timing is created. For example, Routine X_7 and X_{10} violate C_{msgid}, while C_{sync} is satisfied in Lulesh. Therefore, the routines are still *safe*. If C_{sync} is not satisfied, Lulesh can encounter the same race bug as that of Hypre's. As scientific MPI applications become more com-

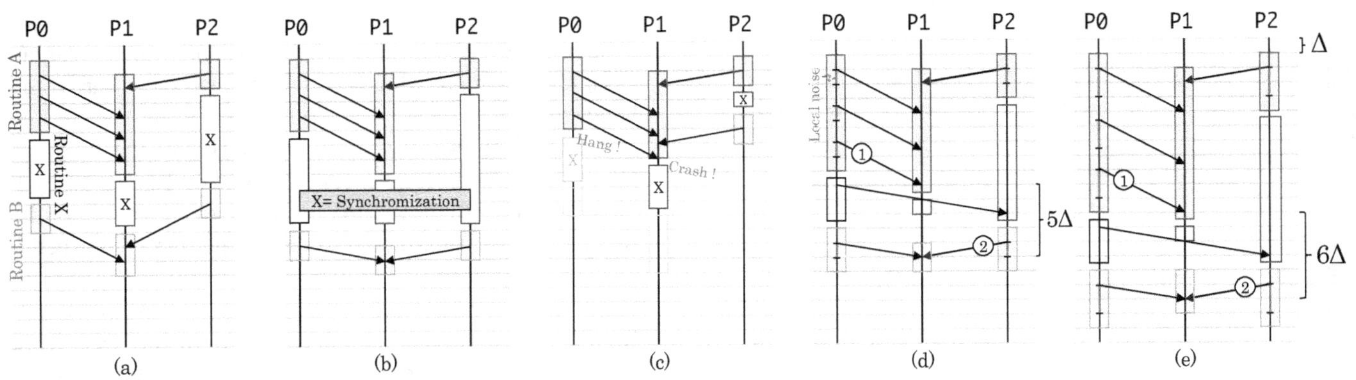

Figure 4. Message race conditions in MPI applications

plex and larger, ensuring the condition, $C_{msgid} \cup C_{sync}$, has been becoming increasingly challenging.

In this example, if Routine A and B are unsafe, then unintended message races can happen, as shown in Figure 4-(c), which can result in an application crash or hang. In practice, the manifestation of unintended message races depends on the execution time of interleaving routines (Routine X) between the two unsafe communication routines (Routine A and B). For example, if Routine X is a computation routine in a strong-scaling problem in which each MPI process operates on an increasingly smaller piece of data, a larger process count leads to a proportionally shorter execution of Routine X. Under such circumstances, message races would only begin to show up at or above a certain process count. However, the same races would not occur at small scales because Routines A and B will never be overlapped in practice as they are separated by a larger running time of Routine X.

We refer to the difficulty in reproducing unintended races due to a relatively large distance between unsafe routines as well as other relevant issues (e.g., noise effects), collectively as the *separation problem.*

3.3 Why Races Disappear under a Tool's Control?

In addition to a problem in existing debugging tools described in Section 2.2, another disadvantage of these tools is that they tend to introduce an extra runtime overhead (*node-local noise*). The occurrence of message races is highly subject to any *noise*, and therefore they can disappear due to the noise introduced by these approaches. Figure 4-(d) illustrates this problem. If processes in Routine X send and receive messages, then the node-local noise propagates through this communication, and Routine A and B can be even further separated if P2 can only transition into Routine B after receiving a message from P0 in Routine X. Nevertheless, message 2 still can arrive at P1 earlier than message 1 if message 1 is significantly delayed (Figure 5-(a)).

In practice, introducing more node-local noise separates the unsafe routines further, therefore making it harder to reproduce message races because Routine X typically contains

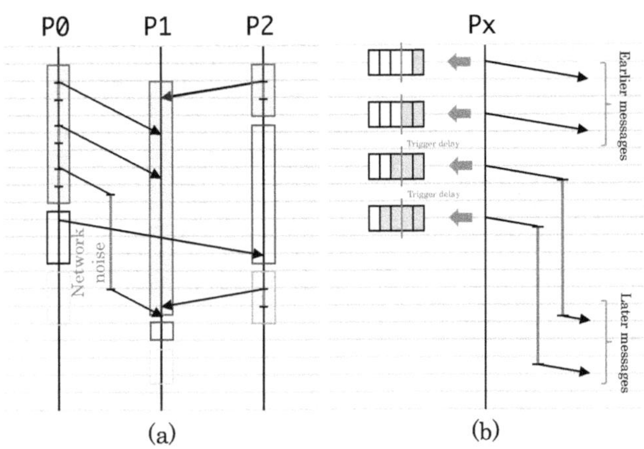

Figure 5. (a) Noise injection can overlap; (b) Noise Triggering Criteria

interleaving communications between the two unsafe routines, as shown in Figure 2 and 3. For example, if each node-local noise unit is Δ, then the interval between the arrival of message 1 and 2 is 5Δ, as shown in Figure 4-(d). However, if the node-local noise unit is 2Δ, then the interval becomes 6Δ ,as shown in Figure 4-(e).

We refer to the difficulty in reproducing this class of races due to the runtime overhead introduced by tools collectively as the *tool overhead problem.*

4. Noise Injection Techniques

When debugging message races, it is necessary to observe the bugs in debug runs. To assist programmers with observing the message races, we need practical approaches to the aforementioned problems of *separation* and *tool overhead.* Our approach is to use noise injection techniques to enable frequent manifestation of message races, and we codified this approach in a prototype called NINJA.

NINJA uses *network noise injection* techniques to control the communication behaviors of the MPI application with the goal of manifesting subtle message races more frequently. Unlike *node-local noise* (Figure 4-(d)), a right amount of *network noise* can expose unintended message races (Figure 5-(a)). NINJA provides two noise injection modes: *system-centric* and *application-centric*. In system-centric mode, NINJA induces message races by reconstructing noise signatures. In application-centric mode, NINJA first analyses the application's behavior to then directly enforce the overlapping of certain communication routines. It achieves this goal by building the application-specific knowledge into its noise injection scheme.

4.1 System-Centric Noise-Injection Mode

When injecting network noise in the system-centric mode, NINJA considers two important factors to maximize the chance for an incorrect message matching to manifest itself due to races, while limiting the application slowdown: which MPI sends to inject noise into; and how much noise to inject.

4.1.1 Noise Triggering Criteria

To induce message races in the example shown in Figure 4-(d) or (e), the ideal approach would be to delay message 1, but not message 2, as illustrated in Figure 5-(a). In general, if we delay later messages in an unsafe communication routine while not delaying earlier messages in the next unsafe routine, we can overlap two unsafe communication routines, thereby, inducing message races Figure 5-(b).

To implement such behavior, each MPI process manages a *virtual* buffer queue (VBQ) at the user level. NINJA regards MPI messages as a sequence of fixed-size chunks, i.e., packets, which are all funneled thought the VBQ of the MPI process. If the number of packets in the VBQ exceeds the configurable *VBQ threshold* (N_s), then NINJA injects a delay to all of the subsequent sends until this congestion condition is cleared. Since the buffer queue is *virtually* managed by NINJA itself, NINJA does not actually buffer the packets, but instead only keeps track of the number of packets that are expected to be in the VBQ and triggers delays as necessary.

4.1.2 Noise Amount

The second factor is the amount of each delay that should be injected. When the number of packets exceeds the threshold, NINJA computes how long the subsequent messages should wait until the VBQ is sufficiently freed up below the threshold, N_s.

More precisely, when sending an MPI message, which will be packetized into N_m packets, with the length and threshold of VBQ being configured to be N_l and N_s respectively, NINJA blocks the issuing of the send operations until N_m packets fit into the VBQ under the VBQ threshold, i.e., until $N_m + (N_l - N_s)$ packets are transmitted, as shown in Figure 6. Finally, we estimate the delayed time it takes to transmit $N = N_m + (N_l - N_s)$ packets, D, which is given

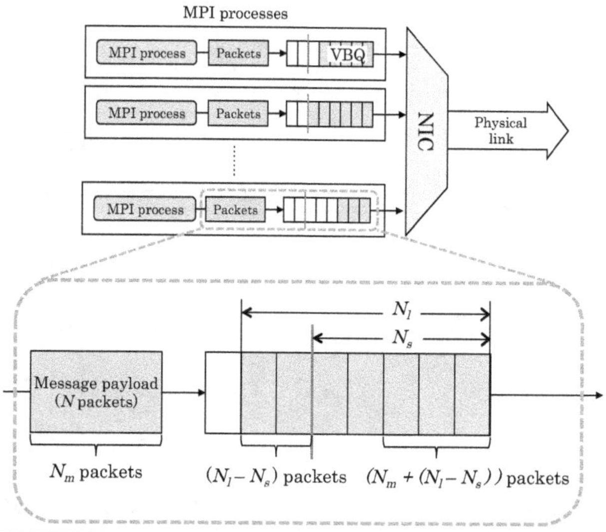

Figure 6. To enqueue all N_m packets of the message in the VBQ, N_m and $N_l - N_s$ packets must be dequeued and transmitted.

by:

$$D = \left\{ \sum_{i=1}^{N} (P_s[i]/B + C) \right\} \times S_p \tag{1}$$

where $P_s[i]$ and B are the size of the i-th packet (the 1st packet being at the head of the VBQ) and network bandwidth respectively, and S_p denotes the noise scaling factor.

This algorithm is also based on our observation that the more the system is congested and the more noisy the network, the more unintended message matchings occur (detailed results are in Figure 11 and 12). Actually, this queue model described in Section 4.1.2 and 4.1.1 is similar to general network flow controls [4, 11]: when a destination buffer do not have enough space, the congestion control engine suspends packet transmission until enough buffer space is freed up to avoid packet losses. Therefore, one can emulate more noisy environment by delaying more messages with lower VBQ threshold, N_s, and by delaying messages longer by higher noise scale factor, S_p. By using the NINJA's system-centric model, users can observe an unintended message matching more frequently than ones without using NINJA.

4.2 Application-Centric Noise-Injection Mode

The system-centric mode is useful to manifest an unintended message matching problem while minimizing overhead to the application. However, this mode cannot guarantee that all pairs of unsafe communication routines will be overlapped. As described in Section 3.2, for example, the smaller the scale is, the longer the time between two unsafe communication routines, thereby making the *separation problem* worse. For a small scale at which message races have never been observed during production runs, our system-centric noise mode will still be unlikely to manifest the race problem.

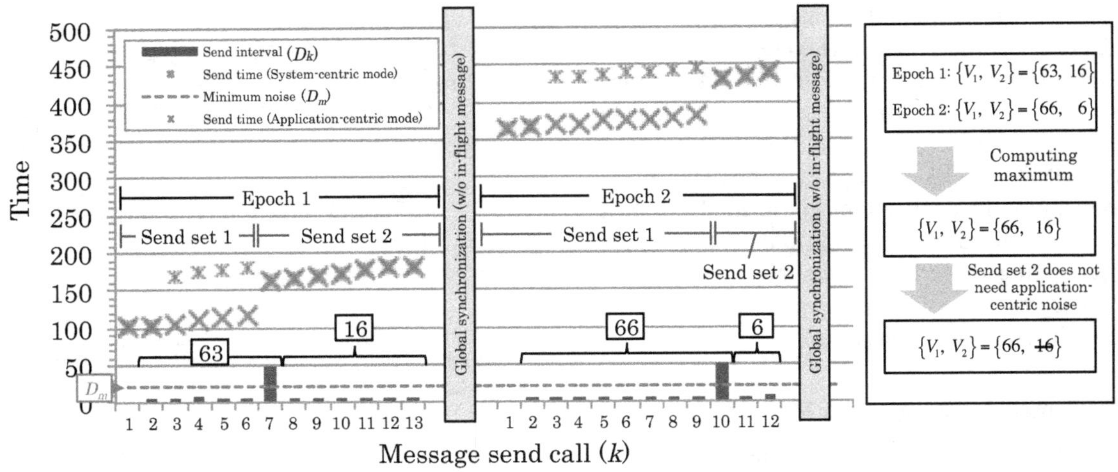

Figure 7. Example: Message send timestamps in system-centric (blue plots) and application-centric mode (red plots)

One can set a significantly large scale factor for S_p to enforce any pairs of unsafe communication routine to be overlapped. However, this configuration would introduce prohibitively large overhead to the application. In addition, debugging an application at a smaller scale is much more preferred than doing it at large scale. Thus, NINJA also provides an alternative way to enforce an overlapping between all pairs of unsafe communication routines.

4.2.1 Enforcing Message Races

To enforce an overlapping, NINJA provides an application-centric mode that uses knowledge about the application's own communication patterns even under a debugging tool's control. During a run in system-centric mode, NINJA traces and analyzes the time intervals between successive message sends, detects unsafe communications violating both C_{msgid} and C_{sync}, and finally dumps the analysis data at the end of execution (if this run in system-centric mode does not hang nor crash due to message races). During successive runs in application-centric mode, NINJA then loads the analysis data and uses this information to inject appropriate amounts of noise to enforce the overlapping of each detected unsafe communication routine.

More specifically, NINJA keeps track of injected *minimum noise* (D_m) during the system-centric mode in its the analysis file. If the time interval between two consecutive sends is larger than D_m, NINJA regards the rest of the message sends (before the next large interval is detected) as the next distinct communication routine. In Figure 7, for example, NINJA regards Send sets 1 and 2 each as a distinct communication routine and also deems that message races have not occurred between Send set 1 and 2. Because the time between Send set 1 and 2 is larger than D_m, it's not guaranteed that Send set 1 and 2 were overlapped during the run in system-centric mode.

After detecting the distinct Send sets, NINJA computes how long messages in Send set 1 should be delayed to be able to be overlapped with Send set 2 (application-centric noise amount). More precisely, NINJA computes the amount of application-centric noise for Send set i, V_i, as follows:

$$V_i = \left\{ \sum_{k=m_i}^{m_{i+1}-1} D_k \right\} \times S_a \tag{2}$$

where D_k is the time interval between send $k+1$ and k, and m_i denotes the first message of Send set i, and finally S_a denotes an application-centric noise scaling factor. NINJA computes V_i at the end of each *epoch*. An epoch consists of a set of routines detected by our *epoch detection* algorithm. Messages sent in an epoch are solely received within the same epoch. As such, they cannot cross the epoch boundary and be received within the next epoch. Figure 7 shows an example where V_1 and V_2 are computed as 63 and 16 respectively in Epoch 1, and 66 and 6 in Epoch 2.

For the epoch detection, each MPI process counts the number of sends and receives. Whenever a global synchronization is called by the application, all of the processes call `MPI_Allreduce` to compute the global sum of the number of sends and receives. If the send count is equal to the receive count, NINJA infers that the application progressed into the next epoch because the global synchronization holds the condition C_{sync}, i.e., synchronization without in-flight messages. Whenever an epoch ends, NINJA updates V_i if new V_i is larger than old V_i to compute the maximum. By updating the maximum of V_i, NINJA ensures that it enforces an overlapping between Send set i and $i+1$ with arbitrary i in every epoch. In Figure 7, V_1 and V_2 become 66 and 16 at the end of Epoch 1.

We note that NINJA does not inject application-centric noise to the last Send set in each epoch, to avoid unnecessary noise injection: Message races will never occur between two

```
10:  int MPI_Isend (…) {
11:    if (is_delayed) {
12:      PMPI_Send_init(…);
13:      /* Enqueue request for Send thread
14:         with timer t_s */
15:    } else {
16:      PMPI_Isend(…);
17:    }
18:  }
 :
30:  int MPI_Wait (…) {
31:    while (!flag) MPI_Test(…);
32:  }
 :
50:  int MPI_Collective (…) {
51:    PMPI_Icollective(…, &reqest);
52:    MPI_Wait(&request, …);
53:  }
```

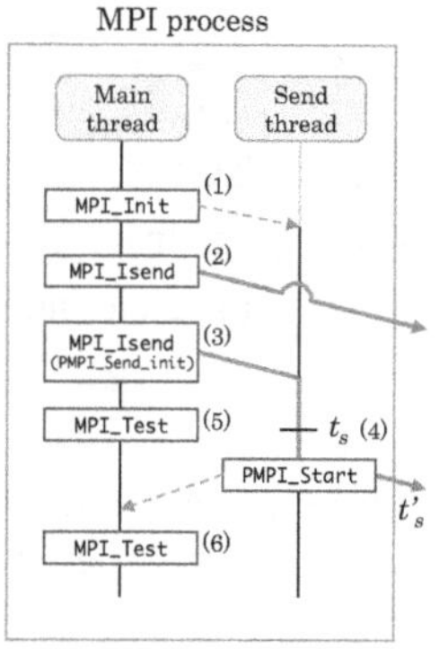

Figure 8. NINJA implementation

Send sets separated by a global synchronization. Figure 7 shows the example where NINJA injects application-centric noise by 66 time units to only Send set 1 when the VBQ gets congested at the third message. Because an application may have multiple unsafe communication routines, NINJA separately computes V_i for each message ID, i.e., a pair of tag and communicator. In addition, since each process independently computes application-centric noise, computing the application-centric noise amount minimally affects the application's scalability.

The analysis file also includes a list of message IDs violating both C_{msgid} and C_{sync}, and can be used for validating correctness of MPI programs.

5. Implementation

NINJA is implemented on top of the PMPI profiling interface, and thus can inject noise into the target application without requiring any modification to its source. In the following, we describe the implementation details of NINJA.

5.1 Send-dedicated thread

To inject network noise, we use a send-dedicated thread, one per MPI process (shown in Figure 8). In `MPI_Init`, each MPI process spawns this send-dedicated thread (*send thread*) as shown in (1) in Figure 8. The send thread is the actual initiator of the send calls for all delayed messages. When the application thread calls `MPI_Isend`, the main thread checks whether this message should be delayed based on the VBQ threshold, N_s. If the VBQ does not reach the threshold, the application thread simply calls `PMPI_Isend` ((2) in Figure 8). Otherwise, the application thread calls `PMPI_Send_init`, computes the amount of delay for either system- or application-centric noise, and then requests the send thread to call `PMPI_Start` at a scheduled send time, t_s ((3) in Figure 8). Meanwhile, the send thread periodically checks the presence of a delayed send request. If the send thread finds any delayed send request whose scheduled send time (t_s) is smaller than the current time, the send thread calls `PMPI_Start` for this message. After that, when the application thread calls one of the matching functions (e.g., `MPI_Test`) before the send thread calls `MPI_Start`, NINJA returns `flag` = 0 ((5) in Figure 8). If the matching function call is after `MPI_Start`, NINJA simply calls `PMPI_Test` ((6) in Figure 8). However, in most of MPI implementations, if the message payload size is less than the *eager limit*, `MPI_Test` immediately returns `flag` = 1 before the message is delivered to the destination. To implement this behavior, if the message payload size is less than the eager limit, the application thread copies the message payload data to its buffer space on `MPI_Isend` and returns `flag` = 1 even before the send thread calls `PMPI_Start`.

MPI guarantees that if an MPI process sends two messages in succession to the same destination and the two messages match the same MPI receive at the destination MPI process, then two messages are ordered, *non-overtaking*. Our network noise injector also abides by the *non-overtaking* rule. MPI also ensures that point-to-point communications within a collective call do not race with other communications. Therefore, we do not inject network noise to MPI collective calls.

5.2 Modification to Blocking Operations

In NINJA, two threads (application and send threads) concurrently call MPI functions. Thus, NINJA requires the underlying MPI implementation to support `MPI_THREAD_SERIALIZED` or `MPI_THREAD_MULTIPLE`. In an `MPI_THREAD_SERIALIZED` mode, NINJA locks and unlocks a mutex before and after each PMPI function call.

However, a simplistic approach can cause a deadlock. For example, consider a condition:

- An application thread of MPI process A locks a mutex in order to call `PMPI_Wait` to wait for Message B from MPI process B;
- A send thread of MPI process A has a delayed send request (Message A);
- Message B is sent after MPI process B receives Message A.

Under this condition, a deadlock occurs because a mutex is acquired by the application thread of MPI process A and the send thread is unable to grab the mutex to send Message A.

To avoid a deadlock, we re-implemented the `MPI_Wait` call family (i.e., `MPI_Wait`, `MPI_Waitany`, `MPI_Waitsome` and `MPI_Waitall`) by using the corresponding `PMPI_Test` calls (i.e., `PMPI_Test`, `PMPI_Testall`, `PMPI_Testany` and `PMPI_Testsome`). For example, the application thread periodically locks and unlocks the mutex, and the send thread can eventually acquire the lock and send Message A (Line 30-32 in Figure 8). Similarly, we also re-implement blocking collective calls by using the corresponding non-blocking collective operations (Line 50-53 in Figure 8).

Table 1. Node specification of Cab and Catalyst

	Cab	Catalyst
Nodes	1,200 batch nodes	304 batch nodes
CPU	2.6 GHz Intel Xeon E5-2670 (16 cores per node)	2.4 GHz Intel Xeon E5-2695 v2 (24 cores per node)
Memory	32 GB	128 GB
HCA	InfiniBand QDR4X (QLogic)	InfiniBand QDR4X (QLogic) x2

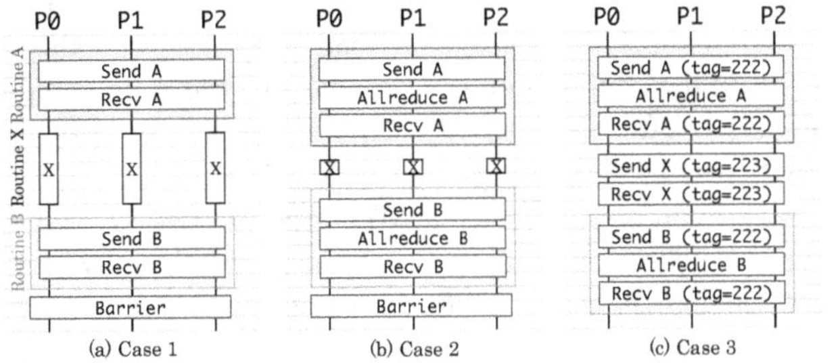

Figure 9. Case 1 and 2: Synthetic cases to capture common unintended message races. Case 3: Hypre communication pattern

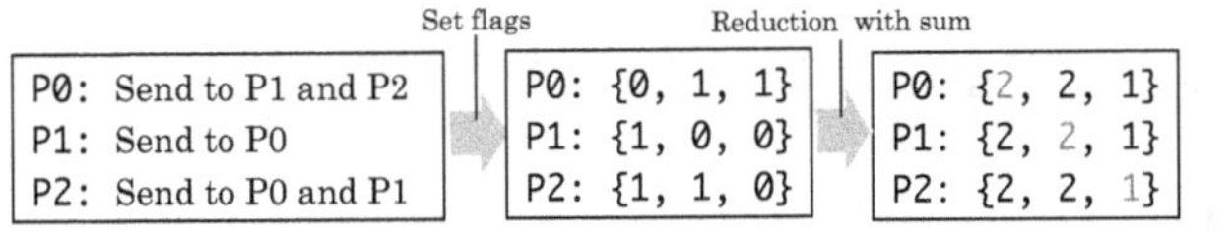

Figure 10. Typical communication patterns needed to determine the exact number of messages to receive at runtime

6. Evaluation

In this section, we present our evaluation results showing the effectiveness and performance overhead of our injection techniques. Our evaluation is conducted on two large systems sited at Lawrence Livermore National Laboratory (LLNL): Cab and Catalyst. The main differences between two systems are: 1) Cab is larger in terms of the number of compute nodes in the machine and 2) as a production system it is more heavily utilized with more users than Catalyst. In terms of the capabilities within each node, however, Catalyst contains a higher number of compute cores than Cab (24 versus 16), and one additional InfiniBand rail that is only used for system management purposes. Taken together, applications are more subject to network congestion when they run on Cab than on Catalyst. For all our evaluation, we used MVAPICH-2.1 as the underlying MPI implementation.

6.1 System-Centric Mode

The main purpose of the system-centric mode is to inject network noise to emulate a highly congested environment for the application. Even on a quiet network system, therefore, this mode can increase the manifestation rate of unintended message races. In contrast to the application-centric mode, the system-centric mode can achieve this without obtaining the application's messaging patterns.

6.1.1 Synthetic Benchmarks For Unintended Races

To evaluate the effectiveness we created two synthetic cases capturing common race conditions (Case 1 and 2), as shown in Figure 9.

In Case 1, each process first sends messages to a randomly selected destination process (`Send A`), receives the messages from the random senders (`Recv A`), and then performs a computation followed by the same random sends and receives, i.e., `Send B` and `Recv B`. Then, each process cycles through this communications and computations for the configurable number of iterations. In Case 2, each process performs the same random sends and receives as Case 1, but this time all processes are synchronized with `MPI_Allreduce` after the random sends. In fact, this captures a common communication pattern that can emerge when each process does not know exactly from which other process(es) the messages will be sent to it. In this case, after sending messages (`Send A`), each process fills in the send array by setting the index corresponding to each destination rank, and calls `MPI_Allreduce` with `MPI_SUM` to compute how many messages should be received. Then, each process calls wild-card receives with `MPI_ANY_SOURCE` (Figure 10). This case is created to evaluate the effectiveness of NINJA when the target application is being under a debugging tool's control and hence is subject to the *tool overhead problem* described in Section 3.3. Because processes are synchronized after `Send A`, the tool's overhead introduced at `Send A` can propagate across all of the processes. Unlike Cass 1, Case 2 can decrease the frequency of exposing unintended message races.

In the experiments for manifestation of message races, we evaluate the manifestation of message races at both small and large scales. However, we only show results at a small scale, 64 processes distributed across 4 compute nodes, because of the following reasons. First, the results are same between small and large scales. Second, if we use a higher number of processes, Routine A can become more load-imbalanced, and this can cause unintended message races between Routine A and B to occur more frequently at large scale. Message races at large scale is more easy to appear than ones at small scale. Third, when debugging unintended message races, it is highly desired to be able to observe the races at small scale, as debugging is much easier and more cost-effective. In summary, we desire to evaluate the effectiveness of NINJA at small scales in more difficult and challenging scenarios to NINJA. We use 3.14 GB/s, 0.25 μsec and 1 for B, C and S_p to emulate a congested environment in system-centric mode.

6.1.2 System-Centric (S-Centric) Mode

Figures 11 and 12 show the number of iterations executed until an incorrect match occurs due to unintended message races in Case 1 and 2, respectively (a message sent in Rou-

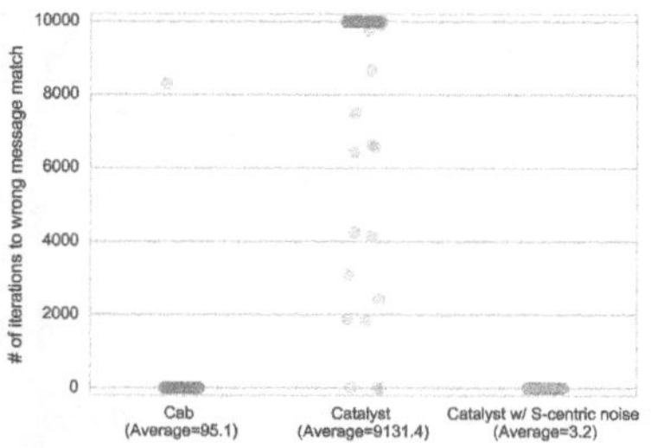

Figure 11. Case 1: # of iterations executed until an incorrect matching appears (Routine X = 1 msec computation; Max iteration = 10,000)

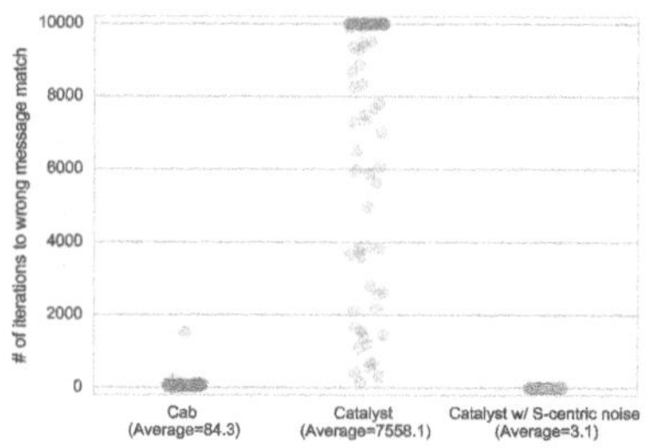

Figure 12. Case 2: # of iterations executed until an incorrect matching appears (Routine X does nothing; Max iteration = 10,000)

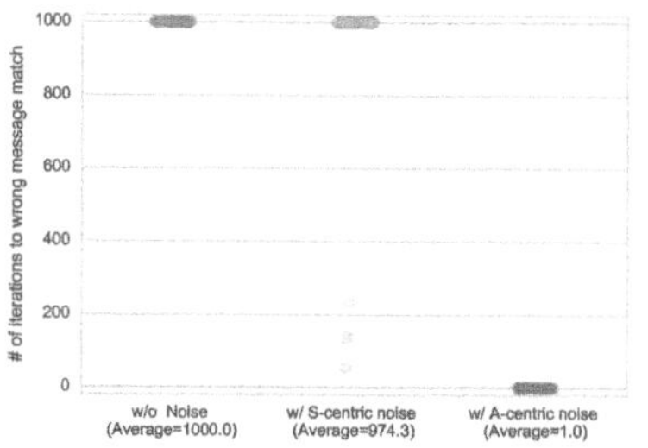

Figure 13. Case 2: # of iterations executed until an incorrect matching appears with 10 usec tool overhead in Cab (Routine X does nothing; Max iteration = 1,000)

tine B is received in Routine A). Here, we configure the maximum number of iterations to be 10,000.

Then, we run this benchmark 100 times and plot the iteration-count distributions as show in these figures. We add 1 msec computation in Routine X for Case 1 in order to emulate the phenomena described in Section 2.1, i.e., to create an scenario where unintended message races frequently manifest themselves in a congested network environment (Cab), but not in a quiet environment (Catalyst). As shown in the both figures, the incorrect message matching occurs more frequently in Cab while not appearing as easily in Catalyst. With NINJA in system-centric mode, however, we can frequently manifest the incorrect matching problem even on Catalyst with an iteration-count distribution similar to that of the experiments on Cab.

With NINJA, we also observe that the incorrect matching occurs in a few iterations. This is important because an HPC application can spend a large amount of time per iteration. The quicker the unintended message race becomes manifested, the more a programmer's productivity will increase. Our evaluation suggests that NINJA in system-centric mode not only can allow programmers to observe the bugs more frequently, but also more quickly, compared to the runs without it.

6.2 Application-Centric (A-Centric) Mode

In this evaluation, we first run our synthetic benchmarks in system-centric mode. For the cases where we cannot observe unintended message races, we use the application-centric mode by using an analysis file generated from the system-centric mode. We set the application-centric scaling factor, S_a to 1.2.

6.2.1 Overcoming Tool Overhead Problem

First, we evaluate how effectively application-centric noise can expose incorrect message matching when an amount of node-local noise akin to a debugging tool's overhead is introduced. We choose the overhead amount assuming that the programmer used `printf` statements to output necessary debug information after send, receive and matching functions complete. Thus, we add fixed 10 μsec overhead after these MPI function calls to Case 2.

Figure 13 shows the results on Cab. While message race bugs manifest themselves in the absence of tool overhead as shown in Figure 12, the same message race bugs are never captured due to the 10 μsec of tool overhead. Even in system-centric mode, the message race bugs rarely manifest themselves. However, in application-centric mode, we observe that NINJA can still frequently uncover the unintended message races. With application-centric noise, we also observe that the message race bugs typically occur at the first iteration in most of the runs. We also confirmed that the same results are achieved with even larger amounts of tool overheads: 100 μsec and 1 msec.

6.2.2 Noise Injection for Separation Problem

We also evaluate NINJA on the separation problem described in Section 3.2. For this evaluation, we add 1 msec computation in Routine X. Figure 14 shows the results. Similarly to Figure 13, the application-centric mode can efficiently uncover the message race bugs even if we introduce a far worse separation problem than the original condition. Because the application-centric mode enforces an overlapping between two unsafe communication routines by tailoring the delays to the application, this mode can even more frequently uncover the unintended message races within the application.

6.2.3 Real-World Bug in Hypre 2.10.1

Finally, we apply NINJA to a known bug in Hypre-2.10.1. Hypre is a library for solving sparse linear systems of equations for MPI applications. A non-deterministic message race bug exists in one solver that computes a sparse approximate inverse pre-conditioner. We use an example code of the solver, `ex5.c`, in the Hypre-2.10.1 package. Case 3 in Figure 9 depicts the two unsafe communication routines that are used in this solver based on Figure 3. Although this solver calls a global synchronization (`Allreduce A`) before receive calls (`Recv A`), an unintended message matching can

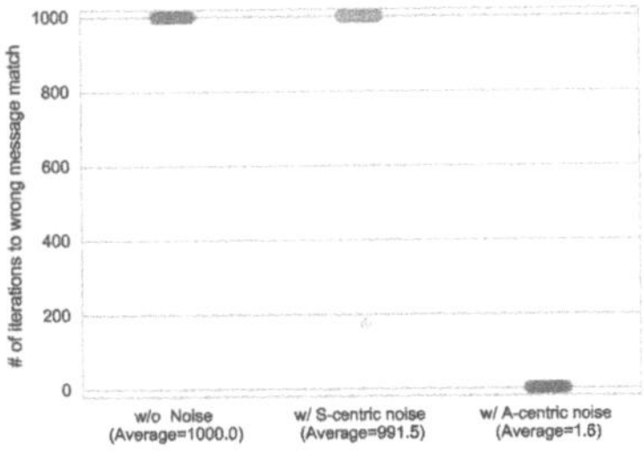

Figure 14. Case 2: # of iterations executed until an incorrect message matching occurs in Cab (Routine X = 1 msec computation; Max iteration = 1,000)

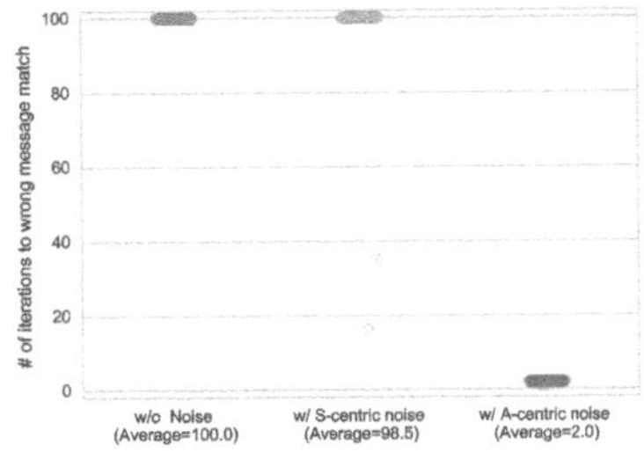

Figure 15. Case 3: # of iterations executed until an incorrect message matching appears (Max iteration = 100)

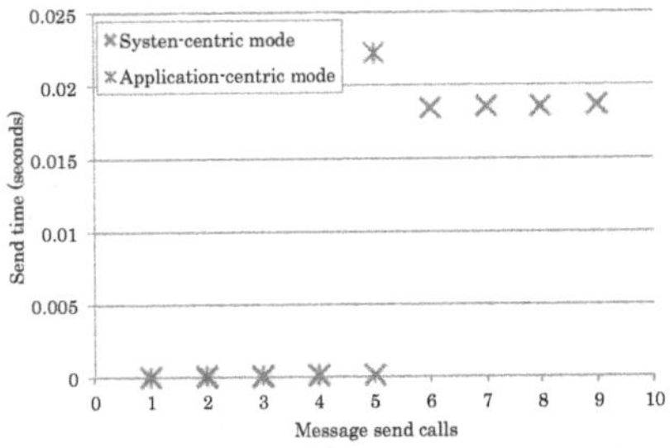

Figure 16. Case 3: Send time in system-centric vs. application-centric mode

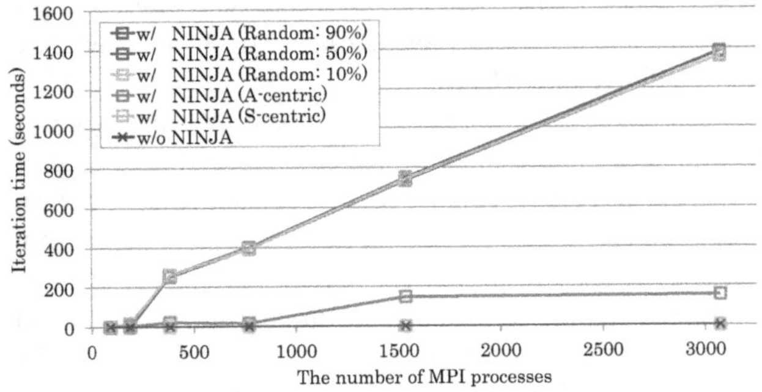

Figure 17. A single iteration time

still occur between Routine A and B because C_{sync} is not held. However, this race infrequently occurs in practice because there exist several communication and computations routines, significantly separating these two unsafe communication routines. Because of this pattern, the message race bugs in Hypre have not been fixed during the 14 years of its history. Figure 15 shows the results. Similarly to the results in Figure 13 and 14, NINJA can successfully uncover this race at small scale in application-centric mode.

Figure 16 shows the actual send time profile of one of the MPI processes, contrasting system- and application-centric modes. The first set of sends belongs to Routine A, and the second set of sends to Routine B. We normalize the send time of these modes such that the time stamp of the first send is 0. As shown in this figure, NINJA injects sufficient amounts of delay to overlap Routine A with B.

6.3 NINJA Performance Overhead

NINJA can expose unintended message races by injecting network noise. One could attempt to achieve the same objective by injecting large amounts of noise to randomly selected messages in order to overlap all pairs of unsafe communication routines. However, the naive random approach can introduce a large runtime overhead to applications with no clear notion of *target communication patterns*. In contrast, NINJA's targeted injection schemes do not incur high overheads.

Figure 17 shows the average iteration time of running the Hypre code with or without NINJA (Random, System-centric and Application-centric noise) as shown in Table 2. We can observe that a random noise injection scheme significantly impacts the code's running time. On the other hand, the application-centric mode injects noise to only unsafe communication routines with noise amount just good enough to expose a race. This limits the performance impact to the application. Further, the system-centric mode only emulates a congested network environment with very small network noise, and thus its overhead is even smaller to the point where it is negligible. Although the system-centric mode cannot provide a guarantee to overlap all pairs of unsafe communicating routines, this mode is useful if one wants to test a large number of codes with bare-minimum overhead for message races.

7. Related Work

Debugging non-deterministic bugs is a challenging task, since these bugs can manifest themselves in production runs, but may disappear in debugging runs. With trends towards asynchronous communications with wild-card receives, MPI applications are becoming increasingly complex and non-deterministic. Debugging tools are critical to observing, finding and fixing bugs, but most of the exiting debugging tools cannot cope well with unintended message races as they cannot help much if the bugs do not occur under their control.

MPI formal verifiers such as ISP [24] and DAMPI [25] explore all possible message-receive patterns so that the tools can eventually hit a target bug. However, these tools are not practical for large-scale applications because they need to run for a significantly large number of iterations to examine all possible message interleavings until a message race is hit. In contrast, NINJA prioritizes examining communication patterns for overlapping two unsafe communication routines

Table 2. NINJA noise trigger, noise amount and target message ID

	Random noise	System-centric	Application-centric
Noise trigger	90, 50, 10% of messages	Method described in Section 4.1.1	Method described in Section 4.1.1
Noise amount	Iteration time	Formula 1 (in Section 4.1.2)	Formula 2 (in Section 4.2.1)
Target matching ID	All	All	Only matching ID in unsafe communication routines (Section 4.2.1)

so that the unintended message races can manifest within a few iterations, which is a more practical solution for large-scale applications.

Record-and-replay is an attractive approach that can ease the efforts needed to debug non-deterministic bugs, as the tool can repeatedly reproduce incorrect message matching once it observes and records this misbehavior. Mainly, two common approaches, data-replay and order-replay, exist: Data-replay [2, 3, 17] records all the received messages including the message receive order and payloads. With data-replay, programmers can replay the buggy behavior with a single MPI process. An alternative approach is order-replay [14–16, 20]. Order-replay only records message-receive order. Although order-replay requires programmers to run the application at the identical number of process count for replay as the record run, the approach can significantly reduce tool overhead. However, both approaches can only deterministically replay incorrect message matching only when the unintended message races manifest themselves during the record phase. By contrast, NINJA can significantly help exposing these errors even with the recording overhead. Hence, NINJA complements existing record-and-replay approaches.

There are several data race detection techniques in shared-memory [6, 18, 21, 22]. The lockset algorithm in Eraser [21] and Active-testing [18] analyzes mutex-lock/unlock behaviors. State-of-the-art data-race detectors such as FastTrack [9] and ThreadSanitizer [22] exploit *happens-before* relations around the lock/unlock concept. However, techniques to analyze and control schedules to uncover unintended races are fundamentally different between the message-passing and shared-memory paradigms. Events in shared-memory, such as memory reads/writes, occur in a single-memory space, whereas message sends/receives occur in distributed-memory spaces. Because of these differences, data-race detection techniques cannot be directly applied to message races. Delay-bounded scheduling explores possible task/thread schedules until buggy behaviors are hit. However, simply delaying MPI processes using such a technique would have a similar effect as injecting node-local noise. Node-local noise does not always work as described in Section 3.3. Instead of node-local noise, NINJA employs a novel network noise injection technique to the message-passing paradigm. To the best of our knowledge, no data-race analysis technique delays memory accesses at the level of channel-to-memory itself.

There exists a strong body of work on the effects of system and network noise [1, 7, 8, 13, 23]. Ferreira et al. [8] developed a noise injection functionality at the OS level, and other works [1, 7, 23] inject noise at the user level. However, these approaches are only capable of injecting OS jitters, i.e., node-local system noise. To adequately delay message sends for our purposes, network noise is necessary. Hoefler et al. [13] investigated the impact of network noise to the application's *performance* by using a *simulator*. In contrast, we developed a *noise injection tool using PMPI* for *debugging* message race bugs. To the best of our knowledge, our work (the NINJA network-noise injection tool) is the first application of network noise to uncover correctness problems in MPI applications.

8. Conclusions

An ability to observe non-deterministic bugs is the critical prerequisite to finding and fixing them. To assist in this, we developed a novel noise injection technique (NINJA) that can uncover subtle and untended message races based on comprehensive analysis on non-deterministic MPI applications. NINJA injects network noise into the application execution in order to expose message race bugs more frequently and quickly during debugging runs. Our evaluation showed that NINJA is highly effective to expose bugs in representative synthetic benchmark codes as well as a real-world bug within Hypre, one of the mostly widely used sparse matrix solver libraries.

NINJA has a promising future to support programming models beyond MPI, which include tasking models. Because non-deterministic bugs often occurs as a function of specific timings of parallel interaction, we believe that our approach can be extended and generalized for other programming models. Indeed, that is a significant part of our future direction.

Acknowledgments

This work was performed under the auspices of the U.S. Department of Energy by LLNL under contract DE-AC52-07NA27344 (LLNL-CONF-699343).

References

[1] P. Beckman, K. Iskra, K. Yoshii, and S. Coghlan. The influence of operating systems on the performance of collective operations at extreme scale. In *Cluster Computing, 2006 IEEE International Conference on*, pages 1–12, Sept 2006. .

[2] A. Bouteiller, G. Bosilca, and J. Dongarra. Retrospect: Deterministic Replay of MPI Applications for Interactive Distributed Debugging. In F. Cappello, T. Herault, and J. Dongarra, editors, *Recent Advances in Parallel Virtual Machine*

and Message Passing Interface, volume 4757 of *Lecture Notes in Computer Science*, pages 297–306. Springer Berlin Heidelberg, 2007. ISBN 978-3-540-75415-2. . URL http://dx.doi.org/10.1007/978-3-540-75416-9_41.

[3] C. Clemencon, J. Fritscher, M. Meehan, and R. Ruhl. An Implementation of Race Detection and Deterministic Replay with MPI. In *EURO-PAR '95 Parallel Processing*, volume 966 of *Lecture Notes in Computer Science*, pages 155–166. Springer Berlin Heidelberg, 1995. ISBN 978-3-540-60247-7. . URL http://dx.doi.org/10.1007/BFb0020462.

[4] D. Comer. *Internetworking with TCP/IP: Principles, Protocols, and Architecture*. Prentice-Hall, Inc., Upper Saddle River, NJ, USA, 1988. ISBN 0-13-470154-2.

[5] CORAL. Collaboration of Oak Ridge, Argonne, and Livermore benchmark codes. https://asc.llnl.gov/CORAL-benchmarks.

[6] M. Emmi, S. Qadeer, and Z. Rakamarić. Delay-bounded scheduling. In *Proceedings of the 38th Annual ACM SIGPLAN-SIGACT Symposium on Principles of Programming Languages*, POPL '11, pages 411–422, New York, NY, USA, 2011. ACM. ISBN 978-1-4503-0490-0. . URL http://doi.acm.org/10.1145/1926385.1926432.

[7] C. Engelmann. Investigating operating system noise in extreme-scale high-performance computing systems using simulation. In *Proceedings of the http://www.iasted.org/conferences/home-795.html* 11th *IASTED International Conference on Parallel and Distributed Computing and Networks (PDCN) 2013*, Innsbruck, Austria, Feb. 11-13, 2013. http://www.actapress.comACTA Press, Calgary, AB, Canada. ISBN 978-0-88986-943-1. . URL http://www.christian-engelmann.info/publications/engelmann12investigating.pdf.

[8] K. B. Ferreira, P. Bridges, and R. Brightwell. Characterizing application sensitivity to os interference using kernel-level noise injection. In *High Performance Computing, Networking, Storage and Analysis, 2008. SC 2008. International Conference for*, pages 1–12, Nov 2008. .

[9] C. Flanagan and S. N. Freund. Fasttrack: Efficient and precise dynamic race detection. In *Proceedings of the 30th ACM SIGPLAN Conference on Programming Language Design and Implementation*, PLDI '09, pages 121–133, New York, NY, USA, 2009. ACM. ISBN 978-1-60558-392-1. . URL http://doi.acm.org/10.1145/1542476.1542490.

[10] M. P. Forum. MPI: A Message-Passing Interface Standard. Technical report, Knoxville, TN, USA, 1994. URL http://www.mpi-forum.org/.

[11] M. Gusat, D. Craddock, W. Denzel, T. Engbersen, N. Ni, G. Pfister, W. Rooney, and J. Duato. Congestion control in infiniband networks. In *High Performance Interconnects, 2005. Proceedings. 13th Symposium on*, pages 158–159, Aug 2005. .

[12] T. Hilbrich, J. Protze, M. Schulz, B. R. de Supinski, and M. S. Müller. Runtime error detection with must: Advances in deadlock detection. In *Proceedings of the International Conference on High Performance Computing, Networking, Storage and Analysis*, SC '12, pages 30:1–30:11, Los Alamitos, CA, USA, 2012. IEEE Computer Society Press. ISBN 978-1-4673-0804-5. URL http://dl.acm.org/citation.cfm?id=2388996.2389037.

[13] T. Hoefler, T. Schneider, and A. Lumsdaine. The impact of network noise at large-scale communication performance. In *Parallel Distributed Processing, 2009. IPDPS 2009. IEEE International Symposium on*, pages 1–8, May 2009. .

[14] J. C. d. Kergommeaux, M. Ronsse, and K. D. Bosschere. MPL*: Efficient Record/Play of Nondeterministic Features of Message Passing Libraries. In *Proceedings of the 6th European PVM/MPI Users' Group Meeting on Recent Advances in Parallel Virtual Machine and Message Passing Interface*, pages 141–148, London, UK, UK, 1999. Springer-Verlag. ISBN 3-540-66549-8. URL http://dl.acm.org/citation.cfm?id=648136.746462.

[15] D. Kranzlmüller and J. Volkert. NOPE: A Nondeterministic Program Evaluator. In P. Zinterhof, M. Vajteršic, and A. Uhl, editors, *Parallel Computation*, volume 1557 of *Lecture Notes in Computer Science*, pages 490–499. Springer Berlin Heidelberg, 1999. ISBN 978-3-540-65641-8. . URL http://dx.doi.org/10.1007/3-540-49164-3_47.

[16] D. Kranzlmüller, C. Schaubschläger, and J. Volkert. An Integrated Record & Replay Mechanism for Nondeterministic Message Passing Programs. In *Recent Advances in Parallel Virtual Machine and Message Passing Interface*, volume 2131 of *Lecture Notes in Computer Science*, pages 192–200. Springer Berlin Heidelberg, 2001. ISBN 978-3-540-42609-7. . URL http://dx.doi.org/10.1007/3-540-45417-9_28.

[17] R. H. B. Netzer and B. P. Miller. Optimal Tracing and Replay for Debugging Message-passing Parallel Programs. In *Proceedings of the 1992 ACM/IEEE Conference on Supercomputing*, Supercomputing '92, pages 502–511, Los Alamitos, CA, USA, 1992. IEEE Computer Society Press. ISBN 0-8186-2630-5. URL http://dl.acm.org/citation.cfm?id=147877.148058.

[18] C.-S. Park, K. Sen, P. Hargrove, and C. Iancu. Efficient data race detection for distributed memory parallel programs. In *Proceedings of 2011 International Conference for High Performance Computing, Networking, Storage and Analysis*, SC '11, pages 51:1–51:12, New York, NY, USA, 2011. ACM. ISBN 978-1-4503-0771-0. . URL http://doi.acm.org/10.1145/2063384.2063452.

[19] M.-Y. Park, S. J. Shim, Y.-K. Jun, and H.-R. Park. *MPIRace-Check: Detection of Message Races in MPI Programs*, pages 322–333. Springer Berlin Heidelberg, Berlin, Heidelberg, 2007. ISBN 978-3-540-72360-8. . URL http://dx.doi.org/10.1007/978-3-540-72360-8_28.

[20] K. Sato, D. H. Ahn, I. Laguna, G. L. Lee, and M. Schulz. Clock delta compression for scalable order-replay of non-deterministic parallel applications. In *Proceedings of the International Conference for High Performance Computing, Networking, Storage and Analysis*, SC '15, pages 62:1–62:12, New York, NY, USA, 2015. ACM. ISBN 978-1-4503-3723-6. . URL http://doi.acm.org/10.1145/2807591.2807642.

[21] S. Savage, M. Burrows, G. Nelson, P. Sobalvarro, and T. Anderson. Eraser: A dynamic data race detector for multi-

threaded programs. *ACM Trans. Comput. Syst.*, 15(4):391–411, Nov. 1997. ISSN 0734-2071. . URL `http://doi.acm.org/10.1145/265924.265927`.

[22] K. Serebryany and T. Iskhodzhanov. Threadsanitizer: Data race detection in practice. In *Proceedings of the Workshop on Binary Instrumentation and Applications*, WBIA '09, pages 62–71, New York, NY, USA, 2009. ACM. ISBN 978-1-60558-793-6. . URL `http://doi.acm.org/10.1145/1791194.1791203`.

[23] G. Shipman, P. M., Cormick, K. Pedretti, S. Olivier, K. B. Ferreira, R. Sankaran, S. Treichler, A. Aiken, and M. Bauer. Analysis of application sensitivity to system performance variability in a dynamic task based runtime. In *The Workshop on Runtime Systems for Extreme Scale Programming Models and Architectures*, 2015.

[24] A. Vo, S. Vakkalanka, M. DeLisi, G. Gopalakrishnan, R. M. Kirby, and R. Thakur. Formal verification of practical mpi programs. In *Proceedings of the 14th ACM SIGPLAN Symposium on Principles and Practice of Parallel Programming*, PPoPP '09, pages 261–270, New York, NY, USA, 2009. ACM. ISBN 978-1-60558-397-6. . URL `http://doi.acm.org/10.1145/1504176.1504214`.

[25] A. Vo, S. Aananthakrishnan, G. Gopalakrishnan, B. R. d. Supinski, M. Schulz, and G. Bronevetsky. A scalable and distributed dynamic formal verifier for mpi programs. In *Proceedings of the 2010 ACM/IEEE International Conference for High Performance Computing, Networking, Storage and Analysis*, SC '10, pages 1–10, Washington, DC, USA, 2010. IEEE Computer Society. ISBN 978-1-4244-7559-9. . URL `http://dx.doi.org/10.1109/SC.2010.7`.

[26] R. Xue, X. Liu, M. Wu, Z. Guo, W. Chen, W. Zheng, Z. Zhang, and G. Voelker. Mpiwiz: Subgroup reproducible replay of mpi applications. In *Proceedings of the 14th ACM SIGPLAN Symposium on Principles and Practice of Parallel Programming*, PPoPP '09, pages 251–260, New York, NY, USA, 2009. ACM. ISBN 978-1-60558-397-6. . URL `http://doi.acm.org/10.1145/1504176.1504213`.

Thread Data Sharing in Cache: Theory and Measurement

Hao Luo *
Google
Mountain View, CA

Pengcheng Li
University of Rochester
Rochester, NY

Chen Ding
University of Rochester
Rochester, NY

Abstract

On modern multi-core processors, independent workloads often interfere with each other by competing for shared cache space. However, for multi-threaded workloads, where a single copy of data can be accessed by multiple threads, the threads can cooperatively share cache. Because data sharing consolidates the collective working set of threads, the effective size of shared cache becomes larger than it would have been when data are not shared.

This paper presents a new theory of data sharing. It includes (1) a new metric called the *shared footprint* to mathematically compute the amount of data shared by any group of threads in any size cache, and (2) a linear-time algorithm to measure shared footprint by scanning the memory trace of a multi-threaded program. The paper presents the practical implementation and evaluates the new theory using 14 PARSEC and SPEC OMP benchmarks, including an example use of shared footprint in program optimization.

1. Introduction

Many programs spend most of the time accessing data, and most of these accesses happen in cache. In the case of a multi-threaded program, threads interact in cache. The interaction can produce opposite effects. The effect may be *collaborative*: if one thread loads a data item that is also needed by another thread, the latter thread can take the data from the cache directly. On the other hand, the effect may be *interfering*: if the fetched item is not used by other threads, the data consumes cache space and leaves less room for others to use. We may also call these two effects *constructive* and *destructive*. The distinction is whether the data is shared.

* The work was done when the author was a graduate student at University of Rochester.

PPoPP '17, Feb. 4–8, 2017, Austin, Texas, USA..

ACM 978-1-4503-4493-7/17/02... $15.00.
http://dx.doi.org/10.1145/3018743.3018759

Figure 1 exemplifies these effects. In this experiment, we test two programs from the PARSEC suite [9] and SPEC OMP [34]. We use a dual-socket machine, run each program first on both sockets and then on just one socket, and measure how the miss ratio and running time change. Changing from two sockets to one cuts the available space of last-level caches (LLCs) by half. The figure shows opposite effects on the two programs: `facesim` has little data sharing and loses performance from the reduction in available cache, but `ilbdc` has significant data sharing and actually benefits from using just one LLC.

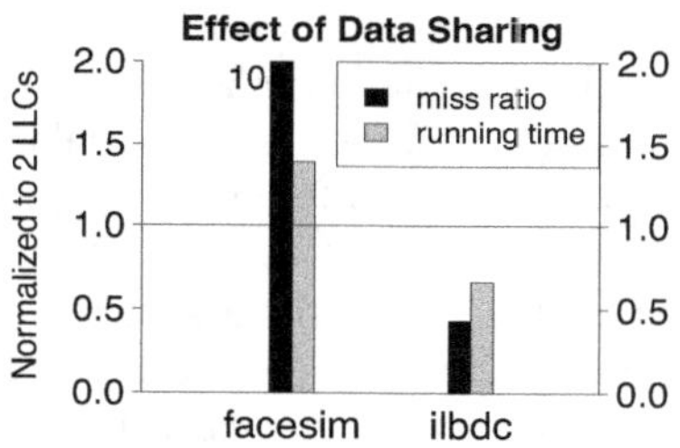

Figure 1: Thread data sharing in cache causes opposite effects when the size of the last level cache (LLC) is reduced by half: the miss ratio and running time are increased in `facesim` but decreased in `ilbdc`.

This paper presents a new theory of data sharing. In particular, the paper defines a new metric called *shared footprint*, formulates its mathematical properties, solves the problems of efficient measurement, and gives several uses in the analysis and optimization of data sharing in cache.

The shared footprint refers to the amount of memory that have been accessed by more than one threads within a time window. It has two important properties. First, it is *composable*. The data sharing by any group of threads can be computed from each thread's shared footprint. Second, it is *machine independent*. It is defined using the data access trace and does not depend on the cache size. Moreover, the miss ratio of any size cache can be computed from the shared footprint. Because of these two properties, a programmer can compute the miss ratio curve of any group of threads using shared footprint and can therefore mathematically derive the best thread grouping without exhaustive testing or repeated trials.

Data sharing in cache has long been studied since the invention of shared-memory processors and distributed shared memory (DSM). Early studies focus on common patterns of data sharing seen at the system or hardware level [4, 23]. They do not account for all manners of data sharing or the aggregate effect. Other studies use simulation, and the results are cache specific [10, 48]. To study multicore processors, several machine-independent models have been developed. The concurrent reuse distance (CRD) can derive the miss ratio of threaded code for all cache sizes [32, 39, 49, 50]. Other models such as StatStack [24] and the high-order theory of locality (HOTL) [28, 53] compute the miss ratio for independent co-run programs (that do not share data). The concurrent reuse distance models data sharing but is not composable. StatStack and HOTL are composable, only if there is no data sharing. CounterStack [47], Shards [45] and AET [29] are recent techniques to measure the miss ratio curve efficiently through sampling. However, they do not solve the problem of composing miss ratio curves when there is data sharing between threads. The shared footprint is the first composable model to handle data sharing.

The new theory has several limitations. First, the shared footprint is specific to thread scheduling. This is both a weakness, i.e. the sharing may change in another run, and also a strength, i.e. the sharing in all thread groups is captured for the same execution. It is like taking one group photo and producing a photo for every sub-group as if they were all taken at the same instant. Second, the miss ratio calculation of shared footprint assumes fully associative LRU cache. The effect of cache associativity and non-LRU replacement can often be estimated using reuse distance, which we can compute using shared footprint (Section 2.4). In addition, the calculation assumes a single-level, shared cache and does not consider the effect of a cache hierarchy or coherence between multiple caches. Finally, even knowing the exact miss ratio does not mean knowing the performance. The latter depends on many other factors, e.g. prefetching. We will evaluate the effect on performance and demonstrate the benefits of machine independence (Section 5)

The main contributions of the paper are as follows:

- Formal definitions and properties of the shared footprint including the miss ratio prediction for all thread groups in cache of any size in Section 2
- A one-pass algorithm to measure the shared footprint and its efficient implementation in Section 3
- Evaluation of the efficiency and accuracy of the shared footprint using 8 PARSEC [9] and 6 SPEC OMP benchmarks [34] in Section 4
- Demonstration in optimizing thread placement and quantifying constructive and destructive thread interaction in Section 5

2. Shared Footprint Theory

We first formalize the new metric shared footprint and then discuss the conversion between shared footprint and miss ratio.

2.1 Data Sharing Spectrum

Two parameters can be used to describe data sharing in cache: the number of sharers and the cache size. Figure 2 shows a description of data sharing of a multi-threaded benchmark, *dedup* [8]. For each cache size, it shows what portion of the cache is shared by how many threads, averaged over the entire execution. Across cache sizes, it shows how the sharing changes as the cache size increases. If we consider the cache of an infinite size, the sharing would be measured for the whole execution. The *cache sharing spectrogram* of Figure 2 shows that in finite size cache (up to 32MB), most data is either not shared or shared by no more than two threads, even if the benchmark uses 8 threads to process data [9].

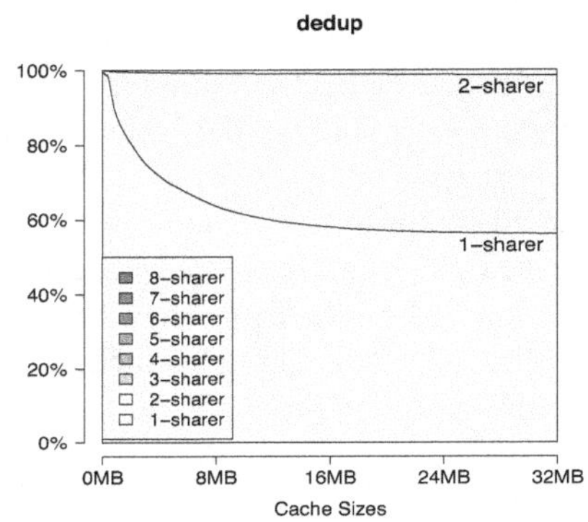

Figure 2: Cache data sharing of *dedup* by different numbers of threads for different cache sizes, shown by a spectrogram.

2.2 Quantify Data Sharing in Timescales

During multi-threaded program's execution, we assume the memory references of each thread can be timed and ordered by a general clock. The clock can be CPU cycles, or a counter of memory references. The referred memory addresses (at a granularity of cache line) ordered by this clock form a *memory trace*. We call a time range in the memory trace a *window*. The quantity of shared data depends on the window in consideration. Longer windows are likely to contain more shared data than shorter windows.

The metric, *shared footprint*, measures *the number of distinct data accessed by more than one thread within a given window*. For instance, in window W_1 of Figure 3, there is only one datum, a, accessed by more than one threads, therefore the shared footprint of this window is 1. Shared footprint can be further parameterized by data's sharing degree. The amount of data accessed by k or more threads ($k \geq 1$) is called k+ *sharers footprint*.

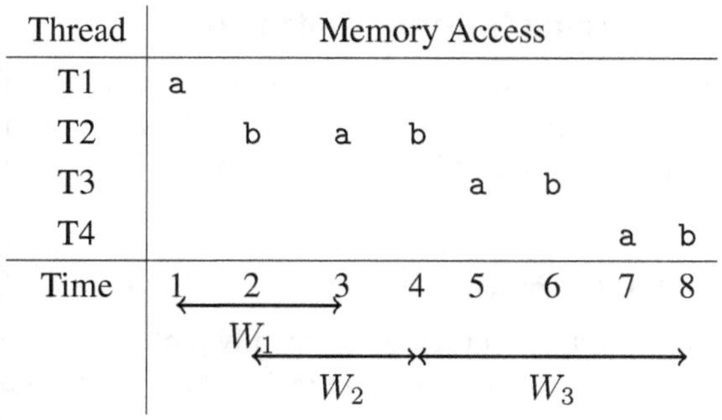

Figure 3: An example multi-threaded execution trace

$sfp_{k+}(l)$	l=0	l=1	l=2	l=3	l=4	l=5	l=6	l=7	l=8
k=1	0	1	2	2	2	2	2	2	2
k=2	0	0	0	0.83	1.60	1.75	2	2	2
k=3	0	0	0	0	0	0.75	1.33	1.50	2
k=4	0	0	0	0	0	0	0	0.50	1

Table 1: $sfp_{k+}(l)$ of the example trace in Figure 3. For any trace, $sfp_{k+}(l)$ is non-decreasing in window length l and non-increasing in thread count k.

Figure 3 shows an example memory trace. Letters are used to represent data blocks. In window W_1, there is only one data block accessed by two threads, a, which contributes to the 2+ sharers footprint. In W_2, two data blocks, a and b, are accessed but not shared, therefore its shared footprint is 0. Similarly in W_3, the contribution is one data block to the 2+ sharers footprint, a, and o ne data block to the 3+ sharers footprint, b.

To represent the sharing throughout the entire execution, we use average shared footprint, which is the average of the shared footprints of all same-length windows. Throughout this paper, we focus on the average k+ sharers footprint, which is denoted as $sfp_{k+}(l)$, where l is window length. Table 1 summarizes all $sfp_{k+}(l)$ of Figure 3. It shows the data sharing in all time scales and of all sharing degrees. Take window length 3 as an example. There are 6 length-3 windows. In every window except W_2, there is exactly one data block accessed by two threads. The 2+ sharers footprint is therefore $\frac{1+0+1+1+1+1}{6} = 0.83$. Successive columns are for window lengths from 1 to 8. As the window lengthens, the footprint is monotone and non-decreasing. Successive rows are for sharer counts k from 1 to 4. As k increases, the footprint is also monotone and non-increasing.

2.3 The Shared Footprint

The shared footprint has following variations:

- ***k+ sharers footprint*** $sfp_{k+}(l)$: the average amount of data accessed by k or more threads in length-l windows, as defined in Section 2.2.
- ***k sharers footprint*** $sfp_k(l)$: the average amount of data accessed by *exactly* k threads in length-l windows, computed by $sfp_k(l) = sfp_{k+}(l) - sfp_{(k+1)+}(l)$.
- ***read-only shared footprint*** $sfp_{ro,k/k+}(l)$: the average amount of read-only data accessed by k or more threads.
- ***read-write shared footprint*** $sfp_{rw,k/k+}(l)$: the average amount of shared data with at least one thread writing to it, computed using the read-only shared footprint by $sfp_{rw,k/k+}(l) = sfp_{k/k+}(l) - sfp_{ro,k/k+}(l)$.
- ***thread-group footprint*** $sfp_g(l)$: the amount of data accessed by and only by the thread group g.

The thread-group footprint is a finer partition of the k sharers footprint. Let Ω be the set of all threads and g be a subset, $sfp_k(l) = \sum_{g \subseteq \Omega \text{ s.t. } |g|=k} sfp_g(l)$, for all $1 \leq k \leq |\Omega|$.

The shared footprint has two important properties:

Machine independence All variations of the shared footprint are defined entirely by the data access trace of a program and not specific to cache parameters. In comparison, the actual data sharing in cache changes with the cache size. The shared footprint is defined for all window length $l \geq 0$. We will show that all-length l allows us to compute the miss ratio of cache of all sizes, and the shared footprint can be measured once and reused on any machine regardless of its cache size.

Composability The shared footprint is *composable*. With different parameters, the shared footprint decomposes the working set of each execution window into disjoint subsets based on the pattern of sharing. For example in any execution window, each k sharers footprint contains a disjoint set of data for different k. The disjointness enables simple additive composition: the footprint of two sets of data is the arithmetic sum of the footprint of each set. Furthermore, the addition between the shared footprint preserves the window length l and hence its machine independence.

2.4 From Shared Footprint to Miss Ratio

From Shared Footprint to Footprint Xiang et al. introduced a metric, footprint, $fp(l)$, to denote the average amount of distinct data accessed in all windows of length l [21, 51, 52]. For a group of threads G, its footprint can be computed from the shared footprint as follows:

$$fp(l) = \sum_{g \subseteq G} sfp_g(l)$$

From Footprint to Miss Ratio The metric footprint can be converted to miss ratio. The conversion is the higher-order theory of locality (HOTL) developed by Xiang et al. [53] HOTL computes the miss ratio curve $mr(c)$, for all cache sizes $c \geq 0$, from the footprint $fp(l)$ as follows:

$$mr(c) = mr(fp(l)) = \frac{fp(l + \Delta l) - fp(l)}{\Delta l}$$

where Δl is a time increment. We take the smallest increment, $\Delta l = 1$, and compute the miss ratio as:

$$mr(c) = mr(fp(l)) = fp(l+1) - fp(l)$$

In other words, *the miss ratio function is the discrete derivative of the footprint function.* The derivative can be interpreted as a fractional miss, incurred every time we increase the window size by 1. The essence of this conversion by HOTL is to equate the average increase of working-set size, i.e. the fractional miss, with the increase of average working-set size, i.e. the footprint.

Consider as an example the sequence `abcdeffedcba`, which has 12 accesses to 6 data blocks. Table 2 shows three rows. The first row give the window length l from 0 to 3 and then to 11 and beyond. The second row gives the footprint $fp(l)$ from 0 to 6. These values are also cache sizes. At each size c, the converted miss ratio $mr(c)$ is the difference between two consecutive footprints, shown in the third row.

access trace: `abcdeffedcba`

l	**0**	**1**	**2**	**3**	...	**10**	**≥ 11**
$c = fp(l)$	0	1	1.9	2.8	...	5.6	6
$mr(c)$ (%)	100	91	89	76	...	33	0

Table 2: Conversion from timescale locality to cache locality: l is the window length, $fp(l)$ the footprint, c the cache size, and $mr(c)$ the miss ratio, computed by the HOTL equation $mr(c) = mr(fp(l)) = fp(l+1) - fp(l)$.

For the example, the conversion is fairly accurate. When the cache size is 0, the miss ratio is 100%. When the cache size is 1 and 1.9, the miss ratio is 91% and 89%. When the cache size increases to 2.8, the miss ratio drops to 76%. If we compute the miss ratio accurately, we have $mr(0) = 100\%, mr(1) = 92\%, mr(3) = 75\%$.

Set Associative and Non-LRU Cache HOTL shows that after the footprint is used to compute the miss ratio, the miss ratio can be used to compute the reuse distance as follows [53]:

$$P(rd = c) = mr(c-1) - mr(c)$$

From the reuse distance, prior techniques can be used to estimate the effect of cache associativity, including the early model by Smith which assumes uniform access to cache sets [27, 41] and recent extensions of per-set reuse distance by Nugteren et al. [36] and Sen and Wood [40] which handles the general access, uniform or not. In addition, Sen and Wood show techniques to model PLRU, RANDOM and NMRU policies [40]. The shared footprint may be calculated per cache set, although the extension is outside the scope of this paper.

3. Measuring Shared Footprint

In this section, we formalize a set of concepts to establish an important theorem which leads to an algorithm to measure shared footprint and its variations in one pass over the memory trace.

3.1 Counting Data Sharing in All Windows

Key Observations It is computationally prohibitive to enumerate all windows and measure their data sharing. The efficient solution we will present next is based on two high-level ideas. First, compared to counting window by window, it is easier to take the perspective of data and count the *contribution* of each datum to the average. Its contribution is the number of windows within which the datum is accessed (present). Second, compared to measuring the presence of data, it is easier to first measure the number of windows when a datum is not accessed (absent) and then obtain the presence count by subtracting the absence count from the total count.

Throughout the rest of this section, we denote the trace length as N and the set of all accessed data as D. The window ending at time i and j in the trace (excluding both endpoints) is denoted as (i, j). Let $W_d^k(l)$ be the number of length-l windows in which the datum d is accessed by at least k threads. The shared footprint can be computed by adding W_d^k from all data and dividing by the number of windows:

$$sfp_{k+}(l) = \frac{\sum_{d \in D} W_d^k(l)}{N - l + 1} \quad (1)$$

For datum, a window either has at least k sharers or has less than k sharers, therefore $sfp_{k+}(l)$ can equivalently be obtained by counting the windows with less than k sharers. To help count such windows, we select two types of special windows:

Definition For datum d, a window is a ***sub-k interval*** ($k > 0$) if (1) inside the window, d is accessed by $k-1$ threads, and (2) the window is maximal in that any window enclosing it must have k or more threads accessing d.

Excluding the windows ending at trace boundaries, for an interval to be sub-k, its both ends, i.e. at times i and j, must access d, and the accessing threads at i and j, t_i and t_j, must not access d inside the window.

Example 1. *In Figure 3, W_1 is sub-1 interval to* $\mathfrak{a}$ *and W_2 is sub-1 to* $\mathfrak{b}$. *W_3 a sub-2 interval.*

Lemma 3.1. *Let datum d be accessed by k or more threads in an execution. d has at most $k-1$ sharers in a window W if and only if W is nested in a sub-k interval of d.*

Proof Assume d has at most $k-1$ sharers in W. We can expand W as much as possible. When it stops, we have a sub-k interval covering W. On the other hand, by definition, any part of a sub-k interval has at most $k-1$ sharers. ∎

Another special type of windows is a sub-type of sub-k intervals called *switch* as follows:

Definition A sub-k interval (i, j) for datum d is called a ***sub-k switch*** $(k > 0)$ if the accesses to d at times i, j are by two different threads, i.e. $t_i \neq t_j$.

Example 2. *W_3 in Figure 3 is a sub-2 switch and W_1 is a sub-1 switch. But W_2 is not a switch.*

Two sub-k intervals may overlap. In Figure 3, window $(1, 5)$ and window $(3, 7)$ are sub-2, to datum a, and they overlap at $(3, 5)$. The next lemma proves that $(3, 5)$, as the overlap of two sub-k intervals, is a switch.

Lemma 3.2. *For datum d, a window is covered by n sub-k intervals if and only if it is covered by $n-1$ sub-$(k-1)$ switches.*

Proof

$\Rightarrow$: Suppose the n sub-k intervals that cover the window are (a_1, b_1), (a_2, b_2),...,(a_n, b_n) and $b_1 < b_2 < ... < b_n$. Because they are maximal, they can not nest each other. Therefore, $a_1 < a_2 < ... < a_n$. Since they all contain the window, we have $a_n < b_1$. We next show that (a_2, b_1), (a_3, b_2), ..., and (a_n, b_{n-1}) are $n-1$ sub-$(k-1)$ switches.

Without loss of generality, consider the sub-k interval (a_i, b_i). Thread t_{b_i} accesses d at the trailing end but not inside the interval. Thread $t_{a_{i+1}}$ accesses d inside the interval, so $t_{a_{i+1}} \neq t_{b_i}$.

Let a' be the leftmost position in the interval (a_i, b_i) such that (a', b_i) has exactly $k-2$ sharers for d. a' must exist and $a_i < a'$, since (a_i, b_i) already has $k-1$ sharers. Thread $t_{a'}$ accesses d at a' and must differ from any sharers in (a', b_i); otherwise, a' would not be the leftmost position.

We now prove that a' is a_{i+1} by contradiction. If the two are not the same, there are two cases with regard to their relative position:

- If $a_{i+1} < a'$, then (a_{i+1}, b_i) contains (a', b_i), and the two are not equal. (a', b_i) has $k-2$ sharers and $t_{a'}$ adds a new sharer. Since (a_{i+1}, b_{i+1}) is sub-k interval, $t_{a_{i+1}}$ differs from those $k-1$ sharers. In this case, the interval (a_i, b_i) would have k sharers, contradicting the assumption that it is a sub-k interval.

- If $a' < a_{i+1}$, then (a', b_i) contains (a_{i+1}, b_i), and the two are not equal. Since (a', b_i) contains $k-2$ sharers, we can expand it to the right to form a sub-k interval by including at least one position to include b_i. Since t_{b_i} differs from $t_{a'}$ and these $k-2$ sharers, the sub-k interval can be formed. This sub-k interval is not any of the (a_k, b_k), contradicting the fact that the window is covered by n sub-k intervals.

Therefore, a' is a_{i+1}. There are exactly $k-2$ sharers between a_{i+1} and b_i. Since $t_{a_{i+1}}$ must differ from t_{b_i}, (a_{i+1}, b_i) is a sub-$(k-1)$ switch.

$\Leftarrow$: Suppose that the $n-1$ sub-$(k-1)$ switches are (a_1, b_1), ..., (a_{n-1}, b_{n-1}). Because t_{a_j} differs from t_{b_j} and from every thread accessing d in (a_j, b_j), intervals (a_j, b_{j+1}) with $j = 1, ..., n-2$ are $n-2$ sub-k intervals. In addition, stretching (a_1, b_1) to the left to include a_1 and (a_{n-1}, b_{n-1}) to the right to include b_{n-1} yield two more and a total of n sub-k intervals covering the window. ∎

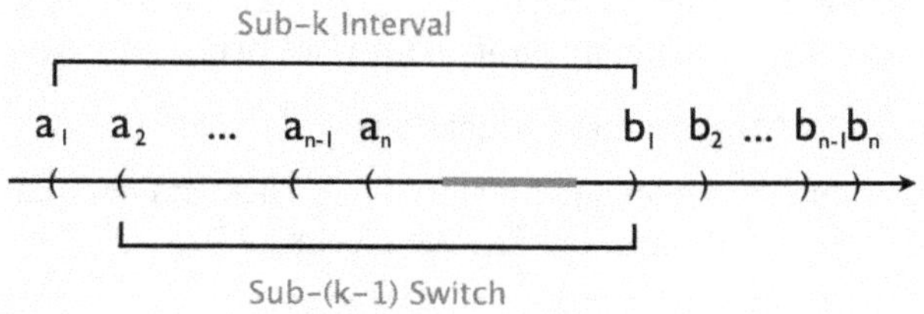

Figure 4: Illustration for the first part of the proof of Lemma 3.2, The red segment is the window of concern. Each (a_i, b_i) is a sub-k interval. The proof shows that (a_{i+1}, b_i) is a sub-$(k-1)$ switch.

For datum d, a sub-k interval of length L will cover exactly $L-l+1$ length-l windows, which have at most $k-1$ sharers. In Figure 3, for length 4, the sub-3 interval of a, (1,7), has $5-4+1=2$ length-4 windows, (2,5) and (3,6), in which a has at most 2 sharers. By Lemma 3.1, any window with at most k sharers must be covered by a sub-k interval. The windows not covered by any sub-k interval then must have k+ sharers. Hence counting k+ sharers footprint can be converted to accumulating all windows nested in all sub-k intervals. Due to the overlap of sub-k intervals, the same window may be overcounted. But by Lemma 3.2, the effect of overcounting can be canceled using sub-k switches.

Let $SI_k^d(l)$ and $SS_k^d(l)$ be the count of datum d's length-l sub-k intervals and sub-k switches respectively. Then we have the following result:

Theorem 3.3. *The total count of length-l windows with fewer than k sharers of d is*

$$\sum_{i=l}^{N} [SI_k^d(i) - SS_{k-1}^d(i)] \times (i-l+1)$$

Proof $\sum_{i=l}^{N}[SI_k^d(i) \times (i-l+1)]$ is the number of length-l windows with fewer than k sharers, but with overcounting. The overcounting is removed by subtracting $\sum_{i=l}^{N}[SS_{k-1}^d(i) \times (i-l+1)]$. The result counts the windows covered by a sub-k interval exactly once. By Lemma 3.1, it is the number of the length-l windows with less than k sharers. ∎

Let D_{k+} be the set of the data with k+ sharers and $|D_{k+}|$ be its cardinality. We denote $\sum_{d \in D_{k+}} SI_k^d(i)$, the cumulative sub-$k$ intervals for all data in D_{k+}, as $SI_k(i)$. Similarly

$\sum_{d\in D_{k+}} SS_k^d(i)$ is denoted as $SS_k(i)$. By Theorem 3.3 and Equation (1), the k+ sharers footprint is:

$$sfp_{k+}(l) = |D_{k+}| - \frac{\sum\limits_{d\in D_{k+}}\sum\limits_{i=l}^{N}[SI_k^d(i) - SS_{k-1}^d(i)](i-l+1)}{N-l+1}$$
$$= |D_{k+}| - \frac{\sum\limits_{i=l}^{N}[SI_k(i) - SS_{k-1}(i)](i-l+1)}{N-l+1} \qquad (2)$$

Algorithm 1 shows that all $|D_{k+}|$, $SI_k(i)$ and $SS_k(i)$ can be obtained by scanning through the trace once.

3.2 The Measurement Algorithm

Algorithm 1 profiles the memory trace once and computes the shared footprint using Equation 2 (line 27).

Algorithm 1 Algorithm of k+ sharers footprint

Require: A memory trace of length N
Ensure: None

1: **procedure** MEMORY_REFERENCE_CALLBACK(d, *tid*) ▷ This routine is called upon reading in a new element in the trace, d is the datum, *tid* is its accessing thread
2: $t_{now} \leftarrow$ current time
3: $k \leftarrow 1$
4: **for** e in d's list **do**
5: $SI_k[t_{now} - e.time] \leftarrow SI_k[t_{now} - e.time] + 1$
6: **if** *tid* equals to e.tid **then**
7: **break**
8: **end if**
9: $SS_k[t_{now} - e.time] \leftarrow SS_k[t_{now} - e.time] + 1$
10: $k \leftarrow k + 1$
11: **end for**
12: **if** *tid* is not found in d's list **then**
13: $SI_k[t_{now}] \leftarrow SI_k[t_{now}] + 1$
14: **end if**
15: promote *tid* and t_{now} to the list head
16: **end procedure**
17: **procedure** COMPLETION ▷ This routine is called after reading all elements of the trace
18: **for** every datum d having appeared in trace **do**
19: $k \leftarrow 1$
20: **for** every element e in d's list **do**
21: $SI_k[N - t_{now}] \leftarrow SI_k[N - t_{now}] + 1$
22: $|D_{k+}| \leftarrow |D_{k+}| + 1$
23: $k \leftarrow k + 1$
24: **end for**
25: **end for**
26: **end procedure**
27: $sfp_{k+}(l) = |D_{k+}| - \frac{\sum_{i=l}^{N}[SI_k(i) - SS_{k-1}(i)]\times(i-l+1)}{N-l+1}$

The algorithm maintains a sorted list for each datum d, which stores each thread's last access time to d. At every memory access, this list will be traversed (line 4-11). For each element e in the list, the difference between the current time t_{now} and the recorded time of the element $e.time$ is accumulated in the histograms SS and SI accordingly (line 5 and line 9). The routine *Completion* accumulates the maximal intervals ending at the trace boundary. (line 21).

Complexity The time complexity is $\mathcal{O}(NT+MT)$, where M is the total footprint, N is the trace length, and T is thread count. The space complexity is $\mathcal{O}(2NT + MT)$ if we compute the shared footprint for every window length. However, it is sufficient to maintain logarithmically many window lengths in practice by grouping the N window lengths in $\mathcal{O}(\log N)$ ranges. $SI_k(i)$ and $SS_k(i)$ now count the windows in the ith range. $i \times SI_k(i)$ and $i \times SS_k(i)$ are also profiled in $\mathcal{O}(\log N)$ ranges independent of $SI_k(i)$ and $SS_k(i)$. The space overhead is reduced to $\mathcal{O}(2T\log N + MT)$.

Measuring Thread-group Footirnt Thread-group footprint is measured similarly as k+ sharers footprint. Instead of profiling SS_k and SI_k based on the sharing degree, we can refine them into specific thread groups. By doing so, the space overhead becomes ($\mathcal{O}(2^T N)$), which is too expensive. To balance precision and cost, we choose to maintain per-group SS_k and SI_k for only a few window lengths, for example, all lengths of 2^i ($i > 12$). This choice compresses the profile and requires only $\mathcal{O}(2^T)$ space. To recover the full profile for all window lengths, we use interpolation to estimate between the selected lengths. Interpolation has a stable accuracy because shared footprint averages over all sliding windows and therefore produces smooth curve.

Measuring Read-only and Read-write Shared Footprint To measure the k+ sharers read-only footprint, we can profile the *read-only* sub-k intervals and switches, which exclude all the write accesses. These two types of windows have the same properties as given in the two lemmas in Section 3. By combining with Theorem 3.3, we can count the windows with fewer than k read-only sharers. Using Equation (2), we have the read-only k+ sharers footprint. By taking the difference between sfp_{k+} and its read-only sub-part, we have the read-write k+ sharers footprint.

3.3 Implementation Details

Clock Algorithm 1 requires reading the time at each memory reference (line 2). We could have used a globally synchronized software counter to denote time, but its cost would increase linearly with the number of threads. As an optimization, we use a loosely synchronized, per-core hardware time stamp counter (TSC) [30], which are available on most modern processors and sufficient for our analysis.

Sampling Bursty sampling has been effective in reducing the cost of profiling [3, 11, 17], including recent uses in measuring the footprint [28, 29, 53]. We use bursty sampling and see two benefits. The first is greater efficiency. In our experiments, some OpenMP benchmarks take several hours in a native parallel run, and the profiling on full trace would take too long to finish. Their parallel behavior is repetitive and could be captured by a few samples. The second is the more accurate miss ratio prediction for programs with phase behavior. In comparison, full-trace analysis measures the average of the entire trace and does not capture phase behavior. Sampling is effective in addressing this problem. We will evaluate sampling analysis in the next section.

4. Evaluation

We implemented Algorithm 1 using Intel's binary rewriting tool Pin [33]. The computed shared footprint is used to guide the optimization as discussed in Section 2.3. We evaluate shared footprint analysis on (1) its time/space overhead, (2) the sensitivity of its profiled results on different machines and (3) the accuracy of its miss ratio prediction.

4.1 Experimental Setup

To evaluate shared footprint analysis itself, we profile 8 pthread benchmarks from PARSEC [9]. To evaluate miss ratio prediction, another 6 OpenMP benchmarks from SPEC OMP 2012 [34] are included. The selected benchmarks represent a wide range of parallel programming patterns such as data-parallel (*blackscholes*), pipeline-style (*dedup*) and task-parallel (*facesim*). The OpenMP benchmarks are widely used for evaluation of OpenMP applications. We exclude some benchmarks because they 1) are not memory-intensive (*swaptions*); or 2) require too much memory that does not fit in our test machine (*mgrid331* and *ilbdc* on ref size); 3) or launch too many threads that our analysis can not handle for now (*x264*); or 4) fail to compile on our testbed (*bt331*).

Two different platforms were set up in the experiment. One was used for shared footprint collection and the other for performance testing. The machine for collection has 12 cores (Intel Xeon E5649 "Westmere") with each 6 sharing a 12MB LLC and the performance-test machine is featured with 8 cores (Intel Xeon E5520 "Nehalem"), with each 4 sharing an 8MB LLC.

4.2 Profiling Cost

Table 3 summarizes the time for measuring k+ sharers footprint and thread-group footprint. The baseline is the execution time on 8 threads without profiling shared footprint.

The slowdown of performing k+ sharers analysis is between 142x and 503x for 7 benchmarks and 747x for *streamcluster*. Thread-group analysis may be twice as long. The slowdown factors are larger than other tools in locality profiling. For example, the cost of reuse distance analysis is between 52x and 426x (153x average) for SPEC INT 2006 as reported in [53]. However, the previous work profiles sequential programs. In our experiment, the baseline is 8-threaded parallel execution time. The relative overhead would be much closer if we compared with the sequential running time.

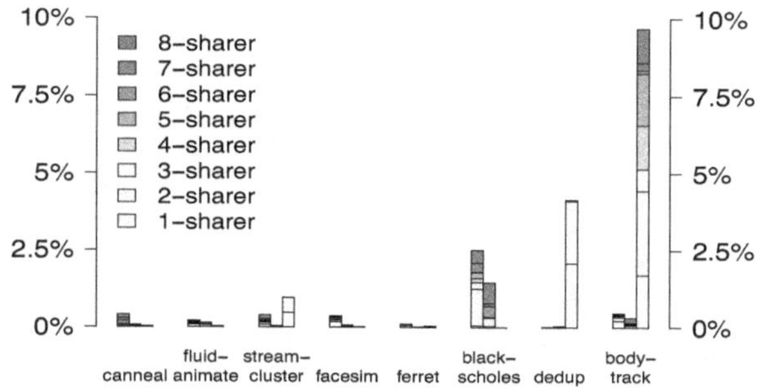

Figure 5: The difference between sharing spectrums due to different thread interleaving (on two different machines). The three bars for each benchmark represent three cache sizes (from left): 32KB, 256KB, and 8MB.

The overhead can be dramatically reduced by sampling. We periodically sample contiguous memory accesses at runtime. Each sampling phase terminates when 32MB memory has been profiled. Between two sampling phases is a fixed time interval. Its specific length depends on the desired sampling rate and its value ranges from 10^8 to 10^{10} memory accesses, as shown in Table 4. The overhead of sampling analysis can be contained in 250x except for *bodytrack*. Five benchmarks are within 100x. *Bodytrack* shows one limitation of our sampling approach: if the memory footprint of the application is small, it would take too long for one single sampling phase to terminate and the sampling will degenerate into full profiling.

4.3 Effect of Interleaving

A parallel execution has many sources of non-determinism due to hardware and OS scheduling. Pin's instrumentation and our analysis also perturb the parallel execution, and the effect has been shown to reduce the speed difference between threads in relative terms since all threads spend most time in the instrumentation code [32].

Our analysis forcefully serializes memory accesses from different threads whenever it is necessary. Such interleaving is one source of the non-determinism that our analysis introduces among others. To quantify how the interleaving affects the validity of results obtained from the analysis, we draw and compare the *cache sharing spectrums* on the two testbeds. An example cache sharing spectrum of the benchmark *dedup* has been given in Figure 2, which shows the portion of sharing of different degrees in all cache sizes.

Figure 5 shows the absolute difference between the spectrums on the two machines. Each bar is the Manhattan distance of the two spectrums. One previous conjecture was that the non-deterministic effect was more visible in short time periods than in long time periods, and more in small cache than in large cache. The spectrum results show that

benchmarks	input	native exec. time (sec.)	k+ sharers time (sec.)	k+ sharers slow-down	thread group time (sec.)	thread group slow-down
blackscholes	simlarge	0.460	146	317x	189	411x
bodytrack	simlarge	0.860	241	280x	650	755x
canneal	simlarge	0.404	57	142x	83	207x
dedup	simlarge	6.649	1730	260x	2372	356x
facesim	simlarge	1.974	828	419x	1263	639x
ferret	simlarge	2.100	750	357x	1067	508x
fluidanimate	simlarge	0.679	342	503x	595	876x
streamcluster	simlarge	1.627	1216	747x	2336	1435x

Table 3: Cost of measuring k-sharers and thread-group footprints using full-trace profiling

benchmarks	interval between two sampling phases (No. mem. accesses)	slow-down
blackscholes	10^{10}	19x
bodytrack	N/A	778x
canneal	2×10^8	14x
dedup	2×10^9	245x
facesim	2×10^9	114x
ferret	2×10^9	47x
fluidanimate	10^{10}	57x
streamcluster	10^{10}	10x

Table 4: Cost of measuring thread-group footprints using sampling

this intuitive view is not true. While the largest cache sees the smallest variation (under 0.3%) in 6 programs, the variation is largest (4% to 10%) in the other 2 programs.

Prior work collects sharing results using cache simulation. Bienia et al. found that because of different thread interleaving enforced by the simulator, the number of memory accesses varies by $\pm 4.7\%$, and the amount of sharing changes by $\pm 15.2\%$ in 4-way set associative 4MB cache [9]. Simulation is cache specific. Shared footprint, however, captures the effect of different interleaving on all cache sizes in particular in the exact impact on the miss ratio.

As we see in these results, data sharing in cache changes from program to program, cache size to cache size, execution to execution, and input to input (which we don't evaluate in this paper). Through the derived metric of sharing spectrum, shared footprint enables quantitative analysis of these variations.

4.4 Thread Group Composition

To evaluate the composition of shared footprint, we compare the thread-group footprint composed from the shared footprint (Section 2.4) against the directly measured footprint by running Xiang et al.'s algorithm [52]. The comparisons were done in two different executions, so the difference in the results may be partly due to the difference in trace interleaving. We examined all 4-thread groups in each of the benchmarks on 8-threaded runs. For the sake of clarity in plotting, we only plot two special 4-thread groups, the maximal one and the minimal one, in Figure 6. Between these two curves lies the other 68 groups' results.

The composition results are close to direct measurement. We found similar accuracy for other thread groups. The benefit of composition is significant: instead of measuring different 4-thread groups 70 times (once for each group), shared footprint measures the execution once and derives all 70 footprints. In fact, it derives the footprint for all thread groups. The benefit increases exponentially as we analyze programs with more threads.

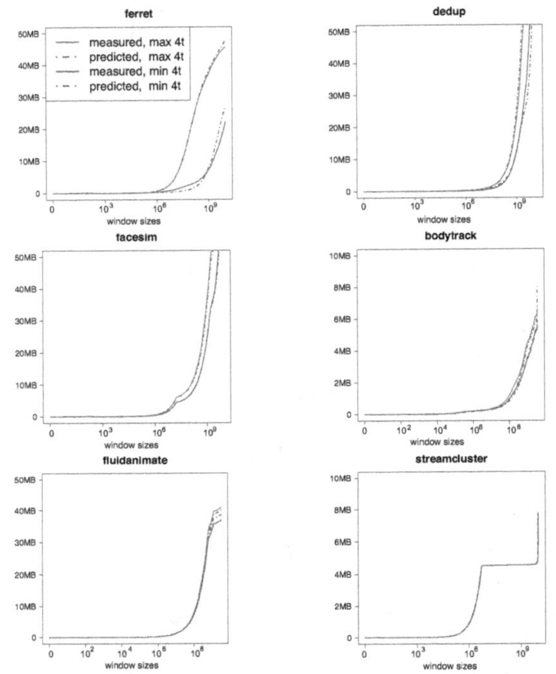

Figure 6: Footprint composition for all 4-thread groups. The x-axis is the window length in logarithmic scale and y-axis is the footprint. Only the two groups with the smallest and largest footprints are shown. The other 68 groups fall between the two extremes. *Canneal* and *blackscholes*, not shown here, are similar to *streamcluster*.

The benchmarks in Figure 6 are grouped horizontally for 3 types of parallelism: pipeline-parallel (*ferret* and *dedup*), task-parallel (*facesim* and *bodytrack*) and data-parallel (*fluidanimate* and *streamcluster*). We discovered that these three categories correspond to different degrees of thread symmetry. The threads' memory behavior is most asymmetrical among pipeline workloads but most symmetrical among data-parallel programs. Shared footprint is an effective way to check for thread symmetry or asymmetry.

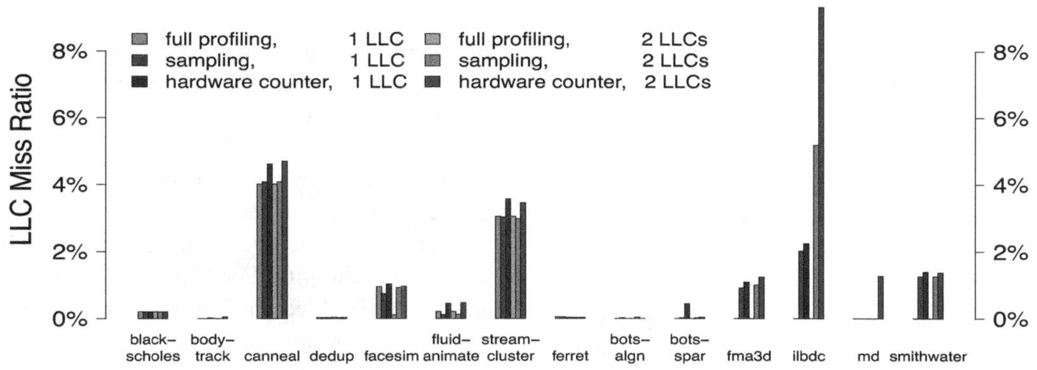

Figure 7: Comparison of the predicted and measured miss ratio for 14 programs using 1 and 2 LLCs. For each program, the first 3 bars (blue) are miss ratios for one LLC, while the next 3 bars (red) are miss ratios on two LLCs. Each LLC is 8MB. The full-trace analysis is used for the first 8 programs (up to *ferret*).

4.5 Miss Ratio Prediction

Shared footprint can be converted to the miss ratio curve as discussed in Section 2.4. We also compared the miss ratios predicted using shared footprint against the results read from hardware performance counters [30]. The following performance events were measured:

- `MEM_INST_RETIRED.LOADS`,
- `MEM_INST_RETIRED.STORES`
- `OFFCORE_RESPONSE_0.DATA_IN.L3_MISS`

Figure 7 shows the 8-thread executions of 14 benchmarks from PARSEC and SPEC OMP. For applications with symmetric threads, we show the miss ratio of a single thread. For applications with asymmetric threads, e.g. *ferret* and *dedup*, only the thread with heaviest workload is shown. We run the SPEC OMP benchmarks on the *ref* input size (except *ilbdc*, which we run *train* size) only with sampling.

The shared footprint predicts the miss ratio accurately except in 4 tests, *bots-spar* with 1 LLC, *md* with 2 LLCs and *fluidanimate* with 1 LLC and 2 LLCs. The full-trace shared footprint also has a large error in *facesim* at 2 LLCs, but the error is corrected by sampling.[1] The errors are unlikely due to footprint composition, which we have shown in Section 4.4 to be accurate. The likely cause is program phase behavior, as it is the case for *facesim*.

In predicting the miss ratio of sequential (SPEC 2006) programs, previous work has shown improvements over full-trace footprint analysis by different sampling techniques. While fixed-interval sampling did not show a significant improvement on a single cache size [53], adaptive bursty sampling (ABF) showed clear improvement for one program (*perlbench*) for a fixed range of cache sizes (up to 8MB) [28], and average eviction time (AET) sampling for four programs for all cache sizes [29]. Among the 16 tests (of the 8 parallel programs) where the full-trace analysis is used, sampling improves significantly only *facesim* at 2 LLCs. We leave it a future study whether the phase effect differs in parallel code than in sequential code and whether more advanced sampling can further improve the prediction accuracy.

[1] Note that *facesim* in Figure 1 is different because it was tested on 12MB LLCs, although the miss ratio on 8MB LLCs is similar, so is the performance.

5. Applications

This section shows two uses of the shared footprint: optimizing thread placement and quantifying constructive and destructive thread interaction.

5.1 Optimizing Thread-Core Mapping

It is beneficial to let the threads that share data to share cache. For example, a technique called faithful scheduling separately schedules threads from different applications [38]. Within the same application, it is still a difficult task to find the best way to group threads since the number of possible placements grows exponentially with the number of threads. On the other hand, optimization may significantly improve performance, especially for programs with asymmetric threads like *dedup*. *Dedup* is a 5-stage data-processing pipeline, where three stages are parallel and every stage shows dramatically different locality.

Figure 8 summarizes *dedup*'s throughput under different thread placements on a two-hyperthreading quad-core processor. The performances vary as high as 60%. The difference is largely due to the use of per-core L2 cache. Shared footprint analysis can quickly evaluate *dedup*'s cache performances for all placements. More specifically, we label each placement with its predicted four L2 cache miss ratios through shared footprint composition and then select

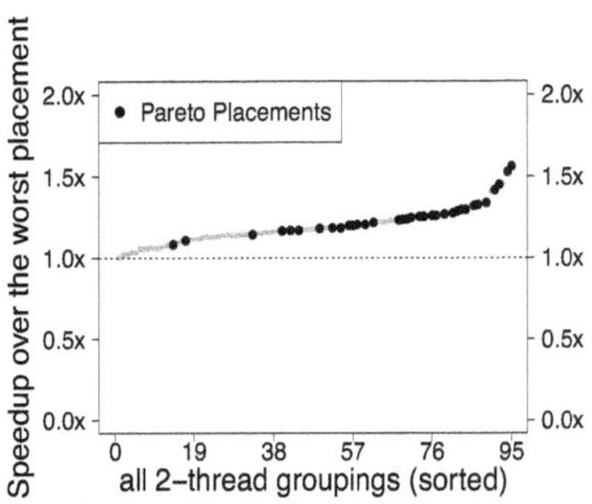

Figure 8: Performances of thread-core mappings, sorted by their speedup over the worst mapping. Shared footprint analysis identifies Pareto mappings without testing.

the *Pareto* placements for further evaluation [54]. In our scenario, a placement is Pareto if *no other placement can reduce the miss ratio in one cache without increasing it in the other cache*. We use shared footprint to find Pareto placements and show them as black solid dots in Figure 8. Only 1/3 placements are Pareto. We then tested them to find the optimal one. Compared to testing all mappings, this method is 37% faster.

5.2 Effective Cache Occupancy

In the shared cache, the thread interaction may be constructive and destructive. Under the assumption of single-level fully associative LRU cache, the shared footprint can precisely quantify these two types of interaction.

Let $\Omega = \{T_i\}$ be the set of threads sharing a fully associative LRU cache of size c. Let the size of program data be larger than c and the window length l_0 exist such that the total footprint is the cache size, $sfp_{1+}(l_0) = c$. For each thread T_i, we compute its *effective cache occupancy* $eco(T_i)$ by the amount of data T_i accesses in the total footprint at l_0, $sfp_{1+}(l_0)$. We may compute it in different ways based on the thread-group footprints and their composibility (Section 4.3). One way is to start with the amount of data only T_i accesses and then add in the amount of data T_i shares with every peer group. The equation is as follows:

$$eco(T_i, c) = sfp_{\{T_i\}}(l_0) + \sum_{g \subseteq (\Omega - T_i)} sfp_{g+T_i}(l_0)$$

where $sfp_{1+}(l_0) = c$, g is every peer group of threads of T_i, and $sfp_{g+T_i}(l_0)$ the average amount of data T_i shares with g in a window of length l_0. We may compute the total occupancy from the individual occupancy. Alternatively, it is simpler to use the k sharers footprints by taking each k sharers footprint and multiplying it with k:

$$eco(\Omega, c) = \sum_{k=1}^{|\Omega|} k\ sfp_k(l_0)$$

It is easy to prove $eco(\Omega, c) \geq c$, because $eco(\Omega, c) \geq \sum_{k=1}^{|\Omega|} sfp_k(l_0) = sfp_{1+}(l_0) = c$, i.e. every data in the total footprint $sfp_{1+}(l_0)$ is accessed by at least one thread, and any data shared by k threads is counted exactly k times. Earlier in Section 2.1, we use $sfp_k(l)$ as the sharing spectrum. In the spectrum, a vertical line at the cache size c shows the portions of data accessed by different number of threads. The portion used by k threads is counted k times in the total occupancy, which makes the occupancy greater than c.

West et al. modeled the cache occupancy in random replacement cache [46]. For LRU cache, Brock et al. showed through HOTL (Section 2.4) that for a set of independent programs that share the cache of size c (but do not share data), there exists of a cache partition for each program P_i, called the *natural cache partition (NCP)* $ncp(P_i, c)$, such that the miss ratio of P_i in the shared cache equals to the miss ratio of P_i in a private cache of size $ncp(P_i, c)$, and the total size of natural partitions is c, i.e. $\sum_i ncp(P_i, c) = c$ [12].

If threads do not share data, the effective cache occupancy is the same as the natural cache partition, i.e. $eco(T_i, c) = ncp(T_i, c)$. In the absence of data sharing, the total occupancy is $eco(\Omega, c) = c$.

The constructive thread interaction is quantified by the total occupancy, $eco(\Omega, c)$. The more data is shared, the greater this total is, and the better the threads uses the cache as a group.

The destructive thread interaction is shown by the individual occupancy, $eco(T_i, c)$. If a thread has a large working set but a much smaller individual occupancy, the thread has trouble keeping its data in cache because of the interference from other threads.

6. Related Work

We focus the discussion on the theory and techniques that model the performance of general rather than specific configurations of shared cache.

Reuse Distance without Data Sharing The earlier models were given by Suh et al. [42] for time-sharing systems and Chandra et al. [15] for multicore processors. Although different terminology was used, the common design is to compose the reuse distance of a program with the footprint of its peers, as explained by Xiang et al., who also showed that just mere reuse distance and (by inference) miss ratio are not composable [51]. Reuse distance is expensive to measure precisely [2, 37], although the cost can be reduced by approximation algorithms [47, 56], sampling [7, 24, 39, 55], static analysis [6, 14, 16], OS and hardware support [5, 13, 43, 57] and parallelization [18, 26, 35, 39]. Recent theories use reuse time. CAPS and StatStack are first models to analyze shared cache entirely from reuse time and have a linear-time complexity. In CAPS, the composition is based on distinct data blocks per cycle (DPC) [31]. In StatStack, the composition is done by first composing the private reuse time and then converting it to reuse distance [24].[2]

When used to analyze shared cache, these techniques must assume independent programs without data sharing. The reason is fundamental — the composition, whether between reuse distance and footprint or between reuse times, is invalid when there is data sharing.

Footprint without Data Sharing The study of memory sharing was pioneered by Denning and others through the development of the working set theory [19]. Thiebaut and Stone defined *footprint* as a program's data in cache [44]. Falsafi and Wood redefined it to mean data blocks accessed by a program, so the data in cache is its "projection" [25]. Early studies used footprint to model interference in time-shared cache [1, 25, 44]. The footprint was measured for a single window length [25, 44] or estimated for all lengths [15, 42], including the working set theory (property P2 in [20]) in 1972 and recently DPC in CAPS [31]. Xiang et al. gave a linear-time algorithm to precisely measure the footprint for all-length windows [52]. Their higher-order theory (HOTL) converts between the footprint and the miss ratio and reuse distance [53], so the footprint models are now as efficient as CAPS and StatStack.

Shared footprint solves the more difficult problem than Xiang et al. [52], because it measures not just the footprint but also the number of sharers. It subsumes the footprint of Xiang et al. as a sub-case, i.e. $fp(l) = sfp_{1+}(l)$. Furthermore, shared footprint gives the read-only and read-write footprint for sequential applications as it does for parallel code.

Concurrent Reuse Distance Early studies focus on common patterns of data sharing seen at the system/hardware level [4, 23]. They did not account for all manners of data sharing, nor for the aggregate effect. Other studies use simulation, and the results are cache specific [10, 48].

Recent solutions developed the concept of concurrent reuse distance [22, 32, 49, 50], also called multicore reuse distance [39]. Concurrent reuse distance gives the shared cache performance for all cache sizes. The miss-ratio prediction is accurate and not affected by phase behavior (unlike shared footprint). Data sharing is modeled by first measuring the amount of shared data between threads in the entire run and then inferring its effect in smaller windows through probabilistic models [22, 32]. For loop-based code, Wu and Yeung developed scaling models to predict the the concurrent and private reuse distances (CRD/PRD) profiles for different thread counts and data input sizes [49]. They used the model to study the scalability of multicore cache hierarchies, to separate the shared cache locality into interference-based and sharing-based components, and to construct a new profile type to model the effect of cluster caches [50].

[2] The naming in StatStack is different. Its reuse distance is our reuse time, and its (LRU) stack distance is our reuse distance.

Reuse distance considers the accesses from multiple threads together. It focuses data reuse rather than data sharing. It does not measure the number of sharers.

Shared Footprint Falsafi and Wood gave a simple model of sharing where all processes share the same footprint, measured for a single window-length [25]. Shared footprint in this paper measures it for all window-lengths. More importantly, it counts the number of threads accessing the same data, adding a new type of locality — the thread-count locality. Thread-count locality is necessary for thread-group composition. In addition, it is necessary to derive metrics of cache occupancy and cache sharing spectrum (Section 5.2). The former is important for understanding performance scaling on multicore, while the latter is important for cache analysis since it shows precisely how interleaving, program input, and other factors affect data sharing in cache.

Thread-count locality in this work extends both window- and access-based locality, for the first time making both types of metrics composable for multi-threaded code. We have shown this in composing thread-group footprint (Section 4.4) and thread-group miss ratio (Section 4.5), both are new and impossible with previous techniques.

7. Summary

We have defined shared footprint, a collection of metrics parameterized by the number of sharers, thread groups, access types, and by derivation, cache of all sizes. We have developed a linear-time algorithm to measure all these metrics in a single pass. The efficiency is further improved by parallelization and sampling. We have measured and analyzed data sharing in 14 multi-threaded applications from PARSEC and SPEC OMP, including sharing spectrum, effect of interleaving, and optimization of thread-core mapping to improve performance by up to 60%. Shared footprint adds the missing piece in the locality theory and augments previous theories of reuse distance and footprint to use thread count, thread composition and access-type analysis.

Acknowledgment

Michael Scott suggested the use of the hardware time stamp counter (Section 3.3), and a PPOPP reviewer measuring the destructive effect of thread cache sharing (Section 5.2). The authors also thank Jacob Brock, Dong Chen, Sandhya Dwarkardas, Michael Gage, Rahman Lavaee, Chencheng Ye, Peng Zhao and other PPOPP reviewers for their comments which have helped the development and the presentation of the paper. The research is supported in part by the National Science Foundation (Contract No. CCF-1629376, CNS-1319617, CCF-1116104), IBM CAS Faculty Fellowship, and a grant from Huawei. Any opinions, findings, and conclusions or recommendations expressed in this material are those of the author(s) and do not necessarily reflect the views of the funding organizations.

References

[1] Anant Agarwal, Mark Horowitz, and John L. Hennessy. An analytical cache model. *ACM Transactions on Computer Systems*, 7(2):184–215, 1989.

[2] George Almasi, Calin Cascaval, and David A. Padua. Calculating stack distances efficiently. In *Proceedings of the ACM SIGPLAN Workshop on Memory System Performance*, pages 37–43, Berlin, Germany, June 2002.

[3] Matthew Arnold and Barbara G. Ryder. A framework for reducing the cost of instrumented code. In *Proceedings of PLDI*, pages 168–179, Snowbird, Utah, June 2001.

[4] John K. Bennett, John B. Carter, and Willy Zwaenepoel. Adaptive software cache management for distributed shared memory architectures. In *Proceedings of ISCA*, pages 125–134, 1990.

[5] Erik Berg and Erik Hagersten. StatCache: A probabilistic approach to efficient and accurate data locality analysis. In *Proceedings of ISPASS*, pages 20–27, 2004.

[6] Kristof Beyls and Erik H. D'Hollander. Generating cache hints for improved program efficiency. *Journal of Systems Architecture*, 51(4):223–250, 2005.

[7] Kristof Beyls and Erik H. D'Hollander. Discovery of locality-improving refactoring by reuse path analysis. In *Proceedings of High Performance Computing and Communications. Springer. Lecture Notes in Computer Science*, volume 4208, pages 220–229, 2006.

[8] Christian Bienia. *Benchmarking Modern Multiprocessors*. PhD thesis, Princeton University, January 2011.

[9] Christian Bienia, Sanjeev Kumar, Jaswinder Pal Singh, and Kai Li. The PARSEC benchmark suite: characterization and architectural implications. In *Proceedings of PACT*, pages 72–81, 2008.

[10] Christian Bienia and Kai Li. Fidelity and scaling of the PARSEC benchmark inputs. In *Proceedings of the 2010 International Symposium on Workload Characterization*, December 2010.

[11] Michael D. Bond, Katherine E. Coons, and Kathryn S. McKinley. PACER: proportional detection of data races. In *Proceedings of PLDI*, pages 255–268, 2010.

[12] Jacob Brock, Chencheng Ye, Chen Ding, Yechen Li, Xiaolin Wang, and Yingwei Luo. Optimal cache partition-sharing. In *Proceedings of ICPP*, 2015.

[13] Calin Cascaval, Evelyn Duesterwald, Peter F. Sweeney, and Robert W. Wisniewski. Multiple page size modeling and optimization. In *Proceedings of PACT*, pages 339–349, 2005.

[14] Calin Cascaval and David A. Padua. Estimating cache misses and locality using stack distances. In *Proceedings of ICS*, pages 150–159, 2003.

[15] Dhruba Chandra, Fei Guo, Seongbeom Kim, and Yan Solihin. Predicting inter-thread cache contention on a chip multi-processor architecture. In *Proceedings of HPCA*, pages 340–351, 2005.

[16] Arun Chauhan and Chun-Yu Shei. Static reuse distances for locality-based optimizations in MATLAB. In *Proceedings of ICS*, pages 295–304, 2010.

[17] T. M. Chilimbi and M. Hirzel. Dynamic hot data stream prefetching for general-purpose programs. In *Proceedings of PLDI*, pages 199–209, 2002.

[18] Huimin Cui, Qing Yi, Jingling Xue, Lei Wang, Yang Yang, and Xiaobing Feng. A highly parallel reuse distance analysis algorithm on GPUs. In *Proceedings of IPDPS*, 2012.

[19] Peter J. Denning. Working sets past and present. *IEEE Transactions on Software Engineering*, SE-6(1), January 1980.

[20] Peter J. Denning and Stuart C. Schwartz. Properties of the working set model. *Communications of the ACM*, 15(3):191–198, 1972.

[21] Chen Ding and Trishul Chilimbi. All-window profiling of concurrent executions. In *Proceedings of PPoPP*, 2008. *Poster paper*.

[22] Chen Ding and Trishul Chilimbi. A composable model for analyzing locality of multi-threaded programs. Technical Report MSR-TR-2009-107, Microsoft Research, August 2009.

[23] Susan J. Eggers and Randy H. Katz. A characterization of sharing in parallel programs and its application to coherency protocol evaluation. In *Proceedings of ISCA*, pages 373–382, 1988.

[24] David Eklov, David Black-Schaffer, and Erik Hagersten. Fast modeling of shared caches in multicore systems. In *Proceedings of HiPEAC*, pages 147–157, 2011. *Best paper*.

[25] Babak Falsafi and David A. Wood. Modeling cost/performance of a parallel computer simulator. *ACM Transactions on Modeling and Computer Simulation*, 7(1):104–130, 1997.

[26] Saurabh Gupta, Ping Xiang, Yi Yang, and Huiyang Zhou. Locality principle revisited: A probability-based quantitative approach. In *Proceedings of IPDPS*, 2012.

[27] Mark D. Hill and Alan Jay Smith. Evaluating associativity in CPU caches. *IEEE Transactions on Computers*, 38(12):1612–1630, 1989.

[28] Xiameng Hu, Xiaolin Wang, Yechen Li, Yingwei Luo, Chen Ding, and Zhenlin Wang. Optimal program symbiosis in shared cache. In *Proceedings of CCGrid*, June 2015.

[29] Xiameng Hu, Xiaolin Wang, Lan Zhou, Yingwei Luo, Chen Ding, and Zhenlin Wang. Kinetic modeling of data eviction in cache. In *Proceedings of USENIX ATC*, pages 351–364, 2016.

[30] Intel Corporation. *Intel® 64 and IA-32 Architectures Software Developer's Manual*. Number 325462-051US. June 2014.

[31] Yunlian Jiang, Kai Tian, and Xipeng Shen. Combining locality analysis with online proactive job co-scheduling in chip multiprocessors. In *Proceedings of HiPEAC*, pages 201–215, 2010.

[32] Yunlian Jiang, Eddy Z. Zhang, Kai Tian, and Xipeng Shen. Is reuse distance applicable to data locality analysis on chip multiprocessors? In *Proceedings of CC*, pages 264–282, 2010.

[33] Chi-Keung Luk, Robert S. Cohn, Robert Muth, Harish Patil, Artur Klauser, P. Geoffrey Lowney, Steven Wallace, Vijay Janapa Reddi, and Kim M. Hazelwood. Pin: building customized program analysis tools with dynamic instrumentation. In *Proceedings of PLDI*, pages 190–200, 2005.

[34] Matthias S. Müller, John Baron, William C. Brantley, Huiyu Feng, Daniel Hackenberg, Robert Henschel, Gabriele Jost, Daniel Molka, Chris Parrott, Joe Robichaux, Pavel Shelepugin, Matthijs van Waveren, Brian Whitney, and Kalyan Kumaran. SPEC OMP2012 – an application benchmark suite for parallel systems using OpenMP. In *Proceedings of the International Workshop on OpenMP*, pages 223–236, Berlin, Heidelberg, 2012. Springer-Verlag.

[35] Qingpeng Niu, James Dinan, Qingda Lu, and P. Sadayappan. PARDA: A fast parallel reuse distance analysis algorithm. In *Proceedings of IPDPS*, 2012.

[36] Cedric Nugteren, Gert-Jan van den Braak, Henk Corporaal, and Henri E. Bal. A detailed GPU cache model based on reuse distance theory. In *Proceedings of HPCA*, 2014.

[37] F. Olken. Efficient methods for calculating the success function of fixed space replacement policies. Technical Report LBL-12370, Lawrence Berkeley Laboratory, 1981.

[38] Kishore Kumar Pusukuri, Rajiv Gupta, and Laxmi N. Bhuyan. No more backstabbing... a faithful scheduling policy for multithreaded programs. In *Proceedings of PACT*, pages 12–21, 2011.

[39] Derek L. Schuff, Milind Kulkarni, and Vijay S. Pai. Accelerating multicore reuse distance analysis with sampling and parallelization. In *Proceedings of PACT*, pages 53–64, 2010.

[40] Rathijit Sen and David A. Wood. Reuse-based online models for caches. In *Proceedings of SIGMETRICS*, pages 279–292, 2013.

[41] A. J. Smith. On the effectiveness of set associative page mapping and its applications in main memory management. In *Proceedings of ICSE*, 1976.

[42] G. Edward Suh, Srinivas Devadas, and Larry Rudolph. Analytical cache models with applications to cache partitioning. In *Proceedings of ICS*, pages 1–12, 2001.

[43] David K. Tam, Reza Azimi, Livio Soares, and Michael Stumm. RapidMRC: approximating L2 miss rate curves on commodity systems for online optimizations. In *Proceedings of ASPLOS*, pages 121–132, 2009.

[44] Dominique Thiébaut and Harold S. Stone. Footprints in the cache. *ACM Transactions on Computer Systems*, 5(4):305–329, 1987.

[45] Carl A Waldspurger, Nohhyun Park, Alexander Garthwaite, and Irfan Ahmad. Efficient mrc construction with shards. In *13th USENIX Conference on File and Storage Technologies (FAST 15)*, pages 95–110, 2015.

[46] Richard West, Puneet Zaroo, Carl A. Waldspurger, and Xiao Zhang. Online cache modeling for commodity multicore processors. *Operating Systems Review*, 44(4):19–29, 2010.

[47] Jake Wires, Stephen Ingram, Zachary Drudi, Nicholas JA Harvey, Andrew Warfield, and Coho Data. Characterizing storage workloads with counter stacks. In *Proceedings of OSDI*, pages 335–349. USENIX Association, 2014.

[48] Steven Cameron Woo, Moriyoshi Ohara, Evan Torrie, Jaswinder Pal Singh, and Anoop Gupta. The SPLASH-2 Programs: Characterization and Methodological Considerations. *The 22nd annual international symposium on Computer architecture (ISCA '95)*, pages 24–36, 1995.

[49] Meng-Ju Wu and Donald Yeung. Coherent profiles: Enabling efficient reuse distance analysis of multicore scaling for loop-based parallel programs. In *Proceedings of PACT*, pages 264–275, 2011.

[50] Meng-Ju Wu, Minshu Zhao, and Donald Yeung. Studying multicore processor scaling via reuse distance analysis. In *Proceedings of ISCA*, pages 499–510, 2013.

[51] Xiaoya Xiang, Bin Bao, Tongxin Bai, Chen Ding, and Trishul M. Chilimbi. All-window profiling and composable models of cache sharing. In *Proceedings of PPoPP*, pages 91–102, 2011.

[52] Xiaoya Xiang, Bin Bao, Chen Ding, and Yaoqing Gao. Linear-time modeling of program working set in shared cache. In *Proceedings of PACT*, pages 350–360, 2011.

[53] Xiaoya Xiang, Chen Ding, Hao Luo, and Bin Bao. HOTL: a higher order theory of locality. In *Proceedings of ASPLOS*, pages 343–356, 2013.

[54] Seyed Majid Zahedi and Benjamin C. Lee. REF: resource elasticity fairness with sharing incentives for multiprocessors. In *Proceedings of ASPLOS*, pages 145–160, 2014.

[55] Yutao Zhong and Wentao Chang. Sampling-based program locality approximation. In *Proceedings of ISMM*, pages 91–100, 2008.

[56] Yutao Zhong, Xipeng Shen, and Chen Ding. Program locality analysis using reuse distance. *ACM TOPLAS*, 31(6):1–39, August 2009.

[57] Pin Zhou, Vivek Pandey, Jagadeesan Sundaresan, Anand Raghuraman, Yuanyuan Zhou, and Sanjeev Kumar. Dynamic tracking of page miss ratio curve for memory management. In *Proceedings of ASPLOS*, pages 177–188, 2004.

Exploiting Vector and Multicore Parallelism for Recursive, Data- and Task-Parallel Programs

Bin Ren
College of William and Mary
bren@wm.edu

Sriram Krishnamoorthy
Pacific Northwest National Laboratories
sriram@pnnl.gov

Kunal Agrawal
Washington University at St. Louis
kunal@wustl.edu

Milind Kulkarni
Purdue University
milind@purdue.edu

Abstract

Modern hardware contains parallel execution resources that are well-suited for data-parallelism—vector units—and task parallelism—multicores. However, most work on parallel scheduling focuses on one type of hardware or the other. In this work, we present a scheduling framework that allows for a unified treatment of task- and data-parallelism. Our key insight is an abstraction, *task blocks*, that uniformly handles data-parallel iterations and task-parallel tasks, allowing them to be scheduled on vector units or executed independently as multicores. Our framework allows us to define schedulers that can dynamically select between executing task-blocks on vector units or multicores. We show that these schedulers are asymptotically optimal, and deliver the maximum amount of parallelism available in computation trees. To evaluate our schedulers, we develop program transformations that can convert mixed data- and task-parallel programs into task block–based programs. Using a prototype instantiation of our scheduling framework, we show that, on an 8-core system, we can simultaneously exploit vector and multicore parallelism to achieve 14×–108× speedup over sequential baselines.

Keywords Task Parallelism; Data Parallelism; General Scheduler

PPoPP '17 Feb. 4–8, 2017, Austin, Texas, USA.
Copyright © 2017 ACM 978-1-4503-4493-7/17/02...$15.00
DOI: http://dx.doi.org/10.1145/3018743.3018763

1. Introduction

The two most common types of parallelism are *data parallelism*, arising from simultaneously executing the same operation(s) over different pieces of data, and *task parallelism*, arising from executing multiple independent tasks simultaneously. Data parallelism is usually expressed through parallel loops, while task parallelism is often expressed using fork-join parallelism constructs.

These types of parallelism are each well-matched to different types of parallel hardware: data parallelism is well-suited for vector hardware such as SIMD units. The paradigm of executing the same computation across multiple pieces of data is exactly what SIMD units were designed for. While multicore hardware is more flexible (and many programming models allow mapping data-parallel execution to multiple cores), the independent execution context provided by multicores are well-matched to the task parallelism in languages such as Cilk [4].

Increasingly, however, both kinds of parallel hardware coexist. Modern machines consist of multicore chips, with *each* core containing dedicated vector hardware. As a result, it is important to be able to write programs that target both types of hardware in a unified manner.

Unfortunately, when programming data- or task-parallelism, the two paradigms are often treated separately. While programming models such as OpenMP [11] support both data- and task-parallelism, the coexistence is uneasy, requiring very different constructs, used in very different contexts. Indeed, Cilk "supports" data parallelism through constructs such as `cilk_for`, which, under the hood, translate data parallelism to task parallelism [6]. In recent work, Ren et al. developed transformations that work in the opposite direction [15]: given a task parallel program, they extract *data* parallelism for execution on vector units. None of these approaches cleanly support both multicore and vector execution *simultaneously*, especially for programs that mix data- and task-parallelism.

In this paper, we develop a system that unifies the treatment of both types of parallelism and both types of parallel hardware: we develop general schedulers that let programs mix data- and task-parallelism and run efficiently on hardware with both multicores and vector units. Importantly, our schedulers allow exploiting data- and task-parallelism at all levels of granularity: task parallel work can be decomposed into data-parallel work for execution on vector units, and data-parallel work can be forked into separate tasks for load balancing purposes through work-stealing. This grain-free treatment of parallelism allows our system to effectively and dynamically map complex programs to complex hardware, rather than "baking in" a particular execution strategy.

The key insight behind our work is a unifying abstraction for parallel work, the *task block*. Task blocks contain multiple independent tasks that can arise from both data parallel loops and from task parallel fork-join constructs. We develop a general scheduling framework that allows task blocks to be used as a unit of scheduling for both data parallelism (essentially, by executing a data-parallel for loop over the task block) or task parallelism (by allowing task blocks to be stolen and executed independently). Importantly, each of these execution modes produce new task blocks that make independent scheduling decisions, allowing for the free mixing of data- and task-parallel execution.

To evaluate our schedulers, we present a simple language that allows programmers to express task parallelism nested within data parallelism. We then extend Ren et al.'s transformations [15] to generate task block–based programs from algorithms written in our language. Programs written in our specification language (or in general-purpose languages restricted to use analogous constructs) and run using our scheduling framework can simultaneously exploit data- and task-parallelism (rather than one or the other) on both vector and multicore hardware.

In this paper, we make several contributions:

1. We develop a general scheduling framework based on task blocks for SIMD and multicore execution of computation trees. Using this scheduling framework, we make three advances: (i) we show that Ren et al.'s approach to executing task-parallel programs on vector hardware is a special case of our framework; (ii) we use our framework to develop a new class of scheduling policies, *restart* that expose more data parallelism; (iii) we provide mechanisms to support Cilk-style work-stealing between cores, unifying execution on data-parallel and task-parallel hardware.
2. We provide theoretical bounds on the parallelism exposed by our various scheduling policies. We show that our new scheduling policies can expose more parallelism than Ren et al.'s original policies, and are *asymptotically optimal* (though in practice, scheduling overheads may dominate). This represents the first theoretical analysis of vector execution of mixed task- and data-parallel programs.
3. We evaluate on eleven benchmarks, including all the benchmarks from Ren et al., as well as new benchmarks that exhibit more general structures (e.g., nesting task- and data-parallelism).

We implement a proof-of-concept instantiation of our scheduling framework. Overall, on an 8-core machine, our system is able to deliver combined SIMD/multicore speedups of $14\times$–$108\times$ over sequential baselines.

2. Background

We now provide some background on previous work on vectorizing task parallel programs and how task parallel programs are scheduled using work stealing.

2.1 Vectorizing Task Parallel Programs

Vectorization of programs has typically focused on vectorizing simple, dense *data parallel* loops [10]. It is not immediately apparent that SIMD, which is naturally data parallel, can be applied to recursive task-parallel programs. Such programs can be thought of as a computation tree, where a task's children are the tasks that it spawned and the leaves are the base-case tasks.[1] Any effective vectorization of these programs must satisfy two constraints:

1. *All of the tasks being executed in a vectorized manner must be (substantially) identical.* This criterion is naturally satisfied because the tasks arise from the same recursive code.
2. *Data accesses in the tasks must be well structured.* Vector load and store operations access contiguous regions of memory. If a SIMD instruction operates on data that is not contiguous in memory, it must be implemented with slow scatter and gather operations.

To understand why this second restriction is problematic, consider trying to vectorize the standard Cilk-style execution model, with each SIMD lane representing a different worker. Because the workers execute independent computation subtrees, their program stacks grow and shrink at different rates, leading to non-contiguous accesses to local variables, and consequently inefficient vectorization.

SIMD-friendly execution: Ren et al. developed an execution strategy that satisfies both constraints for efficient vectorization [15]. The key insight of their strategy was to perform a more disciplined execution of the computation, with the restriction that all tasks executed in a SIMD operation be at the same recursion depth—this allows the stacks of these tasks to be aligned and interleaved so that local variables can be accessed using vector loads and stores.

[1] This formulation does not work once we have computations with syncs. However, those programs can also be represented using a tree; albeit a more complex and dynamic one.

```
void foo(int x)
  if (isBase(x))
    baseCase()
  else
    l1 = inductiveWork1(x)
    spawn foo(l1)
    l2 = inductiveWork2(x)
    spawn foo(l2)
```

(a) Simple recursive code. spawn creates new tasks.

```
void bfs_foo(TaskBlock tb)
  TaskBlock next
  foreach (Task t : tb)
    if (isBase(t.x))
      baseCase()
    else
      l1 = inductiveWork1(t.x)
      next.add(new Task(l1))
      l2 = inductiveWork2(t.x)
      next.add(new Task(l2))
  bfs_foo(next)
```

(b) Blocked Breadth-first version of code in Figure 1(a).

```
void blocked_foo(TaskBlock tb)
  TaskBlock left, right
  foreach (Task t : tb)
    if (isBase(t.x))
      baseCase()
    else
      l1 = inductiveWork1(t.x)
      left.add(new Task(l1))
      l2 = inductiveWork2(t.x)
      right.add(new Task(l2))
  blocked_foo(left)
  blocked_foo(right)
```

(c) Blocked depth-first execution.

Figure 1: Pseudocode demonstrating vectorization transformations.

Ren et al.'s approach targets programs written using a Cilk-like language (or programs in other languages that adhere to similar restrictions). The programs they target consist of a single, k-ary recursive method:

$$f(p_1, \ldots, p_k) \textbf{ if } e_b \textbf{ then } s_b \textbf{ else } s_i$$

This method evaluates a boolean expression to decide whether to execute a base case (s_b, which can perform *reductions* to compute the eventual program result) or to execute an inductive case (s_i), which can *spawn* additional tasks by invoking the recursive method again. As in Cilk, these spawned methods are assumed to be independent of the remainder of the work in the spawning method, and hence can be executed in parallel. Ren et al.'s transformations target single recursive methods; Section 5 describes how we extend the language to handle data-parallel programs with task-parallel iterations.

Figure 1(a) shows a simple recursive program that we use to explain Ren et al.'s execution strategy[2]. The steps of execution are as follows:

1. As shown in Figure 1(b), the computation is initially executed in a breadth-first, level-by-level manner where tasks at the same level are grouped into a *task block*. Crucially, by executing block by block, the code structure is a dense loop over the block allowing one to use standard vectorization techniques [10]. If a task spawns a new task, the newly-spawned task is placed into the next task block representing the next level of tasks. Once the task block finishes, execution moves on to the next block.
2. While breadth-first execution satisfies the two constraints outlined above, it suffers from excessive space usage. A TaskBlock contains all the tasks at a level in the computation tree; therefore, its size can be $\Omega(n)$ where where n is the number of tasks. To control this space explosion, Ren et al. switch to *depth-first* execution once a TaskBlock reaches a sufficient size: each task in the task block simply executes to completion by calling the original recursive function. This limits space usage, as each of these tasks will only use $O(d)$ space to execute (where d is the depth of the tree).

To recover vectorizability, Ren et al. apply *point blocking* [7], yielding the code in Figure 1(c). This strategy proceeds by (recursively) first executing *each task's* left subtask in a blocked manner and then each task's right subtask. Note that the code still operates over a dense block of tasks and all the tasks in any TaskBlock are at the same level, facilitating vectorization.

Because not all tasks have identical subtrees, as execution proceeds, some threads will "die out" and the TaskBlock will become empty. If there are fewer than Q tasks in a TaskBlock (Q is the number of lanes in the vector unit), it is impossible to effectively use the SIMD execution resources. To tackle this problem, Ren et al. proposed *re-expansion*: if a TaskBlock has fewer than Q tasks, they can *switch back to breadth-first execution*, generating more work and making the next-level block larger. Re-expansion is the key to effective vectorization. In Section 3, we show that re-expansion is a specific instance of a class of scheduling policies that our general scheduling framework supports.

2.2 Work-Stealing Scheduler Operation

Work-stealing schedulers are known to be efficient both theoretically and empirically for scheduling task parallel programs [1, 3]. In a work-stealing scheduler, each worker maintains a work *deque*, which contains *ready tasks*. When a task executing on worker p creates two children, the worker places its right child on its deque and executes its left child. When a worker p finishes executing its current task, it pops a task from the bottom of its own deque. If p's deque is empty, then p becomes a *thief*. It picks a *victim* uniformly at random from the other workers, and *steals* work from the top of the victim's deque. If the victim's deque is empty, then p simply performs another random steal attempt.

3. General Schedulers for Vector and Multicore Execution

This section presents our general scheduler framework for efficient vectorized execution. We first describe three mechanisms that can be combined in various ways to produce dif-

[2] Reductions, computations, etc., are hidden in the baseCase and inductiveWork methods. Here, we use Java-like pseudocode, rather than the original specification language.

ferent classes of schedulers. We next show that re-expansion is an instantiation of this framework. We then describe a new, more flexible, scheduler policy, *restart*. Finally, we explain how the framework can be extended to support multicore execution for both re-expansion and restart-based schedulers. Our schedulers are general, and apply to any type of computation tree.

Notation: We assume P cores and Q SIMD lanes per core. We assume that the recursive method has two recursive spawns; the framework readily generalizes to more spawns.

3.1 Scheduler Mechanisms

We first describe mechanisms for a "sequential" scheduler—a scheduler that supports vectorized execution on a single core. The unit of scheduling of the scheduler is *task blocks* (TaskBlock) which contain some number of tasks—nodes in the computation tree—that can be executed in a SIMD manner: if a TaskBlock has t tasks in it, the scheduler can use Q lanes to execute the t tasks in $\lceil t/Q \rceil$ SIMD steps. The scheduler has a deque, with multiple levels. Each level represents a particular level of the computation tree.

The deque starts with a single TaskBlock at the top level that contains a single task: the task generated by calling the recursive method for the first time. At any time, when *scheduling* a block b for execution, the scheduler can take one of three actions:

Breadth-first expansion (BFE): Block b is executed in a SIMD manner. Any new tasks that are generated (spawned) are placed in a block b', which is scheduled next. Note that b' can contain up to twice as many tasks as b. If b' is *empty* (has no tasks), another block is chosen for scheduling from the deque according to the scheduling policy.

Depth-first execution (DFE): Block b is executed in a SIMD manner. For each task that is executed, all new tasks generated by the first spawn call are placed in block b', and all new tasks generated by the second spawn call are placed in block b''. Note that b' and b'' contain at most as many tasks as b. If not empty, block b'' is pushed onto the deque, and block b' is scheduled next. If b' is empty, then another block is chosen for scheduling from the deque according to the scheduling policy.

Restart: The scheduler pushes block b onto the deque (without executing it). If there is already a block on the deque at the same level (e.g., if b is the sibling of a block that was pushed onto the deque), then b is merged with the block at that level. Some block is chosen from the deque for scheduling next, according to the scheduling policy.

Note the distinction between "scheduling" a block, which means choosing an action to take with the block, and "executing" a block, which means running the tasks in the block using SIMD. For brevity, we say e.g., a block is "executed using DFE" to mean that the block was scheduled, a DFE action was chosen, and then the block was executed.

Various schedulers can be created by combining these mechanisms in various ways, and changing the policies that dictate which mechanism is used at each scheduling step.

3.2 Re-expansion

Ren et al.'s re-expansion policy is, in fact, in the class of scheduling policies that can be described using our scheduling framework. Re-expansion only uses the BFE and DFE actions. In the context of the pseudocode of Figure 1, breadth first expansion is akin to executing the code in Figure 1(b)—a single new TaskBlock is generated—while depth-first execution is akin to executing the code in Figure 1(c)—two new TaskBlocks are generated.

Re-expansion schedulers have two thresholds,t_{dfe}[3] and t_{bfe}[4]. A re-expansion scheduler executes its first block in BFE mode. As long as the next block has fewer than t_{dfe} tasks, the scheduler keeps performing BFE actions. If the next block has more than t_{dfe} tasks, the scheduler switches to DFE actions to conserve space. The scheduler then remains in DFE mode until the block has fewer than t_{bfe} tasks, at which point it switches back to BFE mode. If the current block has no work to do, it grabs work from the bottom of the deque. Intuitively, the scheduler uses BFE actions to generate parallel work and DFE actions to limit space usage. However, because BFE actions can only draw from the bottom of the deque, they can only find parallelism "below" the current block, limiting the effectiveness of re-expansion, as Section 4 shows.

3.3 Restart

We now define a new class of schedulers that we call *restart* schedulers. These schedulers take advantage of the restart mechanism to be more aggressive in finding more parallel work, which can lead to better parallelism with smaller block sizes, as Section 4 shows.

The basic pattern of a restart scheduler is as follows: the scheduler starts in BFE mode, and switches to DFE mode when the t_{dfe} threshold is hit, just as in a re-expansion scheduler. However, once in DFE mode, the scheduler behaves differently. If the current block, b, has fewer than $t_{restart}$ tasks on it, the scheduler takes a restart action. b is merged with any other blocks at the current level, and the scheduler looks for more work to be done. Unlike re-expansion schedulers, which would be constrained to begin executing the bottom block on the deque, a re-start scheduler scans up from the bottom of the deque. As the scheduler works its way up through the deque, it merges (concatenates) all blocks at a given level together (there might be more than one block at a given level due to multiple restart or DFE actions that leave blocks on the deque). After merging, if a block has at least $t_{restart}$ tasks on it, the scheduler begins execution of that block in *DFE* mode. If the restart scheduler reaches the

[3] Trigger to switch to depth-first execution

[4] Trigger to switch to breadth-first expansion

top of the deque without finding $t_{restart}$ work, it executes the top block in BFE mode. Intuitively, if a particular part of the computation tree runs out of work, the restart scheduler will look higher up in the tree and try to merge work from different portions of the tree that is at the same level to generate a larger block of work.

A restart scheduler maintains two invariants: (i) at each level *above* the currently executing block, there may be up to two blocks on the deque—one left over from a restart (that must have fewer than $t_{restart}$ tasks), and the other left over from a DFE (that may have more than $t_{restart}$ tasks, but does not have to); (ii) at each level *below* the currently executing block, there is at most one block on the deque, and that block must have fewer than $t_{restart}$ tasks.

3.4 Creating Parallel Schedulers

Both schedulers described above are sequential; though TaskBlocks can be used for vector-parallel execution, the schedulers are for single-core execution; there is just one deque of TaskBlocks. We now extend the scheduling framework to support multicore execution by adding support for multiple workers (cores), each with their own deque, and adding one more action that a scheduler can take:

Steal: The scheduler places block b onto the deque without executing it (b might be empty). The thread then steals a TaskBlock from another worker's deque. The stolen TaskBlock is added to the worker's deque at the appropriate level and, if necessary, merged with any block already on the worker's deque. The choice of which deque to steal from, which block on the deque to steal, and which block to schedule next, is a matter of scheduler policy.

Using this new action, we can extend re-expansion and restart schedulers to support multicore execution:

Re-expansion: A worker never attempts to steal until its deque is empty (i.e.. it is completely out of work). It then steals the *top* TaskBlock from random worker's deque, adds it to its deque, and executes that block as usual; that is, with DFE if it has more than t_{bfe} nodes and with BFE otherwise. Note that only right blocks generated during DFE are placed on deques and are available for stealing.

Restart: Stealing in restart schedulers is more complicated. In the sequential scheduler, a worker that is unable to create a block with at least $t_{restart}$ tasks in its deque executes the top block in its deque with a BFE action. In the parallel scheduler, that worker would instead perform a steal action. Note that at the time it performs the steal, the worker has an invariant that all of the blocks in its deque have fewer than $t_{restart}$ tasks (because it was unable to restart from its own deque). During the steal, the current worker (thief) chooses a random worker (victim) and looks at the *top* of that deque (note that the victim could be the thief itself).

The top of the victims deque contains one or two blocks. If one of them has at least $t_{restart}$ tasks, the thief steals it, adds it to its deque, and executes it with a DFE action. If the block has fewer than $t_{restart}$ tasks, the thief steals it, adds it to its deque, and executes a constant number of BFE actions starting from that block (to generate more work). If this generates a block with at least $t_{restart}$ tasks, the thief switches to DFE. Otherwise, it tries a restart action and, if that fails, steals again.

3.5 Setting the Thresholds

In producing various schedulers, there are three thresholds of importance: t_{dfe}, t_{bfe}, and $t_{restart}$. The first threshold, t_{dfe} places an upper bound on the block size: a TaskBlock has at most $2t_{dfe}$ tasks. The latter two thresholds dictate when a scheduler looks for more work: if a TaskBlock is below one of the thresholds, the scheduler performs some action to find more work— re-expansion schedulers switch to BFE, restart schedulers perform a restart. These thresholds are less constrained and should be set between Q and t_{dfe}.

4. Theoretical Analysis

This section analyzes the performance of various scheduling strategies described above, namely: a) The basic strategy that performs BFE and then switches to DFE; b) re-expansion strategy; and c) restart strategy. We prove asymptotically tight upper and lower bounds on the SIMD running time T_s for computation trees with n unit time tasks. (Utilization bounds are implied by these bounds.) We first analyze the three sequential strategies on a core with Q SIMD lanes. These results indicate that restart can provide linear speedup as long as the block size (t_{dfe}) is larger than Q. On the other hand, the basic strategy and re-expansion both require large block sizes to guarantee linear speedup; however, re-expansion requires significantly smaller block sizes. We then also analyze the parallel performance of restart where we have P cores each with Q SIMD lanes and show that restart is *asymptotically optimal* for these programs. Our theoretical results hold for any computation tree where the elements of a task block are vectorizable, and hence our restart schedulers can guarantee asymptotically optimal speedup regardless of computation tree structure.

Preliminaries: For the theoretical bounds, we model the execution of the program as a walk of a computation tree with n nodes. Each node in the computation tree is a unit time task and each edge is a dependence between tasks (tasks of longer length can be modeled as a chain). We also assume that all nodes at the same level in the tree are similar in that they can be part of a SIMD block, since, in our computations, they have the same computation and aligned stacks. We also assume that each node has at most 2 children.[5] Therefore, the tree's height h is at least $\lg n$ and at most n.

In each *step*, a core executes between 1 and Q nodes. The step is a *complete step* if the core executes Q nodes; otherwise it is *incomplete*. Recall that in our strategies, the

[5] This assumption is for simple exposition; all the results generalize for larger (but constant) out-degrees.

scheduler operates on TaskBlock of size between 1 and $kQ = t_{dfe}$. If the TaskBlock is of size larger than Q, then it may take multiple SIMD steps to execute it. We call the entire execution of a TaskBlock to encompass a *superstep*.

T_s denotes the SIMD execution time of the program on a single core with Q simd lanes; alternatively, we can think of T_s as the number of steps executed by a scheduling strategy. Some relatively obvious bounds on T_s: (1) $T_s < n$, since each step executes at least 1 node. (2) $T_s \geq n/Q$ since each step executes at most Q nodes. (3) $T_s \geq h$, since each step executes only nodes at a particular level. We will, later, also analyze the parallel execution where we have P cores each with Q SIMD lanes. We say T_{sp} is the execution time of the program on these P cores. Again, we have the obvious lower bounds of $T_{sp} \geq n/(QP)$ and $T_{sp} \geq h$.

We first state some straightforward structural lemmas.

Claim 1. *Each superstep has at most one incomplete step.*

Claim 2. *In the entire computation, the number of complete steps is at most n/Q since each complete step executes exactly Q nodes.*

Claim 3. *The breadth first expansion of a tree (or subtree) of height h has at most h supersteps, since each superstep completes an entire level of the tree.*

4.1 Sequential Strategies with and without Re-expansion

For this section, we state the theorems without proof; proofs will be provided in an extended technical report. The following theorem for the basic strategy, with no re-expansion and no restarts, implies that it guarantees linear speedup iff $k = \Omega(2^\epsilon)$; either the block size must be very large or the computation tree very shallow.

Theorem 1. *For any tree with height $h = \lg n + \epsilon$, the running time is $\Theta(\min\{2^\epsilon n/kQ + n/Q + \lg n + \epsilon, n\})$.*

Now consider the strategy with re-expansion, as described in Section 3.2. We assume $t_{dfe} = kQ$ for some k, and $t_{bfe} = k_1 Q$, where $1 \leq k_1 \leq k$.

Theorem 2. *For any tree with height $h = \lg n + \epsilon$, the running time is $\Theta(\min\{(\frac{(\epsilon - \lg k)}{k_1} + 1)n/Q) + \lg n + \epsilon, n\})$.*

Comparing Theorems 1 and 2, we see that dependence on ϵ is linear instead of exponential in the strategy with re-expansion. Therefore, re-expansion provides speedup for larger values of ϵ and smaller values of k than the strategy without re-expansion. In addition, we should make $k_1 \approx k$; that is we switch to BFE as soon as we have enough space in the block to do so since that decreases the execution time.

4.2 Sequential Execution with Restart

We now prove that the restart strategy, as described in Section 3.3, is asymptotically optimal. We set $t_{restart} = k_2 Q$, where $1 \leq k_2 \leq k$. At this point, we start depth first expansion again. We say that a superstep that executes a block of size smaller than $k_2 Q$ is a partial superstep and a block of size greater than $k_2 Q$ is a full block.

The following lemma is obvious from Claim 3.

Lemma 1. *There are at most h partial supersteps during the computation.*

Theorem 3. *The running time is $\Theta(n/Q+h)$ for a computation tree with n nodes and depth h, which is asymptotically optimal for any scheduler.*

Proof. There are at most $n/(k_2 Q)$ full supersteps and at most h partial supersteps; thus, we have at most $n/(k_2 Q)+h$ incomplete steps by Claim 1. Adding the bound of n/Q for complete steps (by Claim 2), gives us the total bound. This is asymptotically optimal due to lower bounds mentioned in the preliminaries section. □

Note that, unlike the previous strategies, the execution time of the restart strategy does not depend on k or k_2; therefore, we can make the block size as small as Q and still get linear speedup.

4.3 Work-Stealing with Restart

We now bound the running time of the parallel work-stealing strategy with restart, as described in Section 3.4.

We can first bound the number of partial supersteps by observing that a partial block is only executed as part of a breadth first execution, which only occurs either at the beginning of the computation or after a steal attempt.

Lemma 2. *The number of partial supersteps is at most $h + O(S)$.*

For the purposes of this proof, we will assume that a steal attempt takes 1 unit of time. The proof can be generalized so that a steal attempt takes c time for any constant c, but for expository purposes, we stick to the simple assumption. We can then bound the total completion time in terms of the number of steal attempts:

Lemma 3. *The completion time of the computation is at most $O(n/QP + S/P)$.*

Proof. Each step is either an incomplete step, a complete step, or a steal attempt. There are a total of $O(n/Q)$ complete steps by Claim 2. Each full superstep has at least k_2 complete steps. Combining this fact with Lemma 2, we can conclude that there are at most $O(n/k_2 Q + S)$ supersteps. By Claim 1, we can bound the number of incomplete steps by the same number. Since there are P total processors, we can add the number of complete steps, the number of incomplete steps, and the number of steal attempts and divide by P to get a bound on the completion time. □

From the above lemma, we can see that the crux of this proof will depend on bounding the total number of steal attempts S. We will bound the number of steal attempts using an argument very similar to the one used by Arora et. al [1] (henceforth referred to as ABP). Similar to that paper, we will define a potential function on blocks which decreases geometrically with the depth of the block (in ABP, the potential function is on nodes).

For any block b, we define $d(b)$ as the depth of the block, which is equal to the depth of all nodes in the block. We define $w(b) = h - d(b)$. We can now define various potentials:

- The potential of a full ready block is $4^{3w(b)}$, the potential of a partial ready block is $4^{3w(b)-1}$. The potential of a block that is executing is $4^{3w(b)-1}$.
- The potential of any processor is the total potential of all the blocks on its deque added to the potential of the block it is executing (if any).
- The potential of the computation is the sum of the potential of all processors.

Like the ABP proof, we show that the potential never increases and that a certain number of steal attempts decrease the potential by a constant factor, allowing us to bound the number of steal attempts. However, the proof also differs due to the following reasons: 1) Unlike standard work-stealing, where there is one node at each depth on the deque, we can have up to two blocks at each depth, necessitating a change in the potential function. 2) In standard work-stealing, a worker only steals when its deque is empty; here it may steal even if its deque contains partial blocks. 3) In work-stealing, all the nodes on a processor's deque have a larger potential than the one that the worker is executing; this may not be the case for our scheduler. 4) Each node takes unit time to execute in the ABP model, while our blocks can take up to k time steps to finish executing; this changes the bound on the number of steal attempts.

The following three lemmas prove that the potential never increases, and that steal attempts reduce potential by a significant amount.

Lemma 4. *The initial potential is 4^{3h} and the final potential is 0. The potential never increases during the computation.*

Proof. Potential changes due to the following reasons:

1. A block starts executing: The potential decreases since an executing block has a lower potential than a ready block.
2. An executing block with weight w finishes executing: This block generates at most 2 ready blocks with lower weight. The potential decreases the least when both are full blocks. In this case, the change in potential is $4^{3w-2} - 2 \times 4^{3(w-1)} \geq 0$.
3. Two blocks with weight w merge: If the result of the merge is a partial block, the potential obviously decreases. If the result is a full block, it immediately starts executing. Therefore, the potential also decreases. □

Lemma 5. ***(Top Heavy Deques Lemma)*** *The heaviest block on any processor is either at the top of the processor's deque or it is executing. In addition, this heaviest block contains at least $1/3$ of the total potential of the processor.*

Proof. By construction, the deque is ordered by depth and the weight decreases as depth increases. Therefore, the heaviest node has to be on the top of the deque or executing.

Let x be the heaviest block (if there are two, we pick one arbitrarily). The potential of this block is at least $\Phi(x) = 4^{3w-1}$ (if it is executing or partial); otherwise it is higher. If there is another node at the same depth, its potential is also 4^{3w-1} since it must be a partial block. Other than this, there may be 2 blocks each with all weights lower than w; one full and one partial. Therefore, the total potential of the processor is$\Phi(p) \leq 2 \times 4^{3w-1} + \sum_{y=1}^{w-1}(4^{3(y-1)} + 4^{3(y-1)-1}) \leq 3 \times 4^{3w-1} = 3\Phi(x)$ Thus, the heaviest block has at least a third of the potential. □

Lemma 6. *Between time t and time t', if there are at least kP steal attempts, then* $\Pr\{\Phi_t - \Phi_{t'} \geq 1/24\Phi_t\} \geq 1/4$

Proof. We divide the potential of the computation into two parts. $\Phi(D_t)$ is the potential of the workers where the heaviest block is on the deque and $\Phi(A_t)$ is the potential of the workers where the heaviest block is executing at time t.

First, let us consider a processor p whose potential is in $\Phi(A_t)$ and let us say that the currently executing block is x. From Lemma 5, we know that $\Phi(x) = 4^{3w(x)-1} \geq 1/3\Phi(p)$. For kP steal attempts to occur, at least k time steps must have passed (since each steal attempt takes 1 time step). Therefore, by time step t', x has finished executing. In the worst case, it enables two full blocks with a cumulative potential of $2 \times 4^{3(w(x)-1)} = 1/8\Phi(x)$. Therefore, the potential of p reduces by at least $7/8 \times 1/3 = 7/24$.

Now consider the processors whose potential is in $\Phi(D_t)$, and say p is one of these processors. If p is a victim of a steal attempt this time interval, then the heaviest block x will be stolen and assigned. From Lemma 5, we know that $\Phi(x) \geq 1/3\Phi(p)$. Once x is assigned, its potential drops by a factor of $1/4$. Therefore, the potential that used to be on p has reduced by a factor of $1/12$.

We use Lemma 7 (Balls into Bins) from ABP to conclude that with probability $1/4$, after P steal attempts, the $\Phi(D_t)$ reduces by at least a factor of $1/24$. □

Lemma 7. *The expected number of steal attempts is $O(kPh)$. In addition, the number of steal attempts is $O(kPh + P\lg(1/\epsilon))$ with probability at least $(1-\epsilon)$.*

Proof. The initial potential is 4^h and the final potential is 0. From Lemma 6, we conclude that after $O(kP)$ steal attempts, the potential decreases by a constant factor in expectation. Therefore, the expected number of steal attempts is $O(kPh)$. The high-probability bound can be derived by applying Chernoff Bounds. □

The final theorem is obvious from Lemmas 3 and 7.

Theorem 4. *The running time is $O(n/QP + kh)$ in expectation and $O(n/QP + kh + \lg(1/\epsilon))$ with probability at least $(1-\epsilon)$.*

Corollary 1. *Since n/QP and h are lower bounds on the completion time, restart mechanism provides an asymptotically optimal completion time.*

4.4 Space Bounds and Discussion

Since each worker can have at most 2 blocks at each depth level in its deque, we get the following bound for space for both restart and re-expansion.

Lemma 8. *The total space used is $hkQP$.*

We can now compare the different strategies in terms of the performance they provide. First, let us consider the strategies on a single processor. The above theorems hold for all values of $h = \lg n + \epsilon$. However, different strategies require different block sizes in order to provide speedup. Here we look at the implications of various block size values on speedup provided by the various strategies. Since the restart strategy always provides optimal speedup, we only compare the strategies with and without re-expansion. In addition, as we mentioned earlier, for the restart strategy, it is not advantageous to make k_1 large; so for the following discussion, we make $k_1 \approx k$.

1. If $k > 2^{h-\lg n}$, all schemes give an asymptotically optimal parallelization.
2. If $k \leq 2^{h-\lg n}$, but $k > 2^{h-\lg n}/Q$ then we see very little speedup without re-expansion. With re-expansion, we get optimal speedup if $k \geq \lg Q$ (a reasonable assumption since k is already so large).
3. For smaller k, where $k > h - \lg n$, we get no speedup without re-expansion, but continue to get speedup with re-expansion as long as $k > \lg Q$.
4. For smaller k, re-expansion provides some speedup until k reaches $(h - \lg n)/Q$. After that, it provides no speedup.

Therefore, while the basic strategy requires very large block sizes to provide speedup, re-expansion can provide speedup with moderate block sizes, which nevertheless increase with the height of the tree.

We also implement parallelism using both restart and re-expansion. However, we only prove the bounds for the restart strategy in this section, since that is the more complicated bound. We can use a similar technique to prove the following bound on re-expansion: $O((\frac{(h-\lg n-\lg k)}{k} + 1)n/PQ) + kh)$ (assuming we make k_1 as large as we can). However, while with restart, we can set $k = 1$ to get asymptotically optimal speedup, this is not possible for re-expansion. As we can see from the bounds, there is a trade-off between multicore parallelism and SIMD parallelism. Larger k reduces the first term, and increases the second term — thereby increasing SIMD parallelism at the cost of reducing multicore parallelism. Smaller k does the opposite. As for space, for a given k, both strategies have the same bound. However, since restart can provide linear speedup at smaller block sizes, it may use less space for the same performance.

```
void c_f(Node p, Node r, float d)
  x = root.c_x − p.c_x
  /∗ similarly y and z∗/
  dr = x ∗ x + y ∗ y + z ∗ z
  if dr >= d || (r.isLeaf && p!=r)
    //update p using reduction
  else
    for (Node c: r.children)
      if c != null //task ||
        spawn c_f(p, c, d/4)

void comp_f_all(ps, root)
  foreach (Node p: ps) //data ||
    c_f(p, root, d)
```

Figure 2: Barnes-Hut, with data and task parallelism

5. Extended language specification

To evaluate our scheduling framework, we can simply target the same type of recursive, task-parallel programs that Ren et al.'s approach targets. However, we also want to validate our schedulers for more general computation trees. To do so, we extend Ren et al.'s specification language to target a broader class of applications: those that combine data- and task-parallelism by nesting task-parallel function calls inside data-parallel loops. We then extend Ren et al.'s transformation so that programs written in this extended specification language generate the TaskBlocks required by our scheduling framework.

5.1 Mixed data- and task-parallel programs

Ren et al.'s model captures classical programs such as those for solving n-queens or min-max problems. However, many interesting task-parallel programs have a different pattern. In particular, in many domains, the application performs task-parallel work for each item in a set of data; this is often expressed as a *data*-parallel loop with each iteration consisting of task-parallel work.

For instance, consider the Barnes-Hut simulation algorithm (Figure 2) [2]. In it, a series of bodies in space (typically, stars in a galaxy) are placed into an octree. Each body then traverses the octree to compute the gravitational forces exerted by each of the other bodies. At its heart, Barnes-Hut consists of a data-parallel loop: "for each body in a set of bodies, compute the force." However, the force computation can be parallelized using task parallelism by visiting subtrees of the octree in parallel [16]. Many other benchmarks follow this general pattern [8, 14].

Prior work on vectorizing such applications, including Barnes-Hut [8] and decision-tree traversal [14], have focused on the data-parallel portion of the computation and do not exploit the task parallelism. Moreover, these attempts have relied on special-purpose transformations targeted specifically at data-parallel traversal applications, rather than general data-parallel applications with embedded task parallelism.

5.2 Extending the language

Ren et al.'s work, and hence their language specification, does not admit task-parallelism nested within data-parallelism: it targets single recursive calls. We can extend the specification language to admit two types of programs: a single recursive method, as before, or a data-parallel loop enclosing a recursive method; this simple extension to the language allows us to express programs such as Barnes-Hut.

$$\textbf{foreach}\ (d : data) f(d, p_1, \ldots, p_k)\ \textbf{if}\ e_b\ \textbf{then}\ s_b\ \textbf{else}\ s_i$$

Note that the non-recursive functions from Ren et al.'s language specification—such as `baseCase` and `isBase` from Figure 1—can include data-parallel loops. This means that our modified language supports programs that nest data-parallelism inside task-parallelism inside data-parallelism.

5.3 Extending the transformation

In these programs, Ren et al.'s transformation framework treats each iteration of the outer data parallel loop as a single task-parallel program and hence execute the data-parallel outer loop sequentially. Therefore, *only* task-parallelism is exploited, not data-parallelism (the opposite problem of that faced by prior work [8, 14]).

To exploit both data- and task-parallelism, we can readily extend the transformation described in Section 2.1. Note that the transformed program in Figure 1(b) operates on a block of tasks. The initial call to this code consists of a TaskBlock with a single task in it, representing the initial call to the recursive method. When transforming data parallel enclosing task parallel code, we can iterate over the data parallel work to construct *multiple* tasks, one for each iteration of the data-parallel loop. These tasks can then be placed into a TaskBlock, which is passed to the initial breadth-first, task-parallel code. If the initial TaskBlock is too big (i.e., if the data-parallel loop has too many iterations), strip mining can be used to create smaller TaskBlocks that are then sequentially passed to the vectorized, task-parallel code.

If there are data-parallel loops within the non-recursive functions of the task-parallel body (i.e., if a single task has a nested data-parallel loop), the iterations of the data-parallel loops are placed into a TaskBlock generated from the enclosing task. Because these data-parallel loops do not have any further nesting, no further transformations are necessary to handle this additional level of parallelism.

6. Implementation

In this section, we present our Cilk implementation—using *spawn* and *sync*—of the re-expansion and restart strategies to schedule recursive task-parallel programs.

Vectorization: We do not discuss the specifics SIMDization in this paper. At a high level, the data parallel loops over task blocks can be vectorized using the same techniques as in Ren et al.'s work [15], such as *AoS to SoA transformation*, together auto-vectorization and SIMD intrinsics when the auto-vectorizer fails, and the process of adding new tasks to blocks can be vectorized using *Streaming Compaction*.

Re-expansion: Figure 3(a) shows the parallel, blocked re-expansion version of the example in Figure 1(a). If re-expansion is triggered, the left and right TaskBlock are merged together. Otherwise, they are executed independently. This code demonstrates that re-expansion can be naturally expressed as a Cilk program by marking recursive function calls (`blocked_foo_reexp`) in lines 13, 15, and 16 as concurrent using the `spawn` keyword. Other aspects of TaskBlock management, such as the stack of task blocks, are handled by the default Cilk runtime.

Restart: Figure 3(b) shows the parallel blocked re-start execution for the same example according to the strategy explained in Section 3.4. This figure illustrates an ideal implementation. Each thread maintains a deque of TaskBlock and RestartBlock (`tbs` and `rbs` in the figure), with at most one task block and restart block per level in the computation tree. Until termination, each thread steals a TaskBlock or RestartBlock (lines2–4), places it in a TaskBlock at the corresponding level in its local deque, and processes it recursively until no level has a non-empty TaskBlock. At the end of this working phase, a worker's local deque only consists of restart blocks. For conciseness, we do not show the BFE step on a steal as explained in Section 3.3. While efficient, this strategy does not naturally map to Cilk-like programming models. A particular challenge of the strategy in Figure 3(b) is that both the continuation of the TaskBlock being executed and the RestartBlock are pushed to the deque and made available for stealing. Rather than modifying the implementation of the spawn-sync constructs in Cilk, we use a simpler strategy that does not guarantee the same space or time bounds, but nevertheless provides good performance.

Simplified restart: The implementation of our simplified restart strategy is illustrated in Figure 3(c). Rather than maintain the restart blocks in the deque, they are maintained in an explicitly managed RestartBlock stack. The restart stack is implemented as a RestartBlock linked-list consisting of an array of tasks at the current level and a pointer pointing to RestartBlock at the next level. The blocked recursive function (`blocked_foo_restart`) takes a TaskBlock stack and a RestartBlock stack as input and returns a RestartBlock stack. If the total number of tasks in the TaskBlock and RestartBlock is less than the restart threshold, the tasks in the TaskBlock are moved into the RestartBlock, which is returned. Otherwise, we fill up the TaskBlock with tasks from the RestartBlock and spawn the TaskBlock for the next level. This spawn only exposes the task block's continuation—not the restart stack—for stealing by other worker threads. The returned RestartBlock stacks from all spawned instances of next level are merged into one RestartBlock stack (`merge(rleft, rright)`), which is then returned. The merge function is also implemented as a blocked func-

```
void blocked_foo_reexp(TaskBlock tb)
  TaskBlock left, right
  foreach (Task t : tb)
    if (isBase(t.x))
      baseCase()
    else
      l1 = inductiveWork1(t.x)
      left.add(new Task(l1))
      l2 = inductiveWork2(t.x)
      right.add(new Task(l2))
  if (/*do re−expansion*/)
    left.merge(right)
    spawn blocked_foo_reexp(left)
  else /*depth−first execution*/
    spawn blocked_foo_reexp(left)
    spawn blocked_foo_reexp(right)
```

(a) Re-expansion

```
/*tbs/rbs: task/restart block stack */
while (not done)
  tb = steal(); lvl = tb.lvl; tbs[lvl] = tb
  blocked_foo_restart(lvl)
void blocked_foo_restart(int lvl)
  if (tbs[lvl].size + rbs[lvl].size < t_restart)
    /* empty tasks in tbs[lvl] into rbs[lvl]*/
    return
  /*fill tbs[lvl] with tasks from rbs[lvl]*/
  TaskBlock left, right
  foreach (Task t : tb)
    if (isBase(t.x)) baseCase()
    else left.add(new Task(inductiveWork1(t.x)))
  tbs[lvl+1] = left; blocked_foo_restart(lvl+1)
  foreach (Task t : tb)
    if (not isBase(t.x))
      right.add(new Task(inductiveWork2(t.x)))
  tbs[lvl+1] = right; blocked_foo_restart(lvl+1)
```

(b) Ideal restart

```
1  RestartBlock blocked_foo_restart(TaskBlock tb,
        RestartBlock rb)
2    if (tb.size + rb.size < t_restart)
3      /*move tasks from tb into rb*/
4      return rb
5    /*fill tb with tasks from rb*/
6    TaskBlock left, right
7    foreach (Thread t : tb)
8      /*Figure 5(a) lines 4−10*/
9    RestartBlock rleft, rright
10   rleft= spawn blocked_foo_restart(left, rb.next)
11   rright = spawn blocked_foo_restart(right, NIL)
12   sync
13   rb.next = spawn merge(rleft, rright)
14   sync
15   return rb
```

(c) Simplified restart

Figure 3: Pseudocode demonstrating blocked, parallel, vectorized execution with different scheduling strategies

tion that recursively merges the input restart stacks, and invokes `blocked_foo_restart` if the number of tasks at a level exceeds the restart threshold.

Frequent restart stack merges may be expensive. To minimize this cost, we introduce an optimization to directly pass the restart stack from one `spawn` to next if *no steal* happened. As shown in Figure 3(c) lines 9–13, in normal case, each `spawn` takes as input a distinct input restart stack and returns a distinct restart stack. These restart stacks are merged together after the `sync`. To reduce the cost, we test whether the a steal immediately preceded the given `spawn` statement. If not, the previous `spawn`'s output restart stack is provided as the input restart stack to this `spawn`, and the merge operation between them is eliminated. In terms of the pseudo-code, the *spawn* in the `blocked_foo_restart` function (line 11) is replaced by the following:

```
if NO_INTERVENING_STEAL:
  rright = spawn blocked_foo_restart(right, rb.next)
else:
  rright = spawn blocked_foo_restart(right, NULL)
```

Limitations of simplified restart: As shown in Figure 3(c), the simplified restart strategy can be directly translated into a Cilk program. While simpler to implement than the restart strategy formulated in Section 4.3, this simplified strategy suffers from significant limitations. These arise from the fact that the RestartBlock stack returned by the function is not available for further processing until all work preceding the immediately enclosing sync scope complete. We briefly discuss these limitations, but do not present concrete proofs due to space limitations. First, passing restart stacks through the return path can lead to an important source of concurrency being stashed away, unavailable for execution by idle workers. In the worst case, this can lead to a fully serialized execution. Second, consider a execution of a TaskBlock at depth h. At each level 0 through $h-1$, a restart stack can be suspended, requiring a total space of $h^2 t_{restart}$ space, which is worse than the space overhead for the ideal restart strategy. Despite these limitations, we observe in Section 7 that this restart strategy achieves competitive performance for the benchmarks considered.

7. Experimental Evaluation

We conduct our experiments on an 8-core, 2.6 GHz Intel E5-2670 CPU with 32 KB L1 cache per core, 20 MB last-level cache, and 128-bit SSE 4.2 instruction set. The input recursive program, re-expansion (`reexp`), and restart (`restart`) variants are parallelized as Cilk programs and compiled using MIT Cilk [5][6]. All program variants are compiled using the Intel icc-13.3.163 compiler with `-O3` optimization. We report the mean of 10 runs. We do not report the negligible standard deviation observed due to space constraints. We observed little difference in performance between enabling and disabling compiler vectorization for the input program, despite some loops getting vectorized. We use execution times of the sequential runs with compiler auto-vectorization as the baseline.

Table 1 list the basic features of the benchmarks: problem input, number of levels in the computation tree, and total number of tasks. The sequential version of each benchmark is obtained by removing the Cilk keywords (spawn and sync). The execution time for this sequential execution time (T_s) serves as the baseline for all evaluation in this section. The benchmarks have varying computation tree structures: `knapsack` is a perfectly balanced tree with all base case tasks at the last level. `fib`, `binomial`, `parentheses`, `Point correlation`, and `knn` (k-nearest neighbor) are unbalanced binary trees with varying numbers of base case tasks in the middle levels. All other benchmarks are more unbalanced with larger fan-outs. `uts` is a binomial tree and much deeper than `nqueens`, `graphcol`, `minmax`, and `Barnes-Hut`[7].

The benchmarks show various mixing of *task parallelism* and *data parallelism*: `knapsack`, `fib`, `parentheses`,

[6] The non-parallelized version of `reexp` is, effectively, Ren et al.'s vectorization strategy [15].

[7] A more detailed characterization can be found in [15]

Benchmark	Problem	#Levels	#Tasks	T_s(s)	T_1(s)	T_{16}	Block size	RB size	T_s/T_1	1-worker		T_s/T_{16}	16-worker	
										T_s/T_{1x}	T_s/T_{1r}		Ts/T_{16x}	Ts/T_{16r}
knapsack	long	31	2.15B	9	61	3.9	2^{12}	any	0.14	1.68	1.69	2.2	24.8	24.6
fib	45	45	3.67B	9	99	6.7	2^{14}	4096	0.09	1.57	1.58	1.3	22.9	22.7
parentheses	19	37	4.85B	10	134	8.8	2^{13}	4607	0.08	1.42	1.40	1.2	20.3	19.4
nqueens	15	16	168M	233	267	16.7	2^{12}	2040	0.89	4.00	4.08	14.2	61.6	60.9
graphcol	3(38-64)	39	42.4M	31	37	2.4	2^{10}	473	0.85	8.74	8.78	13.0	108	107
uts	30	228	19.9M	146	152	9.6	2^{11}	2047	0.97	1.58	1.59	15.4	23.0	23.8
binomial	C(36,13)	36	4.62B	8	126	8.1	2^{13}	4096	0.07	1.00	0.97	1.0	14.9	14.1
minmax	4×4	13	2.42B	19	58	3.7	2^{10}	32767	0.31	1.65	1.57	4.9	20.6	17.1
Barnes-Hut	1M	18	3.00B	81	227	53.8	2^{9}	511	0.35	1.34	1.48	1.5	16.0	17.5
Point corr.	300K	18	1.77B	132	197	13.1	2^{10}	256	0.74	1.89	1.74	11.1	29.9	27.9
knn	100K	15	1.36B	71	105	7.6	2^{9}	128	0.65	1.24	1.20	8.9	19.3	18.4
Geo. mean									0.31	1.89	1.87	4.2	26.7	26.0

Table 1: Benchmark characteristics and performance. T_s: sequential execution time; T_1: single-threaded execution time of the input Cilk version; T_{1x}, T_{1r}: single-threaded SIMD execution time of re-expansion and restart versions, respectively; T_{16}, T_{16x}, T_{16r}: execution time of input, re-expansion, or restart versions on 16 workers, respectively. All re-expansion and restart implementations use 16-wide vector operations, except 8-wide for knapsack,and 4-wide vector operations for uts, Barnes-Hut, Point correlation, and knn. Block size: Best block size for re-expansion and restart, except 16-worker nqueens (2^{11}), graphcol (2^9), and minmax (2^{15} for re-expansion and 2^9 for restart). RB size: Restart block size used by the restart versions.

	scalar	reexp			restart		
		Block	SOA	SIMD	Block	SOA	SIMD
1-worker	0.3	0.5	0.6	1.9	0.5	0.6	1.9
16-worker	4.2	6.4	9.5	26.7	8.2	9.3	26.0
Scalability	13.6	11.7	15.3	14.2	16.2	15.2	13.9

Table 2: Geometric mean of speedup with respect to T_s for implementation variants on 1 and 16 workers. scalar: input Cilk program; Block: Blocked using re-expansion or restart strategy; SOA: Blocked version transformed to struct-of-arrays layout to enable vectorization; SIMD: SIMD vectorized version of the benchmark in SOA form. Scalability shows the relative performance of the same implementation running on 16 workers as compared to 1 worker.

`uts`, `binomial`, and `minmax` only show *task parallelism* in the form of recursions; `nqueens` and `graphcol` have nested *data parallelism* within their outer *task parallel* recursions; `Barnes-Hut` has a for-loop outside recursive function calls, i.e., *task parallelism* is nested in *data parallelism*; and `Point corr.` and `knn` are more complex, with three levels of parallelism, *data parallel* base cases nested within *task parallel* recursion, which is, in turn, nested within *data parallel* outer loops.

To improve vectorization potential, we use the smallest possible data type, without affecting generality, for each benchmark: `knapsack` and `uts` use `short` and `int`, respectively. `Barnes-Hut`, `Point correlation`, and `knn` use `float`. Other benchmarks use `char`.

7.1 Speedup from Blocked SIMD Execution

Table 1 shows the effectiveness of various strategies to exploit task and data parallelism on both single core (1-worker) and multi-cores (16-worker). Even on one thread, re-expansion and restart strategies, coupled with SIMD vectorization, improve (1.8× average) over sequential execution times. Combining compiler vectorization with Cilk parallelization achieves a speedup of 4.2 (average) over sequential execution. Re-expansion and restart significantly improve upon this default parallelization, achieving 26× (average) speedup over T_s. This shows the overall efficacy of the re-expansion and restart strategies. Re-expansion and restart strategies exhibit similar performance across all the benchmarks considered. For `restart`, we select the optimum $t_{restart}$ threshold, shown as *RB Size* in the table.

Our speedup primarily benefits from three sources: first, the reduction of recursive function calls from pure task parallelism to the combination of both task parallelism and data parallelism; second, the vectorization optimization, and associated efficient data layout transformations such as *AoS to SoA*; and third, good scalability from one worker to multiple workers. The first effect is important for kernels with little sequential work. In these kernels, the Cilk recursive scheduling incurs relatively large overheads. Our blocked execution can efficiently reduce such overhead, because our task blocks coarsen the granularity of spawned tasks. This is also why we may get more than `SIMD-width` times speedup for some of these benchmarks' 1-worker version. Table 2 demonstrates the relative speedup of each transformation on the input benchmark from the input version to the blocked, layout transformed to struct-of-arrays form so as to enable SIMD vectorization (`SOA`), and the final vectorized version.

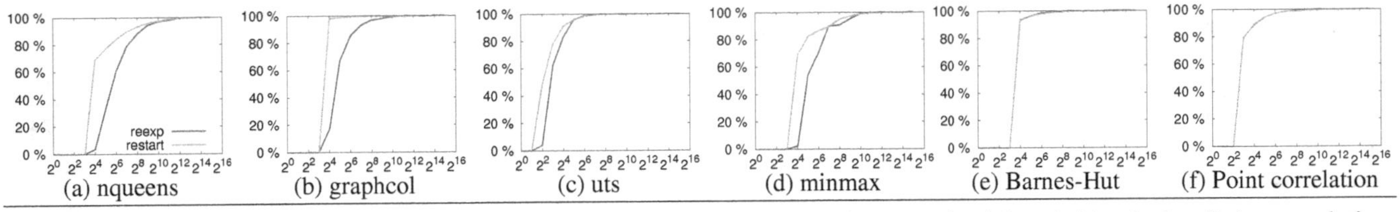

Figure 4: SIMD utilization. x-axis: block size; y-axis: %age of tasks that can be vectorized. knn is identical to Point correlation.

For both re-expansion and restart strategies, we see that the SOA transformation to enable vectorization improve performance on top of blocking. However, we observe even greater improvements from vectorizing this layout-transformed version. In general, comparing to the first effect, the second and third effects are more important. Therefore, in the following sections, we evaluate the impact the `reexp` and `restart` strategies have on vectorization efficiency and scalability.

7.2 Impact of Block Size on SIMD Utilization

Increasing the block size can expose more work to be executed by the vector unit, increasing *SIMD utilization* (the ratio of complete SIMD steps to total steps during execution). However, larger block sizes consume more space and increase cache pressure. A good scheduling strategy should achieve good SIMD utilization with small block sizes.

Figure 4 shows the SIMD utilization of `reexp` and `restart` at various block sizes (for space reasons, we present results only for the larger benchmarks). SIMD utilization grows with increasing block size, and, consistent with the theoretical analysis, at each block size `restart` matches or exceeds the SIMD utilization achieved by `reexp`. For smaller block sizes, `restart` performs better than `reexp` for all benchmarks except for `knapsack`, `Barnes-Hut`, `Point correlation`, and `knn`, where both strategies achieve similar performance improvements. For benchmarks like `graphcol` and `uts`, `restart` can achieve $> 90\%$ SIMD utilization at block size of 2^4, while `reexp` requires 2^7 and 2^5. For benchmarks such as `nqueens` and `minmax`, SIMD utilization improves more slowly for both `reexp` and `restart`. However, SIMD utilization for `restart` continues to exceed that for `reexp` for smaller block sizes. In the case of `Barnes-Hut` and `Point correlation`, both `restart` and `reexp` achieve identical SIMD utilization for all block sizes considered.

7.3 Scalability of Blocked SIMD Execution

The scalability for the best block size is shown in Table 1. For the best block size, `reexp` and `restart` achieve comparable speedups for most benchmarks, and the performance difference is within 5%.

Given the difference in SIMD utilization between re-expansion and restart at smaller block sizes, we show scalability of of `reexp` and `restart` with various numbers of Cilk workers for a small block size (2^5) in Figure 5. For this small block size, we find that `restart` performs better if it can improve the SIMD utilization (such as `nqueens`,

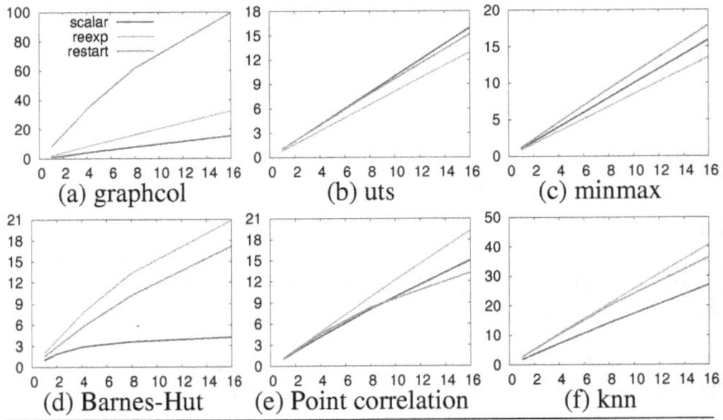

Figure 5: Xeon E5 scalability for block size 2^5. x-axis: number of workers; y-axis: speedup relative to 1-worker Cilk baseline.

`graphcol`, `uts` and `minmax`). Otherwise, it may result in some slowdown due to the implementation complexity and the cost of manipulating the restart stacks. For `nqueens` and `minmax`, `restart` can provide a reasonable speedup whereas `reexp` still results in some slowdown relative to the non-SIMD version. For benchmarks such as `Barnes-Hut`, `Point correlation`, and `knn`, the relatively poor scalability from 8-worker to 16-worker is due to the interference between hyper-threaded workers executed on the same core in the 8-core system.

In summary, both scheduling strategies have their advantages: `reexp` is easier to implement and has very low scheduling overhead, while `restart` has good theoretical bounds and can potentially improve the SIMD utilization for smaller block sizes. With either scheduling method, we can transform our candidate codes to achieve good speedup.

8. Related Work

In many programming systems, parallelizing recursive programs involves user identification of concurrent function invocations coupled with a runtime system that dynamically maps concurrent function invocations to the processing cores. Variants of the spawn-sync construct used in this paper constitute the most common subset of many such programming systems (Cilk [3, 4], Thread Building Blocks [13], OpenMP [11], X10 [18], etc.). These programming systems also allow programmers to write programs that mix task- and data-parallelism, and are not necessarily tied to SIMD architectures, so they are more general. However, they focus on mapping that parallelism to multicores, rather than tackling SIMD; thus, they typically decouple vectorization considerations from multicore parallelism and attempt to use SIMD instructions primarily in the base case. These approaches hence exploit SIMD less thoroughly than ours, which vectorizes the recursive steps in addition to base cases, taking advantage of SIMD at all steps of the computation.

Intel's ispc [12] is another existing effort closely related to our work. It targets programs that have task- and data-parallelism, and also attempts to exploit SIMD units in addition to multicores. However, its handling of nesting of task- and data-parallelism differs substantially from ours. In particular, given a data-parallel for loop, different iterations are mapped to individual lanes of a SIMD unit. If that for loop contains nested task-parallelism, that task parallelism is not exploited: the entire iteration is executed within a single SIMD lane, underexploiting parallelism, causing divergent execution, and incurring unnecessary *gather* and *scatter* memory operations among all SIMD lanes.

Optimizations to improve recursion overhead include partial recursive call inlining [17] and transforming the program to a loop program [9]. Partial inlining indirectly helps vectorization by adding more instructions to the inductive work basic block, but often not enough to keep wide SIMD units busy.

Similar to our approach, Jo et al. [7] optimized tree traversal algorithms by vectorizing across multiple root-to-leaf traversals. The nodes of the tree, rather than the call stack, are used to track execution progress. Also, their work did not consider multi-core parallelization. Ren et al. [15] presented the re-expansion strategy to vectorize recursive programs. However, as discussed in the introduction, they provide no theoretical analysis of the benefits of their strategy, do not deal with multicore execution, and do not consider the restart strategy.

9. Conclusions

We presented a unified approach for executing programs that exhibit both task- and data-parallelism on systems that contain both vector units and multicores. Rather than "baking in" execution strategies based on programming models (e.g., converting data parallelism to task parallelism in Cilk [6], or vice versa [15], or choosing to only exploit one type of parallelism in programs that contain both [8, 14]), our unified scheduling framework allows programs to execute in the manner best suited to the current context and hardware: if there is enough data parallelism at a particular point in an execution, vector units can be exploited, while if there is too much load imbalance at another point, data parallelism can be traded off for task parallelism to allow for work stealing. This *grain free* execution strategy allows for the free mixing and arbitrary exploitation of both types of parallelism and both types of parallel hardware. By using our framework, we are able to achieve 14×–108× speedup (23×–259× over 1-worker Cilk) across ten benchmarks by exploiting both SIMD units and multicores on an 8-core system.

10. Acknowledgments

The authors would like to thank our shepherd, Mary Hall, as well as the anonymous reviewers for their helpful suggestions and comments. The authors would also like to thank Youngjoon Jo for contributing to several benchmarks. This work was supported in part by the U.S. Department of Energy's (DOE) Office of Science, Office of Advanced Scientific Computing Research, under DOE Early Career awards 63823 and DE-SC0010295. This work was also supported in part by NSF awards CCF-1150013 (CAREER), CCF-1439126, CCF-1218017, and CCF-1439062. Pacific Northwest National Laboratory is operated by Battelle for DOE under Contract DE-AC05-76RL01830.

References

[1] N. S. Arora, R. D. Blumofe, and C. G. Plaxton. Thread Scheduling for Multiprogrammed Multiprocessors. In *SPAA*, pages 119–129, 1998.

[2] J. Barnes and P. Hut. A hierarchical $o(nlogn)$ force-calculation algorithm. *Nature*, 324(4):446–449, December 1986.

[3] R. D. Blumofe and C. E. Leiserson. Scheduling Multithreaded Computations by Work Stealing. *J. ACM*, 46(5):720–748, 1999.

[4] R. D. Blumofe, C. F. Joerg, B. C. Kuszmaul, C. E. Leiserson, K. H. Randall, and Y. Zhou. Cilk: An Efficient Multithreaded Runtime System. *Journal of Parallel and Distributed Computing*, 37(1):55–69, August 25, 1996.

[5] Cilk. Cilk 5.4.6. `http://supertech.csail.mit.edu/cilk/`.

[6] I. Corp. Intel Cilk Plus Language Extension Specification, 2011.

[7] Y. Jo and M. Kulkarni. Enhancing Locality for Recursive Traversals of Recursive Structures. In *OOPSLA*, pages 463–482, 2011.

[8] Y. Jo, M. Goldfarb, and M. Kulkarni. Automatic Vectorization of Tree Traversals. In *PACT*, pages 363–374, 2013.

[9] Y. A. Liu and S. D. Stoller. From Recursion to Iteration: What are the Optimizations? In *PEPM*, pages 73–82, 2000.

[10] S. Maleki, Y. Gao, M. J. Garzarán, T. Wong, and D. A. Padua. An Evaluation of Vectorizing Compilers. In *PACT*, pages 372–382, 2011.

[11] OpenMP Architecture Review Board. OpenMP Specification and Features. `http://openmp.org/wp/`, May 2008.

[12] M. Pharr and W. R. Mark. ispc: A SPMD Compiler for High-performance CPU Programming. In *Innovative Parallel Computing (InPar), 2012*, pages 1–13. IEEE, 2012.

[13] J. Reinders. *Intel Threading Building Blocks: Outfitting C++ for Multi-Core Processor Parallelism.* O'Reilly, 2007.

[14] B. Ren, G. Agrawal, J. R. Larus, T. Mytkowicz, T. Poutanen, and W. Schulte. SIMD Parallelization of Applications that Traverse Irregular Data Structures. In *2013 IEEE/ACM International Symposium on Code Generation and Optimization (CGO)*, pages 1–10. IEEE, 2013.

[15] B. Ren, Y. Jo, S. Krishnamoorthy, K. Agrawal, and M. Kulkarni. Efficient Execution of Recursive Programs on Commodity Vector Hardware. In *PLDI*, pages 509–520, 2015.

[16] M. Rinard and P. C. Diniz. Commutativity analysis: a new analysis technique for parallelizing compilers. *ACM Trans. Program. Lang. Syst.*, 19(6):942–991, 1997. ISSN 0164-0925. doi: http://doi.acm.org/10.1145/267959.269969.

[17] R. Rugina and M. C. Rinard. Recursion Unrolling for Divide and Conquer Programs. In *LCPC*, pages 34–48, 2000.

[18] X10. The X10 Programming Language. `www.research.ibm.com/x10/`, Mar. 2006.

Isoefficiency in Practice: Configuring and Understanding the Performance of Task-based Applications

Sergei Shudler
Technische Universität Darmstadt
Darmstadt, Germany
shudler@cs.tu-darmstadt.de

Alexandru Calotoiu
Technische Universität Darmstadt
Darmstadt, Germany
calotoiu@cs.tu-darmstadt.de

Torsten Hoefler
ETH Zurich
Zurich, Switzerland
htor@inf.ethz.ch

Felix Wolf
Technische Universität Darmstadt
Darmstadt, Germany
wolf@cs.tu-darmstadt.de

Abstract

Task-based programming offers an elegant way to express units of computation and the dependencies among them, making it easier to distribute the computational load evenly across multiple cores. However, this separation of problem decomposition and parallelism requires a sufficiently large input problem to achieve satisfactory efficiency on a given number of cores. Unfortunately, finding a good match between input size and core count usually requires significant experimentation, which is expensive and sometimes even impractical. In this paper, we propose an automated empirical method for finding the isoefficiency function of a task-based program, binding efficiency, core count, and the input size in one analytical expression. This allows the latter two to be adjusted according to given (realistic) efficiency objectives. Moreover, we not only find (i) the actual isoefficiency function but also (ii) the function one would yield if the program execution was free of resource contention and (iii) an upper bound that could only be reached if the program was able to maintain its average parallelism throughout its execution. The difference between the three helps to explain low efficiency, and in particular, it helps to differentiate between resource contention and structural conflicts related to task dependencies or scheduling. The insights gained can be used to co-design programs and shared system resources.

PPoPP '17, February 4–8, 2017, Austin, Texas, USA.

DOI: http://dx.doi.org/10.1145/3018743.3018770

Categories and Subject Descriptors C.4 [*Performance of Systems*]: Modeling techniques; D.1.3 [*Concurrent Programming*]: Parallel programming; D.2.8 [*Metrics*]: Performance measures; D.4.8 [*Performance*]: Modeling and prediction

Keywords parallel programming; tasking; isoefficiency; performance modeling; performance analysis; co-design

1. Introduction

Task-based programming models, such as Cilk [7] or OpenMP [28], are well known and as the number of cores per node continues to increase, they gain more and more attention. One major advantage of task-based programming is that it allows parallelism to be expressed in terms of tasks, which are units of computation that can be either independent, dependent on a previous task, or a prerequisite to a subsequent task. Explicitly expressing parts of the code as tasks allows the compiler to take care of all the thread management intricacies, thereby sparing the user from tedious low-level details. Good task delineation also helps the scheduler better exploit the inherent parallelism and can lead to improved load balance. For these reasons, task-based programming will play an even more prominent role in exascale systems.

Normally, when the user receives an allocation of computing resources, the nodes are not shared. This means the user has to use all of the cores on each node efficiently, otherwise, computing resources are wasted. In an exascale system this problem will be even more pronounced because the available node concurrency is predicted to be larger by at least one order of magnitude compared to the systems available today [34].

Although the optimization of task-based algorithms has been studied extensively in the past [12, 14, 21, 27, 33], the size of the input in these studies usually remained fixed. Since the critical path length in a task dependency graph limits the speedup of the algorithm [8], fixed input size means that no matter how well the algorithm is optimized, the speedup, and thus the efficiency, is limited. Starting from a certain core count the speedup will stop increasing unless the input size increases as well. Moreover, scaling is often not perfect, meaning that the speedup rate is too slow to maintain constant efficiency. Figure 1 is an example of this phenomenon. It shows the speedup and efficiency for the applications Sort and Strassen from the Barcelona OpenMP Tasks Suite (BOTS) [14]. Although the inputs for these applications are 128M integers and 8,192 × 8,192 doubles, respectively, their speedup does not increase fast enough, leading to a sharp drop in efficiency. Even if we try to optimize the code and achieve better speedups, the effect will not last at higher scales, as an optimized version will still be limited by the length of the critical path. The only way to ensure that efficiency remains constant, as the number of cores increases, is to increase the input size as well. This concept is embodied in the isoefficiency relation [20], which binds the number of processing elements (PEs) the application uses to the input size. It specifies by which factor the input size has to increase, with respect to the increase in the number of PEs, to maintain constant efficiency. Isoefficiency can be generalized to a two-parameter efficiency function that provides efficiency values as a function of both the PE count and the input size. The contour lines of this function are exactly isoefficiency lines (cf. Section 3).

Although isoefficiency analysis is useful in understanding the scalability behavior of algorithms, it is not straightforward to apply and requires deep knowledge of the algorithm. Moreover, it only provides theoretical insight, much like traditional complexity analysis. In practice, however, task-based algorithms experience hardware limitations in the form of resource contention in general and memory contention in particular. Resources such as cache and memory controllers are limited and can negatively impact application scalability [35]. These might render theoretical isoefficiency functions not accurate enough to be used in practice. To be able to make informed decisions as to how big the input size should be in order to use all of the allocated cores efficiently, the user not only has to have a realistic isoefficiency model but also needs to understand the severity of resource contention at higher scales.

In this study, we propose a novel practical method to automatically model the empirical efficiency functions of task-based applications and their contention-free replay runs. Modeling the efficiency function allows us to easily derive an isoefficiency relation for any realistic target efficiency. To this end, we developed a task replay engine that executes empty task skeletons, thereby emulating execution without resource contention. Resource contention includes cache accesses, memory bandwidth, coherence traffic, network com-

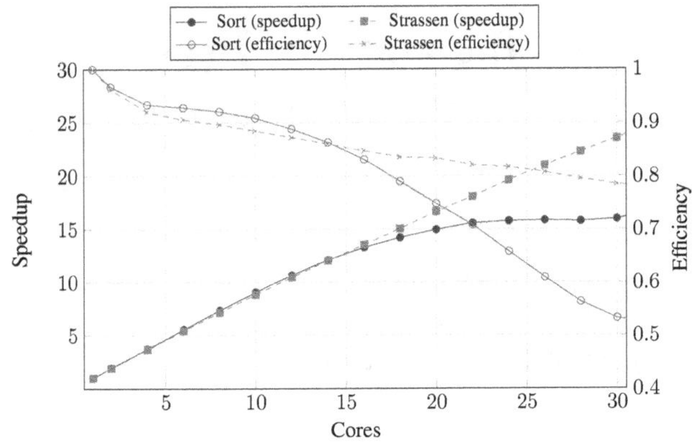

Figure 1: Speedup and efficiency for Sort and Strassen applications from BOTS benchmark.

munication, and disk I/O. After performing the replay runs we derive the efficiency function from the results and compare the models we obtain with the models of normal runs. A big discrepancy suggests that resource contention overhead is a major scalability bottleneck. We also analyze the task dependency graph (TDG) and model an upper bound efficiency based on TDG metrics. A discrepancy between the upper bound efficiency and the contention-free efficiency suggests that there is still room to improve either the algorithm itself or the scheduler. Our approach is applicable to both pure shared memory applications, as well as to task-based parts of hybrid applications (e.g., OpenMP parallel regions in hybrid MPI / OpenMP applications). Our approach helps users, application developers, and hardware designers answer the following important questions, related to both application analysis and deployment:

1. Are there any fundamental scalability limitations in the algorithm or the implementation of a task-based application? This is helpful to compare implementation alternatives independently of the target system.
2. Is poor scaling of a task-based application a result of resource contention overhead? The answer helps application developers analyze the causes of bottlenecks in their applications and system designers to respond to pressure on shared resources.
3. Is there any optimization potential, in terms of task dependencies, scheduling, and granularity in a task-based application? The answer helps application developers optimize their applications on the level of the task graph and its execution.
4. What is the required input size for a given core count such that we maintain a constant, given efficiency? The answer helps users efficiently utilize all the computing resources they have. They can aim for the right problem sizes based on the number of available cores.

5. What is the required core count for a given input size such that we maintain a constant, given efficiency? Which efficiency can we expect for a given number of cores and input size? Both questions are related to the co-design process when hardware designers have to understand how to make future systems suitable for both existing and future applications.

The remainder of this paper is organized as follows. In Section 2, we describe the task dependency graph analysis in greater detail. In Section 3 we describe the efficiency modeling approach and present the task replay engine. Section 4 evaluates our technique, analyzes the results, and, at the end, shows examples of deriving application input sizes for a target machine. Finally, we review related work in Section 5, before drawing our conclusion in Section 6.

2. Task Dependency Graphs and Efficiency Analysis

There is an important difference between tasks and threads: a task is a work package containing a collection of instructions to be executed, whereas a thread is a light-weight process that executes given instructions in an independent context. A task-based code can be executed by one or more threads running on one or more cores. Each instance of a task is executed at any given time by only one thread. For the purpose of our discussion, we will assume that the number of threads is equal to the number of cores, and that each thread runs on a separate core.

A task dependency graph (TDG) is a directed acyclic graph (DAG) that represents the execution of a task-based application. The nodes of this graph are tasks, and the edges represent dependencies between tasks, meaning that a task cannot begin execution before the tasks connected to it via incoming edges have been completed. Except for some trivial cases, most of the interesting and useful problems have dependencies in their algorithm flow, thereby producing complex TDGs.

In the process of execution, the scheduler assigns tasks, which are ready to be executed, to threads. Depending on the scheduler, tasks might be stopped (i.e., preempted) and resumed later. In this regard, tasking environments, including OpenMP, distinguish between *tied* and *untied* tasks. A tied task can only be executed by the thread that started executing it. This implies that if this task is preempted it can only be resumed by the thread that executed it before. An untied task, on the other hand, can be resumed by any available thread after preemption. Both types of tasks have advantages—tied tasks provide guarantees for private data (i.e., data on the stack), whereas untied tasks provide more flexibility to the scheduler. In this study we use applications with both types of tasks.

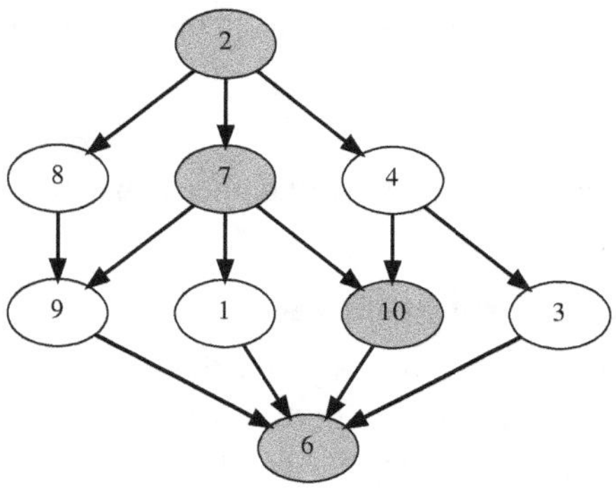

Figure 2: Task dependency graph; each node contains the task time and the highlighted tasks form the critical path.

2.1 TDG Metrics and Laws

We characterize TDGs using a set of key metrics [6, 11]. The *work* of the computation is the total execution time on one core, or the sum of all the task times. The *depth* of the computation (also known as *span*) is the total sum of all task times on the *critical path*, which is the longest path, in terms of task times, from any source node to any target node. A source node is a node with no incoming edges, and a target node is a node without any outgoing edges. Figure 2 shows an example of a TDG in which work equals 50 and depth equals 25. In the rest of the paper, we use the following notations:

- p, n: the number of threads and the input size, respectively.
- $T_p(n)$: the execution time of a computation with p threads with input size n.
- $T_1(n)$: the work of the computation, or the computational effort for input size n.
- $T_\infty(n)$: the depth of the computation for input size n.
- $S_p(n) = \frac{T_1(n)}{T_p(n)}$: the speedup of the computation for specific p and n.
- $\pi(n) = \frac{T_1(n)}{T_\infty(n)}$: the *average* parallelism of the computation for n.

From these TDG metrics we can derive important laws [11] and boundaries on speedup and efficiency.

Work law The execution cannot be faster than when we divide the whole work $T_1(n)$ equally between cores:

$$T_p(n) \geq \frac{T_1(n)}{p} \tag{1}$$

A direct consequence of the work law is an upper bound on the speedup: $S_p(n) \leq p$. We ignore super-linear speedups for the sake of simplicity.

Depth law Since the critical path is a chain of dependencies, the tasks on this path must be executed one after the other, giving us another lower bound on the execution:

$$T_p \geq T_\infty \quad (2)$$

In this case we can derive another upper bound on the speedup: $S_p(n) \leq \pi(n)$.

2.2 Efficiency and Isoefficiency

The two-parameter efficiency function is defined as efficiency $E(p,n) = \frac{S_p(n)}{p}$ with two parameters p and n. The isoefficiency, which binds together the core count and the input size [19, 20] for a specific, constant efficiency, is simply a contour line on the surface of $E(p,n)$. To clarify this point, we first define the total overhead time:

$$T_o(p,n) = pT_p(n) - T_1(n) \quad (3)$$

This is the total amount of time that all of the threads spend without contributing to the solution of the problem, including resource contention, idle time, and scheduling overhead. Rearranging Eq. 3 and using the efficiency definition (i.e., $E = \frac{S_p(n)}{p}$) yields the isoefficiency relation:

$$T_1(n) = \frac{E}{1-E} T_o(p,n) \quad (4)$$

This relation binds $T_1(n)$, p, and E. Normally, in isoefficiency analysis, the efficiency E is constant and we are able to form an expression that relates the core count p to the work of the computation $T_1(n)$. However, if we rearrange Eq. 4 such that $E = f(p,n)$, we obtain an expression that relates the core count p and the input size n to the efficiency E. In other words, we obtain the efficiency function. It is easy to see now that isoefficiency is a special case of the more general efficiency function limited to a specific, constant efficiency.

Isoefficiency is a useful tool in the theoretical analysis of parallel algorithms. It allows users and developers to compare different alternatives and choose the one in which the problem size grows more slowly in relation to the core count. In practice, however, resource contention overhead might overshadow other types of overheads and render a thought-to-be-scalable algorithm unscalable. Our methodology tackles this problem by modeling the empirical efficiency functions of both the application itself and the contention-free replay of the application. We can identify three different efficiency functions for a task-based application:

1. $E_{ac}(p,n)$: The actual efficiency function of the application, modeled after the empirical results of runtime benchmarks. In this case the application runs as it is and experiences contention. Therefore, this function reflects realistic application performance including resource contention and scheduling overhead.
2. $E_{cf}(p,n)$: The contention-free efficiency function, modeled after the results of replaying empty task skeletons according to the application's TDG. The replay uses the same TDG and scheduling policy as in the original runs that were benchmarked to produce $E_{ac}(p,n)$. Since the replay is free of resource contention, this efficiency function reflects an ideal situation in which the application does not experience resource contention caused by threads accessing the same resource simultaneously.
3. $E_{ub}(p,n)$: An upper bound on the efficiency of the application. Since efficiency is defined as $\frac{S_p(n)}{p}$, an upper bound on the speedup also limits the efficiency. From Section 2.1 we know that $S_p(n) \leq \min\{p, \pi(n)\}$, thus we define $E_{ub}(p,n) = \min\{1, \frac{\pi(n)}{p}\}$. This function describes an ideal situation of maximum speedup that is hardly achievable in practice.

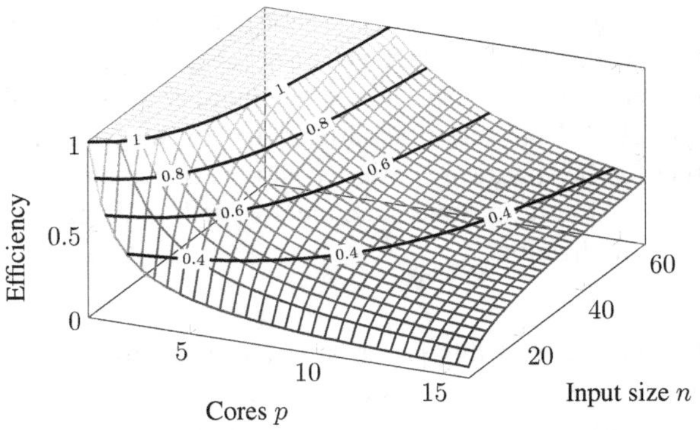

Figure 3: Upper-bound efficiency function $E_{ub}(p,n) = \min\{1, \frac{\log n}{p}\}$. The contour lines are isoefficiency functions for the efficiency values 1.0, 0.8, 0.6, and 0.4.

As a concrete example for an efficiency function, consider the task-based version of the Mergesort algorithm. A theoretical analysis of its TDG, for increasing input size n, gives us: $T_1(n) = \Theta(n \log n)$ and $T_\infty(n) = \Theta(n)$ [11]. Without loss of generality, we assume that the constant factor is 1 and get: $\pi(n) = \log n$. Figure 3 depicts the upper-limit efficiency function $E_{ub}(p,n) = \min\{1, \frac{\log n}{p}\}$ that we obtain in this case. It is a 3D surface graph in which the X and Y axes are the core count and the input size, respectively; whereas, the Z-axis, limited to the range $[0,1]$, gives us the efficiency values. The contour lines at Z-axis values of $E=1$, $E=0.8$, $E=0.6$, and $E=0.4$ are isoefficiency functions for these efficiencies.

By analyzing the differences between the efficiency function we can gain a number of important insights:

- $\Delta_{con} = E_{cf}(p,n) - E_{ac}(p,n)$: The contention discrepancy between actual and contention-free efficiencies characterizes how severe the resource contention overhead is. Essentially, it tells us whether this overhead is a significant obstacle to application scalability. A big discrepancy suggests that optimization efforts should focus

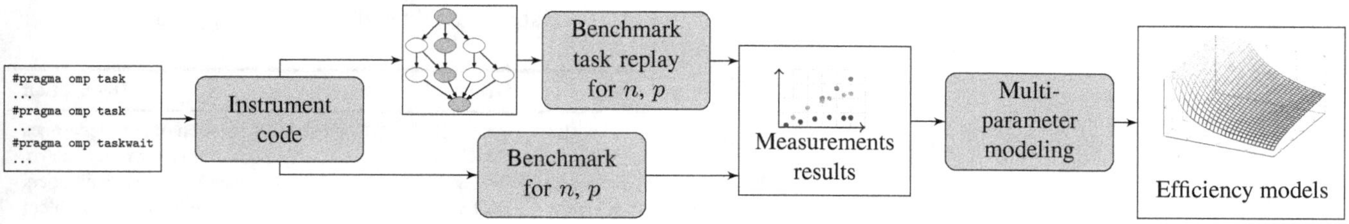

Figure 4: The modeling workflow for actual and replay efficiency models.

on reducing the resource contention either on the level of the application or the underlying system.

- $\Delta_{str} = E_{ub}(p,n) - E_{cf}(p,n)$: The structural discrepancy between upper bound and contention-free efficiencies characterizes the optimization potential of the application on the level of the task graph. A big discrepancy suggests that developers should explore optimization steps beyond reducing resource contention, such as reducing task dependencies, adjusting the task granularity, or using a more efficient scheduler. A small discrepancy, on the other hand, means that – disregarding contention – an algorithm's implementation is close to the maximum efficiency that it can achieve. Δ_{str} can only provide insights into an observed behavior of an application's algorithm. However, there might be other, possibly better algorithms that would produce different TDGs with different $E_{ub}(p,n)$ functions, and potentially, even a better maximum efficiency.

3. Modeling Approach

In this section we present our approach to modeling the efficiency functions, and consequently, the isoefficiency functions. Performance modeling, and automated performance modeling in particular, was shown to be useful and practical for analyzing the performance of parallel applications [9, 23, 26, 31, 32]. In this work, we combine multi-parameter performance modeling with benchmarking of real task-based applications to automatically generate the empirical efficiency functions of both the application and the contention-free replay of the application's TDG.

Figure 4 shows the modeling workflow. It starts with instrumenting the code, continues with the construction of the code's TDG, and then proceeds with benchmarking the code for increasing n and p. The TDG is used as an input to the replay engine, which we will present later in this section, and the replay is benchmarked in the same way as the code itself. After benchmarking both the application and the replay, we continue with producing empirical models using the performance-modeling tool Extra-P [2].

For our study we use the OmpSs [15] threading environment. Similar to OpenMP, OmpSs offers the ability to annotate functions or blocks of code as tasks. Although task dependencies were already introduced in OpenMP 4.0, not all compilers support them in full yet. OmpSs, on the other hand, provides a more mature task dependency support that allows experimentation with more complex TDGs. The OmpSs runtime, Nanos++, provides an instrumentation plugin that instruments the code, measures the task execution times, generates the TDG, and saves it as a Graphviz [3] `.dot` file. We modified the instrumentation plugin to compute T_1 and T_∞, and produce a simplified `.dot` file, better suited as an input to the replay engine.

Moreover, OmpSs and OpenMP offer the same syntax for task creation and synchronization, namely, `#pragma omp task` and `#pragma omp taskwait` work in both environments. This allows the OmpSs compiler to compile OpenMP task-based applications, and it also allows the Nanos++ runtime to successfully instrument them.

OmpSs provides a number of choices for task scheduling policies during application execution. Using the *breadth first* scheduler (`--schedule=bf` flag) for tied tasks and the *work first* scheduler (`--schedule=wf` flag) for untied tasks was shown to produce good runtimes [13]. The breadth first scheduler uses a single, FIFO-ordered global ready queue for the tasks. Whenever a task is ready (i.e., its dependencies are fulfilled) it is enqueued in the queue and later dequeued to be executed by an available thread. The work first scheduler, on the other hand, uses one ready queue per thread. Whenever a task is created by a thread, the thread begins to execute it immediately, preempting the current task and placing it in the queue. If a thread becomes idle and its queue is empty, it attempts to steal tasks from the queues of the other threads to improve load balance. This scheduling policy is similar to the default scheduling policy used in Cilk [7].

3.1 Task Replay Engine

The goal of the task replay engine is to emulate the execution of a task graph without resource contention. The TDG, constructed by the instrumentation plugin, contains task times when the code is executed by one thread. Since a single thread does not have to share memory bandwidth or wait for other threads to access shared data structures, these times are free of resource contention overhead.

Instead of specifying the tasks implicitly using pragmas, the replay engine uses the OmpSs runtime API to specify the tasks and their dependencies explicitly. This API is defined in the `nanox/nanos.h` file that is part of the OmpSs installation. Each task is specified as a function that receives the

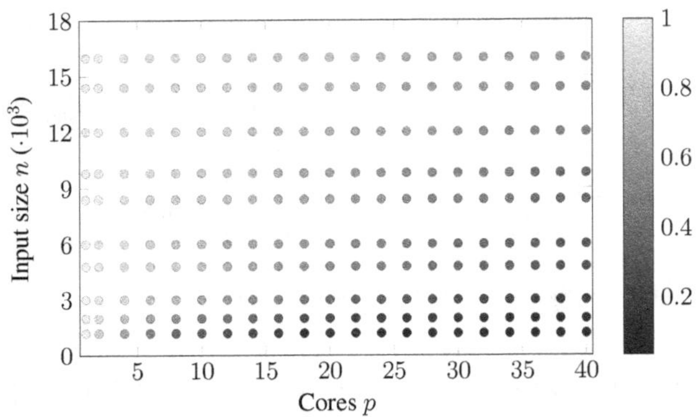

Figure 5: Typical benchmark results; the color of each point represents the measured efficiency.

task time as an argument and then busy-waits in a loop for the duration of this time. To query the time efficiently and with minimal overhead we use the timer of the *LibSciBench* library [22]. The library provides high-resolution timers for a number of common architectures. For the x86 architecture, on which we tested our methodology, the timer of the library uses the RDTSC register, and in order to prevent problems with out-of-order execution it issues the `CPUID` instruction before querying the register. The overhead in the function that emulates task execution is minimal. It only includes querying the time, repeating a loop counter, and accessing one local variable to store the accumulated time.

Since we use the same OmpSs runtime for the replays as we use for the normal runs, we ensure that the combination of the scheduler and tied/untied tasks during the replay is the same as it is during the normal runs.

3.2 Multi-Parameter Modeling with Extra-P

We start by selecting a range of threads p and a range of input sizes n. The benchmark then runs the application for each combination of p and n from these ranges. The results can be viewed as a 2D grid of points: the X-axis is the number of threads and the Y-axis is the input size. Figure 5 shows an example of such a 2D grid. Each point represents a single result and its color the measured efficiency.

After the benchmarking is done we run Extra-P [2] to produce two-parameter models of efficiency. These models are a special case of the more general multi-parameter models that aim to capture how a number of independent parameters, such as core count, problem size, and algorithmic parameters, influence a target metric, such as runtime, floating-point operations, and so on. The *performance model normal form* (PMNF) for multiple parameters [10] is defined as:

$$f(x_1, x_2, ..., x_m) = \sum_{k=1}^{n} c_k \cdot \prod_{l=1}^{m} x_l^{i_{k_l}} \cdot log^{j_{k_l}}(x_l) \quad (5)$$

In this form, parameters x_l are represented by m combinations of monomials and logarithms, which are summed up in n different terms to form the whole model. The exponents i_{k_l} and j_{k_l} are chosen from sets $I, J \subset \mathbb{Q}$, respectively. Essentially, these sets define the scope of all the possible terms. Consider, for example, $n = 3$, $m = 2$, and $I = \{0, 0.25, 0.5\}$, $J = \{0, 1\}$. In this case, the search space for possible terms would be $\{1, log(x), x^{0.25}, x^{0.25}log(x), x^{0.5}, x^{0.5}log(x)\}$, and an example model could be: $f(x_1, x_2) = c_1 + c_2 \cdot x_1^{0.5} + c_3 \cdot x_1^{0.25} x_2^{0.25} log(x_2)$.

The modeling technique is based on an iterative modeling refinement process that stops when $\bar{R}^2$, the adjusted coefficient of determination – a standard statistical fit factor $\in [0, 1]$ such that a value of 1 indicates an optimal fit – cannot be improved any further. In cases when n and m increase and the search space of possible terms becomes too big, the technique uses a heuristic that greatly reduces the number of candidate models, while retaining a high degree of accuracy. This makes the multi-parameter modeling mechanism a usable technique in practice [10].

4. Evaluation

In this section, we model the efficiency, and hence the isoefficiency, of a number of task-based applications using our methodology and evaluate the results. We start with a discussion of the benchmarking setup, and then continue with the analysis of the results, including depth and parallelism models, isoefficiency models, and co-design use cases.

4.1 Experimental Setup

Table 1 presents the applications we evaluated. Since the focus is on task-based OmpSs/OpenMP applications, we selected our candidates from well known benchmark suites that target these programming models, namely, the Barcelona OpenMP Tasks Suite (BOTS) [14] and the Barcelona Application Repository (BAR) [1]. We were able to use the OmpSs compiler, which supports both the OmpSs and the OpenMP syntax, to successfully compile BOTS. While applications from BAR only have tied tasks, BOTS offers both tied and untied versions of its applications. To have a better coverage of potential use cases, we chose to run untied versions of BOTS applications and selected the scheduling policy accordingly.

Table 1: Evaluated task-based applications.

App.	Origin	Description
Cholesky	BAR	Cholesky factorization of dense matrices
FFT	BAR	Fast Fourier transform of a matrix
Fibonacci	BOTS	Calculates Fibonacci numbers
NQueens	BOTS	Solution of the N-Queens problem
Sort	BOTS	Integer sorting with parallel Mergesort
SparseLU	BAR	LU decomposition over a sparse square matrix
Strassen	BOTS	Strassen's matrix multiplication

We ran our experiments on a single NUMA node that consists of four Xeon E7-4890 v2 processors with 15 cores

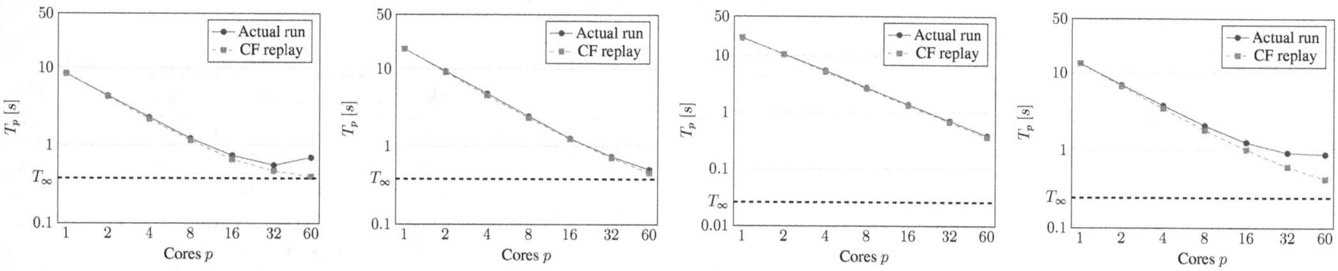

(a) Cholesky (8,400 × 8,400 doubles) (b) Fibonacci (n = 49) (c) NQueens (14 × 14 board) (d) Strassen (4K×4K doubles)

Figure 6: Runtimes of actual runs and contention-free (CF) replays (on log scale) with constant input. The horizontal dashed lines, labeled T_∞, show the depth of the computation for the given inputs.

in each processor. Together they comprise 60 cores in one shared-memory machine.

For measuring both the runtime of each application as well as the task times we used the timer of the *LibSciBench* library [22] (as in the task replay engine). Each execution and replay of a particular combination of (p, n) was repeated multiple times. To reduce the effects of noise and increase the accuracy of the models we measured the confidence intervals of our measurements and increased the number of repetitions accordingly. As a rule of thumb, we deemed the number of repetitions to be enough when the 95% confidence interval was no larger than 5% of the mean. For most of the benchmarked applications, five repetitions was enough, but for some of them ten repetitions were necessary. In the special case of $p = 1$, we ran both the instrumented version of the code to produce the TDG and the uninstrumented version to measure a perturbation-free runtime as input for efficiency calculations.

Some applications have more than one input parameter, and depending on a particular combination of input parameters, the TDG can increase in different ways. In some cases, the number of tasks stays constant, while the task sizes increase; in other cases, the tasks sizes stay constant, but the number of tasks increases. Sometimes both the number of tasks and the task sizes increase. In all these cases, both the work (i.e., $T_1(n)$) and n increase.

In the case of Cholesky, the smallest input was a 1,200 × 1,200 matrix with 200 × 200 blocks, and the largest was a 16,000×16,000 matrix with 800×800 blocks. The inputs for FFT ranged from 5,280×5,280 to 30,000×30,000 matrices.

The input for the Fibonacci application is the index of the Fibonacci number. In our benchmarks, the smallest input was 47 and the largest 53. Smaller inputs resulted in very short runtimes, which did not serve the purposes of this study. The input of NQueens is the board dimension, which ranged from 10 to 15. As in the case of Fibonacci, smaller inputs result in runtimes that are too short.

The application Sort in BOTS is a parallel variant of the Mergesort algorithm that expects the number of elements in the input to be a power-of-two value. Our inputs, therefore,

Table 2: Depth and parallelism models of the evaluated applications.

Application	Model		$\bar{R}^2$
Cholesky	$T_\infty(n)$	$4.31 \cdot 10^{-9} \cdot n^{1.75} \log n$	0.99
	$\pi(n)$	$2.29 + 2.35 \cdot n$	0.98
FFT	$T_\infty(n)$	$0.08 + 1.33 \cdot 10^{-14} \cdot n^{2.75} \log n$	0.92
	$\pi(n)$	$1.19 \cdot 10^{-2} \cdot n^{0.67} \log n$	0.91
Fibonacci	$T_\infty(n)$	0.35	—
	$\pi(n)$	$25.48 + 0.49 \cdot n^{2.75} \log n$	0.99
NQueens	$T_\infty(n)$	$6.57 \cdot 10^{-4} \cdot n^2 \log n$	0.99
	$\pi(n)$	$2.18 \cdot n^{2.875} \log n$	0.98
Sort	$T_\infty(n)$	$3.03 \cdot 10^{-6} \cdot \sqrt{n}$	0.93
	$\pi(n)$	$3.53 + 3.32 \cdot 10^{-2} \cdot \sqrt{n}$	0.94
SparseLU	$T_\infty(n)$	$5.12 \cdot 10^{-5} \cdot n^{0.75} \log n$	0.96
	$\pi(n)$	$5.8 \cdot 10^{-5} \cdot n^{1.75} \log n$	0.99
Strassen	$T_\infty(n)$	$1.47 \cdot 10^{-9} \cdot n^2 \log n$	0.99
	$\pi(n)$	$0.25 \cdot n^{0.75}$	0.99

were arrays with a power-of-two number of integers, which ranged from 1M to 512M. The application SparseLU works on matrices and the inputs, in this case, ranged from 2,500 × 2,500 to 12,500 × 12,500 matrices.

The Strassen application implements a parallel version of the sequential Strassen algorithm. Since this algorithm recursively subdivides each side of the matrix into two, the dimension sizes have to be powers of two. Therefore, the smallest input in this case was a 256 × 256 matrix and the largest a 8,192 × 8,192 matrix.

4.2 Analysis of the Results

Figure 6 shows the runtimes of some of the evaluated applications and their contention-free replays for constant inputs of medium size. In every subfigure, the horizontal dashed line represents $T_\infty(n)$ (the depth), which is a lower bound on the execution time. Note that the Y-axis is on a logarithmic scale. The figure illustrates that in some cases application runtimes reach $T_\infty(n)$ quite quickly.

In the cases of Cholesky and Fibonacci, the convergence is very quick, and by the time p equals 60, the runtime

Table 3: Efficiency models of the evaluated applications. The last column shows the required input sizes (n) for $p = 60$ and an efficiency of 0.8.

Application	Model		rRMSE	Input size for $p = 60$
Cholesky	E_{ac}	$1.09 - 0.51 \cdot \sqrt{p} + 3.11 \cdot 10^{-2} \cdot \sqrt{p} \log n$	9.7%	37,718 × 37,718
	E_{cf}	$1.14 - 0.54 \cdot \sqrt{p} + 3.4 \cdot 10^{-2} \cdot \sqrt{p} \log n$	7.8%	24,685 × 24,685
	E_{ub}	$\min\{1, (2.29 + 2.35 \cdot 10^{-3} \cdot n) \cdot p^{-1}\}$	2.4%	19,500 × 19,500
FFT	E_{ac}	$0.96 - 0.1 \cdot \log p + 5.08 \cdot 10^{-22} n^{4.5} \log p$	19.5%	30,310 × 30,310
	E_{cf}	$1.03 - 0.16 \cdot p^{0.67} + 1.04 \cdot 10^{-2} \cdot p^{0.67} \log n$	4.8%	15,800 × 15,800
	E_{ub}	$\min\{1, (1.19 \cdot 10^{-2} \cdot n^{0.67} \log n) \cdot p^{-1}\}$	4.1%	5,800 × 5,800
Fibonacci	E_{ac}	$0.98 - 5.11 \cdot 10^{-3} \cdot p^{1.25} + 1.76 \cdot 10^{-3} \cdot p^{1.25} \log n$	3.5%	51
	E_{cf}	$0.97 - 1.46 \cdot 10^{-2} \cdot p^{1.25} + 9.26 \cdot 10^{-3} \cdot p^{1.25} \log n$	3.0%	51
	E_{ub}	$\min\{1, (25.48 + 0.49 \cdot n^{2.75} \log n) \cdot p^{-1}\}$	1.5%	49
NQueens	E_{ac}	$1.04 - 0.66 \cdot \sqrt{p} + 0.17 \cdot \sqrt{p} \log n$	13%	14
	E_{cf}	$1.0 - 6.21 \cdot 10^{-2} \cdot p + 1.61 \cdot 10^{-2} \cdot p \log n$	3%	13
	E_{ub}	$\min\{1, (2.18 \cdot n^{2.875} \log n) \cdot p^{-1}\}$	6.6%	12
Sort	E_{ac}	$0.99 - 9.2 \cdot 10^{-3} \cdot p^{1.5} + 2.29 \cdot 10^{-4} \cdot p^{1.5} \log n$	1.9%	350G
	E_{cf}	$1.0 - 4.61 \cdot 10^{-2} \cdot p^{0.75} + 1.62 \cdot 10^{-3} \cdot p^{0.75} \log n$	5.7%	6.6M
	E_{ub}	$\min\{1, (3.53 + 3.32 \cdot 10^{-2} \cdot \sqrt{n}) \cdot p^{-1}\}$	6.7%	1.7M
SparseLU	E_{ac}	$1.02 - 0.46 \cdot p^{0.67} + 3.28 \cdot 10^{-2} \cdot p^{0.67} \log n$	6.3%	12,000 × 12,000
	E_{cf}	$1.05 - 0.48 \cdot p^{0.67} + 3.49 \cdot 10^{-2} \cdot p^{0.67} \log n$	6.1%	11,000 × 11,000
	E_{ub}	$\min\{1, (5.8 \cdot 10^{-5} \cdot n^{1.75} \log n) \cdot p^{-1}\}$	1.7%	7,800 × 7,800
Strassen	E_{ac}	$1.55 - 1.02 \cdot p^{0.25} + 4.59 \cdot 10^{-2} \cdot p^{0.25} \log n$	9.5%	83,600 × 83,600
	E_{cf}	$1.26 - 0.65 \cdot p^{0.33} + 3.89 \cdot 10^{-2} \cdot p^{0.33} \log n$	5.9%	12,680 × 12,680
	E_{ub}	$\min\{1, (0.25 \cdot n^{0.75}) \cdot p^{-1}\}$	2.4%	1,200 × 1,200

would have almost reached $T_\infty(n)$. In other cases, however, the runtime converged more slowly or stagnated due to prohibitive resource contention. For all of these examples, it makes no sense to continue increasing the core count further, unless the problem size is increased as well. This phenomenon is hardly surprising, but the difficult part is to understand what happens to the efficiency when the problem size changes, or how severe the effects of resource contention are. Even if we consider more optimized versions of the applications, the same questions still remain. The figure also shows that in some cases the difference between the actual run and the replay increases as the core count increases, meaning that the resource contention becomes more severe. In some of the benchmarked applications, we observed that the replay time for $p = 1$ is slightly bigger than the execution time of the original code. This happens due to small perturbation effects of task instrumentation [25]; the impact of this effect, however, is minimal.

4.2.1 Scaling of Depth and Average Parallelism

Table 2 presents the models for $T_\infty(n)$ and $\pi(n)$ (average parallelism) that were created using the results from the TDG analysis. In all of the models the logarithms are binary (i.e., base 2 logarithms). The $\bar{R}^2$ column is the adjusted coefficient of determination (cf. Section 3.2). Although theoretical analysis of the average parallelism in an algorithm is an established practice, these results are the first successful attempt to produce empirical $\pi(n)$ models that are able to uncover potential scalability bugs in real implementations. A $\pi(n)$ that grows more slowly than $T_\infty(n)$ indicates that the implementation is asymptotically not scalable, and hence, contains a scalability bug. Surprisingly, the growth of $\pi(n)$ in Cholesky, FFT, and Strassen is slow compared to $T_\infty(n)$. This suggests that there are potential scalability bugs in these applications. Moreover, a fast growing $T_\infty(n)$ is an indication that the algorithm structure could be improved so that the depth would not become the limiting factor as n increases. The $\pi(n)$ models are used as the basis for the $E_{ub}(p, n)$ models in Table 3, since $E_{ub}(p, n) = \min\{1, \frac{\pi(n)}{p}\}$.

The Fibonacci application implements a trivial algorithm in which each task performs very little work. The TDG in this case is a tree, in which the work grows exponentially with n, and the depth linearly with n. The increase in the depth is proportional to the size of a single task, and therefore very small. This is the reason why the $T_\infty(n)$ model for Fibonacci is constant. Since a constant model is essentially an average of the measured values, the $\bar{R}^2$ is undefined in this case. As an alternative, we could consider the model for the height of the tree, which would be exactly $\mathcal{O}(n)$. The parallelism model, however, accurately reflects the fact that Fibonacci has plenty of available parallelism. Since our PMNF does not contain exponential terms, the model in the table is the best approximation of the exponential behavior in the measured data.

The analysis of the models in Table 2 is an example of how we can discover fundamental scalability limitations in

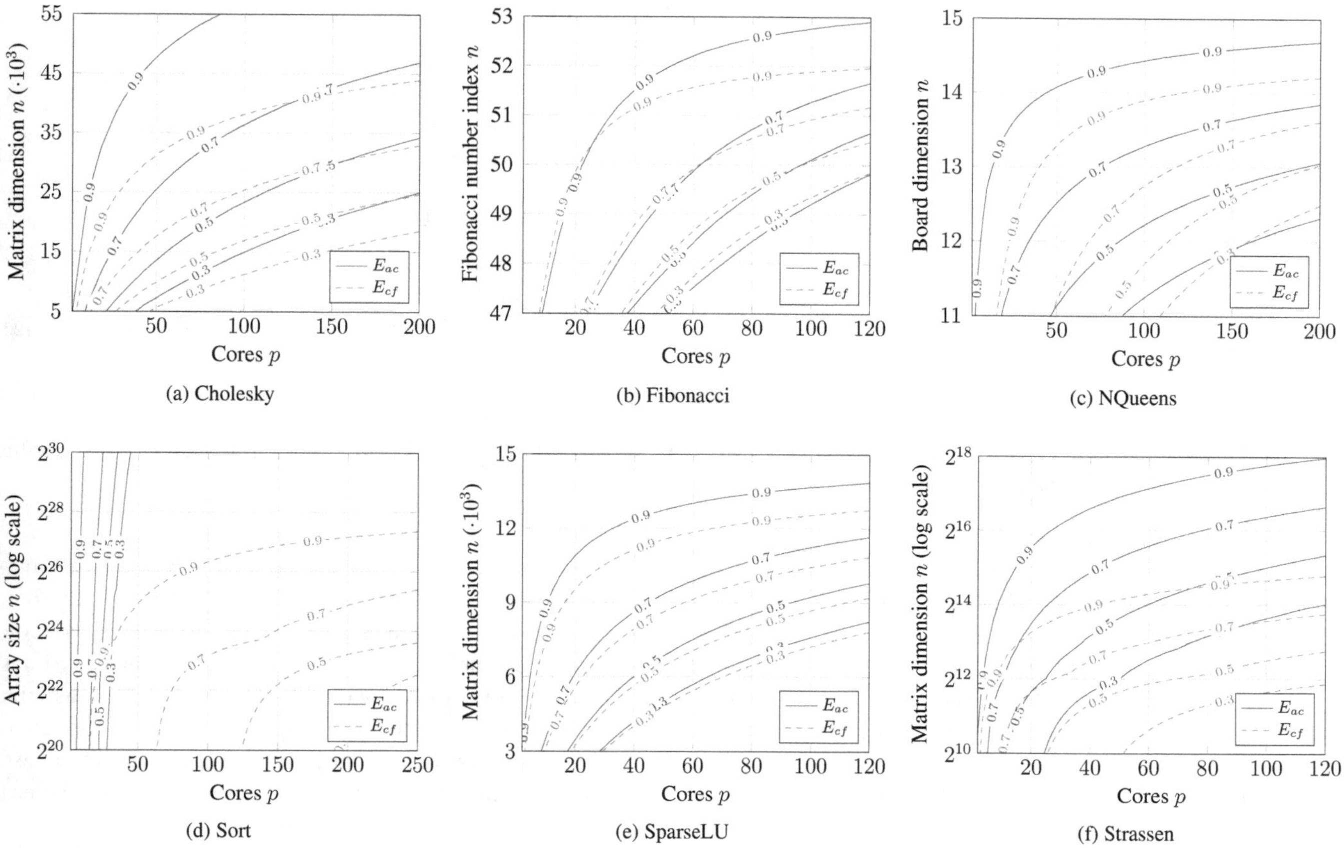

(a) Cholesky (b) Fibonacci (c) NQueens

(d) Sort (e) SparseLU (f) Strassen

Figure 7: Isoefficiency models of evaluated task-based applications and their replays. The label on each line denotes the efficiency of the line. Each model identifies lower-bounds on the inputs necessary to maintain the constant efficiency underlying the model.

task-based applications and help users answer Question 1 in Section 1.

4.2.2 Efficiency Models

Table 3 presents the efficiency models of the evaluated applications. There are three rows for each application listing the three efficiency models that we created (i.e., $E_{ub}(p,n)$, $E_{ac}(p,n)$, and $E_{cf}(p,n)$). In all the models the logarithms are binary. The *rRMSE* column is the relative root-mean-square error. It is a standard statistical factor that measures the relative differences between the observed data and the model, and is defined as: rRMSE $= \sigma/\bar{y}$, where: $\sigma = \sqrt{\sum_{i=1}^{n}(f(x_i) - y_i)^2/n}$, y_i are observed data, and $\bar{y}$ is the mean of the y_i values. For two-parameter models, the rRMSE factor reflects the accuracy of the fit better than $\bar{R}^2$, which is used for the single-parameter models in Table 2. The last column shows the input size n, derived from our models by letting the efficiency E be 0.8 and the core count p be 60, which is the total number of cores on our test machine. In Section 4.2.3, we discuss in greater detail how the input sizes were calculated.

All of the $E_{ac}(p,n)$ and $E_{cf}(p,n)$ models follow the same pattern $C - A \cdot f(p) + B \cdot f(p)g(n)$ that empirically emerged from our measurements. The interpretation of this pattern is that the first term, the constant C, is approximately 1 and it denotes the maximum attainable efficiency. The second term, $-A \cdot f(p)$, reflects the reduction in efficiency that occurs when we increase the core count. The last term, $B \cdot f(p)g(n)$, denotes the efficiency that we gain when we increase the input size. Together these terms reflect the interplay between the core count and the input size, and the effect it has on the efficiency. In the case of FFT, the constant B in the last term of $E_{ac}(p,n)$ is very small, which means that resource contention is a very significant factor and even large increases of the input size are not enough to offset the drop in the efficiency.

Figure 7 depicts the isoefficiency lines $E = 0.9$, $E = 0.7$, $E = 0.5$, and $E = 0.3$ for most of the evaluated applications. The isoefficiency lines start from 0.9, because $E = 1$ is an ideal situation which can hardly be achieved in practice, and therefore has less practical value.

Figure 8 presents the Δ_{con} and Δ_{str} discrepancies for Cholesky, SparseLU, and Strassen. For the sake of brevity,

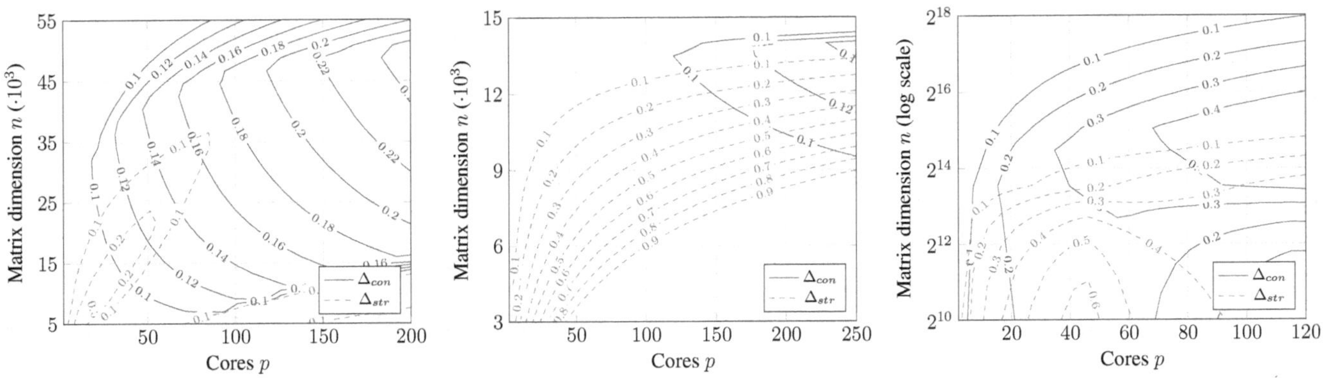

(a) Cholesky (b) SparseLU (c) Strassen

Figure 8: The Δ_{con} and Δ_{str} discrepancies of selected applications plotted as contour lines. The label of each line is the value of the discrepancy along the line.

we chose only these three applications; the other applications exhibit a simpler behavior regarding Δ_{con} and Δ_{str}. Similar to the efficiency functions, Δ_{con} and Δ_{str} are two-parameter functions that range from 0 to 1. The figure depicts the contour lines of these functions at constant intervals, and the label on each line specifies the value of the discrepancy along this line.

In the case of Cholesky, E_{cf} scales better than E_{ac} and, as Figure 8a shows, Δ_{con} exceeds 0.2. For example, consider $p = 100$ and the 0.7 isoefficiency, in this case, E_{ac} yields approximately $n = 36{,}000$, whereas E_{cf} yields approximately $n = 25{,}000$. This is a significant difference between the input sizes required to achieve the same efficiency, and it suggests that contention is a potential scalability bottleneck.

In the cases of Fibonacci, NQueens, and SparseLU, E_{cf} and E_{ac} scale almost at the same rate, and the isoefficiency lines with the same labels (i.e., efficiencies) are close to each other. In Figure 8b, for example, Δ_{con} stays well below 0.2. Considering that Fibonacci and NQueens are not memory-bound, this result is not surprising. It is, however, surprising to see that SparseLU is not affected by resource contention as one might have initially expected. We can conclude that resource contention is not an obstacle to scalability in these cases.

Sort is clearly affected by resource contention as the differences between the isoefficiency lines of E_{cf} and E_{ac} are very big. In the model $E_{ac} = 0.99 - 9.2 \cdot 10^{-3} \cdot p^{1.5} + 2.29 \cdot 10^{-4} \cdot p^{1.5} \log n$, the presence of $p^{1.5}$ in the second term means that the efficiency drops very quickly as the core count increases. Even though $p^{1.5}$ is also present in the third term, the combination of a small coefficient $2.29 \cdot 10^{-4}$ and $\log n$ makes it hard to offset the efficiency drop. It is not surprising that Sort is impaired by resource contention, but the severity of this impact, as evident from the behavior of E_{ac} and E_{cf}, is unexpected.

Not surprisingly, Strassen, which is heavily memory-bound, is also affected by resource contention. In some cases, as Figure 8c shows, Δ_{con} reaches 0.4, and if we consider, for example, $p = 100$ and the 0.7 isoefficiency lines, the input size n in E_{ac} would be about four times as large as in E_{cf}. The discrepancy is big when both the core count and the input sizes are either low or high. In the former case, the threads most likely contend for shared caches; whereas, in the latter case, they contend for memory bandwidth.

From the Δ_{con} analysis we can conclude that, for Cholesky, Sort, and Strassen, poor scaling is a result of a prohibitive contention overhead. This conclusion is an example of how, using our approach, we can answer Question 2 in Section 1.

As suggested by Figure 8a and the example input sizes for E_{ub} and E_{cf} in Table 3, the Δ_{str} of Cholesky, Fibonacci, and NQueens is rather small. However, Figures 8b and 8c show, for SparseLU and Strassen, that Δ_{str} is clearly bigger for certain ranges of p and n. Although this discrepancy becomes smaller as n increases, there is still room for improvement of either task dependencies, scheduling, or granularity. This insight is an example of how our approach helps to answer Question 3 in Section 1.

4.2.3 Co-Design Use Cases

We can use the efficiency models to derive a realistic approximation of the input size n that should be used to run an application with constant efficiency on a given core count p. For example, the actual efficiency model for Strassen is $E_{ac} = 1.55 - 1.02 \cdot p^{0.25} + 4.59 \cdot 10^{-2} \cdot p^{0.25} \log n$. For an efficiency of 0.8 and $p = 60$ we can derive the equation $0.8 = 1.55 - 1.02 \cdot 60^{0.25} + 4.59 \cdot 10^{-2} \cdot 60^{0.25} \log n$, and after solving it we would obtain $n = 83{,}600$, which means the application's input in this case should be a $83{,}600 \times 83{,}600$ matrix. This directly answers Question 4 in Section 1, and helps users efficiently utilize all the computing resources they have. We used the Symbolic Math Toolbox in MATLAB [4] both to solve the equation in this example and to derive the example input sizes in Table 3.

For some of the applications, such as Fibonacci, NQueens, and SparseLU, the example input sizes in the table are within the range of the inputs that we used for benchmarking. This means that the efficiency scaling in these cases is generally good. For other applications, such as Cholesky, we validated the example input size by running the application on all of the 60 cores of our test machine. In the cases of Sort and Strassen, however, validating the input size was impossible due to prohibitive memory requirements.

The inputs in Table 3 provide examples for co-design use cases. By calculating input sizes for future core counts, hardware designers can see whether the inputs are realistic and feasible. The input size for Sort, for example, shows that utilizing all of the 60 cores efficiently also requires adding a substantial amount of memory to a future machine.

Similar to the input size case, we can calculate the required core count, given a specific input size n. In this case, hardware designers can estimate the number of cores they will need for a predefined input size. Unlike the previous case, this approach can provide an answer to how many processing elements and memory controllers in a future machine would be suitable for an existing application with realistic inputs. We can see, for example, that Fibonacci, NQueens, and SparseLU would be suitable for a future machine with higher core counts. This is an example of how our approach can help hardware designers answer Question 5 in Section 1.

Hardware designers could use the generated contention models to design shared resources for future systems-on-chip. For example, the sizes of shared resources such as last-level cache, coherence networks, memory controllers, or input/output channels could be tuned to a specific set of applications using scaling and contention models. We leave details of such micro-architectural discussions for future work, as it lies outside the scope of this paper.

5. Related Work

Directed acyclic graphs, or more specifically task dependency graphs, are an established model of multithreading [6, 8, 11, 16, 18]. They were used in earlier work, even before the emergence of task-based programming models, for analyzing and understanding parallel computations. Perhaps the biggest strengths of the TDG model are its simplicity and that it allows two fundamental metrics to be defined—*work* and *depth*–which provide important bounds on performance and speedup.

An earlier work by Eager et al. [16] used TDGs, as well as work and average parallelism metrics, to investigate the tradeoffs between speedup and efficiency in parallel computations. Blelloch [6] used work and depth metrics to analyze parallel algorithms on a PRAM machine model in the context of the NESL parallel language [5].

The designers of Cilk [7, 17], an early task-based programming model, used TDGs, as well as work and depth metrics, to analyze and understand Cilk's performance. The Cilkview scalability analyzer [21] is a more recent work for profiling and benchmarking Cilk applications. It first instruments the code, and then constructs the TDG once the code has finished running. After benchmarking the code, Cilkview visualizes the measured speedup along with both lower and upper speedup limits (cf. Section 2.2). Although Cilkview is a useful tool for understanding the performance and some limitations of a task-based application, it focuses on just one problem size, ignoring the isoefficiency concept.

Previous studies explored the problem of overheads in task-based applications [27, 33]. The authors identified metrics to characterize the time spent by the threads doing either unrelated work or no useful work at all. They then suggested a number of techniques to improve the runtime of an application on a given number of cores. In another study [35], the authors created low-level models of memory bandwidth that allow the bandwidth usage to be predicted. In our study, in contrast, we take a more general approach to understanding resource-contention effects. The multi-parameter models that we create take both the core count and the problem size into account, allowing the user to understand the interplay between these two parameters.

Our task replay engine shares some similarities with Prometheus [24] and TaskSim [30]. Both tools enable the accurate simulation of task-based codes by either, in the case of Prometheus, constructing a TDG and simulating hardware contention, or, in the case of TaskSim, gathering execution traces. Since our aim is not an accurate reproduction of execution, but a contention-free execution, we used a simpler approach for the task replay.

Although isoefficiency is a well-known concept [19, 20, 29], the empirical analysis of it has not received much attention so far. To the best of our knowledge, there are no studies that explicitly model empirical isoefficiency of task-based applications.

6. Conclusion

In this paper, we propose a novel method that helps users, application developers, and hardware designers identify the causes of limited scalability in task-based applications. The method provides insights into the effects of resource contention on efficiency, and allows users to analyze how severe this contention is. By modeling how the depth and the average parallelism change as the input increases, our method also allows users to identify scalability bugs in task-based applications. Average parallelism that scales poorly compared to the depth indicates that the application would not run optimally for bigger inputs.

We identify three efficiency functions that describe the application behavior in different scenarios, namely, an ideal upper-bound efficiency, actual efficiency reflecting the application behavior, and contention-free efficiency based on the replay of the TDG. By analyzing the discrepancies between these efficiency functions, we are able to provide answers to questions regarding co-design aspects, the connection between poor scaling and resource contention, optimization potential, and the presence of scalability bugs.

We conclude that our methodology is a viable approach for analyzing both the effects of resource contention on efficiency and further optimization potential. It provides users with an insight into whether the obstacle to scaling is resource contention or insufficient parallelism in the structure of the TDG. In addition, users can also calculate the required input sizes to keep efficiency constant on a given core count. This approach can be used in co-design analysis to understand how many processing elements to put in a future machine, such that we can have high efficiency with realistic application inputs. We envision this methodology will be adopted for analyzing present and future task-based applications as many-core hardware becomes ever more ubiquitous.

Acknowledgments

This work was supported in part by the German Research Foundation (DFG) and the Swiss National Science Foundation (SNSF) through the DFG Priority Programme 1648 *Software for Exascale Computing* (SPPEXA). Additional support was provided by the German Federal Ministry of Education and Research (BMBF) through the Score-E project under grant no. 01IH13001G, and by the US Department of Energy under grant no. DE-SC0015524. We would also like to acknowledge the University Computing Center (Hochschulrechenzentrum) of TU Darmstadt for providing us with access to their supercomputers. Finally, we wish to thank the OmpSs team at Barcelona Supercomputing Center (BSC) for their support.

References

[1] BSC Application Repository. `https://pm.bsc.es/projects/bar/wiki/Applications`.

[2] Extra-P – Automated Performance-modeling Tool. `http://www.scalasca.org/software/extra-p`.

[3] Graphviz – Graph Visualization Software. `http://www.graphviz.org`.

[4] MATLAB. `http://www.mathworks.com`.

[5] G. E. Blelloch. NESL: A Nested Data-Parallel Language. Technical report, 1992.

[6] G. E. Blelloch. Programming Parallel Algorithms. *Commun. ACM*, 39(3):85–97, 1996.

[7] R. D. Blumofe, C. F. Joerg, B. C. Kuszmaul, C. E. Leiserson, K. H. Randall, and Y. Zhou. Cilk: An Efficient Multithreaded Runtime System. *Journal of Parallel and Distributed Computing*, 37(8):55–69, 1997.

[8] R. P. Brent. The Parallel Evaluation of General Arithmetic Expressions. *Journal of the ACM (JACM)*, 21(2):201–206, April 1974.

[9] A. Calotoiu, T. Hoefler, M. Poke, and F. Wolf. Using Automated Performance Modeling to Find Scalability Bugs in Complex Codes. In *Proc. of the 2013 ACM/IEEE Conference on Supercomputing (SC '13)*, pages 45:1–45:12. ACM, 2013.

[10] A. Calotoiu, D. Beckingsale, C. W. Earl, T. Hoefler, I. Karlin, M. Schulz, and F. Wolf. Fast Multi-Parameter Performance Modeling. In *Proc. of the 2016 IEEE International Conference on Cluster Computing (CLUSTER '16)*, pages 1–10, September 2016. (to appear).

[11] T. H. Cormen, C. E. Leiserson, R. L. Rivest, and S. Clifford. Multithreaded Algorithms. In *Introduction to Algorithms, Third Edition*, pages 772–812. The MIT Press, 3rd edition, 2009.

[12] A. Duran, J. Corbalán, and E. Ayguadé. An Adaptive Cut-off for Task Parallelism. In *Proc. of the 2008 ACM/IEEE Conference on Supercomputing (SC '08)*, pages 36:1–36:11. IEEE Press, 2008.

[13] A. Duran, J. Corbalán, and E. Ayguadé. Evaluation of OpenMP Task Scheduling Strategies. In *Proc. of the 4th International Conference on OpenMP in a New Era of Parallelism (IWOMP '08)*, pages 100–110. Springer-Verlag, 2008.

[14] A. Duran, X. Teruel, R. Ferrer, X. Martorell, and E. Ayguadé. Barcelona OpenMP Tasks Suite: A Set of Benchmarks Targeting the Exploitation of Task Parallelism in OpenMP. In *Proc. of the 2009 International Conference on Parallel Processing (ICPP '09)*, pages 124–131. IEEE, 2009.

[15] A. Duran, E. Ayguadé, R. M. Badia, J. Labarta, L. Martinell, X. Martorell, and J. Planas. OmpSs: A Proposal for Programming Heterogeneous Multi-core Architectures. *Parallel Processing Letters*, 21(02):173–193, 2011.

[16] D. L. Eager, J. Zahorjan, and E. D. Lazowska. Speedup Versus Efficiency in Parallel Systems. *IEEE Transactions on Computers*, 38(3):408–423, 1989.

[17] M. Frigo, C. E. Leiserson, and K. H. Randall. The Implementation of the Cilk-5 Multithreaded Language. In *Proc. of the ACM SIGPLAN 1998 Conference on Programming Language Design and Implementation (PLDI '98)*, pages 212–223. ACM, 1998.

[18] R. L. Graham. Bounds on Multiprocessing Timing Anomalies. *SIAM Journal on Applied Mathematics*, 17(2):416–429, 1969.

[19] A. Grama, A. Gupta, G. Karypis, and V. Kumar. *Introduction to Parallel Computing*. Addison-Wesley Longman Publishing Co., Inc., 2nd edition, 2002.

[20] A. Y. Grama, A. Gupta, and V. Kumar. Isoefficiency: Measuring the Scalability of Parallel Algorithms and Architectures. *Parallel Distributed Technology: Systems Applications*, 1(3): 12–21, 1993.

[21] Y. He, C. E. Leiserson, and W. M. Leiserson. The Cilkview Scalability Analyzer. In *Proc. of the 22nd ACM Symposium on Parallelism in Algorithms and Architectures (SPAA '10)*, pages 145–156, 2010.

[22] T. Hoefler and R. Belli. Scientific Benchmarking of Parallel Computing Systems: Twelve Ways to Tell the Masses when Reporting Performance Results. In *Proc. of the 2015 ACM/IEEE Conference on Supercomputing (SC '15)*, pages 73:1–73:12. ACM, 2015.

[23] T. Hoefler, W. Gropp, R. Thakur, and J. L. Träff. Toward Performance Models of MPI Implementations for Understanding Application Scaling Issues. In *Proc. of the European MPI Users' Group Meeting (EuroMPI '10)*, pages 21–30. Springer-Verlag, 2010.

[24] G. Kestor, R. Gioiosa, and D. Chavarra-Miranda. Prometheus: scalable and accurate emulation of task-based applications on many-core systems. In *Proc. of the 2015 IEEE International Symposium on Performance Analysis of Systems and Software (ISPASS '15)*, pages 308–317. IEEE, 2015.

[25] D. Lorenz, P. Philippen, D. Schmidl, and F. Wolf. Profiling of OpenMP Tasks with Score-P. In *Proc. of the 2012 41st International Conference on Parallel Processing Workshops (ICPPW '12)*, pages 444–453, September 2012.

[26] M. R. Meswani, L. Carrington, D. Unat, A. Snavely, S. Baden, and S. Poole. Modeling and Predicting Performance of High Performance Computing Applications on Hardware Accelerators. *International Journal of High Performance Computing Applications*, 27(2):89–108, May 2013.

[27] S. L. Olivier, B. R. de Supinski, M. Schulz, and J. F. Prins. Characterizing and Mitigating Work Time Inflation in Task Parallel Programs. In *Proc. of the 2012 ACM/IEEE Conference on Supercomputing (SC '12)*, pages 65:1–65:12. IEEE Computer Society Press, 2012.

[28] OpenMP Architecture Review Board. OpenMP application programming interface, version 4.0. `http://www.openmp.org/mp-documents/OpenMP4.0.0.pdf`.

[29] M. J. Quinn. *Parallel Programming in C with MPI and OpenMP*. McGraw-Hill Education Group, 2003.

[30] A. Rico, F. Cabarcas, C. Villavieja, M. Pavlovic, A. Vega, Y. Etsion, A. Ramirez, and M. Valero. On the simulation of large-scale architectures using multiple application abstraction levels. *ACM Transactions on Architecture and Code Optimization*, 8(4):1–20, 2012.

[31] S. Shudler, A. Calotoiu, T. Hoefler, A. Strube, and F. Wolf. Exascaling Your Library: Will Your Implementation Meet Your Expectations? In *Proc. of the 29th ACM International Conference on Supercomputing (ICS '15)*, pages 165–175. ACM, June 2015.

[32] N. R. Tallent and A. Hoisie. Palm: Easing the Burden of Analytical Performance Modeling. In *Proc. of the 28th ACM International Conference on Supercomputing (ICS '14)*, pages 221–230. ACM, 2014.

[33] N. R. Tallent and J. M. Mellor-Crummey. Effective Performance Measurement and Analysis of Multithreaded Applications. In *Proc. of the 14th ACM SIGPLAN Symposium on Principles and Practice of Parallel Programming (PPoPP '09)*, pages 229–240. ACM, 2009.

[34] U.S. Department of Energy. The Opportunities and Challenges of Exascale Computing. Office of Science, Washington, D.C., 2010. `http://science.energy.gov/~/media/ascr/ascac/pdf/reports/Exascale_subcommittee_report.pdf`.

[35] W. Wang, T. Dey, J. W. Davidson, and M. L. Soffa. DraMon: Predicting Memory Bandwidth Usage of Multi-threaded Programs With High Accuracy and Low Overhead. In *Proc. of the 2014 IEEE 20th International Symposium on High Performance Computer Architecture (HPCA '14)*, pages 380–391, February 2014.

Processor-Oblivious Record and Replay

Robert Utterback Kunal Agrawal I-Ting Angelina Lee
Washington University in St. Louis
{robert.utterback,kunal,angelee}@wustl.edu

Milind Kulkarni
Purdue University
milind@purdue.edu

Abstract

Record-and-replay systems are useful tools for debugging non-deterministic parallel programs by first ***recording*** an execution and then ***replaying*** that execution to produce the same access pattern. Existing record-and-replay systems generally target thread-based execution models, and record the behaviors and interleavings of individual threads. Dynamic multithreaded languages and libraries, such as the Cilk family, OpenMP, TBB, etc., do not have a notion of threads. Instead, these languages provide a ***processor-oblivious*** model of programming, where programs expose task-parallelism using high-level constructs such as spawn/sync without regard to the number of threads/cores available to run the program. Thread-based record-and-replay would violate the processor-oblivious nature of these programs, as they incorporate the number of threads into the recorded information, constraining the replayed execution to the same number of threads.

In this paper, we present a processor-oblivious ***record-and-replay*** scheme for such languages where record and replay can use different number of processors and both are scheduled using work stealing. We provide theoretical guarantees for our record and replay scheme — namely that record is optimal for programs with one lock and replay is near-optimal for all cases. In addition, we implemented this scheme in the Cilk Plus runtime system and our evaluation indicates that processor-obliviousness does not cause substantial overheads.

Categories and Subject Descriptors F.2.2 [*Analysis of Algorithms and Problem Complexity*]: Nonnumerical Algorithms and Problems—Sequencing and scheduling; D.2.5 [*Software Engineering*]: Testing and Debugging—Debugging aids, Tracing

PPoPP '17, February 04-08, 2017, Austin, TX, USA
© 2017 ACM. ISBN 978-1-4503-4493-7/17/02...$15.00
DOI: http://dx.doi.org/10.1145/3018743.3018764

Keywords deterministic replay; dynamic program analysis; reproducible debugging; work stealing

1. INTRODUCTION

Debugging multithreaded programs is challenging, due to non-deterministic effects such as the interleaving of threads' accesses to shared data. Different thread interleavings can produce different results, and a bug that manifests under one interleaving may not manifest under another, making reproducing bugs notoriously difficult. A popular technique for addressing this problem is ***record and replay*** [2, 20, 29, 34, 36, 37, 41–43, 48, 53, 56, 58, 63, 68–70]. One execution ***records*** enough information about its behavior so that a second execution can faithfully ***replay*** that behavior, producing the same outcome. As a result, any bug that manifests during the recorded run will be reproduced during the replay run, easing the task of tracking down bugs.

In particular, we focus on programs where shared objects are protected by locks. A record and replay system for these programs must ensure that critical sections protected by the same lock are executed in the same order during the record run and the replay run. Prior work on record and replay generally records *thread* interleaving, and tracking the behavior of the threads of a program as they execute, ensuring that during replay, threads interleave in the same way when executing critical sections. While this approach succeeds at its goal of replaying recorded behavior, it has the drawback of requiring that the replay run use the same number of threads as the recorded execution.

This concession seems mild: most programming models make the number of threads an explicit parameter. However, a class of parallel programming languages uses ***dynamic multithreading***, where the number of threads is not part of the model at all, such as the Cilk family [18, 32, 40], subsets of OpenMP [6], Threading Building Blocks [39], the Habanero family [8, 23], Task Parallel Library [46], X10 [23, 24], and many others. In these languages and libraries, the program itself is ***processor (or thread) oblivious*** — the programmer specifies the logical parallelism of the program using primitives such as spawn/sync, async/finish, or parallel-for loops. At run time, a scheduler is responsible for efficiently mapping this parallelism to ***worker*** threads that execute the computation in parallel.[1]

Despite the lack of explicit threads, record and replay is still useful for these dynamically multithreaded programs: if multiple parallel tasks access shared data using a lock, different executions might result in tasks' accessing that data in different orders. These sources of non-determinism can lead to difficult-to-identify bugs.

To our knowledge, there exist no record and replay systems for dynamically multithreaded programming models. Even if we keep the number of workers (threads) the same for recording and replaying, standard record and replay mechanisms do not directly work due to the Cilk scheduler's use of ***randomized work stealing***: *which* workers execute *which* tasks *when* is also non-deterministic and can change from one execution of a computation to the next even if the number of workers remains the same. If we record these computations using a standard record and replay scheme, then it would have record all of the decisions of the scheduler and then reproduce these exact decisions during replay significantly increasing cost of both record and replay.

In this paper, we present PORRidge, the first *processor-oblivious* record and replay system, and the first known record and replay system for dynamically multithreaded programs. PORRidge targets ***data-race free*** (DRF) Cilk programs — those whose accesses to shared data are correctly synchronized — and hence focuses on controlling the order in which synchronization operations are performed.[2] We also assume that there are no parallelism within critical sections, which is a standard assumptions for most dynamic multithreaded systems.

Following the processor oblivious model, PORRidge is oblivious to the number of workers. Work stealing is used to schedule the computation during both record and replay. Hence, a program recorded on n workers can be replayed on m workers. Indeed, m can be greater than n — a program can be replayed on more processors than the original recorded run! Replaying on more processors than the recording can be useful during debugging: (i) debugging during replay can be performed with heavyweight instrumentation to aid in bug diagnosis, and replay on more processors can compensate for the additional overhead of instrumentation; (ii) if a bug is seen during recording long after a program has started, replay on more processors can reproduce the bug more quickly.

[1] We use workers and processors interchangeably in this paper.

[2] While data race freedom may seem to be a strong constraint, we note two things. First, DRF is a common assumption for record and replay systems [34, 63], as well as other dynamic analyses [55]. Second, DRF is a limitation of the PORRidge *implementation*, which needs to track sources of non-determinism. PORRidge uses the DRF assumption to allow it to track lock operations only. However, the same *conceptual* record and replay techniques could be applied to racy programs, by using race detection tools (e.g., [25, 30, 31, 45]) to identify races and indicate to PORRidge additional sources of non-determinism (tools like Chimera adopt similar approaches [44]).

The key insight behind PORRidge is as follows: there are multiple sources of non-determinism in scheduling when we execute a dynamic multithreaded program, for instance, the random work stealing decisions that the scheduler makes. However, for a data-race free computation, a recording run needs not record all this information to reproduce it faithfully during replay; it is sufficient to just record the order in which various critical sections acquired a shared lock. To be more precise, a dynamic multithreaded program can be viewed as a directed acyclic graph, with each node in the graph representing a task and edges between nodes represent dependencies. This graph is independent of the number of workers and for race-free computations, the only non-determinism arises from the order that tasks acquire locks. These lock acquires represent additional ***happens-before*** edges in the program DAG and recording these additional edges is sufficient to ensure that the DAG can be replayed faithfully.

Therefore, during a recording run, PORRidge simply records these happens-before edges. More importantly, during the replay run, PORRidge ensures that the happens-before relationships that were recorded are respected: in other words, during replay, PORRidge schedules the ***augmented DAG*** which contains all these happens-before edges in addition to the original dependencies. While this new augmented DAG may have parallelism limited by the happens-before edges, its parallelism is *not* directly limited by the number of threads that the recording run executed on.

Another important property of PORRidge is that the recording system sits *on top* of its runtime. One possible way to record a Cilk computation is to include the Cilk runtime in the scope of what is recorded, recording and subsequently replaying all of the non-deterministic decisions regarding work stealing. But the Cilk runtime is highly parallel and non-deterministic, and including it in the recording scope would dramatically increase the amount of information to be recorded. Instead, PORRidge only records the happens-before relationships.

Replay is more complex. the Cilk runtime system is not designed to obey happens-before edges that are not directly part of the program itself. Therefore, PORRidge adds mechanisms to the Cilk runtime system to respect these dependencies. However, these mechanisms, and generally all of the non-determinism of the scheduler, remain encapsulated separately from the replay itself. By keeping the runtime (both during record and during replay) outside the scope of the system, PORRidge is able to maintain low overhead.

Contributions

This paper makes several contributions:

1. We present PORRidge, the first processor-oblivious record and replay system for dynamic multithreaded programs that keeps track of happens-before relationships between critical sections. To our knowledge, this is the first record

and replay system (processor oblivious or not) for these kinds of programs.

2. We state and prove the theoretical guarantees for PORRidge. Despite the fact that PORRidge requires additional happens-before tracking during record, and requires conforming to those happens-before edges during replay, it can provide strong guarantees. In particular, let W be the ***work*** required by a parallel computation — its serial execution time; let S be the ***span*** (or ***critical path length*** — longest sequence of dependencies in the computation; let P be the number of processors; and let B be the amount of work in critical sections. Then, the runtime of the recorded execution is $O(W/P + S + B)$. For a single lock, this bound is *asymptotically optimal.* While replay incurs slightly higher costs due to the necessity of respecting happens-before edges, its runtime is $O(W/P' + S' \log\log P')$, where S' is the span of the augmented DAG (i.e., with the additional happens-before edges) and P' is the number of processors the *replayed* execution is run on. That means, it is possible for the replay to be *asymptotically faster* than the recorded run by using more processors.
3. We implemented a prototype of our design within the Cilk Plus [40] runtime system. We show across six benchmarks that PORRidge delivers good scalability for both record and replay. In particular, replay can often provide better speedup than record as we increase the number of cores. In addition, despite requiring additional runtime mechanisms in order to respect happens-before edges, the additional overhead of replay over the record is small.

2. PRELIMINARIES

We now provide background on modeling parallel computations, work-stealing schedulers, and some definitions.

Dynamic Multithreading and Computation DAGs. Here we will use Cilk Plus programming keywords, `cilk_spawn` and `cilk_sync`, to explain the dynamic multithreaded programming model; other languages may differ in keywords. Parallelism is created using `cilk_spawn`. When a function instance F ***spawns*** another function instance G by preceding the invocation with `cilk_spawn`, the ***continuation*** of F — the statements after the spawning of G — may execute in parallel with G without waiting for G to return. Instruction `cilk_sync` acts as a local barrier; the control flow cannot move past a `cilk_sync` in function F until functions previously spawned by F have returned.

As is common in the literature, we model the parallel computation as a directed acyclic graph, where each node is a unit time computation and each edge represents a dependence between nodes — a particular node is ***ready*** to execute when all its predecessors have executed. Also, as is common, we assume that each node has an out-degree of at most two. A ***strand*** is a chain of nodes all with in-degree and out-degree 1 — programmatically, a strand is a sequence of instructions that contain no parallel primitives and therefore must execute sequentially. We define two parameters on the dag. ***Work*** W is the total number of nodes in the dag and represents the execution time of the dag on one processor. ***Span*** S is the length of the longest path and represents the execution time on an infinite number of processors.

Work-Stealing Scheduler. During execution, a ***work-stealing*** scheduler [17, 32] dynamically load balances a parallel computation across available ***worker*** threads. Each worker maintains a ***deque***, double-ended queue, to keep track of available work. When a worker creates new strands, they are placed on this worker's deque. When it completes its current strand, it takes work from the bottom of the deque. If its deque becomes empty, the worker turns into a ***thief*** and chooses a ***victim*** worker at random to ***steal*** from. Given a computation with work W and span S, a work-stealing scheduler executes the computation in expected time $\frac{W}{P} + O(S)$ on P processors [17].

Modeling Critical Sections. Since our computations contain critical sections, we must model those. We assume that no parallelism within a critical section, and thus each critical section of length x is simply a strand (chain) of x unit time nodes in the dag. Each node in the chain has in-degree one and out-degree one. The first node of this chain is called a *acquire* node and the last node is called a *release* node. We say B_1 is the total amount of time the lock ℓ_i is held — therefore, it is the sum of the lengths of all chains representing critical sections held by ℓ_i. We say that the ***total blocking time*** is $B = \sum_i B_i$.[3]

Augmented DAG. Once we record the execution of a computation DAG, we must replay it so that all the critical sections protected by the same lock are executed in the same order as the recorded execution. Therefore, additional happens-before edges are added to the computation DAG. We call the new DAG with the happens-before edges an ***augmented dag***. More precisely, if critical section b accesses lock ℓ_i after critical section a that also accesses ℓ_i, with no other critical sections in between accessing ℓ_i, then we say that a is the ***predecessor*** critical section to b, and b is the ***successor*** critical section of a. In the augmented dag, we add an edge from the last node (release node) of a to the first node (acquire node) of b. (Note that since the last node of a has out-degree one from assumption, this still maintains the invariant that no node has out-degree greater than two). The work of this new dag is still W since we haven't added new nodes. However, the span may be larger, and we denote the span of the augmented dag by $\tilde{S}$.

[3] If we are working with racy programs where we instrument the racy accesses as light-weight critical sections, then we must also add those critical sections in the calculation of B.

3. DESIGN OF PORRidge

We now describe the design and implementation of PORRidge. As mentioned in Section 1, since the PORRidge is designed for data-race free programs, it needs to capture only the happens-before edges formed between critical sections protected by the same lock during recording and enforce the same happens-before edges during replay. Consequently, PORRidge has a light-weight recording process that can be implemented entirely outside of the work-stealing scheduler. The replay process, on the other hand, requires modifications to the work-stealing scheduler in order to guarantee the stated theoretical bound.

3.1 Record

Conceptually, during recording, PORRidge stores with each lock an ordered list of successful lock acquires to this lock, henceforth referred to as the ***lock-acquire ordering***. Conceptually, a lock object in PORRidge contains a pointer to the underlying lock defined by the POSIX pthread specification [38] and a data structure recording its lock-acquire ordering. PORRidge provides wrappers for the various thread lock objects and associated acquire / release functions; during recording, the wrapper functions are invoked via compile-time interpositioning [21][Chp. 7.13] to record the necessary information. When a worker successfully acquires a lock, it simply adds the currently executing strand to the end of its lock-acquire ordering. If the lock is not available, the worker spins. At the end of the recorded execution, every lock object writes out the strands in its lock-acquire ordering to a log file in the order inserted.

Identifying Strands. For processor-oblivious replay, the information stored in the list must uniquely identify critical sections in the computation dag, and the identification must be consistent across executions. Here, we use ***pedigree*** [47], a sequence of integers corresponding to the rank ordering of spawn statements in the ancestor functions (including this function) that lead to the current strand. Pedigree uniquely identifies each strand in a consistent manner since it depends only on the computation dag and not on the schedule. Critical sections can be uniquely identified by uniquely identifying the strand they are in and then their ordering within the strand. Therefore, it is sufficient to modify the pedigree mechanism slightly to uniquely identify critical sections.

The open-source Cilk Plus runtime [40] readily provides support for pedigree; however, each read to the pedigree incurs a worst-case $\Theta(d)$ overhead, where d is the maximum ***spawn depth***, the number of spawn statements nested on the stack during serial execution. Since the pedigree must be read in every lock acquire, this causes lock acquires to incur $\Theta(d)$ overhead during record and replay. Ideally, we would like to keep the cost of lock acquire to be constant in order to guarantee both the record and replay time bounds.

To achieve the desired constant overhead, we use a strategy similar to DOTMIX [47] to give each critical section a ***section ID***, which is effectively a hash of a pedigree that can be maintained and derived with constant overhead. DOTMIX works as follows. The runtime generates a size-d vector of random numbers using the seed at the beginning of the computation. Given a pedigree, DOTMIX takes dot-product of the pedigree with the vector and mods the dot-product result with a large prime p; provided that we use the same seed, a pedigree always hashes to the same random number. Moreover, two random numbers generated via two different pedigree have a low probability of collision [47]. Using a similar strategy as DOTMIX, we obtain unique section IDs with constant overhead per lock acquire.

Storing Strand IDs. The drawback of section IDs is the (rare) possibility of collision. We can detect these collisions by maintaining the lock-acquire ordering for each lock using a ***hash-list*** representation, which is a combination of hash table and list. The hash list implicitly maintains a linked list and records lock-acquire ordering using this linked-list, but in addition hashes each list node in a hash table using the corresponding section ID as the key so that the hash table disambiguates lock acquires with the same section IDs.

During record, when a new lock acquire occurs, its section ID gets inserted into the end of the implicit list. PORRidge then checks the section ID in the hash table; if there are no collisions (no entry with the same section ID exists in the hash table), entry for this acquire is simply inserted to the hash table. If there is a collision, it marks the first entry with the same section ID in the hash table as "has collision," reads the full pedigree of the current section, and stores it in the hash table using chaining. Therefore, each entry in the hash table has two "next" pointers: one for the implicit list ordering (points to the next section to acquire the lock) and one for chaining (points to the full pedigree of a section that has the same section ID).

3.2 Replay

At the beginning of the replay, the runtime reads in the previously recorded log and recreates the lock-acquire ordering represented using a hash list. PORRidge maintains invariant that the head of the implicit list always points to the next strand that should successfully acquire the given lock. Each list node also contains a pointer to the runtime data necessary to enable suspending and resuming the strand. During replay, if a worker encounters a lock acquire for critical section a, and its predecessor — a lock release of the critical section b that was executed immediately before a during the recording run — has not executed yet, the worker suspends the execution of the strand, since it is not ready in the augmented dag. On the other hand, when some worker (in this case, the worker that executed b) releases a lock, it may enable critical section a (which was tried earlier and suspended); this worker must then resume this suspended critical section.

Lock Acquire. When a worker encounters a lock acquire, it checks the head of the list to see if this is the strand that should get the lock next. If so, it acquires the lock and continues execution. Otherwise, the worker hashes its section ID and marks the corresponding hash list entry to indicate that the corresponding lock acquire has been tried and suspended. It then suspends the execution of its current deque and work steals.

During process-oblivious replay, a worker must never spin or wait to acquire a lock — spinning not only leads to bad performance, it can also lead to deadlocks. Consider an example where we record an execution on multiple workers and replay it on one worker. Say the computation contains two critical sections x and y, protected by the same lock, that are logically in parallel with each other except for the happens-before dependence. If x comes before y during sequential execution, during replay on one worker, the worker will encounter x first. However, since record is done on multiple processors, y could have gotten the lock before x during record, and thus replay must execute y before it can execute x. If during replay, the worker simply spins when it encounters x, it can spin indefinitely since no other workers are around to execute y. Similar examples can also be created for multiple-processor replay. Therefore, when a worker encounters a lock that it cannot yet acquire during replay, it is essential that it suspends and finds other work to do.

Lock Release. The worker first advances the head of the list and checks to see if the next lock acquire has been tried and suspended. If not, the worker simply continues the execution after the lock release. If the next lock acquire has been tried and suspended, the worker performing the lock release now has two continuations that it can potentially work on — the continuation after the lock release, and the suspended lock acquire enabled by this lock release. Both choices lead to the same theoretical guarantees. In our implementation, we chose to have the worker suspend the continuation after the lock release and resume the next lock acquire in the list to reduce contention. Note that it is possible for a worker to release a lock while a different worker is concurrently suspending the next lock acquire in line — the synchronization is coordinated using a Dekker-like protocol [28], since there are at most two workers concurrently operating on a given list node.

Handling Section-ID Collisions. When a worker encounters a lock acquire and tries to determine if this lock acquire is at the head of the lock-acquire ordering, it may find the head list node marked as"has collision," — in this case, multiple sections with the same ID acquired this lock. Recall that during recording, the runtime stores full pedigrees only when it discovers a section-ID collision; therefore, the first lock acquire involved in the collision has its section ID stored, and the remaining lock acquires involved in the collision have their full pedigrees stored. Thus, if a worker finds a head list node with the same section ID but marked as "has collision," it must read its full pedigree and compare it against other list nodes hashed with the same section IDs (for which the full pedigree is stored). Only if none of them match the current pedigree, the worker can conclude that it is at the head of the list and proceed with getting the lock; otherwise, it must suspend.

Runtime Modifications. The fact that a lock acquire causes a worker to suspend its current execution causes the PORRidge scheduler to diverge from the vanilla work-stealing scheduler used by Cilk Plus without locks. The vanilla work-stealing scheduler maintains the invariant that there are at most P deques containing ready work throughout execution, where P is the number of workers used, and this fact is important for proving the scheduling bound. The PORRidge scheduler no longer maintains the P-deque invariant, since a worker can suspend execution of a non-empty deque. Thus, the runtime must handle multiple deques per worker, and additional care must be taken to provide the provably-scalable time bound for replay.

During replay, a a worker can suspend execution 1) upon a lock acquire if the lock acquire is not ready, or 2) upon a lock release, if the lock release in turn enables a suspended lock acquire. In the first case, if the worker suspends its current (non-empty) deque, it work steals and allocates a new deque for the stolen work, thereby increasing the total number of deques. In the second case, the worker suspends the continuation of the lock release, and resumes the deque containing the lock acquire that it just enabled; in this case, the overall number of deques in the system does not increase.

One important thing to note is that, a suspended lock acquire is never on top of any deque and therefore no one ever steals it. When a worker suspends a deque due to a lock acquire that is not ready, the suspended lock acquire is at the bottom of the deque, and everything above it in the deque is ready. If the suspended deque contains only the lock acquire, the PORRidge runtime frees the deque. The suspended lock acquire, in turn, is always resumed (or enabled) by the lock release that unblocks it. In particular, if r and s are critical sections for the same lock, and r acquired the lock immediately before s during recording, then there is an edge from the lock release in r to the lock acquire in s in the augmented dag. Therefore, if the lock acquire in s is suspended during replay, then s is resumed by the processor that executed the lock release in r. This ensures 1) that no worker ever waits or spins to acquire a lock, and 2) stealing into a suspended deque always results a successful steal.

Since the PORRidge scheduler does not maintain the P-deque invariant during replay, we need to make a few changes to the scheduler to provide the provably good replay bound. First, we maintain the invariant that all P processors have approximately the same number of deques by the following mechanisms: (1) When a worker w suspends a non-empty deque, it picks two workers uniformly at random and gives the deque to the worker with the smaller number of deques; and (2) on every steal attempt, the thief looks at two workers (chosen randomly), takes a suspended deque from the worker with a larger number of deques and gives it to the worker with the smaller number of deques. Second, given that all workers have approximately the same number of deques, we modify the steal protocol to ensure that workers steal from all deques uniformly at random. When a thief steals, it not only selects a victim at random, it also chooses among all the deques that the victim has to steal from at random. We shall see how these changes allow us to provide a provably-scalable replay time bound in Section 4.

3.3 Performance Optimization

Thus far we have been discussing the design assuming that the lock-acquire ordering for a given lock is represented using a hash list. The hash-list representation works, but it can incur large overhead in practice for benchmarks that are already memory-bound (such as the graph benchmarks described in Section 5), since random accesses to the hash list inherently lack locality and incur additional cache misses. We optimized the implementation of the record phase in PORRidge by using a small bloom filter to detect section-ID collisions in place of a hash table. Doing so allows the PORRidge to store the bloom filter with the lock object itself, leading to better spatial locality, and it uses much less space than keeping an actual hash list. The trade-off is that a bloom filter can report false positives (i.e., detecting collisions between section IDs with different values) and thus may lead to reading and logging the full pedigrees unnecessarily. In our experiment, however, we find that using the bloom-filter outperforms the hash list due to cache effects.

Even though we were able to use a bloom filter during recording, the same optimization does not work during replay, since a worker uses the hash table not to identify collision but rather to find the list node corresponding to the encountered lock acquire quickly. During replay, a worker encountering a lock acquire that is not yet at the head of the list needs to find the corresponding list node in order to mark it suspended. If the corresponding section ID is marked to have collision during recording, the worker also needs to search through the list nodes with the same section ID to precisely identify the correct list node. A bloom filter is not sufficient for these purposes. Nevertheless, for many benchmarks, the number of lock acquires for a give lock is small; thus, keeping the lock-acquire ordering in a simple array and searching through the array suffices. For such benchmarks, the spatial locality and decrease in memory usage when using a simple array outweighs the benefit of constant-time search via a hash-list. Since the number of lock acquires per lock is known at the beginning of the replay, in our implementation, we optimized the replay to choose between the two representations — PORRidge keeps the lock-acquire ordering in a simple array if the number is small, and it uses a hash-list otherwise.

Finally, in the PORRidge scheduler, we perform the following optimization that is not necessary for the scheduling bound but which improves performance in practice. Recall that there are two types of suspended deques. (1) When a worker suspends a deque due to lock acquire, the bottom node of this deque is a suspended node. (2) When a worker suspends a deque after a lock release, all the nodes in the deque are ready to resume and there are no suspended nodes. When another worker steals from the second type of deque with no suspended nodes, instead of stealing just the top strand, it ***mugs*** the entire deque and resumes the bottom node. This optimization reduces the number of deques faster, making replay more efficient.

4. THEORETICAL ANALYSIS

In this section, we will prove theoretical upper bounds on the running time of our record and replay strategy. Recording and replaying are done in different processes and we will provide separate bounds for them. The bound on the record process follows directly from the bounds for work-stealing. For replay, we analyze the scheduling strategy provided in Section 3. In the analysis, we will extensively use the analysis of work stealing using a potential function provided by Arora, Blumofe and Plaxton [3] (abbreviated as ABP).

4.1 Running Time of Record

THEOREM 1. *Given a computation with work W, span S, and blocking B (defined in Section 2), if we record the computation on P processors, the running time is $O(W/P + S + B)$ in expectation.*

Record analysis directly follows from work-stealing analysis. The only additional factor is that a worker spins when waiting on a lock, making no progress towards completing the computation. Thus, we shall divide the computation into two types of phases and bound them separately. A phase is ***non-blocking*** if no processor is waiting on a lock, otherwise it is ***blocking***.

LEMMA 2. *The total amount of time spent in blocking phases is at most B.*

Proof. Obvious from the fact that the total time any processor could be holding the lock is at most B.

LEMMA 3. *The total expected time spent in non-blocking phases is $W/P + O(S)$. The time spent in non-blocking phases is $W/P + O(S + \lg 1/\epsilon)$ with probability $1 - 1/\epsilon$.*

Proof. During non-blocking phases, the processors are either working or stealing. The total number of work steps is at most W, since each work step consumes a unit of work in the computation dag. From an argument very similar to that in ABP [3], one can show that the total number of steal steps when no worker is blocked is $O(PS)$ in expectation and $O(PS + P\lg 1/\epsilon)$ with probability at least $(1 - 1/\epsilon)$. Since there are a total of P processors executing these work or steal steps, the total time spent on non-blocking phases is as stated. Note that some work may also be done during blocking phases; however, this only over-estimates the running time.

Combining Lemmas 2 and 3 gives us the stated theorem.

4.2 Running Time of Replay

THEOREM 4. *Given an augmented dag with work W and span $\tilde{S}$, the replay process completes in expected time $O(W/P + \tilde{S} \lg \lg P)$.*

As with the analysis of replay, we divide time steps into work steps and steal steps. No worker ever waits on a lock, so there are no blocking steps. The total work is still bounded by W. Therefore, it only remains to bound the number of steal attempts.

We will use the ideas from the ABP analysis to bound the number of steal attempts. The main difference between vanilla work stealing and our replay strategy is that we now have more than P deques. In particular, the high-level idea in the ABP analysis is the following. If there are X deques in the system, then X steal attempts are likely to reduce the critical path by a constant amount. Therefore, the total number of steal attempts is ((number of deques) $\times$ S) in expectation. Since our scheduler can have an arbitrarily large number of deques (as large as the number of critical sections in the program), we would get a very bad bound if we directly applied that technique. We use additional insights to bound the number of steal attempts for a replay scheduler. We first make the following observation.

OBSERVATION 5. *A steal from a suspended deque always succeeds since it is never empty. Since a successful steal is followed by a unit of work by the thief, the total number of steals from suspended deques is bounded by W.*

Note also that when the number of suspended deques is small, i.e. still on the order of $O(P)$, we can use an analysis similar to ABP to bound the steal attempts. We only run into issues when the number of suspended deques is not small.

A ***work-bounded phase*** begins when at least $P/2$ workers have at least one suspended deque. During a work-bounded phase, about a quarter of the steal attempts are likely to succeed (since that many of the steals occur from a suspended deque). Thus we can bound the total number of steal attempts in these phases by the work of the computation. A ***steal-bounded*** phase begins with fewer than $P/2$ workers having any suspended deques. Recall, as described in Section 3, we try to keep the number of deques across workers roughly balanced by throwing deques to workers at random. Therefore, if fewer than $P/2$ workers have suspended deques, the total number of deques in the system are likely to be small. Therefore, we will bound the steal attempts occurred during steal-bounded phases using analysis similar to that in ABP. Note that a phase is either work-bounded or steal-bounded.

LEMMA 6. *The expected number of steal attempts during work-bounded phases is $O(W)$.*

Proof. In work bounded phases, at least $P/2$ processors have suspended deques. Since a thief chooses a victim uniformly at random, we have $1/2$ probability of stealing into these processors with suspended deques. In addition, since these workers have at most one active deque and at least one suspended deque, about half of the steals from these workers are expected to be successful. Therefore, the expected number of steals attempts during work-bounded phases is $4X$ where X is the number of steal attempts from suspended deques. Combining with Observation 5 gives the lemma.

We now consider bounding the steal attempts in steal-bounded phases. Although we now potentially have more than P deques, we can still use analysis similar to APB to bound the steal attempts. At a very high level, the APB analysis works as follows. The computation starts out having bounded "potential," which is a function of the computation's span. Note that the important node that one needs to execute in order to make progress on the span always sits on top of some deque. The key point in the ABP analysis is that, if there are X deques in the system, and we steal uniformly at random from them, then after $O(X)$ number of steal attempts, some worker steals and executes the important node at the top of some deque and thus make progress on the span. Hence we can bound the number of steal attempts to be $O(XS)$ in expectation.

Similar to ABP, we define a potential function based on the depth of nodes in the augmented dag. The depth of a node $d(u)$ is recursively defined as 1 plus the maximum depth of all its parents. The weight of a node is $w(u) = \tilde{S} - d(u)$. Then, we define a potential as follows:

DEFINITION 1. *The* ***potential*** *$\Phi(u)$ of a node u is $3^{2w(u)-1}$ if u is assigned, and $3^{2w(u)}$ if u is ready.*

The total potential of the computation is the sum of the potentials of all its ready and assigned nodes, and the follow lemma follows from the APB analysis in a straightforward manner.

LEMMA 7. *The initial potential is $3^{2\tilde{S}-1}$ and it never increases during the computation.* □

The following lemma is a straightforward generalization of Lemmas 7 and 8 in ABP [3].

LEMMA 8. *Let Φ_i denote the potential at time t and say that the probability of each deque being a victim of a steal attempt is* at least $1/X$. *Then after X steal attempts, the potential is at most $\Phi(t)/4$ with probability at least $1/4$.* □

In ABP, X would be P. In our case, we need to analyze what X is. To bound X, we define the number of suspended deques a worker has as its ***load***, and we are concerned with the ***maximum load***, i.e., highest number of suspended deques a worker can have. We consider two scenarios. First scenario is where there are at most $2P$ suspended deques in the system, and we can bound the maximum load in this case.

LEMMA 9. *Say there are at most $2P$ suspended deques over all processors. With probability at least $1 - 1/P^2$, the processor with the largest load has at most $k = \lg\lg P + O(1)$ suspended deques.*

Proof. The lemma follows from the Azar et. al's [5, 7] classic balls into bins results. They prove that if we throw K balls into P bins by checking two bins and throwing the ball into the less loaded bin, then the maximum load is $\lg\lg P + O(K/P)$ with high probability. That is, the loads in bins are mostly balanced within an additive factor of $\lg\lg P$. If we think of suspended deques as balls and processors as bins, by performing the load balancing of suspended deques described at the end of Section 3, this result guarantees that when deques are suspended, they are distributed evenly. We will say that a distribution is ***balanced*** if the processor with the largest number of deques has fewer than $2\lg\lg P$ deques, otherwise, we will say that the distribution is unbalanced. We must also worry about imbalance creeping in as processors steal from suspended deques and suspended deques disappear. However, the proof of Theorem 4.1 from Azar et. al's paper [7] implies that if we start from an imbalanced distribution, and on each step, pick two random bins, and move a ball from the more loaded bin to the less loaded bin, then after $P^2 \lg\lg P$ steps, bins will be balanced again. Since our strategy for steals from Section 3 follows exactly this strategy, the following claim follows:

CLAIM 10. *If we start from a balanced distribution, it becomes imbalanced after $P^2 \lg\lg P$ steal attempts with probability at most $1/P^2$. If the distribution becomes imbalanced, it becomes balanced again after $P^2 \lg\lg P$ steal attempts with probability at least $(1 - 1/P^2)$.*

In the other scenario, where there are more than $2P$ suspended deques in the system, we cannot readily bound the maximum load, but one can show that such a scenario falls under the work-bounded phase with high probability:

LEMMA 11. *Say there are more than $2P$ suspended deques. At least $P/2$ workers have at least one suspended deque with probability at least $1 - (e/8)^{P/2} \geq 1 - 1/P^2$ for large enough P.*

Proof. The probability that $P/2$ workers have no suspended deques is $\binom{P}{P/2}(1/2)^{2P} \leq (2e/16)^{P/2}$.

We will divide each steal bounded phase into rounds with $2P\lg\lg P$ steal attempts. We say that a round is ***good*** if the maximum load is at most $2\lg\lg P$ throughout the round and bad otherwise.

LEMMA 12. *Let $\Phi(t)$ denote the potential at the beginning of a good round. After $P\lg\lg P$ steal attempts, at the end of the round, the potential is at most $3\Phi(t)/4$ with probability at least $1/4$.* □

Proof. There are at most $2P\lg\lg P$ deques during the round. Therefore, the probability that a particular steal attempt hits a particular deque is at least $1/(2P\lg\lg P)$ (it may be higher since some workers have fewer than $\lg\lg P$ suspended deques). Therefore, we can apply a small modification to Lemma 8 generalized from ABP and argue that the total potential decreases.

LEMMA 13. *The total number of good rounds is $O(\tilde{S})$ in expectation.*

Proof. Similar arguments to ABP. At a high level, from Lemma 12, a constant number good rounds suffice to decrease the potential by a constant factor in expectation. Therefore, the number of rounds needed to reduce the potential to one is log of the initial potential, which is $3^{2\tilde{S}}$. Therefore, after $O(\tilde{S})$ rounds, the potential disappears and the computation completes.

We still need to bound the number of bad rounds, however.

LEMMA 14. *The number of bad rounds is $O((1/P)X)$ where X is the number of good rounds.*

Proof. A round is good with probability at least $1 - 1/P^2$ from Lemma 9, Claim 10, and Lemma 11. If we ever get into a bad round, things become balanced again after $O(P^2 \lg\lg P)$ steal attempts, or $O(P)$ rounds from Claim 10. Therefore, it takes P^2 good rounds before a bad round occurs and then there can be at most P bad rounds before a good round occurs again. The following lemma follows from Lemmas 13 and 14 and the fact that each round has $P\lg\lg P$ steals.

LEMMA 15. *The expected number of steal attempts in steal bounded phases is at most $O(\tilde{S}P\lg\lg P)$.*

The following lemma follows from Lemmas 6 and 15

LEMMA 16. *The total number of steal attempts across all phases is $O(W + \tilde{S}P\lg\lg P)$.*

Lemma 16 and the facts that the total amount of work is W implies Theorem 4.

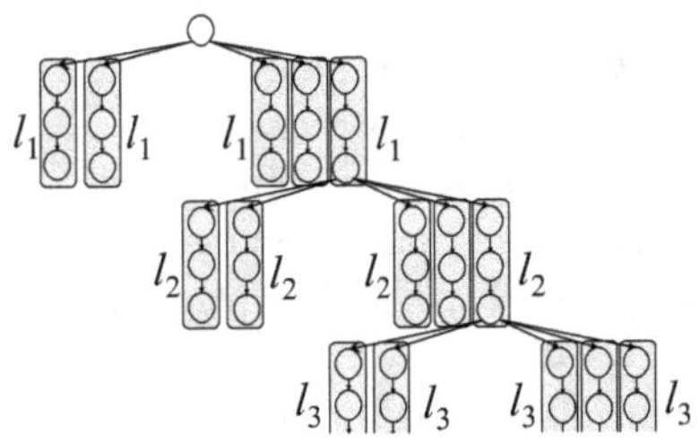

Figure 1: An example DAG with multiple locks where getting a tight bound for recording is impossible for an online scheduler. The offline scheduler can always schedule the "important" (in this case, the right-most) critical section first, but an online scheduler has no way of knowing which critical section is "important", and therefore may execute it last.

4.3 Discussion

We now discuss how good or bad these bounds are, theoretically. For a single lock, note that W/P, S, and B are all lower bounds on the execution on P workers; therefore, the bound is tight. For multiple locks while W/P and S are still lower bounds, B is not a lower bound for all dags. Nevertheless, this bound is existentially tight — there exist dags for which it is tight. In general, it is difficult for online schedulers to get tight bounds on all computation dags with multiple locks without knowing what the future DAG looks like. Consider the dag shown in Figure 1. Gray rectangles represent critical sections, and all critical sections in the same layer access the same lock. An optimal offline scheduler will schedule the right-most critical section of each layer first so it can schedule the next layer in parallel with the previous layers and can get good speedup. However, an online scheduler cannot know which critical section of each layer leads to more future work and may execute them in an order that gets no speedup. In general, an online scheduler cannot guarantee optimality, since for any online strategy S, there is a bad dag where the next layer is always created by the critical section this strategy S executes last.

Let us now consider replay. In this case, W/P, and $\tilde{S}$ are lower bounds; therefore the replay bound of $O(W/P + \lg\lg P\tilde{S})$ is nearly tight — it just has an additional $\lg\lg P$ factor on the span term which is tiny for most machines. In addition, since it is on the span term, according to the work-first principle [32], this overhead does not affect computations with sufficient parallelism.

On series-parallel (or more generally, fully-strict) computations, depth-first work stealing (of the kind we use) also guarantees a space bound; in particular, if the sequential execution uses S_1 stack space, work-stealing uses $O(PS_1)$ when using P workers. Since record uses vanilla work-stealing, it also provides this space bound. However, the replay scheduler executes the augmented DAG which is not a fully-strict DAG. In fact, one can generate augmented DAGs for which it would be impossible to simultaneously provide good speedup and space bounds; the construction is similar to the lower bound in Section-3.1 in [16]. Since our replay scheduler provides an good speedup, it can not guarantee low space usage.

5. EMPIRICAL EVALUATION

This section empirically evaluates PORRidge. The main benefit of a processor-oblivious record-replay system is that one can replay an execution on a different number of processors from that used during the recording — including a larger number — allowing the replay to benefit from parallel execution. There are inherent overheads in the record and replay in order to allow processor-oblivious replay, however. Specifically, during record, PORRidge must record happens-before edges via section IDs in a schedule-independent fashion; during replay, PORRidge may need to suspend and resume strands upon lock acquires and releases.

application	*number of locks*	*number of lock acquires* *total*	*min*	*max*	*mean*	*std. dev.*
`chess`	4	2.8e4	0	2.8e4	7.1e3	1.4e4
`dedup`	1	7.3e5	7.3e5	7.3e5	7.3e5	n/a
`ferret`	1	256	256	256	256	n/a
`matching`	5e6	5e7	5	25	10	2.23
`MIS`	5e6	2.8e6	3	27	5.63	2.73
`refine`	4.8e7	1.2e7	0	27	0.26	0.56

Table 1: Application benchmarks used and their execution characteristics measured when running on one worker. The total column shows the total number of lock acquires across all locks during execution. The min column shows the minimum number of lock acquires invoked on a given lock across all locks; similarly, the max column shows the maximum. The last two columns show the average number of lock acquires per lock and the standard deviation.

We empirically evaluated the overhead and scalability of the record phase and replay phase across six benchmarks with different execution characteristics. Our results indicate that, for benchmarks that have a sufficiently large work-to-critical-section ratio, record and replay incur negligible overhead. For benchmarks whose work is dominated by critical sections, record and replay can incur up to $3.73\times$ overhead, with replay incurring slightly higher overhead than record. In terms of scalability, recording scales similarly compared to the baseline. As long as there is sufficient parallelism in the recorded execution, the replay scales similarly. Moreover, due to its non-blocking execution model, the replay continues to get speedup beyond P_{rec} workers, where P_{rec} is the number of workers used during recording.

Benchmarks. We used the following six benchmarks to evaluate the PORRidge system. The first one, `chess`, is a Cilk Plus program published by Intel [62] that solves a chess puzzle — given eight chess pieces excluding pawns, it counts the number of configurations where the pieces can attack all squares on an 8×8 chess board. The original program uses reducers [33] to keep the count of the number of such configurations found and to perform I/O; we modified the program to use locks instead. Two benchmarks, `dedup` and `ferret`, are from the PARSEC benchmark suite [13, 14]; they can be implemented as Cilk Plus programs that use locks for performing file I/O. Finally, we converted several nondeterministic versions of graph algorithms from the Problem Based Benchmark Suite [65] to use locks instead of Compare-And-Swap (CAS): `MIS` (Maximal Independent Set), `matching` (Maximal Matching), and `refine` (Delaunay Refinement). These benchmarks cover a wide spectrum of behaviors. Their runtime characteristics when executing on one worker are shown in Figure 1. Note that the characteristics during parallel execution may differ slightly for some of the graph benchmarks as they are non-

	baseline	*record*	*replay*
`chess`	64.43	64.38 (1.00×)	65.11 (1.01×)
`dedup`	48.04	48.20 (1.00×)	48.16 (1.00×)
`ferret`	8.92	8.89 (1.00×)	9.10 (1.02×)
`matching`	3.06	9.64 (3.15×)	10.07 (3.29×)
`MIS`	1.01	3.42 (3.39×)	3.77 (3.73×)
`refine`	11.70	14.73 (1.26×)	13.63 (1.16×)

Table 2: Execution times running on one worker ($P_{base} = P_{rec} = P_{rep} = 1$) for six benchmarks, in seconds. The `replay` column shows the replay execution time for replaying the run recorded with one worker. The numbers shown in parenthesis indicate the overhead compared to the baseline.

deterministic by nature. The first three benchmarks use few locks, but still have plenty of critical sections; however, they do a significant amount of work outside of critical sections. The graph benchmarks use a much larger number of locks, since there is one lock per vertex in the input graph. In addition, they do almost all of their work within critical sections.

Experimental Platform. We ran our experiments on an Intel Xeon E5-2665 with 16 2.40-GHz cores on two sockets; 64 GB of DRAM; two 20 MB L3 caches, each shared among 8 cores; and private L2- and L1-caches of sizes 2 MB and 512 KB, respectively. Both hyperthreading and dynamic frequency scaling are disabled in order to get consistent results across runs. For recorded runs, running times are in seconds as the mean of five runs, and we used a 64-bit bloom filter in our implementation (see Section 3). For a given number of workers, the recording with the median running time is chosen for the replay runs. For the most part, the standard deviation was within 5% of the mean for both record and replay. A few data points were the exception — graph algorithms that are memory-bound (`matching` and `MIS`) have higher standard deviation during some replay, up to 12% for `MIS`.

Notation. We use the following notations in this section. The label ***baseline*** refers to executions of the benchmarks with ordinary spin locks (i.e., without PORRidge). The label ***record*** refers to the executions with recording enabled using PORRidge. The label ***replay*** refers to the executions with replay enabled using PORRidge. We use P_{base} to refer to the number of workers used during baseline execution, P_{rec} to refer to the number of workers used during record and P_{rep} to refer to the number of workers used during replay.

5.1 Overhead of Record

To evaluate the recording overhead, we compare the running time of PORRidge recording on one worker with the baseline running on one worker. Table 2 shows the execution times of six benchmark for these configurations. The recording overhead ranges from 1–3.39× with a geometric mean of 1.62×. Since PORRidge incurs overhead only upon lock operations, the overhead is in part dictated by how much work is done per lock acquire. For programs that perform sufficient amount of work outside of critical sections, such as `chess`, `dedup`, and `ferret`, the overhead is negligible. The graph algorithms, especially `matching` and `MIS`, incur higher overhead. For these applications, almost all of the work occurs inside critical sections. In addition, each critical section does a very small amount of work. Their executions mostly involve repeatedly traversing some edge, acquiring a lock corresponding to the vertex at the end of the edge, updating a field in the vertex, and releasing the lock. Hence, the execution time of these programs is dominated by the cost of acquiring and releasing locks. Moreover, these applications are memory bound — they have large working sets and display very little locality in accessing data. The additional space used for logging during recording puts additional pressure on the memory hierarchy. In the initial implementation, we have used a hash list to detect collisions of section IDs (discussed in Section 3), and the additional cache misses incurred by accessing the hash list incurred much larger overhead in these applications (8–9×). By reordering the bookkeeping data layout to obtain better spatial locality and using a bloom filter instead of a hash list, we were able to reduce the overhead drastically.

5.2 Overhead of Replay

Replay has two types of overheads. Replay, like record, incurs overhead upon lock acquires and releases. When a worker tries to acquire a lock, it must search the lock-acquire array or query the hash list with the current section ID to see if this lock acquire is the next in line to obtain the lock. If so, it can acquire the lock. Otherwise, it must suspend. Upon a release, the worker advances the head of the lock-acquire list; if the next lock acquire has been tried and suspended, the worker suspends its current execution and resumes the execution of the next lock acquire. In addition, replay also incurs overheads due to maintaining more deques than the vanilla Cilk runtime system.

If we record on one worker and replay on one worker, the record and replay executions proceeds in exactly the same order. Therefore, the replay execution never has to suspend. Essentially, the work done by replay is the same as the work done by record except that replay may need to search through the lock-acquire arrays if there is ever any collisions in the section IDs. Thus, for most benchmarks, replay exhibits similar overhead as in recorded run when $P_{rec} = P_{rep} = 1$ as shown in Figure 3

The more interesting case is when we record on more than one worker and replay on one worker ($P_{rec} > 1$ and $P_{rep} = 1$). In this case, process-oblivious replay has additional overheads — namely the overhead of suspending and resuming lock acquires. Note that when we replay (on one worker) an execution recorded on multiple workers, the worker likely encounters critical sections in a different order than the recorded execution did. When a worker encounters a critical section that it cannot execute yet, it must suspend its current deque and work steal. In addition, since it steals work

application	*replay on one, recorded on P* P = 1	P = 2	P = 4	P = 8	P = 12	P = 16
chess	65.14 (1.01×)	65.13 (1.01×)	65.11 (1.01×)	65.17 (1.01×)	65.20 (1.01×)	65.13 (1.01×)
dedup	48.16 (1.00×)	48.15 (1.00×)	48.16 (1.00×)	48.21 (1.00×)	48.11 (1.00×)	48.20 (1.00×)
ferret	9.10 (1.02×)	8.95 (1.01×)	8.95 (1.01×)	8.94 (1.01×)	8.93 (1.00×)	8.93 (1.00×)
matching	10.07 (1.04×)	10.13 (1.05×)	10.13 (1.05×)	10.17 (1.05×)	10.37 (1.08×)	10.43 (1.08×)
MIS	3.77 (1.11×)	3.90 (1.15×)	3.94 (1.16×)	3.93 (1.16×)	3.97 (1.17×)	4.04 (1.19×)
refine	13.63 (0.93×)	13.67 (0.93×)	13.47 (0.91×)	13.73 (0.93×)	13.70 (0.93×)	13.73 (0.93×)

Table 3: Execution times, in seconds, when replaying on one worker executions recorded on different number of workers. The numbers shown in parenthesis indicate the overhead compared to the execution time of that recorded on one worker.

at random, the next critical section it acquires may again not be ready. Therefore, the worker may suspend many deques before encountering a critical section it can execute.

We can gauge such an overhead by comparing the overhead of executions with $P_{rec} > 1$ and $P_{rep} = 1$ with the overhead of executions with $P_{rec} = P_{rep} = 1$ shown in Figure 3. It turns out that for the most part, the additional overhead incurred by suspending and resuming lock acquires is negligible — at most a few percent increase for the memory-bound benchmarks.

5.3 Scalability of Record

To analyze the scalability of PORRidge for recording, we compare the speedup of record to the baseline's. The speedup is computed with respect to their respective one-worker execution counterpart. Table 4 shows scalability of both the baseline and recorded runs across benchmarks (the first two columns). The scalability profile for record tracks that of the baseline closely across all benchmarks. This is especially surprising for memory-bound benchmarks since the workers spend longer within critical sections during recording compared to the baseline. In spite if this, it appears that the additional overhead is distributed across processors evenly and did not reduce the overall parallelism by much.

5.4 Scalability of Replay

Table 4 also shows scalability of replay runs that replay executions recorded on $P_{rec} = 1, 2, 4, 8, 12, 16$ processors. Here, we measure the speedup of a replay run by comparing it against the time replaying the same recorded execution on one worker (i.e., $P_{rec} = 1$).

Recall the time bound for replay: its expected execution time on P workers is $O(W/P + \tilde{S} \lg\lg P)$, where W is the overall work in the computation and the $\tilde{S}$ is the span in the augmented dag. Since $S \leq \tilde{S} \leq S + B$, replay should scale as long as record scales if we ignore the $\lg\lg P$ term. For most benchmarks, we do see that the replay scales similarly to the recorded execution when $P_{rec} = P_{rep}$ (the highlighted cells in Figure **??**), indicating that it is generally safe to ignore the $\lg\lg P$ term and that the overheads of suspending and restarting in replay is small.

The two exceptions are data points in `matching` and `MIS`. There are two possible explanation. The first is that the augmented dag is running out parallelism. We don't believe that this is the case, since if replay uses more workers $P_{rep} > P_{rec}$, we continue to see the execution scales (i.e., by looking at the scalability of data points below the highlighted cells). The more likely explanation is the following: these benchmarks are already memory bound, and replay has a much larger memory footprint than record, causing additional cache misses, and the higher memory latency slows down the parallel execution. Indeed, these executions incur higher cache misses during replay than during record. There are two reasons for these additional cache misses. First, during replay, workers suspend their current deque from time to time (discussed in Section 3) and thus can create large number of suspended deques. Second, while record can use a bloom filter and do without a hash list, replay must use either an array or a hash list. While arrays have fewer cache misses than the hash list, both of these have a larger memory footprint than the bloom filter. Indeed, recall that one of the optimizations that we implemented for replay is to use a lock-acquire array instead of a hash list if the number of lock acquires per lock is small (which is the case for these benchmarks). The overhead of replay was much higher when we used a hash list in our initial implementation, which requires even more memory than the array.

The additional memory footprint also in part explains the data points with higher standard deviation. How many additional deques created during replay is a function of scheduling, and the number of suspended deques can differ from run to run. Execution times for benchmarks that are already memory bound will be more sensitive to this changes in the number of suspended deques.

5.5 Benefits of Processor Obliviousness

As our experimental data indicates, processor-oblivious record and replay can be implemented efficiently. The only time PORRidge exhibits non-negligible overhead is when the benchmark is already memory bound. For dynamic multithreaded computations, a processor-aware record-and-replay system would need to log additional information to record the inherent non-determinism in the scheduler, which would further increase the memory footprint of the recording.

Moreover, the strategy used by PORRidge has the additional benefit of scaling the replay beyond the number work-

bench	P	baseline	record	replay on P workers ($P_{rep} = P$) an execution recorded on P' workers ($P_{rec} = P'$) P' = 1	P' = 2	P' = 4	P' = 8	P' = 12	P' = 16
chess	1	64.49 (1.00×)	64.36 (1.00×)	65.14 (1.00×)	65.13 (1.00×)	65.11 (1.00×)	65.17 (1.00×)	65.20 (1.00×)	65.13 (1.00×)
	2	32.20 (2.00×)	32.20 (2.00×)	32.60 (2.00×)	32.60 (2.00×)	32.61 (2.00×)	32.64 (2.00×)	32.63 (2.00×)	32.66 (1.99×)
	4	16.11 (4.00×)	16.11 (4.00×)	16.50 (3.95×)	16.36 (3.98×)	16.35 (3.98×)	16.37 (3.98×)	16.35 (3.99×)	16.34 (3.99×)
	8	8.15 (7.91×)	8.13 (7.92×)	8.55 (7.62×)	8.31 (7.84×)	8.42 (7.73×)	8.45 (7.71×)	8.34 (7.82×)	8.31 (7.84×)
	12	5.38 (11.99×)	5.38 (11.96×)	5.91 (11.02×)	5.65 (11.53×)	5.75 (11.32×)	5.75 (11.33×)	5.66 (11.52×)	5.63 (11.57×)
	16	4.04 (15.96×)	4.11 (15.66×)	4.52 (14.41×)	4.50 (14.47×)	4.47 (14.57×)	4.57 (14.26×)	4.32 (15.09×)	4.35 (14.97×)
dedup	1	48.04 (1.00×)	48.20 (1.00×)	48.16 (1.00×)	49.15 (1.00×)	48.16 (1.00×)	48.21 (1.00×)	48.11 (1.00×)	48.20 (1.00×)
	2	24.43 (1.87×)	24.44 (1.94×)	24.58 (1.92×)	24.44 (1.88×)	24.44 (1.95×)	24.43 (1.95×)	24.45 (1.96×)	24.42 (1.94×)
	4	12.43 (3.86×)	12.40 (3.89×)	12.61 (3.82×)	12.55 (3.84×)	12.51 (3.85×)	12.40 (3.89×)	12.40 (3.88×)	12.41 (3.88×)
	8	6.43 (7.47×)	6.49 (7.43×)	6.72 (7.17×)	6.69 (7.20×)	6.61 (7.29×)	6.46 (7.47×)	6.45 (7.46×)	6.46 (7.46×)
	12	4.52 (10.63×)	4.53 (10.64×)	4.88 (9.87×)	4.83 (9.97×)	4.75 (10.14×)	4.63 (10.41×)	4.55 (10.57×)	4.55 (10.59×)
	16	3.61 (13.31×)	3.65 (13.32×)	3.95 (12.19×)	3.94 (12.22×)	3.89 (12.38×)	3.76 (12.82×)	3.69 (13.04×)	3.64 (13.24×)
ferret	1	8.92 (1.00×)	8.89 (1.00×)	9.10 (1.00×)	8.95 (1.00×)	8.95 (1.00×)	8.94 (1.00×)	8.93 (1.00×)	8.93 (1.00×)
	2	4.52 (1.97×)	4.57 (1.95×)	4.53 (2.01×)	4.54 (1.97×)	4.56 (1.96×)	4.52 (1.98×)	4.53 (1.97×)	4.52 (1.98×)
	4	2.31 (3.86×)	2.33 (3.82×)	2.32 (3.92×)	2.34 (3.82×)	2.32 (3.86×)	2.32 (3.85×)	2.31 (3.87×)	2.32 (3.85×)
	8	1.27 (7.02×)	1.24 (7.17×)	1.24 (7.34×)	1.24 (7.22×)	1.27 (7.05×)	1.26 (7.10×)	1.26 (7.09×)	1.26 (7.09×)
	12	0.91 (9.80×)	0.91 (9.77×)	0.93 (9.78×)	0.90 (9.94×)	0.91 (9.84×)	0.92 (9.72×)	0.92 (9.71×)	0.91 (9.81×)
	16	0.76 (11.74×)	0.78 (11.40×)	0.75 (12.13×)	0.75 (11.93×)	0.75 (11.93×)	0.75 (11.92×)	0.75 (11.91×)	0.74 (12.07×)
matching	1	3.06 (1.00×)	9.64 (1.00×)	10.07 (1.00×)	10.13 (1.00×)	10.13 (1.00×)	10.17 (1.00×)	10.37 (1.00×)	10.43 (1.00×)
	2	1.92 (1.67×)	5.78 (1.46×)	6.88 (1.49×)	6.82 (1.49×)	6.93 (1.46×)	6.64 (1.53×)	6.68 (1.55×)	6.63 (1.57×)
	4	0.96 (3.19×)	3.03 (3.18×)	3.95 (2.55×)	3.90 (2.60×)	3.75 (2.70×)	3.64 (2.79×)	3.63 (2.86×)	3.62 (2.88×)
	8	0.50 (6.12×)	1.68 (5.74×)	3.77 (4.31×)	3.99 (4.57×)	4.22 (4.61×)	2.22 (4.58×)	2.21 (4.69×)	2.11 (4.94×)
	12	0.32 (9.56×)	1.13 (8.53×)	2.57 (3.92×)	2.42 (4.19×)	2.21 (4.58×)	1.89 (5.38×)	1.77 (5.86×)	1.68 (6.21×)
	16	0.25 (12.24×)	0.89 (10.83×)	2.56 (3.93×)	2.41 (4.20×)	2.11 (4.80×)	1.79 (5.68×)	1.58 (6.56×)	1.57 (6.64×)
MIS	1	1.02 (1.00×)	3.40 (1.00×)	3.77 (1.00×)	3.90 (1.00×)	3.94 (1.00×)	3.93 (1.00×)	3.97 (1.00×)	4.04 (1.00×)
	2	0.65 (1.57×)	2.03 (1.67×)	2.57 (1.47×)	2.54 (1.54×)	2.48 (1.59×)	2.47 (1.59×)	2.45 (1.62×)	2.52 (1.60×)
	4	0.32 (3.19×)	1.03 (3.30×)	1.63 (2.31×)	1.52 (2.57×)	1.36 (2.90×)	1.34 (2.93×)	1.33 (2.98×)	1.32 (3.06×)
	8	0.16 (6.38×)	0.58 (5.86×)	1.38 (2.73×)	1.14 (3.42×)	0.93 (4.24×)	0.79 (4.97×)	0.81 (4.90×)	0.79 (5.11×)
	12	0.13 (7.85×)	0.22 (8.10×)	1.54 (2.45×)	1.26 (3.10×)	0.89 (4.43×)	0.69 (5.70×)	0.61 (6.51×)	0.67 (6.03×)
	16	0.14 (7.29×)	0.38 (8.95×)	1.50 (2.51×)	1.28 (3.05×)	0.94 (4.19×)	0.73 (5.38×)	0.61 (6.51×)	0.63 (6.41×)
refine	1	11.70 (1.00×)	14.73 (1.00×)	13.63 (1.00×)	13.67 (1.00×)	13.47 (1.00×)	13.73 (1.00×)	13.70 (1.00×)	13.73 (1.00×)
	2	7.36 (1.59×)	9.32 (1.58×)	9.38 (1.45×)	9.11 (1.50×)	9.19 (1.47×)	9.32 (1.47×)	9.13 (1.50×)	9.17 (1.50×)
	4	4.40 (2.66×)	5.53 (2.66×)	5.60 (2.43×)	5.49 (2.49×)	5.35 (2.52×)	5.36 (2.56×)	5.26 (2.60×)	5.34 (2.57×)
	8	3.15 (3.71×)	3.87 (3.81×)	4.29 (3.18×)	3.99 (3.43×)	3.90 (3.45×)	3.77 (3.64×)	3.74 (3.66×)	3.66 (3.75×)
	12	2.73 (4.29×)	3.32 (4.44×)	3.91 (3.49×)	3.62 (3.78×)	3.44 (3.92×)	3.36 (4.09×)	3.36 (4.08×)	3.31 (4.15×)
	16	2.45 (4.78×)	3.04 (4.86×)	3.61 (3.78×)	3.39 (4.03×)	3.21 (4.20×)	3.04 (4.52×)	3.00 (4.57×)	2.96 (4.64×)

Table 4: Execution times on $P = 1, 2, 4, 8, 12, 16$, in seconds, and their scalability profile for all benchmarks. Each of the replay columns shows the replay time with $P_{rep} = P$ workers replaying the same recorded execution (with $P_{rec} = P'$, as shown in the column heading). The numbers in the parenthesis indicate the speedup comparing to its single-worker execution counterpart, which has the 1.00 speedup. The highlighted cells indicate replay runs that uses the same number of workers as in the recording.

ers used in record, which a processor-aware record and replay system cannot provide. If a recording is done on P workers and takes x time, in a processor-aware system, the replay cannot run in less than x time (asymptotically) no matter how many workers we give it. In fact, it would likely be slower since it would spin when it encounters a lock acquire that is not ready and would have to exactly replicate the steal patterns of the record, causing potentially more idleness. On the other hand, PORRidge never spins during replay and uses suspension to explore all the possible parallelism in the augmented dag. Therefore, as the experiments indicate, replay often runs just as fast as the record when $P_{rep} = P_{rec}$, and can continue to scale when $P_{rep} > P_{rec}$.

6. RELATED WORK

Record and Replay. To our knowledge, all software-based record and replay systems are tied to thread-based programming models: a runtime system records the behavior and interleaving of the threads in the program, and on replay reruns the same threads with the same behavior. Recording and replaying on the same number of threads simplifies both the recording process (as thread-based identifiers can be used to identify operations) and the replay process (as there is no need to map operations from the recorded run onto a different number of threads). RecPlay [63] and JaRec [34] do not handle racy accesses, and have reasonable overhead, but, as with PORRidge, are unsound in the presence of races.

Racy accesses are more challenging, since accesses to shared memory result in happens-before edges that must be preserved during replay. For systems that handle racy accesses, there are several approaches. Some speculate that races are infrequent or irrelevant to keep recording overhead down [43, 68]. Some preserve a limited amount of information during record and rely on offline search or constraint-solving approaches to generate the information required for replay [2, 37, 48, 56]. Some systems track racy interleavings directly, which either add large overhead [42, 70], use coarse-granularity communication tracking (such as page-based conflict detection) that can be overly-conservative [29, 41], or rely on carefully modified virtual machines [20].

One could apply a traditional thread-based record-and-replay system on dynamic multithreaded computation directly, and record all sources of nondeterminism in order to replay deterministically. PinPlay [57] is such a general record and replay system based on Pin, a popular dynamic binary instrumentation framework [50], that captures all sources of nondeterminism including racy memory accesses, thread interleavings, and results from system calls. We ran PinPlay on Delaunay Refinement (`refine` described in Section 5) and find that it has 96.8× overhead for recording and 16.1× overhead for replay when executing the computation on one worker — 1-2 orders of magnitudes worse than the PORRidge overheads of 1.26× and 1.16×, respectively. When we tried recording and replaying on multiple workers, the executions with PinPlay slowed down and showed no speedup. This result in part speaks to the performance advantage of PORRidge's approach, because PORRidge does not need to reproduce the runtimes non-determinism while traditional thread-based record-and-replay systems must. Reproducing the runtimes non-determinism requires logging all inter-thread interactions among worker threads and causing a worker thread to spin wait (instead of doing useful work) when it reaches a recorded inter-thread interaction before the other thread gets there. Note that such inter-thread interactions include all failed steal attempts between a thief and a victim worker, since a failed steal attempt is communicated through shared memory accesses. Chimera [44], another record-and-replay system for pthreaded code, on the other hand, uses static race detection to identify potentially-racing pairs of accesses, and uses lightweight synchronization, as well as lock coarsening, to enable a simple record and replay technique. Such an approach, could be adapted to make PORRidge applicable to racy Cilk programs.

Another strategy is to record information at the *hardware* level [36, 53, 58, 69], by piggy-backing on cache-coherence protocols to record communication between different hardware contexts. While these systems could, in principle, be used to record the behavior of Cilk programs and to capture the non-determinism introduced by the scheduler, they have two drawbacks: 1) like existing software-based models, their (hardware) context-based recording system constrains replay to run with the same level of parallelism as record; 2) they require hardware modifications, and hence do not work in any existing commodity systems.

Determinism. A related technique is *deterministic execution*, where a combination of programming model constraints and runtime checks ensures that an application always produces the same behavior when presented with the same input. Note that this is subtly different than record and replay: in record and replay, different *recorded* runs can exhibit different behaviors; replay must replicate whichever recorded run it is replaying. One approach to determinism is to mandate it through programming model restrictions [12, 15, 19, 22, 54, 61] which generally preclude general use of locks and other synchronization mechanisms. Moreover, while some of these approaches can provide determinism independent of the number of threads [15, 54], most do not. Another approach is to enforce determinism through hardware [26, 27], compiler [10], OS [4, 11] or runtime approaches [49, 55]. While these techniques do not require specialized programming models, these techniques are usually not processor oblivious.

Dynamic Analyses for Dynamic Multithreading. The most common analysis tool for dynamic multithreading programming models is *on the fly race detection* — for a given input, these tools run the program on that input *once* while keeping track of enough information that allows them to report a race if and only if the program contains a race on that input. Over the years, researchers have proposed algorithms for doing this both sequentially [30, 59] and in parallel [9, 51, 60, 67]. Some of these have led to implementations [30, 60, 67]. The parallel tools are generally processor-oblivious; a single run on any number of workers gives the correct answer. Another important class of tools is *performance profilers*, that either measure work and span of the program directly during execution [35, 64] or use sampling to determine where in the code causes workers to be idle [66].

Work-stealing Runtime with Multiple Deques. Prior work-stealing designs have used more than P deques for supporting concurrent data structures [1, 67] or blocking I/O operations [52, 71]; some provide theoretical scheduling bounds [1, 52, 67], but their modifications are for a different purpose and require different modifications and analyses.

7. CONCLUSION

This paper presented the first processor oblivious record and replay scheme for data race-free dynamic multithreaded programs. This scheme is provably good, efficient in practice, and provides good scalability. There are many directions of future work. First, we could target a richer set of primitives that induce happens-before relationships; for instance, `try-lock` and `compare-and-swap`. These require rethinking the exact semantics we want from a happens-before edge, since, in some cases, programs use the non-determinism induced by these mechanisms to enable efficiency, complicating which edges we want to record. Second, we could try to expand to programs with data races — this would involve recording happens-before relationships not just between critical sections, but also between accesses to memory locations that could be involved in races. As mentioned in the introduction, this does not require conceptual changes to PORRidge, just the ability to indicate to PORRidge where non-determinism due to races might occur. Finally, we can explore other mechanisms to enable processor-oblivious record and replay to see if some of them will give better performance.

Acknowledgments

This research was supported in part by National Science Foundation grants CCF-1150036, CCF-1218017, XPS-1439062,

CCF-1150013, CCF-1439126, CCF-1527692, and Department of Energy grant DE-SC0010295. We thank the referees for their excellent comments.

References

[1] K. Agrawal, J. T. Fineman, K. Lu, B. Sheridan, J. Sukha, and R. Utterback. Provably good scheduling for parallel programs that use data structures through implicit batching. In *Proceedings of the 26th ACM Symposium on Parallelism in Algorithms and Architectures*, SPAA '14, pages 84–95, New York, NY, USA, 2014. ACM. ISBN 978-1-4503-2821-0. doi: 10.1145/2612669.2612688. URL `http://doi.acm.org/10.1145/2612669.2612688`.

[2] G. Altekar and I. Stoica. Odr: output-deterministic replay for multicore debugging. In *Proceedings of the ACM SIGOPS 22nd Symposium on Operating systems principles*, SOSP '09, pages 193–206, New York, NY, USA, 2009. ACM. ISBN 978-1-60558-752-3. URL `http://doi.acm.org/10.1145/1629575.1629594`.

[3] N. S. Arora, R. D. Blumofe, and C. G. Plaxton. Thread scheduling for multiprogrammed multiprocessors. In *10th Annual ACM Symposium on Parallel Algorithms and Architectures*, pages 119–129, 1998.

[4] A. Aviram, S.-C. Weng, S. Hu, and B. Ford. Efficient System-Enforced Deterministic Parallelism. In *USENIX Symposium on Operating Systems Design and Implementation*, pages 1–16, 2010.

[5] B. Awerbuch, Y. Azar, S. Leonardi, and O. Regev. Minimizing the flow time without migration. In *Proceedings of the 31st Annual ACM Symposium on Theory of Computing*, pages 198–205, May 1999.

[6] E. Ayguade, N. Copty, A. Duran, J. Hoeflinger, Y. Lin, F. Massaioli, X. Teruel, P. Unnikrishnan, and G. Zhang. The design of OpenMP tasks. *IEEE Transactions on Parallel and Distributed Systems*, 20(3):404–418, Mar. 2009. URL `http://dx.doi.org/10.1109/TPDS.2008.105`.

[7] Y. Azar, A. Z. Broder, A. R. Karlin, and E. Upfal. Balanced allocations. *SIAM Journal Comput.*, 29(1):180–200, Sept. 1999. ISSN 0097-5397. doi: 10.1137/S0097539795288490. URL `http://dx.doi.org/10.1137/S0097539795288490`.

[8] R. Barik, Z. Budimlić, V. Cavè, S. Chatterjee, Y. Guo, D. Peixotto, R. Raman, J. Shirako, S. Taşırlar, Y. Yan, Y. Zhao, and V. Sarkar. The Habanero multicore software research project. In *Proceedings of the 24th ACM SIGPLAN Conference Companion on Object Oriented Programming Systems Languages and Applications*, OOPSLA '09, pages 735–736, Orlando, Florida, USA, 2009. ACM. ISBN 978-1-60558-768-4.

[9] M. A. Bender, J. T. Fineman, S. Gilbert, and C. E. Leiserson. On-the-fly maintenance of series-parallel relationships in fork-join multithreaded programs. In *16th Annual ACM Symposium on Parallel Algorithms and Architectures*, pages 133–144, 2004.

[10] T. Bergan, O. Anderson, J. Devietti, L. Ceze, and D. Grossman. CoreDet: A Compiler and Runtime System for Deterministic Multithreaded Execution. In *ACM International Conference on Architectural Support for Programming Languages and Operating Systems*, pages 53–64, 2010. doi: http://doi.acm.org/10.1145/1736020.1736029.

[11] T. Bergan, N. Hunt, L. Ceze, and S. D. Gribble. Deterministic process groups in dos. In *Proceedings of the 9th USENIX Conference on Operating Systems Design and Implementation*, OSDI'10, pages 177–191, Berkeley, CA, USA, 2010. USENIX Association. URL `http://dl.acm.org/citation.cfm?id=1924943.1924956`.

[12] E. D. Berger, T. Yang, T. Liu, and G. Novark. Grace: Safe Multithreaded Programming for C/C++. In *ACM Conference on Object-Oriented Programming, Systems, Languages, and Applications*, pages 81–96, 2009. doi: http://doi.acm.org/10.1145/1640089.1640096.

[13] C. Bienia and K. Li. Characteristics of workloads using the pipeline programming model. In *Proceedings of the 3rd Workshop on Emerging Applications and Many-core Architecture*, June 2010.

[14] C. Bienia, S. Kumar, J. P. Singh, and K. Li. The PARSEC benchmark suite: Characterization and architectural implications. In *Proceedings of the 17th International Conference on Parallel Architectures and Compilation Techniques*, October 2008.

[15] G. E. Blelloch, J. T. Fineman, P. B. Gibbons, and J. Shun. Internally deterministic parallel algorithms can be fast. In *Proceedings of Principles and Practice of Parallel Programming*, pages 181–192, 2012.

[16] R. D. Blumofe. *Executing Multithreaded Programs Efficiently*. PhD thesis, Department of Electrical Engineering and Computer Science, Massachusetts Institute of Technology, Cambridge, Massachusetts, Sept. 1995. Available as MIT Laboratory for Computer Science Technical Report MIT/LCS/TR-677.

[17] R. D. Blumofe and C. E. Leiserson. Scheduling multithreaded computations by work stealing. *Journal of the ACM*, 46(5): 720–748, Sept. 1999.

[18] R. D. Blumofe, C. F. Joerg, B. C. Kuszmaul, C. E. Leiserson, K. H. Randall, and Y. Zhou. Cilk: An efficient multithreaded runtime system. *Journal of Parallel and Distributed Computing*, 37(1):55–69, 1996.

[19] R. L. Bocchino, Jr., V. S. Adve, S. V. Adve, and M. Snir. Parallel Programming Must Be Deterministic by Default. In *USENIX Conference on Hot Topics in Parallelism*, pages 4–9, 2009.

[20] M. D. Bond, M. Kulkarni, M. Cao, M. Fathi Salmi, and J. Huang. Efficient Deterministic Replay of Multithreaded Executions in a Managed Language Virtual Machine. In *ACM International Conference on Principles and Practice of Programming in Java*, pages 90–101, 2015.

[21] R. E. Bryant and D. R. O'Hallaron. *Computer Systems: A Programmer's Perspective*. Pearson, USA, 3rd edition, 2015.

[22] S. Burckhardt, A. Baldassin, and D. Leijen. Concurrent programming with revisions and isolation types. In *Proceedings of the 25th Annual ACM SIGPLAN Conference on Object-Oriented Programming, Systems, Languages, and Applications*, pages 691–707, Reno/Tahoe, Nevada, USA, Oct. 2010. URL `http://doi.acm.org/10.1145/1869459.1869515`.

[23] V. Cavé, J. Zhao, J. Shirako, and V. Sarkar. Habanero-Java: the new adventures of old X10. In *Proceedings of the 9th International Conference on Principles and Practice of Programming in Java*, PPPJ '11, pages 51–61, 2011.

[24] P. Charles, C. Grothoff, V. Saraswat, C. Donawa, A. Kielstra, K. Ebcioglu, C. von Praun, and V. Sarkar. X10: An object-oriented approach to non-uniform cluster computing. In *20th Annual ACM SIGPLAN Conference on Object-Oriented Programming, Systems, Languages, and Applications*, pages 519–538, 2005. URL `http://doi.acm.org/10.1145/1094811.1094852`.

[25] G.-I. Cheng, M. Feng, C. E. Leiserson, K. H. Randall, and A. F. Stark. Detecting data races in Cilk programs that use locks. In *Proceedings of the 10th ACM Symposium on Parallel Algorithms and Architectures*, SPAA '98, 1998.

[26] J. Devietti, B. Lucia, L. Ceze, and M. Oskin. DMP: Deterministic Shared Memory Multiprocessing. In *ACM International Conference on Architectural Support for Programming Languages and Operating Systems*, pages 85–96, 2009. doi: http://doi.acm.org/10.1145/1508244.1508255.

[27] J. Devietti, J. Nelson, T. Bergan, L. Ceze, and D. Grossman. RCDC: A Relaxed Consistency Deterministic Computer. In *ACM International Conference on Architectural Support for Programming Languages and Operating Systems*, pages 67–78, 2011. doi: http://doi.acm.org/10.1145/1950365.1950376.

[28] E. W. Dijkstra. Co-operating sequential processes. In F. Genuys, editor, *Programming Languages*, pages 43–112. Academic Press, London, England, 1968. Originally published as Technical Report EWD-123, Technological University, Eindhoven, the Netherlands, 1965.

[29] G. W. Dunlap, D. G. Lucchetti, M. A. Fetterman, and P. M. Chen. Execution Replay of Multiprocessor Virtual Machines. In *ACM/USENIX International Conference on Virtual Execution Environments*, pages 121–130, 2008. doi: http://doi.acm.org/10.1145/1346256.1346273.

[30] M. Feng and C. E. Leiserson. Efficient detection of determinacy races in Cilk programs. In *SPAA*, 1997.

[31] J. T. Fineman and C. E. Leiserson. Race detectors for Cilk and Cilk++ programs. In D. Padua, editor, *Encyclopedia of Parallel Computing*, pages 1706–1719. Springer, 2011.

[32] M. Frigo, C. E. Leiserson, and K. H. Randall. The implementation of the Cilk-5 multithreaded language. In *ACM SIGPLAN Conference on Programming Language Design and Implementation*, pages 212–223, 1998.

[33] M. Frigo, P. Halpern, C. E. Leiserson, and S. Lewin-Berlin. Reducers and other Cilk++ hyperobjects. In *21st Annual ACM Symposium on Parallelism in Algorithms and Architectures*, pages 79–90, 2009.

[34] A. Georges, M. Christiaens, M. Ronsse, and K. De Bosschere. JaRec: A Portable Record/Replay Environment for Multi-threaded Java Applications. *Software Practice & Experience*, 34(6):523–547, 2004. ISSN 0038-0644. doi: 10.1002/spe.579.

[35] Y. He, C. E. Leiserson, and W. M. Leiserson. The Cilkview scalability analyzer. In *Proceedings of the Twenty-Second Annual ACM Symposium on Parallelism in Algorithms and Architectures (SPAA'10)*, pages 145–156, Santorini, Greece, June 13–15 2010. doi: 10.1145/1810479.1810509.

[36] D. R. Hower, P. Montesinos, L. Ceze, M. D. Hill, and J. Torrellas. Two Hardware-Based Approaches for Deterministic Multiprocessor Replay. *Communications of the ACM*, 52:93–100, 2009. ISSN 0001-0782. doi: http://doi.acm.org/10.1145/1516046.1516068.

[37] J. Huang, C. Zhang, and J. Dolby. CLAP: Recording Local Executions to Reproduce Concurrency Failures. In *ACM Conference on Programming Language Design and Implementation*, pages 141–152, 2013. doi: 10.1145/2491956.2462167.

[38] Institute of Electrical and Electronic Engineers. Information technology — Portable Operating System Interface (POSIX) — Part 1: System application program interface (API) [C language]. IEEE Standard 1003.1, 1996 Edition.

[39] TBB. *Intel(R) Threading Building Blocks*. Intel Corporation, 2009. Available from `http://www.threadingbuildingblocks.org/documentation.php`.

[40] Intel. *Intel Cilk Plus Language Specification*. Intel Corporation, 2010. Document Number: 324396-001US. Available from `http://software.intel.com/sites/products/cilk-plus/cilk_plus_language_specification.pdf`.

[41] O. Laadan, N. Viennot, and J. Nieh. Transparent, Lightweight Application Execution Replay on Commodity Multiprocessor Operating Systems. In *ACM SIGMETRICS Joint International Conference on Measurement and Modeling of Computer Systems*, pages 155–166, 2010. ISBN 978-1-4503-0038-4. doi: 10.1145/1811039.1811057. URL `http://doi.acm.org/10.1145/1811039.1811057`.

[42] T. J. LeBlanc and J. M. Mellor-Crummey. Debugging Parallel Programs with Instant Replay. *IEEE Transactions on Computers*, 36:471–482, 1987. ISSN 0018-9340. doi: http://dx.doi.org/10.1109/TC.1987.1676929.

[43] D. Lee, B. Wester, K. Veeraraghavan, S. Narayanasamy, P. M. Chen, and J. Flinn. Respec: Efficient Online Multiprocessor Replay via Speculation and External Determinism. In *ACM International Conference on Architectural Support for Programming Languages and Operating Systems*, pages 77–90, 2010. doi: http://doi.acm.org/10.1145/1736020.1736031.

[44] D. Lee, P. M. Chen, J. Flinn, and S. Narayanasamy. Chimera: Hybrid Program Analysis for Determinism. In *ACM Conference on Programming Language Design and Implementation*, pages 463–474, 2012. doi: 10.1145/2254064.2254119.

[45] I.-T. A. Lee and T. B. Schardl. Efficiently detecting races in cilk programs that use reducer hyperobjects. In *Proceedings of the 27th ACM on Symposium on Parallelism in Algorithms and Architectures (SPAA'15)*, pages 111–122, Portland, OR, USA, June 2015. doi: 10.1145/2755573.2755599.

[46] D. Leijen and J. Hall. Optimize managed code for multi-core machines. *MSDN Magazine*, 2007. Available from `http://msdn.microsoft.com/magazine/`.

[47] C. E. Leiserson, T. B. Schardl, and J. Sukha. Deterministic parallel random-number generation for dynamic-multithreading platforms. In *PPoPP*, 2012.

[48] P. Liu, X. Zhang, O. Tripp, and Y. Zheng. Light: Replay via Tightly Bounded Recording. In *ACM Conference on Pro-*

gramming Language Design and Implementation, pages 55–64, 2015. ISBN 978-1-4503-3468-6. doi: 10.1145/2737924.2738001.

[49] T. Liu, C. Curtsinger, and E. D. Berger. Dthreads: Efficient Deterministic Multithreading. In *ACM Symposium on Operating Systems Principles*, pages 327–336, 2011. doi: http://doi.acm.org/10.1145/2043556.2043587.

[50] C.-K. Luk, R. Cohn, R. Muth, H. Patil, A. Klauser, G. Lowney, S. Wallace, V. J. Reddi, and K. Hazelwood. Pin: building customized program analysis tools with dynamic instrumentation. In *Proceedings of the ACM SIGPLAN 2005 Conference on Programming Language Design and Implementation (PLDI'05)*, pages 190–200, Chicago, IL, USA, June 11–15 2005. doi: 10.1145/1065010.1065034.

[51] J. Mellor-Crummey. On-the-fly detection of data races for programs with nested fork-join parallelism. In *Proceedings of the 1991 ACM/IEEE Conference on Supercomputing (Supercomputing '91)*, pages 24–33, Albuquerque, NM, USA, Nov. 18–22 1991. doi: 10.1145/125826.125861.

[52] S. K. Muller and U. A. Acar. Latency-hiding work stealing: Scheduling interacting parallel computations with work stealing. In *Proceedings of the 28th ACM Symposium on Parallelism in Algorithms and Architectures*, SPAA '16, pages 71–82, New York, NY, USA, 2016. ACM. ISBN 978-1-4503-4210-0. doi: 10.1145/2935764.2935793. URL `http://doi.acm.org/10.1145/2935764.2935793`.

[53] S. Narayanasamy, C. Pereira, and B. Calder. Recording Shared Memory Dependencies Using Strata. In *ACM International Conference on Architectural Support for Programming Languages and Operating Systems*, pages 229–240, 2006. doi: http://doi.acm.org/10.1145/1168857.1168886.

[54] D. Nguyen, A. Lenharth, and K. Pingali. Deterministic galois: On-demand, portable and parameterless. In *Proceedings of the 19th International Conference on Architectural Support for Programming Languages and Operating Systems*, ASPLOS '14, pages 499–512, New York, NY, USA, 2014. ACM. ISBN 978-1-4503-2305-5. doi: 10.1145/2541940.2541964. URL `http://doi.acm.org/10.1145/2541940.2541964`.

[55] M. Olszewski, J. Ansel, and S. Amarasinghe. Kendo: Efficient Deterministic Multithreading in Software. In *ACM International Conference on Architectural Support for Programming Languages and Operating Systems*, pages 97–108, 2009. doi: http://doi.acm.org/10.1145/1508244.1508256.

[56] S. Park, Y. Zhou, W. Xiong, Z. Yin, R. Kaushik, K. H. Lee, and S. Lu. PRES: Probabilistic Replay with Execution Sketching on Multiprocessors. In *ACM Symposium on Operating Systems Principles*, pages 177–192, 2009. doi: http://doi.acm.org/10.1145/1629575.1629593.

[57] H. Patil, C. Pereira, M. Stallcup, G. Lueck, and J. Cownie. PinPlay: A framework for deterministic replay and reproducible analysis of parallel programs. In *Proceedings of the 8th Annual IEEE/ACM International Symposium on Code Generation and Optimization*, CGO '10, pages 2–11, Toronto, Ontario, Canada, 2010. ACM. ISBN 978-1-60558-635-9. doi: 10.1145/1772954.1772958. URL `http://doi.acm.org/10.1145/1772954.1772958`.

[58] G. Pokam, C. Pereira, K. Danne, R. Kassa, and A.-R. Adl-Tabatabai. Architecting a Chunk-based Memory Race Recorder in Modern CMPs. In *IEEE/ACM International Symposium on Microarchitecture*, pages 576–585, 2009. doi: http://doi.acm.org/10.1145/1669112.1669183.

[59] R. Raman, J. Zhao, V. Sarkar, M. Vechev, and E. Yahav. Efficient data race detection for async-finish parallelism. In H. Barringer, Y. Falcone, B. Finkbeiner, K. Havelund, I. Lee, G. Pace, G. Rosu, O. Sokolsky, and N. Tillmann, editors, *Runtime Verification*, volume 6418 of *Lecture Notes in Computer Science*, pages 368–383. Springer Berlin / Heidelberg, 2010. ISBN 978-3-642-16611-2.

[60] R. Raman, J. Zhao, V. Sarkar, M. Vechev, and E. Yahav. Scalable and precise dynamic datarace detection for structured parallelism. In *Proceedings of the 33rd ACM SIGPLAN Conference on Programming Language Design and Implementation*, PLDI '12, pages 531–542, 2012.

[61] M. C. Rinard and M. S. Lam. The Design, Implementation, and Evaluation of Jade. *ACM Transactions on Programming Languages and Systems*, 20:483–545, 1998. ISSN 0164-0925. doi: http://doi.acm.org/10.1145/291889.291893.

[62] A. D. Robison. Cilk Plus solver for a chess puzzle or: How i learned to love fast rejection. `https://software.intel.com/en-us/articles/cilk-plus-solver-for-a-chess-puzzle-or-how-i-learned-to-love-rejection`, Feb. 2013.

[63] M. Ronsse and K. De Bosschere. RecPlay: A Fully Integrated Practical Record/Replay System. *ACM Transactions on Computer Systems*, 17:133–152, 1999. ISSN 0734-2071. doi: http://doi.acm.org/10.1145/312203.312214.

[64] T. B. Schardl, B. C. Kuszmaul, I.-T. A. Lee, W. M. Leiserson, and C. E. Leiserson. The Cilkprof scalability profiler. In *Proceedings of the 27th ACM on Symposium on Parallelism in Algorithms and Architectures (SPAA '15)*, SPAA '15, pages 89–100, Portland, Oregon, USA, June 2015. doi: 10.1145/2755573.2755603.

[65] J. Shun, G. E. Blelloch, J. T. Fineman, P. B. Gibbons, A. Kyrola, H. V. Simhadri, and K. Tangwongsan. Brief announcement: the Problem Based Benchmark Suite. In *Proceedings of the 24th ACM Symposium on Parallelism in Algorithms and Architectures*, SPAA '12, 2012.

[66] N. R. Tallent and J. M. Mellor-Crummey. Effective performance measurement and analysis of multithreaded applications. In *Proceedings of the 14th ACM SIGPLAN Symposium on Principles and Practice of Parallel Programming*, PPoPP '09, pages 229–240, Raleigh, NC, USA, 2009. ACM. ISBN 978-1-60558-397-6. doi: 10.1145/1504176.1504210. URL `http://doi.acm.org/10.1145/1504176.1504210`.

[67] R. Utterback, K. Agrawal, J. T. Fineman, and I.-T. A. Lee. Provably good and practically efficient parallel race detection for fork-join programs. In *Proceedings of the 28th ACM Symposium on Parallelism in Algorithms and Architectures*, SPAA '16, pages 83–94, New York, NY, USA, 2016. ACM. ISBN 978-1-4503-4210-0. doi: 10.1145/2935764.2935801. URL `http://doi.acm.org/10.1145/2935764.2935801`.

[68] K. Veeraraghavan, D. Lee, B. Wester, J. Ouyang, P. M. Chen, J. Flinn, and S. Narayanasamy. DoublePlay: Parallelizing Sequential Logging and Replay. In *ACM International Confer-*

ence on Architectural Support for Programming Languages and Operating Systems, pages 15–26, 2011. doi: http://doi.acm.org/10.1145/1950365.1950370.

[69] M. Xu, R. Bodik, and M. D. Hill. A "Flight Data Recorder" for Enabling Full-system Multiprocessor Deterministic Replay. In *ACM/IEEE International Symposium on Computer Architecture*, pages 122–135, 2003. doi: http://doi.acm.org/10.1145/859618.859633.

[70] Z. Yang, M. Yang, L. Xu, H. Chen, and B. Zang. ORDER: Object Centric Deterministic Replay for Java. In *USENIX Annual Technical Conference*, pages 30–30, 2011.

[71] C. S. Zakian, T. A. K. Zakian, A. Kulkarni, B. Chamith, and R. R. Newton. *Concurrent Cilk: Lazy Promotion from Tasks to Threads in C/C++*, pages 73–90. Springer International Publishing, Cham, 2016. ISBN 978-3-319-29778-1. URL `http://dx.doi.org/10.1007/978-3-319-29778-1_5`.

A. Artifact Evaluation

PORRidge is open source and currently available at `https://gitlab.com/wustl-pctg-pub/porridge.git`. The library is provided under The MIT License, while the runtime modifications are licensed separately under a BSD license. The repository contains complete instructions for compiling and using PORRidge, in addition to scripts that reproduce most of the empirical results. Please send feedback or file issues at our gitlab repository to help us continually improve the project.

Simple, Accurate, Analytical Time Modeling and Optimal Tile Size Selection for GPGPU Stencils

Nirmal Prajapati
Waruna Ranasinghe
Sanjay Rajopadhye
Colorado State University
first.last@colostate.edu

Rumen Andonov
IRISA, Rennes
Rumen.Andonov@irisa.fr

Hristo Djidjev
LANL, Los Alamos, NM
djidjev@lanl.gov

Tobias Grosser
Department of Computer Science
ETH, Zurich
tobias.grosser@inf.ethz.ch

Abstract

Stencil computations are an important class of compute and data intensive programs that occur widely in scientific and engineering applications. A number of tools use sophisticated tiling, parallelization, and memory mapping strategies, and generate code that relies on vendor-supplied compilers. This code has a number of parameters, such as tile sizes, that are then tuned via empirical exploration.

We develop a model that guides such a choice. Our model is a simple set of analytical functions that predict the execution time of the generated code. It is deliberately optimistic, since we are targeting modeling and parameter selections yielding highly tuned codes.

We experimentally validate the model on a number of 2D and 3D stencil codes, and show that the root mean square error in the execution time is less than 10% for the subset of the codes that achieve performance within 20% of the best. Furthermore, based on using our model, we are able to predict tile sizes that achieve a further improvement of 9% on average.

1. Introduction

As we move to address the challenges of exascale computing, one approach that has shown promise is *domain specificity:* the adaptation of application, compilation, parallelization, and optimization strategies to narrower classes of domains. An important representative of such a domain is called *Stencil Computations*, and includes a class of typically compute bound parts of many applications such as partial differential equation (PDE) solvers, numerical simulations in domains like oceanography, aerospace, climate and weather modeling, computational physics, materials modeling, simulations of fluids, and signal and image-processing algorithms. One of the thirteen Berkeley dwarfs/motifs [2], is "structured mesh computations," which are nothing but stencils. Many *dynamic programming* algorithms also exhibit a similar dependence pattern. The importance of stencils has been noted by a number of researchers, indicated by the recent surge of research projects and publications on this topic, ranging from optimization methods for implementing such computations on a range of target architectures, to Domain Specific Languages (DSLs) and compilation systems for stencils [11–13, 29, 30, 32, 34, 38, 42, 48, 50, 51, 53]. Workshops and conferences devoted exclusively to stencil acceleration have recently emerged. Stencils belong to a class of programs called *uniform dependence computations*, which are themselves a proper subset of "affine loop programs." Such programs can be analyzed and parallelized using a powerful methodology called the polyhedral model [5, 10, 15–17, 35, 44, 46].

A second aspect of domain specificity is reflected in the emergence of specialized architectures, called *accelerators*, for executing compute intensive parts of many computations. They include GPGPU, general purpose computing on graphics processing units (GPUs), and other co-processors (Intel Xeon Phi, Knight's Landing, etc.). Initially they were "special purpose," limited to highly optimized image rendering

PPoPP '17, February 04-08, 2017, Austin, TX, USA

DOI: http://dx.doi.org/10.1145/3018743.3018744

libraries (aka. graphics processing). Later, users realized that they could be used for other computations. Eventually, the emergence of tools like CUDA and OpenCL enabled general purpose parallel programming on GPUs.

Exploiting the specificity of the applications and the specificity of target architectures leads to domain-specific tools to map high level programs to highly tuned and optimized implementations on the target architecture. Many such tools, both academic research prototypes and productions systems, are widely available. One example is PPCG, developed by the group at ENS, Paris [54]. PPCG includes a module that targets GPUs and incorporates a sophisticated, compiler developed by Grosser et al. [22]. We call it the HHC compiler because it employs a state-of-the-art tiling strategy called *hybrid hexagonal classic tiling*.

A number of parameters can be specified as inputs/flags to the HHC compiler, e.g., the tile sizes, and the number of threads in each dimension. These parameters have a tremendous influence on the performance of the code. An important element of such tools is a step called *auto tuning*: empirical evaluation of the actual performance of a, hopefully small, set of code instances for a range of mapping parameters. This enables the system to choose these parameters optimally for actual "production runs" on real data/inputs.

Modern architectures are extremely complicated, with sophisticated hardware features that interact in unpredictable ways, especially since the latency of operations is stochastic due to the deep memory hierarchy. It is widely believed that because of this, auto tuning is unavoidable in order to obtain good performance. In this paper, we make the case that domain specificity enables us to develop *good* analytical models to predict the performance of specific codes on specific target architectures. This allows a significant reduction in the autotuning search space. Our contributions are:

- **Contribution 1.** We develop a simple analytical model to predict the execution time of a tiled stencil program and apply it to codes generated by the HHC compiler. It is deliberately *optimistic*, ignores the effect of some parameters, and is an analytic function of
  - program, machine, and compiler parameters that are easily available statically, and
  - one stencil-specific parameter, obtained by running a *micro-benchmark* derived from the loop body.
- **Contribution 2.** Although our model may not accurately predict the performance for all tile size combinations, it is very accurate for the ones that matter, i.e., those that give top performance. To show this, we generated more than 60,000 programs for
  - two modern **target platforms** (NVIDIA GTX 980 and Titan X),
  - four 2D and two 3D **stencil codes** (Jacobi, Heat, Laplacian, and Gradient)
  - over a range of ten input data **sizes**, and
  - for each such *platform-stencil-size* combination, a wide range of tile sizes and thread counts (the HHC compiler inputs).

  As we expected, the RMS error over the entire data set was—"seemingly disappointingly"—over 100%. However, our model is very accurate where it matters. When we restricted ourselves to codes whose performance is within 20% of the best, the RMSE is less than 10%.[1]
- **Contribution 3.** To test the predictive abilities of the model, we evaluated the model over the entire feasible space (for each platform-stencil-size combination) and obtained the tile sizes that were within 10% of the best predicted execution time. There were less than 200 such points. We called the HHC compiler with these tile sizes and were able to observe among this set a performance improvement of 9% on average (max improvement was 17%). We also observed that the "conventional wisdom" to choosing tile sizes so as to maximize shared-memory footprint is not always optimal.

The remainder of this paper is organized as follows. After a discussion of related work and backend (Sections 2 and 3) we describe the domain specific parallelization used for stencils and, in particular, the strategies used by the HHC compiler. Then, Section 4 develops our analytical model. Section 5 describes our experimental results on validating the model on a baseline set of tile sizes. Section 6 illustrates the predictive power of the model. Finally, we discuss our results, describe ongoing and future work, and conclude in Sections 7 and 8.

2. Related Work

At the algorithmic level, most stencil applications are *compute bound* in the sense that the ratio of the total number of *operations* to the total number of *memory locations* touched can always be made "sufficiently large" because it is an asymptotically increasing value. We may expect that such codes can be optimized to achieve very high performance relative to machine peak. However, naive implementations turn out to be memory-bound. Therefore, many authors seek to exploit data locality for these programs [6, 31, 43]. One successful technique is called *time tiling* [5, 6, 19, 20, 52, 56, 58, 59], an advanced form of loop tiling [56, 57, 60]. Time tiling first partitions the whole computation space into tiles extending in all dimensions, and then optionally executes these tiles in a so called "45 degree wavefront" fashion. We assume, like most of the work in the literature, that *dense* stencil programs are *compute bound* after time tiling. However, due to the intricate structure of time tiled code, writing

[1] The restriction to the better performing subset was exactly our motivation. We designed the model to help predict/explore data points that would give *good* performance. It is also why we made optimistic assumptions in developing the model.

it by hand is challenging. Automatic code generation, is an attractive solution, and has been an active research topic.

There has been much work on time modeling and performance optimization. For stencil graphs, which are directed acyclic graphs (DAGs) of non-iterated stencil kernels, various DSLs compilers have been proposed. Halide [45] and Stella [24] are two DSLs from the context of image processing and weather modeling that separate the specification of the stencil computation from the execution schedule, which allows for the specification of platform specific execution strategies derived either by platform experts or automatic tuning. Both DSLs support various hardware targets, including CPUs and GPUs. Polymage [39] also provides a stencil graph DSL—this time for CPUs only—but pairs it with an analytical performance model for the automatic computation of optimal tile size and fusion choices. MODESTO [23] proposes an analytical performance model in the context of Stella, for multiple cache levels and fusion strategies, for both GPUs and CPUs.

For iterative stencils a large set of optimizing code generation strategies have been proposed. Ahmed et. al [1] describe time tiling as part of their work on synthesizing transformations for imperfectly nested loops. Li and Song [33] consider fusion and skewing in a unified framework and derive minimal skewing factors for exploiting data reuse along the time dimension of an iterative stencil. Both works do not consider GPU performance. Patus [9] provides an auto-tuning environment for stencil computations which can target CPU and GPU hardware. It does not use software managed memories and also does not consider any time tiling strategies. Pochoir [53] is a CPU-only code generator for stencil computations that exploits reuse along the time dimension by recursively dividing the computation in trapezoids. Diamond tiling [3], Hybrid-hexagonal tiling [22], and Overtile [26] are all tiling strategies that allow to exploit reuse along the time dimension, while ensuring a balanced amount of coarse-grained parallelism throughout the computation. While the former has only been evaluated on CPU systems, the last two tiling schemes have been implemented to target GPUs. Overtile uses redundant computation whereas hybrid-hexagonal tiling uses hexagonal tiles to avoid redundant computation and the increased shared memory that would otherwise be required to store temporary values. Another time tiling strategy has been proposed with 3.5D blocking by Nguyen et. al [41], who manually implemented kernels that use two dimensional space tiling plus streaming along one space dimension with tiling along the time dimension to target both CPUs and GPUs. A slightly orthogonal stencil optimization has been proposed by Henretty et. al [25], who use data-layout transformations to avoid redundant non-aligned vector loads on CPU platforms. All of the previously discussed frameworks either come with their own auto-tuning framework or require auto tuning to derive optimal tile sizes.

For stencil GPU code generation strategies that use redundant computations in combination with ghost zones an analytical performance model has been proposed [37] that allows to automatically derive "optimal" code generation parameters. Yotov et. al [61] showed already more than ten years ago that an analytical performance model for matrix multiplication kernels allows to generate code that is performance-wise competitive to empirically tuned code generated by ATLAS [55], but at this point no stencil computations have been considered. Shirako et al. [49] use cache models to derive lower and upper bounds on cache traffic, which they use to bound the search space of empirical tile-size tuning. Their work does not consider any GPU specific properties, such as shared memory sizes and their impact on the available parallelism.

In contrast to tools for tuning, Hong and Kim [27] present a precise GPU performance model which shares many of the GPU parameters we use. It is highly accurate, but low level, and requires analyzing the PTX assembly code. It is therefore unsuitable for use in a compiler.

3. Stencils and their Parallelization

We now describe the class of computations we tackle, the overall parallelization strategy, and how the HHC compiler implements it.

In codes that implement *dense iterative stencils*, values of array elements are updated iteratively at every time step using the values of some of their neighbors from previous time steps[2] according to a fixed pattern. We consider stencil codes of the following kind. Let $\mathcal{S} = \{(i_1, \ldots, i_k) \mid 1 \leq i_j \leq S_j, \text{ for } j = 1, \ldots, k\}$ be a k-dimensional *space index set* and $\mathcal{T} = \{1, \ldots, T\}$ be a *time index set.* Then, given a set $\mathcal{N}$ defining the "neighborhood" of any point in terms of a pattern of relative coordinates and a coefficient w_a associated with each element $a \in \mathcal{N}$, a (convolutional) stencil code defines an iterative evaluation of the following weighted sum

$$A^t(s) = \Big(\sum_{a \in \mathcal{N}} w_a * A^{t-1}(s+a) \Big) + c\,, \qquad (1)$$

$s \in \mathcal{S}$, $t \in \mathcal{T}$, where we assume that appropriate values are given for the "initial value" (when $t = 0$) and the "boundary values" (when the points $s + a$ fall outside $\mathcal{S}$). Stencils are usually implemented as nested loops with the loop body evaluating the rhs of (1) and storing it in a data array.

Efficient parallelization of stencils on GPUs requires careful consideration of at least two factors at two separate levels, and there is significant interplay between them: parallelism and data locality/reuse, at the fine grain (threads, synchronization, shared and/or scratchpad memory) and at the coarse grain (thread blocks, and global memory). Tiling

[2] Stencils where some updates may use values from the current time step (called Gauss-Seidel stencils) are not included in the definition, as the HHC compiler does not consider these.

is a widely used technique that has been developed to manage this, and it is applied at multiple levels and to both data and iterations of the loop. In a typical implementation, data, initially stored on the CPU, is first transferred to the GPU, subsequently a sequence of *kernel calls* is issued on the CPU to perform the computation on the GPU-resident, and finally the result is moved back to the CPU. For ease of explanation, it is convenient to view the entire stencil computation as defined by its *iteration space*: the set of legal values of the space and time coordinates.

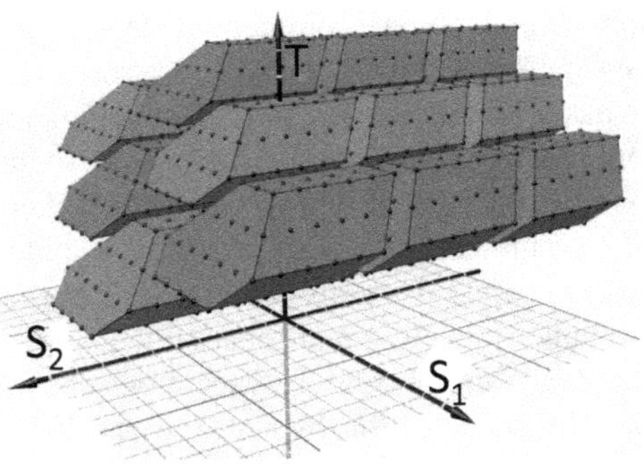

Figure 2: Hybrid-hexagonal tiling for 2D stencils.

3.1 Hybrid Hexagonal/Classical Tiling

The HHC compiler [22], which we are using, implements a hybrid of two strategies: *hexagonal* tiling of the outer two loops/dimensions, and the *classic* time skewing of the remaining (inner/space) dimensions. A 1D stencil is thus, a special case (the iteration space is 2D, and only hexagonal tiling is applicable). For more than two nested loops, it tiles the inner loops using the classic time skewing approach.

Therefore, we first explain hexagonal tiling. The iteration space, a $S \times T$ rectangle, is partitioned into a set of "staggered" hexagons, as shown in Figure 1.a, and we view a "row of hexagons" as those whose (leftmost) corners have the same value of t. Each row is independent, accesses distinct data, and can, hence, be executed in a single kernel call. The main program is just a sequence of such kernel calls.

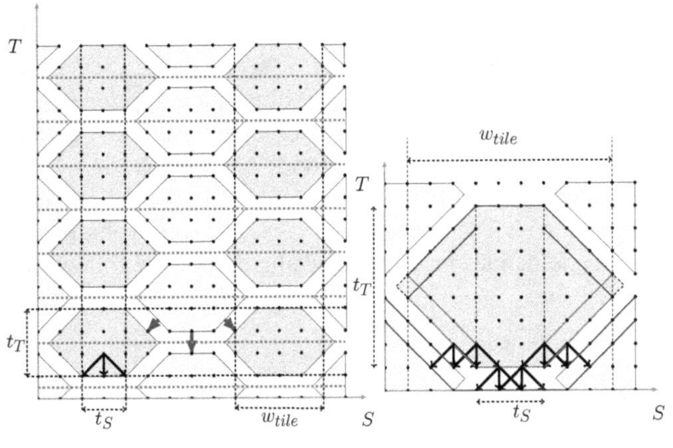

Figure 1: Hexagonal tiling for 1D stencils: the $S \times T$ iteration space is partitioned into hexagons (left). The Jacobi 1D inter and intra-tile dependencies are illustrated as blue and black arrows, respectively. There are two kinds of "tile rows" colored green and yellow. The tiles in each row are independent, and can executed in a single GPU kernel call. A single tile (right) and its I/O (red: iterations reading data from global memory; blue: iterations writing to global memory).

Now consider a 3-D iteration space (see Figure 2) where each hexagon on the outer two (t-k) dimensions now becomes a "prism" extending along the i dimension. Stencil dependences precludes directly blocking this prism. Rather, *time-skewing* has to be applied (illustrated by the oblique hexagonal faces above). After this, the HHC compiler generates code that executes the tiles in the prism via a sequential loop—executed within a single kernel call—whose body is the execution of a tile, the outer loop structure remains the same. The idea is extended to higher dimensions, where the prisms become "slabs" and "hyper-slabs" and the sequential loop iterating over tiles becomes a nested loop.

3.2 Details of the HHC Compiler

HHC generates highly tuned code for specific stencils, problem sizes, and tile size parameters, taking advantage of properties of the "hybrid-hexagonal schedule". The HHC compiler is one module within a complete polyhedral tool suite, PPCG, developed by the group at ENS, Paris [54]. Independently of the tiling scheme, PPCG automatically simplifies generated loop bounds and index expressions, taking into account problem sizes and tile-size parameters.

When generating HHC tiled code, the effectiveness of PPCG's specialization can be largely improved by unrolling the global-to-shared memory copy code as well as the per-tile compute code. When unrolling both, all control flow within a tile is eliminated such that only a sequence of (possibly predicated) instructions remains to be executed by each thread. When using HHC tiling, it is also possible to take advantage of data-reuse between two tiles that are run in sequence by the same threadblock. In this situation, a subset of the data that is loaded by each tile is already in shared memory and does not need to be loaded again. However, as PPCG derives for each tile an optimal data-mapping strategy, the reusable data is not always placed such that it can be immediately reused between tiles. To still exploit this property, PPCG provides two different options. Option 1) enforces a shared (commonly less optimal) memory placement strategy. Option 2) moves reusable data within shared memory to account for different data placement between tiles before loading the remaining data from global memory.

Name	Type	Description
$\mathtt{S_i}$	EP	i-th space dimension
$\mathtt{T}$	EP	time dimension
$ts_{\mathtt{i}}$	ES	tile size along the i-th space dimension
t_T	ES	tile size along time dimension
$n_{\mathrm{thr,i}}$	ES	number of threads per threadblock in the i-th dimension/loop
n_{SM}	EH	number of SMs in the device
n_{V}	EH	number of vector units per SM
R_{SM}	EH	number of registers per SM
M_{SM}	EH	size of shared memory per SM
MTB_{SM}	EH	max threadblocks per SM
L	EH	time per word of global memory access
τ_{sync}	EH	time for a single synchronization
T_{sync}	EH	time for a host-GPU synchronization
N_w	CS	number of wavefronts
m_i	CS	input memory footprint of a tile (amount of data read from global memory)
m_o	CS	output memory footprint of a tile (amount of data written to global memory)
m'	CS	time for global↔shared data transfer for a tile
c	CS	time to perform the computation in a tile (collectively by all the threads)
k	CS	"hyper-threading" factor (threadblocks per SM)
$T_{\mathrm{tile}}(k)$	CS	time to compute a tile (accounting for k-way "hyper-threading")
$w(i)$	CS	width of the i-th wavefront (number of threadblocks in the i-th kernel call)
w_{tile}	CS	width of (number of iterations in) a tile
R_{tile}	CS	number of registers needed per tile
M_{tile}	CS	shared memory needed per tile
M_{io}	CS	I/O volume per tile (global↔shared)
C_{iter}	CSH	(optimized) execution time of one iteration
T_{alg}	C	total execution time of stencil
T_{exec}		observed execution time (not a model parameter)

Table 1: The execution time model parameters. E/C denote Elementary/Composite, and S/H/P denote Software/Hardware/Problem; M_{io} is measured in 4-byte words.

4. Execution Time Model

We now develop a model for the execution time of a stencil computation on the GPU as a function of software, hardware, and problem parameters. These parameters are shown in Table 1. Some of these have to be measured or are chosen by the compiler, we call them *elementary*, while others, called *composite*, are functions of elementary and other composite parameters. In addition to this distinction, we also divide them into three classes, hardware, software, and problem, depending on their origin. Hardware parameters are specific to the machine. Software parameters such as tile size, number of threads per tile, etc., are determined by the user or the compiler. And the problem parameters are determined by the type of stencil, the computation in the loop body, number of variables, nature of memory accesses, etc.

4.1 Model for Hexagonal Tiling

We first derive the execution time for an 1D stencil, Jacobi 1D (for which we drop the subscript on S_1, using just S). Later we extend the model to higher dimensions.

The $T \times S$ rectangular iteration space is tiled into hexagons with a base of size t_S and a height of size t_T (see Figure 1.a). In the following, we suppose that t_T is even, since the HHT compiler only supports this case.

The total execution time for the tiled code can be evaluated by adding the time spent by the GPU in each kernel call and the total synchronization time spent between kernel calls

$$T_{\mathrm{alg}} = \sum_{i=1}^{N_w} \left(\left\lceil \frac{1}{n_{SM}} \left\lceil \frac{w(i)}{k} \right\rceil \right\rceil T_{\mathrm{tile}}(k) + T_{\mathrm{sync}} \right). \quad (2)$$

The ith kernel computes the tiles from the ith *wavefront*. The ith wavefront consists of the tiles that intersect the ith red dashed horizontal line. Note that they contain either yellow tiles only (for odd wavefronts indexed from one) or green tiles only (for even wavefront indices). Let us estimate the number n_0 of even-indexed wavefronts (colored in green). Since the height of each tile is t_T and the height of the iteration space is T, then $n_0 = \lceil T/t_T \rceil$. For estimating the total number of wavefronts, we note that for any even-indexed wavefront (say j) we can associate exactly one, possibly partial, odd-indexed wavefront—the one whose index is $j-1$. Moreover, depending on the relative values of T and t_T, the last wavefront may be even (green) and numbered $2n_0$, or odd (yellow) and numbered $2n_0+1$. Which case holds depends on the relationship between $T - \lfloor T/t_T \rfloor t_T$ and $t_T/2$. More precisely, the total number of wavefronts is equal to

$$N_w = 2\left\lceil \frac{T}{t_T} \right\rceil + \epsilon \approx 2\left\lceil \frac{T}{t_T} \right\rceil, \quad (3)$$

where $\epsilon = 0$ if $0 < T - \lfloor T/t_T \rfloor t_T \leq t_T/2$, otherwise $\epsilon = 1$.

To estimate the tile width, w_{tile}, we decompose each hexagon into a rectangle of size $t_S \times t_T$ and two right isosceles triangles with a hypotenuse t_T, each of which spans $t_T/2$ columns (see Figure 1.b). Adding these, we get

$$w_{\mathrm{tile}} = t_S + t_T - 2. \quad (4)$$

Furthermore, the distance between two consecutive tiles in a wavefront, called *pitch*, can be derived as $w_{\mathrm{tile}} + t_S + 2 = 2t_S + t_T$. Now, there may be one more or less tile in alternate wavefronts, so the number of tiles in a wavefront (i.e., the width of a wavefront) is

$$w(i) = \left\lceil \frac{S}{2t_S + t_T} \right\rceil + \epsilon' \approx \left\lceil \frac{S}{2t_S + t_T} \right\rceil, \quad (5)$$

where ϵ' is 1 or 0, and is ignored. Since $w(i)$ is actually independent of i, the summation in (2) can be simplified to yield

$$T_{alg} = N_w T_{\mathrm{tile}}(k) \left\lceil \frac{1}{n_{SM}} \left\lceil \frac{w}{k} \right\rceil \right\rceil + N_w T_{\mathrm{sync}}. \quad (6)$$

4.1.1 Execution Time of a Tile

In the case of hexagonal tiling, the amount of data read from global memory is the sum of the bottom base (t_S) plus the data needed to compute its two adjacent oblique sides. Each of these oblique sides has $t_T/2$ points, and there are *two* such lines of points that need data from *two* oblique lines (shown in red in Figure 1.b). Collectively, this data comes from *two* other (blue) line segments in a neighboring south-east or south-west tile. The blue points thus depict the input footprint of the tile, m_i, which can be shown to be $t_S+4t_T/2 = t_S+2t_T$. In the case of Jacobi 1D, this amount also equals the output tile memory footprint m_o. The later is depicted in blue (north-oriented tile's facets) in Figure 1.b. Therefore, for the total input/output tile memory footprint we obtain

$$m_{io} = m_i + m_o = 2(t_S + 2t_T). \tag{7}$$

To obtain m' we multiply m_{io} by L and add twice the synchronization time. Hence

$$m' = m_{io}L + 2\tau_{sync} = 2(t_S + 2t_T)L + 2\tau_{sync}. \tag{8}$$

Finally, for these hexagonal tiles, $M_{\text{tile}} = 2(w_{\text{tile}} + 2) = 2(t_S+t_T)$. To determine T_{tile} we consider two cases: a single tile per SM (no hyperthreading) and multiple tiles per SM (hyperthreading).

4.1.2 No Hyperthreading

In this case $k = 1$ and only one tile is executed on each SM at a time. To compute a tile, a read operation, a compute operation, and a write operation are performed in sequence with synchronizations in between them. We assume that both read and write operations take an equal amount of time.

The iteration space dependences indicate that the computations in a tile can be done in parallel in each row, and in a sequential manner between rows from bottom to top. Since C_{iter} denotes the computation time per iteration and, considering the shape of each hexagon, we find that the computation time of a tile is given by

$$\begin{aligned} c &= 2 \sum_{x=t_S,step=2}^{w_{\text{tile}}} \left(\left\lceil \frac{x}{n_V} \right\rceil C_{\text{iter}} + \tau_{sync} \right) \\ &= 2C_{\text{iter}} \sum_{x=t_S,step=2}^{w_{\text{tile}}} \left\lceil \frac{x}{n_V} \right\rceil + t_T\tau_{sync}. \end{aligned} \tag{9}$$

Combining (8) and (9), the total time to process a tile is

$$T_{\text{tile}} = m' + c. \tag{10}$$

When $n_V \geq w_{\text{tile}}$, each tile row can be computed in C_{iter} time and the computation time c of a tile is just $c = t_T(C_{\text{iter}}+\tau_{sync})$. However, note that this is a very inefficient use of the fine grain resources of the SMs, and we expect that for the optimal solution, $n_V \ll w_{\text{tile}}$.

4.1.3 Hyperthreading

Consider the case k > 1, where more than one tile is executed on each SM at a time. The value of k, the number of tiles per SM, depends on the available resources, shared memory and registers in a SM as well as the resources consumed by a tile (thread block), and is bounded as follows:

$$1 < k \leq \min\left(\left\lfloor \frac{R_{SM}}{R_{\text{tile}}} \right\rfloor, \left\lfloor \frac{M_{SM}}{M_{\text{tile}}} \right\rfloor \right). \tag{11}$$

Read/write operations can now overlap with computations. Therefore, reading of the second tile input data can be synchronized and overlapped with the first tile computation. However, the very first read and the very last write cannot overlap with anything. Thus the execution time is the sum of this and the dominant one between $(k-1)$ read-writes and computes. The time to compute k tiles is then

$$T_{\text{tile}}(k) = m' + c + (k-1)\max(m', c). \tag{12}$$

4.2 Hybrid Hexagonal/Classic Tiling for 2D Stencils

Here, the outer two loops are tiled with hexagons, and the inner dimension(s) are tiled using classic time skewing techniques. We illustrate this for the Jacobi2D stencil.

4.2.1 Total Execution Time of Jacobi 2D

As illustrated in Figure 2, each hexagon from Figure 1 now becomes a "prism" with a hexagonal cross section, whose length is S_2 along the S_2-axis. Its data footprint may be too large for the entire prism to be executed as a single tile, so it needs to be tiled. To respect the dependences, time skewing is applied to each prism (notice how the front face is oblique in the S_1-T plane), and then each prism is partitioned using vertical cuts (other than the front face, all the inter-tile faces are vertical). A threadblock executes the entire *sequence of tiles* in a single kernel call. Let T_{prism} denote the time that this takes, and postpone its derivation for now.

The formulæ for the number of wavefronts (N_w), the tile width (w_{tile}), the width of a wavefront in respect to the S_1-axis (w), as well as the total execution time (T_{alg}), are identical to the Jacobi 1D case, and are given by equations 3, 4, 5 and 6 respectively, where the parameters S, t_S are replaced by S_1 and t_{S_1} while the term T_{tile} is substituted by T_{prism}.

4.2.2 Execution Time of a Tile

Since tiles chosen as above could be very large and inconvenient for the shared memory size, we need to further partition them into smaller chunks. In the Jacobi 2D hybrid approach these are hexagonal (non-orthogonal) sub-prisms with a length t_{S_2} and bases defined by the normal vector $(1, 0, 1)$ where time is the first dimension (vertical axis in Figure 2). The number of these sub-prisms in an entire prism is $\left\lceil \frac{S_2+t_T}{t_{S_2}} \right\rceil$ and the dependencies allow to compute them sequentially from bottom to top (right to left in Figure 2). We therefore assume from now on that one tile is computed by a single SM which iterates $\left\lceil \frac{S_2+t_T}{t_{S_2}} \right\rceil$ times for a given prism, and at each iteration computes one of the above sub-prism.

Since the data belonging to the oblique hexagonal faces are allocated in the local SM memory, the amount of data to be transferred from global to shared memory is simply the amount of data as for Jacobi 1D case (7) multiplied by the tile's length t_{S_2}. Hence

$$m_i = m_o = t_{S_2}(t_{S_1} + 2t_T). \tag{13}$$

For the corresponding time we obtain respectively

$$m^{'} = (m_i + m_o)L + 2\tau_{\text{sync}}. \tag{14}$$

The iteration space dependences indicate that the computations in a tile can be done in parallel in each row, and in a sequential manner between rows from bottom to top. We therefore find that the computation time for a **non-boundary/steady state** tile is given by

$$\begin{aligned} c &= 2 \sum_{x=t_{S_1},step=2}^{w_{\text{tile}}} \left(\left\lceil \frac{x t_{S_2}}{n_v} \right\rceil C_{iter} + \tau_{\text{sync}} \right) \\ &= 2C_{iter} \sum_{x=t_{S_1},step=2}^{w_{\text{tile}}} \left\lceil \frac{x t_{S_2}}{n_v} \right\rceil + t_T \tau_{\text{sync}}. \end{aligned} \tag{15}$$

Now, the execution time of an entire prism depends on whether or not hyper-threading is performed. If we have a single tile on each SM, $T_{\text{tile}}(k) = m^{'} + c$. On the other hand, with hyper-threading enabled, $T_{\text{tile}}(k)$ is dominated by $\zeta = \max\{m^{'}, c\}$, and so,

$$T_{prism}(k) = \begin{cases} k = 1 & : \quad \left(m^{'} + c\right) \left\lceil \frac{S_2 + t_T}{t_{S_2}} \right\rceil \\ k > 1 & : \quad m^{'} + k\zeta \left\lceil \frac{S_2 + t_T}{t_{S_2}} \right\rceil. \end{cases} \tag{16}$$

Plugging this into (2) and simplifying we get

$$T_{\text{alg}} = N_w T_{\text{sync}} + N_w T_{\text{prism}} \left\lceil \frac{1}{n_{SM}} \left\lceil \frac{w}{k} \right\rceil \right\rceil. \tag{17}$$

Finally, we extend the analysis for the 1D case to determine $m_i = m_o$ and M_{tile} as

$$m_i = t_{S_2}(t_{S_1} + 2t_T) \tag{18}$$

$$M_{\text{tile}} = 2(t_{S_1} + t_T + 1)(t_{S_2} + t_T + 1). \tag{19}$$

4.3 Hybrid Hexagonal/Classic Tiling for 3D stencils

Here, the outer two loops are tiled with hexagons, and the inner dimension(s) are tiled using classic time skewing techniques. We illustrate this for the Jacobi 3D stencil.

4.3.1 Total Execution Time of Jacobi 3D

Each hexagon from Figure 1 now becomes an $S_2 \times S_3$ "slab" with a hexagonal cross section. Its data footprint is surely too large for the entire slab to be executed as a single tile, so it needs to be further tiled in the two inner dimensions. Indeed, even a single dimensional slice out of this slab, i.e., a 3-dimensional prism, will most likely have too large a data footprint. To respect the dependences, time skewing is applied to each slab (notice how the front face is oblique in the S_1-T plane (see Figure 2 that illustrates the 2D case) and then each slice is partitioned using vertical cuts (other than the front face, all the inter-tile faces are vertical). A threadblock executes the entire *sequence of tiles* in a single kernel call. Let T_{slab} denote the time that this takes, and postpone its derivation for now.

The formulæ for the number of wave-fronts (N_w), the tile width (w_{tile}), the width of a wave-front in the t_{S_1}-axis (w), are identical to the Jacobi 1D case, and respectively, are

$$N_w \approx 2 \left\lceil \frac{T}{t_T} \right\rceil \tag{20}$$

$$w_{\text{tile}} = t_{S_1} + t_T - 2, \tag{21}$$

$$w \approx \left\lceil \frac{S_{s_1}}{t_{S_1} + t_T} \right\rceil. \tag{22}$$

The total execution time is hence similar to the one of Jacobi 1D 6 with the unique difference that the term T_{tile} is substitute now by T_{slab}.

4.3.2 Execution Time of a Slab

Since slabs chosen as above could be very large and inconvenient for the shared memory size, we need to further partition them into smaller chunks. In the Jacobi 2D hybrid approach (see Figure 2) these are hexagonal (non-orthogonal) sub-slabs with a length t_{S_2} and bases defined by the normal vector $(1, 0, 1)$, where time is the first dimension (vertical axis). In case of Jacobi 3D the number of these sub-slabs in an entire slab is

$$N_{sslabs} = \left\lceil \left(\frac{S_2 + t_T}{t_{S_2}} \right) \left(\frac{S_3 + t_T}{t_{S_3}} \right) \right\rceil \tag{23}$$

and we assume from now on that one slab is computed by a single SM, which iterates N_{sslabs} times for a given slab, and at each iteration computes one of the above sub-slab.

Since data belonging to the oblique hexagonal faces are allocated in the local SM memory, the amount of data to be transferred from global to shared memory is simply the amount of data as for Jacobi 1D case (7) multiplied by the tile's length in the S_2 and S_3 axes. Hence

$$m_i = m_o = t_{S_2} t_{S_3} (t_{S_1} + 2t_T). \tag{24}$$

For the corresponding time we obtain respectively

$$m' = (m_i + m_o)L + 2\tau_{\text{sync}}. \tag{25}$$

To obtain the volume of a sub-slab, we multiply the hexagon area by its length in the S_2 and S_3 axes and we obtain

$$V_{\text{tile}} = t_{S_2} t_{S_3} \frac{t_T(w_{\text{tile}} + t_{S_1})}{2}. \tag{26}$$

The iteration space dependences indicate that the computations in a tile can be done in parallel in each row, and in a sequential manner between rows from bottom to top. We therefore find that the computation time for a **non-boundary/steady state** tile is given by

$$\begin{aligned} c &= 2 \sum_{x=t_{S_1},step=2}^{w_{\text{tile}}} \left(\left\lceil \frac{x t_{S_2} t_{S_3}}{n_V} \right\rceil C_{iter} + \tau_{\text{sync}} \right) \\ &= 2C_{iter} \sum_{x=t_{S_1},step=2}^{w_{\text{tile}}} \left\lceil \frac{x t_{S_2} t_{S_3}}{n_V} \right\rceil + t_T \tau_{\text{sync}}. \end{aligned} \tag{27}$$

Now, the execution time of an entire slab depends on whether or not hyper-threading is performed. If we have a single tile on each SM (i.e. $k = 1$) we obtain

$$T_{\text{slab}}(1) = (m' + c) N_{sslabs}. \tag{28}$$

On the other hand, with hyper-threading enabled (i.e. $k > 1$), $T_{\text{tile}}(k)$ is dominated by $\max(m', c)$, and so,

$$T_{slab}(k) = m' + k \max(m', c) N_{sslabs}. \tag{29}$$

Plugging this into (2) and simplifying yields

$$T_{\text{alg}} = N_w T_{\text{sync}} + N_w T_{\text{slab}}(k) \left\lceil \frac{1}{n_{SM}} \left\lceil \frac{w}{k} \right\rceil \right\rceil. \tag{30}$$

All the equations developed here hold true for all stencil codes generated by HHC compiler. However, the parameter C_{iter}, which corresponds to computation time of the loop body, varies with number and type of computations. Again, the model is not restricted to HHC style codes. It can be applied to other parallelization strategies. Consider, wavefront parallel Jacobi1D stencil. The total execution time is the sum of the times for each wavefront. The time for each kernel call (or wavefront) is the sum of the time needed for the SM with maximum number of tiles assigned to it to finish. Hence, equation 6 holds for wavefront parallel codes.

5. Experimental Validation

To validate the model, we perform a number of experiments on two NVIDIA platforms: GTX 980 and Titan X. Our benchmarks include four 2D stencils: Jacobi, Heat, Laplacian and Gradient, all first order stencils. The benchmarks also include two 3D stencils: Heat and Laplacian. All 2D stencils have two space dimensions and one time dimension. The two space dimension sizes we explore are 4096^2 and 8192^2. For each such size, we explore five problem sizes in time dimension (T): 1024, 2048, 4096, 8192 and 16384. In total, we explore 10 different combinations of problem size parameters. With 4 benchmarks, 10 size combinations, and 2 machines, we have a total of 80 combinations, which we refer to as *2D stencil experiments*. Similarly, all 3D stencils have three space dimensions and one time dimension. The three space dimension sizes are 384^3, 512^3 and 640^3. For each such size, we explore five problem sizes in time dimension (T): 128, 256, 384, 512 and 640 where $T \leq S$. In total, we explore 12 different combinations of the problem size parameters. With 2 benchmarks, 12 size combinations, and 2 machines, we have a total of 48 combinations, which we refer to as *3D stencil experiments*.

5.1 Baseline Experiments

We maximize the memory footprint of the tile subject to capacity constraints. Hence, we obtain tile sizes, which are as large as shared memory capacity M_{SM}. This means we execute only one tile per SM at a time. However, both GPUs allow $48K$ shared memory per thread block. This constraint is enforced such that we experience the benefit of hyperthreading factor of two. In HHT paper [22], the authors suggests tile sizes that maximize the compute to IO ratio. We use similar strategies to construct what we call the *baseline experiments* that enable a good exploration of the feasible space.

The shared memory requirement of a tile is given by M_{tile}, which is a function of tile size parameters. Shared memory constraints limit the feasible number of tile sizes. We take data points that maximize M_{tile} over M_{SM} per thread block. To explore hyperthreading, we add data points that allow multiple thread blocks to execute concurrently on one SM. Using this approach, for each experiment we select a set of tile sizes t_{T}, t_{S_1}, and t_{S_2} for 2D stencils. In addition to these tile sizes, we select t_{S_3} for 3D stencils. We generate 85 unique tile size combinations per experiment and, for each of them, we explore 10 different values of $n_{\text{thr,i}}$. Each unique combination of an experiment with the parameters t_{T}, t_{S_1}, t_{S_2}, and $n_{\text{thr,i}}$ is called a *data point*. Hence, our baseline-experiment set contains 850 data points for each experiment.

The HHC compiler generates a separate program (code) for every data point (it cannot produce codes with parametric tile sizes), a total of $850 \times (80+48) = 108,800$ data points. We measure execution time of each data point over five runs, and select the *smallest* of the five measurements. We made this choice of the minimum (rather than the average) as this is a common strategy in performance tuning/optimization and, also, since our model makes optimistic assumptions regarding run time behavior, choosing the smallest time is consistent with our modeling objective.

In order to complete the time model, additional hardware parameters need to be specified. Some of the needed values can be taken from vendor-provided hardware specifications. Table 2 shows such parameters for our two platforms. We also need values of the remaining parameters L, τ_{sync}, T_{sync} and C_{iter}, which could not be obtained from hardware specifications. We conduct the following microbenchmark experiments to gather these values.

5.2 Microbenchmarks

For L, τ_{sync} and T_{sync}, the micro-benchmarks are implemented such that the execution time is dominated by the op-

Table 2: GPU configuration

Architecture Parameters	Type	GTX 980	Titan X
n_{SM}	EH	16	24
n_{v}	EH	128	128
M_{SM} [KB]	EH	96	96
R_{SM}	EH	65536	65536
shared memory banks	EH	32	32
max threadblocks per SM	EH	32	32

Table 3: Parameter values for the micro-benchmarks

Parameter [unit]	GTX 980	Titan X
L [s/GB]	7.36×10^{-3}	5.42×10^{-3}
τ_{sync} [s]	7.96×10^{-10}	6.74×10^{-10}
T_{sync} [s]	9.24×10^{-7}	9.00×10^{-7}

eration of interest. The experimental parameter values that we empirically determined are listed in Table 3.

Another crucial component in our model is C_{iter}. The parameter C_{iter} denotes the execution time of one iteration of the loop body per vector unit provided that all the necessary data is available in shared memory. Its value depends on the types and number of operations in the loop body and on the platform. Since we have 6 benchmarks and 2 platforms, we need to determine 12 values for C_{iter}, one per combination. This is because C_{iter} is independent of the problem size parameters.

Notice that C_{iter} is not a simple function of the number of arithmetic operations of each type, but is quite complex, depending also on the instruction fetch/issue/execution latency, instruction issue pipeline, control flow, shared memory bank conflicts, data dependency, and many other factors. Analytically determining the execution time of a single iteration considering all these factors is a difficult problem. Thus, we estimate the value of C_{iter} empirically. For this purpose, we remove all global⇔shared memory data transfers, while making sure that the computations we want to measure do not get optimized away. The execution time is measured for 70 randomly picked problem and tile sizes and is determined by dividing the execution time per vector unit by the number of iterations of the particular instance. Finally, we take the average over all 70 runs to compute the value of C_{iter} for a benchmark-machine combination. The resulting values are given in Table 4.

Now that we have the values of all parameters in our model, we can use them to validate the model.

5.3 Validation Results

Using the parameter values from the previous subsection, we compute the predicted execution time T_{alg} for each data point. For each benchmark-machine combination we have 10 problem sizes and 850 data points, which overall are 8500

Table 4: Values of C_{iter} in seconds

Benchmark	GTX 980	Titan X
Jacobi2D	3.39×10^{-8}	3.83×10^{-8}
Heat2D	3.68×10^{-8}	4.23×10^{-8}
Laplacian2D	3.11×10^{-8}	3.81×10^{-8}
Gradient2D	6.09×10^{-8}	7.60×10^{-8}
Heat3D	1.55×10^{-7}	1.64×10^{-7}
Laplacian3D	1.36×10^{-7}	1.44×10^{-7}

data points. We compute the root mean square error (RMSE) and observe that the RMSE is in the range of 45%–200% when considering the whole set of data points. However, as our model is designed to optimistically predict the execution time, these inaccuracies are expected. In fact, they are inevitable as our model is not designed to precisely predict the performance of data-points that result in inefficient implementations.

However, when restricting the analysis to the top performing (in terms of GFLOPS per second) data points, our model turns out to be very accurate. Out of the 850 points for each benchmark-platform combination, we observe that for all the data points that are within 20% of the top performing one, the RMSE is for all stencils on both GPUs below 10%. Figure 3 shows the correlation between the predicted and the measured time over the top performing points.

In the following section, we show that the time model can be used for tile size optimization.

6. Tile Size Optimization

The model we developed in Section 4 can be used to predict the efficiency of a code for given values of size parameters, such as S and T, but more importantly, it can be used to select the compiler parameters, in our case, the tile sizes, that lead to the best performance. We first formulate the optimization problem mathematically, describe the limitations that prevent a standard non-linear solver from finding an optimal solution, and then describe how we solved the problem via a simple exhaustive enumeration. Finally, we present our experimental results.

6.1 The Optimization Problem

We formulate the problem of finding optimal tile sizes as a mathematical optimization problem of the following type:

$$\begin{aligned} \underset{t_{S_1}, t_{S_2}, t_T}{\text{minimize}} \quad & T_{\text{alg}}(t_{S_1}, t_{S_2}, t_T) \\ \text{subject to} \quad & M_{\text{tile}} \le M_{\text{SM/threadblock}} \\ & k \le MTB_{\text{SM}} \\ & kM_{\text{tile}} \le M_{\text{SM}} \\ & t_{S_1}\text{–integer}, t_{S_2}\text{–multiple of } 32, t_T\text{–even} \end{aligned} \tag{31}$$

where M_{tile} and k are functions of the tile sizes. We require t_T to be even, as necessary for hybrid-hexagonal tiling [22],

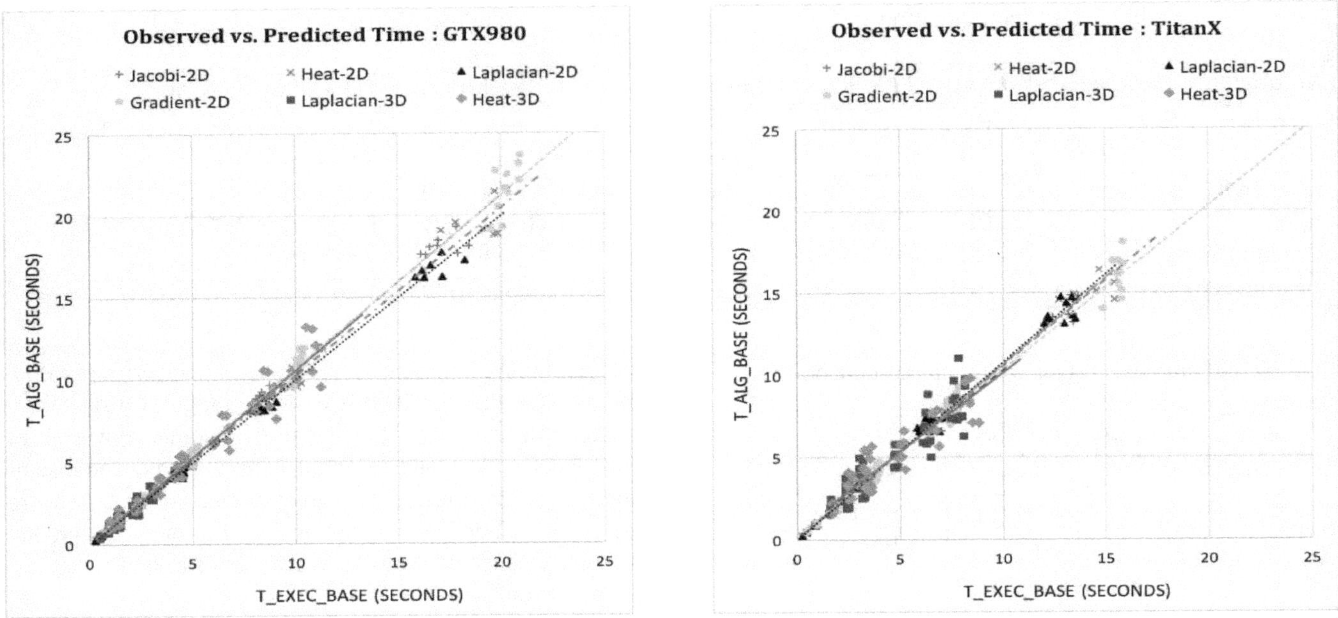

Figure 3: Observed execution time vs. model predicted time on GTX 980 and on Titan X, where $T_{\text{alg\_base}}$ denotes the model predicted time and $T_{\text{exec\_base}}$ denotes the measured execution time for the baseline experiments.

and t_{S_2} to be a multiple of 32 to ensure that neighboring threads in S_2 fill complete warps (groups of 32 threads).

The optimization problem at hand is of a type that does not allow very efficient solution methods as it is non-linear and non-convex and has integer variables. On the other hand, it has a small number of variables (only three). Also, despite the problem being non-continuous due to the ceiling and floor functions, it can be made continuous by replacing these functions with new variables and inequality constraints, e.g., the ceiling in $\lceil x \rceil$ can be eliminated by introducing a new integer variable xc to replace $\lceil x \rceil$ and adding the inequality $x \leq xc$, assuming T_{alg} is a non-decreasing function with respect to $\lceil x \rceil$. Figure 4 illustrates the shape of T_{alg} as a 2D function (the 3D plot is sliced at $t_{S_1} = 8$) and shows that T_{alg} varies significantly with the tile sizes, so careful tile size selection is indeed important for getting good performance.

We encoded the optimization problem in the modeling language AMPL [18] and solved it using several non-linear solvers, including commercial ones. The best results were obtained using the open-source solver Bonmin [7]. All those solvers use heuristics that allow relatively good (but sub-optimal) solution to be found for large problems, but for small problems like ours they do not offer an option to do an exhaustive search that would find the optimal solution.

One of the main reasons for the somewhat disappointing performance is that the feasible space of the optimization problem 31 does not capture an important pragmatic aspect of the GPU code, as we are unable to model it, namely the number of physical registers that the generated code uses: this information is only available *after the generated code is compiled*. It is well known that if the number of registers

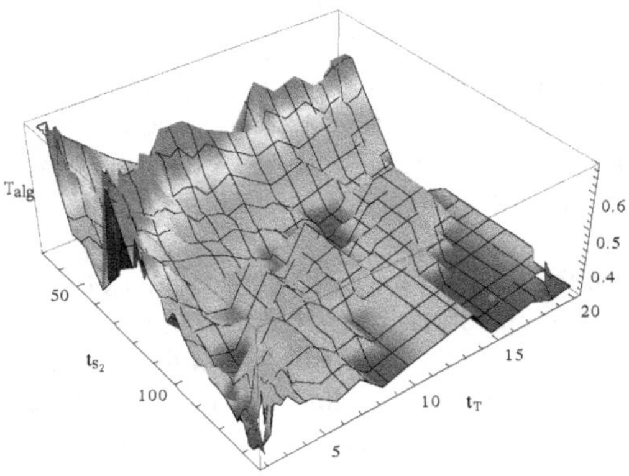

Figure 4: T_{alg} for Heat2D and GTX 980 as a function of t_T and t_{S_2} and with t_{S_1} fixed at 8. The red dot shows $T_{\text{alg\_min}}$, the point of minimum over all T_{alg}.

exceeds the number of physical registers in the SM, namely the hardware parameter R_{SM}, the additional registers are implemented as "virtual registers" and get spilled and restored from global memory. This is known to be extremely inefficient and slows down the generated code.

In our model, we do not have a function for R_{tile}, since this is very difficult to model analytically. Because of this, we used the following approach.

- We evaluate our objective function within the entire feasible space of of Eqn 31.
- We keep all points that yield execution times within 10% of model predicted minimum value of T_{alg}. Many of these were not in our set of 850 baseline experiments.

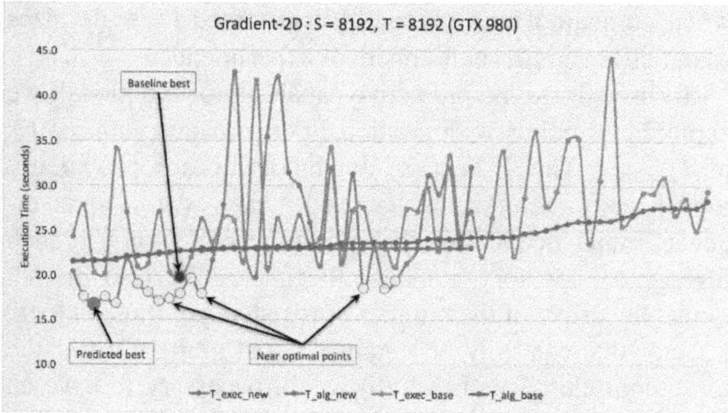

Figure 5: Predicted tile size performance of Gradient-2D for $S_1 = 8192$, $S_2 = 8192$ and $T = 8192$ on GTX 980.

- We generated codes for the new tile sizes in this set and evaluated their performance.

6.2 Experimental Results

We observe that the new tile sizes perform better than those obtained in baseline. Figure 5 shows the execution times and model-predicted times for the Gradient-2D stencil for a problem size of $S_1 = 8192$, $S_2 = 8192$ and $T = 8192$. Clearly, the optimal tile sizes predicted by the model outperform the best baseline tile sizes. As we search within the 10% vicinity of $T_{\text{alg\_min}}$, we find multiple near-optimal points. Baseline observed best is at *19.8 seconds*, whereas our model predicted optimal gives us a tile size that takes 16.5 *seconds*, which is a 17% improvement in performance. This model predicted tile size was not explored in our set of baseline tile sizes. Moreover, we observe multiple near optimal points in the range of *16.5-19.8 seconds*. We get similar performance improvements for all 2D stencils on both platforms over all different problem sizes.

We compare the performance of different tile sizes obtained from HHC, $T_{\text{alg\_min}}$, Exhaustive search and best within 10% of $T_{\text{alg\_min}}$. Figure 6 shows the average GFlops per second achieved by different tile size selection strategies for 2D stencils over ten different problem sizes. It is clear that tile sizes corresponding to $T_{\text{alg\_min}}$ have poor performance in all cases. Another important conclusion is that the conventional wisdom of using large tile sizes does not yield best performance. The tile sizes that are within 10% of $T_{\text{alg\_min}}$ give the best performance with improvement of 60% over HHC and 9% over Baseline.

Finally, note that exhaustive searching over the entire feasible space is not practical, and no autotuner does this. HHC does not have an established autotuner. Comparing against a generic autotuner (e.g., opentuner) could be interesting, but tuning without good domain knowledge will be difficult, as the search space isn't easy to navigate. The feasible space is at least 200 times larger than the number of experiments we ran, and these took many weeks of dedicated machine time.

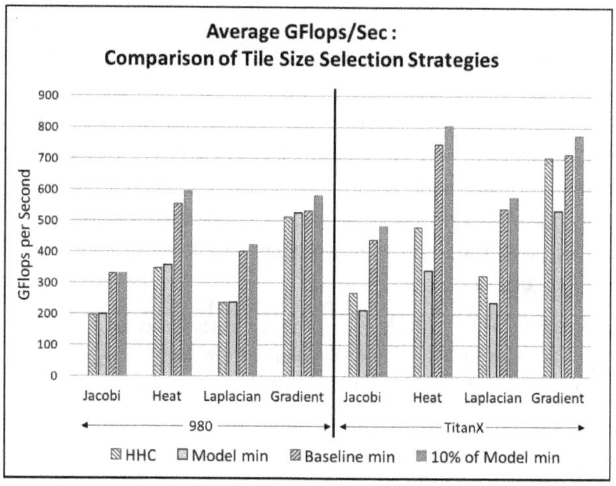

Figure 6: Average (over 10 problem sizes) GFlops/Sec achieved by different tile size selection strategies for 2D stencils.

7. Discussion

There are many "rules of thumb" used to optimize GPU programs. Expert programmers strive to ensure "high occupancy," avoid control-divergence, "coalesce" their memory accesses, and tune the number of threads. They also suggest maximizing the shared-memory footprint, while ensuring latency-hiding of memory accesses (usually by virtualizing multiple threadblocks per physical core). While all these parameters are very difficult to tune, many of these conditions are already ensured by a highly tuned domain specific compiler like HHC. Moreover, our model deliberately ignores some of these. We now discuss the limitations, and also the generality of our approach.

Execution of full warps without thread divergence (except on data-space boundaries) is guaranteed by the HHC compiler, if tile sizes in the innermost dimension are multiples of 32. So we use this to ensure divergence-freedom for all configurations that we predict/model/generate. Similarly, the HHC compiler generates code that guarantees coalesced accesses. This justifies some of our optimistic assumptions.

Limitations The two key limitations of our model are in register usage and the number of threads-per-block (in possibly multiple dimensions). Both are very difficult to model analytically. Although the register usage does not feature directly in our objective function, it appears in a constraint of the feasible space: our optimistic model holds only if register spills do not slow down the execution. However, this can only be known after the back-end `nvcc` compiler is called. Because of this, the results using an off-the-shelf solver like Bonmin were disappointing, and we used the script-driven exhaustive analytical evaluation described in Section 6.1.

The threads-per-block parameter(s) have a significant impact on performance, and this is also hard to model. Largely because of this, our tile selection could not be accomplished using only model-based optimization, but needed additional exploration of the search space in the vicinity of the model-predicted optima. However, we did take it into account during experimentation. Among the high-performing instances, we found that the values of this parameter that yielded the locally best performance was easily predictable—empirically, rather than analytically. The threads-per-block parameter used in our final, optimization experiments use this empirically predicted value.

Generality Our model can be extended to other stencil types for e.g., higher order stencils (provided they can be handled by HHC-compiler). When dependences change, the slopes of the hexagons change by constant factors, the memory footprints change similarly, etc. These are exactly the terms that a polyhedral compiler like HHC manipulates when allocating memory buffers, and constructing loop bounds. Our ongoing work is in incorporating the model into the compiler itself.

We reiterate that although the model is specific to HHC, the approach itself, which involves the choice of parameter hierarchy and the methods of their estimation/approximation, is extensible. For rectangular tiles, for instance, the formulae for N_w, m_i, m_o, etc., will be different, but the elementary software and hardware parameters will be the same, and the methods for deriving the formulae will be similar.

Revisiting conventional wisdom A commonly used "rule of thumb" suggests that the optimal tiling strategy is to choose the "largest possible tile size that fits" i.e., its memory footprint matches the available capacity. Our results suggest that we should question this. First of all, this strategy precludes overlapping of computation and communication (the "hyperthreading effect"). But this can be avoided by explicitly accounting for hyperthreading. Indeed, many modern GPU platforms preclude such large size by limiting the maximum data footprint of a thread block to only *half* the shared memory capacity. So the "hyperthreading-adjusted conventional wisdom" would seek to maximize tile volume subject to the half-capacity constraint—the best strategy is the largest tile volume for the given footprint.

Our experimental data suggests otherwise—an even higher hyperthreading factor turns out to yield best performance in a wide range of our experiments. We still don't know why, and this is the subject of our ongoing investigation.

8. Conclusion

We developed a model for the execution time of stencil codes on the GPU platform and used it for tile size selection for stencil codes generated by the HHC polyhedral compiler. Our model is very accurate for predicting the times of problem instances whose performance is within 20% of the optimal and, hence, it can be used to find values for tunable parameters that will give near optimal performance. We applied our model for optimizing the tile sizes and experimentally observed a noticeable improvement in performance when compared with manually determined best tile sizes found after significant numbers of experiments.

To investigate the predictive capability of the model, we explored all points with predicted performance within 10% of $T_{\text{alg\_min}}$. This is because our model does not explicitly model many architectural and code features: thread divergence, imbalance among threads in the same warp, branch divergence, memory bank conflicts, etc. We also do not model the effect of the number of registers per thread block, a factor that can only be obtained "post mortem" after the `nvcc` compiler. This is why it is still necessary to have an empirical tuning phase, but we have shown that the number of points that need to be explored is relatively small.

Finally, we would like to note that a large part of the time and effort of conducting our experiments was the code generation effort. The HHC compiler generated codes where the tile size and many other parameters are fixed at compile time, necessitating a separate call to the compiler for each data point in our experiments. For some of the points this ran into several tens of seconds, and was a significant fraction of the total time that the experimentation took. We are therefore also exploring the use of parametric tiled code generation, where a single parametric code is generated once for a given input program, and can be reused for different tile sizes. Here, tile sizes may be set a launch time or even dynamically during execution. The trade-off this brings between code efficiency and compilation time is the subject of our ongoing research.

References

[1] N. Ahmed, N. Mateev, and K. Pingali. Synthesizing transformations for locality enhancement of imperfectly-nested loop nests. *International Journal of Parallel Programming*, 29(5): 493–544, 2001.

[2] K. Asanovic, R. Bodik, B. C. Catanzaro, P. Gebis, J. J. abd Husbands, K. Keutzer, D. A. Patterson, W. L. Plishker, J. Shalf, S. W. Williams, and K. A. Yelick. The landscape of parallel computing research: A view from Berkeley. EECS Tech Report EECE-2006-183, UC Berkeley, Decembeer 2006.

[3] V. Bandishti, I. Pananilath, and U. Bondhugula. Tiling stencil computations to maximize parallelism. In *Proceedings of the International Conference on High Performance Computing, Networking, Storage and Analysis*, SC '12, pages 40:1–40:11, Los Alamitos, CA, USA, 2012. IEEE Computer Society Press.

[4] C. Bleck, R. Rooth, D. Hu, and L. T. Smith. Salinity-driven Thermocline Transients in a Wind- and Thermohaline-forced Isopycnic Coordinate Model of the North Atlantic. *Journal of Physical Oceanography*, 22(12):1486–1505, 1992.

[5] U. Bondhugula, A. Hartono, J. Ramanujam, and P. Sadayappan. A practical automatic polyhedral program optimization system. In *ACM SIGPLAN Conference on Programming Language Design and Implementation (PLDI)*, June 2008.

[6] U. Bondhugula, V. Bandishti, A. Cohen, G. Potron, and N. Vasilache. Tiling and optimizing time-iterated computations on periodic domains. In *Proceedings of the 23rd International Conference on Parallel Architectures and Compilation*, PACT '14, pages 39–50, New York, NY, USA, 2014. ACM.

[7] Bonmin 2016. *Bonmin Project Page*. `https://projects.coin-or.org/Bonmin`, 2015 (accessed March 11, 2016).

[8] R. A. Chowdhury, H.-S. Le, and V. Ramachandran. Cache-oblivious dynamic programming for bioinformatics. *TCBB*, 7 (3):495–510, July-September 2010.

[9] M. Christen, O. Schenk, and H. Burkhart. Patus: A code generation and autotuning framework for parallel iterative stencil computations on modern microarchitectures. In *Parallel Distributed Processing Symposium (IPDPS), 2011 IEEE Int.*, pages 676–687, May 2011.

[10] A. Darte, Y. Robert, and F. Vivien. *Scheduling and Automatic Parallelization*. Birkhaüser, 2000.

[11] K. Datta, M. Murphy, V. Volkov, S. Williams, J. Carter, L. Oliker, D. Patterson, J. Shalf, and K. Yelick. Stencil computation optimization and auto-tuning on state-of-the-art multicore architectures. In *SC08: Proceedings of the 2008 ACM/IEEE conference on Supercomputing*, pages 4:1–4:12, Austin, TX, November 2008. http://portal.acm.org/citation.cfm?id=1413370.1413375.

[12] H. Dursun, K. Nomura, L. Peng, R. Seymour, W. Wang, R. K. Kalia, A. Nakano, and P. Vashishta. A multilevel parallelization framework for high-order stencil computations. In *Euro-Par 09*, pages 642–653, Delft, The Netherlands, August 2009.

[13] H. Dursun, K. Nomura, W. Wang, M. Kunaseth, L. Peng, R. Seymour, R. K. Kalia, A. Nakano, and P. Vashishta. Incore optimization of high-order stencil computations. In *PDPTA*, pages 533–538, Las Vegas, NV, July 2009.

[14] J. F. Epperson. *An Introduction to Numerical Methods and Analysis*. Wiley-Interscience, 2007.

[15] P. Feautrier. Dataflow analysis of array and scalar references. *International Journal of Parallel Programming*, 20(1):23–53, Feb 1991.

[16] P. Feautrier. Some efficient solutions to the affine scheduling problem. Part I. one-dimensional time. *International Journal of Parallel Programming*, 21(5):313–347, 1992.

[17] P. Feautrier. Some efficient solutions to the affine scheduling problem. Part II. multidimensional time. *International Journal of Parallel Programming*, 21(6):389–420, 1992.

[18] R. Fourer, D. M. Gay, and B. W. Kernighan. *AMPL: A Modelling Language for Mathematical Programming*. Duxbury Press, Brooks/Cole Publishing Company, 2nd edition, 2002.

[19] M. Frigo and V. Strumpen. Cache oblivious stencil computations. In *Proc. of the 19th Annual Int. Conf. on Supercomputing*, ICS '05, pages 361–366, New York, NY, USA, 2005. ACM.

[20] M. Frigo, C. E. Leiserson, H. Prokop, and S. Ramachandran. Cache-oblivious algorithms. In *FOCS: IEEE Symposium on Foundations of Computer Science*, pages 285–297, New York, NY, October 1999.

[21] S. M. Griffies, C. Bning, F. O. Bryan, E. P. Chassignet, R. Gerdes, H. Hasumi, A. Hirst, A.-M. Treguier, and D. Webb. Developments in Ocean Climate Modelling. *Ocean Modelling*, 2:123–192, 2000.

[22] T. Grosser, A. Cohen, J. Holewinski, P. Sadayappan, and S. Verdoolaege. Hybrid hexagonal/classical tiling for GPUs. In *CGO*, page 66, Orlando, FL, Feb 2014.

[23] T. Gysi, T. Grosser, and T. Hoefler. Modesto: Data-centric analytic optimization of complex stencil programs on heterogeneous architectures. In *Proc. of the 29th ACM on Int. Conf. on Supercomputing*, ICS '15, pages 177–186, New York, NY, USA, 2015. ACM.

[24] T. Gysi, C. Osuna, O. Fuhrer, M. Bianco, and T. C. Schulthess. Stella: A domain-specific tool for structured grid methods in weather and climate models. In *Proc. of the Int. Conf. for High Performance Computing, Networking, Storage and Analysis*, SC '15, pages 41:1–41:12, New York, NY, USA, 2015. ACM.

[25] T. Henretty, R. Veras, F. Franchetti, L.-N. Pouchet, J. Ramanujam, and P. Sadayappan. A stencil compiler for short-vector simd architectures. In *Proceedings of the 27th International ACM Conference on International Conference on Supercomputing*, ICS '13, pages 13–24, New York, NY, USA, 2013. ACM.

[26] J. Holewinski, L.-N. Pouchet, and P. Sadayappan. High-performance code generation for stencil computations on GPU architectures. In *Proc. of the 26th ACM Int. Conf. on Supercomputing*, ICS '12, pages 311–320, New York, NY, USA, 2012. ACM.

[27] S. Hong and H. Kim. An analytical model for a GPU architecture with memory-level and thread-level parallelism awareness. In *Proceedings of the 36th Annual International*

Symposium on Computer Architecture, ISCA '09, pages 152–163, New York, NY, USA, 2009. ACM.

[28] C. John. *Options, Futures, and Other Derivatives*. Prentice Hall, 2006.

[29] S. Kamil, K. Datta, S. Williams, L. Oliker, J. Shalf, and K. Yelick. Impact of modern memory subsystems on cache optimizations for stencil computations. In *MSPC 2005: Workshop on Memory Systems Performance*, pages 36–43, Chicago, IL, June 2005. ACM Sigplan.

[30] S. Kamil, K. Datta, S. Williams, L. Oliker, J. Shalf, and K. Yelick. Implicit and explicit optimizations for stencil computations. In *MSPC 2006: Workshop on Memory Systems Performance and Correctness*, pages 51–60, San Jose, CA, October 2006. ACM Sigplan.

[31] S. Kamil, C. Chan, L. Oliker, J. Shalf, and S. Williams. An auto-tuning framework for parallel multicore stencil computations. In *Parallel Distributed Processing (IPDPS), 2010 IEEE International Symposium on*, pages 1–12, April 2010.

[32] S. Krishnamoorthy, M. Baskaran, U. Bondhugula, J. Ramanujam, A. Rountev, and P. Sadayappan. Effective automatic parallelization of stencil computations. In *PLDI 2007: Proceedings of the 2007 ACM SIGPLAN Conference on Programming Language Design and Implementation*, pages 235–244, San Diego, CA, June 2007. ACM.

[33] Z. Li and Y. Song. Automatic tiling of iterative stencil loops. *ACM Trans. Program. Lang. Syst.*, 26(6):975–1028, Nov. 2004.

[34] P. Liu, R. Seymour, K. Nomura, R. K. Kalia, A. Nakano, P. Vashishta, A. Loddoch, M. Netzband, W. R. Volz, and C. C. Wong. High-order stencil computations on multicore clusters. In *IPDPS 2009: IEEE International Parallel abd Distributed Processing Symposium*, pages 1–11, Rome, Italy, May 2009.

[35] C. Mauras, P. Quinton, S. Rajopadhye, and Y. Saouter. Scheduling affine parameterized recurrences by means of variable dependent timing functions. In S. Y. Kung and E. Swartzlander, editors, *International Conference on Application Specific Array Processing*, pages 100–110, Princeton, New Jersey, Sept 1990. IEEE Computer Society.

[36] W. Mei, W. Shyy, D. Yu, and L. S. Luo. Lattice Boltzmann Method for 3-D Flows with Curved Boundary. *Journal of Computational Physics*, 161(2):680–699, 2000.

[37] J. Meng and K. Skadron. Performance modeling and automatic ghost zone optimization for iterative stencil loops on GPUs. In *Proceedings of the 23rd International Conference on Supercomputing*, ICS '09, pages 256–265, New York, NY, USA, 2009. ACM.

[38] P. Micikevicius. 3D finite difference computation on GPUs using CUDA. In *GPPGPU*, pages 79–84, Washington, DC, March 2009.

[39] R. T. Mullapudi, V. Vasista, and U. Bondhugula. Polymage: Automatic optimization for image processing pipelines. In *Proceedings of the Twentieth International Conference on Architectural Support for Programming Languages and Operating Systems*, ASPLOS '15, pages 429–443, New York, NY, USA, 2015. ACM.

[40] A. Nakano, R. K. Kalia, and P. Vashishta. Multiresolution Molecular Dynamics Algorithm for Realistic Materials Modeling on Parallel Computers. *Computer Physics Communications*, 83(2-3):197–214, 1994.

[41] A. Nguyen, N. Satish, J. Chhugani, C. Kim, and P. Dubey. 3.5D blocking optimization for stencil computations on modern CPUs and GPUs. In *Proceedings of the 2010 ACM/IEEE International Conference for High Performance Computing, Networking, Storage and Analysis*, SC '10, pages 1–13, Washington, DC, USA, 2010. IEEE Computer Society.

[42] A. Nitsure. Implementation and optimization of a cache oblivious lattice boltzmann algorithm. Master's thesis, Institut fr Informatic, Friedrich-Alexander-Universitt Erlangen-Nrnberg, July 2006.

[43] L. Peng, R. Seymour, K. ichi Nomura, R. K. Kalia, A. Nakano, P. Vashishta, A. Loddoch, M. Netzband, W. R. Volz, and C. C. Wong. High-order stencil computations on multicore clusters. In *IPPS*, 2009.

[44] P. Quinton and V. Van Dongen. The mapping of linear recurrence equations on regular arrays. *Journal of VLSI Signal Processing*, 1(2):95–113, 1989.

[45] J. Ragan-Kelley, C. Barnes, A. Adams, S. Paris, F. Durand, and S. Amarasinghe. Halide: A language and compiler for optimizing parallelism, locality, and recomputation in image processing pipelines. In *Proceedings of the 34th ACM SIGPLAN Conference on Programming Language Design and Implementation*, PLDI '13, pages 519–530, New York, NY, USA, 2013. ACM.

[46] S. V. Rajopadhye, S. Purushothaman, and R. M. Fujimoto. On synthesizing systolic arrays from recurrence equations with linear dependencies. In *Proceedings, Sixth Conference on Foundations of Software Technology and Theoretical Computer Science*, pages 488–503, New Delhi, India, December 1986. Springer Verlag, LNCS 241.

[47] G. Rizk, D. Lavenier, and S. Rajopadhye. *GPU accelerated RNA folding algorithm*, chapter 14. Morgan Kauffman, 2010. in GPU Computing Gems 4, editor: W-M. Hwu.

[48] M. Shaheen and R. Strzodka. Numa aware iterative stencil computations on many-core system. In *26th IEEE International Parallel and Distributed Processing Symposium (IPDPS)*, Shanghai, China, 2012.

[49] J. Shirako, K. Sharma, N. Fauzia, L.-N. Pouchet, J. Ramanujam, P. Sadayappan, and V. Sarkar. *Analytical Bounds for Optimal Tile Size Selection*, pages 101–121. Springer Berlin Heidelberg, Berlin, Heidelberg, 2012.

[50] R. Strzodka, M. Shaheen, D. Pajak, and H.-P. Seidel. Cache oblivious parallelograms in iterative stencil computations. In *24th ACM/SIGARCH International Conference on Supercomputing (ICS)*, pages 49–59, Tsukuba, Japan, June 2010.

[51] R. Strzodka, M. Shaheen, and D. Pajak. Time skewing made simple (poster). In *Proceedings of the 16th ACM Symposium on Principles and Practice of Parallel Programming*, PPoPP '11, pages 295–296, New York, NY, USA, 2011. ACM.

[52] R. Strzodka, M. Shaheen, D. Pajak, and H. P. Seidel. Cache accurate time skewing in iterative stencil computations. In

Parallel Processing (ICPP), 2011 International Conference on, pages 571–581, Sept 2011.

[53] Y. Tang, R. A. Chowdhury, B. C. Kuszmaul, C.-K. Luk, and C. E. Leiserson. The pochoir stencil compiler. In *Proceedings of the Twenty-third Annual ACM Symposium on Parallelism in Algorithms and Architectures*, SPAA '11, pages 117–128, New York, NY, USA, 2011. ACM.

[54] S. Verdoolaege, J. Carlos Juega, A. Cohen, J. Ignacio Gómez, C. Tenllado, and F. Catthoor. Polyhedral parallel code generation for CUDA. *ACM Transactions on Architecture and Code Optimization (TACO)*, 9(4):54, 2013.

[55] R. C. Whaley, A. Petitet, and J. J. Dongarra. Automated empirical optimizations of software and the atlas project. *Parallel Computing*, 27(1):3–35, 2001.

[56] M. E. Wolf and M. S. Lam. A data locality optimizing algorithm. In *ACM Sigplan Not.*, volume 26, pages 30–44. ACM, 1991.

[57] M. J. Wolfe. Iteration space tiling for memory hierarchies. *Parallel Processing for Scientific Computing (SIAM)*, pages 357–361, 1987.

[58] D. Wonnacott. Time skewing for parallel computers. In *Languages and Compilers for Parallel Computing, 12th International Workshop, LCPC'99, La Jolla/San Diego, CA, USA, August 4-6, 1999, Proceedings*, pages 477–480, 1999.

[59] D. Wonnacott. Achieving scalable locality with time skewing. *International Journal of Parallel Programming*, 30(3):1–221, 2002.

[60] J. Xue. *Loop Tiling for Parallelism*, volume 575 of *Kluwer International Series in Engineering and Computer Science*. Kluwer, 2000.

[61] K. Yotov, X. Li, G. Ren, M. Cibulskis, G. DeJong, M. Garzaran, D. Padua, K. Pingali, P. Stodghill, and P. Wu. A comparison of empirical and model-driven optimization. In *Proceedings of the ACM SIGPLAN 2003 Conference on Programming Language Design and Implementation*, PLDI '03, pages 63–76, New York, NY, USA, 2003. ACM.

Combining SIMD and Many/Multi-core Parallelism for Finite State Machines with Enumerative Speculation

Peng Jiang   Gagan Agrawal

Department of Computer Science and Engineering
The Ohio State University
Columbus, OH 43210, USA
{jiang.952, agrawal.28}@osu.edu

Abstract

Finite State Machine (FSM) is the key kernel behind many popular applications, including regular expression matching, text tokenization, and Huffman decoding. Parallelizing FSMs is extremely difficult because of the strong dependencies and unpredictable memory accesses. Previous efforts have largely focused on multi-core parallelization, and used different approaches, including *speculative* and *enumerative* execution, both of which have been effective but also have limitations. With increasing width and improving flexibility in SIMD instruction sets, this paper focuses on combining SIMD and multi/many-core parallelism for FSMs. We have developed a novel strategy, called *enumerative speculation.* Instead of speculating on a single state as in speculative execution or enumerating all possible states as in enumerative execution, our strategy speculates transitions from several possible states, reducing the prediction overheads of speculation approach and the large amount of redundant work in the enumerative approach. A simple lookback approach produces a set of guessed states to achieve high speculation success rates in our enumerative speculation. We evaluate our method with four popular FSM applications: Huffman decoding, regular expression matching, HTML tokenization, and Div7. We obtain up to 2.5x speedup using SIMD on one core and up to 95x combining SIMD with 60 cores of an Intel Xeon Phi. On a single core, we outperform the best single-state speculative execution version by an average of 1.6x, and in combining SIMD and many-core parallelism, outperform enumerative execution by an average of 2x.

1. Introduction

The essential computations in many practical applications, including regular expression matching [1], dictionary-base decoding, XML validation, text tokenization, and network intrusion detection, can be expressed as state transitions on finite state machines (FSMs). Thus, the performance of FSMs is critical to the performance of these popular applications. Figure 1a shows an example FSM that checks if a binary number is divisible by 7. This FSM has 7 states labeled from 0 to 6, indicating the remainder when the number is divided by 7. From a given state i, we transition to state $(2i \ mod \ 7)$ after processing a 0, and to state $((2i+1) \ mod \ 7)$ after processing a 1. A straightforward implementation of the state transition is shown in Figure 1c, and the state transition table is shown in Figure 1b.

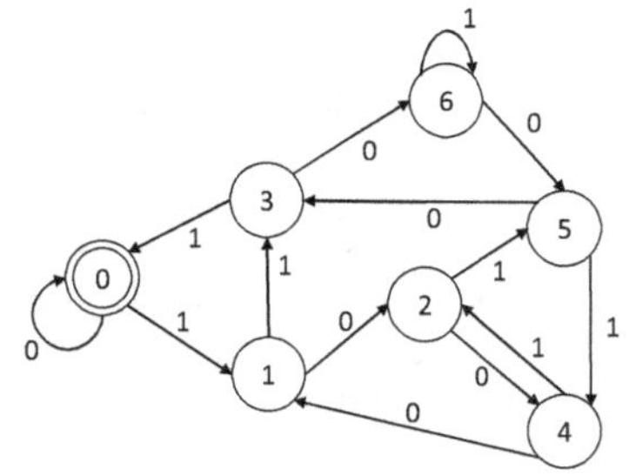

(a)

input \ state	0	1	2	3	4	5	6
Bit 0	0	2	4	6	1	3	5
Bit 1	1	3	5	0	2	4	6

(b)

```
state = 0;
for(i in input_text) {
  state = T[i][state];
}
```

(c)

Figure 1: An example of FSM and its state transition

An FSM is clearly an example of irregular application because of the data-dependent execution. They have even been referred to as *embarrassingly sequential* applications, as it is extremely hard to parallelize them [1]. More specifically, the iterations in the state transition loop are data-dependent because the next iteration must wait for the current iteration to produce the state. In addition, the memory accesses are non-continuous and input-dependent, i.e., the address of the

PPoPP '17, February 04-08, 2017, Austin, TX, USA

DOI: http://dx.doi.org/10.1145/3018743.3018760

state read from the state transition table is determined by the current state and input character in each iteration.

Despite the characterization as an embarrassingly sequential application, many efforts have been made to parallelize state transitions on FSMs. An intuitive way, referred to as *speculative execution*, involves dividing the input into several parts and performing the computation on different parts speculatively [15, 20, 25, 26]. Since the starting state for a given part is unknown until the execution on the previous part finishes, the algorithm needs to *guess* or *speculate* a starting state for each part. After the execution on the previous part ends, the algorithm checks if the the predicted starting state is identical to the correct state. If not, the computation of that part needs to be re-executed with the correct state. This simple idea has been extended to form more nuanced techniques. For example, looking back characters at the end of preceding part can help improve the prediction [20]. More recently, Zhao *et al.* [25, 26] propose a principled speculation method and eliminate the overheads of offline training in state prediction, making speculative execution of FSMs applicable on the fly.

The problem of speculation is that guessing a good starting state can be expensive, and even impossible in certain cases. Moreover, the overheads of starting speculation and checking correctness can be high in a thread or process-based implementation. Another way to parallelize FSMs is to replace the single-state transition in a straightforward implementation with *enumerative-state* transitions. Enumerative-state transition is a binary operation with the associative property, which allows the entire computation to be parallelized similar to parallel prefix sum [2, 13]. The intuition here is to process an input part with every state in the FSM as the starting state since its correct starting state is unknown. The problem of enumeration is that the redundant computations associated with every state in the FSM can easily outweigh the benefits of parallelization. Mytkowicz *et al.* [17] effectively reduce the redundant work by removing converged states periodically during the computation.

In this paper, we propose an *enumerative speculation* approach that combines and enhances the ideas of speculative and enumerative execution of FSMs. Instead of speculating with one state as in speculative methods, our approach speculates with multiple potential states (but not all states) in the FSM. As the number of guessed states is limited in our approach, the redundant work is limited. Based on the observation of Mytkowicz *et al.* [17] that the number of active (distinctive) states the enumerative execution of a FSM converges in is less than 16 – and even less than 8 almost always. Thus, the motivation behind our approach is that guessing a set of active states is much easier than guessing a single state. Specifically, with a set of states guessed by a simple prediction method, our approach can achieve high speculation success rates while eliminating the need for time-consuming profiling and training procedure(s).

The existing efforts on speculative execution of FSMs have been at thread or process level, exploiting multiple cores or MIMD parallelism for improving performance. Another form of parallelism has become ubiquitous over the last 2 decades – the SIMD parallelism. The most common SIMD or fine-grained data-parallel hardware, Streaming SIMD Extentions (SSE), has been part of the x86 since 1999. There have been significant recent developments in this area, including increasing width of SIMD lanes and enhanced instruction sets that provide more flexibility. Since the introduction of SSE, it has been widely used for graphics [8], image, video, signal processing [4], and regular scientific and engineering applications [5, 22]. More recent works such as [3, 19] have shown that several irregular applications including graph algorithms and particle simulations can also benefit from SIMD parallelization. For enumerative computation of FSMs, Mytkowicz *et al.* [17] exploit SIMD *gather* operation to accelerate multiple state transitions. However, SIMD itself does not bring parallelization to the computation in their work since the concurrent processing of different input parts are still performed by multiple threads. In fact, the total body of work on parallelizing irregular applications on SIMD is quite limited [3].

In this work, we combine SIMD and multi/many-core parallelism in implementing *enumerative speculation* of FSMs. With execution on a single core, the SIMD vector is divided into *groups*, with each group responsible for a different input blocks, and each unit within a group operating with different speculated values. Since the number of states speculated is always less than the length of SIMD vector, which is typically 16 or 8 in today's architectures, our approach limits the redundant work while fully utilizing SIMD capacity in the (co)processors. With execution on multi/many-cores, different input blocks are processed by different threads in parallel. Similar to conventional thread-based speculative execution, a main thread maintains the correct state of the program, while each of several speculative threads processes different input blocks. SIMD parallelism within each thread is used to execute with different speculated starting states, increasing chances that at least one of the states is the correct one.

We evaluate our method with four FSM applications: Huffman decoding, regular expression matching, HTML tokenization, and Div7. The results show that our enumerative speculation has high speculation success rates and achieved 2.2x to 2.5x speedups over the serial code on a single core of Intel Xeon Phi coprocessor. With the same prediction method, our enumerative speculation approach has a much higher success rate than conventional single-state speculation, and achieves an average 1.6x speedup compared with the best single-state speculation for the four applications. We also show good scalability on many/multi-cores – combined with SIMD parallelization, we have up to 95x speedup with 60 cores on an Intel Xeon Phi, and we outperform enumerative execution by an average of 2x.

2. Background

This section provides background on both speculative and enumerative computation methods for FSM parallelization. In addition, we also discuss the key features of the Intel Xeon Phi coprocessor, a commercial release of the Intel Many Integrated Core (MIC) architecture, and the main platform where we conduct our experiments.

2.1 Speculative Computation of FSM

A finite state machine can be represented as a tuple $(Q, \Sigma, q_0, \delta, F)$ where Q is a finite set of states, Σ is a fixed alphabet, $q_0 \in Q$ is the initial state, $F \subset Q$ is the set of final states, and δ is the transition function with type $Q \times \Sigma \rightarrow Q$. We focus on deterministic FSMs – a finite state machine is *deterministic* if given a state and an input character, which cannot be empty, there is only one output state.

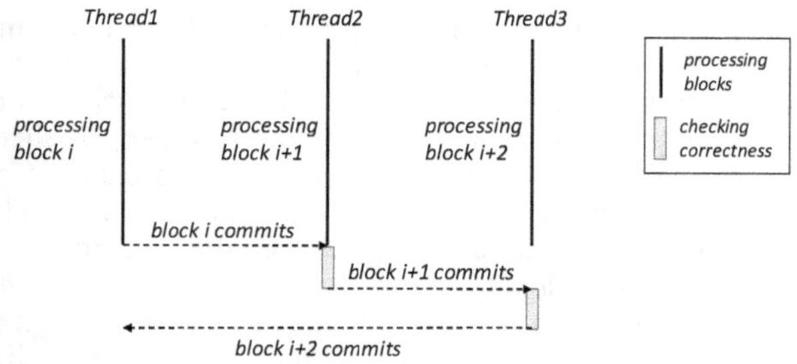

Figure 2: An illustration of speculative computation of FSM

As we stated in the previous section, data dependency is the critical challenge in parallelizing FSM applications. To break the data dependency in state transitions, an intuitive approach is to divide the input data into *blocks*. While one thread is working through a block, another thread can start computing on the next block from what is referred to as a *speculated starting state*. This approach is referred to as *speculative computation* of FSMs [15, 20, 25, 26].

Figure 2 shows an example of speculative computation of FSMs. There are three blocks of input that are processed by three threads. Block i starts from a correct state, while blocks $i+1$ and $i+2$ start from speculated states. When block i finishes the computation, it commits its final state to the block $i+1$. If the speculated starting state of the block $i+1$ is not the same as what block i commits, the computation of the blocks $i+1$ and $i+2$ need to be *rolled back*, and another round of computation for the blocks $i+1$, $i+2$, and $i+3$ will be launched – this time with the block $i+1$ starting from correct state and the other two starting from speculated states. On the other hand, if the guessed starting state of block $i+1$ is identical to what block i commits, then the final state of block $i+1$ is correct and will be committed to the block $i+2$. Now, block $i+2$ repeats the same comparison and so on. If all three blocks are processed successfully, the program will launch another round of computation with the final state of block $i+2$.

The efficiency of the process depends on the success of speculation. Let the size of the *speculation group*, or the number of blocks/threads we attempt concurrent execution on, be denoted by s. Suppose it takes m rounds of execution to finish n iterations, and x_i is the number of iterations computed correctly in the round i. Then, we have, $1 \leq x_i \leq s$, and $\sum_{i=1}^{m} x_i = n$. The best performance is achieved when $x_i = s$ for all iterations, in which case m is the lowest possible, i.e., n/s. The worst case is $m = n$ when all $x_i = 1$. Further, we define the *speculation success rate* α as the number of successful iterations divided by the product of execution rounds and speculation group size, i.e, $\alpha = \frac{\sum_{i=1}^{m} x_i}{s \times m} = \frac{n}{s \times m}$.

2.2 Enumerative Computation of FSMs

As we stated previously, enumerative execution is an alternative to speculative execution. In enumerative execution, instead of computing one state transition, we compute state transitions from every state of the FSM in each iteration. Let $T[c]$ be a state array such that $T[c][i]$ is the state transitioned from state i on the input c. Now, we use $\otimes$ to denote a binary operator such that $i \otimes T[c]$ is $T[c][i]$. Thus, the state transitions in the entire processing of a given string $c_1 c_2 \ldots c_n$ can be represented as a sequence of binary operations:

$$s_{final} = s_{start} \otimes T[c_1] \otimes T[c_2] \ldots \otimes T[c_n]$$

The key idea of enumerative execution is that the binary operator $\otimes$ is associative, and thus, the entire process can be parallelized in the way similar to the parallelization of a prefix sum [2, 13]. A simple implementation involves dividing the input into several blocks and computing $T[c_i] \otimes \ldots \otimes T[c_j]$ for each block concurrently, where c_i and c_j are the start and end character of that block, respectively.

The straightforward implementation described above has a large amount of redundant work, and likely will not deliver speedups in most cases. Mytkowicz *et al.* [17] observed that the states in the enumeration actually converge during the computation. For example, when computing $T[c_i] \otimes \ldots \otimes T[c_j]$, suppose the result of $T[c_i] \ldots \otimes T[c_k] (k < j)$ is S, it is likely that S has a number of *identical states*. Now, only one of these identical states need to be considered in the following computation, i.e, the computation of $T[c_k{+}1] \otimes \ldots \otimes T[c_j]$. Building further on this idea, Mytkowicz *et al.* propose a *convergence detection procedure*, which can be invoked periodically, to reduce the redundant work. More precisely, an interim result S can be factored as a a pair (L, U) such that $S = L \otimes U$ and U contains only the unique elements of S. A consequence of this is that the convergence detection procedure does not impact the associative property of $\otimes$, and thus the correctness of parallelization is maintained.

2.3 SIMD Instructions

Modern (co)processors have a feature where one can apply an operation on several data elements in a single instruction – referred to as SIMD (Single Instruction Multiple Data) parallelism. The basic SIMD operations include loading/storing data elements from consecutive memory addresses, and adding/multiplying a vector of data elements. In order to apply SIMD parallelism to irregular applications, recent architectures have added more flexible SIMD instructions. Most prominently, *gather/scatter* operations load and store data at non-contiguous memory addresses that are specified by an *index vector*. These instructions can allow loading and storing data for irregular applications where non-contiguous accesses are common. The performance of *gather/scatter* is very close to that of (contiguous) SIMD load/store when the elements to be accessed are close to each other [3], but can be significantly slower otherwise.

These gather and scatter instructions are supported on Xeon Phi processors. Unlike the previous SSE (Streaming SIMD Extension) that was supported on Intel CPUs, Intel Xeon Phi coprocessor has a new 512 bit SIMD instruction set referred to as IMCI or Intel Initial Many Core Instructions. In addition to gather and scatter operations, Intel Xeon Phi also supports a *mask* data type and a set of *mask* operations including *mask-read*, *mask-write*, *mask-add*, and *mask-compare*, which are able to apply an operation on a specified subset of lanes within a SIMD vector.

3. Enumerative Speculation

In the last section, we had described the two sets of existing approaches for parallelizing FSMs, i.e., the speculative and the enumerative methods. It turns out that both the methods have their own drawbacks, which we summarize below.

The speculative methods likely have difficulty in guessing the correct starting state even though sophisticated prediction mechanisms have been developed and used. For example, Div7, which we had shown earlier, is an extreme case in the sense that none of its state pairs converge – in other words, state transitions can be considered *input-insensitive*. More precisely, any state in the FSM can be reached with equal probability on a given input string from different starting states. Thus, profiling the FSM cannot determine which state is more likely to be reached without knowledge of the starting state. The prediction techniques, which are typically based on profiling the FSM and training with inputs (online or offline), can very well fail and result in low speedups in this case, as has been acknowledged by certain studies [25]. Also, the normal implementation for a speculation system is either thread or process based, and there are overheads in checking conflicts and rollback for both thread and process implementations. Since the processing of one input character is simply one read operation, the block length needs to be long enough so that most of the processing cycles are spent on computing rather than on checking the conflicts. This, however, implies larger rollback overheads.

The enumerative methods, on the other hand, have the overhead of redundant computations. Every possible state needs to be computed for the next state, making the amount of computation proportional to the number of states in the FSM. When the FSM is large, the computation can be hundreds (or even thousands!) times higher than a straightforward serial implementation. Mytkowicz *et al.* [17] focus on eliminating this redundancy, observing that the states are actually converging during the enumerative computation in many real applications. Exploiting this property, they devise a redundancy checking and elimination procedure that is invoked periodically during the computation. However, the redundancy eliminating procedure can itself be time-consuming because it relies on a *factor* operation that is not supported in architectures currently.

In this section, we first describe our *enumerative speculation* idea that overcomes the drawbacks of both speculation and enumeration by combining them. Next, we show the benefits of enumerative speculation for increasing speculation success rates – we present a simple method to predict starting states that obtains high speculation success rates with enumerative speculation. Moreover, by evaluating enumerative speculation on different types of FSMs, we observe two important properties for parallelizing FSMs: 1) there is a tradeoff between the redundant work and the parallelism (speculation success rate) for FSMs, and 2) the speculation success rate is insensitive to the block size with multiple speculating states.

3.1 Speculating with Multiple Starting States

In speculative parallelization, an unknown variable is usually assigned only one guessed value for execution. Intuitively, if the program tries multiple guessed values for an unknown variable, it is more likely to get a correct speculation, as compared to only trying one guessed value. Based on this simple observation, we propose the concept of *enumerative speculation*. The idea is to speculate with multiple guessed values and select the correct one from the different speculative executions (or rollback when none of them is correct). More specifically, enumerative speculation uses multiple values as the starting state of an input block and executes with each of these guessed values.

Now, enumerative methods can be viewed as an extreme case of enumerative speculation since every state of the FSMs is tried for each input block. The difference is that there is no speculation in enumerative methods because there must be a correct starting state in all of the states of a FSM. Thus, there is no rollback in enumerative methods. Our method, enumerative speculation, has the advantage that the amount of redundant work is reduced. However, like any speculative method, we may be required to rollback. A key enabler to our method work is a simple method to predict starting states. This method, presented in next subsection, can achieve high speculation success rates in FSM applications with no more than 16 guessed states.

We observe that enumerative speculation is well suited for SIMD execution. With 16-way parallelism, we can easily work with multiple different guessed states. Note that the current state-of-the-art is that SIMD lanes are simply unused for an irregular application like FSM. Thus, achieving a factor of 2 or 3 speedup over serial execution will still be a significant improvement.

3.2 Predicting Starting States

Previous studies on speculative execution of FSMs [20, 26] have shown that a *lookback* technique can improve speculation success rate in applications such as Huffman decoding and XML parsing. The idea of a lookback approach is to examine several characters at the end of the preceding block, perform state transition from an arbitrary state on these characters and choose the resulting final state after these transitions as the guessed starting state for the next block. Not surprisingly, this heuristic performs poorly on a FSM with a large number of states and/or if the states do not converge (as is the case with as Div7 – Figure 1a). Zhao *et. al* [26] attribute the inconsistent performance of lookback approach to two factors. First, the length of suffix to examine impacts the performance – a longer suffix usually produces better guessed state but also causes more overheads. Second, the state used for lookback affects the performance – a good state for lookback can lead to correct guess while a bad one does not. Zhao *et. al* [26] introduce an all-state lookback scheme and propose a *principled speculation* approach based on the observation that the likelihoods for different states to be the actual starting state at a speculation point are usually non-uniform. Though their approach effectively improves the performance of speculation in many applications, it incurs more overheads for online and offline learning.

Now, intuitively, enumerative speculation should avoid these problems, since the probability of a successful speculation is the sum of the likelihoods of each state in the set of guessed states to be the actual starting state. We simplify the all-state lookback approach in [26] to produce a set of guessed states that is very likely to contain the correct starting state. Let v_0 be the vector of all states in an FSM and v_i be the vector of resulting states obtained from v_0 on the input character i, i.e., $v_i[j] = T[i][v_0[j]]$, where T is the transition table. We define the likelihood for $v_i[j]$ to be the correct starting state after input character i, denoted as $L_i[j]$, as its frequency of appearance in v_i. More specifically, suppose the number of states in an FSM is m and $v_i[j]$ appears t times in v_i, then $L_i[j] = t/m$. Similarly, suppose the vector of result states transited from v_0 on input characters a and b is v_{ab}, i.e., $v_{ab}[j] = T[b][T[a][v_0[j]]]$. Now, $L_{ab}[j]$, which is the likelihood for $v_{ab}[j]$ to be the correct starting state after

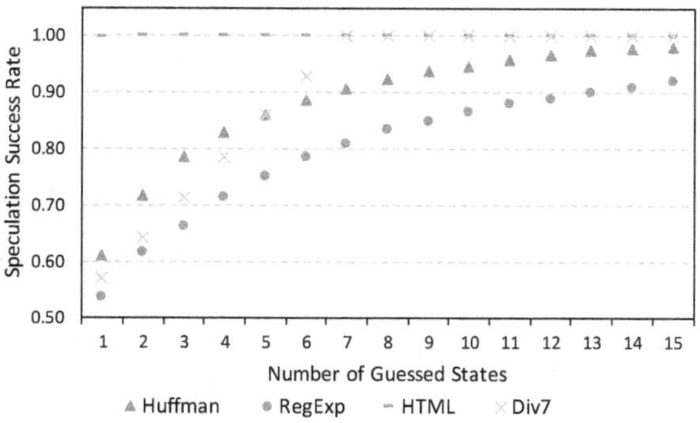

Figure 3: Speculation success rates for four applications: Huffman Decoding, Regular Expression Matching, HTML Tokenization, and Div7 (varying number of guessed states obtained by looking back two input characters)

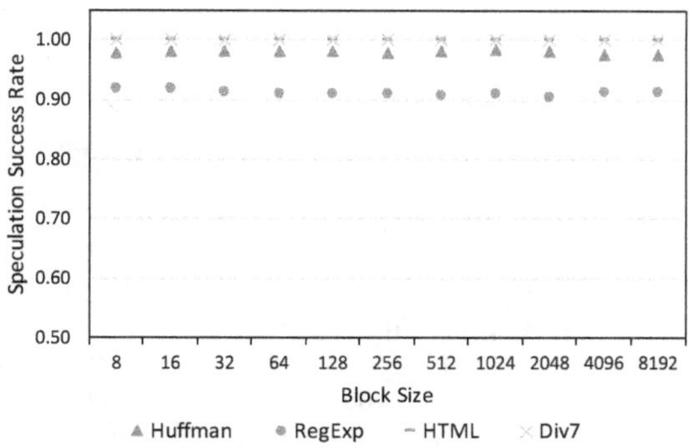

Figure 4: Speculation success rates for four applications: Huffman Decoding, Regular Expression Matching, HTML Tokenization and Div7 (using different block sizes and 15 guessed states)

input character a and b, is p/m, where p is the number of appearance of $v_{ab}[j]$ in v_{ab}.

The single-state speculation approach assumes that the likelihoods for different states to be the correct starting states are non-uniform, so that the most likely one has a high probability of success. In comparison, multiple-state speculation does not require the most likely one to have a high probability. Instead, it assumes that the sum of the few most likely ones have a high probability. Figure 3 shows the speculation success rates of four applications: Huffman decoding (*Huffman*), regular expression matching (*RegExp*), HTML tokenization (*HTML*) and Div7, with different number of guessed states obtained by *lookback-2*, which calculates the likelihoods of states by examining two preceding characters. Here, the number of states is 100+, 200, 38, and 7, respectively, for the four applications. The results show that with only one guessed state, lookback-2 achieves good speculation success rate only for HTML tokenization, and is not effective in the case of the other three applications. Despite the different size of FSMs, the speculation success rates of the other three applications increase as more guessed states are used. All of the four applications achieve speculation success rates of more than 90% when using 15 guessed states.

Figure 4 shows the speculation success rates of four applications running with different block sizes using 15 guessed states produced by lookback-2. We also find that block size has no effect on the speculation success rates, i.e, the set of the 15 states of greatest likelihoods calculated by multiple lookback-2 has a stable and high probability of containing the correct starting state independent of the length of the input characters. These results validate that lookback-2 is effective in achieving good speculation success rates in enumerative speculation.

4. SIMD Implementation of Enumerative Speculation

In this section, we first discuss about how state transitions can be accelerated using SIMD features. Next, we describe a SIMD implementation of enumerative speculation that performs speculation across input blocks. Finally, we discuss an important optimization, which is block size selection.

4.1 SIMD State Transitions

Consider the straightforward FSM implementation shown in Figure 1c. A state is represented by an integer and state transition is implemented by reading a new state from the appropriate position in the transition table (based on the current state and the input character). There are two parts to the computation involved in the process of state transition – the first is the calculation of memory address based on the current state and the input character, and the second is the actual memory access to the transition table based on the calculated address. Assuming we have speculated correctly and are executing different blocks concurrently, the first part can be perfectly parallelized with SIMD and gain speedup proportional to the width of SIMD vector. For example, with a state vector $vstate$, an input vector $vinput$, and a transition table of m states and n input characters as shown in Figure 5, the position of the new state for $vstate[i]$ will be $vinput \times m + vstate$. (assuming characters correspond to the rows and the states correspond to the columns in the transition table).

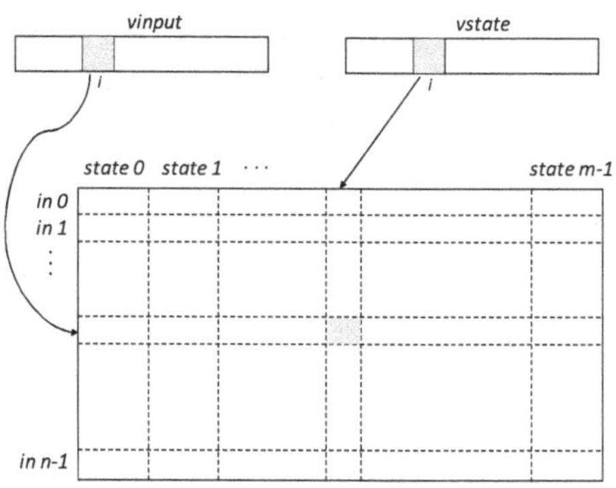

Figure 5: An example of SIMD state transition

The second part, i.e., the actual lookup, can also benefit from SIMD operations. However, the performance now depends on the memory access patterns, as we are loading a set of values using a *gather* operation. To study how this step will perform, we did the following experiment. From the loop we are focusing on, we remove the address calculation part and make the memory accesses to be based only on the current state. In other words, we have a loop that starts from an initial state and uses the current state as the address in an array to access the next state. A version of such a loop,

```
// serial-single version
int x = 0;
for(int i=0;i<N;i++) {
  x = A[x];
}

// SIMD version
__m512i vx = {15,14,…,0};
for(int i=0;i<N;i++) {
  vx = _mm512_i32gather_epi32(vx, A, 4);
}
```

(a)

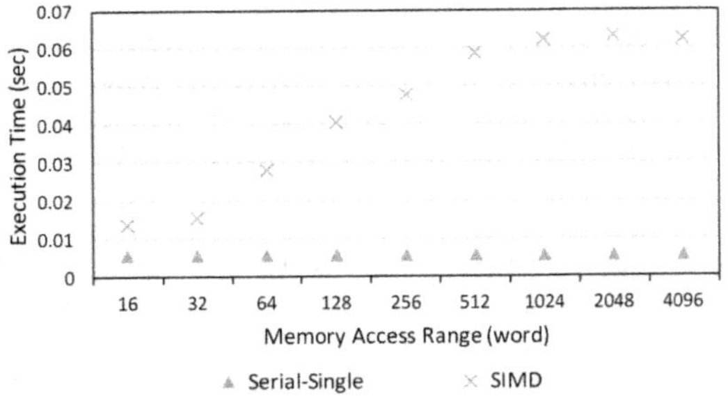

(b)

Figure 6: Three versions of state transition and their execution time with different memory access ranges

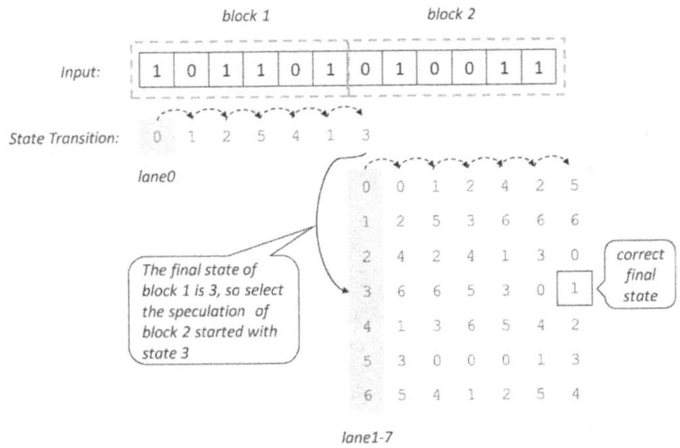

Figure 7: An example of SIMD speculation on FSM for determining if a binary number is divisible by 7

which we refer to as the *serial-single* version, is shown in Figure 6a – here, A is an array of size r comprising random integers ranging from 0 to $r - 1$. The SIMD version of the same loop, also shown in Figure 6a, uses SIMD gather operation to perform state transitions for 16 states in a SIMD vector in each iteration.

Figure 6b shows the running time of these two versions, reporting execution over one million iterations on an Intel Xeon Phi – we vary the *memory access range* for each version. We observe that a SIMD gather is as fast as a single load operation when the memory access range is small. Thus, if multiple state transitions in FSMs can be performed *independently* in SIMD and the memory locality is good, FSMs can be accelerated.

4.2 SIMD Speculation

In the existing research, speculative parallelization of FSMs are executed across cores. In such cases, one speculates with a single guessed state for each block and execution starting with the speculated value is processed by a thread or a process. With SIMD state transition described above, and using our idea of enumerative speculation, one can consider a different approach. We can put the determined state for the block i in the first lane of a SIMD vector and several speculated starting states for the block $i + 1$ in the rest of lanes. In each step, a single state transition for block i is performed in the first lane with correct state on the current input character, while multiple state transitions on block $i+1$ are performed in other lanes with several speculated states, but using the same input character on each. Because there is no dependence among the lanes in the SIMD vector, all this work can be performed simultaneously. After all of the input characters in the block i are processed, the final state of block i is the correct starting state for the block $i + 1$. The program needs to check if the final state of block i is in the set of speculated states for the block $i + 1$, and if so, the program needs to find the lane with the correct speculation.

Figure 7 shows an example of SIMD speculation on the FSM in Figure 1a (the one that determines if binary number 101101010011 is divisible by 7). Assume that the SIMD vector length is 8 and the input binary string is divided into two blocks. The first lane stores the starting state for the block 1, which is known to be 0. The rest of lanes store the speculated starting states for the block 2, which is the set (0, 1, 2, 3, 4, 5, 6). In this example, for simplicity of demonstration, the guessed starting states happen to be all of the states in the FSM, but in most real cases the guessed starting states are obtained using the multiple lookback approach described in Section 3.2. The program processes block 1 and block 2 simultaneously. The state in the first lane will be 1 after reading the bit "1", while the states in the rest of lanes will turn into the set (0, 2, 4, 6, 1, 3, 5) after reading the bit "0". In each iteration, one bit each in block 1 and 2 are processed. The final state of block 1 is 3. So, the correct final state after processing the entire binary number is the final state of block 2 obtained with starting state of 3, which is 1. Therefore, the binary number is not divisible by 7.

The SIMD speculation described above, in which one SIMD vector performs *speculative* state transition for exactly one block, is called *1-way* SIMD speculation. Our idea of enumerative speculation also allows for alternatives to this approach. Specifically, with wide SIMD vectors, it is even possible to divide the vector lanes into more than one *speculation sets*. For example, the first lane can be used for correct execution of the block i, while half of the remaining lanes can be used for the block $i+1$ and the other half used for the block $i + 2$. In this case, three blocks are processed simultaneously, and we call it *2-way* SIMD speculation. Dividing the vector lanes into more than one speculation sets (*k-way* SIMD speculation) provides the opportunity to obtain higher speedup, while also requiring a more complicated logic for checking the correctness of speculation. In the extreme case, a vector of w lanes can perform state transitions for w blocks simultaneously with a single guessed state for each block. This is an extreme case of enumerative speculation, making it identical to simple speculative execution.

4.2.1 Correctness Checking Procedure

We now describe the details of the *correctness checking* procedure for checking the success of speculation. Suppose we are processing block i with a correct state and execution block $i+1$ with a set of speculated states. Let vs be the *starting vector*, i.e., a vector with first element being the actual state for the block i and the remaining elements being the speculated states for the block $i+1$. Similarly, let vf be the *final vector*. Suppose the vector width is w. Now, the correctness checking procedure needs to check if $vf[0]$, which is the final state of block i, is in $vs[1 \ldots w-1]$, which is the set of speculated states for the block $i+1$.

We implement it as follows. Intel MIC architecture supports *mask* data type and SIMD comparison operations. A general approach of correctness checking is to generate a vector with values of $vf[0]$ repeated, and compare it with vs, as shown in Figure 8. The result is a SIMD *mask*, in which each bit indicates whether the corresponding lanes in the two vectors are equal. If all bits (not including the first bit) in the result *mask* are 0, then none of the guessed states is correct. Otherwise, the position of the non-zero bit in the result *mask* is the place of the correct guessed state in vs and the correct final state in vf for the block $i+1$. Though the position can be calculated by $O(w)$ shift operations, an even faster way is to store the positions in an array indexed by the result *mask* and read the value directly from the array.

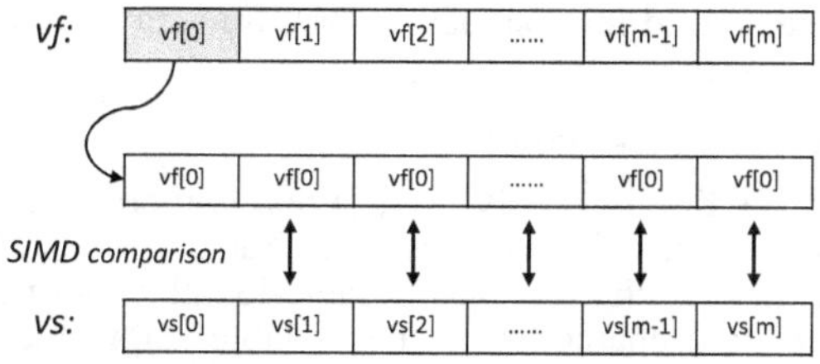

Figure 8: SIMD correctness checking with mask operations

Correctness checking for k-way speculations is similar to that for 1-way speculation. The correctness checking procedure needs to find $vf[0]$, which is the the final state of block i, in the first group of speculation states in vs. If the final state of block i is in the first group, then the corresponding value in vf will be the correct final state of the block $i+1$. With the final state of block $i+1$, the procedure continues to check if the speculation for the block $i+2$ is correct by comparing it with the second group of speculated states. The procedure stops when it finds the first incorrect speculation or if all of the speculations are correct.

4.2.2 Starting A New Speculation

Once the correctness checking procedure determines whether the current round of speculated state has been successful, the program needs to start a new round of speculation. If the speculation for the block $i+1$ is successful, its final state will be available when we are done processing the block i. The next round of speculation will process the block $i+2$ while speculating the block $i+3$ with vs. More specifically, the program will load the final state of the block $i+1$ into the first lane of vs and the guessed states for the block $i+3$ produced by *lookback* into the rest of lanes. If the speculation for the block $i+1$ fails, the program needs to *rollback* and reprocess block $i+1$ with the correct starting state, which is the final state of block i. The program will load the final state

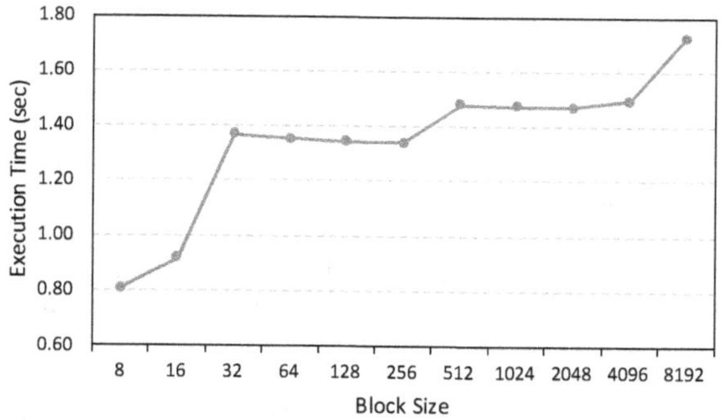

Figure 9: Execution time of reading two consecutive blocks in a text of fixed size simultaneously using SIMD gather with different block sizes

of block i into the first lane of vs and the speculated states for the block $i+2$ in the remaining lanes. The next round of speculation will process the block $i+1$ while speculating the block $i+2$ with vs.

For starting new speculation in k-way speculations, suppose the number of speculation sets in a vector is k, the program needs to load the final state of the last block that is correctly speculated, say block g, into the first lane of vs, and load the guessed states for the next k blocks into the rest of lanes. The next round of speculation will process the block $g+1$ while speculating the blocks $g+2$ to $g+k+1$ with vs.

4.3 Selecting Block Size

Though block size does not change speculation success rates, as shown in Section 3.2, it can impact speculation performance in two ways. First, a small block size can lead to better cache performance when reading input text – this is due to hardware prefetching. Second, as there are overheads of predicting starting states and correctness checking for each block, a larger block size implies fewer blocks and thus lower overheads. Figure 9 shows the running time of a program that simulates reading two consecutive blocks simultaneously, varying block size but keeping the total input size the same. We use SIMD gather on Intel Xeon Phi coprocessor. As the block size increases, the time for reading the entire input text increases, and in fact, the execution with a block size of 8 can be twice as fast as the execution of larger block sizes. However, in our evaluation, the programs using multiple lookback-2 prediction have poor performance with a block size of 8, and the best performance is always achieved with a block size between 1024 to 8192. It is because that the overhead of examining 2 characters out of 8 for predicting starting states outweigh the benefit of better cache performance. In cases where the guessed states are simply assigned in order or selected arbitrarily, there is no overhead for predicting starting states, and the logic for checking correctness is simple, a block size of 8 can always achieve the best performance.

5. MIMD Parallelization

Our discussion in the previous section focused on SIMD implementation. Our enumerative speculation method for FSMs can also easily benefit from many/multi-cores, using multiple threads to process different input blocks. We now describe some of the details of the implementation here.

Since the starting state for the first input block is known, the thread for processing the first input block executes the same way as in a single-threaded implementation. Specifically, the first thread divides the first input block into multiple sub-blocks and applies enumerative speculation as described in Section 3. The starting states for the other input blocks are unknown, so the threads for processing these input blocks need to speculate with multiple starting states. The number of states for speculation is usually the length of a SIMD vector so that multiple state transitions can be done by a single SIMD instruction.

Among the different threads, the speculative execution on multiple input blocks is done in parallel, while the correctness checking is sequential. When the correct final state of the block i is available, the program checks if that state is among the set of speculated states the execution of block $i+1$ started with. If so, the final state of the block $i+1$ is obtained and the program proceeds to the block $i+2$. Otherwise, the program needs to reprocess the block $i+1$ with the correct final state of the block i.

A thread can also aggressively process several input blocks simultaneously with k-way speculations. Specifically, the SIMD lanes can be divided into k groups, with each group storing the speculative states for each input block. For example, on a 16-lane SIMD architecture, 2-way speculation will process two input blocks in one SIMD vector with the first 8 lanes being the speculative states for the block i and the other 8 lanes for the block $i+1$.

6. Evaluation Results

6.1 Applications and Baseline Versions

In this section, we evaluate the effectiveness and efficiency of our enumerative speculation for FSM parallelization using four popular FSM-based applications: Huffman decoding (*Huffman*), regular expression matching (*RegExp*), HTML tokenization (*HTML*), and *Div7*. For each application, we implemented a straightforward serial version, a single-threaded 1-way enumerative speculation version, and several k-way enumerative speculation (k>1) versions for both single core and many-core executions.

In addition, to show the advantages of our approach over (pure) speculation, we implemented a single-state speculation version (`PureSpec`) to compare against single-threaded enumerative speculation (we are not aware of any work applying speculation for combining multi-threaded and SIMD parallelization). The pure speculation versions also perform speculation within SIMD vectors and use the lookback-2 prediction – however, only one SIMD lane is used to process the block with a single speculated state. For example, with 1-way SIMD speculation, enumerative speculation uses the first lane for correct state of block i and all of the remaining lanes to execute with 15 different speculated states for the block $i+1$, while pure speculation uses the first lane for the correct state of block i and the second lane storing one guessed state for block $i+1$.

Next, to show the benefits of our approach over (pure) enumeration, we created a version with convergence optimization (referred to as `EnumConv`), following details from the paper by Mytkowicz *et al.* [17]. This version starts execution with all states in the FSMs, and after a certain number of iterations invokes a convergence checking procedure to eliminate redundant states in execution, and subsequently processes with the remaining *active states*. SIMD instructions are used to perform multiple state transitions to hide the overhead of enumeration. As different applications achieve best performance with convergence checking after different numbers of iterations, this parameter was manually tuned to obtain the best performance for comparing against our approach. For all applications, our comparison against pure speculation is with a single-core execution, whereas comparison against enumeration is on single and multi/many-cores.

Our experiments are conducted on an Intel Xeon Phi SE10P coprocessor which has 61 cores (1.1 GHz) with each core incorporated with 512-bit SIMD units. We use Intel ICC compiler 13.1.0 to compile all the codes with -O3 optimization enabled. For the applications where we experimented with k-way speculation, the vector lanes are divided evenly into k groups. For example, with 2-way speculation, the vector lanes are divided as 1-8-7 on single core, which means the first lane processes with the correct state, the following eight lanes process the next block with eight different speculated values, and the remaining seven lanes process yet another block with seven different speculated states for the second speculation. For 2-way speculation with multi/many-cores, the vector lanes are simply divided as 8-8. For higher values of k, vector lanes are divided as 1-5-5-5 in 3-way SIMD speculation and as 1-3-2-2-2-2-2-2 in 7-way speculation on single core, and divided as 6-5-5 in 3-way and 3-3-2-2-2-2-2 in 7-way with multi/many-core execution. The extreme case is single-core 15-way SIMD speculation where each lane is used for conducting state transition on a different input block.

6.2 Huffman Decoding

Huffman coding is widely used in text compression. It utilizes non-uniform frequencies of characters found in texts and encodes the characters to variable-length bit strings. The mapping from characters to the variable-length bit strings is obtained by the *Huffman encoding procedure*, which is a greedy algorithm that builds a Huffman tree. Huffman decoding, which is the reverse process of Huffman encoding, interprets the bit strings back to the characters based on the Huffman tree – this process is very similar to the process of executing state transitions in an FSM. Thus, we have experimented with the decoding part of this method. The input texts we use are from the most downloaded books from the Project Gutenberg[1]. Table 1 lists the names of the downloaded text files and the number of states in their corresponding FSMs built by Huffman encoding. The number in the filename is the index of that book on the website.

File Name	Number of States in FSM
76.txt.utf-8	179
50247.txt.utf-8	203
98.txt.utf-8	177
74.txt.utf-8	179

Table 1: Input texts used in evaluating Huffman decoding with the number of states in their corresponding FSM built by Huffman encoding

Figure 10 shows the execution time of a straightforward serial implementation (`Serial`) and three versions that use SIMD lanes. These three versions are 1-way enumerative

[1] `http://www.gutenberg.org/`

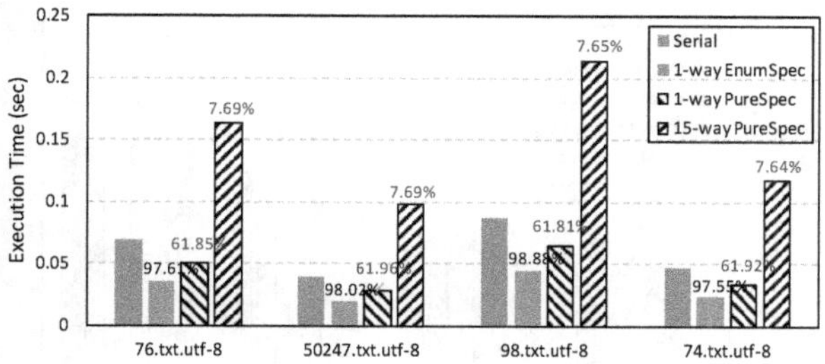

Figure 10: Execution time of different versions of Huffman decoding on a single core (raw numbers are the speculation success rate)

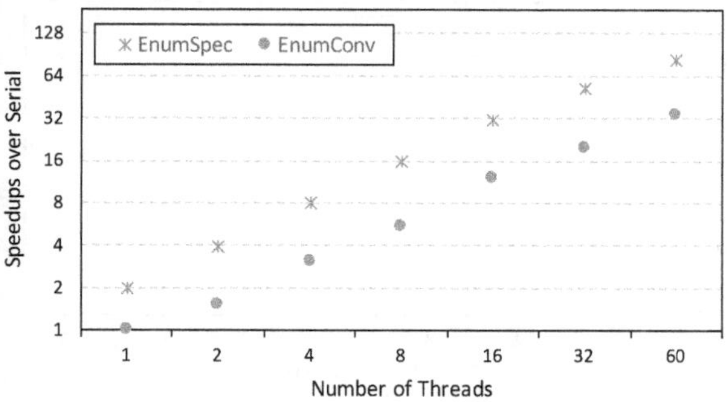

Figure 11: Speedups over serial code – Huffman decoding with 2-way speculation and pure enumeration

speculation version (`EnumSpec`), a 1-way pure speculation version (`PureSpec`) (which uses only 2 SIMD lanes) and a 15-way pure speculation. We did not use k-way speculation as it had lower performance. Also, comparison against enumeration will be reported later. The speculation success rates of each execution, calculated as in Section 2.1, are also labeled on the top of each column. The 1-way enumerative speculation reaches 2x speedup over serial version on all of the input texts. The 1-way pure speculation has a lower success rate, and thus, runs slower than 1-way enumerative speculation. The 15-way runs even much slower than the serial code because the prediction of speculative states incurs overheads while the speculation success rate with lookback-2 is quite low.

For evaluating many-core performance, we use a 100 MB input text so that the input block per core is large enough to justify the cost of invoking more threads. We implemented a multi-threaded version (`EnumSpec`) with 2-way speculation (each thread processes two input blocks simultaneously) and lookback-4 prediction (looking back four preceding characters) – this combination had the best performance among all options. Figure 11 shows the speedups of multi-threaded 2-way enumerative speculation (and 1-way enumerative speculation with a single core). Both x and y-axis in the figure are formatted as base-2 logarithmic scale. The multi-threaded 2-way enumerative speculation reaches 99.99% speculation success rate with lookback-4 prediction. It has linear speedups with increasing number of cores and can achieve $2n$ times speedup with n cores over the serial code. We also see that `EnumConv` also has a near-linear speedup with increasing number of cores, but is slower than our approach by a factor of 2.

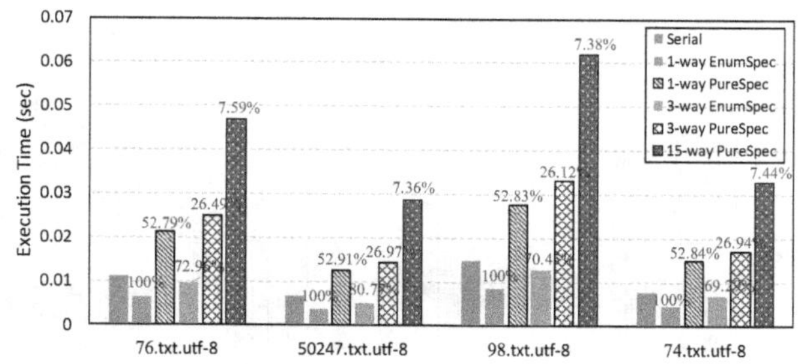

(a) Results for regular expression$(.*l.*i.*k.*e)|(.*a.*p.*p.*l.*e)$

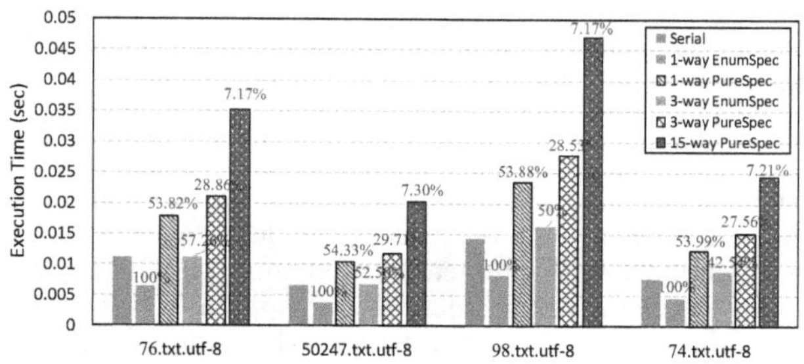

(b) Results for regular expression $(.+,.+\backslash.)^4|(.+,)^4|(.+\backslash.)^4$

Figure 12: Execution times of different versions of Regular Expression Matching

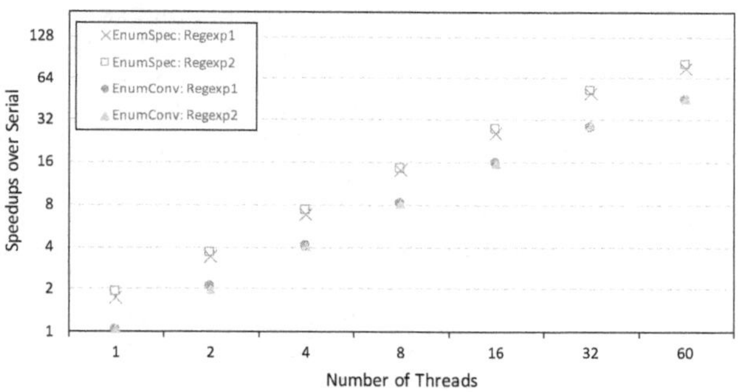

Figure 13: Speedups over serial code for regular expression matching – 4-way speculation and pure enumeration

6.3 Regular Expression Matching

The application we experimented with reads in a text file and searches for all the strings that matches a given pattern. Once a match is found, the program outputs the position of the match in the text file. For comparisons on a single core, we implemented enumerative speculation and pure speculation versions – both 1-way and 3-way – as well as a 15-way pure speculation. The input texts we use here are the same as in Huffman decoding (listed earlier in Table 1). We test the performance with two regular expressions: "$(.*l.*i.*k.*e)|(.*a.*p.*p.*l.*e)$" and "$(.+,.+\backslash.)^4|(.+,)^4|(.+\backslash.)^4$", which are used also by Zhao *et al.* [26]. The "." in the patterns represents any character, "\." represents the period, and the superscripts indicates repetitions.

The results with two regular expressions are shown in Figures 12a and 12b, respectively. The 1-way enumerative speculation has a 100% success rate and reaches 1.73x speedup over the serial version with both regular expressions. In comparison, 1-way pure speculation has a much

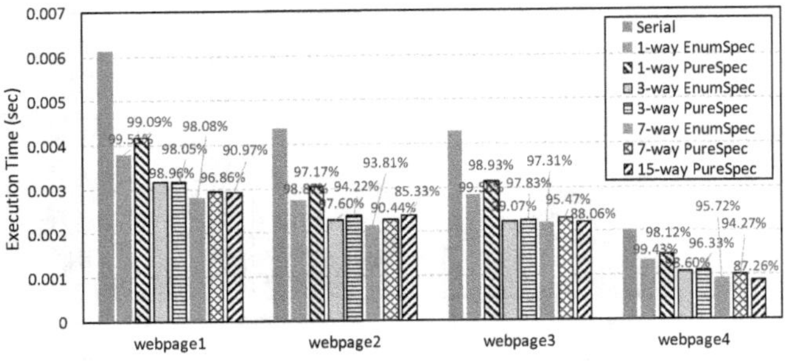

Figure 14: Execution times of different versions of HTML tokenization on a single core

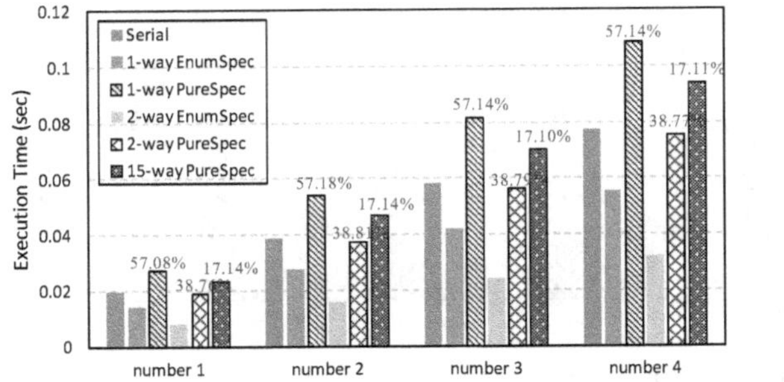

Figure 15: Execution time of different versions of Div7 on a single core

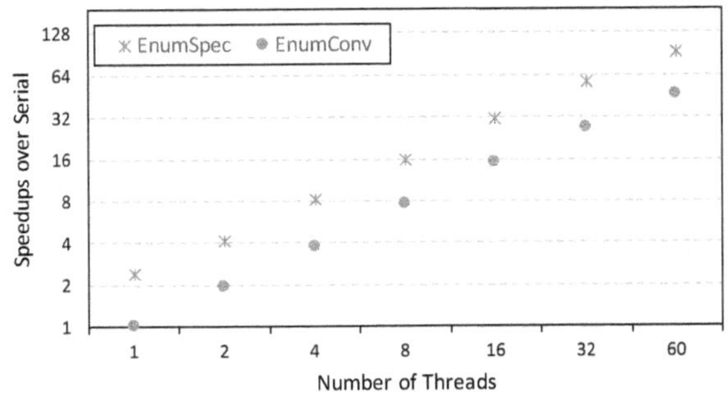

Figure 16: Speedups over serial code – Div7 with 2-way speculation and pure enumeration

lower success rate (53%) and runs even slower than the serial code. The speculation success rate decreases with 3-way speculation for both enumerative and pure speculation. With 3-way enumerative speculation, our approach still outperforms the serial code on the first regular expression, and is slightly slower than the serial code on the second regular expression. The 15-way pure speculation has the worst performance among all of the six versions due to a low speculation success rate.

For evaluating performance on many-cores, we implemented a multi-threaded version (`EnumSpec`) with 2-way speculation (each thread processes two input blocks simultaneously) and lookback-2 prediction. We match the two regular expressions above with a 1GB input text. Figure 13 shows the speedups (for 1-core execution, we use 1-way enumerative speculation). With lookback-2, the multi-threaded 2-way enumerative speculation reaches 100% speculation success rate on both regular expressions. The results show that our approach scales well on many-cores, and we achieve at least $1.6n$ times speedup with n cores over the serial code. The speedups of pure enumeration is near linear on many-cores, but is also a factor slower than our approach due to weak performance on a single core.

6.4 HTML Tokenization

HTML tokenization is widely used in web browsers and web crawlers to extract HTML tokens. Our implementation uses a FSM with 38 states, and the texts used in our evaluation are web pages from New York Times website. For single core performance comparisons, We also implement single-threaded 1-way, 3-way, 7-way, and 15-way SIMD speculation versions.

Figure 14 shows the running time of the different versions on a single core, using different web pages. The 1-way enumerative speculation has 1.5x to 1.6x speedup over the serial version. The speculation success rates in 3-way and 7-way progressively decrease as fewer number of lanes are used for each speculation, but the program runs faster as more input blocks are processed simultaneously. The pure speculation versions have lower speedups due to slightly lower speculation success rates. The success rates of pure speculation turn out to be close to those of enumerative speculation because the states tend to converge to the state 0, and thus, prediction is easy. The performance of 7-way enumerative speculation is the best for most inputs, achieving 1.96x to 2.21x speedups over serial code. The 15-way pure speculation, which uses only one guessed state for each input block, still keeps high speculation success rates (about 90%) and achieves a comparable speedup with enumerative speculation. Note that for this application, we do not evaluate the performance of HTML tokenization on many-cores because webpages are usually small (less than 1 MB).

6.5 Div7

The FSM that Div7 uses was shown earlier in Figure 1a. Though there are only seven states in the FSM, it is hard to predict the starting state for a given block. However, with our enumerative speculation, it is easy to put all the states to a SIMD vector (of length 8 or 16), and the speculation success rate of 100% is easily obtained. We implement a serial version similar to Figure 1c as the baseline, and single-threaded 1-way and 2-way enumerative and pure speculation for comparison. The binary numbers given to the programs are randomly generated, and are of varying length.

Figure 15 shows the running time of the six versions on a single core of Intel Xeon Phi. The 1-way enumerative speculation has 1.85x speedup over serial version, whereas 2-way enumerative speculation achieves speedups up to 2.45x. Both 1-way and 2-way enumerative speculation have guaranteed success rate of 100%. The corresponding pure speculation versions have much lower speculation success rates and poor performance.

To evaluate many-core performance, we implemented a multi-threaded 2-way speculation (each thread process two input blocks simultaneously) version (`EnumSpec`) and a pure enumeration version with convergence optimization (`EnumConv`). Since the FSM has only 7 states which can fit in the 16 lanes of SIMD vector, there is actually no speculation in "2-way speculation". Also, since the FSM does not converge, there is also no convergence optimization in the enumeration. The only difference between our 2-way speculation and the pure enumeration is that our method takes full advantage of the 16 lanes in a SIMD vector for processing two input blocks simultaneously. Figure 16 shows the speedups of Div7 brought by our speculation approach and pure enumeration approach over serial code. It shows that our approach scales well on many-cores and achieves $1.6n$ to $2n$ times speedup with n cores, while the pure enumeration version is slower than our approach by a factor of 2.

7. Related Work

There has been a lot of work on accelerating irregular applications on various parallel platforms, including multi-core machines, GPUs, as well as vector instruction sets. Because of the very large volume of work in this area, this section summarizes closely related efforts on accelerating FSMs (which are one type of irregular applications), and the efforts on mapping irregular applications on the modern SIMD hardware.

Enumerative Methods for FSM As described in Section 2.2, the basic idea here is to apply parallel prefix sum algorithm [2, 6, 13]. However, the challenge is the large amount of redundant work. Several optimizations [7, 17, 18] are proposed to reduce the amount of redundant work. Pan *et al.* [18] construct a powerset of a FSM, which implicitly eliminates the redundant states, to emulate the enumerative computation. As the entire powerset needs to be constructed statically, and the number of states in the powerset can be extremely large, their approach is limited. Holub *et al.* [7] present an optimized implementation based on the assumption that FSM is *k-local*, i.e., any two states in the FSM converge to the same state on any input of length k. However, more recently, Mytkowicz *et al.* [17] have shown that most FSMs seen in practice are not k-local. Instead, their conclusion is that that states in most FSMs converge to no more than 16 distinct states after a certain length of input, and their work includes a periodical convergence checking technique to eliminate the redundancy. They also exploit both SIMD and MIMD units on processor to accelerate the computation, though use of SIMD is limited to gathering inputs only. We have compared our work against an implementation of the technique described in their paper, and shown that we outperform them because of better utilization of SIMD lanes.

Speculative Methods for FSM Speculation is a common strategy to break dependence in computation. Klein *et al.* [12] present a speculative parallelization of Huffman decoding. Luchaup *et al.* [15] propose a speculative parallelization of regular expression matching. Prabhu *et al.* [20] show that a lookback approach can be helpful to predict the starting state in FSMs. Zhao *et al.* [26], however, argue that a simple fixed length lookback approach is not always sufficient. They propose a *principled speculation method* that pre-analyzes FSMs to get the application-specific information and use this information in a probabilistic model. They further propose an *on-the-fly* principled speculation technique [25] to remove the overheads of offline training. Both the efforts still require that the states in an FSM are likely to converge. Also, all of these efforts use multi-threading or multi-processing, and not SIMD. We have implemented speculation on SIMD hardware and demonstrated that our method, enumerative speculation, performs better. More recently, Qiu *et al.* [21] provide a rigorous analysis among three types of parallelism that can be exposed at the fine-grain level for FSMs. Though they discuss using SIMD to conduct multiple speculations, the tradeoff between redundant work and parallelism is not explored in their work.

SIMD Acceleration for Irregular Applications Pennycook *et al.* implemented *Moldyn* on the Xeon Phi, using both MIMD and SIMD parallelism [19]. This is a very initial investigation, using a relatively straight-forward implementation specific to a single application. Saule and Catalyurek [23] provided a preliminary evaluation on graph applications on the Xeon Phi architecture, but without particular optimizations specific to the applications and the hardware. Liu *et al.* [14] used ELLPACK sparse block format, to optimize SpMV kernel on the Intel MIC. Similarly, Tang *et al.* [24] utilized a hybrid storage format with jagged partitioning to optimize SpMV, also for the Intel MIC. Kim *et al.* [11] compile irregular application to use SIMD features of the Cell processor, with vector units that do not support modern SIMD operations such as *gather/scatter*. More recently, Chen *et al.* [3, 9] proposed a tiling-and-grouping approach that improves the data locality and applies SIMD processing in a series of applications including graph algorithms, irregular reduction, molecular interaction and matrix multiplication.

There have been several studies mapping irregular applications to SIMT processing on GPUs. For example, Merrill *et al.* [16] parallelized breadth-first search on the GPUs by focusing on fine-grained task management, and CuSha [10] optimizes graph processing on GPUs with intensive usage of shared memory and by re-organizing the graph data in shards.

8. Conclusions

This paper has presented a novel enumerative speculation method for parallelizing FSM applications. Instead of speculating on a single state, this approach uses multiple states as guessed starting states to achieve higher speculation success rates. We also describe a lookback approach for generating the set of guessed states and show that the approach is efficient and effective. We focus on parallelizing using SIMD instruction sets, as multiple state transitions can be performed simultaneously on different lanes of SIMD vectors, and in combining SIMD processing with multi/many-cores. Our experiments validate that the enumerative speculation method has higher speculation success rates than pure speculation using the same prediction method. The comparison of different versions of SIMD speculation on a single core shows that our approach achieves 2.2x to 2.5x speedups over the serial code and an average 1.6x speedup over the best pure speculation code. Comparison between enumerative speculation and pure enumeration over many/multi-cores shows good scalability of our approach and an average 2x speedup over pure enumeration.

Acknowledgements

This work was supported by NSF award CCF-1526386.

References

[1] K. Asanovic, R. Bodik, J. Demmel, T. Keaveny, K. Keutzer, J. Kubiatowicz, N. Morgan, D. Patterson, K. Sen, J. Wawrzynek, D. Wessel, and K. Yelick. A view of the

parallel computing landscape. *Commun. ACM*, 52(10):56–67, Oct. 2009. ISSN 0001-0782. doi: 10.1145/1562764.1562783.

[2] G. E. Blelloch. Prefix Sums and Their Applications. Technical Report CMU-CS-90-190, School of Computer Science, Carnegie Mellon University, Nov. 1990.

[3] L. Chen, P. Jiang, and G. Agrawal. Exploiting Recent SIMD Architectural Advances for Irregular Applications. In *Proceedings of the 2016 International Symposium on Code Generation and Optimization*, CGO 2016, 2016.

[4] F. Franchetti and M. Puschel. A SIMD Vectorizing Compiler for Digital Signal Processing Algorithms. In *Proceedings of the 2002 IEEE International Parallel and Distributed Processing Symposium (IPDPS 2002)*, pages 20 –26. IEEE, 2002.

[5] C. Garca, R. Lario, M. Prieto, L. Piuel, and F. Tirado. Vectorization of Multigrid Codes Using SIMD ISA Extensions. *Proceedings of the 2003 IEEE Inernational Parallel and Distributed Processing Symposium (IPDPS 2003)*, 0:58a, 2003.

[6] W. D. Hillis and G. L. Steele, Jr. Data Parallel Algorithms. *Commun. ACM*, 29(12), Dec. 1986.

[7] J. Holub and S. Štekr. On Parallel Implementations of Deterministic Finite Automata. In *Proceedings of the 14th International Conference on Implementation and Application of Automata*, CIAA '09, 2009.

[8] N. Ide, M. Hirano, Y. Endo, S. Yoshioka, H. Murakami, A. Kunimatsu, T. Sato, T. Kamei, T. Okada, and M. Suzuoki. 2.44-GFLOPS 300-MHz Floating-Point Vector-Processing Unit for High-Performance 3D Graphics Computing. *IEEE Journal of Solid-State Circuits*, 35(7):1025 –1033, Jul 2000.

[9] P. Jiang, L. Chen, and G. Agrawal. Reusing data reorganization for efficient simd parallelization of adaptive irregular applications. In *Proceedings of the 2016 International Conference on Supercomputing*, ICS '16, 2016.

[10] F. Khorasani, K. Vora, R. Gupta, and L. N. Bhuyan. CuSha: Vertex-centric Graph Processing on GPUs. In *Proceedings of the 23rd International Symposium on High-performance Parallel and Distributed Computing*, HPDC '14, 2014.

[11] S. Kim and H. Han. Efficient simd code generation for irregular kernels. In *Proceedings of the 17th ACM SIGPLAN Symposium on Principles and Practice of Parallel Programming*, PPoPP '12, pages 55–64, New York, NY, USA, 2012. ACM. ISBN 978-1-4503-1160-1. doi: 10.1145/2145816.2145824. URL `http://doi.acm.org/10.1145/2145816.2145824`.

[12] S. T. Klein and Y. Wiseman. Parallel Huffman Decoding with Applications to JPEG Files. *THE COMPUTER JOURNAL*, 46:487–497, 2003.

[13] R. E. Ladner and M. J. Fischer. Parallel prefix computation. *J. ACM*, 27(4), Oct. 1980.

[14] X. Liu, M. Smelyanskiy, E. Chow, and P. Dubey. Efficient Sparse Matrix-vector Multiplication on x86-based Many-core Processors. ICS '13, 2013.

[15] D. Luchaup, R. Smith, C. Estan, and S. Jha. Speculative Parallel Pattern Matching. *IEEE Transactions on Information Forensics and Security*, 6(2):438–451, June 2011.

[16] D. Merrill, M. Garland, and A. Grimshaw. Scalable gpu graph traversal. In *Proceedings of the 17th ACM SIGPLAN Symposium on Principles and Practice of Parallel Programming*, PPoPP '12, pages 117–128, New York, NY, USA, 2012. ACM. ISBN 978-1-4503-1160-1. doi: 10.1145/2145816.2145832. URL `http://doi.acm.org/10.1145/2145816.2145832`.

[17] T. Mytkowicz, M. Musuvathi, and W. Schulte. Data-parallel finite-state machines. In *Proceedings of the 19th International Conference on Architectural Support for Programming Languages and Operating Systems*, ASPLOS '14, pages 529–542, New York, NY, USA, 2014. ACM. ISBN 978-1-4503-2305-5.

[18] Y. Pan, Y. Zhang, and K. Chiu. Simultaneous Transducers for Data-Parallel XML Parsing. In *Parallel and Distributed Processing, 2008. IPDPS 2008. IEEE International Symposium on*, pages 1–12, 2008.

[19] S. J. Pennycook, C. J. Hughes, M. Smelyanskiy, and S. A. Jarvis. Exploring simd for molecular dynamics, using intel xeon processors and intel xeon phi coprocessors. In *Proceedings of the 2013 IEEE 27th International Symposium on Parallel and Distributed Processing*, IPDPS '13, 2013.

[20] P. Prabhu, G. Ramalingam, and K. Vaswani. Safe Programmable Speculative Parallelism. In *Proceedings of Programming Language Design and Implementation (PLDI)*. Association for Computing Machinery, Inc., June 2010.

[21] J. Qiu, Z. Zhao, and B. Ren. Microspec: Speculation-centric fine-grained parallelization for fsm computations. In *Proceedings of the 2016 International Conference on Parallel Architectures and Compilation*, PACT '16, pages 221–233, New York, NY, USA, 2016. ACM. ISBN 978-1-4503-4121-9. doi: 10.1145/2967938.2967965. URL `http://doi.acm.org/10.1145/2967938.2967965`.

[22] T. Rognes and E. Seeberg. Six-Fold Speed-up of Smithwaterman Sequence Database Searches Using Parallel Processing on Common Microprocessors. 16(8):699–706, 2000.

[23] E. Saule and U. V. Catalyurek. An early evaluation of the scalability of graph algorithms on the intel mic architecture. In *Proceedings of the 2012 IEEE 26th International Parallel and Distributed Processing Symposium Workshops & PhD Forum*, IPDPSW '12, pages 1629–1639, Washington, DC, USA, 2012. IEEE Computer Society. ISBN 978-0-7695-4676-6. doi: 10.1109/IPDPSW.2012.204. URL `http://dx.doi.org/10.1109/IPDPSW.2012.204`.

[24] W. T. Tang, R. Zhao, M. Lu, Y. Liang, H. P. Huynh, X. Li, and R. S. M. Goh. Optimizing and Auto-tuning Scale-free Sparse Matrix-vector Multiplication on Intel Xeon Phi. In *Proceedings of the 13th Annual IEEE/ACM International Symposium on Code Generation and Optimization*, CGO '15, 2015.

[25] Z. Zhao and X. Shen. On-the-Fly Principled Speculation for FSM Parallelization. *SIGARCH Comput. Archit. News*, 43(1), Mar. 2015.

[26] Z. Zhao, B. Wu, and X. Shen. Challenging the "Embarrassingly Sequential": Parallelizing Finite State Machine-based Computations Through Principled Speculation. *SIGPLAN Not.*, 2014.

A. Artifact Description

A.1 Abstract

The artifact includes all of the programs that are needed to reproduce the evaluation results in the paper. The programs should be executed on an Intel Xeon Phi SE10P coprocessor with 61 cores. An Intel ICC compiler is required for compiling. Python is also require for executing the scripts that generate some of the inputs. The artifact will print out the execution time of different versions of the evaluated applications on different datasets, which can be expected to be close to the results reports. The artifact will also print out the speculation success rates of different versions of applications, and the rates should be exactly the same as reported in the paper.

A.2 Description

A.2.1 Check-list (artifact meta information)

- **Program:** (1) Huffman decoding, (2) Regular expression matching, (3) HTML tokenization, (4) Div7, each stored in a separate directory with different versions
- **Compilation:** Intel ICC compiler 13.1.0
- **Datasets:** four text files, four webpages, and two python scripts that generate some inputs, all included in the artifact
- **Hardware:** an Intel Xeon Phi SE10P coprocessor with 61 cores
- **Output:** program results including the execution time are printed out to the console
- **Experiment workflow:** a bash script is provided to automatically start the compilation and execution, or simply run every version of every application individually
- **Publicly available?:** Yes

A.2.2 How delivered

The artifact is publicly available at `https://github.com/jiangohiostate/ppopp17_artifact.git`. The initial package is about 4MB. After all datasets are generated, it consumes about 1.2GB disk space.

A.2.3 Hardware dependencies

An Intel Xeon Phi SE10P coprocessor with 61 cores is required.

A.2.4 Software dependencies

Intel ICC compiler 13.1.0 and Python2.x are required.

A.2.5 Datasets

All datasets are included in the package, or can be generated by the scripts in the package.

A.3 Installation

In each of the four directories, there is a 'run.sh' script, which builds the programs, generates the inputs, and run the tests automatically. You can also compile the programs with the Makefile that provided in each directory.

A.4 Experiment workflow

There are three steps to conduct the experiments:

1) Compile the programs. This can be done by make in each of the four directories in the package.

2) Generate the input data. The small input files are already included in the package, while the large ones are generated by python scripts, which reside in the 'datasets' subdirectory of each application's directory. The data will be generated by executing the scripts as "python gen_data.py".

3) Execute the programs. Each of the application has a baseline named 'serial', several single-core versions named 'enumspec*/purespec*' and two multi-core versions named 'enumspec_mimd/enumconv_mimd' (except for HTML tokenization). The programs are executed with command line arguments that specify the input files and number of cores to be used. Detailed usage can be found in the 'run.sh' script in the directory.

Alternative to the above three steps, you can simply execute the 'run.sh' script in each directory. It will automatically compile the programs, generate the inputs, and execute the programs.

A.5 Evaluation and expected result

The execution time of the programs will be printed out in the console, and they should be very close to those reported in the paper. The programs will also print out the final state of the FSM, which should be the same for different versions of an application given the same input. It can verify the correctness of the different versions.

The speculation success rates are also printed out, and they should be the same as reported in the paper.

A.6 Notes

Intel Xeon Phi SE10P is a coprocessor. The 'run.sh' scripts in the package assume you have logged in the coprocessor, so that the binaries can be directly executed in the bash.

Submission and reviewing methodology: `http://cTuning.org/ae/submission-20161020.html`

S-Caffe: Co-designing MPI Runtimes and Caffe for Scalable Deep Learning on Modern GPU Clusters

Ammar Ahmad Awan
Dept. of Computer Science and Engg. The Ohio State University
awan.10@osu.edu

Khaled Hamidouche
Dept. of Computer Science and Engg. The Ohio State University
hamidouc@cse.ohio-state.edu

Jahanzeb Maqbool Hashmi
Dept. of Computer Science and Engg. The Ohio State University
hashmi.29@osu.edu

Dhabaleswar K. Panda
Dept. of Computer Science and Engg.
The Ohio State University
panda@cse.ohio-state.edu

Abstract

Availability of large data sets like ImageNet and massively parallel computation support in modern HPC devices like NVIDIA GPUs have fueled a renewed interest in Deep Learning (DL) algorithms. This has triggered the development of DL frameworks like Caffe, Torch, TensorFlow, and CNTK. However, most DL frameworks have been limited to a single node. In order to scale out DL frameworks and bring HPC capabilities to the DL arena, we propose, S-Caffe; a scalable and distributed Caffe adaptation for modern multi-GPU clusters. With an in-depth analysis of new requirements brought forward by the DL frameworks and limitations of current communication runtimes, we present a co-design of the Caffe framework and the MVAPICH2-GDR MPI runtime. Using the co-design methodology, we modify Caffe's workflow to maximize the overlap of computation and communication with multi-stage data propagation and gradient aggregation schemes. We bring DL-Awareness to the MPI runtime by proposing a hierarchical reduction design that benefits from CUDA-Aware features and provides up to a massive 133x speedup over OpenMPI and 2.6x speedup over MVAPICH2 for 160 GPUs. S-Caffe successfully scales up to 160 K-80 GPUs for GoogLeNet (ImageNet) with a speedup of 2.5x over 32 GPUs. To the best of our knowledge, this is the first framework that scales up to 160 GPUs. Furthermore, even for single node training, S-Caffe shows an improvement of 14% and 9% over Nvidia's optimized Caffe for 8 and 16 GPUs, respectively. In addition, S-Caffe achieves up to 1395 samples per second for the AlexNet model, which is comparable to the performance of Microsoft CNTK.

Keywords MPI_Reduce; CUDA-Aware MPI; Caffe; Deep Learning; Distributed Training

PPoPP '17 Feb. 4–8, 2017, Austin, Texas, USA.

DOI: http://dx.doi.org/10.1145/3018743.3018769

1. Introduction

We are witnessing the era of rapid advances in Artificial Intelligence (AI) fueled by the resurgence of Deep Learning (DL) algorithms and techniques. With widespread applications like Image Recognition, Speech Processing, Textual Analysis, Breast Cancer Detection [49], and Self Driving cars [11], DL has become one of the hottest topics of interest for both academic research groups as well as prominent companies like Google, Baidu, Facebook, and Microsoft. There are two main driving forces behind the momentum that DL has recently gained; first is the public availability of versatile training data sets like ImageNet [25] and CIFAR [35], and second is the affordability of modern high-performance and data-parallel hardware like GPUs and accelerators. This has triggered the development and adoption of DL frameworks like Caffe [33], Torch [21], Theano [17], TensorFlow [14], and Microsoft CNTK [12]. Research efforts from DL and AI communities have been mostly geared towards designing better, bigger, and deeper neural networks (DNN) for improving the accuracy of trained models like AlexNet [36], CaffeNet [7], GoogLeNet [45], Network in Network [38], and VGG [44]. While these models differ in their science and the order of computational layers, they commonly share the need for faster computation and communication capabilities of the system they run on.

At the heart of the Deep Learning resurgence, accelerators like NVIDIA GPUs have seen a phenomenal adoption by the community to accelerate parallel training. Interestingly, GPUs are increasingly becoming popular in the HPC community as well. This is evident from the Top500 [40] supercomputers list where 22% of top 50 systems are GPU based. Due to their high throughput support and an architecture designed specifically for data parallel workloads, GPUs are considered a very good match for DL computational requirements. As a matter of fact, the operations involved in training a DL model have a very high arithmetic intensity [9, 20] thereby making GPU hardware a great match. Thus, most of the DL frameworks including Caffe, TensorFlow, CNTK, and various others are being designed to take advantage of the GPU capabilities. Using NVIDIA's Compute Unified Device Architecture (CUDA) [43] API, these frameworks boost their scale-up (single address space) efficiency using threads to utilize multiple GPUs in a single node [16]. However, the performance of single-node multi-GPU training is nearing saturation for large DL data sets and models as highlighted in Section 3. Thus, scale-out (distributed address space) efficiency for DL frameworks is an emerging requirement. The importance of training for DL frameworks has been stressed by many in the DL community. In particular, Jeffrey Dean from Google highlights in his keynote address [32]: *"training time is a key challenge at the root of the development of new DNN architectures."*

Thus, to develop distributed training support for DL frameworks, we first need to understand and utilize prevalent parallelization approaches for distributed-memory HPC clusters. We can clearly see that in the HPC world, Message Passing Interface (MPI) is perhaps the most popular and widely used parallel programming model for developing large-scale applications. Furthermore, MPI runtimes themselves have witnessed rapid changes and optimizations with the advent of GPUs and accelerators. As the CUDA API matured, several features like Unified Virtual Addressing (UVA) have led MPI researchers to propose the "CUDA-Aware" concept. The idea is to transparently provide support for GPU-based data transfers within and across cluster nodes. Several MPI implementations like MVAPICH2 [41], OpenMPI [47], and CrayMPI [22] now provide efficient CUDA-Aware support. This support includes direct transfer of data from the GPU's (device) memory to improve performance of GPU-GPU communication using techniques like CUDA IPC, GPUDirect RDMA [8], and pipelining. This achieves better performance and programmability for hybrid MPI+CUDA applications. In this context, a lot of traditional HPC applications have been successfully redesigned to scale-out using a hybrid programming model mixing MPI and CUDA [15, 18]. In such cases, CUDA is used to offload computation to the GPU device while MPI is responsible for inter-processes communication. However, most of the current DL frameworks have not been designed with such CUDA-Aware (MPI+CUDA) techniques.

Along with the broad challenge of *efficiently scaling-out a DL framework to take advantage of HPC resources*, we highlight the following design challenges that need to be addressed in order to provide a scalable and efficient DL framework:

- What are the performance and portability bottlenecks when moving from a shared address space DL framework to a distributed address space environment for a data-parallel design?
- How to design a scalable and distributed framework that provides both efficient scale-up performance for a single node and scale-out performance for multiple nodes in a distributed manner?
- What are the new requirements that DL frameworks bring forward for distributed communication runtimes?
- Can co-design of MPI runtimes and DL frameworks be exploited to boost performance and scalability for modern multi-GPU HPC systems?
- What are the performance trends and benefits that can be observed for a distributed and co-designed DL framework like S-Caffe?

In order to address the above challenges, using a co-design methodology, we propose *S-Caffe*; a novel and scalable DL framework that provides efficient scale-up and scale-out for distributed training on accelerated HPC systems. We investigate a co-design approach of S-Caffe and MPI runtimes to bring the distributed-memory space efficiency and CUDA-Awareness of MPI semantics to the S-Caffe framework. We redesign and enhance MPI protocols to satisfy the new requirements pertaining to movement of very large messages in DL frameworks. Table 1 positions the S-Caffe framework in the DL framework design and features space. To the best of our knowledge, this is the first study that provides an in-depth analysis of fundamental system-level bottlenecks being faced by DL frameworks like Caffe and highlights novel co-designed solutions to achieve high performance and scalability.

We make the following key contributions:

- Analyze and identify new requirements brought forward by DL frameworks, especially for large message communication and reductions in MPI runtimes.
- Co-Design, implement, and evaluate S-Caffe; a scalable and distributed CUDA-Aware MPI enabled DL framework.
- Propose novel exploitation of MPI-3 Non-blocking Collective (NBC) operations via multi-stage data propagation and helper-thread based gradient aggregation in DL frameworks.
- Co-design, implement, and evaluate a GPU-kernel based hierarchical CUDA-Aware reduction primitive (MPI_Re-

Deep Learning Frameworks	Framework Features and Platforms Supported							
	Distributed Address Space Systems				Shared Address Space Systems		Parallelization Strategy / Implementation	
	Basic MPI Support	CUDA-Aware MPI	Overlapped Designs (NBC Support)	Co-Designed with MPI runtimes	Single GPU Training	Multi-GPU Training	Model Parallel (MP) / Data Parallel (DP)	Parameter-Server (PS) / Reduction-Tree (RT)
Caffe [33]	×	×	×	×	✔	✔	DP	RT
FireCaffe [30]	✔	Unknown	×	Unknown	✔	✔	DP	RT
MPI-Caffe [37]	✔	×	×	×	✔	✔	MP	N/A
CNTK [12]	✔	×	×	×	✔	✔	MP/DP	PS
Inspur-Caffe [31]	✔	✔	×	×	✔	✔	DP	PS
S-Caffe (proposed)	✔	✔	✔	✔	✔	✔	DP	RT

Table 1. Design and Features Space for Modern Deep Learning Frameworks

duce) for supporting large-scale reductions in DL frameworks like S-Caffe.

- Evaluate and analyze performance of the proposed S-Caffe with small and large data sets like CIFAR10 and ImageNet using various networks like AlexNet and GoogLeNet on different GPU Clusters including a Cray CS-Storm dense multi-GPU system.

The rest of the paper is organized as follows. Section 2 contains important preliminaries including architecture of DL frameworks like Caffe. In section 3, we highlight the challenges and requirements for designing scalable DL frameworks like S-Caffe. In Section 4, we describe at length, the proposed S-Caffe co-design schemes and design alternatives. The details of the proposed hierarchical multi-level MPI_Reduce are provided in Section 5. In section 6, we present a comprehensive performance evaluation. Section 7 covers related DL frameworks and research efforts. We conclude the paper in Section 8.

2. Preliminaries: DL Frameworks, Caffe, and CUDA-Aware MPI

In this section, we provide an overview of different DL frameworks, a detailed description of Caffe's architecture followed by a brief discussion of CUDA-Aware MPI runtimes.

2.1 Architecture of Deep Learning Frameworks

DNNs like AlexNet, GoogLeNet, and VGG have several architectural variations ranging from the number of layers, filter dimensions, among others. Single GPU or CPU based DNN training broadly comprises of iterations over two compute intensive passes; the Forward pass for training the sample data, and the Backward pass for performing gradient computation w.r.t the weights and samples used in the forward pass. In general, all the DNN structures try to model high-level abstractions in a layered manner.

2.2 Caffe: Design and Implementation

We now define major design and implementation components of the Caffe framework; the Net (or the Model), the Layers, the Solvers, and the Forward/Backward computational passes. We discuss them in the context of this work but a detailed description of these can be obtained from [6]. Figure 1 highlights different phases of the Solvers and their interactions with Layers of a Net.

Net, Solvers, and Layers: Caffe's Net class is the base that holds important components of computation, commu-

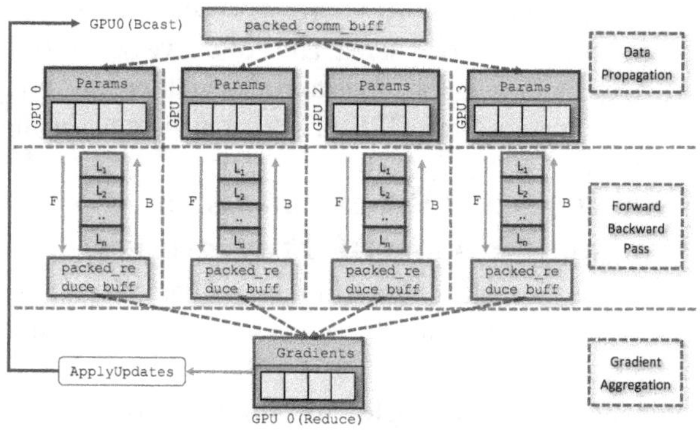

Figure 1. Caffe Architecture: Data Propagation, Forward/Backward Computation, and Gradient Aggregation

nication, and I/O. Net is an abstraction for a DL network like AlexNet or GoogLeNet. Net is sometimes also called the Model. The heart of the framework that orchestrates the execution of different computations using layers is called a Solver. The Solver class is an abstraction that provides an interface that can be implemented by different solvers e.g., a Stochastic Gradient Descent (SGD) solver. Caffe uses a Solver object for each of the GPU. Each Solver has its own Net object that operates on the Layer data. Layers are abstractions for a defined set of computations on the data. It is an interface that can be implemented by DL scientists for specific functionalities. Examples include Convolution, Pooling, and Data Layers. Caffe layers contain two important data structures for communication between Solvers; the parameter data used in the Forward pass and the parameter gradients calculated during the Backward pass.

Major Computation and Communication Phases: Caffe trains a Net in multiple iterations. Each iteration consists of three main phases; the data propagation phase, the Forward/Backward computational passes, and the gradient aggregation phase. Data propagation provides the required parameters. The packed_comm_buffer in Figure 1 shows the combination of data for different layers that is packed onto a buffer at the root solver (GPU 0). The root solver then communicates this buffer to all of the other solvers on different GPUs. The Forward pass of layers 1 to n generates a loss value that is propagated back in the Backward pass to calculate gradients. The gradients place on the packed_reduction_buffer are reduced back to the root solver during the gradient aggregation phase. The root solver then calls the ApplyUpdate() function and updates the parameter data for the next iteration.

2.3 CUDA-Aware MPI

Before the arrival of UVA and GPUDirect, MPI application developers used explicit copies of data between GPU and CPU memory. To use the Send primitive, an explicit device to host copy was required. Similarly, a CPU to GPU copy was needed after receiving the data using a Receive primitive. For supporting such kind of operations transparently, several MPI implementations including MVAPICH2 and OpenMPI provide CUDA-Aware MPI primitives for performing point-to-point, one-sided, and collective operations. This concept enables applications to perform direct and efficient communication from GPU buffers transparently using MPI primitives.

3. Challenges and Requirements for Designing Scalable DL Frameworks

In this section, we elaborate specific challenges, requirements, and issues that need to be addressed in order to design a scalable DL framework on modern GPU systems.

3.1 Parallelization Strategies and Implementation Styles

DL community has explored at least two parallelization approaches [34]: data-parallel approach and model-parallel approach. In this paper, we focus on the data-parallel approach where the same model is replicated for every processing element (a CPU core or a GPU), but is fed with different parts of the training data. To implement the data-parallel approach, there are two different design choices; first is called the parameter-server approach and second is called reduction-tree approach. As shown in Table 1, one of the most recent Caffe adaptation [31] by Inspur, Microsoft CNTK [12], and Intel-Caffe [3] follow the parameter-server design. This is analogous to a classical master-worker design pattern where each of the workers operate on a piece of data and each one of them sends it to a server. The server then aggregates the gradients and sends updated gradients to each of the workers. Parameter-server has also been implemented by frameworks like DistBelief [24]. More recently, Project Adam [19], GeePS [23], and Distributed TensorFlow [14] have also used variants of the parameter-server paradigm.

However, we argue that this design paradigm provides limited scalability. Using a single GPU as the master to perform the aggregation of very large buffers (order of megabytes) for every iteration renders the server to be the bottleneck. Using multiple servers may take away the GPUs from performing the actual training operation especially in the case of GPU-based parameter servers like GeePS [23]. Multiple servers may also pose additional overheads due to the second layer of synchronization between servers. Further, limited GPU memory may pose additional restrictions on the scalability of this approach. Inspur-Caffe, for instance, has only been able to work up to 16 processes. On the other hand, researchers have shown clear benefits of the reduction-tree approach [30]. The original Caffe maintained by BVLC as well as the Nvidia's fork, despite being multi-threaded (non-MPI) implementation, use a symmetric parallelization approach where all GPUs (solvers) communicate using a tree-like pattern. Hence, for the proposed S-Caffe, we investigate the data-parallel approach and its implementation using symmetric SPMD-style solvers where each GPU performs the same amount of work and the communication is performed in a collective fashion before the start and end of each iteration.

3.2 Distributed Address-Space Design and Parallel Data Reading

While GPU systems with multiple GPUs per node are very popular in HPC centers, the number of GPUs in a node is limited and it is common to have 2 or 4 GPUs per node. Hence, in order to satisfy the computing requirement of DL models, distributed frameworks are needed. Indeed, Caffe has been designed primarily for a single address space system where a single process can use multiple threads to take advantage of multiple GPUs in a node. This approach is limited by design to only work for an intra-node scale-up system.

On the other hand, HPC systems usually use a parallel file system (PFS) and storage nodes. In order to limit the I/O overhead in reading large size datasets available in the DL field, frameworks need to be redesigned with parallel reading capabilities to take advantage of PFS like Lustre [39]. Indeed, one of the challenges in developing a distributed system is feeding the training data efficiently to all the solvers. For Caffe, the training data is image files maintained in an LMDB [10] database. Caffe uses a Data Reader thread to constantly bring data from disk to memory queues. A single reader can share the data with the different solvers using a shared queue in Caffe. However, for a distributed framework, we need to design an efficient parallel data reading mechanism.

3.3 Exploiting Overlap of Computation and Communication

DL frameworks like Caffe are both computation and communication intensive. Hence, in order to scale out such frameworks, it is mandatory to overlap the computation with the communication. Indeed, Caffe orchestrates the training process in clearly marked phases like data propagation, forward/backward passes, and gradient aggregation. The issue with marked phases that block for the completion of the previous phase is the sequential nature of workflow. Such separation of computation and communication phases severely limits the system efficiency and scalability. In order to alleviate such limitations, a total redesign of the workflow to bring overlap between the different phases is required. Such a redesign requires: 1) an in-depth analysis of the workflow and its different phases, 2) a fine-grain restructuring of the coarse-grain phases to multiple fine-grain phases thereby exposing potential for overlap, and 3) exploitation of new communication semantics to perform computation/communication overlap.

3.4 Designing DL-Aware Communication Runtimes

MPI, as the defacto programming model for distributed system, has been optimized for HPC workloads. MPI communication protocols and runtimes including the CUDA-Aware ones, are optimized for small and large message sizes up to 4 MB. However, DL frameworks, with their extensively large message sizes (256 MB), bring forward new requirements and entail designing new DL-Aware communication runtimes and protocols. Further, as hinted earlier, DL frameworks are targeting GPU systems. Hence, the new runtime should be GPU/CUDA-Aware in addition to being DL-Aware. For instance, in most of HPC applications, a Reduce operation is performed on 16-64 byte buffer so MPI runtimes can use the CPU to perform such small reductions. However, for DL frameworks, where the aggregation phase requires a reduction on a 256 MB buffer, new algorithms, and runtime-level communication infrastructure are needed that can take advantage of GPU computing capabilities and features like GDR and IPC.

4. S-Caffe: Proposed Architecture and Co-designs

We now describe how we tackled the above challenges in designing S-Caffe. Figure 2 illustrates the architectural overview of the proposed S-Caffe framework at an abstract level. First, we illustrate our experiences in designing a basic CUDA-Aware MPI version. Then, we describe how to push the performance frontiers of such a framework via a co-design approach of the different computational layers (Caffe) and the communication runtime (MPI). Our approach includes: 1) re-designing S-Caffe workflow to maximize the overlap potential by taking advantage of MPI-3 semantics and features including non-blocking collective (NBC) operations in a multi-staged fashion to overlap the computation and communication; and 2) a new CUDA-Aware MPI parallel reduction design that combines GPUDirect RDMA and GPU kernels to efficiently support large-size GPU based reduction operations.

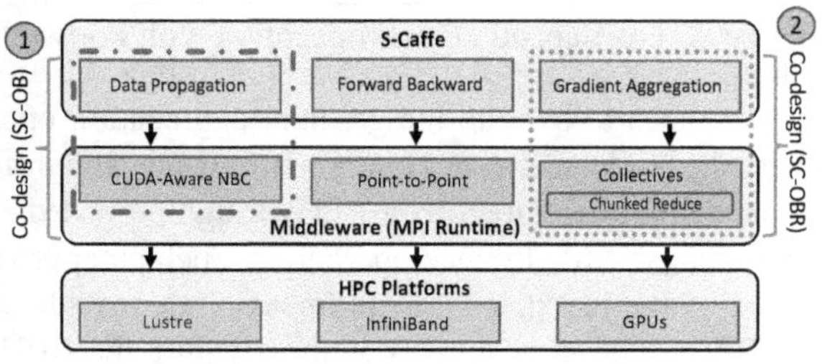

Figure 2. Architectural Overview of S-Caffe

4.1 Basic CUDA-Aware MPI Design (SC-B)

As mentioned earlier, Caffe has been designed using the single-process multi-threaded programming paradigm. Moving from a single address space to a distributed address space is a challenging process that requires a significant code analysis and reorganization effort due to the complexity of Caffe's layered architecture. Further, re-designing an object oriented code where threads share objects across heterogeneous CPU and GPU memory spaces increases the complexity of the work. Below, we highlight how we tackled these challenges. *We note that this design is called S-Caffe Basic (SC-B) in the results section.*

Explicit Data Movement Operations: To move from the shared data access pattern with *Parent-Child* relationship between the solvers to a distributed system, an explicit communication between different processes (solvers) is required. A naive implementation can serialize the different C++ objects and exchange them with MPI operations. This can introduce a significant overhead. To avoid this, we identify minimal data exchange that is required, utilize existing GPU-based communication buffers, and communicate them across processes in a CUDA-Aware fashion. This avoids unnecessary copies between the CPU and GPUs.

Parallel Readers: The second design goal for S-Caffe is to optimize file access operations. To make it possible, we investigated two alternative design choices; first is to use a single data reader thread and communicate the data to other processes, and second is to use parallel data reader threads for each of the processes and maintain separate distributed queues. We chose the second option because it can be optimized for parallel file systems like Lustre where parallel reads from disk can be faster than exchanging images using MPI-level communication. The proposed design is presented in Figure 3. In addition, the parallel reader design can readily be used with both LMDB and ImageDataLayer of Caffe. It is pertinent to mention that even-though LMDB allows parallel accesses, its scalability is very limited. Indeed as discussed later in Section 6, LMDB does not scale for more than 64 parallel readers. On the other hand, ImageDataLayer allows reading image files directly from Lustre storage and can scale to any number of processes. The results section (Figure 8) highlights how our proposed parallel data reading combined with ImageDataLayer achieves scalability up to 160 GPUs.

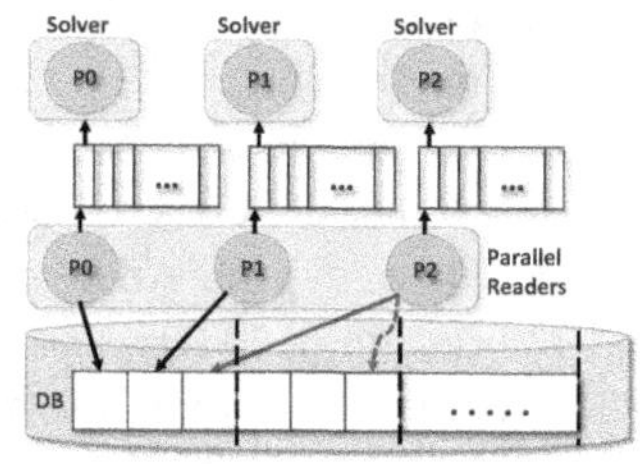

Figure 3. S-Caffe: Proposed Parallel Data Reader Design with Distributed Queues

Collective Operation Patterns for Data Propagation and Aggregation: After extracting the different memory access patterns to shared buffers and changing them to explicit MPI point-point communication as described earlier, with extra analysis of the MPI communication pattern, we noticed an opportunity for improvement. Thus, we enhanced the on_start() data propagation phase to use the MPI broadcast primitive (MPI_Bcast). It is worth mentioning that we use the CUDA-Aware version of this operation. In a similar fashion, for the gradient aggregation part, we use an MPI_Reduce operation. Even-though such designs can be efficient for small scale and especially for small data sets like MNIST and CIFAR, to push the scalability and efficiency for large DL models, a co-design approach is required as discussed in the next section.

4.2 Multi-stage Non-blocking Collectives for Maximal Overlap (SC-OB)

The CUDA-Aware MPI design presented in the previous section provides reasonable performance for small and medium scale data sets like MNIST and CIFAR10. However, as the data set sizes and communication parameters increase with scale, the basic design (SC-B) becomes communication-bound where communication overhead gets significant. To minimize the overhead of this communication, we re-designed S-Caffe workflow to provide opportunities for overlap and co-designing with MPI runtimes.

Figure 1 shows how Caffe performs communication and computation in clearly marked phases that proceed after the completion of one another. This phase based computation and communication is intuitive but limits the efficiency of the system. On the other hand, MPI-3 has introduced Non-Blocking Collective (NBC) operations that provide support for overlapping computation and communication. Naively using NBC may result in performance degradation if the computation/communication overlap ratio is small. In order to efficiently co-design the communication and computation using NBCs, we did a deeper investigation of the data structures and re-designed the core workflow. First, we have moved from a coarse-grain workflow with mainly three successive phases to a fine-grain workflow with multiple phases. We proposed a new workflow which maximizes the overlap of computation and communication phases. The proposed S-Caffe workflow communicates the model parameters and the gradient data in an *on-demand* fashion instead of a coarse-grained approach that performs communication of the entire data in a single operation.

The new workflow overlaps the data propagation with the Forward pass using MPI_Ibcast() calls to send the required data before starting the Forward pass. An Ibcast call is a non-blocking call that returns immediately and MPI runtimes typically progress the communication in the background using different strategies [28, 29]. An MPI_Wait() call is made to complete the operation. Wait call blocks until the progression and completion of the corresponding request. The challenge is to find the best place to use the MPI_Wait() operation. Calling this operation too soon will lead to poor computation/communication overlap as the communication will be mainly progressed during this call. On the other hand, calling it too late might lead to degradation as it limits the potential of overlapping future computation phases. To overlap the propagation with the forward layers, we investigated two designs. As shown in Figure 4, a naive design tries to overlap the communication of layer $i+1$ with the computation phase of layer i. However, this limits the asynchronous progress and hence the overlap potential. To maximize the overlap potential, as shown in Figure 5, we propose a multi-stage on-demand design. It starts all Ibcast operations at the beginning and posts the appropriate Wait operation of ith Ibcast just before the ith Forward pass of a layer that actually needs the corresponding data. *This co-design approach is called S-Caffe Optimized Broadcast (SC-OB) in the results section.*

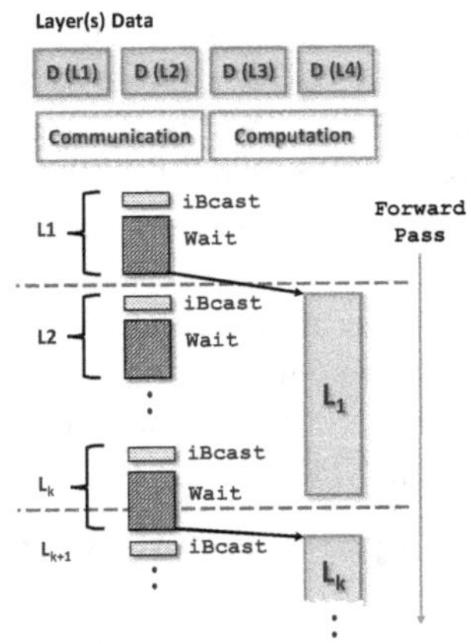

Figure 4. Naive NBC Design for Data Propagation

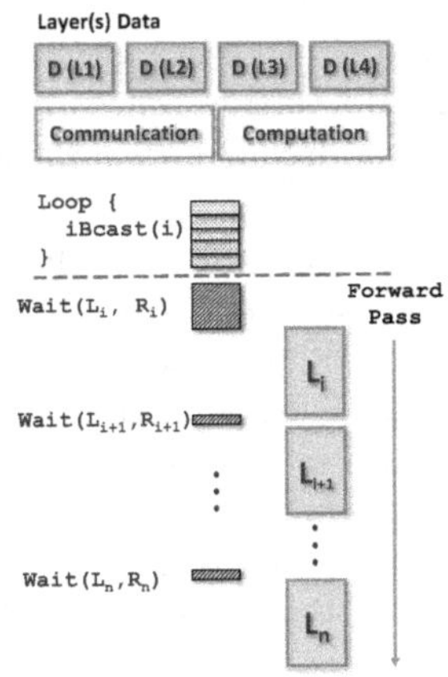

Figure 5. Overlapped Data Propagation with Forward

Taking such overlapped design one step further, we investigated schemes to overlap the gradient aggregation operation with the Backward pass. However, this is not straightforward and cannot exploit an Ibcast-like design proposed earlier that can use MPI_Ireduce operations. Such an approach is limited by the fact that MPI runtimes do not provide efficient NBC reduction primitives as they require the CPU to progress and perform the computation, which clearly nullifies the overlap potential. Further, falling back to a blocking reduce operation and trying to take advantage of a multi-stage scheme to split the reduce operation to multiple reduce operations interleaved between the different backward phases will not provide any overlap as: 1) the number of steps in performing N medium sized reductions are equivalent to a single big reduction, and 2) Even-though the CPU is free, each reduce call is required to wait for the completion of the GPU based backward layer before performing the reduce operation.

To overcome these bottlenecks, we propose a different co-design approach to overlap the gradient aggregation with the backward passes. Our approach includes two main parts: 1) a helper thread to separate the kernel completion and wait for communication progress in order to achieve overlap, and 2) A novel DL-Aware MPI Reduce design that exploits multi-level communicators and kernel-based computation to efficiently reduce large size buffers. Helper-thread co-design is discussed in the next sub-section while the DL-Aware Reduce Design is presented at length in Section 5.

4.3 Co-design Gradient Aggregation for Maximal Overlap and Performance: Helper control thread (SC-OBR)

To split the control flow between the communication and computation phases, we have offloaded the invocation of a layers' backward pass to a helper thread. The helper thread signals the main thread to invoke the reductions in a multi-stage fashion. In this layered design, the $n'th$ layer's reduce requires the completion of the $n'th$ layer's computation. We have designed the two threads to synchronize using a C++ condition flag. This design ensures the overlap of $n'th$ reduce with the layer $n-1's$ compute. While this scheme gives an opportunity for an overlap, however, in order to maximize its efficiency, the reduce operation needs to be optimized as well. Figure 6 shows how the overlapped gradient aggregation hides the latency of reductions under the large computation of layers in the Backward pass.

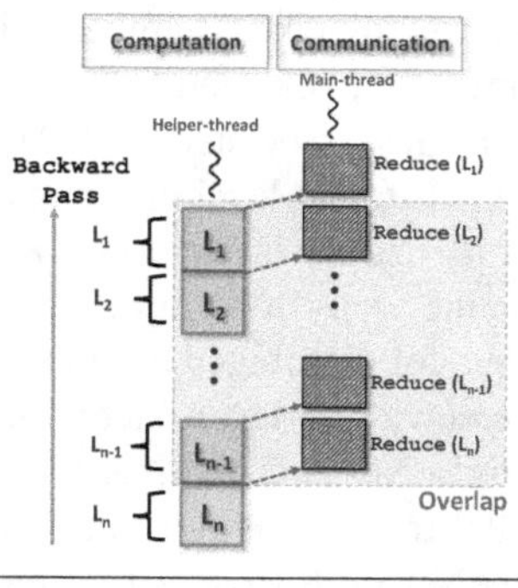

Figure 6. Overlapped Gradient Aggregation with Backward

5. Efficient DL-Aware Hierarchical Reduce (HR):

In modern MPI runtimes like MVAPICH2 and OpenMPI, we typically observe that large-scale collective communication and reduction primitives are implemented using a flat single algorithm like Binomial Tree (and many others), or a hierarchical algorithm with intra-node and inter-node communication. However, this simple intra- and inter-node hierarchical scheme is not sufficient in the context of GPU-based communication and large-scale reductions, especially on systems that contains only 2-4 GPUs per node. Thus, we need to design a hierarchical mechanism for MPI communicators such that a lower level communicator can also span multiple nodes. Detailed discussion about multi-level communicators and their implementation is beyond the scope of this paper. Thus, we present the relevant details for Hierarchical Reduce (HR) and S-Caffe co-design only. Figure 7 presents a two-level design where the lower level communicator spans two nodes and each node has four GPUs. Thus, a total of eight GPUs are in the lower level communicator. We call the number of GPUs in the communicator as the chain-size. We note that chain-size is a runtime parameter that can be dynamically tuned for different systems and configurations. The upper level communicator, in this case, uses a binomial tree algorithm. The selection of algorithms for both upper and lower level communicators can be controlled using runtime parameters.

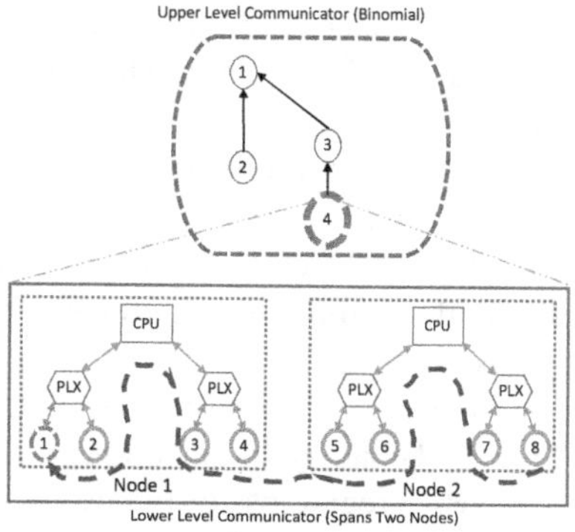

Figure 7. Hierarchical DL-Aware Reduction Design with a Chain-Binomial Combination

To reinforce the need for multi-level communicator design, we now present a mathematical model that governs and verifies the performance benefits of our proposed reduce design alternatives.

Let,

P = number of processes
n = number of chunks
$t(b)$ = time to reduce buffer of size b
$t(c)$ = time to reduce buffer of size c [$c = b/n$]

And,

$T(CC)$ = Total Time for Chunked Chain Algorithm
$T(Bin)$ = Total Time for Binomial Tree Algorithm

Then, the total time for reducing a buffer of size b for P processes for both approaches can be understood by the following equations:

$$T(Bin) = log(P) * t(b) \; .... \; (1)$$
$$T(CC) = (P-1) * t(c) + (n-1) * t(c)$$
$$T(CC) = (n+P-2) * t(c) \; .... \; (2)$$

Analyzing equations (1) and (2) for different number of processes P and buffer size b, we observe:

for small P and large b, $T(CC) << T(Bin)$

But,

for large P and small b, $T(CC) >> T(Bin)$

Thus, the ideal choice is a trade-off between the two algorithms as we can clearly see that P becomes a significant factor in the time of reduction for a chunked chain (CC) while $t(b)$ becomes the dominant time factor for the binomial tree reduction (Bin) as we move towards larger b. Hence, we need a hybrid of the two approaches where the final design is both skew-tolerant (process count) as well as size-tolerant (buffer size).

To implement the above schemes in an efficient manner that provides best performance for all cases, we experimentally determine the ideal P and b for each of the cases and then apply the aforementioned two-level communicator design to realize an efficient and skew-tolerant reduction design. The chunked-chain algorithm is essentially a single-sided pipeline that transfers and overlaps the communication and reduction of successive chunks of a large buffer. The last process in the chain divides the buffer into n chunks and sends the chunk to the process on the left. The receiving process reduces this chunk with its own chunk and forwards it to its left neighbor. This process continues till the chunk reaches the root process. Hence, the entire chain is a directed chain of chunks starting from the last process and terminating at the root process.

For buffer sizes greater than eight megabytes (8M), we observed that chunked chain (CC) performs much better than the binomial tree (Bin) regardless of the number of chunks. However, the performance of CC degrades as we increase the number of processes (P) in the chain. Experimental evaluation for our platform also suggests that eight is the ideal P for CC approach. The benefits start to decrease beyond P >8. Thus, we resort to a two-level design that can scale beyond 8 GPUs. The addition of two-level communicator allows us to scale well beyond 8 GPUs even if we apply a chain of chain approach, i.e., both the upper level communicator and lower level communicator use CC as the desired algorithm. However, as expected, the two-level chains can only scale to a process count of 64 (eight being the ideal size of one chain). For larger process counts, we utilize a hybrid of the two approaches where the upper level communicator uses a binomial tree based reduction while the lower level communicator uses the chunked-chain algorithm as shown in Figure 7. We note that, we have tuned the selection of the appropriate combination, chain-of-chain or chain-binomial depending on the system size. Further, it is worth noting that the proposed design is very extensible. Thus, in future, we can exploit multi-level combinations like chain-of-chain combined with a top level binomial for very large scale reductions. The hierarchical reduction designs have been made publicly available with the MVAPICH2-GDR 2.2 [41] release. Detailed performance evaluation is presented in Section 6.5.

6. Performance Evaluation

6.1 Computational Testbed and Environment

We have used a Cray CS-Storm based GPU cluster called KESCH [2] located at the Swiss National Supercomputing Center. This a dense GPU cluster consisting of 12 hybrid nodes each containing 8 NVIDIA K-80 GK210GL GPUs. This makes a total of 192 GPUs for the 12 nodes and just 24 conventional CPUs. Please note that each K-80 is a dual-GPU card which means that a total of 16 CUDA devices are available in one node. The nodes are connected with the InfiniBand Connect-IB dual-port network cards (HCAs). We refer to this cluster as Cluster-A. To illustrate that the proposed designs are generic and applicable for different types of GPU clusters, we have also used a small 20 nodes GPU cluster containing one K-80 GPU per node. The total number of GPUs we can utilize are 40 for this cluster. The nodes are connected to each other using InfiniBand EDR HCAs. This cluster is henceforth referred as Cluster-B.

6.2 Evaluation Metrics and Data Sets

In DL community, scientists and DL model designers strive for achieving the best accuracy and minimum loss. To achieve this, various hyper-parameters like base learning rate (lr), weight decay, momentum, and learning policy are tuned for the best accuracy. However, training time is one of most crucial metrics for comparing performance of DL frameworks. Large-scale DL networks like AlexNet and CaffeNet can take several days of training to reach the desired accuracy. Thus, training time becomes a decisive factor in using a DL framework. In this paper, we present the parallel training time trend observed for a fixed number of iterations. This can help DL scientists to tweak and tune hyper-parameters. We note that challenges associated with Hyper-parameter Search (HS) are at a different level of granularity compared to S-Caffe. HS parallelization is performed at the SGD algorithm's level while the focus of S-Caffe is on synchronizing parallel SGD solvers for distributed training.

In order to cover a wide variety of networks and data sets, we have used **GoogLeNet** and **AlexNet** for comparing performance of parallel training on the ImageNet dataset. We use the term ImageNet in this paper to refer to the widely used ILSVRC 2012 [5] data set. ImageNet contains over a million images spread across 1,000 categories. For smaller scale, we present results using the CIFAR10 network as well. We present **strong** scaling results, where the batch-size is divided by the number of GPUs (or solvers). E.g. if we specify a batch-size of 1,024 for 32 GPUs, the effective batch-size for a single GPU becomes 32 (as 1,024/32 = 32). For weak scaling, the batch-size of 1,024 remains constant for each of the GPUs. These results are not presented but can be obtained using the public version of S-Caffe [46] by specifying *-scal weak* command line option. We have used default hyper-parameters (lr, momentum, etc.) provided by the reference Caffe and CNTK models for all the experiments. Caffe reports accuracy during the Testing phase only. Therefore, we obtained accuracy for CIFAR10 only as it is possible to train and test fairly quickly. We observed no difference in accuracy between Caffe and S-Caffe. Similarly, the decrease in loss (reported every iteration) for AlexNet and GoogLeNet was similar to the multi-GPU training of Caffe. This validates that S-Caffe's distributed training indeed works as expected.

6.3 S-Caffe: Primary Highlights

GoogLeNet: We first present the primary benefits observed for the proposed S-Caffe co-designs for the GoogLeNet model. In Figure 8, we present strong scaling results for GoogLeNet network up to 160 GPUs. The numbers presented in this figure compare the performance of Caffe with different configurations of S-Caffe. **S-Caffe-L** means that we have utilized LMDB database to access the ImageNet data set. **S-Caffe**, on the other hand, exploits the parallelism in Lustre file system and directly accesses image files through the ImageDataLayer. Caffe, being a single process code, has been run with LMDB as it does not require parallel access. In fact, ImageDataLayer with Caffe suffers degradation, so we have omitted those results. We report speedups of 3.3x over 16 GPUs and 2.5x over 32 GPUs for GoogLeNet training with 128 and 160 GPUs, respectively. We note that this scaling, unlike conventional HPC applications, is considered very promising as large DL models are notoriously hard to scale. This has been a major problem for the DL community as highlighted in [1, 9].

The numbers presented are with different batch sizes written in parentheses. We ran the training for 100 iterations. Beyond 64 GPUs, we experienced severe degradation or race conditions for LMDB. Thus, we present ImageDataLayer based results for process counts larger than 64. Missing data points are for the cases where solvers ran out of memory. It is important to note that a larger batch divided over a smaller number of solvers renders the effective batch-size to be too large to fit inside a GPU's memory. Thus, an added motivation to develop multi-process frameworks like the proposed S-Caffe is to enable training using very large batch-sizes for current as well as upcoming DL models that are expected to deal with much larger data sets and networks.

CIFAR10 Quick Solver: Figure 9 highlights the performance of CIFAR10 Quick Solver, provided as a reference solver for CIFAR10 dataset in the Caffe repository. We note that Caffe numbers are only available for 1 node (up to 16 GPUs). Since S-Caffe can scale beyond one node, the results presented here are for a total of 64 GPUs on 4 nodes. We observed a decent scale-out performance considering the size of CIFAR10 dataset. We run the solver for 1,000 iterations and the batch-size is for 8,192. It is pertinent to mention that this is a dense GPU system, so the results presented are for 4 nodes only. On a conventional GPU cluster, 64 GPUs can mean anywhere between 32 and 64 nodes. We observed similar speedup for CIFAR10 on Cluster-B as well but we have omitted the graph to save space. The overall

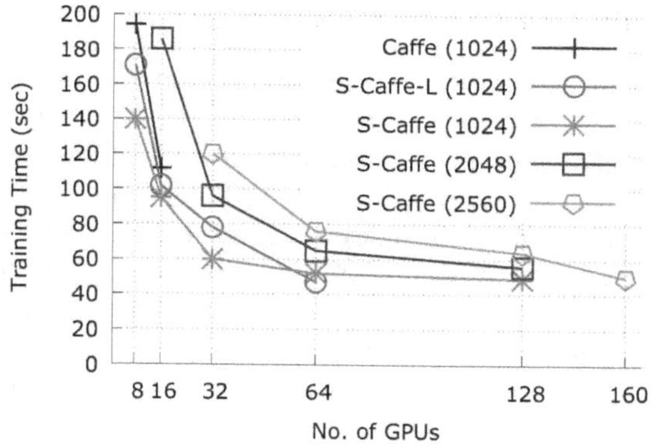

Figure 8. GoogLeNet: Comparison of S-Caffe (up to 160 GPUs) and Caffe (up to 16 GPUs) on Cluster-A

speedup S-Caffe has achieved is 32x over single GPU training. We note that S-Caffe and Caffe perform very similar up to 16 GPUs as CIFAR-10 is a compute-intensive model with small-scale communication between solvers. Thus, it is an encouraging highlight that S-Caffe does not suffer any overhead. This trend was reversed and we saw benefits for S-Caffe over Caffe when training GoogLeNet because it is a communication-intensive model.

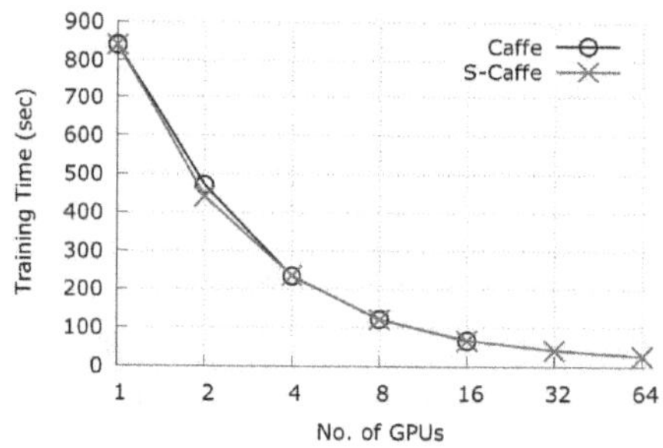

Figure 9. CIFAR10: Comparison of S-Caffe (up to 64 GPUs) and Caffe (up to 16 GPUs) on Cluster-A

Discussion: We note that the results presented above are on the fastest Tesla GPUs available i.e. Kepler K-80, which provides at least 3X faster performance than the K-20x [13] cards. It is pertinent to mention that the largest state-of-the-art scaling presented in [30] is for 128 K-20x GPUs. Thus, the scaling we present here is different and not directly comparable to K-20x level scaling because of the much faster GPUs used for parallel training. As Fire-Caffe [30] is not publicly available for download, we are currently unable to compare our results with them. We plan to do so when the software becomes available.

6.4 Performance Comparison of S-Caffe, CNTK, and Inspur-Caffe

In order to provide a comparison of S-Caffe with different DL frameworks that support distributed training, we have identified three main frameworks: 1) Inspur-Caffe, which is an MPI-based parameter-server implementation, 2) TensorFlow, which is a gRPC based distributed training framework, and 3) Microsoft CNTK, which is also an MPI-based framework. Due to some technical difficulties [27], we were not able to run TensorFlow on our cluster. Therefore, we only compare S-Caffe with Inspur-Caffe and CNTK. We have used the AlexNet network and Cluster-B for this comparison. Results are presented in Figure 10. We note that we present this result in Samples Per Second (SPS) instead of the training time. A higher SPS denotes better performance. For Inspur-Caffe and S-Caffe, we have used LMDB for file reading while default file reading mechanism was used for CNTK. Inspur-Caffe results are shown only for 2 and 4 GPUs as it didn't run for less than 2 GPUs and more than 16 GPUs. For other cases, we were not able to report numbers because the execution hangs after completing a few iterations. We plan to report this to Inspur-Caffe developers. For CNTK, we used their 32-bit SGD design that uses MPI-based communication among workers. A detailed discussion of differences between CNTK, TensorFlow, and S-Caffe can be seen in Section 7.

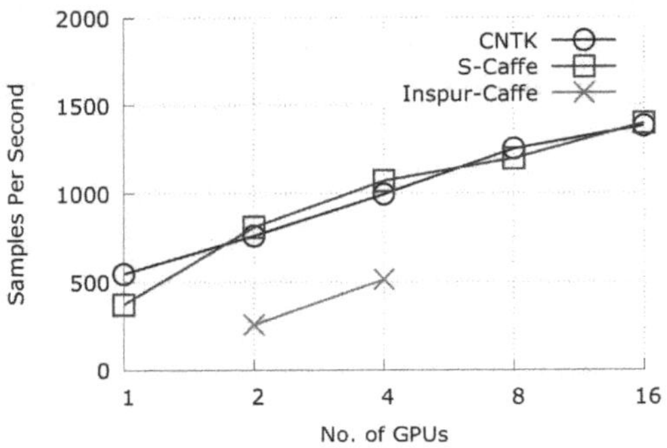

Figure 10. AlexNet: Comparison of S-Caffe, CNTK, and Inspur-Caffe (up to 16 GPUs) on Cluster-B

6.5 Performance of Hierarchical Reductions

We now present the performance evaluation of Hierarchical Reduce (HR) designs. These have been tuned for best performance for all message sizes and process counts. The results are labeled with appropriate design/implementation category. Lower level chain communicator (C) combined with upper level binomial (B) is labeled as **CB**. Upper level chain combined with lower level chain is called **CC**. **MV2** is used for existing MVAPICH2 reduce implementation. **HR (Tuned)** is the new tuned design that builds on top of the tuning infrastructure in MVAPICH2 and efficiently uses the fastest combination for the desired message size and process count range. The numbers in the legend e.g. (-4) represent the size of the chain used. For instance, **CC-4** means that Chain algorithm is applied for both upper and lower level communicators. This micro-benchmark level evaluation has been performed using the OMB [42] suite and is presented in Figure 11.

In addition, we separately present the performance comparison for our proposed design (HR) versus MVAPICH2 and OpenMPI using a log scale for the sake of clarity. Figure 12 shows this comparison. It worth noting that we use OpenMPI v1.10.2 and MVAPICH2 2.2RC1 with their performance features enabled including GDR and IPC (and GDRCOPY for MVAPICH2). As can be seen from the figure, our proposed design is almost 3X faster than MVAPICH2 and up to 133X faster than OpenMPI.

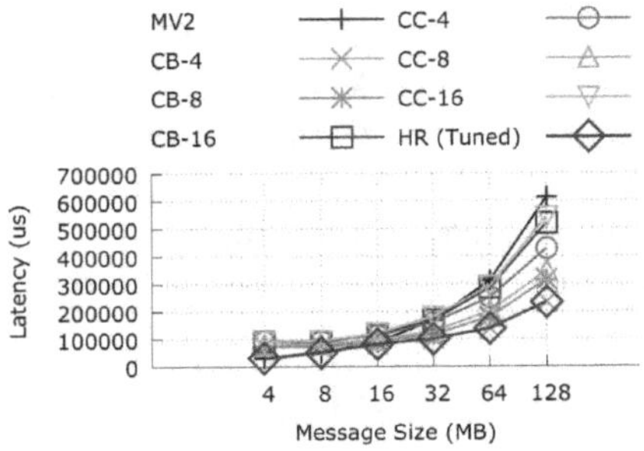

Figure 11. Performance for 160 Processes (GPUs): MVAPICH2, Chain-Binomial, Chain-Chain, and Proposed HR (Tuned) on Cluster-A

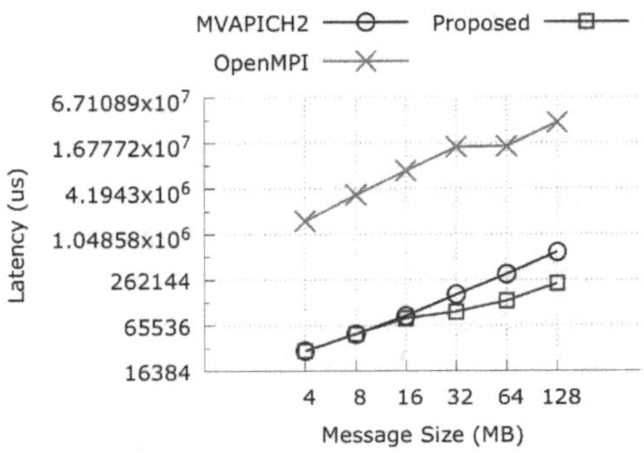

Figure 12. Performance Comparison: MVAPICH2, OpenMPI, and Proposed on Cluster-A

6.6 Impact of Various S-Caffe Co-designs

We now provide further insights on the performance and scalability of the proposed S-Caffe framework and its different co-designs. We compare CUDA-Aware MPI design (SC-B), the overlapped data propagation design (SC-OB), and the overlapped gradient aggregation (SC-OBR) + hierarchical reduce (HR) co-design. We note that numbers presented in this section are not comparable to the overall numbers presented in Section 6.3 as the configuration, batch-size, and number of iterations are different for these runs.

Overlapped Data Propagation (SC-OB): Benefits of SC-OB are shown in Figure 13 by comparing the time required for data propagation and F/B compute passes. We can see that SC-OB co-design provides an excellent overlap of the communication and hides the large latency behind compute intensive Forward pass of layers. Time taken by the reduce phase is not shown as it does not have any effect on the SC-OB design. We report up to 15% improvement for SC-OB design.

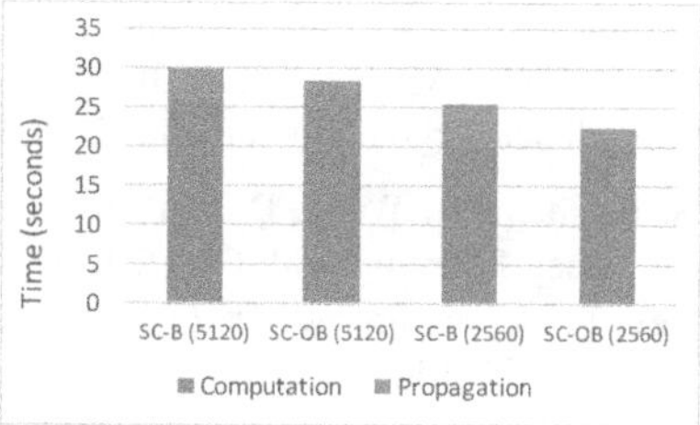

Figure 13. Comparison of SC-B with SC-OB

Overlapped Gradient Aggregation (SC-OBR) and HR: To further illustrate the benefits we achieved by using HR co-designs, we present a comparison of SC-B vs. SC-B (+HR) in Table 2. SC-B (+HR) means that the hierarchical reduction co-design has been applied to improve performance. Furthermore, the configuration of communicator and chain-size has been varied to illustrate the details. We achieve a 2.3x speedup for SC-B (+HR) with optimal chain-size and communicator selection (CB-8). For SC-OBR, we saw a 20% improvement over SC-B for CaffeNet on 8 GPUs and 12% improvement for 16 GPUs.

Algorithm / Communicator	SC-B SC-B (+HR)	Aggregation Time	Total Time	Speedup for Aggregation	Overall Speedup
N/A	SC-B	40.6	113.6	1	1
CC-8	SC-B (+HR)	28.6	101.6	1.47	1.11
CB-4	SC-B (+HR)	19.8	92.8	2.04	1.22
CB-8	SC-B (+HR)	17.6	90.6	2.3	1.25

Table 2. Comparison of SC-B vs. SC-B with HR

7. Related Work

We now compare S-Caffe with prevalent research and development efforts. FireCaffe [30] is one of the most recent efforts in scaling out Caffe using MPI. It discusses scaling of DL models to multi-GPU clusters with prime focus being on observing the behavior of model parameters e.g., batch-size in conjunction with training accuracy for large-scale runs. However, S-Caffe provides a systems' perspective of new co-designs and highlights strategies to accelerate and better scale communication phases in Caffe. Inspur-Caffe [31] is an MPI-based Caffe fork that exploits parameter-server approach with stale asynchronous gradient updates. S-Caffe, on the other hand, uses synchronous gradient aggregation using a reduction-tree. Microsoft CNTK [12] uses MPI to provide distributed training support as well. CNTK, however, does not take advantage of CUDA-Aware MPI and/or co-designed DL-Aware collectives like the proposed reduce (HR). As reported in Section 6, CNTK and S-Caffe achieve comparable performance.

Distributed frameworks can also exploit task-based programming models and scheduling frameworks. StarPU [4] is one such framework to schedule tasks on heterogeneous systems where some tasks are scheduled on GPUs and some on the CPU. However, in S-Caffe, all the computation (solver) is performed on the GPUs in a deterministic fashion. Hence, StarPU will always provide the same configuration with little benefits. In addition, StarPU may still require the MPI communication to be defined. Google TensorFlow is another widely used DL framework that uses a task-based model where computation can be performed on either a CPU or a GPU using the *tf.device* abstraction. The initial release of TF only supported single node training but recent versions (0.8 and onwards) provide distributed training support using the Google RPC [26] library. An MPI version of TensorFlow has recently been proposed in [48] but the current version only supports CPU-based training. Thus, the design challenges for S-Caffe and [48] are different because the primary contribution and focus of S-Caffe is on GPU-based training and that too for large DL models like AlexNet.

Designs presented in GeePS [23] focus on DL models that don't fit well in a GPU's memory as they used K20 GPUs with limited memory (5 GB). However, recent GPUs by Nvidia, like the K-80 and P100 have 12 and 16 GB memory, respectively. Thus, the memory problem is being solved at a hardware level as well. In contrast, we are focusing on scaling distributed training for models that 'do fit' on a GPU's memory.

8. Conclusion

With an increasing interest in accelerating Deep Learning frameworks through GPU-based systems, in this paper, we tackled the challenge of designing a scalable and distributed DL framework called S-Caffe. Using a co-design approach, we fully exploit the resources available in modern GPU clusters to accelerate training of both medium and large scale DL networks. S-Caffe is a culmination of an extensive co-design process that addresses bottlenecks in the sequential phase-based workflow of Caffe. Through data propagation co-design (SC-OB) that provides maximal overlap using MPI-3 Non-blocking Collectives, we reported 15% improvement over the basic CUDA-Aware MPI design (SC-B). We pushed the envelope of performance further with aggressive co-design of gradient aggregation through a helper-thread based overlap of communication and computation (SC-OBR) and an MPI runtime level hierarchical reduction design (HR). Exploiting SC-OBR and HR, we achieve 20% improvement for GoogLeNet-based training on 160 GPUs. We report encouraging speedups for two different solvers; 33X speedup over 1 GPU training for CIFAR10 quick solver utilizing 64 GPUs and 3.3X speedup over 32 GPU training for CaffeNet solver using 128 GPUs. S-Caffe provides comparable performance to Microsoft CNTK for the AlexNet model. S-Caffe has been made publicly available under the OSU HiDL project [46].

Acknowledgments

We would like to thank the anonymous reviewers for the invaluable feedback that helped us in improving this paper. We also extend thanks to our colleague Hari Subramoni for his significant efforts in making the public release of S-Caffe possible. This research is supported in part by National Science Foundation grants #ACI-1450440, #CNS-1513120, and #CCF-1565414.

References

[1] Caffe: Multi-GPU Usage and Performance. https://github.com/yahoo/caffe/blob/master/docs/multigpu.md.

[2] KESCH: Cray CS-Storm System. http://www.cscs.ch/computers/kesch_escha/index.html.

[3] Intel Caffe. https://github.com/intelcaffe.

[4] A Unified Runtime System for Heterogeneous Multicore Architectures. http://starpu.gforge.inria.fr.

[5] ILSVRC2012 Dataset. http://image-net.org/challenges/LSVRC/2012/index, 2012. [Online; accessed Dec-2016].

[6] Caffe Website. http://caffe.berkeleyvision.org/, 2015. [Online; accessed Dec-2016].

[7] CaffeNet. http://papers.nips.cc/book/advances-in-neural-information-processing-systems-25-2012, 2015. [Online; accessed Dec-2016].

[8] GPU Direct RDMA. http://docs.nvidia.com/cuda/gpudirect-rdma/, 2015. [Online; accessed Dec-2016].

[9] HPC: Powering Deep Learning. http://computing.ornl.gov/workshops/SMC15/docs/bcatanzaro_smcc.pdf, 2015. [Online; accessed Dec-2016].

[10] LMDB. http://symas.com/mdb/, 2015. [Online; accessed Dec-2016].

[11] Nvidia Development Platform for Autonomous Cars. http://www.nvidia.com/object/drive-px.html, 2016. [Online; accessed Dec-2016].

[12] CNTK. http://www.cntk.ai/, 2016. [Online; accessed Dec-2016].

[13] Nvidia GPUs Comparison. http://www.extremetech.com/computing/194391-nvidias-new-tesla-k80-doubles-up-on-gpu-horsepower, 2016. [Online; accessed Dec-2016].

[14] M. Abadi, A. Agarwal, P. Barham, E. Brevdo, Z. Chen, C. Citro, G. S. Corrado, A. Davis, J. Dean, M. Devin, et al. TensorFlow: Large-Scale Machine Learning on Heterogeneous Systems, 2015. *Software available from tensorflow. org*.

[15] J. A. Anderson, C. D. Lorenz, and A. Travesset. General Purpose Molecular Dynamics Simulations Fully Implemented on Graphics Processing Units. *Journal of Computational Physics*, 227(10):5342–5359, 2008.

[16] S. Bahrampour, N. Ramakrishnan, L. Schott, and M. Shah. Comparative Study of Caffe, Neon, Theano, and Torch for Deep Learning. *CoRR*, abs/1511.06435, 2016.

[17] F. Bastien, P. Lamblin, R. Pascanu, J. Bergstra, I. Goodfellow, A. Bergeron, N. Bouchard, D. Warde-Farley, and Y. Bengio. Theano: New Features and Speed Improvements. *arXiv preprint arXiv:1211.5590*, 2012.

[18] D. Case, J. Berryman, R. Betz, D. Cerutti, T. Cheatham III, T. Darden, R. Duke, T. Giese, H. Gohlke, A. Goetz, et al. AMBER 2015. *University of California, San Francisco*, 2015.

[19] T. Chilimbi, Y. Suzue, J. Apacible, and K. Kalyanaraman. Project adam: Building an efficient and scalable deep learning training system. In *Proceedings of the 11th USENIX Conference on Operating Systems Design and Implementation*, OSDI'14, pages 571–582, Berkeley, CA, USA, 2014. USENIX Association. ISBN 978-1-931971-16-4. URL http://dl.acm.org/citation.cfm?id=2685048.2685094.

[20] A. Coates, B. Huval, T. Wang, D. Wu, B. Catanzaro, and N. Andrew. Deep Learning with COTS HPC Systems. In *Proceedings of the 30th international conference on machine learning*, pages 1337–1345, 2013.

[21] R. Collobert, S. Bengio, and J. Mariéthoz. Torch: A Modular Machine Learning Software Library. Technical report, IDIAP, 2002.

[22] Cray. http://docs.cray.com/books/004-3689-001/html-004-3689-001/004-3689-001-toc.html, 2016. [Online; accessed Dec-2016].

[23] H. Cui, H. Zhang, G. R. Ganger, P. B. Gibbons, and E. P. Xing. Geeps: Scalable deep learning on distributed gpus with a gpu-specialized parameter server. In *Proceedings of the Eleventh European Conference on Computer Systems*, EuroSys '16, pages 4:1–4:16, New York, NY, USA, 2016. ACM. ISBN 978-1-4503-4240-7. doi: 10.1145/2901318.2901323. URL http://doi.acm.org/10.1145/2901318.2901323.

[24] J. Dean, G. Corrado, R. Monga, K. Chen, M. Devin, M. Mao, A. Senior, P. Tucker, K. Yang, Q. V. Le, et al. Large Scale Distributed Deep Networks. In *Advances in Neural Information Processing Systems*, pages 1223–1231, 2012.

[25] J. Deng, W. Dong, R. Socher, L.-J. Li, K. Li, and L. Fei-Fei. Imagenet: A Large-Scale Hierarchical Image Database. In *Computer Vision and Pattern Recognition, 2009. CVPR 2009. IEEE Conference on*, pages 248–255. IEEE, 2009.

[26] Google. Google's Remote Procedure Call Library (gRPC). http://www.grpc.io, .

[27] Google. Distributed TensorFlow: Github Issues. https://github.com/tensorflow/models/issues/698, .

[28] R. L. Graham, S. Poole, P. Shamis, G. Bloch, N. Bloch, H. Chapman, M. Kagan, A. Shahar, I. Rabinovitz, and G. Shainer. Overlapping Computation and Communication: Barrier Algorithms and ConnectX-2 CORE-Direct Capabilities. In *Parallel & Distributed Processing, Workshops and Phd Forum (IPDPSW), 2010 IEEE International Symposium on*, pages 1–8. IEEE, 2010.

[29] T. Hoefler, A. Lumsdaine, and W. Rehm. Implementation and Performance Analysis of Non-Blocking Collective Operations for MPI. In *Supercomputing, 2007. SC'07. Proceedings of the 2007 ACM/IEEE Conference on*, pages 1–10. IEEE, 2007.

[30] F. N. Iandola, K. Ashraf, M. W. Moskewicz, and K. Keutzer. FireCaffe: Near-Linear Acceleration of Deep Neural Network Training on Compute Clusters. *arXiv preprint arXiv:1511.00175*, 2015.

[31] Inspur. https://github.com/Caffe-MPI/Caffe-MPI.github.io, 2016.

[32] J. Dean. Keynote: Large Scale Deep Learning.

[33] Y. Jia, E. Shelhamer, J. Donahue, S. Karayev, J. Long, R. Girshick, S. Guadarrama, and T. Darrell. Caffe: Convolutional Architecture for Fast Feature Embedding. *arXiv preprint arXiv:1408.5093*, 2014.

[34] A. Krizhevsky. One weird trick for parallelizing convolutional neural networks. *CoRR*, abs/1404.5997, 2014.

[35] A. Krizhevsky and G. Hinton. Learning Multiple Layers of Features from Tiny Images, 2009.

[36] A. Krizhevsky, I. Sutskever, and G. E. Hinton. ImageNet Classification with Deep Convolutional Neural Networks. In F. Pereira, C. J. C. Burges, L. Bottou, and K. Q. Weinberger, editors, *Advances in Neural Information Processing Systems 25*, pages 1097–1105. Curran Associates, Inc., 2012. URL http://papers.nips.cc/paper/4824-imagenet-classification-with-deep-convolutional-neural-networks.pdf.

[37] S. Lee, S. Purushwalkam, M. Cogswell, D. J. Crandall, and D. Batra. Why M Heads are Better than One: Training a Diverse Ensemble of Deep Networks. *arXiv*, 2015. URL http://arxiv.org/abs/1511.06314.

[38] M. Lin, Q. Chen, and S. Yan. Network in Network. *arXiv preprint arXiv:1312.4400*, 2013.

[39] Lustre. Parallel File System. http://lustre.org.

[40] H. Meuer, E. Strohmaier, J. Dongarra, and H. Simon. TOP 500 Supercomputer Sites. http://www.top500.org.

[41] MVAPICH2: MPI over InfiniBand, 10GigE/iWARP and RoCE. https://mvapich.cse.ohio-state.edu/.

[42] Network Based Computing Laboratory. OSU Micro-Benchmarks. http://mvapich.cse.ohio-state.edu/benchmarks/, 2016.

[43] C. Nvidia. Programming Guide, 2008.

[44] K. Simonyan and A. Zisserman. Very Deep Convolutional Networks for Large-Scale Image Recognition. *arXiv preprint arXiv:1409.1556*, 2014.

[45] C. Szegedy, W. Liu, Y. Jia, P. Sermanet, S. Reed, D. Anguelov, D. Erhan, V. Vanhoucke, and A. Rabinovich. Going Deeper with Convolutions. In *Proceedings of the IEEE Conference on Computer Vision and Pattern Recognition*, pages 1–9, 2015.

[46] The HiDL Team. High Performance Deep Learning (HiDL) Project. http://hidl.cse.ohio-state.edu.

[47] The Open MPI Development Team. Open MPI : Open Source High Performance Computing. http://www.open-mpi.org.

[48] A. Vishnu, C. Siegel, and J. Daily. Distributed TensorFlow with MPI. *arXiv preprint arXiv:1603.02339*, 2016.

[49] D. Wang, A. Khosla, R. Gargeya, H. Irshad, and A. H. Beck. Deep Learning for Identifying Metastatic Breast Cancer. *ArXiv e-prints*, June 2016.

Model-based Iterative CT Image Reconstruction on GPUs

Amit Sabne
Microsoft *
amsabne@microsoft.com

Xiao Wang
School of Electrical and Computer Engineering, Purdue University
wang1698@purdue.edu

Sherman Kisner
High Performance Imaging LLC
kisner@ecn.purdue.edu

Charles Bouman
School of Electrical and Computer Engineering, Purdue University
bouman@purdue.edu

Anand Raghunathan
School of Electrical and Computer Engineering, Purdue University
raghunathan@purdue.edu

Samuel Midkiff
School of Electrical and Computer Engineering, Purdue University
smidkiff@ecn.purdue.edu

Abstract

Computed Tomography (CT) Image Reconstruction is an important technique used in a variety of domains, including medical imaging, electron microscopy, non-destructive testing and transportation security. Model-based Iterative Reconstruction (MBIR) using Iterative Coordinate Descent (ICD) is a CT algorithm that produces state-of-the-art results in terms of image quality. However, MBIR is highly computationally intensive and challenging to parallelize, and has traditionally been viewed as impractical in applications where reconstruction time is critical. We present the first GPU-based algorithm for ICD-based MBIR. The algorithm leverages the recently-proposed concept of SuperVoxels [1], and efficiently exploits the three levels of parallelism available in MBIR to better utilize the GPU hardware resources. We also explore data layout transformations to obtain more coalesced accesses and several GPU-specific optimizations for MBIR that boost performance. Across a suite of 3200 test cases, our GPU implementation obtains a geometric mean speedup of 4.43X over a state-of-the-art multi-core implementation on a 16-core iso-power CPU.

Categories and Subject Descriptors I.4.5 [*Image Processing and Computer Vision*]: Reconstruction—Transform methods; D.1.3 [*Programming Techniques*]: Concurrent Programming—Parallel Programming

Keywords Computed Tomography, Model Based Iterative Reconstruction, Iterative Coordinate Descent, Graphics Processing Units

* Author conducted this work while at Purdue University

PPoPP '17, February 04-08, 2017, Austin, TX, USA
 ISBN 978-1-4503-4493-7/17/02...$15.00
DOI: http://dx.doi.org/10.1145/3018743.3018765

1. Introduction

Computed tomography (CT) is an imaging technique that makes it possible to visualize the internals of an object (including the human body) from a limited number of lower-dimensional projections. Model-based iterative reconstruction, or *MBIR* [2, 3], is a CT technique in which a model based upon the geometry of the equipment is used to perform the reconstruction. MBIR, and more generally regularized iterative reconstruction methods, are known to produce better quality images compared to the alternative class of direct methods, which are commonly referred to as *filtered back projection* (FBP) [4, 5, 6, 7, 2, 3, 8]. Unfortunately, MBIR can require up to two orders of magnitude more compute operations than FBP, and is therefore regarded as impractical in scenarios where reconstruction time is paramount.

The MBIR method we focus on in this work is based on an Iterative Coordinate Descent (ICD) algorithm [2, 9, 10]. This algorithm iteratively updates voxels (3D-pixel) in the reconstructed image. A voxel update requires reads and writes of data that are shared among multiple voxels, and so the ICD algorithm does not exhibit explicit data parallelism. Fortunately, the iterative nature of the algorithm makes it error resilient, and a careful choice of voxels allows them to be updated in parallel [11, 12].

We are unaware of any previous effort to port ICD-based MBIR to GPUs. We attribute this to the stringent requirements GPU architectures impose to obtain high performance, such as the need for a high degree of parallelism, coalesced memory accesses, and minimal synchronization and control divergence.

The first challenge in porting MBIR to GPUs is parallelism exploitation. Broadly speaking, there are two key levels of parallelism in MBIR: the computation of a single voxel and the computation of different voxels in parallel. The former involves reduction-style parallelism and the latter requires updating shared data structures; hence, it is fair to say that MBIR lacks explicit, GPU-friendly data parallelism. The state-of-the-art parallel MBIR algorithm exploits inter-voxel parallelism on multi-core CPUs [1]. However, the CPU algorithm employs a much lower degree of parallelism than is needed to exploit the thousands of cores that GPUs offer. Restricting the synchronization cost in the presence of high thread counts is a challenge. The first contribution of this paper is a parallel algorithm that exploits multiple levels of parallelism on the GPU so as to achieve high GPU utilization.

The second challenge results from the irregular memory access pattern. MBIR is known to be a memory bandwidth intensive algorithm. Unfortunately, the memory accesses in MBIR are inherently irregular. Each voxel accesses locations within a 2D array in a sinusoidal pattern (Fig. 1), greatly limiting the caching benefits. Past research [1] has shown that grouping neighboring voxels into larger chunks, called SuperVoxels (*SVs*), and copying the data for a SuperVoxel into a dedicated buffer, called an SVB, can greatly improve cache locality and prefetching benefits on CPUs. GPUs, however, do not benefit much from automatic caching because the cache size per thread is very small. Moreover, GPUs lack hardware prefetching. The second contribution of this paper is a data layout transformation that obtains coalesced accesses for MBIR on GPUs. This transformation involves padding parts of the data, and obtains higher performance, despite performing additional computations, due to significantly improved GPU compute efficiency.

Since MBIR is a memory-bandwidth limited algorithm, the third contribution of this paper is a set of GPU-specific optimizations to improve memory bandwidth. First, a large number of active threads are required to utilize memory bandwidth. However, the MBIR GPU kernel requires a high register count per thread, limiting the number of active GPU threads. To overcome this issue, we migrate thread-local variables from registers into the GPU shared memory (on-chip programmer-managed L1 cache), and thereby obtain higher multi-threading. We also explore the use of the texture cache and improve the bandwidth of L2 cache accesses.

Although we demonstrate an ICD-based MBIR implementation on GPUs, the aforementioned issues and solutions are characteristic of ICD based optimization methods, which are used in a broader range of applications [1].

In summary, the contributions of this paper are as follows:

- This paper presents GPU-ICD, the first GPU algorithm for ICD-based MBIR, which exploits three levels of parallelism : i) inside a voxel's computation, ii) across multiple voxels inside an SV, and iii) across multiple SVs.
- The paper proposes data layout transformations that substantially increase coalesced memory accesses.
- The paper proposes a set of GPU-specific optimizations for MBIR.

With the above contributions, the GPU implementation achieves a geometric mean speedup of 4.43X over the state-of-the-art parallel implementation on an iso-power 16-core CPU [1].

The rest of this paper is organized as follows. Section 2 describes CT, the MBIR method, and the fastest-known CPU implementation. It also provides background on the architectural and programming model for GPUs. Section 3 describes our approach of mapping MBIR parallelism to GPUs, and presents the corresponding algorithm. Section 4 details our data layout transformations and GPU-specific optimizations. Section 5 describes experimental results that evaluate the proposed GPU implementation of MBIR. Section 6 discusses how GPU-ICD can be applied to a broader range of applications. Section 7 discusses related work, while Section 8 concludes the paper.

2. Background

This section begins with a brief description of the CT process. Next, it presents an outline of the fastest CPU implementation. The section ends with an overview of the GPU architecture and programming.

Fig. 1a illustrates a simple representative parallel beam X-ray CT apparatus. An X-ray source and a sensor array that detects X-rays are mounted on a rotating gantry, while the object to be imaged remains stationary. For each view angle, or θ, the recorded measurements from the sensors (which represent the attenuated X-rays that have passed through the object) are stored in a single column of a data structure, called the *sinogram* (Fig. 1b). Different sensors pick up data for different sets of voxels according to the position of the projection rays terminating on each sensor at each θ.

2.1 Computed Tomography and MBIR

Fig. 1b shows the captured measurements for the voxels V_1 and V_2 for different values of θ. The trajectories of the voxels in the sinogram show a sinusoidal pattern. The objective of MBIR is to reconstruct the object from the sinogram data.

Alg. 1 shows the mechanism to update a single voxel, which forms the core of ICD [2, 9, 10], the algorithm traditionally used in MBIR. The algorithm computes two values, theta1 and theta2. The error sinogram, e, represents $y - Ax$, where y is the measurement sinogram, x is the image to be reconstructed, and A represents the system matrix that encodes the CT equipment geometry. Intuitively, the A matrix entries capture the radio density incident upon a voxel, which is proportional to the distance from the X-ray source. The weighing matrix, w, contains the inverse variance of the scanner noise. The theta1 and theta2 values are then used to find the new value of the voxel v, which belongs to x. Finally, the error sinogram is updated to reflect the changed value of v. Alg. 1 repeatedly updates voxels until convergence is reached. Faster convergence is achieved by updat-

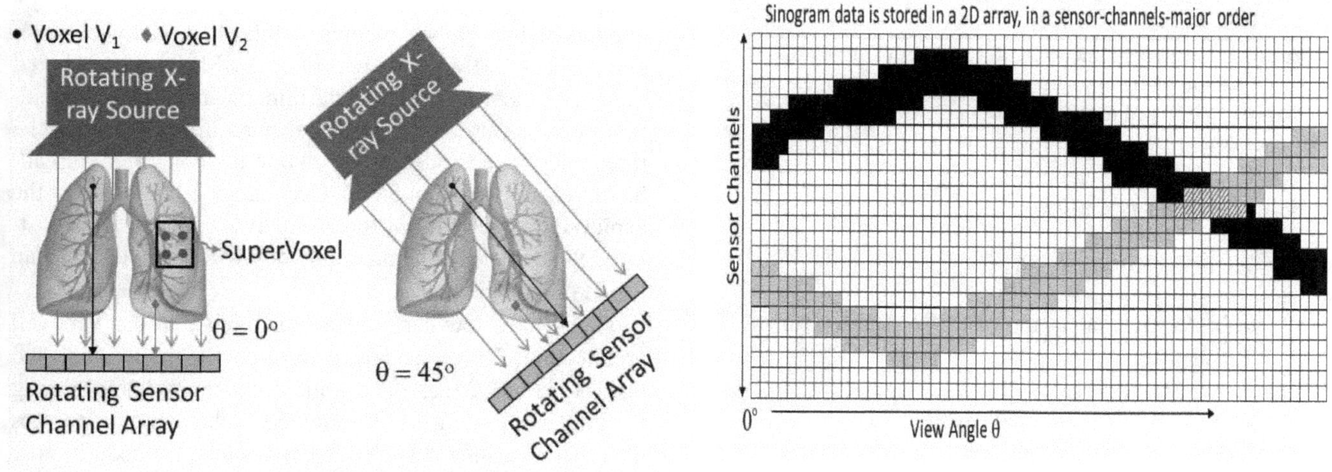

(a) CT Equipment Operation : Different sensors may collect data belonging to a given voxel, depending upon θ

(b) Data collected (sinogram) for voxels V_1 and V_2 : Only a partial sinogram is shown here

Figure 1: Computed tomography geometry and measurement data organization

---

Algorithm 1: Updating Single Voxel (Foundation of all ICD-based techniques)

Input: v - the voxel value to be updated, e- error sinogram, w - weights, A - system matrix representing the CT equipment geometry
Output: v - updated voxel value, e - updated error sinogram

theta1=0;
theta2=0;
`// Calculate theta1, theta2`
foreach $i \in \theta$ **do**
  foreach *($j \in$ sensors containing measurements for the voxel at angle i)* **do**
    theta1 += -$w_{ij} \times$ A[voxel number]$_{ij} \times e_{ij}$;
    theta2 += $w_{ij} \times$ A[voxel number]$^2_{ij}$;
`// func is computationally inexpensive`
delta ← func(v, theta1, theta2, neighbors of v);
v ← v + delta; `// update the voxel`
`// Update error sinogram`
foreach $i \in \theta$ **do**
  foreach *($j \in$ sensors containing measurements for the voxel at angle i)* **do**
    e_{ij} -= A[voxel number]$_{ij} \times$ delta;

---

ing voxels in a randomized order [13] and by *zero-skipping*, *i.e.*, skipping voxels whose values, along with all of their neighbors, are zero.

2.2 Parallel MBIR on the CPU

Several challenges arise in obtaining high performance from the ICD algorithm. We now describe the state-of-the-art adaptation of ICD, Parallel SuperVoxel ICD (PSV-ICD) [1] which was proposed to improve performance on multi-core CPUs.

The sinusoidal access pattern (Fig. 1b) makes caching and prefetching ineffective. Because neighboring voxels access access neighboring sinogram data, PSV-ICD groups to-

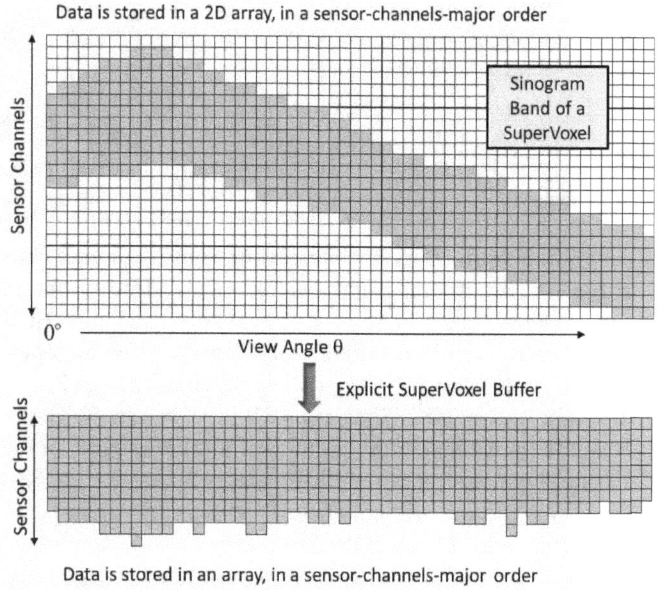

***Figure 2: SuperVoxel buffer (SVB):** linearizes data accesses to a great degree, achieving better cache locality and prefetching on CPUs*

gether neighboring voxels into a *SuperVoxel* (SV). PSV-ICD then creates an explicit buffer, the SuperVoxel buffer (SVB), for each SV and copies the SV's sinogram data into it. This improves locality of the data, and increases the linearity of accesses, which makes prefetching more effective. Fig. 2 shows a SuperVoxel, and it also displays the corresponding sinogram accesses for the SuperVoxel. The weights also display the sinusoidal access pattern and are allocated in a similar data structure. When appropriately sized, SVBs can often fit in the CPU's L1 cache.

Multiple voxels can potentially be simultaneously updated using multi-core parallelism; however, because of the sinusoidal access pattern, any two voxels are bound to par-

Algorithm 2: PSV-ICD Algorithm

```
Input: A - system geometry matrix, e - error sinogram, w -
       weight sinogram
Output: Converged reconstructed image
Create SVs;
iter = 1;
while image not converged do
    if iter == 1 then
        setOfSVsToUpdate ← all SVs;
    else if iter is even then
        setOfSVsToUpdate ← top 20% SVs by the update
          amount;
    else
        setOfSVsToUpdate ← random 20% SVs;
    foreach sv ∈ setOfSVstoUpdate do // done in
      parallel on CPU cores
        create weights SVB_w;
        create error SVB_e;
        SVB_e' ← SVB_e;
        foreach voxel in sv do
            updateVoxel(voxel, SVB_e, SVB_w, A);
        SVB_Δe ← SVB_e' - SVB_e;
        lock();
        e ← e - SVB_Δe;
        unlock();
    iter++;
```

tially share error sinogram data, as shown by the fainter cells in Fig. 1b. Therefore, simultaneous updates from different voxels to the same sinogram entry must be performed in a critical section. PSV-ICD parallelizes across different Super-Voxels, while sequentially updating voxels within an SV, as shown in Algorithm 2. Since each SV has a private SVB, updating the error sinogram is deferred until all voxels in the SV are done, and then the difference between the updated error SVB and the original error SVB is computed and synchronously added back to the original error sinogram.

2.3 GPU Architecture and Programming Model

We briefly describe the GPU architecture and programming model using the example of NVIDIA's Maxwell Titan X and CUDA, which were used in our work.

The GPU's cores are organized into 24 streaming multiprocessor units (SMMs), each having 128 CUDA cores. High-performance GPU programs are typically written using the CUDA programming model, where the programmer offloads parallel sub-programs, called *kernels*, onto the GPU. The CPU and GPU have separate memory spaces among which programmers perform data transfers explicitly. Threads in a kernel are divided into *threadblocks*, which are subdivided into *warps*. A warp represents the SIMD width of the GPU. Threads of a threadblock can synchronize using the *__syncthreads()* function call. There is no such primitive available for threads belonging to different threadblocks. Each thread in the kernel has access to registers, on-chip programmer-managed cache (shared memory), and the device (global) memory. Multiple threadblocks execute on each SMM. Resources of each SMM, such as shared memory, registers, etc. are partitioned among the threadblocks executing on it. Thus, larger requirements from the threadblocks can constrain the maximum concurrent threadblocks executing on an SMM. Occupancy is the metric of the achieved degree of multi-threading. It is the ratio of coexisting GPU threads to the maximum number of threads that can reside on the GPU.

GPUs have low cache sizes per thread. In the Maxwell architecture, L1 cache and texture cache are unified, and have a size of 24KB. The unified cache is shared among the threads of an SMM. The unified cache can only possess data that remains read-only across kernels. By default, only the local data and textures are stored in the unified cache. There is a common L2 cache for all SMMs, sized 3MB. It caters to all global data accesses. If threads in a warp access neighboring memory locations, these accesses may get coalesced into only a single memory access, improving memory bandwidth.

3. Mapping MBIR Parallelism to the GPU

This section describes the proposed mapping of MBIR parallelism to the GPU. Section 3.1 describes the levels of parallelism that we exploit. Section 3.2 presents our thread-mapping scheme, and the resulting GPU-ICD algorithm.

3.1 Understanding the MBIR Parallelism

Three levels of parallelism exist in the processing of each image through the MBIR algorithm.

Intra-voxel parallelism - Updating each voxel requires computation of theta1 and theta2 (steps 3-6 of Algorithm 1). This process requires a dot-product of size (number of views) × (average channels per voxel per view), which is large in practice (>2000). Reduction-style parallelism is exploited for this operation. Updating the error sinogram after the new voxel value is computed (steps 9-11 of Algorithm 1) can also be performed in parallel.

Intra-SV parallelism - Voxels inside a given SV can be updated in parallel, as long as the updates to the error sinogram entries do not overlap. The number of voxels in an SV can be high, *e.g.*, an SV of side 30 would have 900 voxels, allowing significant parallelism.

Inter-SV parallelism - Multiple SVs can be operated on in parallel as well. However, the degree of available parallelism along this dimension is modest, *e.g.*, for an image of 512×512, an SV side of 30 would lead to 289 SVs.

The PSV-ICD algorithm only exploits the top-most level of parallelism, *i.e.*, inter-SV parallelism. As the number of SVs in a typical reconstruction is higher than the CPU core count, this approach provides sufficient parallelism. Although SVBs can be larger than the CPU L1 cache, since

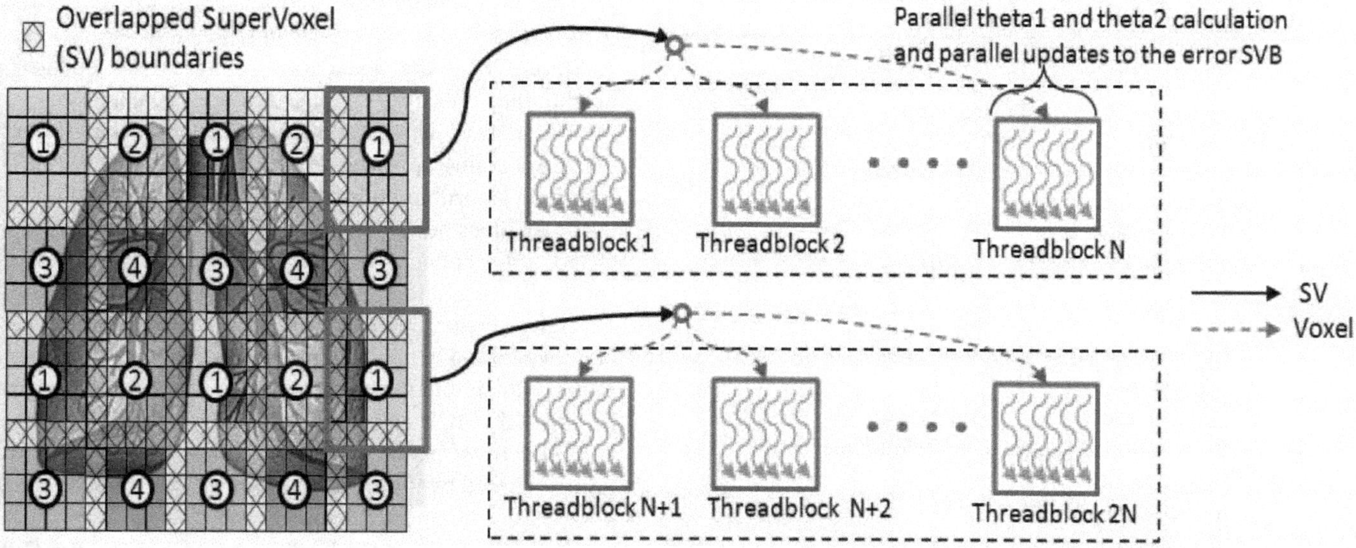

Figure 3: GPU Parallelism Mapping *- SuperVoxels with the same color belong to the same checkerboard group (marked by circled numbers). They do not share any boundaries, and therefore can be concurrently updated. Assigning consecutive threadblocks to the same SV increases achieved L2 bandwidth.*

each CPU core has its own private L2 cache, SVBs for each SV can fit in it, and high locality can be achieved. On the other hand, intra-SV parallelism can lead to false sharing among the CPU cores. The fine-grained intra-voxel parallelism can be exploited by vector instructions, but the irregular memory access pattern hinders autovectorization.

In contrast to the CPU (where a few tens of threads suffice), orders-of-magnitude more GPU threads must be created to ensure that cores are utilized and memory latency is effectively hidden. The number of SVs ranges in the low hundreds. Hence, exploiting only inter-SV parallelism is insufficient. The L1 cache size per thread is fairly small on GPUs (making it difficult to contain an SVB), and no hardware prefetching is present. Unlike CPUs, the L2 cache latency is at least an order of magnitude higher than the L1 latency, lowering SVB caching benefits. One way to gain benefits from inter-SV parallelism alone could be for each SMM to operate on a single SV at a time, so that sufficient L1 cache is available. However, this severely limits the GPU occupancy, leading to poor performance.

Exploiting intra-SV parallelism alone faces similar issues. The voxel count per SV is of the order of a few hundreds, and fails to exploit sufficient GPU parallelism. Similarly, intra-voxel parallelism has a low degree of parallelism. One approach, therefore, would be to use both inter-SV and intra-SV parallelism. Different threadblocks then may operate on different SVs, while threads in a threadblock may update individual voxels in parallel. However, this approach eliminates any possibility of coalesced accesses to the sinograms. Our approach therefore employs all three levels of parallelism, as we describe next.

3.2 Parallelism Mapping

Fig. 3 shows our parallelism mapping scheme, and Alg. 3 describes the corresponding GPU-ICD algorithm. Unlike PSV-ICD, our mapping employs all three levels of parallelism (intra-voxel, intra-SV, and inter-SV) identified above. For each SV, multiple CUDA threadblocks are launched, partitioning the voxels in the SV among themselves. Zero-skipping (Sec. 2) can lead to load imbalance among the different threadblocks, therefore our algorithm performs dynamic scheduling of voxels among threadblocks. Adjacent SVs share boundary voxels, as in PSV-ICD, to obtain faster convergence.

Since SVB size is much larger than the L1 cache size on GPUs, achieving good cache locality via L1 cache or shared memory is impossible. Fortunately, SVB sizes are small enough to fit in the GPU L2 cache. Although GPU L2 latencies are high, our parallelism mapping scheme increases the obtained L2 bandwidth by launching multiple consecutive threadblocks per SV to make the most of the L2 temporal locality. The amount of parallelism in this dimension is limited by the bound on the exploitable intra-SV parallelism.

Each threadblock updates one voxel at a time, exploiting intra-voxel parallelism to compute the theta1 and theta2 values. The partial values computed by each thread are stored into the shared memory, and then reduced using a fast tree-style reduction [14]. Only a single thread of the threadblock updates the voxel value. Writing back to the error sinogram is again performed in parallel by the threads of a threadblock. However, as different threadblocks may be writing to the same sinogram locations, this write-back requires atomic updates.

Algorithm 3: GPU-ICD Algorithm

```
Input: A - system geometry matrix, e - error sinogram, w -
       weight sinogram
Output: Converged reconstructed image
Function MBIR_GPU_Kernel(SVBs, A)
    // Each kernel thread executes this
    tid ← thread identifier;
    svID ← getSVId(tid);
    while (voxel ← atomicFetch(svId)) do // all
     threads in a threablock get the same
     voxel
        Calculate partial theta1 and theta2 and store them in
          shared memory;
        __syncthreads();
        Perform tree-style reduction for theta1 and theta2;
        __syncthreads();
        if tid==0 then
            Update voxel value;
        __syncthreads();
        Atomically write back to the error SVB;
        __syncthreads();

Create SVs;
iter ← 1;
while image not converged do
    if iter == 1 then
        setOfSVsToUpdate ← all SVs;
    else if iter is even then
        setOfSVsToUpdate ← top 25% SVs by the update
          amount;
    else
        setOfSVsToUpdate ← random 25% SVs;
    cb ← makeCheckerBoardGroups(setOfSVsToUpdate);
    for (k=0; k<4; k++) do
        // Launch GPU kernels, each having
           BATCH_SIZE SVs
        for (i=0; i< cb[k].SVCount; i+= BATCH_SIZE) do
            if (cb[k].SVCount - i) < threshold then
                break;
            // done in parallel via GPU kernel
            Create SVBs for the batch in the GPU memory;
            MBIR_GPU_Kernel(SVBs, A);
            // done in parallel via GPU kernel
            Atomically update error sinogram for all SVs in the
              batch;
    iter++;
```

A key distinction of the GPU-ICD algorithm is that unlike PSV-ICD, where the error sinogram is updated with partial deltas ($SVB_{\Delta e}$ in line 18 Algo. 2), immediately after each SV is updated all error sinogram updates are performed once voxel updates across all SVs in a GPU kernel have finished. Similarly, all SVBs are created prior to the execution of the MBIR_GPU_Kernel. The GPU-ICD algorithm does this to avoid cache pollution engendered by $SVB_{\Delta e}$ and SVB'_e accesses during the execution of MBIR_GPU_Kernel. Instead, SVB generation and error sinogram write-backs are performed via separate individual GPU kernels.

Since SVs share boundaries, simultaneous updates of neighboring SVs may lead to erroneous voxel values on the boundaries. This occurs since the error sinogram and the voxel value lose the necessary correspondence. The PSV-ICD algorithm updates fewer SVs in parallel at a time (~16) and does not exploit intra-SV parallelism, making the chances of a boundary voxel being updated simultaneously in parallel negligible. However, the GPU-ICD algorithm generally updates a higher number of SVs concurrently and employs intra-SV parallelism, and therefore is more likely to perform simultaneous boundary voxel updates. To avoid this, the GPU-ICD algorithm partitions SVs into four sets in a *checkerboard* pattern, as shown in Fig. 3. SVs in a given group, marked by the same color in Fig. 3, cannot be neighbors and can be updated in parallel.

Load imbalance is the last issue overcome by the GPU-ICD algorithm. The algorithm launches up to *BATCH_SIZE* SVs at a time on the GPU. However, randomization in the SV ordering, paired with the distribution into four checkerboard sets, may result in fewer SVs than *BATCH_SIZE* getting launched in a GPU kernel. This results in GPU underutilization. To overcome this issue, the GPU-ICD algorithm increases the fraction of SVs to be updated to 25% in each iteration, compared to 20% in the PSV-ICD algorithm. This increases the SV availability in each of the four groups. Furthermore, GPU-ICD only launches a kernel if the number of SVs to be launched is above a *threshold*, which is set to be *BATCH_SIZE/4*.

4. Performance Optimizations for GPU-ICD

In this section, we describe additional optimizations that were explored to improve the performance of GPU-ICD. Section 4.1 presents a data layout transformation to achieve coalesced accesses. Section 4.2 presents a mechanism to exploit the GPU shared memory, while Section 4.3 describes our approach to increase the achieved memory bandwidth.

4.1 Data Layout Transformations to Obtain Coalesced Accesses

The accesses made per voxel to an SVB are not completely linear, as seen in Fig. 4a. For each location in the sinogram associated with a voxel, an associated A-matrix element needs to be accessed. All these A-matrix elements, across all views, are placed in memory in a contiguous fashion, using a sparse matrix format. The data in both the A-matrix and the SVBs are stored in a sensor-channels-major order. In our first naive implementation, threads in a threadblock operate on these data in a sensor-channels-major order as shown by the highlighted cells in Fig. 4a, and therefore fail to obtain coalesced accesses. Moreover, the starting location for each view for each voxel must be pre-calculated and then read before the SVB could be accessed.

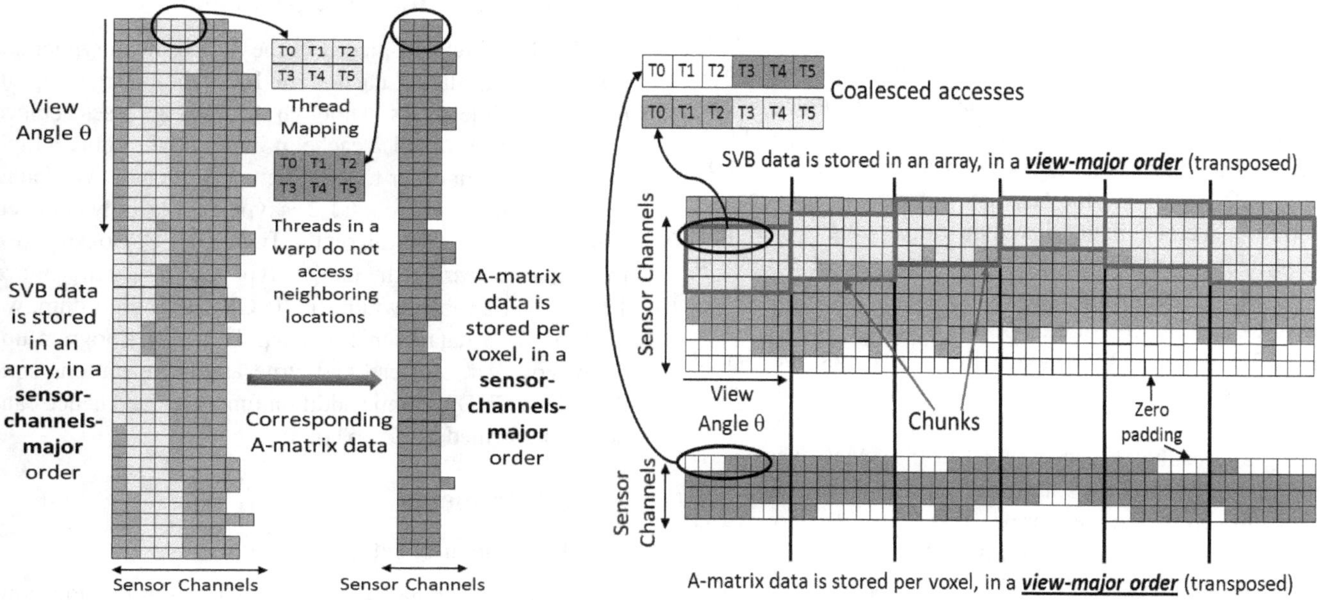

(a) ***Original data layout*** *- Lighter cells contain data for a given voxel in the SVB. Accesses to both the SVB and A-matrix are in the sensor-channels order, and hence are uncoalesced.*

(b) ***Transformed layout*** *- The SVB and A-matrix are both transposed. Data accesses are now in the view order. The A-matrix is zero-padded. Each chunk in an SVB and its corresponding A-matrix chunk are now perfect rectangles.*

Figure 4: Data layout transformation to obtain coalesced accesses

To obtain coalesced accesses, we first transpose the SVB, *i.e.*, data is stored in a view-major order instead of in the sensor-channels-major order. This naturally increases the run-length (length of contiguous accesses per row). However, the number of elements in each row to be operated on is highly variable because of the sinusoidal access pattern, and distributing them fairly among threads becomes difficult. Our scheme overcomes this issue. First, we make the SVB perfectly rectangular by zero-padding, as shown in Fig. 4b, and place each row at an aligned address. Next, the SVB data required per voxel can be conceptually thought of being split into chunks of a given width. Each chunk is a rectangular block, containing few non-voxel-related elements. The next layout transformation zero-pads the A-matrix data so that each SVB chunk can be mapped to an equivalent A-matrix chunk. The computation now simply involves reading each row from the chunks of the SVB and A-matrix, and performing an element-by-element multiplication, achieving coalesced accesses. The zero-padding of the A-matrix ensures that non-voxel-related elements in the SVB do not affect the computation correctness. Although zero-padding increases the amount of computation, and requires additional data to be read, the benefits obtained by coalesced accesses outweigh these costs. In the voxel update mechanism, the chunks get distributed among the warps of the threadblock that is updating the voxel. To do so, only the starting locations and the number of rows for each chunk need to be pre-computed and accessed, overcoming the penalty of per-view starting location look-ups in the naive implementation.

4.2 Achieving High Occupancy via Register Spilling to Shared Memory

GPUs hide their longer (than CPU) memory latency by bringing in a new warp whenever a running warp is waiting on a memory access. Because MBIR performance is largely limited by memory accesses, a large number of warps must be available on each SMM.

Our initial GPU-ICD implementation used 44 registers per thread. Since registers in an SMM are partitioned among threadblocks of the SMM, occupancy is limited by the high register requirement. For a threadblock of 256 threads, occupancy was being restricted to 50%. To achieve higher occupancy, we used the `maxRegCount` flag with `nvcc` and restricted the register count to 32 per thread, achieving 100% occupancy. We observed only a 6% performance improvement by doing this. This was because restricting the register count led to increased accesses to the GPU L1 cache, and the L1 cache hit rate remained poor (30%). The spilled registers were frequently being fetched from the L2 cache, whose high latency was limiting performance.

To address this issue, we manually placed some of the variables from each thread into shared memory. This allowed the MBIR_GPU_Kernel to be compiled with 32 registers per thread. We again achieved 100% occupancy, and obtained a significant performance boost, as will be shown in Section 5.

4.3 Increasing Achieved Memory Bandwidth

Since MBIR is a memory bound algorithm, achieving high memory bandwidth is essential to obtaining high performance. The primary way to achieve high bandwidth is to increase locality, resulting in higher cache hit rates. On the GPU, this is typically achieved by storing reusable data in the shared memory. Shared memory is partitioned across threadblocks. Hence, the larger the shared memory requirement, the smaller the number of concurrent threadblocks. In GPU-ICD, SVBs are the key data structures to be considered for placement in the shared memory owing to their high reuse. Unfortunately, the SVBs are large, and placing them in the shared memory would severely lower the obtained occupancy. *e.g.*, an SV of side 6 voxels results in an SVB of size 135KB for 720 views, which goes beyond the shared memory size. For an SV of side 4, the SVB would require 90KB. As the shared memory size on an SMM is 96KB, only a single threadblock can execute on the SMM. The maximum number of threads a threadblock could meaningfully use is limited by the number of views, i.e., 720, in our case. Hence, the achieved occupancy would only be 35%. Further, since such an SV would have only 16 voxels, intra-SV parallelism, as well as the reuse frequency would get diminished significantly. Therefore, we had to place SVBs in the global memory. To improve the achieved memory bandwidth, we next present two techniques.

4.3.1 Reading the A-Matrix through Texture Cache

The A-matrix is a read-only data structure. Therefore, it makes sense to read it via the combined Texture memory/L1 cache datapath on the Maxwell architecture. This is achieved by explicitly marking the data as read-only, and specifying the `__restrict` keyword that allows the compiler to read the data via the texture cache.

Since A-matrix accesses have little temporal locality, they consume high memory bandwidth, forming a bottleneck. The A-matrix data is stored as `floats`, requiring four bytes per entry. To reduce the memory bandwidth consumed, our scheme converts this data into `unsigned chars`, needing only a byte per entry. Each A-matrix entry is normalized to a byte-long equivalent A-matrix entry as follows:

newAEntry= (unsigned char) (AEntry/maximum of all A-matrix entries for the voxel)*255 + 0.5

The division by the maximum performs normalization, while the multiplication by 255 brings out the MSBs in the 8-bit `unsigned char`. The normalization allows for more bits in the `float` entry to get transferred to the `char`. Adding 0.5 achieves rounding instead of truncation. The maximum A-matrix entry per voxel needs to be stored and referred to when calculating the original `float` value back from the `char`, prior to the actual computation. The overhead of storing and reading this extra data gets compensated for by the reduction in the total data read, as will be shown in Section 5.

4.3.2 Obtaining Higher L2 Bandwidth

The SVBs, which are placed in the global memory, get accessed through the L2 cache. The L2 cache is large enough to hold multiple SVBs. Although the SVB accesses achieve a high hit rate on the L2 cache, it is essential to obtain high L2 bandwidth in order to gain high performance. We found that accessing data through L2 as type `float` only obtained 50% of the L2 bandwidth on the Titan X GPU. However, we found that accessing the data as type `double` can achieve 100% of the L2 bandwidth. In the GPU-ICD algorithm, we read the SVB data in this manner. The error sinogram updates, however, are read-and-write atomic operations conducted via CUDA atomic addition functions, and hence cannot be performed as `double`.

5. Experiments

5.1 Experimental Setup

Inputs: The benchmark data set used in this evaluation comprises 3200 test cases obtained from an Imatron C-300 scanner from ALERT Task Order 3 (TO3) [4]. The slices in this dataset are generated using parallel beam projection, and have reconstruction image size of 512x512. The data is generated using 720 uniformly distributed views between 0 and 180 degrees. The number of sensor array channels used was 1024.

System setup: Our GPU experiments are performed with Nvidia CUDA Titan X GPU which comprises 24 SMMs, each having 128 cores, clocked at 1127 MHz. The GPU has a device memory of 12GB. The GPU node contained an Intel i7-6700K CPU with 16GB RAM. The GPU program was compiled with `nvcc` with *-O3* option. The CPU experiments were conducted on a node with two sockets, each containing Intel Xeon E5-2670 CPU, running at 2.6GHz. The total number of cores was 16, with 64GB RAM. The CPU code was compiled with `icc` with *-O3* option. The TDP of the CPU (230W) is comparable to that of the GPU TDP (250W).

5.2 Overall Performance

Table 1 presents the execution time comparison between the CPU and GPU versions of MBIR. Owing to zero-skipping, neither PSV-ICD, nor GPU-ICD update all voxels in each iteration. Hence, we measure convergence using *equivalent iterations* or *equits*. An update of N voxels, where N is the total number of voxels in the image, is one equit. We first obtain the golden output image by executing the traditional ICD algorithm for 40 equits, by when it is known to converge. For PSV-ICD and GPU-ICD, we evaluate algorithmic convergence by measuring the root-mean-square error (RMSE) with respect to the golden image in Hounsfield Units[1]. We report execution time when the RMSE goes below 10HU, since previous work [15] has found that no visi-

[1] The Hounsfield Unit (HU): a CT measurement unit of the object's radio density compared to the radio density of distilled water.

Table 1: Comparison of PSV-ICD and GPU-ICD MBIR Performance.

	Mean Execution Time (s)	Mean Speedup over Sequential ICD	Std. Dev. of Exec. Time	SV Side Used	Average #Equits to Converge	Time per Equit (s)	Other parameter values
PSV-ICD (CPU)	138.26X	1.801	0.535	13	4.8	0.41	
GPU-ICD	0.407	611.79X (4.43X over PSV-ICD)	0.083	33	5.9	0.07	Chunk Width: 32, #Threadblocks/SV: 40, #SVs/batch: 32

ble artifacts remain at this level. Sequential ICD refers to the publicly available, single-core MBIR implementation [16]. The geometric mean speedup achieved by GPU-ICD over the sequential ICD is 611.79X, while over PSV-ICD is 4.43X. The PSV-ICD time per equit is 5.86X higher than for GPU-ICD. However, GPU-ICD requires more equits to converge. Table 1 also shows that the standard deviation in PSV-ICD runs is much higher than in the GPU-ICD ones. We suspect that GPU-ICD is being limited by the span, lowering the deviation.

Fig. 5 compares the convergence speeds of GPU-ICD and PSV-ICD on a representative image. GPU-ICD achieves convergence much rapidly compared to PSV-ICD.

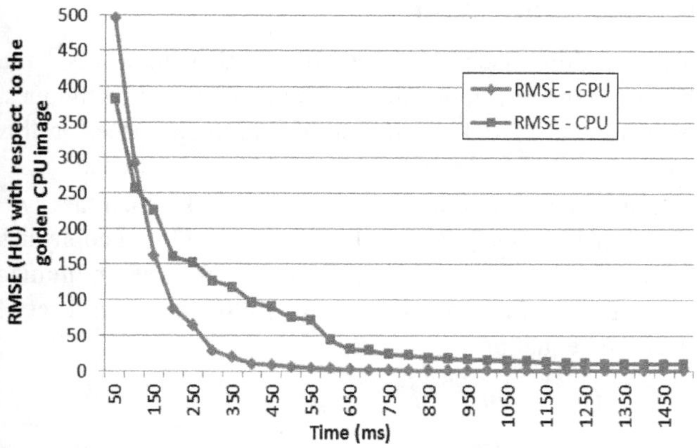

Figure 5: Convergence of PSV-ICD (CPU) and GPU-ICD Algorithms

Table 1 presented several parameters used in the GPU-ICD execution. We tuned these parameters on a representative image, and used those values for rest of the images. We observed however that the best performing parameter values differ across images, with a significant execution time variation. Therefore, the GPU performance in Table 1 can be improved with image-specific parameter selection. Next, we present performance analysis of these parameters on our representative image. To do so, we change one parameter value at a time, while retaining the other parameter values as shown in Table 1.

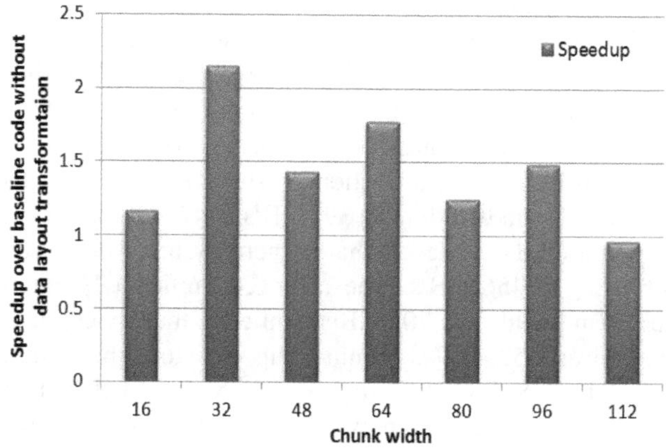

Figure 6: Speedup obtained by data layout transformed code vs. a code with the default data layout

5.3 Performance Impact of the Optimizations

Fig. 6 shows the performance benefits obtained by the proposed data layout transformation (Sec. 4.1). The speedup is calculated over the naive GPU code where the default data layout was employed. For smaller widths, data chunks for a voxel are small in size, lowering the total achieved coalesced access count. For larger chunk widths, the penalty of additional computation and memory accesses becomes prohibitive. The chunk width of 32 performs the best, obtaining a speedup of 2.1X. Widths that are multiples of warp size (i.e 32) perform better because they achieve aligned memory accesses.

Table 2: Impact of shrinking the A-matrix and reading it via Texture cache

Reading A-matrix from (memory, type)	Execution Time (s)	Achieved Bandwidth of Unified L1/Texture Cache (Hit Rate%)
(Global, `float`)	0.48	
(Texture, `float`)	0.45	519GB/s (41.78)
(Global, `char`)	0.44	
(Texture, `char`)	0.41	702GB/s (60.36)

Table 2 summarizes the benefits of compressing and reading the A-matrix via unified L1/texture cache. Shrinking the A-matrix lowers the memory footprint and achieves higher hit rate on the unified L1/texture cache, achieving a 1.17X speedup.

Table 3: Impact of several GPU-specific optimizations

Optimization Turned Off	Slowdown
Reading Sinogram as `double`	1.053X
Placing Variables on the Shared Memory	1.124X
Exploiting Intra-SV Parallelism	6.251X
Dynamic voxel distribution	1.064X
Setting threshold for batch sizes	1.099X

Table 3 measures impact of five optimizations. The impact is measured in terms of the slowdown caused when optimizations were turned off. The first two are i) reading sinograms as `double`, and ii) spilling registers on the shared memory in order to increase occupancy. These optimizations were described in Section 4. The prior increased the achieved L2 bandwidth from 395 GB/s to 472 GB/s. The latter increased the achieved shared memory bandwidth from 398 GB/s to 456 GB/s. The achieved unified L1/Texture cache bandwidth was 702 GB/s, while for the device memory, it was 152 GB/s. Summed up, the total bandwidth achieved is 1802 GB/s, which is 5.36X that of the maximum device memory bandwidth (336 GB/s) for the Titan X GPU. Achieving such high memory bandwidth reduces the memory access bottleneck known to exist in MBIR. The third optimization in Table 3, i.e., intra-SV parallelism, has the highest performance impact measuring about 6X. Exploiting intra-SV parallelism is therefore crucial on GPUs. The last two optimizations (from Section 3) deal with load imbalance issues. The dynamic distribution of voxels of an SV among threadblocks overcomes the load imbalance that arises in static distribution owing to the zero-skipping. Setting a threshold on the number of SVs to be launched in a batch removes the GPU underutilization penalty in cases where only a few SVs are launched.

5.4 Performance Impact of Tuning Parameters

Unlike PSV-ICD, where only the SV side length impacts the achieved performance, several parameters affect the GPU-ICD performance. Fig. 7a measures execution time for different SuperVoxel side lengths. Smaller SV sides result in higher contention during the atomic updates in GPU-ICD. The intra-SV parallelism exploitation worsens this behavior compared to PSV-ICD. For larger SV sides, the SVBs become too large, reducing the L2 caching benefits. An SV side of 33 performs the best, since it achieves the highest L2 throughput. The secondary vertical axis in Fig. 7a displays the number of equits required for each SV side. This number increases with the SV side because updates to the error sinogram occur at coarser granularity, slowing down the algorithmic convergence. We also suspect that the intra-SV parallelism slows the convergence.

Fig. 7b shows the impact of exploited intra-SV granularity. The performance improves with the number of threadblocks used per SV, i.e., intra-SV parallelism. A moderately high number of threadblocks per SV achieves higher L2 temporal cache locality. The performance saturates after 32 threadblocks.

Fig. 7c evaluates performance impact of the exploited degree of intra-voxel parallelism. This degree is determined by the number of threads in a threadblock. Occupancy, which gets affected by the number of threads in a threadblock, plays an important role in the achieved performance, e.g. 384 threads per threadblock result in lower occupancy, leading to lower performance. However, occupancy is not the only factor to consider, e.g., with 64 threads per block, although the occupancy is 100%, the small threadcount per block results in larger active threadblock count. This results in more SVBs being accessed simultaneously, leading to L2 conflicts. A larger threadcount per block (e.g. 512) leads to asymmetric work distribution of the 720 views involved, and increases the reduction cost, resulting in lower performance.

Fig. 7d measures the impact of the (maximum) number of SVs updated in a batch (individual GPU kernel). The lower this number, the higher the total number of kernel launches, resulting in higher overheads occurring from kernel launches. If the number gets too high, then updates to error sinogram start taking place at coarser granularity, leading to slower algorithmic convergence.

6. Generalization

This section discusses how GPU-ICD generalizes to a broader range of applications. The algorithmic techniques, as well as the GPU-specific optimizations proposed in this paper, are applicable to these classes of applications.

For many important sensing problems (such as synchrotron imaging [17], machine learning [18], geophysics sensing [19], radar sensing [20]), it is necessary to minimize a convex cost function given by the following general set of quadratic equations:

$$f(x) = \|y - Ax\|_\Lambda^2 = (y - Ax)^t \Lambda (y - Ax) \qquad (1)$$

where y is a $M \times 1$ vector, A is a very large $M \times N$ matrix, Λ is a diagonal matrix of weights, and x is a $N \times 1$ vector. To find x^* such that $f(x^*)$ is minimized, we can solve Equation (1) by numerical iterative algorithms.

ICD algorithms have received increasing attention as an effective approach to compute the solution to the general optimization problem in Equation (1) because of their fast and robust convergence [2, 1, 10, 11]. In conventional ICD algorithms, every element, $x_j \in x$, is cycled through and updated exactly once in each iteration. The update of each element, x_j, is designed to decrease the value of $f(x)$, so ICD algorithms result in a monotonically decreasing sequence of cost. Under appropriate technical conditions, the ICD algorithms asymptotically reach the value $\lim_{n \to \infty} f(x^n) = f(x^*)$.

Importantly, each update generally requires the evaluation of $A_{*,j} x_j$, and this requires an access to a single col-

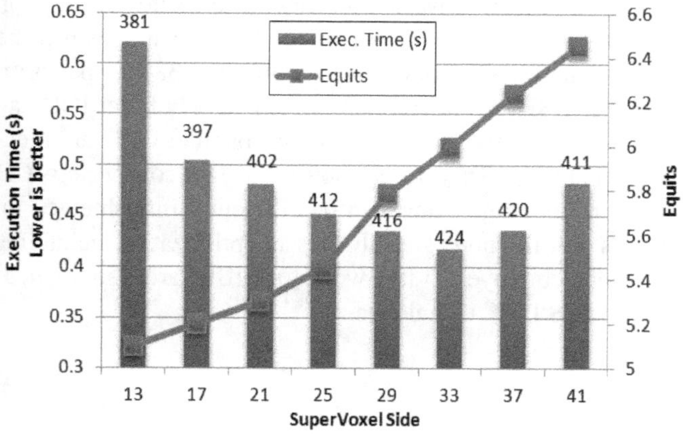

(a) SuperVoxel side length impacts both performance and convergence. The numbers above bars indicate L2 throughput in GB/s

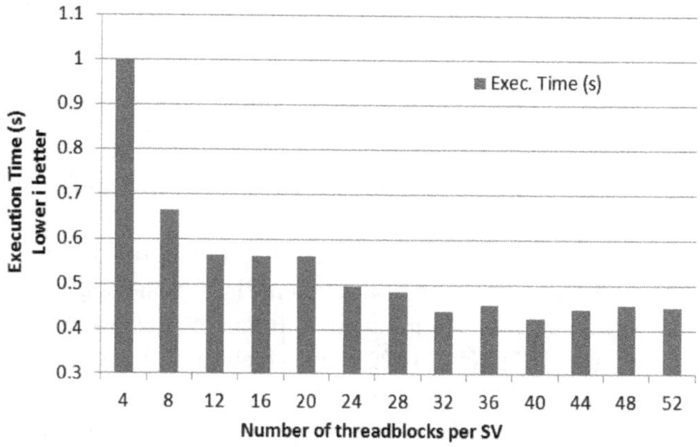

(b) Number of threadblocks used per SV determines the exploited intra-SV parallelism granularity

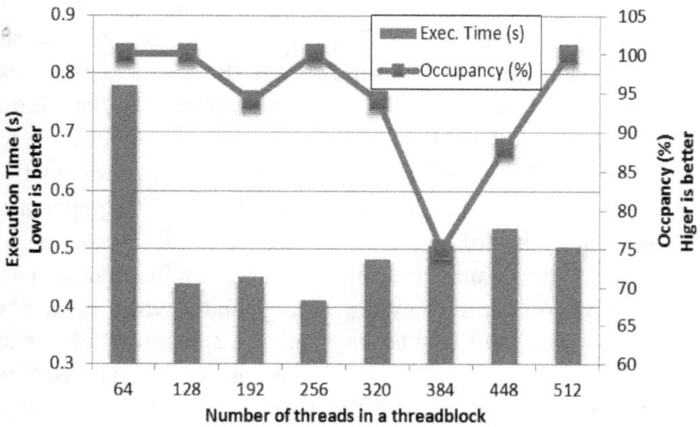

(c) Number of threads in a threadblock determine the exploited intra-voxel parallelism granularity

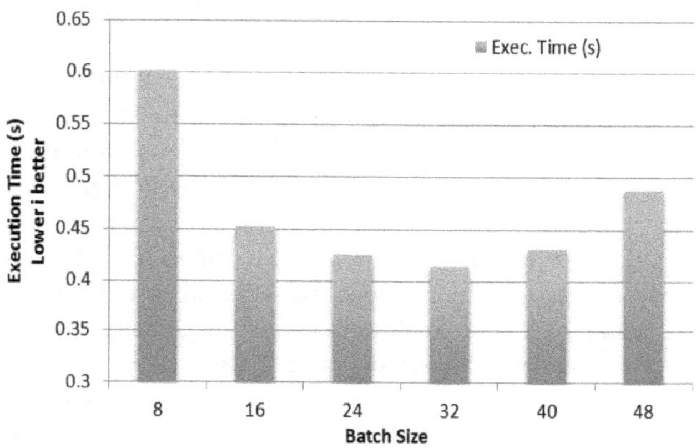

(d) Varying number of SVs processed per kernel launch (batch)

Figure 7: Performance impact of various tuning parameters: *values of these parameters can significantly affect the achieved performance*

umn of the matrix A. While ICD algorithms have been of great theoretical interest, they have been generally assumed to be unsuited for GPUs because of what appears to be their intrinsically serial nature as well as the restriction on how columns of the A matrix are accessed. The GPU-ICD introduced in this paper demonstrates that ICD algorithms can be efficiently implemented on GPUs. Not only does the GPU-ICD show that a large number of parallel operations can run simultaneously for ICD algorithms, but the GPU-ICD algorithm also shows that ICD algorithms can efficiently reuse the GPU memory.

To map such numerical algorithms onto GPUs, not only should vector operations, such as $A_{*,j}x_j$, be parallelized, but different elements of x should be updated simultaneously. GPU-ICD can be perceived as a generalized parallel update framework for such numerical iterative algorithms.[2] Each element of x, x_j, can be perceived as a voxel, as discussed in Section 1. Therefore, the intra-voxel parallelism in GPU-ICD can be generalized for the vector multiplication between $A_{*,j}$ and x_j. A group of x_j, denoted as S, can then perceived as a SV. Voxels of the same SV are chosen to maximize their statistical correlation, so that voxels' updates can exploit cache locality. In other words, if $x_i, x_j \in S$, then $\sum_{k=1}^{M} |A_{k,i}| \cdot |A_{k,j}|$ is maximized. The intra-SV parallelism discussed in Section 3.1 describes how to map the updates for a group of x_j onto a GPU. At the same time, voxels of different SVs are chosen to minimize their statistical correlation, lowering the synchronization overhead. Namely if x_i, x_j belong to different groups, then $\sum_{k=1}^{M} |A_{k,i}| \cdot |A_{k,j}|$ is minimized. The inter-SV parallelism discussed in the paper can be generalized for mapping the updates for different groups of x_j onto a GPU.

[2] Note that if $f(x)$ is a linear system of equations, GPU-ICD is analogous to the parallel Gauss-Seidel algorithm.

7. Related Work

CT image reconstruction techniques can be classified into two major categories: direct methods, such as filtered back projection (FBP), and iterative methods. The iterative method considered in this paper i.e., Model Based Iterative Reconstruction (MBIR) [2, 3], is known to create higher quality images than FBP methods. Past research has studied this for various domains, including medical imaging [2, 3], explosive detection systems (EDS) [4, 5, 6, 7], scientific and materials imaging [8].

There are two prominent approaches to iterative reconstruction. The first approach comprises non-regularized methods, such as Simultaneous Iterative Reconstruction Technique (SIRT) [5, 21, 22] and Algebraic Reconstruction Techniques (ART) [23]. SIRT work by iteratively projecting an entire volume to be reconstructed into the measurement, while ART work by iteratively solving a system of linear equations. However, non-regularized methods lack concrete convergence criteria and rely on stopping times. The other approach is of regularized methods, who generally possess well-defined convergence criteria and generate higher quality images than FBP. Among the regularized methods, Penalized Least Squares (PLS) [24], Penalized Maximum Likelihood (PML) [25], and Model Based Image Reconstrustion (MBIR) are popular. The regularized methods need to minimize a cost function, which is computationally expensive. Two optimization approaches exist to that end. The first is simultaneous methods, which work by using forward/backward projectors. Simultaneous methods are usually slow, and hence need pre-conditioning [26] to converge faster, which is scanner geometry dependent. Ordered subsets [26] is another approach to speed up simultaneous methods. The second approach is of coordinate decent (CD), where methods such as Iterative Coordinate Descent (ICD) [2, 9, 10] and Gradient Coordinate Descent (GCD) [11, 12] are used. The CD methods are preferable since they converge faster than the simultaneous methods, and are geometry agnostic. We consider ICD over GCD in this paper, since it has been highly optimized for multi-core CPUs [1].

Many previous GPU-based efforts of CT reconstruction [27, 28, 29, 30, 31] are based upon the FBP method, since it is easier to parallelize [32]. Cho et. al. [33] present a simultaneous method based on ordered subsets. Flores et. al. [34] show a non-regularized approach where reconstruction is formulated as a least square solver problem and is solved using standard GPU libraries. McGaffin et. al. [35] present an alternating tomography and denoising based regularized MBIR approach on the GPU. In [35], McGaffin and Fessler investigate the use of GPUs for multi-slice helical scan CT reconstruction in medical applications. Their approach uses projection based optimization, rather than ICD, for the tomographic portion of the optimization, and couples it with a separate TV denoising portion for the prior. Importantly, their approach is also based on ordered subset (OS) methods, which are not generally compatible with the sparse view tomography methods that are crucial in many scientific and NDE applications [36, 37, 7].

None of the above approaches have exploited ICD on GPUs. While ICD and its variants have been shown to be robust and rapidly converging algorithms [38] for performing the MBIR reconstruction, there is a belief that ICD can not be efficiently mapped to highly parallel GPU architectures [11, 12]. This paper shows that fast converging ICD optimization algorithms can be efficiently implemented on GPUs. Furthermore, since ICD is an optimization technique, methods employed in this work for MBIR are also applicable to PLS/PML techniques.

8. Conclusion and Future Work

Although ICD-based MBIR (Model-based Image Reconstruction) is known to produce high quality CT reconstruction images, it suffers from a heavy computational cost. This paper presented GPU-ICD, the first GPU-based highly parallel algorithm for this kind of MBIR. The algorithm exploits multiple levels of parallelism in MBIR, namely, intra-voxel parallelism, intra-SV parallelism, and inter-SV parallelism. The paper presented a data layout transformation that obtains coalesced accesses on GPUs. The paper also presented the following GPU-specific optimizations: i) increasing occupancy by spilling registers on the shared memory; ii) compressing system matrix and reading it via texture cache; and iii) obtaining higher L2 bandwidth by reading the data as type `double`. The massive parallelism exploitation combined with the above optimizations results in a mean speedup of 4.43X over the best-known parallel CPU implementation on an iso-power 16-core CPU.

Section 5 showed that various parameters can greatly impact the performance of GPU-ICD. The best values of the parameters are sensitive to the input, and hence are often not catered to by auto-tuning systems [39, 40]. In future, we plan to build a model that automatically selects input-specific high performing parameter values.

Acknowledgments

This research was supported by the U.S. Department of Homeland Security under SBIR Award D15PC00110, subcontracted through High Performance Imaging LLC, and by the Indiana Economic Development Corporation (IEDC). Additional support was provided by the DHS ALERT Center for Excellence supported by the U.S. Department of Homeland Security, Science and Technology Directorate, Office of University Programs, under Grant Award 2013-ST-061-ED0001. The views and conclusions contained in this document are those of the authors and should not be interpreted as necessarily representing the official policies, either expressed or implied, of the U.S. Department of Homeland Security or the IEDC.

References

[1] X. Wang, A. Sabne, S. Kisner, A. Raghunathan, C. Bouman, and S. Midkiff, "High performance model based image reconstruction," in *Proceedings of the 21st ACM SIGPLAN Symposium on Principles and Practice of Parallel Programming*, PPoPP '16, (New York, NY, USA), pp. 2:1–2:12, ACM, 2016.

[2] K. Sauer and C. Bouman, "A local update strategy for iterative reconstruction from projections," *IEEE Transactions on Signal Processing*, vol. 41(2), 1993.

[3] J. B. Thibault, K. D. Sauer, C. A. Bouman, and J. Hsieh, "A three-dimensional statistical approach to improved image quality for multi-slice helical CT," *Medical Physics*, vol. 34(11), 2007.

[4] DHS/ALERT, "Research and development of reconstruction advances in CT-based object detection systems." `https://myfiles.neu.edu/groups/ALERT/strategic_studies/TO3_FinalReport.pdf`, 2009.

[5] S. Degirmenci, D. G. Politte, C. Bosch, N. Tricha, and J. A. O'Sullivan, "Acceleration of iterative image reconstruction for X-ray imaging for security applications," in *Proceedings of SPIE-IS&T Electronic Imaging*, vol. 9401, 2015.

[6] P. Jin, E. Haneda, C. A. Bouman, and K. D. Sauer, "A model-based 3D multi-slice helical CT reconstruction algorithm for transportation security application," in *Second International Conference on Image Formation in X-Ray Computed Tomography*, 2012.

[7] S. J. Kisner, E. Haneda, C. A. Bouman, S. Skatter, M. Kourinny, and S. Bedford, "Model-based CT reconstruction from sparse views," in *Second International Conference on Image Formation in X-Ray Computed Tomography*, pp. 444–447, June 2012.

[8] P. Jin, C. A. Bouman, and K. D. Sauer, "A method for simultaneous image reconstruction and beam hardening correction," in *2013 IEEE Nuclear Science Symposium and Medical Imaging Conference (NSS/MIC)*, pp. 1–5, 2013.

[9] B. D. Man, S. Basu, J.-B. Thibault, J. Hsieh, J. A. Fessler, C. A. Bouman, and K. Sauer, "A study of different minimization approaches for iterative reconstruction in X-ray CT," in *IEEE Nuclear Science Symposium*, vol. 5, pp. 2708–2710, 2005.

[10] Z. Yu, J.-B. Thibault, C. A. Bouman, K. D. Sauer, and J. Hsieh, "Fast model-based X-ray CT reconstruction using spatially nonhomogeneous ICD optimization," *IEEE Transactions on Image Processing*, vol. 20(1), 2011.

[11] J. A. Fessler, E. Ficaro, N. Clinthorne, and K. Lange, "Grouped-coordinate ascent algorithms for penalized-likelihood transmission image reconstruction," *IEEE Transactions on Medical Imaging*, vol. 16(2), 1997.

[12] J. Zheng, S. S. Saquib, K. Sauer, and C. A. Bouman, "Parallelizable bayesian tomography algorithms with rapid, guaranteed convergence," *IEEE Transactions on Image Processing*, vol. 9(10), 2000.

[13] J. E. Bowsher, M. Smith, J.Peter, and R. J. Jaszczak, "A comparison of OSEM and ICD for iterative reconstruction of SPECT brain images," *Journal of Nuclear Medicine*, vol. 79(5), 1998.

[14] J. Luitjens, "Faster parallel reductions on Kepler." `https://devblogs.nvidia.com/parallelforall/faster-parallel-reductions-kepler/`, 2014.

[15] Z. Yu, J. Thibault, C. A. Bouman, K. D. Sauer, and J. Hsieh, "Non-homogeneous ICD optimization for targeted reconstruction of volumetric CT," in *Computational Imaging VI, part of the IS&T-SPIE Electronic Imaging Symposium, San Jose, CA, USA, January 28-29, 2008, Proceedings*, p. 681404, 2008.

[16] P. Jin, S. J. Kisner, T. Frese, and C. A. Bouman, "Model-based iterative reconstruction (MBIR) software for X-ray CT." Available from https://engineering.purdue.edu/ bouman/software/tomography/mbirct/, November 2013.

[17] X. Wang, K. A. Mohan, S. J. Kisner, C. A. Bouman, and S. P. Midkiff, "Fast voxel line update for time-space image reconstruction," in *2016 IEEE International Conference on Acoustics, Speech and Signal Processing (ICASSP)*, pp. 1209–1213, March 2016.

[18] C.-J. Hsieh, K.-W. Chang, C.-J. Lin, S. S. Keerthi, and S. Sundararajan, "A dual coordinate descent method for large-scale linear SVM," in *Proceedings of the 25th International Conference on Machine Learning*, ICML '08, (New York, NY, USA), pp. 408–415, ACM, 2008.

[19] J. F. Claerbout and F. Muir, "Robust modeling with erratic data," *Geophysics*, vol. 38, no. 5, pp. 826–844, 1973.

[20] L. Wu, P. Babu, and D. P. Palomar, "Cognitive radar-based sequence design via SINR maximization," *IEEE Transactions on Signal Processing*, vol. 65(3), 2017.

[21] N. Clinthorne, T. S. Pan, P. C. Chiao, W. L. Rogers, and J. A. Stamos, "Preconditioning methods for improved convergence rates in iterative reconstructions," *IEEE Transactions on Medical Imaging*, vol. 12(1), 1993.

[22] J. Fessler and S. D. Booth, "Conjugate-gradient preconditioning methods for shift-variant PET image reconstruction," *IEEE Transactions on Image Processing*, vol. 8(5), 1999.

[23] R. Gordon, R. Bender, and G. T. Herman, "Algebraic reconstruction techniques (ART) for three-dimensional electron microscopy and x-ray photography," *Journal of Theoretical Biology*, vol. 29, pp. 471–481, 1970.

[24] J. Wang, T. Li, H. Lu, and Z. Liang, "Penalized weighted least-squares approach to sinogram noise reduction and image reconstruction for low-dose X-ray computed tomography," *IEEE Transactions on Medical Imaging*, vol. 25, pp. 1272–1283, Oct 2006.

[25] B. Brendel, M. von Teuffenbach, P. B. Noël, F. Pfeiffer, and T. Koehler, "Penalized maximum likelihood reconstruction for x-ray differential phase-contrast tomography," *Medical Physics*, vol. 43, no. 1, pp. 188–194, 2016.

[26] C. Kamphuis and F. J. Beekman, "Accelerated iterative transmission ct reconstruction using an ordered subsets convex algorithm," *IEEE Transactions on Medical Imaging*, vol. 17, pp. 1101–1105, Dec 1998.

[27] M. Leeser, S. Mukherjee, and J. Brock, "Fast reconstruction of 3D volumes from 2D CT projection data with GPUs," *BMC Research Notes*, vol. 7, no. 1, pp. 1–8, 2014.

[28] V. G. Nguyen, J. Jeong, and S. J. Lee, "GPU-accelerated iterative 3D CT reconstruction using exact ray-tracing method for both projection and backprojection," in *2013 IEEE Nuclear Science Symposium and Medical Imaging Conference (2013 NSS/MIC)*, pp. 1–4, Oct 2013.

[29] G. C. Sharp, N. Kandasamy, H. Singh, and M. Folkert, "GPU-based streaming architectures for fast cone-beam CT image reconstruction and demons deformable registration," *Physics in Medicine and Biology*, vol. 52, no. 19, p. 5771, 2007.

[30] H. Scherl, B. Keck, M. Kowarschik, and J. Hornegger, "Fast GPU-based CT reconstruction using the Common Unified Device Architecture (CUDA)," in *2007 IEEE Nuclear Science Symposium Conference Record*, vol. 6, pp. 4464–4466, Oct 2007.

[31] F. Xu and K. Mueller, "Real-time 3D computed tomographic reconstruction using commodity graphics hardware," *Physics in Medicine and Biology*, vol. 52, no. 12, p. 3405, 2007.

[32] E. Papenhausen and K. Mueller, "Rapid rabbit: Highly optimized GPU accelerated cone-beam CT reconstruction," in *2013 IEEE Nuclear Science Symposium and Medical Imaging Conference (2013 NSS/MIC)*, pp. 1–2, Oct 2013.

[33] J. H. Cho and J. A. Fessler, "Accelerating ordered-subsets image reconstruction for x-ray CT using double surrogates," 2012.

[34] L. A. Flores, V. Vidal, P. Mayo, F. Rodenas, and G. Verdú, "Iterative reconstruction of CT images on GPUs," in *2013 35th Annual International Conference of the IEEE Engineering in Medicine and Biology Society (EMBC)*, pp. 5143–5146, July 2013.

[35] M. G. McGaffin and J. A. Fessler, "Alternating Dual Updates Algorithm for X-ray CT Reconstruction on the GPU," *IEEE Transactions on Computational Imaging*, vol. 1, pp. 186–199, Sept 2015.

[36] S. V. Venkatakrishnan, L. F. Drummy, M. Jackson, M. D. Graef, J. Simmons, and C. A. Bouman, "Model-based iterative reconstruction for bright-field electron tomography," *IEEE Transactions on Computational Imaging*, vol. 1, pp. 1–15, March 2015.

[37] S. V. Venkatakrishnan, L. F. Drummy, M. A. Jackson, M. D. Graef, J. Simmons, and C. A. Bouman, "A model based iterative reconstruction algorithm for high angle annular dark field-scanning transmission electron microscope (haadf-stem) tomography," *IEEE Transactions on Image Processing*, vol. 22, pp. 4532–4544, Nov 2013.

[38] Y. Nesterov, "Efficiency of coordinate descent methods on huge-scale optimization problems," *SIAM Journal on Optimization*, vol. 22, no. 2, pp. 341–362, 2012.

[39] A. Sabne, P. Sakdhnagool, and R. Eigenmann, "Effects of compiler optimizations in openmp to cuda translation," in *International Workshop on OpenMP*, pp. 169–181, Springer Berlin Heidelberg, 2012.

[40] A. Sabne, P. Sakdhnagool, S. Lee, and J. S. Vetter, "Evaluating performance portability of OpenACC," in *International Workshop on Languages and Compilers for Parallel Computing*, pp. 51–66, Springer International Publishing, 2014.

Pagoda: Fine-Grained GPU Resource Virtualization for Narrow Tasks

Tsung Tai Yeh†, Amit Sabne‡*, Putt Sakdhnagool†, Rudolf Eigenmann†, Timothy G. Rogers†
School of Electrical and Computer Engineering, Purdue University†
Microsoft‡
yeh14@purdue.edu, amsabne@microsoft.com, {psakdhna, eigenman, timrogers}@purdue.edu

ABSTRACT

Massively multithreaded GPUs achieve high throughput by running thousands of threads in parallel. To fully utilize the hardware, workloads spawn work to the GPU in bulk by launching large tasks, where each task is a kernel that contains thousands of threads that occupy the entire GPU.

GPUs face severe underutilization and their performance benefits vanish if the tasks are narrow, i.e., they contain < 500 threads. Latency-sensitive applications in network, signal, and image processing that generate a large number of tasks with relatively small inputs are examples of such limited parallelism.

This paper presents Pagoda, a runtime system that virtualizes GPU resources, using an OS-like daemon kernel called MasterKernel. Tasks are spawned from the CPU onto Pagoda as they become available, and are scheduled by the MasterKernel at the warp granularity. Experimental results demonstrate that Pagoda achieves a geometric mean speedup of 5.70x over PThreads running on a 20-core CPU, 1.51x over CUDA-HyperQ, and 1.69x over GeMTC, the state-of-the-art runtime GPU task scheduling system.

CCS Concepts

•Software and its engineering → Runtime environments;

Keywords

GPU runtime system; utilization; task parallelism

1. INTRODUCTION

GPGPU computing has demonstrated an ability to accelerate a substantial class of compute-intensive applications [36, 7]. These applications have a high degree of parallelism, where iterations of large parallel loops are executed on the GPU. The programs see significant performance benefits because they can fully utilize the GPU's hardware resources by launching enough concurrent threads.

The GPU's performance benefits start to diminish as the degree of parallelism lessens. Conventionally, large parallel loops are offloaded to the GPU, while retaining the execution of smaller ones on the CPU. The main thesis of this paper is that despite having a smaller degree of parallelism, applications can benefit from using the GPU, provided that the involved task (or CUDA kernel) count is sufficiently high. Each such task, called a *narrow task*, has limited parallelism ($<$ 500 data parallel threads in practice).

Narrow tasks emerge in a number of scenarios. One set of such applications comprises latency-driven, real-time workloads. For example, online sensors that generate small inputs, resulting in tasks with low parallelism. Online sensors can generate many tasks in quick succession and require immediate processing. These workloads have been characterized as having mixed task and data parallelism [33, 32]. Secondly, *irregular* applications can exhibit narrow tasks. These applications often contain varying amounts of computation among different threads, and/or among loop iterations. To reduce load imbalance, these applications are often represented using many tasks with low degrees of parallelism [24]. Irregular workloads may also arise in multiprogrammed environments. Different applications with low degrees of parallelism can be co-executed on a node to exploit all the computing resources.

GPU underutilization is the key reason why narrow tasks are conventionally executed on CPUs. This paper presents Pagoda[1], a runtime system that greatly improves GPU utilization in the presence of narrow tasks. Pagoda introduces novel elements of a massively parallel OS to virtualize and dynamically schedule GPU core resources at warp granularity, enabling hundreds of tasks to execute concurrently.

Prior work has identified the issue of GPU underutilization [37, 8, 25, 14]. One approach to solve this problem is to statically fuse multiple smaller tasks [37, 8] to accumulate a large kernel. Advanced approaches [28, 25] use a concurrent kernel mechanism, monitoring and time-slicing their execution at runtime to obtain fair sharing. These static approaches require the programmer to fuse tasks *manually* and none of them have been shown to work beyond ten concurrent tasks. These mechanisms also require static knowledge of the kernels to be fused, which is not always possible in multi-programmed or real-time environments. Additionally, individual tasks in a fused tasks receive the same on-chip re-

*Author conducted this work while at Purdue University

PPoPP '17, February 04-08, 2017, Austin, TX, USA
© 2017 ACM. ISBN 978-1-4503-4493-7/17/02...$15.00
DOI: http://dx.doi.org/10.1145/3018743.3018754

[1]Download Pagoda from http://bit.ly/2hmmY5p

Table 1: Pagoda Programming API

CUDA Function	Pagoda Function	Caller	Return Value	Arguments	Description
kernel<<<>>>	taskSpawn	CPU	taskId	#threads, #threadblocks, shared memory, sync flag, kernel pointer, kernel args	Spawn a task from CPU onto Pagoda
cudaEventSynchronize	wait	CPU		taskId	Wait until the specified task is over
cudaEventQuery	check	CPU	true if the task is done, else false	taskId	Returns the status of the task
cudaDeviceSynchronize	waitAll	CPU			Wait until all tasks in Pagoda are over
threadIdx	getTid	GPU	thread Id		Get the thread Id of this thread
syncthreads	syncBlock	GPU			Synchronize all threads in the block
__shared__ char *arr	getSMPtr	GPU	32-byte aligned char pointer		Get shared mem pointer for the threadblock

source allocation, e.g., shared memory and registers, thereby limiting occupancy based on the resource requirements of the largest task.

Dynamic (runtime) solutions can mitigate the above issues of static fusion. NVIDIA's current-generation GPUs employ HyperQ [20], which allows 32 tasks to concurrently execute on the GPU. However, we show that narrow tasks can still cause underutilization, as 32 such tasks may not occupy the entire GPU. We argue that software mechanisms are needed to achieve flexible kernel concurrency. Prior work, *GPU enabled Many-Task Computing* (GeMTC) [14], presents a runtime task scheduling mechanism, where a task executes as a single *threadblock*. *Threadblocks* are sets of threads constituting the GPU kernel. Because GPU architectures limit the concurrent threadblock count, executing narrow tasks in GeMTC may result in poor utilization. In addition, GeMTC uses batch-based task execution, which results in delayed task launching and load imbalance since the completion time of a batch is determined by its longest running task.

Pagoda is designed to overcome these issues. The programmer replaces certain CUDA API calls with equivalent Pagoda calls in the host and device codes, retaining the functionality of the CUDA programming model. Unlike static solutions, the programmer does not have to tediously fuse the available tasks. Pagoda achieves high utilization by continually running a *MasterKernel*, which controls the execution of all GPU *warps* in software. In Pagoda, tasks are spawned by the CPU as soon as they become available, without batching. On the GPU side, the MasterKernel virtualizes the GPU's resource allocation and threadblock scheduling mechanism to allow individual warps to make progress as soon as resources are available. There are three key challenges that must be addressed when attempting to launch and run thousands of short-running tasks on a GPU, the combination of which no previous work has solved.

First, CPU-GPU communication overhead must be minimized, while allowing the GPU to asynchronously schedule new tasks on each Streaming Multiprocessor (SMM). Launching thousands of short-running tasks increases the importance of minimizing the time it takes for each task to begin execution on the GPU. Since the CPU and GPU must coordinate task spawning and scheduling over the PCIe bus, which currently has no support for atomic operations, the handshaking required is expensive or impossible if a traditional data structure, such as a queue [18], is used. Previous work that required OS-like co-ordination over PCIe [12, 31] solved consistency issues using a producer-consumer model but did not have to optimize the system for many, short running tasks. To support narrow tasks, Pagoda presents *TaskTable*, a novel data structure aimed at limiting communication overhead and enabling asynchronous GPU task pulls.

The second challenge is to keep the overheads involved in task spawning and scheduling low. Minimizing both the copying of task parameters and the search for free GPU resources is important when task execution times are short. To limit these overheads, Pagoda performs task scheduling in parallel and pipelines task spawning, scheduling and execution to overlap their operation.

The third issue is supporting native CUDA functionality such as shared memory usage and efficient threadblock synchronization. Since Pagoda's MasterKernel overrides native support for this functionality, we introduce low-overhead software mechanisms to provide it.

In summary, the following contributions enable the efficient execution of narrow tasks on GPUs. This paper

- introduces a continuous task spawning mechanism to reduce CPU-GPU synchronizations and obtains a high spawn rate.
- presents a software mechanism to schedule multiple tasks on the GPU in parallel, and describes a pipelining scheme to overlap several task processing stages.
- describes software solutions for dynamic shared memory management and sub-threadblock synchronizations.
- implements and evaluates the presented methods in a new runtime system, called Pagoda. Pagoda achieves geometric mean speedup of 5.70x over PThreads running on a 20-core CPU, of 1.51x over CUDA-HyperQ, and of 1.69x against GeMTC.

2. GPU PROGRAMMING AND ARCHITECTURE

The GPU cores are organized into 24 Streaming Multiprocessors (SMMs) [2]. Each SMM has 128 CUDA cores and can concurrently schedule up to 64 warps. A *Warp* is the basic Single Instruction, Multiple Thread (SIMT) work unit, which comprises 32 threads that march in lockstep, executing the same instruction. Each SMM has a 96KB on-chip programmer managed cache, known as *shared memory* and 64K, 32-bit registers.

[2]We use terminology from the NVIDIA Maxwell Titan X architecture.

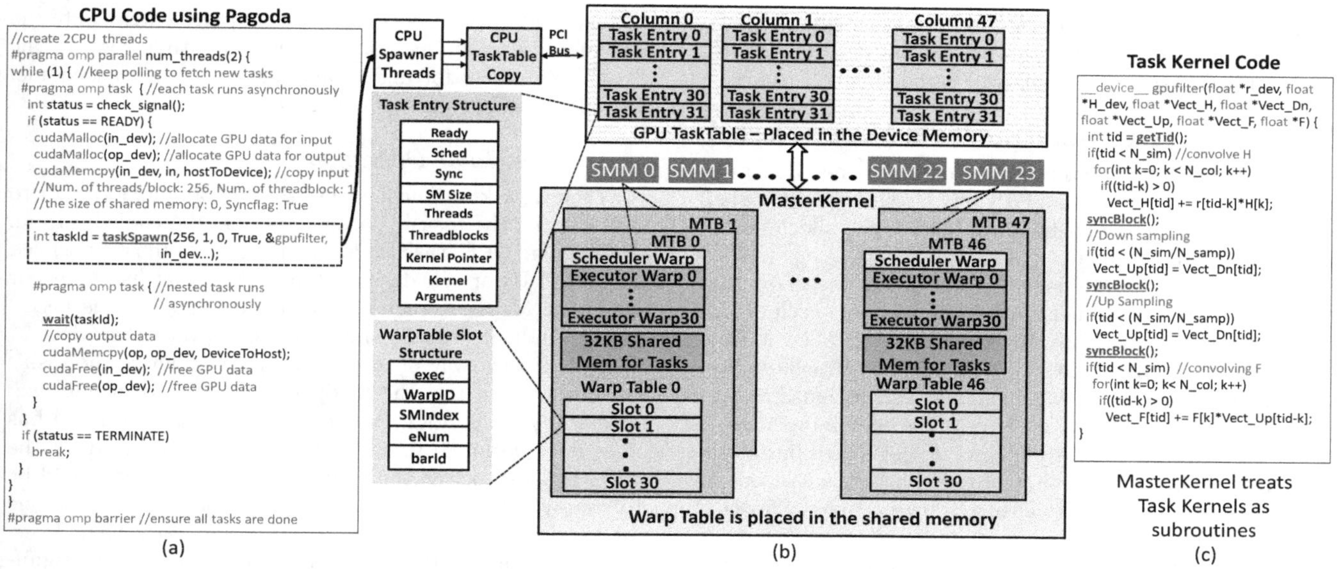

Figure 1: Pagoda runtime system overview: *The source task kernel and CPU code require few changes to an equivalent CUDA code. The MasterKernel design is shown for the Maxwell Titan X GPU. The 48 MasterKernel threadblocks (MTBs) have 1024 threads each. TaskTable is mirrored on both the CPU and GPU. The CPU threads spawn tasks into the CPU TaskTable, which are then sent to the GPU counterpart. Scheduler warps inside each MTB find free executor warps to launch tasks on. The WarpTable performs bookkeeping for each executor warp.*

In the CUDA programming model, the programmer organizes parallel work in *kernels*. Threads of a kernel are grouped into *threadblocks*. Multiple threadblocks can reside on each SMM, the maximum number being 32. The threadblock size is limited to 1024 threads, or 32 warps. Each SMM can hold up to 2048 concurrent threads. Both the shared memory and registers of an SMM are partitioned among the executing threadblocks. There is no CUDA primitive for global, kernel-wide synchronization; however, threads in a threadblock can use the *__syncthreads()* function as a barrier.

A way of measuring the GPU utilization is *occupancy*. Occupancy is the ratio of the total number of resident GPU warps divided by the maximum number of warps that can co-exist in the GPU (i.e. 64 $\times$ the number of SMMs in the GPU). The kernel occupancy is affected by three factors, namely, i) size of threadblocks, ii) kernel's register count, and iii) size of the requested shared memory. Balancing these three factors requires programmer expertise, making high occupancy often difficult to achieve. Consider a scenario of narrow tasks, where one task has 256 threads, or 8 warps. If only one task is executed at a time, the occupancy would be $(8/(64\times24))\times100\% = 0.52\%$. With HyperQ, 32 kernels may co-execute, meaning that 32 narrow tasks can run simultaneously. The achieved occupancy then would still be low, i.e. $(8\times32/(64\times24))\times100\% = 16.67\%$.

3. PROGRAMMING WITH PAGODA

Programmers use Pagoda API functions in their applications to access the Pagoda runtime system. Pagoda supports the CUDA programming model, where-by the Pagoda API functions shown in Table 1 override the corresponding CUDA functions. The Pagoda API functions belong to the following two categories:

CPU-side API: The *taskSpawn* function launches a task from the CPU onto Pagoda. The programmer specifies the number of threads per threadblock, and the number of threadblocks as arguments. The programmer also specifies the kernel to execute, along with the parameters. The size of the shared memory needed per threadblock in bytes may be specified. The *sync* flag indicates if threadblock-level synchronization is necessary for the task. *TaskSpawn* is a non-blocking function. The CPU can synchronize with the spawned task(s) using *wait* and *waitAll* functions, or can check the task status with *check* function. One difference in functionality with respect to CUDA is that Pagoda returns a *taskID* for each task. The taskIDs are essential to use functions such as *wait*.

GPU-side API: Since Pagoda virtualizes the GPU resources, the CUDA-based shared memory allocation and threadblock synchronization cannot be directly used. Pagoda allocates shared memory and barriers for each threadblock when it gets scheduled, and the API provides functions that allow the threadblock to obtain a pointer to its shared memory, and to perform barrier synchronizations. Pagoda also offers a function to obtain the threadId of the current thread.

Fig. 1a shows a possible implementation of Pagoda host code, while Fig. 1c shows the corresponding device code for FilterBank.The two CPU threads spawn tasks and wait for their completion. Calling *wait()* in a nested task allows the CPU thread to progress, without getting blocked. One key distinction from CUDA is that the task kernels are written as `__device__` functions, instead of `__global__`.

4. PAGODA NARROW TASK PROCESSING

This section first describes the MasterKernel design that achieves resource virtualization. Next, it presents the Pagoda task spawning mechanism. The mechanism employs TaskTable, a novel data structure that allows simultaneous updates from both the CPU and GPU, and is mirrored in both their memories. TaskTable drastically reduces the CPU-GPU handshaking communication by allowing lazy aggregate updates. Lastly, the section presents Pagoda's GPU scheduling mechanism that parallelizes the scheduling process, and overlaps various task processing stages.

4.1 Resource Virtualization via MasterKernel

The MasterKernel continually executes on the GPU as a CUDA kernel. It acquires all GPU resources, namely warps, shared memory, and registers, that later get allocated to tasks running on Pagoda.

Fig. 1b describes our MasterKernel design on the Titan X GPU. The MasterKernel acquires all warps of each SMM (64) by launching two, 32-warp threadblocks, called *MTBs* (Master Kernel Threadblocks). Each MTB statically allocates 32KB shared memory, which later gets assigned to different tasks. The MasterKernel uses the remaining shared memory of the SMM to store some of the scheduling data structures. The register count of each thread is capped at 32 (using -maxrregcount) to ensure 100% occupancy for the MasterKernel.

The first warp of each MTB is called a *scheduler warp*, while the rest of the 31 warps are known as *executor warps*. The scheduler warp is responsible for scheduling tasks on the executor warps in the MTB. It also manages shared memory allocations and barriers. The MasterKernel contains two scheduling data structures. The first one, called *TaskTable*, is mirrored on the CPU and GPU, and is used for task spawning. Each entry in the TaskTable holds a task. The GPU TaskTable receives online updates from the CPU TaskTable, and is therefore placed in the GPU device memory. The second data structure is called *WarpTable*. Each MTB contains its own WarpTable, which is placed in the shared memory. Every WarpTable contains 31 slots to maintain the status of each executor warp.

4.2 Continuous Task Spawning

Scheduling algorithms often involve queues that accumulate tasks, where processing elements pull tasks from the queue [31]. To simultaneously schedule several tasks, multiple pulls must take place in a synchronous/atomic manner, which has long been recognized as a critical source of overhead [18]. Performing global synchronizations or atomic operations on GPUs is extremely expensive. Therefore, to reduce this contention, one solution would be to use multiple queues, and only let a smaller set of GPU threads pull from each queue. Even this solution is impractical. As the CPU-GPU memories are discrete, before the CPU could spawn a task on a GPU queue, it must gather the queue *head* and *tail* pointers from the GPU. Such handshaking is expensive because it requires data copies over the PCIe bus. Another way to spawn tasks is to use a batch-based mechanism [14], where CPU sends a batch of tasks to the GPU.However, such mechanisms are susceptible to load imbalance across tasks.

The Pagoda design therefore employs TaskTable, a data structure that as we will show, drastically reduces the amount of CPU-GPU handshaking. Each TaskTable entry contains the following fields describing the task: 1) number of threadblocks, 2) number of threads in a threadblock, 3) task kernel pointer, 4) size in bytes of the shared memory allocation required per threadblock, 5) a flag indicating whether the task needs thread-block-level synchronization, 6) task inputs, 7) *ready* field, and 8) *sched* flag. Each TaskTable column corresponds to an MTB; The scheduler warp in that MTB schedules tasks in the column's entries onto the executor warps of that MTB. Having multiple rows in the TaskTable allows for high availability of tasks to schedule. Pagoda uses 32 TaskTable rows per MTB.

4.2.1 TaskTable Operation

When a task is launched via the Pagoda API (a call to *taskSpawn*), the tasks's parameters must be copied into an entry in the CPU TaskTable, then the entry must be copied to the GPU for scheduling. Since this copy has to occur while the MasterKernel is in flight, a *ready* field is necessary to indicate the finishing of the copy to the GPU. A straightforward way of implementing this, where the task's parameter data and the ready flag are copied in one *cudamemcopy* transaction, cannot work because the PCIe bus does not guarantee that the parameters will arrive in the GPU memory before the ready flag. One solution would be to simply split it into two *cudamemcopy* transactions, one for the parameters, and another for the ready flag. However, this doubles the parameter copying overhead, significantly reducing Pagoda performance. To solve this issue, we pipeline the launching of tasks. The launch of a task prompts a copy of its parameters to the GPU, as well as a pointer indicating which task had its parameters copied in the previous *cudamemcopy* transaction. In the steady-state, we achieve 1 *cudamemcopy* per task table entry and the CUDA streams API guarantees that the parameters are copied before the task is scheduled.

4.2.2 Task Spawning Example

Each task's state comprises its *ready* field and *sched* flag. The *ready* field of each TaskTable entry can be in one of four states: 0 meaning the task is not ready, -1 meaning the task's parameters have been copied to the task table, 1 meaning the task is being considered for scheduling on the GPU, or it can be a taskID which is an integer > 1. The taskID provides the necessary indirection to implement the pipelining, indicating which task has already had its parameters copied to the GPU. The *sched* flag has two states: 1, indicating that the task is ready to begin scheduling on an MTB, and 0 meaning otherwise. Fig. 2a presents a task's state diagram.

Fig. 2b presents an example execution of task A (TA). When the *taskSpawn* function is executed by the CPU, Pagoda finds a TaskTable entry with a cleared *ready* field and copies the task's parameters into the entry. Since TA is the first task, the CPU sets the *ready* field to -1. For all subsequent tasks, it sets the taskId of the last spawned task, e.g., during task B (TB) spawn, TA is set as the *ready* field. The taskIds generated by Pagoda are references to entries in the TaskTable. Next, the CPU clears the *sched* flag, and copies the entry to the GPU. If the *ready* field is a taskID, i.e, > 1, the continually polling scheduler warp for the TaskTable column (S2) sets the state of the previous task (TA) to (1, 1). Next, S2 sets the state of the current task to (-1, 0) (see Algo. 1, lines 5-13). S2 waits for the state of TA to be (-1, 0) before changing it to (1, 1). This is achieved through polling orchestrated with CUDA *threadfence* calls. Now, S1, the scheduler warp for TA, finds that TA has a set *sched* flag, and hence schedules TA. To do so, S1 first clears the *sched* flag and then finds executor warps for the task. Once the task execution is finished, the last finishing executor warp for the task sets the *ready* field to 0, marking the end of the task's execution, and freeing up the task entry

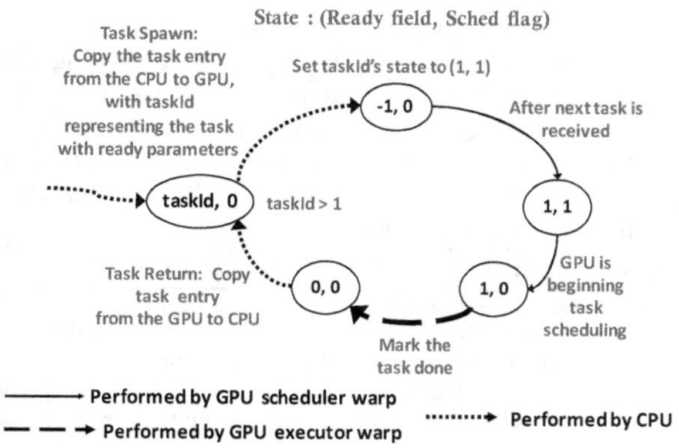

(a) ***TaskTable state diagram :*** *The CPU only touches TaskTable entries with cleared* ready *fields, and the GPU only touches TaskTable entries with non-zero* ready *fields, allowing for simultaneous TaskTable updates from CPU and GPU. The* sched *flag determines when a task gets scheduled to warps.*

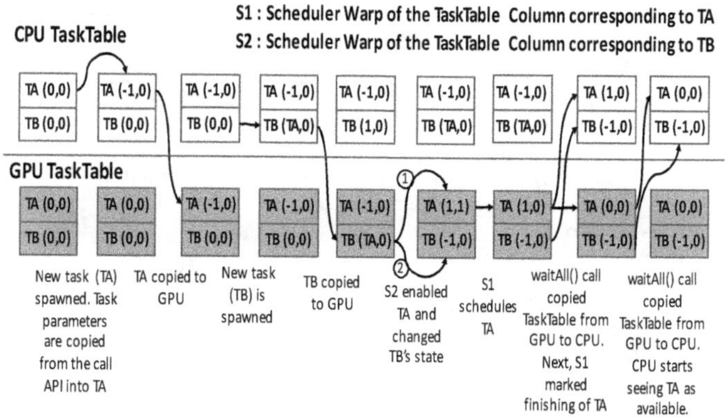

(b) ***Example execution of task TA :*** *TA gets scheduled only after TB is spawned. Our design allows for the CPU and GPU TaskTable entries to contain mis-matching values.*

Figure 2: Obtaining Correct TaskTable Ordering

TA. If the CPU spawner thread observes no new tasks come in, it copies back the status of the last task, i.e. TB, and if it is (-1, 0), then sets it to (1, 1) and copies it to the GPU, ensuring the successful execution of the last task.

Lazy Aggregate TaskTable Updates: The above mechanism allows both the CPU and GPU to simultaneously update the TaskTable. As the CPU only spawns a task if the *ready* field is reset, the CPU can keep spawning as long as it finds an entry with a cleared *ready* field. Similarly, since the GPU only edits TaskTable entries with non-zero *ready* fields, it can keep scheduling as long as it finds a task entry with a set *sched* flag. When the *ready* fields of all CPU-side TaskTable entries are non-zero, the CPU can no longer spawn tasks. In that case, it copies back all the TaskTable entries from the GPU, thereby updating all *ready* fields. It can then realize which tasks have finished, and launch new tasks in entries with cleared *ready* fields. The CPU therefore receives updates from GPU TaskTable in a *lazy aggregate* manner.

This laziness greatly reduces the number of handshaking communication calls. Furthermore, aggregated (bulk) copying achieves better data transfer bandwidth on the PCIe bus. The *wait* and *waitAll* functions return only when the *ready* field(s) of the corresponding task(s) in the TaskTable is/are reset. The laziness of TaskTable updates may block these functions if the CPU is not spawning more tasks; these functions therefore use a timeout, after which they enforce a copy-back of the involved TaskTable entries.

Because the CPU overwrites the TaskTable while the MasterKernel is in flight, coherence issues may arise. We therefore marked the TaskTable as `volatile`, and performed extensive micro-benchmarking to ascertain that the in-flight writes by the CPU to the TaskTable are visible to the GPU and vice-versa on two GPU architectures, Tesla K40 and Maxwell Titan X. This behavior is also confirmed by other researchers [12, 31].

4.3 Concurrent Task Scheduling

Task scheduling in Pagoda involves finding free resources (warps, shared memory) on which to execute a task. All warps of a given task execute in the same MTB. This design stems from the fact that narrow tasks need less threads than those available in an MTB.

We found that task spawning and scheduling are high-overhead operations, especially for narrow tasks, which can be short running. To mitigate this issue, Pagoda overlaps the three task processing stages, namely, spawning, scheduling, and execution. Secondly, multiple scheduler warps across different MTBs schedule tasks concurrently, lowering the time to execution for each task.

Two Pagoda data structures facilitate task spawning and scheduling in parallel: the multi-row TaskTable and the per-MTB WarpTable. While the CPU is spawning tasks on a TaskTable row, scheduler warp(s) on the GPU may schedule tasks from the remaining rows. The status of each executor warp is stored in a WarpTable entry, whose fields are described in Table 2.

Algorithm 1 describes the operation of the scheduler and executor warps. The scheduler warp (Lines 2-28) scans the corresponding column in the TaskTable, and when it finds an entry with a set *sched* flag (Line 14), it attempts to schedule the task. It begins by resetting the *sched* flag. If the task requires shared memory or synchronization, then the scheduler first allocates shared memory/barrier (Lines 19- 24) for them (Section 5.1) and performs scheduling for each individual threadblock of the task. If neither shared memory nor synchronization are required, then execution is based solely on available warp slots (Line 28).

The executor warps remain idle until the *exec* flag in their WarpTable slot is set. Once this flag is set, they execute the task (Line 33). Afterwards, they release the shared memory and the synchronization barriers (Lines 36-39). Lastly, they reset the *ready* flag in the corresponding TaskTable entry, and reset the *exec* flag in the WarpTable element, marking the warp to be free (Lines 41-43). In order for this mechanism to work, the scheduler and executor warps must have a consistent view of the WarpTable, which is achieved by the *threadfences*. The scheduler warp does not explicitly monitor the end of a task execution. Hence, it cannot free the shared memory used by the task's threadblocks immediately after they finish execution. The executor warps cannot themselves deallocate the shared memory, since it may lead

Algorithm 1: Pagoda Task Scheduling : Each MTB Executes this Algorithm

Input: *gTaskPool* - column of task entries in the TaskTable belonging to the given MTB, numEntriesPerPool - #rows in the TaskTable, *ctr[numEntriesPerPool]* and *doneCtr[numEntriesPerPool]* - counters allocated in shared memory, tid - threadID

```
1  while (1) do
2    if tid < warpSize then // scheduler warp does this
3      for (i = 0; i < numEntriesPerPool; i++) do
4        entry ← gTaskPool[i]
5        taskId = entry.ready
6        if taskId > 0 then
7          prevEntry ← taskTable entry for taskId
8          if prevEntry.ready ≠ -1 then
9            threadfence()
10           continue
11         else
12           prevEntry.ready ← 1
13           prevEntry.sched ← 1
14       if entry.sched then // check if sched flag is set
15         entry.sched ← 0
16         doneCtr[i] ← ctr[i] ← getNumWarps(entry)
17         if entry.SMSize > 0 ∨ entry.sync then //
             schedule warps per threadblock
18           for (j = 0; j < entry.numTB; j++) do
19             if (entry.sync) then barId ← getBarId()
20             if (entry.SMSize > 0) then
21               do
22                 deallocMarkedSM() // avoids
                     deadlocking
23                 retVal ← allocSM(entry.SMSize, &index)
24               while (retVal == false)
25             ctr[i]← getNumWarpsPerTB(entry)
26             pSched(ctr[i]×j, i, index, barId, &ctr[i])
27         else // schedule all warps
28           pSched(0, i, 0, 0, &ctr[i])
29   else // executor warps do this
30     if (warpTable[warpId].exec) then
31       entryId ← warpTable[warpId].eNum
32       tEntry ← gTaskPool[entryId]
33       *(tEntry.funcPtr))(tEntry.args) // warp executes the
           task
34       if (laneId == 0) then
35         if lastWarpInBlock() then // only 1 thread per
             threadblock performs this
36           if (tEntry.SMSize > 0) then // dealloc SM
37             markSMForDealloc(warpTable[warpId].SMindex)
38           if (tEntry.sync) then
39             releaseBarId[tEntry.barId]
40         threadfence_block()
41         if (atomicDec(&doneCtr[entryId]))) then
42           tEntry.ready ← 0; // free the task entry
43           warpTable[warpId].exec ← 0 // warp is free now
```

Table 2: WarpTable entry fields

warpId	maintains the warp ID of the warp, for the current task. It is used to generate the threadID in the *getTid()* function.
eNum	refers to the task entry in the TaskTable, which is being executed by the warp. This reference allows each warp to obtain the task kernel arguments.
SMindex	indicates the shared memory starting location for the corresponding threadblock.
barId	maintains the barrier ID that the warp should synchronize on. It is only valid for tasks that request threadblock synchronization.
exec	acts as a flag for the warp to begin task execution. It is also used to query the warp status.

to inconsistencies if the scheduler warp is simultaneously allocating the shared memory. To overcome this issue, the last executing warp of each threadblock requesting shared memory marks the shared memory region to be freed, and before performing any future shared memory allocation, the scheduler warp first deallocates all memory blocks marked for freeing (Line 22). The allocation/deallocation mechanism is described in Section 5.1.

Algorithm 2: Parallel Warp Schedule Function

Input: *tid* - thread number, *baseWarpId* - base warp number getting scheduled, eNum - number of the TaskTable column entry, index - starting address of the shared memory for the threadblock, barId - barrier Id for the threadblock, warpCtr - count of the number of warps to be scheduled

```
1  Function pSched (baseWarpId, eNum, index, barId,
     warpCtr)
2    threadDone ← 1 // private per thread
3    i ← tid; // private per thread
4    while (1) do
5      if (i < numEntriesPerPool) then
6        threadDone ← 0
7        if (!warpTable[tid].exec) then
8          if (id ← (atomicDec(warpCtr)) >= 0) then
9            warpTable[i].warpId ← id + baseWarpId
10           warpTable[i].eNum ← eNum
11           warpTable[i].SMindex ← index
12           warpTable[i].barId ← barId
13           threadfence_block()
14           warpTable[i].exec ← 1
15     if (*warpCtr <= 0) then threadDone ← 1
16     if (__all(threadDone == 1) = true) then //
         Synchronize threads in the scheduler warp
17       break
18     i ← i + 32
19     if (i > numEntriesPerPool) then i ← tid
```

Scheduling is performed by the threads of the scheduler warp in parallel, through the *PSched* function (Algo. 2). Note that the scheduler warps across different MTBs operate concurrently. The threads in the scheduler warp find free executor warps for a given task by checking their *exec* flags. If a free warp is found, a counter holding the number of warps that are yet to be scheduled is decremented atomically. If the result is positive, then the corresponding warp is scheduled (Lines 7-14). This counter resides in the GPU shared memory, speeding up the atomic operations. Note that both branches on lines 7 and 8 are divergent, i.e, different threads may have different branch outcomes. The threads with a false branch outcome may repeatedly execute the outer *while* loop, in spite of the other threads finding free warps. To remedy this problem, all threads in the scheduler warp must be synchronized after each iteration of the *while* loop. We achieve this using *__all()*, a CUDA warp-level vote function, as opposed to the usual CUDA API for synchronization, *__syncthreads()* which will synchronizes all MTB threads.

5. SUPPORTING NATIVE CUDA FUNCTIONALITY

As tasks in Pagoda are launched by the MasterKernel, native CUDA shared memory and synchronization management cannot be used. This section describes how Pagoda supports these functionalities.

5.1 Shared Memory Management

CUDA lacks support for software-driven dynamic shared memory allocation once a kernel has been launched. Tasks in Pagoda piggyback on the MasterKernel, and hence cannot directly use the shared memory. A need therefore arises for software management of the shared memory. Each MTB reserves shared memory when it starts execution, and allocates this memory to threadblocks of one or more tasks, and frees it after the tasks finish execution.

Our software allocator/deallocator manages small, contiguous regions of shared memory with low overhead.

Unlike many general-purpose allocators that rely on freelists [39], Pagoda's algorithm is motivated by the buddy system mechanism [13] to reduce overhead. Threads of the scheduler warp in the MTB are responsible for performing the allocations and deallocations.

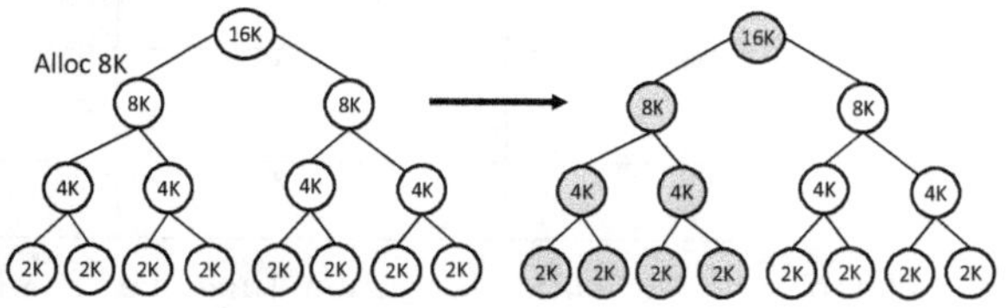

Figure 3: Allocating 8K of shared memory in Pagoda: The value in each node represents the size of the shared memory block. Note that not all levels of the tree are shown here. The white nodes are free blocks and the shaded nodes are allocated blocks.

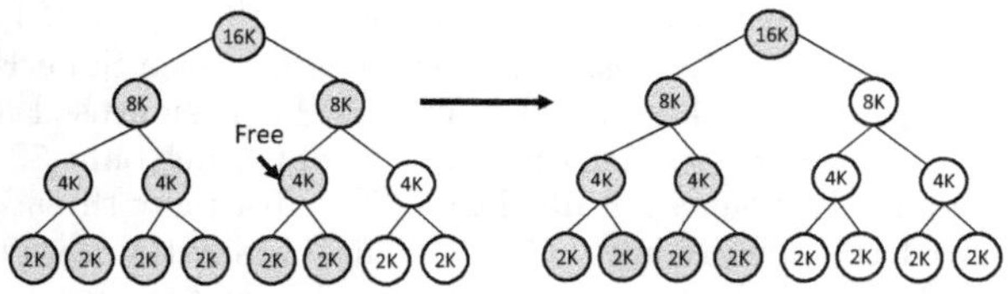

Figure 4: Deallocating 4K of shared memory in Pagoda: Ancestors of the current node are marked free only if the sibling is free.

Data Structure: The memory blocks are represented as nodes in a tree, as shown in Fig. 3. This tree is arranged as an array in the shared memory itself, allowing fast access. Each level in the tree corresponds to memory blocks of a given size. The lowest node in the tree represents 512 bytes of memory, which is the smallest allocation granularity in our mechanism. The parent of a given node represents a memory block twice as large. Thus, the total number of nodes in the tree is 128, small enough to fit in the shared memory. A marked node means the block is allocated, otherwise, it is free. An invariant of this data structure is that if a node is marked, then its parent must be marked as well.

Allocation: Fig. 3 shows a case where a completely free tree receives an 8K allocation request. The first step is to find the tree level at which node sizes are no smaller than the request. The static mapping of blocks allows our mechanism to search for a free node on such a level of the tree, an operation which is performed in parallel by the threads of the scheduler warp. One of these threads that finds such a free node marks it. The next operation is to mark all descendants and ancestors of this node. Since the tree contains only 128 nodes, threads of the scheduler warp each check four nodes, and mark them if they are either the descendants or ancestors of the allocated node.

Deallocation: Fig. 4 shows an example where a block of 4K needs to be freed. First, the threads of the scheduler warp work in parallel to unmark all descendants of this node. Next, the first thread of the scheduler warp unmarks the node itself, and keeps going up the tree unmarking the parent as long as the sibling node is unmarked as well. Recall that both allocation and deallocation are carried out only by the scheduler warp, and hence no locking is necessary while performing them.

5.2 Sub-Thread Block Synchronization

CUDA *__syncthreads()* synchronizes threads within a threadblock. If this function is used directly within the Pagoda kernel code, the synchronization may lead to undefined behavior. This would occur because the MTB may be running two different threadblocks simultaneously, and hence all threads in the MTB may not reach the *__syncthreads()* barrier.

A naive solution to this issue would force all threadblocks running on the MTB to reach the same barrier. However, this would lead to excessive wait times in threadblocks that do not require synchronization. Pagoda presents a sub-threadblock barrier, where only the threads of a given threadblock can synchronize. Pa-goda achieves this using named barriers (using *bar.sync* instruction) in the PTX programming model [23]. Each threadblock of a task that annotates the synchronization requirement in the TaskTable entry is provided a unique barrier ID during the scheduling of the threadblock (Algo. 1, Line 19). When a threadblock encounters the *syncBlock()* function, this barrier ID is used for synchronization. The PTX model allows for only 16 such barriers. The Pagoda design therefore needs to recycle these IDs once the threadblock is finished.

6. EVALUATION

The following subsections detail our experimental setup and results.

6.1 Experimental Setup

The GPU experiments are run on a node with an NVIDIA Maxwell Titan X GPU, which contains 3072 1000MHz GPU cores with 12GB RAM. The machine runs Ubuntu 14.04, with 24GB RAM and an Intel core-i7 4.0GHz quad-core CPU. We enabled 32 concurrent kernels in the HyperQ by setting the CUDA_DEVICE_MAX_CONNECTIONS environment variable to 32. All CUDA and Pagoda benchmarks are compiled using *nvcc* from CUDA 7.5, with *-O3*. The MasterKernel, along with all task kernels, are forced to use at most 32 registers in the Pagoda versions. The PThreads and sequential programs are compiled with *gcc -O3* and are executed on two hyperthreaded Intel Xeon E5-2660 CPUs each having 10 cores running at 2.6GHz.

Table 4 details the applications used in this study. We chose benchmarks from various application domains, such as signal and image processing, network security, and scientific computing where narrow tasks arise often. Table 3 shows the workload characteristics of the benchmarks.

6.2 Comparison against Runtime Mechanisms

Fig. 5 shows that Pagoda obtains higher performance than other runtime schemes, namely, PThreads on the CPU, CUDA-HyperQ and GeMTC on the GPU. The speedup

Table 3: Benchmark Characteristics

Benchmark	Source	Task Type	Input Set per Task(each task is one image, signal, matrix or network packet)	Number of Tasks	% Time spent in data copy (CUDA-HyperQ)	% Time spent in computation (CUDA-HyperQ)	May benefit from Shared Memory	Requires thread-block synchronization	Default Register Count
Mandelbrot(**MB**)	Quinn [27]	Irregular	64 × 64 images	32K	24	76	✗	✗	28
FilterBank(**FB**)	StreamIt [35]	Regular	Signals of width 2K	32K	35	65	✗	✓	21
BeamFormer(**BF**)	StreamIt [35]	Regular	Signals of width 2K	32K	13	87	✗	✗	34
Image Convolution(**CONV**)	CUDA SDK [19]	Regular	128 × 128 images	32K	30	70	✗	✗	25
DCT8x8(**DCT**)	CUDA SDK [21]	Regular	128 × 128 images	32K	81	19	✓	✓	33
MatrixMul(**MM**)	CUDA SDK [22]	Regular	64 × 64 matrix	32K	51	49	✓	✓	30
Sparse LU Decomposition(**SLUD**)	OpenMP Task Suite [4]	Irregular	32 × 32 matrix	273K	3	97	✗	✗	17
3DES	NIST [5]	Irregular	Network packets sized 2K-64K	32K	74	26	✗	✗	26

Table 4: Benchmark Description

MB	Mandelbrot sets are used in fractal analysis [6]. Each pixel value of the image is calculated in parallel; however, the required computation per pixel is highly irregular. Therefore, computation over each pixel is represented as a task that has low degree of parallelism.
MM	This is a standard matrix multiplication implementation, refactored from the NVIDIA SDK samples [22]. We used small matrix sizes, with each multiplication running as a task to simulate the behaviour seen in an earthquake engineering simulator [16]. The behaviour arises from concurrent simulation of various structures, each of which is represented by different but small matrix sizes.
FB	Filterbank is a signal processing algorithm that separates input signals into multiple sub-signals with a set of filters. Multiple radios generate signals, processing each of them represents a task. Each task contains small amount of parallelizable computation.
BF	Beam former is a signal processing method used to control the direction of signal reception and transmission. Many independent signal beams receive inputs asynchronously. Processing individual inputs generate a narrow task.
SLUD	This is a sparse matrix solver using multi-frontal method [15]. A matrix is divided into multiple regular sub-matrices. Sparse LUD is represented as a task-based application owing to the irregularity in the computation size among different iterations of a parallel loop.
3DES	It is used to encrypt electronic data [5]. Network routers encrypt multiple packets as they arrive, each of which is represented as a narrow task. We use NetBench [17] to generate varied sizes of network packets that 3DES encrypts.
DCT	The Discrete Cosine Transform (DCT) [21] is commonly used for compression, e.g, JPEG (image), MP3 (audio), and MPEG (video) use it. Online surveillance systems gather image streams from multiple cameras, and operate on images from different streams in parallel [10]. Processing each image represents a narrow task.
CONV	Convolution filters [19] are used in blur and edge detection mechanisms in image processing. Each filter operation represents a task, which operates in parallel across pixels.
MPE	Pagoda is able to run multi-programmed workloads, where multiple applications generate narrow tasks asynchronously. To evaluate such a setup, we built a multi-programmed benchmark of our own. Multi-programmed environments often encounter heterogeneity in workloads. To simulate that, we chose 1) 3DES and Mandelbrot, which contain irregular computations, 2) Filterbank, which requires threadblock-level synchronization, and 3) Matrix multiplication, which uses shared memory. Each of the benchmarks contained 8K tasks, totalling 32K tasks.

is calculated over the entire execution time, i.e, it measures both compute and data copy times. The performance increase is attributed to the high utilization achieved by Pagoda. The GeMTC versions do not use shared memory, since GeMTC has no support for it. We could not implement SLUD in GeMTC; GeMTC needs the number of tasks to be pre-defined, which is not the case in SLUD. GeMTC launches work in batches, where batch comprises a SuperKernel that runs tasks. The default GeMTC design used 32 threads per SuperKernel threadblock, obtaining only 50% occupancy. We hence modified GeMTC to use more threads; from 64 threads onwards, GeMTC can obtain 100% occupancy. Our evaluation uses 128 threads per task for HyperQ, GeMTC, and Pagoda, which was heuristically chosen because GeMTC performs reasonably well in this configuration (Fig. 7). GeMTC performs worse than HyperQ in MB and 3DES because these applications contain irregular workloads. Speedup achieved by all GPU schemes is low in DCT because the application is data copy bound. For a fair comparison with the CPU, we implemented OpenMP with data parallelism, OS-based task scheduling, Python-based thread pooling, and PThreads-based task parallelism. PThreads obtained the best results, which we include in Fig. 5.

Fig. 6 presents weak-scaling results. It compares execution times when the task count is varied. For low task counts, none of the schemes occupy the entire GPU, and hence HyperQ and GeMTC perform fairly well. However, once the task count grows beyond 512, Pagoda obtains higher performance because of increased utilization.

6.3 Comparison against Static Task Fusion

Static task fusion combines multiple tasks into a monolithic large task [37, 8]. It is clear that such mechanisms perform the best if all tasks start and end together. Benefits from Pagoda come into play when the computations of tasks would not end together, due to irregularities. Here, we compare the speedups achieved by Pagoda, static fusion, PThreads, and CUDA-HyperQ when task compute workloads vary. To obtain such irregularity, we generated input sizes of different tasks in a pseudo-random manner. We

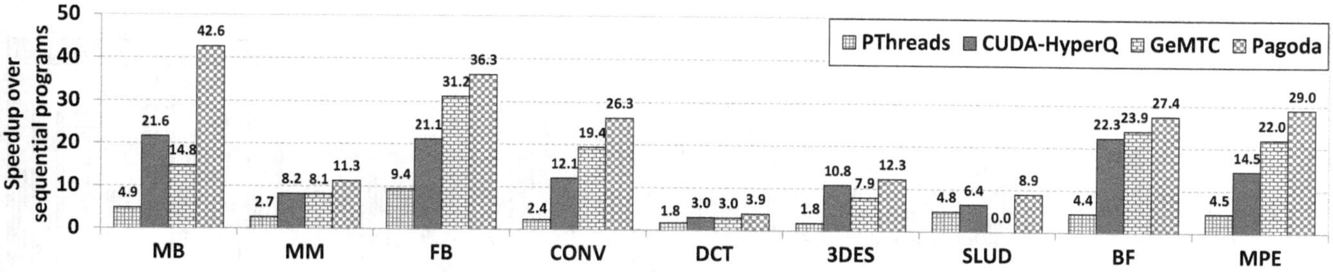

Figure 5: Overall Performance Comparison: The number of tasks in each benchmark is constant (32K), except SLUD, which contains 273K tasks. Each GPU task uses 128 threads. The measurement of execution time contains both data copy and compute times. Pagoda significantly outperforms CUDA-HyperQ(1.51x), 20-core PThreads(5.70x), and GeMTC(1.69x), owing to the higher utilization.

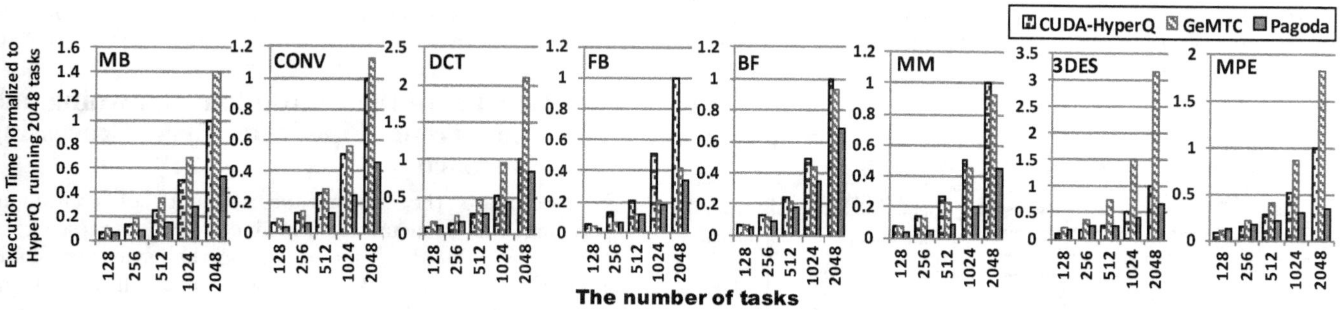

Figure 6: Weak scaling with number of tasks: Each task contains 128 threads, since that configuration works the best for GeMTC. Pagoda versions run faster than HyperQ and GeMTC beyond 512 tasks. The Pagoda execution time scales well with the number of tasks.

could not fuse SLUD since the number of tasks is not known statically. Each application contained 32K tasks. Each subtask in the statically fused task uses 256 threads. We chose this number heuristically, since selecting the best thread count per task is infeasible in static fusion. On the other hand, the runtime schemes of Pagoda/CUDA-HyperQ allow for dynamic thread count selection, based on the size of the irregular task. The tasks in Fig. 9 use between 32 and 256 threads for Pagoda/CUDA-HyperQ. The Pagoda performance is superior to all other schemes. Pagoda achieves a geometric mean speedup of 1.79x over static fusion. Note that the static fusion approach represents the upper-bound performance from batch-scheduling systems such as GeMTC, since the execution time is bounded by the longest running task.

Pagoda's performance gain depends on the input size, thread counts per task, and the number of tasks. Fig. 6 showed the impact of the number of tasks. Next, we analyze the impact of thread counts on the GPU compute time, while keeping the task input sizes fixed and varying the work done per thread. Fig. 7 compares benchmark execution times with a varying number of threads per task. No shared memory was used in either of the program versions because GeMTC does not support it. Pagoda outperforms both CUDA-HyperQ and GeMTC on all configurations. The performance benefits of Pagoda over HyperQ decrease with thread count because the underutilization becomes less severe. Generally, Pagoda performance increases with thread counts owing to the increased pipelined processing benefits. Pagoda's performance on FB decreases at higher thread counts because synchronization in that benchmark incurs a higher penalty when more threads must synchronize. The GeMTC performance does not change much with the thread count. This is explained since each batch, or SuperKernel, contains a fixed number of total threads.

6.4 Understanding Pagoda's Utility

Fig. 8 studies Pagoda's compute time versus HyperQ on two representative benchmarks wherein both the input size and thread counts are varied. The HyperQ configurations use 256 threads per threadblock. The evaluation uses 32K tasks. For most inputs, Pagoda gains significant speedups over HyperQ owing to the increased underutilization, until the thread count is greater than 512. Afterwards, Pagoda benefits diminish, since HyperQ can then better utilize the GPU without having to pay the Pagoda scheduling cost. However, in certain cases after further increasing the thread count, e.g., CONV with input size 256x256 and 64K threads, Pagoda starts to significantly outperform HyperQ. We attribute this behavior to the warp-level scheduling in Pagoda against the threadblock-level scheduling in CUDA. CUDA prohibits a new threadblock from launching until all warps of the previous threadblock finish, where Pagoda can schedule a warp from a new threadblock as soon a warp in a running threadblock completes.

6.5 Task Latency Analysis

Fig. 10 compares the average latency obtained per task in Pagoda with that in a statically fused task. We use two representative applications: 3DES, which contains irregular tasks, and MM, which contains regular tasks. Each task in a statically fused kernel, or in a batch-based system such as GeMTC, can only finish when all tasks in the fused kernel or batch have finished. Therefore, their achieved average latency increases with the number of tasks. On the other hand, the average latency of each Pagoda task remains the same for any number of launched tasks.

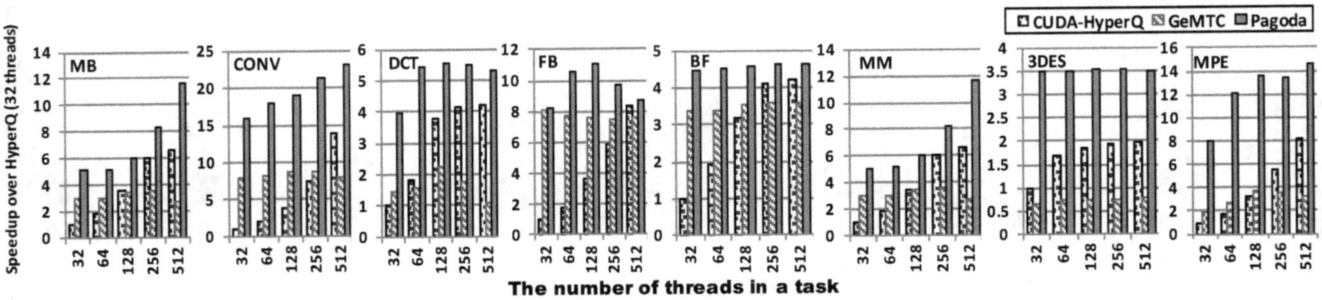

Figure 7: ***Comparison of computation times with different thread counts per task:*** *The number of tasks in each benchmark is 32K. The amount of work per task remains constant in all thread configurations. Pagoda achieves geometric mean speedup of 2.29x over HyperQ, and 2.26x over GeMTC at 128 threads. Pagoda's performance benefit over HyperQ decreases as the number of threads per task increases.*

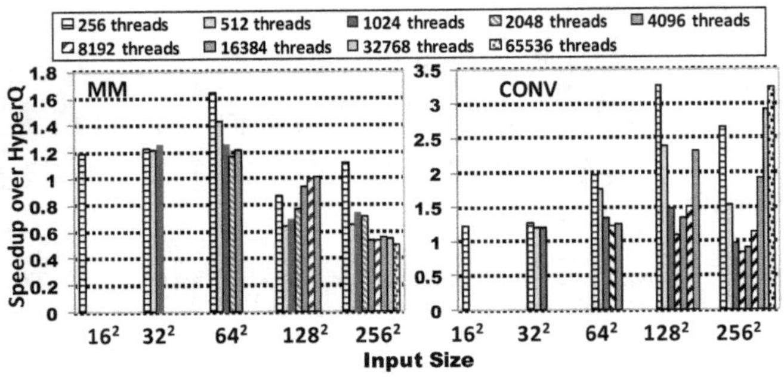

Figure 8: ***Effects of varying threads per task for different input sizes:*** *For small thread counts, Pagoda outperforms HyperQ in all input sizes. For large thread counts, Pagoda may still outperform HyperQ owing to its finer grain of scheduling.*

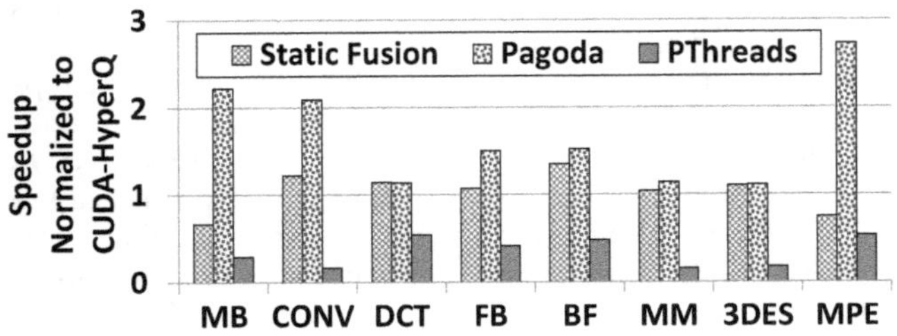

Figure 9: ***Performance comparison of static fusion, CUDA-HyperQ, PThreads, and Pagoda with irregular tasks:*** *Dynamic task spawning mechanism in Pagoda obtains high performance even with irregular workloads.*

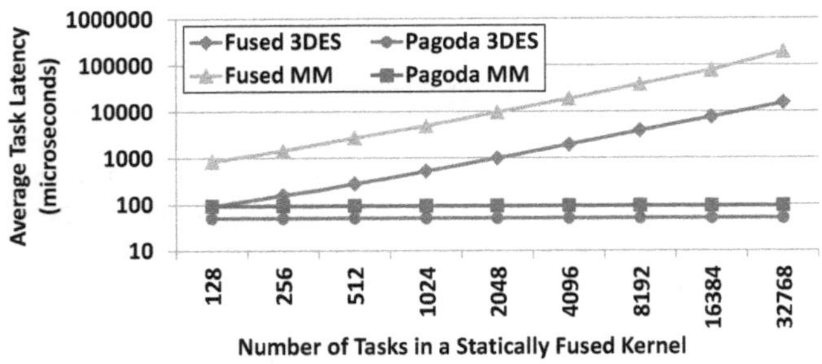

Figure 10: ***Average Latency of Tasks:*** *Pagoda achieves much lower latency compared to static fusion.*

6.6 Benefits of the Continuous Spawning and Concurrent Pipelined Task Processing Approach

To compare the performance benefits of continuous spawning and concurrent pipelined task processing in Pagoda, we created a Pagoda version that spawns tasks in batches, i.e., no new tasks are spawned until all tasks in the previous batch finish. This resembles the task spawning in GeMTC; however, it still performs concurrent task scheduling. We chose the same batch size as GeMTC's. Fig. 11 compares GeMTC, Pagoda Batching, and Pagoda, which performs continuous spawning and concurrent, pipelined task processing. The total task count is 32K, and each task contains 128 threads. The performance difference between GeMTC and Pagoda batching demonstrates the benefits achieved by concurrent task processing. The performance difference between Pagoda and Pagoda Batching demonstrates the benefits achieved by continuous, pipelined task spawning. This mechanism is enabled by Pagoda's TaskTable which offers simultaneous CPU task spawning and GPU task scheduling. Continuous spawning and concurrent, pipelined processing achieve significant benefits. CONV is the only benchmark that does not benefit from continuous spawns, owing its regular, extremely short-running tasks. Multi-Programming Environment(MPE) obtains exceptionally high benefits from continuous, pipelined processing due to its unbalanced tasks.

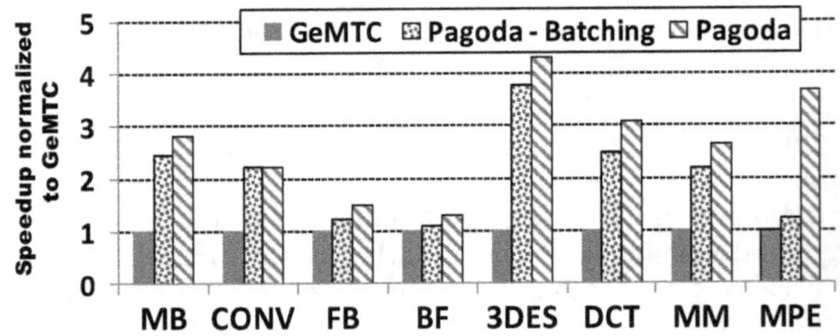

Figure 11: ***Benefits of Pagoda Continuous Spawning and Concurrent, Pipelined Task Processing:*** *Pagoda performs both continuous spawning and concurrent, pipelined task processing. Pagoda-batching only performs concurrent task processing. GeMTC performs neither. Pagoda outperforms GeMTC in all cases.*

*Table 5: **Compute performance comparison of tasks run in Pagoda with and without shared memory allocation:** Each version runs 32K tasks. DCT tasks have 64 threads, MM tasks contain 256 threads. Only the compute time is compared. The shared memory usage offers considerable benefits.*

Bench-mark	Pagoda with Shared Memory		Pagoda without Shared Memory	
	Speedup over HyperQ using Shared memory	Achieved Occu-pancy	Speedup over HyperQ using Shared memory	Achieved Occu-pancy
DCT	1.35x	25%	1.25x	97%
MM	1.51x	97%	1.20x	97%

6.7 Pagoda Shared Memory Analysis

Pagoda performs software management of the GPU shared memory, as described in Section 5.1. To compare the obtainable performance benefits from the use of shared memory, we show performance results on the DCT and MM benchmarks. These two codes can potentially benefit from the use of shared memory. We created two versions for each: with and without using shared memory. Table 5 compares the speedups achieved by these versions over the CUDA-HyperQ versions, which also use the shared memory. The shared memory requirement may reduce the achieved occupancy; yet, Pagoda shared memory versions achieve performance benefits. None of the other static-fusion or runtime batching solution offer shared memory utilization, and miss out on such benefits.

7. RELATED WORK

Task-based models [1, 3] employ a runtime system which governs task executions on various engines, such as CPUs and GPUs. These systems, however, always execute narrow tasks on CPUs, believing that their low parallelism degree cannot overcome the overhead of memory copies.

Static task fusion is the preliminary approach to deal with GPU underutilization. Wang et. al. [37] present a mechanism where such fusion achieves higher utilization, resulting in energy benefits. KernelMerge [8] statically fuses kernels, and explores round-robin and fair-partitioned execution schemes for these kernels. The GPU programming models, such as CUDA and OpenCL, allocate same resources to each thread. Therefore, the resource usage in static fusion schemes gets limited by the requirements of the most resource-hungry task. A more sophisticated approach is therefore to perform fusion at the runtime. Two approaches [28, 25] perform kernel consolidation leveraging concurrent GPU kernel execution. They launch multiple concurrent kernels, where resources not being used by one kernel can be yielded to another. The first approach [28] relies on a threadblock-level launching scheme. The second approach [25] presents a compiler scheme that transforms kernels so that they can automatically support any threadblock configuration. This ability helps in finding the best sharing configuration for different kernels. Zhong et. al. [41] present an approach where a large kernel is split into independent smaller kernels that co-execute to achieve better utilization. Kato et al. [11] propose a software scheduler at the device driver layer to prevent interference among concurrently running GPU applications, trading off response latency for throughput. However, all these approaches are restricted by the 32 kernel limit imposed by CUDA-HyperQ, and fail to efficiently execute narrow tasks.

Runtime systems that virtualize GPU resources can naturally overcome the hardware-imposed kernel limit. Additionally, they offer low execution latencies compared to static fusion. Closest to our work is GeMTC [14]. Like the MasterKernel in Pagoda, GeMTC runs a SuperKernel that virtualizes GPU resources. The use of large dameon-like kernels is similar to persistent threading [9]. Unlike the MasterKernel, the SuperKernel does not guarantee an occupancy of 100%, and therefore may face underutilization. Secondly, the GeMTC design uses a single FIFO queue for its batch-based task launching scheme, resulting in significant task scheduling overhead. Third, GPU-specific functionalities, such as the shared memory and threadblock-level synchronization remain unsupported.

GPU researchers have exploited pipelining [29] to overlap data transfers with kernel computations. The distinguishing factor in the Pagoda pipelined task processing is that it overlaps spawning, which comprises the CPU finding a free task entry and performing a data copy, with GPU scheduling, which is only a sub-part of the overall task processing. Yang et. al. [40] showed that fusing cross-kernel threadblocks can obtain better shared memory performance. Pagoda's shared memory management schedules threadblocks as long as shared memory is found at runtime.

Prior research has explored preemptive hardware techniques to improve GPU utilization in the presence of concurrent low occupancy kernels [38, 26, 34]. In contrast to these works, which require hardware changes, Pagoda provides a software only solution that runs on contemporary GPU hardware and could be applied to any future GPU hardware that supports the CUDA programming model.

Virtualizing GPU resources has also been explored to improve GPU utilization via multi-tenancy in cloud computing. Sengupta et al. [30] focus on virtualizing the GPU as a whole in a cloud with multiple GPUs. Becchi et al. [2] study a virtual memory system that isolates the memory spaces of concurrent kernels and allows kernels whose aggregate memory footprint exceeds the GPU's memory capacity to execute concurrently. By contrast, Pagoda virtualizes the compute resources of a single GPU at the granularity of a warp.

8. CONCLUSION

The paper has presented Pagoda, a GPU runtime system that overcomes underutilization in the presence of narrow tasks. Pagoda virtualizes GPU resources via MasterKernel, a continually executing daemon on the GPU. Pagoda launches tasks on the GPU as long as free warps are available. Unlike previous work, Pagoda supports most functionality of the native CUDA model. A key distinction in Pagoda is the task spawning and scheduling mechanism. It contains a novel data structure, called TaskTable, that greatly reduces CPU-GPU handshaking during task spawning. Pagoda achieves concurrent task scheduling, and overlaps task spawning, scheduling, and execution through pipelining. The experimental evaluation showed that Pagoda achie-ves a geometric mean speedup of 1.51x over CUDA- HyperQ, 1.69x over GeMTC, and 5.70x over 20-core CPU PThreads. The evaluation also showed that Pagoda can outperform static fusion schemes by 1.79x, and achieves much lower latency per task. We believe that the Pagoda design makes it easier for narrow task applications to exploit GPUs, and will encourage the growth of non-traditional workloads on GPUs.

9. REFERENCES

[1] C. A. Augonnet, S. Thibault, R. Namyst, and P.-A. W. Wacrenier. Starpu: A unified platform for task scheduling on heterogeneous multicore architectures. *Concurr. Comput. : Pract. Exper.*, 23(2):187–198, Feb. 2011.

[2] M. Becchi, K. Sajjapongse, I. Graves, A. Procter, V. Ravi, and S. Chakradhar. A virtual memory based runtime to support multi-tenancy in clusters with GPUs. In *Proceedings of the 21st International Symposium on High-Performance Parallel and Distributed Computing*, HPDC '12, pages 97–108, New York, NY, USA, 2012. ACM.

[3] J. Bueno, J. Planas, A. Duran, R. M. Badia, X. Martorell, E. AyguadÃl', and J. Labarta. Productive programming of GPU clusters with ompss. In *Parallel Distributed Processing Symposium (IPDPS), 2012 IEEE 26th International*, pages 557–568, May 2012.

[4] A. Duran, X. Teruel, R. Ferrer, X. Martorell, and E. Ayguade. Barcelona openmp tasks suite: A set of benchmarks targeting the exploitation of task parallelism in openmp. In *Proceedings of the 2009 International Conference on Parallel Processing*, ICPP '09, pages 124–131, Washington, DC, USA, 2009. IEEE Computer Society.

[5] P. FIPS. 46-3: Data encryption standard (des). *National Institute of Standards and Technology*, 25(10):1–22, 1999.

[6] Fraqtive. [Online]. Available: http://fraqtive.mimec.org/, 2016. (accessed March 5, 2016).

[7] N. K. Govindaraju, B. Lloyd, Y. Dotsenko, B. Smith, and J. Manferdelli. High performance discrete fourier transforms on graphics processors. In *Proceedings of the 2008 ACM/IEEE conference on Supercomputing*, page 2. IEEE Press, 2008.

[8] C. Gregg, J. Dorn, K. Hazelwood, and K. Skadron. Fine-grained resource sharing for concurrent GPGPU kernels. In *Proceedings of the 4th USENIX Conference on Hot Topics in Parallelism*, HotPar'12, pages 10–10, Berkeley, CA, USA, 2012. USENIX Association.

[9] K. Gupta, J. A. Stuart, and J. D. Owens. A study of persistent threads style GPU programming for GPGPU workloads. In *Innovative Parallel Computing (InPar), 2012*, pages 1–14. IEEE, 2012.

[10] A. S. Kaseb, E. Berry, Y. Koh, A. Mohan, W. Chen, H. Li, Y. H. Lu, and E. J. Delp. A system for large-scale analysis of distributed cameras. In *Signal and Information Processing (GlobalSIP), 2014 IEEE Global Conference on*, pages 340–344, Dec 2014.

[11] S. Kato, K. Lakshmanan, R. Rajkumar, and Y. Ishikawa. Timegraph: GPU scheduling for real-time multi-tasking environments. In *Proceedings of the 2011 USENIX Conference on USENIX Annual Technical Conference*, USENIXATC'11, pages 2–2, Berkeley, CA, USA, 2011. USENIX Association.

[12] S. Kim, S. Huh, Y. Hu, X. Zhang, E. Witchel, A. Wated, and M. Silberstein. GPUnet: Networking abstractions for GPU programs. In *Proceedings of the 11th USENIX Conference on Operating Systems Design and Implementation*, OSDI'14, pages 201–216, Berkeley, CA, USA, 2014. USENIX Association.

[13] K. C. Knowlton. A fast storage allocator. *Commun. ACM*, 8(10):623–624, Oct. 1965.

[14] S. J. Krieder, J. M. Wozniak, T. Armstrong, M. Wilde, D. S. Katz, B. Grimmer, I. T. Foster, and I. Raicu. Design and evaluation of the GeMTC framework for GPU-enabled many-task computing. In *Proceedings of the 23rd International Symposium on High-performance Parallel and Distributed Computing*, HPDC '14, pages 153–164, New York, NY, USA, 2014. ACM.

[15] J. W. H. Liu. The multifrontal method for sparse matrix solution: Theory and practice. *SIAM Rev.*, 34(1):82–109, Mar. 1992.

[16] F. McKenna. Opensees: A framework for earthquake engineering simulation. *Computing in Science Engineering*, 13(4):58–66, July 2011.

[17] G. Memik, W. H. Mangione-Smith, and W. Hu. Netbench: A benchmarking suite for network processors. In *Proceedings of the 2001 IEEE/ACM international conference on Computer-aided design*, pages 39–42. IEEE Press, 2001.

[18] A. Morrison and Y. Afek. Fast concurrent queues for x86 processors. *SIGPLAN Not.*, 48(8):103–112, Feb. 2013.

[19] NVIDIA. Texture-based Separable Convolution. [Online]. Available: http://docs.nvidia.com/cuda/cuda-samples/#graphics, 2007. (accessed March. 5, 2016).

[20] NVIDIA. Hyper-Q Example. [Online]. Available: http://docs.nvidia.com/cuda/samples/6_Advanced/simpleHyperQ/doc/HyperQ.pdf, 2012. (accessed March. 5, 2016).

[21] NVIDIA. The White Paper of Discrete Cosine Transform for 8x8 Blocks with CUDA. [Online]. Available: http://docs.nvidia.com/cuda/samples/3_Imaging/dct8x8/doc/dct8x8.pdf, 2012. (accessed March. 5, 2016).

[22] NVIDIA. CUDA. [Online]. Available: http://docs.nvidia.com/cuda/cuda-c-programming-guide/, 2015. (accessed March 5, 2016).

[23] NVIDIA. PTX. [Online]. Available: http://docs.nvidia.com/cuda/parallel-thread-execution/, 2016. (accessed March 5, 2016).

[24] K. Ousterhout, A. Panda, J. Rosen, S. Venkataraman, R. Xin, S. Ratnasamy, S. Shenker, and I. Stoica. The case for tiny tasks in compute clusters. In *Presented as part of the 14th Workshop on Hot Topics in Operating Systems*, Berkeley, CA, 2013. USENIX.

[25] S. Pai, M. J. Thazhuthaveetil, and R. Govindarajan. Improving GPGPU concurrency with elastic kernels. In *Proceedings of the Eighteenth International Conference on Architectural Support for Programming Languages and Operating Systems*, ASPLOS '13, pages 407–418, New York, NY, USA, 2013. ACM.

[26] J. J. K. Park, Y. Park, and S. Mahlke. Chimera: Collaborative preemption for multitasking on a shared GPU. In *Proceedings of the Twentieth International Conference on Architectural Support for Programming Languages and Operating Systems*, ASPLOS '15, pages 593–606, New York, NY, USA, 2015. ACM.

[27] M. J. Quinn. *Parallel Programming in C with MPI and OpenMP*. McGraw-Hill Education Group, 2003.

[28] V. T. Ravi, M. Becchi, G. Agrawal, and S. Chakradhar. Supporting GPU sharing in cloud environments with a transparent runtime consolidation framework. In *Proceedings of the 20th International Symposium on High Performance Distributed Computing*, HPDC '11, pages 217–228, New York, NY, USA, 2011. ACM.

[29] A. Sabne, P. Sakdhnagool, and R. Eigenmann. Scaling large-data computations on Multi-GPU accelerators. In *Proceedings of the 27th International ACM Conference on International Conference on Supercomputing*, ICS '13, pages 443–454, New York, NY, USA, 2013. ACM.

[30] D. Sengupta, R. Belapure, and K. Schwan. Multi-tenancy on GPGPU-based servers. In *Proceedings of the 7th International Workshop on Virtualization Technologies in Distributed Computing*, pages 3–10, 2013.

[31] M. Silberstein, B. Ford, I. Keidar, and E. Witchel. GPUfs: Integrating a file system with GPUs. In *Proceedings of the Eighteenth International Conference on Architectural Support for Programming Languages and Operating Systems*, ASPLOS '13, pages 485–498, New York, NY, USA, 2013. ACM.

[32] J. Subhlok, J. M. Stichnoth, D. R. O'Hallaron, and T. Gross. Exploiting task and data parallelism on a multicomputer. In *Proceedings of the Fourth ACM SIGPLAN Symposium on Principles and Practice of Parallel Programming*, PPOPP '93, pages 13–22, New York, NY, USA, 1993. ACM.

[33] J. Subhlok and G. Vondran. Optimal use of mixed task and data parallelism for pipelined computations. *J. Parallel Distrib. Comput.*, 60(3):297–319, 2000.

[34] I. Tanasic, I. Gelado, J. Cabezas, A. Ramirez, N. Navarro, and M. Valero. Enabling preemptive multiprogramming on GPUs. In *Proceeding of the 41st Annual International Symposium on Computer Architecuture*, ISCA '14, pages 193–204, Piscataway, NJ, USA, 2014. IEEE Press.

[35] W. Thies, M. Karczmarek, and S. Amarasinghe. Streamit: A language for streaming applications. In *Compiler Construction*, pages 179–196. Springer, 2002.

[36] V. Volkov and J. W. Demmel. Benchmarking GPUs to tune dense linear algebra. In *High Performance Computing, Networking, Storage and Analysis, 2008. SC 2008. International Conference for*, pages 1–11. IEEE, 2008.

[37] G. Wang, Y. Lin, and W. Yi. Kernel fusion: An effective method for better power efficiency on multithreaded GPU. In *Green Computing and Communications (GreenCom), 2010 IEEE/ACM Int'l Conference on Int'l Conference on Cyber, Physical and Social Computing (CPSCom)*, pages 344–350, Dec 2010.

[38] Z. Wang, J. Yang, R. Melhem, B. Childers, Y. Zhang, and M. Guo. Simultaneous multikernel: Fine-grained sharing of gpgpus. *IEEE Computer Architecture Letters*, PP(99):1–1, 2015.

[39] P. R. Wilson, M. S. Johnstone, M. Neely, and D. Boles. Dynamic storage allocation: A survey and critical review. In *Proceedings of the International Workshop on Memory Management*, IWMM '95, pages 1–116, London, UK, UK, 1995. Springer-Verlag.

[40] Y. Yang, P. Xiang, M. Mantor, N. Rubin, and H. Zhou. Shared memory multiplexing: A novel way to improve gpgpu throughput. In *Proceedings of the 21st International Conference on Parallel Architectures and Compilation Techniques*, PACT '12, pages 283–292, New York, NY, USA, 2012. ACM.

[41] J. Zhong and B. He. Kernelet: High-throughput GPU kernel executions with dynamic slicing and scheduling. *IEEE Trans. Parallel Distrib. Syst.*, 25(6):1522–1532, June 2014.

Groute: An Asynchronous Multi-GPU Programming Model for Irregular Computations

Tal Ben-Nun Michael Sutton

The Hebrew University of Jerusalem, Israel

{talbn, msutton}@cs.huji.ac.il

Sreepathi Pai Keshav Pingali

The University of Texas at Austin, USA

sreepai@ices.utexas.edu pingali@cs.utexas.edu

Abstract

Nodes with multiple GPUs are becoming the platform of choice for high-performance computing. However, most applications are written using bulk-synchronous programming models, which may not be optimal for irregular algorithms that benefit from low-latency, asynchronous communication. This paper proposes constructs for asynchronous multi-GPU programming, and describes their implementation in a thin runtime environment called Groute. Groute also implements common collective operations and distributed work-lists, enabling the development of irregular applications without substantial programming effort. We demonstrate that this approach achieves state-of-the-art performance and exhibits strong scaling for a suite of irregular applications on 8-GPU and heterogeneous systems, yielding over 7x speedup for some algorithms.

Categories and Subject Descriptors D.1.3 [*Programming Techniques*]: Concurrent Programming

Keywords Multi-GPU, Asynchronous Programming, Irregular Algorithms

1. Motivation

Nodes with multiple attached accelerators are now ubiquitous in high-performance computing. In particular, Graphics Processing Units (GPUs) have become popular because of their power efficiency, hardware parallelism, scalable caching mechanisms, and balance between specialized instructions and general-purpose computing. Multi-GPU nodes consist of a host (CPUs) and several GPU devices linked via a low-latency, high-throughput bus (see Figure 1). These interconnects allow parallel applications to exchange data efficiently and to take advantage of the combined computational power and memory size of the GPUs.

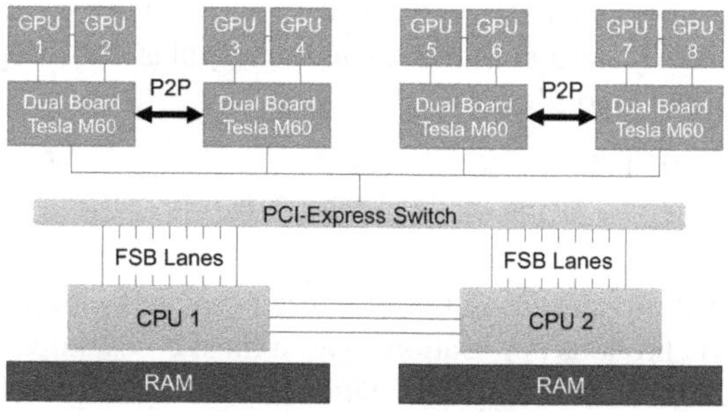

Figure 1: Multi-GPU Node Schematic

Multi-GPU nodes are usually programmed using one of two methods. In the simple approach, each GPU is managed separately, using one process per device [13, 19]. Alternatively, a Bulk Synchronous Parallel (BSP) [32] programming model is used, in which applications are executed in rounds, and each round consists of local computation followed by global communication [6, 26]. The first approach is subject to overheads from various sources, such as the operating system, and requires a message-passing interface for communication. The BSP model, on the other hand, can introduce unnecessary serialization at the global barriers that implement round-based execution. Both programming methods may result in under-utilization of multi-GPU platforms, particularly for irregular applications, which may suffer from load imbalance and may have unpredictable communication patterns.

In principle, asynchronous programming models can reduce some of these problems, because unlike in round-based communication, processors can compute and communicate autonomously without waiting for other processors to reach global barriers. However, there are few applications that exploit asynchronous execution, since their development requires an in-depth knowledge of the underlying architecture and communication network, and involves performing intricate adaptations to the code.

This paper presents Groute, an asynchronous programming model and runtime environment [2] that can be used to develop a wide range of applications on multi-GPU systems.

PPoPP '17, February 04-08, 2017, Austin, TX, USA
© 2017 ACM. ISBN 978-1-4503-4493-7/17/02...$15.00
DOI: http://dx.doi.org/10.1145/3018743.3018756

Based on concepts from low-level networking, Groute aims to overcome the programming complexity of asynchronous applications on multi-GPU and heterogeneous platforms. The communication constructs of Groute are simple, but they can be used to efficiently express programs that range from regular applications and BSP applications to nontrivial irregular algorithms. The asynchronous nature of the runtime environment also promotes load balancing, leading to better utilization of heterogeneous multi-GPU nodes.

The main contributions of this paper are the following.

- We define abstract programming constructs for asynchronous execution and communication.
- We show that these constructs can be used to define a variety of algorithms including regular and irregular parallel algorithms.
- We compare aspects of the performance of our implementations, using applications written in existing frameworks as benchmarks.
- We show that using Groute, it is possible to implement asynchronous applications that in most cases outperform state-of-the-art implementations, yielding up to 7.28× speedup on 8 GPUs compared to a baseline execution on a single GPU.

2. Multi-GPU Node Architecture

In general, the role of accelerators is to complement the available CPUs by allowing them to offload data-parallel portions of an application. The CPUs, in turn, are responsible for process management, communication, input/output tasks, memory transfers, and data pre/post-processing.

As illustrated in Figure 1, the CPUs and accelerators are connected to each other via a Front-Side Bus (FSB, implementations include QPI and HyperTransport). The FSB lanes, whose count is an indicator of the memory transfer bandwidth, are linked to an interconnect such as PCI-Express or NVLink that supports both CPU-GPU and GPU-GPU communications.

Due to limitations in the hardware layout, such as use of the same motherboard and power supply units, multi-GPU nodes typically consist of (~1-25) GPUs. The topology of the CPUs, GPUs and interconnect can vary between complete all-pair connections and a hierarchical switched topology, as shown in the figure. In the tree-topology shown in Figure 1, each quadruplet of GPUs (i.e., 1–4 and 5–8) can perform *direct* communication operations amongst themselves, but communications with the other quadruplet are *indirect* and thus slower. For example, GPUs 1 and 4 can perform direct communication, but data transfers from GPU 4 to 5 must pass through the interconnect. A switched interface allows each CPU to communicate with all GPUs at the same rate. In other configurations, CPUs are directly connected to their quadruplet of GPUs, which results in variable CPU-GPU bandwidth, depending on process placement.

The GPU architecture contains multiple memory copy engines, enabling simultaneous code execution and two-way (input/output) memory transfer. Below, we elaborate on the different ways concurrent copies can be used to efficiently communicate within a multi-GPU node.

2.1 Inter-GPU Communication

Memory transfers among GPUs can either be initiated by the host or a device. In particular, host-initiated memory transfer (*Peer Transfer*) is supported by explicit copy commands, whereas device-initiated memory transfer (*Direct Access*, DA) is implemented using inter-GPU memory accesses. Note that direct access to peer memory may not be available between all pairs of GPUs, depending on the bus topology. Access to pinned host memory, however, is possible from all GPUs.

Device-initiated memory transfers are implemented by virtual addressing, which maps all host and device memory to a single address space. While more flexible than peer transfers, DA performance is highly sensitive to memory alignment, coalescing, number of active threads and order of access.

Using microbenchmarks (Figure 2) we measure 100 MB transfers, averaged over 100 trials, on the 8-GPU system from our experimental setup (see Section 5 for detailed specifications).

Figure 2a shows the transfer rate of device-initiated memory access on GPUs that reside in the same board; on different boards; and CPU-GPU communication. The figure demonstrates the two extremes of the DA spectrum — from tightly-managed coalesced access (blue bars, left-hand side) to random, unmanaged access (red bars, right-hand side). Observe that coalesced access performs up to 21× better than random access. Also notice that the memory transfer rate correlates with the distance of the path in the topology. Due to the added level of dual-board GPUs (shown in Figure 1), CPU-GPU transfer is faster than two different-board GPUs.

In order to support device-initiated transfers between GPUs that cannot access each other's memory, it is possible to perform a two-phase indirect copy. In indirect copy, the source GPU "pushes" information to host memory first, after which it is "pulled" by the destination GPU, using host flags and system-wide memory fences for synchronization.

In topologies such as the one presented in Figure 1, GPUs can only transmit to one destination at a time. This hinders the responsiveness of an asynchronous system, especially when transferring large buffers. One way to resolve this issue is by dividing messages into packets, as in networking. Figure 2b presents the overhead of using packetized memory transfers as opposed to a single peer transfer. The figure shows that the overhead decreases linearly as the packet size increases, ranging between ~1-10% for 1-10 MB packets. This parameter can be tuned by individual applications to balance between latency and bandwidth.

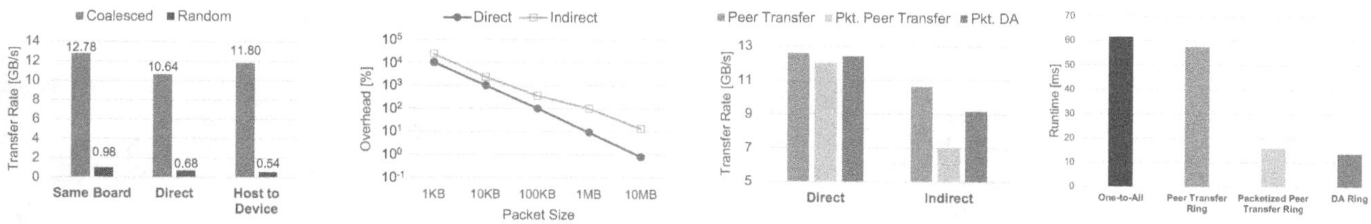

(a) Direct memory access order (b) Packetization overhead (c) Packetized transfer rate (d) Peer broadcast performance

Figure 2: Inter-GPU Memory Transfer M

Figure 2c compares the transfer rate of direct (push) and indirect (push/pull) transfers, showing that packetized device-initiated transfers and the fine-grained control is advantageous, even over the host-managed packetized peer transfers. Note that since device-initiated memory access is written in user-code, it is possible to perform additional data processing during transfer.

Another important aspect of multi-GPU communication is multiple source/destination transfers, as in collective operations. Due to the structure of the interconnect and memory copy engines, a naive application is likely to congest the bus. One approach, used in the NCCL library [24], creates a ring topology over the bus. In this approach, illustrated in Figure 3, each GPU transfers to one destination, communicating via direct or indirect device-initiated transfers. This ensures that both memory copy engines of every GPU are us(to bei

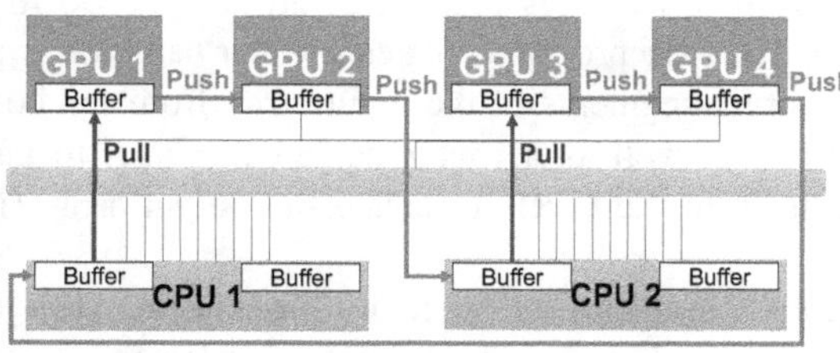

Figure 3: DA Ring Topology

Figure 2d compares the performance of the different methods of implementing one-to-all GPU peer broadcast, ranging from 7 asynchronous transfers from one source, through complete and packetized peer transfers, to the above DA Ring approach. The figure shows that the ring topology consistently outperforms separate direct copies. This can be attributed to the lower amount of indirect peer transfers (one peer transfer to the second quadruplet in ring vs. four in one-to-all). Additionally, packetization induces copy pipelining, which dramatically decreases the running time. DA Ring performs only slightly better than host-controlled ring transfer, consistent with the faster transfer rate in Figure 2c.

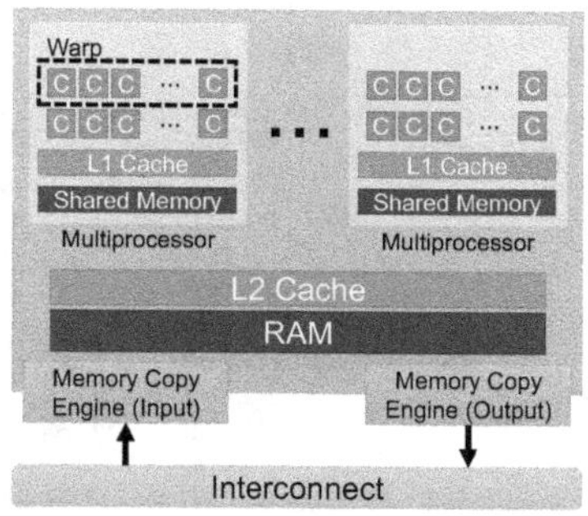

Figure 4: Single GPU Architecture

2.2 GPU Programming Model

The structure of a single GPU device is depicted in Figure 4. As shown in the figure, each GPU contains a fixed set of multiprocessors (MPs) and a RAM unit (referred to as *global memory*). GPU procedures (*kernels*) run on the MPs in parallel by scheduling a *grid* of many threads, grouped to *thread-blocks*. Within each thread-block, which is assigned to a single MP, *warps* (usually comprised of 32 threads) execute on the cores in lockstep. Additionally, threads in the same thread-block can synchronize and communicate via shared memory, as well as use the automatically managed L1 and L2 caches. To support concurrent memory writes, atomic operations are defined on both shared and global memory.

Kernel invocation and host-initiated memory transfers are performed via command queues (*streams*), which can be used to express task parallelism. Stream synchronization between one or more GPUs is usually performed using *events*, which are recorded on one stream and waited for on another.

The GPU scheduler dispatches kernels by thread-blocks, enabling multiple-stream concurrency on the same GPU by scheduling other kernels' thread-blocks when there are no more thread-blocks to schedule for a running kernel. However, high-priority streams allow application developers to immediately invoke kernels, scheduling thread-blocks from a new kernel prior to thread-blocks from a running kernel.

While the stream/event constructs provide fine-grained control over kernel scheduling, difficulties arise when programming higher-level functionality that involves multiple GPUs. In the following section, we present a programming

Table 1: Groute Programming Interface

Construct	Description
Base Constructs	
`Context`	Singleton that represents the runtime environment.
`Endpoint`	An entity that can communicate (e.g., GPU, CPU, Router).
`Segment`	Object that encapsulates a buffer, its size, and metadata.
Communication Setup	
`Link(Endpoint src, Endpoint dst, int packet_size, int num_buffers)`	Connects `src` to `dst`, using multiple-buffering with `num_buffers` buffers and packets of size `packet_size`.
`Router(int num_inputs, int num_outputs, RoutingPolicy policy)`	Connects multiple Endpoints together, enabling dynamic communication.
Communication Scheduling	
`EndpointList RoutingPolicy(Segment message, Endpoint source, EndpointList router_dst)`	A programmer-defined function that decides possible message destinations based on sending Endpoint, and a list of the Router destination Endpoints. The Router will select destinations by availability.
Asynchronous Objects	
`PendingSegment`	Represents a Segment that is currently being received.
`DistributedWorklist(Endpoint src, EndpointList workers)`	Manages all-to-all work-item distribution, consists of a Router and per-GPU links.

abstraction that complements the existing model to facilitate multi-GPU development, using insights from the microbenchmarks to minimize communication latency.

3. Groute Programming Model

The Groute programming model provides several constructs to facilitate asynchronous multi-GPU programming. Table 1 lists a summary of these constructs and their programming interface.

Groute applications consist of two phases: dataflow graph construction and asynchronous computation. A Groute program begins by specifying the dataflow graph of the computation. Nodes in this directed graph, which we call *endpoints*, represent either (i) physical devices like CPUs and GPUs, or (ii) virtual devices called *routers*, which are abstractions that implement complex patterns of communication. Edges in the dataflow graph represent communication *links* between endpoints, and can be created as long as there are no self-loops (endpoints connected directly to themselves) nor multiple identical edges as in multigraphs (i.e., a router can only have one outgoing edge to the same endpoint). Note that to support multitasking, multiple virtual endpoints can be created from the same physical device.

`Send` and `Receive` methods permit endpoints to send and receive data on a link; upon receipt of data, an endpoint may act upon it using a callback. When a router is created, a *routing policy* is specified by the programmer to determine the behavior when an input is received. For example, the input can be sent to a single endpoint, or to a subset of endpoints according to their availability. When a *link* is created,

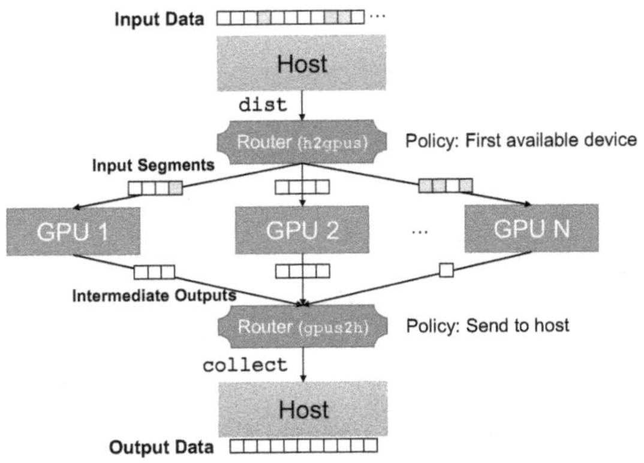

Figure 5: Predicate-Based Filtering Dataflow Graph

the packetization and multiple-buffering policies for that link are specified (Section 2).

To demonstrate the Groute model, we describe the implementation of Predicate-Based Filtering (PBF) using Groute, shown in Figures 5 and 6. PBF is a kernel in many applications such as database management and image processing. The input to PBF is a large one-dimensional array, and the output is an array containing all elements of the input array that satisfy a given predicate. In the Groute program, the host divides the input array into segments, and sends them to free GPUs on demand to promote load-balancing. Processed segments are transferred by the GPUs back to the host, where they are assembled to produce the output. Figure 5 depicts the resulting dataflow graph.

In Figure 6, the code sets up the dataflow graph for PBF in lines 5-20. The physical devices present in the system are determined by accessing a structure of type `Context` (line 5). The PBF program creates a router named `h2gpus` for scattering segments of the input array from the host to the GPUs, as well as a router named `gpus2h` to gather segments from the GPUs to create the output array (lines 9-10).

The code in lines 12-13 specifies the links between these routers and the host, where the link between the host and the `h2gpus` router is created without double buffering. The code in lines 15-20 creates a worker-thread for each GPU using double-buffered links, and input segments are scattered to the devices (line 22). Upon distributing all input segments, the distributor notifies that it will send no further information by sending a shutdown signal (line 23). The result is obtained at the host (lines 25-31) and the program stops once all GPUs send shutdown signals to `gpus2h`, notifying that no additional data will be received (line 27).

The routing policy for both routers is straightforward, selecting the first available device out of all possible router destinations (line 36). On the GPU end, each device asynchronously handles incoming messages (line 45). Once a `PendingSegment` is assigned to the device, it is synchronized with the active GPU stream (line 47) and processing

```
1  std::vector<T> input = ...;
2  std::vector<T> output;
3  int packet_size = ...;
4
5  Context ctx;
6  auto all_gpus = ctx.devices();
7  int num_gpus = all_gpus.size();
8
9  Router h2gpus(1, num_gpus, AnyDevicePolic
10 Router gpus2h(num_gpus, 1, AnyDevicePolic
11
12 Link dist    (HOST, h2gpus, packet_size,
13 Link collect (gpus2h, HOST, packet_size,
14
15 for (device_t dev : all_gpus) {
16   std::thread t(WorkerThread,
17                 Link(h2gpus, dev, packet_
18                 Link(dev, gpus2h, packet_
19   t.detach();
20 }
21
22 dist.Send(input, input_size);
23 dist.Shutdown();
24
25 while(true) {
26   PendingSegment output_seg = collect.Receive().get();
27   if(output_seg.Empty()) break;
28   output_seg.Synchronize();
29   append(output, output_seg);
30   collect.Release(output_seg);
31 }
32 //----------------------------------------------------
33 EndpointList AnyDevicePolicy(
34     const Segment& message, Endpoint source,
35     const EndpointList& router_dst) {
36   return router_dst;
37 }
38
39 void WorkerThread(device_t dev, Link in, Link out) {
40   Stream stream (dev);
41   T *s_out = ...;
42   int *out_size = ...;
43
44   while(true) {
45     PendingSegment seg = in.Receive().get();
46     if(seg.Empty()) break;
47     seg.Synchronize(stream);
48     Filter<<<...,stream>>>(seg.Ptr(), seg.Size(),
49                            s_out, out_size);
50     in.Release(seg, stream);
51     out.Send(s_out, out_size, stream);
52   }
53   out.Shutdown();
54 }
```

Figure 6: Predicate-Based Filtering Pseudocode

is performed (line 48). Line 50 queues a command to the stream, which releases the incoming buffer for future use upon processing completion. The results are then transmitted back to the host using `out` (line 51). When a shutdown signal is received, the worker thread is terminated (line 46) and a shutdown signal is sent (line 53) to `gpus2h`.

Memory consistency and ownership are maintained by the programmer in Groute. The link/router model does not define a global address space or remote memory access operations, but functions as a distributed memory environment. In the paper, algorithms and high-level asynchronous objects implemented over the model (such as Distributed Worklists) define ownership policies, whereas the low-level constructs provide efficient communication and message routing.

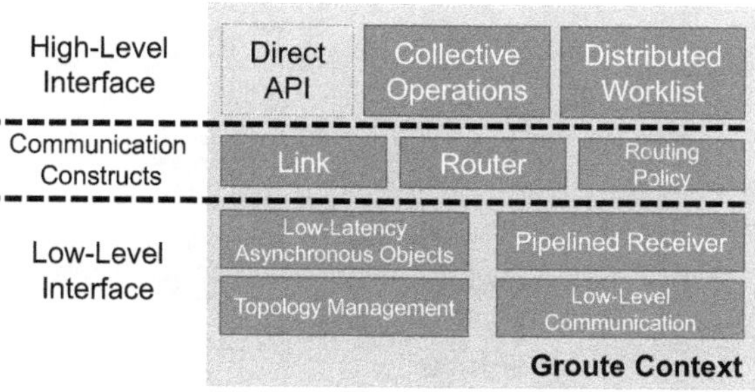

Figure 7: The Groute Library

4. Implementation Details

We realize the Groute programming model by implementing a thin runtime environment [2] over standard C++ and CUDA to enable asynchronous multi-GPU programming. The environment consists of three layers, illustrated in Figure 7. The bottom layer contains low-level management of the node topology and inter-GPU communication, the middle layer implements the Groute communication constructs, using the topology to optimize memory transfer paths, and the top layer implements high-level operations that are commonly used in asynchronous regular and irregular applications. For direct control over the system, each of the layers can be manually accessed by the programmer. In the rest of this section, we elaborate on the implementation of each layer in Groute.

4.1 Low-Level Interface

The low-level layer builds upon insights from Section 2 to provide programmer-accessible interfaces for efficient peer-to-peer transfers. Specifically, the layer provides *Low-Level Communication* APIs for latency reduction; *Pipelined Receivers* to increase computation-communication overlap; *Topology Management* for node interconnect hierarchy introspection; and *Low-Latency Asynchronous Objects* to mitigate system overhead.

The low-level communication interface provides host- and device-initiated memory copy functionality, abstracting packetization and conditional transfer. In Groute, send and receive operations are segmented into packets to increase the overall responsiveness of the node and enable overlapping communication between multiple devices. Without packetization, occasional small transmissions (e.g., GPUs sending counters to the CPU) may suffer from head-of-line blocking behind regular large transfers (e.g., GPU–GPU transfers).

On top of the low-level interface, asynchronous communication is abstracted using a *pipelined receiver* object, which efficiently utilizes the two memory copy engines and the compute engine (Figure 4) by using double- and triple-buffering [35]. The implementation of multiple-buffering allocates read buffers, queuing virtual "future read operations". When data are sent to a pipelined receiver, a read operation is removed from the queue and the corresponding

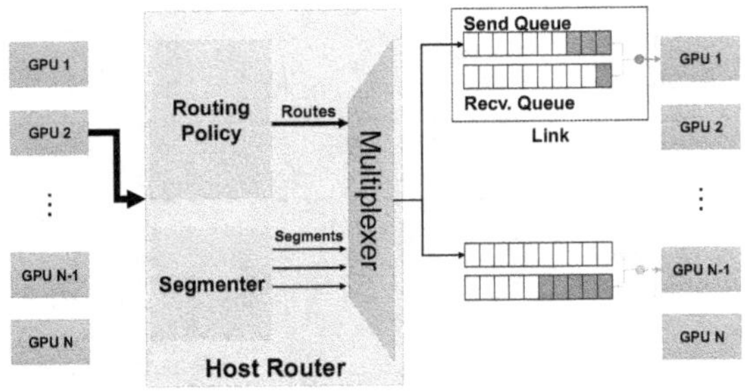

Figure 8: Host-Controlled Router Diagram

buffer is assigned to the sender. Simultaneously, the reader is notified of the incoming pending operation, which can either be waited for or acted upon asynchronously, using the receive stream.

Asynchronous programs often rely on a multitude of fine-grained (non-bulk) synchronization points and impromptu memory allocation to operate correctly. In order to minimize the incurred driver overhead and involuntary system-wide synchronizations, Groute provides several *low-latency asynchronous objects*, among which are *Event Pools* and *Event-Futures*. Event pools facilitate the creation of many short-lived events by way of pre-allocation; whereas event-futures are waitable objects implementing the *future/promise* pattern [18] to maintain two-layered synchronization between the CPUs and GPUs. In particular, event-futures handle situations where GPU events are known to be recorded in the future, but not yet created. These objects are used as the primary building block for queuing various actions, such as future receive operations for devices (CPU and GPU), and can either be synchronized with a CPU thread or a GPU stream.

4.2 Communication and Scheduling

A link can only connect one pair of source and destination endpoints. In Groute, there are two methods to create links: directly, or using an existing router. Specifically, each link specifies its maximal receivable packet size and the number of possible pipelined receive operations. The latter is optional and determined automatically if not given. The `Send` and `Receive` methods initiate memory transfer and return an event-future. In particular, a receive operation returns a future to a `PendingSegment`, which contains an event and a segment that may not yet be ready for processing. Links also provide a socket-like `Shutdown` function, signaling that no further information will be sent.

The internal structure and workflow of a router is depicted in Figure 8. The figure shows that the router contains three main components. The *Segmenter* component controls breaking down messages into segments according to the destination device capabilities; the *Routing Policy* controls the message destination(s); and the *Multiplexer* is responsible for message assignment to available GPUs.

Given a message to send, a routing policy will determine its one or several destinations using the programmer callback. The router then controls send operation scheduling, assigning destinations based on availability. Note that routing performance depends on the underlying topology. For example, in some nodes it is efficient to reduce with all-to-one operations, while in others it is better to use a hierarchical tree for concurrent reductions.

Upon receiving a segmented message and its possible destinations, scheduling is managed by the multiplexer. As shown in the top-right portion of Figure 8, the implementation involves queuing send operations to each of the target devices' send queues. Since links use pipelined receivers, devices also maintain receive queues. If there is a match between a send operation and a receive operation, transfer assignment is performed, dequeuing one item from both the send and receive queues of the link. Additionally, the redundant send operations queued to other devices are marked as stale and removed by each device upon inspection. This ensures that routers do not require a centralized locking mechanism, and per-device queues are the only constructs that should implement thread-safety.

4.3 Distributed Worklists

The high-level interface provided by Groute implements reusable operations that can often be found in multi-GPU applications, such as broadcast and all-reduction. This section details the implementation of distributed worklists, frequently used in irregular algorithms and graph analytics.

Distributed worklists maintain a global list of computations (work-items) that should be processed. Each such computation, in turn, may create new computations that are queued to the same list. For example, breadth-first search traverses a node's neighbors, propagating through the graph by creating new work-items for each neighbor.

Implementing efficient distributed multi-GPU worklists is a challenging task. As each device may contain a different portion of the input data, only certain devices are able to process specific work-items. Thus, distributed worklists require all-to-all communication. Using routers and bus topology, Groute implements distributed worklist management.

In the implementation, global coordination and work counting is centralized and managed by the host. During runtime, devices periodically report produced and consumed work-items for tracking purposes. Once the number of total work-items becomes zero, processing stops and a shutdown signal is sent to all participating devices via router links.

Figure 9 illustrates the implementation of a distributed worklist in Groute, from the perspective of a single device. As seen in the figure, the worklist is implemented over a single, system-wide router. In order to support efficient all-to-all communication, the ring topology is used for the routing policy by default (see Section 2 for evaluation). Apart from the router, each device contains a locally-managed worklist, which comprises one or more multiple-producer-single-

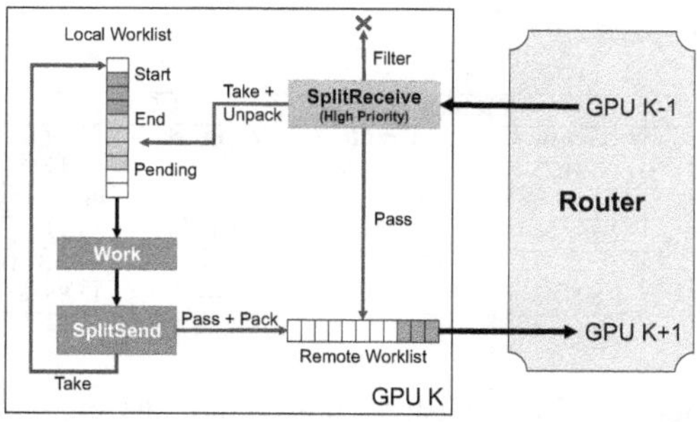

Figure 9: Distributed Worklist Implementation

consumer queues for local tasks. The implementation consists of two threads per device: worker thread and receiver thread, which controls inter-GPU communication and work-item circulation.

Over the ring topology, the workflow presented in Figure 9 is implemented as follows. Each device receives information from the previous device, according to the ring. The received data then undergoes filtering and separation (`SplitReceive`), which passes irrelevant information to the next device. Items that are relevant to the current device are unpacked and "pushed" onto its local worklist, signaling the worker thread that new work is arriving. At the same time, the worker thread processes existing work-items, separating the resulting items to local and remote work (`SplitSend`), and packing outgoing information as necessary. Note that the `SplitReceive` kernel is queued on a separate, high-priority stream. This causes the kernel to be scheduled during existing work processing, increasing the performance and responsiveness of the system.

In order to implement an algorithm over a distributed worklist, five functions must be given by the programmer, listed in Table 2: `Pack`, `Unpack`, `OnSend`, `OnReceive` and `GetPrio`. These functions usually consist of a single line-of-code, but may adversely change work-item propagation. In the `OnSend` and the `OnReceive` functions, the `Flags` return value is a bit-map that controls the work-item destination(s), e.g., pass to the next device, keep, duplicate, or completely remove. The priority of a work-item, obtained using `GetPrio`, is then used for scheduling higher priority work before low priority items, as detailed below.

To implement local worklist queues, Groute uses GPU-based lock-free circular buffers. Such buffers are beneficial for asynchronous applications, as they eliminate the need for dynamic allocation of buffers during runtime.

As shown in Figure 9, each worklist queue consists of multiple producers and a single consumer. Our implementation contains a memory buffer and three fields: `start`, `end`, and `pending`. Work consumption is performed by atomically increasing the `start` field. To avoid consuming items that are not ready, production is controlled by atomically increasing the `pending` field, reserving space in the buffer. After a producer has finished appending its work, `end` is increased by a single writer thread, synchronizing with `pending`.

Table 2: Distributed Worklist Programmer Callbacks

Function	Description
RemoteWork `Pack(`**LocalWork** `item)`	Pack `item` to send to another device.
LocalWork `Unpack(`**RemoteWork** `item)`	Unpack received work-item.
Flags `OnSend(`**LocalWork** `item)`	Determine outgoing `item` destination.
Flags `OnReceive(`**RemoteWork** `item)`	Determine incoming `item` destination.
Priority `GetPrio(`**RemoteWork** `item)`	Obtain priority of incoming `item`.

Additional optimizations to the circular buffers are performed in Groute. If the consuming GPU stream also produces work (as in `SplitSend`), work is pushed to the queue by way of prepending information (i.e., decreasing `start`), which avoids producer conflicts. It is also worth noting that circular buffers use warp-aggregated atomics [4], which increase the efficiency of appending work by limiting the number of atomic operations to one-per-warp.

4.4 Soft Priority Scheduling

A pitfall that should be considered in asynchronous worklist algorithms is excess work resulting from intermediate value propagation. In contrast to bulk-synchronous parallelism, where all devices agree upon a global state in the algorithm, asynchronous concurrency may propagate stale information ("useless work") as a result of lagging devices. Such work-items, in turn, generate additional intermediate work that may increase the overall workload exponentially with the number of devices.

For example, in bulk-synchronous Breadth-First Search (BFS), the current traversed level is a global algorithm parameter. If there are two paths to a given node, where one is longer than the other, only the path with the least number of edges from the source will be registered, writing final values to the nodes. In asynchronous BFS, however, if the path with the least number of edges is located on a lagging device, the "incorrect" path (intermediate value) would be written first. This will, in turn, traverse the rest of the graph using the intermediate value as input. After the device with the short path completes its processing, it will overwrite the node values, essentially recomputing all traversed values.

One way to mitigate this issue is to assign *soft priorities* to each work-item, deferring items that are suspected as generators of "useless work" to a later stage, in which they will likely be filtered out [17].

In Groute, soft priority scheduling is implemented using the programmer-provided `GetPrio` callback. During the runtime of the application, only high priority work-items are processed, where the priority threshold is decided by a system-wide consensus. Upon completion of all processable items, the system modifies the threshold and the distributed worklist will process the deferred items on each device. As

Table 3: Best Performance Comparison

Graph	BFS [ms]			SSSP [ms]		PR [ms]		CC [ms]	
	Gunrock	B40C	Groute	Gunrock	Groute	Gunrock	Groute	Gunrock	Groute
USA	617.85 (1)	**56.83** (1)	128.38 (2)	60,656.91 (8)	**725.93** (3)	1,394.25 (1)	**167.89** (8)	335.65 (1)	**15.11** (5)
OSM-eur-k	3,191.78 (1)	2,177.1 (2)	**616.4** (5)	874,083.5 (4)	**3,513.29** (8)	—	**1,045.33** (8)	—	**160.96** (4)
soc-LiveJournal1	99.11 (2)	**14.07** (4)	24.96 (6)	83.36 (5)	**30.98** (6)	2,782.06 (1)	**371.71** (5)	110.05 (1)	**14.19** (2)
twitter	—	—	**713.6** (8)	1,310.7 (7)	**649.2** (8)	—	**38,549.27** (1)	—	**384.13** (8)
kron21.sym	156.68 (3)	—	**46.55** (7)	**208.43** (2)	213.92 (8)	9,800.43 (1)	**5,342.73** (1)	—	**13.86** (8)

we shall show in Section 5, using soft priority scheduling decreases the amount of intermediate work, increasing overall performance.

4.5 Worklist-Based Graph Algorithms

Using asynchronous Breadth-First Search (BFS), we illustrate how graph traversal algorithms such as Single-source Shortest Path (SSSP) and PageRank (PR) are implemented using distributed worklists.

In BFS, the input graph is given in the Compressed Sparse Row (CSR) matrix format. The graph is first partitioned among the available devices, where each device statically maintains ownership of a contiguous memory segment, corresponding to a subset of the vertices.

When BFS processing starts, the host enqueues a single work-item to the worklist – the source vertex. Groute ensures that the initial work-item is sent to its owner device, where it is processed by setting the vertex value (i.e. *level*) to zero and creating work-items with *level*=1 for each neighboring vertex. If a neighboring vertex is owned by the processing device, it is queued to the device-local worklist (top-left portion of Figure 9). Otherwise, it is asynchronously propagated through the distributed worklist until another device claims ownership on the work-item. The value of *level* is propagated as well. Atomic operations are used to check if the received value is lower, updating the vertex's value and propagating *level*+1 to the neighboring vertices through subsequent work-item processing. After all relevant edges have been traversed, the worklist becomes empty and the algorithm ends.

In addition to owned vertices, each device also stores a local copy of its "halo" vertices, namely, neighboring vertices owned by other devices. The level of a halo vertex can only be updated by the local device, and is used to skip sending irrelevant updates, thus conserving inter-device communication. Skipping such updates does not change the algorithm's behavior, due to the monotonic nature of BFS, i.e., the real vertex value is either equal or lower than the halo value.

5. Performance Evaluation

This section evaluates the performance of five algorithms implemented using Groute:

- **Breadth-First Search (BFS)**: Traverses a graph from a given source node, outputting the number of edges traversed from the source node to each destination node. Implementation is push-based and data-driven, i.e., using distributed worklists.
- **Single-Source Shortest Path (SSSP)**: Finds the shortest path (using edge weights) from a source node to all other nodes. Implementation is push-based and data-driven.
- **PageRank (PR)**: Computes the PageRank measure for all nodes of a given graph using a worklist-based algorithm [34]. Implementation is the push-based variant proposed in the paper.
- **Connected Components (CC)**: Computes the number of connected components in a given graph. Implementation is topology-based, using two routers as explained below.
- **Predicate-Based Filtering (PBF)**: Filters an array of elements according to a given condition. GPU kernel implementation is based on warp-aggregated atomics [4].

Groute is compared to two benchmark implementations of multi-GPU parallel graph algorithms: Gunrock (version 0.3.1) and Back40Computing (B40C). Gunrock [26] is a graph analytics library containing highly optimized implementations of various graph algorithms. Gunrock uses bulk-synchronous parallelism for its multi-GPU implementations of these algorithms. B40C, by Merrill et al. [20], contains state-of-the-art hardcoded BFS implementations, enabling multi-GPU processing by direct memory accesses between peer GPUs.

All implementations, including Groute, contain the following kernel optimizations: warp-aggregated atomic operations, warp-based collectives for inter-thread communication, and intra-GPU load balancing on the warp and thread-block level to exploit Nested Parallelism [25]. Additionally, Groute's asynchronous model allows us to perform kernel fusion (Section 5.2).

Table 3 summarizes the best running times for BFS, SSSP, PR and CC, with the number of GPUs used to achieve the highest performance in parentheses. Asynchronous implementations using Groute clearly dominate over bulk-synchronous implementations and sometimes even outperform hardcoded versions.

Our experimental setup consists of two node types. The first is an 8-GPU server of four dual-board NVIDIA Tesla M60 (Maxwell architecture) cards, each containing 16 MPs with 128 cores; and two eight-core Intel Xeon E5-2630 v3 CPUs. Bus topology is depicted in Figure 1, with 2 QPI links per CPU at 8 GT/s per link for the PCI-Express switch.

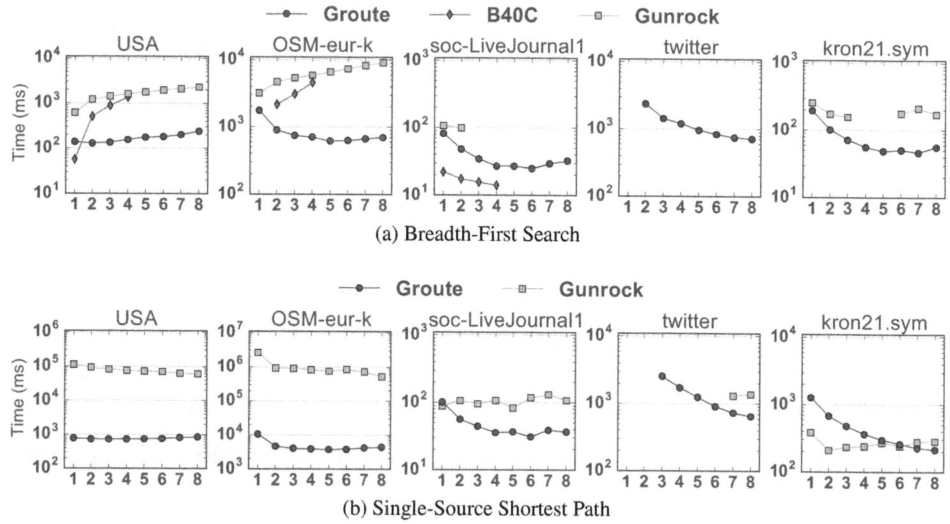

(a) Breadth-First Search

(b) Single-Source Shortest Path

Figure 10: Traversal Algorithm Timing (lower is better)

The second node type is a 2-GPU heterogeneous server that contains one Quadro M4000 GPU (Maxwell, 13 MPs with 128 cores); one Tesla K40c GPU (Kepler architecture, 15 MPs with 192 cores); and one six-core Intel Xeon E5-2630 CPU with 2 total QPI links at 7.2 GT/s per link.

Table 4: Graph Properties

Name	Nodes	Edges	Avg. Degree	Max Degree	Size (GB)
Road Maps					
USA [1]	24M	58M	2.41	9	0.62
OSM-eur-k [3]	174M	348M	2.00	15	3.90
Social Networks					
soc-LiveJournal1 [10]	5M	69M	14.23	20,293	0.56
twitter [8]	51M	1,963M	38.37	779,958	16.00
Synthetic Graphs					
kron21.sym [5]	2M	182M	86.82	213,904	1.40

Table 4 lists dataset information and statistics for input graphs used in the evaluation. All graphs are partitioned between GPUs using an edge-cut obtained from METIS [15] except for *kron21.sym* and *twitter*. METIS fails to partition these two graphs, so we simply partition the node array equally among the GPUs.

5.1 Strong Scaling

Figure 10 presents the absolute runtime of the two graph traversal algorithms (BFS and SSSP), running on 1 to 8 GPUs and comparing with the above frameworks. Missing data points indicate runs that failed due to crashes, out-of-memory failures, or incorrect outputs (compared to externally-generated results).

Overall, observe that in BFS and SSSP, which are communication intensive, the topology of the bus starts affecting the performance of applications when transfers are performed beyond the single 4-GPU quadruplet. While Groute mitigates these issues by optimizing communication paths (Section 2), the phenomenon can still be seen in high-degree graphs such as *soc-LiveJournal1* in BFS, SSSP, and PR.

5.1.1 Breadth-First Search

Figure 10a compares Groute with Gunrock and B40C. B40C's multi-GPU implementation requires direct memory access between all devices, and thus only runs up to 4 GPUs. Additionally, B40C does not use METIS partitioning, failed on *twitter* and *kron21.sym*, and ran out of memory on the single-GPU version of *OSM-eur-k*. The Gunrock implementation of BFS ran out of memory on all *twitter* inputs, and produced incorrect results on *kron21.sym* and *soc-LiveJournal1*.

The figure shows that Groute outperforms Gunrock in all cases, with significant improvements in road networks (*USA*, *OSM-eur-k*). This is due to the kernel fusion optimization enabled by asynchronous processing, which dramatically decreases kernel launch overhead in high-diameter graphs (Section 5.2).

Groute also outperforms B40C on road networks on multiple GPUs. However, B40C is faster on one GPU on the *USA* input and always outperforms Groute and Gunrock on the *soc-LiveJournal1* input. B40C's BFS implementation is highly optimized, containing a hybrid implementation that switches between different kernels as described in their paper [20], an optimization we did not implement due to its highly specialized nature.

5.1.2 Single-Source Shortest Path

Figure 10b presents the strong scaling of SSSP in Groute. In the figure, we see that the multi-GPU scaling patterns are similar to BFS. The multi-GPU scalability of Groute is especially apparent in large graphs, such as *twitter*, in which performance increases even when using more than 4 GPUs. Missing *twitter* results are caused by insufficient memory.

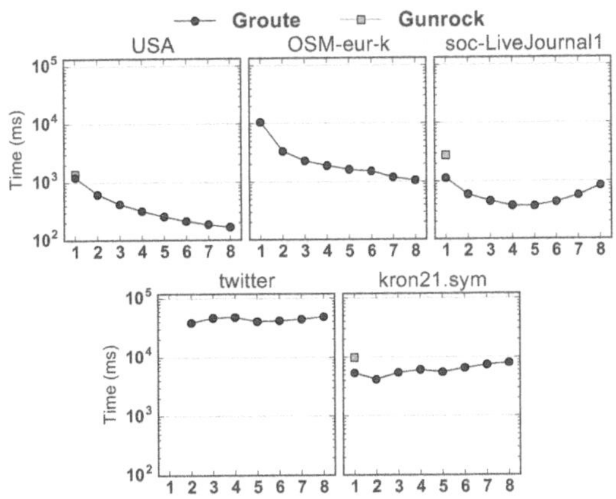

Figure 11: PageRank Execution Time

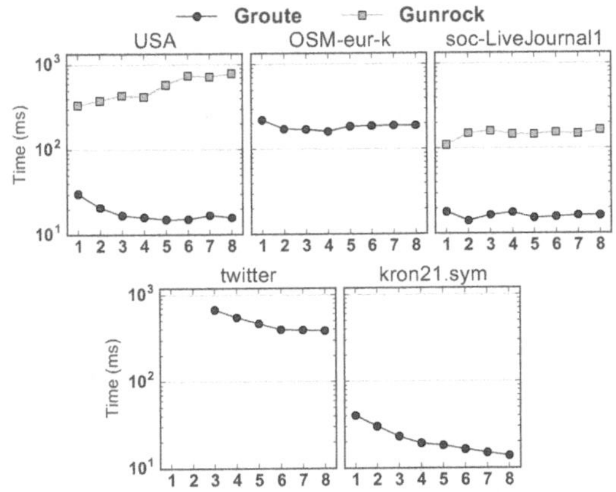

Figure 12: Connected Components Performance

Groute outperforms Gunrock (or matches it on *soc-LiveJournal1*, single GPU) with the sole exception of the *kron21.sym* input. Upon in-depth inspection, it was found that the asynchronous implementation in Groute causes an inflation in the number of performed atomic operations, which increases memory contention and iteration time.

5.1.3 PageRank

The performance of PageRank (PR) is shown in Figure 11. Results are compared with Gunrock in the single GPU case, since the evaluated version of Gunrock's multi-GPU PageRank produced incorrect results. Also, the *twitter* graph does not fit in the memory of 1 GPU.

As opposed to BFS and SSSP, PR is a computationally-intensive problem. In addition, PR starts by processing all the nodes simultaneously, so each GPU can be fully utilized. Observe that in the figure, Groute outperforms Gunrock on all inputs. Additionally, both road networks generate multi-GPU scaling over the single-GPU version, owing to the amount of independent work performed on each device, as well as the communication latency that is hidden by Groute. The same effect is observed in *soc-LiveJournal1* up to a single quadruplet of GPUs.

In particular, the best scaling results are obtained when the ratio of computations to communications is high (i.e., less communications per computation). For example, running PageRank with Groute on *USA* yields a 7.28× speedup on 8 GPUs over one, exhibiting near-linear scaling on all multi-GPU configurations.

As the ratio of computation to communication decreases, scaling becomes less substantial, as in the case of *soc-LiveJournal1*, which exhibits a 3.02× speedup on 4 GPUs over one. Additionally, nearly no speedup is observed in *twitter* and *kron21.sym*, both of which are partitioned randomly (i.e., without METIS) and heavily interconnected.

5.1.4 Connected Components

We implement a topology-driven [27] variant of multi-GPU Connected Components (CC), which does not use a worklist, in order to demonstrate the expressiveness of the Groute asynchronous communication constructs. The performance of CC is shown in Figure 12.

Figure 13 illustrates the dataflow graph of a pointer-jumping topology-driven CC over Groute. In this version, the input graph representation is an edge-list. The edges are distributed to the GPUs, and each GPU keeps note of the parent component of each vertex in its given graph subset. Once a GPU converges locally, its results are merged (using operations called Hook and Compress) with the results of other GPUs to converge to the global component list.

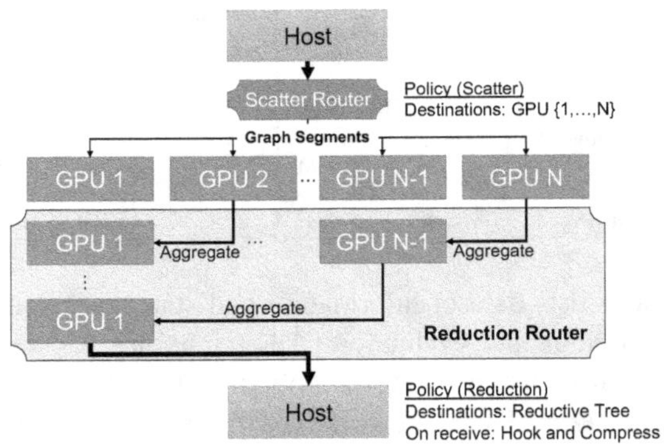

Figure 13: Connected Components Router Structure

With Groute, we create one router to dynamically scatter edges to the GPUs in multiple segments, computing and aggregating local CC results for each segment. Upon completion, each GPU merges its results with the others using an additional reduction router. According to the topology of the measured 8-GPU node, the reduction is implemented as concurrent hierarchical operations. In particular, each GPU merges its results with a designated "sibling" GPU until reaching the first GPU, which sends the information back to the host. The single GPU kernels used in this implementation are based on a state-of-the-art adaptive variant [31] of the pointer-jumping method described by Soman et al. [29].

The results in Figure 12 show that using an asynchronous topology-driven variant is highly beneficial, both in terms of raw performance and scalability, over the implementation found in Gunrock. Specifically, Groute yields 10.99× and 49.6× speedups over Gunrock in *USA* on 1 and 8 GPUs respectively. Furthermore, Groute achieves a strong scaling of up to 2.9× (8 GPUs over 1) in the *kron21.sym* input.

Another advantage apparent in the figure is memory consumption. Since the Groute implementation does not use distributed worklists, the tested multi-GPU system is able to compute CC on large-scale graphs such as *OSM-eur-k*, *twitter* and *kron21.sym*. Gunrock, on the other hand, runs out of memory for all GPU configurations on these three inputs.

5.2 Distributed Worklist Performance

Our distributed worklist uses two optimizations – soft priority scheduling and worker kernel fusion – to significantly improve the performance of asynchronous algorithms.

As explained in Section 4.4, a naive asynchronous irregular application propagates intermediate values from lagging devices, which leads to an increase in work due to redundant computations. Using METIS mitigates this effect somewhat since it reduces the number of paths between the partitions. However, our experiments show that deferring possibly redundant work by using a soft priority scheduler can achieve significantly better performance *even* with good partitions.

Table 5: Distributed Worklist SSSP Performance

Graph	GPUs	Soft Priority Scheduler	Fused Worker
soc-LiveJournal1	1	1.03×	1.03×
	2	0.95×	0.95×
	4	1.29×	1.31×
	8	1.29×	1.09×
kron21.sym	1	1.02×	1.01×
	2	1.10×	1.09×
	4	1.58×	1.57×
	8	1.45×	1.48×
USA	1	71.36×	166.27×
	2	58.11×	142.57×
	4	34.59×	89.94×
	8	16.22×	39.34×

Table 5 compares the performance of the soft priority scheduler and fused worker kernel with the unoptimized version of Groute's distributed worklists. In the table, we see that both versions consistently outperform the original implementation, with the exception of *soc-LiveJournal1* (which slows down 5% on 2 GPUs). The most compelling results can be found in road maps, in which we see performance increase of up to two orders of magnitude.

Soft priorities improve performance by reducing the amount of "useless" work that is performed. This increase in useless work can be dramatic. For example, SSSP works on 13,998M workitems on the *USA* graph in a complete execution on a single GPU. Without soft-priorities, this increases to 15,865M workitems on four GPUs. With soft-priorities, the four GPU version executes only 59M workitems overall. For SSSP, this reduction is comparable to those obtained by using an SSSP algorithm with priorities such as SSSP Near-Far [9]). However, BFS has no notion of priorities, but also exhibits the same effect. Single-GPU BFS on *USA* executes 23.9M work items. Without soft-priorities, this increases to 4,244M work items on four GPUs (27M with METIS). With soft-priorities this reduces to 134M workitems on four GPUs (24.1M with METIS).

Kernel fusion, on the other hand, tackles a problem exhibited by graphs such as road maps which create small workloads with each kernel call (~19 microseconds), causing the GPUs to be under-utilized and increasing the communication management overhead. We augment the worker kernel to include the entire control-flow and communicate with the host and other GPUs using flags shared by both the CPU and GPU. This includes receiving incoming information signals, determining work-item priorities, processing a batch of work-items, running `SplitSend` (Section 4.3), and signaling the router to circulate the outgoing information. By performing this kernel fusion, many of the CPU–GPU roundtrips can be reduced, increasing the overall performance of the system. In practice, kernel fusion in Groute increases the work performed by each kernel invocation, which take between ~10 and 100 milliseconds. Note that the reduction of CPU–GPU roundtrips causes both optimizations to also improve the runtime of a single GPU.

5.3 Load Balancing

Table 6 measures the performance of the PBF implementation from Figure 6 on the heterogeneous 2-GPU node, filtering 250 MB of data. The runtime of each GPU is shown with static scheduling (top three rows) and Groute's "first available device" routing policy (bottom three rows).

Table 6: Heterogeneous PBF Performance

Scheduler	GPU Type	Processed Elements	Time (ms)
Static	Tesla K40c	12.6M	5.73 ms
	Quadro M4000	13.6M	27.04 ms
	Total Time	-	27.37 ms
Groute	Tesla K40c	20.9M	8.84 ms
	Quadro M4000	5.2M	10.90 ms
	Total Time	-	11.26 ms

The table shows that Groute assigns 4 times more tasks to the faster Tesla K40c than the slower Quadro M4000, achieving better load balancing and decreasing overall runtime. Note that the 2 millisecond time difference observed in Groute is within the scheduling quantum, as it is shorter than the runtime of a single kernel on the Quadro M4000.

6. Related Work

The presented link/router programming model can be seen as a close relative of the *Publish/Subscribe* design pattern [11], in which endpoints subscribe to specific channels that other endpoints publish to. The link/router model differs from this model by defining generalized policies, which are more optimized for low-latency communication on multi-GPU nodes than named channels.

Recently, multi-GPU frameworks that simplify programming and provide reusable mechanisms have been proposed. Notable examples include NCCL [24], which implements collective operations on a single node; MGPU [28], which simplifies task partitioning to multiple GPUs; and MAPS-Multi [6], which proposes a scalable programming model based on memory access patterns. Owing to the traditional bulk-synchronous use of multi-GPU nodes, these libraries focus on the efficient implementation of regular computations, such as stencil operators, rather than irregular algorithms.

Data-driven graph algorithm implementations use worklists for processing [22]. These implementations were found, in the general case, to be faster than their topology-driven counterparts on GPUs [21]. These results motivated implementing graph analytics using distributed worklists in this paper.

Other asynchronous graph processing frameworks have been researched. Galois[23] proposes a work-stealing scheduler for asynchronous multi-core CPU processing. Concurrent graph analytics on a single GPU (using multiple streams) has also been proposed in GTS [16], showing that this type of programming is promising for single-GPU applications as well. Additional single-GPU [7, 12, 14, 33] and multi-GPU [20, 26] graph analytics libraries have been proposed. However, as opposed to our asynchronous approach, these implementations all utilize bulk-synchronous parallelism.

The distributed worklist kernel fusion optimization proposed in Section 5 is similar to the Megakernel single-GPU approach, proposed by Steinberger et al. [30], which also transfers portions of the control flow to the GPU.

7. Conclusions

The paper presented a scalable programming abstraction and runtime environment for asynchronous multi-GPU application development. In-depth study of the structure of a multi-GPU node showed that creating such applications requires careful tuning with respect to communication topology and workload processing, particularly in irregular algorithms, where lagging information may have a major impact on scaling. The paper then showed that the programming abstraction is simple yet expressive, enabling the efficient implementation of complex graph analytic algorithms, showing strong scaling results.

This research can be extended in several directions. First, the link/router abstraction concepts can be generalized to other non-GPU architectures, as well as distributed systems. Second, the majority of the router control flow relies on host-based decisions. Similarly to worker kernel fusion, moving these decisions to a device-based router may decrease system overhead by further reducing CPU-GPU copies. Third, load balancing in multi-GPU traversal algorithms may be improved by employing asynchronous work-stealing schedulers and dynamically-changing node ownership.

Acknowledgments

This research was supported by the German Research Foundation (DFG) Priority Program 1648 "Software for exascale Computing" (SPP-EXA), research project FFMK; NSF grants 1218568, 1337281, 1406355, and 1618425; by DARPA BRASS contract 750-16-2-0004; and an equipment grant from NVIDIA.

References

[1] 9th DIMACS Implementation Challenge. URL `http://www.dis.uniroma1.it/challenge9/download.shtml`.

[2] Groute Runtime Environment Source Code. URL `http://www.github.com/groute/groute`.

[3] Karlsruhe Institute of Technology, OSM Europe Graph, 2014. URL `http://i11www.iti.uni-karlsruhe.de/resources/roadgraphs.php`.

[4] A. Adinetz. Optimized filtering with warp-aggregated atomics. 2014. URL `http://devblogs.nvidia.com/parallelforall/cuda-pro-tip-optimized-filtering-warp-aggregated-atomics/`.

[5] D. A. Bader, H. Meyerhenke, P. Sanders, and D. Wagner, editors. *Graph Partitioning and Graph Clustering, 10th DIMACS Implementation Challenge Workshop, Georgia Institute of Technology, Atlanta, GA, USA, February 13-14, 2012. Proceedings*, volume 588 of *Contemporary Mathematics*, 2013. American Mathematical Society.

[6] T. Ben-Nun, E. Levy, A. Barak, and E. Rubin. Memory access patterns: The missing piece of the multi-GPU puzzle. In *Proceedings of the International Conference for High Performance Computing, Networking, Storage and Analysis*, SC '15, pages 19:1–19:12. ACM, 2015.

[7] M. Burtscher, R. Nasre, and K. Pingali. A quantitative study of irregular programs on GPUs. In *Workload Characterization (IISWC), 2012 IEEE International Symposium on*, pages 141–151, 2012.

[8] M. Cha, H. Haddadi, F. Benevenuto, and P. K. Gummadi. Measuring user influence in Twitter: The million follower fallacy. *ICWSM*, 10(10-17):30, 2010.

[9] A. Davidson, S. Baxter, M. Garland, and J. D. Owens. Work-efficient parallel GPU methods for single-source shortest

paths. In *Parallel and Distributed Processing Symposium, 2014 IEEE 28th International*, pages 349–359, 2014.

[10] T. A. Davis and Y. Hu. The university of florida sparse matrix collection. *ACM Trans. Math. Softw.*, 38(1):1:1–1:25, 2011.

[11] P. T. Eugster, P. A. Felber, R. Guerraoui, and A.-M. Kermarrec. The many faces of publish/subscribe. *ACM Comput. Surv.*, 35(2):114–131, 2003.

[12] A. Gharaibeh, L. Beltrão Costa, E. Santos-Neto, and M. Ripeanu. A yoke of oxen and a thousand chickens for heavy lifting graph processing. In *Proceedings of the 21st International Conference on Parallel Architectures and Compilation Techniques*, PACT '12, pages 345–354. ACM, 2012.

[13] P.-Y. Hong, L.-M. Huang, L.-S. Lin, and C.-A. Lin. Scalable multi-relaxation-time lattice Boltzmann simulations on multi-GPU cluster. *Computers & Fluids*, 110:1 – 8, 2015.

[14] S. Hong, S. K. Kim, T. Oguntebi, and K. Olukotun. Accelerating CUDA graph algorithms at maximum warp. In *Proceedings of the 16th ACM Symposium on Principles and Practice of Parallel Programming*, PPoPP '11, pages 267–276. ACM, 2011.

[15] G. Karypis and V. Kumar. A fast and high quality multilevel scheme for partitioning irregular graphs. *SIAM J. Sci. Comput.*, 20(1):359–392, 1998.

[16] M.-S. Kim, K. An, H. Park, H. Seo, and J. Kim. GTS: A fast and scalable graph processing method based on streaming topology to GPUs. In *Proceedings of the 2016 International Conference on Management of Data*, SIGMOD '16, pages 447–461. ACM, 2016.

[17] A. Lenharth, D. Nguyen, and K. Pingali. Priority queues are not good concurrent priority schedulers. In *Euro-Par 2015: Parallel Processing: 21st International Conference on Parallel and Distributed Computing, Vienna, Austria, August 24-28, 2015, Proceedings*, pages 209–221. Springer Berlin Heidelberg, 2015.

[18] B. Liskov and L. Shrira. Promises: Linguistic support for efficient asynchronous procedure calls in distributed systems. In *Proceedings of the ACM SIGPLAN 1988 Conference on Programming Language Design and Implementation*, PLDI '88, pages 260–267, 1988.

[19] E. Mejía-Roa, D. Tabas-Madrid, J. Setoain, C. García, F. Tirado, and A. Pascual-Montano. NMF-mGPU: non-negative matrix factorization on multi-GPU systems. *BMC Bioinformatics*, 16(1):43, 2015.

[20] D. Merrill, M. Garland, and A. Grimshaw. Scalable GPU graph traversal. In *Proceedings of the 17th ACM SIGPLAN Symposium on Principles and Practice of Parallel Programming*, PPoPP '12, pages 117–128, 2012.

[21] R. Nasre, M. Burtscher, and K. Pingali. Data-driven versus topology-driven irregular computations on GPUs. In *Parallel Distributed Processing (IPDPS), 2013 IEEE 27th International Symposium on*, pages 463–474, 2013.

[22] R. Nasre, M. Burtscher, and K. Pingali. Morph algorithms on GPUs. In *ACM SIGPLAN Notices*, volume 48, pages 147–156. ACM, 2013.

[23] D. Nguyen, A. Lenharth, and K. Pingali. A lightweight infrastructure for graph analytics. In *Proceedings of the Twenty-Fourth ACM Symposium on Operating Systems Principles*, SOSP '13, pages 456–471, 2013.

[24] NVIDIA. NVIDIA Collective Communication Library (NCCL), 2016. URL `http://www.github.com/NVIDIA/nccl/`.

[25] S. Pai and K. Pingali. A compiler for throughput optimization of graph algorithms on GPUs. In *Proceedings of the 2016 ACM SIGPLAN International Conference on Object-Oriented Programming, Systems, Languages, and Applications*, OOPSLA '16. ACM, 2016.

[26] Y. Pan, Y. Wang, Y. Wu, C. Yang, and J. D. Owens. Multi-GPU graph analytics. *CoRR*, abs/1504.04804, 2015. URL `http://arxiv.org/abs/1504.04804`.

[27] K. Pingali, D. Nguyen, M. Kulkarni, M. Burtscher, M. A. Hassaan, R. Kaleem, T.-H. Lee, A. Lenharth, R. Manevich, M. Méndez-Lojo, D. Prountzos, and X. Sui. The tao of parallelism in algorithms. In *Proceedings of the 32nd ACM SIGPLAN Conference on Programming Language Design and Implementation*, PLDI '11, pages 12–25. ACM, 2011.

[28] S. Schaetz and M. Uecker. A multi-GPU programming library for real-time applications. In *Proceedings of the 12th International Conference on Algorithms and Architectures for Parallel Processing - Part I*, ICA3PP'12, pages 114–128. Springer-Verlag, 2012.

[29] J. Soman, K. Kishore, and P. J. Narayanan. A fast GPU algorithm for graph connectivity. In *Parallel Distributed Processing, Workshops and Phd Forum (IPDPSW), 2010 IEEE International Symposium on*, pages 1–8, 2010.

[30] M. Steinberger, M. Kenzel, P. Boechat, B. Kerbl, M. Dokter, and D. Schmalstieg. Whippletree: Task-based scheduling of dynamic workloads on the GPU. *ACM Trans. Graph.*, 33(6): 228:1–228:11, 2014.

[31] M. Sutton, T. Ben-Nun, A. Barak, S. Pai, and K. Pingali. Adaptive work-efficient connected components on the GPU. *CoRR*, abs/1612.01178, 2016. URL `http://arxiv.org/abs/1612.01178`.

[32] L. G. Valiant. A bridging model for parallel computation. *Commun. ACM*, 33(8):103–111, 1990.

[33] Y. Wang, A. Davidson, Y. Pan, Y. Wu, A. Riffel, and J. D. Owens. Gunrock: A high-performance graph processing library on the GPU. In *Proceedings of the 20th ACM SIGPLAN Symposium on Principles and Practice of Parallel Programming*, PPoPP 2015, pages 265–266, 2015.

[34] J. J. Whang, A. Lenharth, I. S. Dhillon, and K. Pingali. Scalable data-driven PageRank: Algorithms, system issues, and lessons learned. In L. J. Träff, S. Hunold, and F. Versaci, editors, *Euro-Par 2015: Parallel Processing: 21st International Conference on Parallel and Distributed Computing, Proceedings*, pages 438–450. Springer Berlin Heidelberg, 2015.

[35] D. Wilson. Triple buffering: Why we love it. 2009. URL `http://www.anandtech.com/show/2794`.

A. Artifact description

A.1 Abstract

This artifact contains all the source code necessary to compile the Groute executables and repeat the results of this paper. The package also contains shell scripts to generate the figures and tables as CSVs, obtain code dependencies, and download input graphs for the benchmarks.

A.2 Description

A.2.1 Check-list (artifact meta information)

- **Algorithm:** Micro-benchmarks, Breadth-First Search, Single-Source Shortest Path, PageRank, Connected Components, Predicate-Based Filtering.
- **Compilation:** Using CUDA (nvcc) for GPU code and GCC (gcc, g++) for host code. Both compilers use the following flags: -O3 -DNDEBUG -std=c++11.
- **Binary:** One CUDA executable for each algorithm.
- **Data set:** Publicly-available graphs converted to binary CSR (Galois) format.
- **Run-time environment:** Debian 8 Linux with CMake 3.2, GCC 4.9.3, and CUDA 7.5. Optional requirement (for comparing with Gunrock): Boost 1.55.0.
- **Hardware:** CUDA-capable GPU with compute capability of at least 3.5. Multiple GPUs on the same node are required for multi-GPU tests.
- **Output:** CSV files representing each figure and table.
- **Experiment workflow:** Clone repository, setup environment, run figure-generating shell scripts, review generated CSV files.
- **Publicly available?:** Yes.

A.2.2 How delivered

A Git repository that contains all the Groute code and figure-generating scripts can be found in:
http://www.github.com/groute/ppopp17-artifact
The repository contains shell scripts that set up the environment, obtain and compile external code, download the dataset, and run the figure generators. See additional information in Sections A.3 and A.4.

A.2.3 Hardware dependencies

To run GPU-based tests, Groute requires one or more NVIDIA GPUs with compute capability of at least 3.5. Multi-GPU tests will not run on a single-GPU node. For the test performed in Table 6, a system with two heterogeneous GPUs (i.e., one faster than the other) is recommended to repeat the results.

A.2.4 Software dependencies

To compile Groute, CMake 3.2, GCC 4.9 and CUDA 7.5 are required. Later versions can be used but were not tested by the authors.

The code contained in the above repository includes the following external dependencies: METIS 5.1.0, gflags 2.1.2, MGBench 1.01, NCCL 1.2.3, and Gunrock 0.3.1 (optional).

A.2.5 Datasets

The dataset for this artifact contains all graphs listed in Table 4 of the paper, converted to the Galois CSR binary format (.gr files). The dataset (10.6 GB compressed, 29 GB uncompressed) is automatically downloaded by the setup script. Each graph is located in a separate subdirectory, with three additional files:

1. <graph>/<graphfile>.metadata: Metadata of the graph properties (number of connected components, whether to use METIS partitioning, soft-priority delta).
2. <graph>/bfs-<graphfile>.txt: Externally generated BFS results (source node: 0), used for validation.
3. <graph>/sssp-<graphfile>.txt: External SSSP results (source node: 0), also used for validation.

A.3 Installation

To install, follow the instructions below:

- Clone the Git repository recursively from https://github.com/groute/ppopp17-artifact.git
- Run setup.sh. The script will automatically compile Groute and the external code.
- When prompted whether to download the dataset, respond 'y' or 'n'. The dataset can be downloaded manually by running dataset/download.sh at a later time.

A.4 Experiment workflow

After setting up the environment, either run runall.sh to generate all figures and tables, or run each individual figure separately by calling figures/figureXX.sh, where XX is the figure number. The overall workflow as a list of shell commands is as follows:

```
$ git clone --recursive
  https://github.com/groute/ppopp17-artifact.git
$ cd ppopp17-artifact/
$ ./setup.sh
$ ./runall.sh
$ cat output/figure10b.csv
```

Note: Gunrock execution (for comparison with Groute) is not enabled by default. To enable, export RUN_GUNROCK=1 prior to running the figure-generating scripts.
Note 2: Each individual test may take time, but is limited to 2 hours to avoid waiting forever for a faulty application. For slower GPUs, this timeout can be increased by modifying the TIMEOUT variable from 2h to a different value (line 4 in figures/common.sh).

A.5 Evaluation and expected result

The results, found in output/, are in Comma-Separated Values (CSV) format and represent each figure and table in the paper (e.g., figure2a.csv, table6.csv). Prior to being inserted to the CSV, the results are averaged over at least 3 runs. The results will also be written to the console during the process.

Tapir: Embedding Fork-Join Parallelism into LLVM's Intermediate Representation

Tao B. Schardl William S. Moses Charles E. Leiserson

MIT Computer Science and Artificial Intelligence Laboratory
32 Vassar Street
Cambridge, MA 02139

neboat@mit.edu wmoses@mit.edu cel@mit.edu

Abstract

This paper explores how fork-join parallelism, as supported by concurrency platforms such as Cilk and OpenMP, can be embedded into a compiler's intermediate representation (IR). Mainstream compilers typically treat parallel linguistic constructs as syntactic sugar for function calls into a parallel runtime. These calls prevent the compiler from performing optimizations across parallel control constructs. Remedying this situation is generally thought to require an extensive reworking of compiler analyses and code transformations to handle parallel semantics.

Tapir is a compiler IR that represents logically parallel tasks asymmetrically in the program's control flow graph. Tapir allows the compiler to optimize across parallel control constructs with only minor changes to its existing analyses and code transformations. To prototype Tapir in the LLVM compiler, for example, we added or modified about 6000 lines of LLVM's 4-million-line codebase. Tapir enables LLVM's existing compiler optimizations for serial code — including loop-invariant-code motion, common-subexpression elimination, and tail-recursion elimination — to work with parallel control constructs such as spawning and parallel loops. Tapir also supports parallel optimizations such as loop scheduling.

Keywords Cilk; compiling; control-flow graph; fork-join parallelism; LLVM; multicore; OpenMP; optimization; parallel computing; serial semantics; Tapir.

1. Introduction

Mainstream compilers, such as GCC [68], ICC [24], and LLVM [32], now support ***fork-join parallelism*** [17, 18, 23, 40], where subroutines can be spawned in parallel and iterations of a parallel loop can execute concurrently on modern multicore machines. In particular, these compilers provide support for the Cilk Plus [21] and OpenMP [5, 54] linguistic extensions for fork-join parallelism.[1] The execution of a fork-join program generates a series-parallel dag [14] of logically parallel tasks. The execution and synchronization of parallel tasks is managed "under the covers" by a runtime system, which typically implements a randomized work-stealing scheduler [4, 8, 9, 16] to schedule and load-balance the computation among parallel worker threads. Fork-join programs provide serial semantics [16], and they admit efficient tools to detect "determinacy races" or validate their absence [14, 15, 70].

But although these mainstream compilers support fork-join parallelism, they fail to optimize parallel code as well as they optimize serial code. Consider, for example, the parallel `cilk_for` loop on lines 5–6 in Figure 1a, which indicates that iterations of the loop are free to execute in parallel. In a serial version of this loop, where the `cilk_for` keyword is replaced by an ordinary `for` keyword, each of the compilers GCC 5.3.0, ICC 16.0.3, and Cilk Plus/LLVM 3.9.0 observes that the call to `norm` on line 6 produces the same value in every iteration of the loop, and they optimize the loop by computing this value only once before the loop executes. This optimization dramatically reduces the total time to execute `normalize` from $\Theta(n^2)$ to $\Theta(n)$. Although this same optimization can, in principle, be performed on the actual parallel loop in the figure, no mainstream compiler performs this code-motion optimization. The same is true when the parallel loop is written using OpenMP, as shown in Figure 1b.

This failure to optimize stems from how these compilers for serial languages implement parallel linguistic constructs. The compiler for a serial language, such as C [28] or C++ [69], can be viewed as consisting of three phases: a front end, a middle end, and a back end. The front end parses and type-checks the input program and translates it to an ***intermediate***

PPoPP '17, February 04-08, 2017, Austin, TX, USA
© 2017 ACM. ISBN 978-1-4503-4493-7/17/02...$15.00
DOI: http://dx.doi.org/10.1145/3018743.3018758

[1] Unlike the other compilers, LLVM support for Cilk Plus is not in the main branch, however, but in a separate Cilk Plus/LLVM branch [23].

a

```
01 __attribute__((const)) double norm(const double *A, int n);
02
03 void normalize(double *restrict out,
04                const double *restrict in, int n) {
05   cilk_for (int i = 0; i < n; ++i)
06     out[i] = in[i] / norm(in, n);
07 }
```

b

```
08 __attribute__((const)) double norm(const double *A, int n);
09
10 void normalize(double *restrict out,
11                const double *restrict in, int n) {
12   #pragma omp parallel for
13   for (int i = 0; i < n; ++i)
14     out[i] = in[i] / norm(in, n);
15 }
```

Figure 1. A function that GCC, ICC, and Cilk Plus/LLVM all fail to optimize effectively. **a** A Cilk version of the code. The `cilk_for` loop on lines 5–6 allows each iteration of the loop to execute in parallel. The `norm` function computes the norm of a vector in $\Theta(n)$ time. The call to `norm` on line 6 can be safely moved outside of the loop, but none of these three mainstream compilers perform this code motion, even though they all do so when the `cilk_for` keyword is replaced with an ordinary `for` keyword. **b** The corresponding OpenMP code.

representation (IR), which represents the control flow of the program as a more-or-less language-independent ***control-flow graph (CFG)*** [2, Sec. 8.4.3]. The middle end consists of optimization passes that transform the IR into a more-efficient form. These optimizations tend to be independent of the instruction-set architecture of the target computer. The back end translates the optimized IR into machine code, performing low-level machine-dependent optimizations.

GCC, ICC, and Cilk Plus/LLVM all ***lower*** the parallel constructs — transform the parallel constructs to a more-primitive representation — in the front end. To compile the code in Figure 1a, for example, the front-end translates the parallel loop in lines 5–6 into IR in two steps. (The OpenMP code in Figure 1b is handled similarly.) First, the loop body (line 6) is lifted into a helper function. Next, the loop itself is replaced with a call to a library function implemented by the Cilk Plus runtime system, which takes as arguments the loop bounds and helper function, and handles the spawning of the loop iterations for parallel execution. Since this process occurs in the front end, it renders the parallel loop unrecognizable to middle-end loop-optimization passes, such as code motion. In short, these compilers treat parallel constructs as syntactic sugar for opaque runtime calls, which confounds the many middle-end analyses and optimizations.

Previous approaches

This paper aims to enable middle-end optimizations involving fork-join control flow by embedding parallelism directly into the compiler IR, an endeavor that has historically been challenging [36, 38]. For example, it is well documented [47] that traditional compiler transformations for serial programs can jeopardize the correctness of parallel programs. In general, four types of approaches have been proposed to embed parallelism in a mainstream compiler IR.

First, the compiler can use metadata to delineate logical parallelism. LLVM's parallel loop metadata [41], for example, is attached to memory accesses in a loop to indicate that they have no dependence on other iterations of the same loop. LLVM can only conclude that a loop is parallel if all its memory accesses are labeled with this metadata. Unfortunately, encoding parallel loops in this way is fragile, since a compiler transformation that moves code into a parallel loop risks serializing the loop from LLVM's perspective.

Second, the compiler can use intrinsic functions to demark parallel tasks. (For examples, see [37, 55, 72].) Often, either existing serial analyses and optimizations must be shut down when code contains these intrinsics, or the intrinsics offer minimal opportunities for compiler optimization.

Third, the compiler can use a separate IR to encode logical parallelism in the program. The HPIR [7, 72], SPIRE [29], and INSPIRE [27] representations, for instance, model parallel constructs using an alternative IR, such as one based on the program's abstract syntax tree [2, Sec. 2.5.1]. Such an IR can support optimizations involving parallel constructs without requiring changes to existing middle-end optimizations. But adopting a separate IR into a mainstream compiler has historically been criticized [39] as requiring considerable effort to engineer, develop, and maintain the additional IR to the same standards as the compiler's existing serial IR.

Fourth, the compiler can augment its existing IR to encode logical parallelism, which is the approach that Tapir follows. Unlike Tapir, all prior research on parallel precedence graphs [66, 67], parallel flow graphs [19, 65], concurrent control-flow graphs [34, 53], and parallel program graphs [59, 60] represent parallel tasks as symmetric entities in a CFG. For the parallel `fib` function in Figures 2a and 2b, for example, the parallel flow graph in Figure 2c illustrates how forked subcomputations might be represented symmetrically. Some of these approaches struggle to represent common parallel constructs, such as parallel loops [29, 34], while others exhibit problems when subjected to standard compiler analyses and transformations for serial programs [19, 31, 34, 58, 59, 66, 67]. Existing serial-program analyses in LLVM, for example, assume that a basic block with multiple predecessors can observe the variables of only one predecessor at runtime. For the parallel flow graph in Figure 2c, however, instructions in the `join` block must observe the values of x and y from both of its predecessors, as has been observed by [34]. Parallel loops exacerbate this problem by allowing a dynamic number of tasks to join at the same basic block. Previous research [1, 58] has proposed solutions to these problems, including additional representations of the program and augmented analyses that account for interleavings of parallel instructions, but adopt-

a

```
16 int fib(int n) {
17   if (n < 2) return n;
18   int x, y;
19   x = cilk_spawn fib(n - 1);
20   y = fib(n - 2);
21   cilk_sync;
22   return x + y;
23 }
```

b

```
24 int fib(int n) {
25   if (n < 2) return n;
26   int x, y;
27   #pragma omp task shared(x)
28   x = fib(n - 1);
29   #pragma omp task shared(y)
30   y = fib(n - 2);
31   #pragma omp taskwait
32   return x + y;
33 }
```

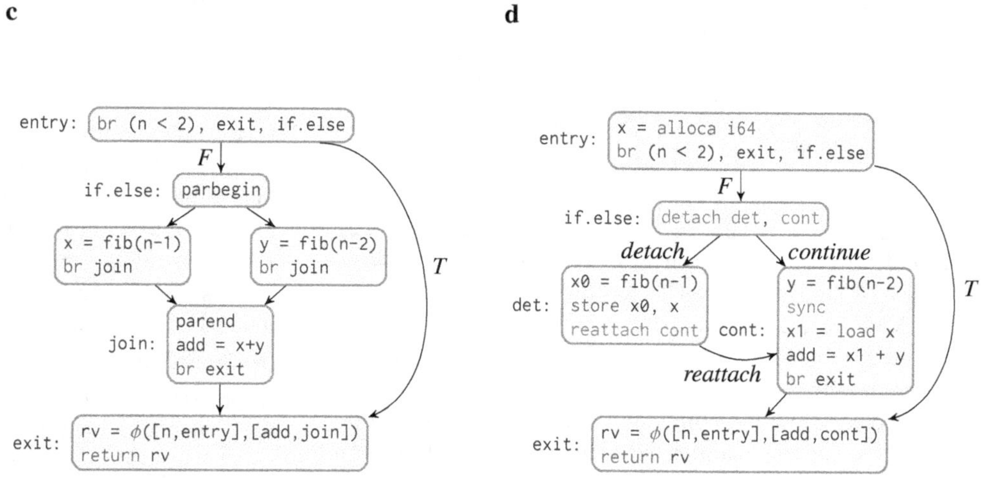

Figure 2. Comparison between a traditional CFG with symmetric parallelism and Tapir's CFG with asymmetric parallelism. **a** The Cilk function `fib` computes Fibonacci numbers. The `cilk_spawn` on line 19 allows the two recursive calls to `fib` to execute in parallel, and the `cilk_sync` on line 21 waits for the spawned call to return. A serial execution of `fib` executes `fib(n-1)` before `fib(n-2)`. **b** A comparable implementation of `fib` using OpenMP task parallelism. **c** A CFG for `fib` that encodes parallelism symmetrically. Rectangles denote basic blocks, which contain C-like pseudocode for `fib`. Edges denote control flow between basic blocks. The `parbegin` and `parend` statements create and synchronize the parallel calls to `fib`. The `br` instruction encodes either an unconditional or a conditional branch. True and false edges from a conditional branch are labeled *T* and *F*, respectively. The ϕ instruction, used to support a static-single-assignment (SSA) form of the program (see Section 2), takes as its arguments pairs that associate a value with each predecessor basic block of the current block. At runtime the ϕ instruction returns the value associated with the predecessor basic block that executed immediately before the current block. **d** The Tapir CFG for `fib`, which encodes parallelism asymmetrically. The `alloca` instruction allocates shared-memory storage on the call stack for a local variable. Section 2 defines the `detach`, `reattach`, and `sync` instructions and the *detach*, *reattach*, and *continue* edge types.

ing these techniques into a mainstream compiler seems to require extensive changes to the existing codebase.

The Tapir approach

This paper introduces Tapir, a compiler IR that represents logical fork-join parallelism asymmetrically in the program's CFG. The asymmetry corresponds to the assumption of ***serial semantics*** [16], which means it is always semantically correct to execute parallel tasks in the same order as an ordinary serial execution.

Tapir adds three instructions — `detach`, `reattach`, and `sync` — to the IR of an ordinary serial compiler to express fork-join parallel programs with serial semantics. Figure 2d illustrates the Tapir CFG for the `fib` function. As with the symmetric parallel flow graph in Figure 2c, Tapir places the logically parallel recursive calls to `fib` in separate basic blocks. But these blocks do not join at a synchronization point symmetrically. Instead, one block connects to the other, reflecting the serial execution order of the program.

The Tapir approach provides five advantages:

1. Introducing fork-join parallelism into the compiler is relatively easy.
2. The IR is expressive and can represent fork-join control constructs from different parallel-language extensions.
3. Tapir parallel constructs harmonize with the invariants associated with existing representations of serial code.
4. Standard serial optimizations work on parallel code with few modifications.
5. The optimizations enabled by Tapir's parallelism constructs are effective in practice.

We discuss each of these advantages in turn.

Ease of implementation

Tapir's asymmetric representation of logically parallel tasks makes it relatively simple to integrate Tapir into an existing compiler's intermediate representation such as LLVM IR [41]. Figure 3 documents the lines of code added, modified, or deleted to implement a prototype of Tapir in LLVM. As Figure 3 shows, Tapir/LLVM was implemented with about 6000 lines, compared to LLVM's roughly 4-million-line codebase. Moreover, fewer than 2000 lines of code were needed to adapt LLVM's existing compiler analyses and transformations to accommodate Tapir.

The breakdown of lines is as follows. The lines for "Instructions" add Tapir's instructions to LLVM IR and adapt LLVM's routines for reading and writing LLVM IR and bitcode files. Conceptually, these changes allow LLVM to correctly compile a Tapir program to a serial executable with no optimizations. The lines for "Memory Behavior" control how Tapir instructions may interact with memory operations, preventing the compiler from creating any races. The lines for "Optimizations" perform any adjustments required

Compiler Component	*LLVM 4.0svn*	*Tapir/LLVM*	
Instructions	105,995	943	}
Memory Behavior	21,788	445	} 1,768
Optimizations	152,229	380	}
Parallelism Lowering	0	3,782	
Other	3,803,831	460	
Total	4,083,843	6,010	

Figure 3. Breakdown of the lines of code added, modified, or deleted in LLVM to implement the Tapir/LLVM prototype.

for LLVM analyses and transformations to compile a Tapir program at optimization level `-O3`. Most of these modifications are not necessary for creating a correct executable but are added to allow the compiler to perform additional optimizations, such as parallel tail-recursion elimination (described in Section 4). The lines for "Parallelism Lowering" translate Tapir instructions into Cilk Plus runtime calls and allow the code to be race-detected with a provably good race detector [14]. The lines for "Other" address a bug in LLVM's implementation of `setjmp` and implement useful features for our development environment.

Expressiveness of Tapir

Tapir can express logical fork-join parallelism in parallel programs that have serial semantics. For example, Figure 2 illustrates how Tapir can express the parallelism encoded by the `cilk_spawn` and `cilk_sync` linguistics from Cilk++ [35] and Cilk Plus [21], as well as the parallelism encoded by OpenMP `task` and `taskwait` clauses [5]. Similarly, Tapir can express the parallelism encoded by OpenMP parallel sections [54] and Habanero's `async` and `finish` constructs [11]. Tapir can also express parallel loops, including `cilk_for` loops and OpenMP parallel loops that have serial semantics (described in Section 2). Other parallel constructs can be represented as well, although parallel operations that cannot be expressed in terms of fork-join parallelism, such as OpenMP's `ordered` clause, cannot be represented directly using Tapir's `detach`, `reattach`, and `sync` instructions.

Tapir makes minimal assumptions about the consistency [10, 56] of concurrent memory accesses. Tapir assumes that memory is shared among parallel tasks and that virtual-register state is local to each task. Parallel instructions in Tapir can exhibit a ***determinacy race***[2] [14] if they access the same memory location concurrently and at least one instruction writes to that location. Tapir itself does not fully define the possible outcomes of a determinacy race, and instead defers to existing compiler mechanisms, such as LLVM's atomic memory-ordering constraints [41], to define whichever memory model they choose. For any targeted runtime system, Tapir relies on a correct implementation of lowering in order to implement the necessary synchronization, but Tapir is oblivious to how that runtime system implements the synchronization.

[2] Determinacy races are also called general races [50] and are distinct from data races, which involve nonatomic accesses to critical regions.

Serial semantics

By grounding its model of parallelism in serial semantics, Tapir enables common compiler optimizations for serial code to work on parallel code. Intuitively, because Tapir always allows parallel tasks to execute in their ordinary serial execution order, the compiler can to optimize parallel code in any manner that preserves the serial semantics of the program and does not introduce new determinacy races. These mild constraints support common optimizations on parallel code, such as sequentialization, which can be invalid under models of parallelism without serial semantics [71].

Optimizations

In practice, we have found that Tapir enables a wide variety of standard compiler optimizations to work with parallel code. The prototype implementation of Tapir/LLVM, for example, successfully moves the call to `norm` in Figure 1 outside of the loop, just as it would for a serial `for` loop. As Section 4 discusses, Tapir enables other optimizations, including common-subexpression elimination [48, Sec. 12.2], loop-invariant-code motion [48, Sec. 13.2], and tail-recursion elimination [48, Sec. 15.1], to work on parallel code. Tapir also enables new optimizations on parallel control flow.

Evaluation of Tapir/LLVM

The compiler optimizations that Tapir enables are effective in practice. We evaluated the Tapir approach by measuring the performance of 20 Cilk application benchmarks compiled using Tapir/LLVM. We compared the performance of these executables to those produced by a comparable reference compiler, called Reference. Conceptually, Reference lowers parallel linguistic constructs directly into runtime calls, as mainstream compilers do today, but otherwise performs the same set of optimization passes as Tapir/LLVM. Section 6 describes our experimental setup in detail, including the design of Reference.

Figure 4 presents the results of comparing Tapir/LLVM and Reference in terms of the "work efficiency" of the compiled benchmarks. To perform this comparison, we compiled each benchmark using each compiler and then ran the executable on a single processing core of a multicore machine to measure its ***work***, the 1-core running time, denoted T_1. We also used each compiler to compile, run, and measure the 1-core running time of the ***serial elision*** [16] of each benchmark, denoted T_S, in which the benchmark is converted into a corresponding serial program by replacing all parallel linguistic constructs with their serial equivalents. We then computed the ***work efficiency*** of each compiled benchmark, which is the ratio T_S/T_1 of the running time T_S of the benchmark's serial elision divided by the work T_1 of the benchmark. In theory, the maximum possible work efficiency is $T_S/T_1 = 1$, but in practice, quirky behaviors of the compiler and multicore architecture can occasionally produce work efficiencies greater than 1. As Figure 4 shows, for most benchmarks, the executables compiled using Tapir/LLVM achieve equal or higher work efficiency than those compiled

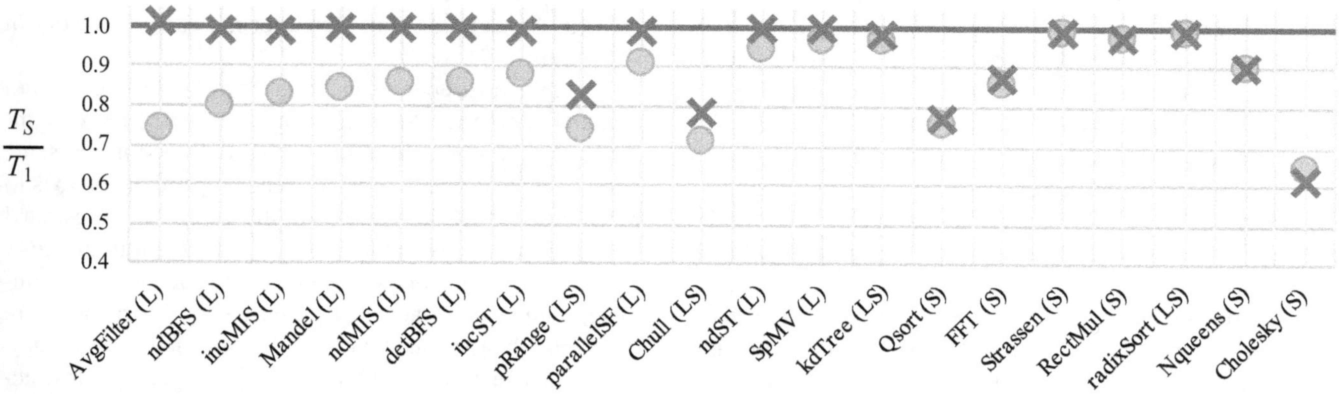

Figure 4. Comparison of the work efficiency of 20 parallel application benchmarks compiled using Tapir/LLVM (X's) and the comparable Reference compiler (O's), described in Section 6, which lowers parallelism in the compiler front end. Each point plots the work efficiency T_S/T_1 of a compiled benchmark, where T_1 is the work of the benchmark and T_s is the running time of the serial elision of the benchmark. Higher values indicate better work efficiency. The horizontal line at 1.0 plots the theoretically maximum work efficiency $T_S/T_1 = 1$. Benchmarks are sorted by decreasing difference in work efficiency between Tapir/LLVM- and Reference-compiled executables. Benchmarks marked with an "L" use parallel loops, and benchmarks marked with an "S" use `cilk_spawn`.

using Reference. Moreover, for many benchmarks, and particularly those implemented using parallel loops, Tapir/LLVM produces executables that achieve nearly optimal work efficiency. Section 6 elaborates on these experiments.

Contributions

This paper makes the following research contributions:

- The design of a compiler IR that represents fork-join parallelism asymmetrically, which enables existing serial optimizations to operate on parallel code and which also enables parallel optimizations.
- The implementation of Tapir/LLVM in the LLVM compiler by modifying about 6000 source lines of code (0.15% of the 4-million-line LLVM codebase).
- The implementation of parallel optimizations such as unnecessary synchronization elimination and parallel-loop scheduling.
- Experiments that demonstrate the advantage of embedding fork-join parallelism into a compiler's IR, as opposed to dealing with parallelism only in the compiler's front end.

Outline

The remainder of this paper is organized as follows. Section 2 describes Tapir's representation and properties. Section 3 discusses how analysis passes can be adapted to operate on Tapir programs. Section 4 describes various optimizations on parallel control flow that Tapir enables. Section 5 describes auxiliary software we developed to exercise and test Tapir/LLVM. Section 6 discusses our evaluation of the effectiveness of Tapir. Section 7 discusses related work. Section 8 provides some concluding remarks. An appendix describes how to set up Tapir/LLVM and how to download and run our suite of application benchmarks.

2. Tapir

This section describes how Tapir represents logically parallel tasks asymmetrically in the CFG of a program. We define Tapir's three new instructions and how they interact with LLVM's static single-assignment (SSA) form [2, Sec. 6.2.4]. Although we describe Tapir as an extension to LLVM IR [41], we see no reason why other compilers cannot gain similar advantages from Tapir-like instructions.

Like LLVM IR, Tapir treats a program function as a CFG $G = (V, E, v_0)$, where

- the set V of vertices represents the function's ***basic blocks***: sequences of LLVM instructions, where control flow can only enter through the first instruction and leave from the last instruction;
- the set E of edges denote control flow between (basic) blocks; and
- the designated vertex $v_0 \in V$ represents the ***entry point*** of the function.

Tapir instructions

Tapir extends LLVM IR with three instructions: `detach`, `reattach`, and `sync`. The `detach` and `reattach` instructions together delineate logically parallel tasks, and the `sync` instruction imposes synchronization on parallel tasks. The three instructions have the following syntax, where $b, c \in V$:

```
detach label b, label c
reattach label c
sync
```

The `label` keywords indicate that b and c are (labels of) basic blocks in V.

The `detach` and `reattach` instructions together delineate a parallel task as follows. A `detach` instruction terminates the block a that contains it and takes a ***detached*** block b and a ***continuation*** block c as its arguments. The `detach` instruction ***spawns*** the task starting at block b, allowing that task to execute in parallel with block c. The control-flow edge $(a, b) \in E$ is a ***detach*** edge, and the edge $(a, c) \in E$ is a ***continue*** edge. A `reattach` instruction, meanwhile, terminates the block a' that contains it and takes a single ***continuation*** block c as its argument, inducing a ***reattach*** edge $(a', c) \in E$ in the CFG. The `reattach` terminates the task spawned by a preceding `detach` instruction with the same continuation block. Together, a `detach` instruction and associated `reattach` instructions demark the start and end of a parallel task and indicate that that task can execute in parallel with their common continuation block.

For the example in Figure 2d, the `detach` in the `if.else` block and the `reattach` in the `det` block share the same continuation block `cont`. Together, this `detach` and this `reattach` indicate that the `det` block is a parallel task which can execute in parallel with the `cont` block. In general, a parallel task delineated by `detach` and `reattach` can consist of many basic blocks in a single-entry subgraph.

The `detach` and `reattach` instructions in a CFG obey several structural properties. We say a `reattach` instruction j ***reattaches*** a `detach` instruction i if i and j share a common continuation block and there is a path from the detached block of i to j. Tapir assumes that every CFG $G = (V, E, v_0)$ obeys the following invariants on every `detach` instruction i and `reattach` instruction j in G:

1. A `reattach` instruction reattaches exactly one `detach` instruction.
2. If j reattaches i, then every path from v_0 to the block terminated by j passes through the detach edge of i, that is, the detach edge of i ***dominates*** j.
3. Every path starting from the detached block of i must reach a block terminated by a `reattach` instruction that reattaches i.
4. If j reattaches i and a path from i to j passes through the detach edge of another `detach` instruction i', then it must also pass through a `reattach` instruction j' that reattaches i'.
5. Every cycle containing a `detach` instruction i must pass through a `reattach` instruction that reattaches i.
6. The continuation block of j cannot contain any ϕ instructions [2, Sec 6.2.4].

These invariants imply that, at runtime, a `detach` instruction i with detached block b and continuation block c spawns the execution of a ***detached sub-CFG***, which is the single entry sub-CFG starting at b induced by all blocks on paths from b to a `reattach` instruction that reattaches i.

The dynamic execution of the program organizes memory as a tree of ***parallel contexts***. A new parallel context is created as a child of the current context when control enters a function or follows a detach edge. When control executes a `reattach` instruction or leaves a function, the context is destroyed and the parent's context becomes the current context. An `alloca` instruction allocates shared memory in the current context.

The `sync` instruction synchronizes tasks spawned within its parallel context. At runtime, a `sync` instruction dynamically waits for the set of sub-CFG's detached in the same parallel context or any of its descendant parallel contexts to reach a `reattach` instruction. In the Tapir CFG illustrated in Figure 2d, for example, the `sync` instruction in the `cont` block simply waits for the execution of the `det` block to complete. Unlike `reattach` instructions, `sync` instructions are not explicitly associated with `detach` instructions, and they, in fact, can be executed within conditionals. A `sync` instruction j ***syncs*** a `detach` instruction i if i and j belong to the same parallel context and the CFG detached by i cannot be guaranteed to have completed when j executes.

Static single-assignment form

LLVM's static single-assignment (SSA) form [2, Sec. 6.2.4] must be adapted for Tapir programs. SSA form ensures that each virtual register is set at most once in a function. LLVM IR employs the ***ϕ instruction*** [2, Sec 6.2.4] to combine definitions of a variable from different predecessors of a basic block. In adapting SSA to Tapir, one concern is that a ϕ instruction might allow registers defined in the detached sub-CFG to be used in the continuation. A basic block containing a ϕ instruction must avoid inheriting register definitions from predecessors that are connected by reattach edges. Otherwise, a register in the detached sub-CFG might not have been computed by the time the continuation executes.

We implemented this constraint by simply forbidding reattach edges from going into basic blocks with ϕ instructions. But what if the continuation c of a `detach` instruction begins with a ϕ instruction? In this case, we create a new basic block c' containing only a branch instruction to c. We reroute the reattach and continuation edges originally going to c so that they go instead to c'. All other edges going to c are left in place.

The reason this solution works is as follows. No reattach edges in the resulting CFG go to blocks containing ϕ instructions. Because a detached sub-CFG does not dominate any outside block, registers in the detached CFG can only be used in ϕ instructions of the immediate successors of the detached sub-CFG. Since the continuation is the only immediate successor of the detached sub-CFG and it contains no ϕ instructions, no registers from the detached sub-CFG may be accessed in the continuation.

Asymmetry in Tapir

The `detach` and `reattach` instructions express parallel tasks asymmetrically both syntactically in the structure of the CFG and semantically in the way memory state is managed. Both asymmetries are illustrated in Figure 2d.

First, the CFG detached by a `detach` instruction is connected by a reattach edge to the continuation block of that instruction, even though they can execute in parallel. For example, the reattach edge between det and cont in Figure 2d breaks the symmetry between them. Reattach edges reflect the serial semantics of a Tapir program, which dictates that a serial execution of the program executes the detached CFG to completion before starting to execute the continuation block. In fact, the parallel task delineated by a detach and a reattach instruction can be ***serialized*** by replacing the detach instruction with an unconditional branch to its detached block and replacing the reattach with an unconditional branch to its continuation block. In contrast, parallel flow graphs and similar previously explored representations join logically parallel tasks in the CFG at a synchronization point. By supporting separate reattach and sync instructions, Tapir decouples the termination of a parallel task from its synchronization.

Second, although memory state is shared among all parallel tasks in Tapir, a virtual register defined in a detached sub-CFG is not accessible in its parent parallel context. For example, the continuation block cont in Figure 2d cannot assume that the register value x0 returned by fib(n-1) in block det is accessible, because the two basic blocks belong to different parallel contexts. Thus, cont must load it again after the sync instruction.

Parallel loops in Tapir

Figure 5 illustrates Tapir's default representation of the parallel loops from Figure 1. As Figure 5 shows, Tapir can represent a parallel loop in the CFG as an ordinary loop, where the head block repeatedly spawns the body block, and the exit block syncs the detached CFG's. Section 4 describes how this representation of parallel loops allows existing compiler loop optimizations to operate on Tapir parallel loops with only minor modifications. Although this loop structure can exhibit poor parallel performance when the loop body is small, separate optimization passes in Tapir/LLVM (see Section 4) transform this parallel-loop representation into a divide-and-conquer form that exhibits good performance.

3. Analysis passes

This section describes how LLVM's analysis passes can be adapted to operate on Tapir programs. We first discuss constraints on how Tapir programs can be safely transformed. Implementing these contraints on LLVM optimization passes primarily involves adapting standard compiler analyses — specifically alias analysis [2, Ch. 12], dominator analysis [2, Ch. 9], and data-flow analysis [2, Ch. 9] — to accomodate Tapir's instructions. We describe how each of these analyses was minimally modified to support Tapir.

Constraints on transformations

To be correct, a code transformation on a Tapir program must preserve the program's serial semantics, and it must not introduce any new behaviors into the program's set of behaviors. A program can exhibit more than one behavior if it contains a determinacy race. In general, the result of a determinacy race can vary nondeterministically from run to run depending on the order in which the participating instructions access the memory location. To avoid introducing new behaviors, code transformations must not create determinacy races, although they can eliminate determinacy races. Many existing serial optimizations can be adapted to respect these properties by adapting the standard compiler analyses they rely on. We now describe how LLVM's alias, dominator, and data-flow analyses were adapted for Tapir.

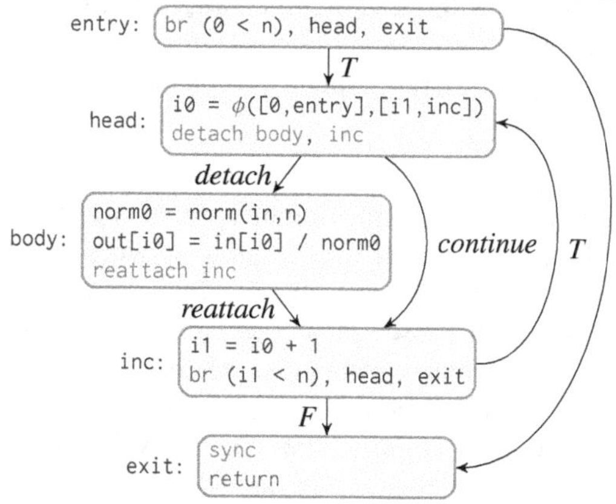

Figure 5. Tapir CFG for the parallel loops in Figure 1, using a format similar to the CFG's in Figure 2.

Alias analysis

LLVM uses alias analysis [2, Ch. 12] to determine whether different instructions might reference the same locations in memory, and in particular, to restrict the reordering of instructions that access the same memory. Tapir/LLVM modifies LLVM's alias analysis to prevent optimizations that move code around from introducing determinacy races. In particular, Tapir adapts LLVM's alias analysis to treat the instructions as if they access memory. For example, consider an instruction k that performs a load or a store. There are four cases to consider when moving k around either a detach instruction i or a sync instruction j:

1. The instruction k moves from before i to after i.
2. The instruction k moves from after i to before i.
3. The instruction k moves from before j to after j.
4. The instruction k moves from after j to before j.

Neither Case 2 nor Case 3 can introduce a determinacy race, because both motions serialize the execution of k with respect to the sub-CFG detached by i. Cases 1 and 4 might introduce a determinacy race, however, if k loads or stores a memory location that is also accessed by the CFG detached by i. To handle Case 1, i is treated as if it were a function call that accesses all memory locations accessed in the CFG detached by i. Similarly, for Case 4, j is treated as if it were a function call that accesses all memory locations accessed by all instructions that j might sync. A reattach instruction is treated as a compiler fence that prevents instructions from moving across it. With these modifications, existing rules in LLVM that restrict reordering of loads and stores properly restrict memory reordering around Tapir's instructions.

Dominator analysis

Optimization passes determine what values are available to an instruction in part by using dominator analysis [2, Ch. 9], which deduces the dominance relation between all basic blocks and edges in a CFG. To handle Tapir programs correctly, optimization passes must not mistakenly cause instructions to use virtual registers that are defined in logically parallel tasks. If instruction i dominates instruction j, than an optimization pass might assume that the value produced by i is always available when j executes.

The asymmetry of Tapir's representation allows LLVM's dominator analysis to analyze Tapir programs correctly without any changes. Ignoring the names of edges, the difference between the CFG $G = (V, E, v_0)$ of a Tapir program and the CFG $G' = (V, E', v_0)$ of its serial elision is the set $E - E'$ of continue edges, each of which connects a `detach` instruction to its continuation. A continue edge short-cuts a detached sub-CFG, changing the continuation's immediate dominator from the detached sub-CFG to the block containing the `detach` instruction itself. This configuration of detach, reattach, and continue edges looks much like an ordinary `if` construct in which the detached sub-CFG is conditionally executed. As a result, dominator analysis never concludes that an instruction in a detached sub-CFG can execute before the corresponding continuation block.

Data-flow analysis

A wide class of code transformations, including those that might move instructions across a reattach edge, rely on data-flow analysis [2, Ch. 9] to examine the propagation of values along different paths through a CFG $G = (V, E, v_0)$. Fundamental to data-flow analysis is an understanding of the set of possible program states at the beginning and end of each basic block $b \in V$, denoted $\text{IN}(b)$ and $\text{OUT}(b)$, respectively.

To illustrate how LLVM's data-flow analyses were adapted to Tapir, let us examine the particular case of forward data-flow analysis. (Backward data-flow analysis is similar.) In an ordinary serial CFG, forward data-flow analysis evaluates $\text{IN}(b)$ as the union of $\text{OUT}(a)$ for each predecessor block a of b:

$$\text{IN}(b) = \bigcup_{(a,b)\in E} \text{OUT}(a) .$$

To handle Tapir CFG's, data-flow analyses must be adapted specifically to handle reattach edges. Because Tapir's asymmetric representation propagates virtual registers and memory state differently across a reattach edge, the modifications to LLVM data analyses consider registers and memory separately.

For variables stored in shared memory, the standard data-flow equations remain unchanged. Thus, LLVM need not be modified to handle them for Tapir.

a

```
34 void search(int low, int high) {
35   if (low == high) search_base(low);
36   else {
37     cilk_spawn search(low, (low+high)/2);
38     search((low+high)/2 + 1, high);
39     cilk_sync;
40 } }
```

b

```
41 void search(int low, int high) {
42   if (low == high) search_base(low);
43   else {
44     int mid = (low+high)/2;
45     cilk_spawn search(low, mid);
46     search(mid + 1, high);
47     cilk_sync;
48 } }
```

Figure 6. Example of common-subexpression elimination on a Cilk program. **a** The function `search`, which uses parallel divide-and-conquer to apply the function `search_base` to every integer in the closed interval [`low`, `high`]. **b** An optimized version of `search`, where the common subexpression `(low+high)/2` in lines 37 and 38 of the original version is computed only once and stored in the variable `mid` in line 44 of the optimized version.

For register variables, however, LLVM's data-flow analyses must be modified to exclude the values in registers from an immediate predecessor a of a basic block b if the edge $(a, b) \in E$ is a reattach edge. Denote the set of reattach edges in E by E_R. For a Tapir CFG, forward data-flow analyses define $\text{IN}(b)$ for register variables as

$$\text{IN}(b) = \bigcup_{(a,b)\in E-E_R} \text{OUT}(a) ,$$

that is, they ignore predecessors across a reattach edge. With this change, Tapir/LLVM correctly propagates register variables through the CFG, never allowing register values in a basic block to use register values set in a logically parallel detached sub-CFG.

4. Optimization passes

Tapir enables LLVM's existing optimization passes [42] to work across parallel control flow. It also enables new optimization passes that specifically target Tapir's fork-join parallel constructs. This section discusses four representative optimizations. Common-subexpression elimination [48, Sec. 12.2] illustrates an optimization pass that "just works" with the additional Tapir instructions. Loop-invariant code motion [48, Sec. 13.2], and tail-recursion elimination [48, Sec. 15.1] were the only two out of LLVM's roughly 80 optimization passes that required any modification to work effectively on parallel code. Parallel-loop scheduling serves as an example of a new optimization pass.

Common-subexpression elimination

The common-subexpression elimination (CSE) optimization identifies redundant calculations and transforms the code so that they are only computed once. For example, the expression `(low+high)/2` in Figure 6a is computed in both line 37 and line 38. Tapir/LLVM performs CSE on this code, producing code equivalent to that in Figure 6b. Existing mainstream compilers that support fork-join parallelism do not eliminate this common subexpression, however, and they compute `(low+high)/2` twice. Tapir/LLVM can perform CSE across either a continue edge, as in the example, or a detach edge. Like the vast majority of optimization passes in Tapir/LLVM, CSE "just works" on Tapir code without any modifications to LLVM's CSE pass.

Loop-invariant code motion

The loop-invariant code motion (LICM) optimization [48, Sec. 13.2] aims to move computations out of loop bodies if they compute the same value on every iteration of the loop. LICM is responsible, for example, for moving the call to `norm` in the parallel loop in Figure 1a outside of the loop, as described in Section 1. By adapting LICM to handle parallel loops, Tapir/LLVM reduces the asymptotic serial running time of this parallel loop from $\Theta(n^2)$ to $\Theta(n)$.

Tapir/LLVM requires a minor change to LLVM's LICM pass to handle parallel loops. Consider the CFG illustrated in Figure 5, which models the parallel loops in Figure 1. For the serial elision of the loop, which would have a similar graph structure except with the continue edge missing, LLVM attempts to find candidate computations to move outside the loop by looking for instructions in the basic blocks of the loop body that dominate the exit block of the loop, such as the block `inc` in Figure 5. (The block labeled `exit` is the exit of the function, not the loop exit.) For a parallel loop, however, this analysis fails to identify any code to move due to the existence of the continue edge. As Figure 5 shows, with the continue edge, blocks in the loop body can never dominate the exit block `inc` as they could for the serial elision.

Tapir/LLVM modifies LLVM's LICM pass to handle a parallel loop by analyzing the serial elision of the loop, which essentially means ignoring continue edges. For simple parallel loop structures with a single continue edge, such as that shown in Figure 5, this modification is implemented by finding blocks in the loop body that dominate the predecessors of the loop exit. The modification required changing only 25 lines of LLVM's LICM pass.

Tail-recursion elimination

Tail-recursion elimination (TRE) [48, Sec. 15.1] aims to replace a recursive call at the end of a function with a branch to the start of the function. By eliminating these recursive tail calls, TRE can avoid function-call overheads and reduce the stack space they consume. This optimization can especially benefit fork-join parallel programs, as many parallel runtime systems impose additional setup and cleanup overhead on a spawned function.

LLVM's existing TRE pass can perform the TRE optimization on Tapir programs with just a minor modification. Specifically, the modified TRE pass ignores `sync` instructions after the tail-recursive call. Further, if TRE is applied and ignores a `sync` instruction, it must then insert a `sync` instruction before any remaining returns. This modification to LLVM's TRE pass required changing only 68 lines.

a

```
49 void pqsort(int* start, int* end) {
50   if (begin == end) return;
51   int* mid = partition(start, end);
52   swap(end, mid);
53   cilk_spawn pqsort(begin, mid);
54   pqsort(mid+1, end);
55   cilk_sync;
56   return;
57 }
```

b

```
void pqsort(int* start, int* end) {
  if (begin == end) return;
  int* mid = partition(start, end);
  swap(end, mid);
  cilk_spawn pqsort(begin, mid);

  start = mid+1;
  // Begin inlined code
  if (begin == end) goto join;
  mid = partition(start, end);
  swap(end, mid);
  cilk_spawn pqsort(begin, mid);
  pqsort(mid+1, end);
  cilk_sync;
  // End inlined code

join:
  cilk_sync;
  return;
}
```

c

```
void pqsort(int* start, int* end) {
pqsort_start:
  if (begin == end) {
    cilk_sync;
    return;
  }
  int* mid = partition(start, end);
  swap(end, mid);
  cilk_spawn pqsort(begin, mid);
  start = mid+1;
  goto pqsort_start;
}
```

Figure 7. Example of tail-recursion elimination on a parallel quicksort program. **a** The Cilk function `pqsort` sorts an array of integers in the range specified by the `start` and `end` pointers. **b** A version of `pqsort` where the recursive tail call on line 54 has been replaced by one round of inlining. **c** A version `pqsort` where tail-recursion elimination has removed the recursive tail call on line 54.

To see why these `sync` instructions can be safely ignored, consider Figure 7, which illustrates how Tapir/LLVM's TRE pass operates on the `pqsort` function, a parallel version of Hoare's quicksort algorithm [20]. The original tail-recursive code is shown in Figure 7a. Figure 7b illustrates the result of simply inlining the tail-recursive call. For the inlined code, all `return` statements are replaced with branches to the `join` label. Because there is a `cilk_sync` at the start of `join`, the `cilk_sync` on line 71 can be eliminated. call an arbitrary number of times, TRE can safely ignore a `cilk_sync` instruction after the final tail-recursive call, assuming that it inserts a `cilk_sync` instruction before all remaining returns.

Parallel-loop scheduling and lowering

As discussed above and in Section 2, Tapir effectively represents a parallel loop as a serial loop over a body that is spawned every iteration. Depending on the number of iterations of the loop and the amount of work inside each loop, however, statically scheduling loop iterations in this way may be inefficient. For a parallel loop with a large number of iterations, for instance, it is faster to schedule the iterations in a recursive divide-and-conquer fashion, which produces more parallelism (see [46, Sec. 8.3]. For parallel loops with few iterations, however, the additional function calls required to perform the parallel divide-and-conquer can make the loop run slower than simply spawning off the iterations.

Tapir/LLVM implements a parallel optimization pass that schedules the iterations of a parallel loop using recursive divide-and-conquer, but only if that loop contains sufficiently many iterations. This pass is implemented as part of Tapir/LLVM's 3800-line lowering pass, which translates `detach`, `reattach`, and `sync` instructions into appropriate Cilk Plus runtime calls [22]. In particular, Tapir/LLVM uses the Cilk Plus runtime calls for `cilk_for` loops [22, Sec 10.7] to schedule parallel loops. Although we could have separated parallel-loop scheduling from lowering, we chose to combine these two passes so that we could perform fair comparisons between Tapir/LLVM and compilers that lower parallel constructs in their front end. We plan to separate the parallel-loop-scheduling and lowering passes in a future version of Tapir/LLVM.

Other optimization passes

Tapir/LLVM implements two minor parallel optimization passes: unnecessary-synchronization elimination and puny-task elimination. ***Unnecessary-synchronization elimination*** identifies and eliminates `sync` instructions that could not possibly sync a detached sub-CFG. ***Puny-task elimination*** serializes detached sub-CFG's that perform little or no work. If the runtime overhead of creating a parallel task outweighs the work in the task, the task might as well be run serially. Both of these optimization passes were implemented in 52 lines of code by augmenting LLVM's SimplifyCFG pass.

5. Auxiliary software

This section describes auxiliary software that we developed to exercise and test Tapir/LLVM. Although our research focuses on the middle end of the compiler, we implemented a front end for Cilk Plus. In addition, we developed compiler instrumentation that allows the compiler to interface to a race detector to verify the correctness of the Tapir/LLVM implementation.

To create the front end, we created a modification of the Clang front end called PClang, which translates Cilk Plus codes to Tapir. We also created a version of Clang that can handle some OpenMP codes. PClang handles most of the fork-join control constructs specified by the Cilk Plus programming model, and specifically, enough to run all the benchmarks described in Section 6.

We augmented Tapir/LLVM in two ways to test the correctness of the implementation. First, we modified LLVM's internal verification pass to check that Tapir's invariants are also maintained. Second, we added an instrumentation pass to Tapir/LLVM to allow parallel executables to be tested for determinacy races using a provably good determinacy race detector. This race detector, based on the SP-bags algorithm [14], is guaranteed to find a determinacy race if an only if one exists in the program execution. The verification pass and race detector helped us locate and fix bugs in Tapir/LLVM, both within our code and within the underlying LLVM codebase. Tapir/LLVM now passes all tests in LLVM's regression test suites and correctly compiles our own suite of parallel test programs.

The instrumentation pass has proved useful for supporting other dynamic-analysis tools based on Tapir/LLVM. Genghis Chau of MIT adapted the Cilkprof scalability profiler [61] to use Tapir/LLVM and this instrumentation in order to build an integrated development environment with always-on race detection and scalability profiling facilities.

6. Evaluation

To evaluate the effectiveness of the Tapir approach, we evaluated Tapir/LLVM on 20 benchmarks. The experiments support the contention that Tapir's approach of embedding parallelism in the IR is superior to lowering parallelism in the compiler front end. We could not simply run Tapir/LLVM against another compiler, such as Cilk Plus/LLVM [23], which lowers parallelism in the front end, because Cilk Plus/LLVM and Tapir/LLVM differ in more ways than just where they lower parallel constructs. Consequently, to perform an apples-to-apples comparison of these two approaches, we implemented a compiler called "Reference," which is as close to identical to Tapir/LLVM as we could muster, except for where lowering occurs. Figure 8 illustrates the compilation pipelines for Clang/LLVM, Tapir/LLVM, and Reference.

The first pipeline, Clang/LLVM, has the traditional three-phase structure. The Clang front-end takes serial C/C++ code and emits LLVM IR. The `-O3` middle-end optimizes the IR, and the CodeGen back-end lowers LLVM IR to machine code for a particular hardware platform.

The second pipeline shows how Tapir/LLVM is organized. The PClang front end takes parallel Cilk Plus code as input and emits Tapir. The middle-end now consists of three steps: `-O3` optimization, a Lower pass to lower Tapir to LLVM IR, and another pass at `-O3` optimization. The first `-O3` pass performs optimizations on the Tapir representation,

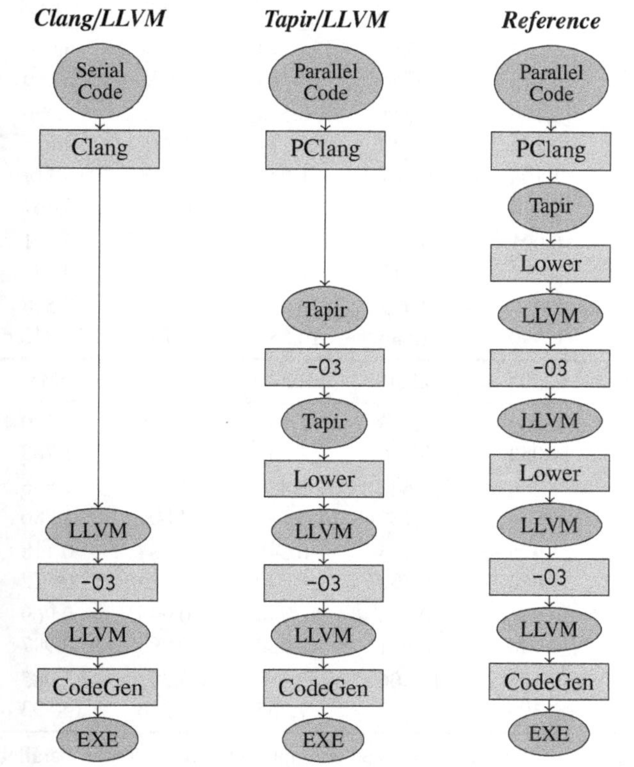

Figure 8. The compilation pipelines for Clang/LLVM, Tapir/LLVM, and Reference. Each block represents a compiler transformation, and each oval designates the format of the code at that point in the pipeline.

the lowering pass translates all the Tapir-specific constructs to LLVM IR, and the second `-O3` pass performs optimizations on the LLVM IR. Finally, the CodeGen back end lowers LLVM IR to machine code.

The third pipeline, called Reference, models how mainstream compilers work today, where parallel constructs are transformed into runtime calls before any optimization can take place. The only difference between Reference and Tapir/LLVM is that the Tapir code emitted by the PClang front end is immediately lowered to LLVM IR before the rest of the Tapir pipeline is invoked. (The second Lower pass in the Reference pipeline therefore has no effect.) Although Reference lowers the parallel constructs early, two iterations of `-O3` are included to ensure that the Tapir/LLVM gains no advantage from optimizing twice. Although one might think that a second pass of `-O3` would be redundant, it is not. For example, a simple matrix-multiplication code runs 13% faster after two rounds of optimization compared to just one. And although most benchmarks run faster after two `-O3` passes, some actually run slower. Thus, we implemented Reference with the same passes as Tapir/LLVM, except for the initial Lower pass in Reference. This difference only affects parallel code. Serial code passes through both pipelines identically.

Suite	*Benchmark*	*Description*
Cilk	Cholesky	Cholesky decomposition
	FFT	Fast Fourier transform
	NQueens	n-Queens solver
	QSort	Hoare quicksort
	RectMul	Rectangular matrix multiplication
	Strassen	Strassen matrix multiplication
Intel	AvgFilter	Averaging filter on an image
	Mandel	Mandelbrot set computation
PBBS	CHull	Convex hull
	detBFS	BFS, deterministic algorithm
	incMIS	MIS, incremental algorithm
	incST	Spanning tree, incremental algorithm
	kdTree	Performance test of a parallel k-d tree
	ndBFS	BFS, nondeterministic algorithm
	ndMIS	MIS, nondeterministic algorithm
	ndST	Spanning tree, nondeterministic algorithm
	parallelSF	Spanning-forest computation
	pRange	Compute ranges on a parallel suffix array
	radixSort	Radix sort
	SpMV	Sparse matrix-vector multiplication

Figure 9. Descriptions of the 20 benchmarks used to evaluate Tapir/LLVM. These benchmarks were taken from the MIT Cilk benchmark suite [16], Intel Cilk Plus example programs [25], and the CMU Problem-Based Benchmark Suite [63]. "MIS" denotes the computation of a maximal independent set of a graph. "BFS" denotes the breadth-first search of a graph.

Benchmarking

To benchmark the compiler pipelines, we assembled a collection of benchmark programs taken from the MIT Cilk benchmark suite [16], Intel Cilk code samples [25], and the CMU Problem-Based Benchmark Suite [63]. From these collections, we selected stable programs that tend to exhibit little performance difference when the number or order of optimization passes is changed. Figure 9 describes the suite of benchmarks tested.

We compiled each program in our benchmark suite with both Tapir/LLVM and Reference, and we ran them on both 1 and 18 cores of our test machine. Additionally, we compiled the serial elision of each benchmark with each compiler. Each running time is the minimum of 10 runs on an Amazon AWS `c4.8xlarge` spot instance, which is a dual-socket Intel Xeon E5-2666 v3 system with a total of 60 GiB of memory. Each Xeon is a 2.9 GHz 18-core CPU with a shared 25 MiB L3-cache. Each core has a 32 KiB private L1-data-cache and a 256 KiB private L2-cache. The system was "quiesced" to permit careful measurements by turning off Turbo Boost, dvfs, hyperthreading, extraneous interrupts, etc.

Overall performance

The results of our tests are given in Figure 10. For the first pair of rows, Reference and Tapir/LLVM produce essentially identical executables when compiling the serial elision of a benchmark. Differences in running times in these rows

		Cholesky	FFT	NQueens	QSort	RectMul	Strasssen	AvgFilter	Mandel	CHull	detBFS
T_S	Ref.	2.935	10.304	3.084	4.983	10.207	10.105	1.751	25.779	0.938	5.670
	Tapir	2.933	10.271	3.083	4.984	10.207	10.119	1.750	25.780	0.935	5.666
T_1	Ref.	4.572	11.919	3.409	6.581	10.413	10.196	2.355	30.520	1.316	6.596
	Tapir	4.739	11.733	3.419	6.461	10.415	10.196	1.730	25.774	1.187	5.673
T_{18}	Ref.	0.387	0.788	0.196	0.648	0.609	1.106	0.708	1.847	0.124	0.517
	Tapir	0.396	0.774	0.197	0.709	0.611	1.124	0.615	1.559	0.120	0.467
$\frac{T_S}{T_1}$	Ref.	0.642	0.862	0.904	0.757	0.980	0.991	0.743	0.845	0.710	0.801
	Tapir	0.619	0.875	0.902	0.771	0.980	0.991	1.012	1.000	0.788	0.992
$\frac{T_S}{T_{18}}$	Ref.	7.579	13.034	15.730	7.690	16.760	9.137	2.472	13.957	7.540	9.518
	Tapir	7.407	13.270	15.650	7.028	16.705	8.990	2.846	16.536	7.792	10.942

		incMIS	incST	kdTree	ndBFS	ndMIS	ndST	parallelSF	pRange	radixSort	SpMV
T_S	Ref.	4.993	4.190	5.473	3.950	9.210	4.069	5.136	2.564	3.775	1.780
	Tapir	5.006	4.173	5.466	3.956	9.253	4.053	5.136	2.559	3.775	1.783
T_1	Ref.	6.030	4.733	5.640	4.930	10.760	4.286	5.646	3.438	3.795	1.836
	Tapir	5.043	4.203	5.546	3.980	9.246	4.063	5.183	3.083	3.800	1.786
T_{18}	Ref.	0.559	0.352	0.342	0.415	0.774	1.925	0.414	0.348	0.284	0.118
	Tapir	0.527	0.329	0.339	0.361	0.701	1.692	0.392	0.330	0.285	0.112
$\frac{T_S}{T_1}$	Ref.	0.828	0.882	0.969	0.801	0.856	0.946	0.910	0.744	0.995	0.969
	Tapir	0.990	0.993	0.986	0.992	0.996	0.998	0.991	0.830	0.993	0.997
$\frac{T_S}{T_{18}}$	Ref.	8.932	11.855	15.982	9.518	11.899	2.105	12.406	7.353	13.292	15.085
	Tapir	9.474	12.684	16.124	10.942	13.138	2.395	13.102	7.755	13.246	15.893

Figure 10. Comparison between executables compiled using Reference and using Tapir/LLVM. Each column refers to a different parallel benchmark described in Figure 9. Rows labeled "Ref." describe executables compiled using Reference, and rows labeled "Tapir" describe executables compiled using Tapir/LLVM. Each measured running time is the minimum over 10 executions, measured in seconds. The pair of rows labeled T_S gives the running time of the executable compiled from the serial elision of each benchmark. The pair of rows labeled T_1 gives the work of each benchmark. The pair of rows labeled T_{18} gives the 18-core running time of each benchmark. The pair of rows labeled T_S/T_1 gives the work efficiency of each compiled benchmark, derived from the first and second pairs of rows. The pair of rows labeled T_S/T_{18} gives the parallel speedup of each compiled executable on 18 cores, derived from the first and third pairs of rows.

are due to system noise. The second pair of rows shows that Tapir/LLVM produces executables with better work than Reference on 15 of the benchmarks. Of the remaining 5 benchmarks, 4 demonstrate less than a 1% difference between their work relative to Tapir/LLVM or Reference. The fourth pair of rows elaborates on the results in the second pair to show that Tapir/LLVM produces executables with nearly optimal work efficiency (within 1%) on 12 of the benchmarks, whereas Reference does so on only 2. The third and fifth pairs of row show that Tapir/LLVM generally produces executables with similar or better parallel speedups than those produced by Reference.

The biggest slowdown created from Tapir/LLVM's compilation occurs on Cholesky, for which the executable produced by Tapir/LLVM has 4% more work than that produced by Reference. In investigating this benchmark, we found that LLVM runs a handful of optimizations on each function before the middle-end optimization and lowering passes in either Tapir/LLVM or Reference. Although these early optimizations have little effect on most programs, they reduce the work of the Reference-compiled Cholesky executable by approximately 20%. Although we experimented with several ways to implement lowering in Reference before these early optimizations, the resulting compilers consistently exhibited bugs on other benchmarks in the suite. In our final design for Reference, we placed the initial lowering pass as early as we could muster while still ensuring that Reference could compile all benchmarks correctly.

7. Related work

This section describes related work in representing parallelism in a compiler IR and in analyzing and optimizing parallel programs.

Various prior research explores compiler optimizations on unstructured parallel threads. For example, some researchers have explored how to find and remove unnecessary synchronization in Java programs [3, 57]. Joisha *et al.* [26] present a technique to detect instructions that are unaffected by parallel threads and can be safely optimized across unstructured parallel control flow. In contrast, our work on Tapir focuses on compiler optimizations for structured parallelism, namely fork-join parallel programs with serial semantics. Although fork-join parallelism may be more restricted than unstructured parallel threads, Tapir demonstrates that many of the optimizations for serial code easily extend to fork-join parallelism. Enabling similar optimizations for unstructured parallel threads appears to be a much harder problem.

Some previous work on compiler optimizations for fork-join parallel programs evaluate which instructions can safely execute in parallel [1] based on concurrency mechanisms supported by a particular memory model. For example, Barik *et al.* [6, 7] use interprocedural analysis to perform various optimizations affecting critical sections of X10 and Habanero-Java programs. Rather than dealing with the complexities of general concurrency mechanisms, Tapir enables compiler optimizations for an easy-to-understand situation: when the optimization respects the serial semantics of the program and does not introduce determinacy races. Compared with general concurrency mechanisms, well-structured parallelism seems to offer a less onerous path to performance.

Khaldi *et al.* [30] modify LLVM IR to support OpenSHMEM parallel programs with the aim of achieving performance in modern network interconnects that support efficient data transfers for partitioned global address spaces (PGAS). Based on the SPIRE methodology [29] for representing parallel code, they augment functions, basic blocks, instructions, identifiers, and types in LLVM IR with execution, synchronization, scheduling, and memory-layout information. In contrast, Tapir models fork-join parallelism for shared-memory multicores, a conceptually simpler context than PGAS systems, and extends LLVM IR minimally using only three instructions. Once again, the Tapir's strong assumption of a fork-join programming model with serial semantics that compiles to a flexible multicore architecture seems to provide both performance and simplicity, albeit at the cost of scalability to huge cluster-based supercomputers that lack strong memory-consistency guarantees.

In contrast with much of the work referenced above, Chatarasi *et al.* [12] focus, as Tapir does, on fork-join programs with serial semantics. Specifically, they examine polyhedral optimizations on OpenMP programs with serial semantics. By combining dependency and happens-before analyses, they manage to enable traditional polyhedral optimizers to work on parallel loops, much as Tapir enables common middle-end compiler optimizations to work on parallel code.

8. Conclusion

To conclude, we would like to leave the reader with three interesting considerations regarding the nature of asymmetry in parallelism, the future of parallel optimizations, and extensions of Tapir-like systems to other models of parallel programming.

Reasoning about logically parallel tasks asymmetrically based on serial semantics can sometimes simplify the understanding of a parallel program's behavior. When a task is spawned to execute in parallel with another, it is natural to reason about the logically parallel tasks as symmetric, because their instructions can execute in any relative order. For parallel programs with serial semantics, however, it is always valid to execute the program on a single processor, which asymmetrically executes one parallel task to completion before starting the other. Serial semantics encourage an asymmetric representation of parallel control flow that is similar enough to its serial elision that most common analyses and transformations for serial programs work on parallel constructs with little or no modification. In particular, serial semantics enables common optimizations on parallel code that can be invalid under other models of parallelism [71].

One of the great benefits of Tapir is that its strategy for representing parallelism makes it easy to write optimization passes specifically for parallel code. Section 4 briefly mentioned some parallel optimization passes we implemented, including parallel-loop scheduling and unnecessary-sync elimination. In addition to helping close the performance gap between serial and parallel versions of code, we hope that the introduction of Tapir will encourage the development and implementation of many more parallel-optimization passes.

Finally, Tapir allows fork-join parallel programs to benefit from both serial and parallel optimizations. Moving forwards, it is natural to wonder whether other models of parallelism, such as pipeline parallelism [13, 33, 49] or data-graph computations [43–45, 51, 52, 62, 64], can take advantage of the Tapir approach.

Acknowledgments

William S. Moses was supported in part by an MIT EECS SuperUROP. This research was supported in part by NSF Grants 1314547 and 1533644, in part by a MIT CSAIL grant from Foxconn, and in part by the Intelligence Advanced Research Projects Activity (IARPA) via Department of Interior/ Interior Business Center (DoI/IBC) contract number D16PC00002. The U.S. Government is authorized to reproduce and distribute reprints for Governmental purposes notwithstanding any copyright annotation thereon. Disclaimer: The views and conclusions contained herein are those of the authors and should not be interpreted as necessarily representing the official policies or endorsements, either expressed or implied, of IARPA, DoI/IBC, or the U.S. Government.

Many thanks to our master bug-finder Tim Kaler of MIT, who also helped us with cloud technology for the artifact evaluation. Shahin Kamali of MIT and Bradley Kuszmaul, formerly of MIT and now of Oracle, were involved in many helpful discussions. Thanks to Johannes Doerfert and Simon Moll of Saarland University, Germany, for their feedback and insights. Thanks to Larry Hardesty of the MIT News Office for asking questions that helped us to simplify Figure 3. We are grateful to the students and staff of the Fall 2016 MIT class 6.172/6.871 *Performance Evaluation of Software Systems* for their patience in using the Tapir/LLVM compiler throughout the semester and reporting bugs. We thank the reviewers for their feedback.

References

[1] S. Agarwal, R. Barik, V. Sarkar, and R. K. Shyamasundar. May-happen-in-parallel analysis of X10 programs. In *PPoPP*, pages 183–193, 2007.

[2] A. V. Aho, M. S. Lam, R. Sethi, and J. D. Ullman. *Compilers: Principles, Techniques, and Tools*. Addison-Wesley, second edition, 2006.

[3] J. Aldrich, C. Chambers, E. Sirer, and S. Eggers. Static analyses for eliminating unnecessary synchronization from Java programs. In A. Cortesi and G. Filé, editors, *Static Analysis*, volume 1694 of *Lecture Notes in Computer Science*, pages 19–38. 1999.

[4] N. S. Arora, R. D. Blumofe, and C. G. Plaxton. Thread scheduling for multiprogrammed multiprocessors. In *SPAA*, pages 119–129, 1998.

[5] E. Ayguade, N. Copty, A. Duran, J. Hoeflinger, Y. Lin, F. Massaioli, X. Teruel, P. Unnikrishnan, and G. Zhang. The design of OpenMP tasks. *IEEE Transactions on Parallel and Distributed Systems*, 20(3):404–418, 2009.

[6] R. Barik and V. Sarkar. Interprocedural load elimination for dynamic optimization of parallel programs. In *PACT*, pages 41–52, 2009.

[7] R. Barik, J. Zhao, and V. Sarkar. Interprocedural strength reduction of critical sections in explicitly-parallel programs. In *PACT*, pages 29–40, 2013.

[8] R. D. Blumofe and C. E. Leiserson. Scheduling multithreaded computations by work stealing. *Journal of the ACM*, 46(5): 720–748, 1999.

[9] R. D. Blumofe, C. F. Joerg, B. C. Kuszmaul, C. E. Leiserson, K. H. Randall, and Y. Zhou. Cilk: An efficient multithreaded runtime system. *Journal of Parallel and Distributed Computing*, 37(1):55–69, 1996.

[10] H.-J. Boehm and S. V. Adve. Foundations of the C++ concurrency memory model. In *PLDI*, pages 68–78, 2008.

[11] V. Cavé, J. Zhao, J. Shirako, and V. Sarkar. Habanero-Java: the new adventures of old X10. In *PPPJ*, pages 51–61, 2011.

[12] P. Chatarasi, J. Shirako, and V. Sarkar. Polyhedral optimizations of explicitly parallel programs. In *PACT*, pages 213–226, 2015.

[13] W. Du, R. Ferreira, and G. Agrawal. Compiler support for exploiting coarse-grained pipelined parallelism. In *SC*, pages 8–21, 2003.

[14] M. Feng and C. E. Leiserson. Efficient detection of determinacy races in Cilk programs. *Theory of Computing Systems*, 32(3):301–326, 1999.

[15] J. T. Fineman and C. E. Leiserson. Race detectors for Cilk and Cilk++ programs. In D. Padua, editor, *Encyclopedia of Parallel Computing*, pages 1706–1719. 2011.

[16] M. Frigo, C. E. Leiserson, and K. H. Randall. The implementation of the Cilk-5 multithreaded language. In *PLDI*, pages 212–223, 1998.

[17] GCC Team. GCC 4.9 release series changes, new features, and fixes. Available at `https://gcc.gnu.org/gcc-4.9/changes.html`, 2014.

[18] GCC Team. GOMP — an OpenMP implementation for GCC. Available at `https://gcc.gnu.org/projects/gomp/`, 2015.

[19] D. Grunwald and H. Srinivasan. Data flow equations for explicitly parallel programs. In *PPoPP*, pages 159–168, 1993.

[20] C. A. R. Hoare. Algorithm 64: Quicksort. *CACM*, 4(7):321, 1961. ISSN 0001-0782.

[21] Intel Corporation. *Intel Cilk Plus Language Specification*, 2010. Document Number: 324396-001US. Available from `http://software.intel.com/sites/products/cilk-plus/cilk_plus_language_specification.pdf`.

[22] Intel Corporation. *Intel Cilk Plus Application Binary Interface Specification*, 2010. Document Number: 324512-001US. Available from `https://software.intel.com/sites/products/cilk-plus/cilk_plus_abi.pdf`.

[23] Intel Corporation. Cilk Plus/LLVM. Available from `http://cilkplus.github.io/`, 2013.

[24] Intel Corporation. *Intel C++ Compiler 16.0 User and Reference Guide*, 2015.

[25] Intel Corporation. Intel Cilk Plus samples. Available from `https://software.intel.com/en-us/code-samples/intel-compiler/intel-compiler-features/intelcilkplus`, 2016.

[26] P. G. Joisha, R. S. Schreiber, P. Banerjee, H. J. Boehm, and D. R. Chakrabarti. A technique for the effective and automatic reuse of classical compiler optimizations on multithreaded code. In *POPL*, pages 623–636, 2011.

[27] H. Jordan, S. Pellegrini, P. Thoman, K. Kofler, and T. Fahringer. INSPIRE: The Insieme parallel intermediate representation. In *PACT*, pages 7–18, 2013.

[28] B. W. Kernighan and D. M. Ritchie. *The C Programming Language*. Prentice Hall, Inc., second edition, 1988.

[29] D. Khaldi, P. Jouvelot, C. Ancourt, and F. Irigoin. SPIRE, a sequential to parallel intermediate representation extension. Technical report, Technical Report CRI/A-487, MINES ParisTech, 2012.

[30] D. Khaldi, P. Jouvelot, F. Irigoin, C. Ancourt, and B. Chapman. LLVM parallel intermediate representation: Design and evaluation using OpenSHMEM communications. In *LLVM*, pages 2:1–2:8, 2015.

[31] J. Knoop, B. Steffen, and J. Vollmer. Parallelism for free: Efficient and optimal bitvector analyses for parallel programs. *ACM TOPLAS*, pages 268–299, 1996.

[32] C. Lattner and V. Adve. LLVM: A Compilation Framework for Lifelong Program Analysis & Transformation. In *CGO*, pages 75–87, 2004.

[33] I.-T. A. Lee, C. E. Leiserson, T. B. Schardl, Z. Zhang, and J. Sukha. On-the-fly pipeline parallelism. *ACM TOPC*, 2(3): 17:1–17:42, 2015.

[34] J. Lee, S. P. Midkiff, and D. A. Padua. Concurrent static single assignment form and constant propagation for explicitly parallel programs. In *LCPC*, pages 114–130, 1997.

[35] C. E. Leiserson. The Cilk++ concurrency platform. *Journal of Supercomputing*, 51(3):244–257, 2010.

[36] LLVM Developer List. LLVMdev discussions on Intel OpenMP proposal. Available from `http:`

//lists.llvm.org/pipermail/llvm-dev/2012-September/053861.html, September 2012.

[37] LLVM Developer List. LLVMdev Parallelization metadata and intrinsics in LLVM (for OpenMP, etc.). Available from http://lists.llvm.org/pipermail/llvm-dev/2012-September/053792.html, September 2012.

[38] LLVM Developer List. LLVMdev discussions on OpenCL SPIR proposal. Available from http://lists.llvm.org/pipermail/llvm-dev/2012-September/053293.html, September 2012.

[39] LLVM Developer List. LLVMdev discussions on parallel IR. Available from http://lists.llvm.org/pipermail/llvm-dev/2015-March/083314.html, March 2015.

[40] LLVM Project. OpenMP®: Support for the OpenMP language. Available at http://openmp.llvm.org/, 2015.

[41] LLVM Project. *LLVM Language Reference Manual*, 2015. Available from http://llvm.org/docs/LangRef.html.

[42] LLVM Project. *LLVM's Analysis and Transform Passes*, 2015. Available from http://llvm.org/docs/Passes.html.

[43] Y. Low, J. Gonzalez, A. Kyrola, D. Bickson, C. Guestrin, and J. M. Hellerstein. GraphLab: A new framework for parallel machine learning. In *UAI*, pages 340–349, 2010.

[44] Y. Low, D. Bickson, J. Gonzalez, C. Guestrin, A. Kyrola, and J. M. Hellerstein. Distributed GraphLab: a framework for machine learning and data mining in the cloud. *Proceedings of the VLDB Endowment*, pages 716–727, 2012.

[45] G. Malewicz, M. H. Austern, A. J. Bik, J. C. Dehnert, I. Horn, N. Leiser, and G. Czajkowski. Pregel: a system for large-scale graph processing. In *SIGMOD*, pages 135–146, 2010.

[46] M. McCool, A. D. Robison, and J. Reinders. *Structured Parallel Programming: Patterns for Efficient Computation*. Elsevier Science, 2012.

[47] S. P. Midkiff and D. A. Padua. Issues in the optimization of parallel programs. In *ICPP*, pages 105–113, 1990.

[48] S. S. Muchnick. *Advanced Compiler Design and Implementation*. Morgan Kaufmann, 1997.

[49] A. Navarro, R. Asenjo, S. Tabik, and C. Cascaval. Analytical modeling of pipeline parallelism. In *PACT*, pages 281–290, 2009.

[50] R. H. B. Netzer and B. P. Miller. What are race conditions? *ACM Letters on Programming Languages and Systems*, 1(1): 74–88, 1992.

[51] D. Nguyen, A. Lenharth, and K. Pingali. A lightweight infrastructure for graph analytics. In *SOSP*, pages 456–471, 2013.

[52] D. Nguyen, A. Lenharth, and K. Pingali. Deterministic Galois: On-demand, portable and parameterless. In *ASPLOS*, pages 499–512, 2014.

[53] D. Novillo, R. Unrau, and J. Schaeffer. Concurrent SSA form in the presence of mutual exclusion. In *ICPP*, pages 356–364, 1998.

[54] OpenMP Architecture Review Board. *OpenMP Application Program Interface, Version 4.0*, July 2013. Available from http://www.openmp.org/mp-documents/OpenMP4.0.0.pdf.

[55] A. Pop and A. Cohen. Preserving high-level semantics of parallel programming annotations through the compilation flow of optimizing compilers. In *CPC*, 2010. URL https://hal.inria.fr/inria-00551518.

[56] W. Pugh. Fixing the Java memory model. In *JAVA*, pages 89–98, 1999.

[57] E. Ruf. Effective synchronization removal for Java. In *PLDI*, pages 208–218, 2000.

[58] R. Rugina and M. C. Rinard. Pointer analysis for structured parallel programs. *TOPLAS*, pages 70–116, Jan. 2003.

[59] V. Sarkar. Analysis and optimization of explicitly parallel programs using the parallel program graph representation. In *LCPC*, pages 94–113, 1998.

[60] V. Sarkar and B. Simons. Parallel program graphs and their classification. In *LCPC*, pages 633–655, 1994.

[61] T. B. Schardl, B. C. Kuszmaul, I.-T. A. Lee, W. M. Leiserson, and C. E. Leiserson. The Cilkprof scalability profiler. In *SPAA*, pages 89–100, 2015.

[62] J. Shun and G. E. Blelloch. Ligra: A lightweight graph processing framework for shared memory. In *PPoPP*, pages 135–146, 2013.

[63] J. Shun, G. E. Blelloch, J. T. Fineman, P. B. Gibbons, A. Kyrola, H. V. Simhadri, and K. Tangwongsan. Brief announcement: the Problem Based Benchmark Suite. In *SPAA*, pages 68–70, 2012.

[64] J. Shun, L. Dhulipala, and G. E. Blelloch. Smaller and faster: Parallel processing of compressed graphs with Ligra+. In *DCC*, pages 403–412, 2015.

[65] H. Srinivasan and D. Grunwald. An efficient construction of parallel static single assignment form for structured parallel programs. Technical report, Technical Report CU-CS-564-91, University of Colorado at Boulder, 1991.

[66] H. Srinivasan and M. Wolfe. Analyzing programs with explicit parallelism. In *LCPC*, pages 405–419, 1991.

[67] H. Srinivasan, J. Hook, and M. Wolfe. Static single assignment for explicitly parallel programs. In *POPL*, pages 260–272, 1993.

[68] R. M. Stallman and the GCC Developer Community. *Using the GNU Compiler Collection (for GCC version 6.1.0)*. Free Software Foundation, 2016.

[69] B. Stroustrup. *The C++ Programming Language*. Addison-Wesley, 4th edition, 2013.

[70] R. Utterback, K. Agrawal, J. T. Fineman, and I.-T. A. Lee. Provably good and practically efficient parallel race detection for fork-join programs. In *SPAA*, pages 83–94, 2016.

[71] V. Vafeiadis, T. Balabonski, S. Chakraborty, R. Morisset, and F. Zappa Nardelli. Common compiler optimisations are invalid in the C11 memory model and what we can do about it. In *POPL*, pages 209–220, 2015.

[72] J. Zhao and V. Sarkar. Intermediate language extensions for parallelism. In *SPLASH*, pages 329–340, 2011.

A. Artifact description

A.1 Abstract

This guide describes how to set up Tapir/LLVM and how to download and run our suite of application benchmarks. In particular, this guide focuses on setting up and running three software components:

- the Tapir/LLVM compiler,
- the PClang front end to Tapir/LLVM, and
- the suite of 20 Cilk application benchmarks described in Figure 9.

We provide instructions to download and build Tapir/LLVM and PClang. We also provide instructions to download the application benchmark suite and run the Tapir/LLVM compiler on that suite.

We have built and tested Tapir/LLVM, PClang, and the test suite on an `x86_64` shared-memory multicore machine running Linux. We provide instructions for obtaining Tapir/LLVM and PClang from our GitHub repositories and setting up the compiler on such a machine. Due to the complexity of the LLVM compiler on which Tapir/LLVM is based, building Tapir/LLVM requires significant computational resources: approximately 50 GiB of disk, 12 GiB of RAM, and anywhere from a few minutes to a couple of hours, depending on the machine. We also provide instructions for obtaining a copy of our test suite from a tarball.

We provide scripts to run all application benchmarks and evaluate the performance results to produce a table of Tapir/LLVM results similar to those in Figure 10. Running all of the tests takes approximately 7 hours. Because we are continuing to develop the Tapir/LLVM compiler, the performance results will not precisely match those in Figure 10.

A.2 Description

Check-list (artifact meta information):

- **Program:** The application benchmark suite includes the 20 Cilk programs described in Figure 9. Packaged with this suite are scripts for compiling and running the tests using the Tapir/LLVM compiler and PClang front end. This suite is publicly available through a tarball, which is approximately 12 GiB in size.
- **Compilation:** Our main software artifact is the Tapir/LLVM compiler. The source code for both Tapir/LLVM and its associated PClang front end are publicly available from GitHub. Due to the complexity of the underlying LLVM and Clang codebases, building Tapir/LLVM and PClang from source requires significant computational resources, even though the changes to implement Tapir/LLVM amount to only about 6000 lines of code.
- **Data set:** The application benchmark suite includes all necessary data sets to run the applications.
- **Run-time environment:** Both Tapir/LLVM and the benchmark suite employ the Intel Cilk Plus runtime system, which is available on several modern Linux distributions via a mainstream package. The evaluation also employs several Linux commands which are similarly available through mainstream packages. We have built and tested Tapir/LLVM on Ubuntu 16.04 and Fedora 24. Root accesses is not required to install Tapir/LLVM, PClang, or the application benchmark suite, but it is required to install the Intel Cilk Plus runtime system and auxiliary Linux commands.
- **Hardware:** We have built and tested Tapir/LLVM on an `x86_64` system. A shared-memory multicore system is required to execute the compiled benchmarks in parallel.
- **Output:** Running the benchmark tests produces a table of performance results similar to Figure 10. These performance results are likely to vary between machines. Moreover, because we are continuing to develop Tapir/LLVM and PClang, these performance results will not perfectly match the values in Figure 10.
- **Experiment workflow:** We provide scripts with the application benchmark suite to run the tests and aggregate the results. The total running time of this experiment is approximately 7 hours on an AWS `c4.8xlarge` instance, but can vary between machines.
- **Experiment customization:** You can run separate sets of tests within the benchmark suite. You can also write your own programs to compile using Tapir/LLVM and PClang. The PClang front end supports a variant of the Cilk programming language and produces Tapir code that can be processed and optimized by Tapir/LLVM.
- **Publicly available?:** Tapir/LLVM and PClang are publicly available on GitHub. The test suite is publicly available via a tarball.

How delivered: You can download and build Tapir/LLVM and PClang from our GitHub repositories, and you can download the application benchmark test suite from a tarball. Although Tapir represents a relatively small modification to the LLVM compiler, it inherits a good deal of complexity from the underlying LLVM software infrastructure. The instructions below aim to streamline the process of building and testing Tapir/LLVM in spite of this complexity.

Hardware dependencies: Tapir/LLVM, PClang, and the test suite have been built and tested to run on `x86_64`. A shared-memory multicore system is needed to evaluate the parallel performance of programs compiled using Tapir/LLVM.

Software dependencies: We have tested Tapir/LLVM, PClang, and the test suite on Ubuntu 16.04 and on Fedora 24. Building Tapir/LLVM and PClang requires `cmake` and a C/C++ compiler. The test script uses `taskset` and `numactl` to quiesce the system for running each benchmark, specifically, to mitigate the effects of hyperthreading and NUMA on the execution of the tests. The test script also uses `bc` to calculate derived values from the measured running times of the tests.

Datasets: The tarball of application benchmarks includes all necessary data sets to execute these applications.

A.3 Building Tapir/LLVM from source

This section describes how to download the source code for Tapir/LLVM and PClang from GitHub and build them. These instructions assume you are building Tapir/LLVM on an `x86_64` system running Linux.

System requirements. Building Tapir/LLVM and PClang involves building the LLVM and Clang systems that they extend. Because of the size of the underlying LLVM and Clang codebases, you need a relatively powerful machine in order to build the compiler in a timely fashion. Approximately 50 GiB of disk space and 12 GiB of memory are needed to compile LLVM and Clang. A fresh build of LLVM and Clang can take substantial time to complete, e.g., approximately an hour on one processor of an AWS `c4.8xlarge` instance. The build script will attempt to use parallel processors to speed up compilation. See `http://llvm.org/docs/CMake.html` for more information on building LLVM and Clang.

1. Install the requisite software to build Tapir/LLVM and PClang, namely, `cmake`, `gcc`, and `git`.
2. Download the sources of Tapir/LLVM and PClang from GitHub:

```
$ git clone --recursive \
> https://github.com/wsmoses/Tapir-Meta.git
```

   The source is approximately 800 MiB in size.

3. Compile Tapir/LLVM and PClang:

```
$ cd Tapir-Meta/
$ bash ./build.sh
```

   This script will build Tapir/LLVM and PClang and store the compiled binaries in `Tapir-Meta/tapir/build`. If the build succeeds, the final line of output will be `Installation successful`.

4. Set up your environment variables to use Tapir/LLVM and PClang:

```
$ source ./setup-env.sh
```

   This script will add the `Tapir-Meta/tapir/build/bin/` subdirectory to your path, so that the `clang` command will refer to Tapir/LLVM and PClang.

A.4 Running the benchmark suite

This section describes how you can download the application benchmark suite described in Figure 9 and test Tapir/LLVM on these benchmarks.

1. Install the requisite software to download and run the tests, namely, `bc`, `libcilkrts`, `numactl`, `python`, `taskset`, and `wget`.
2. Download the tarball containing the application benchmark suite and unpack it:

```
$ wget http://tinyurl.com/TapirLLVMTesting -O testing.tar
$ tar -xvf testing.tar
```

   This tarball is approximately 12 GiB in size. Unpacking the tarball creates the `testing/` subdirectory of the current working directory that contains the application benchmark suite.

3. Run the test script:

```
$ cd testing
$ ./test.sh
```

   The test script takes approximately 7 hours to run. The script compiles each benchmark in the test suite twice using Tapir/LLVM: once as a parallel program, and once as the program's serial elision. All compilations use optimization level `-O3`. The test script runs each compiled executable 10 times using 1 worker thread and 10 times using 18 worker threads.

A.5 Evaluation and expected result

Once the test script finishes running, the results can be summarized into a table similar to Figure 10 as follows:

```
$ ./results.sh > results.csv
```

This command will produce `results.csv`, a table of tab-separated values that contains the minimum running time from each set of 10 runs of a particular executable on a particular worker count. The table also contains derived work-efficiency and parallel speedup values for each benchmark program.

Because these results are performance measurements, they are likely to vary from run to run and from system to system. Moreover, we are continuing to develop the Tapir/LLVM compiler and PClang, meaning that your results will not pecisely match those in Figure 10.

A.6 Experiment customization

We provide scripts for running individual sets of tests within the test suite. The `testCilk.sh`, `testIntel.sh`, and `testPBBS.sh` scripts recompiles and reruns all tests from the MIT Cilk benchmark suite, the set of Intel Cilk Plus example programs, and the CMU Problem-Based Benchmark Suite, respectively. Running any of these scripts updates the performance results for the designated subset of tests. Rerunning the `results.sh` script produces a new table with the latest test results from each subset.

You can write your own programs and compile them using PClang and Tapir/LLVM. The PClang front end is *not* a fully featured Cilk front end, however. For more information on the source language parsed by PClang, please see `testing/PClang-README.txt`.

A Multicore Path to Connectomics-on-Demand

Alexander Matveev * Yaron Meirovitch * Hayk Saribekyan
Wiktor Jakubiuk Tim Kaler Gergely Odor
David Budden Aleksandar Zlateski Nir Shavit
Massachusetts Institute of Technology

Abstract

The current design trend in large scale machine learning is to use distributed clusters of CPUs and GPUs with MapReduce-style programming. Some have been led to believe that this type of horizontal scaling can reduce or even eliminate the need for traditional algorithm development, careful parallelization, and performance engineering. This paper is a case study showing the contrary: that the benefits of algorithms, parallelization, and performance engineering, can sometimes be so vast that it is possible to solve "cluster-scale" problems on a single commodity multicore machine.

Connectomics is an emerging area of neurobiology that uses cutting edge machine learning and image processing to extract brain connectivity graphs from electron microscopy images. It has long been assumed that the processing of connectomics data will require mass storage, farms of CPU/GPUs, and will take months (if not years) of processing time. We present a high-throughput connectomics-on-demand system that runs on a multicore machine with less than 100 cores and extracts connectomes at the terabyte per hour pace of modern electron microscopes.

CCS Concepts **• Computing methodologies → Concurrent algorithms; • Computer systems organization → Multicore architectures; • Computing methodologies → Neural networks; • Applied computing → Computational biology**

Keywords Multicore Programming, Machine Learning, Big-Data, Connectomics

*These authors contributed equally to this work

PPoPP '17, February 04-08, 2017, Austin, TX, USA

DOI: http://dx.doi.org/10.1145/3018743.3018766

1. Introduction

The conventional wisdom in machine learning is that large scale "big-data" problems should be addressed using distributed clusters of CPUs, GPUs or specialized tensor processing hardware in the cloud [6, 11, 20–22, 36, 63]. This paper presents a solution to one of the most demanding big-data machine learning areas: connectomics. It provides a case study in how novel algorithms combined with proper parallelization and performance engineering, can reduce the problem from a large cluster to a single commodity multicore server (that can be placed in any neurobiology lab), eliminating the crucial bottleneck of transferring data to the cloud at terabyte-an-hour rates.

1.1 High-Throughput Connectomics

Perhaps neuroscience's greatest challenge is to provide a theory that accommodates the highly complicated structure and function of neural circuits. These circuits, found in flies, in mammals, and ultimately, in humans, are conjectured to be the substrate that enables the complex behavior we call "thought." However, to this day, our ability to provide such a theory has been hampered by our limited ability to view even small fragments of these circuits in their entirety. Neurobiologists have had sparse circuit maps of mammalian brains for over a century [57]. However, as surprising as this may seem, no one has seen the dense connectivity of even a single neuron in cortex, that is, all of its input and output connections (called synapses) to other neurons. No one has been able to map the full connectivity among even a small group of neighboring neurons, not to mention the tens of thousands of neurons that constitute a "cortical column." Without such maps, it would seem hard to understand how a brain consisting of billions of interconnected neurons actually works. Would you believe that someone understood how a modern microprocessor worked if they could tell you in great detail how individual transistors operated but were unable to describe how these transistors are interconnected?

Mapping brain networks at the level of synaptic connections, a field called *connectomics*, began in the 1970s with a study of the 302-neuron nervous system of a worm [67].

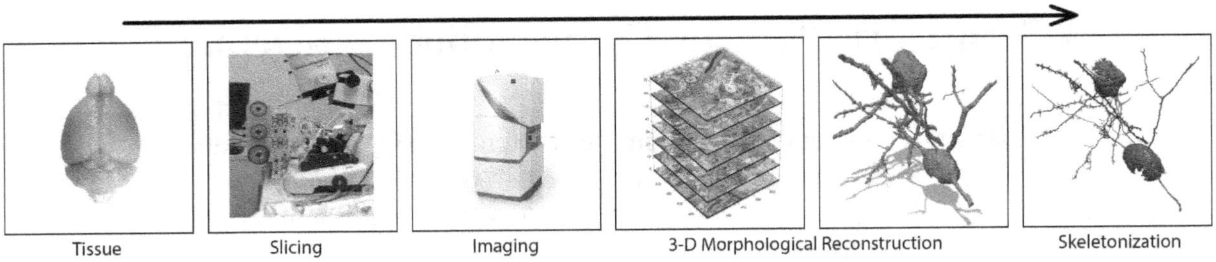

Figure 1: The Stages of a high-throughput connectomics pipeline.

This study, which required capturing and combining hundreds of electron microscopy images, was done by hand and took 8 years. Manual mapping of minute volumes of neural tissue have recently produced breakthrough results in neuroscience [28, 34, 49]. However, extending the approach to the millions and billions of neurons in higher animals seems an unattainable goal without a fast and fully automated pipeline.

Recent advances in the design of multi-beam electron microscopes now allow researchers to collect the nanometer resolution images, necessary to view neurons and the synaptic connections between them, at unprecedented rates. A cubic millimeter of brain tissue, enough to contain a mouse cortical column, is within reach. This is only a tiny sliver of brain, about the size of a grain of sand, but it will contain about 100 thousand neurons and a billion synapses. The cubic millimeter will constitute about two petabytes of imagery that will be collected in about 6 months using a 61-beam electron microscope that generates half a terabyte of imagery per hour [15, 38].

A modern connectomics pipeline [40], as depicted in Figure 1, consists of a physical part and a computational part. The physical part takes a piece of stained brain tissue embedded in a resin, slices it thousands of times using a special microtome device, and feeds these minute slices into an electron microscope that scans them and produces separate images of the slices [15, 61]. The computational part of the pipeline, the focus of this paper, then takes the thousands of separate 2-dimensional images, reconstructs the 3-dimensional neurons within them, and produces skeletonizations or graphs that capture their morphological and connectivity properties.

However, a viable solution to the computational problem of extracting the skeletonizations and connectivity maps from the image data still seems far away. Using existing algorithms and at the present computing rates, the common assumption is that extracting the connectivity of the circuits within two petabytes of data may take years and require supercomputing clusters [38, 66]. It is even unclear how to efficiently move the vast amounts of data from the microscope to a large scale storage and compute facility where it will be processed [40]. The prospect of connectomics-on-demand, where neurobiology labs around the world each run their own microscopes and extract connectomes "as needed" seems far far away.

This paper takes a first step towards proving the feasibility of designing a high-throughput connectomics-on-demand system that runs on a multicore machine with less than 100 cores and extracts connectomes at the terabyte-per-hour pace of modern microscopes. Such a system, once achieved, will eliminate the need to transfer and store petabytes of data in special warehouses. It could be readily deployed in labs across the world, allowing scientists to view connectomes as they come off the scope. Down the road, such efficient connectomics systems could make it feasible for neurobiologists to extract the complete connectome of a mouse cortex of about 12 million neurons and 120 billion synapses from about 100 petabytes of data, and eventually make it possible to analyze exabyte-scale parts of the connectome of both healthy and diseased human brains (Human brain has roughly 100 billion neurons and a quadrillion synapses).*

1.2 Towards an Automated Terabyte-Per-Hour Connectomics Pipeline

The "proof of concept" connectomics system we present here processes a terabyte of data, from image-stack to detailed skeletons, in less than **4 hours** on a single 72 core Haswell-based multicore machine with 500GB of memory. The upcoming generation of both GPU and CPU chips, with some further optimizations (see our performance section), easily place it within the target terabyte-an-hour performance envelope of todays fastest electron microscopes. One should contrast this with the recent connectomics system of Roncal *et al.* [58] that uses a cluster of 100 AMD Opteron cores, 1 terabyte of memory, and 27 GeForce GTX Titan cards to process a terabyte in **4.5 weeks**, and the state-of-the-art distributed MapReduce based system of Plaza and Berg [56] that uses 512 cores and 2.9 terabytes of memory to process a terabyte of data in **140 hours** (not including skeletonization). Importantly, the speed of our pipeline does not

*These numbers may sound like science fiction, yet as Lichtman and Sanes note by analogy [39], sequencing the first human genome took multiple labs around the world a concerted effort over 15 years, while today a single lab can sequence a human genome within hours.

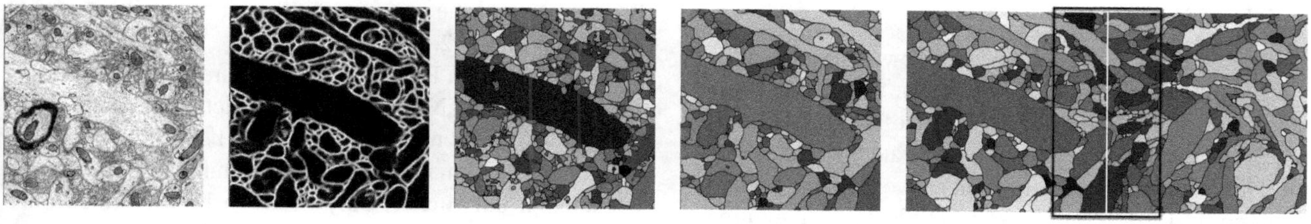

Figure 2: 2D visualization of connectomics pipeline stages: (1) Electron microscope (EM) image. (2) Membrane probabilities generated by CNN. (3) Over-segmentation generated by Watershed. (4) Neuron reconstruction generated by agglomeration. (5) Pipeline inter-block merging: for each two adjacent blocks, the pipeline slices a boundary sub-block and executes agglomeration.

come at the expense of accuracy, which is on par or better than existing systems in the literature [29, 56, 58] (using the accepted *variation of information* (VI) measure [44]).

Our high-level pipeline design builds on prior work [29, 42, 51, 52, 55, 56]. It passes the data through several stages as seen in Figure 2. The image data is split into blocks. The pipeline first runs a convolutional neural network (CNN) on the separate image blocks to detect the boundaries of neurons. The neuronal objects defined by the boundaries are then segmented into objects by a watershed algorithm. At this point the image is over-segmented, that is, neuronal objects are fragmented. The next step in the reconstruction is to run an agglomeration phase that merges all the fragments in a block into complete objects. Then the blocks are merged, so that objects now span the entire volume. Finally, as depicted in Figure 8, the objects are skeletonized.

1.3 Our Contributions

- A new CPU execution engine for CNNs that scales well on multicore systems, processing 1024x1024 images 70x faster than previous state-of-the-art [72] on a single 18-core Haswell CPU. Our code applies GCC-Cilk (a state-of-the-art work-stealing scheduler [3]), is optimized to leverage Intel AVX2 instructions [68] and maximizes memory reuse in L1, L2 and L3 cache subsystems. Analysis shows that this code achieves 80% utilization of the peak theoretical FLOPS of the system on a single-thread and scales almost linearly, compared to previous approaches (Caffe CNN framework with Intel MKL [10, 65]) that exhibit only 20% utilization and no scalability beyond 4 threads. The remaining performance gap is obtained by implementing minimal "dense" (fully-convolutional) CNN inference, which involves 284x fewer computations than naive implementations.
- A new GPU execution engine for CNNs that leverages custom fast Fourier transforms (FFTs) and the latest cuDNN primitives [53]. The system performs ~2x faster for our CNN benchmarks than previous state-of-the-art [50] on a Titan X GPU.
- Parallelized and performance engineered version of NeuroProof, a system originally developed in Janelia Research Labs by Parag, Chakrobarty and Plaza [54]. This system implements an agglomeration procedure that reconstructs 3D neurons from the watershed oversegmentation. Specifically, we redesigned the Regional Adjacency Graph (RAG) algorithm as an augmented merge-sort, efficiently defer expensive operations that occur during constructions and traversals of RAGs, and batch computations for lazy execution. Our implementation is 2.3x faster on a single-thread, and has 85x scalability factor on our 72-core server (super-linear factor due to Hyper-Threading).
- Two new algorithms for the connectomics domain: (1) a new inter-block merging algorithm that, unlike prior approaches, applies parallelized NeuroProof to optimize object-pair merges, and (2) a parallel skeletonization algorithm that uses novel techniques and GCC-Cilk based chromatic scheduling [25, 26] to execute efficiently on multicores. We describe the algorithmic side in more detail in [46].

We believe that our work departs from existing systems by showing that a combination of new algorithms, proper parallelization of existing algorithms, modern scheduling using languages like Cilk, and performance engineering of code to fully utilize CPU resources, can move the connectomics problem from the large scale distributed systems space to run on a commodity shared-memory multicore system. This might be true for other big-data machine-learning based problems in medicine and the life sciences, and even for problems where big systems are necessary, our approach may provide insights on how to make individual system elements much faster and scalable.

1.4 Related Work

The image segmentation approach we use was developed by [1] and suggested for automatic electron microscopy segmentation by [51]. It is used by most of todays systems [29, 42, 51, 52, 55, 56]. Increasingly accurate membrane predictors based on convolutional neural networks have recently been proposed [8, 59]. Our system implements a solution that is inspired by these algorithms, is on-par with their current accuracy levels, and yet is simpler and faster to execute. Other studies have focused on new approaches to segmentation of supervoxels (e.g., [42]). Further research however is required to benchmark their accuracy on even gigabyte size datasets, so at this time their scalability cannot be addressed.

We are aware of three previous connectomics pipelines: the original RhoAna pipeline by Kaynig *et al.* [29], the system by Roncal *et al.* that extends RhoAna [58], and state-of-the-art Plaza and Berg's Spark-based system [56] that uses NeuroProof.

2. System Overview

This is the story of how one can replace the use of a large distributed system with a single multicore machine. Although a large distributed system may have tremendous computational resources at its disposal, its raw computing power comes with a cost of additional overheads and system complexity, e.g. data must be moved over the network, and the system must support a degree of fault tolerance [6, 12, 37, 56, 70, 71]. These overheads tend to be small for problems that are embarrassingly parallel, but can come to dominate the execution time of more complex computations that need to operate on shared data. In addition, the opportunities to obtain performance within a single multicore are abundant, and can result in performance improvements that rival or even dwarf those obtained through horizontal scaling. As we will see, the connectomics problem requirements can be satisfied using a single multicore machine to execute a pipeline of carefully designed multicore algorithms that efficiently utilize a machine's available computing cycles, take advantage of the low shared-memory communication overheads, and parallelize across cores using efficient task scheduling tools.

2.1 Pipeline Structure

The input to our pipeline is a sequence of aligned 2D images each of which represents a single slice of a 3D volume of brain that was captured at high resolution (~3-4nm) by an electron microscope. These images are broken down into smaller sub-images with a standardized size of 1024x1024 pixels, which are then grouped into blocks of 1024x1024x100 pixels. The pipeline executes a segmentation procedure that extracts the neuronal objects within each block, and then executes an inter-block merging procedure that "combines" the per-block segmentations to obtain a complete segmentation of the original input volume [46]. These stages of the connectomics pipeline are illustrated in 2D within Figure 2.

First, as seen in Parts 1 and 2 of Figure 2, a convolutional neural network (CNN) is executed to detect membranes (or cell borders). This network was trained using "ground truth" annotation by human experts. The training process is time-consuming, but since it only needs to be performed once on an annotated subset of the dataset it does not impact the pipeline's throughput. The result of applying the CNN to a subvolume is a new 1024x1024x100 block where each pixel indicates a membrane probability between 0 and 1. Since the CNN may run on blocks independently, this stage of the pipeline may be executed in a distributed manner. It turns out, however, that careful performance engineering enabled this stage of the pipeline to execute sufficiently fast on a single multicore machine. In fact, we found that our optimized code for executing the CNN was able to significantly outperform existing state-of-the-art CPU [10, 65, 72] and GPU [50] implementations. In Section 3 we describe the design of this CNN, and the steps taken to ensure that the our implementations made efficient use of the machine's compute cycles, L1/L2/L3 caches, and disk.

Next, as seen in Part 3 of Figure 2, a 3D watershed algorithm executes on the membrane probability map. The watershed algorithm performs a BFS-style flood from "seed" pixels that have 0 probability of being a membrane, to pixels with higher probability. The result of the watershed execution is a new block in which segments (3D objects) have been formed around seeds, each with a segment identifier. Methods of parallelizing watershed have been described in the literature (e.g. [48]), but it turned out that our pipeline was able to achieve better performance by engineering an efficient sequential algorithm with low-memory consumption. This strategy allowed us to obtain a watershed algorithm that is an order of magnitude faster than the code provided in the popular OpenCV [23] library, and whose low-memory requirements permit us to run many independent instances of the algorithm on a shared memory machine. Section 4 describes the design of this serial watershed algorithm in greater detail.

The segments produced by the watershed algorithm represent an over-segmentation of the true neuronal objects; i.e. each neuron might be fragmented into many smaller parts, as shown in Part 3 of Figure 2. To obtain segments that represent whole neurons an agglomeration algorithm is employed that merges segments that lie within the same 3D object. The result of the agglomeration procedure is a collection of larger segments that each represent a whole neuronal object, as is illustrated (in 2D) in Part 4 of Figure 2. The agglomeration procedure used by the pipeline is based upon the serial NeuroProof agglomeration algorithm of Parag *et al.* [54]. We reformulated the Neuroproof procedure to use parallel algorithms, and performed a variety of performance optimizations to reduce the total work and memory usage. These optimizations obtained a 2.3x improvement in serial runtime, and a 6.5x improvement when executing on 4-cores. Moreover, we achieve near-linear scalability (when running multiple 4-core instances simultaneously) which provides an additional 82x speedup over the optimized serial code on our 72-core server with HyperThreading. Section 5 describes, in greater detail, the parallelization techniques and performance optimizations that were employed to optimize the agglomeration stage of the pipeline.

After a segmentation has been obtained for each block, the pipeline executes an efficient inter-block merging procedure on the reconstructed blocks [46]. Here we utilize the shared memory properties of the machine in which I/O operations are automatically cached by the OS kernel. Thus, for every two adjacent blocks, our block merging algorithm carves out a thin sub-block near the shared boundary and employs a variant of our parallel agglomeration procedure to identify and merge objects across this boundary. Part 5 of Figure 2 is a two dimensional rendering of this merging process. The result of each merging is a small file containing pairs of segment identifiers that should be combined, and it is straightforward (and inexpensive) to combine all of them into a full segmentation. This contrasts with the approach of Plaza and Berg [56] where a sophisticated merge algorithm must be executed across many machines in the network. In our case, there is no need to perform expensive data-transfers over the network and to support a complex failure detection and recovery mechanisms, since the whole system executes on a single server. The design of the inter-block merging procedure is discussed further in Section 6.

The final step of the pipeline skeletonizes the volume segmentation (see Figure 8) on a per-block basis. A skeleton provides a space-efficient one dimensional representation of a 3D volume that runs a long the volume's medial axis, allowing for faster and easier analysis of the biological structures. It is also an intermediate step on the way to creating a graph representation of the neuronal objects. We experimented with various skeletonization algorithms and found out that a subfield "thinning" algorithm [2] fits our purposes best. Thinning starts with points on the object boundary and repeatedly removes ones that do not affect overall topological connectivity. We devised a simple and efficient parallel algorithm for extracting volume skeletons using chromatic scheduling [25, 26] to efficiently schedule the parallel order of which points are considered for deletion doing the thinning process. The details of the skeletonization algorithm are discussed further in Section 7.

3. CNN-based Membrane Detection

The first stage of the pipeline employs a *convolutional neural network* (CNN) [31] to identify cell membranes within the *electron microscopy* (EM) images obtained from the microscope. The output of this stage is a new set of images whose pixels (ranging from 0 to 1) denote the probability that a particular pixel is part of a membrane. A CNN system is typically composed of two components: the *network architecture* which defines layers of perceptrons and their connectivity, and the *computational framework* that executes an architecture's forward propagation over a trained network. In Section 3.1 we describe the *MaxoutNet* CNN architecture that is used in our pipeline to compute membrane probabilities [46]. In Sections 3.2 and 3.3 we describe CPU and GPU-based implementations of our computational framework for executing CNNs.

There are a variety of methods for devising efficient computational frameworks for fully-convolutional neural networks: *e.g.* patch-based sliding windows [8], dilated convolution [69], strided kernels [64], max filtering [32, 72] and filter rarefaction [41]. In our framework, we utilize "maxpooling fragments," which apply the traditional maxpooling operation of CNNs to different offsets of the input image [19, 43]. The resultant images are then recombined to produce the final dense result. The advantage of this approach is that maxpool fragments generate independent matricies that are contiguous in memory, which is leveraged for improved parallelization and memory-locality in both of our CPU and GPU-based implementations.

3.1 Our Network Architecture

The pipeline uses a CNN architecture called *MaxoutNet* that we recently proposed in [46] based on prior work in connectomics [28, 30]. The *MaxoutNet* architecture consists of 4 *ConvPool* layers of alternating convolution/maxpool pairs aggregated with a maxout function, and a final convolution that implements an inner-product. Convolutional layers use 4×4 kernels with stride 1 and either 8 or 32 channels, which combined with stride 2 max-pooling yields a 105×105 field-of-view for each output pixel. For our benchmarks, described in Sections 3.2.4 and 3.3.1, we simplify this network and execute only the last 3 layers of *ConvPool*.

In our pipeline execution, *MaxoutNet* leverages the fact that our input EM images are 3nm resolution (2048×2048) by performing subsampling of the input by executing standard pooling in the first ConvPool layer, while executing "dense" poolings in the next layers. This produces a 2-fold subsampled 1024×1024 output image, and accelerates the network by a factor of 4 without a significant loss of accuracy.

3.2 A Fast CPU framework for CNNs

We introduce *XNN*, a CNN framework implemented in C and inline assembly for Haswell CPUs. The CPU architecture provides support for AVX2 instructions and includes two FMA units, allowing the chip to execute 32 floating point operations per cycle [68]. As a result, a single 2.5 GHz 18-core Haswell chip can theoretically produce 1.44 TFLOPS (compared to state-of-the-art GPU, like NVIDIA's Titan X, that theoretically produces 6TFLOPS). It is, of course, quite challenging to achieve these peak floating point utilizations on either CPU or GPU architectures, and approaching this ideal requires careful engineering techniques that take into account the hardware specifics.

The remainder of this section describes the techniques we applied to optimize *XNN* for the Haswell CPU architecture which enable *XNN* to achieve $70 - 80\%$ FLOP utilization for direct convolutions. Note that FFT-style convolutions can provide additional speedups, as we describe in [4], however, here we focus on low-level performance-engineering of direct convolutions.

3.2.1 Haswell AVX2 SIMD Parallelization

We initially adopted Intel's MLK convolution primitives [10]. However, our results showed that the CPU FLOPS utilization for MKL was only ~20%, so we reimplemented this critical component with hand-crafted AVX2 assembly.

One of the hurdles that must be overcome to use AVX2 instructions is that one must ensure memory operands have properly aligned addresses. This constraint complicates or even precludes the use of AVX2 instructions in standard convolutional windows that slide over a 2D matrix since the window will contain unaligned memory locations. This led us to an alternate strategy that is based on the observation that a CNN's internal matrices are typically 3D, where the first two dimensions are spatial and the third dimension denotes the channels of the CNN. Instead of vectorizing along the spatial dimension, we vectorize along this channel dimension. This strategy assumes that the number of channels is a multiple of the AVX width, but this constraint is not problematic for CNNs that already use many channels.

Our first implementation was a simple loop over the channel dimension, which did not provide a high CPU floating point utilization, since the GCC compiler could not unroll it optimally. To improve this, we manually unrolled the loops with AVX2 C-inline assembly so that the most inner loop computes 6 convolutions. We interleaved the inner loop's AVX register load, FMA compute, and store vector operations of the 6 convolutions, in a way that maximizes the usage of the two FMA units of the Haswell CPU. In addition, we made the inner and outer loop bounds and counter increments constant at compile-time, to allow maximal usage of GCC's automatic code vectorization and loop unrolling for both inner and outer loops that wrap the manually unrolled convolutions.

3.2.2 Cilk-based Concurrency and Caching

We used Cilk [18, 35], a work-stealing scheduler that is supported by GCC 4.8, to dynamically generate multi-core fine-grained tasks. The key advantage of Cilk is that it provides a "fork-join" primitive that scales well to many cores and retains the serial semantics of the program (*i.e.* the removal of parallel control constructs does not change the behavior of the code on 1-core). Cilk uses a sophisticated combination of per-thread double-ended queues, and a clever work-stealing

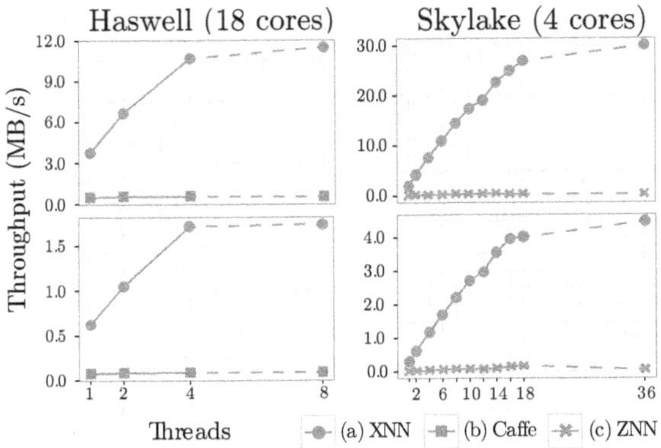

Figure 3: Throughput of the three CPU-based CNN implementations evaluated using 8 and 32-channel MaxoutNet.

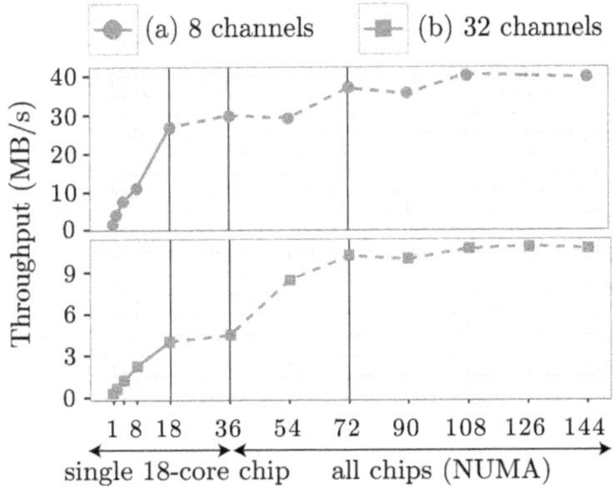

Figure 4: Throughput of the XNN up to 144 hardware threads on our 4 socket system.

algorithm that is provably efficient, and has low memory-contention on shared memory systems.

Our implementation applies the Cilk "fork-join" primitive to all "for-loops" that have no loop iteration dependencies, simplifying our parallelization effort. However, we still require that memory accessed by executing Cilk threads fits into the L3 cache. The L3 cache is much faster than main memory, and having threads working on data that resides in L3 is key to ensuring a high ratio of compute to memory access, which is important for scalability. For example, large matrix operations (*e.g.* convolution) are executed over sub-matrices that each fit into the L3 cache, with a set of threads operating over this sub-matrix before proceeding to the next. We observed that this approach improves scalability by a factor of 3-4x.

3.2.3 Memory Usage

Another important aspect of the implementation is the amount of memory used to compute the forward propagation pass of the CNN network. Since we are only concerned with the performance of forward propagation, we optimized the memory usage significantly by allocating only two large matrix buffers, one for input and one for output, and then reuse (swap) these buffers between layers. As a result, the memory usage is bounded by the largest input/output size of a single CNN layer, which reduces cache trashing and OS paging effects. Note that memory is only allocated at the start, *i.e.* there are no dynamic memory allocations during the computation itself that could introduce contention and bottlenecks.

3.2.4 CPU Benchmarking

Benchmarking was performed on the same shared memory server we use to run our pipeline: a 4-socket machine with Intel *Haswell* 18 core chips and 512 GB of RAM. We also benchmarked a machine equipped with a single 4-core Intel *Skylake* CPU with 64 GB RAM.

We benchmarked our XNN framework against the most efficient known multicore CNN frameworks: the Caffe framework of Yangqing *et al.* [24] and the ZNN framework of Zlateski *et al.* [72]. Throughput was evaluated using 1024×1024 (6 nm) images. We benchmarked all three using a lightweight version of MaxoutNet with 3 fully convolutional ConvPool layers (field-of-view = 53) because the sub-sampling required for the fourth layer (3 nm data) is available only in our XNN framework. We benchmark for both 8 and 32 channels. To ensure best performance, we compiled with the Intel C++ Compiler (ICC) version 16.0.0, optimized for maximum speed (`-O3`), linked against Intel Threading Building Blocks (TBB) version 4.4 (`libtbbmalloc`, `libtbbmalloc_proxy`), and Intel Math Kernel Library (MKL) version 11.3 with enabled FFT caching, and single-precision floating-point arithmetic.

The results of this benchmarking are presented in Figure 3. In this execution, we perform a scalability test on a single 18-core chip: an input is set to a fixed size and we increase the number of threads. By binding multi-threading to one chip we disable the NUMA-effects for this test (expensive inter-chip communication). It is evident that our XNN CPU framework exhibits substantial throughput improvement over Caffe and ZNN. First, one can see that there is a significant difference in single-threaded performance, which is the effect of the hand-crafted assembly of XNN that utilizes the two FMA AVX2 units of Haswell CPU. Second, the scalability of XNN is almost linear, 15x over a single thread on 18 cores. This is achieved by constraining active threads to operate on memory sets that fit into the L3 cache while using Cilk to manage short-living jobs.

Figure 4 presents the results of XNN executed as a single instance (fixed input) on all 72 cores across 4 sockets, running up to 144 threads to utilize hyperthreading. As can be seen, for the 32 channel execution (green) linear scalability is evident up to 18 cores and plateaus all the way to 36 cores, as hyperthreading provides only 10-20% boost in performance. Increasing threads from 36 to 72 utilizes additional cores to again provide pseudo-linear scalability. Beyond 72 cores, additional threads leverage hyperthreading for a minimal further improvement. For 8 channels (red), the smaller network size generates low latency Cilk tasks that introduce more pressure on the software implementation. There is still linear scalability up to 18 threads, but only small improvement is evident beyond 36 cores. This is because the overhead of threading (NUMA side effects) is substantial compared to the performance benefit from adding additional cores.

In our pipeline execution, we overcome these NUMA overheads by combining multi-processing with multi-threading. Specifically, we execute multiple instances of XNN (each bound to a specific chip) with a empirically optimized number of threads, resulting in a 2.8x speedup. Generating these instances increases the RAM requirements (not problematic for our 512 GB RAM system).

3.3 A Fast GPU Framework for CNNs

In this section we present *gpuZNN*, a GPU-based CNN framework that improves upon the previously published ZNN [72] to optimize forward propagation throughput.

The SIMT programming model and limited amount of memory available on a GPU require a different implementation than our XNN CPU framework. To saturate the GPU, we process multiple input images simultaneously. We also leverage the fact that all sub-samplings of the "dense" computation have equal size, which is equivalent to processing multiple inputs of a layer at the same time.

Most of our convolutional primitives use cuDNN's low level implementations [53]. To address the large memory overhead of some primitives, we allow the computation to be split into multiple stages, computing a subset of results at the time. This is accomplished by computing a subset of input batches and/or subset of output images (feature maps). This can reduce the parallelization potential, but reducing the memory overhead can allow for using a computationally cheaper primitive. We also implement optimized FFT-based convolutional primitives with very low memory overhead. Batched 1D FFTs and memory reshuffling was used to efficiently utilize the GPU.

Sub-sampling layers (maxpooling and maxout) were implemented using cuDNN's maxpooling primitive. We minimized the number of calls to the primitives such that each primitive performs more computation and can thus saturate the GPU. To allow this, we implicitly gathered the inputs and scattered the results for each call. Implicit gather/scatter is performed by providing the shapes and strides for all inputs/outputs from which the memory location of each element can be computed.

3.3.1 GPU CNN Benchmarking

We benchmarked our gpuZNN implementation relative to the fastest available GPU frameworks [7] on an NVIDIA GeForce GTX Titan X (3072 cores, 1.0 GHz, 12 GB memory). Specifically, we benchmarked the MaxoutNet network with both 8 and 32 channels for three GPU frameworks: (a)

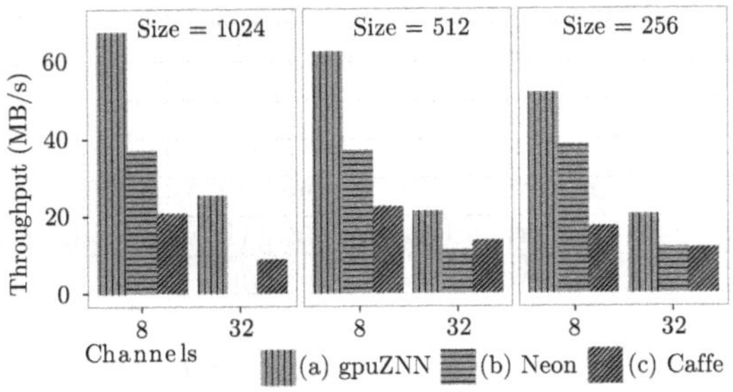

Figure 5: Throughput of GPU-based CNNs using 8 and 32-channel MaxoutNet architectures.

Method	Type	8-channel MaxoutNet Throughput (MB/s)	32-channel MaxoutNet Throughput (MB/s)
XNN	CPU (72-core)	111.1	16.67
gpuZNN	GPU (Titan X)	67.61	25.28
Neon	GPU (Titan X)	37.06	(exceeds memory)
XNN	CPU (4-core)	11.49	1.74

Figure 6: A comparison of CNN throughput for the best-performing CPU and GPU-based implementations using the MaxoutNet architecture.

gpuZNN, our modified version of ZNN [72]; Caffe [24], compiled with cuDNN v4; and Neon by Nervana [50], which outperformed Caffe and other alternatives on several recently published benchmarks [7]. Throughput was evaluated using 6 nm images presented with different sizes ($1024^2, 512^2, 256^2$) in batches of size 32 (a constraint of Neon's GPU backend), while using max-pool layers with a stride of 1. This eliminates "sub-sampling" effects of max-pooling and simulates the same number of floating point computations as a "dense" inference (not supported by Caffe or Neon).

The results of this benchmarking are presented in Figure 5. It is evident that gpuZNN provides the best throughput on both 8 and 32-channels for all image sizes: 1.8x and 2.9x faster than Neon and Caffe for 8 channels respectively, and 1.8x faster than Caffe for 32 channels. The 32-channel MaxoutNet could not be benchmarked on Neon as the memory usage exceeded the 12 GB available on the Titan X. The main reason for gpuZNN's improvement is its low-memory overhead FFTs that allows it to aggregate large sub-computation units and minimize the amount of calls to primitives of the GPU (each such call involves host-device memory transfers on the PCI-E bus). We note that the actual speed difference between 32 and 8 channels for gpuZNN is 2.6x (and not 32/8=4), which is an effect of the overheads of PCI-E host-device memory transfers that become more significant as the network becomes smaller.

3.3.2 A Comparison of CPUs and GPUs

Figure 6 shows the maximum throughput that we could achieve for XNN, gpuZNN and Neon for 8 and 32 channel CNNs. For 72-cores, we found that the best combination of multi-threading and multi-processing is 8 instances (2 per chip), where each is using 18 threads. One can see that for a network with 32 channels, the GPU is faster than the CPU. However, this is not the case for 8 channels, where the CPU is twice as fast as the GPU. This is because an 8 channel CNN implies less compute for the GPU and makes the PCI-E bus memory transfers more expensive.

4. Watershed

The next stage in the connectomics pipeline involves producing an over-segmentation of neuron candidates from the CNN membrane probability output. Over-segmentation ensures that no supervoxel straddles more than one true segment and is later resolved by agglomeration. Specifically, we apply a custom 3D implementation of the popular linear-time watershed algorithm that yields an 11x speed-up on previous implementations [23]. In general, the key idea is to take into account that probability maps are allowed to take only 8-bit values, which allows us to implement the priority queue as a set of 2^8 FIFO queues. The FIFO queues are implemented using simple arrays with an amortized cost of $O(1)$ for both *push* and *pop* operations. As a result, queue access are cache and pre–fetcher friendly. In addition, we reduce the memory overhead by an order of magnitude compared to OpenCV, which is an important factor for the watershed algorithm that exhibits low ratio of compute-to-memory.

5. Agglomeration

The agglomeration stage refines the over-segmentation generated by the watershed algorithm by merging regions it identifies as belonging to the same neuronal volume. Our pipeline's agglomeration stage is based on Neuroproof [54], a state of the art tool for graph-based image segmentation. Serial optimizations and shared memory parallelization techniques were employed to enhance the performance of Neuroproof on our shared memory multicore system, with the results summarized in Figure 7.

5.1 Regional Adjacency Graphs

Agglomeration is performed on a higher-level representation of the labeled volume called a *regional adjacency graph (RAG)*. A RAG is a graph with a vertex for each distinctly labeled region, and an edge connecting each pair of adjacent regions. Each vertex within the RAG maintains several regional features such as histograms of membrane-probabilities and multiple image moments. These features are typically associative with respect to the agglomeration's merge operation, and thus enable the agglomeration procedure to operate directly on the RAG instead of the much larger input volume.

The initial construction of the RAG requires analyzing the entire input volume, and is thus the most expensive component of this stage. Prior to our performance engineering efforts, RAG construction required 124 seconds on a 1024x1024x100 input stack and was responsible for 70% of the total time spent in the stage.

5.1.1 Serial Optimizations

Several optimizations were performed to reduce the total work performed during RAG construction. These optimizations fell into three categories: optimizations to feature computation, eliminating layers of indirection, and improving memory locality.

Feature computation was optimized by providing a batched version the feature computation function, so that it could process multiple pixels at once. In addition, a significant opportunity for optimization was uncovered in the portion of the program that computed image moment features. The ith image moment feature computes the sum of p^i for all pixels p in a region. The standard library `pow` function was used to compute these features for 4 moments, and was to blame for over 50% of the runtime in RAG construction. We modified the function computing moment features to perform iterative multiplication, and reduce the per-pixel-cost to 3 floating point multiplications. These modifications to feature computation resulted in a 2.5x improvement in serial runtime for RAG construction, resulting in a total runtime of 50 seconds.

Another class of changes involved eliminating unnecessary layers of indirection in matrix and hashtable access. The labeled input volume was loaded into an OpenCV `Mat` object and was accessed through a provided interface. We modified all accesses to operate directly on matrices underlying arrays to eliminate unnecessary indirection to the OpenCV library. This resulted in a further 1.6x improvement in RAG construction time, reducing the total runtime of RAG construction to 30 seconds.

The last major optimization was the design of a divide-and-conquer RAG construction algorithm that takes advantage of the associativity of region features. Given a 3D volume, the largest dimension of the volume was divided in half and the RAG was computed for each half recursively. These RAGs were then merged with their regional features combined according to each of their associative update rules. The base-case of the recursion was coarsened so that the total volume would fit into an L2 cache of approximately 256 KB.

5.1.2 Parallelization

The divide-and-conquer implementation of RAG construction was especially amenable to efficient parallelization. In particular, the method of merging RAGs can be performed efficiently by thinking of the algorithm as a parallel merge sort with an augmented merge operation [9, Ch 27.3]. In other words, the RAG construction algorithm can be parallelized in the same fashion as merge sort by considering a RAG to be a sorted edge-list. We represent regions with a self-edge and store the region's computed features as meta data. After performing a merge of two RAGs' edge lists, the edge list is scanned in parallel to identify and merge duplicated edges. These steps can all be performed in parallel using logarithmic-depth algorithms. On 4 cores, the parallel RAG construction algorithm achieves speedup of 3.5x, reducing the time of RAG construction to 6.8s.

	Baseline (s)	**Fast 1-core** (s)	**Fast 4-core** (s)
Input/Output	11.2	10.5	6.7
RAG Construction	123.2	24.2	6.8
RAG Agglomeration	42.5	40.2	13.4
Total	176.9	75.0	27.0

Figure 7: Performance improvements to agglomeration stage.

After RAG construction, RAG agglomeration analyzes edges to determine which node pairs to merge. We observed that most of the work was performed by a random-forest classification library within OpenCV that computes edge weights. To parallelize RAG agglomeration, we defer the computation of edge weights, and mark effected nodes and edges as *dirty* [54]. A dequeued edge is ignored if it is dirty or incident to a dirty node. When the priority queue is empty, the edge weights are all computed in parallel as a batch, and reinserted into the queue. This strategy resulted in 3x speedup for agglomeration, reducing its runtime from 40.2 to 13.4 seconds.

6. Merging

In this section we describe how our pipeline merges all of the per-block segmentations produced by the earlier stages to obtain a segmentation for the entire volume. Prior work by Plaza and Berg [56] describe a method of performing such a merge operation by generating overlaps between adjacent blocks and identifying pairs of segments to merge based on a set of complex hand-crafted heuristics. As reported in [56], this approach is made difficult by the substantial number of edge cases that must be handled correctly to obtain a high quality segmentation. Our approach is of similar spirit, but simplifies the problem of identifying merge-pairs by treating it as a special case of agglomeration.

Our inter-block merge procedure operates in two phases that each perform an agglomeration over the block boundaries. These phases reuse the optimized agglomeration algorithms described in Section 5, but use a random forest classifier that is trained specifically on inter-block segmentations. Segments identified as merge-pairs are then recorded on-disk, and processed into equivalence classes using a disjoint-set data structure. The performance of the merge stage was further optimized by tuning the ordering and parallelism degree to ensure that the machine's caches and disks were used efficiently.

6.1 Merge Pair Decisions.

Merge pairs are determined for all adjacent blocks in the volume in two phases. First, the segments in the block boundary are agglomerated using our parallel agglomeration algorithm. This phase is conservative, to avoid incorrect mergers, but since neuronal objects are large (spanning many blocks) most merge-pairs are found in this phase. In the second phase, the algorithm generates a synthetic ground-truth by re-executing the watershed and agglomeration stages on the block boundaries. This synthetic ground-truth allows for the remaining merge-pairs to be identified via a straightforward optimization procedure. This procedure merges a pair and computes the associated VI score relative to the synthetic ground-truth. If accuracy decreases, it aborts the merge and tries a different pair.

6.2 Combining and Relabelling.

After merge-pairs are identified for pairs of adjacent blocks, the next step is to actually relabel the volume so that each distinct object has a distinct label.

To identify equivalent labels, we operate on the lists of merge-pairs generated for pairs of adjacent blocks and use a disjoint-set data structure to form equivalence classes of segment identifiers (i.e. where two segments are equivalent if they appear as a merge-pair). This process is straightforward since all merge-pairs are present on the machine's local disk, and the total size of all merge-pairs is miniscule in-comparison to other data sets in the pipeline. Finally, the algorithm executes a parallel pass over all segmented blocks and relabels them based on their equivalence class. This relabeling step is I/O bound, but this is mitigated by ordering blocks to be relabeled such that all of the machine's disks are well utilized.

7. Skeletonization

A skeleton is a one dimensional space-efficient representation of a 3D volume that runs along the segments's medial axis. There are a vast number of algorithms to compute skeletons for a variety of purposes in computer graphics [60]. We found that for connectomics a thinning algorithm would be most fitting because it is the fastest algorithm that still preserves the connectivity of the objects. Their algorithms remove all so-called *simple points*, voxels whose removal does not change the topology. Checking if a point is simple or not is non-trivial, especially when multiple voxels are deleted in parallel.

Our parallel thinning algorithm is implemented as a chromatically scheduled dynamic data-graph computation [25, 26]. A grid graph represents the labeled 3D volume and a statically-computed distance-2 coloring is used to identify sets of voxels that may be processed in parallel.

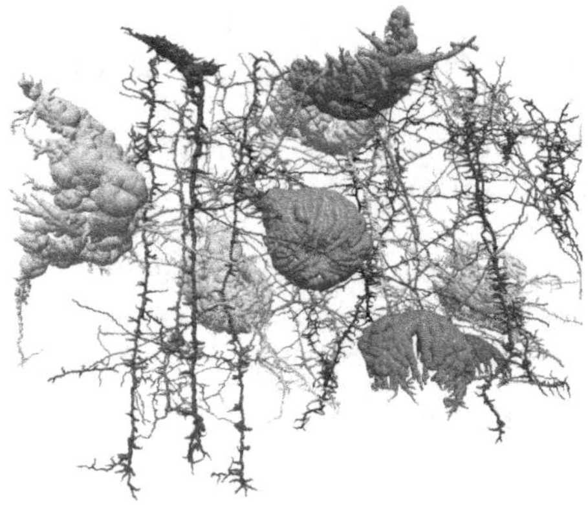

Figure 8: Skeletonization of 20 objects from the Kasthuri *et al.* dataset (as one large block) [28] (473 GB $\approx$ 100,000 cubic microns of cortex).

Initially updates are scheduled on all surface points, which check if a given point satisfies the *simple point* criterion based on their 26-neighborhood. An update that deletes a point schedules an update dynamically for all non-deleted neighbors. Since there are only 2^{26} possible 26-neighborhoods, the simple point criterion can be pre-computed. Our simple point criterion is based upon the 38 templates of [62] and ensures local connectedness. Since our algorithm uses chromatic scheduling, it is equivalent to a standard 8-subfield thinning algorithm and thus provably preserves the topology of the objects [2].

After skeletonization, we transform the 3D segments into tree graphs based on 26-connectivity. If cycles exist in the graph they are broken up arbitrarily, however, large cycles are detected and are reported for further analysis and error detection. After performing a one-pass pruning step the trees are outputted as .swc files and visualized using the neuTube software [17]. Our pipeline currently generates skeletons per-block, but the same algorithm can be applied (with additional engineering effort) to the entire volume (Figure 8).

8. Pipeline Performance

The earlier portions of the paper focused on improving the performance and scalability of individual machine learning algorithms that consume a large fraction of the computation in existing connectomics systems [56, 58]. In this section, we focus on the combined performance of our pipeline elements. The main workhorse for our experiments is the previously described 4-socket shared memory machine equipped with 4 18-core Intel Xeon CPUs with 512 GB of RAM running Ubuntu 14.04.

We tested our pipeline on a 473 GB (3x3x30 nm resolution) electron microscopy dataset of mouse somatosensory cortex [27], containing 1850 pre-aligned 16,384x16,384 (256 MB) 2D EM brain scans.

The total time to process the entire 473 GB EM dataset was **1.7 hours**, implying a throughput of **3.6 hours / TB**.

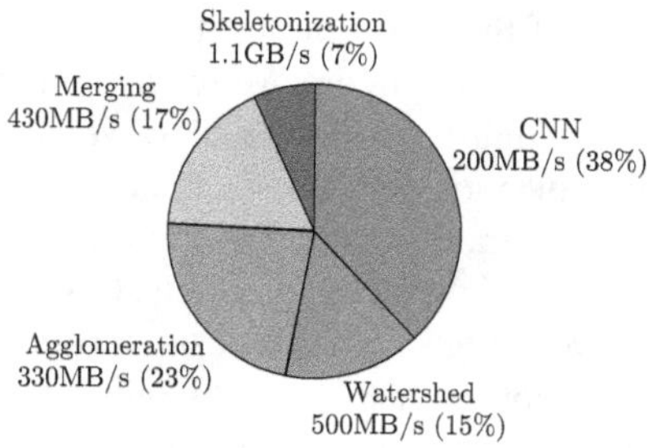

Figure 9: Proportion of the execution time spent on each stage.

Figure 9 provides a breakdown illustrating each stage's contribution to the total execution time. Notably, we have managed to improve the machine-learning-based segmentation component to be on par with the other stages, which alleviates a previously constraining bottleneck in the throughput of connectomics pipelines [56].

To analyze the efficiency of using a 72-core system, we compared the throughput of our pipeline on a single core against our throughput on all 72 cores. On a single core, our pipeline processes data at a speed of 1.11s / MB, compared to 0.013s / MB on 72 cores. This implies that our pipeline achieves an 85x factor speedup, which is greater than 72 since hyper-threading provides our machine with 144 hardware threads.

The number of concurrent instances and the degree-of-parallelism used within each instance varies depending on the pipeline stage. To achieve maximum throughput in the CNN phase, we execute 8 instances of XNN (2 per chip), where each instance uses 18 threads. This eliminates any NUMA side-effects that could introduce contention and bottlenecks. In the watershed phase, we simply spawn 144 instances since the implementation we have is a fast sequential code with low memory consumption (each instance <1 GB, and total memory is 512 GB). In the agglomeration phase, we execute 36 instances (9 per chip) of parallel NeuroProof, where each instance uses 4 threads. A similar scheme is applied to merging and skeletonization.

8.1 Reconstruction Accuracy

To evaluate the reconstruction accuracy of our pipeline we followed the benchmark described by Kaynig *et al.* [29]. We partitioned a total of 150 images (a region of the data called AC3 in [29]) at 2048x2048 and 3 nm resolution into three sets; 10 for training, 65 for validation and 75 for testing. Ground truth neuron segmentation was provided by expert neurobiologist annotators.

Our measure of segmentation accuracy is *variation of information* (VI) [45], that captures the statistical difference between two segmentations. In a typical segmentation there are split errors (neurons split erroneously) and merge errors (neurons merged erroneously), and the VI is an indicator to the extent of such errors in the data set. We benchmarked our 8-channel MaxoutNet CNN architecture (described in Section 3.1) and the state-of-the-art reconstruction of RhoAna described by Kaynig *et al.* [29] using the same evaluation benchmark on our test dataset described above. We note that our comparisons with the RhoAna-based pipeline described in [29] are only with respect to accuracy, since it was not extensively engineered for performance (it requires several weeks and thousands of machines to process a terabyte).

On the AC3 dataset, our pipeline achieved an accuracy score of VI = 1.6483 which is, surprisingly, an improvement over the VI = 1.99 score reported for RhoAna (lower VI means improved reconstruction). This comparison indicates that our pipeline's efficiency does not inherently come at the expense of reconstruction quality, albeit we caution that reconstruction accuracy is a complex metric and that accuracy comparisons performed on a single data set should be taken with a grain of salt.

9. Lessons Learned

In this section we discuss some of the general lessons learnt from our effort to reduce a high-throughput, big-data problem to the domain of a single shared-memory multicore system. Some of these may be known to the reader, but others were counter-intuitive, at least to us, and therefore worth explicit mention.

9.1 Scalable software saves memory

Writing multicore code is generally hard – it is far simpler to write a single-threaded program that avoids concurrency "nightmares," and scale horizontally by launching one instance per core. While this may work for simple tasks, we observed that this approach can be seriously flawed for complex software. In the case of both the agglomeration and membrane-detection stages of our pipeline, the large memory footprint of each instance caused the OS to frequently swap between memory and disk, thus increasing I/O bandwidth requirements. Moreover, performance degraded due to L3 cache pollution caused by multiple instances populating the shared L3 cache with disjoint memory accesses. By engineering our software to scale to multiple cores, we obtained a degree of freedom in our pipeline design that allowed us to run a smaller number of instances, where each uses multiple cores to operate on data fitting into L3 cache. For example, our pipeline runs 8 instances (two per socket) of the CNN code for membrane detection, where each instance uses 9 cores. This enabled efficient use of the caches on each socket and eliminated the need to handle complex NUMA overheads [5, 13, 14, 16, 47].

9.2 Disk I/O is scalable on a single machine

Once computation is sufficiently optimized, disk-to-memory I/O for a single machine can become a bottleneck. This is often part of the motivation to migrate computation to a cluster of machines, and is a problem we encountered in the watershed and agglomeration pipeline phases (where the disk I/O 100 MB/s read and 200 MB/s write were reached). Instead, we resolved this bottleneck by horizontally scaling our disk drives – data was sharded across a set of 5 drives that were installed on the same machine, yielding 500 MB/s read and 1000 MB/s write for the system. Adding more disks to improve I/O bandwidth in this manner is far cheaper and simpler than migrating to a distributed cluster.

9.3 Dynamic multithreading simplifies cache-aware parallelization

A potential criticism of a multicore-centric approach is that it simply shifts from one set of programming complexities (networking, failure detection and recovery schemes on a distributed system) to the unique challenges posed by shared-memory concurrency. Our experience is that writing cache-efficient multicore code can be simple, if using the right tools. Our multicore programs are written using GCC-Cilk which employs an efficient work-stealing scheduler, and allows parallelism to be expressed while retaining the semantics and many performance properties of serial code. As a result, our techniques to make our programs cache and pre-fetcher friendly largely mirror those used in serial code. This allowed us to achieve good cache efficiency without needing to write complex cache-aware scheduling logic.

9.4 A GPU is not 100X faster than a CPU

It is widely believed in the machine learning community that a single GPU can perform orders of magnitude faster than a single CPU. This is supported empirically by popular machine learning packages – if one compares Caffe (bound to Intel MKL and Nvidia cuDNN libraries) execution times on GPU versus CPU, the speed-up is approximately 50 to 100-fold. Following our multicore performance engineering efforts, we observe substantially different results. On a single 18-core 2.4 GHz Haswell chip, our XNN execution is only 2-3x slower than both gpuZNN and the previous fastest CNN framework (Neon [50]) executed on a Titan X GPU. Moreover, XNN execution on a commodity 4-core Skylake chip (a standard desktop/laptop processor) was only 4-6x slower than this top-end GPU. These observations are consistent with the findings reported in [33], but here we support the claim on a modern CPU.

9.5 Multicores enable new efficient algorithms that are expensive on clusters

A common belief of Hadoop/Spark programmers is that coding for a distributed cluster is simpler than for a multi-core, and therefore, shifting software to multicores is not worth the effort. However, our experience shows that this not true. A key point that needs to be emphasized is that coding for clusters is simple as long as the parallelization of the problem is "trivial". In other words, as long as one can break the problem into small parts that can be processed without communicating, then it is easy to do map-reduce style programming. However, if this is simple for the cluster, then it will also be simple for the multicore. Moreover, cluster-based algorithms exhibit high network latencies, which forces them to avoid communication between machines. As a result, programmers are constrained to coding patterns that are "trivially parallelizable" in the context of clusters, since it is the only way to avoid high network costs and get scalability. However, this is not the case for multicores: inter-core communication is orders of magnitude less expensive than network cluster communication, which allows programmers to design more sophisticated approaches that involve complex communication patterns.

10. Conclusion

We presented a "proof of concept" connectomics pipeline that can extract a full skeletonization from an EM image stack in less than 4 hours on a commodity multicore machine and with a VI accuracy on par or better than any existing system. This has the potential to move the connectomics problem, a big-data research problem in the natural sciences, from the realm of distributed data and warehouse storage, to that of on-demand processing in labs across the world. Given current trends in multicore CPU and GPU architectures, we venture to predict that a single socket machine, perhaps with a single attached GPU card, will be able to provide a solution for many connectomics pipelines around the world.

The domain-specific results we report on Kashturi dataset [28], constitute a case-study on the role of multicore performance engineering in large-scale image processing pipelines. The lessons learnt from our experiences designing this system are of great import to those in the multicore and cluster computing communities. Through careful performance engineering, we show that a single commodity multicore machine can not only compete, but significantly outperform, existing CPU- and GPU- based clusters solving the same problem. This, of course, is not intended to advocate that all "big data" problems are best solved on a single multicore, but rather to serve as a reminder of the importance and dramatic benefits that can be obtained through multicore performance engineering.

Acknowledgments

Support is gratefully acknowledged from the National Science Foundation (NSF) under grants IIS-1447786 and CCF-1563880, and the Intelligence Advanced Research Projects Activity (IARPA) under grant 138076-5093555. In addition, we would like to thank the MIT SuperTech group for helpful discussions. In particular, Quan Nguyen, William Hasenplaugh, Bradley Kuszmaul, and Charles Leiserson. Finally, we would like to thank the Harvard connectomics group for reviewing our work and providing useful feedback. Specifically, Daniel Berger, Adi (Suissa) Peleg, Thouis R. Jones, Hanspeter Pfister, David Cox, and Jeff Lichtman.

References

[1] P. Arbelaez, M. Maire, C. Fowlkes, and J. Malik. Contour detection and hierarchical image segmentation. *Pattern Analysis and Machine Intelligence, IEEE Transactions on*, 33(5): 898–916, 2011.

[2] G. Bertrand and Z. Aktouf. Three-dimensional thinning algorithm using subfields. volume 2356, pages 113–124, 1995. doi: 10.1117/12.198601.

[3] R. D. Blumofe, C. F. Joerg, B. C. Kuszmaul, C. E. Leiserson, K. H. Randall, and Y. Zhou. Cilk: An efficient multithreaded runtime system. In *Proceedings of the Fifth ACM SIGPLAN Symposium on Principles and Practice of Parallel Programming*, PPOPP '95, pages 207–216, New York, NY, USA, 1995. ACM. ISBN 0-89791-700-6. doi: 10.1145/209936.209958. URL http://doi.acm.org/10.1145/209936.209958.

[4] D. Budden, A. Matveev, S. Santurkar, S. R. Chaudhuri, and N. Shavit. Deep tensor convolution on multicores. *CoRR*, abs/1611.06565, 2016. URL http://arxiv.org/abs/1611.06565.

[5] I. Calciu, D. Dice, Y. Lev, V. Luchangco, V. J. Marathe, and N. Shavit. Numa-aware reader-writer locks. In *Proceedings of the 18th ACM SIGPLAN Symposium on Principles and Practice of Parallel Programming*, PPoPP '13, pages 157–166, New York, NY, USA, 2013. ACM. ISBN 978-1-4503-1922-5. doi: 10.1145/2442516.2442532. URL http://doi.acm.org/10.1145/2442516.2442532.

[6] T. Chilimbi, Y. Suzue, J. Apacible, and K. Kalyanaraman. Project adam: Building an efficient and scalable deep learning training system. In *Proceedings of the 11th USENIX Conference on Operating Systems Design and Implementation*, OSDI'14, pages 571–582, Berkeley, CA, USA, 2014. USENIX Association. ISBN 978-1-931971-16-4. URL http://dl.acm.org/citation.cfm?id=2685048.2685094.

[7] S. Chintala. Convnet benchmarks. https://github.com/soumith/convnet-benchmarks.

[8] D. Ciresan, A. Giusti, L. M. Gambardella, and J. Schmidhuber. Deep neural networks segment neuronal membranes in electron microscopy images. In *Advances in neural information processing systems*, pages 2843–2851, 2012.

[9] T. H. Cormen, C. E. Leiserson, R. L. Rivest, and C. Stein. *Introduction to Algorithms*. The MIT Press, third edition, 2009.

[10] I. Corporation. Intel math kernel library, 2016. URL https://en.wikipedia.org/wiki/Math_Kernel_Library.

[11] H. Cui, H. Zhang, G. R. Ganger, P. B. Gibbons, and E. P. Xing. Geeps: Scalable deep learning on distributed gpus with a gpu-specialized parameter server. In *Proceedings of the Eleventh European Conference on Computer Systems*, EuroSys '16, pages 4:1–4:16, New York, NY, USA, 2016. ACM. ISBN 978-1-4503-4240-7. doi: 10.1145/2901318.2901323. URL http://doi.acm.org/10.1145/2901318.2901323.

[12] J. Dean and S. Ghemawat. Mapreduce: Simplified data processing on large clusters. *Communications of the ACM*, 51(1): 107–113, Jan. 2008.

[13] D. Dice, V. J. Marathe, and N. Shavit. Flat-combining numa locks. In *Proceedings of the Twenty-third Annual ACM Symposium on Parallelism in Algorithms and Architectures*, SPAA '11, pages 65–74, New York, NY, USA, 2011. ACM. ISBN 978-1-4503-0743-7. doi: 10.1145/1989493.1989502. URL http://doi.acm.org/10.1145/1989493.1989502.

[14] D. Dice, V. J. Marathe, and N. Shavit. Lock cohorting: A general technique for designing numa locks. In *Proceedings of the 17th ACM SIGPLAN Symposium on Principles and Practice of Parallel Programming*, PPoPP '12, pages 247–256, New York, NY, USA, 2012. ACM. ISBN 978-1-4503-1160-1. doi: 10.1145/2145816.2145848. URL http://doi.acm.org/10.1145/2145816.2145848.

[15] A. Eberle, S. Mikula, R. Schalek, J. Lichtman, M. K. TATE, and D. Zeidler. High-resolution, high-throughput imaging with a multibeam scanning electron microscope. *Journal of microscopy*, 259(2):114–120, 2015.

[16] F. Ellen, Y. Lev, V. Luchangco, and M. Moir. Snzi: Scalable nonzero indicators. In *Proceedings of the Twenty-sixth Annual ACM Symposium on Principles of Distributed Computing*, PODC '07, pages 13–22, New York, NY, USA, 2007. ACM. ISBN 978-1-59593-616-5. doi: 10.1145/1281100.1281106. URL http://doi.acm.org/10.1145/1281100.1281106.

[17] L. Feng, T. Zhao, and J. Kim. neuTube 1.0: a New Design for Efficient Neuron Reconstruction Software Based on the SWC Format. *eneuro*, Jan. 2015. ISSN 2373-2822.

[18] M. Frigo, P. Halpern, C. E. Leiserson, and S. Lewin-Berlin. Reducers and other cilk++ hyperobjects. In *Proceedings of the twenty-first annual symposium on Parallelism in algorithms and architectures*, pages 79–90. ACM, 2009.

[19] A. Giusti, D. C. Ciresan, J. Masci, L. M. Gambardella, and J. Schmidhuber. Fast image scanning with deep max-pooling convolutional neural networks. In *ICIP*, page in press, 2013.

[20] Google. Google cloud platform blog: Google supercharges machine learning tasks with tpu custom chip, 2016. URL https://cloudplatform.googleblog.com/2016/05/Google-supercharges-machine-learning-tasks-with-custom-chip.html.

[21] J. Hauswald, Y. Kang, M. A. Laurenzano, Q. Chen, C. Li, T. Mudge, R. G. Dreslinski, J. Mars, and L. Tang. Djinn and tonic: Dnn as a service and its implications for future warehouse scale computers. In *Proceedings of the 42Nd Annual International Symposium on Computer Architecture*, ISCA '15, pages 27–40, New York, NY, USA, 2015. ACM. ISBN 978-1-4503-3402-0. doi: 10.1145/2749469.2749472. URL http://doi.acm.org/10.1145/2749469.2749472.

[22] IBM. Introducing a brain-inspired computer, 2016. URL http://www.research.ibm.com/articles/brain-chip.shtml.

[23] itseez. Open source computer vision library, 2016. URL http://opencv.org/.

[24] Y. Jia, E. Shelhamer, J. Donahue, S. Karayev, J. Long, R. Girshick, S. Guadarrama, and T. Darrell. Caffe: Convolutional architecture for fast feature embedding. In *Proceedings of the ACM International Conference on Multimedia*, pages 675–678. ACM, 2014.

[25] T. Kaler, W. Hasenplaugh, T. B. Schardl, and C. E. Leiserson. Executing dynamic data-graph computations deterministically using chromatic scheduling. In *Proceedings of the 26th ACM Symposium on Parallelism in Algorithms*

and Architectures, SPAA '14, pages 154–165, New York, NY, USA, 2014. ACM. ISBN 978-1-4503-2821-0. doi: 10.1145/2612669.2612673. URL http://doi.acm.org/10.1145/2612669.2612673.

[26] T. Kaler, W. Hasenplaugh, T. B. Schardl, and C. E. Leiserson. Executing dynamic data-graph computations deterministically using chromatic scheduling. *ACM Trans. Parallel Comput.*, 3(1):2:1–2:31, July 2016. ISSN 2329-4949. doi: 10.1145/2896850. URL http://doi.acm.org/10.1145/2896850.

[27] N. Kasthuri, K. Hayworth, J. C. Tapia, R. Schalek, S. Nundy, and J. W. Lichtman. The brain on tape: Imaging an ultra-thin section library (utsl). In *Soc. Neurosci. Abstr*, 2009.

[28] N. Kasthuri, K. J. Hayworth, D. R. Berger, R. L. Schalek, J. A. Conchello, S. Knowles-Barley, D. Lee, A. Vázquez-Reina, V. Kaynig, T. R. Jones, et al. Saturated reconstruction of a volume of neocortex. *Cell*, 162(3):648–661, 2015.

[29] V. Kaynig, A. Vazquez-Reina, S. Knowles-Barley, M. Roberts, T. R. Jones, N. Kasthuri, E. Miller, J. Lichtman, and H. Pfister. Large-scale automatic reconstruction of neuronal processes from electron microscopy images. *Medical image analysis*, 22(1):77–88, 2015.

[30] S. Knowles-Barley. Rhoana git. https://github.com/Rhoana/membrane_cnn/tree/master/maxout.

[31] A. Krizhevsky, I. Sutskever, and G. E. Hinton. Imagenet classification with deep convolutional neural networks. In *Advances in neural information processing systems*, pages 1097–1105, 2012.

[32] K. Lee, A. Zlateski, V. Ashwin, and H. S. Seung. Recursive Training of 2D-3D Convolutional Networks for Neuronal Boundary Prediction. In *Advances in Neural Information Processing Systems*, pages 3559–3567, 2015.

[33] V. W. Lee, C. Kim, J. Chhugani, M. Deisher, D. Kim, A. D. Nguyen, N. Satish, M. Smelyanskiy, S. Chennupaty, P. Hammarlund, R. Singhal, and P. Dubey. Debunking the 100x gpu vs. cpu myth: An evaluation of throughput computing on cpu and gpu. In *Proceedings of the 37th Annual International Symposium on Computer Architecture*, ISCA '10, pages 451–460, New York, NY, USA, 2010. ACM. ISBN 978-1-4503-0053-7. doi: 10.1145/1815961.1816021. URL http://doi.acm.org/10.1145/1815961.1816021.

[34] W.-C. A. Lee, V. Bonin, M. Reed, B. J. Graham, G. Hood, K. Glattfelder, and R. C. Reid. Anatomy and function of an excitatory network in the visual cortex. *Nature*, 532(7599): 370–374, 2016.

[35] C. E. Leiserson. The cilk++ concurrency platform. *The Journal of Supercomputing*, 51(3):244–257, 2010.

[36] H. Li, A. Kadav, E. Kruus, and C. Ungureanu. Malt: Distributed data-parallelism for existing ML applications. In *Proceedings of the Tenth European Conference on Computer Systems*, EuroSys '15, pages 3:1–3:16, New York, NY, USA, 2015. ACM. ISBN 978-1-4503-3238-5. doi: 10.1145/2741948.2741965. URL http://doi.acm.org/10.1145/2741948.2741965.

[37] Y. Li and Z. Lan. Exploit failure prediction for adaptive fault-tolerance in cluster computing. In *Cluster Computing and the Grid, 2006. CCGRID 06. Sixth IEEE International Symposium on*, volume 1, pages 8–pp. IEEE, 2006.

[38] J. W. Lichtman and W. Denk. The big and the small: challenges of imaging the brains circuits. *Science*, 334(6056): 618–623, 2011.

[39] J. W. Lichtman and J. R. Sanes. Ome sweet ome: what can the genome tell us about the connectome? *Current Opinion in Neurobiology*, 18(3):346–353, June 2008. ISSN 0959-4388. doi: 10.1016/j.conb.2008.08.010. URL http://www.sciencedirect.com/science/article/pii/S0959438808000834.

[40] J. W. Lichtman, H. Pfister, and N. Shavit. The big data challenges of connectomics. *Nature neuroscience*, 17(11): 1448–1454, 2014.

[41] J. Long, E. Shelhamer, and T. Darrell. Fully convolutional networks for semantic segmentation. In *The IEEE Conference on Computer Vision and Pattern Recognition (CVPR)*, June 2015.

[42] J. Maitin-Shepard, V. Jain, M. Januszewski, P. Li, J. Kornfeld, J. Buhmann, and P. Abbeel. Combinatorial energy learning for image segmentation. *arXiv preprint arXiv:1506.04304*, 2015.

[43] J. Masci, A. Giusti, D. Ciresan, G. Fricout, and J. Schmidhuber. A fast learning algorithm for image segmentation with max-pooling convolutional networks. In *Image Processing (ICIP), 2013 20th IEEE International Conference on*, pages 2713–2717. IEEE, 2013.

[44] M. Meilă. Comparing clusteringsan information based distance. *Journal of multivariate analysis*, 98(5):873–895, 2007.

[45] M. Meilă. Comparing clusteringsan information based distance. *Journal of multivariate analysis*, 98(5):873–895, 2007.

[46] Y. Meirovitch, A. Matveev, H. Saribekyan, D. Budden, D. Rolnick, G. Odor, S. K.-B. T. R. Jones, H. Pfister, J. W. Lichtman, and N. Shavit. A Multi-Pass Approach to Large-Scale Connectomics. *ArXiv e-prints*, Dec. 2016.

[47] J. M. Mellor-Crummey and M. L. Scott. Algorithms for scalable synchronization on shared-memory multiprocessors. *ACM Trans. Comput. Syst.*, 9(1):21–65, Feb. 1991. ISSN 0734-2071. doi: 10.1145/103727.103729. URL http://doi.acm.org/10.1145/103727.103729.

[48] A. N. Moga, B. Cramariuc, and M. Gabbouj. Parallel watershed transformation algorithms for image segmentation. *Parallel Comput.*, 24(14):1981–2001, Dec. 1998. ISSN 0167-8191. doi: 10.1016/S0167-8191(98)00085-4. URL http://dx.doi.org/10.1016/S0167-8191(98)00085-4.

[49] J. L. Morgan, D. R. Berger, A. W. Wetzel, and J. W. Lichtman. The fuzzy logic of network connectivity in mouse visual thalamus. *Cell*, 165(1):192–206, 2016.

[50] Nervana. Neon. https://github.com/NervanaSystems/neon.

[51] J. Nunez-Iglesias, R. Kennedy, T. Parag, J. Shi, and D. B. Chklovskii. Machine learning of hierarchical clustering to segment 2D and 3D images. *PloS one*, 8(8):e71715, 2013.

[52] J. Nunez-Iglesias, R. Kennedy, S. M. Plaza, A. Chakraborty, and W. T. Katz. Graph-based active learning of agglomeration (gala): a python library to segment 2d and 3d neuroimages. *Frontiers in neuroinformatics*, 8, 2014.

[53] NVIDIA. Nvidia cudnn - gpu accelerated deep learning, 2016. URL https://developer.nvidia.com/cudnn.

[54] T. Parag, A. Chakrobarty, and S. Plaza. A context-aware delayed agglomeration framework for em segmentation. *CoRR*, 2014.

[55] T. Parag, A. Chakraborty, S. Plaza, and L. Scheffer. A context-aware delayed agglomeration framework for electron microscopy segmentation. *PloS one*, 10(5):e0125825, 2015.

[56] S. M. Plaza and S. E. Berg. Large-scale electron microscopy image segmentation in spark. *arXiv preprint arXiv:1604.00385*, 2016.

[57] S. Ramón and S. Cajal. *Textura del Sistema Nervioso del Hombre y de los Vertebrados*, volume 2. Madrid Nicolas Moya, 1904.

[58] W. R. G. Roncal, D. M. Kleissas, J. T. Vogelstein, P. Manavalan, K. Lillaney, M. Pekala, R. Burns, R. J. Vogelstein, C. E. Priebe, M. A. Chevillet, et al. An automated images-to-graphs framework for high resolution connectomics. *Frontiers in neuroinformatics*, 9, 2015.

[59] O. Ronneberger, P. Fischer, and T. Brox. U-net: Convolutional networks for biomedical image segmentation. In *Medical Image Computing and Computer-Assisted Intervention–MICCAI 2015*, pages 234–241. Springer, 2015.

[60] P. K. Saha, G. Borgefors, and G. Sanniti di Baja. A survey on skeletonization algorithms and their applications. *Pattern Recognition Letters*, 76:3–12, June 2016. ISSN 0167-8655. doi: 10.1016/j.patrec.2015.04.006.

[61] S. Seung. *Connectome: How the brain's wiring makes us who we are*. Houghton Mifflin Harcourt, 2012.

[62] F. She, R. Chen, W. Gao, P. Hodgson, L. Kong, and H. Hong. Improved 3d Thinning Algorithms for Skeleton Extraction. In *Digital Image Computing: Techniques and Applications, 2009. DICTA '09.*, pages 14–18, Dec. 2009. doi: 10.1109/DICTA.2009.13.

[63] I. Sutskever, O. Vinyals, and Q. V. Le. Sequence to sequence learning with neural networks. In *Advances in neural information processing systems*, pages 3104–3112, 2014.

[64] F. Tschopp. Efficient convolutional neural networks for pixelwise classification on heterogeneous hardware systems. *arXiv preprint arXiv:1509.03371*, 2015.

[65] B. Vision and L. Center. Caffe deep learning framework. http://caffe.berkeleyvision.org/.

[66] J. Vogelstein. Machine intelligence from cortical networks (microns), 2016. URL https://www.iarpa.gov/index.php/research-programs/microns.

[67] J. G. White, E. Southgate, J. N. Thomson, and S. Brenner. The structure of the nervous system of the nematode caenorhabditis elegans. *Philosophical Transactions of the Royal Society B: Biological Sciences*, 314(1165):1–340, 1986. ISSN 0080-4622. doi: 10.1098/rstb.1986.0056. URL http://rstb.royalsocietypublishing.org/content/314/1165/1.

[68] Wiki. Advanced vector extensions, 2016. URL https://en.wikipedia.org/wiki/Advanced_Vector_Extensions.

[69] F. Yu and V. Koltun. Multi-scale context aggregation by dilated convolutions. *arXiv preprint arXiv:1511.07122*, 2015.

[70] M. Zaharia, M. Chowdhury, M. J. Franklin, S. Shenker, and I. Stoica. Spark: cluster computing with working sets. *HotCloud*, 10:10–10, 2010.

[71] M. Zaharia, M. Chowdhury, T. Das, A. Dave, J. Ma, M. McCauley, M. J. Franklin, S. Shenker, and I. Stoica. Resilient distributed datasets: A fault-tolerant abstraction for in-memory cluster computing. In *Proceedings of the 9th USENIX conference on Networked Systems Design and Implementation*, pages 2–2. USENIX Association, 2012.

[72] A. Zlateski, K. Lee, and H. S. Seung. ZNN-A fast and scalable algorithm for training 3D convolutional networks on multicore and many-core shared memory machines. *arXiv preprint arXiv:1510.06706*, 2015.

SC-Haskell: Sequential Consistency in Languages That Minimize Mutable Shared Heap

Michael Vollmer[1] Ryan G. Scott[1] Madanlal Musuvathi[2] Ryan R. Newton[1]

Indiana University (USA)[1], Microsoft Research (USA)[2]

{vollmerm, rgscott, rrnewton}@indiana.edu madan@microsoft.com

Abstract

A core, but often neglected, aspect of a programming language design is its memory (consistency) model. Sequential consistency (SC) is the most intuitive memory model for programmers as it guarantees sequential composition of instructions and provides a simple abstraction of shared memory as a single global store with atomic read and writes. Unfortunately, SC is widely considered to be impractical due to its associated performance overheads.

Perhaps contrary to popular opinion, this paper demonstrates that SC is achievable with acceptable performance overheads for mainstream languages that minimize mutable shared heap. In particular, we modify the Glasgow Haskell Compiler to insert fences on all writes to shared mutable memory accessed in nonfunctional parts of the program. For a benchmark suite containing 1,279 programs, SC adds a geomean overhead of less than 0.4% on an x86 machine.

The efficiency of SC arises primarily due to the isolation provided by the Haskell type system between purely functional and thread-local imperative computations on the one hand, and imperative computations on the global heap on the other. We show how to use new programming idioms to further reduce the SC overhead; these create a virtuous cycle of less overhead and even stronger semantic guarantees (static data-race freedom).

Keywords memory models, functional programming, sequential consistency

1. Introduction

The prospect of sequential consistency (SC) [21] as a concurrency abstraction for programmers has been debated against a backdrop of mainstream C++ and Java programs. These languages have settled on memory models based on DRF0 [26, 8] that guarantee SC for data-race-free programs. However, as Adve and Boehm point out [3], this is far from a satisfying solution due to the inherent difficulties in enforcing data-race-freedom and in pinning down the semantics of programs with data races.

This paper rests on the hypothesis that high-level languages should shield all programmers from the counter-intuitive effects of compiler and hardware reorderings by providing SC. The key challenge is that doing so requires the language runtime to insert hardware fences to counter the relaxed memory models of current hardware architectures. Doing so for shared-memory imperative languages, such as C++ and Java, either incurs unacceptable overheads or requires sophisticated whole-program analyses [36, 38, 5] that modern language runtimes are loath to implement.

This is not necessarily true for language paradigms that deemphasize access to shared mutable heap when possible. For instance, consider Haskell, Erlang, and Rust, which are designed for functional programming, message passing, and linear ownership, respectively. Programs in these languages naturally use fewer shared heap locations. Moreover, the language type system provides a clean separation between pure or thread-local computation and shared-mutable state. Thus, these languages provide an opportunity to make SC mainstream with acceptable overheads. The goal of this paper is to evaluate this hypothesis for the Haskell language. As functional programming primitives are gradually introduced into mainstream imperative languages, we believe that lessons learned from our efforts here could influence future efforts to tighten the memory models of Java and C++.

Despite its fundamental importance, memory model considerations are usually an afterthought during language design. The current Haskell specification does not formally specify a memory model, a sore spot in a language that otherwise provides a mathematically grounded semantics. We show that this oversight is more than a minor annoyance and demonstrate how a weak memory model can break the fundamental abstractions of Haskell. In particular, in Section 3 we show that the current GHC implementation on ARM is *type-unsafe* — a particular sharing pattern in the imperative parts of a Haskell program can break the type safety of the functional parts of the program, a core language guarantee.

To comprehensively resolve such issues, this paper proposes *SC-Haskell*, a refinement of the existing Haskell lan-

PPoPP '17 Feb. 4–8, 2017, Austin, Texas, USA.

ACM 978-1-4503-4493-7/17/02... $15.00
DOI: http://dx.doi.org/10.1145/3018743.3018746

guage semantics. We implement SC-Haskell in the context of the mature Glasgow Haskell Compiler (GHC), which is the mainstay of the Haskell ecosystem.

Haskell contains threads and mutable references. Thus, in principle, SC-Haskell shares the same problems as a hypothetical "SC-Java." But unlike Java, the Haskell type system isolates pure computations from effectful ones—writing to a global mutable reference is an action with "IO" type. Additionally, Haskell provides a menu of options to minimize sharing of mutable references between threads, including:

1. (parallel) functional programming [28],
2. thread-private references (ST type) [22],
3. software transactional memory (STM type) [17], and
4. libraries that encapsulate alias-free partitions of shared mutable state [19].

In all these cases, the type system serves as a firewall preventing code using these mechanisms from modifying unsynchronized (non-transactional, non-atomic) shared mutable variables. Thus, program transformation to ensure SC can be **type directed** by systematically ignoring all store operations that originate from the four alternate facilities above. Thus our first question is whether the presence of these facilities has *already* made reliance on unsynchronized shared-heap writes statistically rare in existing Haskell programs, and thus the surface area for SC-enforcement small.

The answer to this question is a resounding "yes". As described in section 7.2 we find occurrences of unsynchronized, global-heap-mutating code in less than two percent of one hundred thousand publicly available Haskell modules in the Hackage package manager, representing 17 million lines of open source code. Targeting x86-64 architectures, if we attach memory barriers to all writes to shared mutable memory, only 483 benchmarks of 1,279 we surveyed issued any barriers at all (Section 7.3). For the 483 with barrier overhead, the geometric mean slowdown was only 0.4%. Further, only 12 benchmarks slow down more than 10%.

We believe SC is the right choice for the Haskell language moving forward, and, further, that SC-Haskell showcases a methodology for language design that emphasizes *modular* construction of effects on memory regions. Mixed-paradigm functional and object-oriented languages of the future have the option of reducing reliance on a monolithic shared memory, and instead using separate mechanisms for immutable data, thread-local state, and transactional state, just as Haskell does. The memory models for these languages can be much simpler to specify and simpler for the programmer to use. Finally, for the language designer, separate, modular memory effects can make *proving* sequential consistency easier, by showing that a specialized memory area is disjoint from the global heap (Section 4).

The contributions of this paper are:

- A formal operational semantics for core Haskell against a weak memory model following total-store-order (TSO). Using this we can show that our implementation strategy for global mutable state preserves SC while not adding overhead to thread-private or transactional state in the ST and STM types, respectively (Section 4).
- To our knowledge, the first practical demonstration that a mainstream concurrent language can provide SC with low overheads on a wide swath of application code. We demonstrate this with an empirical evaluation over a thousand benchmark programs (Section 7).
- A case study where we seek out examples of SC-Haskell adding barriers to core libraries, then demonstrate how these libraries can be rewritten to both avoid synchronization overheads *and have much stronger semantic guarantees*. In Section 6, we introduce two novel techniques for enforcing locking discipline and thread-private memory respectively.

2. Background: Mutability in Haskell

The first thing to know about Haskell is that functions and expressions are *pure*, i.e. lacking externally visible side effects. Thus a function of type `Int → Int` takes and returns a number but cannot print to the screen or modify memory.

Ultimately, such effects are a necessary part of programming, and they appear in Haskell in a manner explicitly marked in the types. Specifically, they are expressed in Haskell using *monadic* actions: explicit, first-class descriptions of effects to perform. Thus a function of type `Int → IO Int` takes and returns an integer, while *also* performing additional input/output side effects. Semantically, we view this function is as producing an "`IO Int`" object: an abstract description of the actions to perform later on. IO actions are realized only at the "`main`" function of a complete program. The main function provides the "imperative spine" of a program, even if the vast majority of the work happens in pure functions called from this spine.

Because they are first class values, IO actions can be put in a list or passed as inputs to functions. But for most programs this is irrelevant. Rather, a function in the IO monad (i.e., returning an `IO` action) is compiled to assembly code very similar to that produced from imperative code in other managed languages. From the point of view of the compiler, the monadic treatment is not very different than a type-effect system [24].

Mutable heap locations Within the IO monad, Haskell programmers use a simple library API to build and use mutable references:

```
newIORef   :: a → IO (IORef a)
readIORef  :: IORef a → IO a
writeIORef :: IORef a → a → IO ()
```

In these type signatures, the lower case "`a`" is a *type variable* indicating that the above functions are polymorphic and a `IORef a` is a mutable reference to an object of type `a`. Thus, `newIORef` takes an object of type a and returns a reference to a, with the side effect (indicated by `IO`) of allocating memory to hold the reference. The function `readIORef` takes such a reference and returns the value of the object. Haskell functions are usually *curried*, but the type of `writeIORef` could just as well be written `(IORef a, a) → IO()`; it takes a reference and a value and returns a *monadic action* that writes the value to the reference. Here, `()` is the *unit type*, equivalent to "void" or an empty tuple.

The monadic actions returned by the above functions are typically combined using `do` notation, e.g.:

```
-- A multi-line do-expression with type "IO Int":
do r ← newIORef 0  -- Initial value is zero
   writeIORef r 3  -- Modify value
   readIORef r     -- Returns three
```

When Haskell gained concurrency [32], IORefs could be accessed by multiple threads, by using forkIO to create language-level lightweight threads:

```
forkIO :: IO () → IO ThreadId
```

Unfortunately, no memory model was defined to specify which return values can be obtained from a `readIORef`. Indeed, to this date, the documentation[1] says only that:

> *IORef operations may appear out-of-order to another thread, depending on the memory model of the underlying processor architecture*

Our position is that `writeIORef`, **with these semantics, is harmful and unnecessary**: harmful because of debugging difficulties and even bugs on some architectures (Section 3); unnecessary, because it is possible to simply rely on other mechanisms. For starters, atomic operations are already provided for IORefs:

```
atomicWrite  :: IORef a → a → IO ()
atomicModify :: IORef a → (a → (a, b)) → IO b
```

Both were implemented in GHC with compare-and-swap. Both incur significant overhead and should be used sparingly, but they need not change to support SC.

Intercepting mutable state modifications Because mutable references do not have built-in syntax, it is straightforward to modify their behavior by modifying the library that exposes the above API. The same argument applies to Haskell's other mutable heap objects: (un)boxed arrays. By intercepting all calls that write to mutable, potentially-shared memory, we can enforce a new memory model. For example, in this work, we attach a store-load barrier to each `writeIORef` (turning it effectively into `atomicWrite`), which yields sequential consistency on any TSO architecture.

2.1 Thread-local state: ST monad

Before we go further in changing the semantics of IO-based state, first we look at the alternative mechanisms that allow programmers to *avoid* IO-based state in the first place. If a programmer needs to, e.g., implement an efficient in-place sort, then there are other monads to turn to in place of `IO`.

[1] `https://hackage.haskell.org/package/base-4.9.0.0/docs/Data-IORef.html`

A State Thread (ST) computation [22] enables private, thread-local mutable state. An action of type `ST s a` returns a value `a` while performing side effects on a memory region identified by `s`. Mutable memory managed by the ST monad includes references and arrays, but these data are not allowed to *escape* the state thread. That is, they cannot be read or changed by another ST computation with a different `s` parameter. Furthermore, ST computations cannot fork new threads, so mutable data structures in an ST computation are guaranteed to be used by only one thread.

In order to enforce this, the mutable datatypes—such as the `STRef` counterpart of `IORef`—must also be tagged with an `s` parameter, becoming `STRef s Int` instead of `IORef Int`. The function for mutating a reference then becomes:

```
writeSTRef :: STRef s a → a → ST s ()
```

Here the reference's `s` parameter must match the returned ST action. Eventually, we can eliminate the `s` parameter and embed an ST computation in pure code using `runST`:

```
runST :: (∀ s. ST s a) → a
```

Here is the old trick at the heart of the ST technique: the higher-rank type (indicated by the explicit "`∀ s.`" quantifier) is what *enforces* the requirement that no mutable data may escape the scope of the ST computation. That is, because of the limited *scope* of the `∀ s.` quantifier, if the programmer attempts to *return* a value such as an `STRef s Int`—i.e. smuggled inside of `runST`'s `a` return value—the compiler will report a type error. The `s` cannot escape its scope.

Critically, in order to enforce an SC memory model for Haskell, we do *not* need to add any additional synchronization to `STRef` operations, because they are guaranteed by the type system to be used in one thread, in which case SC is already preserved by all major architectures[2], including the x86 TSO architectures we focus on in our experiments.

Indeed, as we will see in Section 6 and Section 7, shifting most of the work in a program to (1) pure functions, or (2) ST computation, reduces the overhead of SC. But there's also a third category of mutable memory in Haskell—memory which *already* includes implicit synchronization.

2.2 Synchronized mem: STM, MVars, and beyond

In addition to the ST monad, Haskell programmers have at their disposal the STM monad, for *software transactional memory* [17]. Like other STM systems, transactions execute atomically. They are also restricted by the type system to be of a distinct type: `STM a` rather than `IO a`, and they mutate only references of type `TVar t`, never `IORef t`.

STM requires its own synchronization and retry strategy, and a correct implementation naturally preserves sequential consistency. As one of the major concurrency mechanisms in modern Haskell we include it in our formal treatment (Section 4) to show how it interacts with our language-level model of relaxed memory.

[2] by the *program order* relation

Haskell also has other forms of data with built-in synchronization, such as MVars, which include a full/empty bit and blocking operations, or the synchronization variables supported by a family of `Par` monads [28, 25, 20] that complement the existing ST and STM monads. We omit these from our formalism, though the treatment for MVars and Par would follow that of STM and ST respectively—no additional synchronization is needed to achieve SC. The real target of our SC-enforcement effort must be IO actions.

2.3 Safe Haskell

Ideally, the scope for enforcing a memory model would be "every program written in language X", i.e. all IO actions in all Haskell programs. However, even "safe" languages typically contain backdoors. For instance, Rust has the `unsafe` block, and Java has the JNI, which allows programmers to run unsafe C code. Haskell also has backdoors and under-the-hood primitives. In particular, GHC exposes several functions which can subvert programmer expectations, such as `unsafePerformIO`, which can break purity.

To avoid these pitfalls (except in specialized expert code), GHC has a Safe Haskell mode [40]. Safe Haskell is a subset of Haskell code for which the compiler verifies that certain key properties of a safe programming language holds, including type safety, referential transparency, and encapsulation of modules, by disallowing certain exotic language features and restricting the use of certain unsafe modules[3].

Safe Haskell provides a natural target for enforcing our memory model. We guarantee that compiling a module or package with the `-XSafe` flag results in an SC program. Libraries that use raw, lower level primitives (which may *leak* the weak memory model) are by default considered "Unsafe" and thus not available to Safe programs. On the other hand, select libraries can be marked as "Trustworthy", and become part of the trusted code base if they use unsafe features internally but expose only safe external interfaces.

3. Example: GHC type unsafety bug

In general, the "leave it to the architecture" approach to memory models is unacceptable, particularly for languages such as Haskell that otherwise provide a mathematically grounded semantics. However, this oversight is more than a specification problem. We found that the current version of GHC is **not type safe on ARM**. To see why, let's look at two ways that values can flow between threads.

First, purely functional computation can contain parallelism, where multiple threads share the same (pure) data structures. Due to lazy evaluation, a delayed computation (thunk) updated on one thread can issue writes that mutate the heap, which are then read by another thread. This scenario is correctly handled, with a memory fence preceding the write that commits a thunk update. Thus writes that initialize a data structure will be visible.

A second way data can flow between threads is IORefs:

```
-- Force allocation/initialization to happen on the child thread:
{-# NOINLINE mk #-}
mk x = MkMyStruct x
go = do r ← newIORef 0
        -- The $! operator is strict application, no thunks:
        forkIO (writeIORef r $! mk 3)
        readIORef r
```

In this program the `readIORef` may or may not observe the new value written to `r`. Unfortunately, here GHC has a bug as of version 7.10.3. The `MkMyStruct` heap value must be allocated and its initialization visible to the parent thread's `readIORef`. Yet GHC does *not* currently generate a fence on IORef update in the ARM backend. Thus the read may return an uninitialized value. We plan to fix the bug in GHC 8.2.

Java handles the similar problem of initializing final fields in object constructors by adding a fence at the end of such constructors. This solution, however, is unacceptable in our case as most objects are created in pure computations that never escape to the imperative spine of a Haskell program. Note that our fix erases the difference between `writeIORef` and `atomicWriteIORef` and automatically provides SC semantics on TSO architectures.

4. Formal semantics

In this section we introduce a formal model for SC-Haskell *as implemented on a weak-memory, TSO architecture*. In contrast, the simplest high-level model of SC-Haskell would take for granted a global, sequentially consistent memory and *not* address the question of how writes and reads are implemented. Here, we instead expose the *store buffer* which enables relaxed memory and closely follows current x86 hardware[4]. This enables us to explicitly model the implementation strategy of attaching barriers to IO writes (but not ST or STM writes). The "lower level" relaxed-memory operational semantics in this section would also be useful for explicitly reasoning about unsafe code or new extensions.

SC-Haskell is designed such that all well typed programs are sequentially consistent, that is, all programs would produce the same observable behavior under a semantics without store-buffers. The language we present is a combination of a core, purely functional language with a series of extensions for performing different kinds of side effects: IO, ST, and STM. Both purely functional and imperative programs are expressable in this language. To keep the size of the model reasonable, the only kind of mutable memory in the semantics we present are mutable references (not arrays).

[3] In fact, Safe Haskell can be used for untrusted code execution. A Haskell server receives untrusted code over the wire, specifies its expected type, and compiles it in Safe mode [40] together with runtime resource limits [42]. In this way it supports type-system-enforced safety rather than modified runtimes for sandboxing, such as found in Javascript [41].

[4] As shown in previous work on x86-TSO [35], the store-buffer based operational semantics is equivalent to an axiomatic semantics based on happens-before event graphs.

Further, we omit features of Haskell that do not directly relate to concurrency.

4.1 Abstract syntax

The abstract syntax for SC-Haskell is given in Figure 2. It is mostly standard. As in [28] and other semantics for subsets of Haskell, we consider monadic actions—e.g., writing to a mutable reference—to be *values*.

Our subset of SC-Haskell has syntax for `fork`, `runST`, operations on mutable references, and syntax for STM computations. The operations on references are parameterized by a subscript `m`, which is the monad in which the action occurs. Thus $\texttt{write}_{IO}$ is a shorthand for `writeIORef`, and so on.

States in SC-Haskell consist of a parallel composition of threads, $P \mid\mid \ldots \mid\mid Q$, where each thread contains a store buffer and a program term. While relaxed memory models are often formalized in a processor-centric rather than thread-centric fashion, it is reasonable to treat store buffers as per-thread (as previous authors have [9]). This is because a realistic implementation issues a memory fence when context switching between threads, which prevents sharing or aliasing of thread-local store buffers.

No special syntax is necessary for introducing fences. The `atomic` syntax, which is used to launch an STM transaction from within the IO monad, is used also wherever a memory fence is needed. Essentially, fence can be defined as an empty transaction: `fence = atomic (return ())`.

4.2 Static semantics for SC-Haskell

The static semantics for SC-Haskell are given in Figure 1. It is straightforward, and is similar previous formulations [22].

To support the $\forall$ quantifier in the typing judgment for `runST`, the static semantics have both types T and type schemes S:

$$
\begin{aligned}
& t, s \in \textsf{Type Variables} \\
\textsf{Types}\ T\ &::= t \mid T_1 \to T_2 \mid () \mid \\
&\quad \texttt{ST}\ T_1\ T_2 \mid \texttt{STRef}\ T_1\ T_2 \mid \\
&\quad \texttt{IO}\ T \mid \texttt{IORef}\ T \mid \\
&\quad \texttt{STM}\ T \mid \texttt{TVar}\ T \\
\textsf{Schemas}\ S\ &::= T \mid \forall t.S
\end{aligned}
$$

Type judgments could be included for reading and writing to references, but they are generally not interesting. Reading an IORef, for example, is a function that takes an r of type `(IORef a)` and returns a value of type `IO a`. `runST` is given its own typing judgment (`RUN`) to simplify the type system.

4.3 Dynamic Semantics

The main semantics for SC-Haskell are given as a small-step operational semantics via two relations: $\longrightarrow$ for pure computation, and $\underset{m}{\Longrightarrow}$ for monadic computation (Figure 4).

Structural congruence and structural transitions for states P, Q are given in Figure 3, ensuring that parallel composition is both associative and commutative. States obey an equivalence relation $\equiv$, defined up to α-equivalence.

APP
$$\frac{\Gamma \vdash M_1 : T_1 \to T_2 \qquad \Gamma \vdash M_2 : T_1}{\Gamma \vdash (M_1\ M_2) : T_2}$$

LAM
$$\frac{\Gamma, x : T_1 \vdash M : T_2}{\Gamma \vdash \lambda x \to e : T_1 \to T_2}$$

ATOMIC
$$\frac{\Gamma \vdash M : \texttt{STM}\ T}{\Gamma \vdash \texttt{atomic}\ M : \texttt{IO}\ T}$$

VAR
$$\Gamma, x : S \vdash x : S$$

SPEC
$$\frac{\Gamma \vdash M : \forall t.S}{\Gamma \vdash M : S[T/t]}\ t \notin FV(T)$$

GEN
$$\frac{\Gamma \vdash M : S}{\Gamma \vdash M : \forall t.S}\ t \notin FV(\Gamma)$$

RETURN
$$\frac{\Gamma \vdash M : T}{\Gamma \vdash \texttt{return}\ M : m\ T}$$

BIND
$$\frac{\Gamma \vdash M : m\ T_1 \qquad \Gamma \vdash N : T_1 \to m\ T_2}{\Gamma \vdash (M \texttt{ >>= } N) : m\ T_2}$$

RUN
$$\frac{\Gamma \vdash M : \forall t.\, \texttt{ST}\ t\ T}{\Gamma \vdash \texttt{runST}\ M : T}\ t \notin FV(T)$$

FORK
$$\frac{\Gamma \vdash M : \texttt{IO}\ ()}{\Gamma \vdash \texttt{fork}\ M : \texttt{IO}\ ()}$$

Figure 1: Static semantics for SC-Haskell

The pure relation $M \to N$ maps terms to terms, while the monadic relation $P; \Delta, \Theta \underset{m}{\Longrightarrow} Q; \Delta'; \Theta'$ maps a state, name environment, and global store to a new state, name environment, and global store. A state is either a thread (a term M and a thread-local buffer $\langle \Phi \rangle$) or a parallel composition of states $P \mid\mid Q$. Different syntax is used to express stores and buffers: buffers are *ordered*, and the semantics needs to, at various points, distinguish between accessing elements from the front (newer elements) or from the back (older elements) of the buffer. The store is an unordered map.

The main semantics for the monadic relation are given in Figure 4. A simple evaluation context $\mathcal{E}$ is used to drill into `>>=` (monadic bind):

$$\mathcal{E}\ ::=\ [\cdot] \mid \mathcal{E} \texttt{ >>= } M$$

4.3.1 Reduction rules

Most of the reduction rules in Figure 4 are straightforward, but we nevertheless explain them in turn below. For brevity we omit additional features of the STM monad, such as retrying or transaction composition. A full operational semantics for STM is given in [17].

Reading from mutable references happens in one of two ways. In READ-LOCAL, if `r` is mapped to `M` in the thread's local buffer Φ, then $\texttt{read}_m\ r$ evaluates to $\texttt{return}\ M$ (and a side condition ensures that the most recent occurence of `r` is used). Otherwise, in READ-GLOBAL, when `r` does *not* occur in Φ, it is looked up in the heap, Θ.

A FLUSH rule non-deterministically moves entries from a thread's local buffer to the global store. It pulls elements out of the right side of Φ, which acts as a FIFO buffer. The only way entries are added to the global store in the language is through FLUSH, so only this rule must be considered when reasoning about writes to the store.

When creating a new reference in NEW, a fresh reference r is created, and local buffer Φ is extended on the left with a new mapping. This is where Δ is needed, to enable globally unique names that do not occur in the store or any thread's store buffer. The NEW serves for all three monads.

WRITEIO reduces a write action $\texttt{write}_{IO}\ r\ \ M$ to `atomic (return ())`, while appending the write of M to r to the local buffer. Because writes are performed purely for side effects, they return a unit value, or `()`.

In rule FORKIO, on `fork` M a single thread forks into two threads, with the child thread added to the pool to execute the term M. Child threads are executed for effect—they never return a value, and there is no thread-join. Before forking, a thread must have flushed its buffer.

Rule WRITEST(M) is similar to WRITEIO, but leaves out the memory fence. Because the type system ensures that STRefs are thread-local, it is not necessary to ensure that writes to STRefs move to the global store. Likewise, STM writes are synchronized by other means, whose implementation is not modeled explicitly, but is abstracted into the ATOMIC rule.

RUNST states that if a term M reduces to a result N via some ST computation, then the pure term `runST` M can be reduced to to N, effectively turning an ST computation into a pure computation. One interesting aspect is that when a `runST` completes, all remaining state in the store buffer and the (local) store become garbage.

In ATOMIC, if M reduces via a multi-step STM computation to `return` N, then `atomic` M can be reduced in the IO monad to `return` N. The rule also enforces that the thread-local buffer was flushed during the STM computation.

4.4 Sequential Consistency: Proof sketch

Toward proving SC, we propose a new reduction relation $\underset{m}{\Rrightarrow}'$, which corresponds to reduction relation $\underset{m}{\Rrightarrow}$ minus the use of local store buffers. A translation function takes a configuration $P; \Delta; \Theta$ to an equivalent configuration that lacks a store buffer:

$$\begin{aligned} \mathcal{T}[\![P \mid\mid Q]\!] &= \mathcal{T}[\![P]\!] \mid\mid \mathcal{T}[\![Q]\!] \\ \mathcal{T}[\![\langle\cdot\rangle M; \Delta; \Theta]\!] &= M; \Delta; \Theta \\ \mathcal{T}[\![\langle\Phi(r, N)\rangle M; \Delta; \Theta]\!] &= \mathcal{T}[\![\langle\Phi\rangle M; \Delta; \Theta[r \mapsto N]]\!] \end{aligned}$$

It is important that $\mathcal{T}[\![]\!]$ collapses Φ into Θ by copying elements from right-to-left, just as FLUSH moves writes from the right of the buffer into the store. A buffer may contain several writes to a reference r, and the final state of Θ should reflect those writes happening in the correct order.

$$x, y \in \textsf{Variables} \quad r \in \textsf{Refs}$$

$$\begin{aligned} \textsf{Terms}\ M, N &::= x \mid V \mid M\ N \mid \texttt{runST}\ M \mid \cdots \\ \textsf{Values}\ V &::= \lambda x \to M \mid \texttt{return}\ M \mid M\ \texttt{>>=}\ N \\ &\mid \texttt{fork}\ M \mid \texttt{atomic}\ M \\ &\mid \texttt{new}_m\ M \mid \texttt{write}_m\ r\ N \mid \texttt{read}_m\ r \\ \textsf{Monads}\ m &::= IO \mid ST \mid STM \\ \textsf{States}\ P, Q, R &::= \langle\Phi\rangle M \mid P \mid\mid Q \\ \textsf{Buffer}\ \Phi &::= \cdot \mid \Phi\ \Phi \mid (r, M) \end{aligned}$$

Figure 2: Abstract syntax for SC-Haskell programs, and for abstract machine states.

$$P \mid\mid Q \equiv Q \mid\mid P \qquad P \mid\mid (Q \mid\mid R) \equiv (P \mid\mid Q) \mid\mid R$$

$$\frac{P; \Delta; \Theta \underset{m}{\Rrightarrow} Q; \Delta'; \Theta'}{P \mid\mid R; \Delta; \Theta \underset{m}{\Rrightarrow} Q \mid\mid R; \Delta'; \Theta'}$$

$$\frac{P \equiv P' \qquad P'; \Delta; \Theta \underset{m}{\Rrightarrow} Q'; \Delta'; \Theta' \qquad Q' \equiv Q}{P; \Delta; \Theta \underset{m}{\Rrightarrow} Q; \Delta'; \Theta'}$$

Figure 3: Congruence rules for states

For simplicity we omit most of the details of $\underset{m}{\Rrightarrow}'$. The rules are a direct simplification of those in Figure 4. For example, translating the ATOMIC rule simply involves removing the barriers from the configurations:

$$\text{ATOMIC'}\quad \frac{M; \Delta; \Theta \underset{STM}{\Rrightarrow}'^{*} \texttt{return}\ N; \Delta'; \Theta'}{\texttt{atomic}\ M; \Delta; \Theta \underset{IO}{\Rrightarrow}' \texttt{return}\ N; \Delta'\Theta'}$$

Lemma 4.1 *$\mathcal{T}[\![\langle\Phi\rangle \texttt{read}_m\ r; \Delta; \Theta]\!]$ is equivalent to $\texttt{read}_m\ r; \Delta; \Theta$ in $\underset{m}{\Rrightarrow}'$.*

PROOF Follows from the definition of $\mathcal{T}[\![]\!]$.

Lemma 4.2 *$\mathcal{T}[\![\langle\Phi\rangle \texttt{write}_{ST}\ r\ M; \Delta; \Theta]\!]$ is equivalent to $\texttt{write}_{ST}\ r\ M; \Delta; \Theta$ in $\underset{m}{\Rrightarrow}'$.*

PROOF Follows from the definition of $\mathcal{T}[\![]\!]$.

Lemma 4.3 *`atomic (return ())` is equivalent to `return ()` under the $\underset{m}{\Rrightarrow}'$ relation.*

PROOF Follows from the ATOMIC' rule.

Theorem 4.4 *Given a term M and a name environment Δ such that $\langle\cdot\rangle M; \Delta; \cdot \underset{ST}{\Rrightarrow}^{*} \langle\Phi\rangle \texttt{return}\ N; \Delta; \Theta$, then $\mathcal{T}[\![\langle\cdot\rangle M; \Delta; \cdot]\!] \underset{ST}{\Rrightarrow}'^{*} \mathcal{T}[\![\langle\Phi\rangle \texttt{return}\ N; \Delta; \Theta]\!]$.*

PROOF SKETCH RUNST is defined so that non-interference is "baked in"—we start with an empty buffer and store, and the types ensure that only thread-local references are written to them. From lemma 4.1 and lemma 4.2, reading from and writing to the local buffer is equivalent to reading from and

$$\frac{M \longrightarrow M'}{MN \longrightarrow M'N} \qquad (\lambda x \to M)N \longrightarrow M[x/N]$$

PURE
$$\frac{M \longrightarrow N}{\langle\Phi\rangle\mathcal{E}[M];\Delta;\Theta \underset{m}{\rightrightarrows} \langle\Phi\rangle\mathcal{E}[N];\Delta;\Theta}$$

BIND-RETURN
$$\langle\Phi\rangle\mathcal{E}[\texttt{return}\ M\ \texttt{>>=}\ N];\Delta;\Theta \underset{m}{\rightrightarrows} \langle\Phi\rangle\mathcal{E}[N\ M];\Delta;\Theta$$

NEW
$$\begin{array}{l}\langle\Phi\rangle\mathcal{E}[\texttt{new}_m\ M];\Delta;\Theta \underset{m}{\rightrightarrows} \\ \langle(r,M)\ \Phi\rangle\mathcal{E}[\texttt{return}\ r];\Delta,r;\Theta\end{array} \quad r \notin \Delta$$

READ-LOCAL
$$\begin{array}{l}\langle\Phi_1\ (r,M)\ \Phi_2\rangle\mathcal{E}[\texttt{read}_m\ r];\Delta;\Theta \underset{m}{\rightrightarrows} \\ \langle\Phi_1\ (r,M)\ \Phi_2\rangle\mathcal{E}[\texttt{return}\ M];\Delta;\Theta\end{array} \quad r \notin Dom(\Phi_1)$$

READ-GLOBAL
$$\begin{array}{l}\langle\Phi\rangle\mathcal{E}[\texttt{read}_m\ r];\Delta;\Theta[r \mapsto M] \underset{m}{\rightrightarrows} \\ \langle\Phi\rangle\mathcal{E}[\texttt{return}\ M];\Delta;\Theta[r \mapsto M]\end{array} \quad r \notin Dom(\Phi)$$

FLUSH
$$\langle\Phi\ (r,N)\rangle\mathcal{E}[M];\Delta;\Theta \underset{m}{\rightrightarrows} \langle\Phi\rangle\mathcal{E}[M];\Delta;\Theta[r \mapsto N]$$

WRITEIO
$$\begin{array}{l}\langle\Phi\rangle\mathcal{E}[\texttt{write}_{IO}\ r\ M];\Delta;\Theta \underset{IO}{\rightrightarrows} \\ \langle(r,M)\ \Phi\rangle\mathcal{E}[\texttt{atomic (return ())}];\Delta;\Theta\end{array}$$

FORKIO
$$\langle\cdot\rangle\mathcal{E}[\texttt{fork}\ M];\Delta;\Theta \underset{IO}{\rightrightarrows} (\langle\cdot\rangle\mathcal{E}[\texttt{return ()}] \mid\mid \langle\cdot\rangle M);\Delta;\Theta$$

WRITEST(M)
$$\begin{array}{l}\langle\Phi\rangle\mathcal{E}[\texttt{write}_m\ r\ M];\Delta;\Theta \underset{m}{\rightrightarrows} \\ \langle(r,M)\ \Phi\rangle\mathcal{E}[\texttt{return ()}];\Delta;\Theta\end{array} \quad m \in \{ST, STM\}$$

RUNST
$$\frac{\langle\cdot\rangle M;\Delta;\cdot \underset{ST}{\rightrightarrows}{}^{*} \langle\Phi\rangle\texttt{return}\ N;\Delta';\Theta}{\texttt{runST}\ M \longrightarrow N}$$

ATOMIC
$$\frac{\langle\Phi\rangle M;\Delta;\Theta \underset{STM}{\rightrightarrows}{}^{*} \langle\cdot\rangle\texttt{return}\ N;\Delta';\Theta'}{\langle\Phi\rangle\texttt{atomic}\ M;\Delta;\Theta \underset{IO}{\rightrightarrows} \langle\cdot\rangle\texttt{return}\ N;\Delta';\Theta'}$$

Figure 4: Reduction rules for the pure and monadic relations

writing to the store after translation. Reads directly from the store are unchanged.

Theorem 4.5 *Given a state* P *and store* Θ *such that* $P;\Delta;\Theta \underset{STM}{\rightrightarrows}{}^{*}Q;\Delta;\Theta'$, *then* $\mathcal{T}[\![P;\Delta;\Theta]\!] \underset{STM}{\rightrightarrows}{}'^{*}\mathcal{T}[\![Q;\Delta;\Theta']\!]$.

PROOF SKETCH Similar to theorem 4.4.

Theorem 4.6 *Given a state* P*, a name environment* Δ*, and store* Θ *such that* $P;\Delta;\Theta \underset{IO}{\rightrightarrows}{}^{*}Q;\Delta';\Theta'$*, then* $\mathcal{T}[\![P;\Delta;\Theta]\!] \underset{IO}{\rightrightarrows}{}'^{*}\mathcal{T}[\![Q;\Delta';\Theta']\!]$.

PROOF SKETCH We proceed by induction on the monadic reduction relation $\underset{IO}{\rightrightarrows}$. Assuming, for all reductions R of size N in the relation $\underset{IO}{\rightrightarrows}$, there exists an equivalent reduction R' in the relation $\underset{IO}{\rightrightarrows}{}'$:

The cases for reduction rules BIND-RETURN, NEW, FLUSH, FORKIO, WRITEST(M), and PURE are straightforward.

In the case of rules READ-LOCAL and READ-GLOBAL, either a reference r occurs in Φ, or it is absent from Φ and present in Θ. The latter case is trivial, and the former case follows from lemma 4.1.

In the case of WRITEIO, we know by lemma 4.3 that WRITEIO' is equivalent to WRITEST(M)'. From there we can use lemma 4.2.

The ATOMIC case can be proven from theorem 4.5.

5. Implementation

Our changes to GHC were relatively minor. It is possible to narrow down the `Safe` uses of global heap mutation to a handful of functions in the Haskell standard libraries. Therefore, patching those functions to insert memory barriers is sufficient to make GHC sequentially consistent. This precisely follows the formal model of the previous section.

The abstraction of SC is useful to the programmer only if the provided granularity is at least as large as individual program variables. Haskell IORefs have the nice property that sharing occurs at the granularity of a reference and all hardware architectures enable (properly-aligned) addresses to be read and written atomically. Implementing unboxed arrays (`Data.Vector.Unboxed`) requires care, e.g., to provide atomic 64-bit accesses on 32-bit architectures. In GHC, vectors use *type families* (type-level functions), so their representation can be changed based on the element type. This makes it straightforward to implement an additional level of boxing for `Vector Double` on 32-bit architectures.

5.1 Barrier insertion

We added a new primitive operation to GHC 7.10.3 called `storeLoadBarrier#`, which, when compiled down to x86 assembly, emits a `lock` instruction followed by an `addq`. Although `storeLoadBarrier#` can work in any state-transforming monad, which includes ST, in practice we only use `storeLoadBarrier#` in the presence of IO. Hence, we need only introduce one more function, `storeLoadBarrier :: IO ()`, which encapsulates `storeLoadBarrier#` in an IO context.

Equipped with `storeLoadBarrier`, we searched through `base`, Haskell's standard library, for any `Safe` or `Trustworthy` modules with functions that expose the ability to mutate the global heap. This includes the API for IORefs as well as other primitive data structures, such as mutable arrays. For each function that directly writes to global memory, we inserted a `storeLoadBarrier` to ensure that SC is upheld.

5.2 Low-level libraries

Patching `base` is not the end of the story, since many Haskell libraries bypass `base` and use mutable references from another library called `primitive`. Libraries which utilize `primitive` include the widely used `vector` library. To ensure that we obtained an accurate picture of how SC affects Haskell libraries in the wild, we also patched the `primitive` library to make use of `storeLoadBarrier` after writes.

Crucially, `primitive` abstracts over both `ST` and `IO` with a type parameter `m`. In our modification, we emit barriers only when `m` ultimately equals `IO`. A consequence of this is that programmers can use `primitive` to write functions that are polymorphic over whether they will need a barrier on writes to enforce SC. For the most part, adding barriers did not effect the existing Safe Haskell properties of `base` (though we did need to change the type of `stToIO`, as described in Appendix A.1).

6. Case studies: auditing fenced references

Before diving into the results, we examine uses of non-atomic writes found in commonly used Haskell code. While uses of mutable memory are relatively rare (see Section 7.2) in both core libraries and large-scale applications, one can still find code which mutates memory in the IO monad.

Our large-scale evaluation in Section 7, shows a *worst case* SC-scenario—*only* adding the barriers described in Section 5, nothing more. We believe that while the basic technique is already low overhead, that this is only the *beginning* of a transition for the Haskell ecosystem as a whole. Ultimately, it should be possible to rewrite virtually every use of a `writeIORef` to use another alternative that either (1) removes the overhead, and/or (2) enforces even stronger semantics, such as statically-guaranteed data-race freedom. Specifically, there are many techniques one can employ to transition IORef-heavy code over to ST-style mechanisms.

6.1 Buggy uses of `writeIORef`

Auditing the uses of `writeIORef` in Haskell code can reveal bugs (data races) that expose non-SC behavior. One source of problems is APIs which are unclear about thread safety guarantees. The standard `System.Random` library exposes a *global* random number generator (as well as the ability to coin local RNGs). The global RNG can be used and updated atomically, which internally uses `atomicModifyIORef`, and it can be read with `getStdGen` and written with `setStdGen`:

```
setStdGen :: StdGen → IO ()
setStdGen sgen = writeIORef theStdGen sgen
```

Here the update is non-atomic! Yet the documentation makes no mention that this part of the API is *non-thread safe*. Therefore, enforcing SC in GHC fixes a bug in `random`, making the write atomic, and likely fixes bugs in other packages that use `writeIORef` or `modifyIORef` carelessly.

In many cases, the extra memory fence will be enough to provide SC semantics, but *not* enough to statically enforce a correct thread-safe behavior. In those cases, we can build new type-safe mechanisms to ensure stronger safety properties. We cover two examples in the next two subsections.

6.2 Handle: informal, unenforced locking protocols

The `base` library features a `Handle` datatype used for managing file handle operations. `Handle` uses IORefs in a way such that they cannot be trivially converted to STRefs. The (abridged) definition of `Handle` is:

```
data Handle =
  FileHandle FilePath (MVar Handle__)
data Handle__ =
  Handle__ (IORef (Buffer Word8))
           (IORef (Buffer CharBufElem))
           (IORef (BufferList CharBufElem))
```

A file handle is essentially a group of IORefs that are mutated in response to file I/O. These IORefs are used by multiple threads, but they are only reachable from the MVar in a `Handle`, and that the MVar serves as a *lock* that protects the IORefs. As mentioned earlier, an MVar is a synchronization variable which obeys a blocking interface:

```
newMVar  :: a → IO (MVar a)
putMVar  :: MVar a → a → IO ()
takeMVar :: MVar a → IO a
```

An MVar is either full or empty—equivalent to a length-one blocking FIFO. When used as a lock, taking from an MVar is "lock", and putting it back is "unlock". As in most imperative languages, this locking mechanism is not enforced by the type system, and thus nothing prevents a programmer from storing a reference to the `Handle__` outside the MVar and performing non-atomic operations on its IORefs.

While SC-Haskell will ensure that all IORef operations are SC, it's still not a satisfactory solution. Now `Handle` operations must bear the extra overhead of memory fences unnecessarily, since multiple threads shouldn't be modifying mutable state concurrently in the first place! We wish to enforce the *correct* locking behavior and avoid the overhead.

MVarLock solution: Our proposed solution is to introduce a new data type:

```
newtype MVarLock s a = MVarLock (MVar a)
```

This is just an MVar with an extra type parameter `s`. The `s` represents pieces of state, most notably the state in an ST computation. Holding an MVarLock gives the authority to modify both the underlying value inside the MVar as well as any other state tagged with `s`.

We can refactor `Handle` to make use of MVarLocks:

```
data Handle = ∀ s.
  FileHandle FilePath (MVarLock s Handle__)
data Handle__ s =
  Handle__ (STRef s (Buffer Word8))
           (STRef s (Buffer CharBufElem))
           (STRef s (BufferList CharBufElem))
```

Finally, we need a way to modify the state held by an MVarLock. This is accomplished with:

```
withMVarLock :: MVarLock s a
             → (a → ST s (a, b))
             → IO b
withMVarLock (MVarLock mv) fn =
```

```
do x ← takeMVar mv
   (a,b) ← unsafeSTToIO (fn x)
   putMVar mv a
   return b
```

Of course, this function itself must be a part of the trusted codebase due to the use of `unsafeSTToIO`. Likewise, `MVarLock` is an *abstract data type*, such that the end user cannot access the underlying, raw `MVar` value.

In `withMVarLock`, the ST computation serves as a *transaction* to execute while holding the lock. This goes beyond `runST`, because the state lives across multiple sessions, intermixed with IO. But the basic idea is the same: The $\forall s$ in the `Handle` declaration ensures statically that no references to the mutable state can escape. Dynamically, `withMVarLock` ensures that the state is modified only while holding the lock.

While analogous to the formulation of locking in Rust, `MVarLock` is actually more general, because it allows modifying state that is stored *outside* of the value pointed to the lock itself (i.e. the `a` in `MVarLock s a`). To our knowledge, this is a novel formulation of type-enforced locking, which is lighter-weight than static solutions that require full permission types [29] or session types [39].

6.3 A web server with unnecessary IORefs

In the evaluation (Section 7), we use a web server as an example application to measure SC-Haskell's overhead, because it is necessarily IO intensive, and a likely candidate for high SC-overhead. In examining the snap web server[5], we found that because most of the application involves IO, there are in fact several uses of IORefs that could potentially be avoided. For instance, inside the large record type that represent client requests, the request body is an `IORef`:

```
data Request = Request { ···
     rqBody :: IORef SomeEnumerator
      ··· }
```

Following the decision to use this and other IORef fields, there are 29 uses of `writeIORef` across the three core snap packages[6]. The request body is either initialized or rewritten in several places. Because snap is a multi-threaded application, it would increase confidence that accesses to `rqBody` are non-racy by simply using `atomicModifyIORef` to update `rqBody`. But this could introduce substantial overhead because an atomic modification is roughly ten times as expensive as an unsynchronized write (Table 1).

A better solution in this case is to enforce snap's invariant that *separate clients are handled by separate threads*, and each client's data structures are modified only by a *single* thread. We propose a simple solution—not to use locks or atomic updates—but instead to dynamically enforce that the thread accessing the state is the *same thread* that created it:

```
newtype TLState s = TLState ThreadId
newTLState :: (∀ s . TLState s → ST s b)
                      → IO b
withTLState :: TLState s → ST s b → IO b
```

Here we create a token `TLState s`, which binds together the thread ID (dynamic value) and the type of the state. Typically, the `b` value above must use an existential type to capture both the `TLState` and the references it protects. For instance, this data type that stores a token together with a mutable reference to an integer:

```
data Pk = ∀s. Pk (TLState s) (STRef s Int64)
```

We can create a new `Pk` value, hiding `s`, as follows:

```
do e ← newTLState (λtls →
         do r ← newSTRef 3
            return (Pk tls r))
```

And then peek inside the value and modify it:

```
case e of
  Pk t r → withTLState t (writeSTRef r 4)
```

To our knowledge, `TLState` is novel and does not previously occur in the literature or folklore. Yet it is a simply way to enforce that thread-private state stays thread-private. Further, while Table 1 shows that the overhead of `withTLState` is about the *same* as a memory fenced `writeIORef` (7 or 8 nanoseconds), there are several benefits:

1. The measurement for a fenced IORef is *optimistic* because, architecturally, the cost of a fence depends on how full the store buffer is. When benchmarking fenced writes in a loop, the buffer is always empty.
2. The cost of `withTLState` can be *amortized* by checking the token once and then performing an arbitrary number of `ST` operations against the state. E.g. `withTLState` can be lifted outside of loops.
3. `TLState` provides stronger semantics than an SC-preserving IORef, guaranteeing data-race freedom rather than SC.

In summary, `MVarLock` and `TLState`, enable small reductions in overhead. However, *there's limited room to improve*, as most Haskell programs have little performance impact for SC, as we'll see in the next section. Rather, these techniques provide a *continuum* for improvement in *semantic* guarantees: SC becomes the new baseline, and static data-race freedom becomes the goal, with a whole ecosystem full of code that needs to be pushed up the slope.

7. Evaluation

Unless otherwise mentioned, we run our benchmarks on a cluster of identically configured dual-socket Xeons (E5-2670 2.60GHz) with 32GB of memory. Not all benchmarks are parallel, but all are compiled to support parallelism and linked with the threaded runtime system; thus they pay the cost for SC whether or not they are multithreaded.

For all our results, we use the `criterion` package [1] to report the marginal cost of performing one additional operation. This is done by repeatedly measuring 20 seconds worth

[5] http://snapframework.com/

[6] snap-0.14.0.7, snap-core-0.9.8.0, snap-server-0.9.5.1

Method	Cost
writeSTRef	1.67ns
writeIORef (w/barrier)	7.24ns
atomicModifyIORef	11.2ns
MVarLock/writeIORef	28.1ns
TLS Check/writeIORef	7.78ns
read ThreadId only	1.81ns

Table 1: Reference update costs. Here we use linear regression to compute the marginal cost of one loop iteration that writes a boxed integer into a mutable reference.

of a particular computation and fitting a linear-regression model to the timing results. This methodology can perform timing measurements at nanosecond granularities.

We also include limited results from an NVIDIA Jetson TK1 board, with a quad-core ARM Cortex A15 CPU. We were not able to run more extensive benchmarks due to the limited portability of many Haskell libraries.

7.1 Microbenchmarks

Reference overheads First, we look at the overheads of individual IORef operations as shown in Table 1. One takeaway is that MVar-based locks are expensive. A spinlock could probably do somewhat better, but an `atomicModifyIORef` is already more efficient. Thus `MVarLock` should only be used when the program already has MVars, as in the `Handle` case study. The cost of the `TLState` operation depends on how efficiently the thread-ID operation is implemented, and whether storing the token value inhibits other compiler optimizations.

Trust the standard library? We described the `Handle` implementation in Section 6.2. It is one of fourteen components of the standard library that we found which use `IORefs` internally. We audited these and decide that several, including `Handle` can become part of the trusted code base. They need no fences to guarantee SC. Others, like `System.Random`, expose get and set methods and require barriers.

We tested the performance impact of trusting versus not trusting the `Handle/Bytestring` implementations. We tested the overhead of `getLine`, which internally updates several `IORefs` while holding the `MVar` lock. We found that each `getLine` call executes exactly two memory fences if run *untrusted*. In this case, the optimization to eliminate the memory fences—which are redundant with taking the MVar lock—has a small but measurable impact. Using linear regression, we computed the cost of each `getLine` as 220ns with the barriers and 212ns without (with an R^2 fit of 1.000). In this case, we tried to *maximize* the overhead by making the lines themselves very short: two characters. The result reinforces the intuition that "stray" fences are unlikely to incur substantial overhead unless they are inside a tight inner loop: true IO or other substantial work in the loop is likely to amortize the cost of stray fences.

Operation	Lines	Modules
`writeIORef`	4,450 (0.03%)	1,504 (1.47%)
`modifyIORef`	1,631 (0.009%)	564 (0.55%)
Total non-atomic	6,028 (0.03%)	1,767 (1.73%)
`atomicModifyIORef`	1,263 (0.007%)	460 (0.50%)
`atomicWriteIORef`	53 (0.0003%)	22 (0.02%)
Total atomic	1,310 (0.008%)	469 (0.46%)
Total:	17,435,314	102,266

Table 2: Frequency of IORef operations within all packages.

7.2 Static code survey: Hackage

Hackage is the central repository of open-source Haskell packages on the Internet. At the time of writing, Hackage contains 9,017 packages, which contain 17,435,314 lines of Haskell code. We searched all Hackage packages to ascertain the number of uses of unsynchronized `writeIORef` and `modifyIORef` functions, in order to estimate the approximate frequency of packages susceptible to non-SC behavior and to overhead under with SC-Haskell.

Of the 9,017 packages, 379 (4.20%) contain at least one use of `modifyIORef`, and 816 (9.05%) contain at least one use of `writeIORef`. Note that under TSO, SC-Haskell does not insert fences on packages that only contain `readIORef`.

A package typically contains multiple *modules* such as `Data.Map` and `Data.Set`. In Table 2, we measure the occurrences of the IORef operations as a percentage of modules and lines of code. One thing that we see is that even among modules that had `writeIORef`, the number of occurrences per module was less than three on average. `writeIORef` is used sparingly, which is consistent with our expectation that it is usually used for configuration, or coarse-grained communication. Thus we predict that the probability that `writeIORef` is used in an inner loop (such that fence overhead will be substantial) is low. But to evaluate this, we need benchmarks that evaluate a large cross-section of Haskell code.

7.3 `nofib` and Stackage benchmark suites

`nofib` [31] is a collection of Haskell benchmarks that GHC developers use to determine if a new feature results in an appreciable difference in performance. Most `nofib` programs do not mutate global state directly. If the `Handle` implementation is *not* trusted, most benchmarks will perform some memory barriers by virtue of writing to file handles. Here we report on our optimized version with a trusted `Handle`. For details on the savings of this choice, see Appendix A.2 for the full numbers with the unoptimized variant and its additional barriers.

We ran each `nofib` benchmark 20 times with both "stock" GHC and SC-Haskell and calculated the mean runtimes. Within `nofib`, `k-nucleotide` and `n-body` are the only benchmarks which perform (non-file-handle-related) memory barriers, so we focus on those. The total runtime for `k-nucleotide` was 4.0% slower with SC-Haskell than stock GHC, and

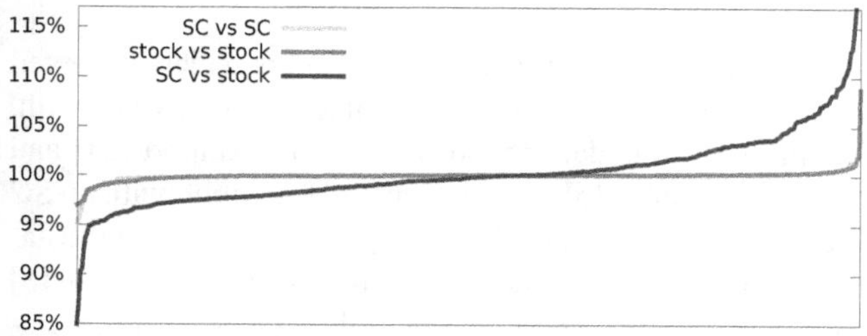

Figure 5: Stackage benchmarks. The X-axis ranges from 1 to 483 benchmarks, sorted by change in runtime. Self comparison allows us to calibrate the degree of variation expected due to noise or inappropriate use of randomness in a large "crowdsourced" benchmark collection.

for `n-body`, the runtime was 0.8% slower. The overall geometric mean runtime for SC-Haskell was 3.3% slower than stock, however. While `k-nucleotide` and `n-body` are long-running, `nofib` unfortunately contains many short-running benchmarks that contribute to noise in this geomean result. For example, the `lcss` benchmark ran for 0.212 seconds on stock GHC and 0.229 seconds on SC-Haskell.

We were also able to evaluate `nofib` on ARM[7]. Here we added additional fences to all `readIORef` operations. The overhead remained low: the overall geomean runtime for SC-Haskell was 1.9% slower than stock.

Noise notwithstanding, the main take away is a *negative result*—that this repository of large benchmark applications does *not* make substantial use of mutable references or arrays in a way that would incur an unacceptable SC penalty.

Stackage: A broader set of benchmarks comes from analyzing Stackage. Stackage is an online repository of curated Haskell libraries that have been confirmed to compile when built against the other libraries in Stackage. Therefore, a simple and effective way to run many working Haskell benchmarks in the wild is to download all packages from Stackage and filter the ones that contain benchmarks. These contain everything from data structure benchmarks to application benchmarks (such as the `pandoc` package).

We ran the benchmarks from the LTS-5.16 Stackage resolver, which uses GHC 7.10.3, the same version of GHC that we modified. From that resolver, we uncovered 61 benchmark suites that ran to completion, with a grand total of 1,279 individual benchmarks. Of those, 19 benchmark suites (483 individual benchmarks) emitted at least one write barrier when compiled with SC-Haskell. In fact, few of these emitted many barriers-per-iteration; the worst offenders are listed in Table 3. We ran benchmarks against stock GHC 7.10.3 (which we refer to as LTS-GHC) as well as SC-Haskell, averaging the results of eight full runs.

Across the 483 benchmarks with added fences, the geometric mean runtime for SC-Haskell was 0.4% slower than LTS-GHC. This is encouraging, but this result hides a large benchmark-specific variance that we discuss below.

[7] One `nofib` test had to be disabled on ARM due to a codegen bug.

Benchmark	Barriers performed
`tls-1.3.7`	278
`incremental-parser-0.2.4.1`	421
`mutable-containers-0.3.2.1`/ref	1,500
`mutable-containers-0.3.2.1`/deque	9,800
`wai-middleware-metrics-0.2.3`	20,000
`conduit-extra-1.1.13.1`	200,156

Table 3: Memory barriers on selected Stackage benchmarks.

There's also one extreme outlier; one of the benchmarks is explicitly designed to measure the cost to modify an IORef 1,500 times. Not surprisingly, SC-Haskell is 182.96% slower than with LTS-GHC. This represents the worst case for SC-Haskell. Fortunately, this anomalous behavior does not occur in other programs. Even with the outlier, it is trivial to replace the non-escaping IORef with an STRef and achieve performance parity between LTS-GHC and SC-Haskell.

Barring the `IORef` benchmark, only 8 benchmarks have an overhead greater than 10% with a maximum of 17.7%. Surprisingly, two benchmarks consistently showed a *speedup* of greater than 10% with the maximum of 15.0%. The overhead for the remaining benchmarks ranged from 10% to -10%, suggesting an inherent noise in our measurements for these benchmarks. To visualize noise effects, in Figure 5 we plot the distribution of overhead among the 483 bechmarks. We compare this variation against that incurred by *self comparison*. I.e. we split the 8 runs into two groups of four and compare LTS-GHC to itself and SC-Haskell to itself. Here we see variation at the tails, even with self-comparison, but *bigger* differences between SC and LTS-GHC. We conclude that while SC makes certain benchmarks slower, and while it causes a general shift in position (slowing down and speeding up), averaging out the noise reveals that SC did not impose too much of a performance hit as a whole.

Finally, while we were not able to build all the dependencies for Stackage benchmarks on ARM, we can *simulate* the expected overhead on an architecture with weaker-than-TSO consistency. We ran all the Stackage benchmarks on our x86 platform with additional fences on all `readIORef` operations. This added an addition 0.2% geomean overhead, with a worst-case of an additional 33% overhead.

7.4 TechEmpower web server benchmarks

The TechEmpower benchmark suite compares over 100 web frameworks implemented in various languages. We choose web servers because they emphasize the `IO` monad and stress the parts of the GHC runtime system (e.g. IO and event manager) that receive extra memory fences. Four Haskell frameworks are included in the TechEmpower suite: wai, snap, spock, and yesod. As a point of comparison, in Round 12 of the official TechEmpower benhcmarks wai ranks 12/195 and snap 88/195 in the "JSON" benchmark, and they rank 23rd and 76th out of 159 entrants in the "Plaintext" benchmark.

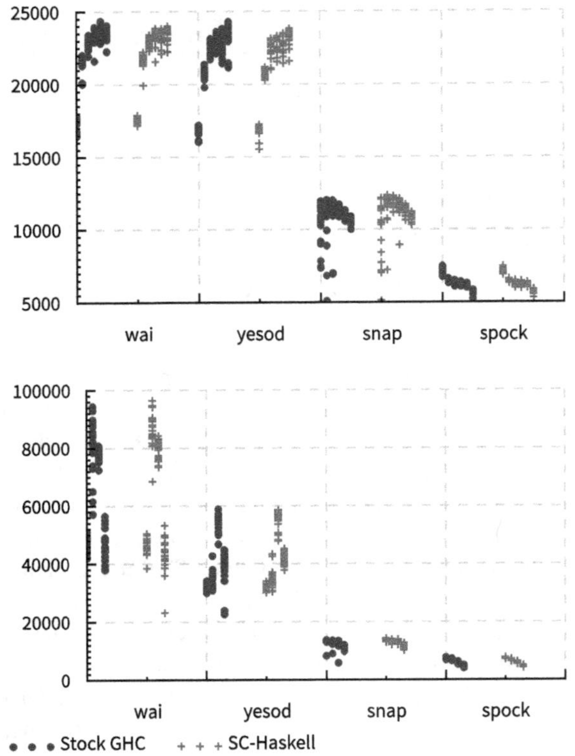

Figure 6: Web server benchmarks; Json serialization benchmark above, Plaintext responses below. Y-axis is throughput in requests/second. Each benchmark runs multiple experiments, which are aligned in slightly offset columns. The large gaps between columns represent different web servers.

The TechEmpower "vagrant-production" environment creates three dual-core virtual machines for the client, server, and database respectively. We run these VMs on one 18 core Xeon E5-2699 (2.3GHz, 64GB) machine, which makes it less likely that networking is a bottleneck rather than CPU. The raw data is shown in Figure 6. Each run of the benchmark suite tests the server in multiple bouts, each of which is shown separately as a slightly offset subcolumn. The whole benchmark suite was run 20 times with stock GHC and 20 times with our SC-Haskell patches, meaning that each vertical column of the scatterplot contains 20 points.

Surprisingly, there is no statistically significant overhead on either benchmark, with wai, yesod, or spock. This was determined by a Mann Whitney U test with a p-value of 0.05. This same test reported that snap had a small difference in performance—it got *faster*. We believe small variations in results are likely due inaccurate timing used by the TechEmpower infrastructure. (The duration of the the benchmarking interval is reported in an *integral* number of seconds. Some report 15 second intervals, some 16.)

8. Related works and conclusion

Defining the memory consistency models of shared-memory programming systems is a long-studied area (see, for instance, [2]). Sequential consistency [21] is widely accepted as the memory model that programmers should work with. For instance, foundational works such as Lamport [21] and Shasha-and-Snir [36] equate "correct" execution with an SC execution. Moreover, DRF0 [4] together with its manifestations in the recent standardization of Java [26] and C++ [8] require programmers to follow a data-race-free programming discipline in order to achieve SC.

One way to provide SC is to build a SC-preserving compiler [27] that targets an SC processor. While efficient research proposals exist for efficient SC hardware [15, 34, 12, 6, 23, 37, 13], current commercial processors do not implement SC and it is unclear if future ones will do so.

Barring hardware SC support, the only option is for programmers, compilers, and/or language runtimes to insert sufficient fences to provide the desired semantics at the programming language interface. Recently, mainstream languages such as C++ and Java have finalized a memory model based on DRF0, with the intention that programmers follow a data-race-free programming discipline. However, enforcing data-race-freedom is hard statically [33, 30] and dynamically [14]. Without tool support, even expert programmers are prone to inadvertently introduce weak-memory-model behaviors in their programs.

Sasha and Snir [36] propose a static program analysis to insert as few fences as needed in imperative programs so as to ensure SC. Building on this, Sura et al. [38] and Kamil et al. [18] present compiler techniques for automatically ensuring SC in Java programs, and Alglave et al. present a scalable tool for automatically inserting fences in C programs [5]. All of these techniques rely on a whole-program analysis that is difficult to scale beyond moderately-sized programs.

Given these difficulties, a viable approach for efficiently providing SC is to restrict the use of shared-memory in programming languages [11, 10, 7, 16]. Boyapati et al. [11, 10] use ownership types to only allow a shared-memory access when holding appropriate locks. Determinstic Parallel Java [7] statically guarantees detereminism and data-race-freedom (and hence SC) through a sophisticated type-and effect system. Similarly, Gordon et al. [16] propose a type system where mutations to objects are only performed by threads that own a unique pointer to that object. However, these approaches create a significant programmer burden in terms of type annotations to ensure SC.

This paper observes that a functional programming language, such as Haskell, naturally controls the mutable updates. The language runtime can guarantee SC by simply inserting fences at *all* potentially shared-memory accesses, because there aren't very many. The language designer can add new memory effects by adding new monads, and can prove SC by proving that the new effects do not interfere with the main, IO monad, evaluation. This paper, to the best of our knowledge, is the first to demonstrate the empirical feasibility of this approach.

References

[1] criterion: a Haskell microbenchmarking library. `http://www.serpentine.com/criterion/`.

[2] S. Adve and K. Gharachorloo. Shared memory consistency models: a tutorial. *Computer*, 29(12):66–76, 1996.

[3] S. V. Adve and H.-J. Boehm. Memory models: A case for rethinking parallel languages and hardware. *Commun. ACM*, 53(8):90–101, Aug. 2010.

[4] S. V. Adve and M. D. Hill. Weak Ordering—A New Definition. In *Proceedings of the Seventeenth International Symposium on Computer Architecture*, pages 2–14, Seattle, WA, May 1990.

[5] J. Alglave, D. Kroening, V. Nimal, and D. Poetzl. Don't sit on the fence - A static analysis approach to automatic fence insertion. In *Computer Aided Verification - 26th International Conference, CAV 2014*, pages 508–524, 2014.

[6] C. Blundell, M. Martin, and T. Wenisch. InvisiFence: performance-transparent memory ordering in conventional multiprocessors. In *ISCA '09*, pages 233–244, 2009.

[7] R. L. Bocchino Jr, V. S. Adve, D. Dig, S. V. Adve, S. Heumann, R. Komuravelli, J. Overbey, P. Simmons, H. Sung, and M. Vakilian. A type and effect system for deterministic parallel java. *ACM Sigplan Notices*, 44(10):97–116, 2009.

[8] H.-J. Boehm and S. V. Adve. Foundations of the C++ Concurrency Memory Model. In *Proceedings of the SIGPLAN 2008 Conference on Programming Language Design and Implementation*, Tucson, AZ, June 2008.

[9] G. Boudol and G. Petri. Relaxed memory models: An operational approach. In *Proceedings of the 36th Annual ACM SIGPLAN-SIGACT Symposium on Principles of Programming Languages*, POPL '09, pages 392–403, New York, NY, USA, 2009. ACM.

[10] C. Boyapati, R. Lee, and M. Rinard. Ownership types for safe programming: Preventing data races and deadlocks. In *OOPSLA '02*, pages 211–230, 2002.

[11] C. Boyapati and M. Rinard. A parameterized type system for race-free Java programs. In *OOPSLA '01*, pages 56–69, 2001.

[12] L. Ceze, J. Tuck, P. Montesinos, and J. Torrellas. BulkSC: bulk enforcement of sequential consistency. In *ISCA '07*, pages 278–289, 2007.

[13] Y. Duan, A. Muzahid, and J. Torrellas. Weefence: Toward making fences free in TSO. In *Proceedings of the 40th Annual International Symposium on Computer Architecture*, ISCA '13, pages 213–224. ACM, 2013.

[14] C. Flanagan and S. N. Freund. FastTrack: Efficient and precise dynamic race detection. In *Proceedings of the 2009 ACM SIGPLAN Conference on Programming Language Design and Implementation*, PLDI '09, pages 121–133, New York, NY, USA, 2009. ACM.

[15] K. Gharachorloo, A. Gupta, and J. Hennessy. Two techniques to enhance the performance of memory consistency models. In *Proceedings of the 1991 International Conference on Parallel Processing*, ICPP '91, pages 355–364, 1991.

[16] C. S. Gordon, M. J. Parkinson, J. Parsons, A. Bromfield, and J. Duffy. Uniqueness and reference immutability for safe parallelism. *SIGPLAN Not.*, 47(10):21–40, Oct. 2012.

[17] T. Harris, S. Marlow, S. Peyton-Jones, and M. Herlihy. Composable memory transactions. In *Proceedings of the Tenth ACM SIGPLAN Symposium on Principles and Practice of Parallel Programming*, PPoPP '05, pages 48–60, New York, NY, USA, 2005. ACM.

[18] A. Kamil, J. Su, and K. Yelick. Making sequential consistency practical in Titanium. In *Proceedings of the 2005 ACM/IEEE conference on Supercomputing*, page 15. IEEE Computer Society, 2005.

[19] L. Kuper, A. Todd, S. Tobin-Hochstadt, and R. R. Newton. Taming the parallel effect zoo: Extensible deterministic parallelism with lvish. In *Proceedings of the 35th ACM SIGPLAN Conference on Programming Language Design and Implementation*, page 2. ACM, 2014.

[20] L. Kuper, A. Turon, N. R. Krishnaswami, and R. R. Newton. Freeze after writing: quasi-deterministic parallel programming with lvars. In *POPL*, pages 257–270, 2014.

[21] L. Lamport. How to make a multiprocessor computer that correctly executes multiprocess programs. *IEEE transactions on computers*, 100(9):690–691, 1979.

[22] J. Launchbury and S. L. Peyton Jones. Lazy functional state threads. In *ACM SIGPLAN Notices*, volume 29, pages 24–35. ACM, 1994.

[23] C. Lin, V. Nagarajan, R. Gupta, and B. Rajaram. Efficient sequential consistency via conflict ordering. In *Proceedings of the Seventeenth International Conference on Architectural Support for Programming Languages and Operating Systems*, ASPLOS XVII, pages 273–286, New York, NY, USA, 2012. ACM.

[24] J. M. Lucassen and D. K. Gifford. Polymorphic effect systems. In *Proceedings of the 15th ACM SIGPLAN-SIGACT Symposium on Principles of Programming Languages*, POPL '88, pages 47–57, New York, NY, USA, 1988. ACM.

[25] P. Maier and P. Trinder. Implementing a high-level distributed-memory parallel haskell in haskell. In *Implementation and Application of Functional Languages*, pages 35–50. Springer, 2012.

[26] J. Manson, W. Pugh, and S. Adve. The Java Memory Model. In *Conference Record of the Thirty-Second ACM Symposium on Principles of Programming Languages*, Long Beach, CA, January 2005.

[27] D. Marino, A. Singh, T. Millstein, M. Musuvathi, and S. Narayanasamy. A case for an SC-preserving compiler. In *Proceedings of the 32Nd ACM SIGPLAN Conference on Programming Lan-guage Design and Implementation*, PLDI '11, pages 199–210, New York, NY, USA, 2011. ACM.

[28] S. Marlow, R. Newton, and S. Peyton Jones. A monad for deterministic parallelism. In *Proceedings of the 4th ACM symposium on Haskell*, Haskell '11, pages 71–82. ACM, 2011.

[29] K. Naden, R. Bocchino, J. Aldrich, and K. Bierhoff. A type system for borrowing permissions. In *Proceedings of the 39th Annual ACM SIGPLAN-SIGACT Symposium on Principles of*

Programming Languages, POPL '12, pages 557–570, New York, NY, USA, 2012. ACM.

[30] M. Naik, A. Aiken, and J. Whaley. Effective static race detection for Java. In *PLDI '06: Proceedings of the 2006 ACM SIGPLAN conference on Programming language design and implementation*, pages 308–319, 2006.

[31] W. Partain. The nofib benchmark suite of Haskell programs. In *Functional Programming, Glasgow 1992*, Workshops in Computing, pages 195–202. Springer-Verlag, 1993.

[32] S. Peyton Jones, A. Gordon, and S. Finne. Concurrent haskell. In *Proceedings of the 23rd ACM SIGPLAN-SIGACT Symposium on Principles of Programming Languages*, POPL '96, pages 295–308, New York, NY, USA, 1996. ACM.

[33] P. Pratikakis, J. S. Foster, and M. Hicks. LOCKSMITH: Context-sensitive correlation analysis for race detection. In *Proceedings of the 2006 ACM SIGPLAN Conference on Programming Language Design and Implementation*, PLDI '06, pages 320–331, New York, NY, USA, 2006. ACM.

[34] P. Ranganathan, V. S. Pai, and S. V. Adve. Using speculative retirement and larger instruction windows to narrow the performance gap between memory consistency models. In *Proceedings of the Ninth Annual ACM Symposium on Parallel Algorithms and Architectures*, SPAA '97, pages 199–210, New York, NY, USA, 1997. ACM.

[35] S. Sarkar, P. Sewell, F. Z. Nardelli, S. Owens, T. Ridge, T. Braibant, M. O. Myreen, and J. Alglave. The semantics of x86-cc multiprocessor machine code. *SIGPLAN Not.*, 44(1):379–391, Jan. 2009.

[36] D. Shasha and M. Snir. Efficient and Correct Execution of Parallel Programs that Share Memory. *TOPLAS*, 10(2), 1988.

[37] A. Singh, S. Narayanasamy, D. Marino, T. Millstein, and M. Musuvathi. End-to-end sequential consistency. *SIGARCH Comput. Archit. News*, 40(3):524–535, June 2012.

[38] Z. Sura, X. Fang, C. Wong, S. Midkiff, J. Lee, and D. Padua. Compiler Techniques for High Performance Sequentially Consistent Java Programs. In *PPoPP*, 2005.

[39] K. Takeuchi, K. Honda, and M. Kubo. An interaction-based language and its typing system. In *In PARLE94, volume 817 of LNCS*, pages 398–413. Springer-Verlag, 1994.

[40] D. Terei, S. Marlow, S. Peyton Jones, and D. Mazières. Safe Haskell. In *Proceedings of the 2012 Haskell Symposium*, Haskell '12, pages 137–148, New York, NY, USA, 2012. ACM.

[41] J. Terrace, S. R. Beard, and N. P. K. Katta. JavaScript in JavaScript (js.js): Sandboxing third-party scripts. In *Proceedings of the 3rd USENIX Conference on Web Application Development*, WebApps'12, pages 9–9, Berkeley, CA, USA, 2012. USENIX Association.

[42] E. Z. Yang and D. Mazières. Dynamic Space Limits for Haskell. In *Proceedings of the 35th ACM SIGPLAN Conference on Programming Language Design and Implementation*, PLDI '14, pages 588–598, New York, NY, USA, 2014. ACM.

A. Appendix

A.1 Safe-Haskell changes: `stToIO`

For the most part, adding barriers did not effect the existing Safe Haskell properties of `base`—that is, modules that were marked `Safe` and `Trustworthy` continued to be so after our changes. There is one exception, though: a function with the type signature

```
stToIO :: ST RealWorld a → IO a
```

that is used within a module marked `Trustworthy`. This poses a problem for an SC-aware definition of trustworthiness, because use of `stToIO` can violate a critical assumption about `ST`. Namely, we have previously assumed that all `ST` computations occur within a single thread, but if `ST` is allowed to be lifted up to `IO`, that assumption no longer holds. Here is an example of problematic code:

```
main :: IO ()
main = do
  x ← stToIO $ newSTRef (0 :: Int)
  y ← stToIO $ newSTRef (0 :: Int)
  forkIO $ do
    stToIO       $ writeSTRef x 1
    y' ← stToIO $ readSTRef y
    putStrLn $ "T2:␣x=1,␣y=" ++ show y'
  stToIO       $ writeSTRef y 1
  x' ← stToIO $ readSTRef x
  putStrLn $ "T1:␣y=1,␣x=" ++ show x'
```

This code contains two threads contending on the values of STRefs, and since `writeSTRef` does not emit barriers, this can result in data races that expose non-SC behavior!

The simplest solution to this problem is to modify the type signature:

```
stToIO :: (∀ s. ST s a) → IO a
```

to disallow the code above, and export the original definition of `stToIO` from a module marked as `Unsafe`.

A.2 `nofib` barriers

The below tables include the largest barrier-counts performed by `nofib` benchmarks, before and after including our optimized version of file handles (both SC-Haskell).

Benchmark	Barriers	Benchmark	Barriers
listcompr	385	para	1,654
listcopy	385	maillist	18,177
compress2	962	hpg	37,172
compress	993	sphere	180,024
cacheprof	1,334	reverse-complement	316,170
treejoin	1,371	fasta	571,685

Table 4: Number of memory barriers performed on selected `nofib` benchmarks, unoptimized mode *including* the barriers upon writing to file handles.

Benchmark	Barriers	Benchmark	Barriers
k-nucleotide	20	n-body	35

Table 5: Number of memory barriers performed on `nofib` benchmarks, *without* the barriers resulting from writing to file handles.

B. Artifact description

The artifact bundled with this paper is a virtual machine image set up with two copies of the Glasgow Haskell Compiler: an unmodified ("vanilla") build of GHC 7.10.3, and a buid of GHC 7.10.3 with the modifications we describe in the paper.

The virtual machine image is based on Ubuntu 16.04 and includes example programs and benchmark programs. Scripts are included in the virtual machine to automatically run benchmarks and compare their results.

The VM is 5.7GB, and can be downloaded from the following location: `http://doi.org/10.5072/FK22J6FG6C` (md5sum 2797486cf47e977b0ef979bc2ebfd660), or by using the DOI to find the current URL.

B.0.1 Hardware dependencies

To successfully complete the benchmarks it is recommended that at least 4GB of RAM is available to the virtual machine (and we have set he default to 8GB, and two cores). Running on one core may require less memory.

B.0.2 Software dependencies

The software dependency is VirtualBox, which is freely available.

B.0.3 Datasets

We used freely available Haskell benchmarks from Stackage, an online source of stable Haskell packages. We used the benchmarks from the LTS-5.16 set, available at `https://www.stackage.org/lts-5.16`.

B.1 Installation

All required software is already installed on the virtual machine image. The virtual machine uses an account whose password matches the account name (and thus it should not be exposed to a network).

B.2 Experiment workflow

The VM contains step-by-step instructions to run the benchmarks mentioned in Section 7. A brief summary is included here, and full instructions are given in `evaluation.md` in the home folder of the virtual machine image.

B.2.1 `nofib` results

The `nofib` test suite (Section 7.3) is located in `~/nofib`. We ran this with both the original and modified versions of GHC. To compute the results, type the following commands:

```
cd ~/nofib
```

```
source use_vanilla_ghc
make run
mv nofib-log nofib-vanilla-log
source use_sc_ghc
make run
mv nofib-log nofib-sc-log
nofib-analyse/nofib-analyse \
    nofib-vanilla-log nofib-sc-log
```

(Note that the "use_" scripts are found in ~/opt/bin and are thus not specific to any directory.)

The `nofib-analyse` command prints out a chart which compares the compilation and performance characteristics of each program in the test suite when compiled with each of the two versions of GHC. It produces a lot of output, but the "Elapsed" column of the first section is what we are primarily interested in. Positive or negative changes represent increases or decreases in runtime in the second log compared to the first.

Note also that the above instructions execute a *single* run of nofib. In Section 7.3 we ran nofib 20 times for both the modified and unmodified compiler, and computed the mean runtime for each benchmark in each mode. This especially helps to compensate for noise from a minority of short-running benchmarks.

B.2.2 Stackage results

Next, instructions for running our Stackage benchmarks from Section 7.3. The `Makefile` we provide runs only a portion of the Stackage benchmarks, as running them all would take about a day. If you want to run all the benchmarks, you can edit `/sc-haskell/benchmarking/Makefile` and remove the parts from the `vanilla` and `sc` targets that say `NODE_NUMBER=1 TOTAL_NODES=67`.

```
cd ~/sc-haskell/benchmarking
make vanilla
make sc
make compare
```

Similarly to `nofib-analyse`, running `make compare` will print out a detailed comparison of the runtime differences between the benchmarks run with the unmodified and modified versions of GHC, and gives a geometric mean runtime difference at the bottom.

B.3 Evaluation and expected result

For both the `nofib` and `Stackage` benchmarks, the expected result will be the difference in runtime between code generated by vanilla GHC and SC GHC.

Limits of virtualized evaluation Be warned that *virtual-machine-based evaluation is non-ideal for this experiment.* The purpose of this experiment is to measure small differences in runtime between two variants of a compiler, with programs executing on dedicated machines under a job control system (as found in HPC deployments). We expect that jitter from virtualization may dominate the differences in runtime. Thus VM-based results can reconfirm that the sequentially-consistent compiler (SC-Haskell) did not add a large amount of overhead, they are unlikely to provide an accurate quantification of the effect.

B.4 Experiment customization

The artifact includes both versions of the compiler, and can thus be reused to evaluate other programs than those we have included.

The instructions on the image also descibe how to inspect the assembly language output of the compiler when called on an arbitrary program. The example program (in the `~/examples` folder) can serve as a starting point to experiment with what code the compiler produces for different Haskell programs.

```
cd ~/examples
source use_sc_ghc
ghc IORefExample1.hs -O2 -ddump-asm
```

B.5 About TechEmpower

We included results from the TechEmpower web benchmarks in section 7.4, but opted to exclude them from the virtual machine, as setting up the benchmarks requires three virtual machines to be running, which makes it impractical to encapsulate within this virtual machine.

Synchronized-by-Default Concurrency for Shared-Memory Systems

Martin Bättig
Department of Computer Science
ETH Zurich, Switzerland

Thomas R. Gross
Department of Computer Science
ETH Zurich, Switzerland

Abstract

We explore a programming approach for concurrency that synchronizes all accesses to shared memory by default. Synchronization takes place by ensuring that all program code runs inside atomic sections even if the program code has external side effects. Threads are mapped to atomic sections that a programmer must explicitly split to increase concurrency.

A naive implementation of this approach incurs a large amount of overhead. We show how to reduce this overhead to make the approach suitable for realistic application programs on existing hardware. We present an implementation technique based on a special-purpose software transactional memory system. To reduce the overhead, the technique exploits properties of managed, object-oriented programming languages as well as intraprocedural static analyses and uses field-level granularity locking in combination with transactional I/O to provide good scaling properties.

We implemented the synchronized-by-default (SBD) approach for the Java language and evaluate its performance for six programs from the DaCapo benchmark suite. The evaluation shows that, compared to explicit synchronization, the SBD approach has an overhead between 0.4% and 102% depending on the benchmark and the number of threads, with a mean (geom.) of 23.9%.

Categories and Subject Descriptors D1.3 [*Concurrent Programming*]: Parallel programming

Keywords Atomic blocks, Concurrency, Parallel programming, Synchronization, Transactional memory

PPoPP '17, February 04 - 08, 2017, Austin, TX, USA

ACM 978-1-4503-4493-7/17/02…$15.00
DOI: http://dx.doi.org/10.1145/http://dx.doi.org/10.1145/3018743.3018747

1. Introduction

Explicit synchronization of threads using locks or atomic blocks is error prone. Missing synchronization may lead to data races or race conditions, while incorrect locking can lead to deadlocks. In this paper, we explore the synchronized-by-default (SBD) approach to concurrency: Instead of requiring the programmer to insert synchronization explicitly, the system synchronizes all shared memory accesses by default. Thus, increasing concurrency requires the programmer to relax synchronization explicitly. To realize this behavior, each thread executes all its instructions within atomic sections, even if the instructions have external side effects. By default, there is a single atomic section per thread. These atomic sections have transactional semantics and therefore are free from concurrency bugs such as data races or race conditions. Furthermore, they can be rolled back to resolve deadlocks. To increase concurrency, a programmer can insert instructions that split the atomic sections dynamically at runtime.

The SBD approach has been explored before [16, 23, 25, 26], to deserve further attention, it must be able to compete with explicit synchronization. The difficulty lies in implementing the approach in a way that reduces the synchronization overhead and supports scalability to the extent provided by explicit synchronization.

Synchronization overhead. Executing all instructions within atomic sections adds a large amount of synchronization overhead. Since atomic sections have transactional semantics, hardware transactional memory (HTM) [21] could be a solution. However, suitable unbounded HTM is not readily available [12], and using simulated HTM makes a comparison against explicit synchronization difficult, as it does not run on the same hardware. An alternative is to use a software transactional memory (STM) [30] as it runs on existing hardware. However, even fast STM implementations [8, 11, 29, 36] are optimized for language integration using the atomic block model [19], i.e., only a fraction of the memory accesses requires synchronization, thus such STMs can tolerate a higher overhead than is acceptable by the SBD approach.

Scalability. The approach must provide the means that allow a programmer to reduce the contention and eliminate deadlocks between concurrently running atomic sections.

Programming effort. The approach should simplify concurrent programming. Thus, it should add only a reasonable amount of additional language constructs over a language using explicit synchronization. Additionally, the approach should be self-contained in that all kinds of parallel programming idioms can be expressed. If a programmer must revert to explicit synchronization, e.g., to execute I/O operations, this step adds additional complexity as the programmer must deal with two concurrency models.

Our claim is that the SBD approach is practicable for realistic application programs because: (i) synchronization became cheaper [9], (ii) shared memory accesses make up only a part of applications, (iii) we can simplify the comparison against explicit synchronization by limiting the number of new language constructs and by adapting and reusing threading constructs known from explicit synchronization, and (iv) the approach can be implemented on existing hardware. The key contributions of this paper are:

- It describes how this approach can be integrated in a realistic, managed language like Java with only few additional language constructs and discusses how to make common concurrency constructs and operations with external side effects compatible with this approach.
- It shows how a special-purpose STM can be combined with compiler optimizations to reduce the synchronization overhead of the SBD approach to enable scalable applications.
- It compares a version of Java adapted for the SBD approach against regular Java with explicit synchronization using locks for six benchmarks from the DaCapo benchmark suite [2]. We made the evaluation in terms of sequential overhead, scalability, programming effort, and memory overhead.

2. Background

The SBD approach is based on previous work [16, 23, 25]: it executes all instructions of a program within atomic sections and uses the concept of splitting atomic sections. Unlike previous approaches, we focus on integrating these two concepts into a managed, object-oriented language using threads. We do this by combining them with the following additional concepts:

- Specific semantics for memory accesses.
- All instructions executed within atomic sections, even those with external side effects, such as I/O.
- Reusing and adapting existing thread control operations.
- Refinement of atomic sections: No nesting, and no splitting within constructors (to reduce overhead).

2.1 Atomic Sections

We describe the additional concepts in Section 3. In this section, we discuss the atomic sections and their integration. An atomic section is opaque [15], i.e., an atomic section S' cannot see any kind of modification (shared memory or I/O) made by a concurrently running atomic section S'' until S'' ends. Thus, atomic sections have transactional semantics, and the system can abort them and undo their modifications. In contrast to atomic blocks [19], a common form of STM language integration, atomic sections do not have a fixed start or end in the program code. Each thread T has a currently active atomic section S_A. Upon start of T, the system creates a new atomic section S and assigns it to T: $S_A \leftarrow S$. Thread T executes all its instructions within its S_A. Further, thread T can execute a `split` operation. Splitting ends S_A, and creates an atomic section S' that becomes the new active atomic section: $S_A \leftarrow S'$. Upon the end of thread T, its atomic section S_A ends as well. The main usage of splitting an atomic section S is to increase the concurrency by releasing resources that S acquired to ensure its transactional execution, and to make modifications as well as external side effects visible.

```
1  class Worker extends Thread {
2   static int processed;
3   void canSplit run() { // atomic section begin
4    for(Request req : getRequests()) {
5      processRequest(req);
6      ++processed;
7      split; // (explicit) atomic section end
8             // new atomic section begin
9      }
10  } // atomic section end
11  // in main:
12  Thread a = new Worker().start();
13  Thread b = new Worker().start();
14 }
```

Figure 1: Example of implicit and explicit atomic sections.

Figure 1 shows a small example of two threads that process requests. Without the `split` operation in line 7, the modification of shared field `processed` in line 6 would serialize the execution of threads `a` and `b`. The `split` instruction in line 7 ensures that resources that protect field `processed` are freed in each loop iteration, and consequently both threads can process requests concurrently (assuming eager conflict detection [28]).

The concurrency provided by SBD approach has the following properties:

Conflict resolution enforced. Simply dividing the work between multiple threads is not necessarily sufficient to enable parallelism. As Figure 1 shows, a programmer is forced to deal with frequently occurring conflicts that limit parallelism.

Asymmetric. The system resolves infrequent conflicts (e.g., program initialization, or configuration changes at runtime) automatically, while frequent conflicts may be more complicated to deal with. Thus, programmer effort with regard to concurrency is asymmetric in SBD compared to explicit locking, where every possible conflict must be found and dealt with.

Incremental. The approach allows to add concurrency incrementally: Missing `split` instructions lead to serialization, but never to data races or race conditions, unlike explicit synchronization, where missing or incorrect synchronization eventually results in a concurrency bug.

Explicit. While concurrency bugs like data races or race conditions can occur nevertheless, splits are the only instructions that can cause them. Splits are visible in the source code, thus, one can check what memory locations are used across a split at places where they should not be used. Therefore, pinpointing the cause of a concurrency bug is more explicit with SBD than with explicit synchronization.

2.2 Preventing unexpected split operations

The presented SBD approach does not allow the nesting of atomic sections. If a method A is in atomic section S' while invoking method B, and B executes a `split` operation, this operation ends atomic section S' and starts section S''. An example is atomic section B_1 shown in Figure 3 that starts in method `run` and ends in method `processPosition`. Therefore, it is necessary to prevent methods, e.g., in a library, from issuing unexpected split operations, as such operations can introduce concurrency bugs.

Modifier canSplit. Only designated methods, which are identified by the method modifier `canSplit` in their signature, may issue a `split` operation either directly, or by invoking a method having the `canSplit` property. Thus, methods not having the `canSplit` property are guaranteed not to issue splits. Thread and task entry points have the `canSplit` property set by default. Constructors cannot have this property to prevent uninitialized instances from escaping an atomic section. And finally, a method that has the `canSplit` property can only override a method that also has the `canSplit` property.

Modifier allowSplit. Further, a method A that has the `canSplit` property requires additional protection. If a method A invokes another method B, it must declare whether it allows B to execute `split` operations, by prefixing the invocation with the keyword `allowSplit`. Checking this at compile time makes it impossible to add the `canSplit` property to an existing method (e.g., in a library) without breaking the API.

Figure 2 shows an example of these modifiers. Here we assume requests contain multiple `Articles`, and conflicts between `Article` instances are frequent. To increase the possible concurrency, we uncomment the modifier `canSplit` of method `processRequest` (line 7) as well as the `split` instruction (line 10). Finally, we uncomment the modifier to the call (line 15). Figure 3 shows atomic sections created for an example execution, with time progressing from top to bottom. Timeline (a) shows the situation for the unmodified case: there is one atomic section per `processRequest`. Timeline (b) shows the situation after uncommenting. Now the system executes each invocation of `processPosition` in a separate atomic section.

```
1  void processPosition(Article a, int num) {
2    if (a.available > num) {
3      a.available -= num;
4      positions.add(a, num);
5    }
6  }
7  void /*canSplit*/ processRequest(Request r) {
8    for(RequestItem ri : r.getItems()) {
9      processPosition(ri.article, ri.quantity);
10     /*split;*/
11   }
12 }
13 public canSplit void run() {
14   for(Request req : getRequests()) {
15     /*allowSplit*/ processRequest(req);
16     ++processed;
17     split;
18   }
19 }
```

Figure 2: Inserting split operations, changes in comments.

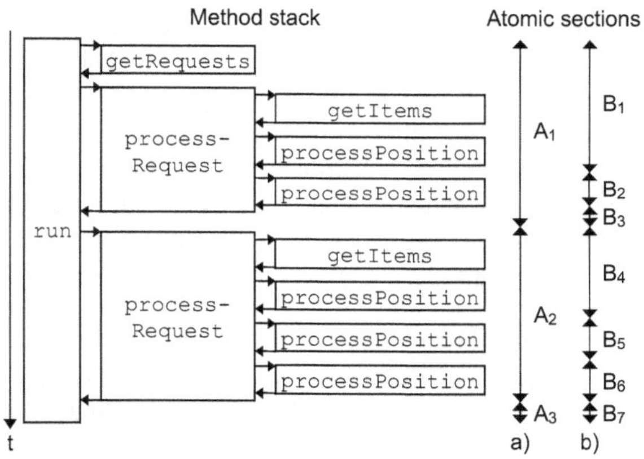

Figure 3: Nested methods vs. non-nested atomic sections.

3. Concepts

In this section, we elaborate the concepts that allow us to address the difficulties described in Section 1. We define the target system, present how we realize the atomic sections using a special-purpose STM system, describe how to reduce the synchronization overhead, and show how to support I/O and thread operations.

3.1 Target applications and programming languages

The first part of the solution is to restrict the class of applications and programming languages that an implementation of the SBD approach should support.

We focus on application programs that use a mix of computations, I/O operations, and memory accesses, e.g., a web server. Many programs fall into this class; the combination of different kinds of activities ensures that shared memory accesses make up only part of the program, thereby reducing the impact of the additional synchronization.

Further, we assume a managed language that uses a garbage collector. Using such a language allows exploiting guarantees regarding memory accesses, e.g., no pointers to arbitrary memory locations. These guarantees allow static analysis to detect and remove superfluous synchronizations.

3.2 Atomic sections

We use transactional memory (TM) to implement the atomic sections. Due to its transactional semantics, an atomic section corresponds directly to a transaction of a TM system. TM systems differ greatly in properties such as conflict detection, version management, etc. In the SBD approach, these properties have a substantial impact on how to implement a program, both from a functional and performance point of view. Thus, they become an integral part of the language semantics, and we cannot choose them arbitrarily. To determine the TM properties, we start by defining the following semantics for memory accesses:

1. Each memory location M that requires synchronization has an associated lock L. Before accessing memory location M, the system acquires lock L if not held already.
2. The system executes memory accesses that require synchronization in the same order as specified in the program.

The first point of this semantics matches pessimistic concurrency control. The second point implicitly allows a programmer to order memory accesses in a way that prevents or reduces the number of transaction aborts due to deadlocks without having to introduce additional language constructs.

To realize atomic sections with the above semantics, we use a special-purpose STM. The reason is that currently available HTM systems (e.g., Intel TSX), or fast STM systems [8, 11, 29, 36] do either not support the combination of the following TM properties, or are not optimized for them:

Conflict detection. Pessimistic concurrency control requires eager conflict detection [28]. The above defined semantics for memory accesses requires visible readers [32] to enforce the ordering of the memory accesses. As conflict detection granularity, we chose field- respectively array element-level granularity. Such a granularity prevents lock contention due to false-sharing compared to instance level locking, thereby avoiding artificial scalability issues that may arise because all instructions execute within a transaction.

Memory access type	Check	Lock	Undo
Non-final field or array element	✓	✓	✓
Final field			
New non-final field / array element	✓		
Local variable (with canSplit)			✓
Local variable (w/o canSplit)			

Table 1: Synchronization per memory accesses type.

Version management. We use eager version management [28], as the system must apply the undo log only in case of an abort. Since we defined a semantics that allows preventing aborts by ordering memory accesses, using eager version management allows manual optimization of a program if required. The overhead of a program with only few aborts consists mainly of locking, updating the undo log, and unlocking.

Progress guarantees. We chose a deterministic deadlock resolution policy since readers are visible. Deadlock resolution already partly ensures progress, but live locks can still occur due to the *friendly-fire* and *starving writers* performance pathologies [4]. To prevent *friendly-fire*, the system uses the following deadlock resolution policy: Always abort the youngest transaction that is part of a deadlock. Thus the oldest transaction, and therefore the program itself, can always make progress. To prevent *starving writers*, the TM uses fair queues: If a thread cannot acquire a lock, the system enqueues it at the end of the waiting queue, regardless of the operation being a read or a write. The only exception to this rule are upgrading readers. The system enqueues them in front of the queue to reduce the number of aborts.

Atomicity guarantees. The STM does not have to provide atomicity guarantees [3]. In the SBD approach all instructions execute within atomic sections. Non-transactional execution is not possible.

3.3 Reducing the synchronization overhead

In the following, we describe the concepts used to reduce the synchronization overhead:

Exploit language level memory access properties. We assume a managed, object-oriented language with the following memory access properties:

- Stack: The stack of a thread is isolated. A thread cannot access stacks of other threads.
- Heap: The language must not allow direct memory access but must provide indirect access to object and array instances via reference pointers. These point either to valid instances or to null. Access to properties of object instances is only possible through their fields. Access to content of array instances is only possible within their bounds and only for complete elements.

Accesses to local variables do not need synchronization because of the isolated stacks. Methods that have the canSplit property, and thus can issue `split` operations, must nevertheless save the old values of modified local variables in the undo log to be able to rebuild the stack in case a transaction is restarted. On the other hand, heap accesses via fields or array elements require synchronization including saving of old values in case of a modification. There are two exceptions: (i) accesses to fields declared as final do not need synchronization, since constructors cannot have the `canSplit` property, other transactions can see only initialized final fields; (ii) accesses to fields or elements of newly instantiated objects or arrays within the same transaction. These accesses do not require synchronization but instead need a dynamic check to determine whether an instance is new or not. Thus non-final field and array element accesses are the main source of synchronization overhead. Table 1 summarizes these rules.

Compile time optimizations. Compile time optimizations can remove unnecessary checks whether a field or array element is already locked. We use the following optimizations:

1. A dataflow analysis to remove redundant checks: An access A to a field or array element X requires synchronization unless the system can prove that X is already synchronized in all possible control flow paths that lead to A. This optimization makes use of the `canSplit` property: As methods without this modifier cannot issue `split` instructions, removal of the synchronization is possible even if such a method lies in a control flow path leading to A.
2. Move lock operations out of loops if the locking order can be preserved.
3. Combination of subsequent field accesses on the same instance to eliminate checks whether an instance is new.

These optimizations are intraprocedural. They benefit from method inlining and are suitable for dynamic compilation.

Combine read- and write-sets with locking information. With pessimistic concurrency control, each access to a non-final field or array element requires synchronization. This involves checking whether the accessed memory location is already in the read- or write-set of the transaction, and if not, to acquire the lock and to update the read- or write-set. We combine these operations by storing the set information directly on the accessed instance instead of storing it in a separate structure. Figure 4 (a) shows the instance layout with the additional locking structures. Each non-final field or array element has its own locking structure. The additional indirection, via the field `locks`, allows lazy allocation of the locking structures of an instance, thereby reducing the amount of memory required in case an instance is transient in a transaction.

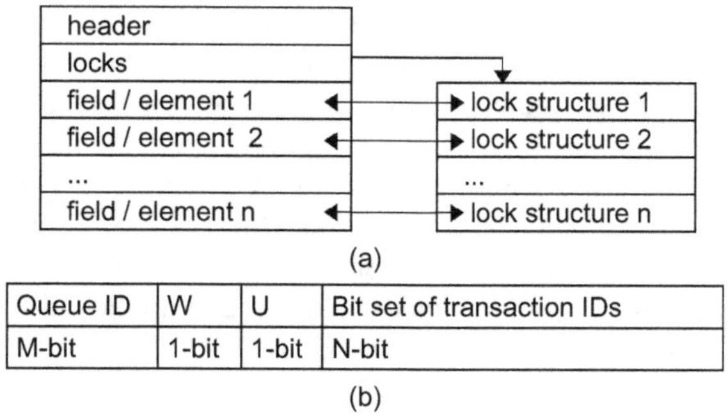

Figure 4: Memory layout of an instance (a) and a locking structure (b).

Figure 4 (b) shows the lock structure. It contains a bit set that encodes whether a transaction has a lock on the associated field or not and whether it is in the read- or write-set of the transaction. Each bit corresponds to a unique, but reusable ID that represents a transaction. The size of the bit set is limited, so that the size of the locking structure does not exceed the limit of a single compare-and-swap (CAS) operation. The fixed bit set size reduces the number of required instructions for a locking operation but also limits the number of transactions that can concurrently be active to the size of the bit set. Beside the bit set, a flag W indicates whether a write lock, or a read lock, is in place. The upgrader bit U [29] is optional but helps to detect *dueling write-upgrades* [4] early. To enable fair scheduling the lock structure includes a queue ID. If a queue ID is set, other transactions are waiting to acquire the lock on the specific queue and directly acquiring the lock is not possible. The maximal number of queues is fixed and equals the maximal number of concurrently active transactions, as in the worst case all concurrently active transactions are enqueued before deadlock resolution begins.

The number of available transaction IDs N limits the achievable actual parallelism. However, this limit only affects systems with P processing units, where $P > N$. On such a system, the actual parallelism of a program cannot exceed N. If no transaction ID is available, a transaction must wait until one becomes free. This strategy works because:

1. No nesting is possible: Once a transaction acquires an ID it is able to finish without acquiring another ID.
2. If a thread T_1 waits for a thread T_2 to update a condition C, T_1 must end its current transaction as otherwise T_2 cannot update C. Ending the transaction, T_1 frees a transaction ID, thus T_2, even if it was waiting for an ID to become free, can complete its work.

The above described locking structure allows to implement a locking operation using very few instructions, as shown in Figure 5: (1) The system checks whether an instance is newly allocated in the current transaction (`a.locks==null`). Newly allocated instances do not require locking. (2) Otherwise, if the lock is unallocated (`a.locks==UNALLOC`), the system performs the lazy allocation. `UNALLOC` is a constant pointer. (3) Then the system checks whether the transaction must acquire the lock (`((lock & trx.mask))==0`). (4) If that is the case, the system acquires the lock by checking whether it is free and then executing a CAS. If the lock is not free or the CAS fails, the thread is enqueued. The system records lock acquisitions in the undo log together with the old value of the field or array element in case of a write.

```
// (1) allocated in previous transaction?
if (a.locks != null) {
 // (2) lazy lock init
 if (a.locks == UNALLOC /*const pointer*/) {
  CAS(a, locksOffs, UNALLOC, new long[size]);
 }
 // (3) already locked?
 long lock = a.locks[lockID];
 if (((lock & trx.mask)) == 0) {
  // (4) try to lock or enqueue
  if ((lock | trx.mask) != trx.mask
    || !CAS(a.locks,offs,lock,lock|trx.mask))
  {
    enqueue(a, lockID); // slow-path
  }
  updateUndoLog(offs, lock, fldOffs, oldVal);
 }
}
```

Figure 5: Locking operation in pseudo code.

3.4 I/O and non-transactional code

In the SBD approach, no code can run outside of an atomic section. This rule applies also to instructions with external side effects, e.g., irreversible I/O operations or (non-transactional) operations invoked using a foreign function interface. There are two viable options to do so: Inevitable (irrevocable) transactions [33], and buffering using transactional wrappers [18].

Implementation of inevitable transactions using pessimistic concurrency control in combination with read/write locks is straightforward [10] but has the problem of limiting actual concurrency. At most one transaction can be inevitable at any given moment in time. E.g., two or more transactions cannot execute I/O at the same time, even if they use different devices. To achieve good scalability, we use transactional wrappers instead, i.e., buffering irreversible actions until an atomic section finishes. Wrappers are hand-written, and must implement an appropriate locking scheme that ensures the atomicity and isolation of the performed external side effects or any returned values.

Using transactional wrappers results in the following two notable changes for a programmer:

1. If an output is made in an atomic section S an observer can see the output only after S ends.
2. All irreversible operations must use transactional wrappers.

The first point causes a small API change for all functionality that has external side effects, as these functions, depending on the situation, may require an additional `split` operation to make the effects visible. Single threaded programs require these additional `split` instructions as well. The second point primarily concerns developers of system libraries but not application developers, as system libraries of a language implementing the SBD approach must already contain such transactional wrappers, e.g., for file system operations.

3.5 Thread operations

Thread operations in the SBD approach work similarly as with explicit synchronization using locks but require minor adaptation. In the following, we describe the adaptations for a number of common operations.

Thread or task start. When an atomic section S' starts a new thread or task T, the start of T is deferred until S' ends. Deferring of T simplifies its reversal, since an instantaneous start of T by S' has the following implications (S'' is the initial atomic section executed by T and is independent of S'):

1. Aborting S' requires aborting T as well, thus S'' of T cannot end until S' ends.
2. If S'' makes modifications, these can become visible only after S' ends.
3. S'' can acquire locks that S' requires after it started T, thus creating a deadlock.

Deferring the start of T until the end of S' avoids this additional complexity (items 1 and 2 above) and the problem (3) of an instantaneous start. Additionally, in many cases an atomic section S' that starts T already holds locks on data that T is supposed to work on. Thus, a deferred thread start does not impose a restriction as only after S' ends, T can start to work on this data. The thread T will always start after S' ends, although its atomic section S'' may be blocked initially, if no free transaction IDs are available. AME [23] uses a similar mechanism to initiate asynchronous method calls.

Thread or task join. A thread or task join operation always issues a `split` operation before waiting. This ensures that the thread or task T to wait for has started. Additionally, the `split` operation causes the waiting thread to release its transaction ID while waiting, thereby ensuring that T can execute.

Sending of a signal. The system defers sending of a signal N until the current atomic section S ends. This deferring avoids unnecessary notifications if the system aborts S after sending. It also ensures that locks on the waiting condition C acquired by S are freed, and the modifications made by S become visible. This allows the threads that are waiting for N to check C and to continue.

Change	Type	Description
Keyword `split`	Add	Ends current atomic section and starts new atomic section.
Modifier `canSplit`	Add	Allows to issue split instructions.
Modifier `allowSplit`	Add	Allows to invoke methods issuing split instructions.
Field access (instance or static)	Change	First lock field (read or write) then access field.
Array element access	Change	First lock array element (read or write) then access array element.
Thread control operations	Change	Change as described in Section 3.5
I/O operations	Change	Use wrapper to execute I/O operations transactionally.
Foreign code execution	Change	Use wrapper to execute non-transactional library operations transactionally.
Explicit synchronization constructs	Remove	Both language-based, and library code.
Direct memory access	Remove	E.g., volatile access properties.

Table 2: Changes required to adapt a managed object-oriented language to the SBD approach.

```
1  class Barrier {
2    private final int expected;
3    private int arrived;
4    public Barrier(int expected) {
5        this.expected = expected;
6    }
7    public canSplit void sync() {
8      arrived++;
9      if(arrived < expected) {
10       while(arrived < expected) {
11         wait(); // split atomic section
12       }
13     } else {
14       notifyAll();
15       split; // split atomic section
16     }
17   }
18 }
```

Figure 6: Example of `notifyAll` and `wait` usage.

Waiting for a signal. A thread T that waits for a signal first issues a `split` operation, thereby releasing all locks it holds, including the ones on the waiting condition C. This step ensures that another thread T' can update condition C. Additionally, the `split` operation causes the T to release its transaction ID thereby ensuring that T' can execute.

Figure 6 shows an example of signaling by way of a barrier implementation. The `notifyAll` (line 14) must release the lock on the field `arrived` to allow the waiters to test the condition (line 10) after signaling. A waiter must release the lock to allow other threads to update the condition `arrived` (line 8).

Thread local memory. The only adaptation to thread local memory is an undo buffer that allows restoring the state in case of an abort.

3.6 Summary

Table 2 summarizes the changes required to adapt a managed object-oriented language using explicit synchronization using locks to the SBD approach.

3.7 Composability

Composability [20] is a feature of TM that allows to combine two or more atomic operations by composing them into a larger atomic operation, i.e., executing them within the same transaction. Extending the SBD approach to allow composition of atomic sections (the smallest atomic operation in SBD) is helpful in case of library methods that perform split operations. A way to compose a function `canSplit f()` and `canSplit g()` into a single atomic section is to extend SBD by adding a block level statement `noSplit{...}`. Within such a `noSplit` block, the system ignores `split` instructions. Care has to be taken because certain methods must be able to split, e.g., a method that sends data over the network and expects a response. Therefore, to be safe, a programmer must explicitly allow execution of a method within such a `nosplit` block, e.g., by an additional property `splitOptional`.

4. Implementation

To evaluate the SBD approach, we use a proof of concept implementation based on the Java language. This implementation runs on an unmodified Oracle JVM. It consists of three components: A bytecode transformation tool to add synchronization, the STM runtime and adapted versions of those classes of the Java Class Library (JCL) that the benchmark programs require. In this section, we describe the relevant parts of this implementation.

4.1 Bytecode transformation

The bytecode transformation tool inserts code to interface with the STM runtime, and performs all code optimizations as described in Section 3.3. The tool uses the Soot framework [34] as basis.

The adaptation of Java arrays to the instance layout as described in Figure 4 (a) requires an additional reference to the locking structures. Altering the array structure is not possible using an unmodified JVM. Therefore, we use wrapper classes to combine an array reference and a reference to an array holding the locking structures of the array elements.

These array wrapper classes replace the regular arrays. To reduce overhead, access to the arrays within the wrappers remains direct (no getters or setters).

Further, to increase the effectivity of the code optimizations, the tool inlines methods statically during transformation. It uses the same inlining decisions for a method as the actual HotSpot Just-in-Time compiler (JIT) of the Oracle JVM would use. The JIT optionally writes its inlining decisions into a compilation log. Based on such a compilation log created during a previous execution, the tool uses the last log of a method for its inline decisions.

Finally, the tool adds support for static initialization. A rollback can revert a static initialization, in which case the system must execute it again. For that, the tool inserts guards before each static access and each constructor call. These guards trigger the static initialization if needed.

4.2 STM details

We implemented the STM as described in Section 3.2. The implementation uses the CAS instruction provided by the `sun.misc.Unsafe` API. The locking structure has a size of 64-bits, the size of the largest CAS operation supported by this API. Therefore, the bit set to store locking information has a size of 56 bits, and the queue ID has a size of 6 bits.

The deterministic deadlock resolution uses a blocking variant of the dreadlocks algorithm [24] modified to work with read-write locks.

4.3 Adaptations of JCL classes

We made the following adaptations to the JCL classes:

- Use the array wrapper classes instead of direct access.
- Implement the changes to the thread operations.
- Implement the transactional wrappers for I/O classes.
- Additional modifications as shown in Table 4.

As the JVM requires some of these classes during startup, we made the modifications to copies of the classes placed under a different namespace to avoid bootstrapping issues. We then redirected the benchmarks to use these copies instead. We only modified JCL classes that we require for the evaluation.

4.4 Implementation of transactional wrappers

For a class C, we manually implemented the transactional wrappers using the following scheme:

1. Implement an adapter class of class C with the same interface, and forward each call.
2. Add a buffer B to save the state before a modification.
3. Before calling a method that queries or modifies the state of an instance, add synchronization to ensure atomicity and isolation. Before modifying, save the state to the buffer B. In case a modification is irreversible or its reversal is nontrivial, the system must defer its execution until the end of the atomic section.
4. Implement commit and rollback operations. Usually, a commit applies deferred operations and clears the buffer B, and a rollback undoes the modifications using data from the buffer B.

E.g., when reading data from a network device, the system places a copy of this data into a buffer B_R. Buffer B_R is associated with the network device. After an abort, the next time the system reads data from the network device it uses the buffer B_R instead. It does this as long as the buffer B_R holds data, then it continues to read from the device. On success, the system discards the buffer B_R. When writing to the network device, the system first writes the data to buffer B_W, thus it defers the write. Only on success, it forwards the data in buffer B_W to the network device. After an abort, the system discards the buffer B_W.

5. Evaluation

To evaluate the SBD approach, we compare it to explicit synchronization using locks with regard to the following four aspects:

1. Programming effort
2. Sequential overhead
3. Scalability
4. Memory overhead

We do this by using multiple benchmarks that originally use explicit synchronization using locks and adapting them to the SBD approach, thus having two variants of each benchmark to compare against each other.

5.1 Setup and testing methodology

The test system has four Intel Xeon E7-4830 CPUs and 64GB RAM. Each CPU runs at 2.13GHz and has eight cores. For all experiments, we enable hyper-threading and disable the turbo mode. We use the Oracle JVM 1.7 for the evaluation. To compare the performance, we measure the steady state performance using the method presented in [13] to reduce the effect of the JIT on the measurements. For each benchmark run, we perform 10 JVM invocations. Per invocation, we require 30 consecutive benchmark iterations with coefficient of variation (CoV) lower than or equal to 0.01. If an invocation does not reach this value after 60 iterations, we use the last 30 iterations.

For testing, we use benchmarks from the DaCapo 09 Benchmark Suite [2] using their default workload. We chose this suite because it contains realistic application programs that we target with the SBD approach (see Section 3.1). We selected six multi-threaded benchmarks with different threading models (task, threads, signaling, custom synchronization, main/worker), and different types of I/O (none, disk, network, database).

We applied the following modifications to all selected benchmarks:

Benchm.	Modification
Tomcat	Use Http11Protocol as Java NIO is not implemented.
	Use statically compiled JSP pages, as dynamic compilation is not implemented.
PMD	Use single-byte charset as support for multi-byte character sets is not implemented.
H2	Allow a variable number of threads.
	Use multi-threaded engine and newer version (1.4.193) to reduce contention.

Table 3: Benchmark modifications not relevant for approach.

- Array wrappers as described in Section 4.1.
- Conversion to Soot internal representation, and back to bytecode.
- Static inlining on bytecode level for the optimizations.
- Additional modifications due to implementation restrictions or benchmark enhancements as shown in Table 3.

The above modifications are necessary due to the bytecode transformation, and not due to the SBD approach. To allow a fair comparison, we applied them to both variants. Table 4 lists custom modifications that increase the scalability of the SBD variant. If one of those modifications also reduced the runtime of the explicit synchronization variant, we applied it there as well. The static inlining uses the identical HotSpot compilation profiles for both variants. To generate the profile, we let each benchmark perform 20 iterations in a single invocation.

5.2 Programming effort

To compare the programming effort of both variants, we adapted the benchmarks from explicit synchronization using locks to the SBD approach. Then, we examined the required modifications. We modified only the parts used by the benchmarks, and not the complete code of the underlying application.

Adapting the benchmarks required functional and non-functional modifications. Functional modifications are additional split operations due to the changed I/O and threading behavior. Non-functional modifications decrease the sequential overhead, and increase the scalability of a benchmark by removing lock contention or by preventing deadlocks. Depending on the situation, we use different solutions for these issues:

1. Split as soon as possible after the contented access.
2. Use thread local memory.
3. Reduce update frequency of contented memory location.
4. Reorder accesses to memory locations.
5. Remove functionality if not needed.

We prefer solutions that do not require additional `split` operations (1), since longer atomic sections reduce the number of locking operations. Table 4 lists the custom modifications that we had to apply to the benchmarks to increase their scalability without a `split` operation (2-5). Only one of the custom modifications (disabling of the string cache, *Tomcat*) had a measurable impact on the *baseline* variant (small speed up). All thread local modifications fix scalability issues and do not reduce sequential overhead.

Table 5 shows the number of modifications we applied for each benchmark. To be able to put the number of modifications in relation, the table lists the number of lines of code (LOC) executed by the benchmark. Columns *Split* (*CanSplit*) show how often this instruction (modifier) is added. Column *Custom* shows the number of custom modifications that we had to implement. Column *Final* lists the number of added final modifiers. The bytecode transformer automatically adds the final modifier to private fields that are modified only in the constructor of a class and thus can be declared as final. Beside being good programming practice, this reduces overhead, as final fields do not need synchronization (see Table 1). Finally, columns *Synchronization* and *Volatile* list the number of synchronization constructs required by the baseline variant, which are not needed for the SBD variant.

Modifications to add `canSplit` and `final` modifiers are quite numerous, the former especially if signaling was used deep down in the method hierarchy. Since both type of changes are rather mechanical, they can benefit from code editor support, e.g., by using static analysis to suggest addition of the modifier. Comparing the combined number of `split` instructions and custom changes to the combined number of synchronized and volatile changes shows that the SBD approach and explicit locking have usually a similar amount of synchronization code. The exceptions are LuSearch, LuIndex, and Tomcat were the SBD approach requires a lower amount of synchronization code but on the other hand requires custom modifications (LuSearch, Tomcat), thus showing the asymmetry of SBD mentioned in Section 2.

5.3 Sequential overhead

The sequential (single thread) overhead of the SBD variant consists of the cost of the executed lock operations (see Figure 5). The cost depends on the effect of the locking operations:

Init: Initialize `locks` field of new instance.

Check New: New instances (check only).

Check Owned: Lock already owned (check only).

Acq. & Rls.: Lock acquire, and release (incl. undo).

The sequential overheads of the examined benchmarks are below 100%, even though the STM uses a CAS operation to implement the reader-writer locks. The reason is not only the performance of the STM, but also its usage. Table 6 shows execution time for a microbenchmark. This bench-

Component	Solution type	Description	Count	LOC
JCL	Frequency	Use separate isEmpty flag (instead of size) in get method for empty check.	1	18
	Thread local	Aggregate output to console per transaction to reduce contention. Uses a reusable thread local `OutputStream` aggregation class.	1	5
LuSearch	Thread local	Make shared message digest instance thread local.	1	20
	Reorder	Frequently updated file system directory cache (resolve read/write conflict)	1	3
PMD	Thread local	Thread local of update statistic counters, aggregate on read. Uses a reusable thread local integer aggregation class.	2	4
Tomcat	Thread local	Made tag handler pool thread local.	1	30
	Thread local	Use a separate connection per client thread, instead of connection pool.	1	1
	Thread local	Thread local update of statistic counters, aggregate on read. Uses a reusable thread local integer aggregation class.	7	3-10
	Frequency	Set initialization flag only once.	1	2
	Remove	Disabled the cache in the string manager class.	1	2

Table 4: Custom Java Class Library (JCL) and benchmark modifications. Column *LOC* excludes aggregation classes.

		Synchronized-by-default				Explicit synchronization	
Benchmark	**LOC**	**Split**	**Custom**	**CanSplit**	**Final**	**Synchronized**	**Volatile**
LuIndex	5222	1		38	76	27	9
LuSearch	2452	4	2	2	46	9	4
PMD	7121	2	2	4	158	2	
Sunflow	3827	3		9	50	3	
H2	1235	1		39	14	1	
Tomcat	29314	15	11	50	333	140	6

Table 5: Number of benchmark modifications. The numbers apply to code executed by the benchmark.

mark executes 100 million read or write operations, on 100 million instances each having a single field. We report time without lock (row *Baseline*) and for lock operations with effects: Check new, check owned, or acq. & rls. (includes undo log). The table shows two different access patterns: pseudo-random and sequential. The results show that the overhead of the checks, both new and owned, is relatively small compared to the overhead of acquire & release, regardless of the access pattern.

The other reason for these overheads are the SBD semantics that allow large transactions sizes. All examined benchmarks allow using such large transactions: Table 5.2 shows the low amount of required split instructions compared to the size of executed LOC. Within such large transactions, lock acquires and releases are relatively infrequent compared to new or owned checks that have a low overhead.

To allow a better understanding of the sequential overhead, Table 7 shows the number of lock operations that the benchmarks execute per second, on average. They are subdivided into four columns based on the effect of the operation (init, check new, check owned, acq. & rls). Note that the lock operation counts and the execution times are from two different executions, and thus may not be completely comparable, as each execution may have invoked the JIT compiler in a different context.

The benchmarks that have an overhead around the geom. mean 35.4% (LuIndex 46.7%, LuSearch 29.9%, PMD 43.3%, Tomcat 24.4%) have a mix of these operations. Sunflow has a high overhead (99.3%), because it executes a large number of lock initializations as well as owned checks. Note that Sunflow does not perform any I/O. On the other hand, H2 experiences a low overhead (13.4%) because it spends most of its time doing I/O operations, i.e., data base accesses via JDBC. As databases use transactions we integrated the JDBC classes using transactional wrappers.

The additional final fields reduce the sequential overhead (geom. mean over all thread counts) for Sunflow by 19.4%, and for PMD by 1.69%. The other benchmarks do not show a measurable reduction.

5.4 Scalability

Figure 7 shows the speedup curves of all benchmarks with the exclusion of LuIndex, which uses a fixed number of threads (main and worker). The speedup curves of Sunflow, PMD and H2 are similar in both variants. For LuSearch and Tomcat, beginning with 32 threads the speedup of explicit synchronization is higher than of the SBD variant. For LuSe-

Effect	Read		Write	
	Random	Seq.	Random	Seq.
Baseline	17.6s	0.92s	32.8s	1.11s
New	17.8s	0.93s	32.9s	1.12s
	(+1.14%)	(+1.09%)	(+0.30%)	(+0.90%)
Owned	28.8s	1.90s	47.5s	2.37s
	(+63.6%)	(+107%)	(+44.8%)	(+114%)
Acq. & Rls.	62.9s	6.75s	68.8s	8.08s
	(+257%)	(+634%)	(+110%)	(+628%)

Table 6: Microbenchmark: 100 million read or write operations on a single core. Avg. over 20 iterations (STD $< 2\%$).

Benchmark	Init	Check New	Check Owned	Acq.
H2	42k	198k	1 036k	520k
LuIndex	46k	186 639k	35 928k	3k
LuSearch	516k	149 164k	18 327k	32k
PMD	940k	56 013k	10 065k	253k
Sunflow	1 596k	66 146k	111 156k	41k
Tomcat	30k	3 078k	7 430k	7 212k

Table 7: Locking operations per second (avg.).

Benchm.	Baseline	SBD			
		Locks	R-W set	Buffers	Init
H2	48 650k	18k	3k	0k	0k
LuIndex	2 664k	75k	13k	1 280k	94k
LuSearch	818k	538k	86k	25k	231k
Pmd	5 758k	831k	56k	171k	2 477k
Sunflow	2 202k	1 034k	159k	0k	3 361k
Tomcat	4 071k	1 146k	511k	5k	0k

Table 8: Memory overhead (avg., single threaded execution).

arch, the reason is the garbage collection (GC) that requires additional time to process the undo log. We consider this an issue of using a Java STM implementation. In a VM-based implementation, the GC could, e.g., avoid processing the undo log, as the lock structures already contain information whether the undo log references an instance. For Tomcat, the reason is that it uses 32 client and 32 server threads thus exceeding the limit of maximal 56 concurrently running threads (restriction of the STM implementation). Table 9 shows the transaction abort rate (abort/success, *Abr.*), the number of contented lock acquires (*Con.*), and the number of CAS-failures (*Fail.*). Synchronization issues are generally low. The exception is the abort rate for Sunflow, but it does not negatively affect the runtime of the benchmark.

5.5 Memory overhead

The memory overhead of the SBD approach consists of the additional memory used by the field level locks and the

Benchm.	Thr.	Base. [s]	Sbd. [s]	Ovr. [%]	Abr. [%]	Con.	Fail.
H2	**1**	4.19	4.75	13.4	0.0	0	0
	2	4.15	4.42	6.6	0.0	7	7
	4	4.24	4.33	1.9	0.0	17	19
	8	5.25	5.31	1.3	0.0	12	13
	16	6.95	7.04	1.3	0.0	14	13
	32	10.12	10.17	0.4	0.0	10	12
LuIndex	**1**	0.92	1.35	46.7	0.0	0	0
LuSearch	**1**	5.68	7.37	29.9	0.0	0	0
	2	2.82	3.71	31.4	0.0	4	0
	4	1.44	1.86	29.3	0.0	11	1
	8	0.72	0.96	32.2	0.0	34	3
	16	0.38	0.5	31.8	0.0	70	5
	32	0.25	0.36	42.7	0.0	76	4
PMD	**1**	3.99	5.72	43.3	0.0	0	0
	2	2.08	2.84	36.2	0.0	4	6
	4	1.4	1.94	38.5	0.0	18	24
	8	1.36	1.84	35.4	0.0	45	69
	16	1.41	1.87	32.8	0.0	78	116
	32	1.5	1.94	29.1	0.0	119	147
Sunflow	**1**	15.11	30.1	99.3	0.0	0	0
	2	7.69	15.15	97.0	3.5	53	11
	4	3.94	7.45	88.8	44.4	209	30
	8	1.98	3.99	102	54.4	264	23
	16	1.17	2.33	98.8	59.9	355	30
	32	0.9	1.82	102	112	666	128
Tomcat	**1**	5.97	7.42	24.4	0.0	0	0
	2	3.04	3.75	23.3	0.0	298	317
	4	1.56	1.91	22.4	0.0	1002	1653
	8	0.82	1.01	24.1	0.1	1605	3030
	16	0.45	0.58	29.0	0.3	1260	2101
	32	0.34	0.51	50.2	0.4	1214	1906

Table 9: Overhead (*Ovr.*) of SBD approach compared to explicit locking (*Base.*). STD of execution times $< 5\%$, except for Tomcat/32/Base: 9.02%.

transaction logs. To measure the memory usage, a separate thread triggers a GC run every 50 ms. The thread samples the memory usage after each GC run. The reported numbers are the average of the samples interpolated linearly. All values are for 20 invocations of a single, sequential execution (STD $< 5\%$). The proof-of-concept implementation of the SBD approach does not allow to measure memory overhead directly. Instead, we report additional memory requirements of the data that is relevant for the SBD approach (largest contributors).

Table 8 shows the results of the measurement. The column *Baseline* lists the average memory usage (heap size after full GC) of the baseline variant. The column *Locks* shows the average additional memory for the lock structures of the SBD variant. Further, columns *R-W set*, *Buffers*, and column *Init* show the size of a transaction, split into the read-write set (incl. old values), undo buffers (reads from streams, and writes to streams/files), and initialization log (list of instances to mark as `UNALLOC` on commit).

Due to the lazy lock structure allocation, additional memory usage of the field level locks is quite low, except for LuSearch (+66%) and Sunflow (+47%). The memory usage of the undo log is in general low, except for LuIndex, which writes a large file in a single transaction, and Tomcat, which has a large R-W set as a result of acquiring many write locks (also visible in Table 7). H2 is mostly using its database interface, thus there is almost no additional memory usage. Benchmarks with large transactions usually also have large initialization logs (Sunflow, PMD).

6. Discussion

Whether the performance overhead associated with the SBD approach is acceptable depends on the use case. We believe that developers that appreciate features like garbage collection (GC), or array index bounds checks, would also appreciate the SBD approach. All these techniques have additional performance overhead but provide in exchange additional safety. The analogy of TM and GC has been observed before [14].

The SBD approach has an impact on the usage of the language itself. However, other features have this as well, e.g., a language that integrates GC would not provide an operation to deallocate memory manually. We consider the transactional external side effects the biggest change of our approach, since it even affects sequential programs. While inevitable transactions remain an alternative, they reduce scalability as explained in Section 3.4.

One concern with the SBD approach is that it is unclear what locks a method acquires. For the examined programs, this was in general a non-issue: Most methods behave as expected, e.g., returning the list size locks the list size, and not arbitrary memory locations. If a method has an unexpected locking behavior, e.g., it uses a cache or an object pool, this can be documented in a similar way as documenting the thread-safety property when using explicit synchronization. Finally, conflicts can be detected dynamically. We implemented a small debug mode in our runtime system that logs the blocked threads, and deadlock situations. This information together with the fact that SBD allows a programmer to incrementally add concurrency allows to resolve these issues mechanically by looking through this log. This was especially helpful as we did not know the benchmark programs beforehand.

7. Related work

The SBD approach relates to various earlier efforts. We group them into three categories.

Synchronized-by-default. Kuszmaul et al. proposed atomicity by default using transactions in combination with language support, i.e., the use of HTM in combination with language extensions to the fork-join mechanism of Clik [25]. Hammond et al. proposed to use HTM and language extensions to loop and fork-join mechanisms. They performed scalability measurements using a simulated HTM [16]. Isard et al. proposed Automatic-Mutual-Exclusion (AME) [23], a system for concurrent asynchronous programming that allows the integration of functionality performing external side effects outside of transactions, and suggested the use of STM. Abadi et al. further investigated the semantics of the AME approach [1]. A proposal to implement atomicity by default without transactions is Coqa [26] by Liu et al., a language that uses message-passing ideas to demark atomic sections and to identify concurrency in a programs. Although not synchronizing by default, the TIC model [31] provides a way to optionally punctuate (split) a transaction, e.g., to perform I/O. The SBD approach shows novel ways to integrate the transactional version of the approach into an object-oriented, managed language based on threads. Further, it shows how to exploit properties of such a language for optimizations and compares a version of Java adapted for the SBD approach against regular Java with explicit synchronization, using several realistic application programs and existing hardware.

STM using readers-writer (RW) locks. Not much attention was paid to these STMs in the past, because they have been slower than STMs using a global clock [29]. Recent work provided examples of well performing STMs using RW locks. Dice et al. show that such an STM can outperform a TL2 global-clock based STM [10, 11] on single-chip multicore processors. Zhang et al. show that a STM using RW locks performs well for low-contention workloads [36], similar to those we used in our experiments. Our approach displays a usage for STMs using RW locks. Unlike previous work, our STM contains only the minimal required features to avoid overhead.

No critical sections. Other techniques that provide synchronization without critical sections are: *Data-centric* approaches such as [7, 35] that infer synchronization from annotations. These annotations group data into atomic units and mark control flow where the system must maintain atomicity. Thus, these approaches require explicit synchronization through annotations. *Effect systems* [5, 22] enable a programmer to annotate a sequence of statements with their effects that a scheduler statically or dynamically can use to execute the statements without conflicts. A further alternative is *isolation* [6, 27] to avoid direct shared memory access by working on copies of data within the context of fork-join parallelism. And finally, Brinch Hansen's Distributed Processes [17] achieve synchronization by forbidding shared memory accesses and by requiring processes (threads) to communicate if shared memory access is needed. All three approaches (effect systems, isolation, and forbidding shared memory accesses) avoid synchronization, but limit the number of expressible parallel programming idioms.

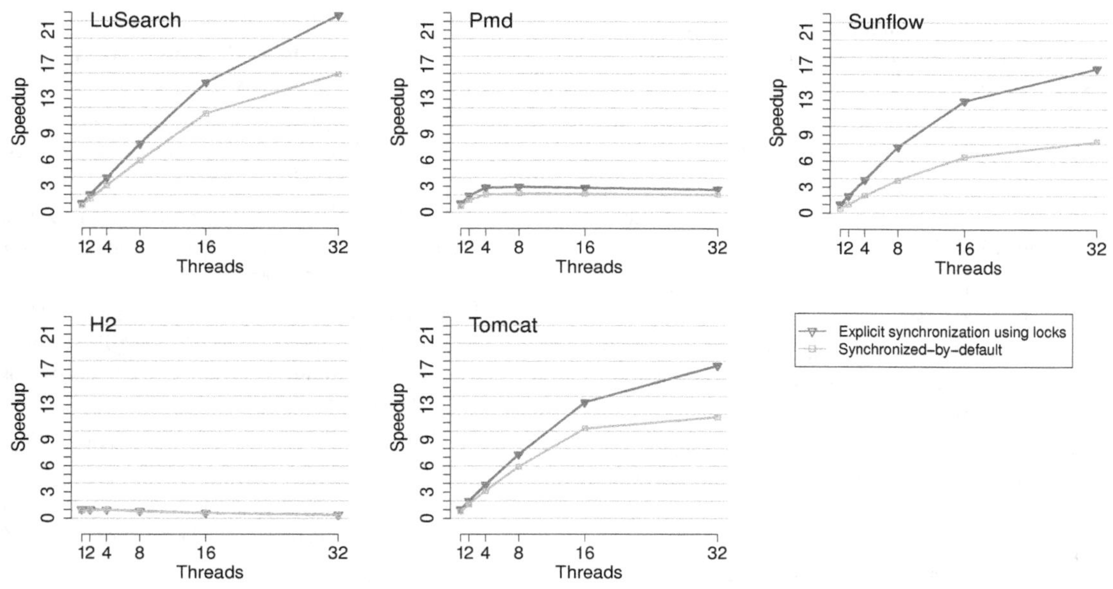

Figure 7: Scalability of the SBD approach vs. explicit synchronization. Base: Single threaded explicit synchronization.

8. Conclusion

The SBD approach for concurrency aims to reduce the occurrence of concurrency bugs due to data races, race conditions, and deadlocks. The approach allows the implementation of realistic applications that are scalable. We measured an overhead of 23.9% (geom. mean) compared to explicit synchronization using locks by executing realistic benchmarks on existing hardware.

The SBD approach requires only a small number of extensions to an existing language. Our prototype implementation is based on Java. There are numerous benefits that are obtained from integrating the SBD approach into an existing framework: it is easy to convert a program to SBD and the result remains similar the version with explicit synchronization using locks, and a comparison is meaningful. Thus, knowledge and experience gained by programmers using explicit synchronization is not lost. An additional benefit is that SBD reuses the existing threading constructs, transactional external wrappers for side effects, and the JIT compiler.

We have not yet studied to what extend SBD eases professional program development outside of an academic setting. However given the difficulty of constructing correct parallel programs, SBD is an attractive option that shows another approach to the development of concurrent programs. To the extend that the execution time of a concurrent program is not dominated by synchronization time, SBD offers an appealing alternative.

Acknowledgments

We thank the anonymous reviewers for their thorough reviews and helpful comments. We acknowledge computing resources provided by SNF grant 206021_133835.

References

[1] M. Abadi, A. Birrell, T. Harris, and M. Isard. Semantics of Transactional Memory and Automatic Mutual Exclusion. In *POPL '08*, pages 63–74, 2008.

[2] S. M. Blackburn, R. Garner, C. Hoffmann, A. M. Khang, K. S. McKinley, R. Bentzur, A. Diwan, D. Feinberg, D. Frampton, S. Z. Guyer, M. Hirzel, A. Hosking, M. Jump, H. Lee, J. E. B. Moss, A. Phansalkar, D. Stefanović, T. VanDrunen, D. von Dincklage, and B. Wiedermann. The DaCapo Benchmarks: Java Benchmarking Development and Analysis. In *OOPSLA '06*, pages 169–190, 2006.

[3] C. Blundell, E. C. Lewis, and M. M. K. Martin. Subtleties of Transactional Memory Atomicity Semantics. *IEEE Computer Architecture Letters*, 5(2), 2006.

[4] J. Bobba, K. E. Moore, H. Volos, L. Yen, M. D. Hill, M. M. Swift, and D. A. Wood. Performance Pathologies in Hardware Transactional Memory. In *ISCA '07*, pages 81–91, 2007.

[5] R. L. Bocchino, Jr., V. S. Adve, D. Dig, S. V. Adve, S. Heumann, R. Komuravelli, J. Overbey, P. Simmons, H. Sung, and M. Vakilian. A Type and Effect System for Deterministic Parallel Java. In *OOPSLA '09*, pages 97–116, 2009.

[6] S. Burckhardt, A. Baldassin, and D. Leijen. Concurrent Programming with Revisions and Isolation Types. In *OOPSLA '10*, pages 691–707, 2010.

[7] L. Ceze, C. von Praun, C. Caşcaval, P. Montesinos, and J. Torrellas. Concurrency Control with Data Coloring. In *MSPC*

'08, pages 6–10, 2008.

[8] L. Dalessandro, M. F. Spear, and M. L. Scott. NOrec: Streamlining STM by Abolishing Ownership Records. In *PPoPP '10*, pages 67–78, 2010.

[9] T. David, R. Guerraoui, and V. Trigonakis. Everything You Always Wanted to Know About Synchronization but Were Afraid to Ask. In *SOSP '13*, pages 33–48, 2013.

[10] D. Dice and N. Shavit. TLRW: Return of the Read-write Lock. In *SPAA '10*, pages 284–293, 2010.

[11] D. Dice, O. Shalev, and N. Shavit. Transactional Locking II. In *DISC '06*, pages 194–208, 2006.

[12] D. Dice, Y. Lev, M. Moir, and D. Nussbaum. Early Experience with a Commercial Hardware Transactional Memory Implementation. In *ASPLOS XIV*, pages 157–168, 2009.

[13] A. Georges, D. Buytaert, and L. Eeckhout. Statistically Rigorous Java Performance Evaluation. In *OOPSLA '07*, pages 57–76, 2007.

[14] D. Grossman. The Transactional Memory / Garbage Collection Analogy. In *OOPSLA '07*, pages 695–706, 2007.

[15] R. Guerraoui and M. Kapalka. On the Correctness of Transactional Memory. In *PPoPP '08*, pages 175–184, 2008.

[16] L. Hammond, B. D. Carlstrom, V. Wong, B. Hertzberg, M. Chen, C. Kozyrakis, and K. Olukotun. Programming with Transactional Coherence and Consistency (TCC). In *ASPLOS XI*, pages 1–13, 2004.

[17] P. B. Hansen. Distributed Processes: A Concurrent Programming Concept. *Commun. ACM*, 21(11):934–941, 1978.

[18] T. Harris. Exceptions and Side-effects in Atomic Blocks. *Sci. Comput. Program.*, 58(3):325–343, 2005.

[19] T. Harris and K. Fraser. Language Support for Lightweight Transactions. In *OOPSLA '03*, pages 388–402, 2003.

[20] T. Harris, S. Marlow, S. Peyton-Jones, and M. Herlihy. Composable Memory Transactions. In *PPoPP '05*, pages 48–60, 2005.

[21] M. Herlihy and J. E. B. Moss. Transactional Memory: Architectural Support for Lock-free Data Structures. In *ISCA '93*, pages 289–300, 1993.

[22] S. T. Heumann, V. S. Adve, and S. Wang. The Tasks with Effects Model for Safe Concurrency. In *PPoPP '13*, pages 239–250, 2013.

[23] M. Isard and A. Birrell. Automatic Mutual Exclusion. In *HOTOS '07*, pages 3:1–3:6, 2007.

[24] E. Koskinen and M. Herlihy. Dreadlocks: Efficient Deadlock Detection. In *SPAA '08*, pages 297–303, 2008.

[25] B. C. Kuszmaul, C. E. Leiserson, and S. Fellow. Transactions Everywhere. Technical report, 2003.

[26] Y. D. Liu, X. Lu, and S. F. Smith. Coqa: Concurrent Objects with Quantized Atomicity. In *CC '08/ETAPS '08*, pages 260–275, 2008.

[27] N. D. Matsakis. Parallel Closures: A New Twist on an Old Idea. In *HotPar '12*, pages 5–5, 2012.

[28] K. E. Moore, J. Bobba, M. J. Moravan, M. D. Hill, and D. A. Wood. LogTM: Log-based Transactional Memory. In *HPCA-12*, pages 254–265, 2006.

[29] B. Saha, A.-R. Adl-Tabatabai, R. L. Hudson, C. C. Minh, and B. Hertzberg. McRT-STM: A High Performance Software Transactional Memory System for a Multi-core Runtime. In *PPoPP '06*, pages 187–197, 2006.

[30] N. Shavit and D. Touitou. Software Transactional Memory. In *PODC '95*, pages 204–213, 1995.

[31] Y. Smaragdakis, A. Kay, R. Behrends, and M. Young. Transactions with Isolation and Cooperation. In *OOPSLA '07*, pages 191–210, 2007.

[32] M. F. Spear, V. J. Marathe, W. N. S. III, and M. L. Scott. Conflict Detection and Validation Strategies for Software Transactional Memory. In *DISC '06*, pages 179–193, 2006.

[33] M. F. Spear, M. Silverman, L. Dalessandro, M. M. Michael, and M. L. Scott. Implementing and Exploiting Inevitability in Software Transactional Memory. In *ICPP 2008*, pages 59–66, 2008.

[34] R. Vallée-Rai, P. Co, E. Gagnon, L. Hendren, P. Lam, and V. Sundaresan. Soot - a Java Bytecode Optimization Framework. In *CASCON '99*, 1999.

[35] M. Vaziri, F. Tip, and J. Dolby. Associating Synchronization Constraints with Data in an Object-oriented Language. In *POPL '06*, pages 334–345, 2006.

[36] M. Zhang, J. Huang, M. Cao, and M. D. Bond. Low-overhead Software Transactional Memory with Progress Guarantees and Strong Semantics. In *PPoPP '15*, pages 97–108, 2015.

A. Artifact Evaluation

The evaluated artifact contained all the necessary code and data to reproduce the performance overhead measurements in Table 9, the locking operations per second in Table 7, and the speedup curves in Figure 7. The results of the microbenchmark in Table 6, and the memory overhead measurements in Table 8 were not part of the evaluation. The artifact is available from the authors upon request.

Function Call Re-Vectorization

Rubens E. A. Moreira
UFMG – Brazil
rubens@dcc.ufmg.br

Sylvain Collange
INRIA – France
sylvain.collange@inria.fr

Fernando Magno Quintão Pereira
UFMG – Brazil
fernando@dcc.ufmg.br

Abstract

Programming languages such as C for CUDA, OpenCL or ISPC have contributed to increase the programmability of SIMD accelerators and graphics processing units. However, these languages still lack the flexibility offered by low-level SIMD programming on explicit vectors. To close this expressiveness gap while preserving performance, this paper introduces the notion of Call Re-Vectorization (CREV). CREV allows changing the dimension of vectorization during the execution of a kernel, exposing it as a nested parallel kernel call. CREV affords programmability close to dynamic parallelism, a feature that allows the invocation of kernels from inside kernels, but at much lower cost. In this paper, we present a formal semantics of CREV, and an implementation of it on the ISPC compiler. We have used CREV to implement some classic algorithms, including string matching, depth first search and Bellman-Ford, with minimum effort. These algorithms, once compiled by ISPC to Intel-based vector instructions, are as fast as state-of-the-art implementations, yet much simpler. Thus, CREV gives developers the elegance of dynamic programming, and the performance of explicit SIMD programming.

Categories and Subject Descriptors D - Software [*D.3 Programming Languages*]: D.3.4 Processors - Compilers

General Terms Languages, Performance

Keywords SIMD, SIMT, Function, Programmability

1. Introduction

New hardware asks for new programming idioms. As an example, the appearance of general purpose Graphics Processing Units (GPUs) has led to a revolution in programming languages [12, 23], which has culminated in the materialization of languages such as C for CUDA [29], OpenCL [22], ISPC [25] and PyCuda [18]. These Multi-Threaded (MT) languages let programmers express computations as single kernels executed by many threads. They target architectures that combine SIMD and multi-threaded execution, like GPUs and multi-core CPUs with vector instructions.

However, such high-level abstractions come at a cost in flexibility and composability. Most programming languages that target hardware accelerators pack threads into SIMD vectors or GPU warps[1] for the whole duration of a kernel call. They also suspend and resume individual threads to simulate thread-dependent control flow. These constraints affect device-side library functions, which cannot assume any particular organization of parallelism nor thread activity. For instance, invoking full SIMD functions within divergent regions might lead to incorrect behavior. Consequently, library functions often contain two versions of each routine, and dynamically dispatch the proper version depending on whether threads diverge at the call site or not[2].

On GPUs, developers circumvent the restrictions listed above in two ways: via *warp-synchronous programming*, or via *dynamic parallelism*. In the first case, programmers use the knowledge that threads are grouped in warps to achieve thread communication without synchronization or memory sharing. Yet, warp-synchronous programming is not easily composable with classic multi-thread programming. Programmers must ensure that every thread in a warp participates in each collective operation; e.g., the CUDA `__shfl` function has undefined behavior when reading data from an inactive thread. However, multi-thread programming puts thread divergences out of the hands of programmers. Consequently, such warp-synchronous functions may not be called from multi-thread code that may have divergent control flow.

CUDA's dynamic parallelism (or OpenCL's device-side enqueue) lets threads already in flight create new groups of threads [36]. This feature gives developers the opportunity to implement strikingly elegant algorithms [21]. However, this construct is too heavyweight for our simpler purpose of re-

PPoPP '17, February 04-08, 2017, Austin, TX, USA

DOI: http://dx.doi.org/10.1145/3018743.3018751

[1] We shall call groups of threads that execute in lock-step a *warp*.

[2] Ex.: see Trove at `https://github.com/bryancatanzaro/trove`.

activating threads within a warp. For instance, invoking new threads from within a thread in CUDA involves the global scheduling of a new grid of threads [16], a very expensive event. In short, currently, either we have the programmability and elegance of the multi-threaded model, or the efficiency of warp-synchronous programming, but not both.

The goal of this paper is to allow the composability of SIMD and MT through a programming construct syntactically similar to dynamic parallelism. To this end, we introduce the notion of *Call Re-Vectorization* (CREV). CREV is a programming idiom that modifies function calls. Functions marked with the **crev** tag, henceforth called *r-functions*, are executed by all the threads in a SIMD unit. This implies a context switch: to run a r-function, the runtime must change the state of all the threads, including those inactive due to divergent control flows. Upon completion, workers return to their previous state, in the same way that a function call is handled. Thus, we achieve a new level of recursion, in which threads can spawn new threads in a stack-based fashion. However, contrary to traditional dynamic parallelism, CREV uses only the accelerator's local memory (registers and call stack) to save thread states; hence, it is cheaper.

To validate our ideas, we have implemented them in ISPC [3, 25][3]. ISPC is a programming language, plus its compiler. This compiler produces industrial quality code for SIMD units such as Intel Streaming SIMD Extensions (SSE), Intel Advanced Vector Extensions (AVX) including AVX-512 for Xeon Phi accelerators [31], or ARM NEON. We chose to implement CREV in ISPC because this framework supports the notion of *unmasked* or *everywhere* blocks [25]: the ability to activate – in a new context – threads that are idle due to divergences. This feature is a requirement of CREV. We have used this new ISPC's extension to implement several classic algorithms using CREV. We show that these implementations are as efficient as warp-synchronous versions of them, and as clear and elegant as if they had been implemented using dynamic parallelism.

Summary of our Contributions. The key contribution of this paper is the notion of Call Re-Vectorization, which comes out of the observation that it is possible to capitalize on divergent threads to help speedup the work of active threads. We explain the concept of CREV through examples, a formal semantics and an industrial quality implementation:

- **Examples:** Section 2 shows examples of algorithms that benefit from our notion of Call Re-Vectorization. Further examples are discussed in Section 4.
- **Semantics:** Section 3.2 formalizes the semantics of μ-SIMD, a low-level instruction set sufficient to implement CREV. We have written a Prolog interpreter to validate that semantics. This interpreter made it easy to prototype different implementations of CREV, until we had a design that we could graft into a state-of-the-art compiler.
- **Translation:** Section 3.3 describes the translation of the high-level "**crev**" keyword into the low-level representation. Core properties of the final, low-level code, as produced by the translator, are listed in Section 3.4.
- **Evaluation:** Section 4 provides an empirical evaluation of our implementation. To perform this evaluation, we have implemented some algorithms, which are faster and cleaner than their original versions without CREV.

[3] The Intel SPMD Program Compiler (ISPC) is available at `https://github.com/ispc/`

2. Overview

The goal of this section is to explain *Warp-Synchronous Programming*, *Dynamic Parallelism* (DP), and our notion of *Call Re-Vectorization* (CREV). To this end, we shall use Algorithm 1 as an example. This program receives a book b_i, plus a pattern p. It then copies out all the lines $l \in b_i$ that match p. Pattern matching is performed by `memcmp`, and memory copying is done by `memcpy`. The book is represented as a matrix of characters; thus, each of its lines, and also the pattern p, is a vector of up to N characters. Algorithm 1 runs in parallel: t_{id} is a thread identifier. Hence, each thread is in charge of matching a line l in b_i against p. In case the match is positive, this thread must copy l to an output matrix b_o. For clarity, we assume a single warp in this example, although the techniques we described can be applied independently to multiple warps. The number of threads that run simultaneously in Algorithm 1 is W, the warp width.

Algorithm 1: SIMD Book Filter

```
W ← warp size; t_id ← thread index;
Function bFilter(mtx b_i, mtx b_o, vec p, int N)
    for k ← t_id to num_lines(b_i) - 1 step W do
        l ← b_i[k];
        if memcmp(l, p, N) == 0 then
            memcpy(l, b_o[k], N);
```

A naive multi-thread implementation of `memcpy` iterates sequentially over the arrays within each thread. This implementation is highly inefficient due to branch and memory divergence. Branch divergence occurs if the number of iterations N differs across threads. Threads with few iteration would finish the loop earlier and wait for threads with more iterations in order to restore convergence at the end of the loop. Memory divergence also happens as threads within a warp access data in unrelated locations. Such accesses, referred to as *uncoalesced* in the CUDA literature or as *gather/scatter* on SIMD platforms, are bandwidth-inefficient compared to accesses to consecutive elements.

2.1 Warp Synchronous Programming

It is possible to write function `memcpy` in a way that distributes operations on contiguous elements across consecutive threads. Algorithm 2 does it. Function `memcpy_shfl` is aware of the SIMD nature of a warp. Variables are stored as vectors, having each position belonging to a specific thread. Instruction $\texttt{shfl}(v, i)$ allows thread t_{id} to read the value stored in variable v, but in the register space of thread i. This implementation give us an efficient way to copy data between arrays, as copies are distributed evenly between threads, removing most of the branch divergence. Memory divergence is also eliminated as threads of a warp access consecutive elements at each iteration of the loop on line 7.

Nevertheless, this function has an important limitation: it requires all threads in the warp to be active. It cannot safely be called from a point that has potential branch divergence. Indeed, the loop on line 7 would skip elements if some threads were inactive. To support calls to `memcpy_shfl` within divergent regions, we need a way to re-activate threads and put them to work on the copy loop. In addition, the warp-synchronous programming construct is more complex and error-prone than the naive implementation.

Algorithm 2: Warp synchronous `memcpy`

```
1 W ← warp size; t_id ← thread index;
2 Function memcpy_shfl(vec s, vec d, int N)
3     for j ← 0 to W − 1 do
4         d_my ← shfl(d, j);
5         s_my ← shfl(s, j);
6         N_my ← shfl(N, j);
7         for i ← t_id to N_my − 1 step W do
8             d_my[i] ← s_my[i];
```

2.2 Dynamic Parallelism in CUDA

In NVIDIA's CUDA and OpenCL 2.0, dynamic parallelism (DP) is the ability to invoke a new kernel K_2 from within a kernel K_1 [32]. In this case, programmers may request a large number of threads, i.e., multiple new warps in multiple thread blocks. As the inner K_2 is a new kernel, all its threads are active upon entry, regardless of branch divergence in K_1. Algorithm 3 shows an implementation of `memcpy` that we could invoke from Algorithm 1 using dynamic parallelism. This algorithm splits, among all the threads in a warp, the work of copying vector s to vector d. Its main advantage is simplicity; its disadvantage is efficiency.

Algorithm 3: Implementation of `memcpy` that could be invoked dynamically from Algorithm 1.

```
W ← warp size; t_id ← thread index;
Function memcpy_dp(vec s, vec d, int N)
    for k ← t_id to N − 1 step W do
        d[k] ← s[k];
```

Wang *et al.* demonstrate that the overhead of a new kernel launch can be as high as one millisecond [32]. The new kernel must be scheduled and wait until there are resources available for its execution. Then, the requested number of warps and memory blocks must be allocated before execution starts. For large workloads, the overhead of launching a nested kernel is paid off by the massive data parallelism available in the GPU [8]. However, for small tasks, this extra cost might degrade performance.

2.3 Call Re-Vectorization

Introducing an inner dimension of parallelism is desirable to implement irregular algorithms such as graph traversal and recursive sorting. Unfortunately, current abstractions based on warp-synchronous programming or Dynamic Parallelism either compromise efficiency or programmability. To solve this conundrum, we introduce Call Re-Vectorization (CREV), a new programming idiom. Syntactically, CREV is akin to CUDA's dynamic parallelism. Semantically, it avoids the cost of scheduling new kernels.

CREV revisits the concept of **everywhere** (also known as **all** or **unmasked**) blocks to temporarily re-enable inactive threads within divergent regions. Such construction was available in programming languages for SIMD machines, such as C* [26], MPL (*MasPar Programming Language*) [20] or POMPC [15] in the late 1980s and early 1990s, and has made a recent comeback in ISPC [25]. In these languages, an **everywhere** block is executed by every processing element, regardless of its divergent state. At the end of that block, threads are sent back to their original state.

The **everywhere** block is a low-level construct to support the implementation of CREV; however, programmers do not deal with it directly – this is the task of the code generator. Algorithm 4 shows how Algorithm 1 looks like, once implemented using CREV. Programmers use the **crev** keyword at line 6 to re-vectorize functions. CREV maintains a stack of thread states to track execution contexts, thus supporting nested calls of r-functions. In terms of performance, a call to a function using the **crev** directive is equivalent to a regular function call – unlike the implementation of dynamic parallelism in CUDA, for instance. Thus, we favour the use of CREV for fine grain nested parallelism. Section 3 will explain the nitty-gritties behind the CREV directive.

Algorithm 4: SIMD Book Filter using CREV

```
1 W ← warp size; t_id ← thread index;
2 Function bFilter(mtx b_i, mtx b_o, vec p, int N)
3     for k ← t_id to num_lines(b_i)-1 step W do
4         l ← b_i[k];
5         if memcmp(l, p, N) = 0 then
6             crev memcpy_crev(l, b_o[k], N);
7 Function memcpy_crev(vec s, vec d, int N)
8     for k ← t_id to N − 1 step W do
9         d[k] ← s[k];
```

3. Semantics of CREV

This section presents the semantics of Call Re-Vectorization. First, in Section 3.1, we state informally key features of CREV. In Section 3.2, we introduce μ-SIMD, a low-level programming language with a set of primitives that lets us implement CREV. In Section 3.3, we show how to implement the **crev** high-level construct using the building blocks available in μ-SIMD. Finally, in Section 3.4, we use our semantics to state some properties of CREV. Before we dive in these details, Example 3.1 arms the reader with some intuition on how CREV works.

Example 3.1 *A function is called with the **crev** prefix to indicate that every thread, whether enabled or disabled, should execute the function. Every thread should execute the r-function multiple times if multiple enabled threads in the warp call it. For instance, if the warp size is 32 and 7 threads are enabled when the program flow hits line 6 in Algorithm 4, all 32 threads execute `memcmp_crev` 7 times. In each case, the 32 threads temporarily take on the local state of the active thread that they are helping. Once done, these workers all get their local state restored.*

3.1 The Cornerstones of CREV

CREV is defined as follows: for each active thread that reaches a call tagged with **crev**, we execute the target function once, forwarding global parameters (scalars) and extracting private ones per active thread (vectors). This principle of Call Re-Vectorization lays on three pillars: *thread re-activation, SIMD function call* and *data distribution.*

Thread Re-Activation. CREV does not lead to the creation of new threads. A function invoked via a CREV call is executed by every thread that is part of a warp, regardless of its threads' state. As mentioned in Section 2, a thread might be inactive due to divergences. However, dormant threads are re-activated to perform work. The former state of the thread is saved into the context stack, used for divergence management. On software context stack implementations such as used on AMD GPUs and Intel AVX-512 platforms, this operation is performed entirely in software. For platforms with hardware context stack implementations, like NVIDIA GPUs, it will require a new machine instruction.

SIMD Function Call. Multi-thread and SIMD languages have different definitions of function calls. In MT, a function call is only performed by active threads. Only register lanes that correspond to active threads are saved. The other threads are guaranteed to stay inactive during execution of the function and need no context save. Although each thread conceptually has its own private call stack, the call stacks of a warp are typically synchronized for performance reasons and to allow the sharing of a single scalar stack pointer for a warp. Implementations of SIMD languages, on the other hand, save whole vector registers on function calls, keeping one stack pointer per warp. Unlike regular MT functions, r-functions follow an SIMD application binary interface. This ensures that all registers in-use are saved before being overwritten inside the function, including lanes of threads that were inactive. Because no threads are created, context switch is similar to the cost of invoking a new function.

branch if zero	`bz` v, l
unconditional branch	`jmp` l
branch if thread previously active	`jmp_mask` t_{id}, l
write to shared memory	$\uparrow v_x = v$
read from shared memory	$v =\downarrow v_x$
binary operations	$v_1 = o_1 \oplus o_2$
copy	$v = o$
shuffle data between lanes	`shfl`(v, v_{lane})
synchronization barrier	`sync`
halt the machine	`stop`
begin `everywhere` *block*	`everywhere`
end `everywhere` *block*	`end_everywhere`

Figure 1. μ-SIMD instruction set. Operands (o) can be either variables or integer constants.

Labels (L)	$::= l \in \mathbb{N}$
Constants (C)	$::= c \in \mathbb{N}$
Variables (V)	$::= T_{id} \cup \{v_1, v_2, \dots\}$
Instructions (I)	::= Figure 1
Active Threads	$\Theta \subset \mathbb{N}$
Local Memory	$\sigma \subset V \mapsto \mathbb{Z}$
Local Memory Bank	$\beta \subset T_{id} \mapsto \sigma$
Shared Memory	$\Sigma \subset \mathbb{N} \mapsto \mathbb{Z}$
Synch Stack	$\Pi \subset (L \times \Theta \times L \times \Theta \times \Pi)$
Context Stack	$\Lambda \subset (\Theta \times \Pi \times \Lambda)$
Program	$P \subset L \mapsto I$
Program Counter	$pc \in \mathbb{N}$

Figure 2. The state of μ-SIMD machine is a septuple $M(\Theta, \beta, \Sigma, \Pi, \Lambda, P, pc)$. Θ is the set of active threads. A thread $t \in \Theta$ has a local memory σ, accessible through a memory bank β. Threads communicate through shared memory Σ. The stack Π tracks control flow divergences. A key component of Call Re-Vectorization is the thread stack Λ. The program counter, pc, keeps track of the next instruction $\iota \in P$ to be executed. The program P is a linear sequence of instructions. Although it never changes, we include it as state for convenience.

Data Distribution. Each formerly active warp thread is serialized to have a full warp operate on its data. As in the warp-synchronous `memcpy` example (Algorithm 2), this requires extracting and broadcasting each thread's register lane. Data distribution will be later detailed in Algorithm 5.

3.2 Low-Level Semantics

We formalize the notion of Call Re-Vectorization on top of a core language, μ-SIMD. This language provides the low-

$$\textbf{split}(\Theta, \beta, v) = (\Theta_0, \Theta_n) \textbf{ where}$$
$$\Theta_0 = \{t \mid t \in \Theta \textbf{ and } \beta[t] = \sigma_t \textbf{ and } \sigma_t[v] = 0\}$$
$$\Theta_n = \{t \mid t \in \Theta \textbf{ and } \beta[t] = \sigma_t \textbf{ and } \sigma_t[v] \neq 0\}$$

$$\textbf{push}([], \Theta_n, pc, l) = [(pc, [], l, \Theta_n)]$$
$$\textbf{push}((pc', [], l', \Theta'_n) : \Pi, \Theta_n, pc, l) = \Pi' \textbf{ if } pc \neq pc'$$
$$\textbf{where } \Pi' = (pc, [], l, \Theta_n) : (pc', [], l', \Theta'_n) : \Pi$$
$$\textbf{push}((pc, [], l, \Theta'_n) : \Pi, \Theta_n, pc, l) = (pc, [], l, \Theta_n \cup \Theta'_n) : \Pi$$

Figure 3. Auxiliar functions used to define μ-SIMD. `split` is a filter, dividing *threads* into two divergent sets (Θ_0 and Θ_n). Auxiliary function `push` updates the synchronization stack Π due to control flow divergences.

level constructs necessary to implement r-functions. Most of the syntax of μ-SIMD comes from Sampaio *et al.* [28], who, in turn, have reused ideas from Bougé *et al.* [2] and Farrell *et al.* [10]. A μ-SIMD program is a sequence of instructions indexed by a *pc*. Figure 1 shows μ-SIMD's syntax.

Operational Semantics. The state M of a program is a tuple $(\Theta, \beta, \Sigma, \Pi, \Lambda, P, pc)$, as described in Figure 2. Threads are uniquely identified by a natural t_{id}, having a local memory $\beta[t_{id}]$, and sharing a global memory Σ. Memory is vectorized, thus, a local address v denotes a vector of variables $v \in \beta[t_{id}]$; hence, each thread sees its private version of v.

To formalize the semantics of μ-SIMD, we use the auxiliary functions shown in Figure 3. The semantics of μ-SIMD is given by Figures 4 and 5. The former shows the behavior of instructions that change the program's control flow; the latter shows the behavior of logic and arithmetic instructions. The result of executing a control flow instruction is a triple (Θ, β, Σ). The interface between Figure 4 and Figure 5 is performed by Rules IT and TL. The result of executing an arithmetic or logic instruction is a pair (β, Σ), i.e., they only update the program memory.

The semantics of control flow divergences. To simulate the effect of divergences, μ-SIMD has a stack Π. Each element in Π is a tuple $(l_{id}, \Theta_{done}, l_{next}, \Theta_{todo})$, which indicates the point where divergent threads must re-converge. A new tuple is pushed onto Π due to a conditional branch, located at l_{id}, that has caused a divergence, as described by Rules BT, BF and BD, in Figure 4. Θ_{done} is the set of threads that have reached the synchronization point. Θ_{todo} is the set of threads waiting to execute. These threads, once active, will resume execution at label l_{next}. The stack is popped by instructions `sync`, whose behavior is given by Rules SS and SP.

The Thread Stack. To implement CREV, we have added a *thread stack* Λ to μ-SIMD. This stack is fundamental to the implementation of **everywhere** blocks. Λ holds pairs (Θ, Π). Figure 4 shows that instructions `everywhere` (Rule EB) push elements onto Λ, and instructions `end_everywhere` (Rule EE) pop it. The first element in this tuple is the set of threads active immediately before the execution of an

$$\text{(SP)} \quad \frac{P[pc] = \texttt{stop}}{(\Theta, \beta, \Sigma, \emptyset, \Lambda, P, pc) \to (\Theta, \beta, \Sigma)}$$

$$\text{(JP)} \quad \frac{P[pc] = \texttt{jmp}\ l \qquad (\Theta, \beta, \Sigma, \Pi, \Lambda, P, l) \to (\Theta', \beta', \Sigma')}{(\Theta, \beta, \Sigma, \Pi, \Lambda, P, pc) \to (\Theta', \beta', \Sigma')}$$

$$\text{(BT)} \quad \frac{\begin{array}{c} P[pc] = \texttt{bz}\ v, l \\ \textbf{split}(\Theta, \beta, v) = (\Theta, \emptyset) \qquad \textbf{push}(\Pi, \emptyset, pc, l) = \Pi' \\ (\Theta, \beta, \Sigma, \Pi', \Lambda, P, l) \to (\Theta', \beta', \Sigma') \end{array}}{(\Theta, \beta, \Sigma, \Pi, \Lambda, P, pc) \to (\Theta', \beta', \Sigma')}$$

$$\text{(BF)} \quad \frac{\begin{array}{c} P[pc] = \texttt{bz}\ v, l \\ \textbf{split}(\Theta, \beta, v) = (\emptyset, \Theta) \qquad \textbf{push}(\Pi, \emptyset, pc, l) = \Pi' \\ (\Theta, \beta, \Sigma, \Pi', \Lambda, P, pc+1) \to (\Theta', \beta', \Sigma') \end{array}}{(\Theta, \beta, \Sigma, \Pi, \Lambda, P, pc) \to (\Theta', \beta', \Sigma')}$$

$$\text{(BD)} \quad \frac{\begin{array}{c} P[pc] = \texttt{bz}\ v, l \qquad \textbf{split}(\Theta, \beta, v) = (\Theta_0, \Theta_n) \\ pc' = pc + 1 \qquad \textbf{push}(\Pi, \Theta_n, pc, l) = \Pi' \\ (\Theta_0, \beta, \Sigma, \Pi', \Lambda, P, pc') \to (\Theta', \beta', \Sigma') \end{array}}{(\Theta, \beta, \Sigma, \Pi, \Lambda, P, pc) \to (\Theta', \beta', \Sigma')}$$

$$\text{(BA)} \quad \frac{\begin{array}{c} P[pc] = \texttt{jmp\_mask}\ T_{id}, l \qquad T_{id} \in \Theta' \\ (\Theta, \beta, \Sigma, \Pi, (\Theta', \Pi') : \Lambda, P, l) \to (\Theta'', \beta', \Sigma') \end{array}}{(\Theta, \beta, \Sigma, \Pi, (\Theta', \Pi') : \Lambda, P, pc) \to (\Theta'', \beta', \Sigma')}$$

$$\text{(BI)} \quad \frac{\begin{array}{c} P[pc] = \texttt{jmp\_mask}\ T_{id}, l \qquad T_{id} \notin \Theta' \\ (\Theta, \beta, \Sigma, \Pi, (\Theta', \Pi') : \Lambda, P, pc+1) \to (\Theta'', \beta', \Sigma') \end{array}}{(\Theta, \beta, \Sigma, \Pi, (\Theta', \Pi') : \Lambda, P, pc) \to (\Theta'', \beta', \Sigma')}$$

$$\text{(SS)} \quad \frac{\begin{array}{c} P[pc] = \texttt{sync} \qquad \Theta_n \neq \emptyset \\ (\Theta_n, \beta, \Sigma, (pc', \Theta_0, l, \emptyset) : \Pi, \Lambda, P, l) \to (\Theta', \beta', \Sigma') \end{array}}{(\Theta, \beta, \Sigma, (pc', \emptyset, l, \Theta_n) : \Pi, \Lambda, P, pc) \to (\Theta', \beta', \Sigma')}$$

$$\text{(SI)} \quad \frac{\begin{array}{c} P[pc] = \texttt{sync} \qquad pc' = pc + 1 \\ (\Theta_n, \beta, \Sigma, (\_, \emptyset, \_, \Theta_0) : \Pi, \Lambda, P, pc') \to (\Theta', \beta', \Sigma') \end{array}}{(\Theta_0 \cup \Theta_n, \beta, \Sigma, \Pi, \Lambda, P, pc) \to (\Theta', \beta', \Sigma')}$$

$$\text{(EB)} \quad \frac{\begin{array}{c} P[pc] = \texttt{everywhere} \\ (\Theta_{all}, \beta, \Sigma, \emptyset, (\Theta, \Pi) : \Lambda, P, pc+1) \to (\Theta', \beta', \Sigma') \end{array}}{(\Theta, \beta, \Sigma, \Pi, \Lambda, P, pc) \to (\Theta', \beta', \Sigma')}$$

$$\text{(EE)} \quad \frac{\begin{array}{c} P[pc] = \texttt{end\_everywhere} \\ (\Theta, \beta, \Sigma, \Pi, \Lambda, P, pc+1) \to (\Theta', \beta', \Sigma') \end{array}}{(\_, \beta, \Sigma, \emptyset, (\Theta, \Pi) : \Lambda, P, pc) \to (\Theta', \beta', \Sigma')}$$

$$\text{(IT)} \quad \frac{\begin{array}{c} P[pc] = \iota \qquad \iota \neq \text{Control Flow Instruction} \\ (\Theta, \beta, \Sigma, \Theta_{mask}, \iota) \to (\beta', \Sigma') \qquad pc' = pc + 1 \\ (\Theta, \beta', \Sigma', \Pi, (\Theta_{mask}, \Pi') : \Lambda, pc') \to (\Theta', \beta'', \Sigma'') \end{array}}{(\Theta, \beta, \Sigma, \Pi, (\Theta_{mask}, \Pi') : \Lambda, P, pc) \to (\Theta', \beta'', \Sigma'')}$$

Figure 4. Semantics of μ-SIMD's control flow instructions.

$$\text{(MM)}\quad \frac{\Sigma(v) = c}{\Sigma \vdash v = c} \qquad \text{(TL)}\quad \frac{(t, \beta, \Sigma, \Theta_{mask}, \iota) \rightarrow (\sigma_t, \Sigma') \qquad (\Theta, \beta \setminus [\beta[t] \mapsto \sigma_t], \Sigma', \Theta_{mask}, \iota) \rightarrow (\beta", \Sigma")}{(\{t\} \cup \Theta, \beta, \Sigma, \Theta_{mask}, \iota) \rightarrow (\beta", \Sigma")}$$

$$\text{(MT)}\quad t, \beta \vdash t_{id} = t \qquad \text{(BP)}\quad \frac{t, \beta \vdash v_2 = c_2 \qquad t, \beta \vdash v_3 = c_3 \qquad \beta[t] = \sigma_t \qquad c_1 = c_2 \oplus c_3}{(t, \beta, \Sigma, \_, v_1 = v_2 \oplus v_3) \rightarrow (\sigma_t \setminus [v_1 \mapsto c_1], \Sigma)}$$

$$\text{(MV)}\quad \frac{\beta[t] = \sigma_t \qquad \sigma_t(v) = c}{t, \beta \vdash v = c} \qquad \text{(SI)}\quad \frac{t, \beta \vdash v_1 = c_1 \qquad t, \beta \vdash v_{lane} = c_{lane} \qquad \beta[t] = \sigma_t \qquad c_{lane} \notin \Theta_{mask}}{(t, \beta, \Sigma, \Theta_{mask}, \mathtt{shfl}(v_1, v_{lane})) \rightarrow (\sigma_t \setminus [v_1 \mapsto \_], \Sigma)}$$

$$\text{(SV)}\quad \frac{t, \beta \vdash v_1 = c_1 \qquad t, \beta \vdash v_{lane} = c_{lane} \qquad \beta[t] = \sigma_t \qquad c_{lane} \in \Theta_{mask} \qquad \beta[c_{lane}] = \sigma_{lane} \qquad \sigma_{lane}(v_1) = c_2}{(t, \beta, \Sigma, \Theta_{mask}, \mathtt{shfl}(v_1, v_{lane})) \rightarrow (\sigma_t \setminus [v_1 \mapsto c_2], \Sigma)}$$

$$\text{(CT)}\quad \frac{\beta[t] = \sigma_t}{(t, \beta, \Sigma, \_, v = c) \rightarrow (\sigma_t \setminus [v \mapsto c], \Sigma)} \qquad \text{(AS)}\quad \frac{t, \beta \vdash v' = c \qquad \beta[t] = \sigma_t}{(t, \beta, \Sigma, \_, v = v') \rightarrow (\sigma_t \setminus [v \mapsto c], \Sigma)}$$

$$\text{(LD)}\quad \frac{t, \beta \vdash v_x = c_x \qquad \beta[t] = \sigma_t \qquad \Sigma \vdash c_x = c}{(t, \beta, \Sigma, \_, v = \downarrow v_x) \rightarrow (\sigma_t \setminus [v \mapsto c], \Sigma)} \qquad \text{(ST)}\quad \frac{t, \beta \vdash v_x = c_x \qquad t, \beta \vdash v = c\beta[t] = \sigma_t}{(t, \beta, \Sigma, \_, \uparrow v_x = v) \rightarrow (\sigma_t, \Sigma \setminus [c_x \mapsto c])}$$

Figure 5. Semantics of arithmetic, logic and data-related instructions. Rule TL loops over every thread $t \in \Theta$, and for each one of them, executes instruction ι. No assumption can be made on the order in which instructions run.

everywhere block. The second element is the divergence stack, also in the state before the execution of the last **everywhere** block traversed by the program flow. In Rule EB (Fig. 4), Θ_{all} represents all the threads available in a warp. The thread stack lets us represent an unbounded number of different thread contexts; hence, programs might contain an arbitrary number of nested **everywhere** blocks. After executing the instruction `end_everywhere`, threads previously inactive will go back into sleeping mode. In other words, after `end_everywhere`, the pair (Θ, Π) at the top of Λ is popped, and the diverging configuration Π becomes part of the current state of threads. If necessary to check if a thread is active due to an **everywhere** block, then μ-SIMD provides a conditinal `jmp_mask`. The statement `jmp_mask`(t_{id}, l) will divert execution to l if t_{id} is active in the mask at Λ's top. Example 3.2 illustrates the behavior of these instructions.

Example 3.2 *Figure 6 shows a program written in μ-SIMD. We assume $|\Theta_{all}| = 4$. This program increments a 4×4 matrix; however, line i is incremented only if $\Sigma[t_{id}] = 0$. The figure shows the initial state of the shared (Σ) and local memory of each thread (σ). The initial state of the variables in the local memory is immaterial for this example. Figure 7 shows a trace of the execution of the program, given its initial state. Only threads $t_{id} = 0$ and $t_{id} = 3$ will enter the **everywhere** section, because $\Sigma[0] = \Sigma[3] = 0$. Nevertheless, all the four threads will execute the commands within that block. Instruction v3 = shfl(v2, v8) lets each thread read into v3 the value of v2 seen by thread v8.*

3.3 High-Level Semantics

The μ-SIMD assembly gives us the primitive building blocks to implement CREV in higher-level languages. As a proof of concept, we have implemented CREV onto ISPC, using instructions of ISPC that are equivalent to those seen in μ-SIMD. By focusing on an abstract notation, μ-SIMD, instead of on a concrete language, such as ISPC, we claim generality: CREV can be implemented in any environment that supports our notions of **everywhere** and shuffle. In this section we show how to implement the **crev** modifier, which marks a function call as an r-function. For simplicity, our high-level language provides only syntax to declare and invoke functions. A function declaration consists of a *name* f, plus a list of *formal parameters*, e.g.: $f(T\, p_1, \ldots, T\, p_n)$. We let T denote a *type modifier*, which can be either *uniform* or *varying*. We have borrowed this notation from ISPC. Other programming languages have different ways to express these

Instructions

```
      v0 = ↓tid
      v1 = (v0 == 0)
      bz v1, Done
      v2 = 4 * (tid + 1)
      everywhere
      v8 = 0
Loop  jmp_mask v8, Call
      jmp Next
Call  v3 = shfl(v2, v8)
      v4 = v3 + tid
      v5 = ↓v4
      v6 = v5 + 1
      ↑v4 = v6
Next  v8 = v8 + 1
      v7 = (v8 == 4)
      bz v7, Loop
      end_everywhere
      ↑tid = 1
Done  sync
```

Shared Memory

Address	0	1	2	3
Contents	0	1	1	0
Address	4	5	6	7
Contents	2	1	3	4
Address	8	9	10	11
Contents	1	5	6	1
Address	12	13	14	15
Contents	2	3	1	7
Address	16	17	18	19
Contents	1	3	4	0

Private Memory

Address	v0	v1	v2	v3
Contents	*	*	*	*
Address	v4	v5	v6	v7
Contents	*	*	*	*
Address	v8			
Contents	*			

Figure 6. Program written in μ-SIMD, plus its initial state.

			Tid				Tid			
	Instructions	**Var**	**0**	**1**	**2**	**3**	**0**	**1**	**2**	**3**
	v0 = ↓tid	v0	0	1	1	0	✓	✓	✓	✓
	v1 = (v0 == 0)	v1	1	0	0	1	✓	✓	✓	✓
	bz v1, Done		F	T	T	F	✓	✓	✓	✓
	v2 = 4 * (tid + 1)	v2	4	*	*	16	✓	•	•	✓
	everywhere						✓	•	•	✓
	v8 = 0	v8	0	0	0	0	✓	✓	✓	✓
Loop	jmp_mask v8, Call		T	T	T	T	✓	✓	✓	✓
	jmp Next		F	F	F	F	✓	✓	✓	✓
Call	v3 = shfl(v2, v8)	v3	4	4	4	4	✓	✓	✓	✓
	v4 = v3 + tid	v4	4	5	6	7	✓	✓	✓	✓
	v5 = ↓v4	v5	2	1	3	4	✓	✓	✓	✓
	v6 = v5 + 1	v6	3	2	4	5	✓	✓	✓	✓
	↑v4 = v6						✓	✓	✓	✓
Next	v8 = v8 + 1	v8	1	1	1	1	✓	✓	✓	✓
	v7 = (v8 == 4)	v7	0	0	0	0	✓	✓	✓	✓
	bz v7, Loop		T	T	T	T	✓	✓	✓	✓
Loop	jmp_mask v8, Call		F	F	F	F	✓	✓	✓	✓
	jmp Next		T	T	T	T	✓	✓	✓	✓
Next	v8 = v8 + 1	v8	2	2	2	2	✓	✓	✓	✓
	v7 = (v8 == 4)	v7	0	0	0	0	✓	✓	✓	✓
	bz v7, Loop		T	T	T	T	✓	✓	✓	✓
Loop	jmp_mask v8, Call		F	F	F	F	✓	✓	✓	✓
	jmp Next		T	T	T	T	✓	✓	✓	✓
Next	v8 = v8 + 1	v8	3	3	3	3	✓	✓	✓	✓
	v7 = (v8 == 4)	v7	0	0	0	0	✓	✓	✓	✓
	bz v7, Loop		T	T	T	T	✓	✓	✓	✓
Loop	jmp_mask v8, Call		T	T	T	T	✓	✓	✓	✓
	jmp Next		F	F	F	F	✓	✓	✓	✓
Call	v3 = shfl(v2, v8)	v3	16	16	16	16	✓	✓	✓	✓
	v4 = v3 + tid	v4	16	17	18	19	✓	✓	✓	✓
	v5 = ↓v4	v5	1	3	4	0	✓	✓	✓	✓
	v6 = v5 + 1	v6	2	4	5	1	✓	✓	✓	✓
	↑v4 = v6						✓	✓	✓	✓
Next	v8 = v8 + 1	v8	4	4	4	4	✓	✓	✓	✓
	v7 = (v8 == 4)	v7	1	1	1	1	✓	✓	✓	✓
	bz v7, Loop		F	F	F	F	✓	✓	✓	✓
	end_everywhere						✓	•	•	✓
	↑tid = 1						✓	•	•	✓
Done	sync						✓	✓	✓	✓

Figure 7. Execution trace of the program in Figure 6. Column **Var** shows contents of last variable assigned. T indicates branch taken; F indicates otherwise. The symbol • marks inactive threads. For the syntax of instructions, we refer the reader to Fig. 1; for their semantics, Figs. 4 and 5.

```
1           everywhere                  ;; begin CREV
2           i = 0                       ;; Loop counter
3   loop :  jmp_mask i, call
4           jmp next                    ;; Skip idle threads
5   call :  extract(t^n, p^n, a^n, i)   ;; Algorithm 5
6           "call" f                    ;; function call
7   next :  i = i + 1
8           bnz(i ≠ W) loop
9           end_everywhere              ;; end CREV
```

Figure 8. Low-level code produced to call r-function f.

modifiers. For instance, in CUDA we have *shared* and *global* allocation filling the role of ISPC's uniform variables.

Figure 8 shows the code that we produce for a r-function call $f(a_1, \ldots, a_n)$, where each $a_i, 1 \leq i \leq n$ is an actual argument of f. Such an r-function call will trigger up to $|\Theta|$ executions of f, one for each active thread $t \in \Theta$. The test

Algorithm 5: Data distribution

```
1 Function declaration: f(p_1, ..., p_n);
2 Function call: f(t_1 a_1, ..., t_n a_n);
3 Function extract(t^n, p^n, a^n, i)
4     for k ∈ 1...n do
5         if t_k == uniform then
6             p_k = a_k;
7         if t_k == varying then
8             shfl(a_k, i);
```

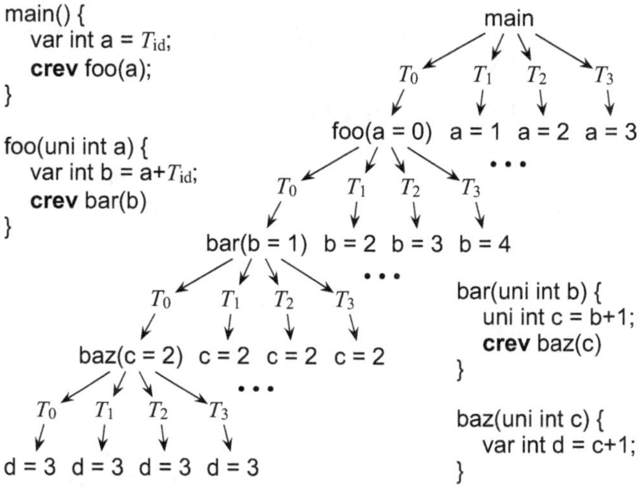

Figure 9. A program written in ISPC, and the tree showing function calls for T_0.

in lines 3 or 8 in Figure 8 are used to single out the function invocation performed by each thread. A different call will happen due to each $handle_t$ label. In another dimension of parallelism, each function call will be executed by Θ_{all} threads, due to the **everywhere** block at lines 10 and 13. Thus, we might have up to Θ_{all}^2 computations.

Algorithm 5 generates code that implements data distribution. Data distribution determines how actual parameters are bound to formal parameters, given that actual parameters can have one of two types: *uniform* or *varying*. By construction, r-functions have only uniform parameters. The loop in line 4 will go over all the function arguments, comparing formal (p) and actual (a) parameters. We let the type of a_i be t_i. If an actual argument is uniform, then parameter passing is trivially implemented as a copy between variables. Line 5 of Algorithm 5 generates code under such circumstance. If an actual parameter has type varying, then we generate code to perform a broadcast, as seen in line 7 of Algorithm 5.

Example 3.3 *The program in Figure 9 shows three functions called via* ***crev****. We are assuming an architecture with four SIMD lanes, i.e.,* $\Theta_{all} = \{T_0, T_1, T_2, T_3\}$*. When foo is in-*

voked, the value of a, main's local variable, is broadcasted to foo's formal parameter. Thus, T_0 sees foo(0), T_1 sees foo(1), etc. When T_0 calls bar from foo, the same behavior is observed. However, when T_0 calls baz from bar, all the four threads activated into this context see baz(2), because baz receives a uniform argument. The fact that baz's local variable d is marked as varying is immaterial in this example, as this variable is initialized with uniform values.

3.4 Properties of CREV

The semantics of CREV, given by μ-SIMD's primitive building blocks, and the translator seen in Section 3.3, lets us establish a few properties that are true about this programming abstraction. In this section we go over a few of these properties. They are valid under the assumption that programs are *well-formed.* We define well-formed programs below:

Definition 3.4 (Well-Formed Program) *A μ-SIMD program is well-formed if any occurrence of an* `everywhere` *instruction at label l_1 is matched by an occurrence of an* `end_everywhere` *instruction at label l_2, and these two labels are* control equivalent.

Definition 3.4 borrows the concept of control equivalence from Ferrante *et al.* [11]. Two points, l_1 and l_2, in a program's control flow graph are said to be control equivalent if l_1 dominates l_2, and l_2 post-dominates l_1. We say that l_1 dominates l_2 if, and only if, any path from the root of the CFG to l_2 must cross l_1. Dually, l_2 post-dominates l_1 if, and only if, any path from l_1 to the end of the CFG must cross l_2. Our translator produces well-formed programs, as long as the program flow cannot leave a function through points other than its return address.

Theorem 3.5 (Well-Formed Translation) *The translator of Figure 8 produces well-formed programs.*

Proof: This result follows trivially from the fact that an **everywhere** block surrounds only Algorithm 5 and the r-function. Well-formedness holds as long as none of these routines let the program flow escape the enclosing `end_everywhere` instruction. This implies that the r-function cannot throw exceptions, for instance. □

Composability. CREV allows the nesting of **everywhere** blocks. Composition happens due to nested function calls. The thread stack Λ ensures that the last invoked r-function will be the first to remove pending computation. In what follows, we visit three consequences of this property.

Composition is multiplicative. An **crev** call will put all the warp threads in active mode. By coupling this observation with *composibility*, we have that, in the absence of divergences, a sequence of n nested **crev** calls will create $|\Theta_{all}|^N$ tasks. Notice that CREV produces new tasks, but not new threads: we still have only $|\Theta_{all}|$ threads to solve these tasks.

Commutativity. The translator of Figure 8 calls an r-function in a lexicographic order defined by thread identifiers. However, μ-SIMD's primitives do not impose any order on the threads pushed onto Λ. Therefore, the multiple SIMD calls of an r-function can be handled in any order.

Synchronization parity. There is no distinction between the top level of parallelism and the inner level of parallelism with regards to the synchronization primitive. In other words, divergences are handled transparently by the synchronization stack Π, and, from a synchronization standpoint, it is not possible to tell if execution exists within the context of an r-function or not. To ensure this property, μ-SIMD's `everywhere` instruction pushes onto Λ, together with the set of active threads, the divergent state Π.

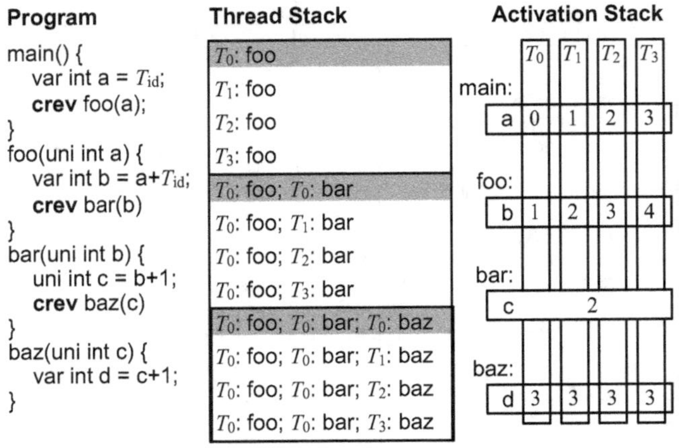

Figure 10. Example of three nested calls to r-functions. Calls currently in the activation stack are highlighted.

The interplay between CREV and nested function calls. The implementation of CREV does not interfere with the implementation of function calls. Programming languages that support recursion use a structure known as *activation stack* to manage function calls. Entries in the activation stack are called *activation records*, and they store functions' local variables, return address, arguments, etc. Upon invocation, the activation record of a function is pushed onto the activation stack. For each thread pushed onto the thread stack there will exist one activation record on the activation stack. The multiplicative nature of CREV also implies on a multiplication of activation records. Therefore, n nested r-calls will generate $|\Theta_{all}|^n$ activation records; however, the maximum depth of the activation stack is still $n+1$: activation records owned by different threads will not exist simultaneously.

Example 3.6 *Figure 10 reuse the program from Example 3.3 to illustrate these points. Again, we assume $|\Theta_{all}| = 4$. Thus, three non-divergent nested r-calls will create $4 \times 4 \times 4 \times 4 = 256$ tasks. At any time, the thread stack will contain at most $4+4+4+4 = 16$ tasks waiting for execution. The activation stack will contain, at any given point, at most 4 activation records, corresponding to the activation of functions main, foo, bar and baz.*

4. Evaluation

To evaluate the ideas presented in this paper, we have implemented CREV on ISPC. We use this implementation to demonstrate that CREV allies the efficiency of warp synchronous programming with the clarity and elegance of dynamic parallelism; hence, avoiding the complexity of the former, and the heavy scheduling cost of the latter.

Experimental Setup. Because CREV is a novel concept within ISPC, this compilation framework does not provide benchmarks that use it. Thus, we have re-implemented seven classic algorithms using the new keyword **crev**. Our seven benchmarks are: (bk) Book Filter (Algorithm 1); (sm) String Matching; (bf) Bellman-Ford [1]; (df) Depth-First Search; (le) Leader Election; (qs) quick-sort; and (ms) merge-sort.

Runtime Environment. We have implemented CREV onto ISPC v 1.9.1, and have used it to target a 6-core 2.00 GHz Intel Xeon E5-2620 CPU with 8-wide AVX vector units, running Linux Ubuntu 12.04 3.2.0. This running environment gives us warps with eight threads, e.g., $|\Theta_{all}| = 8$.

The Competing Approaches. We compare four different ways to implement our benchmarks.

- Seq: serial implementation of each algorithm, as defined in Cormen's book [5]. String-matching was implemented after the Knuth–Morris–Pratt (KMP) [19] algorithm.
- Par: warp synchronous implementation using constructs available in the ISPC language, but without CREV.
- Launch: dynamic parallelism, implemented via the **launch** keyword, which starts a new PThread per function call.
- CREV: the implementation of the algorithms using the ideas introduced in this paper.

The Seq version of each benchmark is implemented in C++, and is compiled with clang version 3.7.1, with the optimization flags -O2/-std=c++11. Benchmarks in the other three categories (Par, Launch and CREV) are compiled with ISPC. The Launch and CREV implementations look the same, except for the keyword that precedes function calls: **launch** in the first case, and **crev** in the second. The implementations in the Par group are different: they do not contain function calls within divergent regions, to ensure correctness.

Implementations are not available for all the programs. Even though it is trivial to implement quick-sort or merge-sort with dynamic parallelism or with CREV, the craft of a warp synchronous implementation of them is not obvious; hence, we omit them. Additionally, we omit a sequential implementation of book filter, because this problem does not have a canonical, textbook-like, solution. Notice, however, that this algorithm reuses two r-functions: string match (sm), and `memcpy` (Algorithm 2). Thus, we show results for sequential string matching, but not for sequential book filter.

How to read our results. Results are measured in millions of execution cycles, as reported by ISPC's testing environment. Numbers are the average of five, out of six samples. We have removed the first, to avoid cold-start discrepancies. The reader must bear four observations in mind, when analyzing our results: (i) speedups of CREV over pure ISPC (Par) are due to the better load distribution that CREV accomplishes by transporting work to inactive threads; (ii) the large slowdowns observed with Launch are due to the heavy cost of scheduling millions of new Posix threads to perform small chunks of work. (iii) CREV's slowdowns are due to the boilerplate code necessary to serialize threads, before invoking r-functions; (iv) we are comparing against an industrial-strength compiler; hence, speedups tend to be modest.

Pg	Seq	Par	Launch	CREV
bk	×	8,530.99	7,857.98	7,405.17
sm	6,649.28	3,576.14	393,166.27	2,737.94
bf	141,088.73	493,619.69	•	529,856.06
df	3,754.10	3,786.26	•	3,790.44
le	4,054.66	3,983.09	5,272.92	3,984.79
qs	2.87	×	204.28	2.87
ms	7.30	×	104.98	4.11

Figure 11. Execution time, in millions of cycles. We use × to indicate that the implementation of a benchmark is not available, and • to indicate that the implementation of the benchmark does not run successfully until completion.

4.1 Results and Discussion

Figure 11 summarizes our results. The table shows runtime, measured as number of execution cycles (in millions), for all the implementations that we have of the seven different benchmarks. These numbers are produced with the largest inputs that we have for each benchmark:

- bk: 10K strings of 0s and 1s, each with 20K bits, and random target pattern with 16 bits.
- sm: 256MB taken from books available in the Project Gutenberg, and a target pattern with 16 characters.
- bf: random Erdös-Rényi [9] graph with 2,048 nodes and 80% edge probability.
- df, le: 8-ary complete tree, depth 5 (root + five full levels).
- qs, ms: 16K random integers in the range $[0, 100000)$.

Figure 11 shows that ISPC, with or without CREV, is competitive against mainstream compilers: Seq is the best C implementation that we could produce of each algorithm; furthermore, these programs are compiled with clang -O2 (which was faster than clang -O3 in this experiment). Nevertheless, CREV and Par outperform these implementations in several cases, although they are not embarrassingly parallel. The table also reveals that Launch is sometimes orders of magnitude slower than the other approaches, being the fastest in only one case: bk. In bf and df, the excessive number of threads created by Launch forced earlier termination.

CREV usually outperforms Par by a small margin. However, the main benefit of the former over the latter is not performance. Rather, it is readability. The Launch and the CREV versions of each benchmark are exactly the same, except that whereas in one case we prepend the call of functions with the launch keywork, in the other we use **crev**.

On the other hand, the Par implementations are very different, because they cannot call functions within potentially divergent regions. To circumvent this restriction, the five Par benchmarks forgo recursion. As an example, the ISPC version of depth-first search uses a stack of tasks, instead of performing recursive functions to traverse the graph.

Algorithm 6: Pattern matching: CREV vs. Naïve

```
1  P ← pattern; T ← target text;
2  W ← warp size; t_id ← thread index;
3  Function memcmp(Offset k)
4      m ← True;
5      for i ← t_id to |P| do
6          if P[i] ≠ T[i + k] then m ← False ;
7      if all (m = True) then Found(k) ;
8  Function StringMatch
9      for i ← t_id to (|T| − |P|) step W do
10         if P[0] = T[i] then crev memcmp(i) ;
11 Function ParStringMatch
12     for i ← t_id to (|T| − |P|) step W do
13         j ← 0; k ← i;
14         while j < |P| and P[j] = T[k] do
15             j ← j + 1; k ← k + 1;
16         if j = |P| then Found(k) ;
```

As another example, Algorithm 6 shows the CREV-based implementation of string matching. This is a warp-synchronous implementation of parallel matching: each thread t_{id} tries to match P at positions $T[t_{id} + n \times W]$, where $n \leq |T|$, and W is the warp size. Thus, in the best scenario, runtime is divided by W. This implementation is irregular: divergences might happen at lines 6 and 10. Each call to `memcmp`[4] will commence a CREV sequence of computations. Figure 12 compares our implementation, seen in Algorithm 6 (`StringMatch`) against the equivalent Par version, which does not perform any function call.

The Impact of Data on Runtime. The numbers seen in Figure 11 are input dependent. However, the overall conclusions remain the same, once we feed our benchmarks with inputs of different sizes. Figure 12 compares the runtime different implementations of string-matching and leader election. In string-matching, we omitted the Launch-based version, as it was too slow. Notice that KMP has lower asymptotic complexity than Algorithm 6. It runs in $O(|T| + |P|)$, whereas Algorithm 6 runs in $O(|T| \times |P|/|W|)$. For this experiment, we searched for prefixes of the pattern "*She had been watching him the la*", of sizes $4, 8, \ldots, 28, 32$ in Jane Austen's book *Pride and Prejudice*, taken from Project Gutenberg[5]. CREV is always faster than `ParStringMatch`, and runs faster than KMP in more than half the cases.

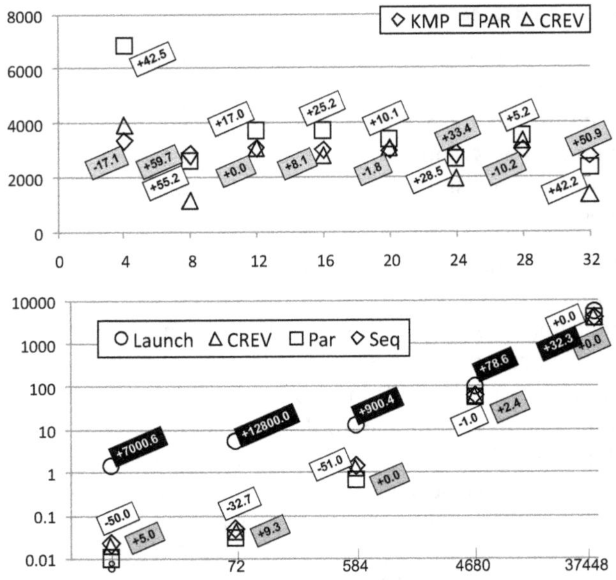

Figure 12. (Top) String-Matching. X-axis shows pattern sizes, in number of characters. Target text contains 256MB divided among 5,058,121 lines. **(Bottom)** Leader-Election. X-axis shows graph size, in number of edges. In both charts, Y-axis shows runtime, in millions of cycles. Boxes show percentage of speedup: white is CREV over Par; grey is CREV over Seq, and black is CREV over Launch.

CREV beats plain parallelism because it distributes function `memcmp` among the eight available vector lanes. On the other hand, `ParStringMatch` has a potentially long divergent block in line 14. In our best result, observed for patterns of size eight, CREV runs in 44% of the time taken by `ParStringMatch`, and in 40% of the time taken by KMP.

Figure 12 (Bottom) shows a comparison between the four implementations of leader-election. Dynamic parallelism is still the slowest, overall; however, we notice that it tends to catch up with the other approaches for very large inputs, in this benchmark. This behavior is expected: if the amount of parallel work is large, then the greater flexibility and independence of pthreads start paying for the cost of creating them. Nevertheless, depending on how the algorithm is implemented, dynamic parallelism might lead to the creation of a very large number of threads, as the size of the input grows. Due to this observation, we have not been able to run the Launch versions of df and bf for the largest available inputs. On the other hand, in the case of leader-election (le), parallelism is coarser: each thread receives the task of finding strong components in a graph. Thus, even though the number of threads grows as the size of the input increases, this growth is less accentuated than in df and bf.

5. Related Work

GPUs' increasing programmability and decreasing costs have made them very popular for the development of gen-

[4] Function memcmp is also used at line 5 of Algorithm 1

[5] https://www.gutenberg.org/ebooks/42671

eral purpose high performance applications [23]. This popularity has attracted the interest of programming language researchers. Control flow divergences have been a particularly important source of attention. Therefore, the compiler-related literature contains a vast body of work describing analyses [6, 27, 28, 30] and optimizations [6, 7, 35, 37] that reduce the effects of divergences in GPGPU code. CREV is not a competitor of these analyses and optimizations. On the contrary, Call Re-Vectorization complements such techniques, giving programmers a tool that lets them deal with divergences at the software level. In the rest of this section we touch work that is more closely related to ours.

Everywhere Blocks. The problem of expressing nested SIMD loops in multi-thread style is not new. Some data-parallel programming languages for SIMD computers in the 80's and 90's allow to re-enable temporarily dormant threads. The C* language [26], the Maspar Programming Language [20] and the POMPC language [15] incorporate a control flow construct named either `everywhere` or `all` to this end. We have re-used these instructions to implement CREV. However, these are low-level primitives: they are not programmer-friendly, nor have any interface with function calls. Using **everywhere** directly is difficult, as this abstraction has no knowledge nor control over the state of dormant threads. CREV, on the contrary, is as easy to use as dynamic parallelism. It manages register saves and restores automatically, relieving the programmer from this task.

Warp-level convergence guarantees. Previous work enforce guarantees on where threads converge after control divergences to make warp-synchronous programming safer. For instance, Pharr *et al.* have proposed the *maximal convergence* guarantee [25], and Gaster has proposed a divergence-aware execution model for OpenCL [13]. CREV goes further by actually *enforcing* convergence at arbitrary program points, allowing warp-synchronous functions to be called from divergent sections. To the best of our knowledge, this is the first attempt to provide developers with such possibility.

Grid-level Dynamic Parallelism. Much effort has been spent to reduce the overhead of dynamic parallelism. Alternatives to CUDA Dynamic Parallelism such as DTBL [33], Free Launch [4] and LaPerm [34] reduce sub-kernel launch overhead or improve cache locality. By relying on global schedulers, they allow load-balancing between GPU stream multiprocessors. We are not competing with these efforts, because CREV is not an alternative to dynamic parallelism. CREV is a static code transformation with no dynamic scheduling; hence, it does not create extra parallelism. In other words, we move work to threads that are already in flight, instead of spawning new threads. The main benefit of CREV, when compared to these previous work comes in terms of programmability and efficiency: by supporting composability of multi-thread and SIMD code, we give developers the chance to benefit from efficient warp-synchronous idioms without neither having to deal with primitives like shuffle, vote and population count, nor having to worry about saving the context of threads.

Thread-level divergence aware optimizations. Compilers may reorder computations across loop iterations within each thread to mitigate branch divergence [6, 14, 17, 24]. However, each thread performs the same set of tasks as in the original version, so divergences induced by load unbalance between threads of a warp remains an issue. CREV is a way to deal with irregular programs whose performance divergences hurt. However, CREV is not an optimization implemented by the compiler: programmers must adapt algorithms to use this construct. CREV deals well with divergences because it lets developers balance workload between threads in flight. In other words, it changes the loop structure by distributing iterations across different threads.

6. Final Thoughts

Primitives such as warp vote and shuffle have given experts the possibility of writing efficient SIMD code, by programming from the point of view of one warp. This coding style has been used in CUB and many other CUDA libraries[6]. However, warp-synchronous code does not play well with branch divergence. Most warp-synchronous algorithms require all threads in a warp to be active. This is a problem for the common usage scenario of a simple MT-style CUDA kernel that calls warp-synchronous library functions. It is our vision that the application developer writing the kernel should not be concerned with the internal implementation of library functions, and should be able to call any function inside divergent program regions. To meet the demands of this vision, this paper has introduced the notion of Call Re-Vectorization(CREV). We have described the building blocks necessary to implement CREV. Looking towards compatibility with future hardware, we have proposed low-level primitives with well-defined semantics and a high-level interface, the **crev** idiom, that makes programmer intent explicit. Thus, our notion of CREV does not rely implicitly on current hardware behavior, which might eventually change. We have implemented CREV into ISPC, using Intel instructions, and have shown how to code irregular algorithms in this environment. Our implementations are not only clearer than non-CREV based approaches, but also more efficient, as they balance work among inactive warp threads.

Acknowledgement

This project is supported by the Inria-Fapemig Associate Team *Prospiel* and by CNPq. We thank the members of the *Dragon Nest* group and the PPoPP referees for their insightful comments and suggestions. Example 3.1 has been suggested by one of the referees. Finally, we thank Albert Cohen for shepherding this paper. Our implementation is publicly available at `http://cuda.dcc.ufmg.br/swan/`.

[6] See `https://nvlabs.github.io/cub/`

References

[1] R. Bellman. On a routing problem. *Quarterly of Applied Mathematics*, 16(1):87–90, 1958.

[2] L. Bougé and J.-L. Levaire. Control structures for data-parallel SIMD languages: semantics and implementation. *Future Generation Computer Systems*, 8(4):363–378, 1992.

[3] J. Brodman, D. Babokin, I. Filippov, and P. Tu. Writing scalable SIMD programs with ISPC. In *WPMVP*, pages 25–32. ACM, 2014.

[4] G. Chen and X. Shen. Free launch: optimizing GPU dynamic kernel launches through thread reuse. In *Micro*, pages 407–419. ACM, 2015.

[5] T. H. Cormen, C. E. Leiserson, R. L. Rivest, and C. Stein. *Introduction to Algorithms*. McGraw-Hill, 2nd edition, 2001.

[6] B. Coutinho, D. Sampaio, F. M. Q. Pereira, and W. M. Jr. Divergence analysis and optimizations. In *PACT*, pages 320–329. IEEE, 2011.

[7] B. Coutinho, D. Sampaio, F. M. Q. Pereira, and W. M. Jr. Profiling divergences in GPU applications. *Concurrency and Computation: Practice and Experience*, 1(10.1002/cpe.285-15):1–15, 2012.

[8] J. DiMarco and M. Taufer. Performance impact of dynamic parallelism on different clustering algorithms. *Modeling and Simulation for Defense Systems and Applications*, 8752(VIII): 87520E–87520E:8, 2013.

[9] P. Erdos and A. Renyi. On random graphs. I. *Publicationes Mathematicae*, 6(1):290–297, 1959.

[10] C. A. Farrell and D. H. Kieronska. Formal specification of parallel SIMD execution. *Theo. Comp. Science*, 169(1):39–65, 1996.

[11] J. Ferrante, K. J. Ottenstein, and J. D. Warren. The program dependence graph and its use in optimization. *TOPLAS*, 9(3): 319–349, 1987.

[12] M. Garland and D. B. Kirk. Understanding throughput-oriented architectures. *Commun. ACM*, 53:58–66, 2010.

[13] B. Gaster. An execution model for OpenCL 2.0. Technical Report 2014-02, Computer Sciences, 2014.

[14] T. D. Han and T. S. Abdelrahman. Reducing divergence in GPGPU programs with loop merging. In *GPGPU*, pages 12–23. ACM, 2013.

[15] P. Hoogvorst, R. Keryell, N. Paris, and P. Matherat. POMP or how to design a massively parallel machine with small developments. In *PARLE*, pages 83–100. Springer, 1991.

[16] S. Jones. Introduction to dynamic parallelism – Invited Talk. In *GPU Technology Conference*, pages 1–33. NVIDIA, 2014.

[17] F. Khorasani, R. Gupta, and L. N. Bhuyan. Efficient warp execution in presence of divergence with collaborative context collection. In *Micro*, pages 204–215. ACM, 2015.

[18] A. Klöckner, N. Pinto, Y. Lee, B. Catanzaro, P. Ivanov, and A. Fasih. Pycuda and pyopencl: A scripting-based approach to gpu run-time code generation. *Parallel Comput.*, 38(3): 157–174, Mar. 2012.

[19] D. E. Knuth, J. H. M. Jr., and V. R. Pratt. Fast pattern matching in strings. *Journal of Computing*, 6(2):323–350, 1977.

[20] MasPar. *MasPar Programming Language (ANSI C compatible MPL) Reference Manual*, 1992.

[21] D. Merrill and A. Grimshaw. High performance and scalable radix sorting: A case study of implementing dynamic parallelism for GPU computing. *Parallel Proceessing Letters*, 21 (2):245–272, 2011.

[22] A. Munshi, B. Gaster, T. G. Mattson, J. Fung, and D. Ginsburg. *OpenCL Programming Guide*. Addison-Wesley, 1st edition, 2011.

[23] J. Nickolls and W. J. Dally. The GPU computing era. *IEEE Micro*, 30:56–69, 2010.

[24] R. Novak. Loop optimization for divergence reduction on GPUs with SIMT architecture. *IEEE Transactions on Parallel and Distributed Systems*, 26(6):1633–1642, 2015.

[25] M. Pharr and W. R. Mark. ISPC: A SPMD compiler for high-performance CPU programming. In *InPar*, pages 1–13. IEEE, 2012.

[26] J. Rose and G. Steele. C*: An extended C language for data parallel programming. In *ICS*, 1987.

[27] D. Sampaio, R. Martins, S. Collange, and F. M. Q. Pereira. Divergence analysis with affine constraints. In *SBAC-PAD*, pages 67–74. IEEE, 2012.

[28] D. Sampaio, R. M. de Souza, S. Collange, and F. M. Q. Pereira. Divergence analysis. *ACM Trans. Program. Lang. Syst.*, 35(4):13, 2013.

[29] J. Sanders and E. Kandrot. *CUDA by Example: An Introduction to General-Purpose GPU Programming*. Addison-Wesley, 1st edition, 2010.

[30] T. Schaub, S. Moll, R. Karrenberg, and S. Hack. The impact of the simd width on control-flow and memory divergence. *TACO*, 11(4):54:1–54:25, 2015.

[31] A. Sodani, R. Gramunt, J. Corbal, H.-S. Kim, K. Vinod, S. Chinthamani, S. Hutsell, R. Agarwal, and Y.-C. Liu. Knights Landing: Second-generation Intel Xeon Phi product. *IEEE Micro*, 36(2):34–46, 2016.

[32] J. Wang and S. Yalamanchili. Characterization and analysis of dynamic parallelism in unstructured GPU applications. In *IISWC*, pages 51–60. IEEE, 2014.

[33] J. Wang, N. Rubin, A. Sidelnik, and S. Yalamanchili. Dynamic thread block launch: A lightweight execution mechanism to support irregular applications on gpus. In *ISCA*, pages 528–540. ACM, 2015.

[34] J. Wang, N. Rubin, A. Sidelnik, and S. Yalamanchili. LaPerm: Locality aware scheduler for dynamic parallelism on GPUs. In *ISCA*, 2016.

[35] J. Wu, A. Belevich, E. Bendersky, M. Heffernan, C. Leary, J. Pienaar, B. Roune, R. Springer, X. Weng, and R. Hundt. Gpucc: An open-source gpgpu compiler. In *CGO*, pages 105–116. ACM, 2016.

[36] Y. Yang and H. Zhou. CUDA-NP: realizing nested thread-level parallelism in GPGPU applications. In *PPoPP*, pages 93–106. ACM, 2014.

[37] E. Z. Zhang, Y. Jiang, Z. Guo, K. Tian, and X. Shen. On-the-fly elimination of dynamic irregularities for GPU computing. In *ASPLOS*, pages 369–380. ACM, 2011.

A. Artifact Evaluation

This artifact consists of a virtual machine, in which we have installed the required software for reproducing our experiments. The file has 9.2 GB uncompressed, 1.6 GB compressed, and is available for download at `http://cuda.dcc.ufmg.br/swan/`. In that webpage we have charts for some experiments that we could not fit in the original paper. We also have a Prolog interpreter for the semantics of μ-SIMD, at `http://cuda.dcc.ufmg.br/swan/src/semantics.zip`. The artifact itself can be downloaded through the link: `http://cuda.dcc.ufmg.br/swan/artifact.tar.gz`.

Hardware Dependencies The hardware requirements are:

- host with x86 64bit processor;
- minimum of 30GB of free space;
- have at least 8 cores available for the virtual machine.

Software Dependencies Our work is entirely implemented on top of Intel's Single Program Multiple Data compiler, namely ISPC. We thus depend on its source code to apply our patch, and thereafter enable our **crev** idiom. ISPC, in its turn, is implemented on top of LLVM, and uses Bison and Flex as parsing tool. Those sum up as all software dependences for our work.

ISPC for Linux 64-bit is available for download at sourceforge: `http://ispc.github.io/downloads.html` (vesion 1.9.1). Bison may be checked-out straight from the linux distro repository, using the command `sudo apt-get install bison`. Notice that the version currently installed is GNU Bison 3.0.2, and a version $\geq$ 2.4 is recommended. If not available from repository, please, try and download it from `https://ftp.gnu.org/gnu/bison/`. Flex may be found at `http://flex.sourceforge.net/` and the version should be $\geq$ 2.5 (currently installed in the VM is version 2.5.39), and can be also checked-out from linux repository using the command: `sudo apt-get install flex`. And as for LLVM, this well-known compiler architecture is available online at `http://llvm.org` (version 3.7.1).

Data sets To validate our approach, we have executed our analysis on our hand-crafted set of benchmarks, namely CREV-ISPC. We targeted as many different applications as possible, ranging from string processing and graph searches to sort algorithms. Our benchmarks are available alongside with this artifact, in the directory `/home/crev/benchmarks`.

A.1 Installation

Our artifact is provided as a virtual machine image. To use it, you need to download and install the VirtualBox VM player[7]. To execute the virtual machine, do the following:

- download and uncompress the VM image;
- open VirtualBox;
- create a new virtual machine, by clicking in `Machine` $\rightarrow$ `New...`;
- give a name to the new VM, by filling the `Name` field;
- in `Type`, select `Linux`;
- in `Version`, select `Ubuntu (64 bit)`;
- click `continue`, select the desired amount of RAM memory, and press `continue` again;
- in the hard drive selection screen, select the option `Use an existing virtual hard drive file`, then select the .vdi file containing the VM image that you just downloaded;
- your virtual machine is ready to use! To start, simply double-click it in the VirtualBox VM list.

At startup, you will be prompted for a username and password. Use the following combination:

login:	`crev`
password:	`crev@ppopp17`

After logging in, a command prompt will appear and the VM is ready to use. Even though the VM image has a command line ready to use, we highly recommend the use of SSH port forwarding, so the user can simply SSH into the Virtual Machine to execute commands. The VM has Ubuntu 15.04 installed on it. There is no graphic interface, so all actions are executed through command line.

A.1.1 LLVM

LLVM is a well-known compiler architecture. In this work, we use LLVM-3.7.1. To proceed with its installation, do the following:

- Download llvm-3.7.1: `codes/s4.3.2-1.sh`
- Download cfe-3.7.1: `codes/s4.3.2-2.sh`
- Extract llvm and cfe: `codes/s4.3.2-3.sh`
- Move cfe folder to the path `llvm/tools/clang`: `codes/s4.3.2-4.sh`
- Create a build directory for llvm, configure, and install it: `codes/s4.3.2-5.sh`

A.1.2 Bison and Flex

Apart from LLVM, ISPC has two other dependences: Bison, a YACC-compatible parser generator; and Flex, a fast lexical analyzer generator. Check if you already have the dependences solved, and otherwise install the required software. Use the following command lines to install from your linux distro repository and check versions installed. Bison must be $\geq$ 2.4, and Flex must be $\geq$ 2.5. `codes/s4.3.3-1.sh`

A.1.3 CREV-ISPC

Before moving ahead with the installation of ISPC, set the path to your LLVM build, so ISPC will be able to use it by

[7] Available at `https://www.virtualbox.org/wiki/Downloads`

default. Add the following lines to your `/home/crev/.bashrc` file. `codes/s4.4-1.sh`

There is a quirk about the dependency with LLVM, which consists of a missing file. It may be related to the version of LLVM being used in our implementation (3.7.1), but it is necessary to copy the file `DiagonosticCommonKinds.inc`, generated after LLVM/Clang build, to the source directory of LLVM. The command below should solve the issue. `codes/s4.4-2.sh`

Now that all dependences have been set up, download our CREV-extended version of Intel's SPMD compiler (ISPC). It is available at http://cuda.dcc.ufmg.br/swan/src/crev-ispc.tar.gz. Once downloaded, extract it and install CREV-ISPC. `codes/s4.4-3.sh`

ISPC's Makefile comes originally configured to automatically fetch the path to LLVM build – as long as it has been informed in variable `${PATH}`. However, in case you step into path problems, set the variables to your needs, as you shall find set in our current version of ISPC's Makefile. The variables below show our specific paths within `ispc/Makefile`. [linenos, firstnumber=65]codes/s4.4-4.sh

A.2 Workflow

To validate our approach, we have executed our analysis on our hand-crafted set of benchmarks, namely CREV-ISPC. Our goal was to target different scenarios in which it may be useful to call SIMD-only function within divergent regions. The selected set of applications implemented is a spread consisting of string matching, graph traversals and sort algorithms. As stated in our paper, our approach provides a facility that helps programmers write efficient code without entangling oneself in complex synchronization-dependent structures. Our benchmarks are available alongside with this artifact, and can be found in the directory `/home/crev/benchmark`.

A.2.1 Runtime Environment

In the core paper, we have implemented CREV onto ISPC v 1.9.1, and have used it to target a 6-core 2.00 GHz Intel Xeon E5-2620 CPU with 8-wide AVX vector units, running Linux Ubuntu 12.04 3.2.0. This running environment gave us warps with eight threads, e.g., $|\theta_{all}| = 8$. In the case of our artifact, we have enabled 4 cores in a computer with two 4-core 2.60GHz Intel i7-3720QM CPU, also with 8-wide AVX vector units, but running Linux Ubuntu 15.04.

A.2.2 Benchmarks

We provide seven benchmarks: (1) Book Filter; (2) String Matching; (3) Bellman-Ford; (4) Depth-First Search; (5) Leader Election; (6) Quick-Sort and (7) Merge-Sort. The numbers in parentheses are used in Section A.2.3 to identify the input data-set of each benchmark. To build up the binaries, simply enter the selected benchmark directory and run `$ make`. Each benchmark varies, be it in the number of binary files generated, output and input format, and input dataset. To this end, we leave, within each folder, a bash script named `run.sh`, which executes the benchmarks. We also have a parser for each of the experiments, in order to extract and list the results in a human-friendly fashion. The parsing script is also a shell script, named `parse.sh`. While compiling, the makefile may raise some warnings, but there is no actual error.

A.2.3 Input Datasets

The table below relates the datasets we have used in the experiments and the associated benchmarks that received the data as input. The datasets are all available in the folder `/home/crev/datasets`. Users of our artifact can produce different inputs to carry out more extensive experiments.

Users	Dataset
1	*Binary strings* 10K strings of 0s and 1s, each with 20K bits, and random target pattern with 16 bits.
2	*Text books* 256MB of text taken from books available in the Project Gutenberg; target pattern is 16 chars.
3	*Erdös-Rényi* random Erdös-Rényi graph with 2,048 nodes and 80% edge probability.
4, 5	*Full octree* 8-ary complete tree with depth up to 5, i.e., root + five full levels.
6, 7	*Random integers* 16K random integers, ranging from $[0, 100000)$.

A.3 Evaluation and Expected Result

During evaluation of the artifact, one may either relate to the paper, in order to validate the results therein presented; or analyze the outputs w.r.t. different implementations: compare execution times for sequential, parallel, crev-based, and launch-based implementations. Either way, the experiments should also take into account the main contribution of the paper: we propose an idiom that combines the simplicity of dynamic parallelism, with the efficiency of warp-synchronous programming. Therefore, as presented in the paper, the results tend to bring up speedups, but this is not expected to hold true for all cases: execution time may vary significantly according to input and algorithm specific parameters. Further information is available online, including graphs with results obtained in the original runtime environment – in which the experiments in the paper were executed. The link to our webpage is http://cuda.dcc.ufmg.br/swan.

B. Reviewing Methodology

This artifact has been reviewed according to the guidelines established by the *Artifact Evaluation Committee of CGO and PPoPP*. This methodology is described at http://cTuning.org/ae/submission-20161020.html

Optimizing the Four-Index Integral Transform Using Data Movement Lower Bounds Analysis

Samyam Rajbhandari Fabrice Rastello + Karol Kowalski *
Sriram Krishnamoorthy * P. Sadayappan

The Ohio State University
INRIA +
Pacific Northwest National Laboratory *

rajbhandari.4@osu.edu fabrice.rastello@inria.fr Karol.Kowalski@pnnl.gov
sriram@pnnl.gov sadayappan.1@osu.edu

Abstract

The four-index integral transform is a fundamental and computationally demanding calculation used in many computational chemistry suites such as NWChem. It transforms a four-dimensional tensor from one basis to another. This transformation is most efficiently implemented as a sequence of four tensor contractions that each contract a four-dimensional tensor with a two-dimensional transformation matrix. Differing degrees of permutation symmetry in the intermediate and final tensors in the sequence of contractions cause intermediate tensors to be much larger than the final tensor and limit the number of electronic states in the modeled systems.

Loop fusion, in conjunction with tiling, can be very effective in reducing the total space requirement, as well as data movement. However, the large number of possible choices for loop fusion and tiling, and data/computation distribution across a parallel system, make it challenging to develop an optimized parallel implementation for the four-index integral transform. We develop a novel approach to address this problem, using lower bounds modeling of data movement complexity. We establish relationships between available aggregate physical memory in a parallel computer system and ineffective fusion configurations, enabling their pruning and consequent identification of effective choices and a characterization of optimality criteria. This work has resulted in the development of a significantly improved implementation of the four-index transform that enables higher performance and the ability to model larger electronic systems than the current implementation in the NWChem quantum chemistry software suite.

PPoPP '17, February 04-08, 2017, Austin, TX, USA
© 2017 ACM. ISBN 978-1-4503-4493-7/17/02...$15.00
DOI: http://dx.doi.org/10.1145/3018743.3018771

1. Introduction

The four-index integral transform is a computationally demanding calculation implemented in numerous computational chemistry suites, including NWChem [4], ACES [1], GAMESS [23], MOLPRO [3], MPQC [2], and PSI [5]. It is used to transform a four-dimensional tensor of coefficients (A), using four applications of a two-dimensional transformation matrix B. The computation can be specified as follows:

$$C[\alpha,\beta,\gamma,\delta] = \sum_{i,j,k,l} A[i,j,k,l]\cdot B[\alpha,i]\cdot B[\beta,j]\cdot B[\gamma,k]\cdot B[\delta,l] \quad (1)$$

However, efficient implementation of this transformation is non-trivial and has been the subject of a number of efforts [6, 8, 10, 11, 16, 19–21, 24–27]. The direct conversion of the above expression into code would result in an implementation with a computational complexity of $O(n^8)$, if all eight indices (α, β, γ, δ, i, j, k, l) range from 1 to n. By utilizing algebraic properties of associativity, commutativity, and distributivity, the transformation can be implemented with a computational complexity of $O(n^5)$ (as discussed in greater detail in the next section) as a sequence of four steps, each involving the tensor product of a 4D tensor with the 2D transformation matrix B. There are a large number of possible ways of partitioning the data and computation across a parallel system, along with fusion/tiling choices to reduce data movement through the memory hierarchy. Further complicating matters is the fact that the tensors have varying degrees of permutation symmetry (elaborated in the next section). It is critical to exploit the savings in space and computational operations by only keeping distinct elements, but this complicates reasoning about the data movement cost of alternative distributed implementations and the numerous fusion/tiling choices. A key challenge is that the intermediate tensors in the four-step index transformation are larger than the final result. This means that either judicious fusion across the steps is required to optimize memory (which complicates the implementation) or that memory use is sub-optimal, limiting the size of the systems that can be modeled.

In this paper, we report on the development of a significantly improved parallel implementation of the four-index transform in NWChem. We pursue a novel approach using data movement lower bounds to guide the optimization process. For the four-index transform, the combination of the number of fusion choices and tile sizes along the loops is prohibitively high. Each tensor contraction in the sequence of four contractions has five nested loops. For each adjacent pair of contractions, four of the five nested loops are common and any combination of these can be selected for fusion. It is also possible to fuse a subset of three common loops across a contiguous set of three contractions, or one of two common loops across all four contractions. Further, we must consider tiling choices for loops. The optimal configuration is not the same for different problem sizes, i.e., auto tuning will require execution of thousands of configurations for each problem size of interest. Thus, neither analytical model-based optimization, nor any successful autotuning approach has been previously reported for the four-index integral transform.

We avoid the combinatorial explosion in the number of modeled code configurations by using a novel and completely different approach towards performance modeling to guide the optimization: *by using lower bounds on data movement complexity*. Lower bounds on data movement (explained in the next section) are schedule-independent assertions on the minimal amount of data movement required for any valid implementation of a given computation (abstracted as a computational directed acyclic graph). This enables identification of effective fusion configurations, along with a characterization of optimality properties with respect to the largest problem sizes that can be transformed, as a function of the aggregate physical memory on the parallel computer system. The resulting implementation of the four-index transform significantly improves on currently implemented versions in NWChem.

The paper makes the following contributions:

- For sequences of loops representing a producer-consumer relationship, it develops the first approach to use data movement lower bounds to reason about the utility of loop fusion to reduce data movement **(Section 4)** and its application to find an optimal fusion choice for the four-index integral transform **(Section 5)**.
- It describes the first use of data movement lower bounds to reason about minimal space requirements for I/O-free computations for the four-index integral transform **(Section 6)**.
- It develops a new parallel implementation **(Section 7)** of the four-index integral transform that improves upon the current state-of-the-art implementations in production computational chemistry codes in two ways: 1) For a given amount of total collective physical memory in a cluster, it can run the provably largest four-index transform that does not use file I/O or redundant re-computation of intermediate tensors; 2) For a given amount of per-process local memory, it minimizes the data movement between non-local and local memory.
- It presents an experimental evaluation of the new parallel implementation, demonstrating significant performance improvement for large problems, and the ability to run larger problems than previously possible with the production NWChem computational chemistry suite **(Section 8)**. For example, we show a practical problem that requires more than 12 Terabytes of collective global memory to execute without fusion. Using our implementation, we execute this problem on a cluster with less than 9 Terabytes of collective global memory.

2. Background and Related Work

In this section, we provide necessary background information before describing the new contributions. We first elaborate on the four-index integral transform and its implementations in NWChem, followed by a brief introduction to data movement lower bounds.

2.1 Four-Index Integral Transform

In equation 1, if all indices $(\alpha, \beta, \gamma, \delta, i, j, k, l)$ range over the integer interval $[1, n]$, a naive implementation of the transform would take $5n^8$ operations. In practice, it is implemented as a sequence of four tensor contractions (shown in Equation 2). Each tensor contraction (higher dimensional analogs of matrix-matrix product) has a computational cost of $2n^5$ operations. The output tensor of a contraction serves as an input tensor for subsequent computation.

$$\begin{aligned} O1[\alpha,j,k,l] &= \sum_i A[i,j,k,l]\cdot B[\alpha,i] \\ O2[\alpha,\beta,k,l] &= \sum_j O1[\alpha,j,k,l]\cdot B[\beta,j] \\ O3[\alpha,\beta,\gamma,l] &= \sum_k O2[\alpha,\beta,k,l]\cdot B[\gamma,k] \\ C[\alpha,\beta,\gamma,\delta] &= \sum_l O3[\alpha,\beta,\gamma,l]\cdot B[\delta,l] \end{aligned} \tag{2}$$

It can be seen that for each adjacent pair of tensor contractions, four of the five loops iterate over common tensor indices, while one loop differs. Thus, many possible fusion choices exist, where loops over the same tensor indices are fused across two or more consecutive contractions.

Symmetry in tensors. Tensors in the four-index transform exhibit permutation symmetry. A tensor is symmetric with respect to a subset of its indices if permuting the indices within the subset does not change the value of the tensor. As an example, consider a tensor $V[a,b,i,j]$. We say that indices a and b are symmetric if $V[a,b,i,j] = V[b,a,i,j]$[1]. A symmetric tensor can have multiple symmetry groups. For example, a, b and i, j are two symmetry groups for V if $V[a,b,i,j] = V[b,a,i,j] = V[b,a,j,i] = V[a,b,j,i]$. This tensor can be represented compactly by only explicitly storing elements $V[a < b, i < j]$ due to the symmetry, denoted $V[ab, ij]$. The symmetry properties imply that only a fraction $(1/d!)$ of the elements of the full tensor need to be

[1] Tensors in quantum chemistry generally possess anti-symmetry rather than symmetry, i.e., $V[a,b,i,j] = -V[b,a,i,j]$, and our codes actually incorporate anti-symmetry. However, for simplicity, we use symmetric tensors in our presentation.

```
/*Memory required: 3n^4/4,
  Computation: 4n^5*/
malloc(A,n^4/4);
malloc(O1,n^4/2)
for a, i, j, k>l
 O1[a,j,k>l] +=
  A[i>j,k>l]*B[a,i] //n^5
delete(A);malloc(O2,n^4/4)
for a>b, j, k>l
 O2[a>b,k>l] +=
  O1[a,j,k>l]*B[b,j]//n^5
delete(O1);malloc(O3,n^4/2)
for a>b, c, k, l
 O3[a>b,c,l] +=
  O2[a>b,k>l]*B[c,k]  //n^5
delete(O3);malloc(C,n^4/32)
for a>b, c>d, l
 C[a>b,c>d] +=
  O3[a>b,c,l]*B[d,j]  //n^5
```

Listing 1: Unfused

```
/*Memory required: n^4/2
  Computation: 4n^5 */
malloc(A,n^4/4);malloc(O1,n^2)
malloc(O2,n^4/4)
for (k>l)
 for (a,i,j)
  O1[a,j]+=A[i>j,k>l]*B[a,i] //n^5
 for (a>b,j)
  O2[a>b,k>l]+=O1[a,j]*B[b,j]//n^5
delete(A); delete(O1)
malloc(O3,n^2); malloc(C,n^4/32)
for (a>b)
 for (c,k,l)
  O3[a>b,c,l] +=
   O2[a>b,k>l]*B[c,k] //n^5
 for (c>d,l)
  C[a>b,c>d] +=
   O3[a>b,c,l]*B[d,j] //n^5
```

Listing 2: First two and last two fused

```
/*Memory required: n^3
  Computation: n^6+ */
malloc(C,n^4/32)
for (a>b)
 malloc(O1,n^3)
 for (i,j,k>l)
  O1[j,k>l] +=
   A[i>j,k>l])*B[a,i]//n^6
 malloc(O2,n^2)
 for (j,k>l)
  O2[k>l]+=O1[j,k>l]*B[b,j]//n^5
 delete(O1); malloc(O3,n)
 for (c,k,l)
  O3[l]+=O2[k>l]*B[c,k]//n^5
 delete(O2,n^2)
 for (c,d,l)
  C[a>b,c>d]+=O3[l]*B[d,j]//n^5
```

Listing 3: With re-computation

Three implementation variants for 4-index transform

Table 1: Sizes of intermediate tensors. s is the factor of storage reduction due to spatial symmetry in tensor C.

Tensors	Sizes
A	$n^4/4$
O1	$n^4/2$
O2	$n^4/4$
O3	$n^4/2$
C	$n^4/(4s)$

stored in the memory, where d is the number of dimensions in a symmetry group. In the above example, V has two symmetry groups of size 2, so that only a fraction $\frac{1}{2} \times \frac{1}{2}$ of the elements need be explicitly stored.

Permutation symmetry in the tensors in equation 2 can be represented as $A[ij, kl]$, $O1[\alpha, j, kl]$, $O2[\alpha\beta, kl]$, $O3[\alpha\beta, \gamma, l]$ and $C[\alpha\beta, \gamma\delta]$. In addition to permutation symmetry, the final result tensor in molecular basis can also exhibit *spatial symmetry*. Spatial symmetry is a structured form of sparsity that causes certain blocks to be zero if the index ranges for that block (corresponding to specific molecular orbitals) satisfy some conditions. Whereas permutation symmetry reduces the size of all tensors—input, intermediate, and output—in the four-index transform, spatial symmetry results in additional size reduction only for the final output tensor C. The sizes of various tensors for the four-index transform are shown in Table 1.

Tensor data structures in NWChem. In NWChem, tensors are blocked along each dimension, resulting in a set of data-tiles representing the tensor. These data-tiles are linearized and distributed using Global Arrays [18], a global address space framework that provides a logical shared view of arrays in a distributed-memory parallel system. Each parallel process in a parallel program can *get*, *put*, or additively *update* any arbitrary data-tile of the tensor.

```
1  int node_id = GA_Nodeid()
2  for l, k, j, alpha
3    if(node_id owns tile C[alpha,j,k,l])
4      malloc (C_buf, Tilesize)
5      for i
6        A_buf = GA_Get(Tile A[i,j,k,l])
7        B_buf = GA_Get(Tile B[alpha,i])
8        DGEMM(A_buf, B_buf, C_buf)
9      GA_Put(C_buf to tile C[alpha,j,k,l])
```

Listing 4: Implementation of the tensor contraction `C[alpha,j,k,l] += A[i,j,k,l] . B[alpha,i]` in NWChem

During a contraction, each distributed processor node is responsible for computing a subset of the tensor tiles. To this end, each processor uses `GA_Get` requests for the input data-tiles required to compute each of its assigned output data-tiles. After accumulating all contributions to an output data-tile, the processor then stores it using `GA_Put`.

Listing 4 depicts the implementation of the first tensor contraction in the four-index transform as performed in NWChem. Here, loop indices represent tile indices in different tensor dimensions. Line 3 checks if the current output-tile is the responsibility of the process. If so, lines 6 and 7 request the required input data-tiles using `GA_Get`. Line 9 stores the computed result using `GA_Put`.

2.2 Related Prior Work

Fusing sequences of tensor contractions to minimize memory use or data movement has been studied using a variety of approaches. Lam et al. [15] viewed individual tensor constractions as loop nests that constitute expression trees and determine the execution order and fusion configuration that minimizes memory used for intermediates, indirectly optimizing data locality. Gao et al. [12] presented an approach to prune the space of candidate fusion and tiling configurations to minimize disk I/O cost. The approach involves computing the disk I/O cost for every valid loop structure for a given sequence of expressions, which grows exponentially with the number of contractions being fused. Sahoo et al. [22] pruned the search space to be explored by casting a part of the choice of fusion configurations as a tile size selection problem, which is then solved using a non-linear optimization solver. Ma et al. [17] extend this approach to deal with multi-level memory hierarchies and further simplify the space by considering only the first-order approximation of the costs. None of these frameworks handled the permutation symmetry in four-index transform. In this paper, we improve upon these approaches by employing lower-bounds analysis on dat amovement costs to identify effective configurations while also handling permutation symmetry.

Over the years, many schemes for the four-index transform have been devised [6, 8, 10, 11, 16, 19–21, 24–27]. These approaches are based on heuristics and experience rather than concrete cost models. Many of these variants have been implemented in the NWChem software suite. the following are the most widely used and performant implementations of four-index transform in NWChem:

Unfused: Fully unfused version, where A, $O1$, $O2$, $O3$, and C tensors are fully created. This form is computationally the most efficient, with an $O(n^5)$ scaling of the algorithm but requires more than $\frac{3n^4}{4}$ words of global memory to fully store the input and output of the largest tensor contraction in the 4-index transform: $(|O1| + |O2|)$. This algorithm is shown in Listing 1.

Fused 12-34: Loop fusion allows significant reduction in the space required for intermediate tensors, since the index corresponding to any common loop over a producer and consumer does not need a corresponding explicit dimension in the tensor – sequential computing over that index is feasible and a lower dimensional intermediate tensor can be repeatedly reused. This algorithm is shown in Listing 2. It can be seen that the previously dominant $O1$ and $O3$ intermediates are now lower dimensional tensors and no longer very demanding of memory. This algorithm requires at least $\frac{n^4}{2}$ words of global memory.

Recompute: This option allows a significant reduction in the memory footprint, at the cost of redundant computation. Generally, this option will be more time consuming but has the lowest memory requirement. The factor of reduction in the global memory required is proportional to the amount of re-computation. Listing 3 shows such an algorithm.

2.3 Data movement lower bounds

Consider matrix-matrix multiplication

$$C[i, j] = A[i, k] \times B[k, j] \tag{3}$$

The standard $O(N^3)$ algorithm is shown in two forms in Figure 1: (a) basic untiled form and (b) tiled form. Both versions require the same number ($2N^3$) of arithmetic operations to compute. However, they differ in the amount of data movement in a hierarchical memory system. Let us consider the simple memory hierarchy containing two levels, with all matrices fitting within the latter level, but too large to fit in the level closer to the processor, which can store only S data elements, $S < N^2$. The untiled version requires the entire matrix B to be accessed for each iteration of the outer i-loop. Therefore, the number of data movement operations from the latter level of memory to the closer level for the untiled version is at least N^3 (ignoring data movement for A and C). However, the tiled version needs much less data movement, $O(\frac{N^3}{T})$, for $T < \sqrt{\frac{S}{3}}$, where T is the tile size.

```
for (i = 0; i <= ni-1; i++)
 for (j = 0; j <= nj-1; j++)
  for (k = 0; k <= nk-1; ++k)
    C[i][j]+=A[i][k]*B[k][j];
```

```
for (ti=0; ti<=floord((ni-1), T); ti++)
 for (tj=0; tj<=floord((nj-1), T); tj++)
  for (tk=0; tk<=floord((nk-1), T); tk++)
   for (i=T*ti; i<min((T*(ti+1)),ni); i++)
    for (j=T*tj; j<min((T*(ti+1)),nj); j++)
     for (k=T*tk; k<min((T*(ti+1)),nk); k++)
      C[i][j]+=A[i][k]*B[k][j];
```

Figure 1: Matrix-matrix multiplication kernel: untiled (left) and tiled (right)

The example shows that unlike the invariance of computational complexity across the two versions ($2N^3$ operations irrespective of the values of S and T), the amount of data movement can depend on: i) which version of the code is used, ii) the size S of fast memory, and iii) the tile size T. A question of interest is: *What is the minimum possible amount of data movement among all equivalent forms of code, to compute the standard matrix-matrix multiplication algorithm?*

In general, this question cannot be answered without examining a combinatorially explosive number of possible valid schedules for a given computation. The foundational work by Hong and Kung [13] developed an approach to provide lower bounds on the data movement required by any valid execution of the set of operations for a given algorithm. They showed that on a system with a two-level memory hierarchy with fast memory capacity of S elements, the minimum I/O for multiplying two $n \times n$ matrices is $\Omega(n^3/\sqrt{S})$. Irony et al. [14] provided a lower bound with scaling constants for multiplication of an $n_i \times n_j$ matrix and an $n_j \times n_k$ matrix to be $\Omega(n_i \times n_j \times n_k/(2\sqrt{2S})$. A much tighter bound was provided by Dongarra et al. [9]: $\Omega(1.73n_i \times n_j \times n_k/\sqrt{S})$.

Tensor contractions represent a generalization of matrix-matrix multiplication. We use the lower bound complexity results for matrix-matrix multiplication in exploring fusion/tiling choices for the four-index integral transform computation.

3. Overview of Approach

The goal of this paper is to construct a distributed four-index transform schedule that optimizes two aspects: i) minimize inter-node communication between distributed memory nodes, and ii) maximize the problem size that can be executed for a given amount of collective physical memory, without going to disk – important because nodes in supercomputers often do not have local disks and the collective bandwidth to the file system disks is very low. Proving the optimality of an algorithm is important because it guarantees that we have arrived at the best possible solution and no further improvement is feasible.

Reducing communication volume between distributed memory nodes, and eliminating disk I/O corresponds to reducing data movement between slow and fast memory at different levels of the memory hierarchy. We use fusion as a tool to reduce the data movement in the 4-index transform. To arrive at the final solution, we develop lower bounds guided fusion analysis. Our lower bound analysis quantifies the maximum possible reduction in data movement via fusion. If the maximum reduction possible is a small fraction of the total data movement of the unfused schedule, then we know that fusion is not very useful and such configurations can be eliminated from consideration. On the other hand if the reduction in data movement is significant, then fusion is useful, and an effort should be made towards finding such a fused schedule. Identifying the utility of fusion is described in detail in Section 4.

In Section 5, we apply the lower bound analysis developed in Section 4 to the 4-index transform and identify the minimum possible data movement for various fusion choices. By quantifying the minimum data movement (or the maximum reduction in data movement) for a fusion strategy, we focus on creating schedules for only those fusion choices that have potential to yield significant reduction in data movement. In section 6, we present a schedule based on an optimal fusion choice that maximizes the reduction in data movement, thus achieving the minimum data movement possible between slow and fast memory.

Our schedule achieves the minimum possible data movement only when the size of the final output tensor fits in fast memory. The next logical question is "Is this schedule optimal in terms of problem size?". In other words, is it possible to create other schedules that might minimize the data movement even when the final output does not fit in fast memory. To answer this question, we derive the necessary conditions for achieving the minimum data movement. We show that it is necessary for the fast memory to be larger than the size of the output to achieve the minimum possible data movement. In other words, if the output size is larger than the size of the fast memory then there can be no schedules that achieve the data movement lower bound. This necessary condition is derived in Section 6.

At the highest level of the memory hierarchy, where disk is the slow memory and collective global memory is the fast memory, the necessary condition described above implies that our schedule maximizes the problem size that can be executed on a given amount of collective physical memory without going to disk. At the next level of memory hierarchy, where global collective memory is the slow memory and local memory is the fast memory, our fusion strategy minimizes communication between local memory and global memory. These details, along with other implementation details are provided in Section 7.

4. Utility of Fusion

In this section, we elaborate on how analysis of data movement lower bounds can be useful in developing high-performance code for the four-index integral transform. As explained earlier, the four-index transform is computed as a sequence of four tensor contractions, with the output tensor from an immediately preceding contraction serving as an input tensor for the immediately following contraction. There are many possible choices of loop permutation and loop fusion, and for each choice of loop permutation/fusion, there is a very large search space of tile sizes for tiled execution (since all loops of a tensor contraction are fully permutable, they are all fully tileable too).

As an aid to eliminating many possible fusion choices and identifying the most promising ones, we develop a necessary condition for the utility of fusion in the context of general sequence of two producer-consumer computations. We first formalize the notion of fusion of computations.

Definition 4.1 (Fusion). *Let $op1$ and $op2$ be two computations where the output of $op1$ is consumed by $op2$. A non-fused schedule of $op1 \cup op2$ is a schedule where all operations constituting $op1$ are fully completed before $op2$ starts. A fused schedule is a schedule where some interleaving of the constituent elementary operations of $op1$ and $op2$ occur.*

Next, we state the Fusion Lemma, which bounds the potential benefit from fusion in terms of the size of the output data from the producer computation used by the consumer computation, and the inherent minimal data movement (we interchangeably use the term I/O for data movement in a memory hierarchy, following the terminology of Hong & Kung [13]) complexity of the producer and consumer computations if executed separately.

Lemma 4.2 (Fusion Lemma). *Let computation $C1$ and computation $C2$ represent a producer-consumer pair, where the output $O1$ produced by $C1$ forms a subset of the input $I2$ of $C2$. Let $IO_{LB}(C1)$ and $IO_{LB}(C2)$ represent known I/O lower bounds for $C1$ and $C2$, respectively. Consider the fused computation $C12$ fusing $C1$ and $C2$, with each output data element from $C1$ serving as an input data element for $C2$. If no element of the output set $O1$ is used internally for any computation in $C1$, any valid schedule for $C12$ has an I/O lower bound given by: $IO_{LB}(C12) = IO_{LB}(C1) + IO_{LB}(C2) - 2 * |O1|$.*

We omit the formal proof of this lemma in the main body of the paper and provide it in Appendix A. The key insight from the Fusion Lemma is that the potential benefit from performing fusion across two computations is dependent on the size of the intermediate data (produced by the first computation and consumed by the second) relative to the "inherent" data movement complexity of the two computations. If the minimal data movement required for each of the producer/-consumer computations is much larger than the size of the intermediate data, fusion is futile since the potential reduction in data volume is bounded by twice the size of the intermediate data. On the other hand, if the intermediate data volume is much larger than the "inherent" data movement requirements for the individual computations, fusion can be very beneficial in reducing data movement.

We illustrate the Fusion Lemma using the example of a sequence of two matrix products: C = AB; E = CD. The output matrix C produced by the first matrix product is used as an input for the second matrix product. Let us first consider the case where all matrices are of the same size, $N \times N$, with the matrices being larger than the cache capacity S. The tightest published lower bound on data movement for matrix multiplication (by Dongarra et al. [9]) is $\Omega(1.73N^3/\sqrt{S})$. An efficient tiled implementation achieves a data movement (for the highest order term) of $2N^3/\sqrt{S}$. From the Fusion Lemma, the minimum possible I/O for any fused algorithm is $2 \times 1.73N^3/\sqrt{S} - 2N^2$. Since efficiently tiled but unfused execution of the sequence of two matrix products can be executed with an I/O cost of $2 \times 2N^3/\sqrt{S}$, the maximum possible reduction in I/O from fusion is limited to be less than $0.54N^3/\sqrt{S} + 2N^2$. Fractionally, the reduction is upper-bounded to be under 0.54/2, or around 27% (ignoring the lower order N^2 term).

Next let us consider a non-square case where A and B are $N \times K$ and $K \times N$, respectively, and D is also $N \times K$, with $N \gg K$. Now, the 'inherent" I/O complexity for each of the two producer/consumer operations is $\Omega(1.73N^2K/\sqrt{S})$, which can be much smaller than N^2. In this case, fusion of the sequence of matrix multiplications can be very beneficial in reducing the total volume of data movement.

5. Analysis: Four-Index Transform

In this section, we develop conditions for establishing tight bounds on I/O for some fusion configurations for the four-index transform.

5.1 Necessary Condition: Utility of Fusion

Consider the four-index transform re-written as shown in Equation 2. Let the extent of the tensor along each index be n. The first two contractions are:

$$O1[\alpha, j, k, l] = \sum_i A[i, j, k, l] \cdot B[\alpha, i] \quad (4)$$

$$O2[\alpha, \beta, k, l] = \sum_j O1[\alpha, j, k, l] \cdot B[\beta, j]$$

Each tensor contraction can be represented as a matrix multiplication (seeing resp. (j, k, l) / (α, k, l) as a "macro-index", ranging over the cross-product of multiple tensor indices in A / $O1$). Thus, each of the contractions in the sequence for the 4-index integral transformation is logically equivalent to a matrix product between a $n^3 \times n$ matrix and a $n \times n$ matrix. We can use the Fusion Lemma to derive conclusions on which combinations of fusion are beneficial. We initially ignore any symmetry, considering all matrices and tensors to be full and dense. However, the final results are based on considering symmetry.

From the result of Dongarra et al. [9], the I/O lower bound for the tensor contraction, i.e., matrix multiplication with the "macro" indices, is $1.73n^5/\sqrt{S}$ if S is sufficiently small. But if S is very large, this bound is lower than the sum of data

```
//  C[alpha,j,k,l] += A[i,j,k,l] . B[alpha,i]
//Does I/O equal to |C|+|A|+|B| if S >= n^2 + n + 1
load B[alpha*,i*]    //requires size n^2
for l, k, j
  copy (A_buf[i*], A[i*,j,k,l]) //requires size n
  for alpha
    scalar c //allocate a scalar
    for i
      c += A_buf[i] * B[alpha,i]
    C[alpha,j,k,l] += c
```

Listing 5: Tensor contraction schedule that achieves I/O equal to sum of its input and outputs

sizes of input and output tensors, which is $n^4 + O(n^2) + n^4$ = $2n^4$ if the lower order $O(n^2)$ term is ignored. Therefore, the I/O lower bound for one tensor contraction in the four-index transform sequence is $max(1.73n^5/\sqrt{S}, 2n^4)$. Considering a sequence of two consecutive tensor contractions from the four-index transform, the size of the intermediate tensor (output from the first contraction that is an input to the second) is n^4 elements. From the Fusion Lemma, an I/O lower bound for any fused schedule is $2 \times max(1.73n^5/\sqrt{S}, 2n^4) - 2n^4$. When S is very small, the $1.73n^5/\sqrt{S}$ term in the max expression is larger than $2n^4$, and the the I/O lower bound for any fused schedule is $3.46n^5/\sqrt{S}$, which is larger than the twice the size of the intermediate tensor if $3.46n^5/\sqrt{S} > 2n^4$, i.e., $S < 3n^2$. Thus, if the size of fast memory is much less than $3n^2$, the Fusion Lemma indicates that fusion would not be worthwhile.

Next let us consider the case where S is larger than n^2. In this case, the I/O lower bound from the Fusion Lemma, $2 \times max(1.73n^5/\sqrt{S}, 2n^4) - 2n^4 = 4n^4 - 2n^4 = 2n^4$, half the minimal unfused I/O cost of $4n^4$ (sum of sizes of input and output tensor for each of the two contractions). Thus, when $S > n^2$, reduction in I/O from fusion is not ruled out by the Fusion Lemma, and we consider that scenario next.

5.2 Tight I/O Bound for Useful Fusion

In this subsection, we identify a tight I/O bound for fusion of two consecutive contractions in the four-index transform when $S \geq 3n^2 + n + 1$. The result are summarized in the following theorem.

Theorem 5.1 (Utility of fusing 2 contractions). *Consider any consecutive pair of tensor contractions op1 and op2 in the four-index transform, where the extent of each tensor dimension is n. Let A/O2 be the input/output of op1/op2. Then, fusion is useful if* $S \geq 3n^2 + n + 1$, *with a tight I/O lower bound of* $IO_{opt}(op1 \cup op2) = |A| + |O2|$ *for the fused schedule.*

Proof. Without loss of generality let us use the first two contractions in the four-index transform (see Eq. 4) to represent any pair of consecutive contractions. We prove the theorem in two steps. First, we show that $|A| + |O2|$ is a lower bound on I/O for a fused schedule when S is sufficiently large. Next, we show that we can construct a fused schedule that achieves this lower bound when $S \geq 3n^2 + n + 1$.

```
//I1[alpha,j,k,l] += A[i,j,k,l] . B1[alpha,i]
//C[alpha,beta,k,l] += I1[alpha,j,k,l] . B2[beta,j]
//if S >= 3n^2 + n + 1
//Total I/O of |C|+|B0|+|B1|+|A|
//requires 2n^2 memory
load B1[alpha*,i*], B2[beta*,j*]
for l, k
  malloc (I1_buf, n^2)
  for j
    malloc (A_buf, n)
    copy (A_buf, A[i*,j,k,l])
    for alpha, i
      I1_buf[alpha,j] += A_buf[i] * B1[alpha,i]
  for beta, alpha, j
     C[alpha,beta,k,l] += I1_buf[alpha,j]*B2[beta,j]
```

Listing 6: Fused pair of tensor contractions that achieves I/O equal to sum of size of its input and outputs

When $S \geq n^2+n+1$, a tight I/O lower bound on individual tensor contractions in the four-index transform is given by the sum of the sizes of the input and output tensors. As each input tensor must be read at least once and the output tensor must be written at least once, this is a lower bound on I/O for the tensor contraction. Listing 5 achieves this I/O. Therefore, it is a tight bound. Now using Lemma 4.2, the lower bound on I/O for a fused schedule is given by:

$$(|A|+|O1|)+(|O1|+|O2|)-2|O1| = |A|+|O2| \qquad (5)$$

Additionally, when $S \geq 3n^2+n+1$, a schedule can be constructed that achieves this bound. Loops k and l can be fused: for any fixed value of k and l, the n^2 values of $A[i,j,k,l]$ can be initially loaded, allowing I/O-free computation of the n^2 values of $O1[\alpha,j,k,l]$. This, in turn, allows I/O-free computation of the n^2 values of $O2[\alpha,\beta,k,l]$, which are then stored. The I/O for such a schedule (shown in Listing 6) is exactly the sum of sizes of inputs and outputs (there is no intermediate I/O in executing the operations). Therefore, $|A|+|O2|$ is a tight I/O bound. □

5.3 Fusion Choices: Four-Index Transform

The optimal fusion strategy is one that minimizes the I/O between slow and fast memory. Different unique ways to fuse the four-index transform are as follows: 1. No fusion; 2. Fuse the first two and last two; 3. Fuse only a single pair; 4. Fuse three contractions; 5. Fuse all four contractions. This section's goal, as summarized in the following frame, is to identify which strategy is the best, i.e., the one with the least I/O.

The I/O lower bound for each of the fusion choices can be computed using Lemma 4.2, in conjunction with the tight I/O bound for individual tensor contractions and the result from Theorem 5.1. We already know that the tight I/O lower bound for each individual (or pair of) contractions is the sum of sizes of its input and output. For fusion of three or more contractions, the sum of its input and output sizes is a correct lower bound but not necessarily a tight bound. Below, we summarize the I/O bounds for each fusion choice.

We use the following notation: *op*1234 (resp., *op*12/34, *op*123/4, etc.) denotes fused computation of all tensor contractions (respectively, first two and last two with forced spilling in between, first three, etc.). Thus (using the sets as in Equation 2):

$$IO_{opt}(op1/2/3/4) = |A|+|O1|+|O1|+|O2|+|O2|+|O3|+|O3|+|C|$$
$$IO_{opt}(op12/34) = |A|+|O2|+|O2|+|C|$$
$$IO_{opt}(op1/23/4) = |A|+|O1|+|O1|+|O3|+|O3|+|C|$$
$$IO_{opt}(op123/4) \geq |A|+|O3|+|O3|+|C|$$
$$IO_{opt}(op1234) \geq |A|+|C|$$

Thus far, we have assumed that the size of all $4D$ tensors is n^4. Hence $IO_{opt}(op123/4) \geq IO_{opt}(op12/34)$. However, in reality, $IO_{opt}(op123/4) > IO_{opt}(op12/34)$ because $|O3|$ is bigger than $|O2|$ due to symmetry (see Table 1). In addition, we also have trivially that $IO_{opt}(op1234) \leq IO_{opt}(op12/34)$. Thus, we get the following total order.

Theorem 5.2 (Order of Fusions). *Consider four consecutive tensor contractions op*1*, op*2*, op*3*, and op*4 *and the previously defined notation for fusion. Let* $S = \Omega(n^2)$. *Then,*

$$IO_{opt}(op1234) \leq IO_{opt}(op12/34) < IO_{opt}(op123/4)$$

In other words, the lower bounds show that fusion of the first two and last two contractions has lower I/O than no fusion, while fusing three contractions does not lower the I/O further. The only way it may be possible to reduce the I/O further is to fuse all four contractions together to achieve I/O of $(|A|+|C|)$, via full reuse of intermediates.

6. Necessary and Sufficient Conditions for Full Reuse

In this section, we develop necessary and sufficient conditions for full reuse of all intermediates in the four-index transform, resulting in an I/O of $|A|+|C|$. If the size of fast memory (S) is larger than the sum of all the intermediates in the four-index transform, then achieving an I/O of $|A|+|C|$ is trivial. Even a schedule that performs each of the tensor contractions individually without any fusion will achieve this I/O. However, when the intermediates are too big to fit in fast memory, is full reuse of intermediates still possible? If so, under what conditions?

We show that $S \geq |C|$ is a necessary and sufficient condition for a tight I/O bound of $(|A|+|C|)$.

6.1 Necessary Conditions

In this subsection, we show that if $IO_{opt}(op1234) = |A|+|C|$, then $S \geq |C|$. We first consider the case without symmetries and then show that the proof holds even with symmetric tensors.

Theorem 6.1 (No symmetry). *Let op*1234 *represent the total computation described by Equation 2.*
Then, $IO_{opt}(op1234) = |A|+|C|$
only if $S \geq \min\left(|A|,|O1|,|O2|,|O3|,|C|\right)$

Proof. To achieve the I/O lower bound $(|A|+|C|)$, the intermediates have to be fully reused without any intervening

I/O in between the operations. Let $C[\alpha, \beta, \gamma, \delta]$ be the first computed element of the output, and the corresponding time stamp right before its computation be T_f. We call the *live set* (also denoted W) the already loaded values of A, partially or fully computed values of $O1$, $O2$, $O3$ and C that are to be used later on. We prove that this live set is at least of size $|C|$. Let $F0, F1, F2, F3$ and $F4$ be the already loaded/computed values of A, $O1$, $O2$, $O3$ and C, respectively (which may or may not be used later on). Let $D0, \ldots, D4$, be the set of values in $F0, \ldots, F4$, respectively, that will not be used later on. Therefore, the size of the live set $|W|$ is given by

$$(|F0| \dashv\vdash D0|)+(|F1| \dashv\vdash D1|)+(|F2| \dashv\vdash D2|)+(|F3| \dashv\vdash D3|)+(|F4| \dashv\vdash D4|)$$

Note that to be spill-free (i.e., without any intervening I/O in between contractions), a schedule must be such that $|W| \leq S$. Indeed, W corresponds to simultaneously live variables: if all of them cannot fit in collective physical memory, it means some need to be stored on disk and retrieved later. We now establish a lower-bound on $|W|$.

Each element of C depends on all values of tensor A. At time step T_f, none of the output elements is yet fully computed. Therefore, at time step T_f, $F0 = A$ and $D4 = \emptyset$. $|W|$ simplifies to

$$(|A| \dashv D0|) + (|F1| \dashv D1|) + (|F2| \dashv D2|) + (|F3| \dashv D3|) + (|F4|) \quad (6)$$

Let us recall the computation of the first tensor contraction:

$$O1[\alpha, j, k, l] = A[i, j, k, l] * B0[\alpha, i]$$

Two key observations are as follows:
1. If a given $A[i, j, k, l]$ is in $D0$, then all $O1[*, j, k, l]$ must be in $F1$;
2. If $D0_{j,k,l}$ denotes all the $A[*, j, k, l]$ (at most n_i elements) in D0 and $F1_{j,k,l}$ denotes all the $O1[*, j, k, l]$ (exactly n_α elements) in $F1$, then $|F1_{j,k,l}|/|D0_{j,k,l}| \geq n_\alpha/n_i$.

Thus, $|F1| \geq |D0| \times n_\alpha/n_i = |D0| \times |O1|/|A|$. Applying the same reasoning on the remaining contractions leads to the following lower bound for $|W|$:

$$\begin{aligned} |W| \geq \quad |A| \quad &+|D0| \times (|O1|/|A| - 1) + |D1| \times (|O2|/|O1| - 1) \\ &+|D2| \times (|O3|/|O2| - 1) + |D3| \times (|C|/|O3| - 1) \end{aligned}$$

This in turn can be bounded by

$$|W| \geq \min(|A|, |O1|, |O2|, |O3|, |C|)$$

, since $|D0| \leq |A|$, $|D1| \leq |O1|$, etc. □

The tensors in the four-index transform contains permutation symmetry that can be represented as $A[ij, kl]$, $O1[\alpha, j, kl]$, $O2[\alpha\beta, kl]$, $O3[\alpha\beta, \gamma, l]$, and $C[\alpha\beta, \gamma\delta]$. While all tensors contain some degree of permutation symmetry, the output tensor C also contains spatial symmetry. Because this makes the output $|C|$ the smallest of all five tensors, we expect the necessary condition for the possibility of full reuse to be: $S \geq |C|$.

Theorem 6.2 (With Symmetry). *Consider the four-index transform computation op1234 (Equation 2 with symmetries in Table 1). Then,*

$$IO_{opt}(op1234) = |A| + |C| \text{ only if } S \geq |C|$$

```
/* In this code a=alpha,b=beta,
   c=gamma,d=delta. If S > |C|,
   then total I/O is
   |C|+|B1|+|B2|+|B3|+|B4|+|A| */
for l
  malloc (O1,n^3); malloc(A_buf,n*3)
  copy (A_buf, A[(i>j)*,k*,l])
  for a, i, j, k
    O1[a,j,k] += A_buf[i>j,k]*B1[a,i]
  delete(A_buf); malloc(O2,n^3/2)
  for a > b, j, k
    O2[a>b,k] += O1[a,j,k]*B2[b,j]
  delete (O1); malloc(O3, n^3/2)
  for a>b, c, k
    O3[a>b,c] += O2[a>b,k]*B3[c,k]
  delete(O2)
  for a>b, c>d
    C[a>b,c>d] += O3[a>b,c]*B4[d,l]
```

Listing 7: Fused four-index transform that achieves I/O equal to the size of input and output

Proof. We note that Equation 6 gives the live-set for both symmetric and non-symmetric contractions. We then prove by contradiction that Equation 6 is greater than $|C|$. To make Equation 6 smaller than $|C|$, each term in Equation 6 must be smaller than $|C|$. This forces $|D0|$ to be greater or equal to $|A| - |C|$, i.e., $|D0| \geq 7|A|/8$ based on Tab. 1. Similar to the previous proof, we have that $D0_{j,kl}$ has at most j elements (exploiting the symmetry $j < i$) and that $F1_{j,k,l}$ has exactly n_α elements. Again, this leads to $|F1| \geq |D0| \times |O1|/|A|$ i.e., $|F1| \geq 7/8|O1| \geq |C|$. In general, enforcing the condition that each term must be smaller than $|C|$ forces Li on the next term to be much larger than $|C|$ for all terms except the last one, where $|F4|$ is forced to be $|C|$. This leads to a contradiction, proving that $S \geq |W| \geq |C|$. □

6.2 Sufficient Condition

Listing 7 shows a fused schedule for *op*1234 with I/O cost of $|A| + |C|$ when $S \geq |C|$, thus establishing that $|A| + |C|$ is a tight I/O bound for *op*1234. Keeping in mind that $S \geq |C|$ must be true, the key idea we used to obtain this schedule was to only consider schedules that retained the output C in fast memory through the entire computation.

In this schedule, we fuse loop `l` across all contractions. Then for each iteration of loop `l`, we compute $O1[*, *, *, l]$, $O2[*, *, *, l]$, and $O3[*, *, *, l]$. Each iteration of `l` thus requires $A[*, *, *l]$ as the input, and no two iterations of `l` depend on the same values of A, $O1$, $O2$, or $O3$. Thus values of the input and the intermediates for a particular iteration of `l` can be discarded before the next iteration as they are fully reused during the iteration. However, each iteration involves a partial contribution to each element of the output tensor C. Therefore, C must be kept in fast memory during all iterations of `l`.

This schedule achieves an I/O of $|A| + |C|$ if $S \geq |C| + 2n^3$, where the first term corresponds to the size of fast memory needed to keep C in fast memory across iterations of l, and the second term the capacity needed to retain intermediates in fast memory without any spilling. Thus, we have a schedule *op*1234 with $IO_{opt}(op1234) = |A| + |C|$, when $S \geq |C|$ (ignoring the lower order term n^3, which is negligible compared to $|C|$).

7. A New Parallel Four-Index Transform

Based on our analysis of fusion for the four-index transform, we next develop a fused schedule for it with the following properties:

1. Largest zero-spill four-index transform: For a given aggregate physical memory capacity of the distributed memory system, the schedule allows for the execution of the largest possible four-index transform problem, without requiring any disk I/O, or redundant recomputation of atomic integrals.
2. Minimization of communication volume: The fused schedule minimizes the communication volume between distributed memory nodes, thus enhancing performance for systems where inter-processor communication overhead is a significant performance bottleneck.

7.1 Largest In-Memory Four-Index Transform

In a distributed-memory system, if we consider the disk-based file system to represent the unbounded slow memory, and the aggregate physical memory as the fast memory, we can apply the results from the previous sections that are based on a two-level abstraction of the memory hierarchy. From Theorem 6.2, the aggregate physical memory in the cluster must be larger than $|C|$, to achieve an I/O of $|A|+|C|$. Our implementation of the four-index transform is based on the Listing 7, which achieves this I/O when the size of global memory is greater than $|C|$. Because $S \geq |C|$ is a necessary condition for complete reuse of the intermediates, it is guaranteed that our solution will allow spill-free execution of the largest possible four-index transform for a given amount of aggregate physical memory in the cluster.

In addition, the I/O for our implementation between disk an global memory is actually zero. The I/O reduces from $|A| + |C|$ to zero because of two reasons:

1. The input tensor is produced on the fly, i.e., elements of it are computed without ever having to store the entire tensor. It is produced in fast memory as needed.
2. For all problems of practical interest, $S \geq |C|$ The output C fits in fast memory, and therefore it can be consumed by the next step in the calculation, without ever having to store it in disk.

Listing 8 shows the details of the implementation. Each loop iterates over tile indices. Loop `l` (line 2) is the fused loop over tile l. Iterations of this loop are executed sequentially, while the computation within this loop is parallelized. Each iteration of loop `l` computes an intermediate sub-tensor of size N^3. In other words, for a fixed value of `l`, a slice of N^3 elements of $O1$, $O2$, and $O3$ are produced. For example, lines 3..14 show the computation of a sub-tensor of $O1$. The sub-tensor is distributed and requires $\mathcal{O}(N^3)$ global memory. Each intermediate sub-tensor is used to compute the next intermediate sub-tensor. This computation is parallelized. Each processor only computes the tiles it owns.

```
1  int node_id = GA_Nodeid()
2  for l
3    GA_Create(A,n^3/2);
4    for i>j, k
5      bufA[i>j,k] = ComputeA(i>j,k,l)
6      GA_Put(bufA,A[i>j,k])
7
8    GA_Create(O1,tilewidth* n^3)
9    for j, k
10     if (node_id owns O1[alpha*,j,k])
11       bufA = GA_Get(A[i*,j,k,l])
12       for alpha
13         for i
14           bufB = ComputeB(alpha,i)
15           DGEMM(bufA[i],bufB,buffO1)
16         GA_Put(bufO1, O1[alpha,j,k])
17   GA_Sync()
18
19   GA_Create(O2,tilewidth*n^3/2)
20   for alpha, k
21     if (node_id owns O2[alpha,beta*,k])
22       bufO1 = GA_Get(O1[alpha,j*,k])
23       for beta //less than alpha
24         for j
25           bufB = ComputeB(beta,j)
26           DGEMM(bufO1[j],bufB,bufO2)
27         GA_Put(bufO2, O2[alpha>beta,k])
28   GA_Sync(); delete O1
29
30   GA_Create(O3,tilewidth*n^3/2)
31   for alpha>beta
32     if (node_id owns O3[alpha>beta,gamma*])
33       bufO2 = GA_Get(O2[alpha,beta,k*,l])
34       for gamma
35         for k
36           bufB = ComputeB(gamma,k)
37           DGEMM(bufO2[gamma],bufB,bufO3)
38         GA_Put(bufO3, O3[alpha>beta,gamma])
39   GA_Sync(); delete O2
40
41   for alpha>beta, gamma
42     if (node_id owns C[alpha>beta,gamma>delta])
43       bufO3 = GA_Get(O3[alpha>beta,gamma])
44       for delta //less than gamma
45         bufB = Compute(delta,l)
46         DGEMM(bufO3,bufB,buffC)
47         GA_Acc(buffC,C[alpha>beta,gamma>delta])
48   GA_Sync(); delete O3
```

Listing 8: Implementation that fuses all four contractions to allow execution of the largest possible problem size without recomputation

Finally, the intermediate sub-tensor $O3$ is used to compute partial contributions to output tensor C. Each iteration of loop `l` computes a partial contribution to the entire output tensor C. Therefore, C must fit in global memory.

The disk to memory communication volume for this implementation is 0, and the total global memory required is:

$$\frac{N_i N_j N_k T_l}{2} + \frac{N_\alpha N_\beta N_k T_l}{2} + \frac{N_\alpha N_\beta N_\gamma N_\delta}{32} \quad (7)$$

7.2 Minimizing Communication Volume

I/O at the second level of the memory hierarchy—between the global (distributed) memory and the local memory—corresponds to communication between distributed memory nodes. At this level of the memory hierarchy, global memory is the unbounded slow memory, while local memory is the bounded fast memory. We can minimize the I/O between global memory and local memory by making the following two observations:

```
//if S > n^2, total I/O = |A|+|O2|+|O2|+|C|
for k > l
  for alpha
    for i, j
      O1[j] += A[i>j,k>l] * B[beta,i]
    for beta //less than alpha
      for j
        O2[alpha>beta,k>l] = O1[j] * B2[beta,j]
for alpha>beta
  for gamma
    for k, l
    O3[l] = O2[alpha>beta,k>l]* B3[gamma,k]
    for delta //less than gamma
      for l
        C[alpha>beta,gamma>delta] +=
          O3[gamma,l]*B4[delta,l]
```

Listing 9: Fused schedule op12/34

1. The computation within the fused loop in Listing 8 is itself a four-index transformation (referred to as the inner four-index transform). By fusing loop l, we have reduced the size of index l within the fused loop to either 1, in absence of tiling, or T_l in the presence of tiling, where T_l is the tile width. However, the fusion analysis presented in this paper still applies to the inner four-index transform.
2. For large problems of interest, the size of the local memory is smaller than the final output C of the inner four-index transform. Thus, full reuse of intermediates is not possible, based on Theorem 6.2. However, from Theorem 6.2 and Theorem 5.2, we know that schedule op12/34 (shown in Listing 9) achieves an I/O bound lower than all other fusion choices, when $S = \Omega(n^2)$ and $S < |C|$. Thus, $op12/34$ can be used to minimize communication volume for the inner four-index transform. Such an implementation is shown in Listing 10. In addition to fusing loop l, this implementation performs additional fusion of the first two and the last two contractions of the inner four-index transform. The k and $alpha$ loops are fused between the first two contractions, and the $alpha, beta$ and $gamma$ loops are fused between the second two contractions, similar to the $op12/34$ schedule shown in Listing 9.

The communication volume between global and local memory for this implementation is $|A| + |O2| + |O2| + |C|$, and the memory required is

$$\frac{N_i N_j N_k T_l}{2} + N_\alpha N_j N_k T_l + \frac{N_\alpha N_\beta N_k T_l}{2} + \frac{N_\alpha N_\beta N_\gamma T_l}{2} + \frac{N_\alpha N_\beta N_\gamma N_\delta}{32} \quad (8)$$

7.3 Mapping to Processors

On a conventional memory hierarchy with a single slow and fast memory, $op12/34$ eliminates I/O corresponding to tensors $O1$ and $O3$. To achieve the same effect on a parallel system with multiple fast memory (corresponding to local memory of individual processors), the mapping of computation to processors must be chosen carefully.

Consider the fused schedule for the first two inner contractions in Listing 10. Inside the fused loop k, each element of A is reused to compute multiple elements of O1 along $alpha$, and each element of $O1$ is reused to compute multiple elements of O2 along $beta$. If different values of $alpha$ (or $beta$) are mapped to different processors, then the same elements of A (or $O1$) must either be recomputed on each processor, or must be communicated. In order to avoid communication or redundant re-computation for A and $O1$, all values of $alpha$ and $beta$ for a given k and l must be computed on the same processor. As a result, only the fused loop k can be parallelized. Similarly, for the last two contractions, only the fused loops $alpha$ and $beta$ can be parallelized.

```
int node_id = GA_Nodeid() //this process's rank
for l
  GA_Create(A,n^3/2)
  for(i>j,k)
    bufA[i>j,k] = ComputeA(i>j,k,l)
    GA_Put(bufA,A[i>j,k])
  GA_Create(O2,tilewidth* n^3/2)
  for k
    if(node_id owns O2[(alpha>beta)*,k])
      bufA = GA_Get(A[(i>j)*,k])
      for alpha
        for j, i
          bufB = ComputeB(alpha,i)
          DGEMM(bufA[i>j],bufB,bufO1[j])

        for beta //less than alpha
          for j
            bufB = ComputeB(beta,j)
            DGEMM(bufO1[j],bufB,bufO2[beta])
          GA_Put(bufO2[beta], O2[alpha>beta,k])
  GA_Sync()
  for alpha > beta
    if(node_id owns C[alpha>beta,(gamma>delta)*])
      bufO2 = GA_Get(O2[alpha>beta,k*])
      for gamma, k
        bufB = ComputeB(gamma,k)
        DGEMM(bufO2[k],bufB,bufO3)

        for delta //less than gamma
          bufB = ComputeB(delta,l)
          DGEMM(bufO3,bufB,bufC)
          GA_Acc(bufC,C[alpha>beta,gamma>delta])
  GA_Sync(); delete O2
```

Listing 10: Implementation that performs outer fusion to maximize problem size and inner fusion to minimize communication.

Parallelism vs communication+load imbalance: For large numbers of processors, there may not be enough parallelism in the inner fused schedule of the first two contractions, since only loop k can be parallelized. We overcome this problem in our implementation by allowing parallelization of $alpha$, which results in increased communication for A, by a factor equal to the parallelization of $alpha$. As this is also true for the unfused inner version, there is still a significant reduction in communication volume due to elimination of data movement for $O1$ and $O3$.

Another side effect of parallelization of $alpha$ is a potential for load imbalance. The load imbalance is due to permutation symmetry between $alpha$ and $beta$. As $alpha \geq beta$, a processor computing $alpha = 2$ only computes for two values of $beta$, while a processor computing for $alpha = 3$ computes three values of $beta$. Thus, there is potential for load imbalance. There are alternative load balancing strategies or strategies to increase parallelism, such as block cyclic-distribution of tensors, or nested tiling of l, allowing loop k and parts of loop l to be parallelized.

7.4 To Fuse or not to Fuse?

When there is enough global memory to store the intermediates of the 4-index transform, the unfused implementation is better than the fused implementation. There are two reasons for this: i) As described in the previous section, the fused schedule is not perfectly load balanced; ii) Fusion leads to a space-time trade-off due to symmetry breaking.

In the absence of any permutation symmetry, the fused four-index transform and the unfused one have the same number of operations (additions and multiplications). However, in the presence of permutation symmetry, fusing loop l across all four contraction in the four-index transform requires breaking the symmetry between k and l indices, which doubles the number of computations for producing O1 and O2. Thus, our fused implementation performs approximately 1.5x more computation than the unfused schedule.

To optimize performance, we choose between the fused and the unfused implementations based on the available global memory. If the problem size is too large for the intermediates to fit in the aggregate physical memory of a system, we always chose the fused implementation. On the other hand, if the problem size is small enough for the intermediates to fit in global memory, we always choose the unfused implementation. We call this the fuse/unfuse hybrid implementation.

8. Experimental Results

In this section, we compare the performance of our fuse/unfuse hybrid implementation (described in Section 7.4) with the 4-index transform implementations in NWChem, for multiple problems sizes ranging from small to very large. We present results on three different distributed memory clusters, each with different characteristics. For each problem on each system, we compare our implementation to the fastest NWChem implementation for that problem on that system.

Platforms: *System A* is a small Infiniband cluster, where each node has two 4-core 2.53 GHz Intel Xeon E5630 (Westmere) processors and 24 GB main memory per node, connected as a full fat tree by QDR Infiniband (40 Gbps). *System B* is another small Infiniband cluster with 18 large memory nodes, where each node has two 14-core Intel Xeon E5-2680v4 2.4GHz processors and 512 GB main memory per node. *System C* is a large supercomputer interconnected via FDR Infiniband (14Gbps), with 1440 2.6GHz dual-socket Intel Xeon E5-2670 processors (8 cores per socket) and 128GB of main memory per node.

We used NWChem 6.5 compiled with GCC 4.4.7 on System A, NWChem 6.6 compiled with GCC 4.8 on System B, and NWChem 6.5 compiled with Intel ICC Compiler on System C.

Benchmarks: We evaluate our implementation using 5 different molecules of varying sizes: Hyperpolar, C60H20, Uracil, C40H56, and Shell-Mixed, consisting of 368 (small), 580 (medium), 698 (large), 1023 (very large) and 1194 (very large) orbitals, respectively. The number of orbitals corresponds to the size of each dimension of the 4-index transform. To compute these 4-index transforms in double precision without fusion requires at least 110 GB, 678 GB, 1.4 TB, 6.5 TB, and 12.1 TB of aggregate physical memory, respectively.

We ran the small, medium benchmarks only on small clusters, System A and System B. We ran the large benchmark on all three systems, and the very large benchmarks only on System B and System C, since only these two systems have sufficient aggregate physical memory to hold the final molecular integral.

Results and Discussion: Figure 2 presents experimental results comparing the fuse/unfuse hybrid implementation to the fastest NWChem implementation. For all problem on all systems, fuse/unfuse hybrid is as fast or faster than the *NWChem Best*, the fastest among available schemes in NWChem that could perform the integral transformation..

When there is insufficient aggregate physical memory to store the intermediates, our fuse/unfuse hybrid strategy uses the fused implementation which is 1.2x-6x faster than NWChem Best. This is demonstrated by i) small benchmark on 32 and 64 cores (4/8 nodes) of System A, and 56 cores (2 nodes) of System B, ii) medium benchmark on 140 cores (5 nodes) of System B, and iii) large benchmark on 140/252 cores (5/9 nodes) of System B and 512/1024 cores (128/256 nodes with 4 ranks per node) of System C.

When there is sufficient aggregate physical memory to store the intermediates, our fuse/unfuse hybrid strategy is as good as NWChem Best because both use the unfused implementation. This is demonstrated by i) small benchmark on 128 cores of System A and 140 cores of System B, ii) medium benchmark on 252 core of System B, and iii) large benchmark on 504 cores (18 nodes) of System B.

For a given amount of aggregate physical memory, our fused implementation can run much larger problems than possible with NWChem implementations. This is demonstrated by the large benchmark on 512 cores of System A, and by the very large benchmarks on 504 cores of System B. In each of these cases, the available aggregate physical memory was insufficient for any of the NWChem implementations to run (marked as "Failed"). However, our fused implementation ran successfully.

9. Conclusions

In this paper, we have addressed the development of a high-performance parallel implementation of the four-index integral transformation, a compute-intensive calculation used in many quantum chemistry models. Loop fusion and tiling are key optimizations, but the space of possible configurations is extremely high. Several implementations have been developed over the last two decades for the four-index transformation in NWChem, successively attempting to improve

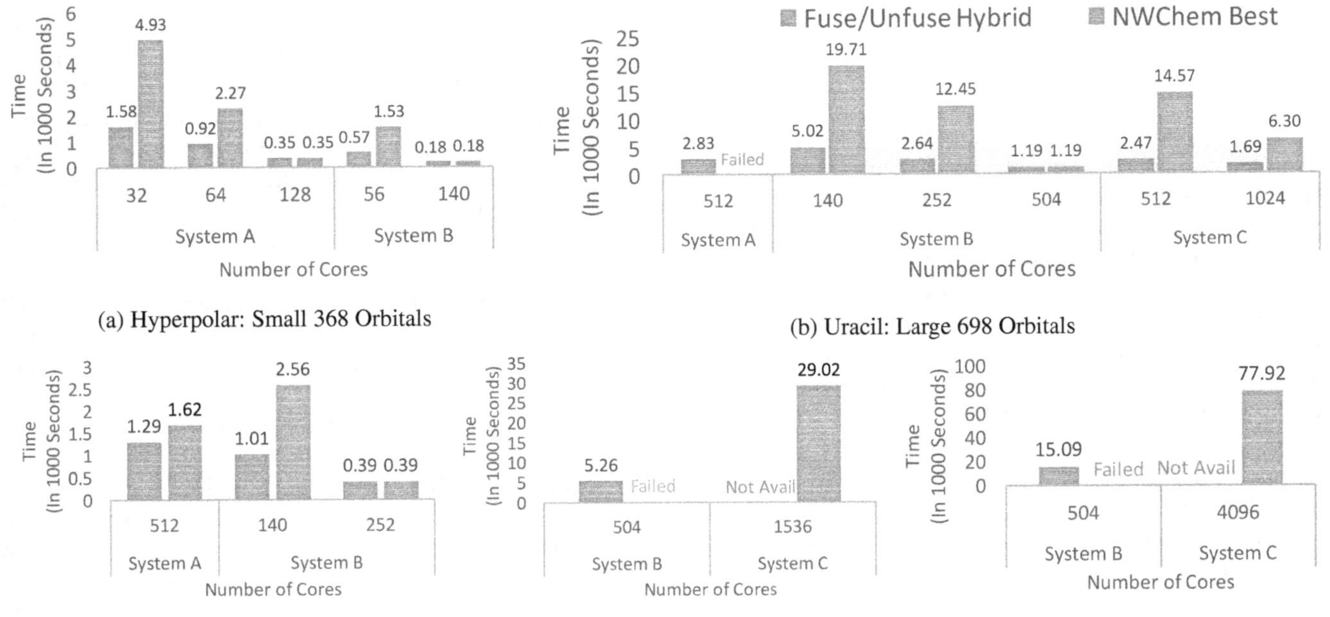

(a) Hyperpolar: Small 368 Orbitals

(b) Uracil: Large 698 Orbitals

(c) C60H20: Medium 580 Orbitals

(d) C40H56: VeryLarge 1023 Orbitals

(e) Shell-Mixed: VeryLarge 1194 Orbitals

Figure 2: This figure shows the execution time for the 4-index transform, for problems of various sizes, on three different distributed memory clusters. It shows a comparison between the new implementation and the best NWChem implementation for the particular problem. Some problems ran out of memory on some systems using all NWChem implementations. Those are marked as failed. On System C, we were not able to acquire resources to run with our implementation for very large problems. Those are marked as Not Avail. However, we show the NWChem results obtained on System C to show the comparsion with the much smaller System B.

on previous versions. In this paper, we pursued a radically different approach to addressing the problem of determining which of many fusion configurations we should consider, using *data movement lower bounds* for analysis. The lower-bounds-based analysis enabled the development of an efficient parallel implementation that was demonstrated to be significantly better than the best current option in the production NWChem code.

Acknowledgment

We thank the reviewers of the paper for their valuable feedback and recommendations. This work was supported in part by DOE award DE-SC0012489, and NSF awards ACI-1440749 and ACI-1404995. Acess to parallel computer resources at the Ohio Supercomputer Center, CSE Department at Ohio State University, and Pacific Northwest national Laboratory are gratefully acknowledged.

A. Appendix: Proof of Fusion Lemma

We use the computational model of the red/blue pebble game [13] to prove the Fusion Lemma. The red/blue pebble game is defined over a computational directed acyclic graph (CDAG), where operations are represented as graph vertices and the flow of values between operations is captured by graph edges.

Definition A.1 (CDAG [7, 13]).
A computational directed acyclic graph (CDAG) is a 4-tuple $C = (I, V, E, O)$ of finite sets such that: (1) $I \subset V$ is the input set and all its vertices have no incoming edges; (2) $E \subseteq V \times V$ is the set of edges; (3) $G = (V, E)$ is a directed acyclic graph; (4) $V \setminus I$ is called the operation set and all its vertices have one or more incoming edges; (5) $O \subseteq V$ is called the output set.

The red-blue pebble game uses two kinds of pebbles: a fixed number (S) of red pebbles that represent small fast local memory (could represent cache, registers, etc.), and an unbounded number of blue pebbles that represent the large slow main memory. Starting with blue pebbles on all inputs nodes in the CDAG, the game involves the generation of a sequence of steps to finally produce blue pebbles on all outputs. The rules of the game are as follows.

Definition A.2 (Red-Blue pebble game (no repebbling)).
Given a CDAG $C = (I, V, E, O)$, S red pebbles and unbounded number of blue pebbles, with a blue pebble on each input vertex, a complete calculation is any sequence of steps using the following rules that results in a final state with blue pebbles on all output vertices:

R1 (Load) *A red pebble may be placed on any vertex that has a blue pebble (load from slow to fast memory),*

R2 (Store) *A blue pebble may be placed on any vertex that has a red pebble (store from fast to slow memory),*

R3 (Compute) *If all immediate predecessors of a vertex of $V \setminus I$ have red pebbles, if not already computed in the* *past, a red pebble may be placed on that vertex (execution or "firing" of operation),*

R4 (Delete) *A red pebble may be removed from any vertex (reuse storage).*

The number of I/O operations for any complete calculation is the total number of moves using rules R1 or R2. We note that although the computational model of the red/blue pebble game abstracts away many features of real hardware, such as cache replacement policy, associativity, non-unit line size, etc., lower bounds established using the formalism of the red/blue pebble game are valid assertions on the minimal number of data elements that must be moved in the memory hierarchy of any real computer system.

Lemma A.3 (Fusion Lemma). *Let computation $C1$ with CDAG $(V1, E1, I1, O1)$ and computation $C2$ with CDAG $(V2, E2, I2, O2)$ represent a producer-consumer pair, where $I2 \cap V1 = O1$. Let $IO_{LB}(C1)$ and $IO_{LB}(C2)$ represent known I/O lower bounds for $C1$ and $C2$, respectively. Consider the fused computation $C12$ fusing $C1$ and $C2$, with CDAG $(V12, E1 \cup E2, I1 \cup I2 - O1, O2)$, where $V12$ represents the union of vertices in $C1$ and $C2$, with each output vertex in $C1$ being merged with some input vertex of $C2$. Then, any valid schedule for $C12$ has an I/O lower bound given by: $IO_{LB}(C12) = IO_{LB}(C1) + IO_{LB}(C2) - 2 * |O1|$.*

Proof. We consider any valid schedule $S12$ for $C12$ and prove that $IO(S12) \geq IO_{LB}(C1) + IO_{LB}(C2) - 2 * |O1|$. 5The schedule $S12$ comprises of some sequence of the four kinds of actions described above. From this schedule $S12$, we first generate a valid augmented schedule $S12^+$ by insertion of additional Loads (rule $R1$) and Stores (rule $R2$) as follows:

Consider each vertex v in $C12$ that represents the merge of an output vertex in $C1$ and an input vertex in $C2$.

- Immediately after the (unique) Compute operation on vertex v, first insert a Store operation to place a blue pebble on the vertex.
- Let o be the earliest Compute operation in the augmented schedule $S12^+$ that uses the value produced in vertex v. Insert a Delete operation for v, followed by a Load operation for v immediately preceding the Compute operation o. This is valid since i) the operation o would have used the value of vertex v in a red pebble in $S12$, so that the Delete operation is valid and also frees a red pebble, and ii) $S12^+$ has a previously inserted Store operations for vertex v, as described above, so that a blue pebble is on v, and a freed red pebble is available to place on v.

The augmented schedule $S12^+$ is a valid schedule for $C12$ since each of the added operations is valid and the relative order of all Compute operations is unchanged from $S12$, i.e., no dependences are violated. From the valid augmented schedule $S12^+$, we construct valid schedules $S1$ and $S2$, respectively, for the unfused computations $C1$ and $C2$.

First, tag as belonging to $S1$, each operation in $S12^+$ on any vertices of $C12$ that correspond to $V1 - O1$. Additionally tag as belonging to $S1$, the Compute operations on vertices belonging to $O1$, as well as the inserted Store operations in $S12^+$ that immediately follow the corresponding Compute operations. By deleting all untagged operations in $S12^+$, the remaining operations form a valid schedule for $C1$. This is because (by induction on the steps of $S1$):

- Every vertex in $C1$ is included in $C12$, and $S12$ (and therefore also $S12^+$) must contain a Compute operation for each such vertex; each such Compute operation has valid operands in $S1$ since any predecessor vertices must belong to $C1$, and all operations on them from $S12^+$ will also appear in $S1$ before it.
- Similarly, every Load, Store, and Delete operation will have valid operands in $S1$ because the relative order of all operations in $S1$ is the same as that in $S12$, which is a valid schedule.
- There will never be any resource violation, i.e., unavailability of a red pebble for any Load or Compute operation because the number of free red pebbles just prior to execution of any operation in $S1$ is greater than or equal to the number of free red pebbles immediately before execution of the corresponding operation in $S12$. This is true at the start (all red pebbles are free) and as we execute operations, the number of free pebbles in $S12$ may go lower due to interleaved operations from vertices in $C2$ but can never be higher than that for $S1$.
- All outputs $O1$ are in blue pebbles at the end of $S1$, due to the explicitly inserted Store operations in construction of $S12^+$.

To construct a valid schedule $S2$ for $C2$, we first remove all $S1$-tagged operations from $S12^+$. We then remove the inserted Delete operations from the Delete/Load pair that was inserted before every first use of a vertex in $O1$ when constructing $S12^+$, as described earlier. This removes all operations pertaining to computation of $C1$ vertices, but if we assume all inputs $I2$ are in blue pebbles before the start of the schedule $S2$, the necessary load operations are all available in $S2$ - for those elements of $I2$ that are in $O1$, explicit Load operations were inserted in constructing $S12^+$, and for other elements of $I2$, $S12$ must already have included the needed Load operations. A similar reasoning as detailed for $S1$ can be carried out for $S2$ to show that each individual operation in $S2$ will not violate any dependences (relative order of operations in $S2$ is the same as $S12$) and that no resource violations can occur, proving that $S2$ is a valid schedule for $C2$.

We now have:

- $IO(S12^+) = IO(S1) + IO(S2)$ (because $S1$ and $S2$ are obtained by a disjoint partition of operations in $S12^+$).
- $IO(S12^+) = IO(S12) + 2 * |O1|$ (because in constructing $S12^+$ from $S12$, exactly $|O1|$ Store operations and $|O1|$ Load operations were inserted, as described above).
- $IO(S1) \geq IO_{LB}(C1)$ (any valid actual schedule must have I/O cost greater than or equal to any valid lower bound for the computation).
- $IO(S2) \geq IO_{LB}(C2)$.

Hence, $IO(S12) + 2 * |O1| \geq IO_{LB}(C1) + IO_{LB}(C2)$, i.e., $IO(S12) \geq IO_{LB}(C1) + IO_{LB}(C2) - 2 * |O1|$.

References

[1] ACES II, a program product of the quantum theory project. *See http://www.qtp.ufl.edu/aces/*, 1996.

[2] The massively parallel quantum chemistry program (MPQC). *http://www.mpqc.org/index.php*, 2004.

[3] MOLPRO, a package of ab initio programs. *See http://www. molpro. net*, 2006.

[4] Nwchem: A comprehensive and scalable open-source solution for large scale molecular simulations. *See http://www. nwchem-sw. org/index. php*, 2010.

[5] Psi4, an open-source ab initio electronic structure program. *See http://www.psicode.org/*, 2012.

[6] M. Abe, T. Yanai, T. Nakajima, and K. Hirao. A four-index transformation in dirac's four-component relativistic theory. *Chem. Phys. Letters*, 388(13):68 – 73, 2004.

[7] G. Bilardi and E. Peserico. A characterization of temporal locality and its portability across memory hierarchies. *Automata, Languages and Programming*, pages 128–139, 2001.

[8] L. A. Covick and K. M. Sando. Four-index transformation on distributed-memory parallel computers. *J. Comp. Chem.*, 11 (10):1151–1159, 1990.

[9] J. Dongarra, J.-F. Pineau, Y. Robert, and F. Vivien. Matrix product on heterogeneous master-worker platforms. In *PPoPP*, pages 53–62, 2008.

[10] G. Fletcher, M. Schmidt, and M. Gordon. Developments in parallel electronic structure theory. *Adv. Chem. Phys.*, 110: 267–294, 1999.

[11] T. R. Furlani and H. F. King. Implementation of a parallel direct scf algorithm on distributed memory computers. *J. Comp. Chem.*, 16(1):91–104, 1995.

[12] X. Gao, S. Krishnamoorthy, S. K. Sahoo, C. Lam, G. Baumgartner, J. Ramanujam, and P. Sadayappan. Efficient search-space pruning for integrated fusion and tiling transformations. *CCPE*, 19(18):2425–2443, 2007.

[13] J.-W. Hong and H. T. Kung. I/O complexity: The red-blue pebble game. In *STOC*, pages 326–333, 1981.

[14] D. Irony, S. Toledo, and A. Tiskin. Communication lower bounds for distributed-memory matrix multiplication. *J. Parallel Distrib. Comput.*, 64(9):1017–1026, 2004.

[15] C. Lam, T. Rauber, G. Baumgartner, D. Cociorva, and P. Sadayappan. Memory-optimal evaluation of expression trees involving large objects. *Comp. Lang. Sys. Struc.*, 37(2): 63–75.

[16] A. C. Limaye and S. R. Gadre. A general parallel solution to the integral transformation and second-order Møller-Plesset energy evaluation on distributed memory parallel machines. *J. Chem. Phys.*, 100(2):1303–1307, 1994.

[17] W. Ma, S. Krishnamoorthy, and G. Agrawal. Practical loop transformations for tensor contraction expressions on multi-level memory hierarchies. In *CC 2011*, pages 266–285, 2011.

[18] J. Nieplocha, B. Palmer, V. Tipparaju, M. Krishnan, H. Trease, and E. Aprà. Advances, applications and performance of the global arrays shared memory programming toolkit. *Int. J. High Perform. Comput. Appl.*, 20(2):203–231, May 2006.

[19] M. Pernpointner, L. Visscher, W. A. de Jong, and R. Broer. Parallelization of four-component calculations. i. integral generation, SCF, and four-index transformation in the Dirac-Fock package MOLFDIR. *J. Comp. Chem.*, 21(13): 1176–1186.

[20] G. Rauhut, P. Pulay, and H.-J. Werner. Integral transformation with low-order scaling for large local second-order Møller-Plesset calculations. *J. Comp. Chem.*, 19(11):1241–1254.

[21] S. Sæbø and J. Almlöf. Avoiding the integral storage bottleneck in LCAO calculations of electron correlation. *Chem. Phys. Let.*, 154(1):83 – 89, 1989.

[22] S. K. Sahoo, S. Krishnamoorthy, R. Panuganti, and P. Sadayappan. Integrated loop optimizations for data locality enhancement of tensor contraction expressions. In *SC 2005*.

[23] M. W. Schmidt, K. K. Baldridge, J. A. Boatz, S. T. Elbert, M. S. Gordon, J. H. Jensen, S. Koseki, N. Matsunaga, K. A. Nguyen, S. Su, et al. General atomic and molecular electronic structure system. *J. Comp. Chem.*, 14(11): 1347–1363, 1993.

[24] R. A. Whiteside, J. S. Binkley, M. E. Colvin, and H. F. Schaefer III. Parallel algorithms for quantum chemistry. i. integral transformations on a hypercube multiprocessor. *J. Chem. Phys.*, 86(4):2185–2193, 1987.

[25] S. Wilson. Four-index transformations. In *Methods in Computational Chemistry*, pages 251–309. Springer, 1987.

[26] T. L. Windus, M. W. Schmidt, and M. S. Gordon. Parallel algorithm for integral transformations and GUGA MCSCF. *Theoretica chimica acta*, 89(1):77–88, 1994.

[27] A. T. Wong, R. J. Harrison, and A. P. Rendell. Parallel direct four-index transformations. *Th. Chim. Acta*, 93(6):317–331.

Using Butterfly-Patterned Partial Sums to Draw from Discrete Distributions

Guy L. Steele Jr.
Oracle Labs
guy.steele@oracle.com

Jean-Baptiste Tristan
Oracle Labs
jean.baptiste.tristan@oracle.com

Abstract

We describe a SIMD technique for drawing values from multiple discrete distributions, such as sampling from the random variables of a mixture model, that avoids computing a complete table of partial sums of the relative probabilities. A table of alternate ("butterfly-patterned") form is faster to compute, making better use of coalesced memory accesses; from this table, complete partial sums are computed on the fly during a binary search. Measurements using CUDA 7.5 on an NVIDIA Titan Black GPU show that this technique makes an entire machine-learning application that uses a Latent Dirichlet Allocation topic model with 1024 topics about about 13% faster (when using single-precision floating-point data) or about 35% faster (when using double-precision floating-point data) than doing a straightforward matrix transposition after using coalesced accesses.

Categories and Subject Descriptors D.1.3 [*Concurrent Programming*]; E.1 [*Data Structures*]: Distributed data structures

Keywords butterfly, coalesced memory access, discrete distribution, GPU, latent Dirichlet allocation, LDA, machine learning, multithreading, memory bottleneck, parallel computing, random sampling, SIMD, transposed memory access

1. Overview

The successful use of Graphics Processing Units (GPUs) to train neural networks is a great example of how machine learning can benefit from such massively parallel architecture. Generative probabilistic modeling [3] and associated inference methods (such as Monte Carlo methods) can also benefit. Indeed, authors such as Suchard *et al.* [23] and Lee *et al.* [14] have pointed out that many algorithms of interest are embarrassingly parallel. However, the potential for massively parallel computation is only the first step toward full use of GPU capacity. One bottleneck that such embarrassingly parallel algorithms run into is related to memory bandwidth; one must design key probabilistic primitives with such constraints in mind.

We address the case where parallel threads draw independently from distinct discrete distributions. This can arise when implementing any mixture model, and Latent Dirichlet Allocation (LDA) models in particular, which are probabilistic mixture models used to discover abstract "topics" in a collection of documents (a *corpus*) [4]. This model can be fitted (or "trained") in an unsupervised fashion using sampling methods [2, chapter 11][7]. Each document is modeled as a distribution θ over topics, and each word in a document is assumed to be drawn from a distribution ϕ of words. Understanding the methods described in this paper does not require a deep understanding of sampling algorithms for LDA. What is important is that each word in a corpus is associated with a so-called "latent" random variable [2, chapter 9], usually referred to as z, that takes on one of K integer values, indicating a topic to which the word belongs. Broadly speaking, the iterative training process works by tentatively choosing a topic (that is, sampling the random latent variable z) for a given word using relative probabilities calculated from θ and ϕ, then updating θ and ϕ accordingly.

In this paper, we focus on the step that, given a discrete distribution represented as a length-K array a of relative probabilities, chooses an integer j such that $0 \leq j < K$ in such a way that the probability of choosing any specific value j' is $a_{j'}/\sigma$, where σ is the sum of all elements of a. (We use zero-based indexing throughout this paper.) This is easily done using a three-step process:

1. Normalize a (divide each entry by the sum of all entries).
2. Let u be chosen uniformly at random (or pseudorandomly) from the real interval $[0, 1)$.
3. Find the smallest index j such that the sum of all entries of a at or below index j is larger than u.

In practice, this sequence of steps may be optimized by doing a bit of algebra and using a binary search:

PPoPP '17, February 04-08, 2017, Austin, TX, USA.

http://dx.doi.org/10.1145/3018743.3018757

1. Compute p, the prefix-sum of a, such that $p_j = \sum_{i=0}^{j} a_i$.
2. Choose u uniformly at random (or pseudorandomly) from the real interval $[0, 1)$, and let $u' = p_{(K-1)} \times u$.
3. Use a binary search to find the smallest index j such that the entry at index p_j is larger than u'.

This works because all elements of a are nonnegative and therefore elements of p are monotonically nondecreasing.

Now suppose that we have many discrete distributions (thousands or millions) and wish to draw one sample from each, using a SIMD-style GPU. An obvious approach is to assign each distribution to a separate thread and have each thread execute the optimized three-step algorithm. However, in the context of the LDA application, a problem arises: when the threads fetch entries from their respective arrays (especially the ϕ arrays), the values to be fetched will likely reside at unrelated locations in memory, resulting in poor memory-fetch performance. A standard technique is to have all the lanes in a warp (a group of threads being executed simultaneously by the SIMD engine) cooperate with each other. For concreteness, suppose there are 32 threads in a warp, and for simplicity, assume that each array a of relative probabilities is also of length 32. We can furthermore assume that the elements of any single a array are stored sequentially in memory (and therefore fit within a small number of cache lines); the problem arises solely because we cannot assume any specific relationship within memory among the 32 a instances to be processed simultaneously. The technique that gets around this problem is *transposed memory access*: as the 32 elements are fetched for each of 32 instances of a, on each step j of 32 steps ($0 \leq j < 32$), lane i ($0 \leq i < 32$) fetches not $a[i][j]$ but instead $a[j][i]$. (Compare, for example, the storage of floating-point numbers as "slicewise" rather than "fieldwise" in the architecture of the Connection Machine Model CM-2, so that 32 1-bit processors cooperate on each of 32 clock cycles to fetch and store an entire 32-bit floating-point value that logically belongs to just one of the 32 processors [10].) In words, on step j all 32 lanes fetch the 32 values needed by lane j; as a result, on each memory cycle all 32 values being fetched are in a contiguous region of memory, allowing improved memory-fetch performance.

It is then necessary for the lanes to exchange information among themselves so that the rest of the algorithm may be carried out, including the summation arithmetic.

The novel contribution of this paper is to observe and then exploit the fact that the binary search of the array p (which is computed from a) does not access all entries of p; in fact, for an array of size K it examines only about $\log_2 K$ entries. Therefore it is not necessary to compute all entries of the prefix-sum table. We present an alternate technique that computes a "butterfly-patterned" partial-sums table, using less computational and communication effort when implemented on a GPU; a modified binary search then uses this table to compute, on the fly, entries that would have been in the original complete prefix-sum table. This requires more work per table entry during the binary search, but because the search examines only a few table entries, the result is a net reduction in execution time. This technique may be effective for collapsed LDA Gibbs samplers [16, 24, 30] as well as uncollapsed samplers, and may also be useful for GPU implementations of other algorithms [32] whose inner loops sample from discrete distributions.

This paper is not about machine-learning algorithms in general or LDA in particular; rather, we use an LDA application as a convenient and practical benchmark for evaluating data-parallel sampling algorithms. The specific LDA algorithm that we use is state-of-the-art [25] and had already been carefully tuned for speed before application of the techniques described in this paper.

2. Background

Suppose we are given a discrete distribution described as an array a of length K such that a_j is the relative probability that sampling the distribution will produce the value j ($0 \leq j < K$, and for purposes of illustration we will use $K = 16$):

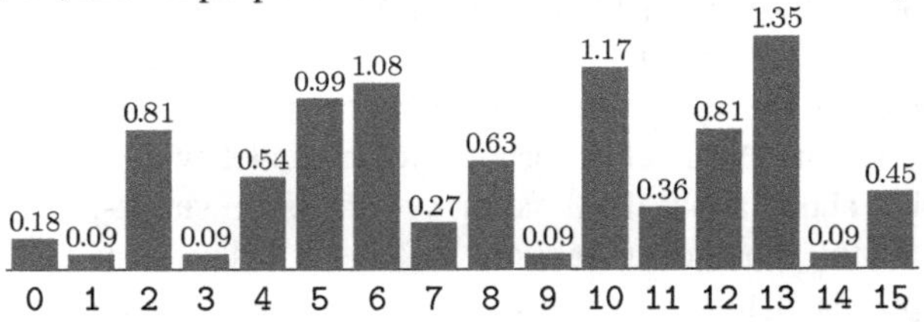

a	0.18	0.09	0.81	0.09	0.54	0.99	1.08	0.27	0.63	0.09	1.17	0.36	0.81	1.35	0.09	0.45

From a, compute the prefix-sum array p:

let $sum = 0.0$
for k from 0 through $K - 1$ **do**
  $sum \mathrel{+}= a[k];\ p[k] := sum$

p	0.18	0.27	1.08	1.17	1.71	2.70	3.78	4.05	4.68	4.77	5.94	6.30	7.11	8.46	8.55	9.00

To sample the distribution, a simple linear search will do:

let $u =$ random value chosen from $[0.0, 1.0)$
let $u' = sum \times u$, $j = 0$
while $j < K - 1$ and $u' \geq p[j]$ **do** $j \mathrel{+}= 1$

Alternatively, one may use a binary search:

let $u =$ random value chosen from $[0.0, 1.0)$
let $u' = sum \times u$, $j = 0$, $k = K - 1$
while $j < k$ **do**
  let $mid = \left\lfloor \frac{j+k}{2} \right\rfloor$
  if $u' < p[mid]$ **then** $k := mid$ **else** $j := mid + 1$

A binary search on an array amounts to walking down a binary tree whose leaves are the array indices and whose internal nodes are labeled with all entries except the last. We can draw such a tree by starting with a drawing of the array and then displacing each entry (except the last) vertically:

p	0.18	0.27	1.08	1.17	1.71	2.70	3.78	4.05	4.68	4.77	5.94	6.30	7.11	8.46	8.55	9.00

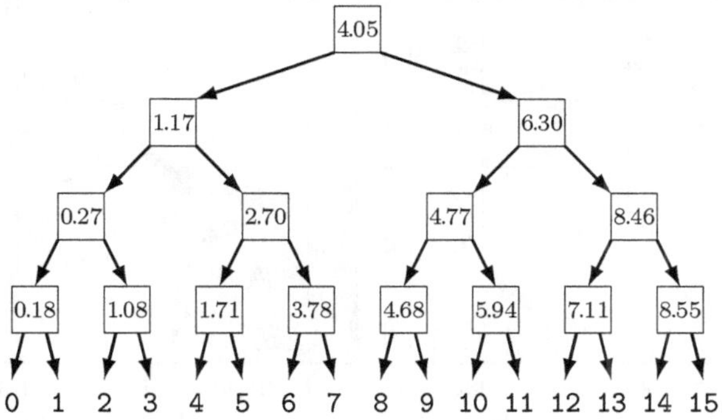

Starting from the root, we compare the quantity we are searching for to the label of each internal node that we encounter; if it is smaller, we descend to the left child, otherwise to the right child.

We can picture the general process by using a convenient abbreviation: a_m^n means $\sum_{m \le i \le n} a_i$. Then array p looks like:

p	a_0^0	a_0^1	a_0^2	a_0^3	a_0^4	a_0^5	a_0^6	a_0^7	a_0^8	a_0^9	a_0^{10}	a_0^{11}	a_0^{12}	a_0^{13}	a_0^{14}	a_0^{15}

and the corresponding binary tree looks like this:

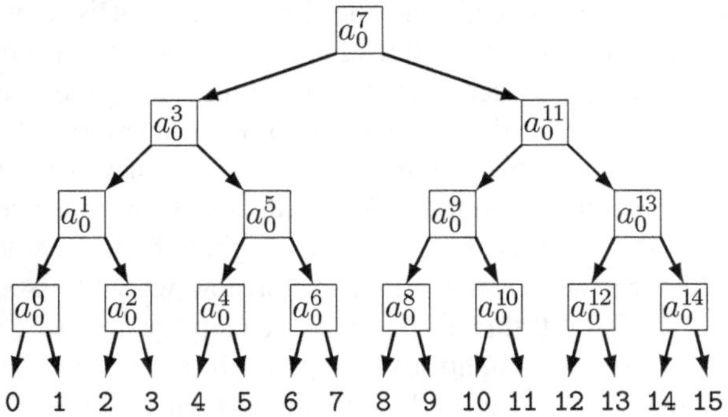

Instead of computing the prefix-sum of a, we can compute a different set of partial sums, which we will call p':

for k from 0 through $K-1$ **do** $p'[k] := a[k]$
for b from 1 through $\log_2 K$ **do**
  for i from 1 through $2^{(\log_2 K)-b}$ **do**
    $p'[(2i)2^{b-1}-1] \mathrel{+}= p'[(2i-1)2^{b-1}-1]$

p'	a_0^0	a_0^1	a_2^2	a_0^3	a_4^4	a_4^5	a_6^6	a_0^7	a_8^8	a_8^9	a_{10}^{10}	a_8^{11}	a_{12}^{12}	a_{12}^{13}	a_{14}^{14}	a_0^{15}

and also treat it as a binary tree to be searched:

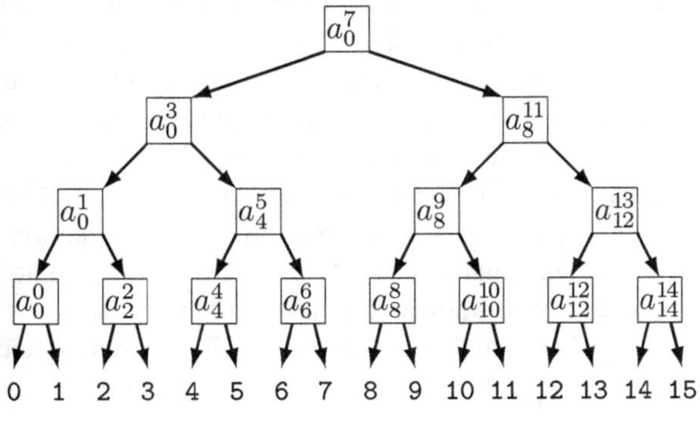

lane	A	B	C	D	E	F	G	H
	A_0	B_0	C_0	D_0	E_0	F_0	G_0	H_0
	A_1	B_1	C_1	D_1	E_1	F_1	G_1	H_1
	A_2	B_2	C_2	D_2	E_2	F_2	G_2	H_2
	A_3	B_3	C_3	D_3	E_3	F_3	G_3	H_3
	A_4	B_4	C_4	D_4	E_4	F_4	G_4	H_4
	A_5	B_5	C_5	D_5	E_5	F_5	G_5	H_5
	A_6	B_6	C_6	D_6	E_6	F_6	G_6	H_6
	A_7	B_7	C_7	D_7	E_7	F_7	G_7	H_7

(a) Normal per-lane arrays

lane	A	B	C	D	E	F	G	H
	A_0	A_1	A_2	A_3	A_4	A_5	A_6	A_7
	B_0	B_1	B_2	B_3	B_4	B_5	B_6	B_7
	C_0	C_1	C_2	C_3	C_4	C_5	C_6	C_7
	D_0	D_1	D_2	D_3	D_4	D_5	D_6	D_7
	E_0	E_1	E_2	E_3	E_4	E_5	E_6	E_7
	F_0	F_1	F_2	F_3	F_4	F_5	F_6	F_7
	G_0	G_1	G_2	G_3	G_4	G_5	G_6	G_7
	H_0	H_1	H_2	H_3	H_4	H_5	H_6	H_7

(b) Transposed arrays

Figure 1. Array storage in lane registers ($W = 8$). Each column represents W consecutive registers in the register file of one lane. Arrays elements are numbered, lanes are labeled by letters; so "C_4" denotes element 4 of the array that logically belongs to (is intended to be processed by) lane C.

Here's the trick: while the internal nodes of this tree do not contain the complete partial sums of p needed for comparison, the values of p that we actually need can be computed from p' on the fly as we walk down the tree.

let u = random value chosen from $[0.0, 1.0)$
let $u' = \mathit{sum} \times u$, $j = 0$, $k = K - 1$
let $\mathit{lowValue} = 0$
while $j < k$ **do**
  let $\mathit{mid} = \left\lfloor \frac{j+k}{2} \right\rfloor$
  let $\mathit{compareValue} = \mathit{lowValue} + p'[m]$
  if $u' < p[\mathit{mid}]$ **then**
    $k := \mathit{mid}$
  else
    $j := \mathit{mid} + 1$
    $\mathit{lowValue} := \mathit{compareValue}$

This tree p' is familiar: it is an intermediate state in one parallel algorithm for computing the prefix-sum array p. Because the iterations of the inner **for** loop used to construct p' are independent, they may be executed in parallel, and so p' can be constructed from a in $\log_2 K$ steps, building the tree from bottom to top; and p can likewise be constructed from p' in $\log_2 K$ steps, passing information down the tree.

3. Parallel SIMD Implementation on a GPU

In the CUDA programming model, as used on GPU products from NVIDIA, one may pretend that one has thousands or millions of threads, each with its own local memory, stack, and registers, and one may assign to each such thread an instance of a computation. The operating system multiplexes the hardware resources to give the illusion of more or less simultaneous execution. For management purposes, threads are grouped into *warps*, each having exactly W threads. In the actual hardware used for our experiments, $W = 32$; however, for purposes of illustration, we will use $W = 8$ or $W = 16$, to make the figures a manageable size while keeping fonts at a readable size. Warps are automatically sched-

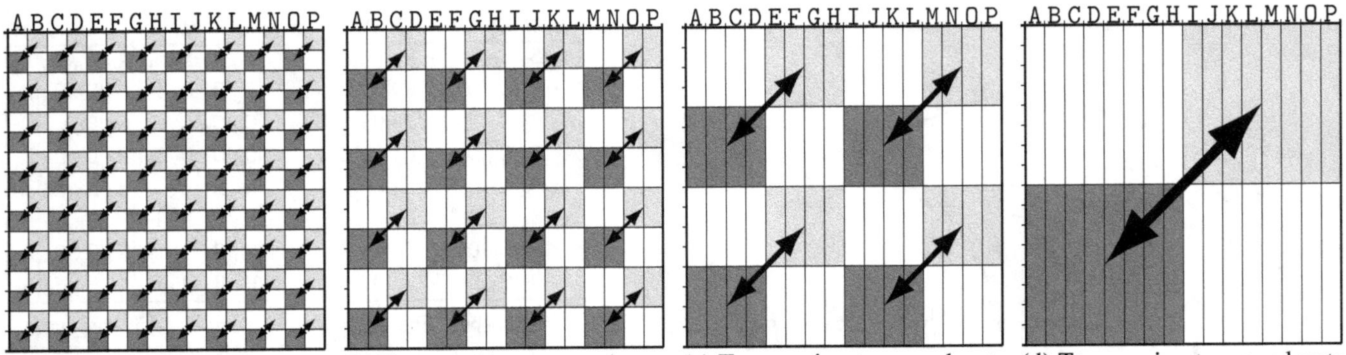

(a) Transposing two elements in each 2×2 block (b) Transposing two quadrants in each 4×4 block (c) Transposing two quadrants in each 8×8 block (d) Transposing two quadrants in the overall 16×16 block

Figure 2. Transposing a matrix consisting of W registers in each of the W lanes of the GPU (shown for $W = 16$)

uled onto multiple SIMD processing engines, where each engine has W *lanes*, and each lane performs the computation for one thread. When an engine has completed computation for one warp, it goes on to process another warp, and so on, until all warps have been processed.

The programmer can count on absolutely simultaneous execution of the W threads that constitute any single warp. There are a few low-level operations that can exchange data synchronously among the lanes of a warp [20, 29]; two are of interest here. The expression `__shfl`$(value, lane)$, when executed (necessarily simultaneously) as a SIMD operation by the threads in a warp, causes each lane to make its computed $value$ available to all lanes, and then returns the $value$ provided by lane $lane$; in short, each lane gets to decide which of the other lanes to read from. The expression `__shfl_xor`$(value, m)$ is, in effect, an abbreviation for `__shfl`$(value, myLaneId \oplus m)$, where $myLaneId$ has the value i in lane i $(0 \leq i < W)$, and where $\oplus$ is the bitwise exclusive-OR operation on unsigned integers. If the same value of m is provided on all lanes, then `__shfl_xor` performs a permutation specified by m; for example, if $m = 2$, then lanes whose numbers differ in exactly one bit position (the second-least-significant bit) will exchange data.

Certain instructions can cause individual lanes of a warp to become conditionally inactive; others can force some or all lanes to become active again. These are typically used by a compiler (such as the CUDA compiler) to implement **if-then-else** statements and loops.

When the lanes of a warp execute a "load" instruction, then W words are read from memory; more precisely, at most W words are read from memory, because the memory controller performs memory reads only for active lanes (but this nicety will not matter for our purposes). The memory controller makes an effort to *coalesce* these read requests, so that if multiple words to be read happen to reside in the same cache line, then the cache line is read only once.

In our LDA application, we have many documents to be processed. each with a different number of words (we presort the documents so that those of any one warp likely have similar lengths). We assign one document to each thread. The thread processes each word in the document; for that word it computes a discrete distribution to be sampled, and then samples it once. All threads in a warp process the kth word of their respective documents simultaneously.

Within each thread, the array a representing the distribution to be sampled is computed on the fly, used once, and then discarded, so a resides in registers. It is the elementwise product of two other arrays, θ and ϕ; θ represents a discrete distribution associated with the document, so it is kept in the local memory of the thread, but ϕ represents a discrete distribution associated with the word type, and comes from a very large table that must reside in main memory. There is no reason to expect significant correlation of word types among the kth words of the W documents in a warp, so very likely their ϕ arrays are scattered throughout main memory.

To keep the discussion simple, for now we will assume $K = W$. (We lift this restriction in Section 5.)

If we use a straightforward approach, every lane loads only the data it needs and computes its own a values. This situation is pictured in Figure 1(a), where for each element the variable name a is replaced with one of the letters `A` through `H` to indicate which lane that particular element logically belongs to. In this case, every a element resides in some register of the lane to which it logically belongs, which logically is just what we want. The downside is poor performance because few memory accesses will be coalesced.

An alternative approach is to use transposed memory access. The lanes work together so that memory accesses are coalesced, then compute the a values for the data they happen to have (the precomputed θ arrays can also be pretransposed, so that every lane will have the elements of θ that it needs in its own local memory). This situation is pictured in Figure 1(b). The downside is that no lane has direct access to all the a values that it needs to compute its p values.

One way out is to arrange to have lanes use `__shfl_xor` operations to exchange data, so as to turn the situation of Figure 1(b) into that of Figure 1(a). This is a well-known problem with well-known solutions; one that works as well as could be expected is illustrated in Figure 2. On step i $(0 \leq i < \log_2 W)$, $W/2$ `__shfl_xor` instructions are used

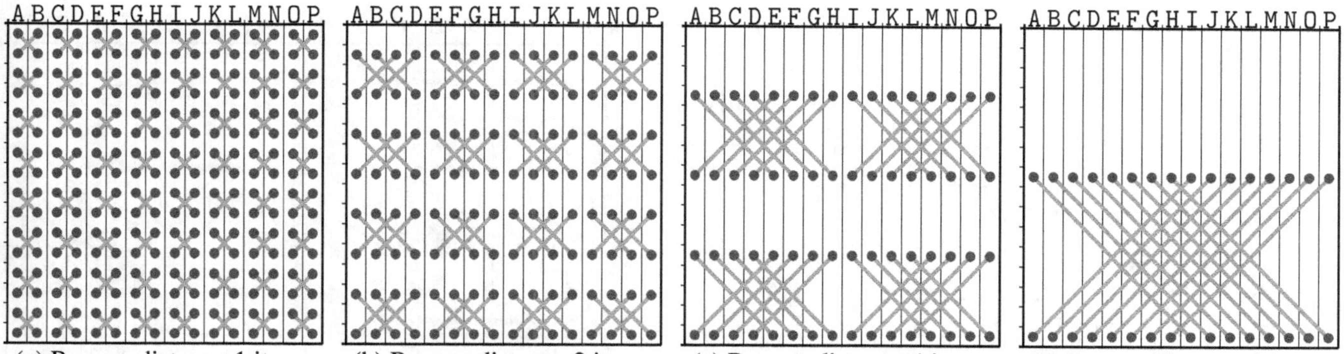

(a) Process distance-1 items (8 __shfl_xor operations) (b) Process distance-2 items (4 __shfl_xor operations) (c) Process distance-4 items (2 __shfl_xor operations) (d) Process distance-8 items (1 __shfl_xor operation)

Figure 3. Patterns of application of butterfly computations to compute butterfly-patterned p' arrays ($W = 16$)

(one for every pair of register positions) to exchange registers whose numbers differ by 2^i between lanes whose numbers differ by 2^i (see Figure 2). First, $W/2$ `__shfl_xor` instructions are used (one for every pair of register positions) to exchange registers whose numbers differ by 1 between lanes whose numbers differ by 1 (Figure 2(a)). Second, $W/2$ `__shfl_xor` instructions are used to exchange registers whose numbers differ by 2 between lanes whose numbers differ by 2 (Figure 2(b)). Third, $W/2$ `__shfl_xor` instructions are used to exchange registers whose numbers differ by 4 between lanes whose numbers differ by 4 (Figure 2(c)). Finally, $W/2$ `__shfl_xor` instructions are used to exchange registers whose numbers differ by 8 between lanes whose numbers differ by 8 (Figure 2(d)). Thus the total number of `__shfl_xor` operations is $\frac{1}{2}W \log_2 W$.

We offer a novel approach that uses $3(W-1)$ shuffle operations[1] and avoids all scattered memory access. The idea is to have the lanes cooperate to construct a partial sums table that is related to the p' arrays discussed in Section 2. Instead of ending up with every lane having all its own p' array elements, each array is distributed across multiple lanes—but instead of every lane containing exactly one element of every p' array, they are distributed in a more complicated way: we call it a "butterfly-patterned partial sums table." The construction of this table requires only $W-1$ `__shfl_xor` operations. During the binary search, an additional $2(W-1)$ `__shfl` and `__shfl_xor` operations are used as the lanes assist each other in accessing array elements.

Here is how the butterfly-patterned table is constructed. There are $\log_2 W$ steps, and during step i ($0 \leq i < \log_2 W$), $2^{(\log_2 W)-i-1)}$ `__shfl_xor` instructions are used to perform $\left(2^{(\log_2 W)-i-1}\right)\frac{W}{2}$ butterfly computations (see Figure 3).

[1] We realize that $3(W-1) > \frac{1}{2}W \log_2 W$ for $W = 16$ or even for $W = 32$. We remark on the algorithmic complexity as a function of the number of shuffle perations as a matter of mathematical principle, but recognize that this comparison does not explain the faster speed observed in practice with the butterfly-patterned partial sums for $W = 32$. Rather, the observed speedup comes from an overall reduction of instructions and the manner in which the CUDA compiler manages to schedule them. In thr future, if GPU chips are ever built with $W \geq 64$, the improvement in algorithmic complexity may also begin to matter.

Each butterfly computation operates on four entries, within the W p' arrays, that are at the intersection of two rows whose indices differ by a power of 2 and two columns whose indices differ by that same power of 2. Suppose the four values in those entries are $\left[\begin{array}{c|c} a & b \\ \hline c & d \end{array}\right]$; they are replaced by $\left[\begin{array}{c|c} a & c \\ \hline a+b & c+d \end{array}\right]$. Each such replacement operation on four entries is symbolized by  in the figures. Here is CUDA code for constructing the butterfly-patterned table:

```
int r = threadIdx.x & 0x1f;      /* lane ID */
for (int b=0; b < W; b+=b) {     /* 1,2,4,8,...*/
  for (int j=0; j < (W>>(b+1)); j++) {
    d = (((j << 1) + 1) << b) - 1;
    h = (r & (1<<b)) ? a[d] : a[d+(1<<b)];
    v = __shfl_xor(h, 1<<b);
    if (r & (1<<b)) a[d] = v;   |These 3 lines are
    else a[d+(1<<b)] = v;       |replaced below to
    a[d+(1<<b)] += a[d];        |make a new version.
    p[d] = a[d]; } }
p[W-1] = a[W-1];
```

The result is shown in Figure 4(a). The rows of this figure are labeled with tree levels (1 through 4) and S. Observe that in the row labeled S, every lane has the sum of its own a array. Observe also in the row labeled 1, every lane has the root of its own binary search tree for p'. The two rows labeled 2 collectively contain all the level-2 internal nodes of the trees, the four rows labeled 3 contain all the level-3 nodes, and the eight rows labeled 4 contain all the level-4 nodes. Figure 4(b) is the same, but highlights entries that logically belong to lane F; one can see the sum (in the bottom row) as well as the entire binary search tree, indicated by the arrows.

Here is a precise description of the pattern: the entry in row i and column j contains the value $\mathtt{X}_v^w$ where $m = i \oplus (i+1)$, $k = \left\lfloor \frac{m}{2} \right\rfloor$, $\ell = (i \,\&\, \neg m) + (j \,\&\, m)$, $\mathtt{X} =$ "ABCDEFGHIJKLMNOP"$[\ell]$, $v = j \,\&\, (\neg k)$, and $w = v + k$. We use "¬" to indicate bitwise NOT, "&" to indicate bitwise AND, and (as earlier) "⊕" to indicate bitwise XOR.

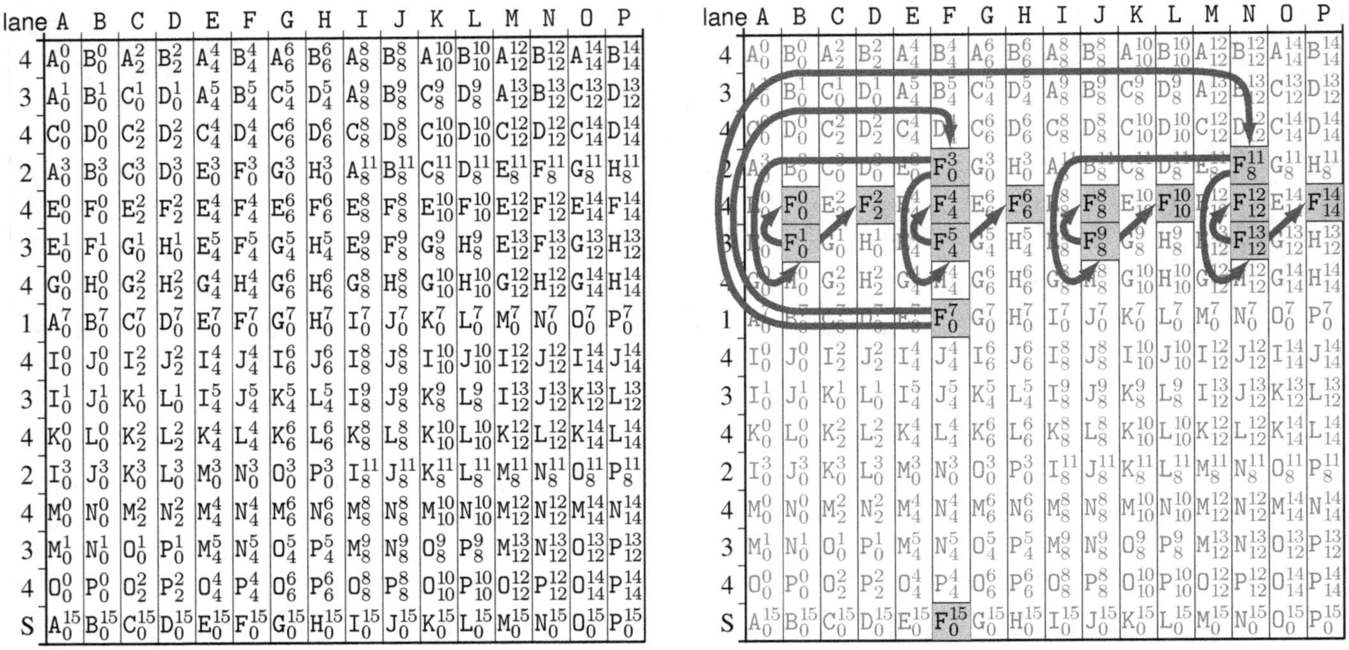

(a) Partial sums resulting from butterfly-pattern summation

(b) The tree and total sum for lane F

Figure 4. The butterfly-patterned table that results from the butterfly computations of Figure 3 ($W = 16$)

Given this table, it's just a matter of making sure that each lane has access to the tree nodes it needs during the binary search. During step i of the binary search ($0 \leq i < \log_2 W$), $2^{(\log_2 W)-i-1}$ `__shfl_xor` instructions are executed so as to make available all entries in rows labeled $(\log_2 W) - i$, and each lane picks off the entry of interest by computing which lane contains it and which `__shfl_xor` instruction will post it; $2^{(\log_2 W)-i-1}$ `__shfl` instructions are also needed to exchange array-address information.

There a variation of this technique that in our experiments turned out to be even faster. It uses a tiny modification of the butterfly computation: instead of replacing $\left[\begin{array}{c|c} a & b \\ \hline c & d \end{array}\right]$ with $\left[\begin{array}{c|c} a & c \\ \hline a+b & c+d \end{array}\right]$, it replaces them with $\left[\begin{array}{c|c} a & d \\ \hline a+b & c+d \end{array}\right]$. This alternate replacement saves one machine instruction at the lowest level in the innermost loop. Merely replace the three lines of CUDA code indicated with these two lines:

```
if (r & (1<<b)) a[d] = a[d+(1<<b)];
a[d+(1<<b)] = a[d] + v;
```

Because the two loops are unrolled (the outer loop we actually unroll manually, and the CUDA compiler then automatically unrolls the inner one), many of the expressions are reduced to constants or hoisted out of the loops at compile time. As a result, the `if` statement represents a single conditional move operation, whereas in the previous version of the code, the `if-else` statement represents two conditional move operations. Eliminating one conditional move operation results in a substantial speed improvement (about 15%).

The resulting table has a slightly more complicated pattern (see Figure 5). It requires a slightly more complicated version of the binary search code, one that either adds or subtracts at each step, and whether to add or subtract at a given step depends on a bit of the lane number (that is, at each step some lanes must add while others subtract).

4. Use in an LDA Application

In Sections 4, 5, and 6 we show how to use these sampling techniques in the context of a kernel for sampling z values for a complete machine-learning application.

For a Latent Dirichlet Allocation model of, for example, a set of documents to which we want to assign topics probabilistically using Gibbs sampling, let M be the number of documents, K be the number of topics, and V be the size of the vocabulary, which is a set of distinct words. Each document is a bag of words, each of which belongs to the vocabulary; any given word can appear in any number of documents, and may appear any number of times in any single document. The documents may be of different lengths.

We are interested in the phase of an uncollapsed Gibbs sampler that draws new z values, given θ and ϕ distributions. Because no z value directly depends on any other z value in this formulation, new z values may all be computed independently (and therefore in parallel to any extent desired).

We assume that we are given an $M \times K$ matrix θ and a $V \times K$ matrix ϕ; the elements of these matrices are non-negative numbers, typically represented as floating-point values. Row m of θ (that is, $\theta[m, \cdot]$) is the (currently assumed) distribution of topics for document m, that is, the relative probabilities (weights) for each of the K possible topics to which the document might be assigned. Note that columns of θ are *not* to be considered as distributions. Sim-

lane	A	B	C	D	E	F	G	H	I	J	K	L	M	N	O	P
4	A_0^0	B_1^1	A_2^2	B_3^3	A_4^4	B_5^5	A_6^6	B_7^7	A_8^8	B_9^9	A_{10}^{10}	B_{11}^{11}	A_{12}^{12}	B_{13}^{13}	A_{14}^{14}	B_{15}^{15}
3	A_0^1	B_0^1	C_2^3	D_2^3	A_4^5	B_4^5	C_6^7	D_6^7	A_8^9	B_8^9	C_{10}^{11}	D_{10}^{11}	A_{12}^{13}	B_{12}^{13}	C_{14}^{15}	D_{14}^{15}
4	C_0^0	D_1^1	C_2^2	D_3^3	C_4^4	D_5^5	C_6^6	D_7^7	C_8^8	D_9^9	C_{10}^{10}	D_{11}^{11}	C_{12}^{12}	D_{13}^{13}	C_{14}^{14}	D_{15}^{15}
2	A_0^3	B_0^3	C_0^3	D_0^3	E_4^7	F_4^7	G_4^7	H_4^7	A_8^{11}	B_8^{11}	C_8^{11}	D_8^{11}	E_{12}^{15}	F_{12}^{15}	G_{12}^{15}	H_{12}^{15}
4	E_0^0	F_1^1	E_2^2	F_3^3	E_4^4	F_5^5	E_6^6	F_7^7	E_8^8	F_9^9	E_{10}^{10}	F_{11}^{11}	E_{12}^{12}	F_{13}^{13}	E_{14}^{14}	F_{15}^{15}
3	E_0^1	F_0^1	G_2^3	H_2^3	E_4^5	F_4^5	G_6^7	H_6^7	E_8^9	F_8^9	G_{10}^{11}	H_{10}^{11}	E_{12}^{13}	F_{12}^{13}	G_{14}^{15}	H_{14}^{15}
4	G_0^0	H_1^1	G_2^2	H_3^3	G_4^4	H_5^5	G_6^6	H_7^7	G_8^8	H_9^9	G_{10}^{10}	H_{11}^{11}	G_{12}^{12}	H_{13}^{13}	G_{14}^{14}	H_{15}^{15}
1	A_0^7	B_0^7	C_0^7	D_0^7	E_0^7	F_0^7	G_0^7	H_0^7	I_8^{15}	J_8^{15}	K_8^{15}	L_8^{15}	M_8^{15}	N_8^{15}	O_8^{15}	P_8^{15}
4	I_0^0	J_1^1	I_2^2	J_3^3	I_4^4	J_5^5	I_6^6	J_7^7	I_8^8	J_9^9	I_{10}^{10}	J_{11}^{11}	I_{12}^{12}	J_{13}^{13}	I_{14}^{14}	J_{15}^{15}
3	I_0^1	J_0^1	K_2^3	L_2^3	I_4^5	J_4^5	K_6^7	L_6^7	I_8^9	J_8^9	K_{10}^{11}	L_{10}^{11}	I_{12}^{13}	J_{12}^{13}	K_{14}^{15}	L_{14}^{15}
4	K_0^0	L_1^1	K_2^2	L_3^3	K_4^4	L_5^5	K_6^6	L_7^7	K_8^8	L_9^9	K_{10}^{10}	L_{11}^{11}	K_{12}^{12}	L_{13}^{13}	K_{14}^{14}	L_{15}^{15}
2	I_0^3	J_0^3	K_0^3	L_0^3	M_4^7	N_4^7	O_4^7	P_4^7	I_8^{11}	J_8^{11}	K_8^{11}	L_8^{11}	M_{12}^{15}	N_{12}^{15}	O_{12}^{15}	P_{12}^{15}
4	M_0^0	N_1^1	M_2^2	N_3^3	M_4^4	N_5^5	M_6^6	N_7^7	M_8^8	N_9^9	M_{10}^{10}	N_{11}^{11}	M_{12}^{12}	N_{13}^{13}	M_{14}^{14}	N_{15}^{15}
3	M_0^1	N_0^1	O_2^3	P_2^3	M_4^5	N_4^5	O_6^7	P_6^7	M_8^9	N_8^9	O_{10}^{11}	P_{10}^{11}	M_{12}^{13}	N_{12}^{13}	O_{14}^{15}	P_{14}^{15}
4	O_0^0	P_1^1	O_2^2	P_3^3	O_4^4	P_5^5	O_6^6	P_7^7	O_8^8	P_9^9	O_{10}^{10}	P_{11}^{11}	O_{12}^{12}	P_{13}^{13}	O_{14}^{14}	P_{15}^{15}
S	A_0^{15}	B_0^{15}	C_0^{15}	D_0^{15}	E_0^{15}	F_0^{15}	G_0^{15}	H_0^{15}	I_0^{15}	J_0^{15}	K_0^{15}	L_0^{15}	M_0^{15}	N_0^{15}	O_0^{15}	P_0^{15}

Figure 5. Alternate "add-subtract" butterfly pattern for p'

ilarly, column k of ϕ (that is, $\phi[\cdot, k]$) is the (currently assumed) distribution of words for topic k, that is, the weights with which the V possible words in the vocabulary are associated with the topic. Note that rows of ϕ are *not* to be considered as distributions. We organize θ as rows and ϕ as columns for engineering reasons: we want the K entries obtained by ranging over all possible topics to be contiguous in memory so as to take advantage of memory cache structure.

We also assume that we are given (i) a length-M vector of nonnegative integers N such that $N[m]$ is the number of words in document m, and (ii) an $M \times N$ ragged array w, by which we mean that for $0 \leq m < M$, $w[m]$ is a vector of length $N[m]$. Each element of w is a word type (a nonnegative integer less than V) and may therefore be used as a first index for ϕ. Our goal, given K, M, V, N, ϕ, θ, and w and assuming the use of a temporary $M \times N \times K$ ragged work array a (which we will later optimize away), is to compute all the elements for an $M \times N$ ragged array z as follows: For all m such that $0 \leq m < M$ and for all i such that $0 \leq i < N[m]$, do two things: first, for all k such that $0 \leq k < K$, let $a[m][i][k] = \theta[m, k] \times \phi[w[m, i], k]$; second, let $z[m, i]$ be a nonnegative integer less than K, chosen randomly in such a way that the probability of choosing the value k' is $a[m][i][k']/\sigma$ where $\sigma = \sum_{0 \leq k < K} a[m][i][k]$. Thus, $a[m][i][k']$ is a relative (unnormalized) probability, and $a[m][i][k']/\sigma$ is an absolute (normalized) probability.

Algorithm 1 is a basic implementation of this process. We remark that a "**let**" statement creates a local binding of a scalar (single-valued) variable and gives it a value, that a "**local array**" declaration creates a local binding of an array variable (containing an element value for each indexable position in the array), and that distinct iterations of a containing "**for**" or "**for all**" construct are understood to create distinct and independent instantiations of such local variables for each iteration. The iterations of "**for** ... from ... through ..." are executed sequentially in a specific order; but the iterations of a "**for all**" construct are intended to be computationally independent and therefore may be executed in any order, or in parallel, or in any sequential-parallel combination. We use angle brackets to indicate the use of a "code chunk" that is defined as a separate algorithm; such a use indicates that the definition of the code chunk should be inserted at the use site, possibly with parameter substitution, as if it were a C macro, but surrounded by **begin** and **end** (this programming-language technicality ensures that the scope of any variable declared within the code chunk is confined to that code chunk).

The computation of the θ-ϕ products (lines 7–8 of Algorithm 1) is straightforward. The computation of partial sums (lines 10–12) is sequential; the variable *sum* accumulates the

Algorithm 1 Drawing new z values

```
1:  procedure DRAWZ(N[M], θ[M,K], φ[V,K],
2:                  w[M][N]; output z[M,N])
3:    local array a[M][N][K], p[M][N][K]
4:    for all 0 ≤ m < M do
5:      for all 0 ≤ i < N[m] do
6:        ▷ Compute θ-φ products
7:        for all 0 ≤ k < K do
8:          a[m][i][k] := θ[m,k] × φ[w[m][i],k]
9:        ▷ Compute partials sums of the products
10:       let sum = 0.0
11:       for k from 0 through K − 1 do
12:         sum += a[m][i][k]; p[m][i][k] := sum
13:       let j = 0
14:       ⟨search the table p[m][i] of partial sums⟩
15:       z[m,i] := j
16: end
```

Algorithm 2 Simple linear search

```
code chunk ⟨search the table P of partial sums⟩:
  let u = random value chosen from [0.0, 1.0)
  let u′ = sum × u
  while j < K − 1 and u′ ≥ P[j] do j += 1
end
```

Algorithm 3 Simple binary search

```
code chunk ⟨search the table P of partial sums⟩:
  let u = random value chosen from [0.0, 1.0)
  let u′ = sum × u, k = K − 1
  while j < k do
    let mid = ⌊(j + k)/2⌋
    if u′ < P[mid] then k := mid
    else j := mid + 1
end
```

Algorithm 4 Drawing z values (transposed access)

```
procedure DrawZ(N[M], θ[M,K], φ[V,K],
                w[M][N]; output z[M,N])
  local array p_local[M][K], a_local[M][W]
  for all 0 ≤ q < M/W do
    local array c_warp[W,W]
    for SIMD 0 ≤ r < W do
      let m = q × W + r
      local array θ_local[K]
      ⟨cache θ values into θ_local⟩
      let i_master = 0
      while any(i_master < N[m]) do
        let i = min(i_master, N[m] − 1)
        ⟨compute partial sums of θ-φ products⟩
        let j = 0
        ⟨search the table p_local[m] of partial sums⟩
        z[m,i] := j
        i_master += 1
end
```

Algorithm 5 Caching θ values (transposed access)

```
code chunk ⟨cache θ values into θ_local⟩:
  let j = 0
  while j < (K mod W) do                ▷ Cache the remnant
    θ_local[j] := θ[m,j];  j += 1
  while j < K do                        ▷ Cache all W × W blocks
    for k from 0 through W − 1 do
      ▷ Next line uses transposed access to θ
      θ_local[j+k] := θ[q × W + k, j + r]
    j += W
end
```

products, and successive values of sum are stored into the array p. A random integer is chosen for $z[m,i]$ by choosing a random value uniformly from the range $[0,0,1.0)$, scaling it by the final value of sum (which has the same algorithmic effect as dividing each $p[m][i][k]$ by that value, for all $0 \le k < K$, to turn it into an absolute probability), and then searching the subarray $p[m][i]$ to find the smallest entry that is larger than the scaled value (and if there are several such entries, all equal, then the one with the smallest index is chosen); the index j of that entry is used as the desired randomly chosen integer. A simple linear search (Algorithm 2) can do the job, but a binary search (Algorithm 3) can be used instead, which is faster, on average, for K sufficiently large [13, exercise 6.2.1-5].

5. Blocking and Transposition

Anticipating certain characteristics of the hardware, we make some commitments as to how the algorithm will be executed. We assume that arrays are laid out in row-major order (as they are when using C or CUDA). Let W be a machine-dependent constant (typically 16 or 32, but for now we do not require that W be a power of 2). For purposes of illustration we assume $W = 8$ and also $K = 19$. We divide the documents into groups of size W and assume that M is an exact multiple of W. (In the overall application, the set of documents can be padded with empty documents so as to make M be an exact multiple of W without affecting the overall behavior of the algorithm on the "real" documents.) We turn the outermost loop of Algorithm 1 (with index variable m) into two nested loops with index variables q and r, from which the equivalent value for m is then computed. We commit to making the loop with index variable i sequential, to treating the iterations of the loop on q as independent (and therefore possibly parallel), and to treating the iterations of the loop on r as executed by a SIMD "thread warp" of size W, that is, parallel and implicitly lock-step synchronized. As a result, we view each of the M documents as being processed by a separate thread. A benefit of making the loop on i sequential is that the array p can be made two-dimensional and non-ragged, having size $M \times K$. We fuse the loop that computes θ-ϕ products with the loop that computes partial sums; this eliminates the need for the array a, but instead (for reasons explained below) we use a_{local} as a two-dimensional, non-ragged array of size $M \times W$ that is used only when $K \ge W$. Within the loop on q we declare a local work array c_{warp} of size $W \times W$ that will be used to exchange information by the W threads within a warp; our eventual intent is that this array will reside in GPU registers. We cache values from the array θ in a per-thread array θ_{local} of length K, anticipating that such cached values will reside in a faster memory and be used repeatedly by the loop on i.

There is, however, a subtle problem with the loop controlling index variable i: the upper bound $N[m]$ for the loop variable may be different for different threads. As a result, in the last iterations it may be that some threads have "gone to sleep" because they reached their upper loop bound earlier than other threads in the warp. This is undesirable because, as we shall see, we rely on all threads "staying awake" so that they can assist each other. Therefore, we rewrite the loop control to use a "master index" idiom and exploit the trick of allowing a thread to perform its last iteration (with $i = N[m]-1$) multiple times, which doesn't work for many algorithms but is acceptable for LDA Gibbs.

The result of all these code transformations is Algorithm 4, which makes use of three code chunks: Algorithm 5, Algorithm 6, and either Algorithm 2 or Algorithm 3. Algorithms 5 and 6, besides using SIMD thread warps of size W to process documents in groups of size W, also process topics in blocks of size W. This allows the innermost loops to process "little" arrays of size $W \times W$. If K (the number of topics) is not a multiple of W, then there will be a *remnant* of size $K \bmod W$. To make looping code slightly simpler, we put the remnant at the *front* of each array, rather than at the end. For $W = 8$ and $K = 19$, topics 0, 1, and 2 form the remnant; topics 3–10 form a block of length 8; and topics 11–18 form a second block. This organization of arrays into

Algorithm 6 Compute partial sums (transposed access)

1: **code chunk** ⟨compute partial sums of θ-ϕ products⟩:
2:   **let** $c = w[m][i]$
3:   **for all** $0 \le k < W$ **do**
4:     $c_{\text{warp}}[k, r] := c$ ▷ Transposed access to c_{warp}
5:   **let** $sum = 0.0$
6:   **let** $j = 0$
7:   **while** $j < (K \bmod W)$ **do**   ▷ Process the remnant
8:     $sum \mathrel{+}= (\theta_{\text{local}}[j] \times \phi[c, j])$; $p_{\text{local}}[m]j] := sum$
9:     $j \mathrel{+}= 1$
10:   **while** $j < K$ **do**   ▷ Process all $W \times W$ blocks
11:     **for** k from 0 through $W - 1$ **do**
12:       ▷ Next line uses transposed access to ϕ
13:       $a_{\text{local}}[m, k] := \theta_{\text{local}}[j + k] \times \phi[c_{\text{warp}}[r, k], j + r]$
14:     **for** k from 0 through $W - 1$ **do**
15:       ▷ Next line uses transposed access to a_{local}, alas
16:       $sum \mathrel{+}= a_{\text{local}}[q \times W + k, r]$
17:       $p_{\text{local}}[m, j + k] := sum$
18:     $j \mathrel{+}= W$
19: **end**

blocks allows reduction of the cost of accessing data in main memory by performing *transposed accesses*.

The simplest use of transposed memory access occurs in Algorithm 5. For every document, a θ value is fetched for every topic. The topics are regarded as divided into a leading remnant (if any) and then a sequence of blocks of length W. The **while** loop on lines 3–4 handles the remnant, and then the following **while** loop processes successive blocks. On line 8 within the inner loop, note that the reference is to $\theta[q \times W + k, j + r]$ rather than the expected $\theta[q \times W + r, j + k]$ (which would be the same as $\theta[m, j + k]$ because $m = q \times W + r$). The result is that when the W threads of a SIMD warp execute this code and all access θ simultaneously, they access W consecutive memory locations, which can typically be fetched by a hardware memory controller much more efficiently than W memory locations separated by stride K. Another way to think about it is that on any given single iteration of the loop on lines 6–8 (which overall is designed to fetch one $W \times W$ block of θ values) instead of every thread in the warp fetching its kth value from the θ array, all the threads work together to fetch all W values that are needed by thread k of the warp. Each thread then stores what it has fetched into its local copy of the array θ_{local}.

Algorithm 6 compensates for this transposition of θ. The idea is also to divide each row of ϕ into blocks (possibly preceded by a remnant) and perform transposed accesses to ϕ. To do this, each thread needs to know which row of ϕ every other thread is interested in; this is done through the $W \times W$ local work array c_{warp}. In line 2, each thread figures out which word is the ith word of its document and calls it c; in lines 3–4 it then stores its value for c into every element of row r of the array c_{warp}. This is not an especially fast

Algorithm 7 Drawing new z values using a butterfly table

1: **procedure** DRAWZ$(N[M], \theta[M, K], \phi[V, K],$
2:         $w[M][N]$; **output** $z[M, N])$
3:   ▷ W (the "warp size") must be a power of 2,
4:   ▷ and M must be a multiple of W.
5:   **for all** $0 \le q < M/W$ **do**
6:     **for SIMD** $0 \le r < W$ **do**
7:       **let** $m = q \times W + r$
8:       **local array** $p'[K], \theta_{\text{local}}[K]$
9:       **register array** $a_{\text{reg}}[W], c_{\text{warp}}[W]$
10:       ⟨cache θ values into θ_{local}⟩
11:       **let** $i_{\text{master}} = 0$
12:       **while** $any(i_{\text{master}} < N[m])$ **do**
13:         **let** $i = min(i_{\text{master}}, N[m] - 1)$
14:         ⟨SIMD compute butterfly partial sums⟩
15:         **let** $j = 0$
16:         ⟨SIMD search butterfly partial sums⟩
17:         $z[m, i] := j$
18:         $i_{\text{master}} \mathrel{+}= 1$
19: **end**

operation, but it pays for itself later on. The loop in lines 7–9 computes θ-ϕ products and partial sums p in the usual way (remember that the remnant in θ_{local} is not transposed), but the loop in lines 11–13 processes a block to compute product values to store into the a_{local} array; the access to ϕ on line 13 is transposed (note that the accesses to θ_{local} and c_{warp} are *not* transposed; because they were constructed and stored in transposed form, normal fetches cause their values to line up correctly with the ϕ values obtained by a transposed fetch). So this is pretty good; but in line 16 we finally pay the piper: in order to have the finally computed partial sums p reside in the correct lane for the binary search, it is necessary to perform a transposed access to a_{local} on line 16; but a_{local} is a local array, so transposed accesses are bad rather than good, and this occurs in an inner loop, so performance still suffers.

6. Using Butterfly-patterned Partial Sums

We avoid the cost of the final transposition of a_{local} by not requiring the partial sums table p for each thread to be entirely in the local memory of that thread. Instead, for each $W \times W$ block we use a butterfly-patterned table p'.

Our final version is Algorithm 7. It is similar to Algorithm 4, but declares all local arrays so as to be thread-local (and specifies that arrays a_{reg} and c_{warp} should reside in registers). It uses Algorithm 5 to cache θ values in θ_{local}, and also uses three new code chunks: Algorithms 8, 9, and 10. For Algorithm 7 to work properly, W must be a power of 2.

Algorithm 8 computes the butterfly-patterned table. The tricky part is the loop on lines 13–23, which is implemented by the alternate (faster) version of the CUDA code shown in Section 3.

Within a butterfly-patterned block of partial sums, Algorithm 9 performs a binary search as follows. The u' value is

Algorithm 8 Compute a butterfly-patterned table of sums

```
code chunk ⟨SIMD compute butterfly partial sums⟩:
  let c = w[m][i]
  for all 0 ≤ k < W do
    c_warp[k] := __shfl(c, k)
  let sum = 0.0, j = 0
  while j < (K mod W) do          ▷ Process the remnant
    sum += (θ_local[j] × ϕ[c, j]); p′[j] := sum
    j := j + 1
  while j < K do                  ▷ Process all W × W blocks
    for k from 0 through W − 1 do
      ▷ Next line uses transposed access to ϕ
      a_reg[k] := θ_local[j + k] × ϕ[c_warp[k], j + r]
    for b from 0 through (log2 W) − 1 do
      let bit = 2^b
      for i from 0 through W/(2×bit) − 1 do
        let d = 2 × bit × i + (bit − 1)
        let h = (if (m & bit) ≠ 0
                   then a_reg[d]
                   else a_reg[d + bit])
        let v = __shfl_xor(h, bit)
        if (r & bit) ≠ 0 then a_reg[d] := a_reg[d + bit]
        a_reg[d + bit] := a_reg[d] + v
        p′[j + d] := a_reg[d]
    sum += a_reg[W − 1]; p′[W − 1] := sum
    j := j + W
end
```

Algorithm 9 Searching within a butterfly-patterned table

```
code chunk ⟨SIMD search butterfly partial sums⟩:
  let u = random value chosen from [0.0, 1.0)
  let u′ = sum × u, j = 0, k = ⌊K/W⌋ − 1
  let searchBase = (K mod W) + (W − 1)
  ▷ Binary search to find correct block of size W
  while j < k do
    let mid = ⌊(j + k)/2⌋
    if u′ < p′[mid × W + searchBase] then k := mid
    else j := mid + 1
  let blockBase = (K mod W) + j × W
  if K ≥ W then
    ⟨SIMD butterfly search one block⟩
  if blockBase > 0 then
    if u′ < p′[m, blockBase − 1] then
      ▷ Not in a block after all, so search remnant
      for i from 0 through (K mod W) − 1 do
        if u′ < p′[i] then { j := i; break }
end
```

computed exactly as in Algorithms 2 and 3, and a block to be searched is identified by performing a binary search on the subarray consisting of just the last row of each block; this identifies a specific block to search. If $K \geq W$, then some

Algorithm 10 Butterfly search within one $W \times W$ block

```
code chunk ⟨SIMD butterfly search one block⟩:
  let lowValue = (if blockBase > 0
                    then p′[blockBase − 1]
                    else 0)
  let highValue = p′[blockBase + (W − 1)]
  let flip = 0
  ▷ Butterfly search within the block of size W
  for b from 0 through (log2 W) − 1 do
    let bit = 2^(((log2 W)−1)−b)
    let mask = ((W − 1) × (2 × bit)) & (W − 1)
    let y = 0
    for i from 0 through W/(2×bit) − 1 do
      let d = (bit − 1) + 2 × bit × i
      let him = (d & mask) + (r & ¬mask)
      let hisBlockBase = __shfl(blockBase, him)
      let t = __shfl_xor(p′[hisBlockBase + d], flip)
      if ((r ⊕ d) & mask) = 0 then y := t
    let compareValue = (if (r & bit) ≠ 0
                          then highValue − y
                          else lowValue + y)
    if stop < compareValue then
      highValue := compareValue
      flip := flip ⊕ (bit & r)
    else
      lowValue := compareValue
      flip := flip ⊕ (bit & ¬r)
  j := blockBase + (flip ⊕ r)
end
```

$W \times W$ block is identified, and it is searched, but it is possible that the desired u' value does not lie within that block; in that case, the remnant is searched using a linear search.

In order to search within a block, Algorithm 10 maintains two additional state variables *lowValue* and *highValue*. An invariant is that if lane m has indices j through k of a block still under consideration, then $lowValue = m_0^{blockBase+j-1}$ and $highValue = m_0^{blockBase+k}$. In order to cut the search range in half, the binary search needs to compare the u' value to the midpoint value $m_0^{blockBase+mid}$ where $mid = \left\lfloor \frac{j+k}{2} \right\rfloor$; in Algorithm 3 this value is of course an entry in the p array, but in Algorithm 10 the midpoint value is *calculated* by choosing an appropriate entry from the butterfly-patterned p' array and then either adding it to *lowValue* or subtracting it from *highValue*. Whether to add or subtract on iteration number b (where the $\log_2 W$ iterations are numbered starting from 0) depends on whether bit b (counting from the right starting at 0) of the binary representation of m is 0 or 1, respectively. Depending on the result of the comparison of the midpoint value with the u' value, the midpoint value is assigned to either *lowValue* and *highValue*, maintaining the invariant, and a bit of a third state variable *flip* (initially 0) is updated. When the binary search is complete, the correct index to select is computed from the value in *flip*.

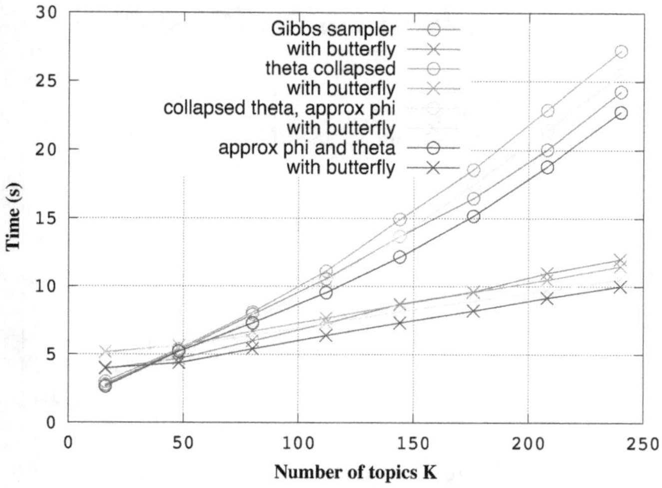

Figure 6. Measurements of execution time, with and without butterfly-patterned partial sums, for four variations of a machine-learning application ($K = 32k + 16, 0 \leq k \leq 7$)

The threads in a warp assist one another in fetching tree nodes using the loop in lines 12–17; the function `__shfl_xor` effects this data transfer in line 16.

7. Evaluation

We coded four versions of a complete LDA Gibbs-sampler topic-modeling algorithm in CUDA 6.5 for an NVIDIA Titan Black GPU ($W = 32$). For each version we tested two variants, one using Algorithm 1 (using the binary search of Algorithm 3) and one using Algorithm 7. (These algorithms are the ones on which we reported at ICML 2015 [25]; that paper includes only a passing mention of this use of butterfly-patterned partial sums, and refers to an early version of this paper [22].) All eight variants were tested for speed using a Wikipedia-based dataset with number of documents $M = 43556$, vocabulary size $V = 37286$, total number of words in corpus $\Sigma N = 3072662$ (therefore average document size $(\Sigma N)/M \approx 70.5$), and maximum document size $\max N = 307$. Each variant was measured using eight different values for the number of topics K (16, 48, 80, 112, 144, 176, 208, and 240), in each case performing 100 sampling iterations and measuring the execution time of the entire application, not just the part that draws z values. Best performance requires unrolling three loops in Algorithm 8; we had to manually unroll the loop that starts on line 13, and the CUDA compiler then automatically unrolled the loops that start on lines 10 and 15. The performance results are shown in Figure 6. The butterfly variants are faster for $K \geq 80$. For $K \geq 200$, for each of the four versions the butterfly variant is more than twice as fast.

In CUDA 7.5 on the same hardware, we measured Algorithms 1, 7, and a variant of 4 that transposes in registers (as in Figure 2) for 32-bit intermediate values (Figure 7(a)) and for 64-bit intermediate values (Figure 7(b)), using the same Wikipedia-based dataset. Each of the three algorithms was measured for $K = 4, 8, 12, 16, \ldots, 1024$, again in each case performing 100 sampling iterations and measuring the execution time of the entire application, not just the part that draws z values. Each data point shown in Figure 7 (and in Figure 8) is an average of five runs; the maximum relative standard deviation was 0.38. One can see that the measurements for Algorithms 4 and 7 have a distinctive sawtooth pattern: the amount by which a measurement dips below an upper-bounding line depends on the number of trailing zero-bits in the bionary representation of the length of the remnant (that is, the value of $K \bmod 32$).

For 32-bit intermediate data (Figure 7(a)), Algorithm 7 is faster than Algorithm 4 for all $K > 576$; moreover, it is also faster for all multiples of 32 greater than 64. For $K = 512$, Algorithm 7 is 8% faster than Algorithm 4; for $K = 1024$, it is 13% faster. For 64-bit intermediate data (Figure 7(b)), Algorithm 7 is faster than Algorithm 4 for all $K > 64$. For $K = 512$, Algorithm 7 is 33% faster than Algorithm 4; for $K = 1024$, it is 35% faster.

Measurements of just Algorithms 4 and 7, for all $480 \leq K \leq 544$ (not just multiples of 4), are shown in Figures 8(a) and 8(b), which exhibit the sawtooth pattern in greater detail in the measurements for both algorithms.

It is difficult to measure GPU memory bandwidth and computational costs directly, because CUDA "abstracts" the hardware architecture, and the optimizing compiler does extraordinarily complex instruction scheduling, so we relied entirely on measuring wall-clock time for entire application executions. Nevertheless, we can draw some inferences.

In each of Figures 7(a) and 7(b), the "register transpose" runs (Algorithm 4) shows the improvement over the baseline (Algorithm 1) that comes from the combination of using transposed (therefore coalesced) memory accesses, compensating for the transposition by shuffling in-register among lanes, and otherwise keeping the computation exactly the same. We may infer that the net improvement over the baseline is attributable entirely to improved use of memory bandwidth (less the cost of in-register shuffling). The "butterfly partial sums" run (Algorithm 7) shows additional improvement from applying the butterfly-patterned partial-sums trick to Algorithm 4, and this additional net improvement is attributable entirely to a combination of reduced computation and reduced register shuffling. Ideally, one would like to "complete the diamond" by evaluating the impact of the butterfly directly over the baseline, but the butterfly makes sense only in conjunction with transposed memory access. For $K = 1024$, then, it is fair to say that for 32-bit intermediate data, taking advantage of memory coalescing provides a 70% speed improvement over the baseline algorithm, and the butterfly-patterned partial-sums technique provides an additional improvement of 4 percentage points relative to baseline, for an overall speedup of 74% over the baseline; and also that for 64-bit intermediate data, taking advantage of memory coalescing provides

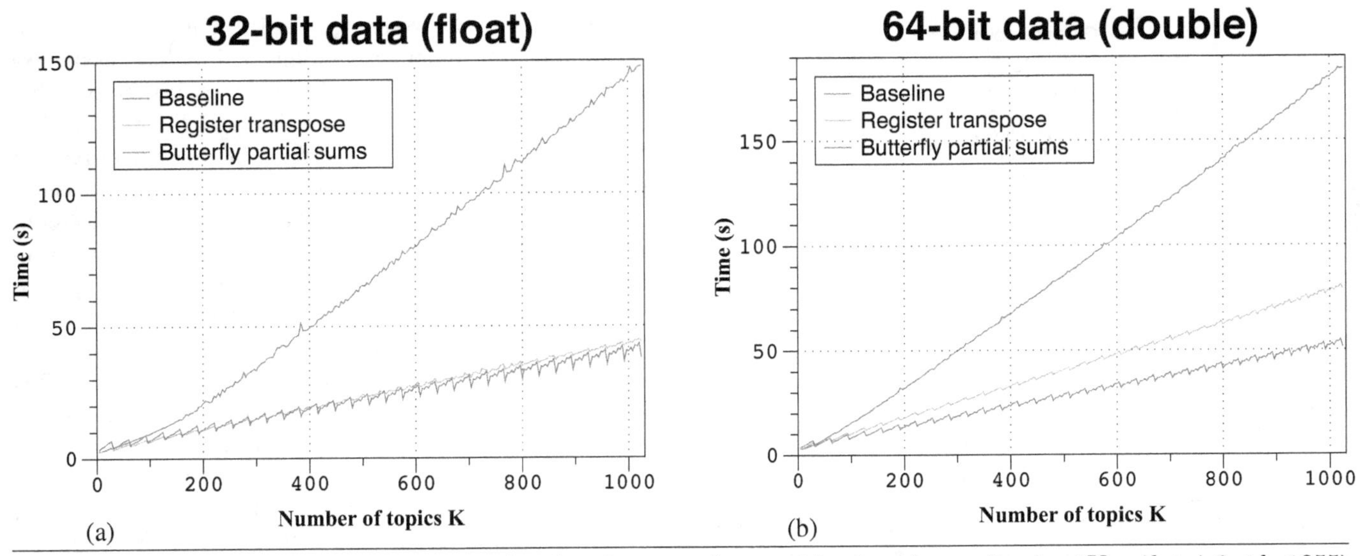

Figure 7. Two sets of measurements of execution time for a complete machine-learning application ($K = 4k + 4, 0 \leq k \leq 255$)

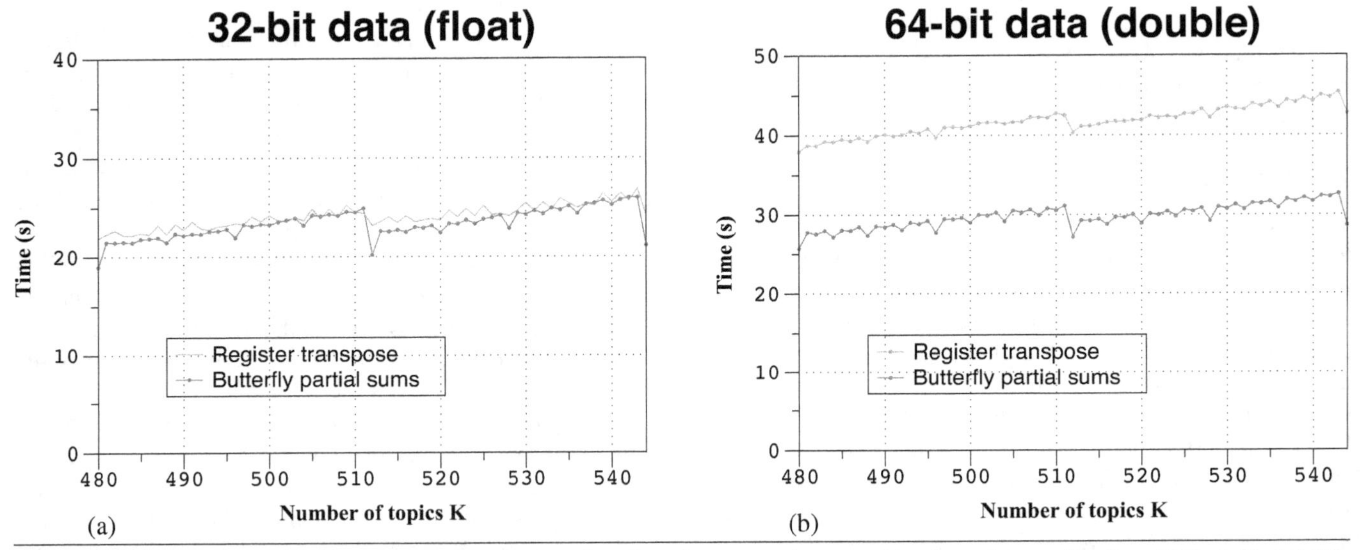

Figure 8. Two more sets of measurements of execution time for a complete machine-learning application ($480 \leq K \leq 544$)

a 56% speed improvement over the baseline algorithm, and the butterfly-patterned partial-sums technique provides an additional improvement of 15 percentage points relative to baseline, for an overall speedup of 71% over the baseline.

8. Related Work

Because the computed probabilities are relative in our LDA application, it is necessary to compute all of them and then to compute, if nothing else, their sum, so that the relative probabilities can be effectively normalized. Therefore every method for drawing from a discrete distribution represented by a set of relative probabilities involves some amount of preprocessing before drawing from the distribution. The various algorithms in the literature have differing tradeoffs according to what technique is used for preprocessing and what technique is used for drawing; some algorithms also accommodate incremental updating of the relative probabilities by providing a technique for incremental preprocessing.

Instead of doing a binary search on the partial sums, one can instead (as Marsaglia [18] observes in passing) construct a search tree using the principles of Huffman encoding [9] (independently rediscovered by Zimmerman[33]) to minimize the expected number of comparisons. In either case the complexity of the search is $O(\log n)$, but the optimized search may have a smaller constant, obtained at the expense of a preprocessing step that must sort the relative probabilities and therefore has complexity $\Omega(n \log n)$.

Walker [27, 28] describes what we now call the "alias" method, in which n relative probabilities are preprocessed into two additional tables F and A of length n. To draw a value from the distribution, let k be a integer chosen uniformly at random from $\{0, 1, 2, \ldots, n-1\}$ and let u be chosen uniformly at random from the real interval $[0, 1)$. Then the value drawn is (**if** $u < F_k$ **then** k **else** A_k). Therefore, once the tables F and A have been produced, the complexity of drawing a value from the distribution is $O(1)$, assuming that the cost of an array access is $O(1)$. Walker's method [28] for producing the tables F and A requires time $\Theta(n^2)$; it is easy to reduce this to $\Omega(n \log n)$ by sorting the probabilities [12, exercise 3.4.1-7] and then using, say, priority heaps instead of a list for the intermediate data structure. Either version heuristically attempts to minimize the probability of having to access the table A.

Vose [26] describes a preprocessing algorithm, with proof, that further reduces the preprocessing complexity of the alias method to $\Theta(n)$. The tradeoff that permits this improvement is that the preprocessing algorithm makes no attempt to minimize the probability of accessing the array A.

Matias *et al.* [19] describe a technique for preprocessing a set of relative probabilities into a set of trees, after which a sequence of intermixed generate (draw) and update operations can be performed, where an update operation changes just one of the relative probabilities; a single generate operation takes $O(\log^* n)$ expected time, and a single update operation takes $O(\log^* n)$ amortized expected time.

Li *et al.* [15] describe a modified LDA topic modeling algorithm, which they call Metropolis-Hastings-Walker sampling, that uses Walker's alias method but amortizes the cost of constructing the table by drawing from the same table during multiple consecutive sampling iterations of a Metropolis-Hastings sampler; their paper provides some justification for why it is acceptable to use a "slightly stale" alias table (their words) for the purposes of this application.

The trees embedded in the butterfly-patterned partial-sums table are reminiscent of Fenwick's binary-indexed trees [6], in that tree nodes containing partial sums are stored as array elements whose addresses are calculated through bit-manipulation of indices. However, the butterfly-patterned table as formulated here differs in three ways: (a) it stores partial sums for multiple distributions in a two-dimensional format rather than partial sums for a single distribution in a one-dimensional format; (b) it requires maintenance of two running values rather than one as a search descends the tree; and (c) at each step of the search it will always perform either an addition to one of the running values or subtraction from the other running value, whereas the Fenwick search always uses subtraction on its single running value, but at each step the subtraction is conditional.

There is a growing literature on interesting and clever techniques for improving the speed of parallel-prefix computations, especially on GPU architectures [5, 17, 31], and these techniques could possibly also be profitably applied to the problem of sampling from discrete distributions. However, we emphasize that, in contrast, the entire point of the butterfly-patterned partial-sums algorithm presented here is not to compute a complete prefix-sum table *faster*, but to *avoid* computing most of it in the first place.

9. Conclusions

This paper focuses on one low-level "utility algorithm": independent sampling from a large number of discrete distributions. The technique presented here can be compared to an optimization that applies "only" to sorting. But sorting is an operation of broad utility that can be exploited in a wide variety of applications. In the same way, drawing from multiple discrete distributions is the most important component of a wide class of machine learning algorithms: discrete latent variable models. This class encompasses mixture models (such as Gaussian mixture models), mixed membership models (such as topic models), mixtures of experts (such as probabilistic decision trees), learning meta-algorithms (such as Bayesian averaging), and more. Just in the specific case of LDA, we are currently aware of more than 50 variants. The currently most scalable and statistically efficient inference training procedures for LDA are based on the Stochastic Expectation Maximization variant of the Gibbs sampling procedure; they all use independent sampling as their most costly step, so improving the speed of independent sampling greatly improves the overall speed of these training algorithms. From an academic perspective, much recent work on Bayesian non-parametrics and hierarchical modeling builds upon LDA (for example, the Pachinko Allocation model and the Chinese Restaurant Franchise model). Speeding up LDA is a fundamental first step toward making such more advanced models practical. From an industrial perspective, LDA and its extensions are now making their way into useful tools and services, for example in product recommendation systems [8], consumer personalization systems [1], audience expansion systems for online advertisement [11], and document summarization [21]. It is precisely as this technology is being deployed that engineering for speed, such as we do in this paper, is most useful. Independent sampling is also used in chemistry and physics, for example to compute the ground state of Ising models (and Potts models) and to simulate Stochastic Cellular Automata.

The technique of constructing butterfly-patterned partial sums appears to be best suited for situations where a SIMD processor is used to compute tables of relative probabilities for multiple discrete distributions, each of which is then used just once to draw a single value, and where each thread, when computing its table, must fetch data from a contiguous region of memory whose address is computed from other data. The LDA application for which we developed the technique has these characteristics. The technique uses transposed memory access in order to allow a SIMD memory controller to touch at most three cache lines on each fetch, then cheaply constructs a butterfly-patterned set of partial sums that are just adequate to allow partial sums actually needed to be constructed on the fly during the course of a binary search. This butterfly-pattern approach provides significant speedup (up to 35%) over a transposition-only approach for our LDA machine-learning application.

References

[1] Amr Ahmed, Linagjie Hong, and Alexander J. Smola. Nested Chinese Restaurant Franchise Processes: Applications to user tracking and document modeling. In *Proc. ICML 2013: 30th International Conference on Machine Learning*, pages 1426–1434, Brookline, MA, June 2015. Microtome Publishing. URL: `http://www.jmlr.org/proceedings/papers/v28/ahmed13.pdf`.

[2] Christopher M. Bishop. *Pattern Recognition and Machine Learning (Information Science and Statistics)*. Springer-Verlag New York, Inc., 2006.

[3] David M. Blei. Probabilistic topic models. *Commun. ACM*, 55(4):77–84, April 2012. `doi:10.1145/2133806.2133826`.

[4] David M. Blei, Andrew Y. Ng, and Michael I. Jordan. Latent Dirichlet allocation. *J. Machine Learning Research*, 3:993–1022, March 2003. URL: `http://dl.acm.org/citation.cfm?id=944919.944937`.

[5] Yuri Dotsenko, Naga K. Govindaraju, Peter-Pike Sloan, Charles Boyd, and John Manferdelli. Fast scan algorithms on graphics processors. In *Proc. 22nd Annual International Conference on Supercomputing*, ICS '08, pages 205–213, New York, 2008. ACM. `doi:10.1145/1375527.1375559`.

[6] Peter M. Fenwick. A new data structure for cumulative frequency tables. *Software: Practice and Experience*, 24(3):327–336, 1994. `doi:10.1002/spe.4380240306`.

[7] Thomas L. Griffiths and Mark Steyvers. Finding scientific topics. *Proc. National Academy of Sciences of the United States of America*, 101(suppl 1):5228–5235, 2004. `doi:10.1073/pnas.0307752101`.

[8] Diane Hu, Rob Hall, and Josh Attenberg. Style in the long tail: Discovering unique interests with latent variable models in large scale social E-commerce. In *Proc. 20th ACM SIGKDD International Conference on Knowledge Discovery and Data Mining*, KDD '14, pages 1640–1649, New York, August 2014. ACM. URL: `http://doi.acm.org/10.1145/2623330.2623338`, `doi:10.1145/2623330.2623338`.

[9] D. A. Huffman. A method for the construction of minimum-redundancy codes. *Proc. IRE*, 40(9):1098–1101, Sept 1952. `doi:10.1109/JRPROC.1952.273898`.

[10] S. Lennart Johnsson, Tim Harris, and Kapil K. Mathur. Matrix multiplication on the Connection Machine. In *Proc. 1989 ACM/IEEE Conference on Supercomputing*, pages 326–332, New York, NY, USA, 1989. ACM. URL: `http://doi.acm.org/10.1145/76263.76298`.

[11] Joon Hee Kim, Amin Mantrach, Alejandro Jaimes, and Alice Oh. How to compete online for news audience: Modeling words that attract clicks. In *Proc. 22nd ACM SIGKDD International Conference on Knowledge Discovery and Data Mining*, KDD '16, pages 1645–1654, New York, August 2016. ACM. URL: `http://doi.acm.org/10.1145/2939672.2939873`, `doi:10.1145/2939672.2939873`.

[12] Donald E. Knuth. *Seminumerical Algorithms* (third edition), volume 2 of *The Art of Computer Programming*. Addison-Wesley, Reading, Massachusetts, 1998.

[13] Donald E. Knuth. *Sorting and Searching* (second edition), volume 3 of *The Art of Computer Programming*. Addison-Wesley, Reading, Massachusetts, 1998.

[14] Anthony Lee, Christopher Yau, Michael B. Giles, Arnaud Doucet, and Christopher C. Holmes. On the utility of graphics cards to perform massively parallel simulation of advanced Monte Carlo methods. *J. Computational and Graphical Statistics*, 19(4):769–789, 2010. URL: `http://arxiv.org/pdf/0905.2441.pdf`.

[15] Aaron Q. Li, Amr Ahmed, Sujith Ravi, and Alexander J. Smola. Reducing the sampling complexity of topic models. In *Proc. 20th ACM SIGKDD International Conference on Knowledge Discovery and Data Mining*, KDD '14, pages 891–900, New York, 2014. ACM. `doi:10.1145/2623330.2623756`.

[16] Mian Lu, Ge Bai, Qiong Luo, Jie Tang, and Jiuxin Zhao. Accelerating topic model training on a single machine. In Yoshiharu Ishikawa, Jianzhong Li, Wei Wang, Rui Zhang, and Wenjie Zhang, editors, *Web Technologies and Applications (APWeb 2013)*, volume 7808 of *Lecture Notes in Computer Science*, pages 184–195. Springer Berlin Heidelberg, 2013. `doi:10.1007/978-3-642-37401-2_20`.

[17] Sepideh Maleki, Annie Yang, and Martin Burtscher. Higher-order and tuple-based massively-parallel prefix sums. In *Proc. 37th ACM SIGPLAN Conference on Programming Language Design and Implementation*, PLDI '16, pages 539–552, New York, 2016. ACM. URL: `http://doi.acm.org/10.1145/2908080.2908089`, `doi:10.1145/2908080.2908089`.

[18] G. Marsaglia. Generating discrete random variables in a computer. *Commun. ACM*, 6(1):37–38, January 1963. `doi:10.1145/366193.366228`.

[19] Yossi Matias, Jeffrey Scott Vitter, and Wen-Chun Ni. Dynamic generation of discrete random variates. In *Proc. Fourth Annual ACM-SIAM Symposium on Discrete Algorithms*, SODA '93, pages 361–370, Philadelphia, PA, USA, 1993. Society for Industrial and Applied Mathematics. URL: `http://dl.acm.org/citation.cfm?id=313559.313807`.

[20] NVIDIA. Developer zone website: Cuda toolkit documentation: Cuda toolkit v6.5 programming guide, section B.14. warp shuffle functions, 2015. Online documentation. Accessed February 6, 2015. URL: `http://docs.nvidia.com/cuda/cuda-c-programming-guide/index.html#warp-shuffle-functions`.

[21] Daniel Ramage, Susan Dumais, and Dan Liebling. Characterizing microblogs with topic models. In *Proc. 4th International AAAI Conference on Weblogs and Social Media*, pages 130–137, Palo Alto, CA, July 2010. Association for the Advancement of Artificial Intelligence.

[22] Guy L. Steele Jr. and Jean-Baptiste Tristan. Using butterfly-patterned partial sums to optimize GPU memory accesses for drawing from discrete distributions. *CoRR (Computing Research Repository at arXiv.org)*, May 2015. URL: `http://arxiv.org/abs/1505.03851`.

[23] Marc A. Suchard, Quanli Wang, Cliburn Chan, Jacob Frelinger, Andrew Cron, and Mike West. Understanding GPU programming for statistical computation: Studies in massively parallel massive mixtures. *J. Computational and Graphical Statistics*, 19(2):419–438, 2010.

[24] Jean-Baptiste Tristan, Daniel Huang, Joseph Tassarotti, Adam C. Pocock, Stephen Green, and Guy L. Steele Jr. Augur: Data-parallel probabilistic modeling. In Z. Ghahramani, M. Welling, C. Cortes, N. D. Lawrence, and K. Q. Weinberger, editors, *Advances in Neural Information Processing Systems 27*, pages 2600–2608. Curran Associates, Inc., 2014. URL: `http://papers.nips.cc/book/year-2014`.

[25] Jean-Baptiste Tristan, Joseph Tassarotti, and Guy L. Steele Jr. Efficient training of LDA on a GPU by mean-for-mode estimation. In *Proc. ICML 2015: 32nd International Conference on Machine Learning*, pages 59–68, Brookline, MA, July 2015. Microtome Publishing. URL: `http://jmlr.org/proceedings/papers/v37/tristan15.pdf`.

[26] M. D. Vose. A linear algorithm for generating random numbers with a given distribution. *IEEE Trans. Software Engineering*, 17(9):972–975, Sept 1991. `doi:10.1109/32.92917`.

[27] A. J. Walker. New fast method for generating discrete random numbers with arbitrary frequency distributions. *Electronics Letters*, 10(8):127–128, April 1974. `doi:10.1049/el:19740097`.

[28] Alastair J. Walker. An efficient method for generating discrete random variables with general distributions. *ACM Trans. Math. Software*, 3(3):253–256, September 1977. `doi:10.1145/355744.355749`.

[29] Nicholas Wilt. *The CUDA Handbook: A Comprehensive Guide to GPU Programming*. Addison-Wesley, Upper Saddle River, New Jersey, 2013.

[30] Feng Yan, Ningyi Xu, and Yuan Qi. Parallel inference for latent Dirichlet allocation on graphics processing units. In *Advances in Neural Information Processing Systems 22*, pages 2134–2142. Curran Associates, Inc., 2009. URL: `http://papers.nips.cc/book/year-2009`.

[31] Shengen Yan, Guoping Long, and Yunquan Zhang. StreamScan: Fast scan algorithms for GPUs without global barrier synchronization. In *Proc. 18th ACM SIGPLAN Symposium on Principles and Practice of Parallel Programming*, PPoPP '13, pages 229–238, New York, 2013. ACM. URL: `http://doi.acm.org/10.1145/2442516.2442539`, `doi:10.1145/2442516.2442539`.

[32] Huasha Zhao, Biye Jiang, and John Canny. SAME but different: Fast and high-quality Gibbs parameter estimation. *CoRR (Computing Research Repository at arXiv.org)*, September 2014. URL: `http://arxiv.org/abs/1409.5402`.

[33] Seth Zimmerman. An optimal search procedure. *American Mathematical Monthly*, 66(8):690–693, Oct 1959.

KiWi: A Key-Value Map for Scalable Real-Time Analytics

Dmitry Basin* Edward Bortnikov* Anastasia Braginsky* Guy Golan-Gueta† Eshcar Hillel* Idit Keidar‡* Moshe Sulamy§

*Yahoo Research, Israel †VMWare Research, Israel ‡Technion, Israel §Tel Aviv University

{dbasin,ebortnik,anastas,eshcar}@yahoo-inc.com ggolangueta@vmware.com
idish@ee.technion.ac.il moshe.sulamy@cs.tau.ac.il

Abstract

Modern big data processing platforms employ huge in-memory *key-value* (KV) maps. Their applications simultaneously drive high-rate data ingestion *and* large-scale analytics. These two scenarios expect KV-map implementations that scale well with both real-time updates and large atomic scans triggered by range queries.

We present KiWi, the first atomic KV-map to efficiently support simultaneous large scans and real-time access. The key to achieving this is treating scans as first class citizens, and organizing the data structure around them. KiWi provides wait-free scans, whereas its put operations are lightweight and lock-free. It optimizes memory management jointly with data structure access. We implement KiWi and compare it to state-of-the-art solutions. Compared to other KV-maps providing atomic scans, KiWi performs either long scans or concurrent puts an order of magnitude faster. Its scans are twice as fast as *non-atomic* ones implemented via iterators in the Java skiplist.

1. Introduction

Motivation and goal. The ordered *key-value* (KV) map abstraction has been recognized as a popular programming interface since the dawn of computer science, and remains an essential component of virtually any computing system today. It is not surprising, therefore, that with the advent of multi-core computing, many scalable concurrent implementations have emerged, e.g., [3, 11, 12, 22, 27, 30].

KV-maps have become centerpiece to web-scale data processing systems such as Google's F1 [33], which powers its AdWords business, and Yahoo's Flurry [5] – the technology behind Mobile Developer Analytics. For example, as of early 2016, Flurry reported systematically collecting data of 830,000 mobile apps [4] running on 1.6 billion user devices [6]. Flurry streams this data into a massive index, and provides a wealth of reports over the collected data. Such *real-time analytics* applications push KV-store scalability requirements to new levels and raise novel use cases. Namely, they require both (1) low latency ingestion of incoming data, and (2) high performance analytics of the resulting dataset.

The stream scenario requires the KV-map to support fast *put* operations, whereas analytics relies on (typically large) *scans* (i.e., range queries). The consistency (atomicity) of scans is essential for correct analytics. The new challenge that arises in this environment is allowing consistent scans to be obtained *while the data is being updated in real-time*.

We present KiWi, the first KV-map to efficiently support large atomic scans as required for data analytics alongside real-time updates. Most concurrent KV-maps today do not support atomic scans at all [3, 9, 11, 12, 22, 27, 28, 30]. A handful of recent works support atomic scans in KV-maps, but they either hamper updates when scans are ongoing [14, 32], or fail to ensure progress to scans in the presence of updates [15]. See Section 2 for a discussion of related work.

The emphasis in KiWi's design is on facilitating synchronization between scans and updates. Since scans are typically long, our solution avoids livelock and wasted work by always allowing them to complete (without ever needing to restart). On the other hand, updates are short (since only single-key puts are supported), therefore restarting them in cases of conflicts is practically "good enough" – restarts are rare, and when they do occur, little work is wasted. Formally, KiWi provides *wait-free* gets and scans and *lock-free* puts.

Design principles. To support atomic wait-free scans, KiWi employs multi-versioning [10]. But in contrast to the standard approach [26], where each put creates a new version for the updated key, KiWi only keeps old versions that are needed for ongoing scans, and otherwise overwrites the existing version. Moreover, version numbers are managed by scans rather than updates, and put operations may overwrite data without changing its version number. This unorthodox approach offers significant performance gains given that

PPoPP '17,, February 04-08, 2017, Austin, TX, USA.

http://dx.doi.org/10.1145/3018743.3018761

scans typically retrieve large amounts of data and hence take much longer than updates. It also necessitates a fresh approach to synchronizing updates and scans, which is a staple of KiWi's design.

A second important consideration is efficient memory access and management. Data in KiWi is organized as a collection of *chunks*, which are large blocks of contiguous key ranges. Such data layout is cache-friendly and suitable for non-uniform memory architectures (NUMA), as it allows long scans to proceed with few fetches of new data to cache or to local memory. Chunks regularly undergo maintenance to improve their internal organization and space utilization (via *compaction*), and the distribution of key ranges into chunks (via splits and merges). KiWi's *rebalance* abstraction performs batch processing of such maintenance operations. The synchronization of rebalance operations with ongoing puts and scans is subtle, and much of the KiWi algorithm is dedicated to handling possible races in this context.

Third, to facilitate concurrency control, we separate chunk management from indexing for fast lookup: KiWi employs an *index* separately from the (chunk-based) data layer. The index is updated lazily once rebalancing of the data layer completes.

Finally, KiWi is a balanced data strucutre, providing logarithmic access latency in the absence of contention. This is achieved via a combination of (1) using a balanced index for fast chunk lookup and (2) partially sorting keys in each chunk to allow for fast in-chunk binary search. The KiWi algorithm is detailed in Section 3 and we discuss its correctness in Section 4.

Evaluation results. KiWi's Java implementation is available in github[1]. In Section 5 we benchmark it under multiple representative workloads. In the vast majority of experiments, it significantly outperforms existing concurrent KV-maps that support scans. KiWi's advantages are particularly pronounced in our target scenario with long scans in the presence of concurrent puts, where it not only performs *all* operations faster than the competitors [14, 15], but actually executes either updates or scans an order of magnitude faster than every other solution supporting atomic scans. Notably, KiWi's atomic scans are also two times faster than the *non-atomic* ones offered by the Java Skiplist [3].

2. Related Work

Techniques. KiWi employs a host of techniques for efficient synchronization, many of which have been used in similar contexts before. Multi-versioning [10] is a classical database approach for allowing atomic scans in the presence of updates, and has also been used in the context of transactional memory [26]. In contrast to standard multi-versioning, KiWi does not create a new version for each update, and leaves version numbering to scans rather than updates.

[1] https://github.com/sdimbsn/KiWi

Braginsky and Petrank used lock-free chunks for efficient memory management in the context of non-blocking linked lists [11] and B^+trees [12]. However, these data structures do not support atomic scans as KiWi does.

KiWi separates index maintenance from the core data store, based on the observation that index updates are only needed for efficiency and not for correctness, and hence can be done lazily. This observation was previously leveraged, e.g., for a concurrent skip list, where only the underlying linked list is updated as part of the atomic operation and other links are updated lazily [13, 23, 25, 35].

Concurrent maps supporting scans. Table 1 summarizes the properties of state-of-the-art concurrent data structures that support scans, and compares them to KiWi. SnapTree [14] and Ctrie [32] use lazy copy-on-write for cloning the data structure in order to support snapshots. This approach severely hampers put operations when scans are ongoing, as confirmed by our empirical results for SnapTree, which was shown to outperform Ctrie. Moreover, in Ctrie, partial snapshots cannot be obtained.

Brown and Avni [15] introduced range queries for the k-ary search tree [16]. Their scans are atomic and lock-free, and outperform those of Ctrie and SnapTree in most scenarios. However, each conflicting put restarts the scan, degrading performance as scan sizes increase. Additionally, k-ary tree is unabalnced; its performance plunges when keys are inserted in sequential order (a common practical case).

Some techniques offer generic add-ons to support atomic *snapshot iterator* in existing data structures [18, 31]. However, [31] supports only one scan at a time, and [18]'s throughput is lower than k-ary tree's under low contention.

Most concurrent key-value maps do not support atomic scans in any way [3, 11, 12, 22, 27, 28, 30]. Standard iterators implemented on such data structures provide non-atomic scans. Among these, we compare KiWi to the standard Java concurrent skip-list [19].

Distributed KV-maps Production systems often exploit persistent KV-stores like Google's Bigtable [17], Apache HBase [1], and others [7, 8]. These technologies combine on-disk indices for persistence with an in-memory KV-map for real-time data acquisition. They often support atomic scans, which can be non-blocking as long as they can be served from RAM [20]. However, storage access is a principal consideration in such systems, which makes their design different from that of in-memory stores as discussed herein.

MassTree [29] is a persistent B^+-tree designed for high concurrency on SMP machines. It is not directly comparable to KiWi as it does not support atomic snapshots, which is our key emphasis. Sowell et. al. [34] presented Minuet – a distributed in-memory data store with snapshot support. In that context, snapshot creation is relatively expensive, which Minuet mitigates by sharing snapshots across queries.

	scans				performance	
	atomic	**multiple**	**partial**	**wait-free**	**balanced**	**fast puts**
Ctrie [32]	✓	✓	✗	✗	✓	✗
SnapTree [14]	✓	✓	✓	✗	✓	✗
k-ary tree [15]	✓	✓	✓	✗	✗	✓
snapshot iterator [31]	✓	✗	✗	✓	✓	✓
Java skiplist [3]	✗	✓	✓	✓	✓	✓
KiWi	✔	✔	✔	✔	✔	✔

Table 1: Comparison of concurrent data structures implementing scans. For range queries, support for multiple partial scans is necessary. Fast puts do not hamper updates (e.g., by cloning nodes) when scans are ongoing.

Algorithm 1 KiWi chunk data structure.

```
immutable minKey                                    ▷minimal key in chunk
array k of ⟨key, ver, valPtr, next⟩                 ▷in-chunk linked list
array v of values                                   ▷values stored in the list
kCounter, vCounter                                  ▷end of allocated (full) prefixes
batchedIndex                                        ▷end of batched prefix in k
  ▷pending put array allowing scans and gets to help puts
array ppa[NUM_THREADS] of ⟨ver, idx⟩
next                                                ▷pointer to next chunk in chunk list
mark                                                ▷indicates whether next is immutable
rebalance data ⟨status, parent, ro⟩                 ▷rebalancing-related data
```

3. KiWi Algorithm

KiWi implements a concurrent ordered key-value map supporting atomic (linearizable) get(key), put(key,value), and scan(fromKey,toKey) operations. Its put operations are lock-free, whereas get and scan are wait-free. A put with a non-existent key creates a new KV-pair, and a put of the $\perp$ value removes the pair if the key exists.

The philosophy behind KiWi is to serve client operations quickly, while deferring data structure optimizations to a maintenance procedure that runs infrequently. The maintenance procedure, *rebalance*, balances KiWi's layout so as to ensure fast access, and also eliminates obsolete information.

In Section 3.1 we explain how data is organized in KiWi. Section 3.2 discusses how the different operations are implemented atop this data structure in the common case, when no maintenance is required. Section 3.3 focuses on rebalancing.

3.1 Data organization

Chunk-based data structure. Similarly to a B$^+$tree, the KiWi data structure is organized as a collection of large blocks of contiguous key ranges, called *chunks*. Organizing data in such chunks allows memory allocation/deallocation to occur infrequently. It also makes the design cache-friendly and appropriate for NUMA, where once a chunk is loaded to local memory, access time to additional addresses within the chunk is much shorter. This is particularly important for scans, which KiWi seeks to optimize, since they access contiguous key ranges, often residing in the same chunk.

The KiWi data layout is depicted in Figure 1, with one chunk zoomed in. The chunk data stucture is described in Algorithm 1.

KiWi's chunks are under constant renewal, as the rebalance process removes old chunks and replaces them with new ones. It not only splits (over-utilized) and merges (under-utilized) chunks as in a B$^+$tree, but also improves their internal organization, performs *compaction* by eliminating obsolete data, and may involve any number of chunks.

In order to simplify concurrency control, however, we do not organize chunks in a B$^+$tree, but rather in a sorted linked list. This eliminates the synchronization complexity of multi-level splits and merges. Yet, to allow fast access, we supplement the linked list with an auxiliary *index* that maps keys to chunks; it may be organized in an arbitrary way (e.g., skip-list or search tree). Each chunk is indexed according to the minimal key it holds, which is invariant throughout its lifespan. (The minimal key of the first chunk in the list is $-\infty$.) The index supports a wait-free lookup method that returns the indexed chunk mapped to the highest key that does not exceed a given key. It further supports conditional updates, which are explained in Section 3.3, as they are done only as part of the rebalance procedure. Such updates are lazy, and so the index may be inaccurate. Therefore, the index-based search is supplemented by a traversal of the chunk linked list.

Intra-chunk organization. Each chunk is organized as an array-based linked list, sorted in increasing key order. KiWi chunks hold two arrays – v with written values, and k with the linked list. Each cell in k holds a key, a pointer valPtr to a value in v, and the index of the cell in k that holds the next key in the linked list. It also has a version number, as we explain shortly. When a chunk is created (as a result of rebalancing), some prefix (typically one half) of each array contains data, and the suffix consists of empty entries for future allocation.

The chunk's full prefix is initialized as sorted, that is, the linked-list successor of each cell is the ensuing cell in k. The sorted prefix is called the chunk's *batched prefix*, and it can be searched efficiently using binary search. As keys are added, the order in the remainder of the chunk is not preserved, i.e., the batched prefix usually does not grow. For example, when a key is inserted to the first free cell, it creates a *bypass* in the sorted linked list, where some cell i in the batched prefix points to the new cell, and the new cell

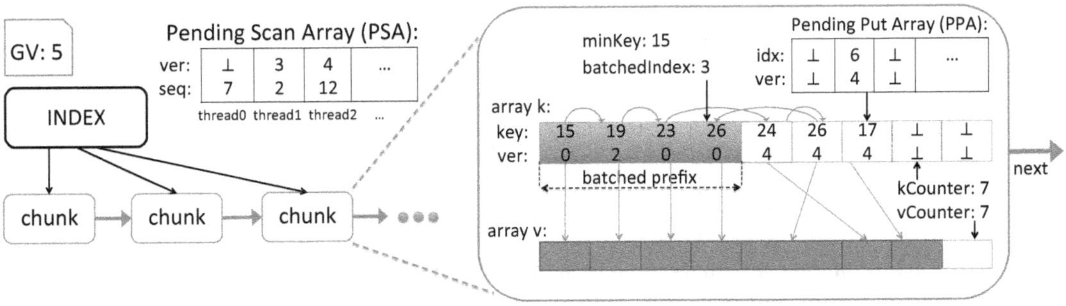

Figure 1: KiWi data structure layout. In the zoomed in chunk (on the right), a pending put by the second thread is attempting to add k[6] to the linked list with key 17 and version 4.

points to cell $i + 1$. We note that in case the insertion order is random, inserted cells are most likely to be distributed evenly in between the batched prefix cells, thus creating fairly short bypasses. Given that the prefix and the remainder are of similar sizes, the expected search time remains polylogarithmic. Nevertheless, in the worst-case, the search time is linear in the size of the remainder of the chunk.

In order to support atomic scans, KiWi employs *multi-versioning*, i.e., sometimes keeps the old version of a key instead of overwriting it. To this end, KiWi maintains a *global version*, GV, and tags each key-value pair with a version, ver. Versions of a key are chained in the linked-list in descending version order, so the most recent version is encountered first. The compaction process that occurs as part of rebalancing eliminates obsolete versions. Unlike traditional multi-versioning, KiWi creates new versions *only* as needed for ongoing scans. This allows us to shift the overhead for version management from updates, which are short and frequent, to scans, which are typically long and therefore much less frequent. Specifically, put operations continue to use the same version (overwriting previous values for written keys, if they exist) as long as no scan operation increases GV.

Coordination data structures. KiWi employs two data structures for coordinating different operations. A global *pending scan array* (PSA) tracks versions used by pending scans for compaction purposes; each entry consists of a version ver and a sequence number seq, as well as the scan's key range. A per-chunk *pending put array* (PPA) maps each thread either to a cell in the chunk that the thread is currently attempting to put into and a corresponding version, or $\langle \perp, \perp \rangle$, indicating that the thread is currently not performing a put. The purpose of the PPA will become evident below.

3.2 KiWi operations

Our algorithm makes use of atomic *compare-and-swap* – CAS(x,old,new), *fetch-and-increment* – F&I(x), and *fetch-and-add* – F&A(x,a) instructions for synchronizing access to shared data; all impose memory fences. A pseudocode of KiWi operations is given in Algorithm 2.

Helping puts. The interaction between put and scan operations is somewhat involved. In a nutshell, a put uses the current value of GV, whereas a scan begins by atomically fetching-and-incrementing GV, causing all future puts to write larger versions than the fetched one. Scan then uses the fetched version, ver, as its scan time, i.e., it returns for each scanned key the latest version that does not exceed ver.

However, a race may arise if put(key,val) reads a global version equal to ver for its data and then stalls while a concurrent scan obtains ver as its scan time and continues to read key before the put writes val for key with ver. In this example, val should be included in the scan (since its version equals the scan time), but it is not (because it occurs late).

We overcome this scenario by having scans *help* pending puts assign versions to values they write. To this end, puts publish their existence in the PPA of the chunk where they write, whereas scans call helpPendingPuts in each chunk where they read, which checks the PPA and helps any relevant pending put threads it encounters (lines 41–46). The helping here is minimal – it consists of a single CAS that assigns a version to the pending put (line 46). For example, in Figure 2, the scan helps put(k1,a) by setting its version to the current global version, namely 8. This orders the put after the scan, so the scan may return the old value.

Since scans use version numbers in order to decide which puts they take into account, the order of put operations is determined by the order of their versions. For consistency, gets also need to rely on version numbers. When a get(key) encounters a pending put(key,v) with no version, it cannot simply ignore the written value, because the put might end up ordered earlier than the get. Gets therefore call helpPendingPuts to help pending puts as scans do. This is depicted in Figure 2, where the get must help put(k2,b) obtain a version, because ignoring it would order the gets inconsistently with the version order that would later be observed by the scan.

Put implementation. The put operation appears in the left column of Algorithm 2. It consists of three phases: (1) locate the target chunk and prepare a cell to insert with the written value; (2) obtain a version while syncrhonizing with

Algorithm 2 KiWi operations – pseudocode for thread t.

```
1: procedure PUT(key, val)
   ▷1. prepare cell to insert
2:     locate target chunk C
3:     if checkRebalance(C, key, val) then
4:         return                      ▷required rebalance completed the put
5:     j ← F&A(C.vCounter, val.size)        ▷allocate place for value
6:     i ← F&I(C.kCounter)                  ▷allocate cell in linked list
7:     if j ≥ C.v.size ∨ i ≥ C.k.size then
8:         if ¬rebalance(C, key, val) then put(key, val)
9:     v[j] ← val
10:    k[i] ← ⟨key, ⊥, j, ⊥⟩        ▷version and list connection not set yet
   ▷2. get version via PPA
11:    C.ppa[t].idx ← i
12:    gv ← GV
13:    CAS(C.ppa[t], ⟨⊥, i⟩, ⟨gv, i⟩)
14:    if C.ppa[t].ver = frozen then          ▷C is being rebalanced
15:        if ¬rebalance(C, key, val) then put(key, val)
16:    C.k[i].ver ← C.ppa[t].ver
   ▷3. add k[i] to linked list
17:    repeat
18:        c← find(key, k[i].ver, C)          ▷search linked list C.k
19:                                 ▷use binary search up to C.batchedIndex
20:        if c = ⊥ then                       ▷not found
21:            link C.k[i] to the list using CAS
22:            if CAS succeeded then break
23:        else if c.valPtr = j'<j then         ▷overwrite
24:            CAS(c.valPtr, j', j)
25:    until c.valPtr ≥ j
26:    C.ppa[t] ← ⟨⊥, ⊥⟩

27: procedure GET(key)
28:     locate target chunk C
29:     helpPendingPuts(C, key, key)
30:     return findLatest(key, ∞, C)

31: procedure SCAN(fromKey, toKey)
    ▷1. obtain version - synchronize with rebalance via PSA
32:     psa[t] ← ⟨?, seq, fromKey, toKey⟩        ▷seq is thread-local
33:     ver ← F&I(GV)
34:     CAS(psa[t], ⟨?, seq, fromKey, toKey⟩, ⟨ver, seq, fromKey, toKey⟩)
35:     ver ← psa[t].ver
    ▷2. scan relevant keys
36:     for each chunk C in query range do
37:         helpPendingPuts(C, fromKey, toKey)
38:         for each key in query range do
39:             return findLatest(key, ver, C)
40:     psa[t] ← ⟨⊥, seq++, ⊥, ⊥⟩

41: procedure HELPPENDINGPUTS(C, fromKey, toKey)
42:     for each entry e in C.ppa do
43:         idx ← e.idx
44:         if C.k[idx].key ∈ [fromKey, toKey] then
45:             gv ← GV
46:             CAS(e, ⟨⊥, idx⟩, ⟨gv, idx⟩)

47: procedure FINDLATEST(key, ver, C)
48:     search key in C.k and C.ppa
49:     if found at least one cell with key and version ≤ver then
50:         return one with highest version, break ties by valPtr
51:     return ⊥
```

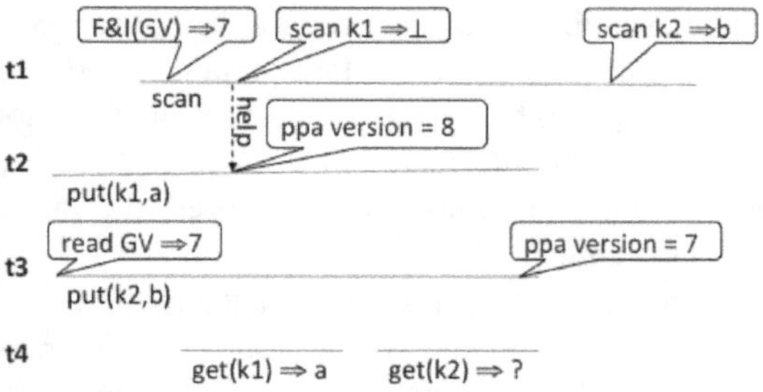

Figure 2: Example of scan operation enforcing order between puts: The scan assigns put(k1,a) a new version (8), whereas put(k2,b) later completes with an old version (7). We see that if get(k2) does not help put(k2,b), the gets see puts in a different order than the scan.

concurrent scans, gets, and rebalances via the PPA; and (3) connect the new cell to the linked list.

The first phase (lines 2–10) locates the target chunk C, traversing the index and the linked list if needed. Later this phase allocates space for the key and the variable-length value, by increasing C's array counters to the next available indices i and j for k and v, resp. This is done using atomic F&I and F&A, so in case of concurrent put operations, each thread gets its own cells.

Before increasing i and j, put checks if rebalancing is needed, because the chunk is full, imbalanced, or immutable, as discussed in the next section. This is done by the procedure checkRebalance given below, which returns false in case no rebalance is needed, and otherwise completes (or restarts) the put. After increasing i and j, put verifies that they are not too large, and if so, proceeds to write values into k[i] and v[j], without a version at this point; note that k[i] is not yet connected to the linked list.

The second phase (lines 11–16) publishes i in the thread's entry in C's PPA, and then uses CAS to set the version to the current value of GV. The CAS may fail in two possible ways. First, if the chunk is undergoing rebalancing, then the reblanacing thread may have set the thread's PPA version to frozen. In this case, the put cannot proceed since the chunk is deemed immutable. Instead, it invokes rebalance, and if rebalance returns false indicating that it did not insert the put's key and value, the put restarts (lines 14–15). (Invoking rebalance on a chunk that is already being rebalanced is done for lock-freedom, given that the original rebalancing thread may be stalled.) Second, a helping thread may have already set the version; to account both for this case and for the case CAS succeeds, put uses the version from the PPA, and copies it to k[i] (line 16).

The third phase, (lines 17–25), adds k[i] to the linked list. To find the insertion point, it first uses binary search on the

	scan	put	rebalance
scan	F&I GV	–	–
put	CAS ppa[t].ver	by version, then F&A vCounter	–
rebalance	CAS psa[t].ver	CAS to frozen ppa[t].ver	CAS rebalanceObj

Table 2: Atomic operations and rendevouz points determining order between KiWi procedures.

batched prefix and then traverses the remaining linked list. If the linked list does not contain a cell with the same key and version, then k[i] is linked to the list (line 21). Otherwise, ties between two puts with the same key and version are broken based on the indices of their allocated cells in v. If the put that allocates cell j finds in the linked list a cell with index j' with the same key and version such that j'<j, it uses CAS to replace that cell's valPtr to point to v[j] (line 24). If j'>j then the put does nothing, since its value has effectively been overwritten. Note that in both cases some cell, either j or j', remains allocated but is not connected to the linked list. Unconnected cells are compacted by the rebalancing process. Finally, the PPA version is cleared (line 26).

Gets and scans. Gets and scans are presented in the right-hand column in Algorithm 2. A get(key) begins by querying the index for key, and then (if needed), traverses the linked-list of chunks until the next chunk's minKey exceeds key (line 28). If there is a pending put to key that does not have a version yet, (i.e., its version is $\perp$), get attempts to help it by setting its version to the current value of GV using CAS (line 46). (CAS may fail in case the put sets its own version or is helped or frozen by another thread). It then calls findLatest() to find the latest version of the searched key.

The findLatest() function (line 47) performs a binary search on the batched prefix, and continues to traverse the in-chunk linked list until it either finds key or finds that it does not exist. In addition, findLatest() checks the PPA for potential pending puts of the target key, ignoring entries with no versions as these were added after the help. In case multiple versions of key exist, it returns the one with the highest version. If a pending put has the same version for the sought key as an entry in the linked list, then the one with the larger valPtr is returned.

A scan first determines its scan time (lines 32–35). It obtains a unique version via F&I of GV, and attempts to set it as its scan time while synchronizing itself relative to helping rebalance operations as described below.

It then reads all the keys in the relevant range (lines 36–39) by traversing the list of chunks, and within each chunk, proceeding as get does to help all pending puts and find the latest version of each key.

Ordering operations. The order among concurrently executing KiWi procedures is determined by atomic hardware operations (F&I, F&A, or CAS) on pertinent memory locations. Table 2 summarizes the rendevouz points for different types of operations. For brevity, we omit gets from the table.

Each scan has a unique version. The order between concurrent scans is determined by the order in which they (or the rebalance threads that help them) perform F&I on GV. Scans (and gets) order themselves relative to a put by thread t via ppa[t].ver in the chunk where the put occurs.

The order between puts that attempt to insert the same key is determined by their versions, which reflects their order wrt ongoing scans. Puts that have the same version, (i.e., the order between them is not determined by scans), are ordered according to the order in which they succeed to fetch-and-add vCounter. Rebalance operations are discussed below.

3.3 Rebalancing

Section 3.3.1 discusses the life-cycle of a KiWi chunk, and in particular, when it is rebalanced. Section 3.3.2 then walks through the stages of the rebalance process.

3.3.1 Triggering rebalance and chunk life-cycle

We saw that put calls checkRebalance(C) in line 3 of Algorithm 2 before adding a new key to C. This procedure triggers rebalance(C) whenever C is full or otherwise unbalanced, according to some specified *rebalance policy*; we refer to C as the *trigger chunk* of the rebalance.

To address the immediate problem, KiWi could, in principle, restrict itself to the trigger chunk: It can free up space by *compacting* C, i.e., removing deleted values, values that are no longer in the linked list because their keys have been over-written, as well as values that pertain to old versions that are not required by any active scan; if this does not suffice (because all the information in C is needed), KiWi may *split* the chunk. Furthermore, it can address the imbalance by *sorting* the chunk.

The problem with this approach is that it may leave under-utilized chunks in the data structure forever. KiWi improves space utilization by allowing chunks to *merge*, or more generally, *engaging* a number of old chunks in the rebalance, and replacing all of them with any number of new ones. The chunks to engage are determined by the rebalance policy.

Rebalance clones the relevant data from all engaged chunks into new chunks, and then replaces the engaged chunks with the new ones in the data structure. Cloning creates a window when the same data resides at two chunks – new and old. In order for get and scan to be wait-free, the chunks remain accessible for reading during this period. But in order to avoid inconsistencies, both chunks (old and new) are immutable throughout the window.

This defines a life cycle for chunks: they are created as immutable *infants* by some *parent* trigger chunk C; they become *normal* mutable chunks at the end of the rebalance process; and finally, they become *frozen* (and again immutable) when they are about to be replaced. (We assume that a complementary garbage-collection mechanism even-

Algorithm 3 The checkRebalance procedure.

```
procedure CHECKREBALANCE(C, key, val)
    if C.status=infant then
        normalize(C.parent)
        put(key, val)
        return true
    if C.vCounter ≥ C.v.size ∨ C.kCounter ≥ C.k.size ∨
        C.status = frozen ∨ policy(C) then
        if ¬rebalance(C, key, val) then put(key, val)
        return true
    return false
```

tually removes disconnected frozen chunks.) The chunk's status (infant, normal, or frozen), the pointer to parent, and the pointer to rebalance object are part of the rebalance data stored in the chunk (see Algorithm 1).

The checkRebalance(C) procedure is given in Algorithm 3. It checks whether C is immutable, and if so, helps complete the process that makes it immutable (C's parent in case C is an infant, and C in case it is frozen). The rebalance procedure consists of two functions, rebalance and normalize; in case the chunk's parent is helped only the latter is perfromed as explained below. In addition, if the chunk is full or if the rebalance policy chooses to do so, it also triggers rebalance on C. Note that put calls checkRebalance before incrementing kCounter and vCounter in order to avoid filling up infant chunks. The reblance procedure takes the put's key and value as parameters, and attempts to piggyback the put on the reblanace, i.e., insert the key and value to the newly created chunk. In case it fails, it returns false, in which case the put is restarted.

The policy will typically choose to rebalance C whenever C is full or under-utilized, as well as when its batched prefix becomes too small relative to the number of keys in C's linked list. In order to stagger rebalance attempts in case of many insertions to the same chunk, the policy can make probabilistic decisions: If a chunk is nearly full or somewhat under-utilized or unbalanced, then the policy may flip a coin to decide whether to invoke rebalance or not.

3.3.2 Rebalance stages

Rebalance proceeds in the following seven stages:

1. *Engage* – agree on the list of chunks to engage.
2. *Freeze* – make engaged chunks immutable.
3. *Pick minimal version* – to keep in compaction.
4. *Build* – create infant chunks to replace engaged ones.
5. *Replace* – swap new chunks for old ones in list.
6. *Update index* – unindex old chunks, index new ones.
7. *Normalize* – make the new chunks *mutable*.

If the first check of checkRebalance() decides to help rebalance a chunk's parent, then rebalance starts in stage 6, since the chunk's reachability implies that stage 5 is complete. In other cases, (a frozen chunk or a new trigger chunk), rebalance cycles through all seven stages. This is safe because all stages are idempotent, and ensures lock-freedom, namely, progress in case the original rebalance stalls. The first five stages are performend in the rebalance procedure, whereas the last two are performed in normalize. Pseudocode for these operations is given in Algorithm 4. The two procedures make use of thread-local variables C_f, C_n, and last. The latter tracks the last chunk engaged in rebalancing, whereas the first two hold pointers to the first and last new chunks, respectively.

1. Engagement. Since multiple threads may simultaneously execute rebalance(C), they need to reach *consensus* regarding the set of engaged chunks. The consensus is managed via pointers from the chunks to a dedicated rebalance object ro. Once a chunk is engaged in a rebalance it cannot be engaged with another rebalance. The engaged chunks in a particular rebalance always form a contiguous sector of the chunks linked list. For simplicity, this sector always starts from the trigger chunk forward, though in principle it is possible to grow the sector backwards from the trigger chunk as well. A rebalance object holds pointers to two chunks, first (the trigger chunk) and next (the next potential chunk to engage in the rebalance). The engagement preserves the following invariant:

INVARIANT 1. *Consider a rebalance object* ro. *If* ro.next$\neq\perp$ *then for every chunk C in the linked list from* ro.first *to the chunk before* ro.next, C.ro=ro.

Engagement begins by agreeing on the ro to use. This is done by (1) creating a rebalance object referring to the trigger chunk C, (2) attempting to set C.ro to the new rebalance object via CAS, and (3) using the ro in C.ro. Note that the latter was set by a successful CAS of some rebalance thread. Next, we try to engage ensuing chunks in the list one by one. In each iteration, we consult the policy whether to engage the next chunk. We then use CAS to change ro.next to either ro.next.next, or $\perp$ indicating that it is time to stop engaging chunks. We exit the loop when ro.next is $\perp$, and then set the local variable last to the last engaged chunk.

2. Freezing. Once the list of engaged chunks is finalized, we freeze them so no data will be added to them while they are being cloned. Recall that puts become visible to concurrent retrievals once they publish themselves in the chunk's PPA, and that before doing so, they check if the chunk is frozen. However, we need to account for the scenario where a chunk becomes frozen after put checks its status and before the put publishes itself in PPA. To this end, rebalance traverses all PPA's entries and attempts to set their versions to frozen using CAS. If the CAS is successful, the put will fail to assign itself a version (Algorithm 2, line 14). Otherwise, the put has already assigned its version, and rebalance can take it into account during cloning.

3. Determining the minimal read version and helping scans. We need to clone all data versions that might still

Algorithm 4 KiWi's rebalance operation.

```
procedure REBALANCE(C, put_key, put_val)
  ▷1. engage
  tmp ← new rebalance object, with first=C, next=C.next
  CAS(C.ro, ⊥, tmp)
  ro ← C.ro
  last ← C
  while ro.next ≠ ⊥ do
    next ← ro.next
    if policy(next) then                          ▷try to engage next
      CAS(next.ro, ⊥, ro)
      if next.ro = ro then                        ▷engaged next
        CAS(ro.next, next, next.next)
        last ← next
      else
        CAS(ro.next, next, ⊥)
    else
      CAS(ro.next, next, ⊥)
  ▷search for the last concurrently engaged chunk
  while last.next.ro = ro do
    last ← last.next
  ▷2. freeze
  for each chunk c from ro.first to last do
    c.status ← frozen
    for each entry e in c.ppa do
      idx ← e.idx
      CAS(e, ⟨⊥, idx⟩, ⟨frozen, idx⟩)
  ▷3. pick minimal version
  minVersion ← GV
  for each psa[t] = ⟨ver, seq, from, to⟩ do
    if ro.first.minKey ≤ to ∧
        last.next.minKey > from then
      if ver=? then add ⟨t, seq, from, to⟩ to toHelp
      else minVersion ← min(minVersion, ver)
  if toHelp ≠ ∅ then
    ver ← F&I(GV)
    for each ⟨t, seq, from, to⟩ ∈ toHelp do
      CAS(psa[t], ⟨?,seq,from,to⟩, ⟨ver,seq,from,to⟩)
      minVersion ← min(minVersion, psa[t].ver)
  ▷4. build
  C_f ← C_n ← new chunk
      with minKey=C.minKey, parent=C, status=infant
  for each chunk C_o from ro.first to last do
    if C_o.minKey ≤ put_key < C_o.next.minKey then
      toPut ← {⟨put_key, GV, put_val⟩}
    else
      toPut ← ∅
    for each k in C_o.ppa ∪ C_o.k ∪ toPut in ascending order do
      if C_n is more than half full then
        C_n.next ← new chunk
            with minKey=k, parent=C, status=infant
        C_n ← C_n.next
      for each version ⟨ ver, val ⟩ of k, in descending order do
        if val = ⊥ then break                     ▷eliminate tombstones
        insert ⟨ k, ver, val ⟩ to C_n
        if ver < minVersion then break
  ▷5. replace
  do
    C_n.next ← last.next
  while ¬ CAS(last.next+mark, C_n.next+false, C_n.next+true)
  do
    pred ← C's predecessor
    if CAS(pred.next+mark, C+false, C_f+false) then   ▷success
      normalize(C)
      return true
    if pred.next.parent = C then                  ▷someone else succeeded
      normalize(C)
      return false
    rebalance(pred, ⊥, ⊥)               ▷insertion failed, help predecessor
  while true                                      ▷ and retry

procedure NORMALIZE(C)
  ▷6. update index
  for each chunk c from C.ro.first to last do
    index.deleteConditional(c.minKey, c)
  for each chunk c from C_f to C_n do
    do
      prev ← index.loadPrev(c.minKey)
      if c.frozen then break
    while ¬ index.putConditional(c.minKey, prev, c)
  ▷7. normalize
  for each chunk c from C_f to C_n do
    CAS(c.status, infant, normal)
```

be needed by scans. To this end, we compute minVersion, the minimum read point among all active and future scans – this is the smallest version among those published in PSA and the current GV.

Since a scan cannot atomically obtain a scan time from GV and publish it in PSA, rebalance cannot ignore scans that have started but did not publish a version yet. We therefore use a helping mechanism: scan first publishes ? in PSA (Algorithm 2, line 32) indicating its intent to obtain a version, then fetches-and-increments the global version and uses CAS to update the version from ? to the one it obtained.

Concurrent rebalance operations help scans install a version in started entries; monotonically increasing counters are used to prevent ABA races where an old rebalance "helps" a new scan. Specifically, rebalance does the following: (1) it scans the PSA for entries with ? whose range overlaps the range covered by the engaged chunks; (2) if any are found, it fetches-and-increments GV and reads its new version into gv; (3) for every psa[t]= $\langle ?, n\rangle$ entry found in (1), it attempts to CAS psa[t] to $\langle gv, n\rangle$. Note that scan's CAS (Algorithm 2, line 34) might fail in case it is helped, but either way, it uses the version written by some successful CAS (line 35).

4. Creating new chunks and completing the put. The next stage creates new chunks to replace the engaged ones. It traverses the list of engaged chunks from ro.first to last. In each chunk, it collects data both from the intra-chunk linked list and from the PPA. Additionally, the key and value of the put that triggered the rebalance is included in the appropriate chunk. Versions associated with deletions (tombstones) are discarded along with all older versions of the same key. All versions of a key that are older than the last version that does not exceed minVersion can be safely discarded, whereas newer versions are cloned into new chunks. New chunks are created one at a time, as infants, with the trigger chunk as their parent. Keys are added, in sorted order, to a new chunk C_n until it is roughly half full, at which point a new chunk C' is created and C_n.next is set to C'. (In case the last chunk is too sparse, for example, only a quarter full, it is discarded and its keys are moved to the penultimate chunk). We assume here that the number of versions is much smaller than the chunk size.

5. Data structure update. Next, rebalance attempts to insert the new section into the linked list instead of the engaged one. This involves two steps: First, the next pointer of the tail chunk in the new section needs to take the value of the next pointer in last. Second, the next pointer of the predecessor of ro.first needs to be set to the head of the new chunks' list. In order to execute the two steps atomically, we do the following: (1) *mark* the next pointer in last as immutable; (2) set the tail of the new chunk sector to its value; and (3) use CAS to set the next pointer of the predecessor of ro.first.

If CAS succeeds, we return true. If CAS fails because another rebalance (using the same rebalance object) has successfully replaced the trigger chunk with a new one, we simply return false (indicating that the new key and value were not added as part of the rebalance, and hence put should restart) without taking any additional actions. But if CAS fails because some other rebalance had marked the next pointer as immutable (step (1) above), then we recursively help that rebalance complete, and then re-attempt to insert the new chunk sector to the list.

In the special case when the new list is empty (because no data is kept), step (3) CASes the next pointer of the predecessor of ro.first to the next pointer of last.

6. Index update. Since the new chunks are already accessible via the linked list and the old chunks are already frozen, the index update can be lazy, and updates of different chunks can proceed without synchronization. Nevertheless, we need to take into account races with old rebalance operations— a thread that wakes up after being stalled must be prevented from indexing a chunk that had already been supplanted.

To this end, we assume that the index supports a form of semantic load-linked and store-conditional; specifically, it provides the following API: (1) loadPrev(k) — returns the indexed chunk mapped to the highest key that does not exceed k; (2) deleteConditional(k,C) — removes key k only if mapped to chunk C; and (3) putConditional(k,prev,C) — maps k to C provided that the highest key in the index that does not exceed k is mapped to prev. Such an index can be implemented in non-blocking ways using low-level atomic operations [12]; in our implementation, we instead use locks.

To index a new chunk C, we first call loadPrev(C.minKey), then verify that C is not frozen, and if so, add it conditionally to the index. Since chunks are frozen before they are unindexed, this check ensures that we do not re-index an unindexed chunk. If the conditional put fails and yet the chunk is not frozen, the put is retried. Index removals call deleteConditional(C.minKey,C).

7. Normalization. Finally, the status of the new chunks is set to normal, and put operations may begin to update them. Though it is possible that old (removed) chunks are still being accessed by old get and scan operations at this point, these operations will be ordered before the new puts, so it is acceptable for them to miss the added data. Once all such old operations complete, the old chunks can be reclaimed.

4. Correctness

We now provide the key arguments for KiWi's correctness. Due to space considerations, we state the main lemmas without proof, while a formal correctness proof is deferred to the full version of the paper. We begin in Section 4.1 by defining the model and correctness notion we seek to prove, and then present the key safety arguments in Section 4.2. The liveness proof is omitted for lack of space.

4.1 Model and Correctness Specification

We consider an asynchronous shared memory model [36], where a finite number of threads execute memory *operations* on shared objects. High-level objects, such as a map, are implemented using low-level memory objects supporting atomic read, write, and read-modify-write (e.g., CAS) operations. High-level operations are *invoked*, then perform a sequence of *steps* on low-level objects, and finally *return*.

Our correctness notion is *linearizability*, which intuitively means that the object "appears to be" executing sequentially. It is defined for a *history*, which is a sequence of operation invoke and return steps, possibly by multiple threads. A history partially orders operations: operation *op*1 *precedes* operation *op*2 in a history if *op*1's return precedes *op*2's invoke; two operations that do not precede each other are *concurrent*. In a *sequential* history, there are no concurrent operations. An object is specified using a *sequential specification*, which is the set of its allowed sequential histories. Roughly speaking, a history σ is *linearizable* [24] if it has a sequential permutation that preserves σ's precedence relation and satisfies the object's sequential specification.

KiWi implements a map offering put, get, and scan operations, and in its sequential specification, get and scan return the latest value inserted by a put for each key in their ranges.

4.2 KiWi's Linearizability

Proving KiWi is linearizable is accomplished by identifying, for every operation in a given history, a *linearization point* between its invoke and return steps, so that the operation "appears to" occur atomically at this point. The linearization point of operation *op* is denoted LP(*op*).

Puts. We saw above that puts in a chunk C are ordered (lexicographically) according to their $\langle v, j\rangle$ pairs, where $\langle v, i\rangle$ is published in their PPA in phase 2 of the put, and C.k[i].valPtr= j; this pair is called the *full version* of the put. We note that in each chunk, the full versions are unique, because threads obtain j using F&A. First, i is published in ppa[t].idx (line 11) and then the location-version pair obtains its final value by a successful CAS of ppa[t].ver, either by the put (line 13) or by a helping thread (line 46). We refer to a step publishing i in ppa[t].idx and to the step executing the successful CAS as the put's *publish time* and the *full version assignment time*, resp., and say that the put *assigned* $\langle v, j\rangle$ for its key in C.

We note that each put assigns a full version at most once. Once a put operation *po* for key k assigns its full version in chunk C at time t, we can define its linearization point. There are two options:

1. If at time t *po*'s full version $\langle v, j\rangle$ is the highest for k in C, (among entries in C's PPA and linked list), then LP(*po*) is the last step reading v from GV before t.
2. Otherwise, let *po*$'$ be the put(k, _) operation that assigns for k in C the smallest full version exceeding *po*'s before time t. Then LP(*po*) is recursively defined to be LP(*po*$'$). Note that *po*'s full version assignment time exceeds that of *po*$'$, so the recursive definition does not induce cycles.

In case multiple puts are assigned to the same point, they are linearized in increasing full version order.

While a chunk is accessible from the chunks list its key range is well-defined. We say that key k is in the *range* of chunk C if $k \geq C$.minKey and $k < C$.next.minKey. C is *mutable* if put operations can assign full version in C, otherwise it is *immutable*. An invariant of the rebalance process is that a chunk is immutable before it is accessible from the chunks list and after the freezing stage is completed. In addition, at any point in time each key is covered by the range of at most one mutable chunk. It is easy to show that a put operation always lands at a mutable chunk with a range that covers the key. Thus, rebalance operations divide puts of key k into disjoint groups; one group per mutable epoch of each chunk covering the key. The following lemma establishes the order among linearization points of puts within one epoch.

LEMMA 4.1. *Consider chunk C accessible as of time t_0, key k in the range of C, and an operation po =put(k, _) that assigns $\langle v, j\rangle$ to C.ppa at time t. Then*

1. *LP(po) is after po allocates location j for its value and before t.*
2. *LP(po) is a read step of GV that returns v.*
3. *LP(po) is after some operation po$'$ (possibly po, but not necessarily) publishes for k to C where later po$'$ assigns a full version equal to or greater than $\langle v, j\rangle$.*
4. *The linearization points of all operations that publish for k to C preserve their full version order.*
5. *At time t_0, the value published to k by the put with the latest linearization point before t_0 is associated with the highest full version in C's linked list.*

Gets and scans. The most subtle linearization is of get operations. A get operation *go* may land in a mutable or immutable chunk. We need to linearize *go* before all concurrent puts that *go* misses while seeking the value. For a get operation *go* for a key k in the range of chunk C, there are three options:

1. If C is not accessible from the chunks list when *go* starts traversing C's PPA, then LP(*go*) is the last step in which C is still accessible from the chunks list.
2. Else, if *go* does not find k in C then LP(*go*) is when *go* starts traversing C's PPA.
3. Else, let *po* be the put operation that inserts the value returned by *go*. LP(*go*) is the latest between when *go* starts traversing C's PPA and immediately after LP(*po*).

The next lemma shows that in the third case no other put writing to k is linearized after LP(*po*) and before LP(*go*). The proof relies on Lemma 4.1 and the rebalance invariants.

LEMMA 4.2. *Consider a get operation go retrieving the value of key k from chunk C. Let t be the step in which go starts traversing C's PPA. Then:*

1. *If go does not find k in C, then for each operation po publishing k in C, LP(po) is after t.*
2. *If go returns the value written by operation po, then LP(go) is after LP(po), and for each po$'$ $\neq$ po publishing k in C, LP(po$'$) is either before LP(po) or after t.*

Scans are linearized when GV is increased beyond their read point, typically by their own F&I, and sometimes by a helping rebalance. Lemma 4.1 helps to prove the following:

LEMMA 4.3. *Consider a scan operation so that acquires version v as its read point. For each key k in the range of the scan, so returns the value of the put operation writing to k that is linearized last before LP(so).*

The definition of the linearization points of scans and get operations imply that these operations are linearized between their invocation and return. Condition 1 of Lemma 4.1 implies the same for puts. It is easy to show that gets and scans land in chunks that contain the saught keys in their ranges. Combined with the rebalancing invariants, Lemma 4.2 shows that get operations satisfy their sequential specification, and Lemma 4.3 proves that scans satisfy their sequential specification. Hence we conclude that KiWi implements a linearziable map.

5. Evaluation

5.1 Setup

Implementation. We implement KiWi in Java, using Doug Lea's concurrent skip-list implementation [3] for the index with added locks to support conditional updates. The code makes extensive use of efficient array copy methods [2]. KiWi's chunk size is set to 1024.

The rebalance policy is tuned as follows: checkRebalance invokes rebalance with probability 0.15 whenever the batched prefix consists of less than 0.625 of the linked list. Rebalance engages the next chunk whenever doing so will reduce the number of chunks in the list. We did not implement the piggybacking of puts on rebalance, and instead restart the put after every rebalance. This does not violate lock-freedom since the number of threads is much smaller than the chunk size, hence it is impossible for pending puts to fill it up.

Methodology. We leverage the popular *synchrobench* microbenchmark [21] to exercise a variety of workloads. The hardware platform features four Intel Xeon E5-4650 8-core CPUs. Every experiment starts with 20 seconds of *warmup* – inserts and deletes of random keys – to let the HotSpot compiler optimizations take effect. It then runs 10 iterations, 5 seconds each, and averages the results. An iteration fills the map with random (integer, integer) pairs, then exercises some workload. Most experiments start from 1M pairs, except those focusing on high scalability that start from 10M.

Competition. We compare KiWi to Java implementations of three concurrent KV-maps: (1) the traditional skiplist [3] which does not provide linearizable scan semantics, (2) SnapTree[14][2], and (3) k-ary tree [15][3]. For the latter, we use the optimal configuration described in [15] with $k = 64$.

5.2 Results

Basic scenarios: get, put, and scan. We first focus on three simple workloads: (1) get-only (random reads), (2) put-only (random writes, half inserts/updates and half deletes), and (3) scan-only (sequential reads of 32K keys, each starting from a random lower bound).

Figure 3 depicts throughput scalability with the number of worker threads. In get-only scenarios (Figure 3(a)), KiWi outperforms the other algorithms by 1.25x to 2.5x. We explain this by the NUMA- and cache-friendly locality of access in its intra-chunk binary search. Under put-only workloads (Figure 3(b)), it also performs well, thanks to avoiding version manipulation. SnapTree, which is optimized for random writes, is approximately 10% faster than KiWi with 32 threads. Note that in general, KiWi's gets are faster than its puts because the latter occasionally incur rebalancing.

KiWi excels in scan performance (Figure 3(c)). For example, with 32 threads, it exceeds its closest competitor, k-ary tree, by over 40%. Here too, KiWi's advantage stems from high locality of access while scanning big chunks.

Concurrent scans and puts. We now turn to the scenario that combines analytics (scan operations) with real-time updates (put operations). This is the primary use case that motivated the design principles behind KiWi. Half of the threads perform scans, whereas the second half performs puts.

Figure 4(a) depicts scan throughput scalability with the number of threads while scanning ranges of 32K keys. Figure 4(b) depicts the throughput for 16 scan threads with varying range sizes. Note that for long scans, k-ary tree's performance deteriorates under contention. This happens because k-ary tree restarts the scan every time a put conflicts with it – i.e., puts make progress but scans get starved. For large ranges, SnapTree has the second-fastest scans because it shared-locks the scanned ranges in advance and iterates unobstructed. Note that KiWi's throughput slightly decreases when the range is particularly big because it takes longer to collect redundant versions, and therefore the scan has to sift through more data. Figure 4(c) depicts similar phenomena for a 10M-key dataset. SnapTree's competitive scan performance comes at the expense of puts, since its locking approach starves concurrent updates. Figures 4(d-f) illustrate this behavior – the latter for a 10M-key dataset.

We study the memory footprints of the solutions in this scenario. We focus on 32-key scans – a setting in which the throughput achieved by all the algorithms except SnapTree is similar. Figure 5 depicts the JVM memory-in-use metric immediately after a full garbage collection that cleans up all the unused objects, averaged across 50 data points. KiWi is on par with k-ary tree and the Java skiplist except with maximal parallelism (16 put threads), in which it consumes 20% more RAM due to intensive version management.

Ordered workload. As a balanced data structure, KiWi provides good performance on non-random workloads. We experiment with a monotonically ordered stream of keys. KiWi achieves a throughput similar to the previous experiments. In contrast, k-ary tree's maximal put throughput in this setting is 730 times slower – approximately 13.6K operations/sec vs KiWi's 9.98M.

6. Discussion

We presented KiWi, a KV-map tailored for real-time analytics applications. KiWi is the first concurrent KV-map to support high-performance atomic scans simultaneously with real-time updates of the data. In contrast to traditional approaches, KiWi shifts the synchronization overhead from puts to scans, and offers lock-free puts and wait-free gets and scans. We demonstrated KiWi's significant performance gains over state-of-the-art KV-map implementations that support atomic scans.

References

[1] Apache HBase – a Distributed Hadoop Database. https://hbase.apache.org/.

[2] Java Array Copy. https://docs.oracle.com/javase/7/docs/api/java/lang/System.html,.

[3] Java Concurrent Skip List. https://docs.oracle.com/javase/7/docs/api/java/util/concurrent/ConcurrentSkipListMap.html,.

[4] http://flurrymobile.tumblr.com/post/144245637325/appmatrix.

[5] Flurry analytics. https://developer.yahoo.com/flurry/docs/analytics/.

[6] http://flurrymobile.tumblr.com/post/117769261810/the-phablet-revolution.

[2] https://github.com/nbronson/snaptree.

[3] http://www.cs.toronto.edu/~tabrown/kstrq/LockFreeKSTRQ.java.

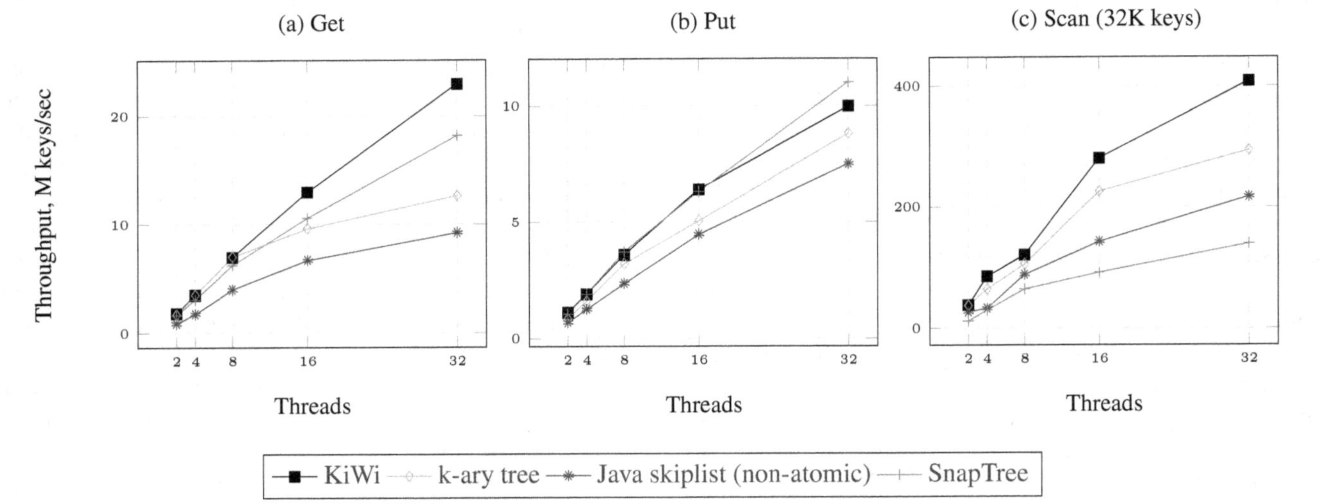

Figure 3: Throughput scalability with uniform workloads, 1M dataset. (a) Get operations, (b) Put operations, (c) Scan operations.

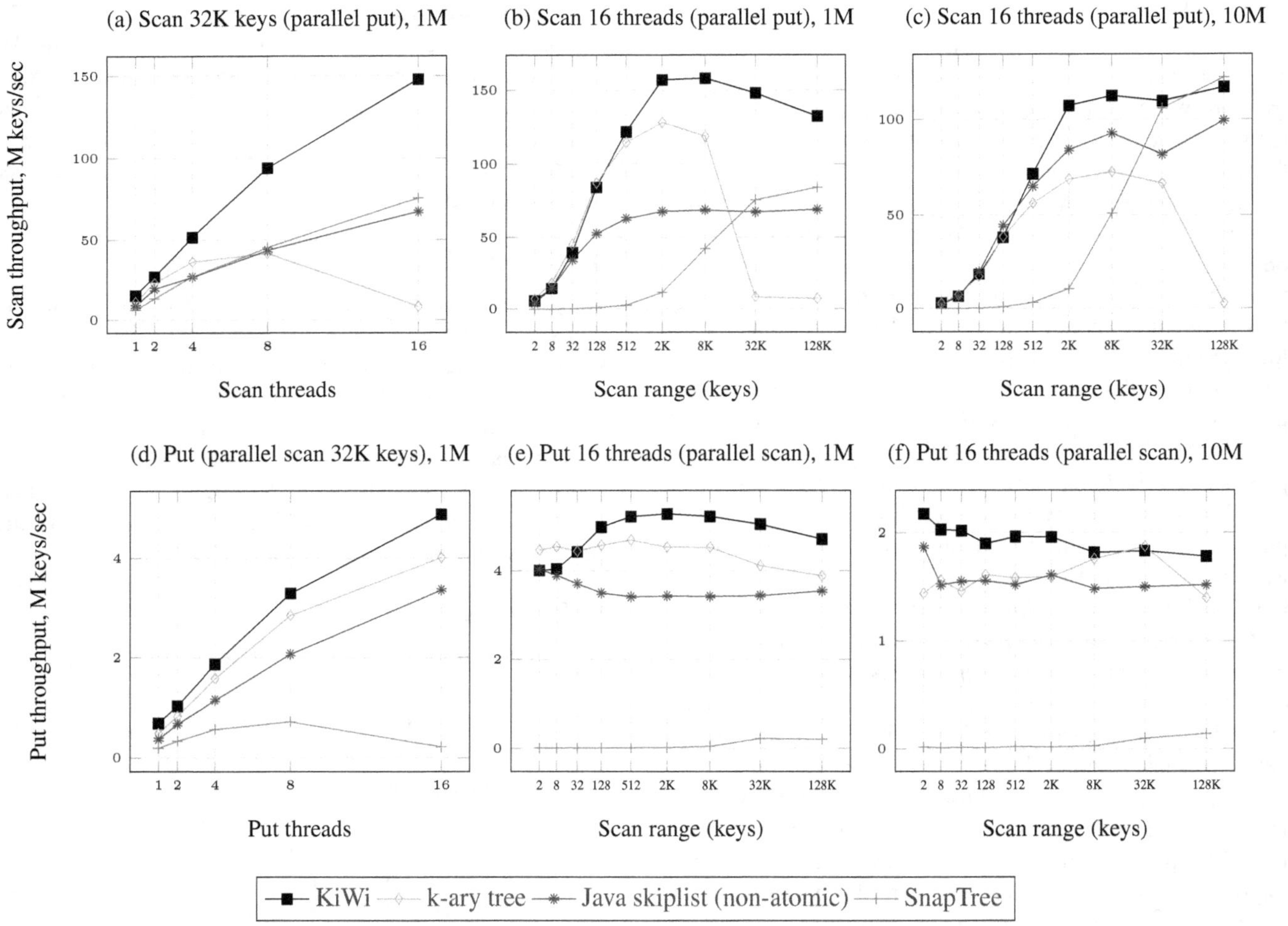

Figure 4: Throughput scalability with concurrent scans and puts. (a,b) Scan operations, 1M dataset. (c) Scan operations, 10M dataset. (d,e) Put operations, 1M dataset. (f) Put operations, 10M dataset.

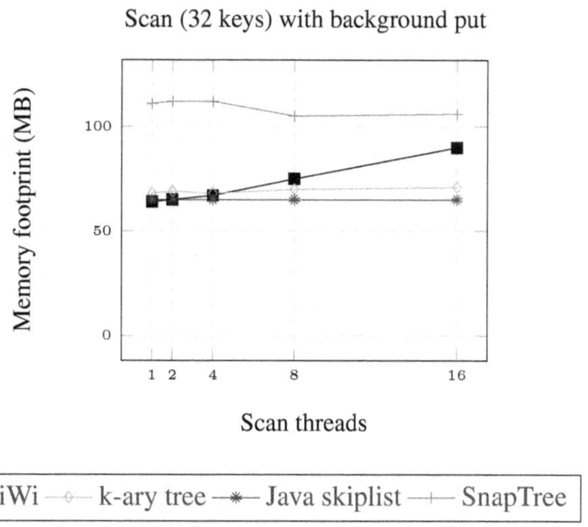

Figure 5: RAM use with parallel scans and puts, 1M dataset.

[7] A persistent key-value store for fast storage environments. http://rocksdb.org/, June 2014.

[8] A fast and lightweight key/value database library by google. http://code.google.com/p/leveldb, Jan. 2014.

[9] M. Arbel, G. Golan-Gueta, E. Hillel, and I. Keidar. Towards automatic lock removal for scalable synchronization. In *DISC*, pages 170–184, 2015.

[10] P. A. Bernstein, V. Hadzilacos, and N. Goodman. *Concurrency Control and Recovery in Database Systems*. Addison-Wesley, 1987. ISBN 0-201-10715-5.

[11] A. Braginsky and E. Petrank. Locality-conscious lock-free linked lists. In *ICDCN*, pages 107–118, 2011.

[12] A. Braginsky and E. Petrank. A lock-free B+tree. In *SPAA*, pages 58–67, 2012.

[13] A. Braginsky, E. Petrank, and N. Cohen. CBPQ: High performance lock-free priority queue. In *Euro-Par*, 2016.

[14] N. G. Bronson, J. Casper, H. Chafi, and K. Olukotun. A practical concurrent binary search tree. In *PPOPP*, pages 257–268, 2010.

[15] T. Brown and H. Avni. Range queries in non-blocking k-ary search trees. In *OPODIS*, pages 31–45, 2012.

[16] T. Brown and J. Helga. Non-blocking k-ary search trees. In *OPODIS*, pages 207–221, 2011.

[17] F. Chang, J. Dean, S. Ghemawat, W. C. Hsieh, D. A. Wallach, M. Burrows, T. Chandra, A. Fikes, and R. E. Gruber. Bigtable: A distributed storage system for structured data. *ACM Trans. Comput. Syst.*, 26(2):4:1–4:26, June 2008. ISSN 0734-2071.

[18] B. Chatterjee. Lock-free linearizable 1-dimensional range queries. In *WTTM*, 2016.

[19] K. Fraser. Practical lock-freedom. In *PhD dissertation, University of Cambridge*, 2004.

[20] G. Golan-Gueta, E. Bortnikov, E. Hillel, and I. Keidar. Scaling concurrent log-structured data stores. In *EuroSys*, pages 32:1–32:14, 2015.

[21] V. Gramoli. More than you ever wanted to know about synchronization: Synchrobench, measuring the impact of the synchronization on concurrent algorithms. In *PPoPP*, 2015.

[22] D. Hendler, N. Shavit, and L. Yerushalmi. A scalable lock-free stack algorithm. In *SPAA*, pages 206–215, 2004.

[23] M. Herlihy and N. Shavit. *The Art of Multiprocessor Programming*. Morgan Kaufmann Publishers Inc., 2008.

[24] M. Herlihy and J. M. Wing. Linearizability: A correctness condition for concurrent objects. *ACM Trans. Program. Lang. Syst.*, 12(3):463–492, 1990.

[25] M. Herlihy, Y. Lev, V. Luchangco, and N. Shavit. A simple optimistic skiplist algorithm. In *SIROCCO*, pages 124–138, 2007.

[26] I. Keidar and D. Perelman. Multi-versioning in transactional memory. In *Transactional Memory; Foundations, Algorithms, Tools, and Applications*, volume 8913, chapter 7, pages 150–165. 2015.

[27] A. Kogan and E. Petrank. A methodology for creating fast wait-free data structures. In *PPoPP*, pages 141–150, 2012.

[28] D. B. Lomet, S. Sengupta, and J. J. Levandoski. The bw-tree: A b-tree for new hardware platforms. In *ICDE*, pages 302–313, 2013.

[29] Y. Mao, E. Kohler, and R. T. Morris. Cache craftiness for fast multicore key-value storage. In *Proceedings of the 7th ACM European Conference on Computer Systems*, EuroSys '12, pages 183–196, 2012.

[30] A. Natarajan and N. Mittal. Fast concurrent lock-free binary search trees. In *PPoPP*, pages 317–328, 2014.

[31] E. Petrank and S. Timnat. Lock-free data-structure iterators. In *DISC*, pages 224–238, 2013.

[32] A. Prokopec, N. G. Bronson, P. Bagwell, and M. Odersky. Concurrent tries with efficient non-blocking snapshots. In *PPoPP*, pages 151–160, 2012.

[33] J. Shute, R. Vingralek, B. Samwel, B. Handy, C. Whipkey, E. Rollins, M. Oancea, K. Littlefield, D. Menestrina, S. Ellner, J. Cieslewicz, I. Rae, T. Stancescu, and H. Apte. F1: A distributed sql database that scales. In *VLDB*, 2013.

[34] B. Sowell, W. Golab, and M. A. Shah. Minuet: A scalable distributed multiversion b-tree. *Proc. VLDB Endow.*, 5(9): 884–895, May 2012.

[35] A. Spiegelman, G. Golan-Gueta, and I. Keidar. Transactional data structure libraries. In *PLDI*, pages 682–696, 2016.

[36] J. L. Welch and H. Attiya. *Distributed Computing: Fundamentals, Simulations and Advanced Topics (2nd edition)*. John Wiley Interscience, 2004.

Grammar-aware Parallelization for Scalable XPath Querying

Lin Jiang, Zhijia Zhao
University of California, Riverside
ljian006@ucr.edu, zhijia@cs.ucr.edu

Abstract

Semi-structured data emerge in many domains, especially in web analytics and business intelligence. However, querying such data is inherently sequential due to the nested structure of input data. Existing solutions pessimistically enumerate all execution paths to circumvent dependencies, yielding sub-optimal performance and limited scalability.

This paper presents GAP, a parallelization scheme that, for the first time, leverages the grammar of the input data to boost the parallelization efficiency. GAP leverages static analysis to infer feasible execution paths for specific contexts based on the grammar of the semi-structured data. It can eliminate unnecessary paths without compromising the correctness. In the absence of a pre-defined grammar, GAP switches into a speculative execution mode and takes potentially incomplete grammar extracted either from prior inputs. Together, the dual-mode GAP reduces the execution paths from all paths to a minimum, therefore maximizing the parallelization efficiency and scalability. The benefits of path elimination go beyond reducing extra computation – it also enables the use of more efficient data structures, which further improves the efficiency. An evaluation on a large set of standard benchmarks with diverse queries shows that GAP yields significant efficiency increase and boosts the speedup of the state-of-the-art from 2.9X to 17.6X on a 20-core machine for a set of 200 queries.

Keywords XML, XPath, Grammar, Parallelization

1. Introduction

Semi-structured data, like XML and JSON, is widely used in many application domains, such as web analytics [42], financial data processing [31], pub/sub applications [27], enterprise data exchanges [8], sensor networks [12], and smart buildings [38]. The volume of semi-structured data grows rapidly. Take Twitter as an example, it produces tweets in semi-structured format at a rate of 600 million per day [20].

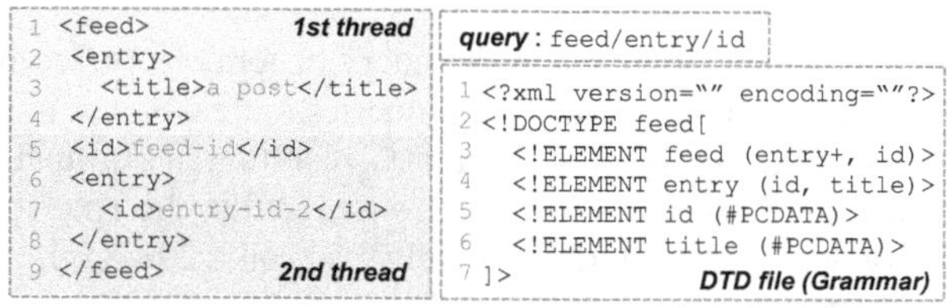

Figure 1. An illustration example (Facebook feed data [1])

To cope with fast data growth, users need efficient querying methods to extract information.

In comparison, the increase of modern CPU frequency has reached a plateau. Hence, exploiting parallelism is key to efficient query processing for semi-structured data. In this work, we focus on XPath queries for their basic roles in semi-structured data processing [1, 18, 23, 30].

However, parallelizing such queries is challenging due to the inherent nested structure of input data. Consider Facebook feed data [13] in Figure 1. Suppose using two threads to process a path query `feed/entry/id`, which aims to find the IDs of entries in the feed. Without examining the tags in the first half of the input, the second thread cannot determine if the `id` at line 5 is a match or not. Because it lacks the "context" of determining the answers to the query. As we will see later, such inherent dependence clearly manifests when the queries are formalized as *pushdown transducers* – a basic computation model for processing data that are defined by context-free grammars (Section 2).

State of The Art. Great efforts have been made on making parallel parsing possible for semi-structured data. With the parsing results, a DOM (Document Object Model) tree, the queries can be easily evaluated by traversing the tree. A practical issue with such methods is that the data could be too large to parse due to the huge memory consumption caused by constructing the parse tree. In addition, the query evaluation after parsing compromises data locality.

In comparison, Odgen and others [30] directly target the parallelization of XPath queries with a novel parallel pushdown transducer. By breaking the input into chunks and enumerating all execution paths for each chunk (except the first one), pushdown transducers are able to process different chunks in parallel. This method shows promising results for single-query processing and processing a small set of con-

[1] For illustration purpose, the data is simplified and slightly reordered.

PPoPP '17 Feb. 4–8, 2017, Austin, Texas, USA.

DOI: http://dx.doi.org/10.1145/3018743.3018772

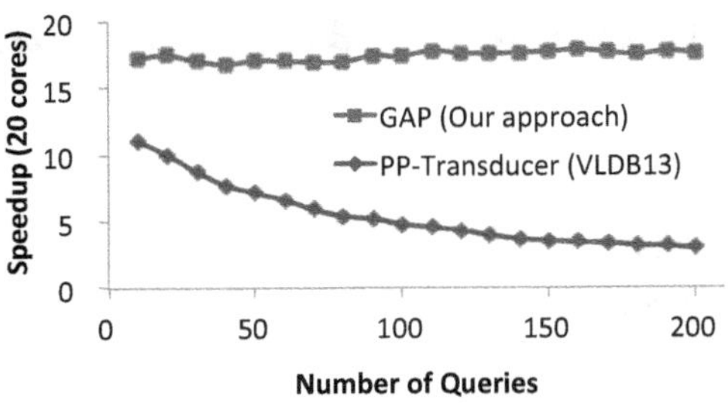

Figure 2. Scalability Comparison

current queries. However, as the query becomes more complex or the number of concurrent queries increases, the total number of execution paths also raises, resulting in a dramatic increase of parallelization cost. Consequently, the speedup quickly drops from 11.1X to merely 2.9X on a 20-core Intel Xeon server, as shown in Figure 2.

In this work, we raise and address some fundamental questions in the parallelization of pushdown transducers: *is it necessary to enumerate all execution paths? If not, how to know which execution paths are unnecessary?*

The key to answering the questions lies in the special properties of input data – *they are defined by (context-free) grammar, either explicitly or implicitly*. For example, XML data are defined by document type definition (DTD) or XML schema. Similar ways are used to define JSON data as well [15]. The grammar not only defines the valid structure of the data, but also adds constraints on the possible execution paths under a specific context. Consider the example in Figure 1. By checking the first element `<id>`, the second thread would be able to infer that it may be under the `<feed>` or an `<entry>`, but definitely not under a `<title>`, as the grammar does not specify an ID for the title.

To leverage these insights, we propose a *grammar-aware parallelization (GAP)* for querying semi-structured data, which can substantially reduce the amount of execution paths up to 200X according to our experiments. It brings in two major benefits. First, a thread only needs to keep a small number of execution paths (typically < 5), hence runs more swiftly. Second, when the number of execution paths drops to one, which happens quite often based on our experiments, it becomes possible to switch to more efficient data structures (from trees to stacks) to execute the pushdown transducers. Together, they dramatically reduce the parallelization cost, making efficient parallelization of larger-scale query processing possible, as shown in Figure 2.

Specifically, depending on the availability of an explicit grammar, GAP works in two modes: non-speculative mode and speculative mode. In non-speculative mode (Section 4), GAP extracts a static syntax tree from the given grammar file (e.g., a DTD file), and symbolically executes the pushdown transducer over the syntax tree to infer feasible execution paths under a specific context (e.g., a token `<id>`). With such knowledge, a parallel pushdown transducer only maintains a set of feasible execution paths and automatically switches to a stack when it detects a unique feasible execution path is left. In certain scenarios, an explicit grammar may not be available. In such cases, GAP enters into the speculative mode, where it first collects some partial grammar from prior runs. As the grammar is partial, the inferred feasible paths might be incomplete. Hence, a pushdown transducer runs speculatively with chances that the correct execution is left uncovered. To guarantee the correctness and reduce the penalty of misspeculation, a pair of validation and selective reprocessing mechanisms are proposed. With the dual-mode GAP, our approach is able to process semi-structured data either with or without a grammar file. Our evaluation results show that both non-speculative GAP and speculative GAP provide sustainable speedup, about 17.6X on a 20-core server, up to a set of 200 concurrent queries.

Contributions. This work makes several contributions:

- To our best knowledge, this work, for the first time, unveils the potential of leveraging input grammar to improve the efficiency of parallelization.
- It offers a rigorous inference of feasible execution paths from input grammar and an adaptive data structure switching mechanism to boost the efficiency of the basic computation model – pushdown transducers.
- It proposes a practical speculation scheme to cover the scenarios where the input grammar is unavailable.
- It, for the first time, enables a scalable parallelization of query processing that yields sustainable speedup as the query complexity increases.

In the following, we will first give the background and motivation (Section 2), then present an overview of GAP (Section 3), followed by the details of GAP in non-speculative mode (Section 4) and speculative mode (Section 5). We show our evaluation results in Section 6, related work in Section 7, and conclusion of this work in Section 8.

2. Background

In this section, we first present some basic concepts for querying semi-structured data. Then we introduce the computation model for processing queries – *pushdown transducer* and its parallelization challenges.

2.1 Querying Semi-Structured Data

Querying semi-structured data is a routine operation in stream processing and many database systems that supports semi-structured data. For instance, YFilter [10] and XMLTK [2] leverage automata to simultaneously process a large number of XPath queries against an XML stream with a constant memory requirement. These studies focus on improving the expressiveness of queries, instead of exploiting data parallelism. On the other hand, database engines, like Microsoft SQL Server [32] and MonetDB [3] provide task-level parallelization for querying XML data, but require pre-computed index to accelerate query processing, which

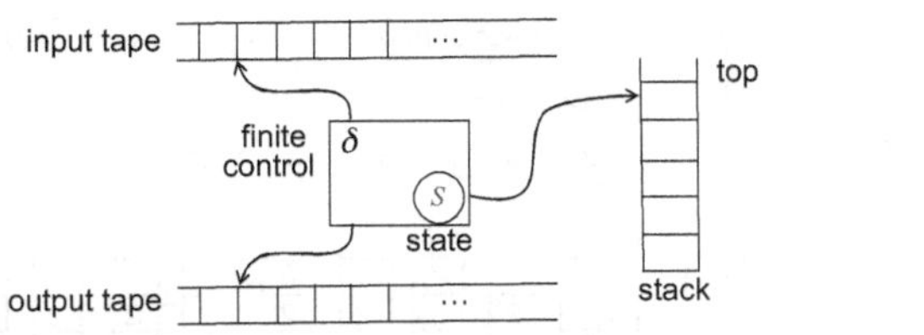

Figure 3. A Diagram of The Pushdown Transducer

becomes unsuitable for single-pass processing model due to the substantial cost of index construction.

Pre-parsing v.s. On-the-fly Querying. There are two basic strategies to process queries: (i) first parse the semi-structure data into a parse tree (i.e., DOM tree in XML context), then answer the queries by searching the tree. (ii) Process the queries on-the-fly without constructing any tree structure. There are three limitations with the first strategy. First, parsing the semi-structured data requires a large memory footprint due to the construction of DOM tree, which is almost infeasible for large semi-structured data or streaming data. Second, parallel parsing itself is quite challenging, existing solutions suffer from either load imbalance or sequential bottleneck caused by a sequential preprocessing. At last, it needs to traverse the data again after the parsing, compromising the data locality. For the above reasons, we choose the second strategy in this work. To enable on-the-fly query processing, queries are implemented using stack-based computation model – pushdown transducers [18, 30], which run over the semi-structured data stream and report matches as it proceeds. We next describe such a computation model.

2.2 Pushdown Transducers

Informally, a pushdown transducer is a finite automaton agumented with a stack and an output tape, as illustrated by Figure 3. With the stack, the pushdown transducer is able to memorize prior states (i.e., history). Such memorization is the essential for processing semi-structured data where certain "context" is needed. A pushdown transducer consumes the input stream by moving a pointer forward along the input tape one by one. Based on the input symbol, the control logic (defined as transitions) examines the current state and the status of the stack, then makes adjustments to the state and stack, and write symbols to the output tape.

A generic pushdown transducer can be defined as follows.

Definition 1. *A pushdown transducer is a 6-tuple (Σ, Γ, Δ, Q, q_0, δ) where Σ is the input alphabet, Q is the set of states, $q_0 \in Q$ is the initial state, Γ is the stack alphabet – a set of symbols that can be pushed onto stack, Δ is the output alphabet, and δ is a mapping $\delta : Q \times \Gamma \times \Sigma \rightarrow Q \times \Gamma \times \Delta$ which is also called the transition function.*

There are three factors that may affect the moving of a pushdown transducer: (i) current input symbol $c \in \Sigma$ from the input tape, (ii) current state $s \in Q$, and (iii) the element $e \in \Gamma$ on top of the stack. As a response, the pushdown transducer may take three actions: (i) move the current state to the next, (ii) update the top of the stack either by `push` or `pop`, and (iii) write a symbol $c' \in \Delta$ to the output tape. Note that, depending on the definition of transitions, the three factors may not always take effects at every transition, and the same is true for the actions.

We next describe the *specific pushdown transducers* for query processing using the running example in Figure 4. It contains a grammar with recursion (between elements `a` and `b`) to demonstrate its generality.

States Q. For any give path query, a corresponding finite automaton can be created based on a simple automaton construction algorithm [18]. The states in the finite automaton are exactly the states in the pushdown transducer. The accept state(s) correspond to the matches of the query. In the running example, a path query `a/b/c` is converted to a finite automaton of five states, as shown in Figure 4-c. `state 4` corresponds to the match of query.

Alphabets Σ ***,*** Δ ***, and*** Γ. In the context of XPath querying, the input alphabet Σ is the set of valid tokens (e.g., XML tags) resulted from a lexer. The output alphabet is actually the same as the input alphabet (i.e., $\Delta = \Sigma$) since the queries only return some parts of the input data stream. As to the stack alphabet, it can be either the state set Q or input alphabet Σ. Based on the convention [30], we set $\Gamma = Q$.

Transitions δ_{plain} ***,*** δ_{push} ***, and*** δ_{pop}. There are three types of transitions in XPath querying pushdown transducers.

1. Plain transitions δ_{plain}: $Q \times \Sigma \rightarrow Q \times \Delta$. They do not influence the stack. For example, the transition after reading a text token `x` is a plain transition.
2. Push transitions δ_{push}: $Q \times \Sigma \rightarrow Q \times \Gamma \times \Delta$. When an start tag (e.g., `<a>`) is read, the transducer first pushes the current state onto the stack, then transition to the next state based on the finite automaton.
3. Pop transitions δ_{pop}: $Q \times \Sigma \times \Gamma \rightarrow Q \times \Delta$. When a close tag (e.g., `</d>`) is met, the transducer pops the stack and sets the current state to the popped state.

Example. Figure 4-d illustrates the transitions of the pushdown transducer for processing query `a/b/a/c`. Among the ten steps, five of them are push transitions and the others are pop transitions. When the pushdown transducer moves to the accept state (`state 5`), it reports a match to the query and outputs the match to its output tape.

Inherent Dependence. Based on the definition of pushdown transducers, it is obvious to notice two types of dependence in its execution depending on the variables: (i) At every step of the transition, the next state depends on either the immediate prior state or the element on top the stack (which is actually an even earlier state). We refer to such dependence as *state dependence*. (ii) Similarly, at each step of the transition, the content of stack depends on stack before the transition and sometimes also depends on the prior state. We refer to this type of dependence as *stack dependence*. In general, a tight dependence chain is formed from the first step to the

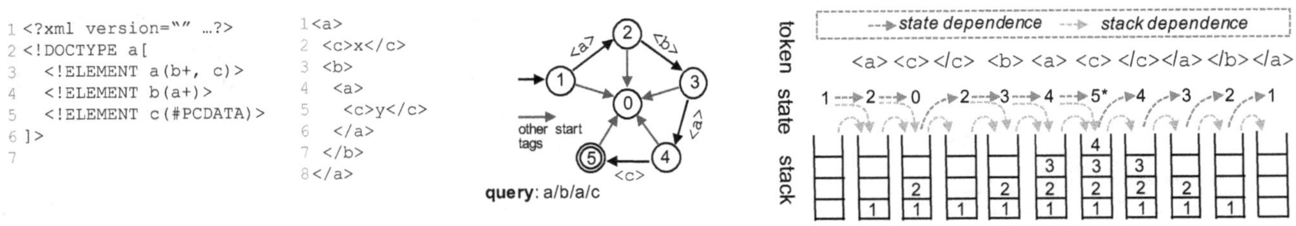

(a) DTD file (Grammar) (b) XML data (c) Query & Finite Automaton (d) Execution of Pushdown Transducer

Figure 4. A running example with a recursive grammar. '*' after state 5 means a match.

current step, making the parallelization of such computation model quite challenging, as illustrated by Figure 4-d.

2.3 Parallel Pushdown Transducers

To circumvent the inherent dependence in pushdown transducers, Ogden and others [30] propose a parallel pushdown transducer. Basically, it works in three major phases:

- *Split phase*. It first cuts the input data into equal-sized chunks, each of which may contain some broken tags.
- *Parallel phase*. For each chunk, except the first one, it enumerates all execution paths, each starting from a different state with an empty stack. A mapping m is maintained from each pair of starting state and stack (q_s, z_s) to a 3-tuple of finishing state, stack and output tape (q_f, z_f, o), that is $m = (q_s, z_s, q_f, z_f, o)$, where $m \in M = Q \times \Gamma^* \times Q \times \Gamma^* \times \Delta^*$. In our running example (Figure 4), it needs to enumerate all the six states (paths) and keeps a mapping for each of them.

  During the processing of a chunk, different execution paths may lead to the same finishing state and stack (called *path convergence*). To improve the efficiency, a double-tree data structure is employed to compress the mapping and reduce some redundant computations when path convergence occurs.

  For a chunk with missing start tags (due to partitioning), it is possible that a pop operation is needed while the stack is empty. In this case, it also has to enumerate every possible element that could be popped out from the stack (i.e. Γ). In such cases, a single path diverges to multiple ones, referred to as *path divergence*. In our running example, if the second thread starts from Line 5, when it processes the end tag </a> at Line 6, it encounters a path divergence, similarly to the end tags </b> and </a> at Lines 7 and 8.
- *Join phase*. Finally, mappings from different chunks are linked by matching the finishing state and stack in a chunk with the starting state and stack of its following.

An additional *filtering* phase may be added to enhance the expressiveness of the transducers (e.g., to handle predicates in XPath queries). Though the split, join and filter phases are sequential, they carry much less computations than the parallel phase and incur marginal cost [30].

Parallel pushdown transducers show promising results for single query or a small set of concurrent queries. However, as the query becomes more complex and as the number of queries increases, enumerating all execution paths tends to be less practical due to large amount of extra computation. To address this question, we propose a new scheme of parallelization, *grammar-aware parallelization (GAP)*, that leverages the grammar of the semi-structured data to guide the design of parallelization. In the following, we first give an overview of GAP before elaborating its major components.

3. Overview of GAP

In this section, we give the high-level design of GAP, a new parallelization scheme that leverages input grammar to boost the efficiency of parallelization.

Grammar Availability and Dual-mode GAP. The key of GAP is the awareness of semi-structured data grammars. A substantial amount of semi-structured data come with grammars, such as the auction data from ebay developer API [9] and the publication data from DBLP [7]. Actually, six out of ten datasets from UW's XML data repository [40] contain some DTD file(s). On the other hand, it is not uncommon that the grammar of some semi-structured data is unavailable, either because there does not exist a pre-defined grammar, or because the access to the DTD or XSD is not granted.

To cover both scenarios, GAP can run in two modes: *non-speculative mode* and *speculative mode*. When the grammar of the semi-structured data is available (e.g., in the form of DTD), GAP enters into non-speculative mode, where the execution correctness is always guaranteed, thanks to the rigorous feasible path inference from a complete grammar (as explained shortly). In another word, there is no speculation or prediction involved in this mode. On the other hand, when the grammar is unavailable, GAP switches into speculative mode. In this mode, GAP first collects some partial grammar by inferring it from previous runs (of the same data corpus). This part is illustrated as the first step of GAP in Figure 5.

Feasible Path Inference. After determining the execution mode, GAP obtains either a complete grammar or a partial grammar. With the grammar, GAP aims to infer which paths are feasible given a specific context, that is, a symbol from the input alphabet Q (e.g., a tag <c> in Figure 4-b).

To achieve this, GAP follows two steps: *static parse tree generation* and *symbolic execution of pushdown transducer*.

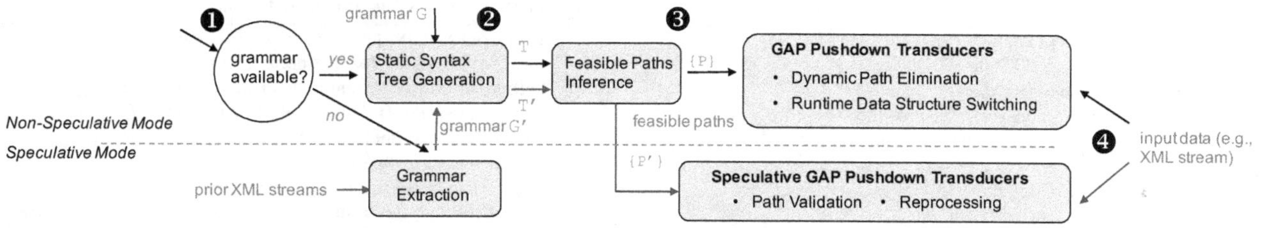

Figure 5. Overview of GAP. Labeled numbers show the major steps when predefined input grammar is available (e.g., DTD or Schema). Blue lines show the speculative execution flow in the absence of a pre-defined grammar.

In the first step, it takes the input grammar G as input and generates a static syntax tree T, which embodies the legal nesting structures of the input data. For example, element b has to be an immediate child of element a (see Figures 4-a and 4-b). In the second step, it executes the pushdown transducer symbolically by executing on every path of the static syntax tree to infer the feasible starting states when meeting a specific input symbol (i.e., the context). The results of the second step is a hash table, called *feasible path table*, where the key is input symbol and the value is the set of feasible paths, as shown in Table 1. Since the syntax tree is static and typically small, a full traversal is affordable. When the grammar is available beforehand, both steps can be done offline.

Input symbol	Feasible paths/states
<a>	{1, 3}
</a>	{2, 4}
<b>	{2}
...	...

Table 1. Feasible Paths Table

GAP Pushdown Transducers. To leverage the results from feasible path inference, we design a new type of parallel pushdown transducer – *GAP pushdown transducers*. First, when it is needed, a GAP pushdown transducer can inquire the feasible path table to determine and remove unnecessary paths, which is referred to as *dynamic path elimination*.

Second, whenever a unique feasible path is left, either caused by path elimination or path convergence, the GAP pushdown transducer switches from the default double-tree data structure to a stack and executes exactly like a sequential pushdown transducer. This makes the GAP pushdown transducer run swiftly without any house-keeping work. This feature is referred to as *runtime data structure switching*.

Speculative GAP. As explained earlier in this section, when a pre-defined grammar is unavailable, only a partial grammar might be collected. Inferring feasible paths from such an incomplete grammar may result in some feasible paths missing. Consequently, feeding such incomplete information to a GAP pushdown transducer may cause the correct execution path being excluded. This scheme is generally referred to as *speculative execution*. There are two basic requirements for effective speculative execution. First, it has to ensure the correctness. GAP pushdown transducers ensure this in the join phase. When no match of mappings is found during the linking of two consecutive chunks, a misspeculation is reported. Under this situation, a reprocessing is initiated immediately on the missepculated chunk to ensure the correctness. Second, the misspeculation penalty should be low enough so that it will not cancel out the benefits of speculation. To achieve this, GAP pushdown transducers carefully divide chunks into even smaller pieces such that reprocessing is done selectively.

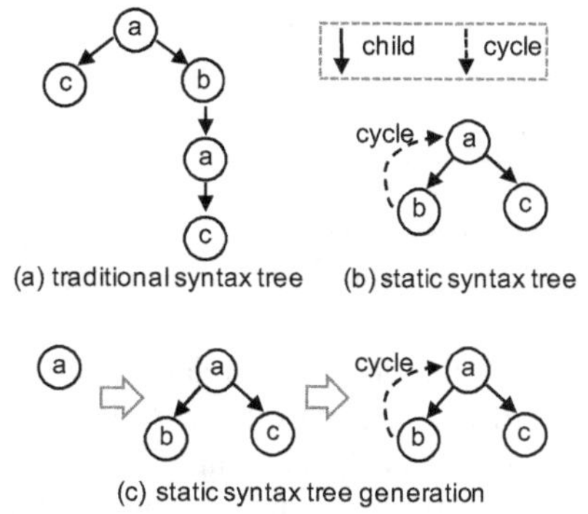

Figure 6. Static Syntax Tree

Figure 5 illustrates both the basic and speculative GAP pushdown transducers. We next elaborate the two modes of GAP in the following two sections.

4. Non-Speculative GAP

When the grammar of the semi-structured data is available, GAP runs in non-speculative mode. In this section, we first describe the two steps to infer feasible paths: static syntax tree generation and symbolic pushdown transducer execution, then present more details about the new features of GAP pushdown transducers.

4.1 Static Syntax Tree Generation

Grammars written in textual rules are hard to interpret directly. To effectively leverage the grammar, we need a data structure to capture all the nesting relations among different input symbols/elements in a concise form.

In fact, the nesting relations can be naturally represented as a tree structure. A traditional syntax tree (or parse tree) indicates the derivation of a concrete sentence based on its (context-free) grammar. Figure 6-a shows the syntax tree of the running example (Figure 4-b). Note that such a syntax

Algorithm 1 Construction of Static Syntax Tree

```
procedure STATIC_SYNTAX_TREE_CONSTRUCTION(DTD)
    for each element el in DTD do
        if el is the first element then
            root = create_node(el); //assume the 1st is root
            root.cycle = null; // represent recursion if exists
            nodes = root;
        else/* search el in tree root */
            nodes = tree_search(root, el);
        for node in nodes do
            for each subelement sub of el do
                if sub.is_ancestor(node) then // recursion
                    node.cycle=sub; // set a backward pointer
                else
                    child = create_node(sub);
                    child.cycle=null;
                    node.add_child(child);
    return root;
```

tree can grow to very large size as the input gets longer, meanwhile it may not capture all the possible derivation of its context-free grammar.

To represent all the derivation relations in the grammar with a concise format, we introduce *static syntax tree* – a tree generated purely based on the input grammar. As shown in Figure 6-b, in a static syntax tree, each child element must appear and only appear once. The size of a static syntax tree depends on the input grammar, rather than input data, hence will not increase as data grows.

The construction of a static syntax tree is straightforward. Basically, a construction algorithm scans the grammar file, identifies the root element and its child/descendant elements iteratively until all leaf elements (elements without any child elements) are included, as shown in Algorithm 1. For recursive grammars, the algorithm labels nodes that refer to an ancestor by setting the field *cycle*. Figure 6-c illustrates the major steps of executing the algorithm on the running example. The time complexity of this algorithm is $O(n^2)$ where n is the number of elements in the DTD file.

4.2 Symbolic Execution of Pushdown Transducer

The goal of symbolic execution is to find out feasible execution paths for each input symbol. Formally, we define the feasible execution path as follows.

Definition 2. *Given an input symbol $c \in \Sigma$, for any syntactically correct inputs, if there exists an input such that the pushdown transducer can transition to state $s \in Q$ right before it reads c, then we call the execution path that starts from state s as a* feasible execution path *for symbol c.*

According to the definition, to infer the feasible paths for an input symbol, it needs to test all the possible inputs of syntactically correct semi-structured data, which is impossible. We address this by running the pushdown transducer symbolically on the static syntax tree. Basically, the transducer walks on every path of the static syntax tree and records the state right before meeting the start tag and end tag of a node on the path. For example, if the current state is `s` and the current node is `n`, then it adds a `key:value` pair of `<n>:s` and `</n>:s'` into the hash table, where `s'` is the next state after consuming symbol `<n>`.

Algorithm 2 Feasible Paths Inference

```
procedure PATH_INFERENCE(root, init_state)
    current = init_state; /* current state in automaton */
    node = root; /* current node in static syntax tree */
    stack.push(root); /* for depth-first traversal */
    while stack is not empty do
        node = stack.pop();
        /* handle a cycle in a recursive grammar */
        if node.cycle != null and node.done == false then
            /* current state and node in the cycle */
            current' = next_state(current, node.start);
            n = node.cycle;
            /* pushdown transducer moves to next state */
            next = next_state(current', n.start);
            if next != null then
                queue.add(n);
                while queue is not empty do
                    n = queue.remove();
                    next = next_state(current', n.start);
                    hash.add(n.start, current');
                    hash.add(n.end, next);
                    current' = next;
                    nodes = DEF_CHILDREN(n, current');
                    if nodes is not empty then
                        queue.add(nodes);
            node.done = true; /* done with this cycle */
        if node.visited == false then
            next = next_state(current, node.start);
            hash.add(node.start, current);
            hash.add(node.end, next);
            current = next;
            node.visited = true;
        for each child of node do
            if child.visited == false then
                stack.push(child);
        if node is a leaf then
            current = next_state(current, node.end);
    return hash;

/* get node's children whose start tags are defined in state */
procedure DEF_CHILDREN(node, state)
    defined_children[];
    for each child of node do
        if next_state(state, node.start) != null then
            defined_children.add(node);
    return defined_children;
```

Recursion Handling. For a grammar with recursion, the static syntax tree contains one or more `cycle`(s). In this case, the algorithm unfolds the cycles. However, a naive unfolding would result in dead loops. To address this, we use the finite automaton to guide the unfolding and only unfold it to the extent that is necessary for revealing feasible states.

Algorithm 2 shows the pseudocode of the symbolic execution. It takes the query automaton and static syntax tree as inputs and outputs feasible path hash table. The time complexity of symbolic execution is $O(n + g \cdot |query|)$, where n is the number of nodes in the syntax tree, g is the number of cycles in the syntax tree, and $|query|$ is the length of the query. The time complexity of dealing with cycles depends on the length the query.

Example. Figure 7 illustrates an execution of Algorithm 2 on the running example with the finite automaton in Figure 4-c and the static syntax tree in Figure 6-c. Note that though there is a cycle in the static syntax tree (labeled at node b), the algorithm terminates quickly after it finds that b is not defined at state 4.

```
/* H: hash table, S: stack, Q: queue */
node=a current=1 S{a} H{}  // line 2-4
node=a current=2 S{b,c} H{<a>:1, </a>:2}  // line 26-34
node=c current=0 S{b} H{<a>:1, </a>:2, <c>:2, </c>:0}  // line 26-34
since c is a leaf node, current=2 (i.e., the next state after </c>)  // line 35-36
node=b (b has a cycle) current'=3 n=a Q{a}  // line 6-15
current'=4, Q{c} H{<a>:{1,3}, </a>:{2,4}, <c>:2, </c>:0}  // line 16-24
/* since b is not defined at state 4, only c added to queue Q{c} */
current'=5 Q{} H{<a>:{1,3}, </a>:{2,4}, <c>:{2,4}), </c>:{0,5}}  // cycle is done
node=b current=2, since b is still unvisited, process b  // line 26
S{} H{<a>:{1,3}, </a>:{2,4}, <b>:2, </b>:3, <c>:{2,4}, </c>:{0,5}}  // finish
```

Figure 7. Algorithm 2 execution on the running example.

4.3 GAP Pushdown Transducers

GAP pushdown transducers are based on the basic parallel pushdown transducers (Section 2.3) with two novel features:

- *Dynamic path elimination*: GAP pushdown transducers leverage feasible path inference to dynamically eliminate impossible execution paths at runtime, based on specific local context.
- *Runtime data structure switching*: Benefited from path elimination and path convergence, GAP pushdown transducers switch between a stack and a double-tree data structure at runtime to maximize the efficiency.

At high-level, GAP pushdown transducers follow the same flow as basic parallel pushdown transducers: (i) *split phase*, (ii) *parallel phase*, and (iii) *join phase*. The main differences between GAP pushdown transducers and basic parallel pushdown transducers lie in the parallel phase. In this phase, each transducer processes an input chunk while maintaining a set of possible execution paths through a set of mappings M. A mapping is defined as follows:

Definition 3. *Given an input chunk i, a mapping m^i for i is a 5-tuple $m^i = (q_s, z_s, q_f, z_f, o)$, $m^i \in M = Q \times \Gamma^* \times Q \times \Gamma^* \times \Delta^*$ where q_s and z_s are the starting state and stack right before processing i, q_f, z_f, and o are the finishing state, stack, and output tape after processing i.*

Basically, a mapping embodies the basic information of an execution path. For example, a mapping (1, ϵ, 4, 1:2:3, 1) says that if the transducer starts from state 1 with an empty stack, then after processing the input chunk, it will end at state 4 with a stack of 1:2:3 (":" separates items in a stack) and an output tape containing a match. Such information is used later for joining the results of different transducers.

Maintaining the mappings brings a significant amount of cost, comparing to a single path execution in a sequential transducer [30]. To reduce such parallelization cost, GAP transducers feature two new optimizations: *dynamic path elimination* and *runtime data structure switching*. Both of them happen in the parallel phase.

Dynamic Path Elimination. A GAP transducer leverages feasible path inference to prune impossible paths in three situations on the fly:

(1) At the beginning of a chunk (except the first one), a GAP transducer uses the first symbol of the chunk as the key to look up the feasible path hash table. In return, it obtains a list of feasible execution paths Q_{hash}, which is often a strict subset of all execution paths Q (i.e., $Q_{hash} \subseteq Q$). Then it processes the chunk with only the paths from Q_{hash}. For example, a GAP transducer that starts at Line 5 of the XML data in Figure 4-b would look up <c> in the hash table (the last line of Figure 7), and keeps only paths $\{2, 4\}$.

(2) During the processing of a chunk, path divergences might happen – when a pop operation is needed while the stack is empty, the parallel transducer has to enumerate all possible states that could be popped out from the stack. Prior work [30] extends the finite automaton by defining the transitions for all end tags, and only includes states that have a defined transition for the given end tag (denoted as Q_{fa}). Since the inference is only based on the finite automaton (i.e., query), regardless the input grammar, the state amount of reduction is limited [2]. In comparison, when a path divergence occurs, a GAP transducer inquires the feasible path hash table that is built based on both the query and the input grammar. Using the given end tag as the key, it can obtain a potentially smaller set of possible states (i.e., $Q_{hash} \subseteq Q_{fa}$). Since the path divergence may happen multiple times during the processing of a chunk, the feasible path inference-based elimination has great potential to reduce the path maintenance cost. Following the example in situation (1), when the GAP transducer processes Line 6, it looks up </a> in the hash table and chooses paths $\{2, 4\}$, instead of $\{2, 4, 0\}$ – the choice of prior work [30].

(3) When processing the first start tag right after a path divergence (e.g., the tag <b> in </d></c><b>, supposing that path divergence happened at both </d> and </c>), a GAP transducer also inquires the feasible path table with the first tag (<b>). The purpose is to further reduce the number of execution paths. This is achieved the taking the intersection between the set of execution paths before the first start tag Q_{old} and the returned path set from feasible path table inquiry Q_{hash} (i.e., $Q_{old} \cap Q_{hash}$).

Runtime Data Structure Switching. To reduce the cost of mapping maintenance, basic parallel pushdown transducers use a double-tree data structure [30], which compresses the mapping and reduces redundant computation in mapping updates. While being more efficient than maintaining each mapping separately, it is much slower than the stack-based execution of a sequential pushdown transducer.

[2] In evaluation, we found it often fails to reduce the possibilities of popped-out states due to the inclusion of a special state that handles unrelated tags (e.g., state 0 in the running example).

An interesting observation we found is that the number of feasible execution paths often drops to one, thanks to the dynamic path elimination and path convergence. To leverage this insight, we allow GAP transducers switch back to stack-based execution once a single feasible path is left.

More specifically, when a path elimination is performed, the GAP transducer checks the number of feasible execution paths. If the transducer finds only one path is left, then it switches to use a stack to continue its execution until the next path elimination check; otherwise it uses a double-tree data structure to maintain multiple execution paths. As discussed earlier, a path may diverge into multiple ones under certain circumstances (see Section 2.3). In such cases, the GAP transducers switch to a double-tree data structure right after the divergence. Since path elimination can happen multiple times for a GAP transducer depending on the contents in the chunk, the data structure switching can also occur multiple times. We hence refer to it as *runtime data structure switching*. Note that the switching cost is usually negligible as the switching typically occurs less than 5 times in millions of transitions, according to our experiments.

Finally, once each GAP pushdown transducer finishes its chunk, the mappings from different transducers are joint pair by pair using the same rules as basic parallel pushdown transducers [30]. Basically, to join a pair of mappings m^1 and m^2, it requires their states and stacks are matched appropriately (e.g., $m^1(q_f) = m^2(q_s)$).

In sum, GAP pushdown transducers are based on basic parallel pushdown transducers and work in three phases. With the two novel features, dynamic path elimination and runtime data structure switching, their execution cost can be potentially reduced.

5. Speculative GAP

In certain scenarios, a pre-defined grammar may not be available. For example, the grammar has not been explicitly defined or its access is not granted. GAP addresses this challenge with speculative execution. In this section, we first describe a method for extracting partial grammars from input data, then introduce the speculative execution of GAP pushdown transducers, including a local reprocessing technique to reduce the misspeculation penalty.

5.1 Partial Grammar Extraction

In the absence of a pre-defined grammar, we leverage the insight that *input data implicitly dictate the grammar to a certain extent, though may not cover the entire grammar.* Specifically, we design a method that automatically extracts a partial static syntax tree from prior inputs.

Many applications process semi-structured data from the same source repetitively. For example, web analytics that receive semi-structured data from a specific social network website or data exchanges between two enterprises. In such scenarios, the input data from run to run tend to follow a similar *structure* as they are all defined by the same "hidden" grammar. Hence, it provides an opportunity to "learn" grammar from earlier runs.

Algorithm 3 shows a straightforward way to extract a (partial) static syntax tree directly from an input stream. More sophisticated grammar learning algorithms are also available from prior studies [35, 36].

Algorithm 3 Static Syntax Tree Extraction from Input Data

```
procedure STATIC_SYNTAX_TREE_EXTRACTION(stream)
    while stream has next tag t do
        if t is the first element then /* root node */
            root = create_node(t);
            stack.push(root);
        else if t is a start tag then
            parent = stack.top();
            /* find a child of parent with tag t */
            child = find_child_by_tag(parent, t);
            if child != null then
                stack.push(child);
            else /* create a new child for parent */
                node = create_node(t);
                parent.add_child(node);
                stack.push(node);
        else if t is an end tag and t == stack.top().end then
            stack.pop();
        else
            print("errors in inputs");
    return root;
```

5.2 Speculative GAP Pushdown Transducers

Speculative GAP pushdown transducers are augmented with the capabilities of validating the speculative execution paths and initiating appropriate reprocessing when speculation fails. Since Section 4.3 already describes the basics of GAP pushdown transducers, here we focus on the aspects of speculative execution.

Speculative Execution. With the extracted grammar, GAP can infer feasible paths in the same way as inferring from a pre-defined grammar. The difference lies in the results – the feasible paths may be incomplete due to missing parts of the extracted grammar. Consequently, GAP transducers run speculatively, with the potential of missing the true path. Similarly to other speculation schemes, speculative GAP transducers first run with speculated data (i.e., feasible paths from extracted grammar), then rely on the validation and reprocessing to guarantee the correctness.

Note that when a speculative GAP transducer looks up an incomplete feasible path table, it may not even find any corresponding feasible paths for the inquired input symbol, simply because the symbol does not appear in the extracted grammar. In such situations, the GAP transducers degrade themselves to basic parallel pushdown transducers and enumerate all execution paths.

Another difference with the non-speculative transducers is about the third scenario of dynamic path elimination (see Section 4.3). When processing the first start tag after a path divergence, it does not take the intersection between two path sets Q_{old} and Q_{hash}. Instead, it simply uses Q_{hash} to replace Q_{old}, for two reasons: first, this creates chances to correct an earlier misspeculation; second, it allows the reprocessing to be performed selectively (as explained next).

Validation and Reprocessing. Once every GAP transducer finishes its chunk (speculatively), they enter into the join phase, where the validation and reprocessing are performed.

According to Section 4.3, the feasible path table is used in three scenarios: (1) at the beginning a chunk (except the first one); (2) in the occurrence of a path divergence; (3) when processing the first start tag after a path divergence. Since the feasible path table is extracted from a partial grammar, it might miss the true execution path. Hence, a validation is required for each of the above three scenarios, respectively. For example, during the joining of a pair of mappings from two consecutive chunks, if the starting states of the latter chunk do not include the correct finishing state of the earlier chunk, a misspeculation is detected. In either case, when a validation fails, a GAP transducer would reprocess the failed part with the corresponding correct starting state. Note that a misspeculation at the beginning of of a chunk does not necessarily mean that the whole chunk needs to be reprocessed. Thanks to the other two dynamic path elimination scenarios, an earlier misspeculation might be corrected by a latter path elimination operation. Hence, the reprocessing of a chunk is usually performed selectively.

6. Evaluation

We evaluate GAP on a set of real-world XML benchmarks and examine its efficiency and scalability on a variety of path queries, including a set of 200 queries.

Implementation. We prototyped GAP in C language. It includes four major components: a static syntax tree generator that takes a DTD/XSD grammar as input and outputs a static syntax tree; a symbolic pushdown transducer executor that runs symbolically over a given static syntax tree; a multi-threaded GAP pushdown transducer implemented using Pthread and can be tuned into either *speculative mode* or *non-speculative mode* (by default, it is set to speculative mode), as well as a grammar extractor that can be enabled either online (for streaming data) or offline (for storage data).

Methodology. We compare GAP with the state-of-the-art parallel pushdown transducers [30], which has shown comparable performance to PugiXML [22], a popular C++ XML processing library and much better performance than Expat [6]. Table 2 summarizes the versions used in our comparison. For speculative GAP versions, we randomly choose a portion of the complete grammar [3].

All experiments run on a 20-core machine equipped with two Intel 2.13 GHz Xeon E7-L8867 processors. The machine runs openSUSE Leap 42.1 and has GCC 4.8.5. All programs are compiled with "-O3" optimization flag. The timing results reported are the average of 10 repetitive runs. We do not report 95% confidence interval of the average when the variation is not significant.

[3] To ensure the partial grammar is meaningful, we randomly and recursively remove leaf elements from the original grammar.

Method Versions	Abbreviation
Parallel pushdown transducer [30]	PP-Transducer
Non-speculative GAP	GAP-NonSpec
Speculative GAP with 20% grammar	GAP-Spec(20%)
Speculative GAP with 40% grammar	GAP-Spec(40%)
Speculative GAP with 80% grammar	GAP-Spec(80%)

Table 2. Method Versions in Evaluation

Benchmarks. Table 3 lists datasets used in our experiments as well as their statistics. Except XMark, all the datasets are from a commonly used UW XML data repository [40], which covers a variety of XML applications. To make a fair comparison with prior work [30], we also use a scaling factor that replicates the datasets, resulting in sizes from 600MB to 6GB. We do not report results for larger datasets because the measurements are stable due to the large amount of repetitive computations involved in semi-structured query processing.

Dataset	#tags	d_{max}	d_{avg}	Dataset	#tags	d_{max}	d_{avg}
Lineitem	34,781,152	3	2.94	DBLP	33,321,292	6	2.9
SwissProt	29,770,302	5	3.55	NASA	237,230,520	8	5.58
Protein	42,597,466	7	5.15	XMark	23,328,398	13	5.55

Table 3. XML datasets (d means depth)

We use queries from XPathMark[14] for its designated purpose of XPath query evaluation and its realistic query structures. As listed in Table 4, the query set covers the whole set of A-type queries as well as two B-type queries in XPathMark. When predicates, parents or ancestors are used, the queries are translated into subqueries or rewritten, such that they can be merged into a single pushdown transducer. The right-most two columns show the number of subqueries and number of matches in the datasets.

Single-Query Performance. The speedup for single-query processing is shown in Figure 8 (left). The baseline is the sequential pushdown transducer.

Among the five versions, GAP-NonSpec yields the best speedup on all tested queries, leading to an average of 15X speedup. In comparison, PP-Transducer achieves least speedup except for benchmarks XM1 and XM2, in which cases the GAP-Spec(20%) performs the worst. It is easy to notice the clear trend among the three speculative versions. As the extracted syntax tree becomes more complete, the performance improves. However, the trend varies across different benchmarks, implying that the performance of speculative versions are less predictable. It is worth to note that even with 20% syntax tree, the GAP-Spec still yields better performance than PP-Transducer (13.2X v.s. 11.6X).

To better understand the performance results, we profiled the average number of starting execution paths, as shown in Table 5. The last row of single query block shows the geometrical mean of the number of starting execution paths for each version. It clearly shows a big discrepancy between PP-Transducer and GAP-NonSpec. The discrepancy confirms the effectiveness of the proposed dynamic path elimination and demonstrates its benefits in improving the performance.

Query	Dataset	Query structure	#sub	#matches
NS1	NASA	/ds/d/tb/ts/tl/tit	1	2,119,760
NS2	NASA	//ds/d/tit	1	3,395,250
PT1	Protein	/pd/pe/r/ri/xs/x/u	1	279,402
PT2	Protein	/p/pe//u	1	1,949,416
DP1	DBLP	/dp/ar/au	1	1,107,323
DP2	DBLP	//dp//ed	1	31,940
DP4	DBLP	/dp/ar[tit]/jn	3	558,046
XM3	XMark	//k/ancestor::li/t/k	3	241,556
NS3	NASA	/ds/d[descendant::tit or descendant::na or descendant::kw]/an	5	1,826,250
NS4	NASA	/ds/d[tit and al]/r/s/o/au/ln	4	191,250
PT3	Protein	/pd/pe/r[aci/acs or at or ct or nt]/ri/ats/at	6	5,668,287
DP3	DBLP	/dp[mt/au or mt/tit or mt/yr or pt/au or pt/tit or pt/yr or ...]/au	43	1,107,323
XM1	XMark	/s/r/*/item/[parent::af]/name	1	3,851
XM2	XMark	//s[r/*/item[parent::au parent::af ... parent:: eu]/mb/m/t/k/ b or ...]/pp/ps/ name	18	178,500

Table 4. XPath queries. #sub shows the number of sub-queries in each query structure.

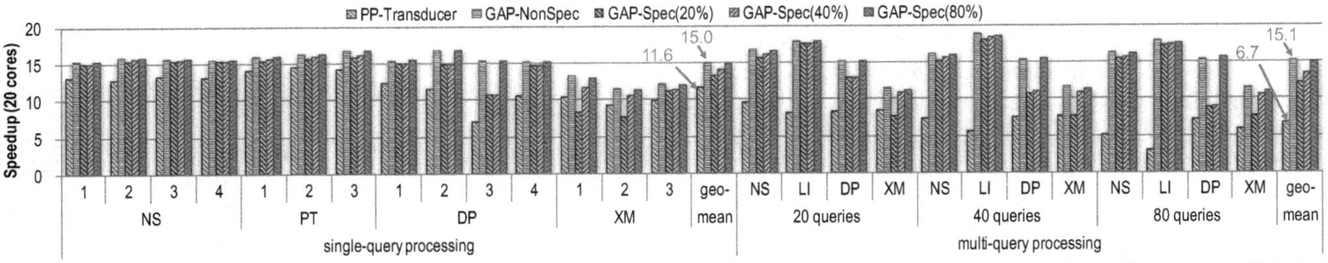

Figure 8. Speedup of Single-Query and Multi-Query Processing on A 20-core Machine

	Query Set	PP-Trans.	GAP-NonSpec	GAP-Spec 20%	GAP-Spec 40%	GAP-Spec 80%
single query	NS	7.7	1.0	5.7	4.8	1.1
	LI	8.4	1.1	5.3	1.3	1.1
	DP	9.0	1.7	3.1	3.1	1.6
	XM	12.4	1.9	6.3	5.5	3.7
	Geo	9.2	1.4	4.9	3.2	1.7
80 queries	NS	275.0	1.1	192.4	157.6	5.3
	LI	166.0	1.0	60.6	51.4	28.5
	DP	96.0	3.2	18.9	17.4	2.5
	XM	285.0	5.4	119.8	75.2	33.4
	Geo	188.0	2.1	71.7	57.0	10.6

Table 5. Average Number of Starting Execution Paths

	Query (set)	GAP-Spec(20%) cost	GAP-Spec(20%) acc.	GAP- Spec(40%) cost	GAP- Spec(40%) acc.
single query	DP1	0.003%	94.12%	0.003%	94.12%
	DP3	0.002%	94.12%	0.002%	94.12%
	DP4	0.003%	94.12%	0.004%	94.12%
	XM1	26.85%	62.50%	0%	100%
	XM2	25.10%	47.83%	0%	100%
query set	DP (20)	0.003%	88.24%	0.002%	88.24%
	DP (40)	0.002%	94.12%	0.003%	94.12%
	DP (80)	0.002%	96.43%	0.002%	96.43%
	XM (20)	24.18%	56.52%	0%	100%
	XM (40)	24.14%	56.52%	0%	100%
	XM (80)	26.02%	54.17%	0%	100%

Table 6. Speculation Accuracy and Reprocessing Cost

Multi-Query Performance. To evaluate the performance of multi-query processing, we use 12 groups of queries, with three different sizes: 20 queries, 40 queries, and 80 queries.

Multi-query processing speedup is shown in Figure 8 (right). Overall, the results follow a similar pattern as single-query processing. However, the performance differences among different versions become larger, especially between PP-Transducer and four GAP versions. Specifically, GAP-NonSpec produces 15.1X, similarly to its single-query performance, while PP-Transducer only yields 6.7X speedup. The reason is that when processing multiple queries concurrently, the pushdown transducers grow larger with more number of states. As a result, PP-Transducer ends up enumerating more paths, causing higher parallelization cost.

Table 5 reports the number of starting paths for all five versions. In single-query processing, the gap between PP-Transducer and GAP-NonSpec is about 10X (9.2 vs. 1.4 on average). While in multi-query processing, the gap quickly increases up to hundreds of times (188 vs. 2.1 on average).

Speculation Accuracy and Cost. Table 6 reports the speculation accuracy and the cost of misspeculation, including both single queries and query sets. The ones that are not listed do not have any misspeculation. The misspeculation cost is typically a very tiny portion of the total execution time, except queries to XM dataset which shows more than 24% misspeculation cost when using 20% grammar (GAP-Spec(20%)). There are two main reasons causing such relatively high cost: First, the speculation accuracy of these queries are relatively low, slightly higher than 50%, resulting in a substantial amount of reprocessing; Second, a few elements that appear quite often in the dataset are missing in the 20% partial grammar, in which cases, the speculative GAP transducers degrade themselves to basic parallel transducers and enumerate all execution paths.

Scalability. We measured the scalabilities in terms of both the number of cores and the number of queries.

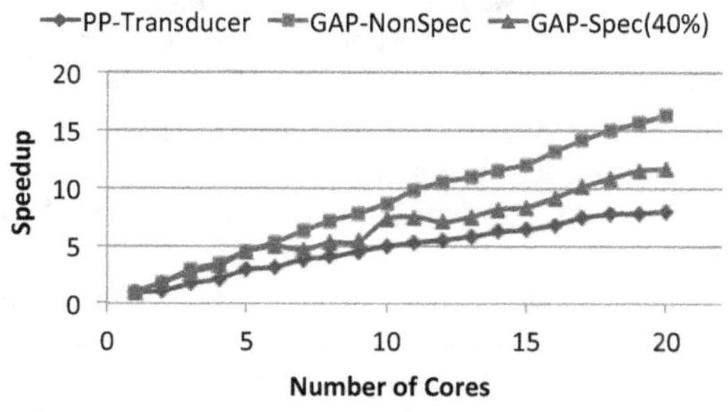

Figure 9. Scalability over Number of Cores

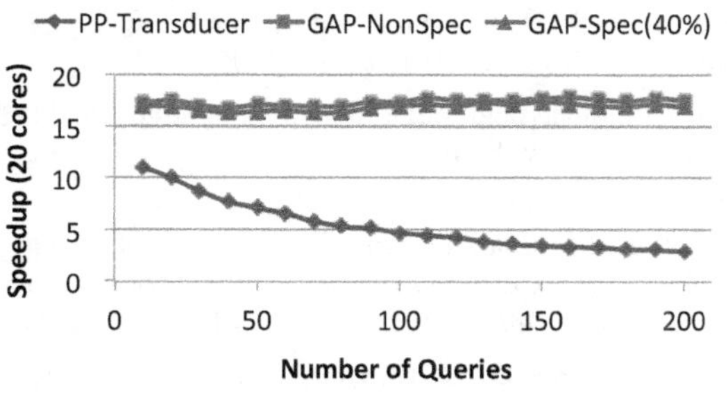

Figure 10. Scalability over Number of Queries

Figure 9 shows the scalability in terms of number of cores. All three versions show good scalability – the speedup linearly increases up to at least 20 cores. Meanwhile, it also clearly shows the trend of their differences – as the number of cores increases the performance gap among these three versions will become even larger.

Figure 10 shows the scalability in terms of number of queries. PP-Transducer shows a sharp decrease as the number of queries increases, which aligns well with the results reported by prior work [30]. In comparison, the two GAP versions show no degradation at all up to at least 200 queries, thanks to the dynamic path elimination.

7. Related Work

There is a large amount of efforts on making parsing parallel for both context-free grammars and non-CFG grammars [16, 17, 29, 37, 41]. They provide valuable insights to this work. In particular, [16] leverages some rules extracted from the input structure to facilitate the parallel expression evaluation. Next, we will focus our discussions on XPath querying and its parallelism exploitation.

XML querying. Many prior work study the expressiveness of XPath querying and the execution of concurrent queries efficiently, including automata-based techniques [2, 44], array-based methods like TurboXPath [21] and stack-based algorithms like Twig2Stack [5]. This work uses an approach that combines a number of small queries into a single DFA and evaluates them simultaneously [19]. Y-Filter [11] and XMLTK [2] are based on this method and address state explosion with lazy DFA.

Some earlier work exploiting data parallelism in XPath queries rewrite an XPath query with predicates into several sub-queries, execute the sub-queries in parallel and merge their results sequentially [4]. However, this approach demands more hardware resources meanwhile exposes limited parallelism. The work by Zhang and others [44] executes multiple states in the NFA in parallel. Although each active state is handled by a different thread, the XML data is still processed sequentially. An alternative method proposed by Liu and others [24] uses a parallel structured join algorithm, where both query and join operations are parallelizable. However, constructing the required data structures is still a sequential step. This work is primarily based on the PP-Transducer [30] which can operate on arbitrarily framed XML chunks. More details are given in Section 1 and 2.3.

Parallel XML Parsing. There are two basic ways of data-level parallel parsing for XML: the partition-oriented and the merging-oriented [25, 33, 39, 43, 45]. The work by Lu and others, for example, first extracts the high-level structure of XML documents through a quick prescan [25], and parses each part of the document in parallel. In comparison, Wu and others [43]'s method cuts XML documents into chunks directly, parses them and merges the result together.

Other Parallelization. Recent work on parallelizing finite automata [28, 34, 46, 47] provides useful insights, but cannot be applied directly to pushdown transducers, due to the involvement of stack. Zhao and others design stack-based automata that predict future function calls to enable parallel Just-in-Time compilation [48]. Saeed and others [26] exploit the rank convergence in parallel dynamic programming, sharing some of the high-level ideas of this work.

8. Conclusion

This paper presents GAP, a novel parallelization scheme that leverages the grammar of semi-structured data to improve the parallelization efficiency. Depending on the availability of a pre-defined grammar, GAP can run in both speculative mode and non-speculative mode. In either case, GAP is able to infer feasible execution paths by generating a static syntax tree and executing the pushdown transducer symbolically on the tree. By feeding such information to the GAP pushdown transducers, unnecessary execution paths can be eliminated on the fly. In addition, GAP transducers feature a runtime data structure switching to further take advantage of path elimination and maximize the efficiency. Evaluation on real-world datasets and queries confirm the benefits of grammar-aware parallelization which yields consistent speedup to a large number of concurrent queries.

Acknowledgments

We thank all anonymous reviewers for their constructive comments and our paper shepherd Armando Solar for his great help with the final preparation. This material is based upon work supported by the National Science Foundation (NSF) under Grant No. 1565928.

References

[1] D. Arroyuelo, F. Claude, S. Maneth, V. Makinen, G. Navarro, K. Nguyen, J. Siren, and N. Valimaki. Fast in-memory xpath search using compressed indexes. *Software: Practice and Experience*, 45(3):399–434, 2015.

[2] I. Avila-Campillo, T. J. Green, A. Gupta, M. Onizuka, D. Raven, and D. Suciu. Xmltk: An xml toolkit for scalable xml stream processing. 2002.

[3] P. Boncz, T. Grust, M. Van Keulen, S. Manegold, J. Rittinger, and J. Teubner. Monetdb/xquery: a fast xquery processor powered by a relational engine. In *Proceedings of the 2006 ACM SIGMOD international conference on Management of data*, pages 479–490. ACM, 2006.

[4] R. Bordawekar, L. Lim, A. Kementsietsidis, and B. W. Kok. Statistics-based parallelization of xpath queries in shared memory systems. In *EDBT 2010, 13th International Conference on Extending Database Technology, Lausanne, Switzerland, March 22-26, 2010, Proceedings*, pages 159–170, 2010.

[5] S. Chen, H. Li, J. Tatemura, W. Hsiung, D. Agrawal, and K. S. Candan. Twig^{2}stack: Bottom-up processing of generalized-tree-pattern queries over XML documents. In *Proceedings of the 32nd International Conference on Very Large Data Bases, Seoul, Korea, September 12-15, 2006*, pages 283–294, 2006.

[6] J. Clark, C. Cooper, and F. Drake. The expat xml parser, 2011.

[7] DBLP Team. Welcome to DBLP. `http://dblp.uni-trier.de/`, 2016. Retrived: 2016-07-01.

[8] F. S. de Boer, M. M. Bonsangue, J. Jacob, A. Stam, and L. Van der Torre. Enterprise architecture analysis with xml. In *Proceedings of the 38th Annual Hawaii International Conference on System Sciences*, pages 222b–222b. IEEE, 2005.

[9] E. developers program. What is the ebay api? `https://go.developer.ebay.com/what-ebay-api`, 2016. Retrived: 2016-07-01.

[10] Y. Diao, P. Fischer, M. J. Franklin, and R. To. Yfilter: Efficient and scalable filtering of xml documents. In *Data Engineering, 2002. Proceedings. 18th International Conference on*, pages 341–342. IEEE, 2002.

[11] Y. Diao, P. M. Fischer, M. J. Franklin, and R. To. Yfilter: Efficient and scalable filtering of XML documents. In *Proceedings of the 18th International Conference on Data Engineering, San Jose, CA, USA, February 26 - March 1, 2002*, pages 341–342, 2002.

[12] A. Dunkels et al. Efficient application integration in ip-based sensor networks. In *Proceedings of the First ACM Workshop on Embedded Sensing Systems for Energy-Efficiency in Buildings*, pages 43–48. ACM, 2009.

[13] Facebook. Public feed API. `https://developers.facebook.com/docs/public_feed`, 2016. Retrieved: 2016-07-01.

[14] M. Franceschet. Xpathmark: Functional and performance tests for xpath. In *Dagstuhl Seminar Proceedings*. Schloss Dagstuhl-Leibniz-Zentrum für Informatik, 2007.

[15] F. Galiegue and K. Zyp. Json schema: Core definitions and terminology. *Internet Engineering Task Force (IETF)*, 2013.

[16] A. Gibbons and W. Rytter. *Efficient parallel algorithms*. Cambridge University Press, 1989.

[17] A. Gibbons and W. Rytter. Optimal parallel algorithms for dynamic expression evaluation and context-free recognition. *Information and Computation*, 81(1):32–45, 1989.

[18] T. J. Green, G. Miklau, M. Onizuka, and D. Suciu. Processing xml streams with deterministic automata. In *International Conference on Database Theory*, pages 173–189. Springer, 2003.

[19] T. J. Green, G. Miklau, M. Onizuka, and D. Suciu. Processing XML streams with deterministic automata. In *Database Theory - ICDT 2003, 9th International Conference, Siena, Italy, January 8-10, 2003, Proceedings*, pages 173–189, 2003.

[20] D. Halstead. What sort of network and storage setup will be required to ingest the entire twitter firehose for 1 year. `http://goo.gl/kFXDH`. Retrieved: 2016-07-01.

[21] V. Josifovski, M. Fontoura, and A. Barta. Querying XML streams. *VLDB J.*, 14(2):197–210, 2005.

[22] A. Kapoulkine. pugixml: a light-weight, simple and fast xml parser for c++ with xpath support. `http://pugixml.org/`. Retrieved: 2016-07-01.

[23] L. Libkin, W. Martens, and D. Vrgoc. Querying graph databases with xpath. In *Proceedings of the 16th International Conference on Database Theory*, pages 129–140. ACM, 2013.

[24] L. Liu, J. Feng, G. Li, Q. Qian, and J. Li. Parallel structural join algorithm on shared-memory multi-core systems. In *The Ninth International Conference on Web-Age Information Management, WAIM 2008, July 20-22, 2008, Zhangjiajie, China*, pages 70–77, 2008.

[25] W. Lu, K. Chiu, and Y. Pan. A parallel approach to xml parsing. In *Proceedings of the 7th IEEE/ACM International Conference on Grid Computing*, GRID '06, pages 223–230, 2006.

[26] S. Maleki, M. Musuvathi, and T. Mytkowicz. Parallelizing dynamic programming through rank convergence. *ACM SIGPLAN Notices*, 49(8):219–232, 2014.

[27] A. Mitra, M. Vieira, P. Bakalov, W. Najjar, and V. Tsotras. Boosting xml filtering with a scalable fpga-based architecture. *arXiv preprint arXiv:0909.1781*, 2009.

[28] T. Mytkowicz, M. Musuvathi, and W. Schulte. Data-parallel finite-state machines. In *ASPLOS '14: Proceedings of 19th International Conference on Architecture Support for Programming Languages and Operating Systems*. ACM Press, 2014.

[29] A. Nijholt. The cyk approach to serial and parallel parsing. 1991.

[30] P. Ogden, D. Thomas, and P. Pietzuch. Scalable XML query processing using parallel pushdown transducers. *Proceedings of the VLDB Endowment*, 6(14):1738–1749, 2013.

[31] S. O'Riain, E. Curry, and A. Harth. Xbrl and open data for global financial ecosystems: A linked data approach. *International Journal of Accounting Information Systems*, 13(2):141–162, 2012.

[32] S. Pal, V. Parikh, V. Zolotov, L. Giakoumakis, and M. Rys. Xml best practices for microsoft sql server 2005. *Retrieved*, 11:2004, 2004.

[33] Y. Pan, W. Lu, Y. Zhang, and K. Chiu. A static load-balancing scheme for parallel xml parsing on multicore cpus. In *Proc. of the 7th International Symposium on Cluster Computing and the Grid (CCGRID)*, 2007.

[34] J. Qiu, Z. Zhao, and B. Ren. Microspec: Speculation-centric fine-grained parallelization for fsm computations. In *Parallel Architecture and Compilation Techniques (PACT), 2016 International Conference on*, pages 221–233. IEEE, 2016.

[35] Y. Sakakibara. Learning context-free grammars from structural data in polynomial time. *Theoretical Computer Science*, 76(2-3):223–242, 1990.

[36] Y. Sakakibara. Efficient learning of context-free grammars from positive structural examples. *Information and Computation*, 97(1):23–60, 1992.

[37] G. Satta and O. Stock. Bidirectional context-free grammar parsing for natural language processing. *Artificial Intelligence*, 69(1):123–164, 1994.

[38] L. Schor, P. Sommer, and R. Wattenhofer. Towards a zero-configuration wireless sensor network architecture for smart buildings. In *Proceedings of the First ACM Workshop on Embedded Sensing Systems for Energy-Efficiency in Buildings*, pages 31–36. ACM, 2009.

[39] B. Shah, P. Rao, B. Moon, and M. Rajagopalan. A data parallel algorithm for xml dom parsing. *Database and XML Technologies, Lecture Notes in Computer Science*, 5679, 2009.

[40] D. Suciu. XML data repository. `http://www.cs.washington.edu/research/xmldatasets/`, 2003. Retrieved: 2016-07-01.

[41] N. Takashi, T. Kentaro, K. Taura, and J. Tsujii. A parallel cky parsing algorithm on large-scale distributed-memory parallel machines. 1997.

[42] A. H. Wang. Don't follow me: Spam detection in twitter. In *Security and Cryptography (SECRYPT), Proceedings of the 2010 International Conference on*, pages 1–10. IEEE, 2010.

[43] Z. Y. Yu Wu, Qi Zhang and J. Li. A hybrid parallel processing for xml parsing and schema validation. In *Balisage: The Markup Conference 2008*.

[44] Y. Zhang, Y. Pan, and K. Chiu. A parallel xpath engine based on concurrent NFA execution. In *16th IEEE International Conference on Parallel and Distributed Systems, ICPADS 2010, Shanghai, China, December 8-10, 2010*, pages 314–321, 2010.

[45] Z. Zhao, M. Bebenita, D. Herman, J. Sun, and X. Shen. Hpar: A practical parallel parser for html–taming html complexities for parallel parsing. *ACM Transactions on Architecture and Code Optimization (TACO)*, 10(4):44, 2013.

[46] Z. Zhao and X. Shen. On-the-fly principled speculation for FSM parallelization. In *Proceedings of the Twentieth International Conference on Architectural Support for Programming Languages and Operating Systems, ASPLOS '15, Istanbul, Turkey, March 14-18, 2015*, pages 619–630, 2015.

[47] Z. Zhao, B. Wu, and X. Shen. Challenging the "embarrassingly sequential": Parallelizing finite state machine-based computations through principled speculation. In *ASPLOS '14: Proceedings of 19th International Conference on Architecture Support for Programming Languages and Operating Systems*. ACM Press, 2014.

[48] Z. Zhao, B. Wu, M. Zhou, Y. Ding, J. Sun, X. Shen, and Y. Wu. Call sequence prediction through probabilistic calling automata. In *Proceedings of the 2014 ACM International Conference on Object Oriented Programming Systems Languages & Applications*, OOPSLA '14, pages 745–762. ACM, 2014.

Eunomia: Scaling Concurrent Search Trees under Contention Using HTM

Xin Wang*†, Weihua Zhang*†, Zhaoguo Wang§, Ziyun Wei*†, Haibo Chen‡, Wenyun Zhao†¶

* Software School, Fudan University

†Shanghai Key Laboratory of Data Science, Fudan University

¶School of Computer Science, Fudan University

‡Institute of Parallel and Distributed Systems, Shanghai Jiao Tong University

§Computer Science Department, New York University

{xin_wang,zhangweihua,weizy14,wyzhao}@fudan.edu.cn zhaoguo@nyu.edu haibochen@sjtu.edu.cn

Abstract

While hardware transactional memory (HTM) has recently been adopted to construct efficient concurrent search tree structures, such designs fail to deliver scalable performance under contention. In this paper, we first conduct a detailed analysis on an HTM-based concurrent B+Tree, which uncovers several reasons for excessive HTM aborts induced by both false and true conflicts under contention. Based on the analysis, we advocate Eunomia, a design pattern for search trees which contains several principles to reduce HTM aborts, including splitting HTM regions with version-based concurrency control to reduce HTM working sets, partitioned data layout to reduce false conflicts, proactively detecting and avoiding true conflicts, and adaptive concurrency control. To validate their effectiveness, we apply such designs to construct a scalable concurrent B+Tree using HTM. Evaluation using key-value store benchmarks on a 20-core HTM-capable multi-core machine shows that Eunomia leads to 5X-11X speedup under high contention, while incurring small overhead under low contention.

Categories and Subject Descriptors D.1.3 [*Concurrent Programming*]: Parallel programming

Keywords Hardware Transactional Memory; Concurrent Search Tree; Opportunistic Consistency

1. Introduction

The emergence of hardware transactional memory (HTM) [18] provides a new opportunity to construct concurrent tree structures. HTM exploits cache coherence mechanisms to protect the consistency of critical sections, which may approach the performance of fine-grained locking or even lock-free schemes while preserving the simplicity of programming with coarse-grained locking. For this reason, there have been plenty of efforts to provide concurrent tree structures (e.g., binary search tree and B-Tree) using HTM [9, 31, 33], which was shown to achieve comparable or higher performance than lock-based schemes under low contention.

However, HTM, as an opportunistic scheme, can have a high abort rate under contention, where access conflicts among multiple cores may collapse the performance of an application. Yet, there are a number of scenarios in which applications may face high contention [20, 21, 32], due to an increased number of processor cores [36], a skewed distribution of key accesses [16], or the contention on shared entities in databases [21]. Consequently, current HTM-based concurrent search tree structures fail to deliver stable and scalable performance when workloads exhibit high contention.

This paper attempts to answer a natural question: with the assistance of HTM, can we construct a concurrent search tree structure that delivers high and scalable performance even under high contention? To answer this paper, we first present a detailed analysis of the performance of a recent concurrent HTM-based B+Tree used in several in-memory databases [9, 31, 33]. We choose the B+Tree [3] because it is a representative concurrent search tree structure widely adopted in databases and file systems. Our analysis uncovers several key issues leading to non-scalable performance under contention.

First, conventional search tree structures store keys in sorted order, which incurs severe false sharing under HTM due to a coarse-grained (i.e., cache line) conflict checking. Second, conventional search tree structures intrinsically contain pervasive shared metadata to maintain semantics, and

PPoPP '17, February 04-08, 2017, Austin, TX, USA

ACM 978-1-4503-4493-7/17/02. . . $15.00

DOI: http://dx.doi.org/10.1145/3018743.3018752

accesses to shared variables usually cause conflicts among transactions. Third, most HTM conflicts occur in common parts, which will abort the entire transaction and incur an expensive retry, leading to excessive re-execution overhead.

Based on the analysis, we present Eunomia, a design pattern that attempts to tackle the above issues with the following design guidelines. First, based on the observation that most HTM conflicts happen in the leaf layer, we partition a monolithic HTM region into multiple parts and protect the atomicity of different parts using HTM respectively. A version-based scheme is utilized to guarantee overall consistency at the boundary of different HTM regions. With this scheme, most conflicts only cause retry within the partitioned transaction pieces, instead of the entire monolithic transaction. Second, to eliminate false conflicts incurred by consecutive data layout and metadata accesses, Eunomia refactors the tree structure in a partitioned way, which dispatches concurrent requests to different segments. Third, to throttle the true conflicting requests, Eunomia adopts an efficient mechanism, which anticipates potential conflicts and avoids them accordingly. Finally, Eunomia adopts an adaptive contention control mechanism, which can detect various contention rates and achieve high performance under both high and low contention.

We have applied these design guidelines to a concurrent B+Tree on Intel's Restricted Transactional Memory (RTM), called Euno-B+Tree. Experimental results using the YCSB benchmark to evaluate key-value store performance show that under high contention, Euno-B+Tree can yield 5X-11X speedup over conventional HTM-based B+Tree and 1.6X speedup over fine-grained lock-based B+Tree, with less than 6% overhead under low and modest contention. The space overhead is lower than 5%.

In summary, this work makes the following contributions.

- A comprehensive analysis of an HTM-based concurrent search tree structure (i.e., a B+Tree) under high contention.
- A design pattern with four design guidelines for scalable concurrent HTM-based tree structures.
- A scalable and concurrent B+Tree that applies the above design pattern, yielding high performance and scalability with contended workloads.

2. Background and Motivation

This section describes the necessary background regarding HTM and uses B+Tree, a widely used concurrent search tree structure, to illustrate the issues of using HTM to construct concurrent search tree structures under contention.

2.1 HTM Semantics and Concurrent B+Tree

With the commercial availability of IBM z- and p-Series [8, 29] and Intel Haswell [11] processors, HTM [18] has been widely available to the mass market. Here we use Intel's RTM[1] as an example to illustrate the semantics and quirks of HTM.

RTM provides *xbegin* and *xend* primitives to enclose a critical region which should be executed transactionally. Memory addresses read and written within an RTM region constitute the read-set and write-set accordingly. A conflicting access occurs if one RTM transaction (i.e., a running instance of an RTM region) has a read set that overlaps with another concurrent transaction's write set or if their write sets overlap. RTM provides strong atomicity [5]. If an RTM transaction conflicts with concurrent memory operations from other transactional or non-transactional code, the processor will abort the transaction. If an RTM transaction is aborted, all its writes will be discarded and the program state will be rolled back to the beginning of the execution. Otherwise, all memory modifications within an RTM region will appear to happen atomically.

However, as a hardware mechanism, RTM provides no forward progress guarantee. Consequently, it is the programmers' responsibility to provide a fallback handler when an RTM transaction retries a predefined threshold. In practice, the fallback handler usually acquires a coarse-grained lock, all other transactionally executing threads eliding the same lock will abort, and the execution serializes on the lock [12]. Hence, the performance of an RTM transaction will fall back to a coarse-grained lock scheme with additional cost of RTM aborts.

2.2 HTM-based B+Tree

Algorithm 1 HTM-Based Put Interface

```
procedure PUT(key, newVal)
XBEGIN()
    node = root
    d = depth
    //1. traversing internal nodes
    while d ≠ 0 do
        node = node.findChild(key)
        d = d - 1
    //2. traversing leaf nodes
    leaf = node
    record = leaf.findRecord(key)
    if record ≠ null then
        record.value = newVal;
    else
        newNode = leaf.insert(key, newVal)
        //3. propagating splits upwards
        while newNode ≠ null do
            parent = newNode.getParent()
            newNode = parent.insertNode(newNode)
XEND()
```

The promising features of HTM like strong atomicity and processor-assisted conflict detection have stimulated the

[1] We will use RTM and HTM interchangeably in this paper

use of HTM to construct concurrent search tree structures. Here, we use an HTM-based B+Tree from DBX [31], an in-memory database, as an example. A B+Tree is a B-Tree in which internal nodes only store keys, and only leaves are associated with values [3]. The HTM-B+Tree adopts HTM regions to protect operations of the B+Tree such as get, put, and delete. This design was later adopted and shown to be effective in other distributed in-memory databases [9, 33]. Since most HTM-B+Tree operations share the major process of accessing B+Tree, we use the *put* operation as an example to illustrate the access algorithm of HTM-B+Tree in Algorithm 1, which comprises the following steps. For brevity, we omit the structural changes and rebalance operations.

(1) Traversing the internal nodes (Lines 6-8). In this stage, the request traverses tree edges from the root to the target leaf node; (2) Traversing the leaf nodes (Lines 10-15). The request first detects if there are duplicate keys in the target leaf. If so, the put operation changes into an update; otherwise it will insert a new record; (3) Propagating splits upwards (Lines 17-19). For a put operation, if the target leaf node is already full, then insertion triggers splits, and propagates the split upwards until encountering an internal node with empty slots.

The three stages are included in a monolithic HTM region marked by *xbegin* and *xend* primitives; such a coarse-grained HTM region eliminates the complexity of maintaining fine-grained locks and makes it easy to reason about correctness. As a result, it was shown to have much better performance compared to a state-of-the-art B+Tree (i.e., Masstree [19]) under low to modest contention [31].

2.3 Issues under High Contention

While the HTM-based concurrent tree structure has high performance under low and modest contention, its performance may collapse under high contention. To illustrate this, we evaluate the throughput of HTM-based B+Tree using the YCSB benchmark with the Zipfian input distribution [16, 24]. We adjust the skew coefficient θ in the Zipfian distribution to simulate different levels of contention. We test it on a 20-core platform with Intel's TSX [11] support. All the performance results are collected using 16 threads (a few cores are reserved for controlling threads). Threads are distributed equally on two sockets (detailed experimental setup in section 5.1).

As shown in Figure 1, with low contention rate (i.e., skew coefficient $\theta < 0.6$), the HTM-based B+Tree achieves high and stable performance. However, when the contention rate increases (e.g., $\theta > 0.6$), performance of an HTM-based B+Tree drops sharply. When $\theta = 0.9$, the performance decreases to lower than 3 million ops/s. To understand the reasons behind the performance collapse, we collect the number of HTM aborts. Since adding performance counters to each HTM region severely hinders the overall throughput, here we set performance counters in every 10 operations, so that the performance with HTM counters deviates little from

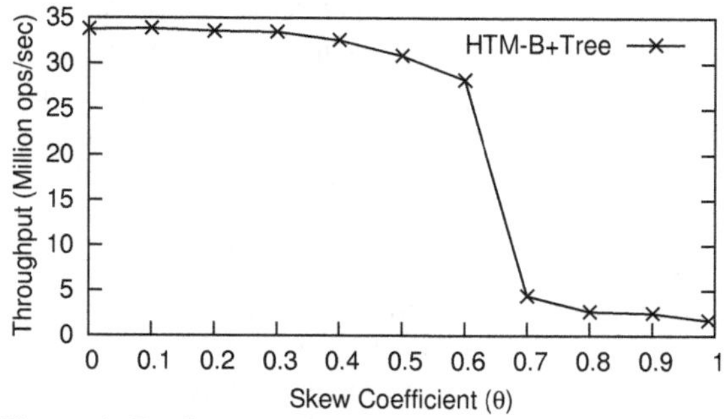

Figure 1: Performance under different contention rates.

that without counters. As shown in Figure 2, the HTM abort rate increases sharply with the contention rate; the HTM abort rate for $\theta = 0.9$ is around 47X higher than that for $\theta = 0.5$. The collected CPU cycles also show that frequent HTM aborts and retries waste more than 94% of the total CPU cycles when $\theta = 0.9$.

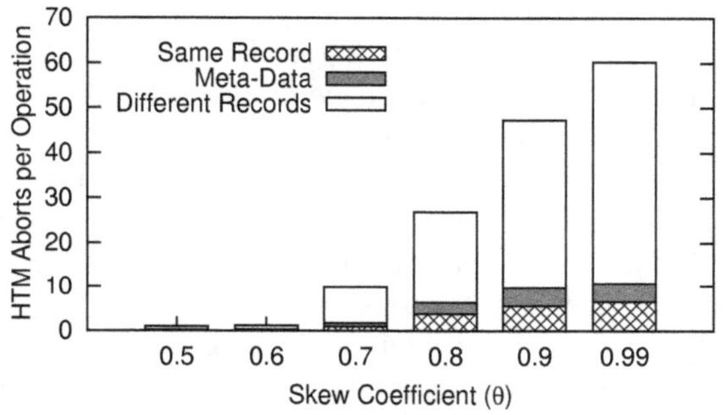

Figure 2: HTM aborts incurred by different reasons.

To understand the underlying reasons for collapsed performance under high contention, we perform a detailed analysis and uncover three main sources of aborts.

- **High retry cost due to monolithic transactions.** While using a monolithic transaction for a critical section provides consistency with trivial effort, it also causes increased abort rates. Even worse, a retry from a leaf node would waste a lot of useful work, causing high retry cost. Our analysis finds that the distribution of conflicts is non-uniform in the B+Tree: more than 90% of conflicts occur in the leaf level. In this case, a conflict in leaf nodes will abort the entire tree traversal from root to leaf, even though there is no conflict in internal nodes.
- **False conflicts.** *False Conflicts* are conflicts incurred by requests accessing different records. False conflicts stem from two major reasons. The first one is *cache line sharing of consecutive records*. B+Tree arranges keys stored in a node in a consecutive manner to provide an ordered store. However, such data layout causes severe conflicts under high contention. Since HTM detects conflicts at cache line granularity, concurrently accessing data in the same cache line would result in increased conflict rates within nodes. The second reason is *accessing the shared metadata in the B+Tree*. A conventional

B+Tree inherently contains pervasive shared variables to maintain tree structure invariants (e.g., number of layers and version number of nodes). We categorize conflicts incurred by shared metadata as false conflicts since their target records are actually different. Since it is difficult to directly measure the exact percentage of false conflicts, we approximate the decomposition by excluding other affected factors and estimating the abort rate. To estimate the impact of "same record," we modified the Zipfian distributed workloads to prevent different threads from accessing the same records and collect the reduction on HTM aborts. We calculate the HTM aborts from accessing different records (e.g., when inserting consecutive records) by subtracting previous rates from the total rate. As to shared metadata, it is hard to remove all shared variables in the tree structure as some are indispensable to proceed with execution. We remove shared variables for version and node status, and estimate the reduction of aborts. As shown in Figure 2, 87%-90% of conflicts are caused by requests to different keys, which is the primary reason for the growth of abort rate. Besides, the conflicts incurred by shared metadata contribute 6%-10%, which is also a non-negligible source.

- **True conflicts.** *True conflicts* are conflicts incurred by requests accessing exactly the same record. For workloads under high contention, the probability that multiple requests access the same record simultaneously is inherently high, which is a significant source of conflict. From Figure 2, we can observe that 9%-12% of conflicts are incurred by requests to the same records.

3. Eunomia Design Pattern

Based on the above analysis, this section describes the Eunomia design pattern, which comprises four design guidelines to scale concurrent search tree structures under contention using HTM:

Splitting large HTM transactions with opportunistic consistency validation. Since retrying a large HTM transaction causes high retry cost, an intuitive way is to decompose a large HTM transaction into a few smaller HTM transactions. Based on the observation that the distribution of conflict aborts may be non-uniform, the decomposition can be guided by the distribution of aborts to reduce the retry code path, e.g., separating the internal nodes from the leaf nodes. However, one key remaining challenge is that there is no longer an atomicity guarantee among the decomposed transactions, which causes inconsistency for a concurrent data structure. To this end, Eunomia uses a version-based opportunistic consistency validation. The idea is based on the observation that for concurrent search trees, the interior tree structure is updated less frequently than the leaf nodes. Eunomia can use a version number to represent the tree's generation and only update it upon a split or rebalance operation. The leaf nodes can then check the version to see if it needs to retry from the root (rare case) or just from the leaf nodes (common case). In this way, Eunomia can ensure the consistency while notably reducing the retry cost.

Partitioning data layout to reduce false conflicts. Consecutive memory layout pervasively exists in concurrent search trees like the leaf nodes in a B+Tree. However, such a layout incurs high false conflict rate when multiple threads access the data in the same cache line. To address this issue, Eunomia first partitions the continuous records in leaf nodes into multiple segments. Then requests to adjacent records will be randomly distributed to different segments located in different cache lines. Since requests to adjacent data are scattered to different segments randomly, the false conflict rate can be reduced. For operations requiring ordered data (e.g., range query in B+Tree), Eunomia uses buffers to store sorted keys gathered from multiple segments temporarily. Hence, the original ordering semantics can still be maintained.

Proactively detecting and avoiding true conflicts. The probability that multiple threads access the same record is high under high contention. Therefore true conflicts also impact performance significantly. To mitigate this, Eunomia proactively detects potential true conflicts and avoids them accordingly. Eunomia adopts two main techniques. First, when a node is nearly full or being split, requests to this node are likely to incur conflicts. Therefore, Eunomia employs a fine-grained advisory lock to serialize concurrent requests to a leaf node if it is near full or in the process of split. Second, detecting potential conflicts of every operation could be a time-consuming process. Eunomia leverages a Bloom filter [4] based mechanism to approximately detect potential conflicts at low cost. For example, with a Bloom filter attached to each leaf node, requests to a non-existent key in the segment will be eliminated, reducing the conflict rate.

Adopting adaptive contention control strategy. While the above design guidelines are helpful for a high contention scenario, applications usually exhibit changing workloads with different levels of contention. As the designs to handle high contention may bring overhead under low contention, Eunomia uses an adaptive contention control strategy to detect contention rates and bypass extra overhead when contention is low.

4. Concurrent B+Tree using Eunomia

This section describes how to apply the Eunomia's design to construct a contention-conscious concurrent B+Tree (namely Euno-B+Tree).

4.1 Design of Euno-B+Tree

Splitting HTM transactions: reducing retry cost. As shown in Figure 3, Euno-B+Tree splits the original HTM region into two parts: *upper region*, protecting the atomicity of index traversing, where conflict rate is low; and *lower*

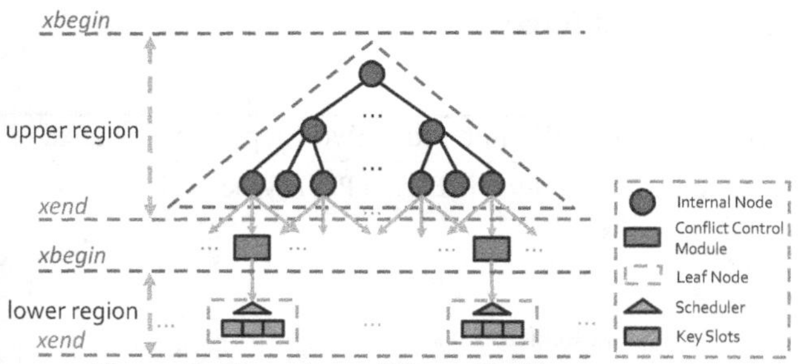

Figure 3: Overview of Euno-B+Tree structure

region, protecting the atomicity of leaf nodes accessing, where conflict rate is high.

Trivially splitting the monolithic HTM region may introduce inconsistency issue when node splits: consider if a thread tries to insert record A, while a concurrent thread tries to read record B. The read request will get the leaf node pointer by traversing the tree index in the upper region. However, before it enters (or retries) the lower region, the leaf node may be split due to the concurrent insertion and record B is moved to the sibling leaf node. The read request will fail to get record B. The problem is the read request gets the leaf node pointer in one HTM region, while it scans the leaf node in another HTM region. As a result, the read request is not aware of concurrent splitting.

Euno-B+Tree adopts the version-based consistency validation approach through a two-step transactional operation. The first step passes a leaf pointer to the latter one. This pointer is the "connection point" between two adjacent transactions. If the pointed leaf splits, the overall atomicity could be violated. Therefore, the overall consistency should be guaranteed by a version number tracking the split operation (Figure 4). At the end of the upper region, the request finds a pointer to the target leaf node, and reads the version number of this node into a local variable before exiting the upper region, while the version number will be checked after entering the lower region (Section 4.2.1). For the above example, after the read request gets the leaf node pointer in the upper region, it also reads its version into a local variable. When a leaf node is split, its version is updated. Therefore, the read request will be aware of the split event by checking the version number at the beginning of accessing the lower region or a new retry. As a result, only when the leaf node splits will a request retry from root; otherwise a conflicting request just retries in the lower region.

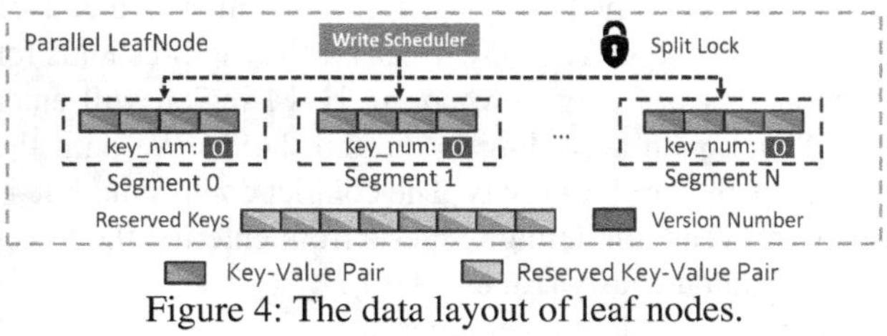

Figure 4: The data layout of leaf nodes.

Scattered leaf nodes: reducing false conflicts. As shown in Figure 4, Euno-B+Tree redesigns the leaf layer in a scattered way. Each leaf node is separated into multiple segments. Only the keys in the same segment are kept sorted and stored consecutively, and the value pointers are combined with keys for the convenience of sorting and reorganization. Each segment has its own metadata to record the number of stored elements. To avoid the conflict in the same segment, we use a *write scheduler* to assign each *put* operation to a random segment. Each leaf node also maintains a version number to ensure the consistency of the separated HTM regions. Each leaf node maintains a lock (split lock) to serialize concurrent split operations. We directly use a per-leaf advisory lock because concurrent split operations on the same leaf node are highly likely to conflict with each other.

In addition, we allocate *reserved keys* in each leaf node as a buffer to hold the sorted keys for operations requiring ordered results (e.g., range query). The reserved keys have the following functions.

(1) Storing old records for a node split. If a node is split, the *reserved keys* in each split node will be used to store old records. The length of reserved keys equals the number of records distributed from the original node. (2) Storing records overflowed from segments. As analyzed in Section 4.2.2, to make room for further concurrent insertions, if an insertion overflows a segment, the *reserved keys* will be dynamically expanded and all records in segments will be moved to it. (3) Storing sorted records for range queries. All of records in segments will be sorted and moved to reserved keys when there is a range query operation.

When *reserved keys* are expand, the total size of segments is shrunk to keep that the size of all segments plus the size of reserved keys equals the size of the original space in a node. The records in *reserved keys* could also be searched and updated. However, the partitioned segments and *reserved keys* work together to scatter different operations, which reduces the probability of false sharing. Such a design sacrifices the performance of search operations. However, since each segment and *reserved keys* are already sorted, performing a merge sort is quick and the sorted results can be reused for consecutive search operations.

Example. For a *get* request, to search a specific record, Euno-B+Tree will compare the first and last elements of each segment and of the *reserved keys* since keys are ordered within each segment while unordered among multiple segments. For an insert operation, Euno-B+Tree uses the write scheduler to assign the operation to a random segment. With the random write scheduler, the probability that multiple requests collide within the same segment is reduced.

Conflict control with fine-grained locking: reducing true conflicts. To proactively detect and eliminate true conflicts, Euno-B+Tree adds a conflict control module above each leaf node. The conflict control module uses fine-

Figure 5: The hash function of conflict control module.

grained atomic locks to detect potential conflicts and avoid two conflicting operations from accessing the same record simultaneously. Figure 5 shows the basic layout of the conflict control module for a single leaf node. It has a hash function and two bit vectors: mark bits and lock bits. The target key of a request will be hashed to a bit in the vector. The lock bits function as fine-grained atomic locks attached to each slot in the leaf node. It detects and serializes all concurrent requests accessing the same key. It can avoid conflicting operations (put vs. get, put vs. put) to enter the HTM region simultaneously. The mark bits vector is used to indicate the existence of the according key, resembling the working mechanism of Bloom filter. If a request searches for a nonexistent key, the mark bits will eliminate it from entering the leaf node; thus fewer threads could enter the leaf node and conflict rate is reduced further. We set the length of the bit vector twice as the leaf node's fanout so that the space overhead is kept below 5% while the false positive rate is kept under 6%.

Example. Consider two concurrent operations on the same record: read and update. In a conventional HTM-B+Tree, the read operation will abort as the concurrent put will update the value of the same record. In contrast, with the conflict control module, the read request will set the lock bit first before entering the HTM region, then the put request will be blocked until the read request finishes. As a result, true conflicts in the HTM region are avoided.

Adaptive concurrency control. To reduce the overhead for low contention rate, we use a *contention detector* in conflict control module, which detects the contention rate and adjust the contention control strategy accordingly. First, the detector predicts the conflict probability of a leaf node based on historical data. When the conflict rate of a leaf node keeps below a threshold for a time period, its contention rate is considered to be low. In such a condition, the new incoming request will bypass the conflict control module and leaf locks, skipping the overhead brought by these modules.

4.2 Algorithms

Based on the above design, we further describe how Euno-B+Tree handles common B+Tree operations, including get, put (it will be changed into a simple update if the target key exists; otherwise it will be changed into an insertion), and range query.

4.2.1 Get/Put Interfaces

Algorithm 2 Get/Put Interface (Two-Step Tree Traversal)

```
21: procedure TRAVERSE(REQ_TYPE, key, newVal)
22: RETRY:
23: XBEGIN() //upper region
24:     node = root
25:     leaf = findLeaf(node, key)
26:     seqno = leaf.seqno
27:     ccm = leaf.CCModule //get the conflict control module
28: XEND()
29:     slot = hash(key)
30:     while !CAS(ccm[slot].lockBit, 0, 1) or leaf.isLocked() do
31:         spin()
32:     exist = ccm[slot].markBit
33:     if !exist then
34:         if REQ_TYPE == GET then
35:             record = null
36:         else //REQ_TYPE == PUT
37:             //insert the key if it does not exist
38:             insert = CAS(ccm[slot].markBit, 0, 1)
39:             if insert and leaf.isNearFull() then
40:                 leaf.lock() //hold the lock for split
41: XBEGIN() //lower region
42:     if seqno != leaf.seqno then
43:         consistent = false //inconsistency happens
44:     else
45:         if exist then
46:             record = leaf.getRecord(key)
47:         if REQ_TYPE == PUT then
48:             if record == null then
49:                 record = INSERT(leaf, key)
50:             record.value = newVal
51: XEND()
52:     if leaf.isLocked() then
53:         leaf.unlock()
54:     ccm[slot].lockBit = 0
55:     if !consistent then
56:         goto RETRY
57:     if REQ_TYPE == GET then
58:         return record
```

Algorithm 2 shows the traversal procedure shared by both *get* and *put* operations. In Euno-B+Tree, the traversal procedure is divided into two phases. The atomicity of each phase is protected by an HTM region, one for the upper region (Lines 23-28) and one for the lower region (Lines 41-51) accordingly. The fallback strategy is similar to that used in DBX [31] and DrTM [33]. We set different thresholds for different types of aborts, where an HTM region will enter the fallback path according to the thresholds. We omit the fallback path here for brevity. The conflict control module is used to prevent conflicting requests from entering the lower region simultaneously (Lines 29-40).

To process a put or a get request:

1. Euno-B+Tree first traverses the tree index from the root to reach the leaf node (Lines 23-28). The atomicity of the traversal is protected by an HTM region. Before exiting the HTM region, it reads the current version number into a local variable (Line 26).
2. Before entering the lower region, Euno-B+Tree uses the conflict control module to serialize conflicting accesses on the same node (Lines 29-40). This is done by atomically checking and setting the lock bit of the corresponding key (Line 30). We use a set of atomic locks to protect the atomicity of each byte in the bit vector. After a request sets the lock bit successfully, it will check if its target key exists or not by checking the mark bit (Line 32). If it does not exist, for a *get* request, it will assign a $null$ value to the record; for a *put* request, it will set its bit in the mark bits vector and begin an insert procedure. For an insertion operation, if the leaf node needs to be split due to the capacity limitation, it will try to acquire the split lock before splitting (Line 40). The subsequent operations will be blocked by the lock from entering a node in split process (Line 30).
3. Scanning the leaf node is protected in the *lower region* (Lines 41-51). At the beginning, it needs to check the version number of the leaf node. If it has changed, it means the node was split by a concurrent request before entering or retrying the *lower region* (Line 43). In this case, a request in the *lower region* could scan the wrong leaf node. Thus it should retry from the root and search for the latest proper leaf node. Otherwise, the leaf node is still valid; the request will search for the target key in this leaf node (Line 46). If the target key is not found in a leaf node, the put request will insert a new key (Line 49); otherwise, it will update the value of an existing key (Line 50).

4.2.2 Insertions

When a *put* request attempts to update a non-existent record, it will include an insertion to the tree structure. As discussed in Section 2, highly-contended workloads usually result in a large amount of highly concurrent operations, and intensive put operations incur highly concurrent insertions. Intensive insertions, combined with consecutive layout of leaf nodes, often generate false conflicts. Retaining concurrency while reducing false conflicts is the starting point of our insertion algorithm.

Based on the partitioned leaf nodes introduced in Section 4.1, Algorithm 3 illustrates concurrent insertions. The important steps are shown in Figure 6.

Algorithm 3 Insertion and Split

```
59: procedure INSERT(leaf, key)
60:     idx = RandomScheduler()
61:     while leaf.segs[idx].isFull() and retries < threshold do
62:         idx = RandomScheduler() //retry with a new idx
63:         retries += 1
64:     if !leaf.segs[idx].isFull() then
65:         record = leaf.insertSegment(idx, key)
66:     else
67:         if leaf.hasSpace() then //the node has sufficient space
68:             //move the keys to reserved space
69:             leaf.moveToReserved()
70:             leaf.shrinkSegs()
71:             record = leaf.insertSegment(idx, key)
72:         else if !leaf.isFull() then
73:             leaf.moveToReserved()
74:             record = leaf.insertSegment(idx, key)
75:         else //node is really full
76:             //move the keys to reserved space
77:             leaf.moveToReserved()
78:             leaf.sortKeys()
79:             newNode = leaf.split()
80:             leaf.seqno += 1
81:             //which one is to insert
82:             toInsert = compareKeys(leaf, newNode)
83:             record = toInsert.insert(key)
84:             while newNode != null do
85:                 parent = newNode.getParent()
86:                 newNode = parent.insertNode(newNode)
87:     return record
```

1. The write scheduler will randomly distribute incoming requests to different segments (Lines 60-66). The random function records the index it generated last time, and guarantees that the current index is not duplicated with the last one (Line 60). If all insertions are distributed to different available segments (segments with empty slots), then multiple insertions can be processed concurrently. Each insertion affects only the local variables within the segment, so that no false conflicts will be triggered by data shifts or shared variables. If the target segment is full, the scheduler will retry the distribution attempt (Figure 6a).
2. If the retry times exceed a threshold, then we can infer the leaf node is near-full or the key-value pairs stored in segments distribute unevenly. In this case, we move the elements in all segments to *reserved keys* (Figure 6b), then clean the segments to accommodate new concurrent insertions. If the retries are incurred by an uneven key-value distribution, after we reorganize the keys to *reserved keys*, there could remain sufficient room in segments to support further concurrent insertions.
    (a) If there is still sufficient room to hold new keys (Figure 6c), the scheduler continues to distribute concurrent insertions to different segments (Lines 67-71).
    (b) If there is not sufficient room for new keys, the advisory lock is acquired for a further split operation (Lines 75-86).

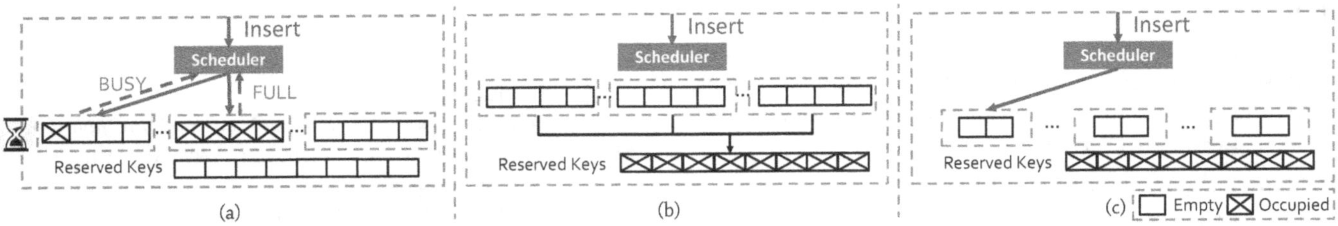

Figure 6: Concurrent insertions to a leaf node

By this means, the leaf node allocates concurrent insertions to different segments, and the shared metadata is naturally divided into several parts. False conflicts are mainly due to put operations (including updates and insertions) to consecutive records. By scattering the accesses to multiple segments and *reserved keys*, the probability of multiple requests accessing adjacent records is reduced; thus the false conflict rate can be decreased.

4.2.3 Splits

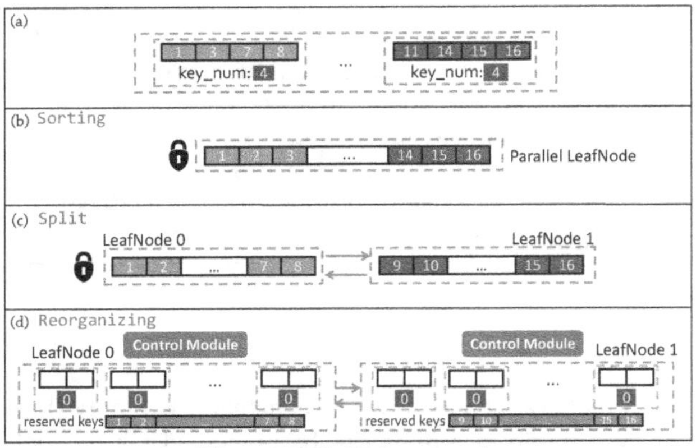

Figure 7: Splitting a node

When a node in a B+Tree is full, a new insertion will trigger a split. The current node is split into two nodes with original keys evenly distributed. The content of the parent node will be adjusted accordingly, and the split propagates upwards if the parent nodes are full themselves.

Given the insertion semantics related in the previous section, the keys in leaf nodes of Euno-B+Tree are arranged in a partially unordered manner (ordered within a segment, unordered among segments). Therefore splitting a node in fact includes both sorting and splitting steps. The procedure of the node split is presented in Lines 75-86 of Algorithm 3.

1. When a node splits, Euno-B+Tree first locks the leaf node to block new incoming insertions; otherwise they are highly likely to conflict when the keys are being reshuffled.
2. Then the keys in the original node are sorted and stashed to *reserved keys* in an ordered manner (Figure 7b and Lines 76-78).
3. The original node is split according to the normal scheme of a B+Tree. The version number increases to keep consistency (Line 80). The parent node also should be adjusted accordingly. (Figure 7c and Lines 83-86).
4. In new nodes, old key-value pairs inherited from the old node are stored in *reserved keys*, and the remaining empty slots are evenly distributed to multiple segments. So that segments will be entirely empty to store new records. (Figure 7d).

In such a *sorting-split-reorganizing* way, we can constrain the randomness of keys within the leaf node layer. The new keys inserted to parent nodes are ordered, and thus the internal nodes are still arranged in an ordered way.

4.2.4 Range Query and Deletion

Range queries, which access a set of consecutive keys, are an important interface for ordered indexes. In Euno-B+Tree, when a range query request reaches a leaf node, the node will be locked by the advisory lock, and key-value pairs stored in all segments will be moved and sorted in *reserved keys*. Hence, the scan iterator can get a sequence of ordered keys.

The traversal process of a deletion is similar to that of a put operation; the tree structure simply labels the status of the record as deleted and clears the corresponding mark bits. The tree will not re-balance instantly. Euno-B+Tree reuses the deletion and garbage collection scheme in DBX [31] to clean up the unused nodes.

Re-balance. Instead of re-balancing the tree on every deletion instantly, we do the re-balance when the number of delete operations exceeds a threshold. Previous research has proved that such a re-balance scheme has theoretical and empirical advantages [26] and has been adopted by many prior systems [19, 31].

4.3 Proof Sketch

This section argues the correctness of our algorithm by showing that the lower region is always consistent with the upper region. More specifically, we need to prove that (1) the version of a leaf node seen in the upper region is mutual consistent with the version seen in the lower region; (2) introducing the conflicting control module does not affect consistency; (3) all the acquired locks will eventually be released.

Version numbers are the key to ensuring the mutual consistency of the leaf node. By comparing the version number at the beginning of lower HTM region (line 42), we ensure that the leaf node has not changed since the upper HTM region committed. Second, adding the conflicting control module only reduces conflict but does not affect overall correctness. To prevent false negatives introduced by the mark bits, the bit locks are used to ensure the mark bits (line 38) are atomically updated with the *insert* operation. Third, to show that all acquired locks will eventually be released, we first argue there is no deadlock among concurrent operations. This is ensured by letting all operations acquire different locks in the same order. We also show every operation makes forward progress. As we use a fallback handler for the HTM to ensure it will not retry infinitely, the operation will eventually execute the code at line 53 and line 54 which release the bit lock and the leaf lock.

5. Tree Evaluation

Our implementation of Euno-B+Tree consists of approximately 600 lines of code in C++. By evaluating the prototype, we try to answer the following questions:

- Does Eunomia solve all the issues discussed in section 2.3?
- Can Eunomia deliver better performance than a fine-grained locking B+Tree even under high contention?
- Can Eunomia achieve performance scalability under different contention levels?
- How does the workload (get/put ratios or input distributions) affect Eunomia's performance?
- How does each design choice affect the performance?

5.1 Experimental Setup

All experiments were conducted on a 20-core server (two 2.30 GHz 10-core Intel® Xeon® E5-2650 chips) running Linux 3.19.0. Each core has private 32 KB L1 data cache, 32KB L1 instruction cache, and 256 KB L2 cache. Each chip has a shared 25 MB L3 cache. The cache line size is 64 bytes. The total DRAM size is 256 GB. We use Intel's Restricted Transactional Memory to implement atomic regions.

We compare Euno-B+Tree with three different concurrent B+Tree implementations: (1) An HTM-based B+Tree adopted by many database systems [9, 31, 33], which uses HTM to protect the atomicity of the entire operation. We reuse the fallback strategy and retry policy in DBX [31]. (2) A highly optimized concurrent B+Tree implementation derived from Masstree [19]. It uses fine-grained locks to achieve good scalability. However, we still use the term "Masstree" for simplicity. (3) An HTM version of Masstree, denoted as HTM-Masstree. It uses HTM region to protect the entire Masstree operation (as in (1)), subsuming multiple elided locks.

We here adopt the Yahoo! Cloud Serving Benchmark (YCSB) [10], which is a representative benchmark for large-scale key-value storage. For each record, both key and value have 8 bytes fixed size. The get/put ratio is set to the default value of 50%/50%. The key range is set to 100 million. The average tree depth is 6 and run duration is set longer than 20 seconds to get stable performance. Unless otherwise specified, we use Zipfian as the default input distribution, private to each thread (intra-thread locality). The Zipfian distribution has a skew coefficient θ, and the probability of accessing a key k is given by

$$P(k) \propto (\frac{1}{k})^{\theta} \quad (1)$$

Thus, we can easily increase the contention rate by increasing θ. With $\theta = 0$, all records are accessed with the same probability (uniform distribution); with $\theta = 0.99$, the "hottest" tenth of the values in the set are accessed by 41% of the requests.

5.2 Throughput

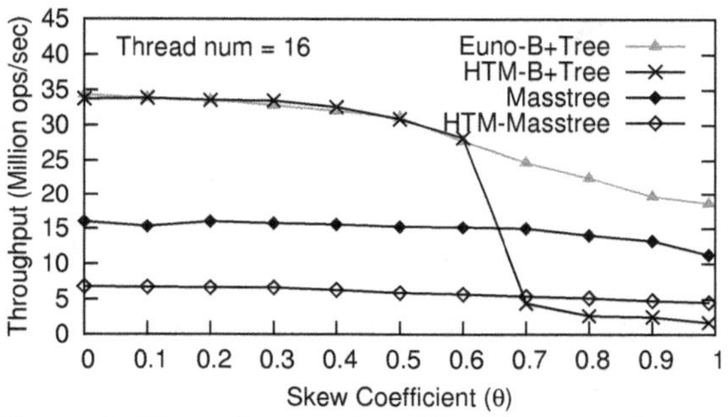

Figure 8: Throughput under different contention rates.

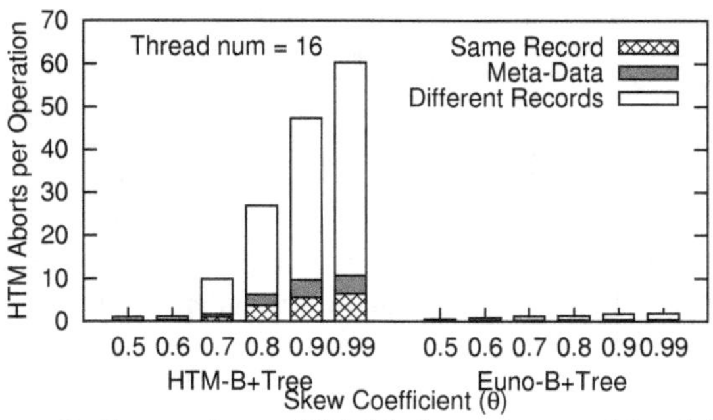

Figure 9: Comparison of HTM aborts incurred by different reasons.

To see whether Eunomia solves the issues discussed in Section 2.3, we repeat the experiment in Figure 1; the data are shown in Figure 8. When the contention is low or even modest ($\theta < 0.6$), Euno-B+Tree can obtain similar performance as HTM-B+Tree about 36.85% higher than Masstree. This is because Euno-B+Tree uses adaptive concurrency control to reduce most overhead under low contention, while Masstree's fine-grained synchronization needs to execute additional instructions. According to our analysis, when θ = 0.5, the amount of instructions executed by Masstree is about 2.10X that of Euno-B+Tree. The extra instructions primarily come from the "before-and-after" version checking mechanism in Masstree (§4.6 of [19]). For example, when θ = 0.5, a put operation in Masstree needs on average to check and manipulate a version number about 15 times while traversing the tree. Under high contention ($\theta > 0.6$), Euno-B+Tree can achieve 11X speedup over HTM-B+Tree (18.6 M vs. 1.7 M Ops/s with θ = 0.99). This is because Eunomia eliminates most aborts compared with HTM-B+Tree (Figure 9): 60.3 vs. 1.9 aborts per Op under extreme high contention. Compared with Masstree, it has 65% better performance even under high contention. This is because Euno-B+Tree executes around 40% fewer instructions under high contention. Performance of the HTM-based Masstree is worse than Masstree under both low and high contention. This is because HTM-based Masstree has shared variable accesses which incurs frequent HTM aborts. This shows that, even for a highly optimized concurrent B+Tree, it is still hard to directly take advantage of HTM.

5.3 Scalability

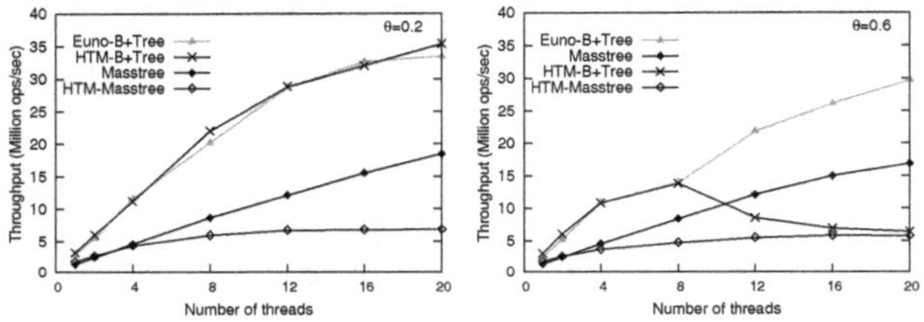

(a) Low Contention (b) Modest Contention

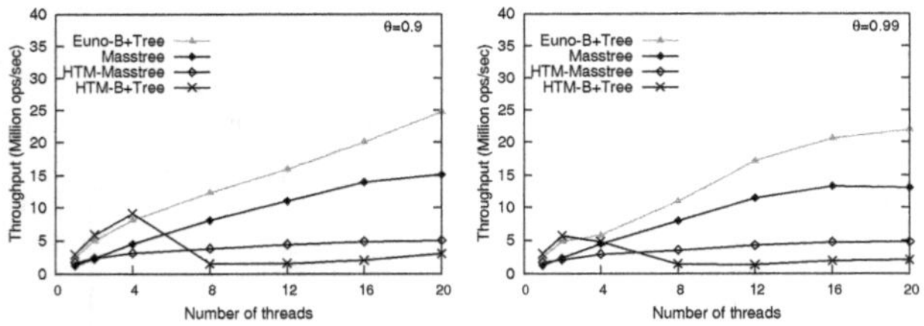

(c) High Contention (d) Extremely High Contention

Figure 10: Performance scalability under different contention levels.

Besides the skew coefficient, an increase in the number of threads also intensifies the contention rate. Here we evaluate scalability with increasing threads under different levels of contention. We set θ by referencing previous research [14, 36]: 0.2 to simulate low contention; 0.6 for modest contention; 0.9 for high contention. We also set θ to 0.99 to simulate extremely high contention. Figure 10 shows the results. Thanks to the adaptive control, under low contention (θ is 0.2), Euno-B+Tree scales smoothly and is very close to HTM-B+Tree. This indicates that the adaptive control can reduce most performance cost under low contention. However, since Masstree needs to execute more instructions for synchronization (40% more instructions per thread), this overhead is amplified by adding more threads. As a result, Eunomia is 52%-63% better than Masstree under high contention. HTM-Masstree fails to scale after 8 cores. Under modest contention (Figure 10b), the performance of HTM-B+Tree begins to collapse after 4 threads due to the increase in abort rate. Masstree still has stable performance as false conflicts do not waste CPU cycles. Under high or even extreme contention, Euno-B+Tree still has reasonable scalability and performs better than Masstree (21.9 M vs. 13.1 M Ops/s with 20 threads) for extremely high contention. This benefit is still from the fact that HTM simplifies the algorithm which makes it execute fewer instructions than Masstree.

5.4 Get/Put Ratio

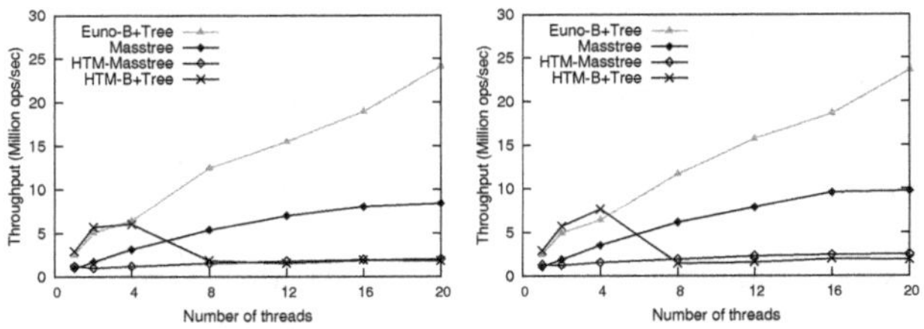

(a) 0% Get/100% Put (b) 20% Get/80% Put

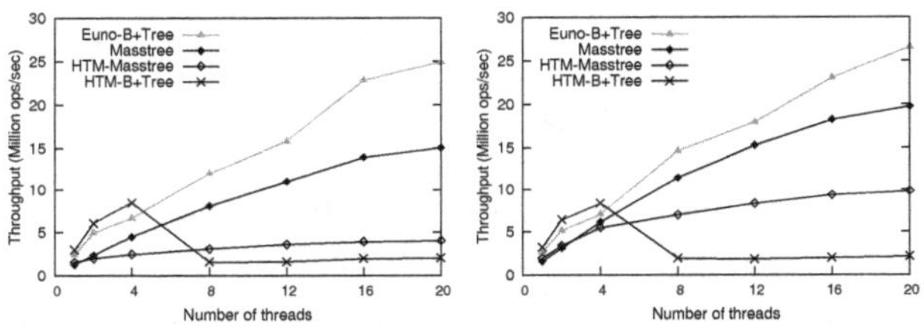

(c) 50% Get/50% Put (d) 70% Get/30% Put

Figure 11: Performance under different get/put ratios in Zipfian Distribution (θ = 0.9).

Get and *put* are the fundamental operations of a key-value store. Interleaved reads and writes often exacerbate contention. Here we measure the impact of the get/put ratio on overall performance. We consider ratios of (1) 0% get/100% put, (2) 20% get/80% put, (3) 50% get/50% put, and (4) 70% get/30% put.

The default ratio of YCSB is 50% get/50% put [10], and we adjust the percentage of get and put to simulate read-heavy and write-heavy situations. Since Eunomia is designed for concurrent tree modifications, we do not consider the all-get case here.

We measure the Zipfian distribution with high contention (θ = 0.9) under these get/put ratios. The performance is shown in Figure 11. From the results, we can observe that Euno-B+Tree can achieve near-linear scalability under various get/put ratios. The speedup increases with put ratio, and the advantage of Eunomia is most obvious with 100% puts

(Figure 11a). This is because the put operations introduce more conflicts, in which case Euno-B+Tree is much better than other alternatives. The performance of Masstree also scales smoothly with threads, but is still 25% lower than Euno-B+Tree on average.

5.5 Different Input Distributions

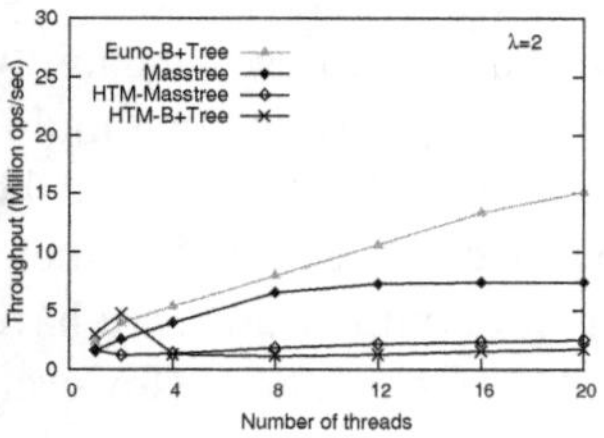

(a) Poisson Distribution

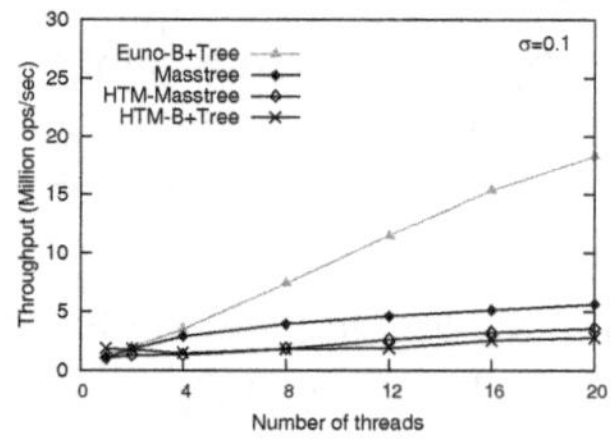

(b) Normal Distribution

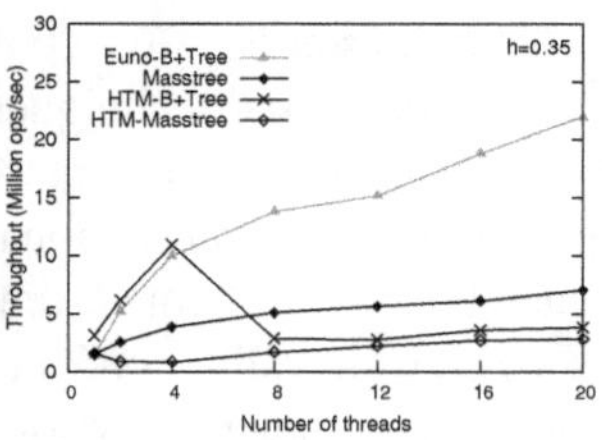

(c) Self-Similar Distribution

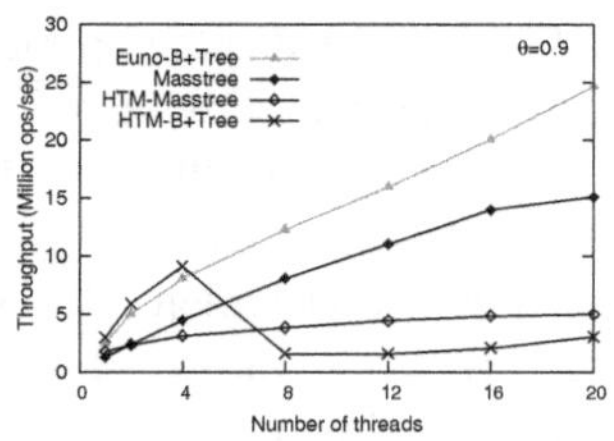

(d) Zipfian Distribution

Figure 12: Performance with different input distributions under high contention.

Since the input keys may follow various kinds of distributions in real use cases, we measure performance with the following mainstream input distributions. Requests with different types of contended keys constitute different input distributions and thus impact the performance of B+Tree systems in different ways.

- **Poisson**: A common distribution in probability and statistics, Poisson expresses the probability of a given number of events occurring in a fixed interval of time or space if such events happen with a known average rate and independently of the time since the last event. The skew coefficient is determined by the expected value λ. Here we set contention such that the 10% hottest records are accessed by 70% of the requests.
- **Normal**: Here the requests are chosen to follow a Normal distribution with mean of N/2, where N is the set to cover a moving range of leaf nodes. The standard deviation is set to 1% of the mean to simulate a skewed situation. Here we set contention such that the 10% hottest records are accessed by 67% of the requests.
- **Self-Similar**: Common in network traffic, the requests in this distribution follow an 80-20 rule [16]. Within any range of the distribution, the skew coefficient is the same as in any other region. Here we set contention such that the 10% hottest records are accessed by 66% of the requests.

The get/put ratio is set to the default 50%/50% in each distribution. The results are shown in Figure 12 (the Zipfian distribution is tested with $\theta = 0.9$). From the figure, we can observe that Euno-B+Tree can achieve scalable performance under various input distributions, higher than HTM-B+Tree and lock-based Masstree. In the Poisson distribution, Self-Similar distribution, and Zipfian distribution, the performance of HTM-B+Tree collapses when threads exceed 2 or 4, due to the CPU time wasted by HTM aborts and retries. Under the normal distribution, the input distributes densely around the expected value; thus, the performance of HTM-B+Tree keeps at a low level, without any obvious trend increasing. The performance of Masstree can scale stably under Zipfian distributions since its contention is comparatively modest among the four input distributions, yet is 38%-51% (40% on average) lower than Euno-B+Tree due to the number of executed instructions.

5.6 Impact of Different Design Choices

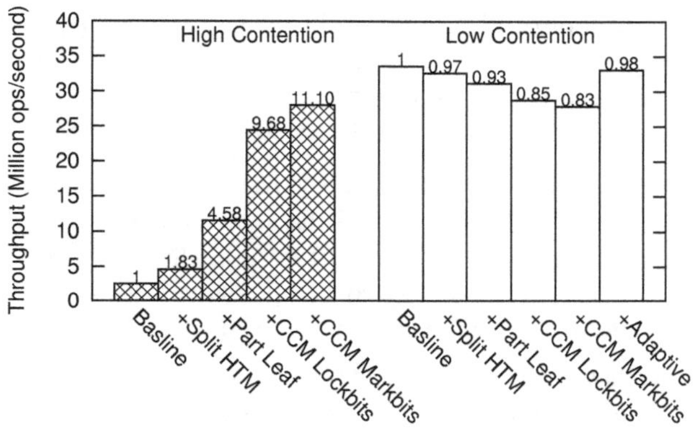

Figure 13: Impact of Different Design Choices. The relative performance is labeled on the top of each column.

To understand the performance improvement and cost from various design aspects, we here present an analysis of multiple factors in Figure 13. The benchmark is the YCSB with Zipfian input distribution with 20 threads under both high contention (θ is 0.9) and low contention (θ is 0.2).

Baseline refers to an HTM-B+Tree using a single RTM region to protect the entire operation. *+Split HTM* means splitting the monolithic HTM region into two parts, and using version numbers to protect consistency. *+Part Leaf* refers to partitioning the leaf nodes to avoid false conflicts. *+CCM lockbits*/*+CCM markbits* refer to adopting the lock_bits/mark_bits in the conflict control module. *+Adaptive* means adopting adaptive concurrency control under low contention.

First, splitting the monolithic HTM region gets 1.83X speedup under high contention, as the overhead of rollback is reduced. Under low contention, it introduces 3% overhead, as it doubles the number of RTM instructions for each operation. Second, partitioned leaf nodes (*+Part Leaf*) generates 4.58X speedup under high contention, as it decreases the false conflict rate caused by accessing the same leaf node. But it incurs 4% performance slow down under low contention by introducing extra overhead on searching. By further reducing false conflicts, *+CCM lockbits* and *+CCM markbits* get 9.68X and 11.10X speedup under high contention. They also introduce overhead (8% and 2%) under low contention due to extra computation. With *+Adaptive*, the overhead introduced by the system is successfully bypassed. As a result, we only have 2% performance overhead under low contention, which is brought by extra HTM instructions and version checking.

5.7 Memory Consumption Analysis

In the design of Euno-B+Tree, two structures would involve additional memory consumption: reserved keys and the conflict control module. The conflict control module consists of two bit vectors for each leaf node and its memory consumption is negligible. Therefore, the main memory overhead comes from reserved keys. Here, we evaluate the memory consumption overhead of Euno-B+Tree using Valgrind toolset [23]. The workload includes getting and putting 10 million keys in a Zipfian distribution with 16 threads. The node fanout is set to 16, and run duration is set to longer than 20 seconds to get stable performance.

1. We have measured the memory overhead under different contention rates. We varied the skew coefficient of the Zipfian Distribution from 0.0 to 1.0. The results show that the average memory consumption overhead is 5.64% (1.79GB v.s. 1.69GB) (from 2.44% to 7.64%).
2. We have also measured the memory overhead with different get/put ratios: 0.2/0.8, 0.5/0.5, and 0.8/0.2. The results show that the average memory consumption overhead is 4.21% (1.62GB v.s. 1.55GB) (from 2.91% to 5.80%).
3. We have also measured the memory overhead with different input distributions. The input distributions include Self-Similar Distribution, Poisson Distribution, and Uniform Distribution. The results show that the average memory overhead is 2.20% (1.81GB v.s. 1.77GB), 6.91% (1.81GB v.s. 1.70GB), and 2.25% (1.77GB v.s. 1.74GB) respectively.

As such analysis results show, the additional memory consumption is small. The major reason is that reserved keys work as a buffer to hold the keys being sorted for split and scan operations. Such data structures are allocated and expanded dynamically and will not hold redundant space.

6. Related Work

Conventional concurrent search tree structures [15] usually adopt fine-grained locks [2, 19, 28] or lock free methods [6, 22, 25, 27] to unleash concurrency and provide consistency. These methods can provide scalability, but incur high performance cost due to thread synchronization. At the same time, lock-free schemes primarily use single-word atomic instructions to coordinate multiple threads, making it difficult to argue correctness. Compared with them, we leverage HTM to simplify the implementation and provide good scalability.

Recent works [30, 31] also try to use HTM to simply the implementation of concurrent data structures. However, it could also exhibit pathological performance if misused. Dice et al. [13] note that memory allocators could incur certain pathological cases. Unlike them, who use HTM intuitively, we figure out more subtle design to achieve scalability under high contention. Brown et al. [7] also find that multi-socket architecture could have a critical influence on the behavior of HTM, as cross-socket cache access lengthens the time to complete a transaction. In our research, we have also noticed the impact of NUMA architecture. However, NUMA architecture only magnifies the impact of transaction conflicts. Our research attempts to find a way to eliminate conflicts, thus solve the problem from the source.

An extensive body of research has discussed techniques to improve HTM efficiency by splitting monolithic transactions. Hassan et al. [17] propose optimistic transactional boosting (OTB), which divides each operation of concurrent data structures into three steps (traversal, validation, and commit). Afek et al. [1] propose consistency oblivious programming (COP), which splits concurrent code to boxes, and allows sections of code that meet certain criteria to execute without checking for consistency. Xiang et al. [34, 35] propose software partitioning of hardware transactions (ParT). It splits common operations into read-mostly *planning phase* and write-mostly *completion phase*. These methods try to reduce conflicts by shrinking transaction size, and our design differs from these works in two aspects: first, we focus on highly-contented workloads; second, we attempt to reduce both true and false conflicts.

7. Conclusions

We have presented Eunomia, a design pattern for concurrent search tree structures under high contention. First, Eunomia provides a new strategy of partitioning monolithic transactions to reduce abort rate. Second, Eunomia scatters the original tree structure to reduce false conflicts. Third, Eunomia adopts fine-grained advisory locks to eliminate true conflicts. Fourth, Eunomia adapts away the overhead under low contention. We have shown the effectiveness of Eunomia by refactoring a concurrent B+Tree according to Eunomia design patterns.

Acknowledgments

We thank our shepherd, Michael Scott, and the anonymous reviewers for their constructive comments. We are grateful to support from the National Key Research and Development Program of China (No. 2016YFB0800104), the National Natural Science Foundation of China (No. 61672160 and 61572314), Shanghai Science and Technology Development Funds (16JC1400801) and NSF award CNS-1218117.

References

[1] Y. Afek, H. Avni, and N. Shavit. Towards consistency oblivious programming. In *OPODIS*, pages 65–79, 2011.

[2] M. K. Aguilera, W. Golab, and M. A. Shah. A practical scalable distributed B-Tree. *VLDB*, 1(1):598–609, 2008.

[3] R. Bayer and E. McCreight. Organization and maintenance of large ordered indexes. In *Software pioneers*, pages 245–262, 2002.

[4] B. H. Bloom. Space/time trade-offs in hash coding with allowable errors. *Communications of the ACM*, 13(7):422–426, 1970.

[5] C. Blundell, E. C. Lewis, and M. M. Martin. Subtleties of transactional memory atomicity semantics. *IEEE Computer Architecture Letters*, 5(2), 2006.

[6] A. Braginsky and E. Petrank. A lock-free B+Tree. In *SPAA*, pages 58–67, 2012.

[7] T. Brown, A. Kogan, Y. Lev, and V. Luchangco. Investigating the performance of hardware transactions on a multi-socket machine. In *SPAA*, pages 121–132, 2016.

[8] H. W. Cain, M. M. Michael, B. Frey, C. May, D. Williams, and H. Le. Robust architectural support for transactional memory in the power architecture. In *ISCA*, pages 225–236, 2013.

[9] Y. Chen, X. Wei, J. Shi, R. Chen, and H. Chen. Fast and general distributed transactions using RDMA and HTM. In *EuroSys*, pages 26:1–26:17, 2016.

[10] B. F. Cooper, A. Silberstein, E. Tam, R. Ramakrishnan, and R. Sears. Benchmarking cloud serving systems with YCSB. In *SOCC*, pages 143–154, 2010.

[11] I. Corporation. Intel® 64 and ia-32 architectures software developers manual, 2015.

[12] D. Dice, Y. Lev, M. Moir, and D. Nussbaum. Early experience with a commercial hardware transactional memory implementation. In *ASPLOS*, pages 157–168, 2009.

[13] D. Dice, T. Harris, A. Kogan, and Y. Lev. The influence of malloc placement on tsx hardware transactional memory. *arXiv preprint arXiv:1504.04640*, 2015.

[14] J. Dittrich, L. Blunschi, and M. A. V. Salles. Dwarfs in the rearview mirror: how big are they really? *VLDB*, 1(2):1586–1597, 2008.

[15] G. Graefe. Modern B-Tree techniques. *Found. Trends databases*, pages 203–402, 2011.

[16] J. Gray, P. Sundaresan, S. Englert, K. Baclawski, and P. J. Weinberger. Quickily generating billion-record synthetic databases. In *SIGMOD*, volume 23, pages 243–252, 1994.

[17] A. Hassan, R. Palmieri, and B. Ravindran. On developing optimistic transactional lazy set. In *OPODIS*, pages 437–452, 2014.

[18] M. Herlihy and J. E. B. Moss. Transactional memory: Architectural support for lock-free data structures. In *ISCA*. ACM, 1993.

[19] Y. Mao, E. Kohler, and R. T. Morris. Cache craftiness for fast multicore key-value storage. In *Eurosys*, pages 183–196, 2012.

[20] S. Mu, Y. Cui, Y. Zhang, W. Lloyd, and J. Li. Extracting more concurrency from distributed transactions. In *OSDI*, pages 479–494, 2014.

[21] N. Narula, C. Cutler, E. Kohler, and R. Morris. Phase reconciliation for contended in-memory transactions. In *OSDI*, pages 511–524, 2014.

[22] A. Natarajan and N. Mittal. Fast concurrent lock-free binary search trees. In *PPoPP*, pages 317–328, 2014.

[23] N. Nethercote and J. Seward. Valgrind: A framework for heavyweight dynamic binary instrumentation. In *PLDI*, pages 89–100, 2007.

[24] D. M. Powers. Applications and explanations of zipf's law. *Joint conferences on new methods in language processing and computational natural language learning*, pages 151–160, 1998.

[25] A. Ramachandran and N. Mittal. Improving efficacy of internal binary search trees using local recovery. In *PPoPP*, pages 42:1–42:2, 2016.

[26] S. Sen and R. E. Tarjan. Deletion without rebalancing in balanced binary trees. In *SODA*, pages 1490–1499, 2010.

[27] J. Sewall, J. Chhugani, C. Kim, N. Satish, and P. Dubey. PALM: Parallel architecture-friendly latch-free modifications to B+Trees on many-core processors. *VLDB*, 4(11):795–806, 2011.

[28] S. Tu, W. Zheng, E. Kohler, B. Liskov, and S. Madden. Speedy transactions in multicore in-memory databases. In *SOSP*, pages 18–32, 2013.

[29] A. Wang, M. Gaudet, P. Wu, J. N. Amaral, M. Ohmacht, C. Barton, R. Silvera, and M. Michael. Evaluation of blue gene/q hardware support for transactional memories. In *PACT*, pages 127–136, 2012.

[30] Z. Wang, H. Qian, H. Chen, and J. Li. Opportunities and pitfalls of multi-core scaling using hardware transaction memory. In *APSys*, pages 3:1–3:7, 2013.

[31] Z. Wang, H. Qian, J. Li, and H. Chen. Using restricted transactional memory to build a scalable in-memory database. In *EuroSys*, pages 26:1–26:15, 2014.

[32] Z. Wang, S. Mu, H. Y. Yang Cui, H. Chen, and J. Li. Scaling multicore databases via constrained parallel execution. In *SIGMOD*, pages 1643–1658, 2016.

[33] X. Wei, J. Shi, Y. Chen, R. Chen, and H. Chen. Fast in-memory transaction processing using rdma and htm. In *SOSP*, pages 87–104, 2015.

[34] L. Xiang and M. L. Scott. Composable partitioned transactions. In *Wkshp. on the Theory of Transactional Memory (WTTM)*, 2013.

[35] L. Xiang and M. L. Scott. Software partitioning of hardware transactions. In *PPoPP*, pages 76–86, 2015.

[36] X. Yu, G. Bezerra, A. Pavlo, S. Devadas, and M. Stonebraker. Staring into the abyss: An evaluation of concurrency control with one thousand cores. *VLDB*, 8(3):209–220, 2014.

A. Artifact Appendix

A.1 Abstract

This artifact contains all the artifacts, data, and shell scripts of Eunomia. It supports the throughput results in Section 5 (Figure 8,10,11,12) of our PPoPP 2017 paper **Eunomia: Scaling Concurrent Search Trees under Contention Using HTM**. To validate the results, build the artifacts, run the test scripts and check the results presented in text output files and tables.

A.2 Description

A.2.1 Check-list (artifact meta information)

- **Algorithm: Eunomia, HTM-B+Tree**
- **Program: C/C++ code**
- **Compilation: gcc 4.8.4 with -O2 flag**
- **Binary: C/C++ executables**
- **Data set: Customized YCSB benchmark**
- **Run-time environment: Ubuntu 14.04 LTS x86-64 or newer Ubuntu versions**
- **Hardware: Dell PowerEdge R730, Intel Xeon CPU E5-2650, 2 sockets, 20 cores, 256GB DRAM**
- **Output: Runtime and/or throughput**
- **Experiment workflow: Install hardware/software dependencies; compile the program; run the scripts; observe the results**
- **Publicly available?: Yes**

A.2.2 How delivered

The artifact is released through GitHub code repository available at: `https://github.com/Eunomia2016/AE`

A.2.3 Hardware dependencies

Eunomia requires Intel CPU with Transactional Synchronization Extensions (TSX) support, NUMA architecture, and at least 2 sockets with 20 hardware cores in total. The artifact uses POSIX threads for concurrency and pins each threads to a specific hardware core with `pthread_setaffinity_np`; hyperthreading is switched off. Eunomia also requires processors support atomic synchronization primitives.

A.2.4 Software dependencies

- jemalloc memory allocator.
- libnuma-dev library.
- gcc with built-in functions for atomic memory access, which are included in gcc 4.1 or later.
- gcc with Intel RTM and HLE intrinsics, which are included in gcc 4.8 or later.
- Linux Kernel 3.19.0 or later versions.
- glibc 2.19 or later versions.
- python 2.7.6 or later versions.

A.3 Installation

- We here provide installation steps to present the build process, including installing all dependent libraries and compiling the programs.
- Enter Top directory

```
$ cd AE/
$ export TOP=$(pwd -P) #default directory
```

- Activate the TSX support of CPU and install the dependent libraries

```
$ cd $TOP/Script/
$ ./install_dependency.sh
```

- Build Eunomia & HTM-B+Tree with ycsb benchmark

```
$ cd $TOP/Code/euno_ycsb/
$ ./make_ycsb.sh
```

A.4 Experiment workflow

For the convenience of the artifact evaluation, we provide a script called `ppopp.sh` which reproduces the results of Section 5 described in the paper. Then the results will be stored in the output text files.

```
$ cd $TOP/Script/
$ ./ppopp.sh <index> <iterations>
```

The first parameter <index> is the index of results to be reproduced. The second parameter <iterations> is the number of iterations to run. The eventual result will be the average value of multiple iterations. Each iterations will be executed for about 20 minutes.

- Results in Section 5.2 (Figure 8)

```
$ cd $TOP/Script/
$ ./ppopp.sh 0 3 #index is 0, iteration is 3
#check results
$ cat $TOP/Data/forms/figure8.txt
#you could run ./check_reference.sh 0 to check
#the pre-generated results for reference
```

- Results in Section 5.3 (Figure 10)

```
$ ./ppopp.sh 1 3
#check results, theta=0.2
$ cat $TOP/Data/forms/figure10_0.2.txt
#check results, theta=0.6
$ cat $TOP/Data/forms/figure10_0.6.txt
#check results, theta=0.9
$ cat $TOP/Data/forms/figure10_0.9.txt
#check results, theta=0.99
$ cat $TOP/Data/forms/figure10_0.99.txt
#you could run ./check_reference.sh 1 to check
#the pre-generated results for reference
```

- Results in Section 5.4 (Figure 11)

```
$ ./ppopp.sh 2 3
#check results, read ratio=0
$ cat $TOP/Data/forms/figure11_0.txt
#check results, read ratio=0.2
$ cat $TOP/Data/forms/figure11_0.2.txt
#check results, read ratio=0.5
$ cat $TOP/Data/forms/figure11_0.5.txt
#check results, read ratio=0.7
$ cat $TOP/Data/forms/figure11_0.7.txt
#you could run ./check_reference.sh 2 to check
#the pre-generated results for reference
```

- Results in Section 5.5 (Figure 12)

```
$ ./ppopp.sh 3 3
#check results, distribution type=Normal
$ cat $TOP/Data/forms/figure12_Normal.txt
#check results, distribution type=Poisson
$ cat $TOP/Data/forms/figure12_Poisson.txt
#check results, distribution type=Self-Similar
$ cat $TOP/Data/forms/figure12_Self-Similar.txt
#you could run ./check_reference.sh 3 to check
#the pre-generated results for reference
```

A.5 Evaluation and expected result

The expected results include both runtime and/or throughput. It should reproduce the results similar to that shown in Section 5 (Figure 8,10,11,12).

Here we provide a sample of expected results and experiment comparison, which reproduces the data shown in Section 5.2 (Figure 8). Figure (a) is the graph presented in the paper. Figure (b) presents the data generated by a random run on a test platform (Dell PowerEdge R730). Due to the difference of hardware, the absolute number is not the same, especially when HTM-B+Tree is under the marginal contention rate (θ=0.7). However, the speedup of Eunomia compared to other versions is clear and stable. Under θ = 0.99, Eunomia in Figure (a) generates 11.04X speedup over HTM-B+Tree; and the speedup is 11.16X in Figure (b), with only 2% deviation.

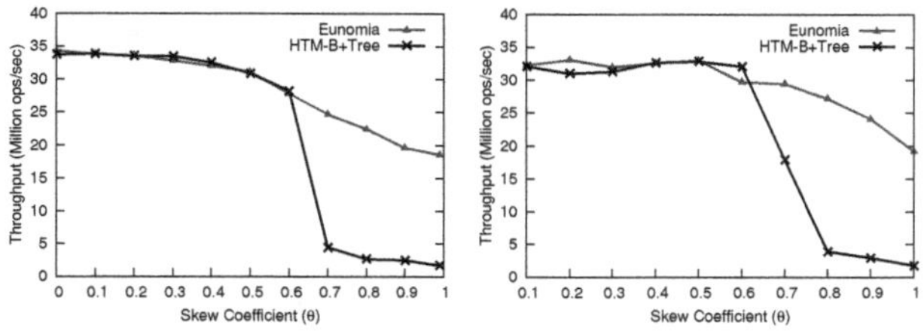

(a) Performance data provided in the paper. (b) Performance data generated by a random test platform.

Figure 1: Performance data comparison of Figure 8.

A.6 Submission and Reviewing Methodology

Please refer to http://cTuning.org/ae/submission-20161020.html for the submission and reviewing methodology.

Self-Checkpoint: An In-Memory Checkpoint Method Using Less Space and Its Practice on Fault-Tolerant HPL

Xiongchao Tang Jidong Zhai Bowen Yu Wenguang Chen Weimin Zheng

Department of Computer Science and Technology
Tsinghua University, Beijing, China
{txc13,yubw15}@mails.tsinghua.edu.cn {zhaijidong,cwg,zwm-dcs}@tsinghua.edu.cn

Abstract

Fault tolerance is increasingly important in high performance computing due to the substantial growth of system scale and decreasing system reliability. In-memory/diskless checkpoint has gained extensive attention as a solution to avoid the IO bottleneck of traditional disk-based checkpoint methods. However, applications using previous in-memory checkpoint suffer from little available memory space. To provide high reliability, previous in-memory checkpoint methods either need to keep two copies of checkpoints to tolerate failures while updating old checkpoints or trade performance for space by flushing in-memory checkpoints into disk.

In this paper, we propose a novel in-memory checkpoint method, called self-checkpoint, which can not only achieve the same reliability of previous in-memory checkpoint methods, but also increase the available memory space for applications by almost 50%. To validate our method, we apply the self-checkpoint to an important problem, fault tolerant HPL. We implement a scalable and fault tolerant HPL based on this new method, called SKT-HPL, and validate it on two large-scale systems. Experimental results with 24,576 processes show that SKT-HPL achieves over 95% of the performance of the original HPL. Compared to the state-of-the-art in-memory checkpoint method, it improves the available memory size by 47% and the performance by 5%.

Keywords Fault Tolerance; In-Memory Checkpoint; Fault-Tolerant HPL; Memory Consumption

PPoPP '17 Feb. 4–8, 2017, Austin, Texas, USA.

ACM 978-1-4503-4493-7/17/02... $15.00
DOI: http://dx.doi.org/10.1145/http://dx.doi.org/10.1145/3018743.3018745

1. Introduction

The substantial growth of system scale in High Performance Computing (HPC) makes fault tolerance increasingly important. A long-running HPC application can run for hours, or even days on an HPC system. Unfortunately, a large-scale system's mean time between failures (MTBF) may be too short to afford a complete fault-free run. For example, large-scale systems such as Blue Waters and Titan have failures everyday [23, 28]. This problem becomes even worse as systems scale up towards exascale computing.

Significant research efforts have been made trying to overcome this problem. A series of algorithm-based fault-tolerant (ABFT) applications [9, 10, 32, 36] have been proposed. The main idea is to modify an application's algorithm for fault tolerance [20]. A recent study, called redMPI [17], employs a strategy of redundant execution to increase system reliability. All computation and communication are duplicated in redMPI. Thus, if there exists any copy that survives a failure, the program can tolerate the failure and continue running. However, since everything is duplicated, the system efficiency is relatively low (no more than 50%).

Although ABFT and redundant execution provide a certain fault tolerance for HPC applications, their ability to tolerate faults highly depends on underlying runtime libraries. Message Passing Interface (MPI) is a *de-facto* standard for HPC applications. In the ABFT and redundant execution, it is assumed that MPI programs can be suspended after a *node failure*. A node failure means that a node is permanently lost, such as power down and network disconnect. Based on our observation, almost all current MPI implementations force the whole program to abort after a node failure is detected. On most MPI runtime, none of ABFT or redundant execution methods can tolerate a permanent node loss, which is quite common on a real HPC system [14, 29]. Some fault-tolerant MPI implementations [5, 6, 12] may support ABFT and redundant execution, with additional performance overhead.

Checkpoint-and-Restart (CR) is a classic strategy [13] that works under extreme cases such as a permanent node loss. Traditional CR methods save checkpoints to underlying storage systems, and leads to significant performance degradation for applications. Since memory has much higher performance than disks, in-memory or diskless CR methods have gained extensive attention recently, which can effectively reduce the overhead of saving checkpoints [18, 27, 38].

Although the in-memory CR significantly reduces checkpoint overhead, it poses a new challenge for applications. Unlike disks, memory is a kind of relatively scarce resource. Checkpoints saved in memory occupy some space so that there is less available memory for applications. What's more, to maintain high reliability, in-memory checkpoint needs to maintain at least two copies of checkpoints [38]. A second checkpoint is used to tolerate failures when updating an old checkpoint. This results in only one third of memory left for applications. A solution is to use memory as a cache of disks, and flush in-memory checkpoints into disks periodically. Several multi-level checkpoint frameworks have already been proposed [3, 23]. However, copying checkpoints from memory into disks also introduces additional overhead thus loses the advantage of in-memory checkpoint.

To address this problem, we propose a novel method for in-memory checkpoint, called **self-checkpoint.** Our method not only achieves the same reliability of in-memory checkpoint using two copies of checkpoints, but also increases available memory for applications by almost 50%. The core idea of our method is to make the workspace of applications also as a checkpoint. For in-memory checkpoint methods, when updating a checkpoint, we need to copy data from the workspace of applications into checkpoint. It means that the data in the workspace and the updated checkpoint are the same, and both of them are in memory. Based on this observation, we propose a novel encoding mechanism, self-checkpoint. With the self-checkpoint, there is no need to save multiple checkpoints in memory, thus more memory is available for applications. Specifically, more available memory has different meanings to different programs. For some programs, more available memory means that the program can run for larger problem sizes with the same nodes. For some others, they can solve fixed-size problems with fewer nodes.

To verify and evaluate the self-checkpoint method, we apply it to a challenging problem, fault-tolerant HPL. **High-Performance Linpack (HPL)** is a prominent benchmark used in the TOP500 ranking list [1] of HPC systems. However, a future large-scale system may not afford a complete HPL test because of decreasing system reliability. Despite previous efforts on fault tolerant HPL, existing approaches either fail to tolerate a permanent node loss on a real system (algorithm-based fault tolerant methods) [32, 36], or introduce too much overhead (traditional CR methods saving checkpoints in disks) [13, 30], thus they are not practical for a performance benchmark.

In-memory checkpoint is a promising solution for fault tolerant HPL. However, HPL has several characteristics that make it even more difficult for in-memory checkpoint. First, the memory usage of HPL is configurable, and generally larger memory is much better for performance. For this reason, HPL needs as much memory as possible for high performance, while checkpoint itself should use as little memory as possible. Second, as the consequence of high memory usage, it will take a long time to flush checkpoints from memory into disks. So multi-level checkpoint methods are not suitable for fault-tolerant HPL. Third, HPL has a big memory footprint. Almost every byte is modified between two checkpoints. As a result, incremental checkpoint methods [2, 26, 31] are not efficient for this problem.

To this end, we implement a fault-tolerant HPL based on the self-checkpoint mechanism, called SKT-HPL[1]. It can not only achieve very high performance but also tolerate a permanent node loss. We evaluate SKT-HPL on two large systems, Tianhe-1A and Tianhe-2 (ranked TOP#2 in TOP500 list). Experimental results show that with 24,576 processes on Tianhe-2, the self-checkpoint method improves the available memory size by 47%. SKT-HPL achieves over 95% of the original HPL's performance, and 5% higher than using previous in-memory checkpoint methods. We also perform powering-off experiments to validate SKT-HPL can tolerate a real node failure.

In summary, we make the following contributions in this work.

- We propose a novel in-memory checkpoint method, self-checkpoint, which can not only keep the same reliability of in-memory checkpoint using two copies of checkpoints, but also significantly increase the available memory space of applications by almost 50%.
- We apply our proposed self-checkpoint method to an important problem, fault-tolerant HPL. We implement a scalable and node failure tolerant HPL (SKT-HPL) on real HPC systems.
- We evaluate SKT-HPL on two large-scale systems, Tianhe-1A and Tianhe-2. Results show that SKT-HPL achieves over 95% of the original HPL's performance and improves the memory usage over the state-of-the-art in-memory checkpoint by 47%.

The remainder of this paper is organized as follows. Section 2 gives basic in-memory checkpoint framework. Section 3 describes the approach of self-checkpoint mechanism. Section 4 discusses the importance of more available memory. Section 5 describes the implementation of SKT-HPL. Section 6 presents our experimental results. Section 7 describes related work. Section 8 gives the conclusion.

2. Basic In-Memory Checkpoint Framework

In this section, we describe some general fundamental techniques for in-memory checkpoint methods. Our work is also constructed on this basic framework.

[1] Source code and documents of self-checkpoint project can be downloaded from https://github.com/thu-pacman/self-checkpoint.git

2.1 Protecting Data with Encoding

For in-memory checkpoint methods, since checkpoints are saved in volatile memory, an error-correcting code is necessary to encode in-memory checkpoints. Calculating error-correcting codes for all processes in a large-scale system is prohibitive due to large communication overhead, so we apply a group encoding strategy [3, 23] to reduce the communication overhead. We partition all the processes into a number of small groups and build error-correcting codes for each group separately. To further reduce communication contention during building error-correcting codes within a group, we perform a stripe-based encoding for each process. The basic idea is that we partition each process data into $N-1$ stripes (each group has N processes), and then each process of the group is in charge of building an error-correcting code for partial stripes. This method can effectively avoid single-node network contention during encoding.

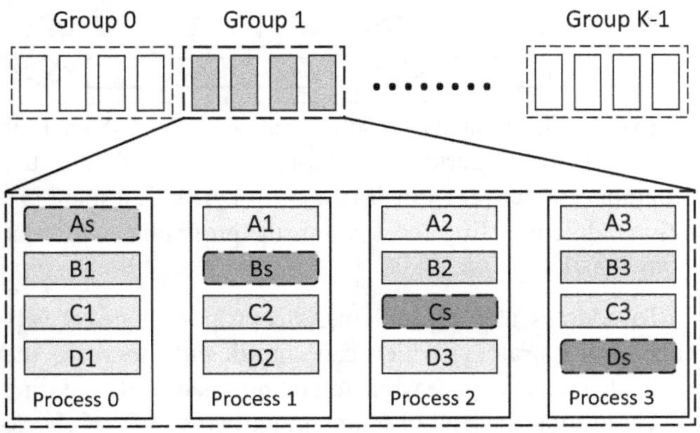

Figure 1. Data encoding. Processes in a large-scale application are partitioned into a number of small groups. We use a stripe-based encoding in each group. A_S, B_S, C_S, and D_S in dashed dark blocks are checksums for A_i, B_i, C_i, and D_i respectively.

Figure 1 shows an example to illustrate above encoding method used in our system, which is similar with the encoding mechanism used in RAID-5 [24]. Suppose that there are four processes, P_0, P_1, P_2, and P_3, in each group. Each process partitions its local data into three stripes and allocates four empty slots. After filling its own three stripes into the slots, each process has an empty slot for the checksum of stripes from the other processes within the same group. For example, we calculate the checksum of A_1, A_2, and A_3 from P_1, P_2, and P_3, then store this checksum A_S into the empty slot of P_0. Other checksums, B_S, C_S, and D_S, are built in the same way. A general encoding method is listed below.

$$X_S = X_1 + X_2 + ... + X_{n-1} \tag{1}$$

X is a stripe in each process. The operator "+" can be either a numerical sum or a logical exclusive-or. Note that the encoding time for each group does not change with the system scale and only depends on the group size, which makes our approach more scalable for a large-scale system.

Using above encoding, each group can tolerate a single node failure. We can apply more complex encoding methods, such as RAID-6 [21] and Reed-Solomon [33], to tolerate more node failures. For a higher degree of fault tolerance, in-memory checkpoint methods can be also combined with a multi-level checkpoint framework [3, 11, 23].

2.2 Calculating Checksums

We use `MPI_Reduce` to calculate checksums of checkpoints, taking full advantage of underlying well-tuned MPI library.

```
MPI_Reduce (datatype, operator, ...)
```

Supported by most MPI implementations, both *exclusive or* (XOR) and *numeric addition* (SUM) encoding methods are supported in our approach:

```
MPI_Reduce (MPI_LONG_LONG, MPI_BXOR, ...)
MPI_Reduce (MPI_DOUBLE, MPI_SUM, ...)
```

On some platforms, the logical XOR operation is much faster than the numerical SUM. Our implementation uses XOR by default, but SUM is also supported.

2.3 Keeping Checkpoints in Memory

Data saved in in-memory checkpoints needs to be accessible after applications restart. However, in most modern operating systems like Linux and Windows, a normal memory region will be freed after its owner exits. The data saved in the freed memory region is no longer accessible. To keep the data always in memory, one method is to mount an in-memory file system (e.g., `ramfs` and `tmpfs` in Linux) and write the checkpoint into that file system. Alternatively, Linux provides a shared memory mechanism (SHM) [2] . A memory region allocated through SHM will not be automatically freed by OS, even though no process is attached to it. In our framework, we use the shared memory mechanism to allocate memory regions for checkpoints. With this mechanism, all the checkpoint data in healthy nodes is still accessible after a node failure.

3. Self-Checkpoint Mechanism

3.1 Methodology

In this subsection, we elaborate our proposed self-checkpoint mechanism. To demonstrate its advantage over previous approaches, we firstly give a short introduction about single checkpoint and double checkpoint mechanisms.

Figure 2 shows the strategy of single in-memory checkpoint. The main advantage of the single checkpoint strategy is its low memory consumption. Almost half of the memory can be used for useful computation. The user's data of the original program is represented by rectangle A. B stands for the memory space for checkpoint, and C is the checksum

[2] More information about SHM can be found at http://man7.org/linux/man-pages/man2/shmget.2.html

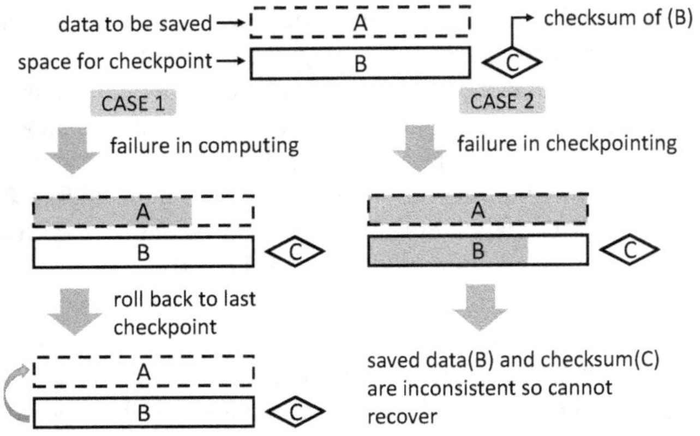

Figure 2. The strategy of single in-memory checkpoint. This method cannot recover data from a failure during checkpoint updating.

of B. The single checkpoint strategy can handle a node failure during the program's computation by rolling back the program using the checkpoint B and checksum C (CASE 1 in Figure 2). However, the single checkpoint cannot tolerate a node failure while updating a checkpoint or a checksum (CASE 2 in Figure 2), because at this time, the checkpoint B and checksum C are in an inconsistent state.

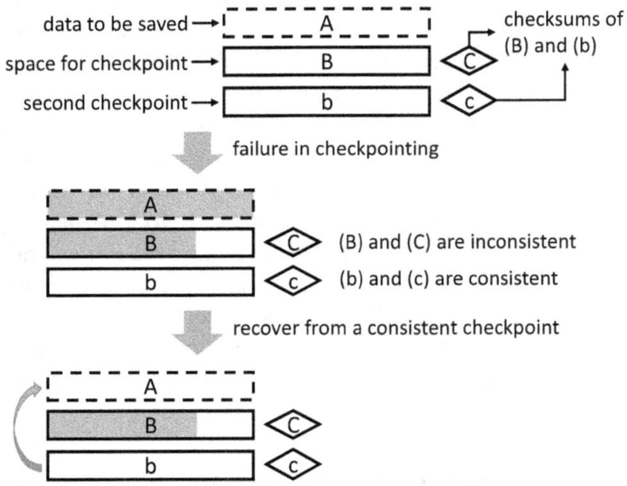

Figure 3. The strategy of double checkpoints. While updating checkpoints, at least one checkpoint and its checksum which are consistent can be used for recovery. Its main disadvantage is that too much memory space is wasted.

To tolerate the node failure during checkpointing, a straight-forward solution is to maintain two copies of checkpoints and overwrite the old one when making a new checkpoint, as shown in Figure 3. Since there are two checkpoints and at least one is available when updating, this strategy can tolerate a node failure at any time. This strategy is widely used in traditional checkpoint methods, which use disks and have sufficient storage space for checkpoints. The state-of-the-art in-memory checkpoint systems [37, 38] also adopt this strategy. However, this strategy has high memory consumption and significantly reduces available memory space for useful computation (only 1/3), which is prohibitive in a system with limited memory resources. Another solution is to flush the old checkpoint into a permanent device like hard-disks, but it will lose the performance advantage of the in-memory checkpoint.

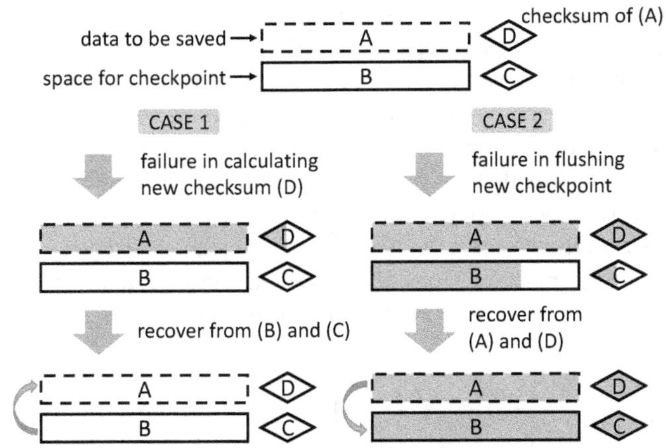

Figure 4. The strategy of self-checkpoint. In CASE 1, if there is a failure during calculating a new checksum, the program can recover from B and C. In CASE 2, if there is a failure while updating checkpoints, the program can recover from A and D

To address above problems, we propose a novel **self-checkpoint** strategy, which can significantly increase the available memory space while tolerating a node failure during checkpointing. Instead of maintaining two copies of checkpoints as shown in Figure 3, we store two copies of checksums in memory. This method is inspired by an observation that a checksum is much smaller than a checkpoint in a group encoding method. More specifically, a checksum is only $1/(N-1)$ of the checkpoint size when a group has N processes. Figure 4 illustrates an ideal case using the self-checkpoint strategy to handle different situations of failures.

When making a new checkpoint, a checksum D is firstly calculated for the user's data A, and then the memory space of A and D is flushed into B and C. As shown in CASE 1 of Figure 4, when a node failure is detected when calculating the checksum D, we can recover the program with the checkpoint B and checksum C. How do we recover the program if a node failure is incurred while updating checkpoints? As shown in CASE 2 of Figure 4, we can recover the program using the user's data A and its checksum D. In other words, the user's memory space for computation itself is served as a checkpoint. Therefore, we call our proposed method a self-checkpoint mechanism.

As discussed in Subsection 2.3, we use SHM to keep data in memory. For dynamic variables allocated in heap, we can change their allocation. For example, a malloc statement `p=malloc(...)` is transferred into an SHM statement `p=shmget(...)`. For statically allocated variables, such as

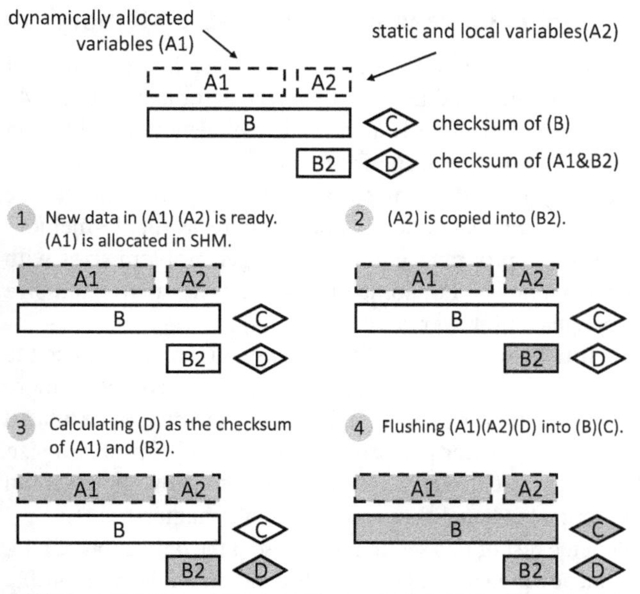

Figure 5. The complete workflow of self-checkpoint strategy. Most data is allocated in the shared memory, represented by $A1$ and little data is stored in the user's space, represented by $A2$. D is the checksum of $A1$ and $B2$.

global and local variables, we can also manually transfer related code to use shared memory. In our experience, large data structures are usually dynamically allocated in heap. For example, almost all data structures of HPL are dynamically allocated. As a result, if the size of statically allocated variables (A2 in Figure 5) is small, such as loop iterators or other scalar variables, we can allocate a small second-buffer (B2 in Figure 5) for simplicity.

Figure 5 illustrates the complete workflow of the self-checkpoint mechanism. $A1$ denotes the data which is stored in the shared memory. $A2$ denotes the data which is stored in the user's space and we need additional checkpoint space for $A2$, but the size of $A2$ can be much smaller than $A1$. The workflow of the self-checkpoint mechanism is listed as below:

1. Most of the user's data $A1$ is stored in the shared memory.
2. Copy the data of $A2$ into $B2$.
3. Calculate D, which is the checksum of $A1$ and $B2$.
4. Copy ($A1$, $A2$) into B, and copy D into C.

Before the last step, we can recover the program from the old checkpoint B and checksum C. Once we get the checksum D, the program can be recovered from $A1$, $B2$, and D. In summary, a single node failure can always be tolerated with our proposed self-checkpoint mechanism.

More detailed analysis about the memory usage is discussed in Subsection 3.2. Section 6 gives the detailed performance data of the self-checkpoint mechanism.

3.2 Analysis of Memory Usage

Selecting a suitable strategy for group partitioning is important for the performance of the self-checkpoint mechanism. In this subsection, we discuss the relationship between the group size and memory usage for different in-memory checkpoint methods.

Suppose that each group has N processes, and each process needs M units of memory for the user's computation. In the self-checkpoint mechanism, as we save most of data in the shared memory ($A1$ in Figure 5) and only partial local variables in the user's space ($A2$ in Figure 5), so the size of $A2$ and $B2$ is negligible.

Item	$A1$+$A2$	B	C	D	Total
Size	M	M	$\frac{M}{N-1}$	$\frac{M}{N-1}$	$\frac{2MN}{N-1}$

Table 1. The memory usage of the self-checkpoint mechanism for each part in Figure 5. The group size is N.

Table 1 lists the memory usage for each part of the self-checkpoint mechanism. Each process uses M of memory size for the original work ($A1$ and $A2$ in Figure 5) and B is also M. Due to the negligible size, B2 is omitted for simplicity. According to the encoding method described in Subsection 2.1, a checksum has the size of $M/(N-1)$. Therefore, the total memory usage of the self-checkpoint mechanism is the sum of $A1$, $A2$, B, C, and D, so it is $2MN/(N-1)$. The available memory for application with the self-checkpoint mechanism is

$$U_{self} \approx \frac{M}{2MN/(N-1)} = \frac{N-1}{2N} \tag{2}$$

Similarly, we can calculate the available memory space of the double checkpoint method shown in Figure 3.

$$U_{2ckpt} = \frac{M}{M + 2MN/(N-1)} = \frac{N-1}{3N-1} \tag{3}$$

And the available memory with the single checkpoint shown in Figure 2 is

$$U_{single} = \frac{M}{M + MN/(N-1)} = \frac{N-1}{2N-1} \tag{4}$$

We illustrate the available memory space of different in-memory checkpoint methods with several typical group sizes in Figure 6. The single checkpoint has the least memory consumption and most available memory space among three methods, but it is not fully fault tolerant and cannot recover from a failure during checkpointing updating. The double checkpoint method is fully fault tolerant but has much less available memory (less than $1/3$). The available memory of our self-checkpoint method is slightly less than the single checkpoint but much higher than the double checkpoint. At the same time, our method is fully fault tolerant. For a large group size, our method has more available memory space than the double checkpoint, up to nearly 50%.

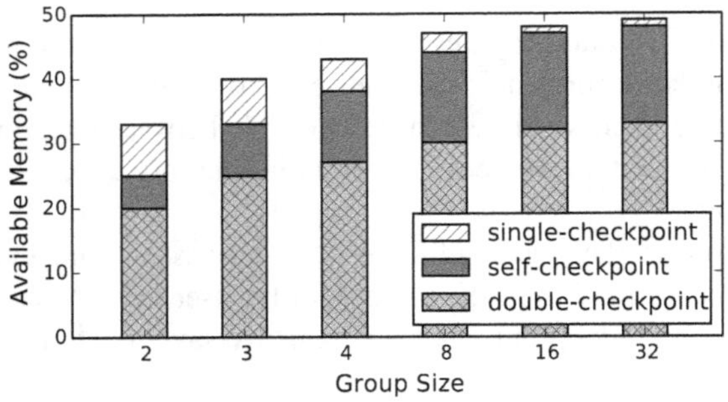

Figure 6. The memory usage of different in-memory checkpoint methods with group sizes of 2, 3, 4, 8, and 16.

3.3 Grouping Strategy

In this subsection, we give our strategies in determining suitable group partitioning in a large-scale system. From Figure 6, we can find that a larger group size always has more available memory, but a larger group is not good for the data encoding. The communication time during the data encoding is positively correlated with the group size. Therefore, a smaller group size introduces much lower communication overhead. Furthermore, a small group size is also beneficial for the system's reliability. Currently, our system only tolerates a single node failure in each group. The more processes a group has, the more likely more than one process will fail. In an extreme case, if a group includes the whole system, only a single failure can be tolerated. If each group has only two processes, the system can tolerate failures for half of the processes at the same time.

As a consequence, a large group is good for the memory space, but increases the communication overhead and is more likely to fail. Conversely, a small group encodes the checkpoint quickly, but less memory space is left for useful computation. In our experiments, we select the group size of 16. The available memory of a group with 16 processes is 47% and is close to the upper bound of 50%. We find that in a large system a larger group size provides little benefit for available memory space but causes much overhead in communication.

For better performance and reliability, an appropriate process mapping strategy should be considered. To tolerate a permanent node loss, processes within a group must be distributed onto different physical nodes. At the same time, for better communication performance, a group tends to select some neighboring nodes. But for high reliability, a group should also spread its nodes as far as possible to tolerate a single rack or switch failure. Based on previous studies [14, 29], as most failures in HPC systems are single node failures, and rack and network failures are minor, we give high priority to the performance in our current grouping strategy. Exploring more mapping strategies within one group is left for future work.

4. Importance of More Available Memory

The core idea of self-checkpoint is to use less memory for fault-tolerance, and leave more memory for applications. As mentioned in Section 1, more available memory has different meanings to different applications. In extreme cases, available memory space determines whether an application can be launched. For some applications, more available memory means that programs can run for larger problem sizes with the same nodes. For some others, they can solve fixed-size problems with fewer nodes.

HPL belongs to the former case. It has an adjustable problem size, thus larger problem can be solved with more available memory. Also, HPL has a characteristic that it can achieve better performance with a larger problem size. Therefore, we use HPL as an example to show the potential performance benefits of more available memory.

In the rest of this section, we present the derivation of HPL efficiency model and give our observation on the relationship between available memory space and HPL efficiency. Our model indicates that more available memory leads to higher performance in HPL. This also confirms our opinion that an in-memory checkpoint method should occupy as little space as possible.

For a given system, the *efficiency* of HPL is a ratio between HPL test performance and the system's theoretical peak performance. For example, if the test performance of HPL is 80 GFlops and the system's theoretical peak performance is 100 GFlops, the efficiency is 80%.

The kernel of HPL is to solve a dense linear equation $Ax = b$, where A is an $N \times N$ matrix. The computational complexity of HPL is $O(N^3)$ and its communication volume and memory access are $O(N^2)$ [25]. Therefore, if we omit the linear and constant computational work in HPL, the main work of HPL can be modeled by an $O(N^3)$ part plus an $O(N^2)$ part.

Since the total computational work in HPL is $O(N^3)$, the theoretical execution time without including any communication or memory access overhead can be modeled as γN^3. Considering various performance overhead and loss, the actual execution time of HPL can be modeled as $\alpha N^3 + \beta N^2$, where $\alpha > \gamma$. And βN^2 is an estimation for memory access and communication overhead. Therefore, the HPL efficiency $E(N)$ can be calculated as follows:

$$E(N) = \frac{\gamma N^3}{\alpha N^3 + \beta N^2} = \frac{N}{aN + b} \quad (5)$$

Here we have $a = \alpha/\gamma > 1$ and $b = \beta/\gamma$. In this model, given an invariant system and fixed process mapping, the parameters a and b are independent of the problem size.

Figure 7 shows that this model fits well with real experimental data on a local cluster. The dots in Figure 7 represent the real data when executing 192 MPI ranks on a local cluster with different problem sizes. The line is fitted with our model.

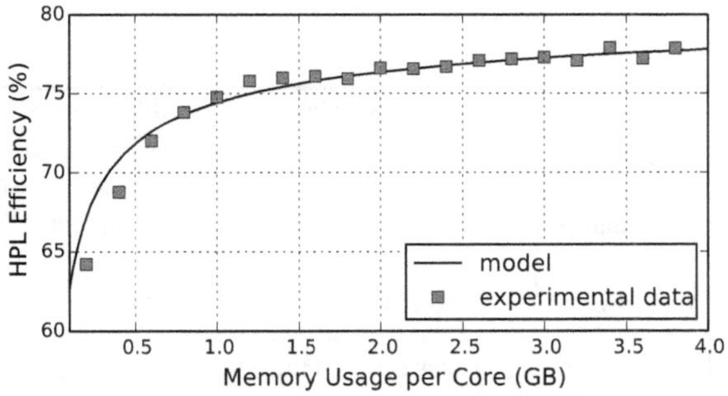

Figure 7. Fitting of the efficiency model with experimental data. Experiments are conducted with 192 MPI ranks on a local cluster with Xeon E5-2670(v3) and 100Gbps Infiniband network.

In Subsection 6.5, we will validate this model in two larger systems.

From above efficiency model, we can get an interesting finding for the HPL performance. For a given system, the HPL performance increases with the input problem size.

Next, we analyze the efficiency of HPL when reducing available memory space. Suppose that a system has an efficiency e_1 for the problem size of N_1 with the total available memory, then we have

$$e_1 = E(N_1) = \frac{N_1}{aN_1 + b} \tag{6}$$

Thus the value of b is

$$b = \frac{(1 - ae_1)N_1}{e_1} \tag{7}$$

If only partial memory is available for HPL, and ratio is $k(0 < k < 1)$, then the problem size N_2 is $\sqrt{k}N_1$. Combining Equation 5, 6 and 7, we have the efficiency for the problem size of N_2 as

$$e_2 = \frac{\sqrt{k}e_1}{1 - (1 - \sqrt{k})ae_1} > \frac{\sqrt{k}e_1}{1 - (1 - \sqrt{k})e_1} \tag{8}$$

The last step is because $a > 1$. Equation 8 gives a lower bound of HPL efficiency for different problem sizes.

To make the relationship between available memory space and HPL efficiency more clear, Figure 8 shows the efficiency of HPL for the top 10 supercomputers in the latest TOP500 list with different available memory space according to our model. We can find that these systems can achieve higher performance using more memory and improve 11.96% of the efficiency on average from one third of the memory to half of the memory. In consequence, it would be much better if an in-memory checkpoint method uses less memory space and leaves more for applications.

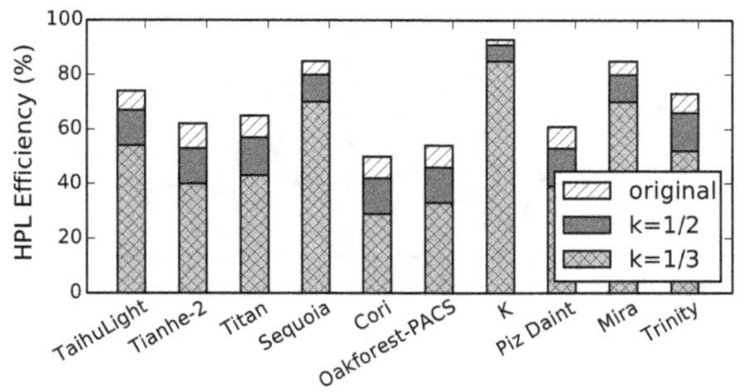

Figure 8. Modeled HPL efficiency of the top 10 supercomputers with different available memory space. The green mesh bars represent officially reported performance. The hatched bars and red bars are results only using one third and half of the memory size respectively, drawn by our model.

5. SKT-HPL Implementation

In this section, we discuss some details of implementing SKT-HPL on a large-scale system.

5.1 SKT-HPL Overview

The kernel of HPL is to solve a linear equation Ax = b, where A is an $N \times N$ matrix. This equation is solved by Gaussian Elimination with Partial Pivoting (GEPP). In general, HPL can be divided into the following four steps:

1. **Initialization** The first step is to initialize MPI runtime, and generate and partition data. The coefficient matrix A and vector b are allocated at runtime and filled by random numbers.
2. **Elimination** The original equation $Ax = b$ is then transformed into an upper triangle equation $Ux = y$. This is the most time-consuming part in HPL, and its computational complexity is $O(N^3)$. This step is done in a loop that iterates over all rows of A.
3. **Back Substitution** This step finally obtains the solution of $x = U^{-1}y = A^{-1}b$. Solving the upper triangle equation $Ux = y$ is much easier, and the computational complexity is only $O(N^2)$.
4. **Report** After solving above equation, HPL verifies the solution of x and then reports the final performance. The computational complexity of this step is $O(N^2)$.

Figure 9 illustrates the workflow of SKT-HPL. The white blocks stand for operations in the original HPL as described above, and the shadow ones are added by SKT-HPL. SKT-HPL makes checkpoints during the elimination step at the end of loop iterations, the main computational step in HPL. After a node failure is detected, some necessary data structures need to be rebuilt in the initialization step and SKT-HPL can restore the program's data from the checkpoint. SKT-HPL do not make checkpoints for the other steps, because they normally take far less time than MTBF and even less than a typical checkpoint interval.

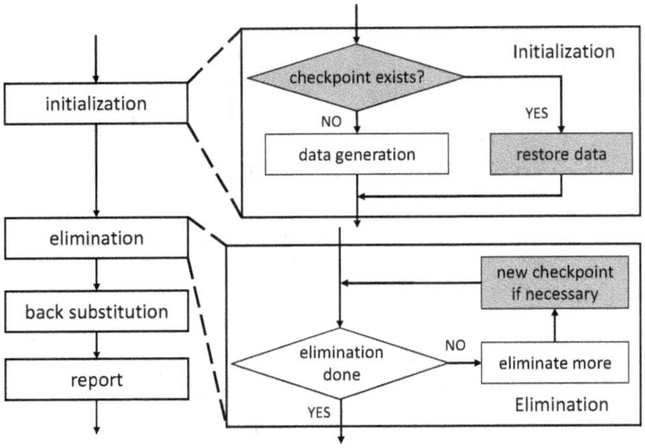

Figure 9. The workflow of SKT-HPL. Checkpoints are made at the end of a certain iteration during the elimination step. If a node failure is detected, SKT-HPL restores the data from the checkpoint in the initialization step.

Although the current implementation of SKT-HPL does not use accelerators, self-checkpoint can be used to implement fault-tolerant HPL that supports accelerators. Accelerators usually have data in their own memory, but operations like checkpointing and recovering are normally performed in main memory. As a result, updated data in accelerators' memory should be explicitly transferred back to main memory before making a new checkpoint.

5.2 Failure Detection and Restart

During an SKT-HPL test, a daemon runs on a master node that is assumed not to fail. Since the master node is a single node, its MTBF is very long and this assumption is reasonable. Deploying the daemon on a reliable distributed system is an alternative choice. If one MPI process aborts, the daemon can detect it by checking the return value of `mpirun` command or the output of a job management system in a typical supercomputer.

To recover the program, SKT-HPL should restart and put each process in the right position. Most MPI implementations support specifying the layout of processes. Normally a ranklist file is used to assign each process to a certain node. After all the MPI ranks exit due to a node failure, the daemon checks the connection for each node in the ranklist. Lost nodes are replaced by other healthy nodes, which can be spare nodes or repaired nodes.

Next, the daemon restarts SKT-HPL according to a new ranklist file. All the processes that ran on healthy nodes continue to run on the same nodes and just attach to the checkpoints saved in their local memory. The processes that ran on the failed node will be restarted on a fresh node where there is no checkpoint. With the same configure file, matrix A and b are always the same since the HPL test uses a fixed random seed. SKT-HPL can skip the generation of matrix A and b, because they are already in the checkpoints. However, some data structures need to be rebuilt in the initialization step.

	Tianhe-1A node	Tianhe-2 node
CPU	Dual Xeon X5670 2×6 cores @2.93GHz	Dual Xeon E5-2692(v2) 2×12 cores @2.20GHz
Peak Performance	140 GFLOPS	422 GFLOPS
Memory	48GB	64GB
P2P Bandwidth	6.9GB/s	7.1GB/s

Table 2. Node configuration of Tianhe-1A and Tianhe-2.

6. Evaluation

6.1 Methodology

We perform our evaluation on two large-scale HPC systems, Tianhe-1A and Tianhe-2 [1]. The configuration of a single node for both platforms is listed in Table 2. Table 2 shows that Tianhe-2 has more powerful CPUs and larger memory size than its predecessor, Tianhe-1A. However, each processor core of Tianhe-1A has more memory than that of Tianhe-2 (4GB/core vs. 2.4GB/core). The bandwidth of point-to-point communication is similar to both systems. Besides these two large systems, we also use a local cluster connected by EDR Infiniband network for experiments that need to power-off computing nodes. Each node is equipped with 2-way Xeon E5-2670 v3 processors (24 processor cores in total) and 64GB of memory size.

Compared to a double-checkpoint method, self-checkpoint provides more available memory for applications. It is a general method and not tied to any specified application. However, some usual benchmarks such as NPB are fixed-size, or have multiple sizes that differ too much. As a result, 50% more available memory does not enable a larger-size problem, so they are not proper for demonstrating our idea. Instead, we use HPL, which has an adjustable problem size, to verify our idea.

6.2 Comparison with State-of-the-Art Methods

In this subsection, we compare SKT-HPL with state-of-the-art methods for fault-tolerant HPL, including an algorithm-based fault tolerant HPL (ABFT-HPL) [36], a traditional checkpoint-and-restart method (BLCR) [19], and a multi-level checkpoint system (SCR) [23]. As some experiments have special requirements, e.g., mounting ramfs, installing SSD (Solid-State Drive), and powering-off computing nodes, which are not allowed on supercomputing centers, we perform these experiments on our local cluster. We compare different methods for fault-tolerant HPL and report their performance. Moreover, to validate the reliability of different methods under a permanent node failure, we power off a computing node during HPL tests. All tests of fault-tolerant HPL are run with 128 MPI processes. Each process has 4GB of memory space, and the group size is set to 8. Table 5.2 shows experimental results.

	Problem Size	Runtime (sec.) (no checkpoint)	Checkpoint Time (sec.)	GFLOPS and Checkpoints (checkpoint per 10min)	Available Memory(GB)	Normalized Efficiency	Recover after node powered-off?
Original HPL	234240	2338.64	-	3669.81 (0 chkpt)	4.00	100.00%	NO
ABFT	212224	2208.55	-	2885.00 (0 chkpt)	3.28	78.61%	NO
BLCR+HDD	234240	2338.64	295.20	2661.83 (3 chkpt)	4.00	72.53%	YES
BLCR+SSD	234240	2338.64	111.92	3209.08 (3 chkpt)	4.00	87.45%	YES
SCR+Memory	129280	426.18	4.33	3380.02 (0 chkpt)	1.22	92.10%	YES
SKT-HPL	154880	709.84	6.21	3467.64 (1 chkpt)	1.75	94.49%	YES

Table 3. Comparison between different methods of fault-tolerant HPL.

In our experiment, ABFT-HPL [36] fails to tolerate a power-off event, because MPI runtime cannot recover the user program's data structures after a node loss. The overhead of such fault-tolerant algorithms is inversely proportional to the number of processes. So its performance is not good in this small-scale experiment and it only achieves 78.61% of the original performance.

BLCR [19] is a classic checkpoint-and-restart framework. We perform our experiments on both hard disk drives (HDDs) and SSD devices. When the checkpoints are written into hard disk drives, the HPL performance is very poor, only achieving 72.53% of the original HPL, shown with BLCR+HDD in Table 5.2. Therefore, it is not practical to use the traditional CR method as a performance benchmark.

When replacing the HDDs with SSD devices, the BLCR method gets much better performance for the HPL test. The performance of BLCR+SSD achieves 87% of the original HPL. In our experiments, both BLCR+HDD and BLCR+SSD write checkpoints into local devices. It would be much slower if a distributed file system is used.

SCR [23] is a state-of-the-art multi-level checkpoint system developed by Lawrence Livermore National Laboratory (LLNL), which can write checkpoints to RAM, Flash, or disk of computing nodes in addition to a parallel file system. In our experiments, we only present its best performance of writing checkpoints into RAM. Because SCR needs to save double in-memory checkpoints to tolerate a node failure during checkpoint updating, there is only 1.22GB available memory (30.5% of the total size) for each process to do the HPL test. Therefore, the problem size SCR solves is the smallest among these methods. Since our local cluster has very large memory size per core, it also achieves 92.1% of the original HPL performance.

Thanks to the self-checkpoint mechanism, SKT-HPL has 1.75GB memory for the HPL test, which is 43% higher than the SCR method. Among these methods, SKT-HPL achieves the best performance for the HPL test and it is 94.49% of the original performance. There are two main reasons for the best performance of SKT-HPL. One is that it has much shorter checkpoint time than traditional checkpoint methods. The other is that it has much more available memory space than previous in-memory checkpoint methods.

6.3 Validation on Large-Scale Systems

Validation experiments on Tianhe-1A and Tianhe-2 are performed by manually removing several computing nodes during SKT-HPL tests. We kill the SKT-HPL processes of those nodes and remove those nodes from the resource pool of the job management system. Those nodes are permanently lost since SKT-HPL can no longer launch processes on them.

In our experiments, SKT-HPL is able to replace the lost nodes using spare nodes, recover the lost data, continue running, and finally pass verification. We therefore argue that SKT-HPL can tolerate real permanent node losses on two systems.

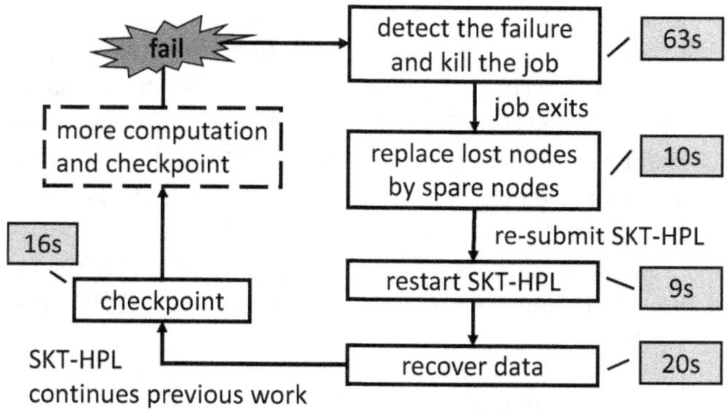

Figure 10. Time for each phase during a work-fail-detect-restart cycle. All results are measured on Tianhe-2 with 24,576 MPI processes. The time value for each phase is presented in the small green rectangles.

We further measure the time for each phase during a work-fail-detect-restart cycle, as shown in Figure 10. The time for detecting a failure depends on underlying job management systems. The failure detection time varies largely on Tianhe-1A, and it is about 30 seconds on average, while the detection time on Tianhe-2 is about 63 seconds. The time for replacing lost nodes and restarting SKT-HPL is about 10 seconds and 9 seconds respectively. The recovery process is similar to that used to calculate the checksum. But due to some additional computation, the recovery time (20 seconds) is a little longer than that to make a checkpoint (16 seconds).

6.4 Performance of SKT-HPL

We perform the original HPL test on both systems with typical configurations. We obtain 15.55 TFLOPS (86.38% of the theoretical peak performance) with 1,536 processes on Tianhe-1A. On Tianhe-2, we do not run HPL from the beginning to the end, since it consumes too much time and power. Instead, we run HPL for minutes and record its actual FLOPS value. The performance on Tianhe-2 is 367.04 TFLOPS (84.94% of the theoretical peak performance), with 24,576 processes.

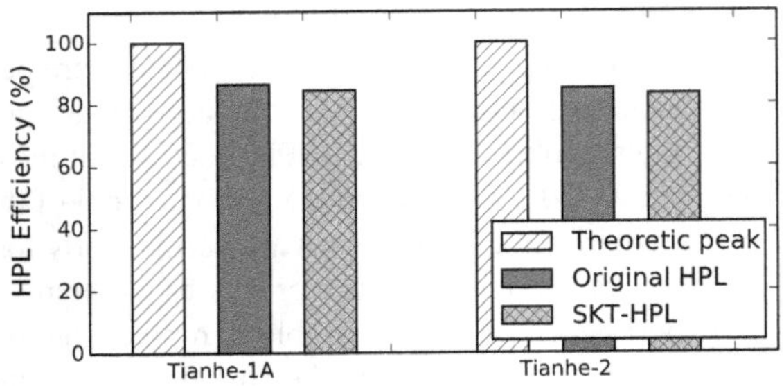

Figure 11. The efficiency of the original HPL and SKT-HPL (without making checkpoint). The original HPL uses full memory and SKT-HPL uses near half of the memory.

To analyze the performance of SKT-HPL, we test SKT-HPL on both systems with near half of the memory, no checkpoint is written. The group size for Tianhe-1A is 16 and 8 for Tianhe-2. Therefore, with the self-checkpoint mechanism, the available memory is 47% and 44% of the total memory on both systems respectively. SKT-HPL obtains 15.21 TFLOPS (97.81% of the original HPL) on Tianhe-1A and 351.60 TFLOPS (95.79% of the original HPL) on Tianhe-2. Figure 11 shows the performance of the original HPL and SKT-HPL.

6.5 Benefits of Self-Checkpoint

To verify the efficiency models presented in Section 4 and demonstrate the benefits of the self-checkpoint mechanism, we run SKT-HPL with different memory size on two large systems. Figure 12 shows test results and fitting results by our model. The squares and triangle dots represent the measured results of Tianhe-1A and Tianhe-2 respectively. Results show that our efficiency models can fit the test results very well and also verify the nonlinear behavior between problem size and HPL efficiency. Using the self-checkpoint can get 5% higher performance than using the double-checkpoint on Tianhe-2 because of its much more available memory (44% vs. 30%).

6.6 Overhead of Building Checkpoints

The time cost of building checkpoints in the self-checkpoint mechanism includes two parts, calculating checksums or encoding (network communication) and overwriting old checkpoints (local memory copying). The local overwriting

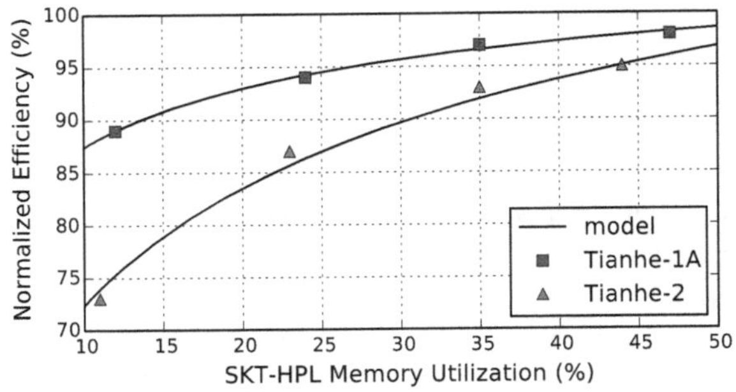

Figure 12. The relationship between Memory space used for computation and the normalized efficiency. The memory space and efficiency are compared with a typical run of the original HPL with full memory. The impact of memory space is more significant on Tianhe-2 than on Tianhe-1A.

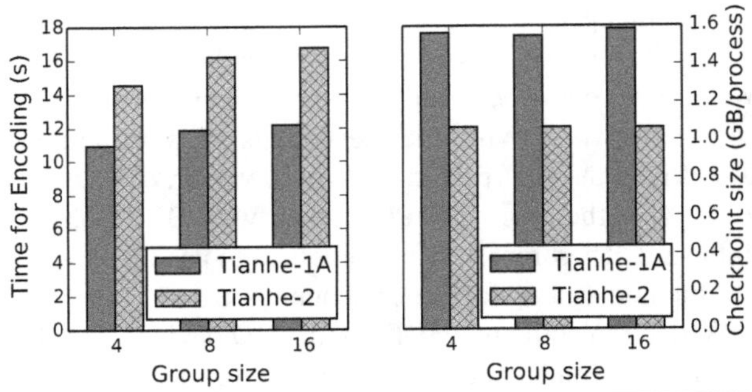

Figure 13. The encoding time of calculating checksums (left) and checkpoint size (right) with different group sizes. Encoding time grows slowly with group size. Checkpoint size is not very sensitive to group size.

time is normally less than one second, and is insignificant compared with the communication time used for the encoding. Figure 13 shows the encoding time and checkpoint size for different group sizes. As a checkpoint is close to half of the memory as shown in Equation 2, the checkpoint size is similar for different group sizes. The encoding time on both systems increases slowly with the group size.

From Table 2 we know that the point-to-point communication performance of Tianhe-2 is better than Tianhe-1A. But the encoding time of Tianhe-2 is much longer even with smaller checkpoints than Tianhe-1. It is because a network port of Tianhe-2 is shared by 24 processes, while in Tianhe-1A one port is only shared by 12 processes. As a result, the bandwidth per process of Tianhe-1A is much higher.

7. Related Work

Checkpoint-and-restart (CR) [13] is a classic fault tolerance method, which saves the intermediate states of an application (i.e., a checkpoint) into a reliable storage, and recovers data from a checkpoint after a failure. As traditional CR methods save checkpoints to a parallel file system [30] and introduce large storage overhead, they are only suitable for medium-scale systems.

Diskless or in-memory checkpoint, which saves checkpoints in memory and uses error-correcting codes to protect data, was proposed since it has much lower overhead than disk-based CR and is a potential solution for large-scale systems [27]. Plank et al. proposed an incremental diskless checkpoint system [26] to reduce memory consumption. In their method, the size of a checkpoint buffer does not need to be equal to workspace. Instead, a buffer should be large enough to save the original version of data modified during a checkpoint interval. This incremental checkpoint method is good for applications with small memory footprint. It is a double-checkpoint method that requires two buffers for checkpoint, while one buffer is needed in our self-checkpoint method. To improve scalability, Zheng et al. proposed an in-memory checkpoint scheme using a buddy system, which is scalable by dividing nodes into many two-node groups [37, 38]. This scheme can only use one third of the memory, making it more suitable for applications with little memory consumption.

Besides in-memory checkpoint, multi-level CR models have been proposed, such as SCR [23], 3D-PCRAM [11], and FTI [3]. Multi-level CR saves checkpoints to fast devices like memory, PCRAM, and local SSD in a short interval, and to slower devices (e.g., global file system) in a long interval. These studies focus on a general CR framework for parallel applications, while our method focuses on improving the available memory space of in-memory checkpoint. Therefore, we can integrate our method into a multi-level CR framework for better performance.

Some numerical algorithms can obtain redundancy by pre-processing the original input data. Huang and Abraham studied algorithm-based fault tolerance (ABFT) for classic matrix operations such as matrix-matrix multiplication and LU decomposition [20]. Yao et al. proposed a fault tolerant HPL [35]. Besides HPL, some other algorithms such as iterative methods and QR decomposition have also been studied with ABFT [7, 34]. Fault tolerant applications based on ABFT usually have low overhead. Chen et al. proposed Online-ABFT [8], which can detect soft errors in the widely used Krylov subspace iterative methods. Li et al. [22] coordinated ABFT and error-correcting code (ECC) for main memory, to improve performance and energy efficiency of ABFT-enabled applications. ABFT methods highly rely on underlying MPI runtime. If the MPI runtime cannot recover from a failure, ABFT has no chance to recover its data.

To the best of our knowledge, no MPI runtime can tolerate node failure with negligible overhead. MPICH-V [5], MPICH-V2 [6], and RADICMPI [12] are implemented based on message logging and checkpoints. Thus the performance overhead is not trivial. Some MPI runtime environments such as Intel MPI can keep running after a process is aborted, instead of forcing all processes to exit. But the aborted process is permanently lost and cannot be recovered. FT-MPI [15] extends the semantic of MPI by trying to repair MPI data structures and restart lost processes after a failure. Based on our experiments, neither Intel MPI nor FT-MPI can restart the lost processes after a node being powered off. Bland et al.'s work [4] shows that a standard MPI runtime can tolerate permanent node losses with the help of network configuration. However, their method introduces overhead to MPI library, and it is not practical for non-privileged users to change the configuration of supercomputers.

The idea of redundant execution uses multiple processes for a logical MPI rank. Both computation and communication are duplicated. Ferreira et al. proposed a prototype system rMPI [16]. Fiala et al. proposed redMPI [17], which can not only tolerate fail-stop errors, but also detect and correct silent data corruption. Similar to ABFT methods, redundant execution is good at detecting soft-errors but also cannot tolerate node failures. Unlike ABFT, a redundant execution model has no requirement on algorithms. Nevertheless, its overhead is much heavier than ABFT. Redundant execution only uses half of the CPU and memory and has an efficiency less than 50%.

8. Conclusion

To reduce the memory usage of in-memory checkpoint, we propose a new strategy, called self-checkpoint. The self-checkpoint not only achieves the same reliability of in-memory checkpoint using two copies of checkpoints, but also increases available memory space for applications by almost 50%. Based on the self-checkpoint mechanism, we further implement SKT-HPL, a fault-tolerant HPL, which can not only tolerate a real node failure on a large-scale supercomputer, but also achieve very close performance with the original HPL. Experimental results show that with 24,576 processes on Tianhe-2, the self-checkpoint method improves the available memory size by 47% than the state-of-the-art in-memory checkpoint. Moreover, SKT-HPL achieves over 95% of the original HPL's performance, and is 5% higher than using previous in-memory checkpoint methods.

Acknowledgments

We would like to thank our shepherd Prof. Narayanasamy and the anonymous reviewers for their insightful comments and suggestions. Also, we thank Yi Yang, Zhen Zheng, Heng Lin, Haojie Wang for their valuable feedback and suggestions. This work is partially supported by National Key Research and Development Program of China 2016YFB0200100, National High-Tech Research and Development Plan of China (863 project) No.2015AA01A301, National Natural Science Foundation of China No.61232008, Tsinghua University Initiative Scientific Research Program, and Microsoft Research Asia Collaborative Research Program FY16-RES-THEME-095. The corresponding author of this paper is Jidong Zhai (Email: zhaijidong@tsinghua.edu.cn).

References

[1] top500 website. http://top500.org/.

[2] S. Agarwal, R. Garg, M. S. Gupta, and J. E. Moreira. Adaptive incremental checkpointing for massively parallel systems. In *Proceedings of the 18th annual international conference on Supercomputing*, pages 277–286. ACM, 2004.

[3] L. Bautista-Gomez, S. Tsuboi, D. Komatitsch, F. Cappello, N. Maruyama, and S. Matsuoka. FTI: High Performance Fault Tolerance Interface for Hybrid Systems. In *Proceedings of 2011 International Conference for High Performance Computing, Networking, Storage and Analysis*, SC '11, pages 32:1–32:32, New York, NY, USA, 2011. ACM. ISBN 978-1-4503-0771-0. doi: 10.1145/2063384.2063427.

[4] W. Bland, P. Du, A. Bouteiller, T. Herault, G. Bosilca, and J. Dongarra. A Checkpoint-on-Failure Protocol for Algorithm-Based Recovery in Standard MPI. In *SpringerLink*, pages 477–488. Springer Berlin Heidelberg, Aug. 2012. URL http://link.springer.com/chapter/10.1007/978-3-642-32820-6_48. DOI: 10.1007/978-3-642-32820-6_48.

[5] G. Bosilca, A. Bouteiller, F. Cappello, S. Djilali, G. Fedak, C. Germain, T. Herault, P. Lemarinier, O. Lodygensky, F. Magniette, V. Neri, and A. Selikhov. MPICH-V: Toward a Scalable Fault Tolerant MPI for Volatile Nodes. In *Supercomputing, ACM/IEEE 2002 Conference*, pages 29–29, Nov. 2002. doi: 10.1109/SC.2002.10048.

[6] A. Bouteiller, F. Cappello, T. Herault, G. Krawezik, P. Lemarinier, and F. Magniette. MPICH-V2: A Fault Tolerant MPI for Volatile Nodes Based on Pessimistic Sender Based Message Logging. In *Proceedings of the 2003 ACM/IEEE Conference on Supercomputing*, SC '03, pages 25–, New York, NY, USA, 2003. ACM. ISBN 1-58113-695-1. doi: 10.1145/1048935.1050176.

[7] Z. Chen. Algorithm-based recovery for iterative methods without checkpointing. In *Proceedings of the 20th International Symposium on High Performance Distributed Computing*, HPDC '11, pages 73–84, New York, NY, USA, 2011. ACM. ISBN 978-1-4503-0552-5. doi: 10.1145/1996130.1996142.

[8] Z. Chen. Online-ABFT: An Online Algorithm Based Fault Tolerance Scheme for Soft Error Detection in Iterative Methods. In *Proceedings of the 18th ACM SIGPLAN Symposium on Principles and Practice of Parallel Programming*, PPoPP '13, pages 167–176, New York, NY, USA, 2013. ACM. ISBN 978-1-4503-1922-5. doi: 10.1145/2442516.2442533. URL http://doi.acm.org/10.1145/2442516.2442533.

[9] Z. Chen, G. E. Fagg, E. Gabriel, J. Langou, T. Angskun, G. Bosilca, and J. Dongarra. Fault tolerant high performance computing by a coding approach. In *Proceedings of the Tenth ACM SIGPLAN Symposium on Principles and Practice of Parallel Programming*, PPoPP '05, pages 213–223, New York, NY, USA, 2005. ACM. ISBN 1-59593-080-9. doi: 10.1145/1065944.1065973. URL http://doi.acm.org/10.1145/1065944.1065973.

[10] T. Davies, C. Karlsson, H. Liu, C. Ding, and Z. Chen. High performance linpack benchmark: a fault tolerant implementation without checkpointing. In *Proceedings of the international conference on Supercomputing*, pages 162–171. ACM, 2011.

[11] X. Dong, N. Muralimanohar, N. Jouppi, R. Kaufmann, and Y. Xie. Leveraging 3d pcram technologies to reduce checkpoint overhead for future exascale systems. In *Proceedings of the Conference on High Performance Computing Networking, Storage and Analysis*, SC '09, pages 57:1–57:12, New York, NY, USA, 2009. ACM. ISBN 978-1-60558-744-8. doi: 10.1145/1654059.1654117.

[12] A. Duarte, D. Rexachs, and E. Luque. An Intelligent Management of Fault Tolerance in Cluster Using RADICMPI. In B. Mohr, J. L. Trff, J. Worringen, and J. Dongarra, editors, *Recent Advances in Parallel Virtual Machine and Message Passing Interface*, number 4192 in Lecture Notes in Computer Science, pages 150–157. Springer Berlin Heidelberg, Sept. 2006. ISBN 978-3-540-39110-4 978-3-540-39112-8. URL http://link.springer.com/chapter/10.1007/11846802_26.

[13] I. P. Egwutuoha, D. Levy, B. Selic, and S. Chen. A survey of fault tolerance mechanisms and checkpoint/restart implementations for high performance computing systems. *The Journal of Supercomputing*, 65(3):1302–1326, Sept. 2013. ISSN 0920-8542, 1573-0484. doi: 10.1007/s11227-013-0884-0.

[14] N. El-Sayed and B. Schroeder. Reading between the lines of failure logs: Understanding how HPC systems fail. In *Dependable Systems and Networks (DSN), 2013 43rd Annual IEEE/IFIP International Conference on*, pages 1–12. IEEE, 2013.

[15] G. E. Fagg and J. J. Dongarra. FT-MPI: Fault Tolerant MPI, Supporting Dynamic Applications in a Dynamic World. In J. Dongarra, P. Kacsuk, and N. Podhorszki, editors, *Recent Advances in Parallel Virtual Machine and Message Passing Interface*, number 1908 in Lecture Notes in Computer Science, pages 346–353. Springer Berlin Heidelberg, 2000. ISBN 978-3-540-41010-2, 978-3-540-45255-3.

[16] K. Ferreira, J. Stearley, J. H. Laros, III, R. Oldfield, K. Pedretti, R. Brightwell, R. Riesen, P. G. Bridges, and D. Arnold. Evaluating the viability of process replication reliability for exascale systems. In *Proceedings of 2011 International Conference for High Performance Computing, Networking, Storage and Analysis*, SC '11, pages 44:1–44:12, New York, NY, USA, 2011. ACM. ISBN 978-1-4503-0771-0. doi: 10.1145/2063384.2063443.

[17] D. Fiala, F. Mueller, C. Engelmann, R. Riesen, K. Ferreira, and R. Brightwell. Detection and correction of silent data corruption for large-scale high-performance computing. In *Proceedings of the International Conference on High Performance Computing, Networking, Storage and Analysis*, page 78. IEEE Computer Society Press, 2012.

[18] L. A. B. Gomez, N. Maruyama, F. Cappello, and S. Matsuoka. Distributed Diskless Checkpoint for Large Scale Systems. pages 63–72. IEEE, 2010. ISBN 978-1-4244-6987-1. doi: 10.1109/CCGRID.2010.40.

[19] P. H. Hargrove and J. C. Duell. Berkeley lab checkpoint/restart (blcr) for linux clusters. In *Journal of Physics: Conference Series*, volume 46, page 494. IOP Publishing, 2006.

[20] K.-H. Huang and J. A. Abraham. Algorithm-based fault tolerance for matrix operations. *Computers, IEEE Transactions on*, 100(6):518–528, 1984.

[21] C. Jin, H. Jiang, D. Feng, and L. Tian. P-code: A new raid-6 code with optimal properties. In *Proceedings of the 23rd international conference on Supercomputing*, pages 360–369. ACM, 2009.

[22] D. Li, Z. Chen, P. Wu, and J. S. Vetter. Rethinking Algorithm-based Fault Tolerance with a Cooperative Software-hardware Approach. In *Proceedings of the International Conference on High Performance Computing, Networking, Storage and Analysis*, SC '13, pages 44:1–44:12, New York, NY, USA, 2013. ACM. ISBN 978-1-4503-2378-9. doi: 10.1145/2503210.2503226. URL `http://doi.acm.org/10.1145/2503210.2503226`.

[23] A. Moody, G. Bronevetsky, K. Mohror, and B. De Supinski. Design, Modeling, and Evaluation of a Scalable Multi-level Checkpointing System. In *High Performance Computing, Networking, Storage and Analysis (SC), 2010 International Conference for*, pages 1–11, Nov. 2010. doi: 10.1109/SC.2010.18.

[24] D. A. Patterson, G. Gibson, and R. H. Katz. A case for redundant arrays of inexpensive disks (raid). In *Proceedings of the 1988 ACM SIGMOD International Conference on Management of Data*, SIGMOD '88, pages 109–116. ACM, 1988.

[25] A. Petitet, R. C. Whaley, J. Dongarra, and A. Cleary. HPL - A Portable Implementation of the High-Performance Linpack Benchmark for Distributed-Memory Computers. `http://www.netlib.org/benchmark/hpl/`.

[26] J. S. Plank and K. Li. Faster checkpointing with N+1 parity. In *Proceedings of IEEE 24th International Symposium on Fault- Tolerant Computing*, pages 288–297, June 1994. doi: 10.1109/FTCS.1994.315631.

[27] J. S. Plank, K. Li, and M. A. Puening. Diskless checkpointing. *Parallel and Distributed Systems, IEEE Transactions on*, 9(10): 972–986, 1998.

[28] Y. Robert. Fault-tolerance techniques for computing at scale. *CCGrid2014*, 2014.

[29] B. Schroeder and G. Gibson. A Large-Scale Study of Failures in High-Performance Computing Systems. *IEEE Transactions on Dependable and Secure Computing*, 7(4):337–350, Oct. 2010. ISSN 1545-5971. doi: 10.1109/TDSC.2009.4.

[30] C. Wang, F. Mueller, C. Engelmann, and S. Scott. A Job Pause Service under LAM/MPI+BLCR for Transparent Fault Tolerance. In *Parallel and Distributed Processing Symposium, 2007. IPDPS 2007. IEEE International*, pages 1–10, Mar. 2007. doi: 10.1109/IPDPS.2007.370307.

[31] C. Wang, F. Mueller, C. Engelmann, and S. L. Scott. Hybrid full/incremental checkpoint/restart for mpi jobs in hpc environments. In *International Conference on Parallel and Distributed Systems*, 2011.

[32] R. Wang, E. Yao, M. Chen, G. Tan, P. Balaji, and D. Buntinas. Building algorithmically nonstop fault tolerant MPI programs. In *High Performance Computing (HiPC), 2011 18th International Conference on*, pages 1–9. IEEE, 2011.

[33] S. B. Wicker and V. K. Bhargava. *Reed-Solomon codes and their applications*. John Wiley & Sons, 1999.

[34] P. Wu and Z. Chen. Ft-scalapack: Correcting soft errors on-line for scalapack cholesky, qr, and lu factorization routines. In *Proceedings of the 23rd International Symposium on High-performance Parallel and Distributed Computing*, HPDC '14, pages 49–60, New York, NY, USA, 2014. ACM. ISBN 978-1-4503-2749-7. doi: 10.1145/2600212.2600232.

[35] E. Yao, M. Chen, R. Wang, W. Zhang, and G. Tan. A New and Efficient Algorithm-Based Fault Tolerance Scheme for A Million Way Parallelism. *arXiv preprint arXiv:1106.4213*, 2011.

[36] E. Yao, R. Wang, M. Chen, G. Tan, and N. Sun. A Case Study of Designing Efficient Algorithm-based Fault Tolerant Application for Exascale Parallelism. pages 438–448. IEEE, May 2012. ISBN 978-1-4673-0975-2, 978-0-7695-4675-9. doi: 10.1109/IPDPS.2012.48.

[37] G. Zheng, L. Shi, and L. V. Kale. Ftc-charm++: an in-memory checkpoint-based fault tolerant runtime for charm++ and mpi. In *IEEE International Conference on Cluster Computing*, pages 93–103, Sept 2004.

[38] G. Zheng, X. Ni, and L. V. Kal. A scalable double in-memory checkpoint and restart scheme towards exascale. In *Dependable Systems and Networks Workshops (DSN-W), 2012 IEEE/IFIP 42nd International Conference on*, pages 1–6. IEEE, 2012.

Silent Data Corruption Resilient Two-sided Matrix Factorizations

Panruo Wu
Department of Computer Science and Engineering
University of California Riverside
pwu011@ucr.edu

Nathan DeBardeleben, Qiang Guan, Sean Blanchard
Los Alamos National Laboratory *
{ndebard,qguan,seanb}@lanl.gov

Jieyang Chen, Dingwen Tao, Xin Liang, Kaiming Ouyang, Zizhong Chen
Department of Computer Science and Engineering,
University of California Riverside
{jchen098,dtao001,xlian007,kouya001}@ucr.edu,chen@cs.ucr.edu

Abstract

This paper presents an algorithm based fault tolerance method to harden three two-sided matrix factorizations against soft errors: reduction to Hessenberg form, tridiagonal form, and bidiagonal form. These two sided factorizations are usually the prerequisites to computing eigenvalues/eigenvectors and singular value decomposition.

Algorithm based fault tolerance has been shown to work on three main one-sided matrix factorizations: LU, Cholesky, and QR, but extending it to cover two sided factorizations is non-trivial because there are no obvious *offline, problem* specific maintenance of checksums. We thus develop an *online, algorithm* specific checksum scheme and show how to systematically adapt the two sided factorization algorithms used in LAPACK and ScaLAPACK packages to introduce the algorithm based fault tolerance.

The resulting ABFT scheme can detect and correct arithmetic errors *continuously* during the factorizations that allow timely error handling. Detailed analysis and experiments are conducted to show the cost and the gain in resilience. We demonstrate that our scheme covers a significant portion of the operations of the factorizations. Our checksum scheme achieves high error detection coverage and error correction coverage compared to the state of the art, with low overhead and high scalability.

1. Introduction

The extreme scale high performance computing (HPC) systems that are expected by the end of this decade poses several challenges including performance, power efficiency, and reliability. Due to the large amount of components in these systems and the shrinking feature size, the probability that an extreme scale application experiences faults during its execution is projected to be non negligible. Resilience to faults have been widely accepted as critical for exascale HPC applications[4, 7, 24].

The focus of this paper is soft error, also frequently called silent data corruption (SDC). Unlike bit flips in memory and storage systems that can be effectively protected by error correcting codes (ECC), logic error is difficult to deal with cheaply, often requiring redundant computations which comes with severe penalties in chip area, energy efficiency, and performance. Furthermore, the silent nature of soft errors make them more difficult to handle than hard errors because the former need active detection. For example, the system hardly knows about a floating point multiplication is carried out erroneously but can usually detect memory access faults or bit flips in memory system. The typical technique to detect soft errors is modular redundancy. The redundancy can be implemented at various levels such as microarchitecture, instruction/register, thread/process, and node level. A successful modular redundancy for large scale MPI program is RedMPI [12]. Modular redundancy has obvious problems: it usually requires 2x resources to detect errors and 3x resources to correct errors. It will also affect execution speed adversely because of the compare operation to detect errors. The strength of modular redundancy is the strong detection and correction capability in the replication sphere.

Algorithm based fault tolerance (ABFT) provides an appealing alternative to modular redundancy for soft error detection and correction. ABFT essentially provides ECC functionality for higher level data that is under certain transformation. Both techniques can detect errors in the encoded data and provide forward error recovery at low cost. The salient difference between ECC and ABFT is that ECC protects invariable data while ABFT must cope with transforming data. For ECC, once the data word is written its codeword is calculated and stored. When the data is read the codeword is checked for integrity. The data are supposed to remain unchanged. Thus ECC protects against bit flips in storage system and communication. However ABFT pro-

* Part of this work was performed at the Ultrascale Systems Research Center (USRC) at Los Alamos National Laboratory. The publication has been assigned the LANL identifier LA-UR-16-26501.

PPoPP '17, February 04 - 08, 2017, Austin, TX, USA

ACM 978-1-4503-4493-7/17/02...$15.00
DOI: http://dx.doi.org/10.1145/http://dx.doi.org/10.1145/3018743.3018750

tects data that are under certain transformations (linear algebra operations). Before computation the target data objects (usually matrix and vector) are encoded and after the computation the encoded data object is checked for integrity. This requires the encoding to remain valid under the computation, and often modification to the algorithms used. It also means that ABFT is algorithm dependent thus not a general fault tolerance method.

Direct eigen solvers including the computation of eigenvalue decomposition and singular value decomposition are prevalent in science, engineering, and more recently in data analytics. In science and engineering, these include common problems such as vibration mode in mechanical engineering and Schrodinger's equation in quantum mechanics. In data analytics, eigen solvers are used in principal component analysis (PCA), Linear Discriminant Analysis (LDA), and spectral graph theory. To solve such eigenproblems the matrix is usually first unitarily reduced to the simplest form possible (Hessenberg for asymmetric matrix, tridiagonal for symmetric matrix, and bidiagonal for SVD decomposition for any matrix) and then is solved iteratively. The first step, the reduction to simple forms, usually dominates in execution time and computing resources. Once reduced, the eigenproblems can be solved iteratively and faster. Therefore we focus on the first phase reduction in this paper.

Two recent publications [16, 17] discussed algorithm based fault tolerance for Hessenberg factorization against fail-stop errors, and bidiagonalization against fail-continue errors, respectively. The algorithmic protection technique used is based on matrix-matrix multiplication similar to [5, 13, 15, 26, 28]. For two sided factorizations that are of interest here, matrix-matrix multiplication only constitutes half of the work in terms of floating point operations (flop) and less than 20%[1] of the execution time. Furthermore, the checksums of the matrices cannot be automatically maintained during the factorizations thus have to be regenerated in every iteration. The checksum regeneration adds overhead and compromises fault coverage, as regenerated checksum cannot be used to verify correctness for prior operations. In contrast, this paper proposes an algorithm based fault tolerance scheme against soft errors that covers all BLAS2 and BLAS3 operations and with automatically maintained checksums. The results are substantially improved fault coverage (almost all floating point operations) with lower overhead. Additionally we consider the complete set of three two-sided factorizations for eigenproblems and analyze them in a unified framework.

The contribution of this paper is as follows:

- We propose the first comprehensive online ABFT schemes against soft errors for three two-sided factorizations without regenerating any checksums.
- We analytically and empirically evaluate the fault coverage and efficiency of the proposed scheme and demonstrate the superiority to the current state of the art.
- We implemented the proposed technique in the Scalable Linear Algebra Package (ScaLAPACK) for easy adoption without changes to the interfaces.

The rest of paper is organized as follows. Section 2 gives brief survey of the most relevant development of algorithmic fault tolerance for matrix factorizations. Section 3 provides necessary background to describe the main idea of this paper. Section 4 introduces the fault tolerance mechanism for the mathematically simple naive two sided matrix factorizations. Section 5 extends the idea to more practical blocked variant of the algorithm used in LAPACK. Section 6 further extend the algorithm to work locally in a distributed version of the two sided factorizations as used in ScaLAPACK. Section 7 analyzes the fault coverage and overhead of various variants of the checksum schemes. Then section 8 presents empirical evaluation of the fault coverage and performance of the proposed method and comparison to state of the art.

2. Related Work

The term algorithm based fault tolerance (ABFT) was proposed by Abraham and Huang [15] for matrix-matrix multiplication on systolic arrays to detect and correct transient errors that have occurred during the computation. The technique was subsequently extended to cover one-sided matrix factorizations (LU, Cholesky, and QR) by [1, 18, 19]. Later developments extend the idea to handle fail-stop errors [3, 11], to tolerate multiple fail-continue errors (soft errors) for LU [9] and QR [10]. For soft errors these developments share the common characteristics that they are offline problem specific. Offline means the error detection and correction happen after the computation is done; problem specific means the technique works regardless of which specific algorithm is used to solve the matrix factorization problems.

To handle multiple soft errors more efficiently, recent research proposed online variant of the ABFT idea on matrix-matrix multiplication [27, 28] one-sided matrix factorizations [6, 26, 29]. The characteristics of these recent developments are that the techniques are online algorithm specific, as opposed to the offline problem specific discussed in the previous paragraph. Online means that the error detection and correction is continuously working during the computation instead of only at the end; algorithm specific means the ABFT scheme has to be designed with a particular matrix factorization algorithm in mind instead of algorithm agnostic.

As for two sided matrix factorizations (Hessenberg, tridiagonalization, bidiagonalization), two recent studies [16, 17] discussed ABFT scheme for Hessenberg factorization against fail-stop errors and bidiagonalization against fail-continue errors. These two works are based on matrix-matrix multiplication and ignore other operations in the factorizations thus only provide partial fault coverage. To provide comprehensive protection for the two sided matrix factorizations, the challenge is that there is no obvious problem specific checksum scheme to base on. It is therefore not obvious to design offline ABFT for two-sided matrix factorizations; algorithm specific online ABFT is necessary. This further entails that substantial algorithm modification must

[1] Assuming BLAS2 speed is 20% of speed of BLAS3, the coverage in time is 16%. For example on Intel Sandy Bridge and AMD Piledriver BLAS2 speed is around 1/5 and 1/7 that of of BLAS3[25].

be incorporated together with the checksum scheme, which will be shown in the following sections.

The first report on soft errors due to alpha particles in computer chips was from Intel in 1978 [20]. The first report on soft errors due to cosmic radiations in computer chips was in 1984 [30]. In 1996, Norman [23] studied error logs of several large computer systems and reported a number of incidents of cosmic ray strikes. In 2005, Hewlett-Packard admitted that the ASC Q supercomputer located in Los Alamos National Laboratory experienced frequent crashes because of cosmic ray strikes to its parity protected cache tag arrays. The machine is particularly susceptible because of the 7000ft altitude of the installation location [21]. The book by Mukherjee [22] surveys extensively the architectural techniques to design architectures for soft errors.

3. Background

This section introduces necessary backgrounds on checksum based fault tolerance and the two sided matrix factorization algorithms.

3.1 Checksums encoded matrix and its operations

Checksum encoded matrix are the basis of algorithm based fault tolerance in linear algebra. Generally speaking checksums are linear combinations of the rows or columns of the matrix. The column checksum of a matrix is a row vector that is the (weighted) sum of all the rows in the matrix; The row checksum of a matrix is a column vector that is the (weighted) sum of all the columns in the matrix. The weights are usually predefined and independent of the matrix. Mathematically, the column checksum of a matrix (denoted with superscript c) can be represented as:

$$A^c = \begin{bmatrix} A \\ e^T A \end{bmatrix}$$

The row checksum can be written as:

$$A^r = \begin{bmatrix} A & Ae \end{bmatrix}$$

The e is a (column) vector with all elements being 1. It is usually used as the default weights; when we want to emphasize a non-uniform weight w is commonly used. The full checksum encoded matrix is a matrix with both row and column checksum:

$$A^f = \begin{bmatrix} A & Ae \\ e^T A & e^T Ae \end{bmatrix}$$

A basic result of checksum based ABFT is as follows: if $AB = C$.

$$\begin{bmatrix} A \\ e^T A \end{bmatrix} \begin{bmatrix} B & Be \end{bmatrix} = \begin{bmatrix} C & Ce \\ e^T C & e^T Ce \end{bmatrix}$$

or using the notation of checksum encoded matrix:

$$A^c B^r = C^f \tag{1}$$

This equation shows the maintenance of checksum in matrix multiplication: column checksum encoded matrix multiply row checksum encoded matrix gives us a full checksum encoded matrix. This property can be used to detect errors in the matrix multiplication.

3.2 Error correction with multiple checksums

The checksums can be used for error detection and it can also be used for error correction if we use multiple checksums with different weights. All the discussions in this paper can be extended to multiple checksums with arbitrary weights. Here is a simple double checksum scheme to locate and correct up to 1 errors per vector. Suppose we encode a vector using two different weights $e_1 = [1, 1, \ldots, 1]^T, e_2 = [1, 2, \ldots, n]^T$. The vector is $a = [a_1, \ldots, a_n]$ and we have two correct encoded checksums of a:

$$r_1 = ae_1 = \sum_{i=1}^{n} a_i, \quad r_2 = ae_2 = \sum_{i=1}^{n} ia_i$$

Now suppose the computed $a' = [a'_1, \ldots, a'_n]$ has up to one erroneous element $a'_j \neq a_j$, where the location j is unknown to us. However when we verify the checksums:

$$\delta_1 = \sum_{i=1}^{n} a'_i - r_1 = a'_j - a_j \neq 0$$

$$\delta_2 = \sum_{i=1}^{n} ia'_i - r_2 = j(a'_j - a_j) \neq 0$$

Then a simple division δ_2/δ_1 gives us the location j. The correct value of a_j can then be recovered using the correct checksum and the other correct elements of a: $a_j = a'_j - \sum_{i=1, i\neq j}^{n} a'_i$. Therefore, if we have two checksums for a vector we can correct up to 1 erroneous element in it. If we have full double checksums for a matrix we can correct up to 1 erroneous element in each column/row. In the following text we only assume single checksum for brevity of notations; extending to multiple checksums with different weights is implied.

3.3 Maintaining checksum for matrix factorizations

There are three common one sided factorizations: LU, Cholesky, and QR. The LU factorization factorizes a matrix A into a lower triangular matrix L and an upper triangular matrix U. It can be shown that (almost) unmodified LU algorithm operating on the full checksum encoded matrix A^f would result in column checksum encoded L^c and row checksum encoded U^r.

$$A = LU, A^f = \begin{bmatrix} L \\ e^T L \end{bmatrix} \begin{bmatrix} U & Ue \end{bmatrix}$$

The same works for Cholesky factorization:

$$A = LL^T, A^f = \begin{bmatrix} L \\ e^T L \end{bmatrix} \begin{bmatrix} L^T & L^T e \end{bmatrix}$$

For QR factorization $A = QR$ because the left factor Q is supposed to be orthogonal, unmodified QR algorithm operating on A^f would *not* result in the desired $Q^c R^r$ as QR produces the orthogonal left factor while Q^c cannot be

$$x = \begin{bmatrix} \times \\ \times \\ \times \\ \vdots \\ \times \end{bmatrix} \quad \xrightarrow{F} \quad Fx = \begin{bmatrix} ||x|| \\ 0 \\ 0 \\ \vdots \\ 0 \end{bmatrix} = ||x||e_1$$

Figure 1. The effect of (left) Householder reflector to a column vector.

orthogonal as Q^c is singular. However if we only perform QR on the row checksum encoded A^r then we have:

$$A = QR, A^r = QR^r$$

We see that the the QR factorization preserves the row checksum. This is possible because the right factor R is supposed to be upper triangular and R^r can conform to this requirement.

For two sided factorizations however the left factor and right factor are both orthogonal thus we cannot hope to use unmodified algorithm to do the factorization that preserves the checksum. For example bidiagonalization factors a matrix into:

$$A = QBP^T, A^f = Q'B'P'^T$$

There is no possibility that $Q' = Q^c$ or $P' = P^c$ as Q', Q, P, P' are all supposed to be orthogonal. Nor can we expect unmodified two sided factorization algorithms to preserve row/column checksums for A^r or A^c. For the other two two-sided factorizations the checksums cannot be automatically maintained without modification to the factorization algorithm, as in both cases the left and right factors are orthogonal.

4. Unblocked version

In this section we describe the checksum based ABFT for unblocked bidiagonal reduction and Hessenberg/tridiagonal reduction. Unblocked algorithms are easy to understand but not practical in practice due to its inefficiency in using modern hierarchical memory system. It will however illustrate the basic technique for further more complex blocked algorithms and distributed algorithms.

4.1 Householder reflector for unitary diagonalization

Householder reflector is an orthogonal matrix that maps a target vector to the first axis. The effect is shown as in figure 1.

The Householder matrix F is constructed based on vector x as follows:

$$v = x + \text{sign}(x_1)||x||_2 e_1, \quad F = I - \frac{2}{v^T v} vv^T \quad (2)$$

in which e_1 is the vector $(1, 0, 0, \ldots, 0)^T$. It can be shown that applying the left Householder matrix to a column vector x will reflect x to the first axis, eliminating all other components except the first one. Note that since the Householder reflector is symmetric and orthogonal, it serves as the primary tool to unitarily triangularize (zero out lower triangular part) a matrix. Likewise, applying a Householder matrix on the right to a row vector will have similar effect and can be used to zero out the upper triangular part.

To simplify notation we normalize the Householder vector v: $v = v/||v||_2$. The Householder matrix thus becomes $F = I - 2vv^T$. Regarding the checksum preserving property of Householder reflection we have the following important lemma that is the basis of all the automatic maintenance of checksums in two-sided factorizations:

Lemma 4.1. *Suppose $(I - 2vv^T)A = A'$, then we have the corresponding checksum result:*

$$A^f - 2v^c v^T A^r = (A')^f$$

Proof.

$$\begin{aligned} \text{LHS} &= \begin{bmatrix} A & Ae \\ e^T A & e^T Ae \end{bmatrix} - 2 \begin{bmatrix} v \\ e^T v \end{bmatrix} v^T [\ A \quad Ae\ ] \\ &= \begin{bmatrix} A' & A'e \\ e^T A' & e^T A'e \end{bmatrix} = \text{RHS} \end{aligned}$$

□

There is a symmetric case that applies F to the right of A. The significance of this lemma is that, if we have the checksum of Householder vector v and the matrix A, we can operate on the checksum augmented vector/matrix to obtain the desired output, *and* its associated checksums. In other words, we have defined a certain application of Householder matrix in such a way that the checksum is preserved. The Householder transformation will be modified in this way in the two sided matrix factorizations in order to maintain the checksum encoding, thus serving as the foundation for checksum based ABFT for them.

4.2 Bidiagonal reduction

Bidiagonal reduction (or bidiagonalization) is the first step in computing singular value decomposition. It is the process of alternating left and right orthogonal transformations to reduce a general $m \times n$ matrix into a upper diagonal form (if $m \geq n$), in which all but the diagonal and first superdiagonal entries are zeros:

$$A = QBP^T, \text{Q and P are orthogonal, B is bidiagonal.} \quad (3)$$

Householder reflectors are usually used to introduce zeros into the subdiagonal. Note that in general no direct methods can reduce A to bidiagonal form. The key method in the factorization is through Householder transformation; applying Householder reflector on the left of the matrix reduces eliminates the entries below diagonal in the current column; applying it on the right eliminate the entries that are right of the first superdiagonal in the current row. The process is shown in figure 2.

Let us first consider the unblocked version of the bidiagonalization algorithm used in LAPACK DGEBD2 subroutine. Suppose we are given a thin matrix A of size $m \times n$

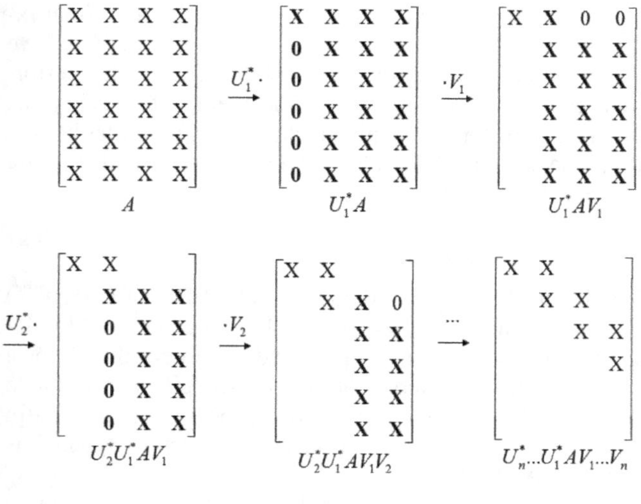

Figure 2. Householder Reduction to Bidiagonal Form

Algorithm 1 Householder Reduction to (Upper) Bidiagonal Form

Require: matrix $A \in \mathbb{R}^{m \times n}, m \geq n$
Ensure: $A \to QBP^T$ where B is (upper) bidiagonal, Q, P are orthogonal

1: **for** $k = 1 : m - 1$ **do**
2: $x = A_{k:m,k}$
3: $q = x + \text{sign}(x_1)||x||_2 e_1$
4: $q = q/||q||_2$
5: $A_{k:m,k:n} = A_{k:m,k:n} - 2q(q^T A_{k:m,k:n})$
6: $x = A_{k,k+1:n}$
7: $p = x + \text{sign}(x_1)||x||_2 e_1$
8: $p = p/||p||_2$
9: $A_{k:m,k+1:n} = A_{k:m,k+1:n} - 2(A_{k:m,k+1:n}p)p^T$
10: Store q, p
11: **end for**

and $m \geq n$. The (upper) bidiagonalization algorithm is described in algorithm 1

Let us walk through the bidiagonalization procedure in algorithm 1. Line 2-4 computes the left Householder vector and matrix; line 5 applies the resulting Householder matrix to the left of the matrix to eliminate the column (see the first and third transformation in figure 2). Note that Similarly, line 6-8 computes the right Householder vector and matrix; line 9 applies the resulting Householder matrix to the right of the matrix to eliminate the row (see the second and fourth transformation in figure 2).

Now it is time to design a checksum scheme and modification to the algorithm 1 in such a way that the checksum encoding will remain valid at certain point during the factorization. In fact we will aim at maintaining checksum encoding at the end of each Householder application (line 5 and 9) in each loop iteration. We summarize the design problem we are facing now:

> Problem: Given a fully checksum encoded original matrix A^f, how do we modify the algorithm 1 such that at the end of line 5 and 9 the matrix A^f or its submatrix is properly encoded?

The basis is the lemma 4.1. Our design is present in the algorithm 2.

Algorithm 2 Modified Householder Reduction to (Upper) Bidiagonal Form

Require: A full checksum encoded matrix $A \in \mathbb{R}^{(m+1)\times(n+1)}, m \geq n$
Ensure: $A \to Q^c B (P^r)^T$ where B is (upper) bidiagonal, Q, P are orthogonal

1: **for** $k = 1 : m - 1$ **do**
2: $x = A_{k:m+1,k}$
3: $q = x + \text{sign}(x_1)||x_{1:\text{last}-1}||_2 e_1^c$
4: $q = q/||q_{1:\text{last}-1}||_2$
5: $A_{k:m+1,k:n+1} = A_{k:m+1,k:n+1} - 2qq^T_{1:\text{last-}1} A_{k:m,k:n+1}$
6: $x = A_{k,k+1:n}$
7: $p = x + \text{sign}(x_1)||x_{1:\text{last}11}||_2 e_1^c$
8: $p = p/||p_{1:\text{last}11}||_2$
9: $A_{k:m+1,k+1:n+1} = A_{k:m+1,k+1:n+1} - 2A_{k:m+1,k+1:n} p_{1:\text{last}+1} p^T$
10: Store q, p
11: **end for**

Theorem 4.2. *In the modified algorithm 2 at the end of line 5 or line 9 in each iteration, the matrix A remains full checksum encoded. At the end of the algorithm, the result will be the full checksum encoded result of that of algorithm 1 performed on the matrix without encoding.*

To see why theorem 4.2 holds intuitively, it is instructive to compare algorithm 2 to algorithm 1 line by line. For example, by induction before line 5 the pre-condition that the matrix A is full checksum encoded. Applying lemma 4.1 to line 5 leads to the post-condition that the after line 5 the matrix A remains full checksum encoded. Also note that by construction q and p in algorithm 2 is the column checksum encoded q and p in algorithm 1. This leads to the conclusion that after line 5 the matrix A in algorithm 2 is the full checksum encoded A in algorithm 1. These two conclusions combined to prove theorem 4.2. We thus illustrated that algorithm 2 provides a solution to our stated problem.

4.3 Hessenberg reduction and tridiagonal reduction

Hessenberg reduction is the first step in computing eigenvalue decomposition. It is the process of applying the same orthogonal transformation to both left and right of the matrix to reduce the a square matrix into upper Hessenberg form in which all but the upper triangular part and the subdiagonal are zero:

$$A = QHQ^T, \text{Q is orthogonal, H is Hessenberg matrix.} \quad (4)$$

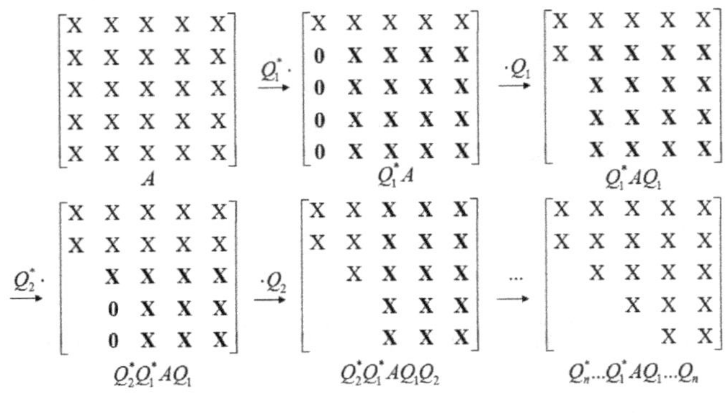

Figure 3. Householder reduction to Hessenberg form

Note the difference from bidiagonal reduction: the left factor and right factor are both Q. The reduction is also carried out through Householder reflectors. The additional constraint that the left factor and right factor must be the same in general prevents direct reduction to bidiagonal as in the case of bidiagonal reduction case; the best we can do is the Hessenberg form. If the matrix A is symmetric then the H is both Hessenberg and symmetric therefore tridiagonal. In our discussion tridiagonal reduction can be treated as a special case of Hessenberg reduction thus will not be discusses separately unless necessary.

To modify the Householder Hessenberg reduction algorithm, again the basis is lemma 4.1. The result is very similar to the bidiagonal reduction case so we only give the modified algorithm 3.

Algorithm 3 Modified Householder Reduction to Hessenberg Form

Require: A full checksum encoded matrix $A^f \in \mathbb{R}^{(m+1)\times(m+1)}$

Ensure: $A^f \to Q^c, H^f, (Q^T)^r$ where $A = QHQ^T$, B is (upper) bidiagonal, Q, P are orthogonal

for $k = 1 : m-2$ **do**

  $x = A_{k+1:m+1,k}$

  $q = x + \text{sign}(x_1)||x_{1:\text{last}-1}||_2 e_1^c$

  $q = q/||q_{1:\text{last}-1}||_2$

  $A_{k+1:m+1,k:m+1} = A_{k+1:m+1,k:m+1} - 2qq^T_{1:\text{last-1}}A_{k+1:m+1,k:m+1}$

  $A_{1:m+1,k+1:m+1} = A_{1:m+1,k+1:m+1} - 2A_{1:m+1,k+1:m+1}q_{1:\text{last-1}}q^T$

  Store q, p

end for

We then have a theorem similar to theorem 4.2 asserting similar checksum maintenance.

5. Blocked version

In contrast to the previous unblocked algorithms for two sided factorizations, in this section we move on to the blocked algorithms which are substantially more efficient and complex. The unblocked algorithms are rich in level 1 and 2 BLAS operations (vector-vector and matrix-vector) which have low computation intensity. The blocked version aggregates some of the BLAS 2 into single BLAS 3 (matrix-matrix multiplication) operations. BLAS 3 operations have much better computation intensity therefore better performance on modern computers. The method to modify the blocked algorithms to maintain checksums is similar but not quite the same as the unblocked algorithms. The details are presented in this section.

5.1 Bidiagonal Reduction

The blocked bidiagonal reduction (xGEBRD in LAPACK) solves the same factorization problem in equation 3 by delaying the application of line 5 and 9 in algorithm 1 for a few iterations and apply the aggregated effect in a single matrix multiplication. The detailed process is illustrated in algorithm 5. The algorithm is summarized from [8] which is used in LAPACK.

The blocked algorithm 5 looks quite a bit more elaborate compared to algorithm 1. The algorithm 5 describes an iteration in a loop. The main complexity is in calculating the temporary matrices X, Y that represent the effect of rank-2 trailing matrix update (line 5 and 9 in algorithm 1). The X, Y "store" the update to the trailing matrix and are used to apply the update in bulk of B rank-2 updates into matrix multiplications, or rank-$2B$ update (step 2, 3 in algorithm 5).

To modify the blocked algorithm 5 such that it maintains checksum encoding when operating on fully checksum encoded matrix A, lemma 4.1 cannot be directly used since the rank-1 Householder transformation is delayed and applied in bulk. An apparent idea is to relate the matrix multiplications in step 2 and 3 in algorithm 5 to equation 1. If we can have a column checksum encoded U, V, X, Y and full checksum encoded A, the trailing matrix update (step 2,3) that subtract $VY^T + XU^T$ from A leaves a fully checksum encoded A as we desired. This approach is used by [17]. The problem with this approach is that the checksums of matrices U, V, X, Y must be recalculated every time before step 2 and 3. The inability to maintain the checksums of U, V, X, Y not only adds additional overheads but also compromises fault coverage: the faulty calculation of U, V, X, Y cannot be detected as they are not encoded. We would like to avoid the recalculation of checksums and develop a automatically maintained checksum throughout the blocked algorithm. The U, V, X, Y should all be encoded throughout the algorithm, and any faulty calculation in the algorithm 5 would lead to inconsistently encoded matrix.

To do that we follow an intuitive guideline similar to the modification we made in algorithm 2: we include the checksums in vector, matrix-vector, and matrix-matrix operations when it makes sense. If the result is supposed to be a full checksum encoded matrix, the left factor should be column checksum encoded and the right factor should be row checksum encoded; if the result is supposed to be column checksum encoded, the left factor should be column checksum encoded and the rest checksum is not included. The resulting modified algorithm is presented in algorithm 4.

We claim that after step 2,3 in algorithm 4, the matrix A is full checksum encoded, and after step 1.(a) or 1.(e) the updated vector in A is row checksum encoded. To see why this is so we need to go into the derivation of

Algorithm 4 Modified Householder reduction to bidiagonal form, Blocked Version in matlab notation. Red color marks the modifications.

Input: Full checksum encoded $A_{1:m+1,1:n+1}$
WHILE $m > 0$:

1. `DLABRD`: REduce the kth panel of the matrix and compute X, Y. [Repeat B times for $i = 1, \ldots, B$.]
   (a) Update the jth column of A: $A_{i:m+1,i} = A_{i:m+1,i} - A_{j:m+1,1:i-1} * Y'_{i,1:i-1} - X_{j:m+1,1:i-1} * A_{1:i-1,i}$.
   (b) Verify $A_{i:m+1,i} = A^c_{i:m,i}$
   (c) Compute the ith column Householder vector of A, $A_{i:m+1,i}$
   (d) Compute $Y_{i+1:n+1,i} = \tau_v(A'_{i:m,i+1:n+1} * A_{i:m,i} - Y_{i+1:n+1,1:i-1} * A'_{i:m,1:i-1} * A_{i:m,i} - A'_{1:i-1,i+1:n+1} * X'_{i:m,1:i-1} * A_{i:m,i})$
   (e) Update the jth row of A: $A_{i,i+1:n+1} = A_{i,i+1:n+1} - A_{i,1:i}Y^T_{i+1:n+1,1:i} - X_{1:i-1,i}A_{1:i-1,i+1:n+1}$.
   (f) Verify $A_{i,i+1:n+1} = A^r_{i,i+1:n}$
   (g) Compute the ith row Householder vector of A, $A_{i,i+1:n+1}$.
   (h) Compute $X_{i+1:m+1,i} = \tau_u(A_{i+1:m+1,i+1:n} * A'_{i,i+1:n} - A_{i+1:m+1,i+1:n} * Y'_{i+1:n,1:i} * A'_{i,i+1:n} - X_{i+1:m+1,1:i-1} * A_{1:i-1,i+1:n} * A'_{i,i+1:n})$.
2. `DGEMM`: Update A with V and Y, $A_{B+1:m+1,B+1:n+1} = A_{B+1:m+1,B+1:n+1} - A_{B+1:m+1,1} * Y'_{B+1m+1,1:B}$.
3. `DGEMM`: Update A with X and U, $A_{B+1:m+1,B+1:n+1} = A_{B+1:m+1,B+1:n+1} - X_{B+1:m+1,1} * A_{1:B,B+1:n+1}$.
4. Verify $A_{B+1:m+1,B+1:n+1} = A^f_{B+1:m,B+1:n}$

$A = A_{B+1:m+1,B+1:n+1}, m = m - B, n = n - B$
END WHILE
Process the remaining A with unblocked algorithm.

Algorithm 5 Modified Blocked Householder Reduction to Bidiagonal Form, Blocked Version in matrix notation.. Red colored marks the modifications.

1. `DLABRD`: Reduce the kth panel of the matrix and compute V, U, X, Y. [Repeat B times for $i = 1, \ldots, B$ (let $j = (k-1)B + i$).]
   (a) Update the jth column of A: $A^c_{:,j} = A^c_{:,j} - V^c_{i-1}y^T_i - X^c_{i-1}u^T_i$
   (b) Compute the ith column Householder vector of A, v^c_i.
   (c) Compute $(y_i)^c = \tau_v((A^r)^T v_i - (Y_{i-1})^c V^T_{i-1} v_i - U^c_{i-1} X^T_{i-1} v_i)$
   (d) Update the jth row of A: $(A^r_{j,:})^T = (A^r_{j,:})^T - Y^c_i(v^T_I) - U^c_{i-1}x^T_{i-1}$
   (e) Compute the ith row Householder vector of A, u^c_i
   (f) Compute $x^c_i = \tau_u(A^c u_i - X^c_{i-1}U^T_{i-1}u_i - V^c_i Y^T_i u_i)$.
2. `DGEMM`: Update A with V and Y, $A^f = A^f - V^c(Y^c)^T$.
3. `DGEMM`: Update A with X and U, $A^f = A^f - X^c(U^c)^T$.

blocked algorithm and the equivalence between unblocked and blocked versions. Carefully applying the basic maintenance of checksums in matrix-matrix/vector multiplication proves this claim. The details are omitted here due to limited space.

5.2 Hessenberg and Tridiagonal Reduction

The Hessenberg and tridiagonal reduction is similar in spirit to the bidiagonal case. We list only the Hessenberg reduction algorithm here in algorithm 6; The tridiagonal reduction is Hessenberg reduction on symmetric matrix.

Algorithm 6 Modified orthogonal reduction to Hessenberg form, blocked version in matrix notation.. Red colored marks the modifications.

1. `DLAHRD`: Reduce the kth panel of the matrix and compute V, Y, T. [Repeat B times for $i = 1, \ldots, B$ (let $j = (k-1)B + i$).]
   (a) Computer the Householder vector v^c_i.
   (b) Compute $y^c_i = \tau(A^c v_i - Y^c_{i-1}V^T_{i-1}v_i)$.
   (c) Compute $t_i = -\tau T_{i-1}V^T_{i-1}v_i$
   (d) Update the $(j+1)th$ column of A if necessary:
      i. Apply the block Householder vector from the right: $A^c_{:,j+1} = A^c_{:,j+1} - Y^c_i[V_i]_{j,:}$
      ii. Apply the block Householder vector from the left: $A^c_{:,j+1} = A^c_{:,j+1} - V^c_i T^T_i V^T_i A_{:,j}$
2. `DGEMM`: Update A with V and Y, $A^f = A^f - Y^c(V^c)^T$.
3. `DLARFB`: Apply the block Householder vector from the left, $A^f = A^f - V^c T^T V^T A^r$.

6. Distributed Blocked Version

In this section we discuss how to adapt the ABFT scheme for the distributed two sided factorizations in the ScaLAPACK package. First we will briefly introduce the 2D cyclic data distribution and how ScaLAPACK implements the blocked factorizations discussed previously on a distributed memory cluster system. Then we discuss the adaption of the ABFT scheme to distributed memory system and the modification to the corresponding distributed algorithm.

6.1 Data distribution

The ScaLAPACK uses the two dimensional cyclic block data distribution [2] for the matrix on distributed memory system because of its efficient support for high performance matrix-matrix multiplication and load balance for parallel speed up and scalability. In many linear algebra algorithms such as the matrix factorizations, the algorithm works on ever smaller submatrix as the algorithm progresses thus posing a load balance problem. To mitigate this problem 2D block cyclic distribution assigns matrix blocks to processes in a round-robin fashion. Therefore each process will possess blocks with a constant stride. Two dimensional means the matrix is partitioned into a 2D array of blocks and the processes are arranged into a 2D grid. The blocks is assigned according to its row and column index, as shown in figure

In the previous section we attach checksums to the global matrix and modify the algorithms to maintain the checksum during factorization. Because ScaLAPACK mostly reuses the LAPACK algorithm and implementation for the two sided factorizations, the same design can be used in ScaLAPACK. However because the matrix is distributed onto multiple computing nodes, the checksum verification procedure would require communication that involves all the processes. To avoid the communication in checksum verification, we would like to attach checksums to the matrix local to each process instead of to the global matrix. In addition, local checksums are desirable in numerical accuracy and scalability in correcting errors. The question is then how to modify the ScaLAPACK two-sided factorizations in such a way that local checksums are maintained in similar way that global checksums are maintained.

The guideline to modify the ScaLAPACK software follows the same principle of LAPACK; the difference is that in LAPACK the matrix-vector and matrix-matrix operations are on global matrix but in ScaLAPACK they are on local matrix. Previously we modify the matrix-vector and matrix-matrix multiplications by including the appropriate checksums global to the matrix/vector, now on the distributed matrix we modify the corresponding operations by including the appropriate checksum local to the matrix/vector. Take matrix-vector multiplication for example as illustrated in figure 4. Suppose we would like to perform a global matrix-vector multiplication $y = Ax$ and the matrices and vectors are distributed as illustrated in 4. First each process owning a part of matrix A would do the matrix-vector multiplication on its local data $y_L = A_L x_L$, and then all processes that contribute to the same part of y would sum up their contribution to form the part of global y. To modify this distributed matrix-vector multiplication to include the

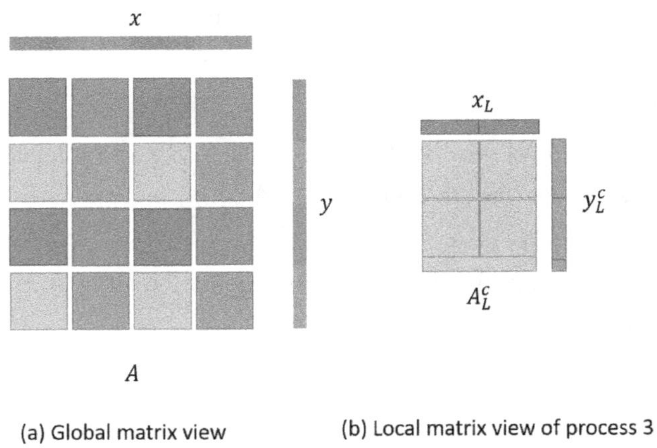

Figure 4. Modification to distributed matrix-vector multiplication to include local checksums

local checksums, we simply include the local checksums in the local matrix-vector multiplication, and then sum up the checksum encoded result vector y_L^c. Modifying distributed matrix-matrix multiplication is similar; the difference is that in matrix-matrix multiplication both row checksums and column checksums are involved.

We now claim that during the modified distributed blocked two-sided factorizations, the process *local* matrix will be properly checksum encoded just like the global matrix is encoded in the non-distributed case. To see why this is true, we note that 1) the checksum is a weighted sum of the participating elements, and all of our discussion will work with any weights; and 2) the following insight:

> Key insight: Each process owns a portion of the global matrix. Checksum of the local matrix is equivalent to checksum of the global matrix with selective weights; see figure 5. This is possible because all the distributions of all the matrices (A, X, Y) are compatible.

This leads to the interesting view that each process in the distributed factorizations use its own selective weights. The global matrix thus have multiple distributed checksums with different weights.

7. Analysis

In this section we analyze three aspects of the algorithms we described in these aspects: 1) the fault coverage; 2) the overhead and scalability.

7.1 Fault coverage

In this section we first attempt to quantify the (detection) fault coverage of different error detection techniques. There are various kinds of error detection techniques; they might have different strength in detecting errors. Intuitively if we only design checksum scheme for part of the data structure and only for some operations, the fault coverage is low be-

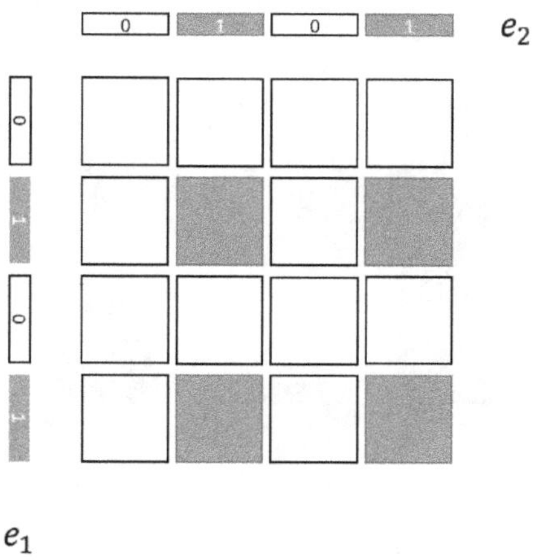

Figure 5. Local checksum equivalent to global checksum with specific weights.

cause corruption to data or operation outside of the protection will not be detected. On the algorithm abstraction layer we can define a metric of (algorithmic) fault coverage as portion of data structures and portion of time for which the data structures are *not* vulnerable. A data structure is vulnerable for a period of time during which a corruption to it cannot in general be detected. The corruption can be in the form of logic error (miscalculation) or bit flips. If all data structures are protected for the whole duration of the algorithm, the fault coverage is 100%. If half the data structures are protected for half of the time in the algorithm, the fault coverage is $50\% \times 50\% = 25\%$. The fault coverage conceptually reflects the probability of error detection if fault happens randomly and uniformly in space and time.

We compare the three checksum schemes for the fault coverage analysis. The first is our proposed checksum scheme without checksum regeneration. The second is the previous checksum scheme from [16, 17] that covers only the matrix-matrix multiplications with checksum regeneration. The third builds upon the second such that covers the matrix-matrix and matrix-vector multiplication with checksum regeneration. We denote the three checksum schemes by FT1, FT2, and FT3 respectively. The checksum regeneration in FT2 and FT3 are necessary because checksums are not automatically maintained across the matrix-vector/matrix operations thus have to be regenerated before the operation begins. The checksums also have to be checked before the result is overwritten and the checksum regenerated, otherwise the fault will elude detection. We will analyze the fault coverage of FT1, FT2, and FT3 based on the LAPACK `dgebrd` subroutine shown as algorithm 5.

For FT1 shown in algorithm 4 all operations except for the four matrix-vector operations in 1.(c) and 1.(f) are covered. The unprotected matrix-vector operations are the four intermediate calculation $V_{i-1}^T v_i, X_{i-1}^T v_i, U_{i-1}^T u_i, Y_i^T u_i$. At each iteration they affect at most $2M \times B$ elements, and takes

$$\sum_{k=1}^{B}(m+n-k+1)(k-1) \leq \frac{mB^2}{2}$$

Summing the above for all iterations ($m = M-N, M-N+B, M-N+2B, \ldots, M$)yields:

$$\sum_{j=1}^{(M-N)/B}(M-N+jB)B^2 \leq \frac{1}{2}BMN$$

Noting that the whole matrix takes space $M \times N$ and the whole algorithm takes FLOPs $\frac{4}{3}N^2(2M-N)$, we can estimate the fault coverage ratio of FT1:

$$\text{Cov(FT1)} \geq 1 - \frac{\frac{1}{2}BMN \times 2MB}{\frac{4}{3}N^2(2M-N) \times MN} \geq 1 - \frac{3}{4}\frac{M}{N}\left(\frac{B}{N}\right)^2$$

We see that the fault coverage of FT1 scheme is in general very high as the blocking size is usually within $[32, 128]$ and the problem matrix can be M, N can be at least 100x that of B. The ratio tends to be larger than 99.9% for reasonably large and square matrix.

For the FT2 scheme that only protects the matrix-matrix factorization, suppose the matrix is a square ($M = N$). In each iteration, the two matrix-matrix multiplication (step 2, 3 in algorithm 5) protects data size n^2 for duration of $4Bn^2$. The whole matrix has size N^2 and duration $\frac{8}{3}N^3$. Taking consideration of all iterations ($n = B, 2B, \ldots, N$) we get:

$$\text{Cov(FT2)} = \frac{\sum_{j=1}^{N/B} 4B(jB)^2 \times (jB)^2}{N^2 \times \frac{8}{3}N^2} = 30\%$$

For the FT3 scheme the fault coverage is almost 100% as the only unprotected parts is the generation of Householder vector (step 1.(b)(e) in algorithm 5) which affect very few elements for very brief time. The problem of this approach is the high overhead due to checksum regeneration and frequent verification to achieve high fault coverage which FT1 does not have. The overhead will analyzed in the next subsection and also empirically shown in the next section.

What about the error correction coverage? Detailed analysis is difficult as whether the error is correctable depends on specific the timing and location of the error. However we note that detection fault coverage is the upper bound for correction fault coverage: errors cannot be corrected unless they are detected. We will explore the correction coverage empirically in the next section.

As a side note, the algorithmic fault coverage discussed here is based on the algorithm abstraction layer; the objects and operations are rather high level and need to be mapped to a program, and subsequently mapped to a computer instructions, and eventually to electrical circuits for execution. Some of the lower abstraction constructs such as the indices, loops, pointers in the programming language layer that are needed to carry out the algorithm are not discussed here; their misbehavior may or may not be covered by higher abstraction layer. The fault tolerance mechanisms for other abstraction layers are important in determining the resilience of the final application execution, but they are out of the scope of this paper. Fault tolerance at different layers have their peculiar trade-offs between complexity, cost, and effectiveness and it is desirable to integrate them to combine their individual advantages.

7.2 Overhead

In this subsection we analyze the overhead in introducing checksum in checksum scheme FT1, FT2, and FT3. The execution time overhead comes from three parts: 1) checksum (re)generation; 2) extra computation/communications that involves the checksums; 3) checksum verification. The memory space overhead comes from the extra space to store checksums. Suppose BLAS2 operation execution rate is α_2 and BLAS3 operation execution rate is α_3. On a typical modern CPU such as Intel Xeon α_3 is about 5x that of α_2.

For FT1, the overhead is

$$O_{\mathrm{FT1}} = \frac{\alpha_2 N^2 + (\alpha_2 + \alpha_3)/2 \times 8N^2 + \alpha_2 \frac{N^3}{3B}}{\frac{4}{3}(\alpha_2 + \alpha_3)N^3} \tag{5}$$

$$O_{\mathrm{FT2}} = \frac{\alpha_2 \frac{N^3}{3B}}{\frac{4}{3}(\alpha_2 + \alpha_3)N^3} \tag{6}$$

$$O_{\mathrm{FT3}} = \frac{\frac{4}{3}\alpha_2 N^3 + \alpha_2 \frac{N^3}{3B}}{\frac{4}{3}(\alpha_2 + \alpha_3)N^3} \tag{7}$$

Under reasonable assumption of $B = 32, N \approx 1000s$, the O_{FT1} and O_{FT2} should be at around a few percent, and O_{FT3} can approach 100% primarily due to the frequent checksum regeneration.

8. Experiments

In this section we empirically study the proposed fault tolerance two sided factorizations for the aspects discussed in the previous section.

8.1 Fault injections

In this subsection we empirically examine the fault coverage of the three checksum schemes FT1(proposed in this paper), FT2, and FT3. We use a fault injector to inject faults into the program and repeat this test to see if the fault can be detected. The fault injection is aimed to assess the algorithmic fault coverage therefore only floating point data and operations are targeted; the indices, pointers, and other control data and operations are not. Corruptions to the matrices and vectors seldom lead to crash of the process thus is almost always a silent data corruption; corruption to control data and operation quite likely will lead to process crash.

The fault injector we use is based on debugger GDB. It works as follows. First the target program is run under the debugger and profiled for its execution time. Then we randomly generate a timer event during the execution to stop the program. The debugger then either randomly decide to corrupt a random element in the numerical data, or modify the current floating point arithmetic instructions. If the current instruction is not a floating point instruction the debugger executes one instruction at a time until it finds a floating point instruction.

We have implemented the three checksums schemes into the blocked serial bidiagonal reduction subroutine `DGEBRD()` in LAPACK 3.6.0. The matrix size is set to 500x500. Each program will be subject to 1000 error injections; each time a single fault is injected and the program will report whether it has detected the fault. All injections will affect the result if untreated. The results are summarized in the figure 6. We can see that FT1 can detect almost all errors and correct a fairly large fraction of them. FT2 can only detect less than 12.5% errors and correct even less. FT3 on the other hand does not perform too well primarily due to the significant added computations of checksum regeneration that are themselves vulnerable, and the non-persistent checksums that cannot detect memory corruptions to already computed data.

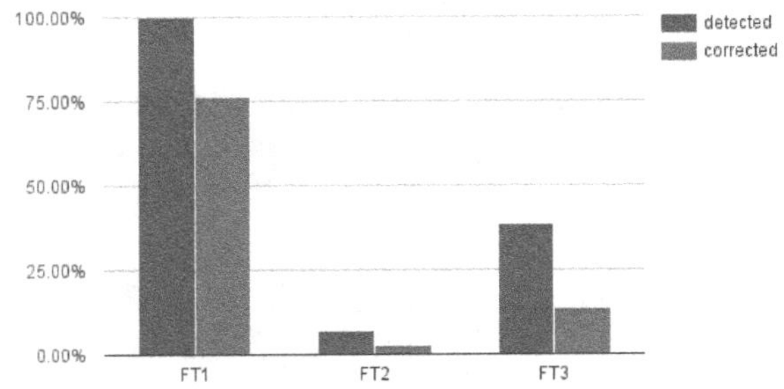

Figure 6. The fault coverage for the three checksum schemes

8.2 Execution time overheads

Here we empirically evaluate the execution time overhead of the checksum schemes. We use the same implementation as the previous subsection but here we enable aggressive optimization flags of compiler and highly optimized BLAS library [25] available on the AMD Opteron system. The problem size is set at 1000x1000 and the block size $B = 32$ as the LAPACK 3.6.0 defaults to. The execution time for the three checksum scheme implementation based on LAPACK `DGEBRD` subroutine is shown in figure 7. From the figure we can see that FT1 as predicted only incurs less than 5% overhead; FT2 has more overhead due to frequent checksum regeneration; and FT3 has almost 200% overhead due to the very frequent checksum regeneration that is BLAS2 operation.

8.3 Overheads and scalability

Now we turn to the distributed memory bidiagonal reduction subroutine `PDGEBRD` in ScaLAPACK 2.0.2 and see how the hardened version scale to more computing cores and nodes. We have two scaling tests. In the first test, we fix the memory usage per processor and scale the number of processors from 4 to 4096. In the second test, we fix the processor grid at 1024 (32x32) and scale the problem size from 500x500 to 1500x1500. This works fills the last major missing parts of dense matrix factorization algorithms in ScaLAPACK. This set of experiments are performed on the TACC Stampede supercomputer, currently ranked at #12 on top500.org list. The Stampede machine consists of Xeon E5-2680 8C 2.7GHz processors and Infiniband FDR fat-tree network. Xeon Phi is not utilized. The compiler is intel/14.0.1.106 and MPI im-

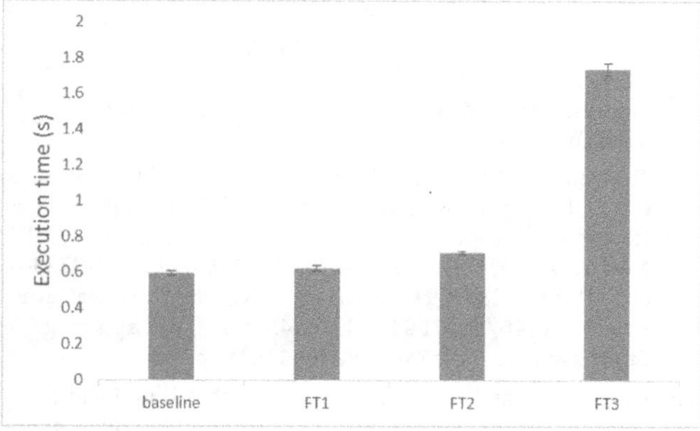

Figure 7. The execution time overhead for various checksum schemes compared to original DGEBRD

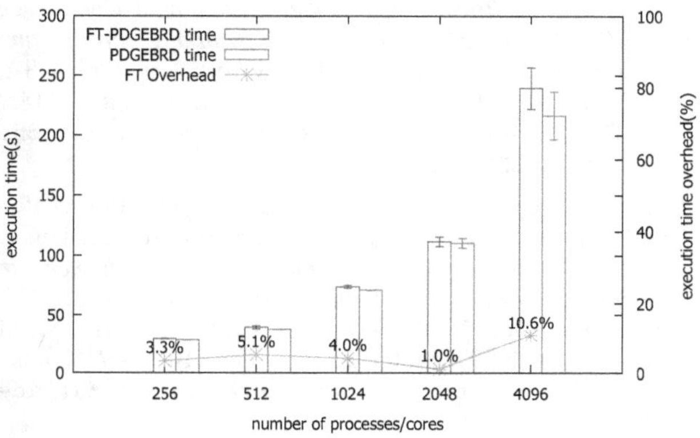

Figure 8. Fault free execution time for fault tolerant FT-PDGEBRD and non-fault-tolerant PDGEBRD from ScaLAPACK. Local matrix is fixed at 1000×1000; the global matrix size scales as the number of processors scales.

plementation is impi/4.1.0.030. The optimized BLAS library is MKL that comes with the Intel compilers. Each time measurement is repeated several times until the 95% confidence interval of the average (indicated as error bar) is within 5% of the average measurements [14], except for the 4096 cores case in figure 8 in which case the variance of the measurements are too high and repeating measurements do not seem to reduce it. The reason might be that allocating 4096 processors has a higher chance of including unhealthy nodes that are slower and drag down the performance. The high overhead 10.6% is therefore of low statistical significance. We see that in figure 8 and 9 in general the hardened FT-PDGEBRD maintains low overhead and the scalability of the original PDGEBRD subroutine in the scaling tests.

9. Conclusion, Limitation, and Future Work

The current state-of-the-art algorithm based algorithm fault tolerance for two-sided matrix factorizations are not not efficient. Since no obvious top-down checksum scheme exist such as those for one-sided factorization, bottom-up check-

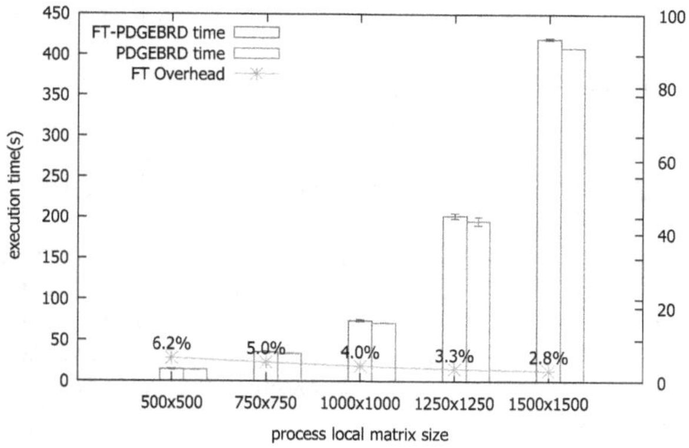

Figure 9. Fault free execution time for fault tolerant FT-PDGEBRD and non-fault-tolerant PDGEBRD from ScaLAPACK. Processor grid is fixed at $1024(32 \times 32)$. The global matrix size scales as the local matrix size scales.

sum schemes are either low in fault coverage or unnecessarily expensive due to the lack of automatic maintenance of checksums across lower level operations. In this work we explore a systematic way to modify three two-sided factorizations used in production codes LAPACK 3.6.0 and ScaLAPACK 2.0.2 to maintain checksums resulting in very low overhead and high fault coverage.

There are two limitations of this work. One is that the proposed technique only works for certain algorithms based on Householder transformations. Another limitation is that the proposed technique only protects numerical data but not control data/flow.

Future works include applying the techniques to other orthogonal transformation based algorithms. In addition, due to the on-line checksum relationship established in this paper, fail-stop errors can also be targeted similar to [13]. Thirdly, the error detection coverage is quite complete but the algorithmic correction coverage is not close to complete using the simply double checksums used. More sophisticated checksums may increase the correction coverage, as explored in [29].

Acknowledgments

The authors would like to thank the anonymous reviewers for their insightful comments and valuable suggestions. This work is partially supported by the NSF ACI-1305624, CCF-1513201, the SZSTI basic research program JCYJ20150630114942313, and the Special Program for Applied Research on Super Computation of the NSFC-Guangdong Joint Fund (the second phase).

References

[1] C. Anfinson and F. Luk. A linear algebraic model of algorithm-based fault tolerance, 1988. ISSN 00189340. URL `http://ieeexplore.ieee.org/lpdocs/epic03/wrapper.htm?arnumber=9736`.

[2] L. S. Blackford, J. Society for Industrial and Applied Mathematics., A. Cleary, E. D'Azeuedo, J. Demmel, I. Dhillon, S. Hammarling, G. Henry, A. Petitet, K. Stanley, D. Walker,

and J. J. Whaley, R. C./Dongarra. *ScaLAPACK user's guide*. SIAM, 1997. ISBN 0898713978.

[3] A. Bouteiller, T. Herault, G. Bosilca, P. Du, and J. Dongarra. Algorithm-based Fault Tolerance for Dense Matrix Factorizations, Multiple Failures and Accuracy. URL http://www.netlib.org/utk/people/JackDongarra/PAPERS/topc.pdf.

[4] F. Cappello, A. Geist, W. Gropp, S. Kale, B. Kramer, and M. Snir. Toward Exascale Resilience: 2014 update. *Supercomputing frontiers and innovations*, 1(1):5–28, jun 2014. URL http://superfri.org/superfri/article/view/14http://superfri.org/superfri/article/download/14/7.

[5] Z. Chen and J. Dongarra. Algorithm-based fault tolerance for fail-stop failures. *IEEE Transactions on Parallel and Distributed Systems*, 19(12):1628–1641, dec 2008. ISSN 10459219. doi: 10.1109/TPDS.2008.58. URL http://ieeexplore.ieee.org/lpdocs/epic03/wrapper.htm?arnumber=4492768.

[6] T. Davies and Z. Chen. Correcting soft errors online in LU factorization. pages 167–178. ACM, 2013. URL http://dl.acm.org/citation.cfm?id=2462920.

[7] N. DeBardeleben, J. Laros, J. T. Daly, S. L. Scott, C. Engelmann, and B. Harrod. High-end computing resilience: Analysis of issues facing the HEC community and path-forward for research and development. *Whitepaper*, 2009.

[8] J. J. Dongarra, D. C. Sorensen, and S. J. Hammarling. Block reduction of matrices to condensed forms for eigenvalue computations. *Journal of Computational and Applied Mathematics*, 27(1-2):215–227, sep 1989. ISSN 03770427. doi: 10.1016/0377-0427(89)90367-1. URL http://linkinghub.elsevier.com/retrieve/pii/0377042789903671.

[9] P. Du and P. Luszczek. High Performance Dense Linear System Solver with Resilience to Multiple Soft Errors. *Procedia Computer Science*, 9:216–225, 2012. ISSN 18770509. doi: 10.1016/j.procs.2012.04.023.

[10] P. Du, P. Luszczek, S. Tomov, and J. Dongarra. Soft error resilient QR factorization for hybrid system with GPGPU. *Proceedings of the second workshop on Scalable algorithms for large-scale systems - ScalA '11*, page 11, 2011. doi: 10.1145/2133173.2133179. URL http://dl.acm.org/citation.cfm?doid=2133173.2133179.

[11] P. Du, A. Bouteiller, G. Bosilca, T. Herault, and J. Dongarra. Algorithm-based Fault Tolerance for Dense Matrix Factorizations. PPoPP '12, pages 225–234, New York, NY, USA, 2012. ACM. ISBN 978-1-4503-1160-1. doi: 10.1145/2145816.2145845. URL http://doi.acm.org/10.1145/2145816.2145845http://dl.acm.org/ft{_}gateway.cfm?id=2145845{&}type=pdf.

[12] D. Fiala, F. Mueller, C. Engelmann, R. Riesen, K. Ferreira, and R. Brightwell. Detection and Correction of Silent Data Corruption for Large-scale High-performance Computing. SC '12, pages 78:1–78:12, Los Alamitos, CA, USA, 2012. IEEE Computer Society Press. ISBN 978-1-4673-0804-5. URL http://dl.acm.org/citation.cfm?id=2388996.2389102http://dl.acm.org/ft{_}gateway.cfm?id=2389102{&}type=pdf.

[13] D. Hakkarinen, P. Wu, and Z. Chen. Fail-Stop Failure Algorithm-Based Fault Tolerance for Cholesky Decomposition. *IEEE Transactions on Parallel and Distributed Systems*, 26(5):1323–1335, 2015. ISSN 10459219. doi: 10.1109/TPDS.2014.2320502. URL http://ieeexplore.ieee.org/ielx7/71/4359390/06805637.pdf?tp={&}arnumber=6805637{&}isnumber=4359390http://ieeexplore.ieee.org/xpls/abs{_}all.jsp?arnumber=6805637.

[14] T. Hoefler and R. Belli. Scientific Benchmarking of Parallel Computing Systems: Twelve Ways to Tell the Masses when Reporting Performance Results. SC '15, pages 73:1–73:12, New York, NY, USA, 2015. ACM. ISBN 978-1-4503-3723-6. doi: 10.1145/2807591.2807644. URL http://doi.acm.org/10.1145/2807591.2807644http://dl.acm.org/ft{_}gateway.cfm?id=2807644{&}type=pdf.

[15] K.-h. Huang and J. A. Abraham. Algorithm-Based Fault Tolerance for Matrix Operations. *IEEE Transactions on Computers*, C-33(6):518–528, jun 1984. ISSN 0018-9340. doi: 10.1109/TC.1984.1676475. URL http://ieeexplore.ieee.org/lpdocs/epic03/wrapper.htm?arnumber=1676475.

[16] Y. Jia, G. Bosilca, P. Luszczek, and J. J. Dongarra. Parallel reduction to hessenberg form with algorithm-based fault tolerance. In *Proceedings of the International Conference for High Performance Computing, Networking, Storage and Analysis on - SC '13*, pages 1–11, New York, New York, USA, nov 2013. ACM Press. ISBN 9781450323789. doi: 10.1145/2503210.2503249. URL http://dl.acm.org/citation.cfm?id=2503210.2503249.

[17] Y. Jia, P. Luszczek, G. Bosilca, and J. J. Dongarra. CPU-GPU hybrid bidiagonal reduction with soft error resilience. In *Proceedings of the Workshop on Latest Advances in Scalable Algorithms for Large-Scale Systems - ScalA '13*, pages 1–5, New York, New York, USA, nov 2013. ACM Press. ISBN 9781450325080. doi: 10.1145/2530268.2530270. URL http://dl.acm.org/citation.cfm?id=2530268.2530270.

[18] F. Luk and H. Park. Fault-tolerant matrix triangularizations on systolic arrays. *IEEE Transactions on Computers*, 37(11):1434–1438, 1988. ISSN 00189340. doi: 10.1109/12.8712. URL http://ieeexplore.ieee.org/xpl/freeabs{_}all.jsp?arnumber=8712.

[19] F. T. Luk and H. Park. An Analysis of Algorithm-based Fault Tolerance Techniques. *J. Parallel Distrib. Comput.*, 5(2):172–184, apr 1988. ISSN 0743-7315. doi: 10.1016/0743-7315(88)90027-5. URL http://dx.doi.org/10.1016/0743-7315(88)90027-5.

[20] T. May and M. H. Woods. Alpha-particle-induced soft errors in dynamic memories. *IEEE Transactions on Electron Devices*, 26(1):2–9, jan 1979. ISSN 0018-9383. doi: 10.1109/T-ED.1979.19370. URL http://ieeexplore.ieee.org/ielx5/16/31785/01479948.pdf?tp={&}arnumber=1479948{&}isnumber=31785http://ieeexplore.ieee.org/xpls/abs{_}all.jsp?arnumber=1479948{&}tag=1.

[21] S. E. Michalak, K. W. Harris, N. W. Hengartner, B. E. Takala, S. Wender, and Others. Predicting the number of fatal soft errors in Los Alamos National Laboratory's ASC Q supercomputer. *Device and Materials Reliability, IEEE Transactions on*, 5(3):329–335, 2005.

[22] S. Mukherjee. *Architecture design for soft errors*. Morgan Kaufmann, 2011. URL http://app.knovel.com/web/toc.v/cid:kpADSE0016https://books.google.com/books?hl=en{&}lr={&}id=wBuyOoLXEuQC{&}oi=fnd{&}pg=PP1{&}dq=architecture+design+for+soft+errors{&}ots=8xRhRBNaaq{&}sig=

Gk6RnKWTcO9HszxcshwNKHVNzCc{#}v=onepage{&}q=architecturedesignforsofterrors{&}f=f.

[23] E. Normand. Single event upset at ground level. *IEEE transactions on Nuclear Science*, 43(6):2742–2750, 1996.

[24] M. Snir, R. W. Wisniewski, J. A. Abraham, S. V. Adve, S. Bagchi, P. Balaji, J. Belak, P. Bose, F. Cappello, B. Carlson, A. A. Chien, P. Coteus, N. A. DeBardeleben, P. C. Diniz, C. Engelmann, M. Erez, S. Fazzari, A. Geist, R. Gupta, F. Johnson, S. Krishnamoorthy, S. Leyffer, D. Liberty, S. Mitra, T. Munson, R. Schreiber, J. Stearley, and E. V. Hensbergen. Addressing failures in exascale computing. *International Journal of High Performance Computing Applications*, 28(2):129–173, may 2014. ISSN 1094-3420, 1741-2846. doi: 10.1177/1094342014522573. URL http://hpc.sagepub.com/content/28/2/129http://hpc.sagepub.com/content/28/2/129.full.pdfhttp://www.mcs.anl.gov/publication/addressing-failures-exascale-computing-0.

[25] Q. Wang, X. Zhang, Y. Zhang, and Q. Yi. AUGEM. In *Proceedings of the International Conference for High Performance Computing, Networking, Storage and Analysis on - SC '13*, pages 1–12, New York, New York, USA, nov 2013. ACM Press. ISBN 9781450323789. doi: 10.1145/2503210.2503219. URL http://dl.acm.org/citation.cfm?id=2503210.2503219.

[26] P. Wu and Z. Chen. FT-ScaLAPACK: Correcting Soft Errors On-line for ScaLAPACK Cholesky, QR, and LU Factorization Routines. HPDC '14, pages 49–60, New York, NY, USA, 2014. ACM. ISBN 978-1-4503-2749-7. doi: 10.1145/2600212.2600232. URL http://doi.acm.org/10.1145/2600212.2600232http://dl.acm.org/ft{_}gateway.cfm?id=2600232{&}type=pdf.

[27] P. Wu, C. Ding, L. Chen, F. Gao, T. Davies, C. Karlsson, and Z. Chen. Fault tolerant matrix-matrix multiplication. In *Proceedings of the second workshop on Scalable algorithms for large-scale systems - ScalA '11*, page 25, New York, New York, USA, 2011. ACM Press. ISBN 9781450311809. doi: 10.1145/2133173.2133185. URL http://dl.acm.org/citation.cfm?doid=2133173.2133185.

[28] P. Wu, C. Ding, L. Chen, T. Davies, C. Karlsson, and Z. Chen. On-line soft error correction in matrix-matrix multiplication. *Journal of Computational Science*, 4(6):165–172, nov 2013. ISSN 18777503. doi: 10.1016/j.jocs.2013.05.002. URL http://www.sciencedirect.com/science/article/pii/S1877750313000641http://www.sciencedirect.com/science/article/pii/S1877750313000641/pdf?md5=740c9447815ceb3ef4e1fc79e3e60af2{&}pid=1-s2.0-S1877750313000641-main.pdf.

[29] P. Wu, Q. Guan, N. DeBardeleben, S. Blanchard, D. Tao, X. Liang, J. Chen, and Z. Chen. Towards Practical Algorithm Based Fault Tolerance in Dense Linear Algebra. In *Proceedings of the 25th ACM International Symposium on High-Performance Parallel and Distributed Computing - HPDC '16*, pages 31–42, New York, New York, USA, 2016. ACM Press. ISBN 9781450343145. doi: 10.1145/2907294.2907315. URL http://dl.acm.org/citation.cfm?doid=2907294.2907315.

[30] J. F. Ziegler and H. Puchner. *SER–history, Trends and Challenges: A Guide for Designing with Memory ICs*. Cypress, 2004.

POSTER: Reuse, don't Recycle: Transforming Algorithms that Throw Away Descriptors

Maya Arbel-Raviv
Technion - Israel Institute of Technology

Trevor Brown
University of Toronto

Abstract

Lock-free algorithms guarantee progress by having threads help one another. Complex lock-free operations facilitate helping by creating *descriptor* objects that describe how other threads should help them. In many lock-free algorithms, a new descriptor is allocated for each operation. After an operation completes, its descriptor must be reclaimed by a memory reclamation scheme. Allocating and reclaiming descriptors introduces significant space and time overhead.

We present a transformation for a class of lock-free algorithms that allows each thread to efficiently reuse a single descriptor. Experiments on a variety of workloads show that our transformation yields significant improvements over implementations that reclaim descriptors.

Keywords Concurrent data structures, Synchronization, Lock-free

1. Introduction

As core counts continue to rise in modern processors, applications' scalability is increasingly important. Designing scalable concurrent software is notoriously difficult, and programmers must rely on efficient concurrent library code. Concurrent data structures represent some of the most fundamental building blocks in these libraries.

Lock-free data structures are beneficial since they guarantee that some thread always makes progress, even if processes halt unexpectedly. This progress guarantee is typically achieved with *helping*. When a thread is blocked by an operation performed by another thread, it helps the other thread to make progress before continuing its own operation.

In complex lock-free data structures (e.g., [2, 3, 5]), threads publish descriptors for their operations, and helpers look at these descriptors to determine how to help. Existing lock-free algorithms that use descriptors fall into two categories: those that initially allocate a fixed number of descriptors and reuse them, and algorithms that allocate many descriptors throughout an execution and rely on garbage collection to reclaim them. We call the former *reusable descriptor* algorithms and the latter *throwaway descriptor* algorithms. Existing reusable descriptor algorithms use complicated adhoc techniques that are difficult to separate from the algorithms that use them. On the other hand, throwaway descriptor algorithms are faced with the limitations of lock-free memory reclamation algorithms, which introduce significant time and/or space overhead.

We introduce a transformation that takes a large class of lock-free throwaway descriptor algorithms and produces lock-free reusable descriptor algorithms with desirable properties. Throwaway descriptor algorithms that use k descriptors *per operation* are transformed into reusable descriptor algorithms that use k descriptors *per thread.*

We applied our transformation to lock-free double-compare-single-swap (DCSS) and k-compare-and-swap (k-CAS) primitives, and to a lock-free binary search tree. We compare our reusable descriptor implementations against throwaway descriptor implementations that use state of the art lock-free memory reclamation algorithms. Our results show that the reusable descriptor implementations perform at least as well as their throwaway descriptor counterparts, and *significantly* outperform them in some workloads.

PPoPP '17 February 04-08, 2017, Austin, TX, USA

ACM ISBN 978-1-4503-4493-7/17/02. . . $15.00

DOI: http://dx.doi.org/10.1145/3018743.3019035

2. Transformation

We start by describing the class of non-blocking algorithms to which our transformation can be applied. Each update operation allocates a new *descriptor* object, and fills it with information that describes any modifications it will perform. This information will be used by any threads that help the operation. (For example, if the non-blocking algorithm performs its modifications with a sequence of CAS steps, then the descriptor might contain the addresses, expected values and new values for the CAS steps.) An operation then "locks" an object by publishing a pointer to its descriptor in the object, typically using CAS.

When a thread encounters a pointer ptr to a descriptor (for a different operation), it may decide to help the other operation by invoking a function $Help(ptr)$. If all accesses to fields of a descriptor occur inside *Help*, then it is straightforward to apply our transformation. Otherwise, some algorithm specific knowledge may be necessary.

In our transformation, each thread has a single descriptor of each type, and these descriptors are reused repeatedly. Conceptually, each of these descriptors has multiple versions. Each time an operation in the original algorithm would create a new descriptor, it instead reuses its single descriptor and increments its version. Whenever a thread tries to access another thread's descriptor, it must specify which version of that descriptor it is trying to access. If the version it specifies does not match the current version of the descriptor, then the thread fails to access the descriptor. Thus, whenever a thread accesses a descriptor, it always sees a consistent view of its contents. This introduces new semantics for reading and writing descriptor fields. In particular, these steps can now fail (due to a descriptor being reused).

Naturally, the original algorithm must be modified to take some special action when these steps fail. A failed step means that the operation being helped has already finished. Since descriptors are accessed only when a thread is helping another operation complete, the failed step means that operation *no longer needs help*, and the correct response is to stop helping.

We implement descriptor versions by storing a sequence number in each descriptor. To avoid the ABA problem with descriptor pointers, we represent a pointer to a descriptor by the concatenation of the thread name (which identifies the location of the descriptor) and the descriptor's current sequence number. Each time a process accesses a descriptor, it verifies that the sequence number has not changed. If it has changed, then the access fails.

3. Experiments

For brevity, we describe a small subset of our experiments. Our experiments were run on a 2-socket Intel E7-4830 v3 with 12 cores per socket and 2 hyperthreads (HTs) per core, for a total of 48 threads.

We compared our reusable descriptor implementation of k-CAS [4] to several implementations that use memory reclamation schemes. Specifically, we implemented k-CAS using a lock-free memory reclamation scheme called *hazard pointers* (HP) [7], and two blocking epoch-based reclamation schemes *DEBRA* [1] and read-copy-update (RCU) [6].

We ran a simple array-based microbenchmark. For each algorithm $A \in \{$*Reuse*, *DEBRA*, *HP*, *RCU*$\}$, array size $S \in \{2^{14}, 2^{20}, 2^{26}\}$ and k-CAS parameter $k \in \{2, 16\}$, we run ten timed *trials* for several thread counts n. In each trial, an array with fixed size S is allocated and each entry is initialized to zero. Then, n concurrent threads run for one second, during which each thread repeatedly chooses k uniformly random locations in the array, reads those locations,

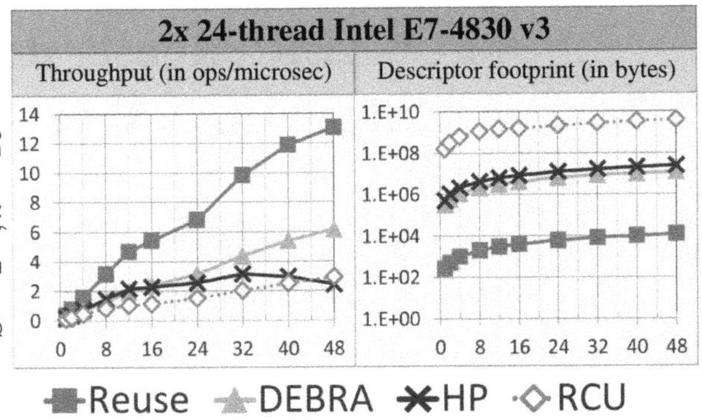

Figure 1: Results for the k-**CAS microbenchmark**. The x-axis represents the number of concurrent threads.

and then performs a k-CAS (using algorithm A) to increment each location by one.

Due to the lack of space, Figure 1 shows only graphs for array size 2^{26} and $k = 16$. The left graph shows the throughput (total number of operation per microsecond). *Reuse* outperforms every other algorithm and its throughput is *2.2 times* that of the next best algorithm at 48 threads. The right graph shows the approximated descriptor footprint, i.e., the largest amount of memory occupied by descriptors at any point during a trial. Note that the y-axis is a logarithmic scale. The results show that *DEBRA* and *HPs* use almost three orders of magnitude more memory than *Reuse* at their peaks, and *RCU* uses nearly three orders of magnitude more memory than *DEBRA* and *HPs*.

Acknowledgments

This work was supported by the Israel Science Foundation (grant 1749/14), the Yad-HaNadiv foundation, the Natural Sciences and Engineering Research Council of Canada, and Global Affairs Canada. Maya Arbel-Raviv is supported in part by the Technion Hasso Platner Institute Research School.

References

[1] T. Brown. Reclaiming memory for lock-free data structures: There has to be a better way. In *PODC '15*, pages 261–270.

[2] T. Brown, F. Ellen, and E. Ruppert. A general technique for non-blocking trees. In *PPoPP '14*, pages 329–342.

[3] F. Ellen, P. Fatourou, E. Ruppert, and F. van Breugel. Non-blocking binary search trees. In *PODC '10*, pages 131–140.

[4] T. L. Harris, K. Fraser, and I. A. Pratt. A practical multi-word compare-and-swap operation. In *DISC '02*, pages 265–279.

[5] S. V. Howley and J. Jones. A non-blocking internal binary search tree. In *SPAA '12*, pages 161–171.

[6] P. E. McKenney and J. D. Slingwine. Read-copy update: Using execution history to solve concurrency problems. In *Parallel and Distributed Computing and Systems*, pages 509–518, 1998.

[7] M. M. Michael. Hazard pointers: Safe memory reclamation for lock-free objects. *IEEE Trans. Parallel Distrib. Syst.*, 15(6): 491–504, June 2004.

An Architecture and Programming Model for Accelerating Parallel Commutative Computations via Privatization

Vignesh Balaji   Dhruva Tirumala   Brandon Lucia
Carnegie Mellon University
{vigneshb,dtirumal,blucia}@andrew.cmu.edu

1. INTRODUCTION

Synchronization and *data movement* are the key impediments to an efficient parallel execution. To ensure that data shared by multiple threads remain consistent, the programmer must use synchronization (e.g., mutex locks) to serialize threads' accesses to data. This limits parallelism because it forces threads to sequentially access shared resources. Additionally, systems use cache coherence to ensure that processors always operate on the most up-to-date version of a value even in the presence of private caches. Coherence protocol implementations cause processors to serialize their accesses to shared data, further limiting parallelism and performance.

Our work is motivated by the observation that while accesses to shared data by different threads *must be serialized*, the order in which those accesses are serialized is often inconsequential. Indeed, in a multithreaded execution, the execution order of such accesses may vary non-deterministically, potentially leading to different – yet correct – outcomes. We refer to operations with this permissible form of order non-determinism as "commutative operations" (or COps) and the data that they access as "commutatively accessible data" (or CData). Figure 1 shows how the results of commutative updates are independent of the interleaving of operations.

The crux of this work is to exploit the commutativity of COps on CData. We describe CCache, a system architecture in which parallel threads can perform COps to *replicated copies* of the same CData without the need for synchronization, coherence, or data movement. Threads that perform parallel COps on replicated CData must eventually *merge* the result of their COps using an application-specific merge function that the programmer writes, to combine independently manipulated copies of CData. Merging combines the CData results of different threads' COps, effectively serializing the execution of the parallel COps. CCache improves parallel performance through *on-demand data duplication*, creating a private copy of CData on which each thread may perform COps independently.

PPoPP '17, February 04-08, 2017, Austin, TX, USA
ACM 978-1-4503-4493-7/17/02.
http://dx.doi.org/10.1145/3018743.3019030

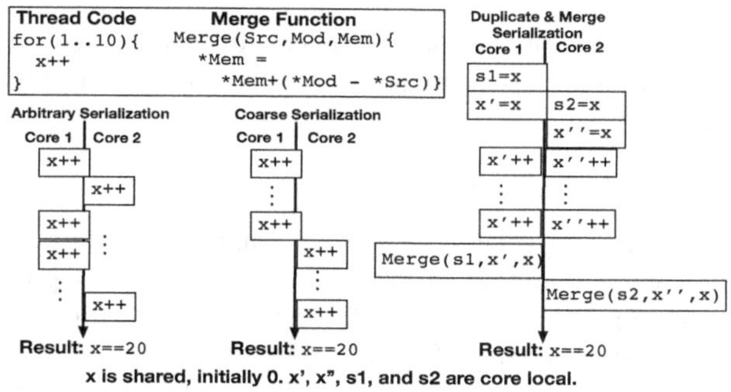

Figure 1: **Three Ways to Serialize Commutative Updates.**

2. CCache: ON-DEMAND PRIVATIZATION

CCache is a new execution model for a parallel program that uses *on-demand* data duplication to increase parallel access to data (CData) that are manipulated by commutative operations (COps).

We implement CCache by introducing ISA extensions. The programmer explicitly identifies the commutatively updated data (CData) via `c_read` and `c_write` instructions. A `c_read` or `c_write` operation creates two copies of the memory location it is accessing, the first is the core-local *source copy*, which cores preserve in a new per-core hardware structure called the *source buffer*. The second copy is the core-local *update copy*, which the core uses to perform its computations, instead of directly referring the location in memory. The update copy is stored in the private cache itself and distinguished from normal data by a per-cacheline *CCache bit*. Each core executes its COps independently on a privatized copy of the shared CData, and then later *merges* its private copy with the value in shared cache. The merge operation uses the *update copy* and *source copy* to compute the core's update and then applies it to the value in shared cache (Figure 1 shows an example merge function for addition op-

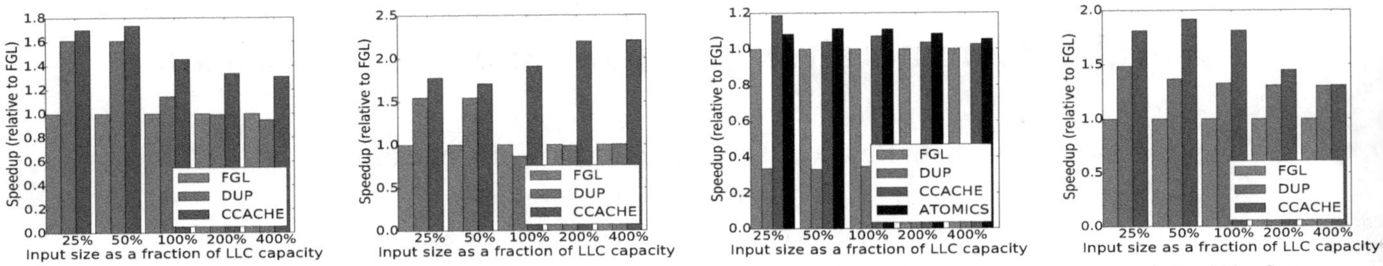

(a) Page Rank (b) K-Means (c) SSSP (d) Key-Value Store

Figure 2: **Performance comparison of CCache and DUP relative to FGL.**

erations). When all the cores in the system have merged their local updates we get the final result that is equivalent to some serialization of COps.

3. EVALUATION

We evaluated CCache to show that it improves performance compared to fine-grained locking (FGL) and data duplication (DUP) versions. Further, CCache provides performance improvements across different working set sizes.

Figure 2 shows the performance improvement by CCache for four benchmarks - Key Value store, Pagerank, K-Means and Single Source Shortest Path (SSSP) - running on an 8 core simulated system. The speedup reported for the DUP and CCache versions are relative to the FGL version. CCache outperforms the FGL and DUP version for input sizes ranging from 25% to 400% of the Last Level Cache (LLC) size.

Our performance characterization study revealed that the performance improvement in the Key Value store benchmark was the result of reduction in L3 misses relative to the FGL version. Additionally, reduction in coherence traffic also contributed to the performance improvement by CCache. For the kmeans benchmark, CCache outperformed the FGL version due to elimination of serialization. The performance improvement over the DUP version was primarily due to reduction in coherence traffic. In the DUP implementation, the main thread merges the thread per-thread copies at the end of each iteration, thereby generating a lot of coherence traffic. CCache avoids this coherence traffic by allowing each core to independently merge its local updates with the global copy. For the pagerank benchmark, we used an optimized DUP implementation where threads shared only one static duplicate. CCache outperformed even this optimized DUP implementation. Finally, for the SSSP benchmark, we observe only marginal improvement in CCache over the FGL version. This is because the benchmark has very few conflicting accesses and, hence, the FGL version does not pay the serialization penalty. We also compared the performance of CCache to an implementation that used atomic instructions instead of locks. Elimination of the overhead to store lock variables and the acquire and release locks, provides the marginal improvement in CCache and atomics versions.

4. RELATED WORK

The closest prior work to CCache is COUP[6]. COUP extends a MESI-like coherence protocol to exploit commutativity. Our system differs from COUP by providing the programmer the control to decide when to merge private updates. Further, we also provide support for the specification of arbitrary merge functions. CCache also has similarities to work done on combining parallel updates [2][3] , *expansion* and *privatization*[4][5] and *speculation*, including transactions[1].

References

[1] C. Blundell, A. Raghavan, and M. M. Martin. Retcon: Transactional repair without replay. In *Proceedings of the 37th Annual International Symposium on Computer Architecture*, ISCA '10, pages 258–269, New York, NY, USA, 2010. ACM.

[2] S. Burckhardt, D. Leijen, C. Sadowski, J. Yi, and T. Ball. Two for the price of one: A model for parallel and incremental computation. In *Proceedings of the 2011 ACM International Conference on Object Oriented Programming Systems Languages and Applications*, OOPSLA '11, pages 427–444, New York, NY, USA, 2011. ACM.

[3] M. C. Rinard and P. C. Diniz. Eliminating synchronization bottlenecks using adaptive replication. *ACM Transactions on Programming Languages and Systems (TOPLAS)*, 25(3):316–359, 2003.

[4] P. Tu and D. A. Padua. Automatic array privatization. In *Proceedings of the 6th International Workshop on Languages and Compilers for Parallel Computing*, pages 500–521, London, UK, UK, 1994. Springer-Verlag.

[5] H. Yu, H.-J. Ko, and Z. Li. General data structure expansion for multi-threading. In *Proceedings of the 34th ACM SIGPLAN Conference on Programming Language Design and Implementation*, PLDI '13, pages 243–252, New York, NY, USA, 2013. ACM.

[6] G. Zhang, W. Horn, and D. Sanchez. Exploiting commutativity to reduce the cost of updates to shared data in cache-coherent systems. In *Proceedings of the 48th International Symposium on Microarchitecture*, MICRO-48, pages 13–25, New York, NY, USA, 2015. ACM.

HythTM: Extending the Applicability of Intel TSX Hardware Transactional Support

Arnamoy Bhattacharyya, Mike Dai Wang, Mihai Burcea, Yi Ding, Allen Deng, Sai Varikooty, Shafaaf Hossain, Cristiana Amza

University of Toronto

{b.arnamoy, dai.wang, burceam, fourfire.ding, allen.deng, s.varikooty, s.hossain, amza}@mail.utoronto.ca

Abstract

In this work, we introduce and experimentally evaluate a new hybrid software-hardware Transactional Memory prototype based on Intel's Haswell TSX architecture. Our prototype extends the applicability of the existing hardware support for TM by interposing a hybrid fall-back layer before the sequential, big-lock fall-back path, used by standard TSX-supported solutions in order to guarantee progress. In our experimental evaluation we use SynQuake, a realistic game benchmark modeled after Quake. Our results show that our hybrid transactional system,which we call HythTM, is able to reduce the number of transactions that go to the sequential software layer, hence avoiding hardware transaction aborts and loss of parallelism. HythTM optimizes application throughput and scalability up to 5.05x, when compared to the hardware TM with sequential fall-back path.

1. HythTM: Layered Design

HythTM extends the standard RTM TSX hardware support solution (Dai Wang et al. 2014) by interposing a hybrid layer between the two existing transactional layers: the RTM hardware-only layer, and the last resort fall-back of locking the software global lock for the execution of the entire critical section. We use an object-based tracking mechanism where each transactional object is assigned an object tag which maintains HythTM statistics for the respective application object. Each tag contains two fields: (1) a version number, and (2) a conflict counter.

Shared accesses in the first layer, which uses RTM for hardware-only speculative execution, do not need to be explicitly tracked in software. However, even in this layer, write operations are trapped and version numbers for each object are incremented. The intermediate hybrid layer traps both reads and writes for the purposes of read set, write set and statistics collection. Finally, the execution of the big-lock fall-back path prevents the concurrent execution of any hardware transaction.

PPoPP '17 Feb. 4–8, 2017, Austin, Texas, USA.

ACM ISBN 978-1-4503-4493-7/17/02

http://dx.doi.org/10.1145/3018743.3019027

2. Mechanism for Varying the Tracking Granularity in HythTM

As mentioned above, HythTM has statistics collection support for detecting the optimal object tracking granularity (Burcea 2015). The version numbers are incremented only inside hardware transactions where the respective object is updated, either in Layer 1, or in the hardware commit transaction of Layer 2. The conflict counter is incremented every time that a read validation check on this object fails.

Varying the tracking granularity of an application object can be done by simply reassigning its tag pointer to point to a different object tag. All objects sharing the same TM-maintained object tag will be tracked as a unit for the purposes of conflict detection by the TM.

For SynQuake, we use two levels of tracking granularity: fine granularity and coarse granularity. High degree of contention between game objects require a fine granularity of tracking while a medium to low contention can utilize a coarser granularity.

For each leaf node in the game tree, we evaluate if the respective conflict counter for that area node is above some threshold and also more than a percentage of the total conflicts generated by all area nodes. A node splitting operation continues to split the newly generated nodes recursively using a pre-computed estimate of the tree depth we wish to achieve. The pre-computed estimate uses the simplifying assumption that each time we split we are halving the number of conflicts, and thus determines the number of times we need to split in order to fall under the conflict counter thresholds.

2.1 Benefits of Automatic Tag Granularity Management

Utilizing the shared version tag mechanism described in Section 2, HythTM creates smaller, software-based read-sets. For HythTM with coarser granularities, the reduction in the number of tags that need to be checked at the read validation stage leads to a shorter read validation phase, hence a shorter commit phase, and therefore a higher chance of successful hardware commit. Additionally, if false sharing is not a problem, then managing a smaller number of version tag objects may gain significant performance improvements in HythTM because of better cache behaviour.

3. Evaluation

Our experiments are run on the same Intel i7-4770 Haswell chip-set with TSX support and are compiled with GCC v4.8.1. All of the results presented are averaged over 3 runs to eliminate the effect of possible statistical errors and run-time anomalies.

3.1 Throughput improvement

Figure 1 shows the percentage of transactions that successfully commit in each layer for different contention levels of Synquake. We show the statistics with both the hybrid layer disabled and enabled for showing the effectiveness of having the hybrid layer. It is clearly seen that in all contention levels, the hybrid layer significantly increases the throughput in hardware layer. The limitation for hybrid disabled version points to the contention for the global single fall-back lock. The HythTM version mitigate and delay such contention throughout transaction execution by introducing additional layers, therefore giving an improved throughput.

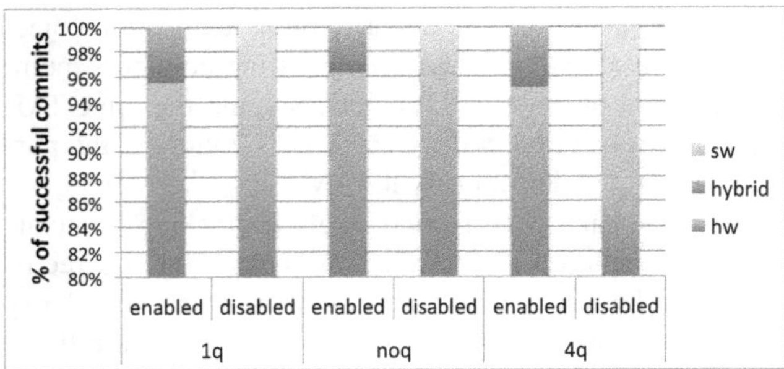

Figure 1: Hardware layer throughput improvement for different contention levels with hybrid layer enabled.

3.1.1 Scalability of Throughput Improvement

Our HythTM system not only improves the throughput from the first hardware layer, but also the improvement scales with increased number of threads. Figure 2 shows the scalability of the relative increase in the number of hardware transactions due to the presence of the hybrid layer for different game contention levels. The relative increase is calculated by normalizing to the number of hardware commits in a single threaded run. The improvement in scalability is best for the noquest scenario, as there is much less contention than in the other game scenarios. For the more realistic 4quest scenario, the scalability is still good. We appreciate that our results show scaling potential, although our evaluation cannot easily be extended to a large number of cores until they become available commercially.

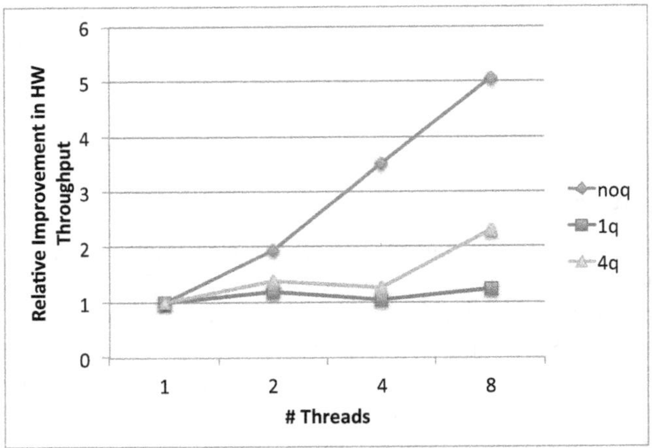

Figure 2: Scalability of Hardware layer throughput improvement for different contention levels with hybrid layer enabled.

4. Conclusion

In this work, we investigate HythTM, which interposes a hybrid transactional fall-back layer between the hardware-only layer and the sequential, software-only fallback layer of the standard Intel TSX solution. Our experimental results with a HythTM supported implementation of SynQuake shows throughput improvements of up to a factor of 5.05x compared to the standard Intel TSX architecture also with good scalability. This combination of performance and programmability would greatly help programmers towards achieving the ultimate desirable for the programming experience: correctness, simplicity, and performance.

References

M. Burcea. *Using Variable Conflict Granularity to Improve the Performance of Transactional Memory Support for Games*. PhD thesis, University of Toronto, 2015.

M. Dai Wang, M. Burcea, L. Li, S. Sharifymoghaddam, G. Steffan, and C. Amza. Exploring the performance and programmability design space of hardware transactional memory. In *ACM SIGPLAN Workshop on Transactional Computing (TRANSACT)*, 2014.

D. Lupei, B. Simion, D. Pinto, M. Misler, M. Burcea, W. Krick, and C. Amza. Transactional memory support for scalable and transparent parallelization of multiplayer games. In *Proceedings of the 5th European Conference on Computer Systems*, EuroSys '10, pages 41–54, 2010.

POSTER: Provably Efficient Scheduling of Cache-Oblivious Wavefront Algorithms

Rezaul Chowdhury[¶] Pramod Ganapathi[¶] Yuan Tang[§] Jesmin Jahan Tithi[*]

[¶]Department of Computer Science, Stony Brook University, New York, USA.
[§]School of Software, Shanghai Key Lab of Intelligent Information Processing, Fudan University, Shanghai, China.
[*]Intel Corporation.

Abstract

Standard cache-oblivious recursive divide-and-conquer algorithms for evaluating dynamic programming recurrences have optimal serial cache complexity but often have lower parallelism compared with iterative wavefront algorithms due to artificial dependencies among subtasks. Very recently cache-oblivious recursive wavefront (COW) algorithms have been introduced which do not have any artificial dependencies. Though COW algorithms are based on fork-join primitives, they extensively use atomic operations, and as a result, performance guarantees provided by state-of-the-art schedulers for programs with fork-join primitives do not apply.

In this work, we show how to systematically transform standard cache-oblivious recursive divide-and-conquer algorithms into recursive wavefront algorithms to achieve optimal parallel cache complexity and high parallelism under state-of-the-art schedulers for fork-join programs. Unlike COW algorithms these new algorithms do not use atomic operations. Instead, they use closed-form formulas to compute at what time each recursive function must be launched in order to achieve high parallelism without losing cache performance. The resulting implementations are arguably much simpler than implementations of known COW algorithms.

Keywords recursive wavefront; cache-oblivious; parallel; divide-and-conquer; dynamic programming

1. Introduction

For good performance on a modern multicore machine with a cache hierarchy, algorithms must have good parallelism and should be able to use the caches efficiently at the same time. Iterative wavefront algorithms for solving *Dynamic programming (DP)* problems on these machines have optimal parallelism but often suffer due to bad cache performance. On the other hand, though standard cache-oblivious recursive divide-and-conquer DP algorithms have optimal serial cache complexity, they often have low parallelism. The tiled-iterative wavefront algorithms achieve optimality in cache complexity and achieve high parallelism but are cache-aware, and hence are not portable and do not adapt well when available cache space fluctuates during execution in a multiprogramming environment. Very recently, *cache-oblivious wavefront (COW) algorithms* (Tang et al. 2015) have been proposed that have optimal parallelism and optimal serial cache complexity. Though COW algorithms are based on fork-join primitives, they extensively use atomic operations for correctness. But current theory of scheduling nested parallel programs with fork-join primitives do not allow such atomic operations. As a result, no bounds on parallel running time and parallel cache complexity could be proved for those algorithms. Those algorithms are also very difficult to implement since they require hacking into a parallel runtime system. Extensive use of atomic locks causes too much overhead for very large and high dimensional DPs.

PPoPP '17 February 04-08, 2017, Austin, TX, USA

ACM ISBN 978-1-4503-4493-7/17/02... $15.00
DOI: http://dx.doi.org/10.1145/3018743.3019031

Source of suboptimal parallelism in standard recursive algorithms. Fastest iterative DP implementations have the following wavefront-like property: if an update on a DP table cell x requires reading from cells $S = \{y_1, y_2, \ldots, y_s\}$, then x is updated immediately after all cells in S are fully updated. But a standard recursive DP algorithm may not update x at the earliest possible time. Consider the standard recursive algorithm $\mathcal{A}$ for computing LCS length given in Figure 1. As per the recursive structure, the top-left quadrants of X_{12} and X_{21}, i.e., $X_{12,11}$ and $X_{21,11}$, respectively, can only start executing when the execution of the bottom-right quadrant of X_{11}, i.e., $X_{11,22}$ completes. These dependencies amomg subtasks are not implied by the DP recurrence but arise from the recursive structure of the algorithm. We call these dependencies *artificial dependencies*.

Recursive wavefront algorithms. One can expect to improve parallelism of a standard recursive DP algorithm by removing artificial dependencies from the algorithm and allowing the smallest recursive subtasks to execute as closely to the iterative wavefront order as possible. We call such algorithms *recursive wavefront algorithms*. Indeed, such algorithms were introduced in (Tang et al. 2015), and named cache-oblivious wavefront (COW) algorithms. However, as we have already mentioned COW algorithms have several limitations that we have overcome in our current work.

In this work, we develop a generic method to schedule recursive wavefront algorithms based on timing functions. These algorithms have a structure similar to the standard recursive divide-and-conquer algorithms, but each recursive function call is annotated with start-time and end-time hints that are passed to the scheduler. Start-time (resp. end-time) is the minimum number of timesteps from the start of the program at which a task can start (resp. end) execution assuming that applying an update operation requires one timestep. The task scheduler will make sure that the algorithms are executed in a wavefront fashion using the timing functions. Indeed, the actions the scheduler is expected to take based on the timing functions is straightforward, and a programmer may choose to make some straightforward transformations of the code herself and use a scheduler that does not accept hints. The transformed code is still purely based on fork-join parallelism, and the performance bounds (e.g., parallel running time and parallel cache complexity) guaranteed by any scheduler supporting fork-join parallelism apply.

2. Deriving recursive wavefront algorithms

In this section, we describe how to transform a standard recursive DP algorithm into a recursive wavefront algorithm. Our transformation involves augmenting all recursive function calls with timing functions to launch them as early as possible without violating any dependency constraints implied by the DP recurrence. The timing functions are derived analytically, and do not employ locks or atomic instructions. Our transformation allows the updates to the DP table proceed in an order close to iterative wavefront, but from within the structure of a recursive algorithm. The goal is to reach the higher parallelism of an iterative wavefront algorithm while retaining the better cache performance (i.e., efficiency and adaptivity) and portability (i.e., cache- and processor-obliviousness) of a recursive algorithm.

Transformation. It is completed in three major steps:

[*Construct completion-time function.*] A closed-form formula for the timestep at which each DP cell is fully updated in wavefront order is derived based on the DP recurrence.

[*Construct start- and end-time functions.*] Cell completion times are used to derive closed-form formulas that give the timesteps in wavefront order at which each recursive function call should start and end execution.

[*Derive the recursive wavefront algorithm.*] Each recursive function call in the standard recursive algorithm is augmented with its start- and end-time functions so that it applies only the updates in any given timestep in wavefront order. We then use a variant of iterative deepening on top of this recursive algorithm to execute all timesteps efficiently.

Example. We will apply our method on the recursive algorithm LCS-OUTPUT-BOUNDARY given in (Chowdhury and Ramachandran, SODA'06) for computing LCS length. Let's call it algorithm $\mathcal{A}$. In LCS DP, a cell in DP table X depends on three of its adjacent cells. The completion time of cell (i, j) is given by $\mathfrak{C}(i, j)$, and the start-time (resp. end-time) of A on DP table X is given by $\mathcal{S}_{\mathcal{A}}(X)$ (resp. $\mathcal{E}_{\mathcal{A}}(X)$).

$$\mathfrak{C}(i,j) = \begin{cases} 0 & \text{if } i < 0 \,||\, j < 0 \,||\, i = j = 0, \\ \max\Big(\mathfrak{C}(i-1,j), \mathfrak{C}(i,j-1), \mathfrak{C}(i-1,j-1)\Big) + 1, & \text{otherwise.} \end{cases}$$

$$\mathcal{S}_{\mathcal{A}}(X) = \mathcal{E}_{\mathcal{A}}(X) = \mathfrak{C}(X) \quad \text{if } X \text{ is a cell,}$$
$$\mathcal{S}_{\mathcal{A}}(X) = \mathcal{S}_{\mathcal{A}}(X_{11}) \text{ and } \mathcal{E}_{\mathcal{A}}(X) = \mathcal{E}_{\mathcal{A}}(X_{22}) \quad \text{if } X \text{ is not a cell.}$$

Solving, $\mathfrak{C}(i, j) = i + j$, $\mathcal{S}_{\mathcal{A}}(X) = x_r + x_c$, and $\mathcal{E}_{\mathcal{A}}(X) = x_r + x_c + 2n - 2$, where, $(x_r, x_c) =$ top-left corner of X.

Figure 1 shows the resulting wavefront algorithm.

```
A(X)
if X is a cell then update X
else
  A(X_11)
  parallel: A(X_12), A(X_21)
  A(X_22)
```

```
RECURSIVE-WAVEFRONT-LCS(X)
w ← 0
while w < ∞ do
  w ← A_wave(X, w)
```

```
A_wave(X, w)
v_i ← ∞ for all i ∈ [1, 4]
if X is an n' × n' matrix then                {for some predetermined n'}
  if w = S_A(X) then A(X)
else
  arg_1..4 ← ⟨X_11, X_12, X_21, X_22⟩
  parallel for i ← 1 to 4 do
    if w < S_A(arg_i) then v_i ← S_A(arg_i)
    elif w ≤ E_A(arg_i) then v_i ← A_wave(arg_i, w)
return min v_i for all i ∈ [1, 4]
```

Figure 1. Transforming standard recursive LCS algorithm $\mathcal{A}$ into recursive wavefront algorithm RECURSIVE-WAVEFRONT-LCS.

3. Experimental results

We present results on LCS, the parenthesis problem, and Floyd-Warshall's APSP (FW-APSP). Table 1 compares ideal parallelism of the following algorithms computed using Intel© Cilkview scalability analyzer: (i) standard 2-way recursive divide-and-conquer (`CO_2Way`), (ii) recursive wavefront that switches to `CO_2Way` at some point (`wave-hybrid`), and (iii) recursive wavefront that directly uses an iterative kernel (`wave`). For `wave-hybrid`, $n' = \max\{256, \text{ power of 2 closest to } n^{2/3}\}$. All implementations for parenthesis and FW-APSP switch to iterative kernels when $n = 64$, and for LCS when $n = 256$.

Algorithm	LCS ($n = 256$K)	Parenthesis ($n = 16$K)	FW-APSP ($n = 16$K)
`CO_2Way`	18	23	148
`wave-hybrid`	152	823	277
`wave`	510	1,916	1,404

Table 1. Projected parallelism.

We ran all implementations including original COW with atomic locks on a 2.7GHz 16-core Intel Sandy Bridge machine with 64GB RAM and two 20MB shared L3 caches. Both `wave` and `wave-hybrid` outperformed `CO_2Way` and COW in all cases. For parenthesis problem, `wave` was $2.6\times$, and `wave-hybrid` was $2\times$ faster than `CO_2Way`. For LCS the factors were $1.5\times$ and $1.7\times$, respectively, and for FW-APSP they were $1.2\times$ and $1.1\times$, respectively.

Acknowledgments

NSF grants CCF-1439084 and CNS-1553510; XSEDE.

References

Y. Tang, R. You, H. Kan, J. J. Tithi, P. Ganapathi, and R. A. Chowdhury. Cache-oblivious wavefront: improving parallelism of recursive dynamic programming algorithms without losing cache-efficiency. In *PPoPP*, pages 205–214, 2015.

POSTER: State Teleportation via Hardware Transactional Memory *

Nachshon Cohen
Technion
nachshonc@gmail.com

Maurice Herlihy
Brown University
mph@cs.brown.edu

Erez Petrank
Technion
erez@cs.technion.ac.il

Elias Wald
Brown University
elias_wald@brown.edu

Abstract

State teleportation is a new technique for exploiting hardware transactional memory (HTM) to improve existing synchronization and memory management schemes for highly-concurrent data structures. When applied to fine-grained locking, a thread holding the lock for a node launches a hardware transaction that traverses multiple successor nodes, acquires the lock for the last node reached, and releases the lock on the starting node, skipping lock acquisitions for intermediate nodes. When applied to lock-free data structures, a thread visiting a node protected by a hazard pointer launches a hardware transaction that traverses multiple successor nodes, and publishes the hazard pointer only for the last node reached, skipping the memory barriers needed to publish intermediate hazard pointers. Experimental results show that these applications of state teleportation can substantially increase the performance of both lock-based and lock-free data structures.

1. Introduction

The emerging widespread availability of *hardware transactional memory* (HTM) [4] on commodity processors, such as Intel's x86 [5], provides an opportunity to rethink how we design and implement concurrent data structures. This paper introduce *state teleportation*, a novel way to exploit hardware transactional memory to improve the performance of existing lock-based and lock-free data structures.

Many data structures, such as lists, skip-lists, B-trees, queues and hash maps, consist of a collection of nodes linked by pointers. Threads navigate through these links, sometimes adding or removing nodes from the structure. Highly-concurrent data structures must typically solve two interrelated tasks: *synchronization*, and *memory management*. For synchronization, we consider data structures that use either *fine-grained locking*, where individual nodes are locked and released, or *lock-free synchronization*, where locks are replaced by atomic instructions such as *compare-and-swap*.

For memory management, we consider data structures that use *lock-free navigation*, such as the *lazy list* [2, 3], where threads traverse the data structure without acquiring locks, but then validate the target nodes (using locks or atomic operations) before making changes. In these data structures, it is not safe to reuse a node immediately after it is unlinked from the data structure, because another thread may still be traversing that node. Instead, each traversing thread publishes the address it is about to read, a so-called *hazard pointer* [6], preventing other threads from recycling that memory. Hazard pointers are expensive, because a thread must execute a memory barrier each time a new node is traversed. Recently, various new memory reclamation schemes were introduced to reduce the overhead of hazard pointers, but those require special compiler and runtime support or require to present the algorithm in a special normalized form.

In highly-concurrent data structures, a high-level operation (such as adding a value to a hash set) is executed as a sequence of atomic state transitions, where each transition may require a memory barrier. Examples of such transitions include critical sections, atomic reads and writes, and read-modify-write operations such as compare-and-swap (CAS).

* This work was supported by the United States-Israel Binational Science Foundation (BSF) grant No. 2012171 and by the National Science Foundation (NSF) grant 1331141.

PPoPP '17, Feb. 4–8, 2017, Austin, Texas, USA..

ACM 978-1-4503-4493-7/17/02.
http://dx.doi.org/10.1145/3018743.3019026

Hardware transactional memory (HTM) [4] is a synchronization mechanism that has recently become available on commodity processors such as Intel's x86 [5] architecture. HTM provides the ability for a thread to execute a sequence of machine instructions as an atomic transaction: the sequence appears to take effect instantaneously, without interleaving with other threads' instructions. For the foreseeable future, however, HTM transactions will be *best-effort*: no transaction is guaranteed to commit. Transactions abort because of data conflicts, cache overflow, or cache associativity issues. As a result, HTM should be considered to be a potentially unreliable short-cut: any data structure or algorithm that uses HTM must have a fallback path that does not rely on HTM for progress.

State teleportation is a simple idea that exploits HTM's short, best-effort hardware transactions to short-cut an operation's state transitions. Starting from one state, a thread launches a hardware transaction that traverses multiple successor states, halting in a state that may not be directly reachable from the start. To an outside observer, that thread appears to have *teleported*, moving instantaneously from the starting state to the final state without visibly traversing the intermediate states.

In this paper we consider two applications of state teleportation. First, we show how state teleportation can be superimposed on a well-known fine-grained locking algorithm: *lock-coupling* [1] (or hand-over-hand locking). By teleporting a lock from one node to a non-adjacent node, we avoid the memory traffic produced by locking and unlocking the intermediate nodes. Next, we show how teleportation can be superimposed on two hazard pointer-based memory management schemes. By teleporting a hazard pointer from one node to a non-adjacent node, we avoid the memory barriers need to publish the intermediate hazard pointers.

2. State Teleportation

The heart of the state teleportation algorithm is the teleport () method. This method takes as an argument an *initial state*: an internal data structure node from which the navigation begins. This node is assumed to be protected by the chosen synchronization primitive, e.g., locked in lock-coupling algorithms or pointed by an hazard pointer for hazard pointer memory reclamation. The teleport () atomically reaches a node which is closer to the target node (on which the operation should be applied); the returned node is protected by the chosen synchronization primitive, while the initial node is released. teleport () employs HTM to avoid the synchronization overhead of traversing intermediate nodes.

Due to the best-effort nature of HTM, it is not possible to assume that a teleportation of any fixed number of nodes would succeed (not even one). On the other hand, it is desirable to teleport over several nodes as this reduces the overhead of synchronization. Toward this end, the teleport () method dynamically adjusts the attempted teleportation distance. Every time a transaction succeeds, the thread increases the attempted teleportation distance by one. When a transaction fails, the teleportation distance is halved. However, we do not let the distance fall below a threshold, because short teleportation distances harm performance. When too many failures occur, the algorithm reverts to standard traversal.

2.1 Evaluation

We measure the effectiveness of teleportation on three linked-list data structures: lock-coupling, lazy, and lock-free. All measurements were done on a 8-core Broadwell processor with hyperthread enabled (total 16 hardware threads). Figure 1 provides the teleportation speedups when applied to hand-over-hand locking and when applied to the hazard pointers with lazy list and lock-free list.

For the hand-over-hand implementation, teleportation yields an an approximate 1.5-fold speedup for a single thread, increasing to a 4-fold speedup at 16 threads. The teleportation scheme is able to avoid most overhead associated with repeated acquiring and releasing the locks. The effect is especially dominant when hyperthreading is enabled (more than 8 threads). For the hazard pointer scheme, teleportation improves the performance by 21% – 65%, while keeping the strong progress guarantee provided by hazard pointers.

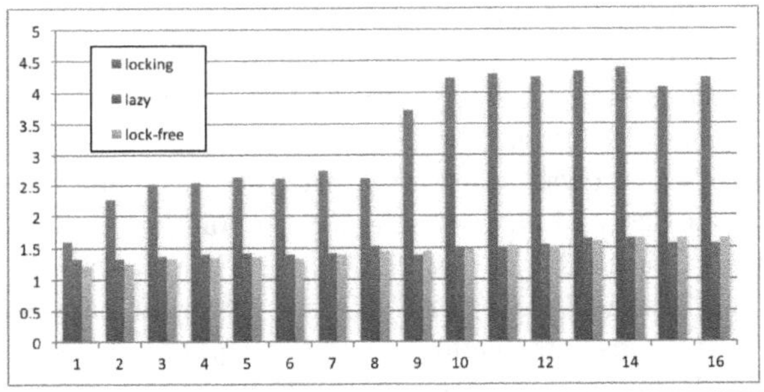

Figure 1. Effects of teleportation on various lists. The bars show the ratio between original list and teleportation. Higher means teleportation is more effective.

References

[1] BAYER, R., AND SCHKOLNICK, M. Concurrency of operations on b-trees. *Acta Informatica* (1977).

[2] HARRIS, T. A pragmatic implementation of non-blocking linked-lists. In *DISC'01* (2001).

[3] HELLER, S., HERLIHY, M., LUCHANGCO, V., MOIR, M., III, W. N. S., AND SHAVIT, N. A lazy concurrent list-based set algorithm. In *OPODIS'05*.

[4] HERLIHY, M., AND MOSS, J. E. B. Transactional memory: architectural support for lock-free data structures. In *ISCA'93*.

[5] INTEL CORPORATION. Transactional Synchronization in Haswell, 2012.

[6] MICHAEL, M. M. Hazard pointers: Safe memory reclamation for lock-free objects. *IEEE Trans. Parallel Distrib. Syst.* (2004).

IOGP: An Incremental Online Graph Partitioning for Large-Scale Distributed Graph Databases

Dong Dai
Texas Tech University
dong.dai@ttu.edu

Wei Zhang
Texas Tech University
X-Spirit.zhang@ttu.edu

Yong Chen
Texas Tech University
yong.chen@ttu.edu

CCS Concepts **• Information systems → Graph-based database models; DBMS engine architectures; Distributed storage**

Keywords Graph Database; OLTP; Graph Partition

1. Introduction

Large-scale graphs databases are designed to serve continuous updates from the clients, and, at the same time, answer complex queries towards current graph in an on-line manner. This is different from another important set of tools, namely graph processing engines, which focus on performing complex analysis on graphs, like Pregel and GraphX. In fact, the boundary between graph databases and graph processing engines is a bit fuzzy. Most graph databases are capable of delivering graph computations through defining complex graph traversal, and, on the other hand, many graph computation engines also allow graphs to be updated and evolved like a database. In this study, we differentiate them according to the workloads they are optimized for. We consider graph databases are optimized for OLTP (online transaction processing) workloads like `INSERT`, `UPDATE`, `GET`, and `TRVEL` queries. Those operations should be performed in an interactive manner and expected to finish fast. On the other hand, graph processing engines are designed for OLAP (online analysis processing) workloads like running PageRank on the whole graph or finding the structure of social graph. Those differences lead to significantly different preferences in performance optimizations and also affect the choices of graph partitioning fundamentally.

First, since graph computation engines run analysis tasks on the whole graph which usually takes a long time, they are allowed to spend a long time in optimally partitioning the graphs. But, this is not the case for graph databases as each transaction is normally short, has to finish fast and takes effect immediately. Second, in graph computation engines, when partition the graph, the graph structure (i.e., graph connectivity) should already be known. In fact, such information is critical to deliver an optimized partitioning in existing algorithms. For example, when a vertex is inserted, most of its connected edges should be known to place the vertex. However, such graph structures are not available to partitioning algorithms in graph databases, where vertex and its connected edges are inserted separately and independently. Third, graph processing engines mainly run analytic tasks applied on the whole graph, so they optimize for the best overall throughput. However, graph databases mostly serve single-point accesses on vertices and edges, or graph traversal starting from several vertices. This leads to different considerations on the efficiency of partitioning. Only considering the goals of minimizing "edge cuts" and maximizing "balance" among partitions, like most existing graph partitioning algorithms did, does not necessarily generate a good partition for graph databases. For example, the best partitioning on a graph that consists of k equal size disconnected subgraphs, would be putting each subgraph to one server to achieve the minimized 'cut' and best load balance. However, from graph databases' perspective, if any of these subgraphs contains high-degree vertices, graph traversal will be significantly slow due to throughput bottleneck of single machine.

2. IOGP Algorithm

In this paper, we introduce a new graph partitioning solution, namely *Incremental Online Graph Partitioning*, for distributed graph databases. It consists of three stages: *quiet*, *vertex reassign*, and *edge splitting*.

Quiet Stage. It is the default stage. A new vertex will be placed into the server chosen by its hashed value; all edges will be placed together with their connected vertices. Hashing calculates fast, hence supports single-point accesses on vertices and edges with minimized overheads. But, it does not consider the locality affinity of vertices, which grows while more edges are inserted. IOGP solves this in *vertex reassign stage*. In addition, as vertices and their edges are placed together, this may lead to hot-spots if vertices are

PPoPP '17 February 04-08, 2017, Austin, TX, USA

ACM ISBN 978-1-4503-4493-7/17/02.

DOI: http://dx.doi.org/10.1145/3018743.3019037

having too many edges, which, in fact, are commonly seen in power-law graphs. We tackle this in *edge splitting stage*.

Vertex Reassign Stage. In quiet stage, vertices have not gotten enough edges to expose connectivity information, hence random hashing is a good option. But, along with more edges are inserted, we should leverage connectivity information to re-assign the vertex to the best partition. The intuition behind vertex reassignment is straightforward: vertex should be moved to the partition that stores the most of its neighbors and all partitions should be balanced to avoid hotspot. To decide which partition is the best choice, we leverage the heuristic score defined in Fennel (Tsourakakis et al. 2014). Basically, for each vertex v, it assign a score for each partition p_i based on the number of v's neighbors in p_i and also the total size of p_i. The best one should be chosen as the location. The key to calculate the heuristic score is to get the number of neighbors of v in a specific partition p_i. However, this is nontrivial while serving OLTP requests. A plain calculation needs to scan vertices stored in each storage servers, which is too time-consuming. In IOGP, we actually maintain such value on each partition, with controllable memory footprint, while new vertices and edges are inserted.

Edge Splitting Stage. In a power-law graph, vertex degree could be extremely large. This may lead to significant performance degradation in OLTP operations like scanning neighbors. We introduce the *edge splitting stage* to handle it. The core idea is to split edges of high-degree vertex into multiple servers to amortize the loads. To decide when to split a vertex, a threshold `MAX_EDGES` is defined. It limits the maximal edges of a vertex can have in one partition. If a vertex exceeds this number, it will switch to edge splitting stage. The splitting is quite simple: it will place an outgoing edge together with its destination vertex and place an incoming edge together with its source vertex. One key observation of such edge splitting is that the overall locality does not change since an edge is moved to either its source vertex or destination vertex, without gaining or losing any locality. However, the performance of scanning high-degree vertex will be significantly improved as these operations now can be carried out in parallel after splitting.

3. Evaluation Results

We evaluate the proposed IOGP graph partitioning algorithm using both real world and synthetic graphs. The evaluations were conducted on the CloudLab APT cluster with up to 32 nodes as the storage servers.

Evaluation Datasets. We use the SNAP dataset and also synthetic graphs generated using the RMAT graph generator. All datasets are power-law graphs.

Partition Quality. We compare IOGP and several state-of-art graph partition algorithms: METIS (Karypis and Kumar 1998), Fennel, and Hash on the quality of partitions. METIS is only ran once on the final graph. Fennel is run after we manually force a vertex and all its edges are inserted together. Hashing and IOGP are conducted in an online manner. The results are shown in Figure 1. The results show the offline METIS achieves the best locality and Hash gives the worst partitioning; IOGP and Fennel are in between of them; and IOGP is better than Fennel in all tested graphs.

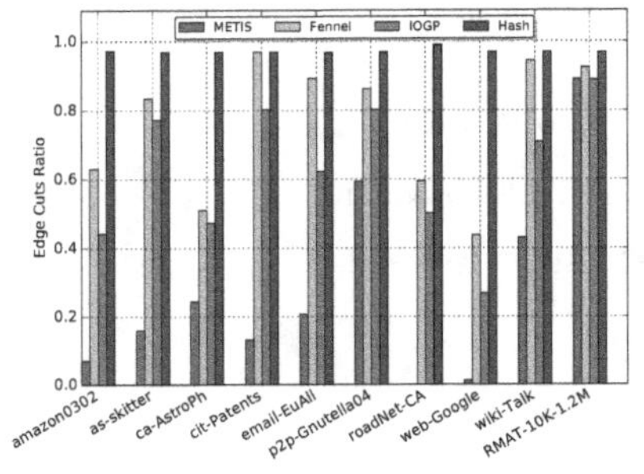

Figure 1. Edge cuts ratio comparison.

OLTP Performance. To show IOGP is a competitive alternation to Hash on OLTP workloads, we compare `INSERT` and `TRAVEL` operations in a 32-node cluster. Our results on `INSERT` performance show a maximal 10% overheads comparing to Hash, due to vertex reassignments and edge splitting in IOGP. In Figure 2, we show the travel performance of IOGP and Hash. All traversals are started from the same randomly chosen vertex. We evaluate 2, 4, 6, 8 steps. IOGP achieves clearly better traversal performance than Hash due to better locality. The performance gaps are also increasing while more traversal steps are needed.

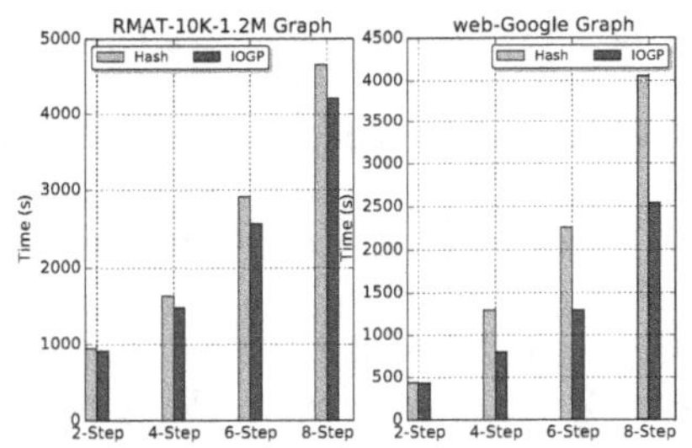

Figure 2. Graph traversal performance.

4. Conclusion

In this study, motivated by the needs of large-scale distributed graph databases, we propose an incremental online graph partitioning algorithms optimized for OLTP workloads. The evaluation and comparisons show its performance advantages and indicate the possibility of using it as the default graph partitioning solution for graph databases.

References

G. Karypis and V. Kumar. A fast and high quality multilevel scheme for partitioning irregular graphs. *SIAM Journal on scientific Computing*, 20(1):359–392, 1998.

C. Tsourakakis, C. Gkantsidis, B. Radunovic, and M. Vojnovic. Fennel: Streaming graph partitioning for massive scale graphs. In *Proceedings of the 7th ACM international conference on Web search and data mining*, pages 333–342. ACM, 2014.

Distributed Control: The Benefits of Eliminating Global Synchronization via Effective Scheduling

In the Context of Graph Applications

Jesun Shariar Firoz[†] Thejaka Amila Kanewala[†] Marcin Zalewski[†]
Martina Barnas[†] Andrew Lumsdaine[♯]

[†]Indiana University
{jsfiroz,thejkane,zalewski,mbarnas}@indiana.edu

[♯]Pacific Northwest National Laboratory
andrew.lumsdaine@pnnl.gov

Abstract

In distributed computing, parallel overheads such as *synchronization overhead* may hinder performance. We introduce the idea of *Distributed Control* (DC) where global synchronization is reduced to *termination detection* and each worker proceeds ahead optimistically, based on the local knowledge of the global computation. To avoid "wasted" work, *DC* relies on local work prioritization. However, the work order obtained by local prioritization is susceptible to interference from the runtime. We show that employing effective scheduling policies and optimizations in the runtime, in conjunction with eliminating global barriers, improves performance in two graph applications: single-source shortest paths and connected components.

Keywords Graph Processing; Distributed Runtimes; Single-Source Shortest Paths; Connected Components

1. Introduction

The irregular nature of graph computation often results in the *straggler effect* where the whole distributed system must wait for the last straggler to move to the next step. To alleviate the problem of stragglers, we consider the class of unordered algorithms with large available parallelism that can be executed *optimistically*. Relaxing the constraints of work optimality, the graph structure can be explored optimistically, correcting results as better information becomes available (*label-correcting* algorithms). Such unbridled parallelism can lead to explosion of work, but it can be controlled by assigning tasks priority based on a metric (e.g., distance, component number). Tasks with higher priority are better, but when resources are available, tasks with lower priorities can be processed optimistically.

Our *distributed control* (DC) [4] approach implements such optimistic computation, mitigating the straggler effect by maintaining *the local view* on the state of the computation and eliminating global barriers and data structures. However, DC can be highly dependent on the task scheduling in the underlying runtime. We use two different asynchronous many task (AMT) runtime systems (AM++ [3] and HPX-5 [1]) to investigate the effect of runtime scheduling on distributed asynchronous implementations of connected components (CC) and single-source shortest path (SSSP).

2. Distributed Control

Distributed control (DC) is a work scheduling method for distributed unordered algorithms that benefit from priority. A distributed system consists of shared memory domains with concurrent workers working on tasks. Tasks are distributed throughout the system, but they can be ordered in an *implicit task priority queue* by collecting all the tasks that exist at any given time and ordering them by a metric . The closer the execution order of tasks is to the oredering in the implicit task priority queue, the more optimal the work the algorithm generates. A task on one domain may generate tasks that depends on data on other domains, and such tasks is sent to data over the network. Workers retrieve tasks from the network and collect them in *private working sets* that are ordered according to work item priority (the local ordering).

3. Algorithms and Runtimes

We evaluate DC using two problems, single-source shortest paths (SSSP) and connected components (CC), on two distributed runtimes, HPX-5 and AM++. Both algorithms rely on local asynchronous updates to vertices. When the updates are propagated to neighbors, they are ordered in priority queues, according to distance for SSSP and to component number for CC. Termination detection is used to discover when no more updates are left, and the algorithms are then terminated.

PPoPP '17 February 04-08, 2017, Austin, TX, USA
ACM 978-1-4503-4493-7/17/02.
http://dx.doi.org/10.1145/3018743.3019036

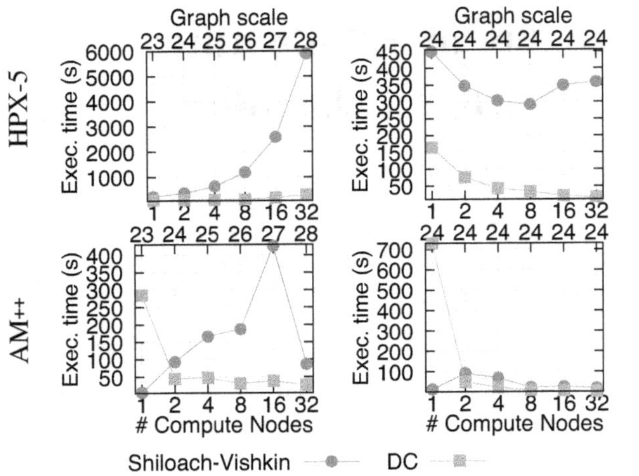

Figure 1: Weak and strong scaling results for CC algorithms with Graph500 input on HPX-5 runtime.

HPX-5 and AM++ represent work as *parcels* and *active messages* respectively. This discrete representation of work allows us to schedule work in thread-local priority queues. Both HPX-5 and AM++ utilize several runtime-level mechanisms (e.g., flow control, interleaving of application and runtime progress work by adopting proper scheduling policy, optimizing parameters of the communication layer, coalescing messages) to make the DC approach feasible.

3.1 Experiments

We ran our experiments with Graph500 input graphs [2], where a graph of scale n designates a graph with 2^n vertices and an average vertex degree of 32 (edges are considered bi-directional). Figure 1 shows weak and strong scaling results for connected component algorithms respectively. The DC-based CC algorithm scales better in both runtimes. In the HPX-5 runtime, CC acutely suffers from the *all_reduction* operations needed to identify whether any hooking or short-cut operation is ongoing. In both scaling experiments, *DC* performs better than Shiloach-Vishkin, except on one node. Due to space constraints we omit the results of SSSP experiments, but the *DC* version performs significantly better than Δ-stepping in both runtimes.

In addition to measuring performance, we perform *workload characterization* experiments. Figure 2 shows the rate at which vertices were completed in SSSP algorithms running on HPX-5. The number of completed vertices is measured in constant time intervals, and two moving averages are plotted (period 2 and 255). Δ-Stepping shows a wide variation in work processing rate, which is expected due to ramp-down periods in the delta buckets. *DC* shows a much more sustained work processing rate. Despite higher long-period moving average rate, Δ-stepping is slower since it's processing rate is much less stable (average of processing rate samples overestimates overall processing rate).

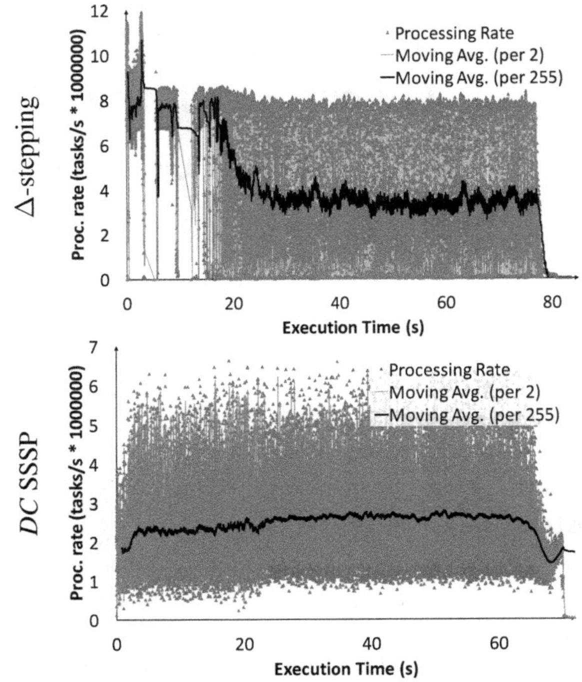

Figure 2: Task execution rate over time for Δ-Stepping and *DC* SSSP with scale 29 graph and 32 compute nodes.

4. Conclusion

We introduce distributed control approach for unordered algorithms that exploits optimistic paralleization by eliminating global barriers and by removing ordering constraint. The time gained by the exclusion of global synchronization can be invested in local ordering and can result in better performance. We discuss runtime parameters that are crucial for realizing full potential of distributed control approach. We demonstrate our approach on two algorithms, showing that distributed-control versions perform better than the state-of-the-art algorithms. Finally, we analyze actual work execution patterns and compare them to our intuitive model explaining the performance gains of distributed-control algorithms.

References

[1] `http://hpx.crest.iu.edu/`. Accessed: 2016-05-25.

[2] Graph500. `http://www.graph500.org/`, Aug. 2016. Accessed: 2016-05-31.

[3] J. J. Willcock, T. Hoefler, N. G. Edmonds, and A. Lumsdaine. AM++: A Generalized Active Message Framework. In *Proce. 19th Int. Conf. on Parallel Architectures and Compilation Techniques*, pages 401–410. ACM, 2010.

[4] M. Zalewski, T. A. Kanewala, J. S. Firoz, and A. Lumsdaine. Distributed Control: Priority Scheduling for Single Source Shortest Paths Without Synchronization. In *Proc. of the Fourth Workshop on Irregular Applications: Architectures and Algorithms*, pages 17–24. IEEE, 2014.

MAPA: An Automatic Memory Access Pattern Analyzer for GPU Applications

Gangwon Jo   Jaehoon Jung   Jiyoung Park   Jaejin Lee

Center for Manycore Programming
Department of Computer Science and Engineering
Seoul National University, Seoul 08826, Korea
{gangwon, jaehoon, jiyoung}@aces.snu.ac.kr, jaejin@snu.ac.kr
http://aces.snu.ac.kr

Abstract

Various existing optimization and memory consistency management techniques for GPU applications rely on memory access patterns of kernels. However, they suffer from poor practicality because they require explicit user interventions to extract kernel memory access patterns. This paper proposes an automatic memory-access-pattern analysis framework called MAPA. MAPA is based on a source-level analysis technique derived from traditional symbolic analyses and a run-time pattern selection technique. The experimental results show that MAPA properly analyzes 116 real-world OpenCL kernels from Rodinia and Parboil.

Categories and Subject Descriptors D.3.4 [*PROGRAMMING LANGUAGES*]: Processors—Compilers, Optimization, Run-time environments

Keywords Auto-tuning, Compiler, GPGPU, Memory access pattern, OpenCL, Optimization, Symbolic analysis

1. Introduction

There have been many proposals that use compiler and runtime techniques to overcome the difficulty of GPU programming, and some of them rely on memory access patterns of GPU kernels[2, 3, 5]. They decide which specific optimization technique needs to be applied to a kernel by observing its memory access patterns on a case-by-case basis. Since most of the memory accesses made in a typical GPU kernel have simple and regular patterns, such pattern-by-pattern approaches are adequate for GPU applications and may outperform a single, generic technique. However, all these techniques force programmers to explicitly annotate the memory access patterns in their code using language extensions and/or API functions. This significantly limits the practicality of the previous approaches.

The goal of this paper is to bridge the missing link between the previous pattern-by-pattern techniques and real-world GPU applications. We present a framework called *MAPA* that automatically determines and extracts memory access patterns of a kernel. It relies on both a source-level compiler analysis technique derived from traditional symbolic analyses for parallelizing compilers[4, 6] and runtime information (*e.g.*, kernel arguments). The current implementation of MAPA supports only OpenCL, but it can be easily extended to support CUDA and other heterogeneous programming models.

2. Categories of Memory Access Patterns

We define ten pattern categories for an OpenCL buffer, say M_A, that are listed below. In the following definitions, we say a memory location is *affine in variables* if the location is determined by an affine function of the variables.

- ⟨***constant***⟩: All work-items access the same element(s) of M_A.
- ⟨***affine in IDs***⟩: Each work-item accesses exactly one element of M_A potentially more than once. The location is affine in local IDs and/or work-group IDs.
- ⟨***affine in IDs and iteration counts***⟩: Each loop iteration of a work-item accesses exactly one element of M_A. The location is affine in local IDs, work-group IDs, and/or iteration counts.
- ⟨***set of offsets + affine in IDs***⟩: Each work-item accesses multiple elements of M_A. However, all of the elements have the same base address, and only constant offsets differ. The base address is affine in local IDs and/or work-group IDs.
- ⟨***set of offsets + affine in IDs and iteration counts***⟩: Each loop iteration of a work-item accesses multiple elements of M_A. The elements have the same base address and different constant offsets. The base address is affine in local IDs, work-group IDs, and/or iteration counts.
- ⟨***indirect, affine in IDs***⟩: Each work-item accesses exactly one element of M_A using an element of another read-only buffer

PPoPP '17, February 04–08, 2017, Austin, TX, USA
ACM 978-1-4503-4493-7/17/02.
http://dx.doi.org/10.1145/3018743.3019034

M_B as the index (*e.g.*, `A[B[...]]`). The location of the index is affine in local IDs and/or work-group IDs.

- ⟨***indirect, affine in IDs and iteration counts***⟩: Each loop iteration of a work-item accesses exactly one element of M_A using an element of another read-only buffer M_B as the index. The location of the index is affine in local IDs, work-group IDs, and/or iteration counts.
- ⟨***contiguous in a work-item***⟩: Every work-item accesses all elements in a contiguous region of M_A. However, the exact location of the region is not analyzable.
- ⟨***indirect, contiguous in a work-item***⟩: Every work-item accesses elements of M_A using all elements in a contiguous region of another read-only buffer M_B as the indices. The exact locations of the indices are not analyzable.
- ⟨***complex***⟩: The access pattern of M_A does not match any of the above categories.

3. Memory Access Pattern Analysis

MAPA uses the static single assignment (SSA) form as internal representation for kernels. Each scalar variable and structure field is represented with an SSA variable unless its address is ever taken. All user-defined function calls in a kernel are inlined to make interprocedural analyses unnecessary. MAPA also identifies induction variables in a kernel and replaces each of their definitions (*i.e.*, a ϕ-function) with a μ-function[1]. This makes control-flow-insensitive symbolic analyses properly recognize the induction variables.

The symbolic analysis algorithm of MAPA consists of two steps. First, it represents the value of each SSA variable in a symbolic expression by performing forward substitution. Then, it determines the target address of each buffer access in a symbolic expression. Since our goal is to discover regular buffer access patterns, we do not need to take all complicated symbolic expressions into account. Instead, we define *canonical symbolic expressions*. If a value cannot be represented in the canonical form, it is just represented in $\perp$ that means the value is too complex to be analyzed.

If at least one target address is not in the form of $buf_x + \langle\langle expr \rangle\rangle$, where buf_x is a buffer pointer passed through a kernel parameter, the access patterns of all buffers become ⟨*complex*⟩ because the unknown address may point to any buffer. Otherwise, MAPA aggregates all buffer accesses that share the same buffer pointer together. Then, the access pattern of each buffer is determined in case-by-case basis.

When a target address is calculated from parameters of a kernel, the access pattern of the kernel *may* vary depending on the actual arguments given at run time. In this case, MAPA generates all possible candidates for the access pattern, and chooses one of the candidates immediately after the kernel arguments are set up at run time. This mechanism can be combined with a memory-access-pattern based optimizer. For example, a kernel compiler can generate multiple optimized versions of the kernel, one for each pattern candidate, and a runtime system can execute a proper version of the kernel on the GPU at run time.

Pattern Categories	# of Buffers	Portion
⟨*constant*⟩	39	8.69%
⟨*affine in IDs*⟩	136	30.29%
⟨*affine in IDs and iter.*⟩	41	9.13%
⟨*set of offsets + affine in IDs*⟩	21	4.68%
⟨*set of offsets + affine in IDs and iter.*⟩	9	2.00%
⟨*indirect, affine in IDs*⟩	10	2.23%
⟨*indirect, affine in IDs and iter.*⟩	0	0.00%
⟨*contiguous in a work-item*⟩	5	1.11%
⟨*indirect, contiguous in a work-item*⟩	10	2.23%
⟨*complex*⟩	178	39.64%
Total	**449**	**100.00%**

Table 1. Analysis result.

4. Evaluation

Table 1 shows how the buffer pointers in all 116 kernels from Rodinia and Parboil are analyzed by MAPA. The result shows that 60% of the buffers are properly classified to 8 pattern categories. Other buffers are classified into ⟨*complex*⟩. Note that most of the ⟨*complex*⟩ buffers really have complicated access patterns and cannot be optimized by the previous manual techniques.

Acknowledgments

This work was supported by the National Research Foundation of Korea (NRF) grant funded by the Korea government (MSIP) (No. 2013R1A3A2003664). This work was also supported by BK21 Plus for Pioneers in Innovative Computing (Dept. of Computer Science and Engineering, SNU) funded by National Research Foundation of Korea (NRF) (21A20151113068). ICT at Seoul National University provided research facilities for this study.

References

[1] R. A. Ballance, A. B. Maccabe, and K. J. Ottenstein. The program dependence web: A representation supporting control-, data-, and demand-driven interpretation of imperative languages. In *Proceedings of the ACM SIGPLAN 1990 Conference on Programming Language Design and Implementation*, pages 257–271, 1990.

[2] M. Bauer, H. Cook, and B. Khailany. CudaDMA: Optimizing GPU memory bandwidth via warp specialization. In *Proceedings of 2011 International Conference for High Performance Computing, Networking, Storage and Analysis*, 2011.

[3] S. Che, J. W. Sheaffer, and K. Skadron. Dymaxion: Optimizing memory access patterns for heterogeneous systems. In *Proceedings of 2011 International Conference for High Performance Computing, Networking, Storage and Analysis*, 2011.

[4] M. R. Haghighat and C. D. Polychronopoulos. Symbolic analysis for parallelizing compilers. In *ACM Transactions on Programming Languages and Systems*, volume 18, pages 477–518, 1996.

[5] B.-N. Tal, E. Levy, A. Barak, and E. Rubin. Memory access patterns: The missing piece of the multi-GPU puzzle. In *Proceedings of the International Conference for High Performance Computing, Networking, Storage and Analysis*, 2015.

[6] P. Tu and D. Padua. Gated SSA-based demand-driven symbolic analysis for parallelizing compilers. In *Proceedings of the 9th International Conference on Supercomputing*, pages 414–423, 1995.

Cache-Oblivious MPI All-to-All Communications on Many-Core Architectures

Shigang Li
SKL Computer Architecture,
Institute of Computing Technology,
Chinese Academy of Sciences
shigangli.cs@gmail.com

Yunquan Zhang
SKL Computer Architecture,
Institute of Computing Technology,
Chinese Academy of Sciences
yunquan.cas@gmail.com

Torsten Hoefler
Department of Computer Science,
ETH Zurich
htor@inf.ethz.ch

Abstract

In the many-core era, the performance of MPI collectives is more dependent on the intra-node communication component. However, the communication algorithms generally inherit from the inter-node version and ignore the cache complexity. We propose cache-oblivious algorithms for MPI all-to-all operations, in which data blocks are copied into the receive buffers in Morton order to exploit data locality. Experimental results on different many-core architectures show that our cache-oblivious implementations significantly outperform the naive implementations based on shared heap and the highly optimized MPI libraries.

Keywords cache-oblivious algorithms, MPI_Alltoall, many-core

1. Introduction

Many-core architectures tend to come with massive intra-node parallelism, deep memory hierarchies, and complex Networks-on-Chip (NoC). The Message Passing Interface (MPI) [5] is used ubiquitously for communication in parallel applications. The performance of MPI collective communications, which often determines the scalability of applications, becomes increasingly dependent on the intra-node component. Intra-node communication is essentially cache line transfer on the NoC. Thus, it is imperative to design algorithms for collective communications with high cache efficiency.

However, designing optimal communication algorithm in terms of cache efficiency is non-trivial. There are two major challenges. Firstly, traditional algorithms for MPI collectives [6] mainly focus on reducing the latency and bandwidth overhead over the network, but ignore the cache complexity. The second challenge comes from the diversity of the many-core architectures: processors may have different memory hierarchies, such as a two-level cache for Intel® Xeon Phi™ KNC or a three-level cache for Intel® Xeon® E7; furthermore, there are various arrangements of main memory, including Uniform Memory Access (UMA) or Non-Uniform Memory Access (NUMA).

Cache-oblivious algorithms [1] are asymptotically optimal in terms of cache complexity without considering any hardware parameters. Thus, these algorithms enable portable performance on different architectures. To carry these benefits towards implementations of MPI collectives, we propose cache-oblivious algorithms for MPI all-to-all style operations. The key idea is to arrange the order of transferring the send buffers to the corresponding receive buffers in Morton order [4]. We also demonstrate the performance advantages of our cache-oblivious algorithms on different many-core architectures.

2. Cache-Oblivious Algorithms for All-to-All Operations

We design the algorithms for intra-node collectives based on a shared heap. The technique of creating a globally shared heap for all MPI processes has been discussed in our previous work [2, 3]. All the send and receive buffers are allocated in a shared heap. Then, each process can directly access all the send and receive buffers, which enables more opportunities to exploit the data locality, and design cache-oblivious algorithms.

For MPI_Alltoall, also known as all-to-all personalized exchange, every process sends a distinct data block to every other process. Each process can view all the send buffers as a 2D matrix, of which each dimension is equal to the number of processes and each element represents a data block; and so do the receive buffers. We name these two matrices as 'send-buffer matrix' and 'recv-buffer matrix', respectively. In a naive implementation of MPI_Alltoall, each process copies a column of the send-buffer matrix into its receive

PPoPP'17 February 04-08, 2017, Austin, TX, USA

ACM ISBN 978-1-4503-4493-7/17/02...$15.00
DOI: http://dx.doi.org/10.1145/3018743.3019025

buffer (i.e., a row of the recv-buffer matrix). The access to the send-buffer matrix exhibits poor spatial locality because of the row-major property of the matrix. To have good spatial locality for both send-buffer and recv-buffer matrices, we use Morton order [4] (also known as Z-order) to guide the copying of data blocks into recv-buffer matrix. Figure 1 shows MPI_Alltoall with 8 processes based on Morton order. The Z-shaped curve is equally divided into 8 segments and each one is handled by a process. Following the Z-shaped curve, the spatial locality of MPI_Alltoall is exploited.

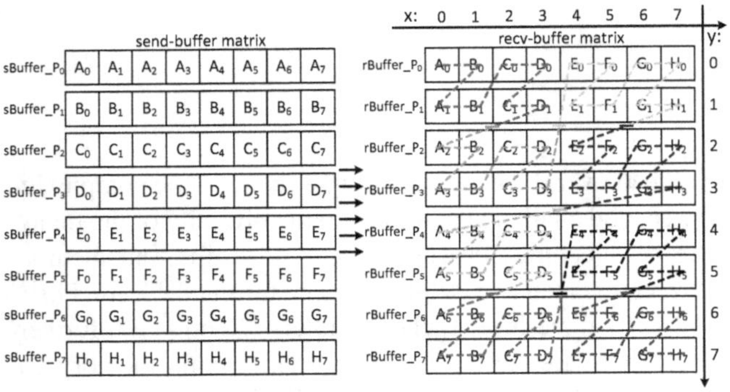

Figure 1. MPI_Alltoall with 8 processes based on Morton order.

For MPI_Allgather, also known as all-to-all broadcast, each process sends the same data block to all other processes. Each process can view all the send buffers as a vector (we call it "send-buffer vector") and the receive buffers as a matrix (we call it "recv-buffer matrix"). In a naive implementation of MPI_Allgather, each process copies the send-buffer vector into its receive buffer (a row of the recv-buffer matrix), which exhibits poor temporal locality. As for MPI_Allgather, we use Morton order to guide the copying of data blocks from send-buffer vector into recv-buffer matrix. In this way, the temporal locality of send-buffer vector is exploited.

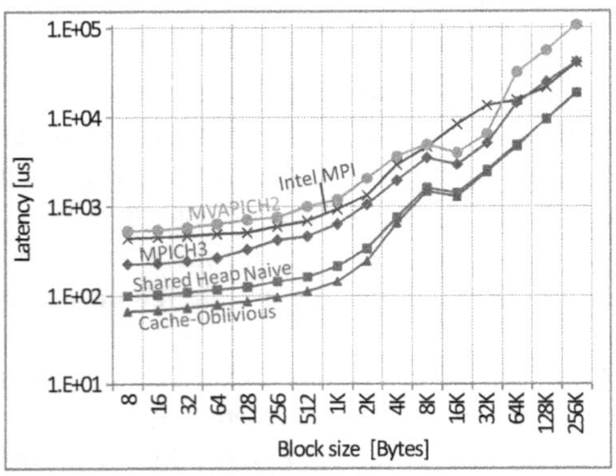

Figure 2. Latency comparison of MPI_Alltoall between traditional MPI, naive shared heap, and the cache-oblivious implementation on Intel Xeon Phi.

Preliminary experiments are conducted on Intel Xeon Phi KNC 5110P and Intel Xeon E7-8890 v3. Xeon Phi is a UMA architecture with 60 cores. Xeon E7-8890 is a NUMA architecture with 72 cores. Figure 2 presents the latencies of MPI_Alltoall with different block sizes on Xeon Phi. On Xeon Phi, our cache-oblivious implementation for MPI_Alltoall outperforms the naive implementation based on shared heap by 40% on average when the block size is less than 16 KB, and outperforms MPICH3 by 211% on average over all the block sizes. On Xeon E7-8890, our cache-oblivious implementation for MPI_Alltoall also has significant performance advantage. These demonstrate that our cache-oblivious algorithms achieve portable performance improvement on different architectures.

3. Conclusion

As supercomputers evolve into exascale, data movement is growingly expensive. We propose cache-oblivious algorithms for MPI all-to-all style collectives to exploit data locality. Experimental results show that our cache-oblivious algorithms achieve portable performance improvement on both UMA and NUMA architectures. Architecture trends indicate massive intra-node cores and deep memory hierarchies will be necessary to reduce power consumption and contention on buses. We foresee that the benefit of our cache-oblivious algorithms will be more significant on such future machines.

Acknowledgments

This work was supported by the National Natural Science Foundation of China under Grant No. 61502450, Grant No. 61432018, and Grant No. 61521092; National Major Research High Performance Computing Program of China under Grant No. 2016YFB0200803.

References

[1] M. Frigo, C. E. Leiserson, H. Prokop, and S. Ramachandran. Cache-oblivious algorithms. *ACM Transactions on Algorithms (TALG)*, 8(1):4, 2012.

[2] S. Li, T. Hoefler, and M. Snir. NUMA-aware shared-memory collective communication for MPI. In *Proceedings of the 22nd international symposium on High-performance parallel and distributed computing*, pages 85–96. ACM, 2013.

[3] S. Li, T. Hoefler, C. Hu, and M. Snir. Improved MPI collectives for MPI processes in shared address spaces. *Cluster Computing*, 17(4):1139–1155, 2014.

[4] G. M. Morton. *A computer oriented geodetic data base and a new technique in file sequencing.* International Business Machines Company New York, 1966.

[5] MPI Forum. MPI: A Message-Passing Interface standard. Version 3.0, September 2012.

[6] R. Thakur, R. Rabenseifner, and W. Gropp. Optimization of collective communication operations in MPICH. *International Journal of High Performance Computing Applications*, 19(1): 49–66, 2005.

Automated Load Balancer Selection Based on Application Characteristics

Harshitha Menon, Kavitha Chandrasekar, Laxmikant V. Kale
University of Illinois Urbana Champaign
gplkrsh2@illinois.edu, kchndrs2@illinois.edu, kale@illinois.edu

Abstract

Many HPC applications require dynamic load balancing to achieve high performance and system utilization. Different applications have different characteristics and hence require different load balancing strategies. Invocation of a suboptimal load balancing strategy can lead to inefficient execution. We propose Meta-Balancer, a framework to automatically decide the best load balancing strategy. It employs randomized decision forests, a machine learning method, to learn a model for choosing the best load balancing strategy for an application represented by a set of features that capture the application characteristics.

1. Introduction

HPC applications are increasingly becoming complex and frequently use dynamic structures and adaptive refinement techniques. Such complex techniques introduce load imbalance and therefore, require dynamic load balancing to achieve good performance. Different applications have different characteristics requiring the use of different load balancing strategies. Optimal strategy depends on a complex combination of various application characteristics making it difficult to select the best one. Further, load balancing algorithms have also grown in number making this choice harder. Using a load balancer that is not well suited for the application will result in loss of performance. Typically, the runtime behavior of the application depends on the problem being simulated and the machine characteristics. As a result, choosing the load balancing strategy that gives the best performance becomes difficult. Most commonly, the application programmer decides which load balancer to use and when to do load balancing based on some educated guess. This may result in a suboptimal solution.

PPoPP '17 February 04-08, 2017, Austin, TX, USA

ACM ISBN 978-1-4503-4493-7/17/02... $15.00
DOI: http://dx.doi.org/10.1145/3018743.3019033

We propose an introspective run-time system component called Meta-Balancer to automate the decision of choosing the best load balancing strategy for an application. Previous works (Pearce et al. 2012; Siegell and Steenkiste 1996) proposes models to predict load balancing period based on the cost benefit of load balancing and (Pearce et al. 2012) predicts load balancing strategy but from a limited set. In constrast our work proposes a framework that makes a selection from six different strategies and uses machine learning technique to do so. Meta-Balancer continuously monitors the application and based on the observed characteristics automatically selects the load balancing strategy. Randomized decision forests, a machine learning method, is used to learn a model for choosing the best load balancing strategy for an application represented by a set of features that capture the application characteristics. Meta-Balancer is implemented on Charm++ runtime system and takes advantage of its support for load balancing.

2. Meta-Balancer Strategy Selection

Meta-Balancer framework monitors the application and system characteristics by automatically collecting statistics about it. It then chooses the load balancing strategy based on the observed characteristics. It is implemented as a part of the Charm++ runtime system. Meta-Balancer consists of two major components, namely, asychronous statistics collection and decision making module for the ideal load balancing strategy.

2.1 Meta-Balancer Statistics Collection

Meta-Balancer collects load and communication information about the application frequently. These statistics are collected at the iteration boundary. The load balancing framework in Charm++ automatically collects the load and communication at each PE and stores it in a distributed manner. The Meta-Balancer uses some of the information stored in the load balancing framework. The statistics that are collected are normalized and used as features for the random forest machine learning technique.

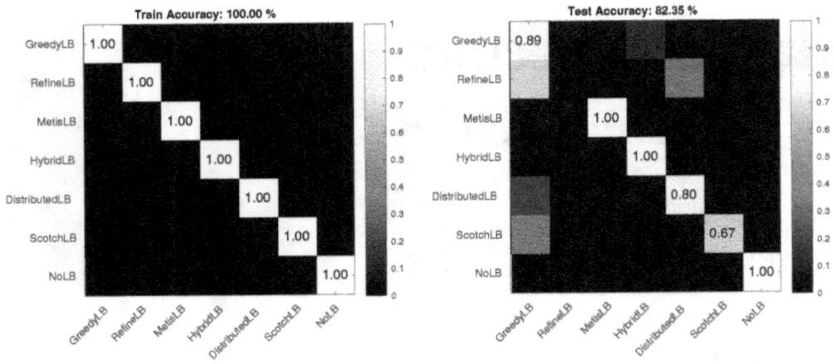

Figure 1: Accuracies on the training and test set along with confusion matrix.

2.2 Load Balancing Strategy Selection

There are a number of load balancing strategies in Charm++. These strategies handle load imbalance for different application characteristics. When no load balancing is required, we refer to it as NoLB. The strategies used are:

GreedyLB: A strategy that uses greedy heuristic to assign heaviest tasks onto least loaded processors iteratively.

RefineLB: A strategy that incrementally transfers the load away from the overloaded processors.

MetisLB: A strategy that passes the load information and the communication graph to METIS graph partitioner.

ScotchLB: A strategy that uses SCOTCH graph paritioning library to make load balancing decisions.

HybridLB: A hierarchical strategy in which at each level of the hierarchy, the root node performs the load balancing for the processors in its sub-tree.

DistributedLB: A refinement based distributed load balancing strategy that does probabilistic work transfer.

2.3 Load Balancing Strategy Selection Using Machine Learning

Machine learning techniques have been used to do pattern recognition. These techniques operate by building a model from a sample input set and learn to predict the outcome. We use a supervised random forest technique to predict the load balancing strategy. In supervised learning algorithms, the tool is presented with example inputs and their desired output.

A benchmark, called *lbtest*, was used to generate the training set for the random forest. This benchmark was run with different parameters to generate different configurations. For each configuration, all the load balancers were run to identify the best performing load balancing strategy. For the training set, the statistics collected were used as input features to the machine learning algorithm. The desired output for the training is the best performing load balancing strategy.

3. Experiments

The benchmark used for the strategy selection is *lbtest*. It was run on Blue Waters, a hybrid XE/XK system located

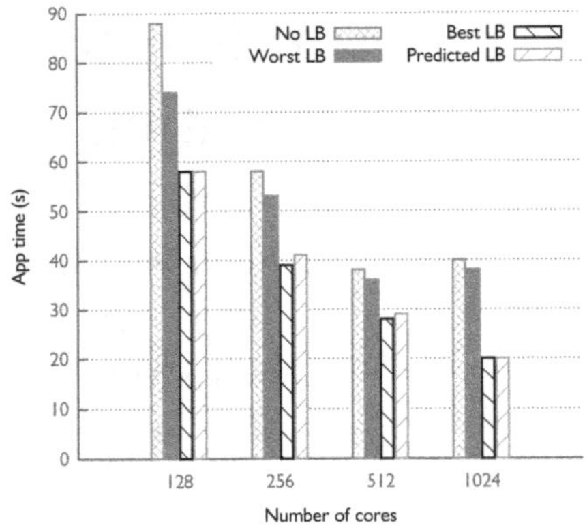

Figure 2: Performance of Lassen using the trained model

at NCSA.More than 200 samples were collected to generate the training set for the machine learning model. The samples were divided into training and test set and the learning algorithm was given the training set and evaluated on the test set. The expected outcome is the best performing load balancing strategy. Figure 1 shows the performance of the machine learning model in predicting the expected outcome. We can see that it is able to achieve an accuracy of 82%. The confusion matrix shows how the expected outcome varied.

We used the trained model on a new application, Lassen, which is a LLNL proxy app to study detonation shock dynamics, to predict the ideal load balancing strategy. Figure 2 shows the total application time with NoLB, worst, best and the predicted load balancing strategies. Meta-Balancer accurately predicts the best performing load balancer for 128 cores to be GreedyLB and for 1024 to be DistributedLB. For 256 and 512 core runs, the predicted (GreedyLB) is very close to the best performing load balancing strategy (DistributedLB). The predicted load balancing strategy gives an improvement ranging from 30% to 100%.

Acknowledgments

This research was supported in part by NCSA PAID - LB (NSF OCI 07-25070) NSF ChaNGa (AST 13-12913) and NSF OpenAtom (ACI 13-39715). This research used resources of the Argonne Leadership Computing Facility at Argonne National Laboratory, which is supported by the Office of Science of the U.S. Department of Energy under contract DE-AC02-06CH11357.

References

O. Pearce, T. Gamblin, B. R. de Supinski, M. Schulz, and N. M. Amato. Quantifying the effectiveness of load balance algorithms. In *26th ACM international conference on Supercomputing*, ICS '12, pages 185–194, 2012.

B. S. Siegell and P. A. Steenkiste. Automatic selection of load balancing parameters using compile-time and run-time information, 1996.

A GPU-Friendly Skiplist Algorithm *

Nurit Moscovici
Technion
nurits86@gmail.com

Nachshon Cohen
Technion
nachshonc@gmail.com

Erez Petrank
Technion
erez@cs.technion.ac.il

Abstract

We propose a design for a fine-grained lock-based skiplist optimized for Graphics Processing Units (GPUs). While GPUs are often used to accelerate streaming parallel computations, it remains a significant challenge to efficiently offload concurrent computations with more complicated data-irregular access and fine-grained synchronization. Natural building blocks for such computations would be concurrent data structures, such as skiplists, which are widely used in general purpose computations. Our design utilizes array-based nodes which are accessed and updated by warp-cooperative functions, thus taking advantage of the fact that GPUs are most efficient when memory accesses are coalesced and execution divergence is minimized. The proposed design has been implemented, and measurements demonstrate improved performance of up to 2.6x over skiplist designs for the GPU existing today.

Keywords GPU; SIMD; Data Structures; Skip List

1. Introduction

In recent years, GPUs have become widely available at a low cost. Todays GPUs provide hundreds of computing cores at high energy efficiency, with more cores added in every generation. The introduction of specialized parallel programming platforms such as CUDA (Nvidia 2015) over the past decade have opened GPUs for general-purpose programming (GPGPU), without need for a background in computer graphics. Interest in GPGPU has surged in recent years, and GPUs are used to accelerate applications in a wide variety of fields such as deep learning, networking abstractions, and file-system services. However, the design and implementation of efficient general-purpose algorithms remains a significant challenge.

GPUs are very effective for regular-access data-parallel computations on large datasets, often utilizing large vectors or matrices. However, irregular access to memory and control-flow divergence in applications can severely impair performance (Burtscher et al. 2012; Nvidia 2015). These behaviors are often exhibited by pointer-based data structures, which are frequently required in general purpose algorithms. While many such data structures have been developed for use on the CPU, attempts to port them directly to the GPU have shown that further GPU optimizations are necessary (Misra and Chaudhuri; Cederman et al. 2012).

Skiplists are popular in concurrent algorithms, as they offer a probabilistic alternative to balanced search trees without costly balancing operations. They have been used as a basis for key-value stores (RocksDB 2014; Carlson 2013) and for other data structures such as priority queues (Shavit and Lotan 2000). However, classic skiplist designs provide little locality of data and have highly irregular access patterns, both of which are significant drawbacks on the GPU in terms of performance. Additionally, synchronization on the GPU is very costly, especially when necessary at the thread-level, as it is in classic skiplists.

In this paper we propose GFSL, a GPU-friendly design for a fine-grained lock-based skiplist. GFSL consists of linked lists of array-based nodes, each of which contains several consecutive keys. Threads in a warp access these nodes in a coalesced fashion and cooperate in the execution of each skiplist operation. As such we reduce the amount of concurrent skiplist operations to gain higher memory coalescence and lower execution divergence, thus playing to the strengths of the GPU.

We compare GFSL to an implementation of a lock-free skiplist algorithm running on the GPU written by Misra and Chaudhuri, which was shown to achieve a speedup over the CPU implementation. Results show that our optimizations offer a performance boost for large key ranges. In a range of 1M keys, our implementation offers a speedup of 2x-2.6x.

* This work was supported by the Israel Science Foundation grant No. 274/14 and by the Nechemya LevZion VATAT scholarship.

PPoPP '17 Feb. 4–8, 2017, Austin, Texas, USA.

ACM 978-1-4503-4493-7/17/02... $15.00
DOI: http://dx.doi.org/10.1145/3018743.3019032

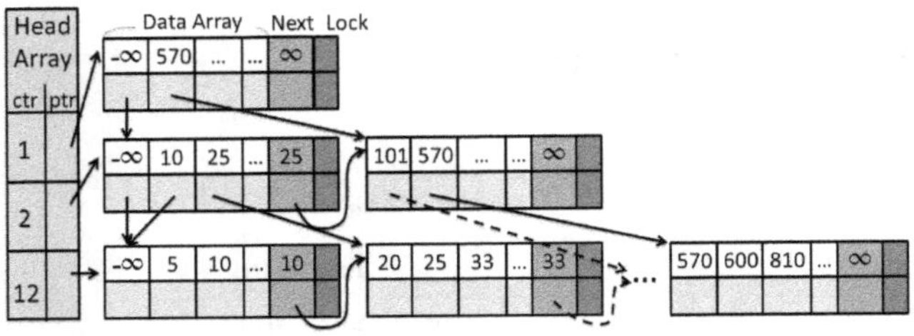

Figure 1. A chunked skiplist (GFSL)

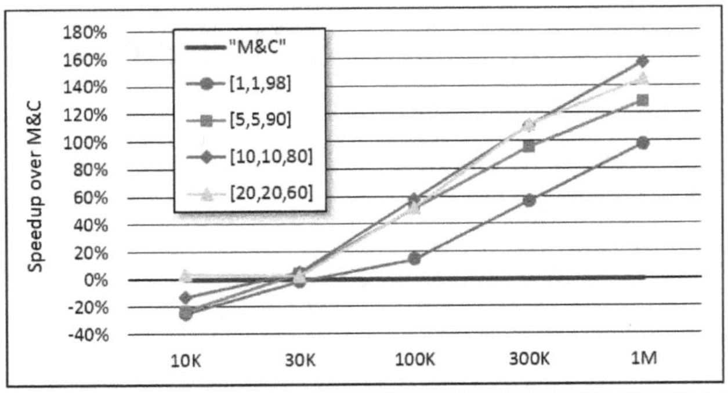

Figure 2. Speedup over M&C as a function of key range.

2. Algorithm Overview

GPU algorithms are most efficient when performing coalesced memory accesses with low divergence (Nvidia 2015). To this end we implemented *chunks*: large cache-aligned skiplist nodes that contain consecutive key-value pairs from the same level. Chunks consist of a sorted array of key-value pairs, along with a lock and a pointer to the next chunk.

Threads are divided into groups called *teams*, which cooperate to perform the skiplist operations. Teams can be the size of a warp or smaller. The number of entries in a chunk is equal to the number of threads in a team, so a team reads an entire chunk in a single kernel instruction (executed in lock-step). Each thread in a team simultaneously reads data from the chunk index corresponding to its place within the team.

GFSL consists of several levels of chunked linked lists, each containing a subset of the keys in the level below, as seen in Figure 1. In the upper levels the value field of each key-value pair points to a chunk in the level below, and in the bottom level this field will hold the data element associated with the corresponding key.

Threads in a team search for a single key, k, by performing a cooperative traversal over the skiplist; similar in spirit to traversal over the classic skiplist. The team reads an entire chunk from memory, then uses intra-warp operations to decide on the next step to be taken. The team takes a lateral step if k is greater than the maximum key in the chunk, and otherwise steps down via the data-entry containing the largest key smaller or equal to k. While traversal is lock-free, insertions and deletions require locks on the affected chunks.

A skiplist implemented to this design contains fewer nodes and levels than the classic version, as each node contains several keys, each of which can point to a node in the level below. The teams process more data for every memory transaction than a single thread does in the original algorithm, enabling faster traversals over the structure, while also causing less divergence within a warp.

3. Evaluation

We tested GFSL compared to the skiplist algorithm ported to the GPU by Misra and Chaudhuri (denoted "M&C" below). The code for their implementation is available online.

Our testing platform consisted of a GM204 GeForce GTX 970 (Maxwell architecture) GPU with CUDA driver 7.5 and compute capabilities 5.2; and a 64-bit Ubuntu Server 14.04 with Linux kernel version 3.13.0-88-generic. We evaluated GFSL and M&C under several mixtures of operations, represented as groups $[i,d,c]$ signifying a set of random operations with a probability of *i% Inserts*, *d% Deletes*, and *c% Contains*. Each test consisted of 1M total operations and was tested on key ranges of sizes 10K, 30K, 100K, 300K and 1M.

Performance Results As can be seen in Figure 2, GFSL is slower than M&C by up to 25% in the 10K range, shows similar or higher performance in the 30K range, and outperforms them by 14%-157% in higher ranges.

The main advantage of GFSL is the usage of coalesced reads, which optimizes accesses to the global memory. In the smaller range (10K), the entire structure fits into the L2 cache in both implementations. This significantly reduces the benefits of the coalesced reads as L2 access is much faster than global memory access. However, in larger key ranges, M&C requires frequent uncoalesced accesses to the global memory that causes a sharp degradation in performance. GFSL does not suffer from this degradation.

In addition to the key range, the performance is also impacted by the operation distribution. For the 10K range, M&C is faster than GFSL by 13%-25% when the percentage of *Contains* operations is high and slower by 4% when there are more *Inserts* and *Deletes*.

References

M. Burtscher, R. Nasre, and K. Pingali. A quantitative study of irregular programs on gpus. In *IISWC*, 2012.

J. L. Carlson. *Redis in Action*. Manning Publications Co., 2013.

D. Cederman, B. Chatterjee, and P. Tsigas. Understanding the performance of concurrent data structures on graphics processors. In *Euro-Par*, 2012.

P. Misra and M. Chaudhuri. Performance evaluation of concurrent lock-free data structures on gpus. In *ICPDS, 2012*, http://www.cse.iitk.ac.in/users/mainakc/lockfree.html.

Nvidia. CUDA C Programming Guide v7.5, september 2015. NVIDIA Developer Zone: website, 2015.

RocksDB. A persistent key-value store for fast storage environments. `http://rocksdb.org/`, 2014.

N. Shavit and I. Lotan. Skiplist-based concurrent priority queues. In *IPDPS*, 2000.

Poor Man's URCU

Pedro Ramalhete
Cisco Systems
pramalhe@gmail.com

Andreia Correia
Concurrency Freaks
andreiacraveiroramalhete@gmail.com

Abstract

RCU is, among other things, a well known mechanism for memory reclamation that is meant to be used in languages without an automatic Garbage Collector, unfortunately, it requires operating system support, which is currently provided only in Linux. An alternative is to use Userspace RCU (URCU) which has two variants that can be deployed on other operating systems, named *Memory Barrier* and *Bullet Proof*.

We present a novel algorithm that implements the three core APIs of RCU: `rcu_read_lock()`, `rcu_read_unlock()`, and `synchronize_rcu()`. Our algorithm uses one mutual exclusion lock and two reader-writer locks with `trylock()` capabilities, which means it does not need a language with a memory model or atomics API, and as such, it can be easily implemented in almost any language, regardless of the underlying CPU architecture, or operating system.

Keywords RCU, locks

1. Introduction

When implementing lock-free and wait-free data structures in languages without an automatic Garbage Collector (GC), or just to manage object lifetime, some kind of memory reclamation technique is required. Several such techniques have been discovered, with RCU (McKenney et al. 2001) one of the most well known. RCU has two interesting properties for its non-reclaiming methods, i.e. `rcu_read_lock()` and `rcu_read_unlock()`, one being its wait-free progress condition, and the other its low impact on latency with high scalability. RCU is unfortunately not a generic technique because it requires operating system support.

Fortunately, Userspace RCU (URCU) (Desnoyers et al. 2012) has two variants that are generic enough to be implemented regardless of operating system support, named Memory Barrier and Bullet Proof. Even so, these two variants of URCU are currently implemented in C99 and although many architectures are supported, the support is not universal, and other languages may have difficulty linking with the library.

We present a new algorithm which we named Poor Man's URCU which can be easily implemented in any language, as long as the language provides a mutual exclusion lock and a reader-writer lock with `trylock()` functionality. This means our algorithm can be implemented across a large number of languages, without need for a memory model, or atomics API, and regardless of the operating system on which it runs. Our algorithm implements only the core functionality of RCU, namely `rcu_read_lock()`, `rcu_read_unlock()`, and `synchronize_rcu()`, and it does so providing only lock-free progress for the first two, while RCU and URCU typically provide wait-free progress.

2. Algorithm

Poor Man's URCU is composed of one mutual exclusion lock and two reader-writer lock instances. Threads that call `rcu_read_lock()` and `rcu_read_unlock()` (readers) will attempt to acquire the reader lock on the first of the reader-writer locks (`rwlock1`) with a `trylock()`, and if it fails, do a `trylock()` on the second reader-writer lock (`rwlock2`), and if that also fails, try again the first rwlock, and so on. This procedure can go on indefinitely, but it will fail only if there is another thread making progress, namely, a thread acquiring the write-lock in one of the reader-writer locks, which means the operation is lock-free.

A thread that calls `synchronize_rcu()` (updater) will start by acquiring the lock on the mutual exclusion lock to guarantee only one updater at a time is present. The updater will then acquire the write-lock on the second reader-writer lock and release it as soon as it has obtained it, followed by acquiring the write-lock on the first reader-writer lock and release it as soon as it has obtained it. This is enough to introduce a linearization point, and it is now safe for the updater to free/delete the memory of the object that is meant to be reclaimed, because it has the guarantee that any ongoing readers can no longer hold a pointer to such object.

Algorithm 1 shows the implementation in C99 of *Poor Man's URCU* using the Pthreads library API. Notice that

PPoPP '17 February 04-08, 2017, Austin, TX, USA

ACM ISBN 978-1-4503-4493-7/17/02... $15.00
DOI: http://dx.doi.org/10.1145/3018743.3019021

Algorithm 1 Pthread implementation of Poor Man's URCU

```
typedef struct {
  pthread_mutex_t   updaterMutex;
  pthread_rwlock_t  rwlock1;
  pthread_rwlock_t  rwlock2;
} poorman_urcu_t;

// The return value should be passed as arg 'whichone'
int rcu_read_lock(poorman_urcu_t* self) {
  while (1) {
    if (pthread_rwlock_tryrdlock(&self->rwlock1) == 0) {
      return 1;
    }
    if (pthread_rwlock_tryrdlock(&self->rwlock2) == 0) {
      return 2;
    }
  }
}

void rcu_read_unlock(poorman_urcu_t* self, int whichone) {
  if (whichone == 1) {
    pthread_rwlock_unlock(&self->rwlock1);
  } else {    // whichone == 2
    pthread_rwlock_unlock(&self->rwlock2);
  }
}

void synchronize_rcu(poorman_urcu_t* self) {
  pthread_mutex_lock(&self->updaterMutex);
  pthread_rwlock_wrlock(&self->rwlock2);
  pthread_rwlock_unlock(&self->rwlock2);
  pthread_rwlock_wrlock(&self->rwlock1);
  pthread_rwlock_unlock(&self->rwlock1);
  pthread_mutex_unlock(&self->updaterMutex);
}
```

in this implementation the `rcu_read_lock()` API returns which reader-writer lock was acquired in the form of an integer, which is then passed to `rcu_read_unlock()` as an argument, so that it knows which reader-writer lock to unlock, but an alternative implementation can be done using a thread-local variable to pass this information.

In our implementation the order of acquiring the lock on `synchronize_rcu()` is first on `rwlock2` then on `rwlock1`, but it would be equally correct to do the opposite order.

3. Benchmarks and Discussion

Figure 1 shows the median for 5 runs of the number of operations per second, on a microbenchmark that iterates for 20 seconds per run. Each read-iteration calls `rcu_read_lock()`, reads all items in an array of 100 user-defined objects (read-critical section), then calls `rcu_read_unlock()`. Each update-iteration creates a new user-defined object, then it replaces a random object in the array of 100 using `compare_exchange_strong()`, calls `synchronize_rcu()`, and then it safely `frees` the memory of the previous instance. The benchmark was ran on a PowerPC Power8E with 8 cores, running Ubuntu Linux 14.04 64 bit, with GCC 4.9.2. The Memory Barrier implementation of URCU requires prior thread registration, but the Bullet Proof does not, therefore, in order to have a fair comparison with Poor Man's URCU which also requires no registration of threads, we compared only against Bullet Proof.

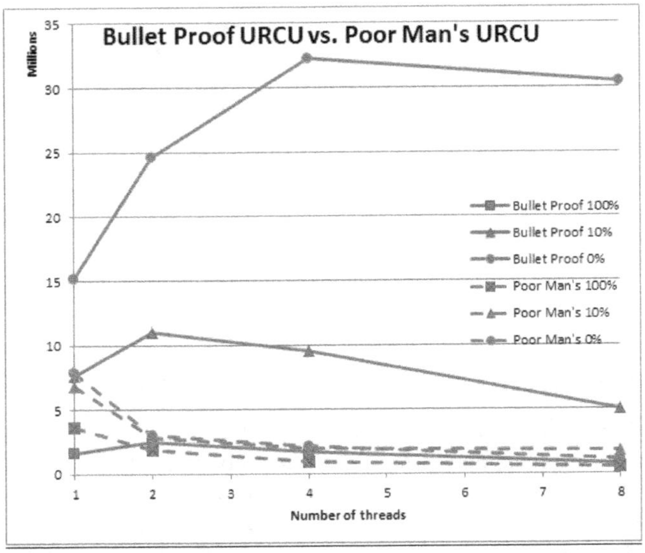

Figure 1. The plot above shows the total number of operations as a function of the number of threads, on a PowerPC machine with 8 cores. The `100%` lines means that each thread would only call `synchronize_rcu()`. The `10%` lines means that each thread would call `synchronize_rcu()` 10% of the times, and the remaining 90% of the times it would call `rcu_read_lock()` followed by `rcu_read_unlock()`.

Even though there is a performance advantage of the Bullet Proof algorithm, the Poor Man's implementation is not that far behind and it surpasses in the special case of 1 thread at 100%, when the thread is doing only calls to `synchronize_rcu()`. We should keep in mind that the performance of Poor Man's URCU is tightly coupled to the underlying implementation of the Reader-Writer Locks used, and recent advances in this area (Calciu et al. 2013) should provide significant improvement in throughput.

Although not particularly efficient, and with a limited API, our *Poor Man's URCU* algorithm is highly portable across Operating Systems and programming languages, does not require linking with an external library, does not require kernel/OS support, and has no licensing constraint. The simplicity and ease-of-use of our algorithm can foster the usage of RCU in domains where before it was impractical.

References

I. Calciu, D. Dice, Y. Lev, V. Luchangco, V. J. Marathe, and N. Shavit. NUMA-aware reader-writer locks. *PPoPP 2013*, 2013.

M. Desnoyers, P. E. McKenney, A. S. Stern, M. R. Dagenais, and J. Walpole. User-level implementations of read-copy update. *Parallel and Distributed Systems, IEEE Transactions on*, 23(2): 375–382, 2012.

P. E. McKenney, J. Appavoo, A. Kleen, O. Krieger, R. Russell, D. Sarma, and M. Soni. Read-copy update. In *AUUG Conference Proceedings*, page 175. AUUG, Inc., 2001.

A Wait-Free Queue with Wait-Free Memory Reclamation

Pedro Ramalhete
Cisco Systems
pramalhe@gmail.com

Andreia Correia
Concurrency Freaks
andreiacraveiroramalhete@gmail.com

Abstract

Queues are a widely deployed data structure. They are used extensively in many multi-threaded applications, or as a communication mechanism between threads or processes. We propose a new linearizable multi-producer-multi-consumer queue we named Turn queue, with wait-free progress bounded by the number of threads, and with wait-free bounded memory reclamation. Its main characteristics are: a simple algorithm that does no memory allocation apart from creating the node that is placed in the queue, a new wait-free consensus algorithm using only the atomic instruction compare-and-swap (CAS), and is easy to plugin with other algorithms for either enqueue or dequeue methods.

Keywords wait-free non-blocking queue, low latency

1. Wait-Free Queue

When it comes to fairness and low latency, the most desirable of the progress conditions is wait-freedom. Wait-free queue algorithms are rare when both enqueue and dequeue operations can be executed by multiple threads (MPMC).

An essential part of any singly-list based queue is the nodes that compose it. The `Node` of Turn queue contains the pointer to the item, the pointer to the next node that follows in the list, and two extra variables, `enqTid` indicates which thread is requesting the enqueue, and `deqTid` indicates which thread will have the node for its dequeue request.

Two arrays are also required, `enqueuers` and `dequeuers`, with size `maxThreads`. In `enqueuers`, the position assigned to a specific thread, will be the index placed in the node's `enqTid`. `enqueuers` is an array of atomic pointers to nodes to be inserted in the queue, where `nullptr` means no active request. The `dequeuers` is in reality two arrays of nodes named `deqself` and `deqhelp`, when equal it represents an active dequeue request.

PPoPP '17 February 04-08, 2017, Austin, TX, USA

ACM ISBN 978-1-4503-4493-7/17/02... $15.00
DOI: http://dx.doi.org/10.1145/3018743.3019022

Algorithm 1 enqueue(T* item, int tid)

```
Node* myNode = new Node(item,tid);
enqueuers[tid].store(myNode);
for (int i = 0; i < maxThreads; i++) {
  if (enqueuers[tid].load() == nullptr) return;
  Node* ltail = hp.protectPtr(kHpTail, tail.load(), tid);
  if (ltail != tail.load()) continue;
  if (enqueuers[ltail->enqTid].load() == ltail) {
    Node* tmp = ltail;
    enqueuers[ltail->enqTid].compare_exchange_strong(tmp, nullptr);
  }
  for (int j = 1; j < maxThreads+1; j++) {
    Node* nToHelp = enqueuers[(j + ltail->enqTid)%maxThreads].load();
    if (nToHelp == nullptr) continue;
    Node* nullnode = nullptr;
    ltail->next.compare_exchange_strong(nullnode, nToHelp);
    break;
  }
  Node* lnext = ltail->next.load();
  if (lnext != nullptr) tail.compare_exchange_strong(ltail, lnext);
}
enqueuers[tid].store(nullptr, std::memory_order_release);
```

At the basis of the Turn queue is a singly-linked list, where enqueing consists of one CAS on the tail's `next` variable and another CAS to advance `tail`, just like on the MS queue (Michael and Scott 1996). Our consensus algorithm is based on the consensus protocol of the Turn starvation-free mutual exclusion lock (Correia and Ramalhete 2015), where each thread publishes its intent, in this case, an intent to enqueue a node, and the decision of who is the next thread is based on who is the next request *to the right* of the current `turn`. The current turn is the `enqTid` of the queue's tail.

The intent to enqueue is signaled with a non-null store of the node's pointer to be enqueued in `enqueuers`. The first non-null entry in the `enqueuers` array that is *to the right* of the current `turn` is the one that all threads will attempt to help next to enqueue, executing a CAS on `Node.next`, similarly to the MS lock-free enqueue algorithm. Each thread calling `enqueue()` will continue helping the next enqueue request until its own request has been completed.

The mechanism that insures a wait-free bounded enqueue relies on the `enqTid` variable of the node referenced by `tail`. This indicates to all threads that are executing an enqueue, that the last request that was satisfied, belonged to the thread that published its request in position `enqTid` of the `enqueuers` array. All threads realize that the thread's

Algorithm 2 dequeue() and helper functions

```
1  T* dequeue(const int tid) {
2    Node* prReq = deqself[tid].load(); Node* myReq = deqhelp[tid].load();
3    deqself[tid].store(myReq);
4    for (int i=0; i < maxThreads; i++) {
5      if (deqhelp[tid].load() != myReq) break; // No need for HP
6      Node* lhead = hp.protectPtr(kHpHead, head.load(), tid);
7      if (lhead != head.load()) continue;
8      if (lhead == tail.load()) {
9        deqself[tid].store(prReq); // Rollback request to dequeue
10       giveUp(myReq, tid);
11       if (deqhelp[tid].load() != myReq) { deqself[tid].store(); break; }
12       return nullptr;
13     }
14     Node* lnext = hp.protectPtr(kHpNext, lhead->next.load(), tid);
15     if (lhead != head.load()) continue;
16     if (searchNext(lhead, lnext) != NOIDX) casDeqAndHead(lhead, lnext, tid);
17   }
18   Node* myNode = deqhelp[tid].load();
19   Node* lhead = hp.protectPtr(kHpHead, head.load(), tid);
20   if (lhead == head.load() && myNode == lhead->next.load())
21     head.compare_exchange_strong(lhead, myNode);
22   hp.retire(prReq, tid); return myNode->item;
23 }
24
25 void giveUp(Node* myReq, const int tid) {
26   Node* lhead = head.load();
27   if (deqhelp[tid].load() != myReq || lhead == tail.load()) return;
28   hp.protectPtr(kHpHead, lhead);
29   if (lhead != head.load()) return;
30   Node* lnext = hp.protectPtr(kHpNext, lhead->next.load());
31   if (lhead != head.load()) return;
32   if (searchNext(lhead, lnext) == NOIDX) lnext->casDeqTid(NOIDX, tid);
33   casDeqAndHead(lhead, lnext, tid);
34 }
```

request on that position was the last to be executed so it will be the next request *to the right* to have its turn and get its request executed. When it reaches the end of the array, it will start processing requests at the start of the array. It can happen that not all threads actively calling `enqueue()` will agree on which is the node immediately to the right of the current turn. Regardless of which node gets enqueued, the new `turn` will be based on the node that was successfully inserted at the tail of the list, from then on, all previously published requests will be seen by current or new threads calling `enqueue()`. *At most* there will be `maxThreads-1` other nodes inserted in front of a request to enqueue, making the enqueue wait-free bounded by the number of threads.

The `dequeue()` algorithm uses the same Turn consensus algorithm. The dequeue operation can have two possible outcomes, it can return an item from the queue, or a null pointer when the queue is empty. When the queue is not empty, the algorithm follows the same approach used in the enqueue, it uses the Turn consensus to determine which request is to be satisfied next. A thread i calling `dequeue()` will *open* a request by setting `deqself[i]` to point to the same node as `deqhelp[i]`. Following the Turn consensus protocol, when a thread j decides that it is thread's i turn, it will assign the next node's `deqTid` to i using a CAS, and if successful, from that moment on, the node belongs to thread i. All threads that see `node.deqTid` different from `NOIDX` will be able to help by doing CAS in `deqhelp[i]`, this will guarantee that the result is visible to thread i and at the same time, it will make `deqhelp[i]` different from `deqself[i]` which closes the request. Representing a logical dequeue request with nodes of the queue, avoids the overhead of allocating a dequeue request object, and subsequently tracking its lifetime.

In case of an empty queue, due to `head` pointing to the same node as `tail`, the dequeue request will have to be rollbacked. This procedure is executed by `giveUp()`.

To rollback the dequeue request, thread i will set `deqself[i]` to its previous value, which was stored in a local variable `prReq`. It can happen that during the rollback, another thread that saw the request of thread i opened, assigned it a node, and that node was present on the list between the read of `head` in line 6 and the read of `head` in line 26. In that case, the result is published in `deqhelp[i]`, and thread i can return the item, thus aborting the giveup. Unfortunately, it is still possible that some thread saw the request opened but has not yet published in `deqhelp[i]`. In this case it is necessary to guarantee that the first node of the queue is assigned to some thread. If there isn't any open dequeue request, thread i will assign the node to it self. Due to happens-before guarantees, once the head advances, all threads seeing the new head will subsequently see the rollback. From this moment on, if there wasn't already a node assigned to thread i, then it is guaranteed that there will not be a node assigned to thread i for this request. The `giveUp()` method will guarantee that it will only return a null pointer if and only if no other helping thread has assigned a node to `deqhelp[i]` and that the head has advanced after the request has been rollbacked. Therefore, all threads will see a closed request for thread i once they realize the head has advanced.

To avoid losing wait-free progress, we used Hazard Pointers (HP) for memory reclamation (Michael 2004). In HP, the protect operation can be wait-free if instead of a load-store-load loop on the pointer that is being read, we do a single load-store-load sequence where the second load validates that the `head` of the queue has not advanced. Otherwise, it will jump to the next iteration in the algorithm's loop.

We have presented the first linearizable memory-unbounded MPMC wait-free queue with wait-free memory reclamation.

References

A. Correia and P. Ramalhete. Mutual exclusion - two linear wait software solutions. `https://github.com/pramalhe/ConcurrencyFreaks/blob/master/papers/cralgorithm-2015.pdf`, 2015.

M. M. Michael. Hazard pointers: Safe memory reclamation for lock-free objects. *Parallel and Distributed Systems, IEEE Transactions on*, 15(6):491–504, 2004.

M. M. Michael and M. L. Scott. Simple, fast, and practical non-blocking and blocking concurrent queue algorithms. In *Proceedings of the fifteenth annual ACM symposium on Principles of distributed computing*, pages 267–275. ACM, 1996.

POSTER: STAR (Space-Time Adaptive and Reductive) Algorithms for Real-World Space-Time Optimality

Yuan Tang *, Ronghui You

School of Computer Science, School of Software, Fudan University
Shanghai Key Lab. of Intelligent Information Processing
State Key Lab. of Computer Architecture, Institute of Computing Technology, Chinese Academy of Sciences
P. R. China
[yuantang, 15210240027]@fudan.edu.cn

Abstract

It's important to hit a space-time balance for a real-world algorithm to achieve high performance on modern shared-memory multi-core or many-core systems. However, a large class of dynamic programs with more than $O(1)$ dependency achieve optimality either in space or time, but not both. In the literature, the problem is known as the fundamental space-time tradeoff. By exploiting properly on the runtime system, we show that our STAR (Space-Time Adaptive and Reductive) technique can help these dynamic programs to achieve sublinear parallel time bounds while still maintaining work-, space-, and cache-optimality in a processor- and cache-oblivious fashion.

Keywords space-time balance, cache-oblivious algorithm, dynamic program, shared-memory multicore system

1. Introduction

It's important to hit a space-time balance for a real-world algorithm to achieve high performance on modern shared-memory multi-core or many-core systems. However, a large class of DP (Dynamic Programming) algorithms with more than $O(1)$ dependency, including the general MM (matrix multiplication), Strassen-like fast MM, LWS, GAP, and Parenthesis [2], achieve optimality either in space or time, but not both.

Let's take the general MM on a closed semiring as an example. The general MM not only is itself a dynamic programming algorithm with $O(n)$ dependency since the full update of each cell of the output matrix requires $O(n)$ reads and computation from the two input matrices, but also serves as a basic building block for more complicated DP algorithms such as LWS, GAP, and Parenthesis to achieve sublinear parallel time bounds (or time bounds for short) [2] [1]. The general MM can be computed in a recursive divide-and-conquer fashion as follows. At each level of recursion, the computation of an MM of dimension n (i.e. n-by-n) is divided into four equally sized quadrants, which require updates from eight sub-MMs of dimension $n/2$ as shown in the Equation (1). Depending on the availability of extra space,

$$\begin{bmatrix} C_{00} & C_{01} \\ C_{10} & C_{11} \end{bmatrix} = \begin{bmatrix} A_{00} & A_{01} \\ A_{10} & A_{11} \end{bmatrix} \otimes \begin{bmatrix} B_{00} & B_{01} \\ B_{10} & B_{11} \end{bmatrix} = \begin{bmatrix} A_{00} \otimes B_{00} & A_{00} \otimes B_{01} \\ A_{10} \otimes B_{00} & A_{10} \otimes B_{01} \end{bmatrix} \oplus \begin{bmatrix} A_{01} \otimes B_{10} & A_{01} \otimes B_{11} \\ A_{11} \otimes B_{10} & A_{11} \otimes B_{11} \end{bmatrix} \quad (1)$$

the computation of the eight sub-MMs can be scheduled to run either completely in parallel (Figure 1a) or in two parallel steps (Figure 1b).

We can calculate the time and space bounds of the two algorithms by recurrences and see that the MM-n^3-SPACE algorithm (Figure 1a) has an optimal time bound of $O(\log n)$ if counting only the data dependency and a poor space bound of $O(n^3)$; By contrast, the MM-n^2-SPACE algorithm (Figure 1b) has a an optimal space bound of $O(n^2)$, but a sub-optimal time bound of $O(n)$. In the literature, it is known as the fundamental space-time tradeoff. A real-world MM algorithm usually employs some tuning technique (e.g. 2.5D MM algorithm) to go somewhere in the middle ground of the two extremes. However, one interesting research question is if it is possible to achieve a sublinear time bound while still

* This work is supported in part by the Open Funding of State Key Laboratory of Computer Architecture, ICT, CAS (No. CARCH201606)

[1] This paper uses the notion "time bound" to stand for the running time of a parallel algorithm on infinite number of processors, or equivalently the critical path length of the computation DAG, and uses the notion "work" to stand for the running time of the same algorithm on a single processor, or equivalently the total number of vertices of the computation DAG.

PPoPP '17 February 04-08, 2017, Austin, TX, USA

ACM ISBN 978-1-4503-4493-7/17/02... $15.00
DOI: http://dx.doi.org/10.1145/3018743.3019029

```
MM-n^3-SPACE(C, A, B)
// C ← A × B
if (C is small enough)
    BASE-KERNEL(C, A, B)
    return
D ← alloc(sizeof(C))
// Run all 8 sub-MMs concurrently
MM-n^3-SPACE(C00,A00,B00) || MM-n^3-SPACE(C01,A00,B01)
|| MM-n^3-SPACE(C10,A10,B00) || MM-n^3-SPACE(C11,A10,B01)
|| MM-n^3-SPACE(D00,A01,B10) || MM-n^3-SPACE(D01,A01,B11)
|| MM-n^3-SPACE(D10,A11,B10) || MM-n^3-SPACE(D11,A11,B11)
; // sync
// Merge matrices C and D into C by addition
MADD(C, D)
free (D)
return
```

(a) The $O(n^3)$ space recursive MM algorithm

```
MM-n^2-SPACE(C, A, B)
// C ← A × B
if (C is small enough)
    BASE-KERNEL(C, A, B)
    return
// Run the first 4 sub-MMs concurrently
MM-n^2-SPACE(C00,A00,B00) || MM-n^2-SPACE(C01,A00,B01)
|| MM-n^2-SPACE(C10,A10,B00) || MM-n^2-SPACE(C11,A10,B01)
; // sync
// Run the next 4 sub-MMs concurrently
|| MM-n^2-SPACE(C00,A01,B10) || MM-n^2-SPACE(C01,A01,B11)
|| MM-n^2-SPACE(C10,A11,B10) || MM-n^2-SPACE(C11,A11,B11)
; // sync
return
```

(b) The $O(n^2)$ space recursive MM algorithm

Figure 1: Recursive Divide-And-Conquer MM algorithms. "||" (Parallel) and ";" (Serial) are symbols for the linguistic constructs of the ND (Nested Dataflow) parallel programming model [1].

bounding the total space requirement to be asymptotically optimal.

We care about an algorithm's space bound not only because the operating system will disable a computation from executing if it exceeds the space quota, but also because it's a good indicator of cache bound, an even more important factor than the computational bound in deciding an algorithm's real performance on any modern computing system with hierarchical caches. By a similar recurrences analysis, we can see that the MM-n^3-SPACE algorithm has a sub-optimal $O(n^3/B)$ cache miss bound [2], in contrast to the optimal $O(n^3/(B\sqrt{M}))$ bound of the MM-n^2-SPACE algorithm. These cache bounds match proportionally to their space bounds. But we have to remind the audience that an algorithm can repeatedly allocate and free space throughout its computation to bound the total space to be some optimal number. This strategy will inevitably incur a lot of cold cache misses. In other words, a good space bound does **not** necessary imply a good cache bound. Thus, we have to calculate both bounds.

Contributions

- We propose the property of "remote-blocking". If a runtime system stands by the property, we show that our STAR (Space-Time Adaptive and Reductive) technique can bound the total space requirement of a large class of DP algorithms with more than $O(1)$ dependency to be asymptotically optimal while still being work-optimal and having a sub-linear time bound.
- We propose a parallel stack-like memory management system for large chunks of space in a multi-threaded setting. By the system, our STAR technique can bound the cache misses to be asymptotically optimal as well in a processor- and cache-oblivious fashion.

  Though our STAR technique has the processor count "P" in the algorithm design, we use this parameter only to bound the total space requirement and cache misses. Our algorithms do **not** partition "statically" according to the parameter, thus still have the full benefits of "scalable to any number of processors without changing a single line of the algorithm" , "dynamic multi-threading" and "dynamic load-balance" as any processor- and cache-oblivious algorithm.
- By combining the STAR and the cache-oblivious wavefront technique [3], or the ND (nested dataflow) in general, we solve one open problem raised in Galil and Park's paper [2]. More precisely, we have a better GAP algorithm with an optimal $O(n^3)$ work, a sublinear $O(P^{1/2}n^{3/4}\log n)$ time bound conditional on that the processor count $P = o(n^{1/2}/\log^2 n)$, an optimal $O(n^2)$ space and optimal $O(n^3/(B\sqrt{M}))$ cache bound.

[2] This paper calculates only the serial cache miss bound under the ideal cache model since the parallel cache complexity is determined in large by the runtime scheduler.

References

[1] D. Dinh, H. V. Simhadri, and Y. Tang. Extending the nested parallel model to the nested dataflow model with provably efficient schedulers. In *SPAA'16*, Pacific Grove, CA, USA, 11 – 13 2016.

[2] Z. Galil and K. Park. Parallel algorithms for dynamic programming recurrences with more than $O(1)$ dependency. *Journal of Parallel and Distributed Computing*, 21:213–222, 1994.

[3] Y. Tang, R. You, H. Kan, J. J. Tithi, P. Ganapathi, and R. A. Chowdhury. Cache-oblivious wavefront: Improving parallelism of recursive dynamic programming algorithms without losing cache-efficiency. In *PPoPP'15*, San Francisco, CA, USA, Feb.7 – 11 2015.

Recovering Performance for Vector-based Machine Learning on Managed Runtime *

Mingyu Wu Haibing Guan Binyu Zang Haibo Chen

Shanghai Key Laboratory of Scalable Computing and Systems
Institute of Parallel and Distributed Systems, Shanghai Jiao Tong University, China
{followmoon, hbguan, byzang, haibochen}@sjtu.edu.cn

1. Introduction

The explosive growth of data and the demand for learning useful information from such data have stimulated a cross-disciplinary area named big learning, which leverages a cluster of commodity machines to run machine learning applications on large datasets. Those applications are usually implemented on high-level programming frameworks [1–4], which are running atop managed runtimes. Since the applications usually involve many iterations of computation over input data, the frameworks will cache them for performance consideration. In this work, we investigate a set of vector-based machine learning applications in Spark MLlib [3] and find that cached datasets have a strong impact on overall efficiency.

To confirm the problem, we design and implement a new data structure in place of original vectors and re-implement some vector-based benchmarks on it. Our evaluation shows that the newly written code can reach as much as 4.31x speedup compared with original one.

Given the observation, we provide *CADANA*, a CAched DAtasets ANAlyzer to automatically optimize the cached datasets. This tool will conduct code analysis to find out the usage of cached datasets and refine their abstractions and layouts. The analysis contains three compiler-like optimization techniques: redundant fields elimination, data batching, and layout transformation. We also provide two analysis engines to make *CADANA* adaptive to various workloads.

* This work is supported by National Key Research and Development Program of China (No. 2016YFB1000104) and NSFC (No. 61572314 and No. 61672345)

PPoPP '17, Feb. 4–8, 2017, Austin, Texas, USA..

ACM 978-1-4503-4493-7/17/02.
http://dx.doi.org/10.1145/3018743.3019039

In summary, the main contribution of our work includes:

- An investigation to indicate that cached datasets are a major root to poor performance for machine learning applications.
- A tool to automatically analyze and refine cached datasets to solve efficiency problem.
- Two analysis engines that adaptively optimize different machine learning workloads.

2. Analysis

Many machine learning applications use vectors as the main data structure. In this work, we investigate a set of vector-based machine learning applications in MLlib [3], the machine learning library in Spark [4]. Spark is an in-memory computing framework and provides simple API for users to cache useful datasets in memory. Thus, we believe that the result in Spark is representative for other frameworks.

In our analysis, we have found three problems in the cached vector datasets:

- Redundant data fields. Applications often use general numeric libraries, which contain useless data fields in those machine learning algorithms. Those redundant data fields could result in costly serialization/deserialization, heavy memory pressure and frequent garbage collections.
- Inefficient computing pattern. Spark adopts a traditional iterator-based computing pattern. During processing, vectors are fetched and computed in an iterative way. Though general and user-friendly, the iterator-based pattern suffers from constant costs (such as virtual calls) and abstraction-related costs (such as box/unbox operations). Meanwhile, the iterator-based pattern increases code complexity and precludes the JIT compiler from optimizations.
- Dimension unawareness. According to our investigation, the dimensions for cached datasets are often not large. For those vectors, a layout transformation can improve locality and enable hardware acceleration, and in turn improving performance. However, cached datasets in Spark

are agnostic about dimensions and many optimization opportunities are missed.

To validate our analysis, we have implemented a new data structure in Spark 1.1.0 to replace the original vectors. We also manually re-implement some benchmarks based on our new data structure, and conduct some experiments against original ones. The result indicates that our manual implementation improves performance for all applications, and it can reach as much as 4.31x speedup. Our result implies that the efficiency of cached dataset is a key to performance.

3. CADANA

Based on our observation, we provide a tool called *CADANA*, the CAched Dataset ANAlyzer, to automatically analyze and optimize cached datasets for vector-based machine learning code. The workflow of *CADANA* starts with locating the cached datasets in the program. Then, it attempts to refine datasets by using three compiler-like optimizations: redundant field elimination, data batching and layout transformation. After refining, the types of cached datasets change. Therefore, *CADANA* will propagate the updated type information through a whole program analysis and find if some violations are impeding the optimization. Optimizations will succeed only if no violation is found. *CADANA* will generate a summary on what optimization techniques could be used before it exits.

CADANA is equipped with two analysis engines so that it is adaptive to various workloads. The static engine will analyze user code together with library code offline and generate new source code. An extra redeployment phase is required since the new code should be merged with original one manually (according to hints provided by *CADANA*).

In contrast, our dynamic engine can eliminate the redeployment phase by collaborating with Spark runtime. When Spark is running, the dynamic engine intercepts its execution plan and searches for optimization opportunities. The dynamic engine further leverages high-level language features like Java Reflect API and Scala ClassTag to conduct on-the-fly code generation so that Spark can continue execution with a modified execution plan. The optimization phase is totally transparent to end users. However, the dynamic engine puts analysis overhead into the runtime, so if application code is complex or contains too many library invocations, users should turn to the static engine instead.

We have implemented *CADANA* on Spark-1.1.0. It mainly leverages Scala ToolBox to convert source code into abstract syntax trees (ASTs), and further exploits Scala Tree API to analyze and refactor the trees.

4. Performance Evaluation

We evaluate *CADANA* with a set of well-known machine learning applications in Spark MLlib on a 6-node cluster. The workload contains various test cases where the dimension of vector ranges between 10 and 100. The result for Linear Regression is illustrated in Figure 1.

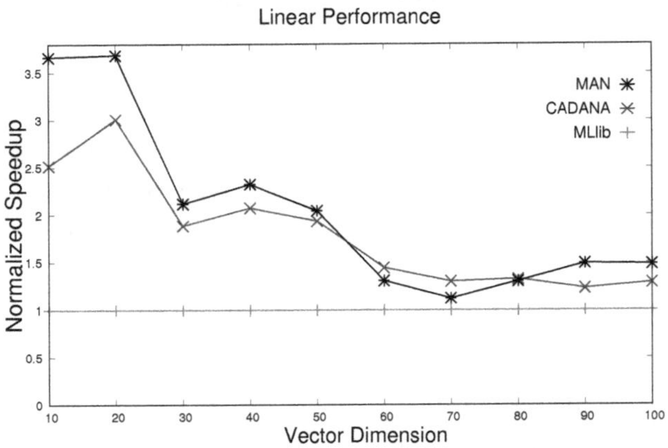

Figure 1: Evaluation for Linear Regression

The result shows that code generated by *CADANA* reaches comparable performance compared with that manually written by us, and the performance speedup against original Spark MLlib implementations ranges from 1.08x to 3.01x. We find that the speedup is quite sensitive with vector dimension and it requires more analysis in the future.

We also provide a breakdown analysis to further investigate where the improvement comes from. We find that *CADANA* can significantly reduce memory footprint (by at most 27.8%) induced by cached datasets, which leads to less GC pause time (reduced by at most 34.3%). Besides, *CADANA* cuts the serialization time nearly in one-third on average for benchmarks relying heavily on data transfer through network. Our evaluation also shows that some benchmark benefits from SIMD acceleration because of layout transformation.

To prove that our mechanism can also be adapted to other frameworks, we manually modify some applications in Apache Flink [1], Apache Mahout [2], and an up-to-date version (2.0.0) for Spark. We observe speedup from 2x to 3.4x among all those frameworks.

References

[1] A. Alexandrov, R. Bergmann, S. Ewen, J.-C. Freytag, F. Hueske, A. Heise, O. Kao, M. Leich, U. Leser, V. Markl, et al. The stratosphere platform for big data analytics. *VLDB*, 23(6):939–964, 2014.

[2] Apache. Apache mahout: Scalable machine learning and data mining. mahout.apache.org.

[3] X. Meng, J. Bradley, B. Yuvaz, E. Sparks, S. Venkataraman, D. Liu, J. Freeman, D. Tsai, M. Amde, S. Owen, et al. Mllib: Machine learning in apache spark. *JMLR*, 17(34):1–7, 2016.

[4] M. Zaharia, M. Chowdhury, T. Das, A. Dave, J. Ma, M. McCauly, M. J. Franklin, S. Shenker, and I. Stoica. Resilient distributed datasets: A fault-tolerant abstraction for in-memory cluster computing. In *NSDI*, 2012.

POSTER: On the Problem of Consistency Exceptions in the Context of Strong Memory Models *

Minjia Zhang
Microsoft Research
minjiaz@microsoft.com

Swarnendu Biswas
Univeristy of Texas at Austin
sbiswas@ices.utexas.edu

Michael D. Bond
Ohio State University
mikebond@cse.ohio-state.edu

Abstract

This work considers the problem of availability for memory models that throw consistency exceptions. We define a new memory model called *RIx* based on isolation of synchronization-free regions and a new approach called *Avalon* that provides RIx. Our evaluation shows that Avalon and RIx substantially reduce consistency exceptions, by 1–3 orders of magnitude and sometimes eliminate them completely. Furthermore, our exploration provides new, compelling points in the performance–availability tradeoff space.

1. Introduction

To achieve high performance, compilers and architectures for shared-memory parallel programs commonly perform optimizations that assume no interactions with concurrent threads. To avoid visibly affecting program semantics, these optimizations are restricted from reordering across synchronization operations (e.g., lock acquire and release). These rules enable shared-memory languages and hardware to provide a strong guarantee—code regions between synchronization operations appear to execute atomically—for program executions that are free of *data races* (conflicting accesses to the same variable that are not ordered by synchronization operations) [1]. However, for executions with data races, compiler and hardware optimizations lead to erroneous, unpredictable, often undefined behavior [1]. These guarantees are formalized in the *DRF0* memory consistency model, which ensures strong semantics for data-race-free executions only. Java, C++, and other shared-memory languages provide variants of DRF0 [5, 7].

To address this semantic hole, researchers have proposed *memory consistency models*, or simply *memory models*, that provide strong semantics for *all* program executions. Notable among these models are those that treat data races as *errors*, potentially throwing a *consistency exception* for a data race, and otherwise ensuring strong consistency [6].

Problem. In a world where programs (with data races) can throw consistency exceptions, programmers will try to identify and eliminate data races that cause consistency exceptions during testing. Dealing with data races is analogous to fixing existing *memory* errors, such as buffer overflows, for which memory- and type-safe languages such as Java provide fail-stop semantics. Regardless, even well-tested software will contain unknown data races that manifest under certain production environments, inputs, or thread interleavings, leading to unexpected consistency exceptions. Unexpected exceptions hurt the *availability* (this work's term for exception freedom) of production systems.

Our approach. To address the availability issue, we introduce a new memory model called *RIx* based on *synchronization-free-region isolation* (RI). We introduce a runtime approach called *Avalon* that provides RIx and avoids throwing consistency exceptions. Our evaluation on benchmarked versions of large, real programs shows that our Avalon design and our extensions to prior work provide significantly better availability, at competitive cost, than existing approaches. To our knowledge, this work is the first to consider and address the problem of availability in memory consistency models that generate consistency exceptions.

Our technical report describes RIx and Avalon in more detail [8].

2. RIx: A New Strong Memory Model

An execution provides *isolation of synchronization-free regions* (RI) if it provides two properties: *write atomicity* and *read isolation* of regions [2, 3]. An RIx execution either provides RI or throws a consistency exception—but only if the execution has a data race. In particular, RIx guarantees that each execution conforms to the following: (1) it generates a consistency exception, but only if the execution has a data race; and (2) it provides RI of all regions, until and if the execution throws a consistency exception.

If an execution is data race free, RIx inherently ensures not only RI but also RS. RIx is strictly stronger than DRF0, and it relaxes semantics from RS to RI only for racy regions, which have undefined or weak semantics under DRF0.

* This material is based upon work supported by the National Science Foundation under Grants CSR-1218695, CAREER-1253703, CCF-1421612, and XPS-1629126. Thanks to Brandon Lucia and the anonymous reviewers for helpful feedback and discussions.

PPoPP '17 February 04-08, 2017, Austin, TX, USA
ACM 978-1-4503-4493-7/17/02.
http://dx.doi.org/10.1145/http://dx.doi.org/10.1145/3018743.3019024

	FastRCD	Valor	Avalon
eclipse6	**14K** ± 24K	**1.8K** ± 3.5K	**0.3** ± 0.6
hsqldb6	**53** ± 5.6	**140** ± 5.4	**0.1** ± 0.1
lusearch6	**0.1** ± 0.1	**0.2** ± 0.2	**0** ± 0
xalan6	**120** ± 5.8	**93** ± 3.4	**5.5** ± 1.5
avrora9	**610K** ± 6.4K	**670K** ± 9.7K	**24K** ± 730
jython9	**0** ± 0	**0** ± 0	**0** ± 0
luindex9	**0** ± 0	**0** ± 0	**0** ± 0
lusearch9	**110** ± 25	**93** ± 13	**21** ± 4.5
pmd9	**3.3K** ± 520	**3.5K** ± 930	**110** ± 51
sunflow9	**23** ± 6.3	**37** ± 14	**0** ± 0
xalan9	**1.5K** ± 220	**6.2K** ± 1.2K	**0.3** ± 0.4

Table 1. The number of consistency exceptions reported by FastRCD, Valor, and Avalon. Reported values are the mean of 10 trials, including 95% confidence intervals.

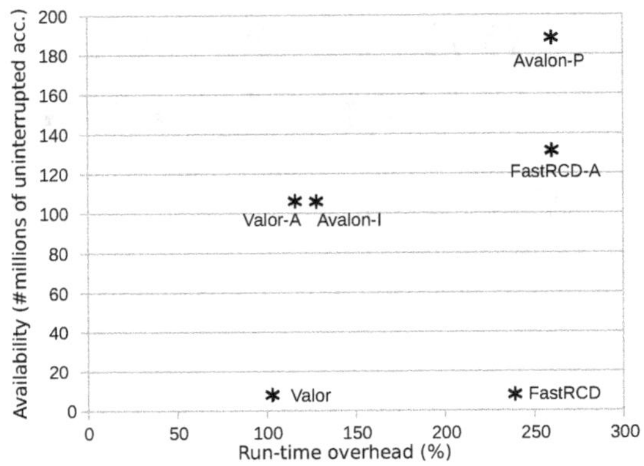

Figure 1. Availability vs. performance for all approaches.

3. Avalon: Transparent Runtime Support for RIx

In order to enforce RIx automatically, we design transparent runtime support called Avalon that ensures that an execution is RI and otherwise throws a consistency exception. At a high level, Avalon detects conflicts by tracking each shared variable's last writer region and last reader region(s), distinguished using per-thread clocks. When Avalon detects a *write–write* or *write–read* conflict, it waits until the conflict no longer exists, thus *avoiding* the conflict. When Avalon detects a *read–write* conflict, it allows the writing thread to *proceed until the end of its current region*, thus *tolerating* the conflict legally under RIx. Interestingly, Avalon provides RI, or else it *deadlocks* due to a dependence cycle of waiting on conflicts; Avalon detects such deadlocks and throws a consistency exception.

Avalon can optionally detect read–write conflicts *imprecisely* (allowing false conflicts but without missing true conflicts) without jeopardizing support for RIx. We introduce a variant of Avalon, called *Avalon-I*, that represents variables' last reader information imprecisely, enabling lower run-time costs and complexity than the precise variant, which we call *Avalon-P*.

4. Evaluation

We have implemented Avalon and compare it with two prior analyses that support RSx: FastRCD and Valor [4]. Table 1 reports the number of consistency exceptions from FastRCD, Valor, and Avalon. Comparing with prior work's FastRCD and Valor, Avalon-P reports substantially fewer consistency exceptions. Avalon-P reduces regions that report an exception and total exceptions by up to three orders of magnitude (e.g., eclipse6, hsqldb6, xalan6, pmd9, and xalan9), or eliminates consistency exceptions completely (e.g., lusearch6 and sunflow9). Avalon's ability to reduce consistency exceptions comes from two aspects: (1) avoiding write–write and write–read conflicts and (2) tolerating read–write conflicts (by exploiting RIx).

We plot the availability and performance results in Figure 1. FastRCD-A and Valor-A are our extensions to *FastRCD* and *Valor* that avoid exceptions by waiting at conflicts. The x-axis is the geomean of run-time overhead across all programs. The y-axis is availability, which is defined as the geomean of memory accesses performed without interruption by a consistency exception. That is, *availability* $= \frac{\#\, memory\ operations}{\#\, consistency\ exceptions + 1}$. Larger values represent better availability. Points closer to the top-left corner represent a better performance–availability tradeoff. Valor performs best, but provides worse availability than FastRCD-A, Valor-A, Avalon-P, and Avalon-I. Avalon-P has the best availability, but its performance overhead is relatively high. Avalon-I and Valor-A arguably each offer the best tradeoff between availability and performance.

Avalon-P, Avalon-I, and RIx thus represent new ways to balance performance, semantics, and availability when providing a memory consistency model.

References

[1] S. V. Adve and H.-J. Boehm. Memory Models: A Case for Rethinking Parallel Languages and Hardware. *CACM*, 53:90–101, 2010.

[2] A. Adya, B. Liskov, and P. O'Neil. Generalized Isolation Level Definitions. In *ICDE*, pages 67–78, 2000.

[3] H. Berenson, P. Bernstein, J. Gray, J. Melton, E. O'Neil, and P. O'Neil. A Critique of ANSI SQL Isolation Levels. In *SIGMOD*, pages 1–10, 1995.

[4] S. Biswas, M. Zhang, M. D. Bond, and B. Lucia. Valor: Efficient, Software-Only Region Conflict Exceptions. In *OOPSLA*, pages 241–259, 2015.

[5] H.-J. Boehm and S. V. Adve. Foundations of the C++ Concurrency Memory Model. In *PLDI*, pages 68–78, 2008.

[6] B. Lucia, L. Ceze, K. Strauss, S. Qadeer, and H.-J. Boehm. Conflict Exceptions: Simplifying Concurrent Language Semantics with Precise Hardware Exceptions for Data-Races. In *ISCA*, pages 210–221, 2010.

[7] J. Manson, W. Pugh, and S. V. Adve. The Java Memory Model. In *POPL*, pages 378–391, 2005.

[8] M. Zhang, S. Biswas, and M. D. Bond. All That Glitters Is Not Gold: Improving Availability and Practicality of Exception-Based Memory Models. Technical Report OSU-CISRC-4/16-TR01, Computer Science & Engineering, Ohio State University, 2016.

An Infrastructure for HPC Knowledge Sharing and Reuse

Yue Zhao
North Carolina State University
yzhao30@ncsu.edu

Chunhua Liao
Lawrence Livermore National Laboratory
liao6@llnl.gov

Xipeng Shen
North Carolina State University
xshen5@ncsu.edu

Abstract

This paper presents a prototype infrastructure for addressing the barriers for effective accumulation, sharing, and reuse of the various types of knowledge for high performance parallel computing.

1. Introduction

Software optimization is a complicated process and making the right optimizations for a program in various contexts requires a wide range of knowledge in the program code,the domain, the hardware, properties of various optimizations, and so forth. The problem is especially important for High Performance Parallel Computing (HPC) due to the high requirement of the desired performance and energy efficiency, as well as the growing complexity in HPC software algorithms and hardware architectures. Currently, HPC knowledge has been expressed in various formats and scattered everywhere. The ad-hoc knowledge representation and organization have created tremendous difficulties for the HPC community to effectively accumulate, share, and reuse HPC knowledge.

Our observations reveal a fundamental issue facing HPC: The lack of a flexible, open infrastructure for the HPC community to effectively share, accumulate, and reuse HPC knowledge has been hampering the progress of HPC development. Take the optimization of stencil computation as an example. As the core computing pattern in many scientific simulations, high-performance stencil computing has drawn a large number of studies in the last decades. Just an incomplete counting on Google Scholar shows that there are 2,490 research papers published on the topic "stencil computation(s)" in the last five years, some on GPU memory performance, some on non-uniform memory access (NUMA), and some on parallel thread scheduling or other aspects of optimizations. A survey of the practices in U.S. National Labs shows that despite the large volume of prior work, there are still many explorations on the topic going on everyday. Many of them are simple repetitions of some others' explorations due to the unawareness of the prior work or the unavailability of their results.

A fundamental reason for the redundant efforts is the difficulty in systematically collecting and leveraging prior experiences. There are some scholarly research databases (e.g., [3]), digital libraries, technical forums (e.g., stackoverflow.com), or general knowledge managing systems (e.g., [1]). None of them allow automatic inference tools to be built upon the knowledge base for HPC or offer a structural representations of knowledge for automatic software optimization agents to easily leverage. The goal of this work is to develop an infrastructure, named *OpenK*, to mitigate the difficulty.

PPoPP '17 February 04-08, 2017, Austin, TX, USA

ACM ISBN 978-1-4503-4493-7/17/02. . . $15.00
DOI: http://dx.doi.org/10.1145/3018743.3019023

2. OpenK Framework

OpenK is an infrastructure to provide a comprehensive way to help the HPC community systematically accumulate, share, and reuse HPC knowledge. Its design tries to meet the following requirements: (1) *Generality:* being able to accommodate a wide range of knowledge of various levels, sources, or forms, due to the nature of HPC. (2) *Deep Inference:* being amenable for automatic logic inferences to make it possible to do sophisticated knowledge exploitation rather than simple search as what common search engines do. (3) *Consistent Conceptualization:* being able to prevent inconsistency in the definition of concepts and terminology. (4) *Usability:* being easy for both the community and automatic software agents to add, update, retrieve, and visualize the HPC knowledge. (5) *Extensibility:* being open and extensible for collaborations cross the HPC community.

Figure 1 depicts the overall structure of the OpenK framework. It consists of three components.

(1) Front End. The front end includes a webpage-based interface, through which, humans input new knowledge, submit queries, visualize the knowledge base or query results, and submit ratings on the quality of some knowledge or new reasoning modules. It is also equipped with a locally installed integrated development environment (IDE), and a SWI-Prolog programming interface for app development.

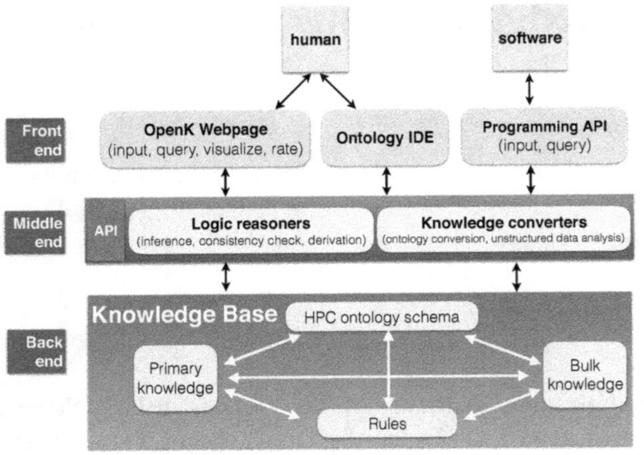

Figure 1. Overall structure of OpenK.

(2) Middle End. The middle end of OpenK consists of two main components. The first is a set of logic reasoners including SWI-Prolog and HermiT [2] , which conduct automatic logic inferences on the OpenK knowledge base to find answers to queries. It further includes the modules for any other types of analysis of the knowledge base (e.g., statistical analysis through Machine Learning) and to derive new insights or relations. The second component is a set of knowledge converters, which take the inputs from various sources and/or in various formats and generates knowledge represented formally (in RDF) and send it to the OpenK knowledge base. Both components are made extensible.

(3) Back End. The back end of OpenK is the actual knowledge base. OpenK uses ontology—a generic format for knowledge representation—to ensure that various types of HPC knowledge can be uniformly represented, and can together form a seamlessly integrated knowledge base. Through some typical logic reasoners (e.g., HermiT [2]), one can conduct inferences across all the knowledge.

3. Use Case Studies

We first use stencil computation as a case study to demonstrate how OpenK helps programmers directly.

Stencil computation refers to a computation pattern and is important in many image processing and scientific simulation programs. However, due to the lack of a systematic way to organize the knowledge, the prior findings are scattered in thousands of papers and reports. It usually costs user a tremendous amount of time to find and leverage these knowledge for high performance stencil computations. Duplicated explorations are common.

We build an ontology schema for the stencil computation subdomain in OpenK. Then we upload the key insights from a number of research papers into OpenK through its interfaces and converters. It emulates the accumulation and sharing of knowledge across the community. The knowledge uploading took less than 10min for a paper (assuming the authors have prior knowledge of the paper already). We then query OpenK for advises for optimizing four arbitrary stencils of different types for a target architecture. Results show that the advices can effectively enhance the performance of the stencil computations, as Table 1 reports.

Table 1. The speedup of different optimizations. (* suggested optimization by the OpenK).

Grids	Points	Cache blocking	SIMD, Padding	Unrolling, CSE
512^3	7	10%*	≈ 0	≈ 0
512^3	27	≈ 0	13%*	30%*
$1024^2 \times 512$	7	22%*	≈ 0	≈ 0
$1024^2 \times 512$	27	8%	14%*	42.5%*

In another case study, OpenK shows significant benefits for easing the creation of tools for guiding data placements on GPU memory. Details omitted.

4. Conclusion

To our best knowledge, OpenK is the first infrastructure that provides a comprehensive way to help the HPC community to systematically accumulate, share, and reuse HPC knowledge. Experiments demonstrate that it is promising for serving as an infrastructure for HPC knowledge management and promoting the HPC community synergy.

This material is based upon work supported by DOE Early Career Award (DE-SC0013700), the National Science Foundation (NSF) under Grant No. 1455404, 1455733 (CAREER), and 1525609, and Google Faculty Award. It was also performed under the auspices of the DOE by Lawrence Livermore National Laboratory under Contract DE-AC52-07NA27344. Any opinions, findings, and conclusions or recommendations expressed in this material are those of the authors and do not necessarily reflect the views of DOE, NSF, LLNL, or Google.

References

[1] Google knowledge graph. `https://www.google.com/intl/es419/insidesearch/features/search/knowledge.html`.

[2] B. Glimm, I. Horrocks, B. Motik, G. Stoilos, and Z. Wang. Hermit: an owl 2 reasoner. *Journal of Automated Reasoning*, 53(3):245–269, 2014.

[3] D. B. Krafft, N. a. Cappadona, B. M. Devare, B. J. Lowe, and J. Corson-rikert. VIVO : Enabling National Networking of Scientists. *Technology*, page 24 months, 2010. URL `http://journal.webscience.org/316/`.

Author Index

www.ingramcontent.com/pod-product-compliance
Lightning Source LLC
LaVergne TN
LVHW080004210926
848481LV00011B/2943